"Ray's *Introduction to Psychological Science* takes a serious, research-based view of the field. It explains current research within the context of the history of the field – classic studies, theories and figures. It is a higher-level textbook for students and instructors that are serious about psychological science."
– **Dennis Miller, University of Missouri, USA**

"This is a well-written book that is applicable to majors from different disciplines. A strong text that should be closely considered when looking for intro psychology course materials."
– **Gary F. Kelly, Clarkson University, USA**

Introduction to Psychological Science

Introduction to Psychological Science provides students with an accessible, comprehensive, and engaging overview of the field of scientific psychology. It expertly incorporates a variety of perspectives ranging from neuroscience to cultural perspectives at an introductory level.

Ray brings together cutting-edge research from traditional psychological literature to modern, evolving perspectives, and creates a unified approach by focusing on three core themes:

- Behavior and Experience: an analysis of behavior and experiences observed across a variety of everyday life situations.
- Neuroscience: an examination of psychological experiences through the neuroscience lens ranging from genetic/epigenetic to cortical networks as related to psychology.
- Evolutionary/Human Origins: an exploration of broader scientific questions by examining psychological processes from the perspective of human and cultural history.

Through these themes, the book delves into topics like social processes, psychopathology, stress and health, motivation and emotion, developmental sequences, and cognitive functions such as memory, learning, problem solving, and language. Throughout it helps students to understand the nature of psychological science by addressing common myths and misconceptions in psychology, showing how psychological science can be applied to everyday life and how new research can be created. Additionally, this student-friendly book is packed with pedagogical features, including "concept checks" to test reader knowledge, "extensions" features which show how to apply knowledge, and a comprehensive glossary.

Reflecting the latest APA Guidelines concerning the essential elements of an introductory psychology course, this text is core reading for all undergraduate introductory psychology students.

William J. Ray is an Emeritus Professor of Psychology at Pennsylvania State University, USA. At Penn State, he was the Director of the SCAN (Specialization in Cognitive and Affective Neuroscience) program and was the Director of the Clinical Psychology Program. His research has focused on approaching clinical questions from a neuroscience perspective.

Introduction to Psychological Science

Integrating Behavioral, Neuroscience, and Evolutionary Perspectives

William J. Ray

NEW YORK AND LONDON

First published 2021
by Routledge
605 Third Avenue, New York, NY 10158

and by Routledge
2 Park Square, Milton Park, Abingdon, Oxon, OX14 4RN

Routledge is an imprint of the Taylor & Francis Group, an informa business

© 2022 William J. Ray

The right of William J. Ray to be identified as author of this work has been asserted by him in accordance with sections 77 and 78 of the Copyright, Designs and Patents Act 1988.

All rights reserved. No part of this book may be reprinted or reproduced or utilised in any form or by any electronic, mechanical, or other means, now known or hereafter invented, including photocopying and recording, or in any information storage or retrieval system, without permission in writing from the publishers.

Trademark notice: Product or corporate names may be trademarks or registered trademarks, and are used only for identification and explanation without intent to infringe.

Library of Congress Cataloging-in-Publication Data
Names: Ray, William J., 1945- author.
Title: Introduction to psychological science : integrating behavioral, neuroscience and evolutionary perspectives/William J. Ray.
Description: 1 Edition. | New York : Routledge, 2021. | Includes bibliographical references and index. |
Identifiers: LCCN 2020056128 (print) | LCCN 2020056129 (ebook) | ISBN 9780367697785 (hardback) | ISBN 9780367693596 (paperback) | ISBN 9781003143192 (ebook)
Subjects: LCSH: Psychology. | Psychology—Study and teaching.
Classification: LCC BF121 .R389 2021 (print) | LCC BF121 (ebook) | DDC 150—dc23
LC record available at https://lccn.loc.gov/2020056128
LC ebook record available at https://lccn.loc.gov/2020056129

ISBN: 978-0-367-69778-5 (hbk)
ISBN: 978-0-367-69359-6 (pbk)
ISBN: 978-1-003-14319-2 (ebk)

Typeset in Bembo
by Apex CoVantage, LLC

Access the companion website: www.routledge.com/cw/Ray

*To Mary K as she approaches 100 years of age,
living independently and experiencing life*

Contents

Preface   xix

Acknowledgments   xxiii

1   Psychology: Historical Roots and Modern Approaches   1

Psychology Is About Behavior and Experience   2
  How to Understand Ourselves and Others   4
Historical Considerations in Understanding Behavior and Experience   5
  From Ancients to Sir Isaac Newton   6
  1700s to the 1900s   9
  The Beginning of a Scientific Psychology   14
  20th-century Trends in Psychology   16
  African American Psychologists Who Shaped our Perspectives   24
The Three Major Themes of This Book   25
  What We Do and What We Experience Is Critical to Psychology   25
  Our Brain and Body Determine What We Do and Experience   26
  Human Behavior and Experience Developed Over a Long Period of Time   28
Levels of Analysis   31
  Different Psychologists Focus on Different Levels of Analysis   34
Summary   37
Study Resources   39
  Review Questions   39
  Web Resources   40
  Key Terms and Concepts   40

2   Scientific Psychology and Its Research Methods   41

What Is Science?   42
  A Human Activity   42
  Science and Doubt   43
  Debunking Superstition and Pseudoscience   44
What Are the Methods of Science?   46
  Descriptive Research: What Can We Observe?   47
  Experimental Research: How Do We Determine Cause and Effect?   55
  Combination Research Designs: When Does It Make Sense?   56
How Do Scientists Evaluate and Analyze Data?   59
  Validity   59
  Reliability   60
  Measurement   61

Descriptive Statistics 62
How Do We Design an Experimental Study? 66
   Select and Group Participants 67
   Plan the Structure 67
   Interpret the Results 68
What Are the Ethics of Scientific Research? 72
   The Pursuit of Knowledge and Avoiding Harm 72
   The Care and Use of Laboratory Animals 75
   Deception Studies 76
Summary 77
Study Resources 79
   Review Questions 79
   Web Resources 80
   Key Terms and Concepts 80

3 The Neuroscience of Behavior and Experience 81

How Does the Nervous System Enable Behavior and Experience? 82
   Neurons 83
   Neural Impulses 84
   Neurotransmission 86
   Neural Networks 89
   Hormones and the Endocrine System 91
What Are the Parts of the Brain? 91
   The Neocortex 92
   The Limbic System 93
   The Brain Stem 96
   The Cerebellum 96
   The Spinal Cord 98
How Do We Investigate the Brain? 99
   Measuring Electrical and Magnetic Activity 99
   Measuring Structure 100
   Measuring Blood Flow Changes 103
   Evaluating Techniques 105
How Does the Brain Develop and Evolve? 108
   From Neural Tube to Brain 108
   Brain Structure Evolved According to Necessity 109
What Is the Link Between Heredity, Behavior,
and Experience? 112
   Genetics Help Explain Evolutionary Change 113
   Patterns of Inheritance Vary 118
   Behavior and Environment Influence Gene Expression 121
   Epigenetic Processes Respond to Changing Environments 122
   Behavior Genetics 126
Summary 130
Study Resources 133
   Review Questions 133
   Web Resources 134
   Key Terms and Concepts 134

4 Developmental Processes — 135

Physical Development   136
    Prenatal Development   137
    Brain Development   138
    Sensory Development   141
    Learning From the Environment   143
    Motor Development   144
Cognitive Development   148
    Piaget and Stages of Development   149
    Vygotsky and the Sociocultural Perspective   151
    Memory   152
    Temperament   154
Learning about Others and the World   156
    Mirror Neurons and Imitation Learning   156
    Theory of Mind   158
    Theories of Attachment   159
Development During Adolescence   165
    Physical Changes in Adolescence   166
    Risk-Taking in Adolescence   166
    Moral Development in Childhood and Adolescence   168
Lifespan Development and Adulthood   170
    Erikson and Psychosocial Stages   171
    Successful Aging   173
Summary   176
Study Resources   178
    Review Questions   178
    Web Resources   179
    Key Terms and Concepts   180

5 Sensation and Perception — 181

Psychophysics   183
    Sensory Measurement Thresholds   184
Vision   184
    The Visual System Is Sensitive to Electromagnetic Energy   185
    A Tour of the Eye   187
    Rods and Cones   189
    Vision and Color   191
    The Eye Connects to the Brain   194
    The Primary Visual Cortex   195
    Depth   197
    Visual Illusions   198
    Gestalt Psychology   199
Hearing   205
    How the Ear Works   207
    Creating Sounds in the Brain   208
    The Vestibular System and Balance   210
The Chemical Senses: Smell and Taste   212
    Olfaction: The Smelling Sense   212

The Gustatory System: A Matter of Taste 214
Touch and Pain 216
  The Sense of Touch 216
  Understanding Pain 219
Summary 221
Study Resources 225
  Review Questions 225
  Web Resources 226
  Key Terms and Concepts 226

6 Consciousness 227

Consciousness 227
  Consciousness and Attention 229
  Types of Awareness 230
  Levels of Consciousness 231
  Variations in Consciousness 232
Sleep and Dreams 238
  Sleep Patterns 240
  Neuroscience Studies of Sleep 246
  Sleep Disorders 250
  Dreams 252
Hypnosis and Meditation 257
  Hypnosis 257
  Hypnotic Effects 258
  Meditation 261
Psychoactive Substances 262
  Addiction 263
  Major Psychoactive Substances 266
  Drugs Found in the Brain 271
Summary 271
Study Resources 274
  Review Questions 274
  Web Resources 275
  Key Terms and Concepts 276

7 Memory 277

Understanding Memory 278
The Temporal Dimension of Memory 279
  Sensory Memory 280
  Short-Term Memory 280
  Long-Term Memory 282
  Processes Involved in Learning and Long-Term Explicit Memories 283
  The Role of Meaning in Memory 285
Memory and the Brain 288
  H.M. and Memory 289
  Brain Areas Involved in Memory 291
Individual Differences in Memory Abilities 294

Mnemonists 296
Memory Disorders 299
False Memories 299
Summary 304
Study Resources 307
Review Questions 307
Web Resources 308
Key Terms and Concepts 308

8 Learning, Ethology, and Language Processes — 309

Classical Conditioning 311
Conditioning in Your Daily Life 312
Drug Reactions 313
Emotional Conditioning 314
Garcia Effect and Food Aversion 315
Conditioning and the Brain 316
Operant Conditioning 319
Thorndike and the Puzzle Box 319
B. F. Skinner and Operant Conditioning 320
Learning as Viewed through Ethology 324
Play as Learning 324
Observational Learning 326
Imitation Learning and Mirror Neurons 327
Learning Takes Place as Part of Life 328
Language 329
Speech Processing and Vocalization in Infants 329
Structure of Language 331
Evolutionary Roots of Language across Species 332
Language Learning in Animals 333
What Is Language? 334
Structure of Vocal Cords 337
Language, Genes, and the Brain 339
Reading 343
Evolution of Language 343
Language and Genes 343
Summary 344
Study Resources 347
Review Questions 347
Web Resources 348
Key Terms and Concepts 348

9 Cognition, Problem-Solving, and Intelligence — 349

How We Think 350
Fast and Slow Thinking 350
Concepts and Categories 351
Making Decisions 352
Analogies 352
Logic 352

Heuristics 354
Behavioral Economics 356
Solving Problems 360
Insight Problems 360
From Problem-Solving to Measuring Intelligence 365
How Do We Measure Intelligence? 365
Psychometric Theories of Intelligence 369
Multiple Intelligences 372
Relationship of "g" to Cognitive Factors 374
Brain Change with Age 375
Genetic Factors Associated with Intelligence 376
APOE Gene and Intelligence 379
Maintaining Intelligence throughout Life 381
Flynn Effect 384
Group Differences in Intellectual Ability 384
Summary 390
Study Resources 392
Review Questions 392
Web Resources 393
Key Terms and Concepts 393

10 Motivation and Emotion   394

Motivation 394
Basic Motivations 395
Intrinsic and Extrinsic Motivation 396
Motivation for Food 397
Experiences of Hunger and Satiety 398
Eating Pattern and Obesity 400
Body Mass Index (BMI) 402
Eating Disorders 403
Sexuality 406
Historical Perspectives 406
Sexual Activities of Americans 407
Understanding Human Sexuality 408
Emotion 415
Darwin and The Expression of Emotions 419
Universal Emotionality 421
Nature of Basic Emotions 426
Underlying Dimensions of Emotionality 427
Historical Theories of Emotionality 428
Physiological Systems Involved in Emotion 429
Summary 435
Study Resources 437
Review Questions 437
Web Resources 438
Key Terms and Concepts 438

11 Stress and Health   439

What Is Stress?   439
Historical Approaches to the Study of Stress   441
Autonomic Nervous System (ANS)   444
    Physiology of Stress   446
    Immune System   449
Social Support Research and Stress   452
    Social Shaping   454
    Individual Differences   454
    Uncontrollable Stress   455
    Trauma and PTSD   456
Health   459
    Improving Health and Managing Stress   462
    Meditation   464
Summary   466
Study Resources   468
    Review Questions   468
    Web Resources   468
    Key Terms and Concepts   468

12 Social Psychology   469

Social Psychology   469
Social Cognition   471
    Attribution   472
    Categorization and Stereotyping   474
    Looking at Others and the Face   477
    The Social Brain Hypothesis   482
    Brain Systems Involved in Social Relations   484
Social Emotions   486
    Prosocial Behavior and Helping   488
    Non-Cooperation   493
Social Influences on Behavior   498
    How We Act in Groups   500
    Social Influences on the Level of the Self   500
    Social Influence and Compliance   501
    Social Influence and Conformity   502
    Social Influence and Persuasion   505
Making Moral Judgments   509
Summary   513
Study Resources   515
    Review Questions   515
    Web Resources   516
    Key Terms and Concepts   516

13 Personality   517

Personality   518

Historical Aspects of the Study of Personality 518
Psychodynamic Perspectives on the Development of Personality 522
 The Structure of Personality 523
 Psychosexual Development 523
 Other Psychodynamic Approaches Influenced by Freud 526
 Using Internal Processes to Understand Personality 527
The Existential-Humanistic Approach to Personality 531
Social Cognitive Theories of Personality 532
Current Perspectives on Personality 533
 Typical Personality Traits 533
 Evolutionary Perspectives on Personality 536
 Genetic Factors in Personality 539
 Physiological Factors Related to Personality 540
 Cultural Factors in Personality 541
Self 544
 Self-Concept 545
 Neuroscience of Self 546
 The Characteristics of a Healthy Self 547
Summary 548
Study Resources 551
 Review Questions 551
 Web Resources 552
 Key Terms and Concepts 552

14 Psychological Disorders   553

Psychological Disorders 554
 Stigma and Mental Disorders 556
 Understanding Psychopathology 557
 Creating a System to Understand Mental Disorders 558
 Universal Psychopathology 563
 Thinking about Psychopathology from an Evolutionary Perspective 564
Common Disorders Involving Emotions or Moods 565
 Anxiety Disorders 565
 Obsessive-Compulsive and Related Disorders 569
 Mood Disorders 571
 Suicide 574
Dissociative Disorders 578
 Depersonalization–Derealization Disorder 580
 Dissociative Amnesia 580
 Dissociative Identity Disorder 581
Schizophrenia 582
 Positive and Negative Symptoms 584
 Factors in the Development of Schizophrenia 586
Personality Disorders and Personality 591
 What Is a Personality Disorder? 592
 Personality Disorders and Typical Personality Traits 593
Neurodevelopmental Disorders 597

Autism Spectrum Disorder (ASD) 597
Attention Deficit Hyperactivity Disorder (ADHD) 599
Summary 601
Study Resources 604
Review Questions 604
Web Resources 606
Key Terms and Concepts 606

15 Treatment 607

Historical Understanding of Psychopathology and Its Treatment 609
The Psychological Treatment Perspectives in
the 20th Century 613
Psychodynamic Perspectives on Treatment 613
Existential-Humanistic Perspectives 615
Behavioral and Cognitive Behavioral Perspectives 618
Biological Approaches to Treating Mental Illness 622
Psychotropic Medications 623
Electroconvulsive Therapy 625
Brain Simulation 625
Effective Treatment of Mental Disorders 627
Treatment for Anxiety Disorders 628
Treatment for Social Anxiety Disorder 630
Treatment for Specific Phobias 630
Treatment for Panic Disorder 631
Treatment for Obsessive-Compulsive Disorder 631
Treatment for Depression 632
Treatment for Bipolar Disorder 637
Treatment for Dissociative Disorders 638
Treatment for Schizophrenia 638
Treatment for Personality Disorders 642
Treatment for Neurodevelopment Disorders 645
Summary 647
Study Resources 651
Review Questions 651
Web Resources 652
Key Terms and Concepts 652

References 653

Glossary 721

Index 753

Preface

This book is based on conversations with a number of faculty who have dedicated their efforts to helping students understand the nature of psychological science. Although psychological science has a rich theoretical and scientific tradition, many students come to the course with misconceptions concerning psychology. Some students think that psychology is not really a science. Others think that psychology is only about helping those with mental disorders. Still others expect an easy course which they already know a lot about. Helping students make the transition into an understanding of psychological science lies at the heart of this book.

Both the Association for Psychological Science (APS) and the American Psychological Association (APA) have addressed the process of teaching psychology. As such, these concerns have informed this book, including the latest *APA Guidelines for the Undergraduate Psychology Major*. Specifically, the book represents the latest psychological knowledge based on a scientific research tradition. Additionally, features are included in each chapter to help students think critically and apply scientific considerations as well as realize the need for understanding diversity and social responsibility. In this way, the book places scientific knowledge within the larger context of human complexity and a worldwide perspective.

Overall, this book represents a history of teaching introductory psychology to both large classes and small honors sections. The book reflects both examples and information that students have found exciting and larger clarifications of topics experienced by students as being difficult. Topics such as processing information without awareness as seen in "split brain" patients or those with "blindsight" as well as experiencing a limb that does not exist are intriguing to students. Likewise, the fact that humans make quick moral judgments or have an internal calculus for social and sexual relations are also fascinating topics. On the other hand, drawing valid conclusions from research findings is often a difficult process and requires more attention.

Over the last hundred years, psychology has developed a rich theoretical and scientific tradition. Historically, particular scientific approaches were developed to answer specific questions. This book seeks to integrate the manner in which various scientific disciplines have sought historically to answer psychological questions. This allows students to understand and integrate information from varying perspectives within psychology and the neurosciences. Early chapters of the book offer basic information to understand the nature of psychological science.

With the advent of the 21st century, questions of importance to psychology were being embraced by the neurosciences. This allowed for both a richness and an integration of scientific information concerning important psychological questions. In the past thirty years, we have seen a shift in focus which has included the "decade of the brain" as well as a real emergence of the cognitive and affective neurosciences. Today, advances within the cognitive and emotional neurosciences are available to add additional understanding to traditional psychological science perspectives.

Whereas many of the earlier perspectives in psychology were attempts to bring a scientific approach to human processes, fundamental human behaviors and experiences were often ignored. For example, although for the larger part of the 20th century, psychology emphasized learning as the basis of behavioral adaptation and change, it did so in a limited manner with organisms that were kept hungry or deprived in some manner. Some basic processes, such as one-trial learning after eating bad food, the migration of birds and butterflies without being taught, and the manner in which experience can influence brain and genetic changes, were often ignored.

Even during the time of John Watson and his conditioning of little Albert, there existed research (cf., Valentine, 1930) showing that it was evolutionarily-important objects that were most susceptible to the conditioning process. That is to say, it was shown to be much easier to condition a child such as little Albert to fear furry animals than to fear an inanimate object such as a wooden toy. Today, research performed by individuals such as Eric Kandel has shown that learning causes actual changes in the brain. Other Nobel Prize winning psychological researchers such as Daniel Kahneman have shown that humans think in very different ways depending on the situation.

Such new research is taking psychology beyond historical debates. The historical genetics vs culture debate was often presented in dichotomous ways in textbooks. As such, this debate was of limited value without an understanding of the manner in which humans both live within a culture and are genetically influenced by historical environments. Further, through epigenetic processes, the environment and previous experience strongly influence the manner in which genes are expressed.

On a cognitive and emotional level, humans talk to themselves and greatly influence their own behavior and experience. Expectations play a large role in the human experience and on a larger level, the current generation can be influenced not only from those around them but also from what was written thousands of years ago.

Our human history also has an important influence. As human beings, we have always lived in groups of individuals and our abilities and processes have evolved to encompass a rich social environment. Humans think differently when considering other humans. Current cultural research has also shown the importance of integrating neuroscience perspectives to fully understand the individual in his or her culture and social group.

Thus, using a broader perspective, the dichotomous positions of nature vs nurture or innate vs learned fuse into the larger question of how aspects of each contribute to an understanding of behavior and experience. On a molecular level, we have come to see that genes must be turned on or off. What this means is that many significant human processes are directed by the environment. The traditional emphasis placed on the environment by psychological science is now being utilized in the neurosciences to understand a number of processes. Other processes such as relationships with our culture and our friends are also critical aspects of psychological science.

We know that a variety of organisms learn and carry behaviors over generations by observing others and adopting these behaviors. With humans an even more impressive process is the active teaching of skills and behaviors to others. If fact, some have suggested that humans are the only species that have formal institutions such as schools and universities to teach the next generation.

Overall, this book presents an integrated perspective. Previous attempts to bring a more integrated perspective to psychology were often interpreted to reflect a biological determinism that ignored critical environmental factors and did not give human plasticity a scientific perspective. Psychology has now moved beyond that perspective. As emphasized by Charles Darwin over 150 years ago, there is a close relationship between an individual's internal and external environments which makes traditional nature/nurture arguments misleading at best and wrong at their worst. Psychology is just now beginning to come to grips with the manner in which evolutionary thinking can impact and shape psychology. Psychology has come to this perspective indirectly through research and theoretical perspectives from cognitive and affective neuroscience including the study of emotional processing, human ethology, and genetics.

In the same way that psychology offers important insights on the systems level in terms of human behavior and experience, it is imperative that introductory psychology texts begin to offer such an integrative perspective. For example, recent perspectives in social neuroscience suggest that it is not productive to teach brain anatomy or emotionality in one chapter and social relationships, influence, and perception in another without noting their interrelationships. With an integrated approach, students come to understand the nature of social relationships including those aspects of our behavior and experience such as empathy, social grouping, and moral judgments that we share with those humans who came before us. Similar considerations can also be seen in terms of cognition, psychopathology, and developmental processes.

The purpose of the present text is to bring together current perspectives concerning the manner in which the human mind, behavior, and experience can be understood. In addition to the traditional psychological literature, the book draws from work in the cognitive and affective neurosciences, ethology, and genetics/epigenetics. The focus is also on a unification and integration of evolutionary understandings within these broader neuroscience considerations. For example, animals largely live within nature. Humans on the other hand are influenced both by nature and by the culture within which they live. Recent research has shown this to be a two-way street for humans. Human cultures are able to influence biological processes at the same time that these processes can influence human culture. In order to achieve this integration, the book focuses on three themes, that of behavior and experience, that of neurosciences understanding, and that of evolutionary perspectives.

Features in Each Chapter

A number of features of the book help faculty facilitate students' transition to appreciating the nature of psychological science. In addition, linkage to scientific research related to studying and learning information are presented to help students study effectively. Every chapter begins with learning objectives. The summary at the end of the chapter is organized around these learning objectives. Throughout each chapter are concept checks. At the end of each chapter are a set of Study Resources that include Review Questions, Books and Articles for Further Reading, Key Terms and Concepts, and Web Resources.

Each chapter also includes three types of feature boxes:

1. **The World Is Your Laboratory**—how psychological scientists can use already occurring events to better understand psychological processes
2. **Applying Psychological Science**—how psychological principles can be applied to create new research and information
3. **Myths and Misconceptions**—what are some common misconceptions among the public

Acknowledgments

Many individuals have contributed to this book. Josh Wede and Brian Crosby discussed both the contents of the book and their experiences with large undergraduate intro courses at a major university. I also appreciate the students in my honors intro class who over the years have given me insight into how to present the information seen throughout this book as well as finding new information and perspectives. Faculty from across the country were extremely helpful in their reviews of this book and suggestions. Three individuals offered insights into the material: Nathan Fox, *University of Maryland*; Andreas Keil, *University of Florida*; and Don Tucker, CEO, *Belco.tech* and *University of Oregon*.

With great appreciation, I thank Vicki Knight, the editor who initially signed this book for her creative insights and intellectual discussions concerning the book. I also appreciate the efforts of Judy Ray for her careful reading and helpful suggestions. At Routledge, a number of editors made important contributions. These include Georgette Enriquez, Hanna Shakespeare, Lucy McClune, and Akshita Pattiyani.

1 Psychology
Historical Roots and Modern Approaches

LEARNING OBJECTIVES
1.1 Define psychology and how the processes of behavior and experience influence how we interact with one another.
1.2 Review the historical concepts that have influenced psychology.
1.3 Summarize the major approaches to psychology in the 20th century.
1.4 Describe the three themes used in this book.
1.5 Describe the different levels of analysis used by psychologists.

On what began as a normal day, Tom was driving home from soccer practice. An oncoming car crossed over into his lane and hit him. The car went out of control and Tom was thrown out of the car. Tom lost his left arm in the accident. However, afterward, he could still feel his arm as if it were there. He even had the sense of moving each finger and being able to grab an object (Ramachandran & Blakeslee, 1998). Strange as it might seem, Tom is not alone in experiencing the sensation of having a limb that is not there. This phenomenon has been reported since antiquity and following the US Civil War, it came to be known as phantom limb. Phantom limb is experienced today in those who have fought in a war or have had industrial or other accidents that resulted in loss of limbs. Not only do individuals with a lost limb experience its presence, more than 70% of them also experience pain in the limb, which can last for years after its loss.

Can you remember where you were on your 15th birthday? How about what you had for lunch two weeks after that? Although most of us can remember what we wore for a special occasion, what we wore or had for lunch three weeks later is next to impossible. However, there is a small number of people who can remember every day of their life after about age 10. This ability is referred to as Highly Superior Autobiographical Memory (LePort et al., 2012).

If you are walking to class and almost get hit by a car, what do you say? If you are like most people, you say the driver is "stupid" or even a more colorful remark. However, if you are driving and almost hit someone, what do you say then? Typically, most people say something like the sun was in my eyes or he ran in front of me or another situational explanation. As you will see in the chapter on social processing, we tend to attribute trait characteristics such as being stupid to others, while using situational explanations such as having the sun in our eyes for ourselves.

As you read about these three experiences described (phantom limb, superior memory, and attribution), a number of questions may come to mind. You might wonder how it happens that some can experience a hand that is not there. This takes us to a larger question of how we come to have the experience of having our own body and knowing where it is in space. In later chapters you will learn about how our brain receives information from our body and creates our experiences of moving through space or picking up an object such as your coffee cup.

You may also wonder if you experience the world the same as others, especially if you see words in colors or can remember every day of your life in detail. One thing you will learn in the memory chapter is that being able to recall every event that happened to you every day in your life will not make it easier to learn academic material for a test. There are, however, things you can do to help you learn new information.

The last example of almost being hit by a car helps us to understand that how we see the world and the importance of the situation influence attributions. As you will see, our social perceptions and social relationships are a critical aspect of our human history. We have always lived with others in groups and this shapes how we treat social relationships. In fact, many of us use much of our day engaging in social relationships in person or through social media. This also brings up the question of how you feel about yourself if you see yourself different from how others see you. These are some of the questions we will be asking in this book.

Psychology Is About Behavior and Experience

This book is a journey to explore who we are as humans, how we think, feel, and do, as well as how we interact with others and ourselves. We will look at ourselves through the lens of psychology. ***Psychology*** is the study of behavior and experience. Behavior is what we do. ***Experiences*** are related to our internal thoughts and feelings. Some of our ***experiences*** are similar to those of others. Other experiences are rare but still can be understood through the scientific methods available to psychologists. Let's begin with a description of behavior and experience.

Behavior is simply the way we act. Behavior includes our actions and those of others in a variety of situations. We see behavior all around us and make inferences about its meaning. Watching others from a distance, we can quickly determine if they are friends, lovers, or even angry at each other without even hearing a word of what they are saying. Quite amazing, isn't it?

How do we do that? We just watch their behavior, which includes facial expressions, gestures, and touching. Humans have had thousands of years of learning to infer the behavior of others. Otherwise, we would not have survived. The fact that we are always making inferences about ourselves and others and the manner that we are able to do this is one important aspect of psychology. Ask yourself, for example, how do the people in the picture below feel about each other?

Another aspect of psychology that will be important in this book is that of *experience*. Unlike actions that we can observe, experiences are internal and take many forms. We have internal feelings as we interact with others. We dream at night. We remember an event we have experienced or a person we have known. We feel moved by music or stories. We may feel excited when we go to a new country. We enjoy gossip. We let our mind wander as we wait for someone or even spontaneously daydream in the middle of an event. We feel hungry or tired. We see and hear a world full of colors and sounds. We also talk to ourselves, which at times is helpful as we plan for what we need to do. Other times what we say to ourselves is not very helpful, as we become negative about ourselves, which separates us from others and our world. The manner in which scientists have sought to study internal processes is another important aspect of psychology.

Behavior and experience always take place within a *context*. Sometimes the context is the present, including the people we are with and the particular tasks we are doing. Sometimes, we remember something that happened to us in the past and this has a profound influence on what we experience in the present. We might remember when a friend left and we

Figure 1-1 Couple sitting on park bench—how do they feel about each other?

feel sad. We can even imagine what might happen in the future and this leads us to see the world differently. That is, we have emotional reactions at this moment based on what might happen in the future. We know, for example, that those individuals with depression can imagine that a future meeting will not work out well. This leads them to withdrawing and not trying.

Although you have no problem knowing how the couple in the picture feel about each other, this is only the beginning in psychology. You could be wrong. Psychological considerations are always tested through science. You will learn some of the exact techniques of science in later chapters. For now, it is important to realize that psychology is a science that covers all aspects of human behavior and experience.

Sometimes our research in psychology emphasizes how we interact with other people. In the real world salespeople often shake our hands or touch us lightly on the shoulder as they tell us how wonderful we will look in that new car. Other salespeople may turn us off if they don't listen to what we say. Psychological scientists can test which factors determine whether we like or dislike another person. Another example is what factors determine whether we obey another person or not. Most of us imagine that we are in charge of our own actions and able to predict our own behavior. However, as you will see later in this book, experiments suggest this is not always the case. Sometimes each of us reacts differently to a new situation than we image we would.

Not only can we consider how people are influenced in the present by their thoughts, feelings, and actions, but we can also consider how our ancestors may have lived life and interacted with others in the past. What would your life have been like if you had lived 100, 1,000, or even 10,000 years ago? This takes us to a larger context that includes the vast scale of human history. If you think about it for a minute, you may realize there has never been a time in our human history that humans have lived alone. We have always lived in groups, whether it is our present-day communities and cities or our previous existence in hunter-gatherer groups.

Given this type of historical cultural perspective you might guess that humans would have developed a variety of ways of interacting with others and even ourselves. You would be correct. It is not surprising that humans today love to be with others, to gossip, to talk on the phone, to send text messages, and to update their social media pages. Scientific psychology is interested in learning more about how our past ways of interacting with others and ourselves play a role in our current life.

Behavior and experience also take place in different types of situations. For example, we often feel different when we work than when we play. With others, we are generally aware of our interactions. At some times these interactions are easy and fun and at other times difficult and tiring. This has led psychologists to ask: what are the characteristics involved when everything seems to be going your way? You can't miss the tennis shot or basketball hoops or play an instrument perfectly. Psychologists are also interested in when we don't reach our potential. Sometimes we are just tired. Other times this results from some type of psychological problem such as anxiety or depression. Much of what you will read in this book discusses how we normally behave and experience the world.

How to Understand Ourselves and Others

As a science, psychology is just over 130 years old, although humans have been thinking about other humans and suggesting reasons for their actions for thousands of years. Psychology is one of the most popular courses in universities in the United States. However, many individuals come into the course expecting something other than a science course (Toomey, Richardson, & Hammock, 2017). It is to be hoped that those individuals will have a new perspective after reading about psychology. This book is about how scientists have come to view human behavior and experience. As humans we create reasons for why a person does a particular behavior. Sometimes we are correct and sometimes not. Thus, we need ways to check out our ideas. Psychologists check their ideas by designing experiments and using other scientific methods.

Those engaged in the science of psychology seek to develop theories that give us insight into human behavior. Having a theory is not enough; we also need to determine if our theories are accurate or not. To do this, psychologists developed specific research methods. These methods help us to understand what factors influence our behavior and experience. Scientific methods also help us to know if our theories are wrong.

In psychology, we ask critical questions as to what makes us human and how are we like other species. Aspects of our genes and physiology are shared by a variety of species. Thus, how are we unique as a species? Are there processes that humans do that other species cannot? One answer to this question is that we produce and understand language in a manner that other species do not. Another answer is that we create institutions such as schools and universities to formally teach others. Part of being human is to actively seek and pass on knowledge.

As humans we also create culture in which we build cities and develop technology. More than 35,000 years ago, humans began to draw pictures of animals on the walls of caves (Aubert et al., 2019). As humans we seek to represent and share the experiences that we encounter. This has a long history, but modern technology has changed and sped up how we communicate with one another. In less than 40 years, computers, cell phones, and how they connect with each other has greatly changed our society and our world. However, we continue to use technology within the context of a culture. For example, some cultures see it as OK to use a cell phone in a restaurant or theater or train or bus, whereas others do not. How our culture influences us as well as which characteristics are common across cultures is another topic important to psychology.

Figures 1-2a and 1-2b Cave art from Lascaux, France, dated more than 17,000 years ago. This art shows humans hunting animals with a bow and arrow. The picture on the right shows realistic depictions of animals.

This text will cover a wide array of psychological approaches and examine human behavior and experience through several different lenses. In order to give you a more complete understanding of psychological science, three major themes will be emphasized in this book: (1) behavior and experience; (2) neuroscience; and (3) human origins and a historical cultural perspective. These three major themes will be described at greater length later in the chapter. Let us now begin with a historical overview of how human behavior has been of great interest to thinkers for more than 2,000 years, and how, much more recently, psychology developed as a science.

CONCEPT CHECK

- What does it mean to say that psychology is the study of behavior and experience? What are some examples of behavior and experience that you would like to learn about from this course?
- What does it mean to say that psychology is a science? What advantages does science bring to the study of psychology?
- Identify the three major themes this book takes in regard to psychology.

Historical Considerations in Understanding Behavior and Experience

Psychology seeks to describe and understand human behavior and experience. In fact, as humans, we have a long history of trying to understand ourselves. In this section, you will be introduced to some of the historical conceptions that have influenced psychology in the United States (see Finger, 2000 or the classic Boring, 1950 for more information). A more complete history would include historical developments in China, India, Africa, and the Middle East. For example, an Egyptian text referred to as the Edwin Smith Papyrus dates from approximately 1600 BC. This was one of the earliest documents that suggested different brain areas are involved in different processes. Overall, it is a medical text describing some 48 case studies and can be seen at the US National Institutes of Health website (https://wayback.archive-it.org/7867/20190220142516/https://ceb.nlm.nih.gov/proj/ttp/books.htm).

You should consider this section as more than just a discussion of history. You will also learn about how you think, feel, and move. This includes the role of the body and its involvement in our mental processes. You will also read about how you create the world around you. Some of these ideas date back thousands of years, yet still influence our views today. Some other ideas we may have rejected, but they still show their influence in our language. For example, no one today would think of the heart being involved in memory as did Aristotle in the 4th century BC, yet we still say that we "learn things by heart."

From Ancients to Sir Isaac Newton

Beginning more than 2,500 years ago—in the 6th century BC—there was an emphasis by Pythagoras (who we know primarily for his theorem concerning the sides of a right triangle), on identifying the underlying scientific principles that may account for all forms of behavior. Pythagoras coined the term *philosophy*, which can be translated as love of meaning or wisdom.

Moving beyond philosophy, he also set the stage for understanding human behavior and experience as related to internal processes and natural causes. As such, Pythagoras was one of the first to see the brain as the structure involved in human intellect and mental disorders. This was in contrast to a common view that human behavior and related disorders reflect the actions of the gods, including the belief that mental illness was a divine punishment. At that time, and even in some places today, *magic* was viewed as the primary way to understand the world.

Hippocrates: Behavior and Experience Come from the Brain

In the next century, Hippocrates moved the science of psychology to the next level with his emphasis on careful observation and a continued articulation of the idea that all disorders—both mental and physical—should be sought within the patient and not supernatural forces. He saw the brain as the source of our internal processes, such as dreams, fears, and irrational concerns. Mental illness and a person's inability to connect appropriately with the environment were also seen as brain processes. Hippocrates is often seen as the father of Western medicine.

Plato: Do We Really See Reality?

Whereas Hippocrates located the brain as an important structure for intellect and reasoning, it was Plato in the next century who was to describe the nature of the human condition. His *allegory of the cave* describes human beings who live in an underground cave. They have been there since childhood and are only able to see the wall in front of them. Behind them is a fire that reflects shadows on the wall in front. As humans they try to make sense of the shadows they see on the wall and give them names and descriptions. Plato then asks, what would happen if after a long time the people were able to turn around and see what was behind them? What would they believe to be real, the images they had seen on the wall all their life or the newly seen environment behind?

Some of the types of questions this allegory raises for those interested in behavior and experience is the degree to which we are limited in our ability to see and interpret the world and our experience of it. The story suggests a variety of ways in which our perceptions of what we believe to be reality may be distorted. Whatever our experiences growing up, our brain creates a world based on the information it has available. Plato's allegory is actually a rich and deep story that continues to have meaning for those who ponder the ideas suggested by it.

Aristotle (384–322 BC) also considered the human condition. He suggested that humans are not totally rational, only potentially so. In fact, Aristotle suggested that humans are "the very worst of animals" when they are separated from reason. For this reason, Aristotle saw studying ethics as critical for human society to function well. He also understood that people are social animals. Overall, Aristotle played a historical role in the debate concerning the nature of human nature and how we differ from other animals.

The Romans through the Renaissance

The Romans built on many of the ideas established by the Greeks. Galen (AD 130–200) was a physician who influenced Western and Islamic thought until the Renaissance. During his lifetime, Galen wrote a large number of treatises on science, medicine, and philosophy—estimated by some to number between 500 and 600. He was largely a champion of empiricism. **Empiricism** is the idea that knowledge should be derived through our sensory processes. That is, it is better to learn from observation than to just believe what one has been told.

Between the time of Galen and the Renaissance, Western science and medicine remained fairly stagnant with little new knowledge being added. Beginning in the 14th century, a new spirit began to emerge in Europe with profound influences on art, literature, politics, and science. In art, there was a desire for a sense of realism, which led artists such as Leonardo da Vinci to carefully study the human body. He performed dissections on animals and human cadavers to carefully reveal the structure of human organs. **Figure 1-3** shows one of Leonardo da Vinci's drawings.

Descartes: Bodies of Animals and Humans Are Mechanical, but Humans Have a Mind

Another influential thinker who utilized mechanical models along with physics and mathematics was the philosopher René Descartes (1596–1650). Descartes was intrigued by mechanical machines. Some of these machines looked like humans that moved their hands and performed actions. Throughout Europe there were large clocks with moving figures or water displays in large fountains. By analogy, he assumed that human and animal reflexes or involuntary actions of organisms were based on similar principles. Thus, moving your hand from a hot stove or even digesting food was seen as a mechanical operation. For Descartes, all animal behavior could be explained by *mechanical principles* as could human involuntary actions.

In **Figure 1-4,** from Descartes's work, you can see the mechanical means by which a hot fire would cause an involuntary or reflexive movement. The important distinction, which continues until today, is that behavior can be categorized as either *voluntary* or *involuntary*. Voluntary actions such as thinking or consciously performing an act were different in that they required a mind, and humans are the only organism to have a mind, according to Descartes. By thinking, humans can know with certainty that they exist. Thus, the famous philosophical statement of Descartes, "I think, therefore I am."

Given the situation that the bodies of animals are totally mechanical and that humans have both a body and a mind, Descartes created a *mind/body distinction* that science has continued to face in its explanations. The problem is how can a material body including the brain be influenced by an immaterial process such as the mind? How can a thought influence a cell in the brain? Although today we generally talk about the mind/body

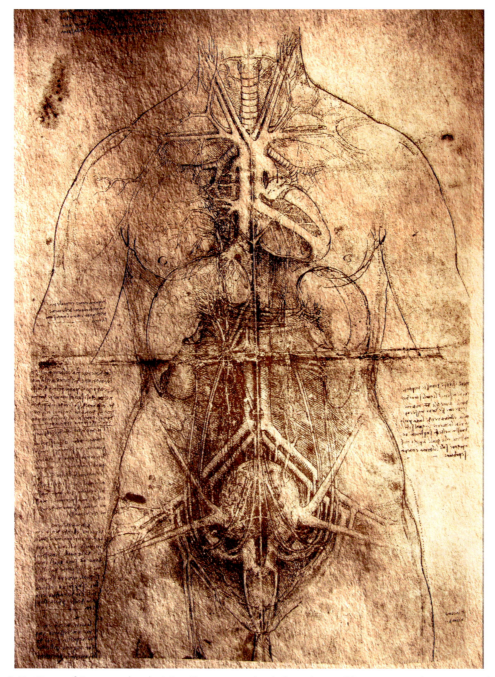

Figure 1-3 One of Leonardo da Vinci's anatomical drawings. These were important in helping scholars learn about the organs of the human body.

problem, the metaphysics of Descartes' era would often make the distinction between body and soul.

The Beginning of Western Science

In the 1600s, science as a way of understanding the world began to emerge. Galileo successfully replaced authority as the main source of knowledge with that of *experimentation* and *science*. This movement toward experimentation was greatly aided by Galileo's own inventions, such as the telescope, the thermometer, an improved microscope, and a pendulum-type timing device.

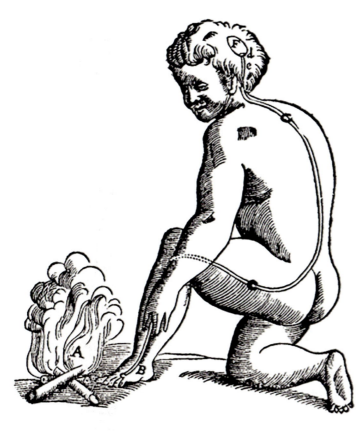

Figure 1-4 Descartes' drawing showing context for involuntary or reflexive movement. The person touching the fire with his foot results in an impulse being sent to the brain.

Isaac Newton's classic work *Principia* was published in the 1860s (Newton, 1729–1969 reprint). In this work, Newton describes his theories of time, space, and motion. As you will see in the chapter on sensation and perception, Newton helped us to understand the nature of light. Specifically, he suggested that white light is made up of different colors. Newton also set out the basic ideas for performing science.

CONCEPT CHECK

- What important contributions did the Ancient Greeks and Romans—including Pythagoras, Hippocrates, Plato, Aristotle, and Galen—make to our current view of psychology?
- Describe the shift from authority to science as a way of knowing that happened during the Renaissance. Specifically, what did da Vinci, Descartes, Galileo, and Newton contribute during this period that led to this shift?
- What contributions to the beginning of Western science did scientists such as Galileo and Isaac Newton provide?

1700s to the 1900s

From the 1700s to the 1900s, there was a period of scientific exploration in which one discovery led to another. The 1700s focused on the electrical activity produced by our nervous system. The 1800s helped to establish how different cognitive functions such as language and spatial abilities are influenced by different parts of the brain. Near the end of the 1800s, the manner in which organisms change in relation to their environment became the focus of evolution. Also, the later 1800s helped to establish the manner in which expectations and psychological processes could influence basic human processes such as what we see and experience.

The Brain and Body Use Electrical Impulses

At the beginning of the 1700s, there was a basic understanding of the structure of the nervous system. The 1700s began a quest to understand how it worked. One of the contributions of this endeavor was the realization that the body created and used electrical activity in its basic processes. By the middle of the 1700s, individuals such as Benjamin Franklin, who experimented with lightning rods and kites, published works on the nature of electrical activity in general. Later in the century such scientists as Luigi Galvani and Emil du Bois-Reymond were able to show that electrical stimulation would cause a frog's leg to twitch. With this demonstration, nerves were beginning to be thought of as wires through which electricity would pass. Further, it was determined that the brain could itself produce electrical activity.

Human Functions Can Be Localized in the Brain

One important realization of the 1700s was that particular functions can be localized to different parts of the brain. One person often cited today is Franz Josef Gall who studied neuroanatomy and physiology. His idea was that brain areas associated with different tasks were reflected on the skull. If one were good at a particular ability, Gall assumed that their skull would look different from someone who was not as talented. To support this idea, he examined the skulls of people at the extremes, such as great writers, statesmen, and mathematicians as well as criminals, the mentally ill, and individuals with particular pathologies. Overall, he defined 19 processes that he thought humans and animals both performed and another 8 that were unique to humans (see **Figure 1-5**). These included such abilities as art, humor, hope, fairness, and curiosity, as well as the ability to murder.

Although Gall and his followers never scientifically tested their ideas, others found that research did not support Gall's ideas about the structure of the head. What Gall did that was supported in later research was to suggest that the brain is capable of performing a variety of functions and that these functions could be localized in different parts of the brain. For example, he was correct in suggesting that the frontal lobes of the brain were related to social and cognitive functioning. He also emphasized that all mental functions come from the brain.

Language Is Composed of Two Processes and These Can Be Located in the Brain

In 1861, Paul Broca, a French physician, examined a patient who could understand language but could not speak. The patient died shortly thereafter. This allowed Broca the opportunity to perform an autopsy and report an abnormality in an area on the left side of the frontal lobe. Based on a variety of cases, Broca was able to show that language is a left-hemispheric process and that damage to the frontal areas of the left hemisphere also resulted in problems in higher executive functions such as judgment, the ability to reflect on a situation, and the ability to understand things in an abstract manner. The area related to language production in the left hemisphere today is called Broca's area and is shown in **Figure 1-6**.

Some 15 years after Broca made his discovery related to language production, Carl Wernicke published a paper in 1874 that suggested that language understanding was related

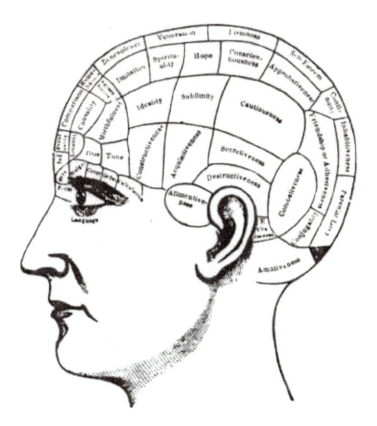

Figure 1-5 Gall's depiction of functional localization in the brain. Each area of the brain was thought to be related to a particular ability, such as art, humor, curiosity, and even the ability to murder another person.

to the left temporal lobe. He studied patients who were unable to comprehend what they heard. However, they were able to produce fluent speech, that is, a continuous string of words, although it was incomprehensible and included nonexistent words. The specific area identified by Wernicke is now called Wernicke's area and is located in the left temporal lobe. The discoveries of Broca and Wernicke helped the scientific community understand that language consists of different processes. These include the ability to understand language and the ability to produce language.

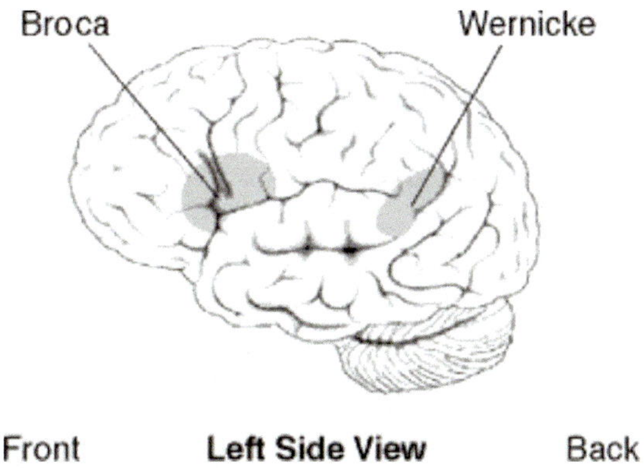

In 1868 Broca went to the UK for a scientific meeting where he met Hughlings Jackson, a well-known British neurologist. Having learned of Broca's work in Paris some four years earlier, Jackson examined some cases of individuals who showed problems with speech. In almost all of these cases, Jackson found that the person had a paralysis on the right side of their body that would suggest that the damage to the brain was in the left hemisphere. This results from the fact that the right side of the body below the neck is controlled by the left hemisphere and left side of the body by the right hemisphere.

Jackson also noted that patients with left hemisphere damage did not show problems in performing perceptual tasks, whereas those with right hemisphere damage did. He reported on one particular patient with right hemisphere damage who could not recognize people—including his wife—and another who had difficulty with finding his way through a town he knew. In doing this, Jackson became the first scientist to realize that

Figure 1-6 Broca's area is a part of the temporal lobe that is involved in speaking a language. Wernicke's area is involved in understanding language.

language is processed by the left hemisphere and spatial abilities by the right hemisphere. You will learn about these differences in later chapters.

Charles Darwin: All Life on Earth Is Evolving

Another big idea that came forth in the 1800s was the idea that all of nature is in constant flow. Charles Darwin (1809–1882) showed how organisms change. His ideas focused on the *evolution* of the species, including both plants and animals. *Variation* was to become one of the major components of Darwin's thinking concerning evolution. Darwin's research is not discussed in detail in many psychology books, yet his work was extremely influential to the beginning of a scientific psychology. His work emphasized the brain as the center for behavior. His work also began a tradition of using the behavior of animals as a way to understand human behavior.

Darwin suggested two mechanisms that influence which physical characteristics are passed on to the next generation. The first mechanism is *natural selection*. Basically, natural selection focuses on characteristics that vary in a given species such as the physical size of the finch's beak or the color of the moth. If these characteristics help an organism survive within a particular environment, they will be passed on to the next generation.

The second mechanism is *sexual selection*. Sexual selection takes place on two levels. The first level involves both genders. Characteristics that make an individual more attractive to a mate will be passed on to future generations. For example, if female peahens prefer male peacocks with larger and more colorful tails, then they will choose them as mates. We now know that the vibrancy of the color also reflects the health of the peacock as well as the underlying genetics. Through mating, these characteristics will be passed on

Figure 1-7 Peahen and peacock. The peahen chooses which male to mate with by the color and shape of the peacock's tail. We now know that these characteristics are related to the health of the male.

to future generations. That is, by choosing who to mate with, she is also choosing which characteristics will be passed on.

The second level involves characteristics within a single gender. Within the same sex, characteristics such as strength or cunning that allow one to compete and control reproduction will also have a greater chance of being passed on to future generations. This is because those individuals without these characteristics will have less opportunity to mate. In many species such as the northern elephant seal off the coast of California, the colossal males (the largest weighing in at more than 5,000 pounds) battle with one another for the ability to mate with the females.

Overall, Darwin helped us understand the close connection between the environment and genetic processes, although Darwin did not know about genes at that time. Today, we know that this close connection makes such questions as what is responsible for our behavior, nature in terms of genes *or* nurture in terms of experiences meaningless. As you will see later, genes influence our environment *and* our environment influences which genes are activated or not.

Hermann von Helmholtz: Perception Is a Constructive Process

During the middle part of the 1800s, the rigid view of the body as a machine was beginning to change. For example, Hermann von Helmholtz (1821–1894), who had measured the speed of the nerve impulse, also began to note that perception is more than just taking in information as a camera would do. In today's language we would discuss perception as a *constructive process* that takes place outside of our awareness. It is constructive in the sense that we create it. We may even see something that does not exist as in the "white triangle" presented here (**Figure 1-8**). We make a distinction between the white of the triangle and the white that surrounds it. However, the distinction is in our experience and not on the physical reality of the printed page.

Other times, when we look at a scene, what we see may be based on our previous experiences. We may actually add information to the scene. Helmholtz called this *unconscious inference*. Given that Helmholtz studied basic sensory processes such as vision and hearing

Figure 1-8 White triangle.

and noted the manner in which humans add a personal element to the creation of their perception, he is often seen as an important founder of what was to become experimental psychology and the study of sensation and perception. Helmholtz added further to the realization that physical reality and psychological reality are not the same.

The Beginning of a Scientific Psychology

The stage was being set for the formal appearance of a *scientific psychology*. Two men are credited with establishing the first psychological laboratories in the world. The first is Wilhelm Wundt (1832–1920) in Germany. Wundt was initially trained as a physician and physiologist. Working as a physiology professor, Wundt published a number of books on sensory and physiological processes. In 1862 he offered a course at Heidelberg University on "psychology from the standpoint of natural science." This material was published the next year as a book entitled *Lectures on the Minds of Men and Animals*. Wundt later published a book on psychology called *Outline of Psychology*.

In 1875, Wundt moved to Leipzig where he set up a psychological laboratory and created a journal that was later to be renamed *Psychological Studies*. In his lab Wundt used a variety of techniques to study such human processes as consciousness, awareness, and perception. One of these techniques was the use of reaction time as a means of denoting speed of mental processes. For example, you could ask a person to press a key when a light came on and measure the time it took to perform this task. You could then ask the person to press the key only if the light was blue. It would then be possible to subtract the light-alone reaction time from the blue-light reaction time to obtain a measure of how long it took the person to process light color.

Another technique was *introspection*. **Introspection** is the examination of one's own mental state, which Wundt referred to as internal perception. Introspection involved training a person to observe his internal state. The person also needed the ability to focus attention on his internal processes. Wundt required that an individual complete 10,000 individual introspective observations before his data could be used for Wundt's research (Schultz & Schultz, 2011). However, even with this training, introspection was not always reliable.

Wundt's laboratory examined feelings and asked how it could be understood. Wundt's answer was to suggest that a feeling can be divided into three separate dimensions. Thus, if I ask you to describe how you feel about a painting or piece of music, your experience could be seen as reflecting these dimensions. The first dimension is pleasantness to unpleasantness. The second dimension ranges from excitement to calmness. The third dimension varies from tension to relaxation. The basic idea was that it was possible to take a complex process such as cognitive processing or feeling and then break it down into its component parts. A variety of scientists from around the world came to work with Wundt and returned to their own countries including the United States to set up psychological laboratories.

One of these individuals was Edward Titchener (1867–1927) who had studied with Wundt in Germany and became a professor at Cornell University in Ithaca, New York. His work was known as **structuralism**, which is the idea that human processes can be broken down into their component parts. Overall, Titchener suggested the first task for psychology was to ask what the basic elements of experience are. The second task is to determine how these elements combine. And, third, the task is to understand the causal relationships. Titchener also used introspection as a way to understand internal processes. It can be noted that Titchener's first graduate student was Margaret Floy Washburn. In 1894, she was the first woman to receive a PhD in psychology in the United States.

The second person credited with establishing the first psychological laboratory is William James (1842–1910). James became a medical student at Harvard in the 1860s. However,

Figure 1-9 Wilhelm Wundt (seated) with colleagues in his psychological laboratory. Wundt is credited with establishing one of the first psychology laboratories in the world. He is identified with structuralism.

he interrupted his studies to read Darwin and go to Europe to visit scientific laboratories including those of Helmholtz and Wundt. In 1869 James received his MD degree and in 1872 was appointed as a physiology faculty member at Harvard and created a laboratory that included psychological studies. Although he was initially appointed in physiology, his title was changed to professor of psychology in 1889. The next year his classic book *Principles of Psychology* was published. For many years, this book served as a psychology text in both America and Europe and is still read today.

In his work, James was particularly interested in the functional aspects of psychological processes, asking the question what purposes specific psychological processes serve. You could ask, for example, what function consciousness serves. This came to be known as ***functionalism***. In his major works, he distinguished between the more long-term cause or function of a behavior and an immediate cause of the behavior.

Functional approaches are also distinguished from structural approaches as a way of describing behaviors. In a structural approach, an experience is divided into its parts. However, James saw human processes such as consciousness as something that was forever changing and are thus impossible to divide into components. James saw our consciousness as a stream that flows and changes. From this James studied the *stream of consciousness*. This includes the ideas and feelings that continually pass through our brains. He was also interested in the manner in which our consciousness or attention is selective and appears to choose what it attends to. For example, at a party you may only notice what those immediately around you are saying. However, if someone across the room says your name, you instantly notice it.

James saw humans as beginning life with a large number of reflexive actions from sneezing, hiccupping, and startling to moving limbs when touched or stimulated. Later, emotional and sexual impulses as described by Darwin come forth and,

Figure 1-10 William James set up one of the first experimental psychology laboratories in the world. His laboratory was at Harvard University. His approach is associated with functionalism.

with experience, humans begin to modify and even create situations for bringing forth instinctual experiences. In the final analysis, these impulses are used in the service of human purposes and goals. Thus, you yell at a football game to bring forth impulses in your team to make them play better and to confuse their opponents. Overall, James's functional psychology had a large influence on the development of psychology in America.

CONCEPT CHECK

- Three early discoveries in the period covered by the 1700s to the 1900s were cited as being important in paving the way for the new science of psychology. Who were the primary scientists working in each area and what were their major contributions?
    - The brain and body use electrical impulses.
    - Language is composed of two processes and they can be located in the brain.
    - Perception is a constructive process.
- What are the primary aspects of Charles Darwin's theory of evolution? How were the concepts of variation, natural selection, and sexual selection critical to Darwin's theory? How does the idea of human evolution fit into Darwin's thinking?
- Which two scientists are considered to be pioneers in the beginnings of a scientific psychology? What were their seminal contributions to the science of psychology?

20th-century Trends in Psychology

At the beginning of the 20th century, there were a number of approaches used to understand human behavior and experience. You will come to learn in more depth about many of these approaches in the specific chapters of this book. The experimental approaches began with an emphasis on how external stimuli became internal sensations. This was followed by an emphasis on mechanisms. That is, how is information learned and how is it forgotten? Further questions looked to how behavior is generated. A somewhat separate focus was on mental disorders and their treatment. Let us now turn to some of these trends in the 20th century.

Behaviorism and the Empirical Study of Observable Behavior

At the beginning of the 1900s, **behaviorism** adopted a strict form of empiricism, the idea that knowledge should be derived through our sensory processes. The idea was that psychology could become a science like physics, but all that should be studied is observable behavior. This was in direct opposition to the use of introspection. This meant that internal processes such as thoughts, images, emotions, and consciousness would not be a part of psychology. It also meant that brain processes were not a focus.

Thus, such concepts as motivation, consciousness, or awareness could not be studied since these processes cannot be directly observed. Behaviorism also carried with it a philosophical position that all behavior is learned. Thus, learning became an important focus of behaviorism.

One of the individuals who is often seen as a forerunner of behaviorism is Ivan Pavlov (1849–1936). Pavlov was a Russian physiologist and medical doctor who won a Nobel Prize in 1904 for his research on digestion. Pavlov is best known in the United States for his demonstration that dogs could be conditioned to salivate by pairing food with a sound such as a bell. After a number of these pairings, the bell alone would produce salivation in the dog. This came to be called *classical conditioning*, which you will learn about in the chapter on learning.

Another person you will read about in the chapter on learning is Edward Thorndike (1874–1949). At about the same time as Pavlov, Thorndike was researching how animals escape from a puzzle box to obtain food. Thorndike would deprive the animals of food so that they were hungry when placed in the puzzle box. He noticed that the animals would make a number of movements until they pushed a lever on the floor or pulled a cord that released the door and allowed the animal to eat. This came to be known as *trial and error learning*. Both Pavlov and Thorndike carefully examined the behaviors and their timing that led to new behaviors.

In 1913, John Watson (1878–1958) published a paper in *Psychological Review* with the title "Psychology as the behaviorist views it." In this paper, Watson emphasized that psychology should only concern itself with observable behavior and give up all attempts to describe consciousness or any internal process. In this paper Watson also emphasized that psychology should focus on the prediction and control of behavior. This led to an overemphasis on the environmental stimuli that were capable of producing behavior and learning. In particular, Watson suggested that psychological processes should be studied in terms of a *stimulus* and a *response*. As you will see in later chapters, behaviorists said that all human behavior, including mental disorders, were learned. Watson's career changed drastically in 1920 when Johns Hopkins University asked him to resign for having an affair with a graduate student. Following this scandal, he became an advertising executive.

Following Watson, B. F. Skinner (1904–1990) became the voice of behaviorism for a large part of the 20th century. His research involved the nature of the learning process in a variety of different animals. One common apparatus, which has come to be known as the *Skinner box*, allowed an animal, often a rat or pigeon, to press a lever to receive food. Skinner would reduce the animal's food intake so that they would be hungry before they were placed in the Skinner box. Skinner then carefully measured the manner in which the animal would learn to press a lever in the box and receive food. One important idea is that behaviors that are followed by rewards (*reinforcement*) will be increased. This came to be called *operant conditioning* and will be discussed in the chapter on learning. Skinner saw almost all human behavior, including the learning of language and the development of mental disorders, as controlled by the laws of learning.

Gestalt Psychology

In Germany a movement developed that sought to offer an alternative to the structuralism based on Wundt's approach and the strong form of behaviorism seen in the United States. This alternative was called **Gestalt psychology**. The German word *Gestalt* refers to such English terms as pattern, form, structure, and a sense of the whole perception.

Figure 1-11 Figure-ground illustration in which either two faces or a vase can be seen. As you view the image, the figure and ground can change depending on what is seen.

Whereas structuralism suggests that a process can be understood as an addition of its parts, Gestalt psychology suggested that the whole is always greater than the sum of its parts. Three important developers of this approach were Max Wertheimer (1880–1943), Kurt Koffka (1886–1941), and Wolfgang Köhler (1887–1967).

As you will see in the chapter on sensation and perception, one important area of Gestalt research was perception. When we look at an object, we tend to see it in certain ways. For example, when you look at **Figure 1-11**, you will either see two faces or one vase. You cannot see both at the same time. What you are focusing on is referred to as the *figure* and the other as the *ground*. One clear message of Gestalt psychology is that perception as well as other cognitive processes rely on more than just what is in the environment. Each person brings a perspective to what they see. There is a dynamic rather than fixed response to our ability to create experiences. One such dynamic process is the *phi phenomenon*. This is the situation in which two fixed lights, such as those seen on railroad crossing signs, can appear to move in between one and the other as they blink. Clearly, in this situation the person is seeing more than what is there in the environment. Other Gestalt perspectives will be discussed in the chapter on sensation and perception.

Cognitive Psychology

By the 1960s, a number of psychologists saw behaviorism as too limiting in the topics that psychology studied. These psychologists sought to understand how thinking, attention, perception, problem solving, and other such internal processes influence both human reasoning and action. This approach came to be called **cognitive psychology**. An important book, *Cognitive Psychology*, was published in 1967 by Ulric Neisser that helped to establish the field.

The cognitive perspective offered a broader approach to understanding human behavior and experience. With behaviorism, the emphasis was on behavior, whereas cognitive psychology also included knowing and reasoning. For example, the Massachusetts Institute of Technology (MIT) linguist Noam Chomsky pointed out that children can understand sentences as well as produce sentences they have never heard before. This would be impossible if you learned language through just learning one word at a time. Infants also show predictable patterns of language learning and other forms of development that cannot be explained by behaviorism. Others have pointed out that animals and humans have spatial maps in their mind that they can use to navigate in their world. Birds and butterflies are known to be able to migrate long distances over areas that they have never seen before. All of these examples show that humans and other animals are able to use mental resources beyond those learned through operant or classical conditioning.

At the same time that psychologists were designing experiments to understand how humans perceive, reason, and make actions, computers were being developed. This led a number of researchers to ask if our cognitive abilities could be understood in terms of computer processing. For some, they looked at the input components, the memory components, and the processing components that led to an output. This came to be called the *information processing approach*. Researchers also went in the other direction and asked whether computers could simulate the way in which the human mind processes information. This developed into the field of *artificial intelligence*.

Near the end of the 20th century, technological developments began to allow scientists to see what was actually happening in the brain during cognitive processing. Such brain imaging techniques allowed researchers to ask totally different types of questions. For example, it was possible to study what happens in the brain when a person hears a noun as opposed to a verb. Areas such as emotionality could also be studied by examining cortical reactions to emotional facial expressions in others. Brain imaging techniques allowed psychology to have a more precise alternative to self-report or introspection techniques. The addition of cognitive psychology with brain imaging and other physiological techniques came to be called **cognitive neuroscience** that is an important aspect of this book.

Development of a Clinical Psychology

Although humans have created theories of mental disorders for centuries, it was Sigmund Freud (1856–1939) who influenced early thinking in **clinical psychology**. His work and that of others became known as the **psychodynamic perspective**. This perspective is based on the idea that psychological problems are manifestations of internal mental conflicts and that conscious awareness of those conflicts is a key to recovery. The psychodynamic approach emphasized clinical observation rather than experimental procedures.

By the beginning of the 20th century, there was an understanding that psychological processes were an important source of information concerning mental illness. The Paris physician Jean-Martin Charcot (1825–1893) studied individuals who would show problems hearing, seeing, or feeling pain without any underlying physical problems. Sigmund Freud had worked with Charcot in Paris and observed individuals with hysteria. In this disorder, the experience, such as not feeling pain in a limb or having difficulty hearing, did not match the underlying physiology. For example, with *glove amnesia* the person would not feel pain in the area of the fingers that would be covered by a glove even when pricked with a pin. What makes this a psychological process is that the lack of sensation does not correspond to the location of nerves in the human hand. This meant that the pain experience could not have a totally physiological cause. These types of experiences led Freud to seek psychological explanations for the cause and treatment of mental disorders.

Freud was an enthusiastic reader of Darwin and credited his interest in science to an early reading of Darwin. A number of Freud's ideas can be seen as coming from Darwin (Ellenberger, 1970; Sulloway, 1979). Although Freud incorporated Darwin's emphasis on instinct into his work, he emphasized sexuality over natural selection. For Freud, the sexual instinct became the major driving force for human life and interaction. Freud was also influenced by the suggestion of the neurologist Hughlings Jackson that in our brains we find more primitive brain areas underlying more advanced ones. The more primitive areas are related to breathing, sleeping as well as primary emotional reactions. We all experience this when we make a plan to diet but feel the pangs of hunger. Thus, it is quite possible for the psyche to be in conflict with itself or at least to have different layers of the brain representing different processes.

To understand the nature of these more primitive processes, Freud looked to the description of dreams and wish fulfillment. One of his works, *The Project for a Scientific Psychology*, utilized these ideas and sought to place psychology on a firm scientific basis (see Pribram & Merton, 1976). The *Project* was based on three separate ideas. The first was *reflex processes*. For example, organisms withdraw when confronted with unpleasant stimuli. Freud extended this idea to cognitive and emotional processes to suggest that, mentally, humans avoid ideas or feelings that are unpleasant to them. The second idea Freud used was *associationism*. That is to say, experiences that are presented together in time will be mentally called forth together. Freud suggested that if as a child you experience a fearful situation such as falling out of a car, then riding in a car could make you feel fearful or anxious. The third idea is that the nervous system is capable of retaining and discharging energy. Freud later identified this energy as *libido* or sexual energy.

Freud's approach to treatment was based on the search for ideas and emotions that are in conflict and the manner in which the person has relationships with other people. His specific treatment came to be called **psychoanalysis**. One basic procedure was free association in which an individual lay on a couch with the therapist behind him and said whatever came to mind. It was the therapist's job to help the client connect ideas and feelings that he was not aware of. One thing Freud was searching for was connections within the person's psyche when external stimulation was reduced. To reduce stimulation he had individuals lie on a couch with no one to look at. Dreams were also analyzed in this way since they are produced outside of daily life and external stimulation. Consistent with others in this time period, Freud often described his ideas in terms of case studies.

In the 1950s, Carl Rogers brought the **humanistic perspective** to the forefront by creating **client-centered therapy or person-centered therapy**. He was also one of the first psychologists to record therapy sessions so that they could be used for research. Rogers emphasized the theme of *human potential* by saying that psychotherapy is a releasing of an already existing capacity in a potentially competent individual. In fact, it was the interaction with the therapist that allowed for the person to experience himself or herself and come to understand his or her potential. In this way, Rogers emphasized the relationship between the therapist and client as a critical key to effective therapy.

Overall, there are three key characteristics of the client-centered approach. The first is *empathic understanding*. As the therapist reflects back what the client says, the client begins to experience their innermost thoughts and feelings. The second is what Rogers referred to as *unconditional positive regard*. That is, the therapist accepts what the client says without trying to change the client. For some individuals who had experienced significant others in their lives as critical of them, to be accepted by the therapist is a new experience. The third characteristic is for the therapist to show *genuineness* and *congruence*. In this way, the therapist models what interactions between two real people could be like. Other individuals such as Abraham Maslow who helped to develop the humanistic movement will be discussed in later chapters of this book. More recently, the humanistic approach can be seen in the field of *positive psychology* that focuses on the strengths of individuals.

In the 1970s, there was a combining of the behavioral approach and its emphasis on careful research with the cognitive approach with its emphasis on reasoning. The result was cognitive behavioral psychology. The **cognitive behavioral perspective** suggests that dysfunctional thinking is common to all psychological disturbances. By learning in therapy how to understand one's thinking, it is possible to change the way one thinks as well as one's emotional state and behaviors. One basic feature of our thinking is that it is automatic. Ideas just pop into our mind such as, "I can't solve this" or "It is all my fault." A number of therapies based on cognitive principles along with behavioral interventions have been shown to be effective (Beck, 2019; Beck & Bredemeier, 2016).

In summary, every person with a mental disorder can be considered from two perspectives—the person responding to his or her own symptoms and mental health professionals treating the disorder. There is now evidence that both aspects are important and that a crucial aspect of treatment is the willingness of the person to be actively involved in his or her own treatment. There are currently three broad approaches for the psychological treatment of mental disorders: the psychodynamic perspective, the humanistic perspective, and the cognitive behavioral perspective. They were developed somewhat independently and often in opposition to one another. Today, each of these three approaches have integrated techniques developed by the other approaches. With this integration, there is also an emphasis on research to show that the treatment is effective.

Beginning in the 1950s and 1960s, there was a movement to determine the effectiveness of both medical and psychological treatments in a scientific manner. Researchers and clinicians began to focus more on approaches and principles for which there was scientific evidence. This approach is referred to as *empirically supported therapies*. This led to developing effective treatments for particular disorders as well as greater integration of techniques from the three different approaches as well as from other perspectives. Today, there is a strong emphasis on using treatment for which there is strong scientific evidence.

There has also been a movement to integrate various approaches in psychology with information from other disciplines. In a paper published in 1977 in the scientific journal *Science*, George Engel introduced the term **biopsychosocial** (Engel, 1977). Biopsychosocial refers to biological, psychological, and social variables. An integrative perspective that includes all three of these domains can offer a fuller picture of human behavior and experience.

In terms of clinical treatment, Engel suggested that those with a medical disorder or mental illness should not be understood from only a single perspective. For Engel, the treatment of a disorder required more than just a biological explanation and treatment. Diabetes is a medical disorder but it is also related to how the person eats and exercises. Likewise, depression and anxiety can be influenced by social and emotional factors. Thus, it is necessary to see the signs and symptoms of the disorder in a larger context. Otherwise, one has a limited perspective that ignores the social, psychological, and behavior dimensions of any disorder.

The biopsychosocial perspective has been an important impetus in psychology. More current perspectives have also emphasized the important role of culture in a person's life (Leong, 2014). As a health care psychologist, for example, you would want to know more about an individual than just the symptoms that the person describes. This could include his or her family life, work conditions, and cultural practices as well as eating habits and exercise. Initially, this led researchers and health professionals to ask questions on three levels: the biological, the psychological, and the social. Since the 1970s researchers have come a long way in understanding how various levels ranging from genetics to culture interact with one another in a complex manner. The box The World Is Your Laboratory—Psychology Takes Place Within a Culture describes the way American culture has influenced our understanding of mental disorders and their treatment.

The World Is Your Laboratory—Psychology Takes Place Within a Culture

Psychology and other sciences are influenced by the culture in which they exist. In fact, many individuals adopt the values of their society without realizing the alternatives. During the Middle Ages, the authority of the church determined what type of questions could be asked and what type of answers could be given. As psychology became a laboratory science at the beginning of the 20th century, psychology sought to answer questions critical to American society. Some of these included the types of schooling needed for specific children in terms of ability and intelligence. With the beginning of World War I, selection procedures were developed to match a person's skills with the jobs the military required. One critical question for society has been how to understand and treat individuals with a mental disorder.

American culture has continued a dynamic tension that has strongly influenced the application of psychology to those with mental illness. On the one hand, we seek to take care of those who are not able to take care of themselves, for example helping the homeless and those with mental disorders. On the other hand, there is also a tradition in America related to our settlement of the frontier—the vast lands that our pioneer forefathers and mothers found before them. This is represented by the pioneer or cowboy spirit in which we support the individual's right to do what he or she wants and to live the type of life desired. One area in which this dynamic tension plays out is our level of willingness to support local and national government programs designed to help others.

During the first half of the 20th century, state mental hospitals were the main source of treatment and care for those with mental disorders in the United States (see Fisher, Geller, & Pandiani, 2009; Torrey, 1997 for overviews). By the 1950s, there were more than a half million individuals in these hospitals. However, during the 1950s and 1960s a number of events occurred that changed the way individuals with mental disorders were treated in the United States.

One significant event was the introduction of antipsychotic medication. Prior to this time, individuals with serious mental disorders such as schizophrenia needed a high level of care and protection. With the introduction of medications that would help treat the disorder, it was possible for some of these individuals to live outside the hospital.

Another significant event was the Community Mental Health Act of 1963, which was signed by President John F. Kennedy. President Kennedy suggested to Congress that all but a small portion of those in mental hospitals could be treated in the community. The basic idea was that community mental health centers would offer a variety of programs to those with mental illness. However, the community facilities for those with mental illness were never fully funded or were not even built.

Although the population of the United States increased by 100 million between 1955 and 1994, the number of individuals in mental hospitals decreased from 550,239 to 71,619. During this time the United States went from a country who used institutions for the treatment of mental illness to one who emphasized deinstitutionalization as its policy.

For some of the individuals today who would have been placed in a hospital in the 1950s, their quality of life in the community is much better than it would have been. However, for many individuals, the ideals of the community mental health movement were never fulfilled. This left many individuals not receiving the type of treatment they needed. Some of these individuals have found themselves homeless and on the streets. Others, who were disruptive or led to concerns in the community, found themselves in jails and prisons with little mental health treatment and care. In the United

States, there are now three times more seriously mentally ill individuals in jails and prisons than there are in hospitals (Torrey et al., 2010).

The dynamic tension between taking care of others and being independent becomes clear when we see homeless individuals in our community who have a mental illness. This raises a number of questions. Can we take these individuals off the street if they don't want to be taken to a shelter? Can we force them to take their medication if this would help them function better in our community, but they do not want the medication? Should it be the police or health care workers who work with these individuals?

Thought Question: What is the dynamic tension in American culture concerning understanding and treating individuals with mental illness? What do you think is the best approach?

Women at the Beginning of Scientific Psychology

At the beginning of the 1900s, American society, like other societies, had specific views on the roles of women and men in society. For many in society, the role of women was in the home as mother and wife. In spite of this, in 1903 Mary Calkins, Christine Ladd-Franklin, and Margaret Washburn were identified as among the 50 most important American psychologists (Fancher, 1996).

Mary Calkins (1863–1930) wrote an introductory psychology textbook in 1901. She set up one of the earliest research laboratories in America at Wellesley College in 1891. She became a professor and published more than 100 scientific articles. Mary Calkins was also the first female president of the American Psychological Association. However, the path to her success was not easy. With some difficulty, as a student she went to William James's lectures at Harvard. When she submitted her PhD dissertation, the psychology faculty approved it, but the administration of Harvard refused to give a PhD degree to a woman.

Christine Ladd-Franklin (1847–1930) became an expert on color vision. She published a critical evolutionary theory that suggested that sensitivity to blue light came before that to red and green. Today, we know that the genes associated with red–green sensitivity are located on a different chromosome than those associated with blue. Like the other pioneering women, she completed her PhD in logic and mathematics at Johns Hopkins University in 1882 before psychology was available. However, since women were not awarded formal degrees at that time, her degree was not formally awarded until 1926 when she was 78 years old.

As noted, Margaret Washburn (1871–1939) was the first woman to be awarded a PhD in psychology in America. She initially went to Columbia University in New York City, but after the first year it became clear that she might not be allowed to receive a PhD there. In 1892, she moved to Cornell and became the first woman to receive a PhD in psychology. After this, she taught at Vassar College and studied animal behavior. She was also interested in movement and mental imagery. She was the second woman to be president of the American Psychological Association.

The role of women in psychology has changed drastically in the last 100 years. In 2018, the number of women who received PhDs in psychology represented 71.4% of all psychology PhDs (http://www.nsf.gov/statistics/srvydoctorates/#tabs-2). This is a change from only a few women at the beginning of the 1900s to about 10% before 1960. Beginning in 1960, there was an increase in women receiving PhDs in psychology every decade until the current rate of about 70%. As you will see throughout this book, today there is a large number of women performing significant psychological research and contributing to psychology as health care professionals.

African American Psychologists Who Shaped our Perspectives

During the first part of the last century, there were many obstacles that made the availability of a college education to non-white populations extremely difficult. Between 1876 and 1920, only 12 African Americans earned a PhD in any field, whereas some 10,000 Caucasian individuals did. In spite of this, Francis Cecil Sumner (1895–1954) became the first African American to be granted a PhD in psychology in the United States. He graduated in 1920 from Clark University and conducted research on race relations, equality, and the psychology of religion (Holliday, 2009). Sumner went on to chair the newly established psychology department at Howard University in Washington, D.C. in 1928. He remained as department chair until 1954.

The first African American woman to receive a doctorate in psychology was Inez Prosser who received an Ed.D. in educational psychology from the University of Cincinnati in 1933 (Benjamin, Henry, & McMahon, 2005). Prior to this, she had been involved in teaching at a number of levels. Her dissertation included issues that would be critical to the later Supreme Court decision on integration in the school, *Brown v. Board of Education*. Unfortunately, she died in a car accident one year after finishing her dissertation at the age of 38.

The next year in 1934 Ruth Winifred Howard (Beckman) (1900–1997) received a PhD in psychology from the University of Minnesota. She wrote her dissertation of the development of triplets and continued doing work in clinical psychology throughout her life. In 1937 Alberta Banner Turner received her PhD in psychology from Ohio State University. Turner worked for the Ohio Bureau of Juvenile Affairs/Ohio Youth Commission for more than 27 years. She began as a clinician and retired as the director of research. During her years with the commission, Turner specialized in research on and treatments for juvenile delinquents, including the operation of a mobile clinic.

Kenneth Clark (1914–2005) was the first African American to become the president of the American Psychological Association in 1970. Before this in 1942, he was the first African American psychologist to be hired by City College of New York. He worked as a team with his spouse, Mamie Phipps Clark (1917–1983) who was the first African American woman to receive a PhD in psychology from Columbia University in New York. You can read more and see photos of Kenneth and Mamie Clark at http://www.apa.org/pi/oema/resources/ethnicity-health/psychologists/clark.aspx.

They performed a series of studies that examined self-esteem in children, which showed that segregation had a profound effect on Black children's self-esteem. These studies were used in the Supreme Court case, *Brown v Board of Education*, to show that segregated schools were problematic and did not benefit the students involved. This was an important use of psychological research to help inform decisions in terms of social policy.

CONCEPT CHECK

- What is the focus of Gestalt psychology? What is its specific contribution to research in perception?
- For the behaviorists, what were the critical areas of focus in psychology? On the other hand, what areas were considered out of bounds?

- What are the primary areas of interest in cognitive psychology? What contributions did this approach make to research in psychology in terms of the scope of inquiry, experimental design, and technological innovation?
- Sigmund Freud was instrumental in the beginning of clinical psychology. What are the primary ideas and techniques of his psychodynamic perspective?
- What are the three key characteristics of Carl Rogers's client-centered therapy?
- In what ways does the cognitive behavioral perspective combine the traditions of the separate behavioral and cognitive approaches?
- What are "empirically supported therapies," and what is their contribution to the field of psychology?
- What is the biopsychosocial perspective, and what is its contribution to the field of psychology?
- What were some early contributions by women in psychology? How does the changing role of women in psychology reflect broader changes in US society?
- Who were some early African American psychologists who shaped our perspectives?

The Three Major Themes of This Book

Psychology's maturing as a discipline over the past 130 years has led to many useful ways to understand and study how we humans think, act, and engage with others. These different approaches will be described, and emphasis will be placed on three major themes in this text: (1) behavior and experience, (2) neuroscience, and (3) human origins and a historical cultural perspective. Let us now look at these three themes.

What We Do and What We Experience Is Critical to Psychology

The first theme takes a ***behavioral and experiential perspective*** and relates to behaviors and experiences observed across a variety of situations. For the most part, we will consider normal situations that you experience in your everyday life. You sleep, you eat, you talk with your friends, you play, and you work. Some of you are also raising children, or serving as a caregiver to a family member. In looking at these various aspects of daily living, we will examine current ways of classifying and describing our behavior and experiences. In fact, this book is organized around these processes including memory, perception, sensation, cognition, social behavior, and so forth.

One way we interact with the world is to expect certain things to happen. If I were to ask you to read the following (in **Figure 1-12**), you would have no trouble reading "The Cat." Although the second letter in each word is exactly the same, you see it as an "H" in the first word and an "A" in the second. We make sense out of our world based on what we know and what we expect.

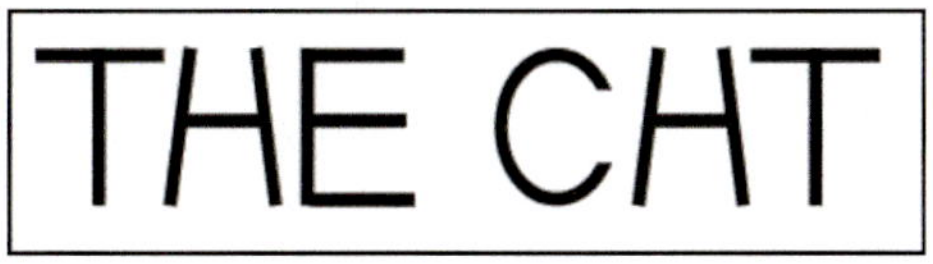

Figure 1-12 "The Cat."

Making sense of the world is what we normally do. A large part of what our brain does is to process the present and make a guess about what will happen next. If you are playing tennis or baseball, your body moves to where it expects the ball to be. We love mystery stories, especially when what we predicted would happen did not. Our brain shows a change in electrical responding when we hear "Mary had a little pizza" rather than "Mary had a little lamb."

In psychology we also consider the non-normal. One aspect of this is *diminished capacity*. You see this both in terms of brain damage and in mental illness. Later in the book, you will read some first-person reports from individuals with particular disorders. You will learn that not everyone who experiences a mental disorder will behave in the same way. You will also see how some of these individuals have restructured their world to let them live productive lives. Another important aspect of this perspective will be the manner in which particular disorders are seen throughout the world and the role culture plays in their manifestations. You will also see how the brain is involved in these disorders.

The opposite of a decreased capacity is an *increased capacity*. Some waiters in restaurants, for example, can remember orders from 10 or 20 people without writing them down. Memory loss is often thought to be a problem of aging, however, some individuals in their 80s and 90s score better on memory tests than those 30 or 40 years younger. These individuals are referred to as *SuperAgers* (Harrison, Weintraub, Mesulam, & Rogalski, 2012).

Another increased capacity is *effortless functioning*. Many of us have had the experience of playing a sport such as basketball or tennis, and everything seems to work perfectly and to require little effort. Some researchers have called the experience of effortless success as *being in the flow* or *flow states* (Csikszentmihalyi, 1990). One critical question is how to change a normal state into an extraordinary one.

In answering questions related to behavior and experience, you will be asked to consider how you are like others and how you are unique. Humans around the world seek to interact with others, seek others to mate with, and solve basic questions of adaptation. Social media also allows us to have connections that were not previously possible. However, studies from around the world show that adolescents and young adults may also feel a fear of missing out (FOMO) when they are away from their social media devices (Alt, 2015; Buglass, Binder, Betts, & Underwood, 2017; Roberts & David, 2020).

Our culture influences the pattern of interactions that we use as well as the language we speak. Although the specifics may vary by culture, there is a universal experience in terms of speaking a language, expressing emotions, and being with others. We also have similar systems that allow us to see the world and hear what is around us. Many of these systems we share with other animals. Most mammal adolescents, no matter what the species, engage in play. Both our uniqueness and our universality are important parts of psychology.

Our Brain and Body Determine What We Do and Experience

The second theme examines what we know about particular psychological experiences from the standpoint of a **neuroscience perspective**. In particular, emphasis will be placed on the structure and function of the brain as it relates to psychology. With the development of brain-imaging techniques in the last few decades, observing greater precision of brain activity is now possible.

Structure refers to which brain areas or networks are involved in a given task such as feeling afraid. We know, for example, that when you process information that is emotionally important to you, a specific brain structure called the *amygdala* becomes active. We also know that particular networks of the brain are involved in processing faces and still others in understanding and producing speech. We can also ask how changes in processes such as learning change structure. For example, you may be surprised to know that learning a new skill can actually change the manner in which neurons in your brain are connected.

Function refers to what role in your life a particular process plays. We can study the function of memory, for example, without asking which brain structures are involved. That is, we can examine how a memory influences our lives. Thus, psychology often asks questions of function. Sleep, for example, not only functions to help you feel refreshed but also to stabilize information you have learned during the day. Sleeping the night before a test after studying actually improves your memory of the information. Staying up all night to study actually may hurt your performance.

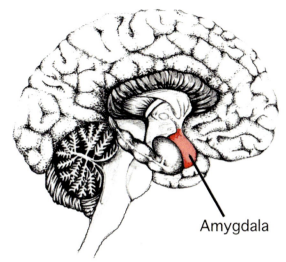

Figure 1-13 The amygdala is involved in our processing of emotional material.

The neuroscience perspective will also help us to consider how certain human processes share similar connections or networks in the brain. For example, knowing that the brain networks involved in social relationships are also involved in particular types of anxiety would help us to better characterize these processes. It may also help us scientifically to understand why most of the anxiety people experience is of a social nature. Knowing that different brain areas are involved when you pay attention from when you daydream may help us to better understand underlying mechanisms for our everyday behavior and experience.

The brain occupies a special position in human functioning. Although it weighs only a few pounds, it uses more than 20% of all the energy our body produces. As you will see later in this book, our brain devotes more of its areas to some body parts than others. How do you think your brain sees your body? That is, what would we look like if our body parts matched the size of the brain areas that control them? The answer is a small person with big hands and a large face. We have a lot of brain devoted to our hands and face but less to our legs and back. The fact that we have a thumb that can work with our fingers allows us to do fine motor tasks such as painting, sewing, or keyboarding that no other animal can do. The brain's control of our hands allows us to perform fine motor movements that you do every day with your cell phone or computer.

Not only does our brain control our movement, but also what we see. As you looked at the white triangle in the section on Perception Is a Constructive Process, you saw a white triangle. However, what you saw was literally not there—the white square in the middle. Part of what you will learn in this book is how our brain creates the world that we experience. This will also help us to understand why you hear some sounds as wonderful music and other sounds as noise. The neuroscience perspective also aids us in understanding how our sensory systems work and how they create meaning. Take a moment and look at this video (https://www.youtube.com/watch?v=2k8fHR9jKVM). Clearly what you see in terms of the person moving his lips determines what you hear. This is referred to as the *McGurk effect*.

It is through the work of brain imaging that the experiences (phantom limb, synesthesia, superior autobiographical memory, and attribution) described at the beginning of this chapter have been understood in a much richer manner. Although our brain is critical for human functioning, we also have some strange ideas about how it works, as you will see in the box: Myths and Misconceptions—You Use Only 10% of Your Brain.

> ### Myths and Misconceptions—You Use Only 10% of Your Brain
>
> Unlike some earlier times in history, most people now believe that their brain is involved in their ability to think and act. Children are told to use their brain when they do something foolish. There are various techniques online for "brain training." The popular media rushes to publish articles on how to improve our abilities.
>
> However, one of the most often repeated claims, that we use only 10% of our brain, is a myth. Movies and TV shows have used the 10% idea as a premise, treating this claim as "fact." Self-help books repeat this idea. The implication is that if we tap into those parts of our brain that are unused, we could be more creative, think better, and accomplish more.
>
> As wonderful as the idea that we could use 90% more of our brain is, there is no research to support it. Our brains are complex. Our brains do use more of our energy than other organs. Different networks of the brain are used for doing different types of tasks. Yet, 90% of the brain is not available to make us superhuman. In fact, during your day, you probably use close to all of your brain.
>
> If the 90% idea is wrong, where did the idea come from? Barry Beyerstein of the Brain Behavior Laboratory at Simon Fraser University in Vancouver, Canada, has sought to find the source of the idea (Beyerstein, 1999). He points initially to a statement by William James. James suggested that we don't achieve all of our potential or use all of our resources. This is not a statement that most people would disagree with. However, in the 1930s, there was an individual named Dale Carnegie who wrote self-help books. One of his best sellers was *How to Win Friends and Influence People*. The writer, broadcaster, and adventurer Lowell Thomas, who made Lawrence of Arabia famous, wrote the foreword to Dale Carnegie's book. In the foreword to this book, James was misquoted to suggest we use only 10% of our brain and the myth became part of the American landscape. Dale Carnegie repeats the 10% idea in some of his later books. Others also attribute the 10% idea to Albert Einstein, although no one at the Einstein archives can find it in his papers.
>
> What is interesting from a psychological point of view is that once a myth is out there and continues to be repeated, it takes on a life of its own. As with the claim that we only use 10% of our brain, it does not matter whether it is true or not, people continue to repeat it.
>
> **Thought Question**: Why do you think it is so difficult for us as humans to give up an incorrect idea?

Human Behavior and Experience Developed Over a Long Period of Time

The third theme asks a much broader scientific question and examines psychological processes from a ***human origins and historical cultural perspective***. In adopting this perspective, we can think about how certain ways of behaving and seeing the world might be adaptive.

We can also think about how the experiences of those who came before us might have influenced how our nervous system functions. It is not often that we think about how our ancestors behaved and reacted to situations. Yet, our ability to form social relationships, to help others, to have children, to survive in different environments as well as consider ourselves, others, and our place in the world can be seen from a human origins and historical cultural perspective. These and many other abilities are directly related to our history as human beings. For example, look at the pictures below.

If I were to ask you what you see, you would probably say two pictures of a woman. At first glance most people see the pictures of the former 1980s British Prime Minister, Margaret Thatcher, as being the same. However, if you turn them upside down, you see something very different. What this suggests is that from a human origins and historical cultural perspective, our perceptual system evolved to recognize human faces including emotional expressions in one orientation, the way in which we normally see another's face—right side up.

Additionally, if you consider that over evolutionary time light came from one major source, the sun, we might assume that our sensory system evolved to reflect this fact. If we see an object with light on top and a shadow on the bottom, we would interpret the image to reflect a ball-like structure (Figure 1-15). What if we viewed the same object upside down? Turn Figure 1-15 upside down and see. What do we now see?

In terms of our evolutionary history with the sun above us, shadows would only occur in one way. For example, if we were looking into a hole in the side of a rock or hill, where would the shadow be? Looking at the figure again, this is indeed what we see. We see a ball or convex surface if the light is on the top and a hole or concave surface if the light is on the bottom. Somewhat amazing since both objects are exactly the same except for rotation! Turn the page upside down and watch your perception change. However, it becomes less amazing when we realize that our sensory systems evolved in relation to the environment in which we lived.

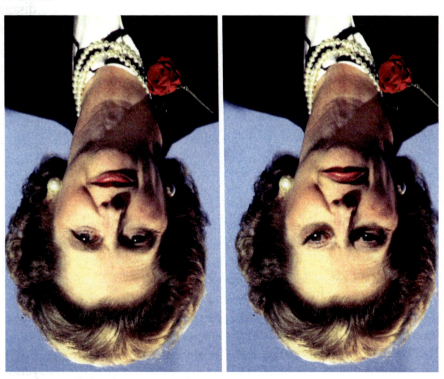

Figure 1-14 Pictures of the former British Prime Minister Margaret Thatcher. Turn them upside down and notice what you see.

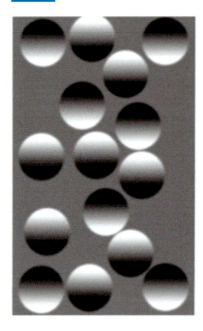

Figure 1-15 Multiple balls with shadow on top or bottom.

The human origins and historical cultural perspective also gives us a way to think about cultural factors. Our culture has a strong influence on us. Sometimes humans all over the world do things in very similar ways and other times specific cultures develop a different way of doing things. We all wear clothes, for example. Yet, the clothes in each culture are often different. Humans in almost every culture dance. However, the nature of dancing is very different. What you will see is that both the similarities and differences in cultures can be related to human origins. Understanding cultural and universal factors is an important part of this perspective. The answer we will discover is that our genes and our environment including our culture function together in a close-knit manner.

We can also think about how humans are both similar and different to other animals with whom we share a variety of genetic and physiological mechanisms. For example, are we the only species to laugh, use tools, use a napkin, feel depressed, or experience anxiety? The answer appears to be no. Research suggests that humans are not the only species to use tools. For example, a number of primates use sticks to pull termites from their nests. They then eat the termites. How about using napkins when eating? Surprisingly, orangutans use leaves as napkins. Thus, many of the characteristics we see in humans are also found in other species.

The human origins and historical cultural perspective leads to some interesting questions related to psychology. For example, given the evolutionary process of survival of the fittest, we ask why particular mental disorders continue to exist. Individuals with schizophrenia, for example, generally have fewer children than those without the disorder. Over long periods of time with fewer children, we would expect to see fewer people with schizophrenia. That is, if schizophrenia is related to genetic processes, we might expect that schizophrenia would have gradually disappeared over our evolutionary history. However, this is not the case.

We can also consider if schizophrenia is related to the environment in which one lives. In fact, schizophrenia occurs at approximately the same percentage (approximately 1% of the population) throughout the world in both developed and developing countries. Thus, such factors as pollution or foods eaten would probably not be related to schizophrenia. As we will see later, this suggests that schizophrenia is an old disorder that has existed since humans migrated out of Africa some 80,000 to 100,000 years ago. That is, if a disorder is found everywhere in the world in equal proportions, then one alternative is that it is a disorder that humans shared some 100,000 years ago in Africa. It also raises the possibility that the genes related to schizophrenia may be associated with more positive, survival-enhancing human traits. Some researchers have suggested, for example, that there exists a relation between families who have a member with schizophrenia and creativity.

These three themes—behavior and experience, neuroscience, and the human origins and historical cultural perspective—give us important perspectives for thinking about psychology. Behavior and experience are the basic data of psychology. The neurosciences help us to understand the mechanisms underlying our experiences and actions. The human origins and historical cultural perspective on the other hand gives us a more functional answer to questions concerning our behavior and experience. That is to say, this perspective helps us to consider "why" we act or feel certain ways and the advantage of doing so. Overall, we begin with the basic data of behavior and experience and ask what the mechanisms that produce these are and what function do they serve.

Levels of Analysis

As we explore together the themes of behavior and experience, neuroscience contributions, and the human origins and historical cultural perspective as related to psychology, you will see that we will move across a variety of **levels of analysis**. In specific, you will be introduced to the level of the individual, the level above that which will include our social groups, society, and culture, and the levels that make up our biological processes. These levels or units of analysis should be seen as ways of understanding human behavior and experience. This book will consider an *integrative approach* that draws on a number of these levels and asks how they interact with one another. No one level should be seen as more important than another. Which level is emphasized depends on the specific psychological process that we wish to describe and research. These levels are shown in **Table 1-1**.

Although it is useful to think in terms of biology, psychology, and social aspects, there are number of other factors that influence us. These range from a cultural understanding to a genetic level. Higher level understandings will include *culture and society* as well as our social relationships. Some psychologists emphasize cultural psychology in their research and seek to understand how culture is related to psychological processes. One such topic would be the manner in which mental disorders are understood in different cultures.

Other psychologists emphasize our *social relationships* with one another. This is the field of *social psychology*, which includes topics such as how we perceive others including stereotyping, prejudice, and discrimination. Historically, social psychologists have also studied what would make us conform to or follow the orders of others. As you will see in the chapter on social processes, how we think we will act in a social situation is not always how we actually do act.

From there we can look at what makes up the social level, which is the *individual level*. This level includes our actions as well as our experiences. We can then ask what makes up the individual in terms of sensory, motor, emotional, and cognitive systems. The field of cognitive psychology focuses on what factors influence what we pay attention to as well

Table 1-1 Level of analysis 1.

Level of Culture and Social Groups	Culture
	Social relations
Level of the Individual	Individual as person
	Cognitive, emotional, motor, and instinctual processes
Level of Biological Processes	Physiological processes of the central and peripheral nervous systems
	Neurons and cortical networks
	Genetics

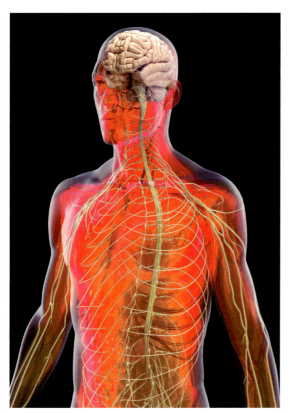

Figure 1-16 Physiological processes of the central and peripheral nervous systems—how does our body work?

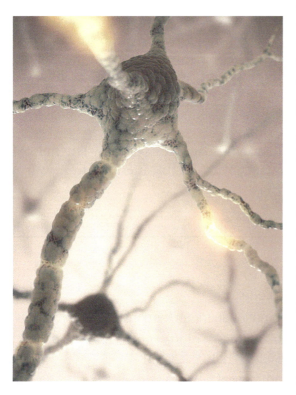

Figure 1-17 Neurons and cortical networks—how does our brain process information?

how we learn and remember information. In this book, we will examine each of these topics as they influence our behavior and experience. We will also consider what happens when cognitive, emotional, or motor processes do not function in an optimal manner. This is the field of *clinical psychology*. An important part of clinical psychology examines how humans may misperceive their world as well as how they internally talk with themselves. Treatment approaches or therapies that seek to correct these misinterpretations is another part of clinical psychology.

From there we can ask how each of these systems works and look at the *physiological processes* that make up our central and peripheral nervous systems. This will take us to the cellular level, and you will see how the neuron forms the basis of information transfer. In psychology, the study of these levels is referred to as *biopsychology*, *physiological psychology*, and *behavioral neuroscience*.

The most basic level you will be introduced to in this book is the *genetic level*, which in turn will require us to understand how environmental conditions influence genetic processes. You will also learn about a related process, *epigenetics*, in which genes can be turned on or off by the environment and passed on to future generations without actually changing the basic genetic structure. Historically, this level has been the domain of *behavioral genetics*. Studies of twins who share similar genetic information has been an important part of this area.

In order to help focus their work, scientists often focus primarily on one of these levels of analysis. However, more recent research has shown the value of drawing from more than one level. For example, both cultural and social psychology researchers have begun to show the value of using brain imaging or genetics in their research. This book will consider an *integrative approach* that draws on a number of these units or levels and asks how they interact with one another. Sometimes we just focus on a few of these levels as illustrated in the box: Applying Psychological Science—The Use of Psychological Principles to Improve Learning.

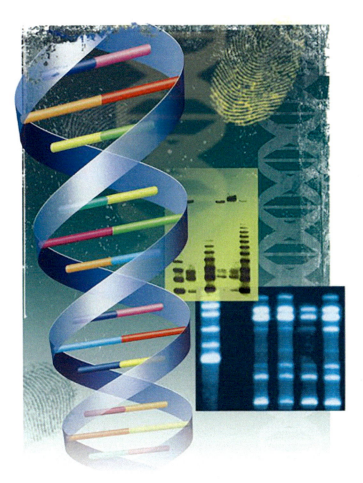

Figure 1-18 Genetic—what are the possibilities of our structure and experience?

Applying Psychological Science—The Use of Psychological Principles to Improve Learning

We all have ideas about what to do if we want to improve our ability to learn new information. As you will learn in this book, we don't always pay attention when we do common tasks such as driving a car, reading a newspaper, or reading a book. Perhaps you can think of times when you space out when you are doing a task. Ask your friends what they read on Facebook or in a newspaper earlier in the day. You may be surprised how many people can't answer with certainty.

Thus, reading a textbook as well as doing any task successfully requires some strategies. These include paying attention and testing yourself. Some people think that if they learn it in small bits, they can remember it better. That may be true if you do not try to learn lots of isolated facts. As you see in the chapter on memory and learning, it is easier to remember information that has meaning to you rather than just isolated facts. It is also true that if you are able to connect different ideas you read into a larger system, you will remember it better. Writing down what you have just read will help you to organize the material.

As you will also see in the chapter on memory, just reading a page of this book does not mean that you have learned it. You need to rehearse it and ask yourself what you just read. Some people find that telling another person the important points of a section helps them to know what they have retained. You can also do this with yourself. To help, you will find concept checks at the end of sections and review questions at the end of the chapter. In this way you can check whether you need to reread certain sections.

What if you have an exam? Some people think that if they stay up all night and read the material, they will know it best. But, is this true?

The answer to what works best is somewhat surprising. The best thing to do is to go to bed. In a number of studies, psychologists have shown that sleep is one important way to enhance learning and memory (Chambers & Payne, 2015). This is true for a number of types of learning including the cognitive material you would learn for a test as well as learning motor skills such as playing video games.

One study that was conducted in the evening had individuals learn word pairs that have no meaning in themselves (Plihal & Born, 1997). For example, if you were in the experiment, you might have learned tree–table, book–bicycle, and video–clouds. To test your ability to remember these at a later time, you would be given the first word of the pair and asked to report the second. After the person was able to remember 60% of the word pairs, half of the participants were allowed to sleep and half stayed awake. After three hours, both groups were tested again. Those individuals that were allowed to sleep were better able to remember the word pairs than those that stayed awake. Further, the greatest benefit of sleep is seen if the words learned are related to one another (Payne, Chambers, & Kensinger, 2012). These and other studies using different types of cognitive material suggest that studying for a test and then going to sleep will benefit your learning.

Not everything you learn is made up of words. Learning images of natural landscapes also improved with a period of sleep (Takashima et al., 2006). Even more interesting, better learning with sleep was still seen after a 30-day lapse from the previous learning. Another study asked people to imagine they were standing on a balcony of an art museum and to imagine ten objects placed in various locations around them (Plihal & Born, 1999). Again, those who were allowed to sleep performed better.

If you have an emotional reaction to what you read or see, you remember that information better than if you have a neutral reaction. However, if you sleep after seeing or reading the emotional information, your learning is improved even more.

As you will see throughout this book, psychologists have performed extensive research related to how individuals learn new information that you can apply to your own life. Some of these studies have been summarized on the Learning Scientists website (https://www.learningscientists.org/).

Thought Question: How can you use the information presented to improve your performance on exams?

Different Psychologists Focus on Different Levels of Analysis

Psychologists are diverse in their areas of interest. They are also diverse in the methods they use. An important part of this book is to introduce you to this diversity in terms of topics of study and levels of analysis. Even if you do not plan to become a psychologist, psychological principles can be useful for understanding your work. This includes making software that is user friendly, improving safety on the part of drivers and pilots, working with social media, improving public policy to involve more community involvement, working with individuals in the health care system to improve their own health, and working with data presentations. Occupations ranging from athletics, to business, to education, to acting, to farming, to literature and art can all utilize psychological principles.

In each chapter of this book, you will learn from psychologists who have focused on different aspects of behavior and experience. As you will see, psychology is a tremendously varied field. Psychologists conduct both applied and basic research. They teach in colleges and universities. Other psychologists serve as mental health professionals. They may be involved in the assessment and treatment of human functioning including mental disorders. These psychologists seek to help individuals lead a productive life whether it is to perform better in sports or to change problems such as anxious or depressive feelings. Psychologists may also work for large corporations. A psychologist was probably involved in determining how easy it is for you to use your cell phone or to find your way around a website. Other psychologists help the courts determine how to interview children and adolescents.

Figure 1-19 shows where psychologists who have a doctoral degree work. As you can see about 25% work in a university or college setting and an equal number work in health services. About 16% work for the government or the Veterans Administration. A little over 10% work in business or the nonprofit sector. About 8% work in schools and non-college educational institutions. Approximately 6% work in medical schools, and another 6% work as independent professionals such as those who offer assessment and treatment of mental disorders.

Clinical psychologists assess and treat mental, emotional, and behavioral disorders. They may focus on a particular disorder such as anxiety or schizophrenia. They may also focus on particular groups such as adolescents who consider suicide, or older individuals who are seeking new experiences, or groups that feel left out by society. Counseling psychologists overlap with clinical psychologists and will often be found working in such locations as university mental health centers.

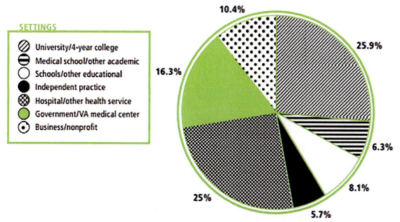

Figure 1-19 The American Psychological Association has surveyed the careers available in psychology and described these on their website (http://www.apa.org/careers/resources/guides/careers.pdf).

School psychologists work in elementary and secondary schools where they assess student abilities and make recommendations for improving the learning environment. Developmental psychologists focus on how individuals develop and the manner in which they see the world. Although initially this area of psychology focused on children, there is currently a lifespan approach that follows individuals from conception to old age.

Industrial/Organizational (I/O) psychologists apply psychological principles to the workplace. Their focus may be helping to choose the leadership of the organization, improve productivity and creativity, reduce workplace accidents, and improve health in the workers, as well as prepare workers for organization change. Whereas I/O psychologists focus on the workplace, community psychologists focus on the community. They seek to influence changes in the community that will improve the well-being of those who live in the community. They examine the manner in which political, cultural, and environmental factors influence the life of the community. They may work with local governments to improve the day-to-day lives of those who live and work there.

Sport psychologists help athletes improve their abilities by helping them to reduce anxiety and focus on their skills. They may also be involved in assessing sports injuries such as concussion. Other psychologists help individuals reduce their anxiety and improve their abilities in a number of different areas where performance is also important including music and the theater.

All psychologists use psychological research to inform their decisions. In the chapter on social processes, you will see how social psychologists study our relationships with others including how we think and feel about people who are different from us. Health psychologists focus on how psychological factors interact with our behaviors and emotions to influence our health status. You will find out that having friends helps your health and that exercise can keep both your body and your brain healthy throughout your lifetime (Fernandes, Arida, & Gomez-Pinilla, 2017). Personality psychologists seek to understand those aspects of our individuality that are enduring and those that change over our lifetime. You may have read in the popular press that college students today feel more entitled and are more narcissistic. To test this idea, personality psychologists examined personality scales from 1992 to 2015 (Wetzel, Brown, Hill, Chung, Robins, & Roberts, 2017). What they found was that narcissism is actually lower in college students today than in the 1990s or 2000s.

In other chapters, you will see how cognitive psychologists study such areas as decision making, learning, memory, producing actions, and perceiving the world. By the way, research shows that texting in class disrupts your ability to comprehend new information (Gingerich & Lineweaver, 2014). Actually, leaving your cell phone at home will improve your grade point average (Katz & Lambert, 2016). However, playing video games at home may actually help you to think better (Stanmore, Stubbs, Vancapfort, de Bruin, & Firth, 2017).

CONCEPT CHECK
- Three major themes—behavior and experience, neuroscience, and the human origins and historical cultural perspective—are presented as giving us important perspectives for thinking about psychology. What are some of the ideas that each of these perspectives offers? What are some of the questions each of these perspectives asks?

- What levels of analysis are important to consider in understanding psychology? What are the advantages of focusing on one level of analysis? What are the advantages of considering multiple levels and taking an integrated approach?

Summary

Learning Objective 1: Define psychology and how the processes of behavior and experience influence how we interact with one another.
Psychology is the study of behavior and experience. *Behavior* is simply the way we act and what we do. Behavior includes our actions and those of others in a variety of situations. We see behavior all around us and make inferences about its meaning. Watching others from a distance, we can quickly determine if they are friends, lovers, or even angry at each other without even hearing a word of what they are saying. *Experiences* are related to our internal thoughts and feelings. Unlike actions, which we can observe, experiences are internal and take many forms. We have internal feelings as we interact with others. We remember an event we have experienced or a person we have known. We feel moved by music or stories. We may feel excited when we go to a new country.

Behavior and experience always take place within a context. Sometimes the context is the present, including the people we are with and the particular tasks we are doing. Sometimes, we remember something that happened to us in the past and this has a profound influence on what we experience in the present. We might remember when a friend left and we feel sad. We can even imagine what might happen in the future and this leads us to see the world differently. That is, we have emotional reactions at this moment based on what might happen in the future. Sometimes our research in psychology emphasizes how we interact with other people. What factors determine whether we like or dislike another person is one example of this type of research.

Learning Objective 2: Review the historical concepts that have influenced psychology.
There is a long timeline of historical conceptions and discoveries that have influenced psychology and brought it to its current state. Important periods along that timeline, as well as the individuals and their contributions, inform our understanding of psychology today. Ancient Greek influences gave psychology both philosophy and scientific exploration. Beginning in the 14th century, a new spirit began to emerge in Europe that influenced art, literature, politics, and science. In the 1600s, science as a way of understanding the world began to emerge. Galileo and Isaac Newton proposed methods for performing scientific inquiry that have directed the physical sciences for the past 300 years. In the 1800s, Charles Darwin's ideas focused on the evolution of the species including both plants and animals. Two men are credited with establishing the first psychological laboratories in the world: Wilhelm Wundt in Germany and William James in the United States at Harvard University. Wundt's work was known as *structuralism*. William James was particularly interested in the functional aspects of psychological processes, asking the question what purposes specific psychological processes serve. This came to be known as *functionalism*.

Learning Objective 3: Summarize the major approaches to psychology in the 20th century.
Psychology was influenced by the early philosophies, but became an influential science during the 20th century. Several schools of thought emerged including behaviorism,

Gestalt, psychodynamic, humanistic, and cognitive behavioral. *Structuralism* suggests that a process can be understood as an addition of its parts. Gestalt psychology suggests that the whole is always greater than the sum of its parts. One important area of Gestalt research was perception. Three important developers of this approach were Max Wertheimer (1880–1943), Kurt Koffka (1886–1941), and Wolfgang Köhler (1887–1967). *Behaviorism* adopted a strict form of empiricism, the idea that knowledge should be derived through our sensory processes, and that all that should be studied is observable behavior. Behaviorism also carried with it a philosophical position that all behavior is learned. Thus, learning became an important focus of behaviorism. Important researchers in behaviorism include Ivan Pavlov (1849–1936), Edward Thorndike (1874–1949), John Watson (1878–1958), and B. F. Skinner (1904–1990). The *cognitive approach* offered a broader approach to understanding human behavior and experience. With behaviorism, the emphasis was on behavior, whereas cognitive psychology also included knowing and reasoning. The addition of cognitive psychology with brain imaging and other physiological techniques came to be called cognitive neuroscience. Sigmund Freud (1856–1939) influenced the beginning of a clinical psychology. By the beginning of the 20th century, there was an understanding that psychological processes were an important source of information concerning mental illness. Freud's work and that of others became known as the psychodynamic perspective. In the 1950s, Carl Rogers brought the humanistic perspective to the forefront by creating client-centered therapy or person-centered therapy. Beginning in the 1950s and 1960s, there was a movement to determine the effectiveness of both medical and psychological treatments in a scientific manner. This approach is referred to as empirically supported therapies.

At the beginning of the 1900s, American society, like other societies, had specific views on the roles of women and men in society. In spite of this, in 1903 Mary Calkins, Christine Ladd-Franklin, and Margaret Washburn were identified as among the 50 most important American psychologists. The role of women in psychology has changed drastically in the last 100 years. Today there is a large number of women performing significant psychological research and contributing to psychology as health care professionals.

Francis Cecil Sumner (1895–1954) became the first African American to be granted a PhD in psychology in the United States. The first African American woman to receive a doctorate in psychology was Inez Prosser in 1933. The next year in 1934 Ruth Winifred Howard (Beckman) (1900–1997) received a PhD in psychology. Kenneth Clark (1914–2005) was the first African American to become the president of the American Psychological Association in 1970. He worked as a team with his spouse, Mamie Phipps Clark (1917–1983), who was the first African American woman to receive a PhD in psychology from Columbia University in New York.

Learning Objective 4: Describe the three themes used in this book.
The first theme takes a *behavioral and experiential perspective* and relates to behaviors and experiences observed across a variety of situations. In looking at various aspects of daily living, we examine current ways of classifying and describing our behavior and experiences. In fact, this book is organized around these processes, including memory, perception, sensation, cognition, social behavior, and so forth.

The second theme examines what we know about particular psychological experiences from the standpoint of a *neuroscience perspective*. With the development of brain-imaging techniques in the last few decades, observing greater precision of brain activity is now possible. The structure and function of the brain as it relates to psychology is described.

The third theme asks a much broader scientific question and examines psychological processes from a *human origins and historical cultural perspective*. In adopting this perspective, we can think about how certain ways of behaving and seeing the world might be adaptive. We can also think about how the experiences of those who came before us might have influenced how our nervous system functions.

Learning Objective 5: Describe the different levels of analysis used by psychologists.
Psychology is a diverse profession that explores behavior and experience from a number of levels using a variety of methods. These range from basic research on genetics to cultural factors that play an important role. Besides research and teaching, a number of professional psychologists seek to apply psychological principles in a number of settings, including the clinic, schools, businesses, and other applied settings.

Study Resources

Review Questions

1. Think of yourself as a scientist during each of the following historical periods. How would you know about yourself and the world? What tools would you have? Who were the individuals, and what were the ideas, critical to each period?
   a. Ancient Greece
   b. Roman Empire
   c. Renaissance to the 1700s
   d. 1700s to 1900s
   e. 1900s to the present
2. Descartes created a mind–body distinction that science since that time has had to address. How can a material body including the brain be influenced by an immaterial process such as the mind? How can a thought influence a cell in the brain? Why is this a core question for psychology? How would you answer the mind–body question?
3. Scientific psychology started in the laboratory. What advantages does laboratory research offer? On the other hand, what kinds of questions might be better studied in other types of environments?
4. The role of women in psychology has changed drastically in the last 100 years—not to mention the last 2,000. What advantages does diversity of researchers and theorists bring to the field of psychology? In what other ways could that diversity be expanded?
5. There are currently three broad perspectives for the psychological treatment of mental disorders that were developed somewhat independently and often in opposition to one another.
   a. What are those perspectives and their core areas of interest?
   b. When were they introduced and what was their impact on the field of psychology?
   c. How are these perspectives in opposition to one another? Are there ways they can be integrated?
6. The title of this chapter is "Psychology: Historical Roots and Modern Approaches." In words or images, depict your view of the developmental timeline of psychology from its historical roots to its modern approaches.
7. Three major themes—behavior and experience, neuroscience, and the human origins and historical cultural perspective—are presented as giving us important perspectives for thinking about psychology. As you approach your own study of psychology, what questions does each of these perspectives raise in your mind? What excites you?
8. Describe the three major levels that will be used in this book and give examples of types of measures used.

For Further Reading

DeWaal, F. (2005). *Our Inner Ape.* New York: Riverhead Books.
Jablonka, E., & Lamb, M. (2014). *Evolution in Four Dimensions, Revised Edition.* Cambridge, MA: MIT Press.
Mook, D. (2004). *Classic Experiments in Psychology.* Westport, CT: Greenwood Press.
Pinker, S. (1997). *How the Mind Works.* New York: Norton.

Web Resources

Women in psychology—http://www.nsf.gov/statistics/srvydoctorates/#tabs-2
McGurk effect—https://www.youtube.com/watch?v=2k8fHR9jKVM
Learning scientist—https://www.learningscientists.org/
Careers in psychology—https://www.apa.org/careers/resources/guides/careers.pdf

Key Terms and Concepts

behavior
behavioral and experiential perspective
behaviorism
biopsychosocial
client-centered therapy or person-centered therapy
clinical psychology
cognitive behavioral perspective
cognitive neuroscience
cognitive psychology
empiricism
experience
functionalism
Gestalt psychology
humanistic perspective
human origins and historical cultural perspective
introspection
levels of analysis
neuroscience perspective
psychoanalysis
psychodynamic perspective
psychology
structuralism

2 Scientific Psychology and Its Research Methods

LEARNING OBJECTIVES

2.1 Summarize how science can help us be part of and explain our world.

2.2 Describe the major research designs used in psychological science.

2.3 Explain the techniques used to understand and evaluate scientific data.

2.4 List the steps involved in designing an experimental study.

2.5 Evaluate the ethical guidelines that psychologists follow when conducting scientific research.

Neuroscientist V. S. Ramachandran treated an individual named David at his medical center in San Diego, California (Ramachandran, 1998). David had no problems with memory, engaged easily in conversation, expressed emotions, and otherwise appeared "normal." However, he did one very puzzling thing. He did not recognize his own mother. When she appeared, he insisted, "That woman looks exactly like my mother, but she is not my mother!"

As a health care professional, how might you understand this? You might ask if this was some type of psychosis in which he had the delusion that his mother was not his mother. However, David showed no other signs of disorganization or problems with functioning. You might also ask if David had any type of emotional conflict with his mother. The answer to that was also no. After more information gathering, it was discovered that David at times also thought his father was not his father. Eventually, it was revealed that David did indeed experience his parents as really his parents when talking to them on the phone. Seeing them resulted in a different experience.

The formal name for this condition is the Capgras syndrome, named after the physician who first described the symptoms in the 1920s. However, the mechanisms involved were not known. Since David had previously had a motorcycle accident, it was possible that normal brain processes were not functioning correctly. In order to understand David, Ramachandran asked himself what was missing in David's experience of his mother. His answer was that there was no emotional response. How can we test the emotional response to seeing a face? Emotion is not only processed in the brain but also in the autonomic nervous system (ANS), which prepares the body for dangerous situations. For example, if we see a bear and start running, it is the sympathetic part of the ANS that makes us feel excited and moves blood to our muscles for a quick getaway. One easy way to measure the sympathetic nervous system is to pass a small electrical current along the skin, usually between the palm and the finger. This procedure is referred to as electrodermal activity (EDA), which has also been used in lie detection. If we are excited, then our skin sweats slightly, this in turn, makes it easier for the electrical current to pass between the two electrodes. Whenever we have an emotional response to what we see, we get changes in the EDA. Not surprisingly, David did not show any EDA differences when viewing pictures of those close to him. This suggested to Dr. Ramachandran that there was a disconnect between David's visual face perception areas and the emotional centers of the brain. Since the auditory system connects to emotional centers of the brain differently than the visual system, then it makes sense that David did not have the same emotional disconnect when talking with his parents on the phone as when he saw them.

To study an unknown condition, as scientists we must logically examine important components of the condition. In David's case, what was important was both what he experienced—not believing his mother was his mother—as well as what he didn't experience—the emotional response to his mother.

What Is Science?

Science is a method for asking questions about the world. The quality of the answers we receive is influenced by several factors, one of the most important being the experimental design that we use. A well-controlled experiment allows us to be more certain of our results. As a scientist you could also ask other questions about David's case. You might begin by investigating what the research literature tells us about the cognitive and emotional factors involved in recognizing and experiencing a parent. As a scientist, you would also want to know:

- What factors are related to experiencing a parent and what factors can be ruled out?
- How would you go about studying the phenomenon of Capgras syndrome?
- What techniques can you use to measure cognition and emotion?

This is a general process called ***science*** that involves experiencing the world and then drawing general conclusions, or ***facts*** from observations. Sometimes these facts are descriptive and can be represented by numbers. For example, we know that the moon is 238,000 miles from Earth and that the brain uses 20% of the energy produced by the body. Other times, knowledge is more general and can describe a relationship or a process, like the fact that it is more difficult to learn a second language after puberty than before, or that following puberty, most adolescents want to be with their friends rather than their parents. Whatever the topic, the known facts about a particular subject are called ***scientific knowledge*** *(see Ray, 2022 for more information)*.

A Human Activity

Science is above all a human activity. Some people perform science as their profession and are known as scientists. Equally accurate is the idea that all people perform science in some form. In fact, science in many ways is similar to the way we have been learning about the world since we were infants. We learn through interacting with our world. In fact, you probably know much more about the scientific method than you think you do. You have been using it in one form or another since you first began toddling about and discovering the world.

Watch a young child. When something catches his or her eye, the child must examine, observe, and have fun with it. Next, the child wants to touch it. Some interactions are fun: "If I tip the glass, I get to see the milk form pretty pictures on the floor." Others are not so much fun: "If I touch the red circles on the stove, my fingers hurt!" From passive observations to active interactions, the child learns a little more about the world.

Figure 2-1 Child playing with blocks and learning about simple principles of physics and spatial abilities.

Like the child, scientists are exploring the unknown—and sometimes the known—features of the world. All basic research strategies are based on one simple notion: *To discover what the world is like, we must experience it.* To have an idea about the nature of the world is not enough. Instead, like the child, scientists experience the world to determine whether their ideas accurately reflect reality. Direct experience is an essential tool because it alone allows us to bridge the gap between our ideas and reality.

Science and Doubt

There is another aspect to science that many people do not think about. This is the aspect of **doubt.** In science we use doubt to question our ideas and our research and ask whether factors other than the ones that we originally considered might have influenced our results. By doing this, we come to see that science is a combination of interaction with the world and logic. The logic of science leads us to the realization that one of the real strengths of science is showing us when we are wrong. If someone says that all swans are white, for example, seeing a white swan—or thousands of swans, all of which are white—does not actually prove this to be the case. However, a black swan would clearly show that the statement was wrong. In this spirit, Einstein is reported to have said, "No amount of experimentation can ever prove me right; a single experiment can prove me wrong." The philosopher of science Sir Karl Popper referred to this approach as ***falsification.*** Thus, one important aspect of doing science is to ask yourself, how would I know if I was wrong? By the way, being wrong also helps researchers to know factors that are not involved.

As you think about falsification and doubt, you begin to realize that doing psychological science is a broad and critical process. It is more than designing an experiment and looking at the results. It is also thinking critically about the experiment and the results. As you will see in this chapter, at every step of performing psychological science, you ask if there could be other explanations for understanding the results. You can also ask if there are other studies that would help you support or better understand your results. You use logic, scientific methods, and your own experience to critically evaluate your ideas.

Debunking Superstition and Pseudoscience

One of the goals in this book is to help you think critically. This is done in the context of psychology as a science. Science emphasizes ways to evaluate information and come to valid conclusions. Experience and doubt form two important characteristics of psychological science.

However, other aspects of our human nature may work against this. Human beings have a long history of relying on magic and superstition to guide our decisions. Even today some hotels do not have a 13th floor, since this is considered by some to be unlucky. Some people carry lucky charms or wear certain clothes to important meetings because they think this will help them succeed. Even our newspapers have daily horoscopes to tell us what types of activities to engage in that day.

Most likely, superstition is part of our long evolutionary history. We may emotionally believe that something is true and hate the thought of giving up that particular idea or belief. Social and cognitive psychology research shows that this is made even more complicated by the fact that when we believe something to be true, we tend to look only for supporting evidence and to dismiss any contradiction to our belief as an exception (Kahneman, 2011). Without a method to test our ideas, we will never know the validity of our conclusions. That is one important aspect of science.

You also know that frequently individuals make claims in the name of science that are not actually based on rigorous scientific procedures. Often these are individuals who want to sell you something. You see this every day on social media. Some of these claims have made their way into popular books and even have been reported as true in the mass media. For example, the idea that you can learn while you sleep was a popular one during parts of the 20th century. This idea found its way into a variety of movies and novels and was even spoofed on an episode of *The Simpsons*.

The Simpsons had it correct, since numerous scientific research studies have not been able to find evidence supporting the claim of learning during sleep (Simon & Emmons, 1955). Despite this, even today you can go on the web and buy materials that claim to help you learn languages, study for exams, and improve a variety of abilities while you sleep. All of these items are supposed to be based on scientific research, or at least that is what the websites say.

The phenomenon of presenting information as if it is based on science when it is not is referred to as **pseudoscience**. Pseudoscience is false science. Often claims of pseudoscience are based on testimonials that present a single side of the issue and have not been evaluated by others studying similar phenomena using valid scientific methods. For this reason, scientists pay particular attention to research that has been evaluated by other scientists before it is published. This process is called **peer review**, and journals that follow this procedure are peer-reviewed journals. One characteristic of pseudoscience is that it is not found in peer-reviewed journals. As we continue throughout the book, you will learn how to identify pseudoscience and develop some of the skills of critical thinking to evaluate its claims.

Just because something is not based on science does not mean that we shouldn't consider it. Many of us love to read science-fiction and other types of fantasy literature. Such writing makes us consider possibilities and other ways of thinking about our world. As we will see in this book, scientists are always considering alternative explanations and sometimes ideas that seem crazy. However, considering that something could be true does not mean that it has scientific support. Thus, we need a means for testing our ideas. We particularly need ways of knowing if we are wrong, which is one of the important aspects of designing scientific research.

Unintended Influence

Besides pseudoscience, sometimes even the person making the claim believes it to be true. "There is a horse that solves correctly problems in multiplication and division." This is the provocative statement that opens a book (*Clever Hans*) that describes the remarkable story of a German horse nicknamed Clever Hans (Pfungst, 1911). People from all over Germany wanted to see this horse as it tapped out the correct answers to math problems. It could even solve problems that involved fractions by first tapping the numerator and then the denominator. If that was not enough, Hans also knew the yearly calendar and was able to give you the date of any day you would present.

As you also can imagine, people who knew horses well and how to train them were skeptical. The book's introduction asserts that thousands of these individuals watched Hans and his owner, a Mr. von Osten, over many months and could not find a trick. Mr. von Osten had assumed that animals were smart and could be taught if only given enough time.

Mr. von Osten taught Hans as if he were a German schoolboy. There were blackboards, flash cards, and all the curriculum subjects available in Germany. Over a period of years, van Osten taught Hans to move his hooves in a way to differentiate between yes and no, and to tap out numbers. Food, praise, and other rewards were given for correct responses. In the Germany of the early 1900s, some thought this was a way to understand animal consciousness. Others thought it was all a fraud. Thus, we are left with a riddle, as the book says.

In order to solve the riddle, Oskar Pfungst, a German psychologist, began a series of experiments that were published in 1911. Pfungst first tells us that we cannot determine Hans's abilities in the ordinary conditions in which he performed. This is because he could not control the environmental factors surrounding the performance. In order to reduce the environmental influences, Pfungst erected a large canvas tent within Mr. von Osten's courtyard in which the horse could freely move. Pfungst then tried to have the horse respond to the questions of others. In fact, he tried some 40 different individuals with inconclusive results.

What does this mean? It means that there is something special about Mr. von Osten that allows the horse to answer. Oskar Pfungst then did a very clever experimental manipulation. He alternated questions to which Mr. von Osten knew the answer with those he did not. If Hans was able to answer both types of questions, then it could be concluded that the questioner was not influencing the horse. If Hans was only able to answer questions that the questioner himself knew the answer to, then Pfungst could begin to look for subtle influences on Hans. To further restrict these influences, Pfungst placed blinders on Hans so he could only see in front of him.

What do you think was found? Pfungst found that if the questioner knew the answer to the question, then Hans was correct nearly all the time. If the questioner did not know the answer, Hans was rarely correct.

How did Mr. von Osten communicate the correct answer to the horse? He did what all of us do when we ask a child to count. We lean forward slightly when the child is answering the question and then lean backwards when the correct answer is given. Hans had learned to keep tapping when the questioner was leaning forward and to stop when he leaned backwards. Mr. von Osten had no idea that he was not teaching the horse to count during the years of training but rather training him to respond to subtle cues that neither he himself nor those watching him work with the horse could see.

The story of Clever Hans shows us that all organisms, including humans, are sensitive to their environment. This is true whether we are interacting with other people or being part of an experiment. Thus, in psychological experiments there are a number of opportunities for those who are researchers to influence those who are participants in ways that were never intended. Participants can also influence researchers. For example, participants in experiments may respond to their own ideas or internal demands rather than those of the experiment itself.

What Are the Methods of Science?

The methods of science closely parallel our ways of learning about the world. We interact with the world and gain new knowledge and understanding of what we experience. However, in doing psychological research, we do this in a more organized and logical manner. We may observe and describe what we see, which is referred to *qualitative research*. We can also measure and report the number of specific factors that can be used in a mathematical manner, which is referred to as *quantitative research*. The scientific approach emphasized in this chapter will describe both qualitative and quantitative approaches. In both, researchers approach a particular question or topic in a logical manner. We can think about a critical approach to science in terms of four stages.

1. Scientists first begin with an idea or expectation. A formally stated expectation is called a **hypothesis**. The scientist says, "I expect this to happen under these conditions," and thus states the hypothesis.
2. Second, scientists look to experience to evaluate the accuracy of their ideas or expectations about the world. That is, they try to find or create the situation that will allow them to observe what they are interested in studying.
3. Through observation and experimentation, scientists can begin to evaluate their ideas and expectations about the world. Learning about the world through observation and experimentation is an example of **empiricism**, which means nothing more than the acceptance of sensory information as valid.
4. Fourth, on the basis of their observations and experiments, scientists seek to draw conclusions or inferences about their ideas and expectations. They reorganize their ideas and consider the impact of the new information on their theoretical conceptualizations.

Figure 2-2 presents a simplified outline of this procedure, which reflects the evolutionary nature of science. The steps include (1) the development of the hypothesis, (2) the translation of this hypothesis into a research design, (3) the running of the experiment, and (4) the interpretation of the results. You will notice that there is also an arrow from step 4

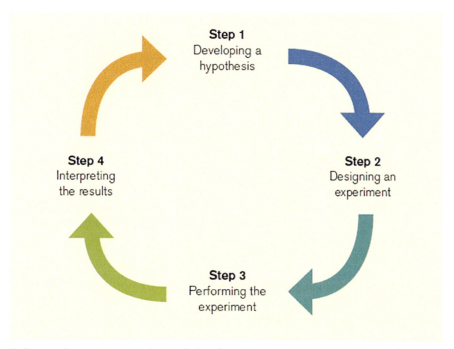

Figure 2-2 Schematic representation of the four major steps in the experimental process. These are developing a hypothesis, designing an experiment, performing the experiment, and interpreting the results.

back to step 1. Researchers take the results and interpretations of their studies and create new research studies that refine the previous hypothesis.

In psychological research, we have some powerful techniques to help us achieve this goal. Unlike the detective, who must always reconstruct events after the fact, the researcher has the advantage of creating a new situation in which to test ideas. This is comparable to a homicide detective's ability to bring a dead man back to life and place him in the presence of each suspect until the murder is reenacted. Such a reenactment might lack suspense, but it would increase the certainty of knowing who committed the murder.

In fact, increased certainty is a large part of the experimental process. Scientists increase certainty by creating an artificial situation—the experiment—in which important factors can be controlled and manipulated. Through control and manipulation, participant variables can be examined in detail, and the influence of one variable on another can be determined with certainty.

Science is a way of determining what we can infer about the world. In its simplest form, the ***scientific method*** consists of asking a question about the world and then experiencing the world to determine the answer. When we begin an inquiry, what we already know about our topic leaves us in one of a number of positions. In some cases, we know little about our topic, or our topic may be very complex. Consequently, our ideas and questions are general. For example, how does our memory work? What causes mental illness? What factors make a fruitful marriage? How can we model the brain? Can experience change our brain?

Descriptive Research: What Can We Observe?

The first way to do psychological science is to observe what we see around us. A developmental psychologist might want to know what type of facial expressions newborn babies make. A clinical psychologist could study the specific words that people use to describe

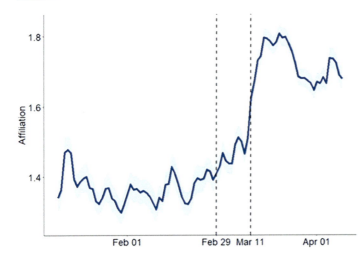

Figure 2-3 Affiliation words during COVID-19 increased when the COVID-19 crisis began.

distress. A cognitive psychologist might seek to understand how individuals make choices in their lives.

We may want to know how a particular event, such as the beginning of the COVID-19 epidemic, influenced people's thoughts and emotions. James Pennebaker, Ashwini Ashokkumar, and their colleagues examined the language that people used to track their thoughts and emotions during the initial months of the COVID-19 epidemic. Using a language analysis program, they calculated how much each of hundreds of thousands of posts on Reddit communities used affiliation words such as "we," "us," "our," "together," and "love," which they saw as a measure of social relationships. As shown in **Figure 2-3**, people began to use affiliation words more in the last week of February, indicating that they started to increasingly focus on their social relationships. Mid-March, at about the time when shelter-in-place directives began, there was a sharp increase in feelings of social connection. Overall, COVID-19 increased people's feelings of social connection.

Observation Studies

If little is known about a particular phenomenon, it is often useful simply to watch the phenomenon occur naturally and get a general idea of what is involved in the process. Initially, this is accomplished by observing and describing what occurs. This scientific technique is called ***observation studies*** or ***naturalistic observation***.

A classic example of this approach is Charles Darwin's observation of animals in the Galápagos Islands. His careful descriptions of their appearance and environment became the basis of his theory of evolution. Since the 1960s, Jane Goodall has observed primates around the world in their natural environments. She was one of the first researchers to describe a chimpanzee using a stem of grass and modifying it so he could poke it into a termite mound to gain food (Goodall, 1990). Other researchers (De Waal, 2008) sought to understand how animals and humans use peacemaking to resolve aggressive episodes (see **Figure 2-4**). For example, the bonobo, another primate, uses sexuality in place of aggression. Like humans, bonobos are sexually active at times other than just when a child can be conceived.

How might you perform research with bonobos to determine how they use sexuality for the purpose of lovemaking? It would first be necessary to find a place where bonobos would interact. You would then watch the interaction and note the behaviors observed. It is important that those being observed do not realize they are being observed, otherwise they might change their behavior.

Figure 2-4 Chimpanzees. Did you know that in addition to bonobos and humans, chimpanzees often kiss their partner on the mouth after a fight?

The naturalistic observation method has four characteristics:

1. Noninterference is of prime importance. Scientists using this method must not disrupt the process or flow of events. In this way they can see things as they really are, without influencing the ongoing phenomenon.
2. This method emphasizes the invariants, or patterns, that exist in the world. For example, if you could observe yourself in a noninterfering manner, you might conclude that your moods vary with the time of day, particular weather patterns, or even specific thoughts.
3. This method is most useful when we know little about the subject of our investigation. It is also particularly helpful for understanding the "big picture" by observing a series of events, rather than isolated happenings.
4. The naturalistic method may not shed light on the factors that directly influence the behavior observed. The method provides a description of a phenomenon; it does not answer the question of why it happened.

Case Studies

The naturalistic method may not shed light on the factors that directly influence the behavior observed. The method provides a description of a phenomenon; it does not answer the question of why it happened. Sometimes, as in the case of David and his experience of not recognizing his mother, professionals encounter a rarer event. The study of such a naturally occurring event that happens to an individual is referred to as a ***case study***.

The case study method has a rich tradition in studying unique situations that do not lend themselves to traditional research procedures. In fact, much of our initial understanding of brain function came from careful study of individuals who had accidents or experienced war injuries. The case study offers a means of examining in some depth the manner in which a person understands his or her experiences. Further, the case study offers a means of helping researchers develop new questions to be asked concerning how a phenomenon developed and might be understood.

In *psychopathology* research, the advantage of the case study is its ability to present the clinical implications of a particular disorder. One classic example is Freud's case study of Anna O, which focused on the treatment of "hysteria," which we now call conversion disorder (Breuer & Freud, 1893–1955). Another example is described in Morton Prince's book *The Dissociation of a Personality* (1913). Prince described a case of "multiple personality," what we currently label dissociative identity disorder, at a time when the existence of that diagnostic category was in question. Initial case studies from battlefield experiences also helped to clarify the nature of post-traumatic stress disorder (PTSD).

A recent example of a case study was reported by four health care professionals in China (Yu, Jiang, Sun, & Zhang, 2015). A 24-year-old patient came into their hospital complaining of dizziness and nausea. She also reported that, for more than 20 years, she had experienced difficulty walking in a steady manner. Further examination showed that this individual could speak and understand language, but that she could not stand by herself before the age of 4 and that she did not walk on her own before the age of 7. Brain-imaging techniques showed that this individual was missing an important part of her brain, the cerebellum. The cerebellum is related to motor functions such as walking. Such non-normal cases of development allow scientists to understand how the lack of a cerebellum affects behavior and experience.

Correlational Research: What Goes with What?

Correlational research helps us understand how things go together. As with much of human behavior, there are complex relationships between psychological variables, or factors. Correlational approaches reveal what factors are related. For example, you can ask if people who have more friends have fewer health-related problems than people who do not. Thus, we ask if one aspect of a system is associated with another aspect.

How would you go about answering this question? Let's begin with the relationship between friends and health. You could start by asking how many Facebook friends an individual has. How does this relate to health? The next step might be to determine the number of times that individual went to the health center. If you did this with a group of people, you would have two numbers for each person—number of Facebook friends and number of health center visits.

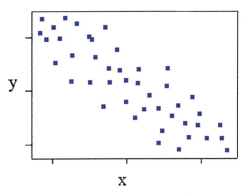

Figure 2-5 Scatter diagram showing negative relationship between two measures. As the number of health care visits increases (*y*-axis), the number of friends decreases (*x*-axis). Correlation alone can only describe the relationship between factors. Correlation cannot determine which factor caused the change in the other factor.

Visualizing the Data

What would you do with these data? One helpful technique is to create a visual of the information. A ***scatterplot*** is a graph on which the data from each person is plotted. We would use the *y*-axis to display the number of friends on Facebook (for example,

0–150) and the *x*-axis to display the number of visits to the health center during the past year (for example, 0–20). We could then look at these measures for each person and plot that point on the graph (**Figure 2-5**). It is now possible to look at the graph and visually determine if there is a relationship. In general, the dots show a pattern that indicates that people with fewer friends tend to have more health center visits, and the subjects with more friends have fewer visits.

Determining Direction and Degree

Correlations have both a direction and a degree, or strength. Although humans are good at determining patterns, the **correlation coefficient,** which indicates both the strength of the relationship and its direction, allows for better precision.

Let's start with the direction. If the number of friends on Facebook were associated with more health center visits, then this relationship would be called a **positive correlation**. That is, they both increase. However, if fewer friends were associated with more visits, then this relationship would be called a **negative correlation**. One increases and the other decreases. **Figure 2-6** shows a variety of relationships.

Of course, as you might guess, few factors or variables are perfectly related to one another. Thus, the correlation statistic is also able to reflect the *degree* of an association between two variables. For example, you might expect that the more hours you study for a test, the higher score you would receive. However, some people who study more will not do as well as some individuals who study less. Thus, it is not a perfect correlation, but a positive one.

Whether the relationship between the variables is positive or negative is denoted by the + and − signs. The correlation statistic can range from −1 to +1. A perfect positive relationship would be +1 and a perfect negative relationship would be −1. If there was no relationship it would be 0. Thus, a low positive relationship could be .3, whereas a stronger

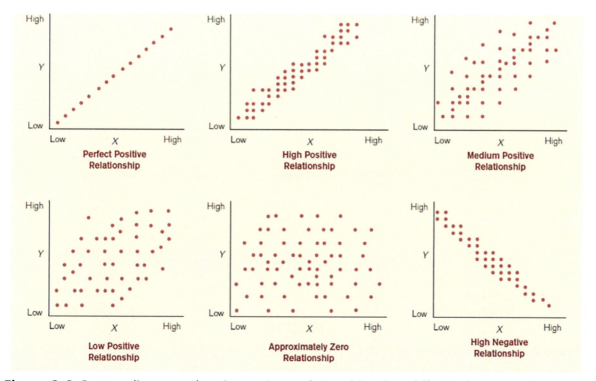

Figure 2-6 Scatter diagrams showing various relationships that differ in degree and direction.

one would be .70. It should be noted that both the statistic and the research approach are referred to as correlational.

Correlation Does Not Equal Causation

In correlational studies, the researcher is interested in asking whether there is an association between two variables, but he or she does not attempt to establish how one variable influences the other, only that a relationship exists. For example, if drinking orange juice at breakfast is associated with better health, it does not mean that the orange juice led to better health. It could be the case that not being in a state of good health would make anyone less likely to want to drink orange juice in the morning.

A *correlational relationship does not mean there is a causal one.* Establishing that such an association exists may be the first step in dealing with a complex problem and discovering what type of causal relationship exists. In Chapter 6, there is a graph that shows the relationship between the weight of an animal and the number of hours that the animal sleeps (**Figure 2-7**). If you were to take these data and create a correlation coefficient, the result is a negative correlation of −.8. That is, the more an animal weighs, the fewer hours it sleeps during a 24-hour period. However, this relationship involves only animals that do not eat meat.

What we cannot know from correlational research is whether either variable influences the other directly. That is, if two variables are related, what might the reason be for the relationship? It might be that there is a direct relationship. Having lots of friends to follow on Facebook might help you to feel cared for and lead you to feeling less sick. In this way, more friends would result in fewer visits. Looking at the other side of the situation, it

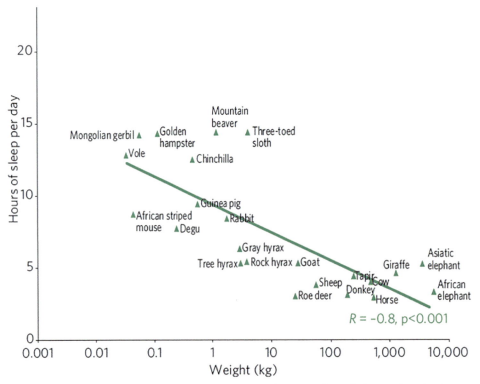

Figure 2-7 Length of sleep each day in relation to the weight of the animal. The more an animal weighs, the less it sleeps. The animals shown are ones that do not eat meat. Note a kilogram (1,000 grams) equals 2.2 pounds.

Source: Siegel (2005).

could be the case that if a person felt sick often, they might not seek others as friends and post on Facebook.

As you begin to suggest factors that might have produced a high degree of relationship, you realize that a third, unspecified variable actually may have influenced the two variables in the correlational study. For example, there is a high correlation between wearing bathing suits and eating ice cream. In this case, they are both determined by the outside temperature. Thus, a third variable determines the relationship. Thus, the nature of a correlational study is to suggest relationships but not to suggest which variable influences which other variable.

The association of two factors does not in itself imply that one influences the other. However, if there is a *low* correlation between the two events, you can infer that one event does *not* cause the other. A high degree of association is always necessary for establishing that one variable influences another. A correlational study is often the first step for providing the needed support for later experimental research, especially in complex areas. At times, correlational research has led to difficult problems for society as you will see in the box: Myths and Misconceptions—Doing Good Science and the Controversy over Childhood Vaccinations and Autism Spectrum Disorder.

Myths and Misconceptions—Doing Good Science and the Controversy over Childhood Vaccinations and Autism Spectrum Disorder

Over the past 20 years, our understanding of autism spectrum disorder has increased tremendously. Autism is a disorder in which children show social difficulties in terms of communication with others. Parents and guardians are paying more attention to the social functioning of their children and even seeking evaluations to identify autism early in a child's life. What are the consequences of this? Given that more children are being evaluated, one consequence of this is that more children are being diagnosed with the disorder. Is there an increase in the disorder? That is an important question.

During the past 20 years, many people in the United States also became concerned with the food they ate. Sales of organic food increased. Now, what if we presented a graph of organic food sales and the diagnosis of autism? As you can see in **Figure 2-8**, there is a close correlation.

You might conclude that eating organic food causes autism. However, you are a better scientist than that! Since the correlation between organic food sales and autism diagnosis was high, you would want to look for the *reason* for the relationship. You could start by researching if those children who ate organic food developed autism. To answer this question, you could note the number of children who ate organic food and developed autism and the number who did not. You would also want to see the number of children who developed autism but did not eat organic food. You might examine if mothers if who ate organic food during their pregnancy had children who later developed autism. You could also look for third variables that were related to both. For example, as society became more interested in health, then both eating better and seeking an early health diagnosis for a disorder such as autism might increase.

As you realize, making the conclusion that eating organic food leads to autism is bad science. However, there are times that fraud and not science leads to society believing in an erroneous conclusion. In 1998, a British surgeon and medical researcher,

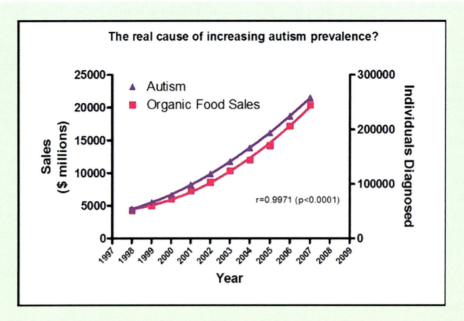

Figure 2-8 This graph shows a close positive correlation (r=.99) between the sale of organic foods and the diagnosis of autism over 20 years.

Dr. Andrew Wakefield, published a paper in the respected medical journal *The Lancet*. The article, based on 12 children, reported a relationship between the measles, mumps, and rubella (MMR) vaccine and autism and a certain bowel disease. The paper suggested that 8 of the 12 children might have shown problems within days of being given the MMR vaccine. As you can imagine, this published report upset many parents, some of whom refused to have their children vaccinated.

Those in the medical profession found the claim of the relationship between the MMR vaccine and autism troubling and began to research this relationship. In studies in other labs, no one was able to find the same relationship. Media investigations discovered that Andrew Wakefield had been given money by a lawyer interested in suing drug companies on behalf of children with autism. The British General Medical Council opened an investigation and concluded that the published report involved dishonesty. Andrew Wakefield lost his medical license. Medical journals and other publications referred to the published paper and other presentations of Wakefield as fraudulent. *The Lancet* retracted the paper.

Yet the initial media discussion of Wakefield's article left a profound "hangover" with chilling effects. In the wake of these allegations, vaccination rates dropped in both England and the United States. As recently as 2015, an outbreak of measles was traced to unvaccinated children visiting Disneyland in California. In 2019, the US had the greatest number of measles cases reported since 1992 and since measles was declared eliminated in 2000.

Thought Question: What are your thoughts concerning the following question for psychology and society at large: Why are people so quick to believe in the initial claim of an MMR vaccination and autism connection and so slow to give up this belief in the presence of overwhelming data?

Experimental Research: How Do We Determine Cause and Effect?

Establishing that a relationship exists between two events does not allow us to determine exactly what that relationship is, much less to determine that one event actually caused the other event to happen. If we want to state that one event produced another event, we need to develop a much stronger case for our position.

To do this, we could see how some single event over which we have control affects the phenomenon we are studying. In this way, we begin to interact with the phenomenon. We structure our question in this form: "If I do this, what will happen?" Numerous questions can be asked in this way, such as, "Will you learn words better in a foreign language if each word is of the same class (for example, food words) instead of coming from different classes (foods, cars, and toys)?"

As our knowledge grows, we may even get to the point of formulating specific predictions. In this case, our questions are structured in the form, "If I do this, I expect this will happen." Sometimes our predictions are more global, and we predict that one factor will be stronger than another. We might predict that more people are likely to help a stranger if they perceive the environment to be safe than if they think it is dangerous. Sometimes, however, we may know enough about an area to make a more precise prediction, or *point prediction*. For example, we might predict that three months of exercise will lead to a 10-mm Hg decrease in blood pressure. These approaches, in which we interact directly with the phenomenon we are studying, are examples of the **experimental method**.

The Experimental Method

What if we want to know whether drinking coffee affected how many words from a list could be remembered? The hypothesis, or idea being tested, is that drinking coffee influenced memory. To test the hypothesis, we could give coffee to one group and not to a second group. The group that received the coffee is called the **experimental group**. The group that did not receive the coffee is called the **control group**. A control group is a group that is treated exactly like the experimental group except for the factor being studied. In this case, the factor being studied is the coffee and its influence on memory.

Since memory can be viewed in a variety of ways, we need a specific definition of what memory means in our study. Memory, for example, could be defined as the number of words that could be remembered from a list of 20 words. An **operational definition** takes a general concept, such as memory, or aggression or effectiveness, and places it within a given context. That is, *it redefines the concept in terms of clearly observable operations that anyone can see and repeat*. For example, we might define *aggression* as the number of times a child hits a toy after watching a violent television show.

In an experimental study, we want to know how one variable—which we manipulate—affects another variable. In the example of coffee affecting memory, whether or not someone drank coffee was the manipulated variable. This is also called the **independent variable (IV)**. Memory, in this example, is the variable influenced by the coffee and is called the **dependent variable (DV)**. That is, it depends on, or is influenced by, the independent variable.

What other factors could influence a memory test? If we suspect that some unintended factor may also be operating, then the truth or validity of the experiment is seriously threatened. Thus, the conclusion that the IV influenced the DV could be questioned.

In the memory experiment, if the control group was run in the morning and the experimental group in the afternoon, then time of day could have an effect. Whenever two or more independent variables are operating, the unintended independent variables (those not chosen by the experimenter) are called *confounding variables*. Other confounding variables may go together with the independent variable and be more difficult to notice. For example, assume that a researcher compared a new medication against a problem-solving approach for the treatment of anxiety. If she found the problem-solving approach to show a greater reduction in anxiety, could she conclude that problem solving produced the reduction?

Although that is one possibility, it also may have been the case that spending time with a professional produced the reduction in anxiety. That is, because giving medications requires less time with a client than discussing problem-solving techniques, the results found may not have been due to the independent variable as planned in the study but rather to the confounding variable of time spent with the patient.

Combination Research Designs: When Does It Make Sense?

Let's examine a specific study in which both experimental and correlational procedures were used. Thomas Elbert and his colleagues began with the idea that experience could change the manner in which connections in the brain were established (Elbert et al., 1995). These researchers needed to find a task that would allow them to measure change and make logical inferences. Since they were interested in long-term changes, they focused on the skill of playing a musical instrument, something people often learn in childhood. Specifically, they chose the violin. Here is where logic and experimental design came in. By focusing on the violin, these researchers were able to compare the differences between the violinists' left and right hands and their representation in the brain.

Violinists use their left hand to continuously finger the strings. The right hand simply moves the bow back and forth. If playing a violin for 20 years would affect the brain, then it should affect those areas involved with the left hand in a different manner than those involved with the right. This is exactly what they found.

To measure neuronal activity in the brain, these researchers used a brain-imaging technique, the magnetoencephalography (MEG), which measures magnetic activity produced in different parts of the brain. In their study, they found that neuronal activity in the brain was different between the areas of the brain related to musicians' left and right fingers. Further, they found that the brain areas of the musicians' right hands were not different from those of the control group who did not play a musical instrument.

Thus, the experimental comparison was between individuals who had played a musical instrument since childhood and the control group was those who had not. There was also a comparison between the brain areas involved with the left and right fingers of the musicians. Further, these researchers examined the correlation between neuronal activity (dipole strength) and the length of time an individual had played an instrument. **Figure 2-9** shows this relationship. As you can see, this is a negative correlation in that the earlier (lower number) one began to play an instrument, the stronger the neuronal activity was. The experimental and correlational aspects of this research helped the researchers logically conclude that previous experience can influence brain organization. We have not always thought that actions could change our brains, as you will see in the box: The World Is Your Laboratory—Science from a Larger Perspective.

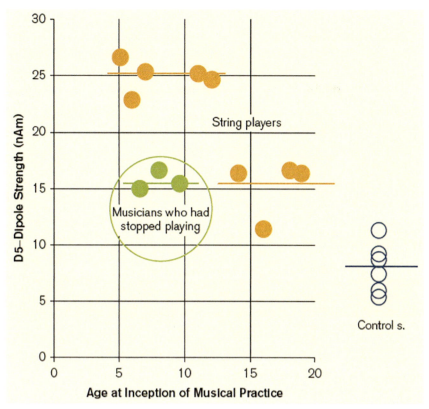

Figure 2-9 Relationship between neuronal activity and the length of time an individual had played an instrument. This graph shows that those who began playing the violin at an early age showed a different pattern of brain activity than those who began playing later or never played the violin.
Source: Elbert, Pantev, Wienbruch, Rockstroh, and Taub (1995).

The World Is Your Laboratory—Science from a Larger Perspective

Science begins with someone saying, "There is something I don't understand and I want to understand it." The task then becomes one of figuring out how to gain this understanding. Sometimes, it is by watching; sometimes it is by interacting with the process. In this sense, science is universal since we, as humans, seek to gain knowledge and understand ourselves and our world.

Although science seeks to add new information, it is also influenced by scientists' own human nature. As humans we live in a culture that influences what we value and how we interact with others. Thomas Kuhn (1970) has examined the larger culture of science. From this perspective, he suggests that science is more than just adding new information to old facts. For Kuhn, over time scientific information reflects a cycle of revolutions followed by periods in which *normal science* takes place. The period of normal science reflects what Kuhn called a *paradigm*.

A *paradigm* is a set of assumptions that guides the activity until a new revolution (a *paradigm shift*) takes place. If you lived in the Middle Ages, when it was assumed that the world was flat and the center of the universe, then all of your activities would reflect this "fact." You would draw maps that showed the world to be flat and never question it. However, with the realization that the world was neither flat nor the center of the universe, your view of the world would change, a paradigm shift.

Psychology and the neurosciences have gone through a number of these revolutions. At the beginning of the 20th century, it was assumed that everything was learned and the infant came into the world as a blank slate. Research today reflects a complex interplay between the environment and genetic processes. For example, we now know that children come into the world ready to absorb the languages available to them. Likewise, it was previously assumed that once you left childhood, your brain no longer could be changed. We now know that everything you do has the potential to make changes in the brain. In short, with new scientific discoveries, paradigms shift.

Thought Question: What "scientific fact" is so taken for granted as true that it might just be ready for a new way of looking at it through a paradigm shift?

CONCEPT CHECK

- Define the following: science, facts, scientific knowledge, doubt, and falsification. How do they fit together?
- What is the difference between science and pseudoscience? What criteria would you use to decide for yourself whether a particular report is science or pseudoscience?
- What are the four major steps in the experimentation process?
- What is the primary value of a case study? In what situations in psychology would it be most appropriate?
- What are the four characteristics of the naturalistic observation method?
- If a research study reports that two variables are correlated, what do you know about their relationship? What don't you know about their relationship?
- How is the experimental method different from naturalistic observation and the correlational approach?
- What is the difference between the experimental group and the control group? Why is the control group important?
- What is an operational definition and why is it important in doing research? Create at least two different operational definitions of "violence on television" and "aggression."
- How are the independent variable (IV), the dependent variable (DV), and confounding variables related?
- Thomas Kuhn's "culture of science" includes revolutions, normal science, and paradigms. What are they and how do they work together?

How Do Scientists Evaluate and Analyze Data?

Perhaps you have heard the story of our friend from Boston who, every morning, went outside, walked around in a circle three times, and yelled at the top of his voice. His neighbor, being somewhat curious after days of this ritual, asked for the purpose behind his strange behavior. The man answered that the purpose was to keep away tigers. "But," the neighbor replied, "there are no tigers within thousands of miles of here." To which our friend replied, "Works quite well, doesn't it?"

How could we demonstrate to our friend that his yelling is not causally related to the absence of tigers? One strategy might be to point out that the absence of tigers is due to other reasons, including the fact that there are no tigers roaming the greater Boston area. In technical terms, we would say that yelling could be a *necessary* condition but not a *sufficient* condition for the absence of tigers.

Logic is particularly important in science when asking, "What question should my experimental study answer to test my ideas about the world?" For example, our friend's reasoning was incorrect because it overlooked many other plausible explanations for the obvious absence of tigers. Although our friend sought to infer a relationship between his yelling and the absence of tigers, his *inference* was weak. **Inference** is the process by which we look at the evidence available to us and then use our powers of reasoning to reach a logical conclusion. Like Sherlock Holmes engaged in solving a mystery, we attempt to solve a problem based on the available evidence. Did the butler do it? No, the butler could not have done it because there was blond hair on the knife and the butler had black hair. But perhaps the butler left the blond hair there to fool us.

Like a detective, scientists try to determine other factors that may be responsible for the outcome of their experiments or to piece together available information and draw general conclusions about the world. Also, like the detective, the scientist is constantly asking, "Given these clues, what inference can I make, and is the inference valid?" Logic is one method for answering these questions.

Validity

Logical procedures also help us understand the accuracy or validity of our ideas and research. **Validity** means that something is true and capable of being supported. There are various types of validity in psychology that arise from differing contexts. These contexts range from developing types of tests to running experiments. The overall question is, "Does a certain procedure, whether it is an intelligence test or an experiment, do what it was intended to do?" There are two general types of validity (Campbell & Stanley, 1963).

- **Internal validity**. The word "internal" refers to the experiment itself. Internal validity asks, "Is there another reason that might explain the outcome of our experimental procedures?" Students are particularly sensitive to questions of internal validity. For example, when it is time for final exams; they can make a number of alternative suggestions about what the exam actually measures and why it does not measure their knowledge of a particular subject. Like students, scientists look for reasons (threats to internal validity) that a particular piece of research may not measure what it claims to measure. In the case of our friend from Boston, the absence of tigers near his house could have reflected a long-standing absence of tigers in his part of the world rather than the effectiveness of his yelling.
- **External validity**. The word "external" refers to the world outside the setting in which the experiment was performed. External validity often is called **generalizability**. External

validity refers to the possibility of applying the results from an internally valid experiment to other situations and other research participants. Thomas Elbert and his colleagues found brain differences between those who played an instrument from an early age and those who did not. External validity asks if these results could be found in other individuals who played musical instruments from an early age.

We logically design our research to rule out as many alternative interpretations of our findings as possible and to ensure that any new facts are applicable to as wide a variety of other situations as possible. In many real-life situations in which external validity is high, however, it is impossible to rule out alternative interpretations of our findings. In a similar way, in laboratory settings in which internal validity is high, the setting is often artificial, and in many cases our findings cannot be generalized beyond the laboratory. Consequently, designing and conducting research is always a trade-off between internal and external validity. Which type of validity we choose to emphasize depends on the particular research question being asked.

Reliability

Whereas validity refers to a measurement being true, reliability refers to the measurement being consistent. For example, a bathroom scale is reliable if it gives you the same weight no matter how many times you stand on it (assuming your weight does not change between weighings). Most of our measures such as intelligence or treatment effectiveness show more variation than a physical measure such as weight. For this reason, when researchers are first designing a measure for a particular construct (for example, depression), it is common for the researchers to give the same measure over a number of occasions under similar conditions. They then examine the consistency of the research participants' responses to determine test–retest reliability, which is the correlation between the scores on each of the testing occasions.

In any study you want to use instruments that show a high positive correlation between these occasions. In addition, we also need the people who make the observations in a research study to be reliable in their ratings of particular behaviors. Like test–retest reliability, we can correlate the ratings of different observers when examining the same behavioral pattern. This is referred to as interrater reliability.

The Importance of Replication

Before we continue, let's clear up one misconception. It is the idea of designing "the one perfect study." Although scientists strive to design good research, there are always alternative explanations and conditions not included in any single study. It is for this reason that Donald Campbell, who introduced scientists to the idea of internal and external validity, also emphasized the importance of replicating studies (Campbell, 1957).

Replication involves repeating the study. If the same study is performed a number of times with similar results, then we can have more assurance that the results were both reliable and valid. Even better, if the study is performed in a variety of settings around the world, we have even more confidence in our results (Koole & Lakens, 2012; National Academy of Sciences, 2019; Shrout & Rodgers, 2018). The American Psychological Society (APS) is supporting such groups as the Center for Open Science (https://cos.io/about/mission/) in getting researchers to register their replication study before it is performed. In this way one can see after a number of the replication studies are completed which ones found data consistent with the original study and which did not. Thus, as an informed consumer of research findings, you want to base your conclusions on findings that have been replicated. There are also statistical techniques that you will learn about in more advanced courses that allow us to combine the data from a number of separate studies examining the same variables. This is referred to as *meta-analysis*. Meta-analysis also lets us know the strength of the relationship between the independent variable and dependent variable.

Measurement

Behavior can be described in many ways. In naturalistic observation studies, descriptions may consist of simple lists of behaviors or behavior sequences. For example, a cognitive psychologist might describe how a person interacts with a computer app. A developmental or clinical psychologist might report the manner in which a family interacts. In experimental studies, behaviors usually are expressed in more quantitative terms. We need a measure that others can use also. In a diet study, a common measure would be weight in pounds. Some other examples of quantitative measurements are the number of millimeters by which an observer overestimates the length of a line in a visual illusion experiment, the number of words recalled in a memory experiment, the change in a person's heart rate as a result of watching an emotionally charged film, and the results of an IQ test taken under different conditions.

Techniques

There are a variety of ways to measure a particular process. If you were interested in emotional responding, for example, you could record facial expression; measure psychophysiological activity, facial muscle activity, brain activity, and heart rate; obtain self-reports of internal states; and so on. Recording more than one measure is of great benefit to understanding what you are studying. Even when you decide which measure or measures to obtain, you still must decide whether to record the frequency of response, the intensity of response, the duration of response, the reaction time to the first response, or some combination of measures most appropriate to the question being asked. But how do we determine the appropriateness of a measure? One answer to this question is related to the conceptual question being asked.

Graphic Description of Frequency Information

A useful way to begin analyzing the results of any experiment is to convert your numerical data to pictorial form and then simply look at them. One way to do this is to draw a *frequency distribution*. In a frequency distribution, you simply plot how frequently each score appears in your data. Suppose you were interested in dreaming. An initial baseline measurement might be to ask 20 people to write down their dreams for a week. To get an idea of how often people dream, you might begin your analysis by seeing how many dreams each person recalls.

To create a pictorial representation, you want to match each participant with the number of dreams they recalled. A first step would be to find the smallest number of dreams recalled (0 in our case) and the largest number of dreams recalled (7). You could then list all the numbers from 0 to 7. Going through all of the responses recorded in **Table 2-1**, you could make a mark by the number of dreams recalled for each person in your study.

Now we have two variables (number of dreams recalled and number of people who recalled a certain number of dreams). This information can be plotted on a graph.

Table 2-1 Table of data from hypothetical dream study. This shows the number of dreams that each of the 20 participants reported.

Hypothetical Dream Study

Participant	Number of Dreams Recalled	Participant	Number of Dreams Recalled
1	1	11	7
2	4	12	1
3	5	12	2
4	2	14	5
5	0	15	6
6	2	16	5
7	0	17	2
8	6	18	6
9	1	19	7
10	3	20	5

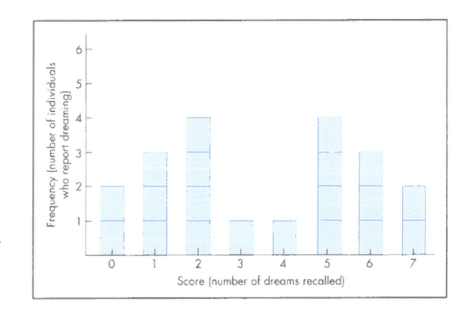

Figure 2-10 Bar graph of dream data. This graph shows the number of individuals who reported a particular number of dreams.

Figure 2-10 is a frequency distribution for these data. The vertical, or *y*-axis (ordinate), labeled "Frequency," is the number of people who fall into each category; the horizontal, or *x*-axis (abscissa), labeled "Score," is the number of dreams recalled. This type of presentation is called a *bar graph*.

Descriptive Statistics

Descriptive statistics are statistics that define the nature of the number that we are examining. You use descriptive statistics all the time in terms of your weight, your grades, and the amount of money you spend. Descriptive statistics allow us to characterize numbers in terms of frequency and variability.

Measures of Central Tendency

If you pay attention to the news, you will notice that certain terms are often used to describe the way we "typically" live. You will hear one report discussing the median income of college professors; another report may discuss the mean price of a new house in different cities in America. Modal (mode) descriptions are used less often, which is simply the most frequently occurring number.

There are three **measures of central tendency**, which is simply a single summary measure that describes a number of scores. These central tendency measures are known as the mean, median, and mode. Of these three, the mean is used most often. The **mean** of a set of scores is the arithmetic average of those scores. It is obtained by adding the scores and dividing the total by the number of scores. In our dream data, 20 people reported a total of 70 recalled dreams:

$$\text{mean} = \frac{\text{sum of scores}}{\text{number of scores}} = \frac{\text{number of dreams recalled}}{\text{number of individuals}} = \frac{75}{20} = 3.75$$

In this particular example, 70 divided by 20 equals exactly 3.75.

The **median** of a set of scores is the middle score—that is, the score that has an equal number of scores both above and below it. To calculate the median of a set of scores, list all the scores in order of magnitude (from largest to smallest or vice versa); the median is the middle score or, in the case of an even number of scores, the score halfway between the two middle scores. In our dream data, the two middle scores are 3 and 4. Consequently, the median is 3.5.

The **mode** is the most frequently occurring score. The only mathematical calculation required to compute the mode of a distribution of scores is to count the frequency of each score. The score that occurs most frequently is the mode. If there are two scores with the same frequency, we report two modes. For example, the dream data presented earlier had two modes: one at two dreams and one at five dreams recalled.

Given these three measures, you may be wondering which provides the best estimate of central tendency. There is no clear-cut answer. The appropriate choice varies with the particular frequency distribution and the intent of the researcher. For example, in a *normal distribution* the mode, median, and mean all have the same value (**Figure 2-11a**). This is not the case in a *skewed distribution* (**Figure 2-11b**). In a skewed distribution, extreme scores affect the mean.

Conceptually, the question asked influences which central tendency measure is used. If you are interested in the scores of a whole group, then the mean is the most appropriate measure. However, if you are more interested in a representative individual score, then the median is more appropriate. For example, before you take a job in a company where the mean salary is $100,000 a year, you might want to find out the median salary. That is, a mean of $100,000 could be produced by 10 people making $10,000 each and 1 person making $1,000,000 (1,100,000/11 = 100,000). Thus, mean salary would not help. If you were a stock market analyst concerned with how much a company pays out in salaries, however, the mean would be the appropriate measure. In other words, if you are interested in the scores of a whole group, then the mean is the most appropriate measure. However, if you are more interested in a representative individual score, then the median is more appropriate.

In psychological research, we tend to use the mean most often both for historical reasons and because it fits into already developed statistical theory. In summary, the measure of central

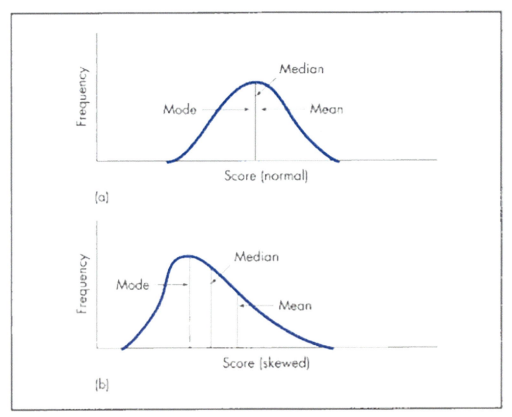

Figure 2-11 Mean, median, and mode of (a) a normal distribution and (b) a skewed distribution. In a normal distribution, the mean, median, and mode are the same. If the distribution is not normal, then the mean, median, and mode can be different.

tendency that you use depends on the question that you are asking. In the final analysis, you must use your judgment to determine which measure of central tendency to use.

Measures of Variability

You probably have completed a science course assignment requiring you to make measurements of some physical dimension, such as the length of a line. The exact readings among students probably differed. If we were to plot each measurement, we would see that the measurements varied around a particular point. We could also imagine that contained within these measurements was the actual length of the line or the *true score*. Any measurement is composed of a true measurement plus the variability associated with that measurement.

For example, your weight may change from day to day while still remaining constant when viewed over a series of measurements. Thus, to describe a set of measurements more accurately, we need a different measure. As we have seen, a measure of central tendency gives us some information concerning a set of scores. However, it does not give any information about how the scores are distributed. To obtain a more complete description of a set of data, we use a second measure in addition to the measure of central tendency. This is a measure of **variability**.

Measures of variability are attempts to indicate the degree to which scores in a data set differ from one another. We can also call this variability *dispersion*. One common measure of dispersion is the **range**, which reflects the difference between the largest and smallest scores in a set of data. The actual computational formula given for the range in most introductory statistics books is the largest score minus the smallest score. (In the dream data presented earlier, the range is 7; that is, 7 − 0 = 7.) Although computing the range is easy,

Scientific Psychology and Its Research Methods

Table 2-2 Data table of two different groups.

Group A	Group B
2	2
3	5
4	5
5	6
6	6
7	6
8	7
9	7
10	10

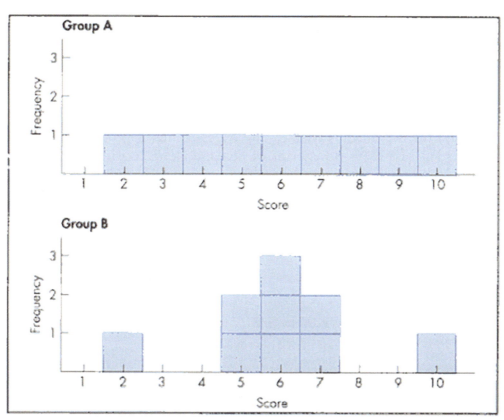

Figure 2-12 Two different distributions with the same range and mean but different dispersions of scores. To fully understand the numbers in your experiment, you would want to consider the distribution of scores.

the range tells us only about the two extreme scores; it provides no information about the dispersion of the remaining scores if we know nothing about the underlying distribution.

Let's now demonstrate this graphically. Consider the following two sets of data for Group A and Group B.

In these two distributions, the ranges are the same (8), and the means are the same (6), yet the actual shapes of the distributions are very different (**Figure 2-12**). The scores in Group B appear more concentrated in the center of the distribution, yet our estimate of range does not reflect this. To provide a more sensitive description of the dispersion of *all* the scores, we use a second measure of the variability of data. This measure is called the variance. The **variance** is a description of how much each score varies from the mean.

Another measure of variance is **standard deviation**. A standard deviation is defined mathematically. It is determined by taking the square root of the variance. The standard deviation is the most common measure of dispersion used in the scientific literature. By knowing the standard deviation, you can know how the scores in your study contribute to the mean. That is, you can know if they fall close to the mean or are widely dispersed.

CONCEPT CHECK

- Identify and describe the two general types of validity. What is the importance of each in conducting good research?
- What are three measures of central tendency? How is each calculated, and when would you use it?
- What are three measures of variability? How is each calculated, and when would you use it?

How Do We Design an Experimental Study?

The goal of experimental research is to determine the relationship between the independent variable and the dependent variable. The experimental approach is all about strong inference. The less bias there is in terms of demand characteristics related to both the participant and the experimenter aids in creating a logical relationship between the IV and DV. How do we infer a relationship between the independent variable and the dependent variable?

There are four factors that are critical to sound inference (**Figure 2-13**):

1. Participant selection
2. Participant assignment
3. Design of experiment
4. Interpretation of relationship of IV to DV

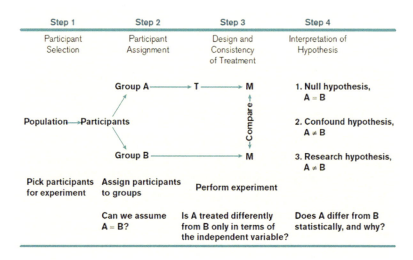

Figure 2-13 The four conceptual steps in experimentation. The first is selecting the people to be in the study. The second is assigning the participant to groups such as the experimental and control group. The third is to perform the experiment. The fourth is to interpret the results.

Select and Group Participants

Selecting participants for an experiment may seem simple, but it is often a bigger problem than it appears. The individuals selected for the study should be directly related to the hypothesis being tested. If you want to know if college students perform better on a memory test after drinking coffee, then of course you select college students. If you want to be able to apply the results to the *population* of all adults, then it is necessary to include adults of all ages in the study. Each study begins by asking who the individuals are that this research will apply to. This is formally known as the population under study. However, in most cases you can't study everyone.

Researchers use a variety of means for selecting participants. The best is some form of *random sampling*. Random sampling is the case in which any person that is part of the population is equally likely to be selected. You might choose every tenth person in the college directory, for example. When the selection is not random, that is, every person is not equally likely to be chosen, then bias can appear. One classic example of this type of bias happened in the surveys of the 1936 presidential election.

In 1936, asking more than 2 million people for whom they would vote in the next presidential election led one magazine to conclude that the Republican nominee, Alfred Landon, would beat the Democratic incumbent, Franklin Roosevelt (Gallup, 1972). To be precise, the magazine predicted that Landon would carry 32 states and 57% of the vote compared to Roosevelt's 43%. In fact, the results were very different, with Landon carrying only 2 states and receiving 37% of the vote in comparison to Roosevelt's 61%.

George Gallup conducted a much smaller survey of only 5,000 voters and correctly predicted the winner. What was the secret of his success? How did Gallup do more with less? The answer was in the sampling procedures. Although the magazine sampled 2,376,523 people, their names were drawn from automobile registration lists and telephone directories.

Realizing that this survey took place in 1936, during the middle of the Great Depression, you can understand, perhaps, what the bias was in this sampling technique. During the Depression, many people did not have money for cars or telephones and thus would not have been included in the survey. Those who did have telephones and cars tended to be wealthy and also to be Republicans. Thus, wealthy Republicans completed the survey in disproportionate numbers, saying they would vote for Landon and against Roosevelt. Gallup used a sampling procedure that did not exclude the poor, who were mainly Democrats and more likely to vote for Roosevelt. Gallup thus had the more accurate representation, and his prediction of a Roosevelt victory was correct.

After the participants have been randomly selected from the larger population under study, they can then be randomly assigned to experimental and control groups. This ensures that the groups are equal before the experiment begins. *Randomization* controls for both known and unknown potentially confounding variables. Randomization leaves solely to chance the assignment of our participants to a group. In this way any differences, even unknown or unsuspected differences, will also be nullified by being randomly distributed between our two groups.

Plan the Structure

Somewhat like a blueprint, the *experimental design* directs the procedures and gives form to the experiment. In essence, an experimental design is a plan for how a study is to be structured. In an outline form, a design tells us what will be done to whom and when. To be evaluated favorably, a design must perform two related functions. First, it must provide a logical structure that enables us to pinpoint the effects of the independent variable on the dependent variable and thus answer our research questions. Second, it must help us to rule out confounds as an alternative explanation for our findings. A sound design must allow us to determine logically the effect of the independent variable on the dependent variable and to rule out alternative explanations.

Imagine a study in which a social psychologist was interested in determining if watching a film about the value of interacting with people (IV) would result in the participant being more sensitive to individuals showing more positive or engaging emotions (DV). After the subject watched the film, he or she could be shown images of a variety of individuals with different facial expressions. The participant could be instructed to press the computer key as soon as he or she could identify the emotion.

If we were to diagram the design of this study, it would be:

Select the group   Watch film   Measure reaction time

If we performed the experiment with just a single group, what could we conclude? We could determine if our participants were faster recognizing positive or negative emotions. However, this would not help us determine if this was related to the film they saw. It may be that humans recognize positive versus negative emotions differently no matter what the situation. Such a design would not be much help in pinpointing the effect of the independent variable on the dependent variable, nor would it rule out confounds.

A stronger design would use a control group. This design would appear as:

| Experimental group | Film | Measure reaction time |
| Control group | No film | Measure reaction time |

Since the control group had not seen the film, then we would have stronger evidence that seeing the film was related to differences in reaction time measures.

In our research design, different participants comprise the experimental group versus the control group. This type of design is called the *between-subjects design*. Between-subjects refers to the fact that different participants are part of each group.

Interpret the Results

Once we have collected our data we want to know how to interpret our experimental results. We do this by considering three separate hypotheses:

1. *Null hypothesis*—this is a statistical hypothesis that is tested to determine if there are differences between our experimental and control groups. Null is similar to being invalid or zero and thus refers to the possibility that there are no differences between groups. Part of this statistical procedure is to ask the question of whether our results could have happened by chance.
2. *Confound hypothesis*—this is a conceptual question that asks if our results could be the result of a factor other than the independent variable.
3. *Research hypothesis*—this asks the question of whether our results are related to the independent variable.

Inferential Statistics

As described previously, descriptive statistics are used to determine characteristics of a group such as mean and variance. You might want to know how many other children 6-year-olds talked to during recess. You might examine how students performed on a particular college quiz. In both of these cases, you are only interested in these specific groups. However, we usually perform research with a limited number of individuals so that we can infer the behavior of all individuals related to the group we are studying. For example, if we study how a group of 3-year-olds produce sentences, then it is our assumption that other 3-year-olds would perform in a similar way.

What are the odds that the 3-year-olds in our group are like all 3-year-olds everywhere? To determine this **probability**, we use **inferential statistics**, which are methods for understanding how the data from an experiment can be generalized to all similar people. Ideally, if the same experiment was run an infinite number of times with a different sample of individuals chosen from the entire population, then the population of estimates would then represent all the possible outcomes of the experiment.

What we need, of course, is a technique for determining whether a set of results is different from what would be expected. One of the common statistical techniques used for this is called the *t-test*. A t-test determines the size of the association between two variables in relation to the number of participants in the study. It was developed near the beginning of the 20th century by William Gosset who worked for the Guinness Brewery in Dublin, Ireland. Since breweries want all of the beer they sell to taste the same, Gosset wanted a method for determining the uniformity of each batch of beer. In this case, he actually wanted the null hypothesis to be true. That is, each beer would be the same.

Confound Hypothesis

The second question asked is could our results be due to a **confound**, something that systematically biases the results of our research, rather than the independent variable. What is a confound? Almost anything can be a confound. Confounds often result from unintended factors. It may be the fact that on the day before we ran the experimental group in a social psychology experiment on conformity there was a television special on how we always do what other people tell us. Or a confound may be introduced into a weight-reduction experiment if one group is asked to lose weight at a time of the year when people eat less and their gastrointestinal systems work faster (summer), whereas another group was started at a time when people eat more (winter). Some confounds can be prevented or controlled, but others cannot. You cannot control world events, but you can ask whether there is any reason to believe that a particular event that took place inside or outside of the laboratory could have influenced one group more than another and thus introduced a confound.

One classic example of an initially overlooked participant factor occurred in an experiment conducted in the 1930s at the Hawthorne plant of Western Electric. It was designed to determine how factors such as lighting and working hours affect productivity (Mayo, 1933). The participants were a group of women who worked at the plant; they were asked to work under varying conditions. The productivity of these women was compared with general productivity. When the data were analyzed, a strange finding emerged. In many cases the productivity of these women increased. It even increased under a condition in which the lighting in the experimental condition was not as good as that in the actual plant. From an experimental design standpoint, it was difficult to understand the data until the experimenters examined how they had treated these women. The answer they came up with was that the

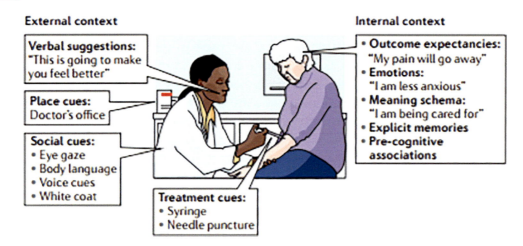

Figure 2-14 The placebo response includes both external and internal factors. External factors can include where the procedure takes place, how the professional appears, and the nature of the social interaction. Internal factors can include expectations, past experiences, and internal reactions to the professional.
Source: Wager and Atlas (2015).

women in the experiment had been given special attention just by being in an experiment. This attention caused the women to consider themselves *special,* and this feeling was reflected in the work they performed. This came to be known as the *Hawthorne effect* after the name of the plant in which they worked. In research terminology, this type of bias is referred to as **demand characteristics**. Demand characteristics occur when a participant's response is influenced more by the research setting than by the independent variable.

A related phenomenon is the **placebo effect**. This occurs when some people show psychological and physiological changes just from the suggestion that a change will take place. The placebo effect is related to prior learning, expectation, and social factors, and also includes a brain component (Wager & Atlas, 2015; Geuter, Koban, & Wager, 2017). It includes both situational factors and what the person tells himself or herself (see **Figure 2-14**). How could this effect be addressed in a treatment study to reduce anxiety?

To control for the placebo effect in research, various procedures have been used. One is to use a control group that receives either no treatment or a treatment previously shown to be ineffective for the particular disorder under study. In medical research, it is common to give a "sugar" pill that looks exactly like the medicine with the active ingredient.

Another procedure to study placebo effects is called the *open-hidden paradigm* (Geuter, Koban, & Wager, 2017). For example, after an operation in a hospital, patients are often connected through a needle in their arm to a machine that delivers various drugs. Since the machine is there constantly, most individuals don't actually know when medication is being delivered. This is the hidden part of the open–hidden paradigm. The open part of the paradigm is for the health care worker to administer the drug in the form of a shot or to place the drug in the machine so that the patient realizes that it is being administered.

With pain patients, open administration has been found to be more effective in reducing pain than hidden administration (Price, Finniss, & Benedetti, 2008; Kaptchuk & Miller, 2018). In one of these studies, which used five different drugs including morphine, pain patients showed more pain reduction when the same drug was administered in the open as opposed to the hidden condition (Amanzio, Pollo, Maggi, & Benedetti, 2001).

During the 1970s, researchers were trying to understand how opiate drugs such as heroin, morphine, and opium worked. To their surprise, they found that there are opiate receptors in our brains. This suggested that our brains use opiate substances for some purpose. To make a long story short, they discovered that not only did the brain have receptors for opiates but also that the brain made opiates. The most well-known of these brain-made opiates are called *endorphins*. The term *endorphin* is a contraction for "endogenous morphine." Like the opiate drugs given by medical professionals for pain, our brain administers endorphins as a way to reduce pain. This helps us to understand how athletes or solders are able to complete an activity even when injured. At times, they don't even know they are injured.

This research with endorphins may lead one to believe that our brain is involved in the placebo effect. However, how do we know that? One way we know that begins with a study from 1978 (Levine et al., 1978). In this study, individuals who had seen the dentist for oral surgery were given medication for pain two hours later. Some of these dental patients were given morphine, some were given a placebo, and some were given a placebo plus naloxone. Naloxone is a chemical that takes away the effects of morphine. Both the morphine and the placebo reduced the pain. However, the group that received naloxone showed an increase in pain. This was clear evidence that the placebo effect for pain involves the opiate substances produced by our brain.

Experimenters also have expectations. For example, knowing that one set of participants has been assigned to one condition rather than another could result in those participants being treated differently. Such situations are referred to as ***experimenter effects***. One important way to control for experimenter effects is to use a ***double-blind experiment*** in which the experimental group is divided into two groups. One group is given the actual treatment, and the other is given a treatment exactly like the experimental treatment but without the active ingredient. Neither the placebo group nor the experimental group would know which medication they are receiving, and in this way these research participants are said to be ***blind controls***. The term double blind indicates that the experimenters giving the medication also do not know which treatment is experimental and which is placebo.

In order to sort through the results of our experiments, we must be like detectives who constantly ask if there is another way to understand what was found. Our way of doing that is through research, logic, and doubt. We use research to design a study to consider alternative possibilities. We use logic to consider if our conclusions follow from the results. We use doubt to ask if there is a way to know if we are wrong.

CONCEPT CHECK

- What are four factors critical to enabling sound inference in determining the relation between the IV and the DV in an experiment?
- Why is randomization important to selecting participants and assigning them to groups in an experimental study?
- What is the difference between descriptive statistics and inferential statistics? What is the primary purpose of each?
- What is a double-blind experiment, and what are researchers trying to control for by using that design?

What Are the Ethics of Scientific Research?

In several Nazi concentration camps during World War II, prisoners were injected with a virus or bacterium and then received drugs to determine the drugs' effectiveness against the injections. Although medical knowledge was gained from these experiments, the world judged the experiments unethical and criminal. Later, these scientist–physicians stood trial in Nuremburg, Germany and were found guilty of war crimes. They were either executed or received long prison sentences. The other result of these trials was a code of ethics for medical experimentation with human participants. It is called the Nuremberg Code, and was adopted as a guideline for future research.

Ethics is the study of proper action that examines relationships between human beings and provides principles regarding how we should treat one another. The ultimate decision in ethical questions resides in judgments of value.

The Pursuit of Knowledge and Avoiding Harm

Ethical considerations of psychological experimentation have at their heart the idea that people participating in research should not be harmed. Of course, no psychological researcher seeks to harm a participant. However, there can be unexpected outcomes. Specifically, at the end of an experiment, participants should not be affected in a way that would result in a lower level of human functioning. This includes emotional distress. Ethical considerations must also look at the other side of the participant–scientist relationship. This includes the scientist's right to know and to seek answers to questions. It would also be considered unethical to prevent a scientist from seeking knowledge without considering his or her rights. Thus, we begin with the rights of the scientist to know and to pursue knowledge and the rights of the participants to be protected from undue harm.

In most cases the scientist has a question that he or she wants to ask and that the participant is willing to help answer. Scientists have the right to study human functioning and answer appropriate questions. Participants have the right to be protected. In some cases, the participants learn something about themselves or about psychology from the experience, and they are glad to have participated. In brain-imaging studies, for example, participants often report that they enjoy seeing their brain activity (for example, functional magnetic resonance imaging (fMRI), electroencephalogram (EEG)) displayed. Other participants, like some travelers to a foreign country, enter the world of experimentation and leave it again without ever realizing it. Although ignorant of the underlying structure, they still leave with the experience of the event and may be changed by it.

If these experiences were always pleasant and any changes in the participant always positive, people would gladly participate in experiments, and scientists would face few ethical questions. However, at times the scientist may want to answer a question that requires that the participant experience psychological or physiological discomfort. These situations raise a number of questions:

1. What are the responsibilities of the scientist toward the participant?
2. What are the rights of the participant?
3. Are there guidelines for reconciling conflicts between the rights of the participant to pursue happiness and the rights of the scientist to pursue knowledge?
4. What type of relationship or dialogue would be most productive for helping the scientist and participant fulfill their needs and desires?

Since the 1950s, the American Psychological Association (APA) has published a set of guidelines. This is available online (http://www.apa.org/ethics). The federal government has adopted similar sets of guidelines for human and animal research, including the manner in which these studies should be reviewed.

Voluntary Participation and Informed Consent

What was unethical about the experiments at the Nazi concentration camps? It was not that human beings were given a virus, as almost all of our current procedures of preventive medicine (the polio vaccine is a historical example) require that the procedure eventually be tested on human beings. These physicians were convicted of conducting experiments *without the consent of their participants*. One of the first principles of research is that the participants must consent to being part of an experiment. Furthermore, they must also be informed of the experiment's purpose and its potential risks. Thus, major ingredients in the dialogue between the scientist and the research participant are *voluntary participation* and *informed consent*.

Although a number of studies worldwide have ignored basic participant rights, the US Public Health Service began one particularly troubling study in 1932 that was originally designed to understand the long-term effects of syphilis. The participants were African-American men in Macon County, Alabama, who had syphilis. The people involved in the experiment were not told that they had syphilis and were denied any form of treatment. Although treatments for syphilis in the 1930s were not very effective, this study continued even after effective treatments were developed in the late 1940s. In fact, the study was not terminated until its existence was publicly exposed in a Washington newspaper in 1972, some 40 years later. This study not only violated basic ethical principles such as informed consent, but also put others, such as the participants' families, at risk. It came to be called the *Tuskegee experiment* (https://www.tuskegee.edu/Content/Uploads/Tuskegee/files/Bioethics/SyphilisStudyCommitteeReport.pdf).

In the initial dialogue between the scientist and the prospective participant, the scientist must ask the participant to be a part of the experiment. This is the principle of **voluntary participation**. In essence, the voluntary participation principle suggests that a person should participate in an experiment only by free choice. In addition, this principle states that a participant should be free to leave an experiment at any time, whether or not the experiment has been completed.

As you think about voluntary participation, you will become entangled in the question of whether anyone can ever make a free decision and, if so, under what circumstances. As you might have realized already, this question becomes even more complicated for someone interested in developmental psychology, which requires research with children, or for someone interested in psychopathology, which requires research with patients who are mentally impaired. In terms of ethical concerns involving research with children, a number of recommendations have been put forward by the National Academies of Science, including how to obtain informed consent and ensure voluntary participation in research (Field & Behrman, 2004).

Assuming for a moment that someone can agree freely to participate in research, the scientist in the initial dialogue should inform the prospective participant about what will be required of him or her during the study. The scientist must also inform the prospective participant about any potential harm that may come from participation. Thus, the prospective participant must be given complete information on which to base a decision. This is the principle of **informed consent**. Consider the Tuskegee experiment—the principle of informed consent raises the issue of how much information about an experiment is enough.

From the principles of voluntary participation and informed consent, we can see that it is the initial task of the scientist to fully discuss the experimental procedure with prospective participants and to remind them that they are human beings who do not give away their rights just because they are taking part in a psychological experiment.

Confidentiality and Anonymity

In our society, research participants have the same rights during an experiment that they have outside the experimental situation, including the **right to privacy**. Most of us may initially consider the right to privacy as the right to spend time by oneself or with others of one's choosing, without being disturbed. This is the external manifestation of the right to privacy. But there is also an internal or intrapersonal manifestation of this right (see Raebhausen & Brim, 1967). This is the right to have private thoughts or, as it is sometimes called, a **private personality**. This means that the thoughts and feelings of a participant should not be made public without the participant's consent. It also means that a conversation between a participant and a scientist should be considered a private event, not a public one.

If that is the case, how can the scientist ever report her or his findings? There are two considerations that are part of the scientist's responsibility to the participant: *confidentiality* and *anonymity*.

- **Confidentiality** requires that the scientist not release data of a personal nature to other scientists or groups without the participant's consent. Even during the experiment, researchers keep any personal data in a secure location and often destroy personal information once the experiment is completed.
- **Anonymity** requires that the personal identity of a given participant be kept separate from his or her data. The easiest way to accomplish this is to avoid requesting names in the first place; however, there are times when this may be impossible. Another alternative is to use code numbers that protect the identities of the participants and to destroy the list of participants' names once the data analysis has been completed.

The Ethical Relationship

Let's remind ourselves that ethical questions have at their base issues of relationships and traditions. As scientists we ask what *is* and what *ought to be* our relationship with our participants and our society with regard to research. To answer this question, we stress that part of our ethical responsibility is to consult with others about our research. In this context, we would include the manner in which internal review committees evaluate the ethics of research and the guidelines (for example, those of the American Psychological Association and the federal government) used to direct our evaluations. With both humans and animals, we are only beginning to develop methods for the study of inner experience that can help to inform our ethical considerations. Part of our ethical responsibility is to use treatment approaches that have been shown to be effective, as described in the box: Applying Psychological Science—Empirically Based Treatments.

Applying Psychological Science—Empirically Based Treatments

Before the middle of the 20th century, very little formal research was performed to determine the effectiveness of psychological or medical interventions. Beginning in the 1950s and 1960s, there was a movement to determine the effectiveness of both in a scientific manner. In medicine, this came to be known as *evidence-based medicine*. This was the beginning of an approach that sought to replace opinion and tradition with solid scientific evidence. In psychology, the terms *empirically based treatments* or *empirically based principles* refer to psychological treatments and their aspects for which there is scientific evidence that the treatment is effective.

Three websites have been developed that list treatments for specific mental disorders.

- The first is maintained by the Clinical Psychology section of the American Psychological Association (APA) (https://www.apa.org/ed/graduate/specialize/clinical).
- The second is maintained by the US Substance Abuse and Mental Health Services Administration (SAMHSA), which is part of the US Department of Health and Human Services. This website contains a searchable online registry of mental health and substance abuse interventions that have been evaluated (http://samhsa.gov).
- The third website is devoted to effective treatments for children and adolescents (http://effectivechildtherapy.com/). This site is maintained by the Society of Clinical Child and Adolescent Psychology section of the APA.

There are a number of different treatments available when you visit a health care professional. You want to know what will work for *you*. That is the purpose of *effectiveness research*. Not all treatments work the same with every person. Thus, clinical researchers test treatments with a diversity of individuals. Such factors as gender, age, socioeconomic level, ethnic diversity, and so forth are important to consider.

As a society we want to focus more on approaches and principles for which there is scientific evidence. In determining what works there has been a willingness to integrate techniques from different theoretical approaches to treatment. The last chapter of this book will examine treatment for psychological disorders in greater detail.

Thought Question: We all act as scientists in our everyday lives. What situations in your life, for example, doing well in your studies or increasing your fitness level, could you tackle with effectiveness research? What series of experiments would you design to come up with empirically based principles for yourself? What would be the independent and dependent variables?

The Care and Use of Laboratory Animals

The issue of animal research has raised a number of questions over the past couple of decades. In fact, the American population is increasingly concerned about how animals are treated. In a 2015 Gallup poll, some 62% of Americans said that animals need protection from harm and exploitation, but it is appropriate to use them for the benefits of humans (http://www.gallup.com/poll/183275/say-animals-rights-people.aspx). Some 32% of Americans took a stronger position and suggested that animals should receive the same protections as humans in terms of harm and exploitation. In specific situations, there was most concern for animals in the circus, sports events, and research. There was less concern for animals used as household pets or raised for food.

To protect animals from undue suffering or harm, a number of professional organizations have issued guidelines concerning the care and use of laboratory animals. The federal guidelines were issued by the US Public Health Service (PHS) in 1985 and updated in

1996 and 2002. In this policy statement, the PHS describes the manner in which animals are to be used and cared for.

It is clear that there are a number of emotional and polarized positions about the use of animals in research. The February 1997 issue of *Scientific American* offered a series of articles relating to animal research that illustrates well the opposing positions. For example, one position suggests that information learned from animal research is often redundant and unnecessary and may be misleading (Barnard & Kaufman, 1997). On the other hand, other researchers suggest that at least since the time of Pasteur, animal research has offered important breakthroughs in the treatment of disorders for both humans and animals (Botting & Morrison, 1997).

Those who support using animals in research point out that animal research is crucial to meet the goals of society. One propaganda poster points out that animal research has added 20 years (through medical research) to the lives of the people who protest against it. Of course, there is no one right answer for all situations. There are situations in which research with animals may not benefit society. As noted previously, even our research with humans has at times been inappropriate.

Today, scientists are seeking alternatives to using animals in laboratory research. One of the alternatives to laboratory research with animals is to study them in their natural environment. Other alternatives include computer simulations or the use of tissue cultures in biomedical research. In this book, you will notice that much of the animal research presented comes from an earlier period in the history of psychology. Technology now allows us to study human processes in ways not possible previously.

Humans and animals have a long-standing bond. Historical records suggest that animals have been kept as pets and used for herding sheep, plowing fields, and transportation for thousands of years. To protect their welfare, various organizations have been formed over the years, including the Society for the Prevention of Cruelty to Animals (SPCA), formed in England in 1824 and in the United States in 1866. Surprisingly, child abuse cases in the 19th century were initially brought to court under the laws against cruelty to animals because there were no similar laws for children!

Deception Studies

Deception research is any study in which the participant is deceived about the true purpose of the experiment or the experimental procedures. For example, if an experimenter wanted to examine the effects of anxiety on performance in college students, he or she might create an anxiety-provoking situation followed by a performance measure. One method used to create anxiety in college students is to administer a so-called IQ test that cannot be completed in the allotted time and to state that most college students who later go to graduate school have no trouble finishing this test. In the chapter on social process, you will be introduced to some classic studies in psychology that have used deception.

Another type of deception often used in medical research is the placebo treatment. For example, participants are given a pill made up of sugar or other inactive ingredients and told that it will cause certain physiological changes, such as reducing the number of headaches they have been experiencing. There is a long history that shows changes with placebos that cannot be explained by the medication itself (see Benedetti, 2009 for an overview). Thus, to give a medication with only inert ingredients could be considered deceptive. For this reason, most placebo studies tell the participants that they will either receive a placebo or a treatment with an active ingredient.

Most psychological studies that use deception try to create a situation in which the participant sees the world and what he or she is being asked to do in a certain way. Because it is impossible to obtain informed consent in deception research without compromising the study, is it unethical to perform this research? This is not an easy question to answer, and the professionals in the field currently fall into two camps.

The first group suggests that any deception is unethical, and thus no deception research is possible. The second group argues that certain types of deception research are necessary. This group further argues that, given appropriate safeguards, deception research is the only way to answer certain questions.

Once the experiment is concluded, however, it would be unethical to allow a participant to leave the experimental situation without a true understanding of what had taken place. The process of explaining the true purpose of the experiment afterward is called ***debriefing***. In the debriefing procedure, the experimenter removes any misconceptions and offers a full discussion of the experiment. It is the goal of this dialogue to ensure that participants leave the laboratory with at least as much self-esteem and as little anxiety as when they came to the experiment (Kelman, 1968).

The debriefing process consists of two major aspects. First, the debriefing is an opportunity for the participants to tell the experimenter how they felt about being part of the experiment. This not only is good feedback for the experimenter but also allows the participants to express any self-doubt about their performance and deal with thoughts and feelings that arose during the experiment. Second, the debriefing is an opportunity for the experimenter to explain the study to the participants in greater detail.

CONCEPT CHECK

- "Ethical considerations of psychological experimentation have at their heart the idea that people participating in research should not be harmed." What four questions does every scientist need to consider in designing a research study?
- What are "voluntary participation" and "informed consent" in the context of scientific research? What are some of the specific issues they raise in terms of psychological research?
- How do confidentiality and anonymity figure into the experimenter's responsibility to protect the research participant's right to privacy?
- Why does the issue of animal research raise questions with the public? What are five reasons for conducting research with animals in biological psychology?

Summary

Learning Objective 1: Discuss the general process called science.
In general, there is no single scientific method, yet there is a general process called *science*. This process consists of experiencing the world and then drawing general conclusions (called *facts*) from observations. Sometimes these conclusions or facts are descriptive and can be represented by numbers. For example, we say that the moon is 238,000 miles from

Earth or that the brain uses 20% of the energy produced by the body or that the average human heart rate is 72 beats per minute unless you exercise a lot and then it is probably about 50 beats per minute. Other times, these facts are more general and can describe a relationship or a process. For example, we say that it is more difficult to learn a second language after puberty than before or that as we age we hear fewer high-frequency sounds. Whatever the topic, the known facts about a particular subject are called *scientific knowledge* (see Ray, 2022 for more information).

Learning Objective 2: List the steps in the scientific method.
There are four stages to the scientific method: (1) develop an idea or expectation (hypothesis), (2) turn this hypothesis into an experiment, (3) evaluate the ideas and expectations about the world through observation and experimentation, and (4) draw conclusions or inferences about the ideas and expectations and consider the impact of the new information on theoretical conceptualizations. This is very different from the phenomenon of pseudoscience—or "fake" science—which presents information as if it is based on science when it is not. There are many research designs and which one to select begins with the question the scientist wants to answer. Some of the research designs used to study psychology include case study, naturalistic observation, correlational approaches, experimental method, and behavioral genetics designs.

Learning Objective 3: Explain how logic and inference are used to reach a conclusion.
Logic can help us answer questions of inference, which is the process by which we look at the evidence available to us and then use our powers of reasoning to reach a conclusion. Logical procedures are also important for helping us understand the accuracy or validity of our ideas and research. Using measures of two types of validity (internal and external), we logically design our research to rule out as many alternative interpretations of our findings as possible and to have any new facts be applicable to as wide a variety of other situations as possible. There is no "one perfect study"; designing and conducting research is always a trade-off between internal and external validity. Behavior can be described or measured in many ways; likewise, there are a variety of ways to measure a particular process. A useful way to begin analyzing the results of any experiment is to convert numerical data to pictorial form and then simply look at them. A second step is to calculate descriptive statistics for the sample—measures of central tendency and variability. The measure of central tendency that you use in your analysis—mean, median, or mode—depends on the question that you are asking. Measures of variability indicate how spread out the scores are. Measures of variability (or dispersion) include range, variance, and standard deviation. One characteristic of human beings is that we seek to determine what will happen next. If participants' expectations (demand characteristics) or researchers' expectations (experimenter effects) interfere with the influence of the independent variable, then the study could give inaccurate results. A related phenomenon is the placebo effect. To control for the placebo effect in research, various procedures have been used, the most powerful of which is to design a double-blind experiment.

Learning Objective 4: Describe the steps involved in designing an experimental study.
There are four steps to the experimental process that reflect the evolutionary nature of science: (1) the development of the hypothesis, (2) the translation of this hypothesis into a research design, (3) the running of the experiment, and (4) the interpretation of the results. Researchers

take the results and interpretations of their studies and create new research studies that refine the previous hypotheses, and the cycle begins anew. One goal of experimental research is to determine the relationship between the independent variable (IV) and the dependent variable (DV). The less bias in terms of demand characteristics related to both the participant and the experimenter aids in creating a logical relationship between the IV and DV. Additional factors critical to sound inference are participant selection and assignment, the design of the experiment, and the interpretation of the relationship of the IV to the DV. The experimenter considers three hypotheses in interpreting whether the DV is related to the IV: null hypothesis, confound hypothesis, and research hypothesis. Scientists pay particular attention to research that has been evaluated by other scientists before it is published in a process called peer review, and journals that follow this procedure are called peer-reviewed journals. Replication of studies in different locations with different participants increases the certainty that the results found reflect the true nature of what is being studied.

Learning Objective 5: Discuss the ethical guidelines that psychologists follow in order to protect the rights of people participating in research projects.
Ethical considerations of psychological experimentation have at their heart the idea that people participating in research should not be harmed. In addition, research participants have a right to privacy including the right to a private personality. To protect those rights, participants must be informed of the experiment's purpose and its potential risks (informed consent) and then voluntarily agree to participate in the experiment (voluntary participation). Confidentiality and anonymity are two additional considerations that are part of the scientist's responsibility to the participant. Deception research and animal research are two areas of study in psychology in which specific ethical concerns have been raised. Guidelines for reconciling all conflicts between the rights of the participant to pursue happiness and the rights of the scientist to pursue knowledge are provided by such resources as the APA, and the federal government.

Study Resources

Review Questions

1. What does the author mean by "science is a combination of interaction with the world and logic"? What key role does doubt play in the process of science?
2. Design a series of research studies around a single question that uses each of the methods of science covered in this chapter: naturalistic observation, correlational approach, and experimental method.
3. Why can't you design "the perfect study"? What trade-offs do you need to consider in designing an experimental study in the real world? What can you do to improve the quality of your study?
4. What roles do the following hypotheses play in interpreting experimental results:
   a. null hypothesis?
   b. confound hypothesis?
   c. research hypothesis?
5. How is a scientist conducting psychology research like a detective solving a mystery? How are they different?
6. If we think about psychology research as an ethical problem, what are the rights of the research participant, and what are the responsibilities of the experimenter in ensuring the protection of those rights? What legal and ethical resources are available to guide this effort?

For Further Reading

Kuhn, T. (1962). *The Structure of Scientific Revolutions.* Chicago, IL: University of Chicago Press.
Mook, D. (2004). *Classic Experiments in Psychology.* Westport, CT: Greenwood Press.
Ray, W. (2022). *Research Methods for Psychological Science.* Thousand Oaks, CA: Sage.

Web Resources

APA ethics—www.apa.org/ethics
Tuskegee experiment—https://www.cdc.gov/tuskegee/timeline.htm
Empirical therapy APA—http://www.div12.org/PsychologicalTreatments
SAMSHA approaches—http://samhsa.gov
Treatment for children—http://effectivechildtherapy.com/
Gallop poll—http://www.gallup.com/poll/183275/say-animals-rights-people.aspx

Key Terms and Concepts

- anonymity
- blind controls
- case study
- confidentiality
- confound
- confound hypothesis
- confounding variables
- control group
- correlation coefficient
- correlational research
- debriefing
- deception research
- demand characteristics
- dependent variable (DV)
- descriptive statistics
- double-blind experiment
- doubt
- empiricism
- ethics
- experimental design
- experimental group
- experimental method
- experimenter effects
- external validity
- facts
- falsification
- generalizability
- hypothesis
- independent variable (IV)
- inference
- inferential statistics
- informed consent
- internal validity
- logic
- mean
- measures of central tendency
- median
- meta-analysis
- mode
- naturalistic observation
- negative correlation
- null hypothesis
- operational definition
- paradigm
- paradigm shift
- peer review
- placebo effect
- population
- positive correlation
- private personality
- probability
- pseudoscience
- random sampling
- randomization
- range
- replication
- research hypothesis
- right to privacy
- scatterplot
- science
- scientific knowledge
- scientific method
- standard deviation
- *t*-test
- validity
- variability
- variance
- voluntary participation

3 The Neuroscience of Behavior and Experience

LEARNING OBJECTIVES

3.1 Describe the basic elements of the nervous system and their connection to behavior and experience.

3.2 Describe the development and evolution of the brain.

3.3 List the key structures of the brain.

3.4 Outline the neuroscience methods that are being used to observe activity in the brain.

3.5 Describe the role that genetics play in helping us understand our psychological processes.

*In 1848, 25-year-old Phineas Gage was a railroad construction supervisor in Vermont. Part of his job was to prepare the charges to blast rocks so that the railroad tracks could be laid. After a hole was drilled in the rock, it was filled by gunpowder and sand, which was then tamped down with a long iron rod. On one occasion, Phineas Gage did not realize that the sand had not been added and began to drop the iron rod into the hole. As the rod went into the rock, a spark ignited the gunpowder and it exploded, sending the fine-pointed 13-pound iron rod through his face, skull, and brain (**Figure 3-1**). The rod landed some 30 feet away.*

After being momentarily stunned, Gage amazingly regained full consciousness. He was taken back to his boarding house by cart and was even able to walk upstairs with help. He was even able to joke and laugh with the local doctor who was treating him. Soon after that he became unconscious and stayed that way for two weeks. Surprisingly, over time Phineas Gage was able to recover from his physical injuries. He continued to be able to speak and perform everyday motor processes. His intelligence and ability to learn new information remained as before the accident.

However, his personality showed such a drastic change that his coworkers said he was "no longer Gage." Whereas he was a mild-mannered person before the accident, afterward he was prone to angry outbursts. He would make a plan but then change his mind. A person who previously had a good sense of money management, he now lacked this ability. Gage also started ignoring social conventions and frequently used profanity. The accident had clearly influenced his emotional processing.

This case study, as described by his physician, Dr. Harlow, has helped scientists understand how brain damage can influence social and emotional processes seen in other types of mental disorders (Harlow, 1868). This knowledge has helped later scientists to consider which areas of the brain might be involved in mental disorders that show deficits in social and emotional processing. The importance of this case has also prompted a number of modern reexaminations of the evidence concerning Phineas Gage (Damasio, Grabowski, Frank, Galaburda, & Damasio, 1994; Van Horn, Irimia, Torgerson,

82 The Neuroscience of Behavior and Experience

Chambers, Kikinis, & Toga, 2012). The iron rod and Gage's skull now reside at the Medical Museum at Harvard University.

How Does the Nervous System Enable Behavior and Experience?

Sir Charles Sherrington, the 1930s Nobel Prize winner for his groundbreaking work on reflexes, suggested that we view the brain as an *enchanted loom*. He was referring to how the cells in the brain become active and form patterns, only to change these patterns as new processes become important. This metaphor helps us to realize that the brain is never constant but always changing. In fact, Sherrington saw these patterns as a dance (**Figure 3–2**).

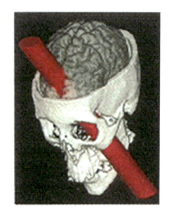

Figure 3-1 Depiction of the rod in Phineas Gage's brain.

Every experienced feeling or thought involves different aspects of our nervous system. The same is true of behavior. For example, we make predictions as to how to catch a ball in the air or when to swerve the car to miss a pothole on the road. This happens when our nervous system, composed of networks of neurons that convey information throughout our bodies, is activated. We have also come to the realization that our brain not only processes information but also makes predictions about what will happen next (Allen & Friston, 2018; Friston, 2018).

Our nervous system can be divided into two major components (**Figure 3–3**). The first division is the **central nervous system (CNS)**, which is composed of the brain and spinal cord. The second division is the **peripheral nervous system (PNS)**. The peripheral nervous system includes the *somatic nervous system*, which sends and receives information to and from the brain. This system allows us to pick up a water bottle, find our keys in a backpack, or go for a run. This system also permits our brains to send information to and receive information from internal organs. For example, when we see a bear in the woods, our heart rate speeds up as we prepare to avoid danger. The chapter on stress

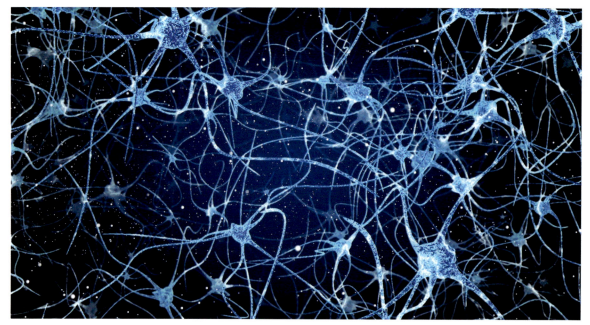

Figure 3-2 The dance of the neurons—sometimes one is more active than another.

The Neuroscience of Behavior and Experience

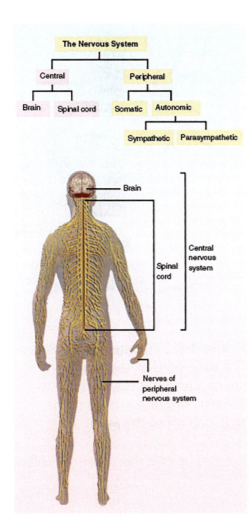

Figure 3-3 Divisions of the nervous system.

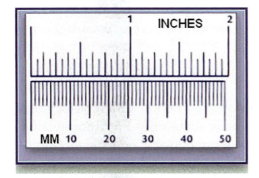

Figure 3-4 Scale showing size of a millimeter. In a box with a millimeter on each side, there can be 100,000 neurons.

and health will describe the *peripheral nervous system (PNS)* and how the body reacts to fear and stress, while this chapter will focus on the central nervous system and its major component, the brain. Many of the topics covered in this chapter, such as parts of the brain, neurotransmitters, and the function of neurons, are available in two-minute videos (www.neurochallenged.com).

Neurons

Santiago Ramón y Cajal (1852–1934), often considered the father of modern neuroscience, was the first to theorize that the nervous system is made up of individual cells. He identified these cells as separate components of the nervous system. These specialized cells are **neurons**, single nerve cells that can transmit information to other neurons. Neurons are central to all brain processes, and are the basis for the brain's communication with the rest of the body.

Neurons—all 86 billion of them—play important roles in learning as well as in transferring information in the brain (Azevedo et al., 2009). If you turn your head, specific neurons are active in your brain. If you feel excited, other neurons are active. Even the act of remembering the fact that there are 86 billion neurons in your brain involves another set of neurons.

Amazingly, the neuron has remained the basic building block of organisms over millions and even billions of years of evolution. Almost all living types of organisms, except some like the sponge or slime mold, have neurons. Neurons are found in the nervous systems of animals ranging from insects to humans. In general, humans have 100,000 neurons in a cubic millimeter of the brain, which is one millimeter on each side (Fried, Rutishauser, Cerf, & Kreiman, 2014).

Although neurons come in a variety of sizes and shapes, they share some basic characteristics (see **Figure 3-5**). The *cell body* contains a nucleus, which includes deoxyribonucleic acid (DNA) and other substances, and also mitochondria that are involved in supplying energy. The **axon** (from the Greek word for axle) comes from the cell body, or *soma*, and is involved in conveying information to other cells. Axons can be fairly short—as found in the human brain—or four or five feet in length, such as those that go from the spinal cord to your arms and legs. There are axons in blue whales that are half the length of a basketball court. Bundles of axons are the *nerves* we refer to when discussing nerve damage in the arms or legs. The **dendrites** (from the Greek word for tree) are attached to the soma and receive information from other cells.

We can also describe neurons in terms of their function.

- **Motor neurons** are involved in moving our muscles, which allows us to walk, throw a ball, or send a text.
- **Sensory neurons** help us to see, feel, and hear the world. Other senses, such as taste and smell, also involve sensory neurons. These neurons send information to the brain that allows us to experience the world. Motor and sensory neurons transfer information to the brain through the spinal cord.
- Finally, neurons that relay information from other neurons are referred to as **interneurons**, which create circuits to process information in the brain. Most of our actions, such as picking up and drinking a cup of coffee, use all three types of neurons. We look at the cup and through our hands determine how much force to use as we pick up the cup. We then taste the coffee through our taste buds and smell.

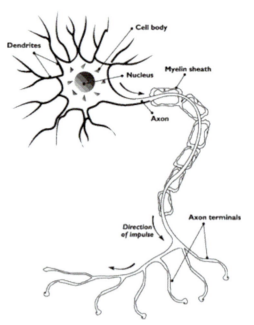

Figure 3-5 Structure of a neuron. The basic parts of the neuron are the dendrites that connect to the cell body, the axon, and the terminals off of the axon.

Besides neurons, another component of the brain is glia. *Glia cells* are different from neurons. Glia cells outnumber neurons by two to ten times in the brains of humans. During the development of the human brain, glia cells are involved in directing neurons to their location and connections. Although the role of glia cells in cognitive processes has been largely ignored, new research suggests that glia does play a part (Bilbo & Stevens, 2017; Koob, 2009; Perea, Sur, & Araque, 2014). Glia cells influence how neurons interact with one another. They also form networks that communicate differently than neurons. A third component of the brain is *arteries and vesicles* that are part of the blood system in the brain. Glucose and oxygen are components of blood and supply energy to the brain. As you will see, being able to measure blood flow in specific areas of the brain can give us insight into how the brain works.

Neural Impulses

The dendrites receive information from other neurons, which end at different locations on the dendrites. Although illustrations in textbooks usually show only a few connections between neurons, there are generally thousands of these connections. The *terminal branche*, also referred to as axon terminals or terminal buttons, from these other neurons do not actually touch but make a biochemical connection through a small gap filled with fluid. That small gap filled with fluid is referred to as a **synapse**. These biochemical connections can release molecules that influence the transmission of information. Synaptic transmission can either be influenced by chemical agents called neurotransmitters or electrical ions to convey information.

The Neuroscience of Behavior and Experience

A neuron is surrounded by a membrane, which separates it from the fluid in which it exists. In the walls of the membrane are small pores called *channels*. These channels can open and close depending on the internal and external chemical structure. Inside the neuron there is a high concentration of ions of potassium (K^+) and other substances. In the fluid surrounding the cell are ions of sodium (Na^+) and others. The electrochemical nature of the inside and outside of the membrane creates a battery-like situation with a resting potential. The resting neuron has an electrical difference of about -50 to -70 mV (millivolts) between itself and the fluid that surrounds it. That is, when the neuron is negative, it is in a resting state. When sufficient information arrives at the dendrites and results in an electrochemical change, then, at a critical point, the neuron becomes positive and an electrical potential is created.

As more of these electrical changes add together, the size of the electrical potential is increased. At a critical point, an electrical signal—called an **action potential**—is produced at a location near the cell body. The brain receives, analyzes, and conveys information by using action potentials. When you see something, hear something, feel something, and even smell something, action potentials are involved. Regardless of the stimuli, each action potential is the same. What determines the experience that you have is the pathway involved. Visual pathways result in seeing, auditory pathways result in hearing, and so forth.

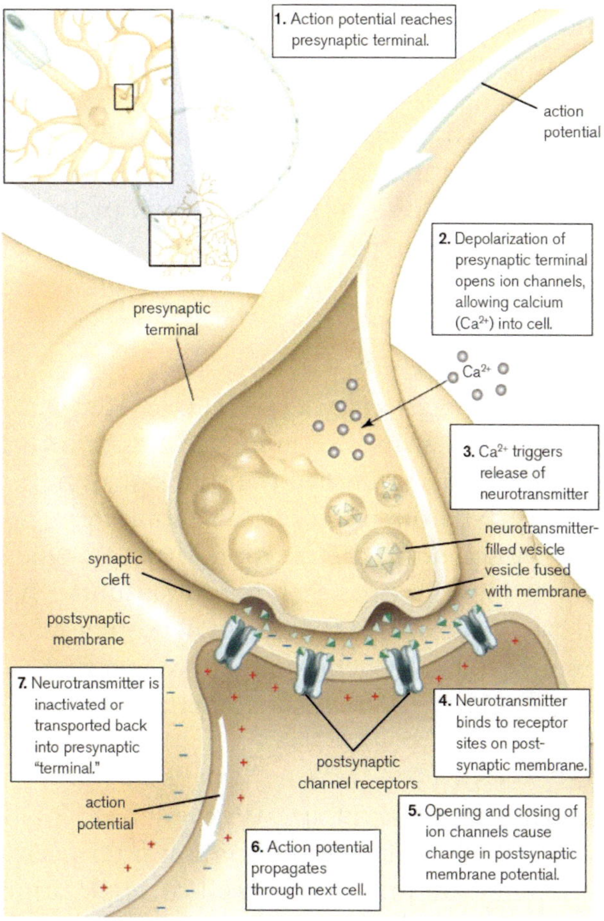

Figure 3-6 Depiction of the structures and processes of synapses.

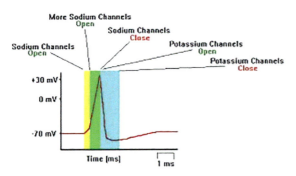

Figure 3-7 Action potential changes over time. These changes allow information to be passed throughout the brain.

More specifically, there is a rapid rise in sodium ion (Na$^+$) permeability in the membrane, which results in the large positive change in the electrical potential. This is followed by a slower rise in potassium ion (K$^+$) permeability resulting in a return to the stable electrical state. This same mechanism moves the action potential along the length of the axon. That is, small spaces along the axon referred to as the *nodes of Ranvier* renew the action potential as it moves along the axon.

When ions are added together in this way to produce the action potential, we refer to it as *excitatory*. It can also happen that the charged ions from the dendrites combine in a manner that prevents the firing of the action potential. This is referred to as *inhibitory*.

After the electrical signal is produced, the action potential then travels quickly down the axon. It travels only in one direction. The speed at which the action potential travels down the axon depends on two factors. The first is the width of the axon. Action potentials travel faster in axons with larger diameters. And the second factor is whether the axon is covered with an insulating material called the *myelin sheath*. Action potentials travel faster in axons surrounded by this myelin sheath, which is made from glia cells. This helps different brain areas to communicate with one another. Without a myelin sheath, the action potential may move at the rate of 1 meter per second. With a myelin sheath, the speed is 10 to 100 times faster. Thus, an axon with a larger diameter and wrapped in myelin will have the fastest conduction times.

An action potential is referred to as an "*all or none*" signal. This is because it is only above a critical value that an action potential is produced. Below that critical value, no electrical activity is sent down the axon. Following the production of an action potential there is a brief period in which the cell cannot fire another action potential. This is referred to as the *refractory period*.

Neurotransmission

In the chemical synapse, *neurotransmitters* play a critical role (Spitzer, 2017). **Neurotransmitters** are chemical molecules of a specific shape that influence how information is transmitted from one neuron to another. Neurotransmitters can transmit signals from one neuron to another and in this way are excitatory. Neurotransmitters can also decrease the information flow, and in this way are inhibitory. Most neurons utilize more than one type of neurotransmitter for their functioning, and the amount of time each neurotransmitter has influence depends on the neurotransmitter. To date, more than 100 different neurotransmitters have been identified. Many of the medications used to treat psychological disorders, such as anxiety, work by influencing neurotransmitters. They have been classified both in terms of structure and function.

Structure of Neurotransmitters

Classifying neurotransmitters in terms of size (Purves et al., 2008) results in two broad categories. The first type is small molecule neurotransmitters that tend to be involved in rapid synaptic functions. They are often composed of single amino acids. One of these small molecule neurotransmitters, which is excitatory, is *glutamate*. Glutamate is the most important neurotransmitter in terms of normal brain function. In abnormal conditions, the firing of rapid glutamate neurons can lead to seizures in a number of areas of the brain.

The other is the inhibitory neurotransmitter *GABA* (gamma-aminobutyric acid). Drugs that increase the amount of GABA available are used to treat such disorders as anxiety. The second type of neurotransmitter in terms of size are larger protein molecules referred to as *neuropeptides*. These can be made up of 3 to 36 amino acids. Neuropeptides tend to be involved in slower ongoing synaptic functions. Endorphins that help your body to not experience pain are an example of neuropeptides.

Function of Neurotransmitters

Neurotransmitters can also be categorized into three broad groups by function (Nadeau et al., 2004). The first category includes those neurotransmitters such as glutamate and GABA, which mediate communication between neurons. The second category includes neurotransmitters such as opioid peptides in the pain system that influences the communication of this information. And the third category includes neurotransmitters such as *dopamine, adrenaline, noradrenaline,* and *serotonin* that influence the activity of large populations of neurons. In later chapters, you will learn about the function of neurotransmitters in greater detail. For example, when you expect something pleasant to happen such as experiences related to food, sex, or drugs, dopamine is involved. If, however, you were to see a bear, then adrenaline would prepare you to quickly run.

The Synaptic Gap

Passing information from one neuron to another involves a number of steps. The first step is that neurotransmitters need to be created and stored. When the conditions described previously occur, an action potential travels down the axon to the terminal. This allows a neurotransmitter to be released into the synaptic gap between the two neurons. The

Table 3-1 Some representative neurotransmitters.

Neurotransmitter	Function
Monoamines	
Serotonin	Involved in mood, sleep, arousal, aggression, depression, obsessive-compulsive disorder, and alcoholism.
Dopamine	Contributes to movement control and promotes reinforcing effects of food, sex, and abused drugs; involved in schizophrenia and Parkinson's disease.
Norepinephrine	A hormone released during stress. Functions as a neurotransmitter in the brain to increase arousal and attentiveness to events in the environment; involved in depression.
Epinephrine	A stress hormone related to norepinephrine; plays a minor role as a neurotransmitter in the brain.
Amino acids	
Glutamate	The principal excitatory neurotransmitter in the brain and spinal cord. Vitally involved in learning and implicated in schizophrenia.
Gamma-aminobutyric acid (GABA)	The predominant inhibitory neurotransmitter. Its receptors respond to alcohol and the class of tranquilizers called benzodiazepines. Deficiency in GABA or receptors is one cause of epilepsy.
Neuropeptides	
Endorphins	Neuromodulators that reduce pain and enhance reinforcement.

88 The Neuroscience of Behavior and Experience

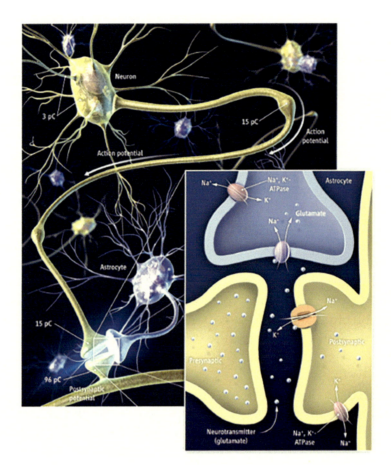

Figure 3-8 The role of neurotransmitters in synaptic processes. Neurotransmitters can increase activity of the neuron or decrease activity depending on the neurotransmitter in the space between two neurons.

neurotransmitter then binds with specific proteins in the next neuron. This either increases (excitatory) or decreases (inhibitory) the possibility that the next neuron will create an action potential. Afterwards, the gap between the two neurons must be made neutral by a variety of mechanisms including making the neurotransmitter inactive, having the neurotransmitter taken up by the first neuron (referred to as *reuptake*), and removing the neurotransmitter from the gap between the two neurons.

Action at the synaptic gap determines how you experience the world. As you will see in later chapters, touching your finger, hearing a sound, or having light come into your eyes results in specific types of receptors setting up the conditions for the generation of action potentials. These action potentials result in information being passed from neuron to neuron. This allows your brain to create the sensations you experience as reality.

Some of these experiences involve a pathway using only a few neurons. Being startled by a loud sound or touching a hot stove are examples of processes that use short pathways. More voluntary and complex processes such as reading this page and examining the diagrams use a much longer series of neuronal connections.

Spike Trains

Frequency determines how action potentials encode information. That is, a loud sound would be encoded by a series of action potentials from the cells sensitive to sound intensity. A soft sound would result in fewer action potentials being fired. When observed in relation to a stimulus, action potentials are also referred to as *spikes,* and a number of spikes over time are referred to as *spike trains.* Understanding the nature of spikes and how they relate to information in the brain has been an important question since the beginning of the 20th century when they were first recorded (see Rieke, Warland, van Steveninck, & Bialek, 1999 for an overview).

The early work on spike trains was performed at the University of Cambridge in the UK by Lord Edgar Adrian (1889–1977) who won the Nobel Prize for his work on the function of neurons (Adrian, 1928). This work led to three important observations. First, although there are a variety of sensory systems (for example, vision, audition, and touch), the neurons connected to them all produce similar action potentials to external stimuli. This universality is seen across a variety of species. Second, the rate of spiking increases as the stimulus becomes larger. This can serve as a measure of intensity. And, third, if a given stimulus is continued for a long period of time, the spiking decreases.

As you will see in a number of other chapters in this book, action potentials and their frequency help to determine how you experience your world. An increased number of spike trains result in a greater experience of intensity in areas such as brightness and loudness. Fewer action potentials in a given period result in a less intense experience. Further, if we experience a consistent set of sounds such as a bell tower on a campus or the sounds of a train, our sensory system produces fewer action potentials over time. This results in our ignoring what was once an obvious experience.

Neural Networks

How neurons work together is an important topic in brain research. Donald Hebb (1904–1985), like Freud before him, considered brain connections to be closely connected with previous experience (Hebb, 1949). Previous experience helps to develop connections between neurons, and the repetition of those behaviors strengthens these connections. We now know that neurons actually grow additional connections with other neurons as learning takes place. Our brains are not static. A **network** is simply a group of neurons that becomes active under certain conditions. Networks allow basic human processes such as learning, memory, thinking, planning, feeling, and decision making to take place (Bassett & Mattar, 2017; Ito, Hearne, Mill, Cocuzza, & Cole, 2020).

Hebb's work suggested a link between the physical processes of neurons and psychological processes. *Networks* allow our brains to efficiently process information (Bassett & Sporns, 2017; Laughlin & Sejnowski, 2003; Sporns, 2011; Logothetis, 2015; Rosenberg, Finn, Scheinost, Constable, & Chun, 2017). Overall, cortical networks are influenced by experience and designed to be efficient in terms of connections between neurons in the network. This efficiency allows for less use of energy. One way energy is conserved is through not having every neuron connect with every other neuron.

How are neurons connected in a network? The answer may seem strange. Neurons are neither totally random in their connections with other neurons nor totally patterned. It appears that neurons are connected to one another in the same way that all humans on this planet are socially connected. In the 1960s, the social psychologist Stanley Milgram (Travers & Milgram, 1969) asked the question, "What is the probability that any two people randomly selected from a large population of individuals such as the United States would know each other?" They answered this question by giving an individual a letter addressed to another person somewhere in the United States. This individual was to send the letter to someone he knew who might know the other person. In turn this person was to send the letter to someone she knew who might know the person. Surprisingly, it only required five or six different people for the letter to go from the first individual to the final individual. This phenomenon has been referred to as the *small world problem* and later the phrase *six degrees of separation* became part of common language.

It turns out that neurons, like humans, can be connected to one another in similar ways. Various studies have shown that the neurons in the brain can be considered within a ***small world framework*** (Sporns, 2011). Neurons have numerous short distance local connections, which taken together, can be considered as a *hub* or module. From these hubs there are more long-distance connections to other hubs.

Local hubs can be made up of neurons that connect with one another over very short distances. Such connections are seen in gray matter. Gray matter appears dark and can be seen in the outer shell of the brain. *Gray matter* contains the synapses, dendrites, cell bodies, and local axons of neurons. Some 60% of gray matter is composed of axons and dendrites. Underlying this are the axons that transfer information throughout the brain. Their myelin sheaths are lighter in color and thus these areas are referred to as *white matter*. Myelin is made up of fats and proteins and wrap around axons like insulation does around electrical cables and results in an increased speed in information transmissions. About 44% of the human brain is white matter. White matter generally represents longer connections between neurons. This allows for cortical networks over larger areas of the brain.

The Brain's Default Network

What does your brain do when you are just sitting and waiting or daydreaming or talking to yourself? This is a question that is just now beginning to be explored. In psychology, most of the research you read about involves a person doing something. Reacting to emotional pictures or solving cognitive problems are common examples. In these cases, one's attention is focused on a task in the external world.

Different networks of your brain are involved when you perform different types of tasks. In the same way that the brain is organized to process spatial and verbal material differently and involve different cortical networks, it also appears that different circuits are involved with internal versus external information. A variety of studies have examined brain-imaging procedures in which individuals performed internal tasks versus external tasks. However, we all know that even without an external task to do, our mind is constantly working. It jumps from one thought to another. William James called this process the *stream of consciousness* (James, 1890). Recent researchers refer to this process as *mind wandering*.

Those neural networks that are active during internal processing have come to be referred to as the brain's ***default or intrinsic network*** (see Bucker, Andrews-Hanna, & Schacter, 2008; Brucker & DiNicola, 2019; Raichle, 2015 for overviews). The default network is separate from, but can be understood as similar to, other networks such as those involved in visual perception or motor activities. It is made up of a set of interacting brain regions that include the medial prefrontal cortex, the posterior cingulate cortex, and the inferior parietal lobe. The default network can be seen in brain imaging when individuals are not engaged in any active task. Engaging in an active task reduces the activity of the default network.

Different Networks Are Involved in Different Tasks

In addition to the default network, the executive and salience networks have been identified (Menon, 2011). The ***central executive network*** is involved in performing such tasks as planning, goal setting, directing attention, performing, inhibiting the management of actions, and the coding of representations in working memory (see Eisenberg & Berman, 2010 for an overview). These are sometimes referred to as *frontal lobe tasks* since damage to the frontal areas of the brain compromise performance in these tasks. These tasks are also referred to as *executive functions* since they are involved in planning, understanding new situations, and having cognitive flexibility. The **salience network**, as the name implies, is involved in monitoring and noting important changes in biological and cognitive systems. That is, a process that is salient is something that stands out. There are also other networks involved with vision, audition, and other sensory experiences.

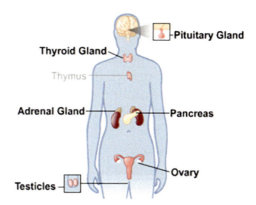

Figure 3-9 Glands of the endocrine system that secrete hormones into our blood.

Hormones and the Endocrine System

Neurons and neurotransmitters are not the only chemical communications that can affect behavior and experience. The **endocrine system** is a system of glands located throughout our body. The **pituitary gland** is a pea-sized gland located at the base of the brain, just below the *hypothalamus*. The hypothalamus controls the glandular system by affecting the pituitary. The pituitary gland is sometimes called the master gland since it affects other glands of the endocrine system (**Figure 3-9**). The endocrine glands release biochemical substances into the bloodstream called **hormones** that change the physiology and behavior of specific organs as they move throughout the body. These hormones can stimulate our immune system, influence male and female sex characteristics, affect blood sugar levels, and perform a number of other functions.

Hormones have a direct effect on our experiences and behaviors. This includes our basic human functions such as eating, emotional responses, including anxiety and depression, sexuality, and the use of energy. They can affect how well we are able to flee from what is perceived as a dangerous situation, to how we experience closeness with our family members. In fact, hormones and neurotransmitters are very similar. If the biochemical substance is released into the gap between neurons in the brain, it is referred to as a neurotransmitter. If it is released into the blood supply, it is referred to as a hormone. Neurotransmitters tend to be fast acting as they facilitate or inhibit the action potential and thus process information in the brain. In contrast, hormones take longer to produce effects. Changes produced by hormones are in the time frame of seconds to days, depending on the particular hormone involved. Hormones and the endocrine system will be discussed further in the chapter covering stress.

What Are the Parts of the Brain?

Neuroscientists share a common conviction—there is something unusual about the human brain that leads to our abilities to perform a variety of tasks (Northcutt & Kaas, 1995; Preuss & Kaas, 1999). The human brain contains billions of neurons and more than 100,000 kilometers of interconnections (Azevedo et al., 2009; Hofman, 2001). It is estimated that in mammals, a given neuron would directly connect to at least 500 and at times thousands of other neurons. This suggests that there are at least 50 trillion or more different connections in the human brain.

Regardless of how exact this estimate may be, we still come away with the conclusion that the human brain is extremely complex. Let's begin with some simple terms. Structures closer to the front of the brain are referred to as *anterior,* whereas those closer to the back are called *posterior*. You will also see the Latin terms *rostral* and *caudal* used in the same way. You can remember that the speaker's rostrum is in the front of the room if you want a way to remember this difference.

The brain appears symmetrical from the top with *left and right hemispheres*. Structures closer to the midline dividing the left and right hemispheres are referred to as *medial*, whereas those farther away from the midline are called *lateral*.

The Neocortex

Looking at the left hemisphere from the side, we can describe four lobes of the brain (see **Figure 3-10**).

- The *frontal lobe*, located at the front of the cortex, is involved in planning, higher order cognitive processes such as thinking and problem solving, as well as moral and social judgments. Scientists also refer to the frontal part of the frontal lobe as the *prefrontal cortex* (PFC). The beginning of this chapter told the story of Phineas Gage, whose frontal lobe was damaged by the iron rod. After that, he had difficulties following a plan and making appropriate social decisions. There is a cavity referred to as the *central sulcus* that separates the frontal lobe from the parietal lobe. In the area of the frontal lobe along the central sulcus is a strip of cortex referred to as the **motor strip**. Different parts of

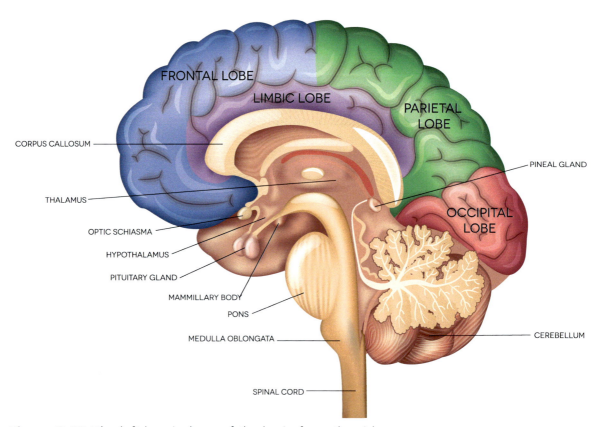

Figure 3-10 The left hemisphere of the brain from the side.

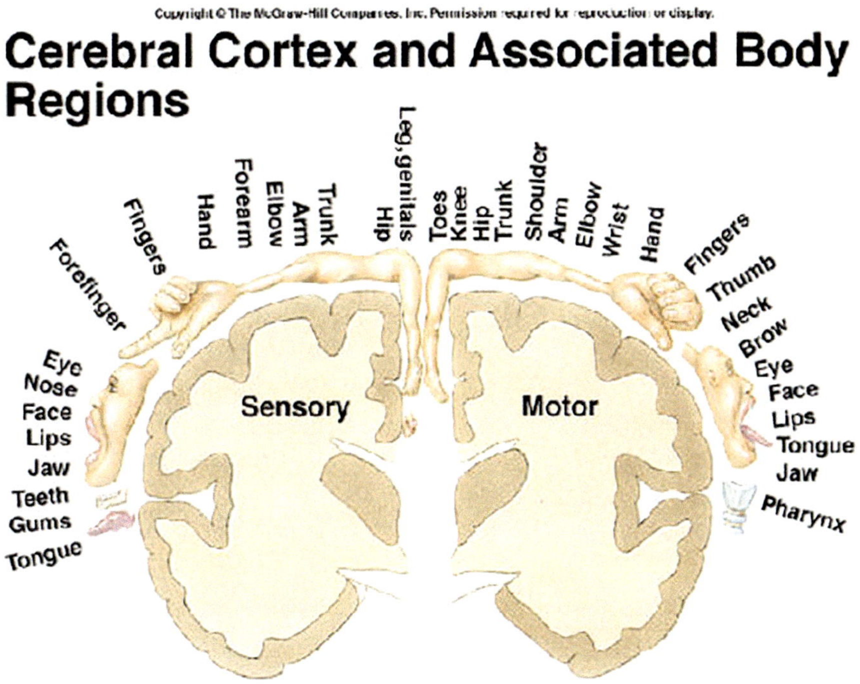

Cerebral Cortex and Associated Body Regions

Figure 3-11 Cerebral cortex and associated body regions. The size of the body part in the figure represents the brain area devoted to that part.

this strip correspond to movements of different parts of the body. As can be seen in **Figure 3-11**, larger parts of the motor strips are involved in movement of the hands and face than other parts of the body.
- The ***parietal lobe***, which is toward the back and at the top of the cortex, is involved in spatial processes such as knowing where you are in space and performing spatial problems. Behind the central sulcus is a strip of cortex in the parietal lobe referred to as the ***somatosensory cortex*** (see **Figure 3-11**). It is this strip that is associated with receiving sensations from various parts of the body. Thus, you experience the feel of your coffee cup through the somatosensory area and then use the corresponding motor process to pick it up and drink from it. Like the motor strip, the size of the area involved in sensations from various parts of the body reflects the sensitivity of that body part. Our hands and face are much more sensitive than our back, and these areas have more cortical representation on the somatosensory cortex than does the back.
- The ***occipital lobe*** is located near the back of the brain and toward the bottom. The occipital lobe is involved with the processing of visual information and receives information from our eyes, which you will learn about in the chapter on sensation and perception.
- Below the frontal and parietal lobes is the ***temporal lobe***. Looking at the brain, you can see that the frontal and temporal lobes are separated by a deep groove that is called the *Sylvian fissure*. The temporal lobe receives information from our ears and is involved in hearing as well as aspects of language. Other parts of the temporal lobe are involved in the naming of objects from visual information processed in the occipital lobes.

The Limbic System

During the 1930s, James Papez suggested that a particular brain network was associated with emotional experience and expression (Papez, 1937). Later, Paul MacLean introduced

The Neuroscience of Behavior and Experience

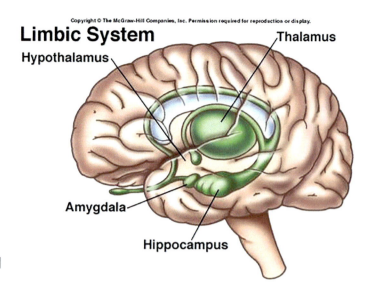

Figure 3-12 Structures and areas in the limbic system. The limbic system is associated with emotional processing.

the term *limbic*, which comes from the Latin *limbus*, which means border. Papez believed that in the same way that the occipital lobe processes visual information, the **limbic system** processes emotional processes. Today, scientists see this system involved in emotion, motivation, memory, and other related processes.

Initially, Papez saw the limbic system being composed of parts of the thalamus, the hypothalamus, the cingulate gyrus, and the hippocampus. The *thalamus* functions as a relay center between subcortical structures and the cortex. Except for the experience of smell, information from all sensory systems passes through the thalamus. The *hypothalamus* is involved in a number of metabolic processes including hormones that influence organs throughout the body. Responses to stress and danger involve the hypothalamus. It is also involved in a variety of basic processes such as hunger, thirst, and temperature control. Neurons in the hypothalamus become active when you are thirsty or when glucose levels are low. The *cingulate gyrus* is involved in a variety of emotional and motivational processes including pain and cognitive control. The *hippocampus* is a critical part of our memory system. You can actually see changes in the hippocampus if you learn to navigate a complex town, as described in the box: The World Is Your Laboratory—Changing the Brain through Experience. Additionally, individuals with smaller hippocampi are more at risk for post-traumatic stress disorder (PTSD), and those with larger structures are shown to recover faster (Apfel et al., 2011).

Later formulations of the limbic system include the *amygdala*. The term "amygdala" comes from the Latin word for "almond," which reflects its shape. Initial brain-imaging studies suggested that the amygdala was involved in the experience of negative emotions such as fear or anger including aggression. The amygdala is also involved in stress related disorders such as post-traumatic stress disorder (PTSD). In individuals with PTSD, a mildly fearful stimulus produces an overreactive amygdala.

Additional research has shown the amygdala to be active whenever any emotional information that is related to one's self is processed. Neuronal connections within the amygdala and its connections to the hippocampus may also be changed in situations of severe stress (Roozendaal, McEwen, & Chattarji, 2009). In this manner, humans would have a heightened memory of severe stress situations. The manner in which these changes relate to the development of anxiety disorders is being studied.

The World Is Your Laboratory—Changing the Brain through Experience

Eric Kandel set out to understand how learning and memory were represented in the brain. For his discoveries, he won the Nobel Prize in 2000. But that is getting ahead of the story. Since no one knew how learning and memory took place in the brain, Kandel needed to choose a simple organism that could learn. For his research, he chose the California sea slug *Aplysia*. Although this sea slug is complicated in many ways (it can be both male and female as needed), it does have a simple reflexive behavior—the withdrawal of its gill. The gill is an external organ that the sea slug uses to breathe. Touching the gill causes it to withdraw.

It turns out that this gill reflex is similar to a number of responses in humans. For example, the first time you hear a clock tower chiming or a plane flying over your house, it seems loud. However, after a time, your response decreases as the sound is repeated. This process is referred to as *habituation*.

Kandel and his colleagues focused on a critical synapse that is located between the neuron that brought sensory information related to being touched and the motor neuron that caused the gill to withdraw. They discovered that with repeated stimulation, habituation took place and the sensory neuron released less of a neurotransmitter. That neurotransmitter was glutamate—the major excitatory neurotransmitter in our brain. Less of the neurotransmitter glutamate reduces the chance that an action potential will be produced.

The opposite of habituation is *sensitization*. For example, if you receive a painful shock, then the next shock would result in a greater response in a number of different systems. The shock could, for example, make a noise seem louder. Kandel and his colleagues found that sensitization results in a greater level of glutamate at the synapse. Thus, this increases the chance that an action potential will be produced. In other studies, Kandel and his colleagues showed that when experiences become part of long-term learning and memory, the connections at the synapse are increased. This shows that with learning the brain connections change (see Kandel, 2006 for an overview).

Does learning also change the human brain? Katherine Woollett and Eleanor Maguire at University College London decided to tackle this question. To become a London taxi driver, you must learn all of the obscure and non-structured roads of the city. As you can see from the map of London (**Figure 3-13**), this is not an easy task.

These researchers performed brain-imaging studies of a group of volunteers at the beginning of their training as well as brain-imaging studies of a control group of non-taxi drivers. At the beginning of the study, the two groups showed no difference in the hippocampus, which is the structure of the brain involved in memory.

After three or four years, brain imaging, along with some tests of memory, was again conducted on these two groups. The researchers found that those who passed the test and became taxi drivers had a greater volume of gray matter in the hippocampus. Since gray matter reflects neurons, this suggests that new nerve cells were created in the brain as new learning was taking place. Long-term learning does change the brain (Woollett & Maguire, 2011). If you want to change your brain, learn something new.

Figure 3-13 Map of London showing the approximately 25,000 irregular streets. How long do you think it would take you to learn these streets?
Source: Woollett and Maguire (2011).

Thought Question: What experiences do you think have changed your brain the most?

The Brain Stem

The **brain stem** includes the *midbrain*, *pons*, and *medulla*. These structures are involved in basic life functions, including breathing, digestion, levels of arousal, pleasure, and physiological processes such as heart rate and blood pressure. Pons and midbrain processes are also associated with eye movements, including the rapid eye movements (REM) seen during sleep. Posture and certain facial expressions are also related to these structures. Movements controlled by the brain stem tend to be whole body movements rather than the finer hand movements connected with neocortical control. Across species, movements related to the brain stem tend to be more of an instinctual nature, such as those seen in a startled organism.

Although not part of the brain stem, one important structure related to movement is the *basal ganglia*, which are located deep within the cerebral hemispheres. Parkinson's disease, which is characterized by tremors, is associated with the degeneration of neurons in the basal ganglia. It is reduction of the neurotransmitter dopamine in the basal ganglia that is associated with Parkinson's disease. Serotonin, another neurotransmitter, was seen in lower levels in the medulla of infants who died of sudden infant death syndrome (SIDS) (Duncan et al., 2010).

The Cerebellum

Involved in the coordination of movement, the **cerebellum** (little brain) is located at the base of the skull (Cerminara, Lang, Sillitoe, & Apps, 2015; Schmahmann, Guell, Stoodley,

& Halko, 2019). It receives inputs from almost all areas of the cortex and allows for the smooth movement of our bodies. When the cerebellum is damaged, a person's movements can appear jerky and uncontrolled. It is also involved in the automation of tasks such as learning to ride a bicycle, typing, or playing a musical instrument. One important aspect of cerebellar control is the timing of motor movement as would be required when you play a musical instrument.

The cerebellum, with its connections to our brain and body, allows for an intricate set of feedback processes. When you decide to shoot a basketball at a hoop, your neocortical motor areas send out messages to your arms and legs. This same information goes to the cerebellum. Once you have made the shot, feedback from limbs and the visual system goes back to the cerebellum. With this information, it is possible to correct your next shot based on the performance of the previous one.

Although it was historically thought that the cerebellum was only involved in movement, more recent research suggests that it is also involved in cognitive processes (King, Hernandez-Castillo, Poldrack, Ivry, & Diedrichsen, 2019; Wagner & Luo, 2020). For example, with its connections to the prefrontal cortex, activity is seen in the cerebellum when learning simple rules for performing a task (Balsters & Ramnani, 2011). Every day we make these types of decisions mainly outside of awareness, such as when we stop and go in relation to traffic lights. Another study performed brain imaging on individuals born in 1936. Brain imaging of these individuals in their 60s was correlated with cognitive abilities. Scanning the frontal areas and the cerebellum showed that gray matter volume in the cerebellum predicted general intelligence (Hogan et al., 2011).

The cerebellum interacts with many different parts of the brain. Pathways to and from the neocortex suggest that a closed loop system includes inputs and outputs to the cerebellum. This allows for coordinated control of motor functions such as playing a musical instrument or throwing darts. In addition to motor movements, cerebellum activity is also

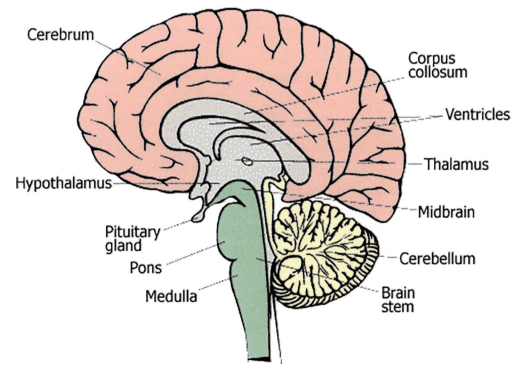

Figure 3-14 Brain stem and cerebellum.

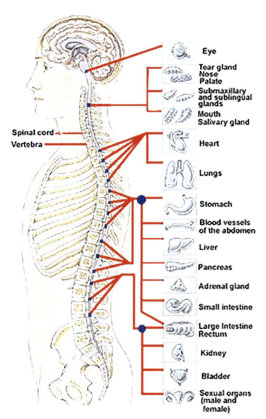

Figure 3-15 Spinal cord and connection to the internal organs.

related to attention, executive control, language, working memory, learning, pain, emotion, and addiction (Strick, Dum, & Fiez, 2009; Wagner & Luo, 2020).

The Spinal Cord

The hind brain is directly connected to the spinal cord. As the second structure of the central nervous system (the brain is the first) the **spinal cord** contains *fiber tracts* within a cavity surrounded by bone through which information from all parts of the body is taken to the brain (*ascending tracts*). Information is also taken from the brain to the muscles and internal organs (*descending tracts*). Damage to the fiber tracts in the spinal cord can result in individuals being unable to move their bodies. The higher up on the spinal cord that the damage occurs, the greater the paralysis.

Besides controlling muscles, information to and from internal organs goes through the fiber tracts in the spinal cord (see **Figure 3-15**). Not only does the spinal cord move information to and from the brain, it is also able to produce simple reflexes. What if you touch a hot stove? You may have noticed you actually move your hand before you realize it. This is because the sensory information goes to the spinal cord and a motor response (withdraw your hand) is produced without involving the brain.

CONCEPT CHECK

- What are the primary structures of the brain, and what is the primary function of each?
- What is the primary function of the limbic system? What are the five major structures that make up the limbic system, and what is the primary function of each?
- Research has shown that the brains of California sea slugs and London taxi drivers were changed by experience. What evidence did the researchers present to support their conclusions?
- What structures are part of the brain stem and what is the primary function of each?
- The cerebellum interacts with many different parts of the brain and the body and is critical for performing a variety of tasks. Describe four of these tasks that are dependent on the functioning of the cerebellum.
- How is the functioning of the spinal cord related to the brain?

How Do We Investigate the Brain?

There are a number of ways we can measure the energy used by the brain. This, in turn, helps us to understand the fascinating manner in which the brain is involved in behavior and experience. With 86 billion neurons and 50 to 200 trillion connections between neurons in the human brain, understanding these connections on a neuronal level would be an impossible task. However, scientists have been able to use the manner in which neurons work together as a window into their function.

Measuring Electrical and Magnetic Activity

Our brain is always active, even when we sleep. This constant activity includes electrical and magnetic changes, and measuring these changes allows researchers to better understand how the brain processes information and which networks are involved.

Electroencephalography

Electroencephalography (EEG) records the electrical activity of the brain at the level of the synapse (Nunez & Srinivasan, 2006). The EEG was first demonstrated in humans by the German psychiatrist Hans Berger in 1924, who initially measured EEG from his teenage children. His work was published five years later (Berger, 1929). It has been used to signal changes in sleep states as well as perceptual, cognitive, and emotional processes (Cohen, 2017). EEG is the product of the changing excitatory and inhibitory currents at the synapse. Action potentials contribute very little to the EEG. However, since changes at the synapse do influence the production of action potentials, there is an association of EEG with spike trains (Mazzoni et al., 2010; Whittingstall & Logothetis, 2009).

Since the neurons of the brain and their connections are constantly active, EEG can be measured during both wake and sleep. EEG can be measured with only two electrodes or as a high-density array of more than 200 electrodes (see **Figure 3-16**).

Some aspects of the EEG may appear almost random while other fluctuations appear periodic. Using signal-processing techniques, it is possible to determine the major frequency and amplitude seen in the signal. *Amplitude* refers to how large the signal is, and *frequency* to how fast the signal cycles measured in cycles per second or Hertz (Hz). Some EEG patterns are extremely reliable and can be

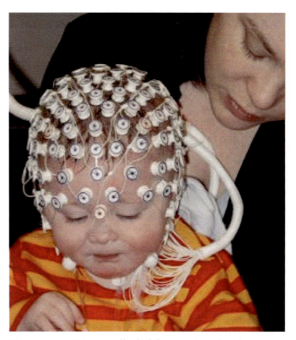

Figure 3-16 Small child wearing high-density array EEG cap with her mother.

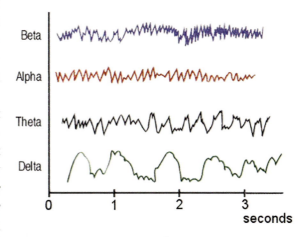

Figure 3-17 Patterns of EEG activity ranging from high to low frequency activity.

visually observed (as would have been required in the days before computer analysis). These patterns have been identified by Greek letters such as α (alpha), ß (beta), and θ (theta). Alpha activity in the 8–12 Hz range was the first pattern of EEG activity Hans Berger noted.

Over the years researchers have noticed that specific patterns of EEG activity are associated with a variety of psychological states. When an individual is relaxed with his or her eyes closed, high amplitude regular activity is seen in the EEG at a frequency of 8–12 Hz called Alpha activity. If the person begins to perform some mental activity such as mental arithmetic, lower amplitude EEG is seen at a higher frequency above 20 Hz, referred to as Beta activity. Delta and Theta activity can be seen during sleep.

Magnetoencephalography

Figure 3-18 Woman sitting in MEG.

Magnetoencephalography (MEG) uses a SQUID (superconducting quantum interference device) to detect the small amount of magnetic activity that results from the activity of neurons. As shown in **Figure 3-18**, the person simply puts her head in a device that contains magnetic sensors.

MEG signals are similar to EEG signals but have one important advantage. This advantage stems from the fact that magnetic fields are not distorted when they pass through the cortex and the skull. This makes it possible to be more accurate with MEG in noting where the signal arises within the brain.

Measuring Structure

In the 1980s a great step forward in brain imaging was made with the introduction of *magnetic resonance imaging (MRI)*. MRI offers a static image of brain structure. This is accomplished by having the person lie on a horizontal bed that is moved into the scanner (see **Figure 3-19**). It is often used for scanning the brain, although it can be used to show any body part. The basic technique is to align the water molecules in the body with an extremely strong field. Radiofrequency current is then used to reflect the structure of the organs of the body. **Figure 3-20** shows an MRI image of the brain of a person looking to your left.

By using software, it is possible to reconstruct any area of the brain. This allows researchers to determine the size of different structures in the brain. They can then compare these between groups of people or changes within a person as in the case of London taxi drivers. Often researchers will reconstruct images of the brain as if they were taking a "slice" at different distances from the front or top of the brain.

It is also possible to use the MRI to measure cortical connections in the brain, which is referred to as *diffusion tensor imaging (DTI)*. DTI is available with most MRI imaging systems. It is a procedure for showing fiber tracts (white matter) in the brain. This information can then be visualized by color coding it, as shown in **Figure 3-21**. This allows the mapping of white matter connections in the brain. In this figure, the connections between different parts of the brain can be seen.

Often DTI is used to note connections in individual regions of the brain in terms of a specific research question. If you were interested in memory changes following concussion,

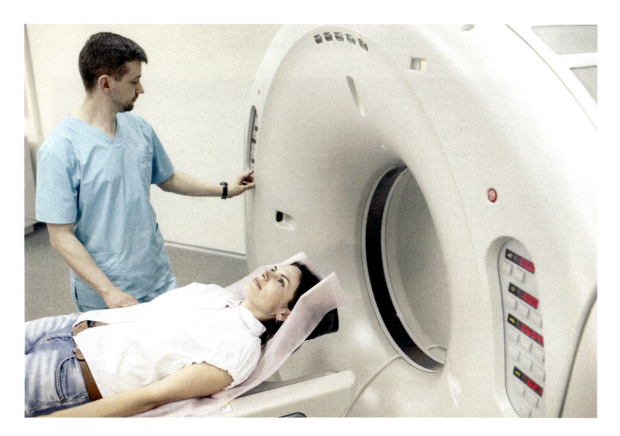

Figure 3-19 Person lying in MRI.

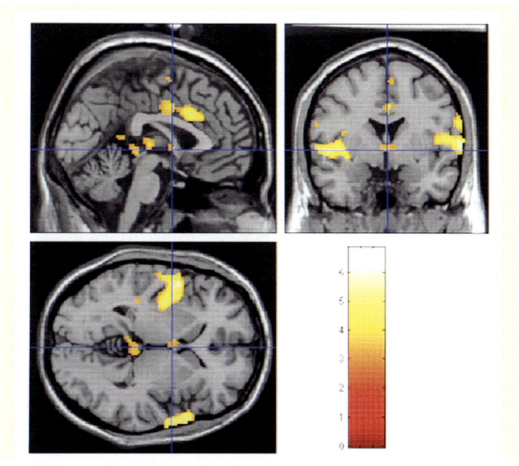

Figure 3-20 MRI image of the brain.
Source: ©iStockphoto.com/CGinspiration.

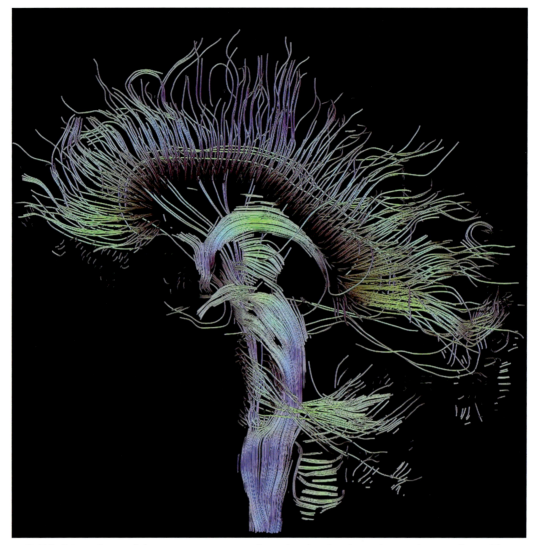

Figure 3-21 Mapping white matter connections in the brain using color coding. These represent the myelin sheath connections in the brain.

for example, you might map the connections with the hippocampus. The brain can also be considered as a whole and the connections with all areas mapped. Analyzing the connections of the whole brain has been referred to as the *connectome*. That is, the connectome is a map of neural connections in the brain.

Currently, ambitious projects to understand the connections in the brain are being developed by the National Institutes of Health in the United States (www.nih.gov/science/brain) and the countries of the European Union (www.humanbrainproject.eu). Some see great potential in the connectome projects (see Seung, 2012 for an overview). Since our experiences help to determine our brain connections, even identical twins with the same genes could have different experiences and brain connections. Describing whole brain connections can be valuable not only in understanding brain differences but also in creating ways to change these connections in order to treat disorders.

One such study looked at the connectome of males and females (Ingalhalikar et al., 2014). As shown in **Figure 3-22**, females showed more connections *between* the hemispheres of the brain, whereas males showed more connections *within* each hemisphere. These researchers suggest that female brains are structured to facilitate communication between analytical and intuitive processing modes, whereas male brains are structured to facilitate connectivity between perception and coordinated action.

Measuring Blood Flow Changes

The human brain weighs only about 3 pounds but uses some 20% of all the energy consumed by our body (see Magistretti, 2009 for an overview). Energy is available to the brain by a complex system of blood that circulates in the brain. For the brain to function efficiently, it needs blood with oxygen and glucose. By measuring changes in blood flow it is possible to estimate which areas of the brain are involved in processing information. The two major techniques are fMRI and PET.

Functional Magnetic Resonance Imaging

In the 1990s the development of ***functional magnetic resonance imaging (fMRI)*** helped to create the field of *cognitive neuroscience*. Whereas MRI shows brain structure, fMRI is able to reflect brain function. With fMRI, it was now possible to measure processing in the brain as well as which brain areas are involved. fMRI is

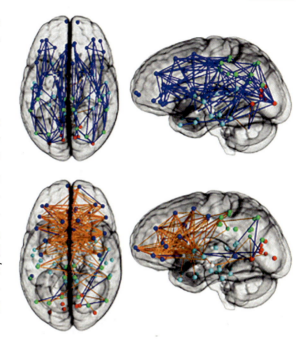

Figure 3-22 Brain networks of males (top) and females (bottom). Connections within the hemisphere are shown in blue and connections between hemispheres are shown in red.

Source: Ingalhalikar et al. (2014).

possible because blood flow increases in active areas of the cortex. That is, if running through math problems in your head, the areas of the brain related to arithmetic require energy that is supplied by the blood. Specifically, *hemoglobin*, which carries oxygen in the bloodstream, has different magnetic properties before and after oxygen is absorbed. Thus, by measuring the ratio of hemoglobin with and without oxygen, the fMRI is able to map changes in cortical blood and infer neuronal activity.

Measurements using fMRI are made by having a person lie on his or her back inside a device that measures changes in blood oxygen levels. Initially a structural image of the brain is created. A common procedure is then to take a baseline in which the person just relaxes. Following this, specific tasks are performed. The fMRI response recorded during the tasks is subtracted from that recorded during baseline. This shows the specific areas of the brain that are involved in performing a task. This information is then placed on the image of the brain. The color used reflects the amount of activity seen in a particular brain area. **Figure 3-23** shows fMRI images reflecting activity of internal brain structures.

In using fMRI, it is necessary to compare activity under one condition with activity under another condition. What if you were interested in the concept of self? You could ask if a person would react differently to his or her own face as compared to a friend's face or to his or her own voice as compared to a friend's voice. To answer this question, it would be important to establish how your brain reacts when it sees a picture or hears a voice. **Figure 3-24** shows brain activity when a person saw a picture or heard a voice compared to a resting baseline (Kaplan, Aziz-Zadeh, Uddin, & Iacoboni, 2008).

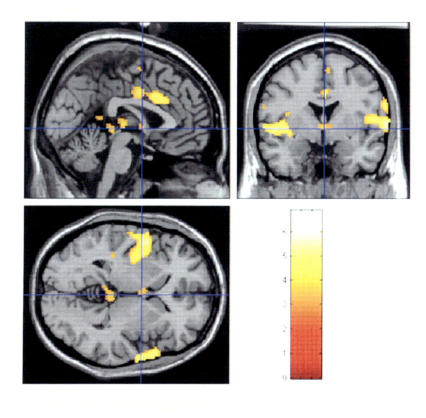

Figure 3-23 FMRI images—color reflects the amount of activity seen in a particular brain area.

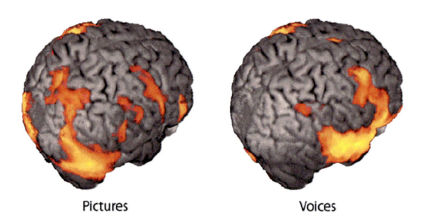

Figure 3-24 Viewing pictures and hearing voices compared with resting baseline. The orange yellow areas represent more brain activity.

Kaplan, Aziz-Zadeh, Uddin, & Iacoboni (2008).

Positron Emission Tomography

Positron emission tomography (PET) is a technique that measures the blood flow in the brain that reflects cognitive processing. In other words, PET systems measure variations in cerebral blood flow that are correlated with brain activity. It is through blood flow that the brain obtains the oxygen and glucose from which it gets its energy. By measuring changes in blood flow in different brain areas, it is possible to infer which areas of the brain are more or less active during particular tasks. Blood flow using PET is measured after participants inhale, or are injected with a tracer (a radioactive isotope) that travels in the bloodstream and is recorded by the PET scanner (a gamma ray detector).

The general procedure is to make a measurement during a control task that is subtracted from the reading taken during an experimental task. It takes some time to make a PET reading that reduces its value in terms of measuring cognitive processes that change quickly. However, it is possible to determine specific areas of the brain that are active during slower changing types of processing. This is referred to as *temporal resolution*, or the speed at which brain changes can be measured. Further, since PET can measure almost any molecule that can be radioactively labeled, it can be used to answer specific questions about neurotransmitters.

Some of PET's main disadvantages include the expense involved in creating radioactive agents and the risk involved in the injection of radioactive tracers. Also, PET has limited temporal resolution. Due to risks associated with exposure to the radioactive tracer elements in a PET study, participants typically do not participate in more than one study per year, which limits the degree to which short-term treatment changes can be studied. With the development of fMRI, PET is no longer the technique of choice for research studies. However, it does offer an advantage for studying specific receptors such as dopamine receptors in the brain, which are particularly active in those with a drug addiction or inactive in those with Parkinson's disorder.

Evaluating Techniques

In summary, there are a variety of neuroscience techniques for measuring physiological changes in your body. There are advantages and disadvantages to each of these techniques. For example, measuring heart rate is easy and inexpensive. Measuring blood flow in the brain is more complicated and much more expensive. These different techniques are presented in **Table 3-2**.

There are a number of trade-offs that researchers must consider when choosing a brain-imaging technique. It begins with the research question you are asking. If you wanted to know whether the areas of the brain associated with memory, such as the hippocampus, are larger or smaller in London taxi drivers, then you would want a measure of structure. If you wanted to know whether those with autism quickly viewed different

Table 3-2 Pros and cons of different neuroscience techniques.

Technique	Pros	Cons
EEG	Reflects quick changes in the brain, inexpensive, not invasive, safe, little discomfort	Difficult to know which brain areas produced the EEG
MEG	Reflects quick changes in the brain, not invasive, safe, no discomfort	Basic equipment is expensive
MRI and fMRI	More exact location of structure and activity, safe, little discomfort	Basic equipment is expensive, cannot be used with people who have any metal in their body (heart pacemaker or metal pins), fMRI not able to measure short-term changes in the brain
PET	Able to measure specific neurotransmitters	Basic equipment is expensive, injection of radioactive tracers limits number of scans per year, not able to measure short-term changes in the brain

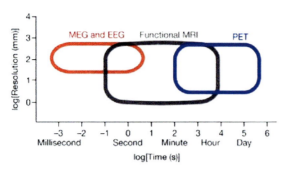

Figure 3-25 Spatial and temporal resolution of imaging techniques.
Source: Meyer-Linderberg (2010, p. 194).

emotional faces in a different way, then you would want a measure that reflects changes in brain processes.

One important question is how fast a particular technique can measure change. This is referred to as temporal resolution. EEG and MEG, for example, can measure quick changes in the brain on the millisecond level. PET, on the other hand, can only record changes that take place in a period of a few minutes or more. Another consideration is spatial resolution—that is, what size of brain area can a technique measure? PET and fMRI are better able to pinpoint the location of activity in the brain, whereas with EEG it is less possible to know specifically where in the brain the activity came from. The relationship between spatial and temporal resolution is shown in **Figure 3-25**. Temporal resolution is important for using brain activity to control artificial limbs as described in the box: Applying Psychological Science—Using Brain Activity to Move Limbs.

Applying Psychological Science—Using Brain Activity to Move Limbs

In the 1960s, researchers were interested in whether or not individuals could learn to discern changes in internal processes such as EEG, heart rate, and muscle potentials. One application of this research was for clinical, or treatment, purposes and was referred to as *biofeedback*. For example, controlling muscle potentials could aid in the treatment of headaches. Likewise, if an individual could learn to control blood flow to the hands, then disorders such as Raynaud's disease, which produces cold and numb hands or feet, could be treated.

Another set of researchers asked if individuals could learn to control their EEG (Wolpaw & Wolpaw, 2012; McFarland & Wolpaw, 2017). It would be somewhat amazing if you could play a video game with your brain. This is exactly what they were able to do. Initially, EEG was used to move objects on a computer screen. With further advances, the person was able to make more refined moves.

Using cortical signals to control devices in this way is known as *brain–machine interface* (BMI). In the last 20 years, a number of research labs have sought to train individuals to control mechanical devices such as artificial limbs. For those who had lost a limb, the artificial limb could be attached to the person. People who were paralyzed could learn to control an external device that could feed the person or move objects. Researchers wanted to know which aspects of EEG, for example, should be used and how we could train someone to control them. Another question was whether we can determine how the brain signals a movement to a muscle and then use this to control an artificial limb.

In June 2014, a 29-year-old paraplegic man literally kicked off soccer's World Cup competition in Brazil. EEG from the man's scalp went to the external movement device on the man's legs. Through intensive training, he learned to imagine leg

The Neuroscience of Behavior and Experience 107

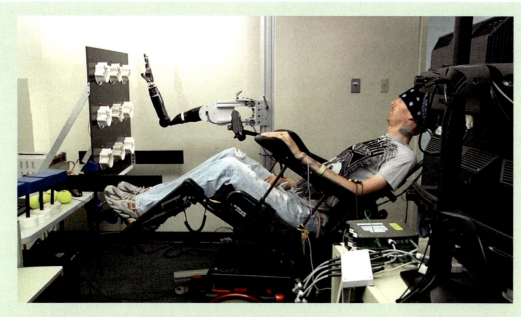

Figure 3-26 Learning to move an artificial limb.

Figure 3-27 Paraplegic kicks soccer ball at 2014 World Cup.

movements, which produced the EEG that was then computer-analyzed to control the device that moved his legs.

The goal of brain–machine interface is to give individuals without the ability to control their limb that ability through their brain activity. One approach is to implant electrodes in the brain. The signals from these electrodes are processed and sent wirelessly to the person's limbs, which can initiate movements. Today, many individuals have implanted pacemakers that keep their heartbeat both regular and able to respond to an increase in production. Perhaps tomorrow, we will see more individuals being able to control problem limbs with brain interfaces.

108 The Neuroscience of Behavior and Experience

Thought Question: Using a brain–machine interface to allow a man with paraplegia to kick a soccer ball to open the World Cup is truly a monumental accomplishment. If you were a researcher in this area, what task would you study that might be more significant to an individual's day-to-day life? Why would you choose that task?

CONCEPT CHECK
- Describe six types of brain-imaging techniques currently being used, and identify a purpose for which each is especially valuable.
- What are some of the trade-offs that researchers and clinicians must consider when choosing a brain-imaging technique? What questions help inform their decision?
- What is brain–machine interface (BMI)? What are some ways it has been used to extend the power of an individual's brain to enhance functioning in his or her body?

How Does the Brain Develop and Evolve?

Our brains represent a long evolutionary history in which different structures and functions have developed at different periods of time. For example, the experience of pain is suggested to have developed before our sense of feeling social rejection. Although most animals, including humans, show similarities in their patterns of development, differences in structure and the connection between these brain structures allow different species to display different abilities. Humans, for example, show language performance not seen in other species. Overall, the development of the brain follows genetic processes, but environmental factors can play a role at any point after conception. Since humans continue to show brain development following birth, environmental factors continue to be an important component of brain development.

From Neural Tube to Brain

The central nervous system, which includes the brain and spinal cord, develops during the first month of pregnancy. At about 18 days post conception, a process begins that results in the creation of the *neural tube* from which the brain and spinal cord develop.

Structurally, the most anterior end of the neural tube becomes the forebrain, the midbrain, the cerebellum, and the hindbrain. The remaining part of the tube becomes the spinal cord (see **Figure 3-28**). The *forebrain* includes the two cerebral hemispheres, the thalamus and the hypothalamus. The *midbrain* contains structures that have secondary roles in vision, hearing, and movement. The *hindbrain* is composed of the pons and the medulla. The cerebellum is located at the back and below the forebrain. These structures will be described in detail later. In general, the areas of the hindbrain are involved in sleep, arousal, and movement. The hindbrain is continuous with the spinal cord. In fact, you may not be able to tell where the hindbrain ends and the spinal cord begins. **Figure 3-29** shows the development of the neural tube into the forebrain, the midbrain, the cerebellum, and the hindbrain.

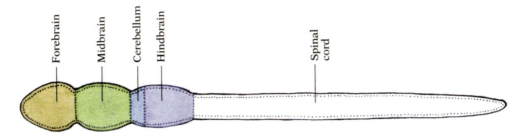

Figure 3-28 Neural tube. The neural tube is the beginning of our brain and spinal cord.
Source: Allman (2000, p. 53).

Different parts of the tube expand differently in different animals under the control of specific genes. For example, as compared to other organisms, primates, including humans, have an extremely large neocortex that develops from the most anterior part of the neural tube. Within mammals, there are extreme differences not only in number of neurons, but also in the surface area of the neocortex. For example, the surface area of a macaque monkey brain is some 100 times that of the mouse. The human brain has about 1,000 times more surface area than the mouse and about 10 times more than the monkey (Blinkov & Glezer, 1968).

Brain Structure Evolved According to Necessity

Along with the expansion of the surface area of the brain during evolution, there was also an increase and expansion of areas involved in processing information. Humans have more than 30 areas devoted to visual processing whereas rodents have only 5. As evolution produced greater diversity in cortical structure, there remained a similarity in the manner in which the nervous system functioned. The basic unit of signal transmission is the axon and the action potential that is generated within it.

Mammals have evolved a brain structure different from other organisms—the six-layered neocortex (see **Figure 3-30**). Each of these layers has a distinct neurological organization and connections. The bottom layers (five and six) have neurons that project to subcortical structures. The next layer (four) contains local circuit neurons. The next two layers (two and three) have neurons that project to other cortical structures. Layer one primarily contains dendrites and almost no cell bodies. Although consistent in structure, among mammals there is great variation in cortical size and organization.

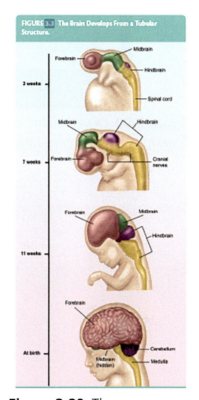

Figure 3-29 The development of the brain from the neural tube. Figure shows the brain at 3 weeks after conception, 7 weeks after conception, 11 weeks after conception, and at birth.

This variation is not just in size but also in area devoted to different types of cortical processing and greater network connectivity. As seen in **Figure 3-31**, connections between neurons increase during a child's early life.

Neurons are also created in humans after birth. A somewhat strange part of this story is that as an adult you actually have fewer neurons than you did as an infant. This may

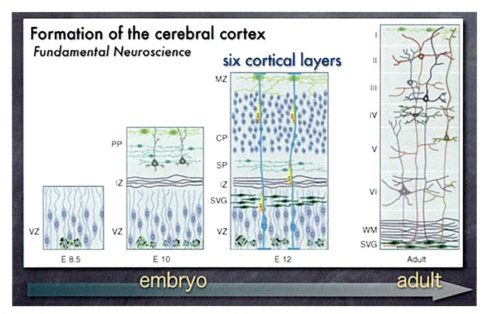

Figure 3-30 Development of the six layers of the brain over time. As we age, our brain develops a more complicated structure.

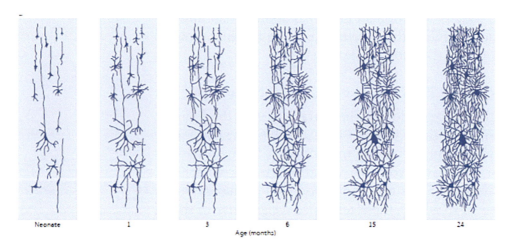

Figure 3-31 There is an increase in the connections between neurons during the early years of a human child's life.

Source: Gilmore, Knickmeyer, and Gao (2018).

seem surprising since neurons are some of the longest living cells in the body. However, this is a normal condition that is connected with a variety of processes. In infancy, use is important. For example, in your first year of life, you could recognize any sound used in any language around the world. However, this ability is lost if that language is not part of your environment. Likewise, if a child is born unable to hear, the normal initial babbling behaviors will be produced during the first year of life but then lost. These types of disuse and loss take place on the neuronal level. Unused neurons die. *Use it or lose it* is the brain's way of being.

Separate cortical areas are devoted to processing specific types of information such as color or motion, which are later combined to give us a coherent image. It is thought that this increase in size allows for additional information processing to occur. However, humans do not have the largest brain, nor do we have a brain with the greatest number of folds or convolutions. Whales, dolphins, porpoises, and elephants all have larger brains than humans.

It should be noted that as brains become larger across species, they also tend to change in terms of internal organization (Striedter, 2005). This change in internal organization allows for new cortical networks, which have evolved to process novel capacities. Language in humans would be one such example. If a brain increases in size, there must also be an increase in energy and ways to supply that energy. Although our brain is only about 2% of our body weight, it uses some 20% of the energy. Further, as a brain evolves to solve the challenges of life, the complexity of the neuronal networks and processing times becomes limited by this very complexity and the related processing time (Hofman, 2014).

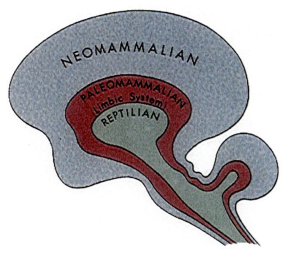

Figure 3-32 The triune brain. Each part is different in terms of structure and function.

We are just beginning to understand the manner in which human brain evolution is built upon a vast history of organic development. Since our understanding is incomplete, scientists have developed large conceptual frameworks upon which to build testable hypotheses. Paul MacLean developed one of the major programs for understanding cortical and behavioral processes from an evolutionary perspective in the 20th century (MacLean, 1990). Examining fossil records along with brains from a variety of organisms, MacLean suggested that our current brain can be viewed as having the features of three basic evolutionary formations—reptiles, early mammals, and recent mammals.

MacLean's formulation, which is referred to as the **triune brain**, suggests that through rich interconnections, our brains can process a variety of information in three somewhat independent, although not autonomous, ways (see **Figure 3-32**). MacLean (1973) emphasized that the three brains intermesh and function together.

The first level MacLean referred to as the *reptilian brain*, the name of which suggests that the basic structure is similar to that found in reptiles. This level includes the brain stem and cerebellum, and processes major life requirements such as breathing, temperature regulation, and sleep–wake cycles regulated through the brain stem. This level of processing represents fairly structured behavioral patterns involving basic activities such as territoriality, courtship, and hunting, and also includes patterned displays related to these behaviors.

The second level of the triune brain is *paleomammalian*, which includes the limbic system and its involvement in emotional processing. The third level of the triune brain is *neomammalian* and is related to the neocortex and thalamic structures. As the name implies, the neocortex and its related structures is the "new brain." This level is generally associated with problem solving, executive control, and an orientation toward the external world with an emphasis on linguistic functions. From an evolutionary perspective, it is the level of the neocortex that would be most influenced by cultural processes and new learning. It would also be at this level that processes involving self-control and self-regulation become apparent.

Although MacLean describes these three levels separately in an evolutionary sense, it is important to recognize the rich interconnections. This allows for information exchange between the structures that compose the various levels. In fact, MacLean notes the manner in which neocortical structures may be involved in regulating emotional and instinctual functions. Structurally, an interesting recent finding in neuroscience research is that there are more inhibitory pathways from the higher brain areas to the lower ones than vice versa, which would allow for more behavioral flexibility than that available to more primitive organisms. This gives us a means to inhibit more basic or primitive responses.

CONCEPT CHECK

- What are the three different types of material in the brain, and what is their function?
- "The brain works in terms of one basic element, the neuron." What are the different parts that form the structure of the neuron, and what roles do they play?
- What are the defining characteristics of neurotransmitters in terms of structure and function?
- What are the steps involved in a neuron passing information on to other neurons, and how is that information encoded?
- What are white matter and gray matter? How are they related to different types of connectivity in the brain?
- How is the brain's default or intrinsic network different from the central executive and salience networks in terms of function and region of the brain?
- How does the central nervous system, including the brain and spinal cord, develop in the human embryo? How is the development process the same, and different, in other species?
- Paul MacLean proposed that our current brain can be viewed as having the features of three basic evolutionary formations—reptiles, early mammals, and recent mammals. What did he call his schema of the brain, and what were its primary characteristics?

What Is the Link Between Heredity, Behavior, and Experience?

Genetic terminology has permeated popular culture. Court cases or police investigations that reference deoxyribonucleic acid (DNA) appear daily in our newsfeeds, and forensic crime procedurals dominate the television networks. In the field of medicine, new discoveries can connect a person's genetic makeup to certain diseases. However, in newspaper and television descriptions of genetic discoveries, the complex turning on and off of our genes is often ignored. It is easy to believe that if a person has a particular gene, then whatever activity is connected with that gene will be evident. This could be a negative experience such as cancer or alcoholism. It could also be a positive experience such as having perfect pitch or having a strong immune system. However, it is just not that simple.

Genes do not exist to make people or animals sick or to give an individual special talents. The manner in which we become sick or display talents is a complex process that involves our genes, but that also involves a variety of environmental factors. Except for blood type, genes display very few traits without a complex interaction with the environment or experience. The link between heredity, behavior, and experience or environment is not a simple one. Genes influence behaviors and behaviors can also influence gene processes. The environment we are in also plays a critical role.

In considering the role of genetic and environmental factors in behavior and experience, we can recall Darwin's reminder that "how infinitely complex and close-fitting are the mutual relations of all organic beings to each other and to their physical conditions of life." That is, genetic and environmental factors are mutually dependent upon one another. In fact, what you experience can determine if a gene influences your behavior (gene turns on) or not (gene turns off).

Environments can determine which genes turn on and off. The National Aeronautics and Space Administration (NASA) in 2019 released results of an astronaut who spent a year in space while his twin brother remained on Earth (https://www.nasa.gov/twins-study). Both twins were astronauts and thus had similar experiences previous to the study. Spending time in space changed the way that specific genes turned on and off (Garrett-Bakelman et al., 2019). Although the twin who spent time in space retained the basic genetic structure as the one who remained home, about 7% of his genes did turn on and off in different ways. Turning a gene on or off can influence behavior and experience. The majority of the genes that did change during the space flight returned to normal functioning within six months after returning to Earth. Thus, the environment can influence genetic expression.

The opposite is also the case. Your genes can influence the type of environments you seek. That is, if you are a person who seeks stimulation, then you are more likely to have a certain set of genes different from those who are happy reading a book at home. In seeking stimulation, you look for environments that allow you to go mountain climbing or sky diving.

Numerous examples of the close fitting of genes and environment also exist in nature, such as a particular butterfly, the *Bicyclus anyana*, which is brightly colored if born in the rainy season, but gray if born in the dry season. The side-blotched lizard of the Mojave Desert will also have different colorings depending on its environment. It will be black if it is raised in a habitat of black lava flow and lighter if raised in light desert sand. The advantage of this tight coupling with the environment is that it offers a means of protection against predators.

Genes, the most basic unit of heredity, carry the instructions that direct the expression of particular traits and behaviors in a complicated process. As you will see, a number of factors influence which genetic programs are expressed.

A basic distinction in terminology is made between the *genotype* (genetic material) and the *phenotype* (organism's observable characteristics). The **genotype** consists of what is inherited through the sperm and the egg at the moment of conception. The **phenotype** represents the observed traits of the individual including structure, physiology, and behavior. The focus of psychology has largely been the study of the phenotype. Current research also seeks to describe how genes are involved.

Genetics Help Explain Evolutionary Change

Genetic transmission is how evolution "works." In his theory of natural selection, the English naturalist Charles Darwin (1809–1882) stressed variations in heritable traits and the manner in which different environments place specific traits at an advantage. Darwin originally showed this with the finches in the Galápagos Islands. In times of plenty, the seeds and nuts from the trees in which the finches ate were well developed and hard. Thus, the birds with strong beaks were able to obtain food. In times of less food, those birds with longer peaks were able to find food that had fallen between rocks. Those birds that survive are able to pass their traits on.

Another example are peacocks that have brightly colored large tails. How did they get these? The female peahen chooses which male peacock to mate with in terms of the quality of the characteristics of his tail. Thus, by choosing males with large and colorful tails, this trait is passed on. After a number of generations, peacock tails became larger with certain colors. We now know that the vibrancy of the color also reflects the health of the peacock as well as the underlying genetics. By choosing the male with the highest quality tail, the female is also choosing the male with better genes. What Charles Darwin did not know at the time he was writing was the specific units involved in this process.

Chromosomes

Long strands of genetic material, including genes, are called **chromosomes**. Different organisms have different numbers of chromosomes. In humans there are 23 separate pairs of chromosomes making 46 in all. Each chromosome has a unique appearance. The chromosomes are numbered in approximate order of size with 1 being the largest and 22 being the smallest. These 22 are referred to as *autosomes*. The remaining chromosome pair is called the *sex chromosome* in that this chromosome differs in males and females. Females carry two copies of the X chromosome while males carry one X and one Y. By treating cells with particular dyes, chromosomes can be seen under a microscope. They appear as long, banded, cylinder-like structures that are pinched in at one point along their length (see **Figure 3-33**).

The image of chromosomes after being isolated, stained, and examined with a microscope is referred to as a *karyotype*. Chromosomes are typically laid out in order of size in pairs with the sex chromosomes being shown last. Thus, a human male would be 46 XY and a human female 46 XX. Through research, each of the chromosomes has been associated with different physiological processes, particularly in terms of genes.

The Job of the Gene

All of us begin as a single fertilized egg, which by the time of birth has given us a body with some trillion cells. These cells can be differentiated both in terms of structure and function. For instance, cells in your muscles do different things from those in your brain. However, each of the cells, regardless of function, has a nucleus that contains the genome. A human genome is a set of some 20,500 genes. Other organisms have different numbers of genes, although the basic mechanism is similar across species. In fact, many of our genes are also found in other organisms and perform similar functions.

The job of a gene is to lay out the process by which a particular protein is made. In other words, each gene is able to *encode* a protein. *Proteins* are involved in a variety of processes. Functionally, proteins in the form of enzymes are able to make metabolic events speed up, whereas structural proteins are involved in building body parts. Similar proteins in insects are involved in creating such structures as spider webs, and butterfly wings. Proteins are diverse and complex and found in the foods we eat as well as made by our cells. Proteins serve as signals for changes in cell activity. Proteins are also involved in health and disease as well as development and aging. Proteins do the work of the body and genes influence their production.

The Neuroscience of Behavior and Experience 115

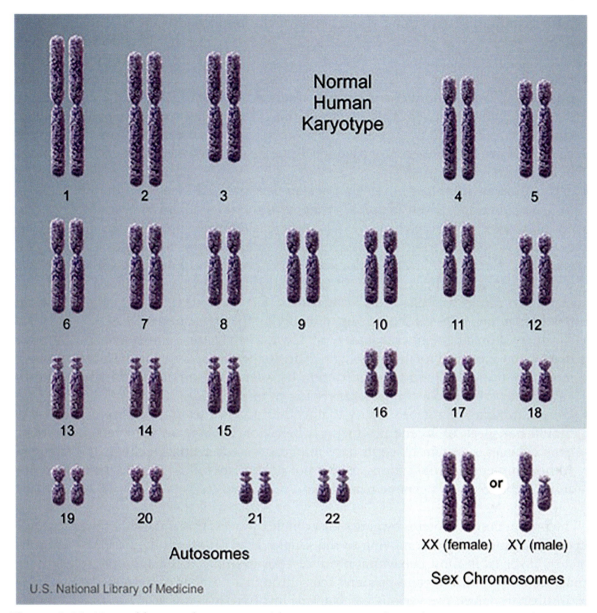

Figure 3-33 Normal human karyotype with autosomes and sex chromosomes. Each chromosome is associated with particular physiological processes.

Although the cells in the body carry the full set of genetic information, only a limited amount is expressed at any one time related to the function of the cell. That is to say, although a large variety of proteins could be produced at any one time, there is selectivity as to what is produced related to internal and external conditions. Further, the location of the genes makes a difference in that cells in your brain produce different proteins from those in your muscles, liver, heart, and so forth.

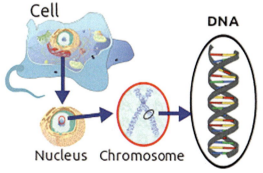

Figure 3-34 Structure of a cell. In every cell there is a nucleus that contains our DNA.

Before continuing, let's think about some of the implications for a gene encoding a protein.

- First, a gene does not produce a protein constantly but in the context of a complex physiological system influenced both by internal bodily processes and events from the external environment. Thus, we can think of a gene being turned on (produce the protein) or turned off (do not produce the protein) relative to specific events. The bottom line is that just because a person has a specific gene does not mean that it will necessarily be expressed.
- Second, the environment in which a person develops and lives plays an important role in gene expression. Even identical twins with the same genotype can display different phenotypes if their environmental conditions differ during their development. For example, if one was to grow up in a high mountain range and the other in a below sea level desert, important physiological differences such as lung capacity and function would be apparent. Thus, as we will see there are few factors in terms of human processes that can be explained totally by genetic factors alone. It is also equally true that few human processes can be explained totally by the environment.
- Third, we should remember that there are few human factors of interest to psychologists that can be explained totally by a single gene. Rather, what we view in human processes represents not only a complex interaction between a person's genetic makeup and the environment, but also a complex expression of many genes.
- Fourth, thinking of a gene's ability to encode a protein, we should also realize that we should not speak of a gene producing a behavior. Rather, we must remember that a gene encodes a protein that can have implications for actions, feelings, and thoughts. Although there are implications, it does not necessarily follow that the behavioral outcome is the result of a genetic plan alone.

The production of proteins by genes is a complex process that involves a variety of levels, especially in humans. Even moving to the simpler level of insects, there are still a number of steps involved in most behavioral processes. For example, if the appropriate genes in a spider do not produce certain proteins, then through a number of steps the web will end up misshapen. Given the various mechanisms involved, it is not accurate to talk about a gene for misshapen spider webs. Thus, when we hear or read about the gene for misshapen spider webs or any of the other traits, we must consider what protein was produced under what conditions as well as the steps required. At this point it will be useful to move to a structural level in our consideration of genetics. Let's begin with DNA.

DNA and RNA

Deoxyribonucleic acid (DNA) provides information necessary to produce proteins. ***Ribonucleic acid (RNA)*** transmits genetic information from DNA to proteins produced by the cell. We can think of proteins as a link between the genotype and the phenotype. The question arises as to how we get from information, which is what DNA and RNA is all about, to actual physiological changes. This is accomplished in two steps:

1. The information in DNA is encoded in RNA.
2. This information in RNA determines the sequence of amino acids, which are the building blocks of proteins.

DNA, which is the information storage molecule, transfers information to RNA, which is the information transfer molecule, to produce a particular protein. Further, change in the rate at which RNA is transcribed controls the rate at which genes produce proteins. The expression rate of different genes in the same genome may vary from 0 to approximately 100,000 proteins per second. Thus, not only do genes produce proteins, but they do so at different rates. The crucial question becomes what causes a gene to turn on or turn off.

In a classic work, Jacques Monod and François Jacob in the 1960s came to an initial understanding of how genes turn on and off. The particular organism they were studying was the bacterium *Escherichia coli*. This organism can switch from a diet of sugar (glucose) to milk sugar (lactose) if glucose becomes scarce in its environment.

To make this happen, these bacteria must produce an enzyme that breaks down lactose. Monod and Jacob discovered that an environmental event—the presence of lactose and the absence of glucose—would cause the genes to turn on and the enzymes to be produced. When this environmental condition was not present, these enzyme-producing genes were inhibited and thus not allowed to turn on.

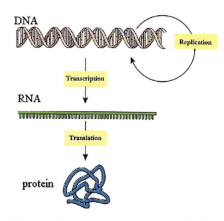

Figure 3-35 DNA, RNA, and the production of proteins. DNA, which is the information storage molecule, transfers information to RNA, which is the information transfer molecule, to produce a particular protein.

Said in the language of genes, the transcription of the DNA into RNA and the resulting proteins was repressed in the environmental condition of lactose presence and glucose absence. What this tells us is that genes are designed to perform specific tasks depending on the presence of certain internal or external environmental conditions. Even the determination of larger organizational structures, such as whether an organism becomes male or female in some species, relates directly to the environmental conditions during its development and the genes that are turned on and off. For example, eggs hatched in warm water produces males in alligators but females in turtles.

In summary, genes form the blueprint that determines what an organism is to become. They are found in every cell of the body. Within each gene, DNA—the information storage molecule—transfers information to RNA—the information transfer molecule—to produce (or encode) a particular protein. The location of the genes in the body makes a difference in that cells in the brain produce different proteins from those in the muscles, or liver, or heart. A gene is turned on (produces the protein) or turned off (does not produce the protein) relative to specific events.

In terms of evolution, one of the real scientific contributions of DNA analysis has been the realization of how similar organisms are in terms of DNA structure. This suggests that all organic life on Earth involves similar building blocks in terms of DNA. Humans have DNA, chimps have DNA, bacteria have DNA, and even flowers have DNA. Given that all organisms have DNA, it is possible to compare how similar different organisms are, and from this make inferences about common ancestors. We know, for example, that the structure of DNA in chimpanzees and humans is about 97% the same. However, how the genes are expressed makes a real difference.

Whereas DNA science began with Watson and Crick and the discovery of DNA structure, it has come of age with the publication of the map of the human genome in 2003.

118 The Neuroscience of Behavior and Experience

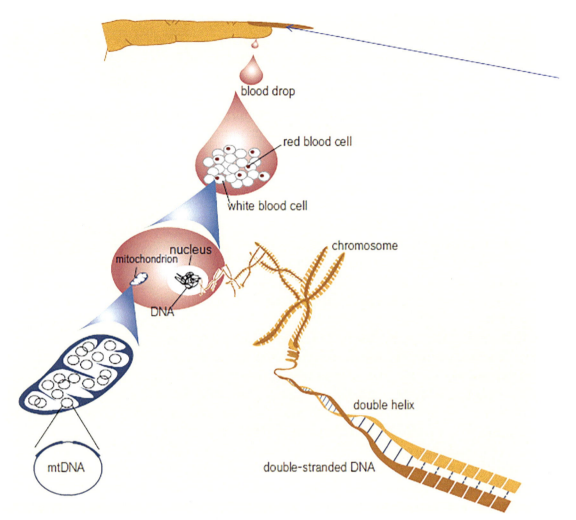

Figure 3-36 Chromosomes, genes, and DNA. In the center of every cell in our body, we have a complete set of genes (DNA). There is also another set of genes passed on from your mother referred to as mitochondrial DNA (mtDNA), which supplies energy to the cell.

Genes are particular stretches of chromosomes that contain all of the heritable bits of information necessary to produce a new individual. On any one chromosome, there can be anywhere from a few hundred to almost 3,000 genes (Lander et al., 2001). In 1990, the *Human Genome Project* was launched with the goal of cataloging the genetic information found in humans. It was completed in 2003 with the identity of all of the approximately 20,500 human genes. The research related to the project can be seen online (http://www.ornl.gov/hgmis/).

Patterns of Inheritance Vary

Genes form the blueprint to describe who you are to become. They determine many physical characteristics such as eye color. Although genes can produce variation over evolutionary history, a majority of our genes have not changed. This is why all humans have two eyes and one nose and one mouth, for example. However, perhaps a fourth of all genes allow for variation, which results in differences between us in physical and psychological characteristics. What makes things interesting is that each of these genes can have pairs in which one is slightly different from the other.

The technical name for the unique molecular form of the same gene is an ***allele***. It has been estimated that of our approximately 20,500 genes, some 6,000 exist in different versions or alleles (Zimmer, 2001). Thus, in each sperm or egg, the alleles inherited from the mother may express different characteristics from those from the father.

It is these structural differences that determine many of your characteristics from the shape of your face to the size of your fingers to whether or not your earlobes are attached. For example, although it is a single gene that determines the development of your earlobes, slight structural differences in this gene determine whether they develop attached or not. Being able to touch your tongue to your nose or curling your tongue are also related to the alleles of two different genes.

Mendelian Genetics

The study of genetics began with the work of Gregor Mendel (1822–1884). Although unknown to each other, at about the same time Darwin was examining heritable traits in finches, Gregor Mendel was describing the initial mechanisms by which genes work. During the latter part of the 19th century, the work of Darwin and Mendel and their followers occupied parallel tracks. However, both emphasized variation and factors that influenced it. It was the publication of Dobzhansky's *Genetics and the Origins of Species* in 1937 that brought together the natural history of organisms with an understanding of genetics. These two lines of research came together in what is now referred to as the *modern synthesis* (Huxley, 1942; Mayr, 1942).

Curious about how plants obtain atypical characteristics, Mendel performed a series of experiments with the garden pea plant. Peas are a self-fertilizing plant, which means that the male and female aspects needed for reproduction develop in different parts of the same flower. Therefore, successive generations of peas are similar to their parents in terms of particular traits such as their height or the color of their flowers.

Mendel found that when combining peas with white flowers with those with purple flowers, the next generation had all purple flowers. Allowing this generation to self-fertilize brought forth plants that had purple flowers but also some that had white flowers. Mendel explained these findings by suggesting that a plant inherits information from each parent, the male and female aspect. Mendel was hypothesizing that information must be conveyed. He further suggested that one unit of information could be *dominant* in comparison to the other. The non-dominant one we now call *recessive*. In this case, the unit of information that coded for purple would be dominant.

Mendel did not know about genes, but hypothesized the existence of a specific structure he called *elements*. From his experiments, he determined the basic principle that there are two elements of heredity for each trait (for example, color in the previous example). Mendel also assumed that one of these elements can dominate the other and if it is present then the trait will be present. Mendel suggested that these elements can also be non-dominant, or recessive. For the trait to appear, both of these non-dominant elements must be present. These ideas are referred to as *Mendel's first law or the law of segregation*.

If your eyes are blue, then you can guess that both of your parents have blue eyes since the allele for blue eyes is recessive. Put in today's language, Mendel suggested that variants of a specific gene exist that account for variations in inherited characteristics and that an organism receives one of these from each parent. Traits are inherited depending on whether the allele is dominant or recessive. The allele for blue eyes is recessive so you need to receive the same allele from both your mother and father to have blue eyes.

However, if you receive the gene associated with brown eyes from one parent and the gene associated with blue eyes from the other, you will have brown eyes since the brown eye allele is dominant.

Mendel also realized that the inheritance of the gene of one trait is not affected by the inheritance of the gene for another trait. In the previous example illustrating the inheritance of eye color, those factors influencing color do not affect height, and vice versa. That is, the probability for each occurs separately. This fact is known as *Mendel's second law or the law of independent assortment.*

As genetic research progressed in the 20th century, it became clear that it was necessary to go beyond the two laws suggested by Mendel to a more complex understanding of how traits are passed from generation to generation. For example, if two genes are located close to one another on the same chromosome, then the result is different from that predicted by Mendel's second law. Additionally, it was initially assumed that one day genes would be able to explain the development of psychopathology (mental disorders), especially schizophrenia. However, after decades of research, it is clear that simple genetic explanations will not be forthcoming. Mental disorders disrupt a variety of cognitive, emotional, and motor processes that develop over a person's lifetime and are guided by thousands of genes (see Plomin, 2018 for an overview).

Sex-Linked Inheritance

In addition to the genetics that Mendel studied, there is also inheritance that is sex-linked. Males and females have partially different genomes—the sex chromosomes are inherited differently for males and females. Human females have two X chromosomes and males have an X and a Y chromosome. One implication of this is that genes on the Y chromosome are expressed only in males. Another implication is that some genes on the X chromosome may be expressed at a higher level in females. Besides physical sexual organs, researchers are just beginning to understand which characteristics of males and females are influenced by genes on the X and Y chromosomes. Given that females have two X chromosomes, they transmit an X chromosome to all of their offspring whether they are males or females. Thus, everyone receives an X chromosome from their mothers. Males, on the other hand, transmit an X chromosome to their offspring who are daughters, but not to their sons. Thus, sons cannot inherit an allele on the X chromosome from their fathers. These male offspring receive only a Y chromosome.

Since the X and Y chromosomes are different and do not contain the same identical genes, this sets up the possibility for transmission of traits that can be different for males and females. One implication is that recessive traits on the X chromosome will be expressed in males, but not as frequently in females. One common X-linked recessive trait is color blindness. The most common form results in the individual being unable to see red or green as distinct colors. Since this is caused by a recessive allele on the X chromosome, females would need to inherit the allele on both X chromosomes for them to be color blind, whereas males, having only one X chromosome, would only need to inherit one recessive allele.

Sex-linked traits also have different patterns of inheritance throughout generations for males and females. Since fathers do not pass X chromosomes to their sons, a color-blind father and a non-color-blind mother are not likely to have a color-blind son. They might, however, pass the allele on to their daughter whose son could be color blind. That is to say, the son would not be color blind but would be a carrier of the color-blind allele, whereas the grandson would be color blind. In this manner the trait would skip a generation.

The Neuroscience of Behavior and Experience 121

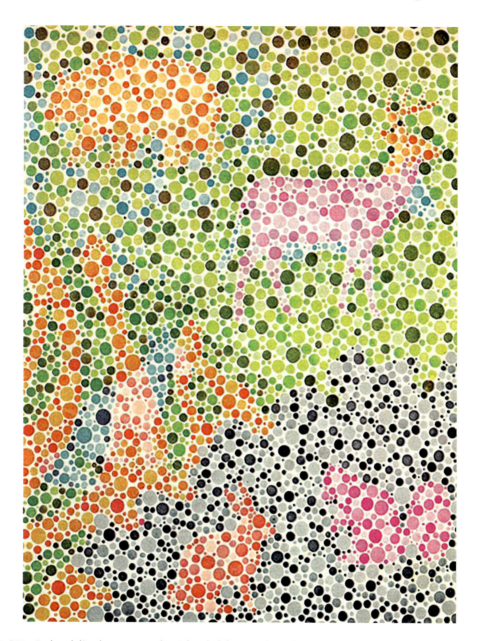

Figure 3-37 Color-blind test used with children. The ability to see the animals in the picture requires that the person can see red and green as separate from gray.

Behavior and Environment Influence Gene Expression

In terms of behavior and experience, changes caused by the production of proteins can be transitory. For example, touching a cat's whiskers causes changes in gene expression in the cells of the sensory cortex of the brain (Mack & Mack, 1992). This is just a momentary change. Changes can also be long term. As we will see when we discuss development, turning on one set of genes may have lasting influence on the ability of other genes to produce specific proteins. For example, when a songbird first hears the specific song of its species, a particular set of genes comes into play that when once set, determines the song produced by that bird for its entire life. This process has been mapped by a number of researchers (Mello, Vicario, & Clayton, 1992). Likewise, raising mice in an enriched environment, that is, one with lots of toys and stimulation, will cause increased gene expression in genes that are associated with learning and memory (Rampon et al., 2000).

How do we know which genes are involved? In this study, the genes of mice in enriched environments were compared with those of control mice who did not have this experience. Another way to know which genes are involved in a process is to actually change the genes in a particular organism. So called "knockout" mice are genetically engineered mice in which particular genes have been turned off by breeding them in specific ways. Research shows that simple genetic changes made experimentally in animals can result in protein changes that influence social behavior. Some examples of such behaviors are increased fear and anxiety, increased grooming, hyperactivity, and even increased alcohol consumption when stressed.

One striking example of the manner in which cultural and environmental change can be mapped along with genetic change is *lactose tolerance* (Tishkoff et al., 2006). Lactose is a sugar found in milk. The infants of most mammals, including humans, can no longer digest milk once weaned. Infants are able to digest lactose due to certain enzymes in their mothers' milk that work with the infant's own genes to break down the lactose. A single dominant gene is involved in the production of the enzyme that breaks the milk sugar down. Without the enzyme, anyone drinking milk can feel sick, including cramps, diarrhea, and nausea. However, some humans currently living in Europe, India, and sub-Saharan Africa and their descendants continue to be able to drink milk into adulthood. How did this happen?

It appears that when cattle were first domesticated some 9,000 years ago, humans began to eat their meat and drink their milk. Some of the people living at that time had a mutation that kept the gene involved in producing the enzyme, which allowed the individual to digest milk sugar permanently, switched on. Given that these individuals did not become sick from drinking milk, they had a certain advantage, particularly in difficult times such as droughts.

In fact, it has been estimated that individuals with the mutation that allowed for milk drinking into adulthood were able to produce almost ten times as many descendants as those without it (Tishkoff et al., 2006). This is demonstrated today by the fact that almost all of the citizens of the Netherlands and Sweden, the area where cattle were originally domesticated in Europe, are lactose tolerant. Further, it is thought that lactose tolerance developed independently in different parts of the world. Overall, this shows the manner in which cultural and environmental changes can produce a shift in the genetics of a specific population.

Environmental couplings may also promote health and well-being. With some genetic disorders, such as phenylketonuria (PKU), simply changing the environmental conditions in terms of the types of food a person eats can actually change the negative outcomes of the disorder. Even more surprising is that if you are a mouse, what your mother ate before you were born can influence the color of your fur and the diseases you are susceptible to. This is the result of epigenetic changes.

Epigenetic Processes Respond to Changing Environments

According to Mendelian genetics, genes are not changed by experience. What is passed on, except in the case of damage to the gene, is exactly the same gene that was received by the organism from its parents. This was known as the *central dogma of molecular biology* as described by neuroscientist Francis Crick, who discovered the structure of DNA. He stated that the information flow was one-directional (Crick, 1970). That is, it went from the gene to the protein. What came to be called *reverse translation* was seen as impossible. Thus, the gene could not be influenced or affected by changes in proteins, and, by implication, experience could not change DNA. This was the basic view from the 1950s until very recently.

However, the story has become more complicated. Researchers examining how genes turn on and off in relation to environmental factors discovered that internal genetic processes could make genes easier or harder to turn on or off. These processes that determine which genes turn on and off could themselves be passed on to the next generation. The factors that turn genes on and off are complex but largely influenced by the environment of the organism. In short, DNA is covered by proteins. Changes in these proteins and the other chemicals associated with them can influence the manner in which nearby genes are turned on or off. Even more surprising was that the tendency for a gene to be turned on easily or not could be passed on to the next generation. Thus, although DNA itself could not be influenced by the environment, it was possible for the environment to influence future generations through its changes to those processes that turn genes on and off.

This possibility of another form of inheritance came to be called **epigenetic inheritance** (see Bagot et al., 2014; Hallgrímsson & Hall, 2011; Nestler, 2011; O'Donnell & Meaney, 2020 for overviews). Instead of actually changing the gene itself, epigenetic modifications *mark* a gene. This alters how it is turned on and off. DNA is wrapped around clusters of proteins called *histones*. These are further bundled into chromosomes. Being tightly packed keeps genes in an inactive state by preventing access to processes that turn genes on. When action is needed, a section of DNA unfurls and the gene turns on. Whether a segment is relaxed and able to be activated or condensed, resulting in no action, is influenced by *epigenetic marks or tags* (see **Figure 3-38**). As a *tag*, histone acetylation tends to

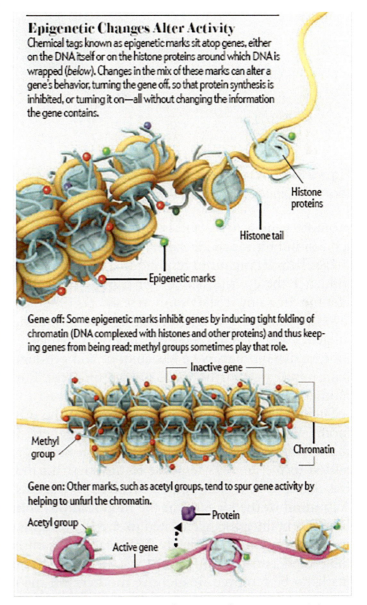

Figure 3-38 Epigenetic changes alter gene activity. When the genes are tightly wrapped, they are more difficult to turn on. When they are not, they are easier to turn on.

Source: Nestler (2011).

Figure 3-39 A mother rat taking care of her pups. This information can be passed on in the form of epigenetic mechanisms.

promote gene activity and is called a *writer*. Histone methylation and DNA methylation tend to inhibit it and are called *erasers*.

Tags help an organism respond to a changing environment. The environment itself can influence these writer and eraser tags. Some tags last a short time while others can last a lifetime. In a now classic study, researchers observed that some rat mothers displayed high levels of nurturing behavior, licking and grooming their pups, whereas others were less diligent (Weaver et al., 2004; Meaney, 2010; Miller, 2010). Behaviorally, the offspring of the more active mothers were less anxious and produced less stress hormone when disturbed than pups cared for by more passive mothers. Further, the females raised by nurturing mothers became nurturing mothers themselves.

The intriguing part of this study was that the offspring of the rat mothers who showed more licking and grooming differed in epigenetic factors. Pups raised by passive mothers showed more DNA methylation than aggressively groomed pups. The pup differences were related to the animal's response to the stress hormone *cortisol*. This excessive methylation was detected in a brain region involved in learning and memory called the *hippocampus*. Activation of the receptor in the hippocampus actually signals the body to slow production of a brain substance related to stress. The epigenetic-related response exacerbates the stress response in the animals. This makes the animals more anxious and fearful. Further, these traits persist throughout their lifetime. Overall, attentive mothers cause the methyl marks to be removed. Inattentive mothers, on the other hand, cause methyl marks to be added. Thus, rats inherit certain behaviors based on experience. The genes had not been changed, but the tags were.

Fathers, including human fathers, can also influence their offspring. It has been shown that a mouse will develop a diabetes-like disease if her father's diet before her conception was high in fat (Skinner, 2010). Also, if a mouse father is overweight, then gene activity in the pancreas of his offspring is abnormal (Ng et al., 2010). Since the pancreas makes insulin, which regulates blood sugar, then this may set up the possibility of future diabetes. The opposite is also the case. If the father's diet results in an underweight condition, then genes in the liver associated with fat and cholesterol synthesis were shown to be more active in their offspring (Carone, 2010). Another study examined human fathers who smoked early in life and determined this was associated with his sons being heavier in weight at age 9 (Pembrey et al., 2006). Stress-related factors can also influence epigenetic processes. For example, the experience of violent events is associated with decreased DNA methylation across human generations (Serpeloni, Nätt, Assis, Wieling, & Elbert, 2019).

Overall, epigenetic research suggests that behavior and environmental experiences at critical periods could later influence characteristics for future generations. Current health research related to such disorders as diabetes and cancer, as well as types of psychopathology, is suggestive of such a relationship (Bagot, 2014; Katsnelson, 2010; O'Donnell & Meaney, 2020). Both addiction and depression have been shown to have an epigenetic component (Nestler, 2011, 2014). Extreme childhood abuse is related to a number of negative outcomes including suicide. Those who committed suicide were shown to have changes in epigenetic mechanisms (see Labonte & Turecki, 2010 for an overview). There is also research to suggest that long-term physical exercise can not only increase cognitive functions of the brain and reduce the possibilities of neurological disorders, but that exercise can influence future generations through epigenetic mechanisms (Fernandes, Arida, & Gomez-Pinilla, 2017).

Thus, epigenetic inheritance, which involves tags or marks that determine when genes are turned off or on, offers a parallel track to traditional Mendelian inheritance for influencing phenotypes. One new area of research uses identical twins to study specific epigenetic mechanisms with the goal of determining how genetic and environmental factors influence *epigenetics* (for example, Bell & Spector, 2011; Tan, 2020). This approach may offer better insight into the expression of complex traits as seen in both normal and psychopathological processes. One example of epigenetics is described in the box: Real World Psychology—Dutch Winter and Epigenetics.

Real World Psychology—Dutch Winter and Epigenetics

In the 1940s, much of Europe was experiencing hardships from World War II and from especially cold winter weather. In the Netherlands, there was an active resistance movement directed against the Nazi occupation. In November of 1944, the Nazi occupiers of Holland sought to punish the population for war resistance activity. To do this, the food supply was cut such that the mean caloric intake went from approximately 2,000 calories a day to less than 800. When the Allies liberated Holland some seven months later, food supplies returned to normal.

This terrible event was referred to as *Hongerwinter* (hunger winter) in which 18,000 people starved to death. Since everyone had their food supplies cut and reinstated at exactly the same time, it is possible to see the effects of this experience. Like much of Europe, hospitals in Holland collected health data from mothers and their children. Using birth data from the hospitals during the period of food deprivation, it was possible to determine which mothers became pregnant after the food was limited and which mothers were already pregnant at this time. Thus, some fetuses would be undernourished at the beginning of the pregnancy and others only at the end of the pregnancy. Those fetuses that were undernourished late in pregnancy had a reduced birth weight. Those fetuses that were undernourished early in pregnancy had a normal birth weight. Even with early malnutrition, these infants were able to catch up in body weight.

The close connection between an infant and its environment influences a number of developmental processes. The body of an infant is structured to live in the same environment that it experienced as a fetus. In periods of famine, one would want a physiological system that could survive in times of less food. However, a different system would be ideal for times of plenty. In the Dutch winter of 1944, there was a brief period of intense deprivation, in an otherwise well-nourished population. This resulted in a mismatch between the infant and his or her environment.

Not only did scientists study the birth weight of those born in the aftermath of the Dutch Winter, but they also followed these individuals throughout their lives. What they found was that those babies who were born small remained that way for the rest of their lives and showed less obesity than the general population. On the other hand, those infants born with a normal body weight were later shown to develop obesity and insulin resistance. Later tests also showed these individuals had higher plasma glucose concentrations after a standard glucose tolerance test. Thus, malnutrition early in pregnancy left these individuals susceptible to future obesity and diabetes.

There is also an epigenetic aspect to the Dutch Winter. With the excellent data collected from parents of the Dutch Winter and their children and grandchildren, it has been possible to explore the consequences of experiencing the famine. In the Dutch Winter, those women who were malnourished in the first trimester had normal weight babies but their grandchildren tended to be heavier. If on the other hand the women were malnourished in the third trimester, their babies were underweight but their grandchildren were of normal weight. Further, some 60 years later researchers looked for epigenetic differences. They did this by comparing the individuals who were in the womb during the Dutch Winter to their older and younger siblings who were born in normal periods of food availability. What was found was that the siblings did not show differences in DNA methylation of particular genes, whereas the Dutch Winter children did. What this and other research suggests is that it is possible for an environmental event to be transmitted to later generations through epigenetic mechanisms (see Ahmed, 2010 and Carey, 2012 for overviews).

Thought Question: What does the Dutch Winter story teach us about how the environment influences developmental processes? What epigenetic changes were found?

Behavior Genetics

Behavioral genetics is the study of genetic and environmental contributions to behavior (see Knopik, Neiderhiser, DeFries, & Plomin, 2017; Plomin, 2018 for overviews). This is an exciting field of research today, and a fundamental question addressed is the manner in which genes and the environment work together to shape behavior. What if you were raised by a different set of parents, would you be different? What if you had an older brother or sister rather than a younger one? What if you were not an only child? In each case you would have grown up with different life experiences. Although interrelated, psychologists interested in behavioral genetics seek to quantify the amount of variance that can

Figure 3-40 Identical twins usually look alike and may display similar preferences.

be attributed to genetic influences and the amount attributed to environmental influences. One of the main approaches used in behavioral genetics is *twin studies*.

Twins offer an occurrence in nature that allows for understanding critical factors related to genetic influences. This is largely based on the fact that there are two types of twins. ***Monozygotic (MZ) twins*** are identical twins resulting from the zygote (fertilized egg) dividing during the first two weeks of gestation. Because they both come from the same egg, their genes are identical. ***Dizygotic (DZ) twins***, on the other hand, result from the situation in which two different eggs are fertilized by two different spermatozoa. These individuals are called fraternal twins since their shared genes are approximately 50%, which is the same as that between any two siblings. DZ twins can be either same sex or opposite sex, whereas MZ twins must always be the same sex. By comparing the psychological traits of MZ and DZ twins it is possible to obtain an estimate of heritability.

A classic research design is to compare the responses of MZ twins with DZ twins on particular behavioral traits such as intelligence or personality characteristics (Bouchard, 2013; Johnson, Turkheimer, Gottesman, & Bouchard, 2010; Segal, 2012). Since it is assumed that both DZ and MZ twins would have had similar environmental influences in their family,

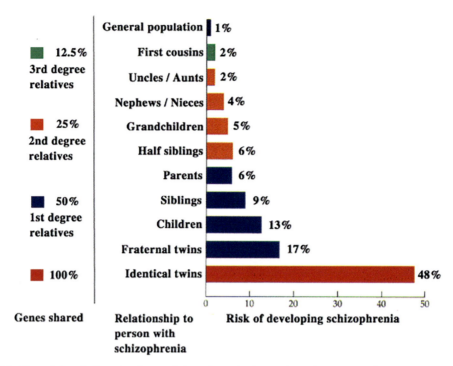

Figure 3-41 The risk of developing schizophrenia based on how another person with schizophrenia is related to you.

then differences between MZ and DZ twins would be seen to be the result of genetic influences.

Gottesman (1991) has studied schizophrenia with this design. In these studies, a particular MZ twin had a 48% chance of developing schizophrenia if the other twin also did. In DZ twins there was only a 17% chance. **Figure 3–41** shows the risk of developing schizophrenia based on another person with schizophrenia related to you.

Statistically, researchers examine the degree to which twins are identical to each other as a function of genetic influences and environmental influences. That is to say, you create correlation coefficients for MZ twins and for DZ twins. This tells you how similar each type of twin is on a particular trait. From this, it is possible to determine the percentage of contribution to the trait that comes from environmental influences and the percentage of contribution that comes from genetic influences. For example, personality factors such as extraversion have been shown to have a 50% contribution of genetic factors and a 50% contribution of environmental factors. Although we use the term identical twins, they can be different, as described in the box: Myths and Misconceptions—Identical Twins: Identical Brains.

Myths and Misconceptions—Identical Twins: Identical Brains

Identical twins look the same. There are even stories about identical twins who grew up apart going into the ocean on vacation in the same way—by walking in backwards. While it is true that identical twins come from the same egg and sperm, after that there are a number of ways they can become different.

One of the first ways they can be different is when they are in the womb. Although we think of life in the womb being the same for both of them, that is not actually the case. Through a variety of situations, one of the twins may receive more nutrients than the other. Even at the beginning, their DNA can be reproduced in slightly different ways. In the process of turning genes on and off, a single gene can produce different proteins. These proteins, in turn, can influence other processes that can lead to differences between the two twins.

One exciting finding in the study of genes is the so-called *jumping gene*. These jumping genes, also known as *transposable elements*, were discovered more than 50 years ago by Barbara McClintock at Cold Spring Harbor Laboratory in New York. As the name implies, these genes move from one location on the genome to another. As such, they can move within and between chromosomes. In their new location, these genes sometimes have no effect at all. However, in some cases they can activate the genes in the new location and influence individual cells in the brain. This in turn can create differences in brain function between individuals, even identical twins.

Given that identical twins may have different brain processes, which include behavior, cognition, and even reaction to stress, this may help to explain how one twin may remain disease-free, and the other not. Even mice who have been bred to be genetically identical and environmentally treated in the same manner will show differences in learning ability and responses to fear and stress. Further, novel situations and exercise in mice, as well as humans, produce new growth of nerve cells and connections in the brain. An intriguing idea is that as we learn new information that increases brain connections, we also increase the activity of jumping genes (see Gage & Muotri, 2012 for an overview). This, in turn, would allow us to solve new problems in different ways. Thus, each person remains unique in his or her brain activity, even identical twins.

Thought Question: What are the different ways identical twins can be different?

Another important type of study is the **adoption study**. This is the situation where DZ and MZ twins have been raised apart. During World War II, for example, children from England were often sent to Canada to allow them to grow up in a less dangerous situation. At times, the twins were split up and raised by different parents. Since the children were raised in different environments, this made it possible to better determine the environmental and genetic influences.

Since 1979, in the United States a series of twins who were separated in infancy and reared apart have been studied by researchers at the University of Minnesota (see Bouchard, Lykken, McGue, Segal, & Tellegen, 1990; Segal, 2012 for overviews). In work with more than 100 pairs of twins, these researchers found that about 70% of the variance in intelligence quotient (IQ) could be associated with genetic factors. Later studies have supported this finding. However, environmental factors such as poverty can greatly reduce the role of genetics as related to IQ. Although it is not surprising to find IQ or temperament to have genetic associations, it was intriguing to see that the leisure time interests of each twin in a pair were similar whether the twins were reared together or reared apart.

CONCEPT CHECK

- Many people think that if a person has a particular gene, then whatever trait or activity is connected with that gene will be seen. What is a better description of the relationship between a gene and the trait or activity to which it is connected?
- What is the role of the environment in turning genes on and off? Give some specific examples.
- What are the concepts of genotype and phenotype, and how are they related?
- "The job of a gene is to lay out the process by which a particular protein is made." What are four implications of this statement?
- What do genes do and how and where do they do it? What are the roles of DNA and RNA in that process?
- How do we know that genes change behavior? What kinds of research have been done with animals to identify the specific genes involved?
- Describe the human genome. In what ways is it similar to, and in what ways different from, the genome of other animals?
- How does the process of sexual reproduction ensure that you will not be a clone of either of your parents or even a 50–50 combination of the two of them? What are the mathematical odds that you ended up with the specific combination of chromosomes that you did?
- What are the two important principles of Mendelian genetics? What evidence led Mendel to their discovery? Give two examples of how Mendel's laws have been modified since he proposed them.
- How does epigenetic inheritance work? Describe the steps in the process using the study on mother rats and their nurturing behavior. What other examples can you cite?
- What is the overall goal of behavioral genetics research? What are the three primary types of research designs used in behavioral genetics research?

Summary

Learning Objective 1: Describe the basic element of the brain and its connection to behavior and experience.
The basic element of the brain is the neuron that is connected to other neurons. Since the human brain has been estimated to contain 86 billion neurons and more than 100,000 kilometers of interconnections, scientists have analyzed them in terms of networks using the small world framework. Neurons have numerous short distance local connections that taken together can be considered as a hub or module. From these hubs there are more long-distance connections to other hubs. Three specific networks have been examined in terms of psychology—the default network (also called the intrinsic network), the central executive network, and the salience network.

The Neuroscience of Behavior and Experience

Learning Objective 2: List the key structures of the brain.
First, the brain has four lobes—frontal lobe (involved in planning, higher order cognitive processes, and moral and social judgments); parietal lobe (involved in spatial processes); occipital lobe (involved in the processing of visual information); and temporal lobe (involved in hearing as well as aspects of language). Two other sections are the motor strip (associated with movements of different parts of the body) and the somatosensory cortex (associated with receiving sensations from various parts of the body). Second, the limbic system is considered to be an important evolutionary system that evolved for the processing of emotional material. Five major structures composed the limbic system: parts of the thalamus, hypothalamus, cingulate gyrus, hippocampus, and amygdala. Third, the brain stem is traditionally considered to include the midbrain, pons, and medulla. These structures are involved in basic life functions. Movements related to the brain stem tend to be more of an instinctual nature. Fourth, the cerebellum, located at the base of the skull, is involved in the coordination of movement and in the automation of physical and cognitive tasks. It interacts with many different parts of the brain using an intricate set of feedback processes.

Learning Objective 3: Discuss the neuroscience methods that are being used to observe activity in the brain.
Scientists have been able to use the manner in which neurons work as a window into their function. A variety of techniques for observing activity in the brain have been developed. Currently, the major types of brain-imaging techniques are EEG, MEG, PET, and fMRI. There are a number of trade-offs that researchers and clinicians must consider when choosing a brain-imaging technique. It begins with the research or clinical question one is asking whether the appropriate measure is one of structure (spatial resolution) or how fast a process can be measured (temporal resolution).

Learning Objective 4: Describe how the networks of the brain process information.
Networks allow our brains to efficiently process information. Overall, cortical networks are influenced by experience and designed to be efficient in terms of connections between neurons in the network. This efficiency allows for less use of energy. One way energy is conserved is through not having every neuron connect with every other neuron. Neurons are neither totally random in their connections with other neurons nor totally patterned. It appears that neurons are connected to one another in the same way that all humans on this planet are socially connected. It turns out that neurons, like humans, can be connected to one another in similar ways.

Various studies have shown that the neurons in the brain can be considered within a *small world framework* (Sporns, 2011). Neurons have numerous short-distance local connections that, taken together, can be considered as a hub or module. From these hubs, there are more long-distance connections to other hubs. Such connections are seen in gray matter. Gray matter appears dark and can be seen in the outer shell of the brain. *Gray matter* contains the synapses, dendrites, cell bodies, and local axons of neurons. Some 60% of gray matter is composed of axons and dendrites.

Underlying this are the axons that transfer information throughout the brain. Their myelin sheaths are lighter in color and thus these areas are referred to as *white matter*. Myelin is made up of fats and proteins and wrap around axons like insulation does around electrical cables and results in an increased speed in information transmissions. About 44% of the human brain is white matter. White matter generally represents longer connections between neurons. This allows for cortical networks over larger areas of the brain.

Those neural networks that are active during internal processing have come to be referred to as the brain's *default or intrinsic network*. Overall, the default network is involved during internal or private considerations that do not require processing external sensory information. In fact, it appears as if there is a negative correlation between activities in the default network versus networks associated with processing information from the environment. That is, when someone begins some cognitive activity, then new networks associated with that task become active and the default mode network becomes less active. Overall, this suggests that separate brain mechanisms evolved for dealing with information involving the external environment as opposed to considerations internal to the person.

In addition to the default network, the executive and salience networks have been identified (Menon, 2011). The *central executive network* is involved in performing such tasks as planning, goal setting, directing attention, performing, inhibiting the management of actions, and the coding of representations in working memory (see Eisenberg & Berman, 2010, for an overview). These tasks are also referred to as *executive functions* since they are involved in planning, understanding new situations, and having cognitive flexibility. The **salience network**, as the name implies, is involved in monitoring and noting important changes in biological and cognitive systems. There are also networks involved with vision, audition, and other sensory experiences.

Learning Objective 5: Describe the development and evolution of the brain.
The human central nervous system (CNS), which includes the brain and spinal cord, begins to develop during the first month of pregnancy with the creation of the neural tube. The most anterior end of the neural tube becomes the forebrain, the midbrain, the cerebellum, and the hindbrain. The remaining part of the tube becomes the spinal cord. Different parts of the tube expand differently in different animals under the control of specific genes. Along with the expansion of the surface area of the brain during evolution, there was also an increase and expansion of areas involved in processing information. As evolution produced greater diversity in cortical structure, there remained a similarity in the manner in which the nervous system functioned. Mammals have evolved a brain structure different from other organisms—the six-layered neocortex. Although consistent in structure, among mammals there is great variation in cortical size and organization in terms of area devoted to different types of cortical processing and greater network connectivity.

We are just beginning to understand the manner in which human brain evolution is built upon a vast history of organic development. In the 20th century, Paul MacLean examined fossil records along with brains from a variety of organisms and proposed that our current human brain can be viewed as having the features of three basic evolutionary formations—reptiles, early mammals, and recent mammals. MacLean's formulation—called the triune brain—suggests that through rich interconnections our brains can process a variety of information in three somewhat independent, although not autonomous, ways. In effect, these three brains—reptilian, paleomammalian, and neomammalian—intermesh and function together.

Learning Objective 6. Describe the role that genetics and evolution play in helping us understand our psychological processes.
Genes form the blueprint that determines what an organism is to become. They are found on chromosomes in every cell of the body. Within each gene, DNA—the information storage molecule—transfers information to RNA—the information transfer molecule—to

produce (or encode) a particular protein. The location of the genes in the body makes a difference in that cells in the brain produce different proteins from those in the muscles, or liver, or heart. A gene is turned on (produces the protein) or turned off (does not produce the protein) relative to specific events. A basic distinction in terminology is made between the genotype (what is inherited through the sperm and the egg at the moment of conception) and the phenotype (the observed characteristics of the individual, including body structure, physiology, and behavior). The focus of psychology has largely been the study of the phenotype. In terms of evolution, one of the real scientific contributions of DNA analysis has been the realization of how similar organisms are in terms of DNA structure. Different organisms have different numbers of chromosomes—humans have 23 separate pairs of chromosomes. Males and females have partially different genomes—the sex chromosomes are inherited differently for males and females. Since the X and Y chromosomes are different and do not contain the same identical genes, this sets up the possibility for transmission of traits that can be different for males and females. Sex-linked traits also have different patterns of inheritance throughout generations for males and females.

Study Resources

Review Questions

1. The connectivity in the brain has been described by some as "an enchanted loom" or a "dance." What characteristics of that connectivity led them to use those metaphors? What metaphor would you use?
2. The human brain is more accessible to science than it has ever been. Brain imaging is a window into the structure and function of the brain. Brain–machine interfaces extend brain functioning to control devices, for example, moving prosthetic limbs directly with thoughts. Another example of these interfaces is deep brain stimulation where electrodes are implanted in specific areas of the brain to regulate abnormal impulses in treating a number of neurological conditions. With all of this capability, what do you think is the next critical brain research area for psychology?
3. How does the small world framework from social science help us understand how neurons are connected in a network? What implications does this have for the transmission of information within a network and across networks?
4. Mammals have evolved a brain structure different from other organisms—the six-layered neocortex. Although consistent in structure, among mammals there is great variation in cortical size and organization. Does the species with the largest brain win? What are the implications for increase in overall size as well as organization and connectivity?
5. Describe the way in which Paul MacLean mapped evolutionary history onto the structure and functioning of the human brain through his theoretical conception of the triune brain. What are the primary implications of this mapping for interpreting previous research results and suggesting future research questions?
6. How have the discoveries of epigenetic inheritance and mitochondrial inheritance enriched our understanding and added to the complexity of Mendel's initial theory of genetic inheritance?

For Further Reading

Andreasen, N. (2001). *Brave New Brain*. New York: Oxford University Press.
Andreasen, N. (2005). *The Creative Brain*. New York: Dana Foundation.

Dingman M. (2019). *Your Brain, Explained.* Boston, MA: Nicholas Brealey Publishing.
Eagleman, D. (2011). *Incognito: The Secret Lives of the Brain.* New York: Pantheon.
Nesse, R. (2019). *Good Reasons for Bad Feelings.* New York: Dutton.
Plomin, R. (2018). *Blueprint: How DNA Makes Us Who We Are.* Cambridge, MA: MIT Press.
Ramachandran, V. (2011). *The Tell-tale Brain.* New York: Norton.
Riddley, M. (2000). *Genome, the Autobiography of a Species in 23 Chapters.* New York: HarperCollins Publishers.
Sapolsky, R. (2017). *Behave, the Biology of Humans at Our Best and Worst.* New York: Penguin Press.

Web Resources

Brain-to-brain interface—http://video.techbriefs.com/video/Brain-to-Brain-Interface-Demons;medical
Two-minute videos—www.neurochallenged.com
NIMH brain—www.nih.gov/science/brain
European brain project—www.humanbrainproject.eu
NASA twin study—https://www.nasa.gov/twins-study
Genome project—http://www.ornl.gov/hgmis/

Key Terms and Concepts

action potential
adoption study
allele
axon
behavioral genetics
brain stem
cell body
central executive network
central nervous system (CNS)
cerebellum
chromosomes
default or intrinsic network
dendrites
deoxyribonucleic acid (DNA)
diffusion tensor imaging (DTI)
dizygotic (DZ) twins
encode
electroencephalography (EEG)
endocrine system
epigenetic inheritance
frontal lobe
functional magnetic resonance imaging (fMRI)
genotype
hormones
interneurons
limbic system
magnetic resonance imaging (MRI)
magnetoencephalography (MEG)
monozygotic (MZ) twins
motor neurons
motor strip
network
neurons
neurotransmitters
occipital lobe
parietal lobe
peripheral nervous system (PNS)
phenotype
pituitary gland
positron emission tomography (PET)
proteins
ribonucleic acid (RNA)
salience network
sensory neurons
small world framework
somatosensory cortex
spinal cord
synapse
temporal lobe
triune brain
twin studies

4 Developmental Processes

LEARNING OBJECTIVES

4.1 Discuss the brain, sensory, and motor developments that take place during infancy.

4.2 Discuss cognitive development based on the theories of Piaget and Vygotsky.

4.3 Describe the aspects of social development and how we make emotional and social connections with others.

4.4 Discuss the physical, psychological, cognitive, and emotional domains that occur during adolescence.

4.5 Discuss the concept of lifespan development and adulthood.

In a research study in the 1960s, preschool children in Palo Alto, California, were first asked to select what they would like as a treat. There were a number of choices available including cookies, little pretzels, mints, and marshmallows. The children were then given a choice: The choice was, "Would you like your treat now or if you wait, you can have more of what you like." That is, eat the treat now or have two treats later. One girl, Amy, chose marshmallows. She sat alone at a table with the single marshmallow on it that she could have immediately. Also on the table were two marshmallows, which she could have if she waited. In some cases she would have to wait alone for up to 20 minutes. Also on the table was a bell that she could use to call the researcher. Then she could say, "I want to eat the single treat now." Otherwise, she must wait for the researcher to return. Different children took various approaches to pass the time and not ring the bell.

Although this was initially a test of delay of gratification, the follow-up results showed differences that most people would not have imagined. For example, the longer a child waited at age 4 or 5, the higher his or her SAT scores were in adolescence, more than ten years later. How can that be? Also, those who waited longer rated their social and cognitive skills as better in adolescence. Just waiting at age 4 is related to how you rate yourself some ten years later. Even more amazing is that more than 20 years later by age 27–32 years old, the children who waited were less obese and had a better sense of self-worth. They were also able to deal more effectively with stress and frustration. Finally, by midlife, there was a difference in brain-imaging patterns related to addiction and obesity in those who were able to delay gratification compared to those who were not. Did these kids learn to delay gratification? Was it inborn? How did it happen? Does it change as the child becomes older? Developmental psychologists seek to answer these types of questions, as you will see in this chapter.

Based on *The marshmallow test* by Walter Mischel (2014).

We are all children who grew up. We began as infants. Most of us had a family. Some of us had brothers and sisters. What factors do you think influenced your development? Parents often think they play the most important role in their child's development. However, many of you would also include the role your friends play. You may also name teachers, youth group leaders, and others vital to your development. What would you see as the really critical factors? Was it a series of single events or a more continuous process? Part of what *developmental psychologists* seek to understand are the factors that influence development and the manner in which they do so.

How might we understand how Amy was willing to wait to eat the marshmallow that she wanted? Was she born with the ability to delay gratification? Did she learn it? Or, was it a combination of factors? Additional research showed that although Amy could wait at age 5, younger children would not be able to consider waiting as an alternative (see Mischel, 2014 for an overview). Also, later research has shown that if the mothers of the children did not complete college, then the relationship between delay and later achievement was not as strong as in the original study (Watts, Duncan, & Quan, 2018). It has also been suggested that the marshmallow test is influenced by social factors such as growing up in a supportive environment (Michaelson & Munakata, 2020). Further, in a replication in China, 3- and 4-year-olds were shown to wait the longest if they were told their teacher would find out how long they waited (Ma, Zeng, Xu, Compton, & Heyman, 2020).

Further, how could a simple activity at age 4 or 5 be related to future success? This is the type of question developmental psychologists seek to answer. **Developmental psychology** is the study of cognitive, emotional, and motor development of humans across their lifespan. As you will see in this chapter, brain development is also an important aspect of human development. As noted in the first chapters of this book, there are a number of levels ranging from genes to culture that play critical roles in shaping our behavior. We know many of these, although we probably have not thought about our own life in a systematic manner.

In studying development, we can look at what is going on at each age (or stage) of our life. As infants, we learn how to walk and talk and see the world. As children, we learn how to play and interact with others as well as develop cognitive skills. As adolescents, we become part of a social group as well as experience our sexuality. As young adults, we consider our alternatives and create a life for ourselves. Some of us will create families as well as pursue a profession. As we continue to age some of us experience children and then grandchildren. At some point we consider retirement and what this stage will require.

In this chapter, you will learn about the development process we are all a part of as humans. You will also become familiar with the questions needed to be answered at each of our ages. These questions can include the languages we speak, the way we move, how we feel, and how we play with others. Later we think about who we should marry, what profession we should pursue, and how do we give meaning to our life. These questions differ at each period of our lifespan. This is referred to as *lifespan development*. As we move through life, our brain changes, and some specific periods are more critical than others.

Physical Development

The development of all our lives began with two cells—a sperm and an egg. Not long after birth we all have 100 billion neurons—the same as you have today. However, by the age that you are today, your brain has increased in size and the connections you have between areas of the brain are much more complex. Your abilities have also increased. You have learned how to speak and understand others. You understand social relations and the intentions of others. You can think logically and solve problems. You understand emotions in yourself and others. You have motor skills and can play games and perform various acts. Although education played an important role, many of these skills developed outside of formal education as you interacted with your environment, including your friends and culture. Let us now turn to the period before birth.

Prenatal Development

There are two critical periods in terms of brain development over one's life. The first occurs in the womb, and the second is during adolescence (Váša et al., 2020). Although most of us understand that the brain develops when we are in the womb, adolescence is not usually considered. As you will see later in the chapter, your brain creates new patterns of organization during adolescence. This means that all types of factors and experiences can have a greater impact during this period. It is also at this time that many mental disorders develop. However, that is getting ahead of our story. Let's return to conception and birth.

Before a child is born, the brain has begun to form the connections necessary to perform basic sensory and motor functions (see Byrge, Sporns, & Smith, 2014; Konrad & Eickhoff, 2010 for overviews of connectivity in the brain). This process begins about two to three weeks after conception with the development of brain tissue. At about 18 days, the neural tube begins to form, which will become the brain and spinal cord. Following this, there are periods of cell division that actually produce more neurons than will be utilized.

During the period three to six months before birth, your brain created as many as 250,000 neurons every minute. Yes, it is 250,000 per minute! Approximately half of all created neurons will die in a programmed manner between about the sixth month in the womb and the second month after birth (see Markant & Thomas, 2013; Zelazo & Lee, 2010 for overviews). At this point, you will have about 86 billion neurons, the same as you have today.

During this period, neurons migrate to the correct place in the brain. Once the neurons arrive at this final position, they continue the growth and development of dendrites that connect to other neurons. However, the number of connections between the neurons are much fewer at birth as compared to the brain of an adult human. At birth the brain is about one-third the size of an adult brain. By one year of age, your brain is about 60% the size of your adult brain and about 90% of adult weight by age 5. It takes until age 16 for the brain to reach its adult weight.

After the development of movement and vision, the brain develops from back to front. The last area to develop is the frontal lobes, which continue to develop into early adulthood. Overall, early environmental experiences have been shown to influence brain development, neurotransmitter functioning, and neuroendocrine function, which in turn can influence different types of behaviors (Burnette & Cicchetti, 2012).

Teratogens Can Change Brain Development

Given the fact that the brain grows so quickly prior to birth, a number of factors can influence this development in both positive and negative ways. Sufficient nutrients and vitamins can help the fetus develop, whereas their lack can negatively influence its development. Other substances such as alcohol, drugs, and lead as well as bacteria, viruses, and extreme temperatures can have terrible consequences on the fetus. These agents are referred to as *teratogens*. The word teratogen comes from the Greek word meaning monster.

Depending on the substance taken by the mother and the length of time and amount consumed, teratogens can influence physical development as well as behavioral, cognitive, and emotional development. One aspect of this influence is through a disruption in connections formed in the brain (van den Heuvel & Thomason, 2016). There are also individual differences in how teratogens influence development, and these can be related to genetic makeup (Cassina, Salviati, Di Gianantonio, & Clementi, 2016).

One well-studied disorder related to the teratogen of alcohol is *fetal alcohol syndrome (FAS)* (Carter & Cunniff, 2016). Actually, there are a number of conditions referred to as fetal alcohol spectrum disorders that occur when the mother drank alcohol during pregnancy. According to the US Centers for Disease Control and Prevention (CDC) (https://www.cdc.gov/ncbddd/fasd/facts.html), fetal alcohol disorders can be prevented if the mother does not drink alcohol during pregnancy. An infant with FAS can have any of the following: abnormal facial features, small head size, shorter-than-average height, low body weight, poor coordination, hyperactive behavior, difficulty with attention, poor memory, difficulty in school (especially with math), learning disabilities, speech and language delays, intellectual disability or low IQ, poor reasoning and judgment skills, sleep and sucking problems as a baby, vision or hearing problems, and problems with the heart, kidneys, or bones. The more alcohol that a woman drinks during pregnancy, especially binge drinking, the more likely that her child will show signs of FAS during his or her lifetime. Although no one has established a safe level of drinking during pregnancy, recent research suggests drinking less than one drink a day may have minimal effects on the fetus (https://www.cdc.gov/ncbddd/fasd/alcohol-use.html). However, most physician groups still suggest having no alcohol during pregnancy. The same is also true for recreational drugs.

Brain Development

During gestation and the early years of life, the brain is establishing its cortical connections and growing neurons at an amazing rate. Within this period, the infant initially develops the ability to process sensory information, which forms the basis of language and cognitive skills. These skills develop in a particular order.

The first areas to develop in an infant are related to movement and vision. There is actually a close connection between movement and the development of visual functions. In looking at the average motor skills developed during the first 16 months of life, consider how each of these new motor skills gives the infant a new perspective and experience of his or her world. These experiences change the connections and networks of the brain. For example, Joe Campos and his colleagues have shown that infants do not show fear of heights until they are able to crawl (Campos, Bertenthal, & Kermoian, 1992).

In this sense, the fear of heights emerges as a complex interaction involving the visual system and the motor system, as well as the feedback and experience that the infant receives as he or she begins to crawl. These factors are further influenced by such environmental factors as when the baby is born. For example, babies born in the winter crawl sooner than those born in the summer. Babies born in the winter need to develop before they can crawl. Thus, they would begin to learn to crawl during the summer, a time that parents are more likely to let them play on the floor.

As you would expect, the areas of the infant's brain with increasing connections involve visual, auditory, and motor processing (Collin & van den Heuvel, 2013). As seen in **Figure 4-1**, language and spatial orientation, which involve the parietal areas, don't fully develop until about puberty. Executive functions involving goals, reasoning as well as integration of information and social processes continue to develop until your 20s.

If you were to use brain imaging such as MRI to look at your brain today, you would see less gray matter than you had as a child. This is because of an increase of white matter connections that increase the speed of processing throughout the brain. Neurons surrounded by white matter (myelin) transmit signals at 50 to 100 times faster than those that are unmyelinated. **Figure 4-2** shows the decrease in gray matter volume from age 5 to age 20.

Brain connections remain stable until about 12 years of age. During adolescence there is another critical period when the brain begins to rewire itself in a different manner (Váša

Developmental Processes 139

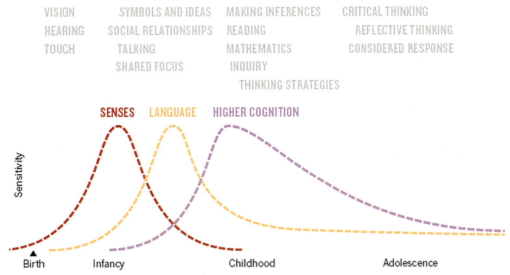

Figure 4-1 Timing of different types of learning in children. Sensory learning comes before language and more advanced cognitive functions such as reading, math, and understanding.

Source: Bardin (2012, p. 25).

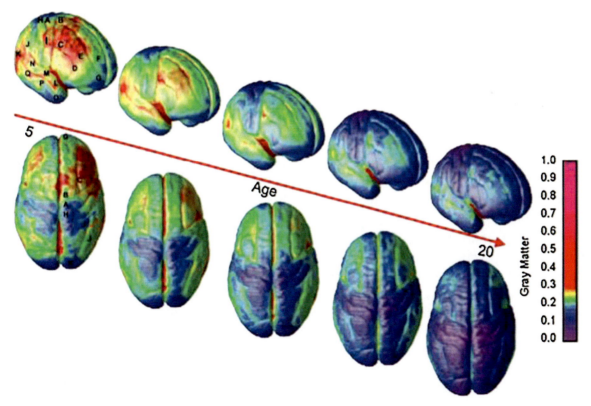

Figure 4-2 Changes in gray matter volume in the brains of those age 5 to age 20. Red color shows the highest gray matter volume and violet the lowest. As a person matures, the brain forms more connections with myelin sheaths (white matter) and thus reduces the gray matter measurements in the brain.

Source: Dennis and Thompson (2013).

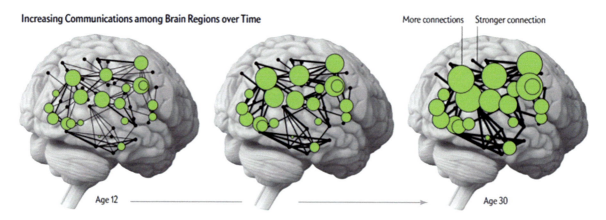

Figure 4-3 Increasing connections in the brain from age 12 to 30. Bigger green circles show more connections. Thicker black lines show stronger connections.
Source: Giedd (2015, p. 35).

et al., 2020). It is suggested that the adolescent brain should not be seen as either an old child brain or an underdeveloped adult brain (Giedd, 2015). Rather, the adolescent brain is unique in its ability to respond to the environment by modifying its network connections.

If we were to examine these connections between the ages of 12 and 30 years, we would see an increase in the connections that neurons make with one another (Dennis & Thompson, 2013). In **Figure 4-3** the size of the node (green balls) reflects the number of connections and the thickness of the line reflects the strength of the connection. Thus, it is not the growth of brain areas that takes place in adolescence, but the connections these areas have with one another that increases communication between different areas in the brain.

These cortical changes particularly involve such higher cognitive functions as reasoning, interpersonal interactions, cognitive control of emotions, risk-versus-reward appraisal, and motivation (Paus, Keshavan, & Ciedd, 2008). These changes are usually positive; however, a disruption can lead to problems. External or internal events, including genetic processes, can happen that may lead to physical or mental disorders. External events can include the use of drugs during adolescence, which can interfere with normal cortical development. The need for sleep is also critical for the adolescent brain during this period of cortical changes (Galván, 2020).

In terms of brain development, developmental psychologists consider the question of which of our psychological processes reflect more stable or invariant processes and which are less fixed and thus open to modification. The term that is often used to describe conditions in which processes are open to modification is referred to as ***plasticity***. As you will see later in the chapter, in terms of development, a variety of studies have shown that both human and other primate infants who are initially deprived of social and emotional stimulation show later difficulties in these areas. However, some of these difficulties can be reversed if the infants are placed in a more caring and stimulating environment. Thus, humans and other organisms possess mechanisms that allow for plasticity in developmental processes.

Although plasticity exists, there are also ***critical or sensitive periods*** during which certain types of experiences must be present for successful functioning. One is with language. As you will learn in the chapter on language, infants by the sixth month of life are able to distinguish any sound (phoneme) in any language on earth. By 12 months of age, infants have more difficulty making these same distinctions in languages that are not their own (Kuhl, 2004, 2010). As an adult you can learn other languages, but you no longer can sound like a native speaker. As you will also see in this present chapter, psychologists have sought to understand the role of sensitive periods in a number of areas of human functions. In fact, at different periods of our development, it is as if our brains expect to receive a certain type of experience.

It is important to understand that a critical or sensitive period represents a close connection between our brain and our environment (Bardin, 2012). For example, when mice after birth first open their eyes, a protein called Otx2 is created in the retina and transported through the optic nerve to the area of the brain related to vision—the visual cortex (Sugiyama, Prochiantz, & Hensch, 2009). This causes cells in the visual cortex to start the process of establishing the critical pathways needed for vision. If the mice are raised in the dark, this entire process does not take place. In human children born with cataracts, three-dimensional vision does not develop. However, not every impairment is permanent. New research is beginning to study whether sensory processes that did not develop in the normal critical period could be improved through using drugs to reopen critical period mechanisms in the brain.

Overall, human infants display an amazing ability to develop brain connections that relate to a number of skills. As you will see, following birth, human infants are able to form connections with their caregivers and maintain a close connection with others. They learn language quickly. They know how to understand nonverbal expressions, and later be part of a larger social community. Every infant learns to talk and walk and express emotions.

Darwin suggested that the infant possesses **intrinsic motivation**. That is to say, the infant and then the child is a curious and interested explorer of the world rather than a passive recipient of environmental influences. We now know that infants actually seek new information on a variety of levels, including motor, emotional, and cognitive responses. He or she feels happy when solving a problem or learning something new, which in turn allows the infant to have a close relationship with its environment as it has new experiences.

Sensory Development

Psychologists often discuss development in terms of human processes. As such, development is considered in terms of motor development, cognitive development, language development, social development, emotional development, and so on (see **Table 4-1**). However, if you watch infants through their first years of life, you will see that there is a complex interaction involving all of these systems. Parents emotionally encourage their child when he or she stands or walks. There is a complex interaction with parents as the child begins toilet training. Part of the problem is that the muscles involved do not give the same feedback to the child as that experienced in other types of motor learning. Other individuals also influence development. With brothers and sisters as well as with day care providers, there are social and emotional interactions that take place on a number of levels. All of these experiences help create the richness seen in each individual's development.

Not only does the infant find himself or herself in a particular environment, but, like a scientist or explorer, the infant wants to know what is there. You may wonder how psychologists can know this in an infant who cannot use language. There are a number of methods. Infants like adults show a change in heart rate when they find something interesting. Infants also suck a pacifier differently when they are engaged with what they see. Further, when infants see something they did not expect, they show a particular facial expression or even cry.

Each of these behaviors can be recorded and used in research. For example, when mothers read Dr. Seuss's *The Cat in the Hat* to their fetuses once a day during the last six weeks of pregnancy, newborns showed a familiarity to the story that they did not show

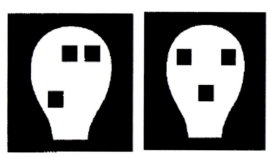

Figure 4-4 Infants prefer more human-looking faces. The left face on top (54 seconds) versus top right (38 seconds), and the right face on bottom (41 seconds) versus left face (35 seconds).

Source: Turati, Simion, Milani, and Umiltà (2002).

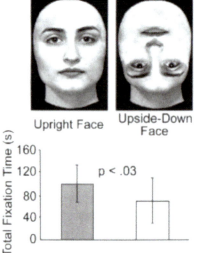

Figure 4-5 Total fixation time for each face seen by newborn infants. They look more at the upright face as opposed to the upside-down face.

Source: Cassia, Turati, and Simion (2004, p. 381).

to other stories (DeCasper & Spence, 1986). How did the researchers know this? They determined it through the patterns of pacifier sucking. A follow-up study also showed heart rate changes to rhymes their mothers had recited during her late pregnancy compared to other rhymes (DeCasper, Lecanuet, Busnel, Granier-Deferre, & Maugeais, 1994).

Human newborns show the ability to make a variety of sensory differentiations (Rakison, 2005). For example, they prefer the taste and smell of sweet nourishment and can differentiate a variety of tastes. Newborns can identify—and prefer—the scent of their mother to the scent of a stranger. They can also recognize their mother's voice, which they prefer.

In terms of visual perception, infants lack the ability to see detail (referred to as *visual acuity*) at birth. By age six months, they see almost as clearly as adults. It is at this age that the infants can connect the emotional responses seen in the face with the voice. Not surprisingly, infants prefer happy faces to angry or fearful ones.

Even with less acuity, newborns prefer more face-like images than those that have the same features but in different places (shown in **Figure 4-4**). Newborn infants from 1 to 3 days old also look longer at a right-side up face as opposed to an upside-down face (see **Figure 4-5**). Further, 1-month-old infants prefer looking at a human face as opposed to a monkey face (Sanefuji, Wada, Yamamoto, Mohri, & Taniike, 2014). This was true irrespective of the race of the person's face. Even more surprising, with new technology that allows images to be projected through the uterine wall, a third trimester human fetus shows preferences to stimuli such as a face rather than an upside-down version of the same stimuli (Reid, Dunn, Young, Amu, Donovan, & Reissland, 2017).

Since these studies have been carried out in laboratories around the world with different ethnic groups, it is assumed that this is a universal characteristic of all human infants. Overall, research suggests that newborns come into the world with mechanisms that predispose them to look at faces. Human newborns also respond to motion and are able to track moving objects. This, of course, is an evolved ability seen across a variety of species that would help track predators and thus increase an organism's chance of survival.

Learning From the Environment

Not only do human infants actively search their environment, they have expectations of what should happen next. How do we know this? We know this by what an infant focuses on and how long they pay attention to a particular action. Like adults, when infants see the same action over and over again, they stop paying attention. This is technically referred to as **habituation**.

Habituation can happen in any sensory modality. If you move into an apartment near a bell tower or train track or airline flight path, you initially notice each time you hear the sound. After a while, you don't even notice the event. Not only do we expect sensory events, but also cognitive and psychological events. We, as well as infants, pay particular attention to those events we do not predict. We will even show surprise when the event is totally beyond our expectation.

Renée Baillargeon and her colleagues used infants' reactions to study their sensory, cognitive, and psychological reasoning (Baillargeon, 2004; Luo & Baillargeon, 2005; Baillargeon, Scott, & He, 2010). In a number of studies over 20 years, we now know that even infants as young as 2.5 months possess expectations about physical events, and that these expectations undergo significant development during the first year of life.

One research design is to show the infant a toy doll. Two structures would then come down—one of which would hide the doll. If the doll were to move from one side to the other, it would be seen in the opening between the two sides. However, if the doll appeared on the other side when the screen was pulled up, the infant would look longer than when it would appear on the expected side. This suggested that young infants have an expectation of how the world works.

Not only do infants have expectations, but they also act as "little scientists" and try to test out their ideas. When their expectations are not met, they try to learn from what they experience. Aimee Stahl and Lisa Feigenson showed 110 infants situations that were consistent with what would be expected and situations that were not (see **Figure 4-6**). To strengthen their research, they included a number of control conditions to rule out alternative explanations (Stahl & Feigenson, 2015).

The main idea of the study was that infants treat unexpected events differently and use these events to learn new things about the world. The conditions compared an expected condition with an unexpected one. In the expected case, a toy such as a car or ball is stopped by a barrier. In the unexpected case, the toy goes through the barrier as if by magic. When the 11-month-old infant is given the toy that went through the barrier, he or she will take the toy and bang it on the highchair tray as if to test whether it will go through the tray as it did with the barrier.

In another condition, the toy is pushed past the end of a box. In the expected condition, the toy falls to the floor. In the unexpected condition, the toy continues as if the box were still below it. When given the toy after this, the infant drops it as if to see whether it will fall. It is as if the infant is trying to make the toy perform the same way as what they observed. However, the infants did not seek to learn from toys that did not violate their expectations. They just treated these toys as they always had (see movies of the different research conditions in http://www.npr.org/blogs/ed/2015/04/02/396812961/why-babies-love-and-learn-from-magic-tricks and the supplemental information published online at http://www.sciencemag.org/content/348/6230/91/suppl/DC1).

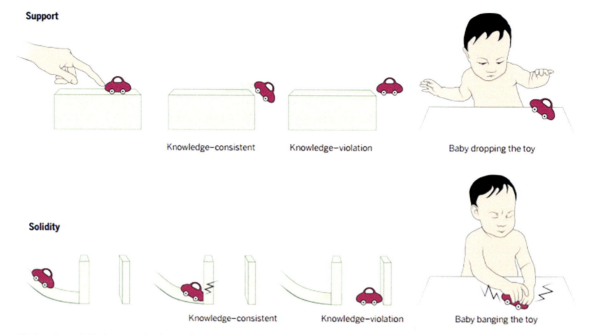

The importance of violating expectation. Stahl and Feigenson show that babies who have previously seen an object behave in an unexpected way are more likely to explore this object. The results help to understand how babies and young children learn.

Figure 4-6 If the infant sees the car violating the law of gravity, he or she will drop it on their highchair. If the infant sees the car appear to go through the barrier, the infant will try to push it through their tray.

Source: Schulz (2015) based on Stahl and Feigenson (2015).

This study shows us that infants already have expectations about the world. Not only do they have expectations, but if their expectations are violated, they try to learn the new information. That is, they drop the toy that did not fall or bang the toy on their tray to see if it will indeed go through as it did with the barrier. In this sense, infants are like scientists. That is, when confronted with unexpected results, they explore and seek to gain new information and create new hypotheses about how the world works.

As psychologists we tend to focus on the cognitive and emotional levels, but we must realize that the infant's nervous system is constantly asking questions concerning what it needs next on the basic levels as well. We know, for example, that if children lack a certain substance in their diet, they will modify their diet, if allowed, to increase those foods in which they are deficient (Davis, 1939). Other species also show similar food preferences for balancing their internal processes (Rozin & Schull, 1988). Overall, this suggests that an infant comes into the world with a series of procedures ready to be exploited for his or her own benefit.

Motor Development

In 1877 Charles Darwin published a description of an infant developing (Darwin, 1877, *Mind*). He began by describing the reflex actions he observed in the infant, such as yawning, stretching, sucking, and screaming. Darwin touched the bottom of the infant's foot and it pulled away. On the ninth day of the infant's life, Darwin reported that the infant focused on a candle. Darwin also noted when different emotions first appeared. This was one of the early case studies that informed what was to become developmental psychology. By the way, this infant was Darwin's own son.

As Darwin noted with his own son, humans come into this world with a number of reflexes. One of these is the *grasping reflex* in which the infant will grab your finger. Since infants can actually hold their own weight, many researchers see this as part of our evolutionary history. If you take your finger and place it near an infant's mouth, he or she will turn toward it and open its mouth. This is referred to as the *rooting reflex*. Infants will also show a *sucking reflex* if something touches their lips. This can also be their own thumb. Sucking one's thumb and moving arms and legs is also the beginning of gaining a sense of one's body and where it exists in space. You actually need to learn that you have arms and legs and that you can control them.

Motor development in infants proceeds in two directions. The first is from head to toe, and the second is from the midline of the body to the periphery. At about 2 months of age, the infant develops the muscles necessary for raising his or her head. About a month later, the infant develops the muscles of the torso necessary to roll over and sit in a highchair. During the next six months, the infant can begin to crawl. At the first year of age, infants can begin to stand while holding on to a low table and take steps on their own. Likewise, development goes from the midline in which infants can move their arms and legs before they can actually use their hands to purposely grab an object. **Figure 4-7** shows the motor milestones that an infant passes through. Interestingly, infants who are born blind go through motor milestones in a similar order to sighted infants. However, blind babies reach these milestones anywhere from a few weeks to a few months later (Adelson & Fraiberg, 1974).

Humans also retain previous physiological structures from our evolutionary history that are neither adaptive nor functional. These are called *vestigial structures*. For example, human babies can grasp and hold their own weight. Other primates, of course, need to hold on

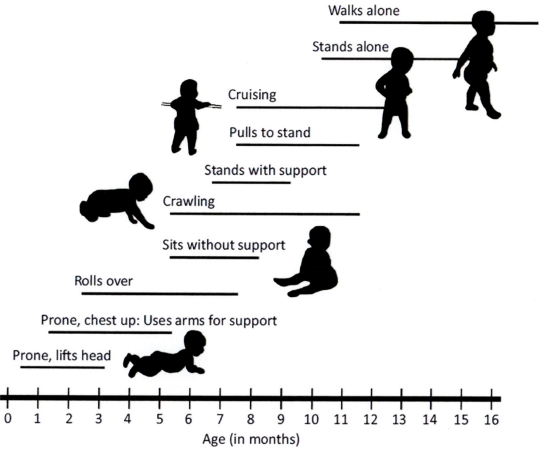

Figure 4-7 Motor skills developed during the first 16 months of life.

to their mother as she moves through the trees. Some people can wiggle their ears. This probably remained from other mammals that make ear movements to localize sounds.

Myrtle McGraw was a developmental psychologist in the 1930s who was interested in the motor development of infants. She was the first to ask if there was a swimming reflex in 2- to 4-month-old infants. Fortunately for the infants, there was. Infants show a *swimming reflex* until about 6 months of age; after that point, it disappears.

One of her research projects was to work with Johnny and Jimmy who were twins (McGraw, 1935). She taught one of the twins a number of motor skills including roller skating, climbing, and swimming. The other twin was not taught these skills until 22 months of age. Her procedure was to watch the first twin and as soon as McGraw saw a motor skill begin to be expressed, she would then start to develop it. One general conclusion from this work is that infants are able to perform a variety of motor tasks but there is no advantage to teaching these tasks earlier. To learn a new motor task still requires a sequence of steps.

Esther Thelen also watched infants as they learned motor skills such as walking. However, she sought to integrate an understanding of motor movement with advances in the neurosciences, biomechanics, and the study of perception and action. Her initial work was summarized in her 1995 book and referred to as **dynamic system theory** (Thelen, 1995; Smith & Thelen, 2003).

Part of her work is based on the Russian movement physiologist Nikolai Bernstein who suggested that there is an important cognitive component in our actions. That is, we perform actions differently in terms of what we expect to happen. We must also put together a number of possible body movements. If you hold a 1-month-old infant under the arms on a moving treadmill, he or she will show stepping movement similar to an adult walking. However, the infant will not show this movement alone until they are 1 year old. In learning movements we are also faced with physical constraints such as gravity. The emphasis for the dynamic system approach is to ask how all of our different

Figure 4-8 Infant showing swimming reflex.

body parts work together to produce stability and change. One conclusion is that the general milestones as shown in **Figure 4-7** reflect the average age norm, but not the only pattern of motor development. **Table 4-1** shows the milestone in four different areas from 15 months to 5 years.

Table 4-1 Milestones achieved in motor, adaptive, language, and social areas during the first five years of life (from Clyman 3rd Psychiatry)

Emerging Patterns of Behavior from 1 to 5 Years of Age*

15 months
Motor:	Walks alone; crawls up stairs
Adaptive:	Makes tower of three cubes; makes a line with crayon; inserts pellet in bottle
Language:	Jargon; follows simple commands; may name a familiar object (ball)
Social:	Indicates some desires or needs by pointing; hugs parents

18 months
Motor:	Runs stiffly; sits on small chair; walks up stairs with one hand held; explores drawers and waste baskets
Adaptive:	Makes a tower of four cubes; imitates scribbling; imitates vertical stroke; dumps pellet from bottle
Language:	10 words (average); names pictures; identifies one or more parts of body
Social	Feeds self; seeks help when in trouble; may complain when wet or soiled; kisses parent with pucker

24 months
Motor:	Runs well; walks up and down stairs, one step at a time; opens doors; climbs on furniture; jumps
Adaptive:	Tower of seven cubes (six at 21 months); circular scribbling; imitates horizontal stroke; folds paper once imitatively
Language:	Puts three words together (subject, verb, and object)
Social	Handles spoon well; often tells immediate experiences; helps to undress; listens to stories with pictures

30 months
Motor:	Goes up stairs alternating feet
Adaptive:	Tower of nine cubes; makes vertical and horizontal strokes but generally does not join them to make a cross; imitates circular stroke, forming closed figure
Language:	Refers to self by pronoun "I"; knows full name
Social:	Helps put things away; pretends in play

36 months
Motor:	Rides tricycle; stands momentarily on one foot
Adaptive:	Tower of 10 cubes; imitates construction of "bridge" of three cubes; copies a circle; imitates a cross
Language:	Knows age and sex; counts three objects correctly; repeats three numbers or a sentence of six syllables
Social:	Plays simple games (in "parallel" with other children); helps in dressing (unbuttons clothing and puts on shoes); washes hands

Emerging Patterns of Behavior from 1 to 5 Years of Age*

48 months
Motor: Hops on one foot; throws ball overhand; uses scissors to cut out pictures; climbs well
Adaptive: Copies bridge from model; imitates construction of "gate" of five cubes; copies cross and square; draws a man with two to four parts besides head; names longer of two lines
Language: Counts four pennies accurately; tells a story
Social: Plays with several children with beginning of social interaction and role-playing; goes to toilet alone

60 months
Motor: Skips
Adaptive: Draws triangle from copy; names heavier of two weights
Language: Names four colors; repeats sentence of 10 syllables; counts 10 pennies correctly
Social: Dresses and undresses; asks questions about meaning of words; domestic role-playing

CONCEPT CHECK

1. What are the two critical periods in terms of brain development over one's life, and what happens that is so critical in each of these periods?
2. On the face of it, developing a fear of heights seems like a simple process. What are the critical factors in the complex interactions that actually take place?
3. Studies have shown that "when infants see something that does not behave in an expected way, they pay more attention to it." What is the evolutionary value of this fact for humans?
4. Define the following concepts in terms of psychological processing and give an example of each:
   a. plasticity
   b. critical or sensitive periods.
5. Infants can't fill out a questionnaire or press a button in an experiment. What are some of the methods researchers have used to assess an infant's "answer" in experimental situations?
6. How did the dynamic system theory of Esther Thelen and Nikolai Bernstein change and expand the traditional understanding of motor development during the first six years?

Cognitive Development

Not everyone at the beginning of the 20th century agreed with the view of infants as *scientists with expectations.* As noted earlier, one of the influences in psychology in the early part of the 20th century came from John Watson and behaviorism (Watson, 1913, 1924). Watson suggested that the environment was the only significant factor needed to understand human development. In fact, he said:

> Give me a dozen healthy infants, well-formed, and my own specified world to bring them up in and I'll guarantee to take any one at random and train him to become any type of specialist I might select – doctor, lawyer, artist, merchant-chief and, yes, even beggar-man and thief, regardless of his talents, penchants, tendencies, abilities, vocations, and race of his ancestors. I am going beyond my facts and I admit it, but so have the advocates of the contrary and they have been doing it for many thousands of years.
>
> (Watson, 1930: 82)

Heredity and instinctual processes were dismissed and largely ignored by Watson. In fact, Watson suggested only three instincts were present at birth: love, fear, and rage. Thus, neither intelligence nor special abilities were seen to be the product of genetic influences. He further suggested that parents were too sentimental to bring up their children properly. Although Watson influenced a number of psychologists during the first half of the 20th century, his ideas have not been supported by critical research.

Other researchers at that time sought to articulate patterns of development across motor, emotional, cognitive, and social domains. Jean Piaget emphasized the interaction with the physical environment and the manner in which a child's mind develops. Lev Vygotsky stressed the social and cultural environment and how this influences development. Let us begin with Piaget.

Piaget and Stages of Development

Jean Piaget studied the cognitive development of children. In fact, Piaget is considered to have created the study of *cognitive development*. **Cognitive development** refers to the way we reason and use language, as well as traditional intellectual abilities such as memory and problem solving. Piaget's work was mainly based on the observation of children at different ages. Piaget initially studied with Alfred Binet in Paris in the early 1900s and worked on the first intelligence tests. Alfred Binet, who you will learn about in the chapter on intelligence, was one of the first to study differing abilities of children who were the same age. One thing Piaget found interesting was that children of the same age tended to make the same mistakes compared to younger or older children. The children also differed in systematic ways from children both older and younger. Piaget developed his ideas by giving children problems to solve and watching the children attempt to solve them.

During this period, it was not uncommon for the average person to see a child as a small adult. What Piaget did was to show that a child understands his or her world differently at different points in life. His theoretical position suggests that a child moves through a series of stages and that these influence how he or she sees the world. The child learns or constructs knowledge of the world through observation and interaction. In this sense, a child is like a scientist who has ideas and seeks to test them.

Piaget introduced the term *schema*, which refers to how the child sees the world. Although schemas influence our actions, it typically works outside of our awareness. One important part of Piaget's contribution was the idea that a child has a different schema or set of assumptions at different periods of his or her life. These schemas can be changed as the child interacts with the world and takes in new information.

The process by which schemas are changed involves two processes. The first is assimilation. *Assimilation* is the process by which new experiences are made part of existing schemas. Of course, not every experience becomes part of existing schemas. The child must first be ready for it. A child, for example, may learn to view fairy tales on a tablet computer such as an iPad and move his or her finger to change the page. If someone else, such as a grandparent, brings a book with the same fairy tale, the child may attempt to also use his finger to change the page. In this way the child tries to use an existing schema such as moving his finger in the new situation of a physical (not electronic!) book.

The child then must use the second process by which schemas are changed—accommodation. **Accommodation** is the process by which existing schemas are modified or new ones created. In the fairy tale example, the child begins to understand that there is another category of media that contains fairy tales—physical books—and physical books work differently than e-books on a tablet computer.

Piaget saw children as not just expressing random ideas. Rather, they are attempting to make sense of the world through a set of rules they have acquired. Through his observations of how children solve problems as well as the mistakes they make, Piaget suggested there were four periods or stages of development. These four stages are (1) sensorimotor, (2) preoperational, (3) concrete operations, and (4) formal operations. Further, these stages were seen to correspond with particular ages of the child.

The *sensorimotor stage* is characterized by the use of motor actions and the senses. The actions you see in an infant are not random but are his or her attempts to understand the environment through sensory and motor processes. This stage lasts from birth to 2 years of life. Looking, touching, and grasping give the infant a sense of her world. Give an infant an object and she will put the object in her month.

Initially, the child understands something exists only while that object is experienced. "Out of sight, out of mind" is the experience of the infant. Parents use this as they play "peek-a-boo" with their infant. Near the end of this stage, infants begin to understand that an object still exists even if it is covered with a cloth or placed in a drawer. This is the beginning of what is referred to as **object permanence**. We now know that object permanence develops as memory develops (Diamond, 1985).

The *preoperational stage* shows the beginning of *symbolic thought*. The thought is symbolic in that it can transcend the objects at hand. A child may take a stick and treat it like a sword, guitar, or rake. Pretend play is an important activity, especially in the early part of this stage. Parents often like playing with their children in terms of these pretend games and enjoy their magical ways of thinking.

The preoperational stage lasts from 2 to 7 years of age. Although children in this stage can use images of doing something before actually performing the act, they have difficulty doing the reverse. That is, they are not able to logically determine what would happen if they did not do the act. Also, their perspective is based on perceptions. This is demonstrated by the liquid conservation task, as shown in **Figure 4-9**.

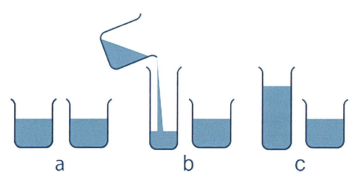

Figure 4-9 Liquid conservation task. The liquid is poured from one of two equal-sized containers into one of a different shape (b). The child is then asked if the liquids in c are equal.

In this task, you first show the child the two containers that have an equal amount of liquid, as shown in **a**. You then pour the liquid from one of those containers into a tall container, as shown in **b**. You then show the child the two containers shown in **c** and ask which has the most liquid. Children in the preoperational stage will say that the taller container in **c** contains more liquid even though they saw it being poured.

Conservation is seen not only with liquids but also with mass. Take two equal balls of clay and roll each out into a snake-like shape. If one is longer than the other, the child will choose that one as the one that contains more clay. Likewise, take candies such as M&Ms and place the same number in each of two rows—six candies, for example. Then you take one of the rows and spread it out so that there is more space between the individual candies. Again, the child will say the longer row contains more. This will happen even if you ask the child to count the number of candies in each row.

The third stage identified by Piaget is **concrete operations**. This stage begins at about 6 or 7 years of age and lasts until the child is about 11 years old. Children in this stage can move their thinking beyond themselves and deal with the nature of concrete objects. Children in elementary school, for example, can perform mathematical operations in terms of adding, subtracting, multiplying, and dividing. They can solve problems based on the example in front of them. However, Piaget suggested that children at this stage could not perform the abstract problems as seen in algebra or computer programming where one variable represents a general class in the abstract.

With the schema to perform abstract operations comes the fourth stage—*formal operations*. This stage begins in adolescents at about 12 years of age. Adolescents can think in abstract terms and solve hypothetical problems. They find it possible to talk about ideas like world peace or justice. They also can imagine worlds that do not exist. They can create theories of how the world should be different, especially how their parents should act. In their school work and other projects, they are able to form hypotheses and consider ways of testing them.

Piaget's ideas played an important role in developmental psychology. His work influenced psychological research as well as educational perspectives. In particular, educators today seek to consider what students of a certain age are able to understand and how they will receive the information that is being taught. There are also more interactive types of problems aimed at students' stage of development. Of course, since Piaget began his observations in the 1930s, a number of research studies have better defined infant and childhood development. We now know that different abilities and ways of thinking, feeling, and doing develop at different rates. We also know that given the correct situation, children may show abilities earlier than suggested by Piaget. There have also been scientific explorations beyond cognitive development to examine social and emotional development. This has led us to think more about the roles of culture, parents, and friends in a person's development.

Vygotsky and the Sociocultural Perspective

It was the Russian psychologist Lev Vygotsky who offered a *sociocultural perspective* to cognitive development. Vygotsky was born in the same year as Piaget, 1896. Both saw the child's interactions with his or her environment as critical to development. However, whereas Piaget emphasized the interaction with the physical environment, Vygotsky stressed the social and cultural environment. It is the child's interactions with others that largely shape the child's development. From our culture we learn a language. From our culture we are also given stories and histories that influence how we view ourselves and others.

Learning facilities differ around the world. Some cultures offer a more technological approach with computers and other devices. Other cultures emphasize a more literary and oral tradition with the learning of critical books. These are referred to as *tools of intellectual adaptation*. Of course, the language that a culture uses is one of the important tools. It is through language with his or her parents and others in the culture that the young child comes to be a social being and understand the world. Further, unlike Piaget, Vygotsky

Table 4-2 Table of Piaget's stages.

Piaget's Stages of Cognitive Development		
Stage	**Description**	**Age Range**
Sensorimotor	An infant progresses from reflexive, instinctual action at birth to the beginning of symbolic thought. The infant constructs an understanding of the world by coordinating sensory experiences with physical actions.	Birth to 2 years
Preoperational	The child begins to represent the world with words and images; these words and images reflect increased symbolic thinking and go beyond the connection of sensory information and physical action.	2 to 7 years
Concrete operational	The child can now reason logically about concrete events and classify objects into different sets.	7 to 11 years
Formal operational	The adolescent reasons in more abstract and logical ways. Thought is more idealistic.	11 to 15 years

saw an important relationship between language and thought. Thought for Vygotsky is internal speech.

Children learn from those around them. As such, children can solve more difficult problems with an adult's help. Less difficult problems they can solve on their own. In between these two situations was an area Vygotsky referred to as the *zone of proximal development*. This zone is the difference between what the child can do independently and what he or she can do with the help of another who is more advanced. The zone of proximal development represents a concept for developmental psychologists that points to how a child can learn from more experienced others. As such, this concept is especially valuable to teachers in considering what skills should be taught next.

In summary, the theories of Piaget and Vygotsky were broad-based theories initially based on observation and theory. By the middle of the 20th century, there was a movement to test development patterns with research. There was also a tendency to focus on particular development processes. One important process that has been extensively researched is memory.

Memory

Developmentally, human infants have an amazing capacity for remembering spoken words and songs as well as faces. However, most of us remember little of our life until we are about 3 or 4 years of age. One influential idea is that we need certain brain networks to develop before we can recall events from our lives. As you will see in the chapter on memory, this is referred to as *autobiographical memory*. Specifically, it is suggested that memory and cognitive systems are organized around infants' experience of events, including their interactions with others.

Social relations play a special role in the life of humans. Flavell (2000) has suggested four ways in which the early predisposition and abilities of infants involve other humans. First, human infants find human faces, voices, and movements highly interesting. Second, infants can perceptually analyze and discriminate human stimuli. Third, infants seek to attend to and interact with other humans. And fourth, infants respond differently to humans than they do to objects. Other humans are special to humans.

Infants are capable of learning new information that involves different types of memory processes. For example, if an infant has learned to solve a simple puzzle, he or she shows improvement when presented with the same puzzle a second time. What happens when you begin a nursery rhyme with an infant? The infant says the next word, which shows the early development of cognitive memory. By age 2, toddlers show the ability to use memory processes to discuss events in their lives. As such they can begin simple narratives. This is illustrated by saying to a 2-year-old, "Tell Mommy what you just did" and she says, "I just threw the ball." By age 3 to 5, most children can describe events and display memory of events. True memory of events is more than just recalling your participation in a particular event, it also includes the ability to do this without any situational cues for its recall in the present. That is to say, you can recall at will particular events that happened in your life at almost any of your previous ages. This, of course, requires that you have a sense of time, that is, past, present, and future. Like language, some researchers view memory of events as unique to humans. However, it should be noted that some cultures do not use the same sense of time in their language as do Western cultures. It should also be noted that just playing music to your baby does not necessarily make him or her a genius, as described in the box: Myths and Misconceptions—Mozart Effect.

Myths and Misconceptions—Mozart Effect

All parents want to help their child develop in superior ways. The media has articles on "ten ways to make your baby smart" or "how to stimulate your baby." One website has an article on "15 signs you will raise a genius." Thus, when you hear about a new technique, you consider trying it out. Yet, not every suggestion has been tested scientifically.

One that was tested is referred to as the *Mozart effect*. In 1993, a study was conducted with college students that reported that listening to music by Mozart for 10 minutes improved performance on three spatial tasks commonly used in intelligence tests (Rauscher, Shaw, & Ky, 1993). Listening to music was compared with listening to a relaxation tape or silence. The Mozart effect was shown to last for a short time, less than 15 minutes.

Although the study was conducted with college students, the idea was presented in the media that playing music by Mozart to your baby would improve his or her intelligence. It sounded reasonable to many since Mozart was a genius and created complex musical patterns. Even the Governor of Georgia, Zell Miller, suggested that the state should send every newborn a CD of classical music. Toy companies began to sell special genius CDs. Somehow, the music was supposed to change and improve the baby's brain.

The popularity of the Mozart effect brought forth a number of research studies seeking to test the idea. Christopher Chabris reviewed 16 of these studies, principally those whose subjects were young adults (Chabris, 1999). Additionally, he used a technique referred to as meta-analysis that statistically combined the results of all the studies that included 714 participants. Chabris found that the so-called Mozart effect showed a change of only a few IQ points rather than the eight or nine originally suggested. Further, listening to a Stephen King story or popular music also increased performance. However, this appeared to be true only for those who enjoyed what they had heard.

Chabris suggested that since spatial tasks rely on the right hemisphere of the human brain, other processes such as enjoyment may also prime this region of the brain. If the right hemisphere was activated by a previous task, then doing a spatial task would not require as much cognitive effort. It would also explain why the original effect was short-lived. Other studies with school-age children have shown that listening to Mozart is not unique in promoting this performance. Listening to popular dance music led to the same changes in spatial performance as Mozart (McKelvie & Low, 2002).

What can we learn from the Mozart effect? The first is that we as human beings are always looking for easy ways to improve ourselves and our children. Of course as you learned previously, you can change your brain by learning to play a musical instrument as a child, but that takes effort and requires a long-term commitment. Another study showed that teaching children to play the piano also improved performance on a spatial task (Rausher, Shaw, Levine, Wright, Dennis, & Newcombe, 1997). Second, the media often presents the results of a scientific study in ways that go beyond the data presented. The authors of the original Mozart effect study, for example, never suggested that listening to music could change your brain or IQ in a long-term manner. And third, it is critical to replicate the study and conduct additional studies in order to understand the conditions under which the effects take place and determine the limits to the effect. By the way, if you go to amazon.com today you will discover a large number of books available to help you heal your body, strengthen your mind, and unlock your creative spirit using the Mozart effect. Perhaps, once the public has accepted a myth, they have a hard time giving it up.

Thought Question: What advertisements have you seen on TV or online that promise miraculous results just by "reading this book," "using this piece of exercise equipment," or "taking this pill"? How could you go about researching the scientific evidence behind the claim?

Temperament

We all come into the world with bodily emotional responses all our own. Some infants are very active and others somewhat quiet. Interestingly enough, the emotional responses seen early in one's life remain fairly stable. This constellation of emotional and behavioral responses is referred to as ***temperament***. Some infants seem happy all the time while others look to outsiders as if they are fearful or anxious. Although temperament has been described for thousands of years, it was reintroduced to the study of infants during the 1960s and 1970s (Chess & Thomas, 1977).

Longitudinal studies of temperament were conducted by Jerome Kagan and his colleagues at Harvard University (see Kagan, 2003 for an overview). These researchers began to follow different groups of infants as they grew. They sought to study the stability of their temperament in terms of behavioral, emotional, and physiological measures. Kagan and his colleagues classified infants in terms of *reactivity*. If the infants are exposed to an unfamiliar event such as a toy that makes noise and moves, about 20% of the 4-month-old infants will show distress and vigorous motor activity. These same high-reactive infants will be shy, timid, and fearful in response to unfamiliar events in their second year of life. One-third of these high-reactive children become very fearful and are referred to as *inhibited* by Kagan. About 40% of the infants Kagan and his colleagues studied showed low levels of reactivity to unfamiliar events. This was also seen during the second year of life as these children appeared sociable and less fearful in unfamiliar situations. One-third of the low-reactive infants show almost no fear and are referred to as *uninhibited*. By age 11, more children who were high-reactive at an earlier age were now shy. On the other hand, more low-reactive children were sociable and emotionally spontaneous in unfamiliar situations. EEG differences were also seen at age 2 and age 11 between high-reactive and low-reactive children.

Temperament is seen as a broad set of emotional and behavioral reactions. Both genetic and environmental factors are seen to play a role. Later in the chapter on personality, you will see which cognitive and emotional responses in childhood remain consistent over the lifespan. Personality, as you will see later, is more of a way of valuing and processing one's world, which shares some components with temperament.

CONCEPT CHECK

1. What did John Watson and those tied to the behaviorism perspective believe were the critical factors in explaining a child's development? Which factors did they think were unimportant?

2. What did Jean Piaget mean by the term "schema"? How do the processes of assimilation and accommodation work together to change schemas during development?

3. Russian psychologist Lev Vygotsky offered a sociocultural perspective to cognitive development. What did he consider the critical factors in a child's development? How did Vygotsky's concepts of "tools of intellectual development" and "zone of proximal development" play a role in his theory of development?

4. Most of us remember little of our life until we are about 3 or 4 years of age, yet aspects of memory development are very active in infants and very young children. What evidence does this chapter present on early memory processes?

5. Well, it turns out we can't improve our cognitive performance by listening to Mozart's music, but what three things can we learn from the "Mozart effect"?

6. What have we learned from the research of Jerome Kagan and his colleagues on the development and stability of temperament during childhood?

Learning about Others and the World

As you have learned so far, infants are able to learn important aspects of motor and cognitive development. They are able to move through their world. They are also able to demonstrate an understanding of basic cognitive processes depending on their level of development. In this next section, you will be introduced to important aspects of social development. In particular, you will learn about how we learn by watching others, how we come to understand their actions and intentions, and how we make emotional and social connections with others, especially our caregivers. The section ends with a discussion of how parents interact with their children.

Mirror Neurons and Imitation Learning

How do you know what someone else is experiencing? What helps us feel empathy for that person? Most of us would answer that we know because it is an experience that has happened to us. While this is true, we now understand more about the mechanisms that allow this to happen. Let's begin with a simple act.

What happens in your brain when you see someone wave or clap her hands? One intriguing answer to this question comes from research that suggests the neurons in your brain fire as if you had performed the same actions. These neurons are called **mirror neurons**. Mirror neurons were first discovered in monkeys. These neurons were shown to fire both when the monkey performs a particular action, as well as when it just observes another monkey, or even a human, perform that action.

These mirror neurons were first discovered in areas of the brain referred to as F5, which is a part of the premotor cortex. Some researchers suggest that this brain process may lie at the basis of **imitation learning**, as well as other human social phenomena, including language and empathy (Rizzolatti & Craighero, 2004; Sinigaglia & Rizzolatti, 2011). Imitation learning is seen in a number of species. You watch someone do something and then you copy it. Children may simply watch a video and then copy what they saw.

The basic idea for imitation learning is simple. Each time an individual sees an action done by another, the neurons that would be involved in that action are activated. This activation in brain circuits in turn creates a motor representation of the observed action. That is, we see an action and our brain considers how we might make it ourselves, although we don't do this consciously. What this means is that our brain turns a visual image into a *motor plan*. A motor plan is nothing more than how we would perform an action.

This process can explain one aspect of how imitation learning can take place. That is, by seeing something, my brain also comes to know how I can do it. Since the same neurons fire in my brain as I watch another do a task, my brain is able to create an action plan when I wish to produce the motor response. Even more important for Rizzolatti and Fogassi (2014) is that such a network puts the organism at an advantage. The advantage is not only do I understand "what" others are doing, but also "why" they are doing it. I am able to make guesses at their motivation and their plan of action. Thus, by having my brain work similarly to another's brain, then I have some understanding of what he or she is experiencing.

It has also been suggested that the mirror neurons not only lead to an understanding of another's actions but also to *empathy* (see Iacoboni, 2009 for an overview). The basic idea is that through connections between the mirror neuron system and the limbic system, which is related to emotional processing, and the insula, which is related to a sense of self, it would be possible to recognize emotions and thus empathy. In a series of studies, it was shown that the more someone imitates your actions, the more you like that person and report that you care about them (Chartrand & Bargh 1999). Thus, imitation, liking, and caring go together. This in turn could be an important part of interpersonal relationships. Although most schools emphasize cognitive development, there are programs based on scientific principles that seek to integrate emotional development with other learning. One of these programs is described in the box: Applying Psychological Science—Early Intervention Programs—The PATHS Curriculum.

Applying Psychological Science—Early Intervention Programs—The PATHS Curriculum

Children come to school influenced by many different experiences. Some have had difficult families where the experience of anger was common. Some have had parents who were not available when needed. Some children lacked basic nutrition. This leaves an important challenge for school teachers to help children with the integration of cognitive, emotional, and motor tasks. As children mature, they begin to talk about their internal processes as well as those of others. Some children do this better than others. As many teachers will tell you, formal social and emotional education for preschool and elementary school students is often not available. Without these skills, children may show behavioral problems and aggressive behaviors. Various programs have been developed to increase social and emotional skills.

One program designed to help children form relationships and monitor their emotions and social needs as well as those of others is Promoting Alternative Thinking Strategies (PATHS). This program was developed by Mark Greenberg, a psychologist at Pennsylvania State University, and his colleagues. They have also tested their program in outcome studies (Greenberg 2018; Greenberg, & Lippoid, 2013; Mahoney et al., 2020). The PATHS curriculum was developed as a preventive program designed to give children more awareness of their own emotions and those of others. In addition, they are taught a way of solving problems from a cognitive perspective and preventing negative emotional and social outcomes. Overall, the children learn about self-control, understanding their emotions, self-esteem, relationships, and how to work with others.

Reviews of the literature have shown a relationship between a child's emotional understanding and the ability to have positive social relationships. Additionally, the ability to inhibit one's actions is associated with successful social and academic performance. In this view, emotional understanding is related to less acting out or negative internal attributions (Upshur, Wenz-Gross, & Reed, 2013).

Across the world, children may not have the family structure that supports problem solving and prosocial relationships. In these situations, programs that support the child being able to regulate emotions and solve day-to-day problems are critical. At this point, the PATHS curriculum has been studied in a number of developing and developed countries. Studies from both Germany and the Netherlands have shown positive effects of the training.

Head Start is the largest provider of early childhood education for disadvantaged children in the United States. One study followed children in Head Start using the PATHS curriculum (Domitrovich, Cortes, & Greenberg, 2007). The preschool children were randomly assigned to either the PATHS curriculum or a control situation on a classroom level. The children in different classrooms were matched so that similar characteristics were present in those children who received the PATHS curriculum and those who did not. The PATHS program was presented once a week for 30 weeks by the Head Start teachers who had been trained. The results suggest that after exposure to PATHS, intervention children had higher emotion knowledge skills and were rated by parents and teachers as more socially competent compared to peers. Further, teachers rated children who received the PATHS curriculum as less socially withdrawn at the end of the school year compared to controls.

An additional study examined 2,937 children over the first three years of elementary school (Conduct Problems Prevention Research Group, 2010). In those classrooms that received the PATHS curriculum, there was a reduction in aggression and an increase in prosocial behavior as reported by teachers. Peer reports also found a reduction in aggression, especially for boys. These researchers concluded that well-implemented multiyear social–emotional learning programs can have significant and meaningful preventive effects on the population-level rates of aggression, social competence, and academic engagement in the elementary school years. Overall, helping children become aware of the emotional and social responses of themselves and others as well as methods to reduce conflict is an important component of a child's successful development.

Thought Question: When you were in elementary school, how were you helped to think about your emotions and solve interpersonal problems?

Theory of Mind

Before mirror neurons were discovered, a number of developmental psychologists studied the ways in which children understood the actions of others. Surprisingly, an important aspect of this work focused on animals. *Theory of mind* was initially researched by Premack and Woodruff in 1978 in relation to primates. As scientists have considered the differences between humans and other primates, the differentiation generally focuses on social aspects of human interaction (see Dunbar, 2003 for an overview). In particular, two important distinctions are the *utilization of language* and the *ability of humans to infer another person's mental state and intentions.*

Theory of mind continues to be an important topic in developmental psychology. Included in theory of mind is the capacity to infer another person's mental state from their behavior. Mental state can include purpose, intention, knowledge, belief, thinking, doubt, pretending, liking, and so forth. Some researchers have suggested that only humans possess this ability, which allows for sophisticated social interactions.

One experimental procedure for understanding theory of mind uses a cereal box. This technique is formally called the "false-belief" task. In this procedure, a cereal box, for example, is shown to the child. The child is then asked what is in the box. Of course, the child responds by naming the type of cereal, such as Cheerios. The experimenter then opens the box and shows the child it contains something else, such as ribbons. The child is then asked what another child out in the hall would think is in the box. Three-year-old children tend to respond "ribbons," whereas four-year-olds would say "Cheerios." Thus, the four-year-olds understand what others would believe, whereas three-year-olds would not. In the final part of the task, the experimenter asks the children what they initially thought was in the box. Four-year-olds say Cheerios, whereas three-year-olds say ribbons. When theory-of-mind type of tasks have been given around the world, it is observed that it develops at about the same time. Few three-year-olds correctly understand what another knows and few five-year-olds are incorrect in their ability to understand what another child would experience.

Theories of Attachment

In the course of development, there are a number of especially sensitive periods in which disruptions can lead to long-term effects. For example, what happens when events such as war or natural disasters interrupt the normal caregiving patterns? The British psychiatrist John Bowlby sought to determine what would happen if a young child had his or her physical needs such as food and housing satisfied, but did not experience a close emotional connection. His early work examined children who became orphans during World War II. They were physically cared for, but lacked the emotional attention given from a caregiver, such as a mother dealing with her own infant. His and later research has shown that these infants display patterns of interpersonal behaviors that have been associated with psychological problems. He referred to the infant–mother relationship as *attachment*.

John Bowlby developed a theoretical understanding of interpersonal relationships based on the interactions of a child with his or her parents. Of course, this type of bonding has great survival value for a human infant who cannot take care of him or herself. Along with a number of other instincts, such as the rooting reflex in which an infant begins sucking when the cheek or mouth are touched, attachment is seen as the basis of early emotional relationships between a mother and her child. It initially begins in terms of nursing as the mother and her child learn how to respond to each other. Both internal and external processes and their constant interplay lead to mother–infant bonding.

Bowlby considered the process of attachment as a *social-emotional behavior* equally as important as *mating behavior* and *parental behavior*. He saw attachment as a multifaceted process involving a variety of developmental mechanisms over the first year of life. For Bowlby, attachment was a process in which the mother was able to reduce fear by direct contact with the infant and provide support, called a *secure base*. This secure base would allow for later exploratory behaviors. Bowlby suggested that there were five universal attachment behaviors in human infants. These are sucking, clinging, crying, following, and smiling. Bowlby assumed that the relative immaturity of the human infant resulted in attachment being a slower process in humans than in other primates.

Specifically, the development of attachment takes place in four phases according to Bowlby. The first phase is *preattachment* and lasts from birth to 6 weeks of age. During this period, the infant produces such behaviors as crying. In turn, the caregiver comes and comforts the infant. The second phase is *attachment in the making* that lasts from about 6 weeks to 8 months. During this phase, infants smile, laugh, or babble in the presence of their caregivers. It is at this time that the infants begin to develop trust or the lack thereof. The third phase is *clear-cut attachment*. Beginning at about 8 months, this phase lasts until about 1 ½ years of age. Infants are happy to see their caregiver and show distress when left. The fourth phase is *reciprocal relationships*, which lasts from 1 ½ or 2 years on. This represents a more mutual relationship based on the infant's abilities to use language and understand emotions.

Attachment in Primates

In a classic series of experiments in the 1950s, Harry Harlow initially examined the mechanisms of attachment with primates. At that time, there was a real debate between whether the infant's response to its mother is learned, or whether certain inherent properties of the mother elicit infant attachment (Harlow, McGaugh, & Thompson, 1971). To better understand the nature of attachment in monkey infants, Harlow (1958) separated infant monkeys from their mothers after birth and placed them in isolated cages. In the cage were two surrogate mothers—one made of wire and the other made of terrycloth (see **Figure 4-10**). The wire surrogates had bare bodies of welded wire, whereas the cloth surrogates were covered by soft, resilient terrycloth. Both surrogates had long bodies that could be easily clasped by the infant rhesus monkey.

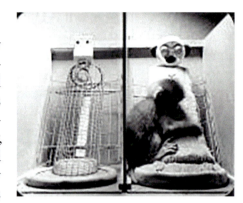

Figure 4-10 Surrogate mothers—one is made of wire and one is made of cloth. Experimenters would change which mother would be able to feed the infant.

Source: Harlow, McGaugh, and Thompson (1971, p. 58).

For half of the infants, a nipple by which they could feed themselves was attached to the wire mother, and for the other half the nipple was attached to the terrycloth mother. In either surrogate mother, the infants had the nutrition that they needed. If one thought that attachment was totally learned through reinforcement, then the infant monkeys should go to the mother from which they were fed. What do you think happened? What happened was a finding completely contrary to the learning theory interpretation. As the infants who fed on the wire mother grew, they showed decreasing responsiveness to her and increasing responsiveness to the cloth mother even though this mother had no food to offer (see **Figure 4-11**). From this, Harlow concluded that it is the contact comfort and not the feeding per se that binds the infant to the mother (see **Figure 4-12**).

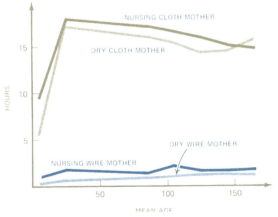

Figure 4-11 Time spent on cloth and wire surrogate. Whether fed or not, the monkey infants like the cloth mothers better.

Source: Harlow, McGaugh, and Thompson (1971, p. 59).

Figure 4-12 Young monkey clinging to cloth mother.

Measuring Attachment

Part of Bowlby's original interest in attachment came from observations of children in orphanages following World War II. Like the primates in Harlow's experiments, these children had all of their physical needs met, but lacked a form of emotional and social connectedness. As part of a World Health Organization (WHO) project, Bowlby concluded that children deprived of their mothers were at risk for physical and mental illness. In particular, he concluded that separation from emotional caregivers could lead to severe anxiety and psychopathic personality (Bowlby, 1951).

Bowlby carefully observed children and recorded his observations in a series of books and articles focused on secure attachment as well as loss and separation anxiety (Bowlby, 1961, 1969, 1982, 1988). Bowlby had been influenced by *ethology*, which is the study of animal behavior. One classic example as described by the ethologist Konrad Lorenz is the *imprinting* of newborn ducks on their mother such that they will follow her wherever she goes. This will be discussed in the chapter on learning. Thus, Bowlby interpreted attachment from an evolutionary perspective emphasizing the survival value of attachment, especially as the human infant is beginning to crawl or walk on his or her own.

In terms of the general characteristics of attachment, Bowlby reported that children who develop a secure bond or attachment with a caregiver or parent, who is usually their mother, display patterns of activity that are especially strong from the end of the first year of life until about three years of age in relation to that caregiver. First, the infant shows distress when the caregiver leaves. Second, the infant smiles, makes noises, or shows other signs of pleasure when the caregiver returns. Third, the infant shows distress when approached by a stranger, unless the caregiver encourages the interaction. And fourth, the infant shows more exploratory behaviors in an unfamiliar situation when the caregiver is present.

Attachment Styles

Based on infants' reactions to their caregiver, Mary Ainsworth developed the **strange situation** to research attachment patterns experimentally (Ainsworth, Blehar, Waters, & Wall, 1978). The basic procedure is to bring the infant and his or her mother into an unfamiliar room with toys. With the infant and mother alone, the infant is allowed to explore without the mother being involved. At this point a stranger enters and talks with the mother and then approaches the infant. During this time the mother leaves inconspicuously. The stranger reacts to the infant as appropriate. The mother then returns and greets and comforts the infant. Following this, the mother leaves the infant alone in the room, and the stranger returns. The mother then returns again and greets and picks up the infant while the stranger leaves. During this procedure, the researchers observe the infant's reaction to the return of the mother.

Initially, Ainsworth described three **patterns of attachment styles** (Ainsworth, Blehar, Waters, & Wall, 1978). The first pattern, which is referred to as the *secure attachment pattern*, is characterized by the following pattern in which the infant: (1) engages in active exploration; (2) is upset when the mother leaves; and (3) shows positive emotions when the mother returns. The second pattern is the *avoidant attachment pattern*. In the avoidant style, the infant shows more interest in the toys than the mother and shows less distress when the mother leaves and less positive emotion when she returns. The third attachment pattern is referred to as *anxious/ambivalent attachment pattern*. In this pattern, the infant appears preoccupied with having access to the mother and shows protest on her separation. When she returns, the infant may show anger or ambivalence to her. This attachment pattern is associated with developing anxiety disorders later in life.

Later, other researchers suggested that a fourth pattern of attachment may exist that is characterized as *disorganized/controlling attachment pattern*. This attachment category was added when it was observed that some infants show disruptions in processing during the strange situation (Main & Solomon, 1990). That is, when their parent is present, these infants show disorganized behavior patterns or disorientation. Children with this attachment style tend to have problems dealing with psychological stress and a tendency to develop dissociative disorders later in life.

Of course, infants do not grow up in a vacuum, so it is also important to characterize the mothering style of the caregiver. With infants displaying secure attachment patterns, the style of the mother is consistent and responsive to her infant's signals. On the other hand, mothers of infants showing avoidant patterns tend to be more rejecting and rigid and, in general, insensitive to the infants' signals, including requests for bodily contact. Anxious/ambivalent patterns tend to be associated with inconsistent mothers who may be intrusive. Disorganized/controlling patterns tend to be associated with parents who show unpredictable abusive behavior or other behaviors that are frightening to the child. Mothers of these children have also been shown to be more likely to experience depression (O'Connor, Bureau, McCartney, & Lyons-Ruth, 2011). The complexity of the situation is highlighted by the fact that some infants are easier to care for than others. That is to say, some infants appear to be temperamentally more irritable than others, and thus could be more difficult for a caregiver to approach positively.

Attachment patterns can be seen as an internal roadmap or schema through which the person interprets his or her social experiences (Dykas & Cassidy, 2011). A secure pattern clearly has both physical and psychological benefits for the infant. There are also psychological values to trusting friends and other individuals as one moves through her lifespan. How about insecure attachment patterns, how are these protective? Bowlby (1980) suggests that these patterns prevent the infant from experiencing psychologically distressful experiences. If a caregiver is absent, inconsistent, and negative, then adopting a style that minimizes psychological pain would be protective. An important long-term research study described the role of attachment in the real world. This is described in the box: The World Is Your Laboratory—Romania Adoption Study.

The World Is Your Laboratory—Romania Adoption Study

Nicolae Ceaușescu was the head of state of Romania from 1967 to 1989. By the end of his rule, he had become brutal and repressive. Not only was he a brutal dictator who enforced his rule with the use of the secret police, but he also instituted strict policies requiring Romanians to have more children. He sought to increase the low birth rate in Romania by making divorce difficult and contraception and abortion illegal. He also dictated that women should have at least five children. To this end, Ceaușescu established the menstrual police. These were state gynecologists who conducted monthly checks of women of childbearing age who had not borne at least five children. To encourage additional children, families received a stipend for having more than two children but were also taxed for having fewer than five children. The number of new births did increase, although a number of these children were abandoned since the families could not afford to keep their children. The state encouraged placing these children in state orphanages.

After the fall of the Ceauşescu regime in 1989, it became clear that some 170,000 children had been placed in state institutions. The international media described these children as being "warehoused." Initially, some of these children were adopted internationally, but this practice was later banned by Romania. The government after Ceauşescu sought to move some of the infants and children in the government facilities to foster families. This made possible a naturalistic study in which attachment relationships and future cognitive, emotional, and physiological development could be assessed and studied. Thus, there were a number of infants and children randomly assigned to be placed with families and others to receive the usual care in orphanages. These groups of children could also be compared to other children who were raised in their own family.

A team of researchers was able to follow a subset of these children over a number of years. Initially, measurements were taken (a baseline assessment) with the children who were assigned to a foster family as well as those who remained in the institution. These measurements allowed the researchers to know if there were later changes in terms of groups. The baseline measurements were followed by a comprehensive follow-up at 30, 42, and 54 months and 8 and 12 years. An initial study showed that those children in the institution displayed less attachment to a caregiver than those who had never been in the orphanages (see **Figure 4-13**).

When assessed at 42 months, more children in foster care showed secure attachment style, whereas those who received care as usual at the orphanage showed more of the other insecure styles. The term "resistant" refers to the anxious/ambivalent attachment pattern (see **Figure 4-14**).

In addition to attachment, cognitive development (as measured in terms of intelligence quotient (IQ)) was higher the earlier the child was placed in foster care. Physiological measures including EEG and brain volume were also shown to be influenced by type of caregiving situation.

Although we have known for more than 50 years that institutional care was associated with cognitive and emotional problems, the Romanian study with its randomized design allowed for greater validity in the results. Children come into the world seeking interactions with others. This interaction helps to develop cognitive, emotional, language, and motor development.

(Based on Nelson, Fox, & Zeanah, 2014.)

Community	Institution
• 76.7% secure	• 16.8% secure
• 3.6% avoidant	• 4.7% avoidant
• 0.0% resistant	• 0.0% resistant
• 19.7% disorganized	• 65.4% disorganized
• 0.0% unclassifiable	• 13.1% unclassifiable

Figure 4-13 Children in the institution displayed less attachment to a caregiver than those who had never been in the orphanages.

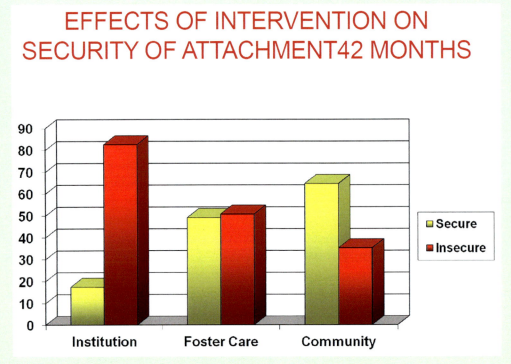

Figure 4-14 Security of attachment by group at 42 months.

Thought Question: There are many situations in the world where orphanages are the only good alternative for caring for children. From what you've read so far, what three principles do you think are most important in designing and running an orphanage that results in psychologically healthy children?

CONCEPT CHECK

1. Describe the basic process of imitation learning in terms of actions. How have researchers extended that idea to understanding another's internal experience and developing empathy?
2. What was the purpose behind creating the PATHS curriculum? What results have been shown with children who have gone through the program?
3. Theory of mind was initially researched by Premack and Woodruff in 1978 and continues to be an important topic in developmental psychology.
   a. How would you define theory of mind?
   b. Describe how experimental procedures have been used to study the theory of mind.
   c. What do theory and research results tell us about theory of mind's developmental process and timeline?
4. From John Bowlby's perspective, why is attachment so critical in human development? Is there a critical period for attachment? What are the phases of the attachment process?

5. What did Harry Harlow's studies with infant monkeys contribute to our understanding of the mechanisms of attachment? How did that, in turn, inform Bowlby's study following World War II that focused on orphans' psychological development?
6. Describe Mary Ainsworth's different patterns of attachment style. How are attachment styles related to the mothering style of the caregiver?
7. From the research presented (including the Romania Adoption Study), in what ways can an individual's attachment style in infancy impact his or her later life? Discuss this in terms of both positive and negative effects.

Development During Adolescence

When I was a boy of 14, my father was so ignorant I could hardly stand to have the old man around. But when I got to be 21, I was astonished at how much the old man had learned in seven years.

(Attributed to Mark Twain)

Adolescence is a time of great change, both in the brain and body, as well as in the relationships with one's friends and parents. Similar changes are seen worldwide related to biological, psychological, and social development (Blakemore, 2019). During adolescence the individual changes from having a close connection with a family to developing a sense of one's independence. Often this comes with emotional rejections and conflict with one's parents. During this period the individual can begin enjoying the privileges allowed by society, such as driving a car, being part of the military, working, voting, and consuming alcohol, although the exact age differs by culture.

Adolescence has been characterized as a time in which an individual moves from a more family-oriented frame of reference to one of peer relations. Peer relationships during this period involve meeting and understanding new individuals as well as determining the types of relationships available. Sexuality and romantic interests develop during this period. Concomitant with these social and emotional changes are large changes in the brain. Overall, adolescents show an increased sensitivity to both positive and negative rewards than do either adults or younger children (Galván, 2013). Adolescents are particularly sensitive to being included in groups in terms of mood changes and anxiety feelings. As the adolescent moves into young adulthood, there is a shift from thinking about the self to taking the perspective of others.

In many cultures, adolescence is considered the time in which a male or female becomes an adult. Commemorating this entry into adulthood often involves a rite of passage or some special celebratory event for the individual. Some of these celebrations are religious, such as the time in which a Christian may join the church through confirmation. Jewish adolescents begin to follow religious rites, and this is celebrated by a Bar or Bat Mitzvah. In Mexico, a *Quinceañera* or *fiesta de quince años* is celebrated when a girl turns 15 years of age. Many other puberty celebrations or rites of passage are found throughout the world.

The word *puberty* actually comes from Latin, *puber*, which refers to being of marriageable age. Historically, rites of puberty marked this passage. As such, adolescence is a time of change to one's body and the awakening of new interests and desires. These changes are associated with brain changes and reorganization (see Sturman & Moghaddam, 2011 for an overview).

Overall, changes during adolescence are seen in every domain, including physical, psychological, cognitive, and emotional (see Towbin & Showalter, 2008). Although the terms *puberty* and *adolescence* are commonly used interchangeably, technically there is a difference. Adolescence is a social, cognitive, and behavioral term developed in relation to society, whereas puberty is a series of biological events. The social and behavioral development of adolescence and the biological development of puberty actually involve different brain circuits (Sisk & Foster, 2004). However, as you can imagine, there is constant interaction between these systems.

Physical Changes in Adolescence

As puberty approaches, there is physical growth in terms of the size of hands and feet, and height and weight. This *growth spurt* is the greatest change in physical growth of the person since infancy. It peaks at about 12 years of age for females and age 14 for males. During this period, girls begin to appear more as they will as adults with wider hips, softer skin related to an increased layer of fat, and the appearance of breasts. Males show more body mass and broader shoulders. Facial features also change, including facial hair in males.

During puberty in both males and females, hormone levels increase throughout the body. For females, the ovaries produce the hormone *estrogen*. With this comes the growth of the breasts and sex organs. The vagina becomes larger and the muscles in the wall of the uterus become stronger. It is these muscles that will be utilized during the birth of a child. Externally, the labia (tissue around the vaginal opening) and the clitoris increase in size and become sensitive to touch. Girls then begin menstruation, although the ability to conceive is typically delayed a year or so.

For males, the testes produce the hormone *testosterone*. This is associated with the enlargement of the testes and growth of pubic hair. As the testes grow, the scrotum that contains them descends and darkens. The penis lengthens and becomes wider. About 13 to 14 years of age, sperm production begins. Although somewhat varied in time course, males show an increase in body hair of the face, arms and legs, and chest. The male voice becomes lower and muscle mass increases. Sexual thoughts and aggressive impulses increase in males.

Girls typically enter puberty about two years earlier than boys. However, there is great variability in the timing of puberty for both males and females. For example, extreme exercise or having an eating disorder will delay puberty. As with other signs of physical growth such as height, puberty is coming earlier today than it did 100 years ago in the industrialized nations. This may be related to better nutrition and public health, although other genetic and environmental factors have been shown to play a role in the timing of puberty.

Risk-Taking in Adolescence

Adolescents take more risk than either children or adults do (see Steinberg, 2007 for an overview). An increase in risk-taking leads to various types of accidents, unprotected sex, use of drugs, and even crime. In fact, automobile accidents are the leading cause of death among adolescents. This risk-taking cannot be seen as the lack of logical reasoning since 15-year-olds do as well as adults in laboratory-type cognitive reasoning tasks. Some risk-taking may be related to a lack of information since knowledge-based programs such as sex education do influence pregnancy rates. However, a more important factor seems to be making decisions in social and emotional situations.

One such social/emotional situation is being with peers. The desire to be with others along with the willingness to take risks, can influence decision making. For example, when schools were closed during the COVID-19 virus epidemic and adolescents were told to stay in place, some adolescents ignored the warning of health care professionals and met with their friends. This put them and others at risk for contracting the virus.

This *risk-taking or impulsivity* involves distinct brain networks related to the ability to *inhibit* (Whelan et al., 2012). Logical reasoning itself (absent social or emotional components) tends to be developed by about 15 years of age. However, frontal lobe development, which is related to planning and goals as well as inhibition, is not fully developed in adolescents and continues to develop well into an individual's 20s. This suggests that adolescents have not yet developed the abilities to protect themselves from risk, especially when they are with their peers.

Overall, research in psychology and the neurosciences has shown that adolescence is a period of development in which the person is particularly sensitive to social environmental cues (see Blakemore & Mills, 2014 for an overview). Our brain networks during adolescence are actually more sensitive to these social cues than during either childhood or adulthood. Interestingly, our ability and sensitivity for cultural learning comes before adolescence.

Risk-Taking with Peers

One of the hallmarks of adolescent risk-taking is that it is more likely to occur in the presence of their peers (Chein, Albert, O'Brien, Uckert, & Steinberg, 2011). One of the risky behaviors seen in adolescents is driving. Using a stoplight driving game in an fMRI, Jason Chein and his colleagues compared the results of adolescents (14–18 years of age), young adults (19–22 years of age), and adults (24–29 years of age). The goal of the stoplight game is to drive through 20 intersections as fast as possible. At each intersection, the driver can either stop for the light and experience a short delay or take a risk and go through the red light without any delay. However, running the red light could result in a crash. All participants were also asked to bring a friend of their same age with them. Compared to young adults and adults, adolescents showed riskier decisions and crashes when they were observed by a friend (see Figure 4-15).

Chein and his colleagues also took functional MRI measures. The fMRI results showed differences in the left prefrontal cortex (PFC) by age. There were also differences in the right ventral striatum (VS) and the left orbitofrontal cortex (OFC) in terms of age and whether a friend was present. These areas are associated with making a decision in a social context. The greater activation of these areas suggests that adolescents saw risk-taking as more rewarding in the presence of a friend. Overall, this research shows that peer presence makes a greater difference in risk-taking, which is also seen in brain processes in adolescents compared with those beyond adolescence.

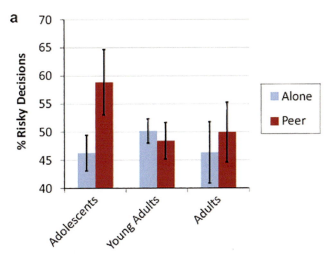

Figure 4-15 Risky decisions on the stoplight driving task when alone or being watched by a friend by age group.

Source: Chein, Albert, O'Brien, Uckert, and Steinberg (2011).

Moral Development in Childhood and Adolescence

Although adolescence is associated with greater risk taking, it is also a time that moral development such as a desire to change the world and make it a better place can be seen. In fact, adolescence is a period of rapid **moral development**. Let's begin with how children make moral judgments. One question is to ask whether children younger than the age of six can differentiate between a moral judgment and a conventional one. An event that would require a *moral judgment* would involve aggression such as hitting or biting another, stealing such as taking another child's possession, and psychological harm such as teasing. Events related to a *conventional judgment* would include not being neat or making a mess and breaking school rules such as playing in an area that is off-limits.

In a classic study, preschool children were asked to evaluate naturally occurring and hypothetical events involving moral and conventional transgressions (Smetana, Schlagman, & Adams, 1993). These researchers found that preschool children did make a distinction between the moral events and the conventional ones. The moral events were seen as more serious, wrong, and more deserving of punishment than the conventional events. Evolutionary psychologists view these types of results as suggesting that cultural and moral judgments rely on different systems of judgment and that moral transgressions are seen as more serious an offense than cultural ones.

When there are limited resources but there are needs, how does one make a decision about one's actions? These resources can be related to time, physical ability, or money. A classic example of moral reasoning is to ask the question—who would you save first in a burning building, a 3-year-old or an 85-year-old? Adults can make a decision quickly. Some moral problems on the other hand are more complex. Would you be willing to hurt another person if it meant that three others would be saved from harm? These types of problems are not solved as quickly and often leave the person feeling uncertain about how to answer. In solving moral problems, children appear to change perspectives as they increase in maturity.

Given that moral and cultural norms are different, when do children begin to express moral decisions (see Colby, Kohlberg, Gibbs, & Lieberman, 1983; Sheskin, Chevallier, Lambert, & Baumard, 2014 for overviews)? In sharing with others, 9-year-olds have no problem sharing with others and selecting fair distributions. Five-year-olds tend to select a spiteful distribution over a fair one. Three-year-olds look to their own desires and do not share equally with others. Supporting the idea that moral reasoning has an emotional component, older children report more positive feelings after they engage in moral behavior. However, it should be noted that some researchers have made a distinction between the cognitive aspect of moral reasoning and moral emotions such as shame and guilt.

Based on the idea of stages of cognitive development suggested by Piaget, Lawrence Kohlberg (1963) asked if there are similar stages in *moral development*. As such, an individual's way of solving a moral dilemma would be different at different ages. The type of reasoning given at one stage would be self-contained and different from that at another stage. Further, with development these stages become more complex and differentiated. Thus, in the same way that a child would solve the water jar conservation task differently at different ages, he or she would solve moral problems differently throughout their development. In terms of moral reasoning, obeying your parents would be a less differentiated answer than suggesting that societies work better if fairness is promoted.

Kohlberg used hypothetical situations to determine the level of moral development. Below are two examples of these moral dilemmas.

- *In Europe, a woman was near death from cancer. One drug might save her, a form of radium that a druggist in the same town had recently discovered. The druggist was charging $2,000, ten times* *what the drug cost him to make. The sick woman's husband, Heinz, went to everyone he knew to borrow the money, but he could only get half of what it cost. He told the druggist that his wife was dying and asked him to sell it cheaper or let him pay later. But the druggist said, "No." The husband got desperate and broke into the man's store to steal the drug for his wife. (Should the husband have done that?)*

- *There was a woman who had very bad cancer, and there was no treatment known to medicine that would save her. Her doctor, Dr. Jefferson, knew that she had only about six months to live. She was in terrible pain, but she was so weak that a good dose of a pain-killer like ether or morphine would make her die sooner. She was delirious and almost crazy with pain, and in her calm periods she would ask Dr. Jefferson to give her enough ether to kill her. She said she couldn't stand the pain and she was going to die in a few months anyway. Although he knows that mercy killing is against the law, the doctor thinks about granting her request. (Should Dr. Jefferson give her the drug?)*

How would you respond to these situations? For Kohlberg, the critical issue was not whether a person said yes or no to the dilemma, but the way in which the person reasoned. In fact, each dilemma could be answered either "yes" or "no" but with a different level of analysis. Based on research and theoretical considerations, Kohlberg outlined three levels of moral development with two stages in each (see **Figure 4-16**).

The first level is *preconventional morality*. At this level, rules are external to the individual. For a child, decisions are based on the rules of parents and teachers. The first stage of this level is *punishment and obedience orientation*. Bad actions are those that result in punishments and good actions are those that do not. The worse the punishment, the worse is the act. The second stage of this level is *instrumental hedonism*. This is the situation where you conform to the rules so that you will be rewarded or you do something for someone else so they will do something for you. This first level is typically seen in preschool children and those in the first few grades of elementary school.

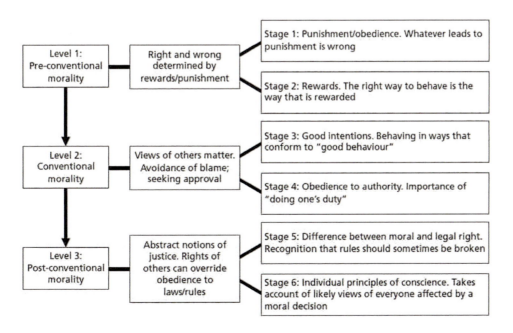

Figure 4-16 Levels of morality according to Kohlberg.

The second level is *conventional morality*. With conventional morality, the individual has begun to internalize the values. As expected from developmental research, the individual is able to understand the perspective of others. The first stage of this level (stage 3) is that of *good boy or good girl*. Being accepted by others is important. People at stage 3 also evaluate others by their intentions. Stage 4 involves *doing one's duty*. In the dilemma of the expensive drug, this type of reasoning would suggest that it is the husband's duty to take care of his wife. This type of reasoning begins in elementary school. By adolescence, another type of reasoning occurs.

The third level is *postconventional morality*. The beginning of postconventional morality occurs as one becomes a young adult. As the name implies, this level uses higher-level moral principles. One might break local laws that are at odds with higher principles such as justice. Gandhi and Martin Luther King, Jr. both went against their conventional societal rules to present a higher purpose. People at this level would also seek to change existing laws if they were seen to violate larger universal principles. The movement for women's vote at the beginning of the 1900s would be another example of this type of reasoning. Kohlberg saw stage 5 as reflecting a *social contract that improves social welfare*. Stage 6 was seen to reflect *universal moral principles*. However, Kohlberg dropped the use of stage 6 since it was so rarely used as a source of moral reasoning.

CONCEPT CHECK

1. Changes during adolescence are seen in every domain including physical, psychological, cognitive, emotional, and relationships. Describe an example of each.
2. What has research found concerning risk-taking in adolescents and the role of peers? How do these results change for individuals in their 20s?
3. There is a debate in our society as to whether adolescents have the psychological ability to understand crime in the same way as adults. Take a position *pro* or *con* and cite evidence to support your position.
4. Based on the idea of stages of cognitive development suggested by Piaget, Lawrence Kohlberg asked if there are similar stages in moral development. Describe the stages and levels Kohlberg proposed, as well as the ages when individuals would typically show that type of moral reasoning.

Lifespan Development and Adulthood

In the 1960s and 1970s, psychologists began to expand the concept of human development (see Lerner & Overton, 2010 for an overview). Prior to this time, the emphasis was on the developmental processes you have read about thus far in the chapter—development in infancy, childhood, and adolescence. To follow an individual across his or her lifespan in a theoretically integrated manner using psychological research was a new approach. This was referred to as **lifespan development**. Of course, many theorists over the years discussed the aging process and the types of questions asked, but these tended to lack a careful research focus.

For example, an early developer of analytic psychology, the Swiss psychiatrist Carl Jung suggested that the first half of life was about the development of one's ego or personality with an emphasis on the external world. In so doing, one pays attention to his or her work, family, and society. On the other hand, for Jung the second half of life was about the self. This includes an understanding of both the positive and negative aspects of one's self and one's world. A person also considers how to pass values and understandings to the next generation. During the second half of life, a person begins to fully integrate his or her life with a focus on internal values. Overall, Jung suggested the first half of life was more about the external world and the second half about the internal world (see Jung, 1989). Although this perspective was based on a clinical practice, these ideas were not designed to be tested with research.

Others such as Daniel Levinson discussed lifespan development in terms of the seasons of one's life (Levinson, 1978). He focused on the challenges you face or will face as you live your life. The initial stage occurs as you move from adolescence to becoming an adult. This is followed by the choices you make in your 20s in terms of who your friends are, what type of lifestyle you will live, whom you will love, and what values you will use to direct your life. Some people in their late 20s and 30s find themselves changing jobs through choice or being laid off. As people move into their 30s, there is a period of settling down. Some will have children and experience a change in focus. This may include a different understanding of who one is and how one fits into society. In one's 40s and 50s, there are new realizations about life, and opportunities may decrease. As people move into their 60s, friends develop health problems such as heart attacks or even die. People may also ask questions concerning what they have accomplished. Some have criticized Levinson's work suggesting that the individuals he studied may not represent current generations. In addition, there is the issue that the lifespan has increased.

Demographic changes during the last 100 years have also made us reconsider the concept of aging. In 1900, life expectancy was less than 50 years of age. In the 1930s, life expectancy in the United States was below 60 years of age, while in 2010 it was more than 78 years of age. That is almost a difference of 20 years of longer life. You even hear in the media that 70 is the new 50! Further, women are expected to live some five years longer than men (averaging 80 versus 75 years of age). **Figure 4-17** shows life expectancy from 1970 to 2010. Some 30 or more countries have longer life expectancies than the United States; for example, Japan has a life expectancy of 83 years. The larger perspective is that those of you who are currently about 20 years of age will have 60 more years of life to live. In fact, it is estimated that by 2050 more than 2 billion people worldwide will be more than 60 years of age (Huentelman et al., 2020). This raises a number of questions as to how to use one's extended lifetime.

Erikson and Psychosocial Stages

One of the first theorists to present a map of lifespan development was Erik Erikson. He was born in Frankfurt, Germany in 1902. He was initially influenced by Sigmund Freud and worked with Freud's daughter, Anna Freud. Erikson expanded psychodynamic concepts through observations of children in several cultures and an understanding of biology. Based on these influences, Erikson suggested that people throughout the world experience eight major *psychosocial stages* (see **Table 4-2**). During each of these stages, there is a major conflict or question that must be answered.

At each stage the person is asking who am I and how do I relate to the world, myself, and others. During the first year of life the infant determines whether he can trust his

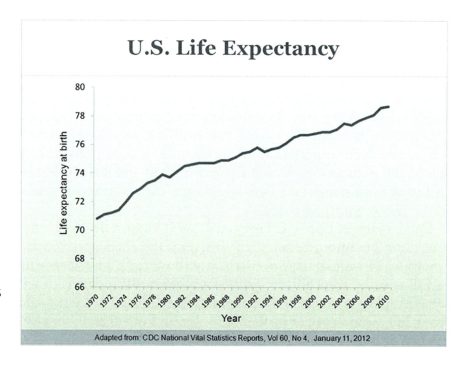

Figure 4-17 Changes in US life expectancy. We continue to live longer.

Table 4-3 Erikson's psychosocial stages

Approximate Ages	Stage	Positive Characteristics Gained and Typical Activities
Birth to 1 year	Trust versus mistrust	Hope; trust in primary caregiver and in one's own ability to make things happen (secure attachment to caregiver is key)
1 to 3	Autonomy versus shame and doubt	Will; new physical skills lead to demand for more choices, most often seen as saying "no" to caregivers; child learns self-care skills such as toileting
3 to 6	Initiative versus guilt	Purpose; ability to organize activities around some goal; more assertiveness and aggressiveness (harsh parental criticism may lead to guilt)
6 to 12	Industry versus inferiority	Competence; cultural skills and norms, including school skills and tool use (failure to master these leads to sense of inferiority)
12 to 18	Identity versus role confusion	Fidelity; a unified and consistent sense of self that integrates pubertal changes into a mature sexual identity, assumes adult social and occupational roles, and establishes personal values and attitudes
18 to 30	Intimacy versus isolation	Love; person develops intimate relationships beyond adolescent love; many become parents
30 to old age	Generativity versus stagnation	Care; people rear children, focus on occupational achievement or creativity, and train the next generation; turn outward from the self toward others
Old age	Integrity versus despair	Wisdom; person conducts a life review, integrates earlier stages and comes to terms with basic identity; develops self-acceptance

environment or not. With good conditions, the infant gets the attention, caring, and food that is needed for development. If this is the case, the infant has a sense that the world is safe and reliable. However, if the caregiving is inconsistent or the infant does not get the attention needed, then he understands the world as unsafe and not a situation to be trusted.

As the infant becomes a toddler, movement and new perspectives become possible. In the family the child is encouraged to become a person with wishes and desires. If this is not available, then doubt in one's own behavior can be seen. Following this, the child becomes part of groups, whether it is family, playschool, or group play. With this come the social emotions, such as guilt for breaking rules. On the individual level, the child can have goals that may be different from the group. A positive resolution to the conflict is for the child to experience purpose more than guilt. Entering elementary school, the child spends more time with other children and begins to see where they stand in terms of physical, emotional, and cognitive abilities. As the child becomes an adolescent, she becomes part of different groups and has the opportunity to try out different social roles. This leads to a sense of identity. If the adolescent is unable to do this, role confusion and identity problems result. In young adulthood, the person begins to make more long-term decisions. When successful, the person is able to experience intimacy in both social and sexual relationships. By middle adulthood, the person can focus on creativity in her world. She can also consider how to teach and mentor others. If this does not happen, there is a sense of stagnation. As one enters old age, the person has the chance to reconsider what is important to him and to look back on his life. It is at this point that the individual can come to value and accept the decisions and accomplishments that he has made. If not, the person will experience despair for the life he wished he had lived.

Successful Aging

At one time, aging was discussed in terms of loss of cognitive functions such as memory and the increase in medical problems (Pluvinage & Wyss-Coray, 2020; Wulff et al., 2019). A common view from the middle of the last century was that a person would work and then retire to a community in a state such as Florida or Arizona. It was often assumed that the person would relax and not engage in high-level intellectual or physical activities. However, today the manner in which people age follows a number of different pathways. Some people do show mental or physical deterioration as they age. Disorders such as Alzheimer's are a common experience of this group. However, others retain both physical and mental abilities as they age. The study of this last group has been referred to as *successful aging*.

One of the early studies of successful aging was conducted in the 1930s. In 1937, the philanthropist William T. Grant gave money to study the lives of "people who are well and do well." These individuals were studied for 35 years (see Vaillant, 2002 for overview). The basic conclusions from this study were that:

- psychopathology is always with us;
- health is the way we react to conflict, not the absence of conflict;
- not one of the people, some of whom were very successful, were without problems.

Although no individual was without problems, the manner in which they coped with their problems was associated with better or worse health outcomes. Immature defenses such as blaming others or taking it out on one's self were associated with the worst health outcomes. More mature defenses such as acceptance or humor were associated with the best health outcomes. These results are shown in **Figure 4-18**.

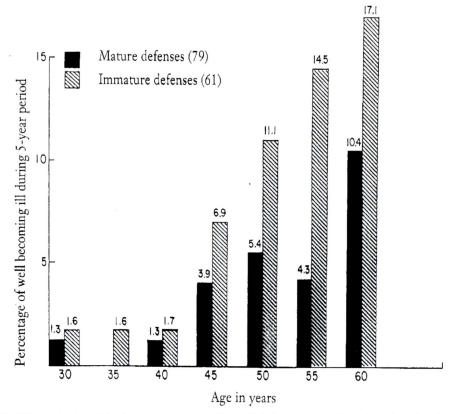

Figure 4-18 The relationship between maturity of defenses and decline in physical health.

Successful aging is now considered one aspect of lifespan development. Successful aging is seen to include three main components (Rowe & Kahn, 1997). The first component is a low probability of disease and disease-related disability. The second component is high cognitive and physical functional capacity. And the third is an active engagement with life. Of course, these components are inter-related. For example, choosing a healthy lifestyle in terms of food and exercise is one way to reduce the likelihood of disease. Also, being involved with other people in terms of social networks or marriage has been shown to be protective. A number of retired people continue working in either a volunteer or self-employed manner, which gives meaning to their lives.

Of course, even in those who age successfully, changes do take place. As we age, the speed of our reactions decreases. Actually, your ability to play video games begins to decrease in your 20s. Your ability to perform tasks that require reasoning and spatial abilities also decreases. As one becomes older, difficulty with hearing and vision becomes more obvious. Many older adults find driving at night to present problems in terms of seeing the edge of the road and reacting to the lights from other cars.

Although all individuals experience changes with aging, older people actually report that they feel younger than they actually are and are satisfied with their aging (Kleinspehn-Ammerlahn, Grühn, & Smith, 2008). Further, people more than 60 who report that they enjoy life had fewer problems in day-to-day abilities some eight years later than those who reported they did not enjoy life (Steptoe, de Oliverira, Demakakos, & Zaninotto, 2008).

One strong finding across the lifespan is that individuals in committed romantic relationships have longer, healthier, and happier lives than unmarried individuals (see Diamond, Fagundes, & Butterworth, 2010). This is also true for those who have a same-sex relationship. One key variable is that the emotional relationship is protective from stress factors. However, over the lifespan, marital satisfaction is highest at the beginning of the relationship and after children leave the house. It is lowest after the birth of the first child. Older and younger couples appear similar in terms of agreements and disagreements over leisure, intimacy, money, housework, and other concerns.

How old will you be in the year 2050 or 2060? As you think about your age at this time, you can ask if there are simple things you can do to help you age successfully. As noted, research has shown an important role for exercise and social support in a healthy lifestyle and successful aging (Voss, Vivar, Kramer, & van Praag, 2013). Exercise is thought to play an important role in aging by promoting healthy cardiovascular function. That is, exercise increases blood flow to the entire brain. Exercise also protects the brain from the adverse effects of aging. Research with animal models has shown that exercise slows the expression of Alzheimer's-like disorders.

In a review of literature from different areas, Kramer and Erickson (2007) suggest that exercise provides multiple routes to enhancing cognitive vitality across the lifespan. These include both the reduction of disease risk as well as improvement in molecular and cellular structures of the brain, including better blood supply to the brain through new capillaries. This, in turn, increases brain function. Exercise also increases the size of the hippocampus and improves memory (McAuley et al., 2011). Further, it is suggested that aerobic exercise affects executive function more than other cognitive processes.

Following more than 700 older individuals without neurocognitive disorders for several years, Aron Buchman and his colleagues (2012) found that daily physical activity slowed cognitive decline. Exercise was also associated with a lower risk for developing Alzheimer's disease. Although performing various types of cognitive tasks such as crossword puzzles or speaking a second language are also associated with successful aging, these brain effects appear to be more localized in those areas of the brain related to the specific task.

In order to better help articulate the causal role of exercise, Lindsay Nagamatsu and her colleagues (2013) randomly assigned older individuals who were beginning to show mild cognitive impairment to one of three groups. The first group received resistance training and lifted weights. The second group received aerobic training and walked outdoors at a level that increased their heart rate. The third group received balance and stretching exercises. The third group served as the control group. After six months of twice-weekly exercise, the first two groups improved in memory functions. This was seen more strongly on a difficult spatial memory test. The aerobic group also improved performance on the verbal memory test. The important point of this study is that six months of exercise can improve memory in 70-year-olds.

Social support has also been associated with a reduced risk for neurocognitive disorders. Two of these factors are the size of one's network of friends and whether one is married or not. As suggested in studies of the social brain, understanding and maintaining networks of friends requires a variety of cognitive resources, which in turn offer a reserve for dealing with brain pathologies. One study followed 16,638 individuals over the age of 50 for six years. Those individuals who were more socially integrated and active showed less memory loss during the six-year period (Ertel, Glymour, & Berkman, 2008).

CONCEPT CHECK

1. In the 1960s and 1970s the concept of human development was expanded to include lifespan development. What changes did this bring to the way

psychologists study human development in terms of scope, theoretical research, and demographic necessity?

2. A number of people have proposed that the concept of lifespan development can be organized around the problems individuals face at different critical periods of their lives and how they solve those problems. What were the life problems and their critical periods presented by the following people:
   a. Carl Jung?
   b. Daniel Levinson?
   c. Erik Erikson?
   d. William T. Grant?

3. What are the three main components of successful aging? Cite evidence that shows the value of exercise and social relationships in successful aging. What will you consider starting now so that you age successfully?

Summary

Learning Objective 1: Discuss the brain, sensory, and motor developments that take place during infancy.

Developmental psychology is the study of the cognitive, emotional, and motor development of humans across their lifespan. This development is influenced by a number of factors including culture, parent and peer involvement, and brain processes.

There are two critical periods in terms of brain development over one's life. The first occurs in the womb, and the second is during adolescence. During gestation and the early years of life, the brain is establishing its cortical connections and growing neurons at an amazing rate. The areas of the infant's brain with increasing connections involve visual, auditory, and motor processing. Language and spatial orientation, which involve the parietal areas, don't fully develop until around puberty. Executive functions involving goals, reasoning, as well as integration of information and social processes continue to develop until your 20s.

Psychologists often discuss development in terms of human processes, including motor development, cognitive development, language development, social development, and so on. However, if you watch infants through their first years of life, you will see that there is a complex interaction involving all of these systems. Not only do human infants actively search their environment, they have expectations of what should happen next. Not only do infants have expectations, but they also act as "little scientists" and try to test out their ideas. When their expectations are not met, they try to learn from what they experience.

Motor development in infants proceeds in two directions. The first is from head to toe, and the second is from the midline of the body to the periphery. At about 2 months of age, the infant develops the muscles necessary for raising his or her head. About a month later, the infant develops the muscles of the torso necessary to roll over and sit in a highchair. During the next six months, the infant can begin to crawl. At the first year of age, infants can begin to stand while holding on to a low table and take steps on their own. Likewise, development goes from the midline in which infants can move their arms and legs before they can actually use their hands to purposely grab an object.

Learning Objective 2: Discuss *cognitive development* **based on the theories of Piaget and Vygotsky.**

Cognitive development refers to the way we reason and use language, as well as traditional intellectual abilities such as memory and problem solving.

Jean Piaget is considered to have created the field of cognitive development. His work was mainly based on the observation of children at different ages. One important contribution was the idea that a child has a different schema or set of assumptions at different periods of his or her life. Through his observations of how children solve problems, as well as the mistakes they make, Piaget suggested there were four periods or stages of development that correspond with a child's age: (1) sensorimotor, (2) preoperational, (3) concrete operations, and (4) formal operations.

Russian psychologist Lev Vygotsky offered a sociocultural perspective to cognitive development. Whereas Piaget emphasized the interaction with the physical environment, Vygotsky stressed the social and cultural environment.

We all come into the world with bodily emotional responses all our own—a constellation of emotional and behavioral responses referred to as temperament. Temperament is seen as a broad set of emotional and behavioral reactions in which both genetic and environmental factors play a role.

Learning Objective 3: Describe the aspects of social development and how we make emotional and social connections with others.

Infants are able to learn important aspects of social development by watching others and making emotional and social connections, especially parents and other caregivers.

What happens in your brain when you see someone wave or clap her hands? One intriguing answer to this question comes from research that suggests the neurons in your brain fire as if you had performed the same actions. These neurons are called *mirror neurons*. Some researchers suggest that this brain process may lie at the basis of *imitation learning*, as well as other human social phenomena, including language and empathy.

Theory of mind is the capacity to infer another person's mental state from their behavior. Mental state can include purpose, intention, knowledge, belief, thinking, doubt, pretending, liking, and so forth. Theory of mind is an important topic in developmental psychology.

John Bowlby developed a theoretical understanding of interpersonal relationships based on the interactions of a child with his or her parents, which he referred to as attachment. Mary Ainsworth described three patterns of attachment styles: (1) secure attachment pattern, (2) avoidant attachment pattern, and (3) anxious/ambivalent attachment pattern. Later researchers suggested a fourth attachment style: (4) disorganized/controlling attachment pattern. Numerous studies have shown attachment patterns to be relatively stable across the lifespan in a number of areas.

Learning Objective 4: Discuss the physical, psychological, cognitive, and emotional domains that occur during adolescence

During adolescence, there is physical growth in terms of the size of hands and feet, and height and weight. This growth spurt is the greatest change in physical growth of the person since infancy. During puberty, in both males and females, hormone levels increase throughout the body. Girls typically enter puberty about two years earlier than boys, however there is great variability in the timing of puberty for both males and females.

Adolescence has been characterized as a time in which an individual moves from a more family-oriented frame of reference to one of peer relations. Concomitant with these social and emotional changes are large changes in the brain. Research suggests that, from childhood to adulthood, the brain goes from a largely undifferentiated system to one composed of specialized neural networks.

Adolescents take more risk than either children or adults do. This risk-taking or impulsivity involves distinct brain networks related to the ability to inhibit. Peer presence makes a greater difference in risk-taking, which is also seen in brain processes in adolescents compared with those beyond adolescence. Overall, adolescents show an increased sensitivity to both positive and negative rewards than do either adults or younger children.

Learning Objective 5: Discuss the concept of lifespan development and adulthood. In the 1960s and 1970s, psychologists began to expand the concept of human development to include lifespan development—following individuals across their lifespans in a theoretically integrated manner using psychological research.

One of the first theorists to present a map of lifespan development was Erik Erikson. He proposed that people experience eight major psychosocial stages—each stage defined by a major conflict or question that must be answered. His eight stages are: (1) trust versus mistrust; (2) autonomy versus shame and doubt; (3) initiative versus guilt; (4) industry versus inferiority; (5) identity versus role confusion; (6) intimacy versus isolation; (7) generativity versus stagnation; and (8) integrity versus despair.

At one time, aging was defined primarily in terms of loss of cognitive functions such as memory and an increase in medical problems. However, today the manner in which people age follows a number of different pathways. Some people do show mental or physical deterioration as they age. However, others retain both physical and mental abilities as they age. The study of this last group has been referred to as successful aging. Research shows an important role for exercise and social support in a healthy lifestyle and successful aging.

Study Resources

Review Questions

1. This chapter opened by saying: "We are all children who grew up." Now that you have come to the chapter's close, how would you answer the following questions based on the ideas and evidence presented:
   a. What factors do you think influenced your development?
   b. What would you see as the critical factors?
   c. Was it a series of single events or a more continuous process?
2. In Walter Mischel's study, will 5-year-old Amy eat the single marshmallow right away or will she be able to wait and receive the reward of two marshmallows? Of course, we don't know, but what would the following researchers say are the critical factors in determining what she will do:
   a. Charles Darwin?
   b. John Watson?
   c. Jean Piaget?
   d. Lev Vygotsky?
   e. John Bowlby?
   f. Harry Harlow?
   g. Mary Ainsworth?
   h. Nelson, Fox, and Zeanah in the Romanian adoption study?

3. In this chapter, most of the coverage of the stages of human development across the lifespan begins at birth. To complete the picture, construct a timeline of the human brain and nervous system development that happens in the womb before birth.
4. In all primates, early development is the foundation from which the rest of an individual's life spins out. Humans share some developmental aspects, for example, certain reflexes, with other primates. However, some capabilities are considered to be uniquely human. From what has been presented in this chapter, create a table showing developmental aspects and processes humans share with other primates and those that are uniquely human.
5. One of the tasks of preschool and elementary school children is the integration of cognitive, emotional, and motor tasks. Mark Greenberg, the lead developer of the PATHS curriculum, has asked you to develop a brief statement to mail to elementary school principals describing the program, its purpose, target audience, and evidence of outcomes. What would you write?
6. This chapter has focused on human development from the perspective of the developing individual. Now take the perspective of the parent. Briefly describe the role of the parent throughout the developmental stages: infancy, childhood, adolescence, and adulthood.
7. Changes during adolescence are seen in every domain including physical, psychological, cognitive, emotional, and relationships. You've just come through adolescence yourself. Given what you've read so far in this book and what you've experienced in your own life, how would you assess the importance of each of these domains and their interrelationships in your own development?
8. Based on what we know about human development through the lifespan, what recommendations would you make to the following organizations to foster successful development during the period they cover:
    a. Mother–baby clinic?
    b. Day care or nursery school?
    c. Primary school?
    d. High school?
    e. College?
    f. Community psychology clinic?
    g. Retirement community?

For Further Reading

Hrdy, S. (1999). *Mother Nature.* New York: Pantheon.
Hrdy, S. (2009). *Mothers and Others.* Cambridge, MA: Harvard University Press.
Nelson, C., Fox, N., & Zeanah, C. (2014). *Romania's Abandoned Children.* Cambridge, MA: Harvard University Press.
Taylor, S. (2001). *The Tending Instinct.* New York: Henry Holt, & Co.

Web Resources

CDC fetal alcohol disorder—https://www.cdc.gov/ncbddd/fasd/facts.html
CDC alcohol during pregnancy—https://www.cdc.gov/ncbddd/fasd/alcohol-use.html
Unexpected event in infants—http://www.npr.org/blogs/ed/2015/04/02/396812961/why-babies-love-and-learn-from-magic-tricks and the supplemental information published online at http://www.sciencemag.org/content/348/6230/91/suppl/DC1

Key Terms and Concepts

- accommodation
- assimilation
- attachment
- cognitive development
- concrete operations
- critical or sensitive periods
- dynamic system theory
- habituation
- imitation learning
- intrinsic motivation
- lifespan development
- mirror neurons
- moral development
- object permanence
- patterns of attachment styles
- plasticity
- preoperational stage
- psychosocial stages
- schema
- secure base
- sensorimotor stage
- strange situation
- successful aging
- temperament
- theory of mind

5 Sensation and Perception

LEARNING OBJECTIVES

5.1 Describe how psychophysics relates to our understanding of how we experience the world.

5.2 Describe key processes in the visual system.

5.3 Explain what happens in the auditory system that allows us to hear.

5.4 Summarize the role that chemical processes play in smell and taste.

5.5 Describe the different senses of touch and how we experience pain.

James Wannerton lives in London and since he was a child, he has experienced sounds as tastes. Every sound he hears, he also involuntarily experiences a taste. He reports that every time he stops or passes through a London Tube (subway) station, he experiences a taste and a feeling in his mouth. Since he has ridden the London Underground often over the past 50 years, he has created a map of each station and the taste he experiences in response to the different sounds as he goes through that station. Although extra sounds at a particular station could be different on a given day, the tracks and shape of each underground station make for the same sound at each unique station (Cook, 2014).

Another person, John, had no problem talking about an object. He could recall the object from memory and describe it. He could even draw it from memory. However, when he looked at the object, he could no longer access this knowledge. He clearly could describe what he was seeing in terms of size and shape and appearance. He could say the object was long and thin with a shiny surface. The connection between what he was seeing and what he knew about the object disappeared when he looked at the object. He also found it difficult to recognize friends and family from their faces. Further, although John found reading a passage to be difficult and slow, he found it easy to write (Humphreys & Riddoch, 2014).

Another individual whom we shall call Laura reported that when she watched an object in motion, she felt sick. Laura said that she no longer saw movement in objects. Rather, the objects appeared as "restless" or "jumping around." She could see objects at different distances and at different locations. However, she could not see them move from one location to another. According to Laura, the objects appeared jumping from one location to another but nothing in between. This caused her real problems when walking in the city. Traffic had become very frightening. Although she could identify cars, she could not tell if they were moving or not (Heywood & Zihl, 1999).

The experiences described can be understood by knowing about our brain and how it creates our experiences. The story of James Wannerton reflects a condition called *synesthesia*. **Synesthesia** is the condition in which the experience of one sense automatically

182 Sensation and Perception

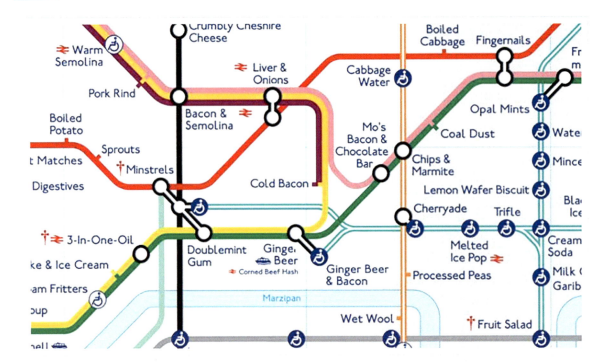

Figure 5-1 Part of the London subway map as experienced by James Wannerton.

Source: Cook (2014); Spiers and Maguire (2006); Hobson and Pace-Schott (2002); Hobson (1989, 2009); Golombek and Rosenstein (2010).

produces experience in another. For Wannerton, sound produced tastes and feelings in his mouth. For others, sounds produce colors. Some people see a color when they look at numbers or words. Synesthesia is present in about 1% of the population. Many people with synesthesia would not want to change the way they experience the world.

The next two stories of John and Laura are not as pleasant. These cases resulted from damage to the brain through a stroke or an automobile accident. In reading these cases, you can see that our vision of people and things is not a single process but a number of different processes that are put together by our brains. We also understand movement and color of objects and people as part of the world outside of us, although it requires a brain to make it happen.

You could also tell your own story as you ride a roller coaster at your favorite theme park. You receive lots of information that create sensations. You hear sounds, see the world moving quickly, and have difficulty determining where you are in space. The roller coaster and other rides are designed to give you experiences that are not part of your everyday life. However, even in your everyday life, your brain is busy creating experiences that are influenced by what is going on in the external world.

This chapter is about understanding how the external world influences what is going on in your brain and giving you basic sensory experiences. The brain is actively doing tasks of its own during these external stimuli changes. Thus, your sensory experiences are a combination of what your brain is doing and what is impacting your senses from the external world. Using this information, your brain creates your reality.

The nature of our nervous system actually determines whether we sense something or nothing at all. You can stand in a big city and see and hear various sensations. However, you don't experience the radio waves or cell phone activity that is all around you. Although similar in nature to the frequency of light that we do see, radio waves and cell phone activity are energies at a different frequency. As humans, we do not have receptors that are sensitive to these frequencies.

In terms of sensory systems across species, we can see how evolution favored one sensory system over the others. In humans, this is seen in the sensory organization in the brain in that the visual connections from the eye to the brain contain more than one million fibers, whereas the auditory system contains only about 30,000 fibers. Thus, it is not surprising that you primarily use vision rather than smell or sound to move around your world. Since seeing is such an important sense for humans, this chapter will focus on vision.

In this chapter, you will learn the basic mechanisms of sensation and perception. It is our nervous system responding to certain types of stimulation that gives us an experience that we interpret as reality. Thus, our experience of reality is based on how our nervous system is constructed. However, as you know from going to the grocery store when you are hungry, our sensory processes can be changed by what is going on in our body. In this chapter, you will see how ongoing activities in the brain are modified by external stimulation to give us experiences.

The manner in which our brain and nervous system take energy that exists around us and turns it into an experience is a critical aspect of sensation and perception. **Sensation** refers to the manner in which our receptor system transforms energy into activity that can be interpreted by the brain. **Perception** is the manner in which the brain makes sense of this activity. Said in other terms, sensation and perception is the study of the way our brain creates a world that we experience external to ourselves or, in other cases such as pain, the location may be internal.

Let's begin with simple sensations. Since the time of Aristotle (384–322 BCE) more than 2,300 years ago, five sensory systems have been described. These are *vision*, *hearing*, *touch*, *taste*, and *smell*. More recently, it has been suggested that *pain* and *temperature* should also be included. Each of the sensory systems uses different biological processes referred to as **transducers** to initiate the sensory process. The transducer in the auditory system turns sound waves into mechanical and then electrical impulses. The transducers in our eye turn light energy into electrical impulses.

There are also connections between the brain areas involved in different sensory processes that give us an integration of sensory processes. Putting these together gives us the feeling of a single event. These specific connections are referred to as *pathways* and **networks**. These pathways and networks allow us to see, hear, and feel the world as if it is a coherent whole. However, our brain begins with information from each of the sensory systems alone. Although there is a relationship between the physical characteristics of the stimulus and the way our sensory system responds, there is not a perfect relationship. This was studied in the 1800s with the establishment of the field of psychophysics.

Psychophysics

The research of Gustav Fechner (1801–1887) in the 1800s helped to establish the field of *psychophysics*. **Psychophysics** is the study of the relationship between the physical characteristics of a stimulus and the manner in which we experience it. Fechner noted that although there is a relationship between the increase in the physical intensity and the subjective experience, it is not a linear relationship. For example, we do not experience a 200-watt light bulb as being twice as bright as a 100-watt bulb. What this suggests is that experiences in the mental world are not the same as changes in the physical world.

Sensory Measurement Thresholds

Part of Fechner's work was based on studies by Ernst Heinrich Weber (1795–1878). Weber had studied how much physical difference is needed for you to detect a change. He had individuals place a weight in their hand. Then they lifted a second weight and noted if it was different from the first. Weber wanted to know how much more the second weight needed to be before people noticed a difference. You can ask a similar question about any of our sensory processes. How much does light need to change in frequency before you notice a different color, or how much louder does a sound need to be before you experience a louder sound. This difference is referred to as the *just-noticeable difference or JND*.

Fechner also noticed that the JND changes as the original weights change. That is, if you had a 100-gram weight (about one-fifth of a pound) and added 2 grams, you could tell a difference. However, if you had a 200-gram weight and added 2 grams, you would not notice the difference, but you would notice a 4-gram change. If you did this over a number of different weights you would notice that there is a constant proportion of the original weight that is required to notice a change. Fechner referred to this relationship as *Weber's law*. The constant proportion described in Weber's law varies by modality. It is .02 in the weight example just described. However, it is larger when determining light intensity or the saltiness of one taste versus another.

Weber also studied our ability to detect differences in tactile stimulation. For example, you could ask how far apart two pin pricks would need to be on your skin before you could experience them as two pins rather one. You may notice that this distance is farther on your back than on your fingers, for example. A measure related to JND is called the *difference threshold*. This is the actual physical measure between the original stimulus and the one first noticed as different.

When there is just one stimulus present, the concept is the *absolute threshold*. The basic question is what amount of stimulation is necessary for you to detect that it is present. In this chapter you will learn that on a dark night you can detect a candle at 20 miles. In order to determine the absolute threshold, you would simply have someone move the candle away from you until it could no longer be detected. The basics for determining thresholds were described in detail in Fechner's 1860 book, *Elements of Psychophysics*.

CONCEPT CHECK

1. Define the terms below including their role in the human sensory system.
    a. Sensation
    b. Perception
    c. Transducer
2. How does psychophysics relate to our understanding of how we experience the world?
3. What is just-noticeable difference (JND), and how are difference threshold and absolute threshold related to it?

Vision

Our ability to see and use visual information has evolved to aid us on a variety of levels. On a survival level, vision helps us survive and avoid danger. On a sexual level, we see others as attractive and desirable and potential sexual partners. On a social level, we have evolved mechanisms related to those people we want to be with and those we want to avoid. Visual processes play an important role in additional cultural processes such as reading and art. We see some images as beautiful while we see others as awful. At least half of our brain is related directly or indirectly to the processing of visual information including areas involved in the recognition of faces.

If you ask most of us what we see when we look at the world, we might respond that we see a blue sky, or green leaves on a tree, or the texture of a building. We can generally go into great detail about what is there. However, if you were to ask physicists what is there, they would tell you that what exists is energy. It is this energy that our nervous system turns into colors, shapes, movement, and a variety of other sensations.

Although we rarely think about it, our visual system is really amazing. If you were in a desert at night with no external light, you could detect candlelight from more than 20 miles away. You can also see stars millions of miles away. The visual system is also able to produce a visual image whether it is a dark night or a bright day. Let us now begin with the structure of the visual system and how this relates to its function.

The Visual System Is Sensitive to Electromagnetic Energy

Let's begin with light. Light is *electromagnetic energy*. Physicists have considered light both as made up of waves and as a stream of particles or photons. Some receptors in our eye require a large number of photons to create a response while other receptors require fewer photons. Researchers interested in vision tend to see light as photons when discussing the firing of individual receptors and as waves when describing the characteristics of light. Both definitions of light are correct.

The light we see is only a small part of the electromagnetic spectrum. Different parts of the overall spectrum are associated with gamma rays, X-rays, ultraviolet rays, infrared rays, radar, microwaves, cell phone activity, and various forms of radio and television broadcasts over the air. The part of the spectrum that we can see is found between ultraviolet rays and infrared rays.

In terms of the visual spectrum, we refer to this light in terms of waves. As such, these waves can be described in terms of two factors. *Amplitude* refers to how large it is. *Frequency* refers to how often it recurs. Frequency is also described in terms of *wavelength*, which is how much distance there is between two consecutive waves (see **Figure 5-2**).

Since graphs of the electromagnetic spectrum may be in terms of frequency or wavelength, it can be noted that a higher frequency is associated with a shorter length between cycles and a lower frequency is associated with a longer wavelength.

When our eye transforms the visual spectrum, we see the lower frequencies (longer wavelengths) as red and orange and the higher frequencies (shorter wavelengths) as blue and violet. The greens and yellows are in between. Why might we humans be sensitive to this particular part of the electromagnetic spectrum?

Evolution offers us one answer to this question. Little more than 500 million years ago, there was an increase in diversity of life forms on Earth. Organisms existing at that time lived in water. One characteristic of water is that it passes some frequencies in the electromagnetic spectrum better than others. As the graph in **Figure 5-3** demonstrates, those frequencies that are least affected when passed through water correspond to those frequencies of light to which our visual system is most sensitive. Thus, although the visual system continued to evolve as organisms lived outside of water, the physical frequencies processed by our visual system harken back to adaptations manifested more than 500 million years

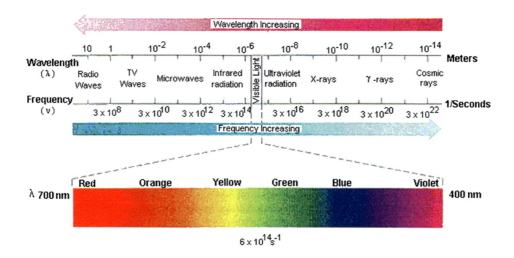

Figure 5-2 Showing wavelengths and frequencies of colors. Wavelength is the length of a single cycle. Frequency is the number of cycles in a given time—usually a second.

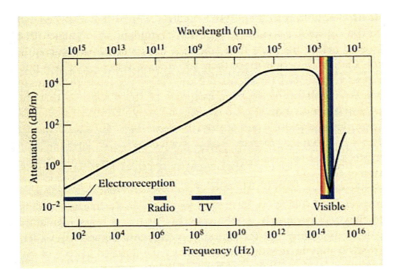

Figure 5-3 Attenuation of wavelength in water. This graph shows those frequencies that are not reduced as they pass through water are the same ones as the colors we see. The higher the line on the *y*-axis, the less of that frequency that could be experienced.
Source: Allman (2001, p. 67).

ago. By the way, you may have also noted in the graph that low frequencies (approximately 100 Hz) were also transmitted without reduction in water. These are frequencies used by electric fish to probe and sense their environment.

It also happened that during this period of increasing diversity more than 500 million years ago, new genetic variations developed that produced different types of *photoreceptors*. A **photoreceptor** is simply a cell that responds when light hits it. One type of photoreceptor was sensitive to low light. These light-sensitive cells, which later evolved as *rods*, allow us to see in dim light.

Another type of photoreceptor was produced that required greater illumination (more photons). Over time, the receptors of this system differentially became sensitive to different frequencies in the visual spectrum. These were the forerunners of the *cones* in our visual system that allow us to experience colors. The genes for cones differ in different species resulting in different sensitivity to different parts of the visual spectrum. In humans, the genes responsible for red and green sensitivity are located close to each other on a single chromosome, whereas the genes for blue sensitivity are located elsewhere. This suggests that blue sensitivity evolved at a different time than red and green sensitivity.

The visual system also evolved to solve a large variety of tasks that differ in different species (Baden, Euler, & Berens, 2020). As humans, we rarely think about how stable the world stays as we move our heads and go through the space around us. If we moved a video camera in the same way, we would see more of a blur. To maintain our visual world in a stable manner, our *vestibular system* senses movement and sends this information to the hindbrain, which in turn sends signals to the eye muscles. You will be introduced to the role of the vestibular system later in the chapter.

The information from the vestibular system allows our eyes to go in the opposite direction from our movement in order to compensate for movement and leave the image on our retina stable. Pretty clever engineering. Further, corrections take place through the cerebellum, which compares changes in eye velocity and head velocity. The front-facing location of our eyes allows us to determine depth, which would have been helpful in human history for both eye–hand coordination and catching animals. Like us, other animals such as owls and cats with flat faces can experience depth using both eyes. Let us now turn to how the eye functions and uses the brain to create the visual world that we experience.

A Tour of the Eye

In this section you will be taken on a tour of the structure and function of the eye. On this tour, you can note what each aspect contributes to our construction of our visual world. Let us begin with the human eye, which is shown in **Figure 5-4**.

Light reaches the *cornea* where it is bent and the *lens* where it is focused. Both are located at the front of the eye. The object we see is focused on the **retina** at the back of the eye. If your eye does not focus the image on the retina exactly, then you are either nearsighted or farsighted. If the image is focused in front of the retina, you are nearsighted (referred

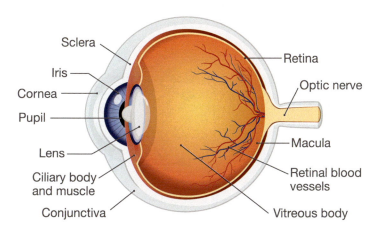

Figure 5-4 Structure of the human eye: note the fovea is located at the center of the macula, which produces the greatest visual acuity.

to as myopia). If it focuses behind the retina, you are farsighted (referred to as hyperopia). Your glasses or contact lenses cause the image to fall on the retina. Also, as most people age, their eyes lose the ability of the lens to change shape as easily as they did before middle age. This results in difficulty to focus on things close to the eye. This condition is referred to as presbyopia.

The physics of this is that when an object is somewhere about 30 feet from our eyes, the reflected light from an object is no longer parallel. This requires greater *refraction* or bending of the light waves to produce a shape image on the retina. This is referred to as *accommodation*. The lens of your eye is actually elastic—when we view objects at a distance, it becomes flatter, and when we view objects close up, it bulges forward. With aging, the lens becomes less elastic and less refraction is possible with close-up objects. Many people by age 50 find it difficult to see clearly close up or read small print without glasses. Quite a change from the 1-year-old infant who can see objects located just beyond his or her nose.

The *pupil* is surrounded by muscles contained in the *iris*, which let the pupil allow in more or less light according to the intensity of the light energy. If you want to see this for yourself, stand in front of a mirror with the lights off. Then, turn them on and watch your pupils change in size. By the way, as light is reflected off the iris, its pigmentation determines the color that you see in someone's eyes. About half of humans worldwide have brown eyes. If you have blue eyes, you probably have an ancestor who lived near the Baltic Sea.

Within the eye there is a clear fluid referred to as the *vitreous*. Light passes through this fluid and reaches the back of the eye that contains the receptors that change the electromagnetic energy of light into electrical energy. It is the job of this electrical energy to create information in the brain. You may note that, from an optics standpoint, the actual image that falls on the retina is turned upside down. This of course is not critical since it is the neuronal information that determines what we see. Although extremely complex, the retina is only about .2 mm thick.

Figure 5–5 shows you the eye with the three main layers of the retina.

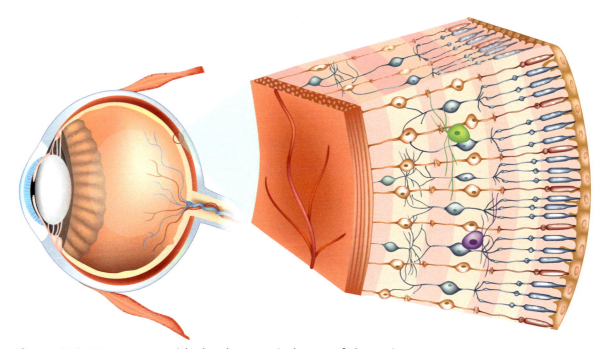

Figure 5-5 Human eye with the three main layers of the retina.

Rods and Cones

If you look at the figure of the retina, you may at first think it is backward. However, it is not. It is more like a medieval castle in which modern wiring was placed outward from the wall rather than behind it. The furthest layer of the retina is composed of some 100 million photoreceptor cells that are sensitive to light. There are some 95 million rods and some 5 million cones. Rods and cones are named for their shape (see **Figure 5-6**).

The easiest way to think about *rods* and *cones* is to consider rods as related to nighttime vision and cones to daytime vision. Rods allow you to see in dim light. They are much more sensitive than cones to the few photons of light energy available on dark nights. When light strikes one of the photoreceptors, the photons of light are absorbed, which in turn modifies the flow of current in the neuron.

There are three types of cones. Historically, these have been referred to as "green," "red," and "blue" cones. This is technically not correct since the experience of color is determined by comparing the activity of each type of cone with that of the other types. In each type of cone, the chemical sensitive to light is sensitive to a different frequency. This gives us the ability to experience color. Cones also allow you to see with high-spatial acuity, which gives you the ability to see detail.

Rods and cones also differ in their location. There are many more rods in the peripheral parts of the retina and more cones located in a more central region of the retina called the

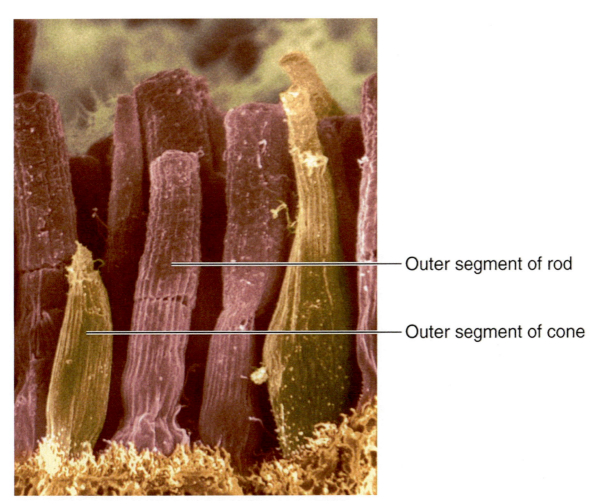

Figure 5-6 Outer segments of rods and cones. Both rods and cones respond to specific frequencies of light.

fovea, although there tend to be fewer of the blue cones at the fovea. One implication of having rods in the periphery is that your peripheral vision is very good on dark nights.

Whether we look at something directly or in the periphery can make a difference. Look at the Leonardo da Vinci portrait of the Mona Lisa. Margaret Livingstone (2000) pointed out that if you look at her forehead or other areas away from her mouth, you will use the lower frequency rods and see her having a smile. If you look at her mouth, you will use your higher frequency cones and the smile will be less apparent.

It is the purpose of the rods and cones to transform light energy into electrical activity. This is accomplished by a chemical process that works differently in rods and cones. The photochemical in rods is called *rhodopsin*, which is very sensitive to light. This is what allows you to see with clarity at night. However, bright light such as daytime sunshine will cause rhodopsin to not function in the same way. Thus, in the daytime you see mainly with cones that contain different photochemicals.

A new device for those who have lost functioning in rods and cones is described in the box: Applying Psychological Science—Bionic Eye Implants Gives Vision to Those with Profound Vision Loss.

Applying Psychological Science—Bionic Eye Implants Give Vision to Those with Profound Vision Loss

Philip Booth first began losing his sight at the age of 7. Booth has an inheritable disease in which the rods and cones in his retina slowly began to stop working. By age 30 he was totally blind. However, in the last few years, he has been testing a device that allows him to see letters and structures such as doors and windows (da Cruz et al., 2013).

The device is referred to as Argus II. Argus II has two major components. The first is a pair of glasses that contains a video camera with a processing unit that can wirelessly transmit the visual signal. The second component is a grid of electrodes that is placed directly on the retina. The wireless connections means that there are no wires going to the person's retina. Additionally, only a single operation is needed to initially implant the electrode grid. When the wireless signals reach the electrodes, the cells in the retina are stimulated in relation to the visual image recorded by the camera. These cells produce action potentials that go to the visual areas of the person's brain.

Argus II has been approved in the United States by the US Food and Drug Administration (FDA) and in some countries of Europe. Research testing the device with a number of participants has shown it to be effective over at least six years (for example, da Cruz et al., 2013). At this point, the Argus II does not produce normal vision. It limits the vision of individuals to letters, words, and some large objects. However, it shows that it is possible to create a prosthesis that improves vision. One would expect that with better visual processors and increased electrode arrays, even better vision would be possible.

Thought Question: Why is it particularly important to augment the sensory capabilities of young children? What ideas do you have for innovations to enhance any of our senses?

CONCEPT CHECK

1. In what specific ways has our ability to see and use visual information evolved to aid us in living in the world?
2. What is the electromagnetic spectrum, and how is it related to vision?
3. Draw your own image of the structure of the human eye. Label the important parts and describe the function of each. Be sure to include at least the following: cones, cornea, iris, lens, pupil, retina, rods, and vitreous fluid.
4. Rods and cones are both photoreceptors. What specific contributions does each provide to visual processing in humans?

Vision and Color

Before leaving the eye to understand visual processing in the brain, let's look at color. Although much of the information in our visual world comes from shapes and edges, color offers richness that lets us quickly determine evolutionarily valuable information such as "is the fruit ripe?" It was Newton who understood that color is not part of the external world itself but something that humans create from specific parameters of the energy of light. At this point let's ask how this energy produces the sensations needed to give us the perception of color.

Wavelengths and Color

The cones in the retina are sensitive to different wavelengths of electromagnetic radiation that the brain is able to change into the experience of color. There are three different cone types in terms of frequency sensitivity.

The first type is sensitive to a wavelength of about 430 nanometers (nm), which we experience as blue. A nanometer is one-billionth of a meter. The second is most sensitive to a wavelength of 530 nm, which we experience as green, and the third is most sensitive to 560 nm, which we see as red. However, if we only had one type of cone, we would not see that color. Why is that?

Our ability to see colors requires that the signals from the different types of cones be compared in the brain. For example, the experience of orange results from the red cones being the most activated, the green cones being less activated, and the blue cones being least activated. In this way we have the experience of seeing orange.

Our experience of color is actually the result of our nervous system comparing the signals from each of the cones against one another. Because of the computation nature of experiencing color, blue, red, and green cones are more accurately referred to in terms of their wavelength sensitivity as S (short), M (middle), and L (long) cones. But we are getting ahead of the story. Let's now look at how we historically came to understand color vision.

Theory of Color

Isaac Newton helped establish our modern understanding of color. He is well known for demonstrating that sunlight could be broken down into a spectrum of colors by using a prism. He further showed that this spectrum could be refracted to produce the original white light.

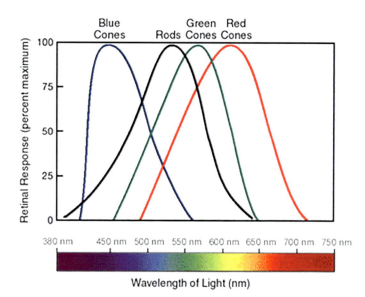

Figure 5-7 Wavelength of light. Each of the receptors in the eye is sensitive to different frequencies of light.

Later, the fact that any color can be produced by mixing red, green, and blue light was demonstrated by the British physicist Thomas Young in the early 1800s. He began by considering the impossibility of the retina to contain receptors for every possible color. Since this would be impossible, Young suggested that there must be a limited number of receptors that respond to a limited number of colors.

Young then suggested that three kinds of "fibers" existed in the eye. One is sensitive to red, another to green, and the third to blue. Young determined that in people with normal color vision, three different color lights (red, blue, green) are necessary to match any other possible color.

In the middle of the 1800s, Hermann von Helmholtz expanded Young's idea and also had individuals match a standard color by varying red, blue, and green light sources. He also sought to elaborate on how the visual system is able to experience color. The idea that variations in three different light colors lies at the bottom of our experience of color came to be known as the ***Young–Helmholtz trichromatic theory of color***.

An alternative theory of color vision was developed by Ewald Hering (1834–1918) who demonstrated that there are some aspects of color perception that the Young–Helmholtz trichromatic theory could not explain. This alternative theory is referred to as the ***opponent-process theory of color vision***. As the name implies, certain colors result in opposite responses in the visual system. Let's begin with an example, as can be seen in **Figure 5-8**. If you look at the center of the American flag for about 30 seconds and then look at a blank white sheet of paper and blink, you will see the real colors of the American flag.

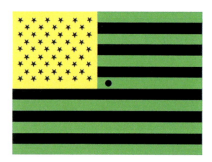

Figure 5-8 Afterimage demonstration—look at the flag for 30 seconds and then look at a white sheet of paper.

The results are that blue produces a yellow afterimage and yellow produces a blue one. Likewise, green produces a red afterimage and red produces a green one. Hering also postulated a third opponent mechanism that involved light and dark, that is, black and white.

Initially seen as opposing theories, the trichromatic and the opponent process are now seen as complementary. In fact, each theory describes physiological mechanisms for color vision at different locations in the visual system. The trichromatic theory reflects early color processing involving the cones and the opponent process theory reflects later processing by the ganglion cells in the retina.

Color Blindness

In performing color-matching studies in the 1800s, it was determined that some individuals used only two of the three light sources to match colors. These individuals are commonly called **color blind**. Some color-blind individuals matched colors to a standard color by using only green and blue light while others used only blue and red light. These individuals are called *dichromats*. Color blindness is found more often in males than females, since it is caused by a recessive allele on the X chromosome as described previously. **Figure 5-9** is one common test of color blindness in which those with normal color vision would see a "2" in the middle of the figure.

At this point, we have discussed the basic structure of the eye as well as how fundamental information such as color is processed. However, basic stimulation of light on the retina

Figure 5-9 Common test of color blindness—you are to tell the number you see in the image.

needs to be processed by our brain to give us the rich and complex information we experience when we see the world. Let us now turn to how visual information is communicated from the eye to the brain.

CONCEPT CHECK

1. If color is not part of the external world, how do we create it?
2. What did each of the following researchers contribute to our understanding of how we process colors:
   a. Isaac Newton?
   b. Thomas Young?
   c. Hermann von Helmholtz?
   d. Ewald Hering?
3. Most humans have three different types of cones. What happens when a genetic variation causes an individual to have two types of cones? What would happen if an individual only had one type of cone?

The Eye Connects to the Brain

We now leave the eye itself and move to its connection with the brain. That is, the next point on our tour is the place where visual information leaves the eye. The axons of the ganglion cells are long and end in the midbrain. The point at which these axons leave the eye is referred to as the **optic disk or blind spot**. This is also the point at which blood vessels enter the eye. Although there are no receptors in this part of the eye to respond to light, the brain fills in the missing information by using information from the other eye and eye movement. Thus, you see a complete scene without a hole in the image.

The demonstration in **Figure 5-10** allows you to experience this lack of receptors at the blind spot. Simply hold this book up to your face with one eye closed. Starting about four inches from your face and focusing on the cross, slowly move the book back until the cow disappears. This is the point at which the cow falls on your blind spot.

Your **visual field** is nothing more than what you see in front of you without moving your head or eyes. Drawing an imaginary vertical line down the middle of this field creates a *right visual field and a left visual field*.

Your left visual field is projected on to the right side of both of your eyes. In turn, the right visual field goes to the left side of each eye. Information from the left and right visual fields is kept separate in the brain and, as shown in **Figure 5-11**, goes to different hemispheres. The left visual field information goes to the right hemisphere, and the information from the right visual field goes to the left hemisphere. Although 90% of the retina neurons go to a part of the thalamus, the lateral geniculate (LGN), information from the eye also goes directly to the *superior colliculus*.

Figure 5-10 To find your blind spot, close one eye and look at the cross. Begin with the image about four inches from your face. Slowly move the image away from you. At one point the cow will disappear as it falls on your blind spot.

Sensation and Perception 195

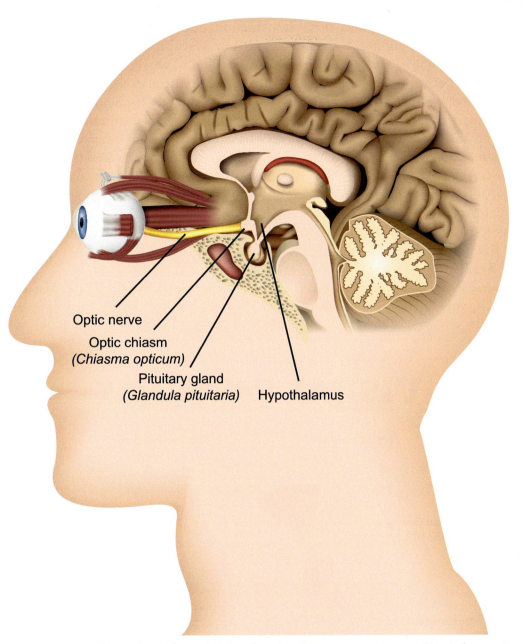

Figure 5-11 Images from the left and right visual fields go to each eye. The information from each visual field is kept separate. Information from the right visual field goes to the occipital lobe of the left hemisphere. Information from the left visual field goes to the occipital lobe of the right hemisphere.

The Primary Visual Cortex

At this point on our tour of the visual system, we have gone from light-sensitive photoreceptors in the retina to ganglion cells capable of producing action potentials. The pathways continue to the LGN and then to the primary visual cortex. At each level, the brain is able to construct greater abstraction in relation to the visual stimuli.

At the primary visual cortex level, the visual stimuli are seen mainly in terms of lines, edges, movement, and color. This information is also interpreted in terms of the context in which it is presented. To continue the tour, we need to move to areas involved in even more abstract processes including motion, depth, form, and color.

It turns out that as we process visual information, our brains want to know two things. The first is what something is. Is it a house, a tree, or a face? It is also at this point that other processes such as our memory becomes involved. That is, we recognize a face because we have seen that person before and stored that information in memory. It can be noted that the *what* pathway is the only visual pathway that leads directly to the hippocampus, an area critically important for memory. This type of connection in the brain allows us to give meaning to basic visual information; we see something and remember what it is.

The second question we seek to answer is where something is located in our world. This pathway has to do with spatially related factors such as motion, depth, and location. Both the what and *where* pathways begin as light stimulates our retina, which sends information to the primary visual cortex also called V1. In technical terms, we say there is a ventral pathway to the temporal lobe involved in processing what something is, and a dorsal pathway to the parietal lobe involved in processing where something is. This can be seen in **Figure 5-12**.

Other researchers have emphasized the role the ventral pathway plays in visual perception and the role the dorsal pathway plays in visual control of action (for example, Milner

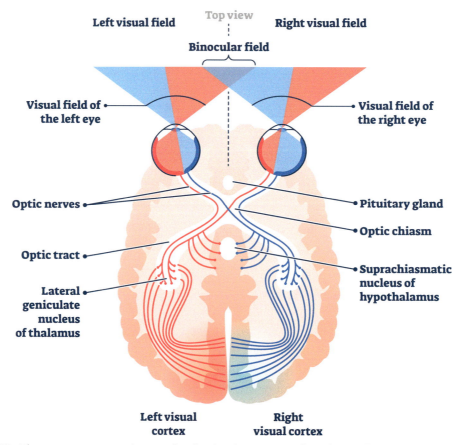

Figure 5-12 There are two pathways in the brain—one related to where an object is and one related to what the object is.

Source: http://www.ssc.education.ed.ac.uk/courses/vi&multi/vmay092ii.html

& Goodale, 2006). In this case the ventral pathway helps an organism know what something is and its relation to space and time. The dorsal pathway is involved in using vision for doing things in the world. When you play tennis or baseball or other sports, you are constantly using visual information to direct your actions. We constantly estimate what will come next.

CONCEPT CHECK

1. What is the blind spot? Since we all have it, how are we able to see a whole scene without a hole in the middle of it?
2. Once visual information has left the eye, what are the primary structures it passes through on its way to and through the brain to be processed?

Depth

If you were asked whether the world is three-dimensional, you would quickly answer "yes." However, as you think about the perception of depth, you have to consider how your visual world began with visual stimuli falling on the retina. That is to say, you begin with a two-dimensional image on the retina, and from that your visual system constructs a three-dimensional world with depth. Somewhat an amazing feat, don't you think?

There are two types of information that humans use to perceive depth. The first is a set of cues that can be determined from using only one eye or *monocular cues*. How we perceive depth was a critical question for artists of the Renaissance such as Leonardo da Vinci. Many of the paintings prior to this time, especially religious paintings, were often two-dimensional and viewed as flat.

Monocular Cues

We use a number of cues to determine depth. Some of the cues we use for determining depth with just one eye are as follows:

1. **Our knowledge of the object**: From experience we know the size of people, trees, houses, buildings, mountains, and so forth. From this information we can determine whether something is close or far.
2. **Occlusion**: If a person or object hides the view of another person or object, we conclude that what is unhidden is closer.
3. **Linear perspective**: Parallel lines such as a railroad track appear to come together as they approach the horizon. This is called the *vanishing point* in art. Greater distance is experienced with a greater convergence.
4. **Size perspective**: If we assume two objects are the same size, we perceive the smaller one to be farther away.
5. **Distribution of light and shadows**: The manner in which light and dark fall give us the impression of depth. Likewise, brighter colors are seen as closer.
6. **Motion**: Even with one eye, we experience objects that move more slowly across our retina to be farther away than objects that move quickly. As you run through the woods, for example, the bushes next to your path move more quickly across the retina than do the trees farther away. An even more classic example is looking out the window of a fast car. You see the area close to the road moving very quickly and that in the distance moving more slowly. This is referred to as *motion parallax*.

Binocular Cues

In humans, our eyes are separated from each other by about 6 cm. What this means is that for distances of less than about 100 feet, each eye receives slightly different information when looking at the same scene. You can see this for yourself by quickly closing one eye after the other while looking at an object 5 or 10 feet away. As you close and open each eye, you will see the object shift slightly from side to side.

An even more graphic illustration is to hold your finger up in front of you and again alternate the closing of one eye and then the other. In comparison to the background image, your finger will move from side to side. This is particularly clear if you line up your finger with some vertical line in the background, such as a utility pole or the edge of a bookcase.

The fact that the image falls on a different place on the retina of each eye is called *binocular disparity*. Thus, the greatest differences or disparity between the images on the two retinas would come from objects that are close, whereas those at a great distance will show almost none at all.

Research has shown that there are cells in V1 that are sensitive to the differences in information received by the two eyes in terms of binocular disparity. Following the *where* or M-pathway from the visual cortex to the parietal area, one can also find cells sensitive to the disparity between the image on the two retinas. Additionally, there appear to be some cells that are sensitive to particular directions of movement and the amount of disparity. For example, some cells fire to a right-moving object that is close to the observer, whereas other cells fire to left-moving objects that are far away.

In the demonstration where you focused on your finger with alternating eyes, another process was at work. To focus on your finger or any other close object requires that each of your eyes moves and turns more inward. When looking at a distant scene, your eyes are more parallel. Whether you focus close or focus far requires different eye-movement positions. The muscle movement of the eyes gives an additional channel of feedback to the brain for determining depth.

Visual Illusions

One aspect of our visual system is that a variety of processes are occurring at the same time. This parallel processing allows us to create an image quickly. However, at times this results in what have come to be called **illusions**. In Chapter 1 you saw a white triangle that was not there. In **Figure 5-13**, we all see a white square, but actually there is no square there. It is the construction of our nervous system.

We see what we expect to see. As you look at **Figure 5-14**, you read "A, B, C" in a horizontal manner and "12, 13, 14" in a vertical manner. Of course, the middle symbol is exactly the same. This is referred to as *a top-down process* since what is expected, or the idea of a particular word, determines what is seen. If you just focus on the "13," you process the information from a *bottom-up perspective*. That is, your brain analyzes the nature of the stimuli such as a vertical line, curves, and so forth to determine that they are the numbers 1 and 3.

We tend to resolve the information that is presented to our sensory system in a *coherent manner*. This is based both on a top-down process in which our expectations help to form what we see and on a bottom-up process by which our sensory system puts together the individual features into a coherent scene (see Bar & Bubic, 2014 for an overview). One common experience of visual information is that we seek to create a *consistent image*. As

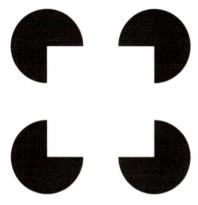

Figure 5-13 Image of white square—it is there, isn't it?

Figure 5-14 Image of A–B–C, 12–13–14—you see 13 or B depending on the context.

you look at the image below, you see either a man playing a saxophone or the face of a woman (**Figure 5-15**).

Not only do we see things (the white square) that are not there, but we are also able to see a world that cannot exist. The artist M. C. Escher enjoyed playing with our sensory systems in many of his etchings. You can see these online (for example, https://www.wikiart.org/en/m-c-escher). We can even make a static figure move (see **Figure 5–16**).

We think of the figures we just looked at as illusions. However, in some ways all of what we "see" is an illusion or construction of our nervous system (Eagleman, 2001). For example, we do not notice the edges of our visual field. That is, we don't notice where the top and bottom or left and right of our field of vision ends. Neither do we notice that our vision in the periphery is not as sharp as that in the center of our visual field. When we watch an old 35mm film at the movies, we "see" continuous motion, whereas what is really there is a sequence of individual still pictures presented one at a time. Illusions are important since they help us understand how the visual system works. In fact, illusions have been studied and described for at least 2,000 years.

Figure 5-15 Image of either a man playing a saxophone or the face of a woman.

Gestalt Psychology

At the turn of the last century, an approach developed in Germany that emphasized the manner in which our perceptual system organizes the visual world in a predetermined manner. The name of this approach was **Gestalt psychology**, which you read about previously. As you remember "gestalt" means *form* or *shape*. The basic idea is that the whole is more than the sum of the parts. That is to say, the parts of a visual scene become organized in a manner such that a whole image emerges. This also happens in music in which the song you experience is more than just the sum of the individual notes. There is a *form quality* to the experience of music that transcends the instrument on which it is played or the musical key in which it is played.

Figure 5-16 Making a static figure "move."

The field of Gestalt psychology was developed by Max Wertheimer, Kurt Koffka, and Wolfgang Köhler. Gestalt psychology emphasized the observance of perceptual phenomena with a small number of individuals. For example, some of Wertheimer's early work examined what he called the *phi phenomenon*, which is the experience of apparent motion when two lights are turned off and on at an interval of 50–60 milliseconds. The experience of motion from one light to the other emerges from the situation and cannot be explained by just knowing that two lights alternatively turn on and off. The individuals see the lights move from one to the other.

In 1915, Edgar Rubin in Denmark showed that our perceptual system organizes ambiguous stimuli in a definite manner. His famous Rubin's vase clearly demonstrates that given this ambiguous set of stimuli, our perceptual system will organize it in one of two ways, either as two faces or as a vase. This came to be known as the ***figure–ground relationship***.

When we see faces, the vase becomes the ground and is no longer viewed as a vase. The opposite is true when we see the vase.

By 1925, Koffka, Wertheim, and Köhler had defined a number of principles that describe the manner in which our sensory system organizes patterns of sensory stimuli. The basic idea is that there are a set number of principles that are part of our evolutionary history. These include:

1. **Similarity**: We tend to see objects that are similar to one another to be grouped together. For example, in **Figure 5-17** we see the dots organized in horizontal lines according to color. It is more difficult to view them as vertical lines.
2. **Proximity**: We tend to see objects that are close together as part of a group. For example, in **Figure 5-18** the four vertical lines in the figure are grouped into two separate groups.
3. **Closure**: We tend to fill in missing parts, even when the lines are not present. We have no problem seeing the panda in the illustration in **Figure 5-19**.
4. **Continuation**: We tend to follow lines to their culmination. We are more likely to see the X figure as composed of two continuous lines in **Figure 5-20**.
5. **Good figure**: We tend to see structures in a manner that makes it as simple as possible. For example, in **Figure 5-21**, we tend to see three boxes rather than three "L" shapes on one side and three upside-down "L" shapes on the other.

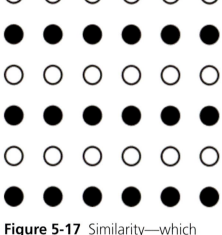

Figure 5-17 Similarity—which dots are alike?

Figure 5-18 Proximity—how do you group the lines?

Figure 5-19 Closure—we fill in the missing lines.

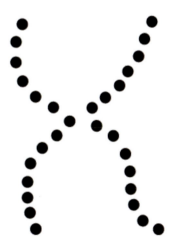

Figure 5-20 Continuation—there is a predictable way that we see the beginning and end of the line.

Figure 5-21 Good figure—we create figures such as the boxes.

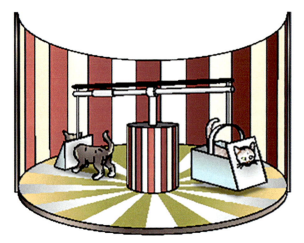

Figure 5-22 Apparatus for equating motion and consequent visual feedback.

Learning to See Requires Movement

Until the middle of the last century, most people thought that you learn to see as the result of looking at the object. External stimulation was seen as the key. Held and Hein (1963) showed us that it was more complicated than just having external stimulation. In a very ingenious study, they took ten pairs of kittens. Each pair was from a different litter. One kitten rode in a gondola-like apparatus with limited ability to move. The other kitten was free to move itself in a number of directions as it pulled the gondola in a circle. This procedure is pictured in **Figure 5-22**.

The kittens were exposed to the apparatus for 3 hours a day from 8 weeks to 12 weeks after birth. When not in the apparatus, the kittens were kept with their mothers and litter mates in a dark environment. What difference did riding versus walking have? Held and Hein looked at three different tasks.

The first task was simply holding the kitten in the experimenter's hand and slowly moving it down toward the edge of a table. Normal kittens anticipate contact with the table and put out their paws. The second task was a visual cliff situation. In this situation, a red checkered tablecloth is placed either directly below a piece of glass or about a yard or so below the piece of glass. The glass is illuminated from below in such a manner that the glass is not apparent. If the animal has depth perception, it will not walk on the glass with the pattern a yard below it. The third task was simply to hold the kitten in a standing position and then for an experimenter to move his or her hand quickly toward the kitten. Normal kittens show an eye blink response.

When the kittens that walked and pulled the gondola were tested on these three tasks, they showed the normal response on each of the tasks. The kittens that rode did not show the normal responses. Overall, this research shows the importance of self-produced movement in the development of visual processes. It can also be noted that human infants do not show a fear response to the visual cliff until they are able to crawl (Campos, Bertenthal, & Kermoian, 1992).

Plasticity

What happens if someone loses his or her vision early in life? Does this result in the person developing a greater sensitivity to sound or touch? This idea has been around at least since the time of the ancient Greeks. Today, a variety of studies have shown that this indeed is the case (Bavelier & Hirshorn, 2010). Individuals who become blind early in life are shown to have increased auditory abilities. Likewise, individuals who become deaf early in life are shown to have superior visual abilities. What happens to these areas in the brain? The unused visual cortex in individuals who are blind is taken over by other sensory processes such as touch or hearing. Some research has shown that the primary visual cortex (V1) in blind individuals may be involved in reading Braille or in hearing. This is also true with deaf individuals with the auditory cortex being taken over by other senses.

The World Is Your Laboratory—Human Sight Returned

The importance of learning to see has been highlighted through the study of unfortunate individuals who lose sight as children through accidents. Some of these have had transplant operations later in life that restored the ability to see. What they saw was of great interest to scientists.

One such case was a man referred to as S.B. born in 1906 who lost sight in both eyes at about 10 months of age (Gregory & Wallace, 1963). Fifty years later, this man received corneal grafts to restore sight. The vision psychologist Richard Gregory worked with the physician who performed the operation to study the manner in which sight was restored. The patient's initial sight was described as follows:

> S.B.'s first visual experience, when the bandages were removed, was of the surgeon's face. He described the experience as follows:—He heard a voice coming from in front of him and to one side: he turned to the source of the sound, and saw a "blur". He realized that this must be a face. Upon careful questioning, he seemed to think that he would not have known that this was a face if he had not previously heard the voice and known that voices came from faces.
>
> At the time we first saw him, he did not find faces "easy" objects. He did not look at a speaker's face, and made nothing of facial expressions. On the other hand, he very rapidly (apparently within a couple of days) distinguished between passing lorries [trucks] and cars, and would get up at six each morning to look at them some way off. He "collected" different types of lorry, and took much pleasure recognizing vans, articulated lorries, and so on. His particular interest in cars and lorries may have been in part that they made familiar sounds, which helped in identification; that they could only be driven by sighted people, and so held out particular promise to him. He had spent many hours trying to visualize the shape of cars while washing them, particularly his brother-in-law's car, which he frequently washed down.

The initial contact with S.B. resulted in Richard Gregory noting that S.B. was able to walk without the need for touching when he went through a doorway. He was also able to tell time from a large clock. S.B. reported that he learned to tell time by feeling the hands on a clock. He had also learned letters of the alphabet through touch. Thus, he was able to make a transition from touch to vision. He could also identify the colors red, white, and black. Other colors confused him.

Later, a variety of illusions such as the *Necker cube*, the *Zöllner illusion*, and the *Poggendorf illusion* were shown to S.B. These are shown in **Figure 5-23**, **Figure 5-24**, and **Figure 5-25.** The Necker cube changes perspective in terms of whether the corner is seen to be close or far away. The vertical lines in the Zöllner illusions are not seen as parallel. The diagonal line in the Poggendorf illusion is not seen as a straight line. In general, S.B. did not see the Necker change perspective, that is, the inside move toward or away from him. Also, he did not see the lines in the Zöllner to be non-parallel or the line in the Poggendorf not to be straight.

Richard Gregory also took S.B. to view particular tools, one of which was a lathe. Gregory notes that S.B. was somewhat agitated and could not identify the parts of the tools. Upon being allowed to touch the lathe, S.B. closed his eyes and correctly understood how it worked. S.B. reported, "Now that I've felt it I can see."

204 Sensation and Perception

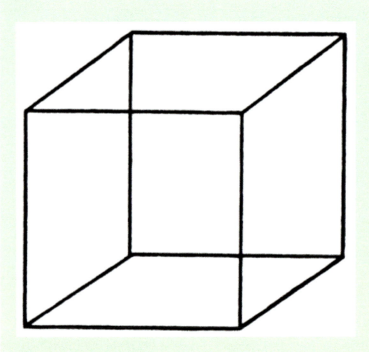

Figure 5-23 Necker cube.

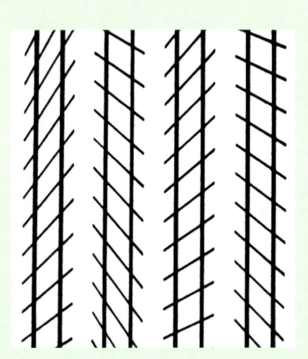

Figure 5-24 Zöllner illusion.

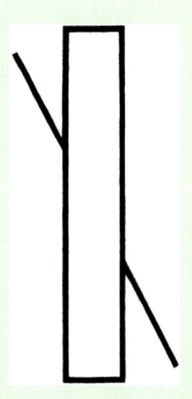

Figure 5-25 Poggendorf illusion.

Thought Question: S.B. reported being able to understand what he was seeing by being able to touch it. What senses could you use to help you understand your world if you could no longer see?

Sensation and Perception

CONCEPT CHECK

1. What characteristics built in to our visual system allow for us to experience illusions?
2. What is the difference between monocular cues and binocular cues for determining depth? Give an example of each.
3. Gestalt psychology is interested in the way our perceptual system organizes ambiguous stimuli in a definite manner. Identify and describe five organizational principles that are part of our evolutionary history.
4. Until the middle of the 20th century, most people thought that you learned to see by merely looking at objects. How have our views changed as a result of the kitten experiments? As a result of this research, what recommendations would you make to parents to provide an environment in which their infants develop their visual systems most effectively?

Hearing

You are sitting and listening to your favorite music. You realize the complexity of the music but have no difficulty picking out the vocal part from that of the instruments. Then, from the next room you hear the sound of plates dropping and breaking as they hit the floor. This may be followed by your friend saying a few words reflecting his or her anger at the event.

Real-world sounds are extremely complex. We have the ability to make a wide variety of discriminations ranging from the sound of the human voice to a babbling brook to rain on the roof or a piece of music with one particular type of guitar or even sounds that signal danger (see Schnupp, Nelken, & King, 2011 for an overview). How do we do it?

Hearing or audition is the manner in which we detect sounds. The auditory system is not only able to detect whether a sound is present but also where the sound is coming from. Unlike vision, in which the receptors in the eye are sensitive to changes in electromagnetic energy, hearing works on a more mechanical basis. It is the *changes in air pressure at particular frequencies* that produce our experience of sound.

As you press a key on a piano, a string is struck. The string then begins to vibrate at a particular frequency. This in turn changes air pressure, which produces waves. Similar to throwing a rock into a still pond, the waves move outward from their source. If it is a large rock, the waves will be big. If it is a small rock, they will be small.

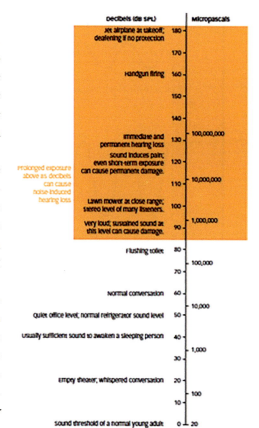

Figure 5-26 Sounds experienced in everyday life and the level associated with each.

Large sound waves or those high in *amplitude* will result in our experience of a loud sound. Small amplitude waves will result in a soft sound. The unit of measure for amplitude is the *decibel (db)*. **Figure 5-26** shows the amplitude expressed in db of common experiences.

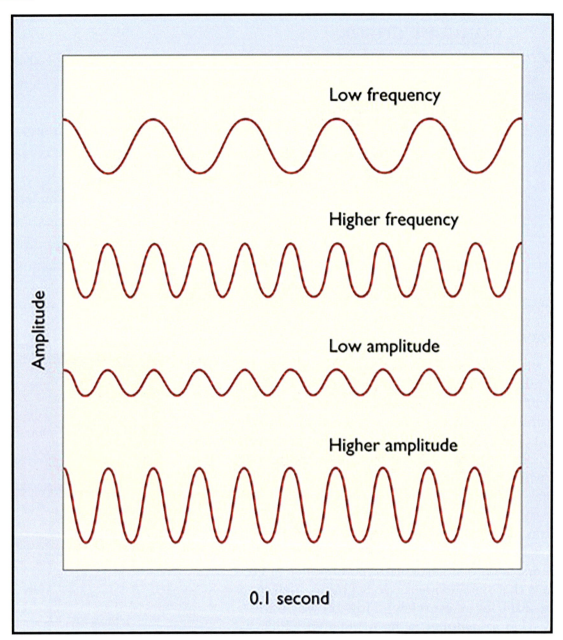

Figure 5-27 Sound is described in terms of frequency and amplitude.

If the waves are fast, we experience a high-pitched sound, whereas slower waves are experienced as lower in pitch. At times, we can both hear and feel sounds as you might in an action movie in a theater. The unit of measure for *frequency* is *cycles per second or hertz*, which is abbreviated *Hz*. The typical young adult can detect frequencies between 20 Hz and 20,000 Hz, whereas your dog can hear up to 40,000 or 60,000 Hz. In fact, most animals can hear higher frequencies than humans with the porpoise, whale, and bat being able to hear above 100,000 Hz. As humans grows older, their hearing becomes less responsive to the upper frequencies.

If you hear the tones shown in **Figure 5-27**, you would hear a simple tone. However, most sounds that we hear are complex. That is, they are made up of a number of sounds. If you think about a violin as it plays a note, what you hear is a complex sound. *Timbre* is the term used to describe complex tones such as a train whistle or a church bell ringing. Each of these is not a single frequency wave but a complex set of waves around a particular frequency.

How the Ear Works

Sound waves enter the ear. It is the pressure of these waves that influences our hearing of sound. The components of a sound wave include *frequency*, *amplitude*, and *complexity*. Frequency determines the pitch that we hear. We hear a high pitch such as that produced by a piccolo or flute differently from the low pitch of a tuba. The intensity or amplitude of the sound wave determines whether we experience it as loud or soft. The complexity of the sound wave determines the richness or timbre of the experience of hearing.

Sound waves are directed through the *ear canal* to the *ear drum* also called the *tympanic membrane*. These structures are referred to as the *outer ear*. Your outer ear is shaped in a particular way. This shape allows for particular frequencies coming from different locations to be differentially acted upon. This allows your brain to use this information to help localize sounds in space and to know where they are coming from.

The sound waves coming from the outer ear move to the ear drum. The ear drum transfers this energy to three bones, the *hammer*, *anvil*, and *stirrup*. The stirrup connects to the *inner ear*. Since the size of the ear drum is larger than the size of the area of the stirrup connecting to the inner ear, there is an increase in pressure. This increase in pressure allows for more sensitivity especially in the middle frequencies of human hearing.

The cavity between the ear drum and the inner ear that contains the three bones is filled with air. In fact, the air comes from the throat through the Eustachian tube. The Eustachian tube is normally closed but will open when the pressure on the outside of the ear drum is different from that of the middle ear. Some people chew gum or yawn when flying in an attempt to equalize the two pressures. The experience is of your ears "popping."

The sound waves from the middle ear are then transferred to the inner ear. The main structure that changes pressure waves into information that can be processed by the brain is the *cochlea*. Cochlea comes from the Greek word for *snail* and, as you can see in **Figure 5-28**, it looks like the shell of a snail. The human cochlea is wound about three times. The diameter of the coil becomes smaller as it progresses.

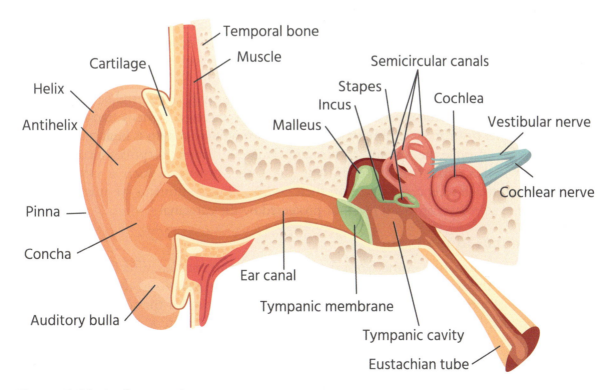

Figure 5-28 Auditory pathway.

When energy from the middle ear moves the stirrup, which is connected to the *oval window* at the end of the cochlea, this energy moves the fluid inside the tube. The oval window is a membrane that is flexible and can be moved to create wave-like action. At the other end of the cochlea is another membrane, the *round window*, which is also flexible. These two flexible membranes allow the fluid in the cochlea to move.

Like waves at the ocean, the pressure from the sound moves throughout the cochlea. However, the movement does not occur in a uniform manner. The movement of the fluid reflects the amplitude and frequency of the sound waves. Because the mechanical nature of the cochlea is that it is more flexible in some areas and more rigid in others, specific frequencies of sound stimulate hair cells in different parts of the tube (see **Figure 5-29**).

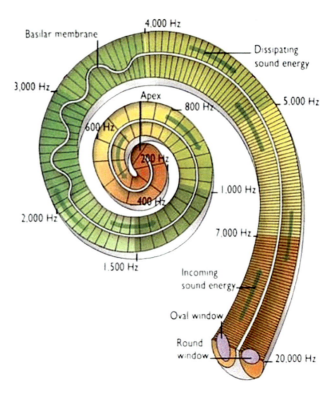

Figure 5-29 Human cochlea.

To summarize, mechanical activity in the environment such as a tree falling produces sound waves. These sound waves are picked up by the ear and channeled down the ear canal. The waves then reach the ear drum, which they cause to vibrate. These sound pressure vibrations move the bones of the middle ear. The third bone, the stirrup, moves the oval window in relation to the frequency and amplitude of the sound waves. This moves the fluid of the inner ear, which in turn stimulates hair cells in the cochlea. The stimulated hair cells release neurotransmitters that result in the firing of neurons that send information to the auditory areas of the brain. Notice that sound waves move through a number of physical structures before an action potential can be produced.

Sound waves in the air become mechanical waves in the air cavity of the middle ear, which in turn creates fluid waves in the inner ear. Why does sound go through so many transformations? One answer is that from an evolutionary perspective, the auditory system is built on a very old system. Fish, for example, are sensitive to pressure changes in water. Porpoises receive sounds through their bodies rather than through their ears. Other organisms such as moths receive sounds through touch receptors located on their bodies. Thus, in humans we might think of the ear drum as a pressure or touch receptor protected by the ear canal.

Creating Sounds in the Brain

Three types of information come from the hair cells in the cochlea. The first is the pitch or frequency of the sound. The second is the amplitude or how loud the sound is. And the third type of information is the temporal nature or duration of the sound also referred to as complexity. From these three types of information, we create a world of music and language.

This information from each ear is initially kept separate as it goes to the initial structure in the brain stem involved with hearing, the *cochlear nuclei*. The information created in the cochlea of the left ear travels along auditory nerve fibers to a group of neurons referred to as the left cochlear nucleus. Information from the right ear goes to a different set of neurons, the right cochlear nucleus. The cochlear nuclei are located in the brain stem at the junction of the medulla and pons (see **Figure 5-30**). The structure of the cochlea neurons is such that pitch information is mapped in terms of neuron location. This is similar to how the keys on a piano go from low-frequency to high-frequency notes.

Creating sounds in your brain is a complicated process as are the pathways that auditory information follows as it moves through your brain (see Kandel, Schwartz, Jessel, Siegelbaum, & Hudspeth, 2013; Schnupp, Nelken, & King, 2011 for more detailed information). Only the basics will be presented here.

Above the level of the cochlear nuclei, information related to sound goes in parallel fashion to a variety of structures. These pathways generally include information from both ears. Since you have two ears, it is possible for a sound to reach one ear slightly before it reaches the other. A sound off to your left would reach the left ear about 700 millionths of a second before it reached the right ear. Of course, a sound from in front of you would arrive at each ear at the same time.

When a sound arrives at the right and left ears, it is processed in the cochlea and then sent to the cochlear nucleus associated with that ear. From the left and right cochlear nuclei, the information is sent to the *superior olive* (see **Figure 5-30**). Information arrives at the superior olive from each ear in the form of action potentials. If an action potential related to sound in one ear is delayed from that related to the other ear, neurons in the superior olive will respond. This set of neurons in humans is able to distinguish time differences as short as 10 millionths of a second (Kandel, Schwartz, Jessel, Siegelbaum, & Hudspeth, 2013).

How do you know where a sound came from in the external world? The superior olive is able to process differential loudness information between the sounds heard at the left and right ears. Using both the time at which a sound arrived at the left and right ears and the loudness of the sound, the superior olive begins to create a map of where in the external world a sound may have originated.

Pathways go from the superior olive to the *inferior colliculus* and then to the *medial geniculate nucleus* and then to the *primary auditory cortex* in the left and right temporal lobes. In the same way that the primary visual cortex is called V1, the primary auditory cortex is called A1. The neurons of the auditory cortex are arranged in a manner that reflects the pitch or frequency of the sound information.

From the auditory cortex, there are two pathways that go to two different prefrontal areas of the cortex. One of the pathways has been called the *what* pathway and is associated with determining what a sound is. The other pathway is the *where* pathway and is involved with determining where in space an object is located.

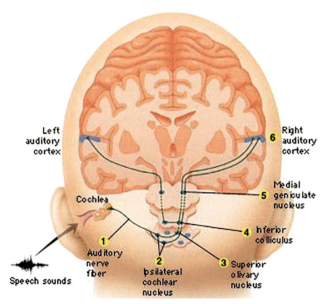

Figure 5-30 The pathway in the brain that creates the experience of hearing a sound.

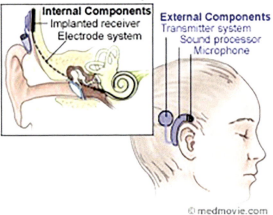

Figure 5-31 With a cochlear implant, external sounds are processed and sent directly to the auditory nerve.

Cochlear Implant

If a person has lost their ability to hear, one approach has been to present information directly to the auditory nerve. This is referred to as a cochlear implant. As seen in **Figure 5-31**, a microphone, sound processor, and transmitter are placed on the skull above the ear. These are the external devices. The internal components include a receiver and an electrode system, which send signals to different parts of the auditory nerve.

It should be noted that a cochlear implant does not restore normal hearing. Rather, it is a means to help the person use the sounds found in the environment, especially in terms of speech. With the advent of small computer chips, researchers are seeking to improve the quality of what is being heard.

Intact hearing makes learning to speak much easier. This is why children who are born deaf are fitted with cochlear implants as early as possible. Adults who have lost their hearing can also benefit from cochlear implants. These implants allow patients to understand the spoken word, but music is more of a problem. Improvements in hearing can be achieved by using cochlear implants in both ears.

According to the Food and Drug Administration (FDA), as of December 2012, approximately 324,200 people worldwide have received implants. In the United States, roughly 58,000 adults and 38,000 children have received them (http://www.nidcd.nih.gov/health/hearing/pages/coch.aspx). In 2017, the FDA approved a device that allows individuals with certain cochlear implants to stream sound directly from an iPhone or iPad. This will allow for phone calls and music to be sent directly to the cochlear implant.

The Vestibular System and Balance

Before we leave the ear, let's look at another system that is contained in the inner ear. This is the *vestibular system*. The **vestibular system** contributes to your experience of movement, head position, and where you are in space in relation to gravity. It also functions as an internal guidance device.

As you saw in **Figure 5-28** previously, there are three semicircular canals that are located near the cochlea. There are also two other structures called the *saccule* and the *utricle*. Like the cochlea, these structures and canals contain hair cell receptors. In fact, the hair cells related to hearing and those related to balance and your movement in space work in the same way. As you look at these canals you will notice that they are located in different *orientations* (see **Figure 5-32**). As such, each is sensitive to movement in different directions. Further, the saccule and utricle are slightly different in size such that one moves faster than the other. In that way you experience *acceleration*. Jumping up and down will influence the fluid in these structures and canals differently than moving your head from left to right. As this fluid moves, it puts pressure on the hair cells, resulting in action potentials being sent to a number of areas in the brain.

Sensation and Perception   211

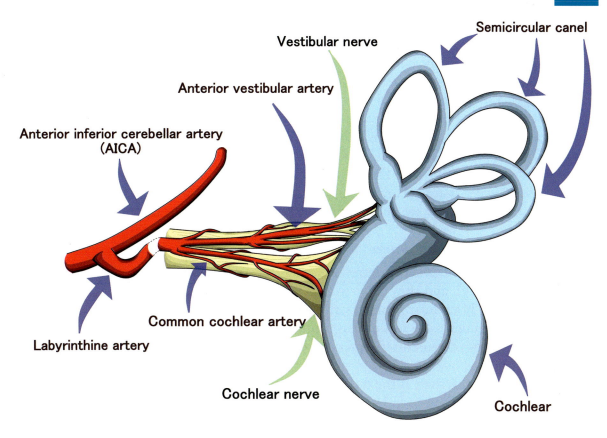

Figure 5-32 The vestibular system of the inner ear.

CONCEPT CHECK

1. The auditory system processes sound waves to result in our experience of hearing. How do the following components of sound waves affect what we hear:
   a. Amplitude?
   b. Frequency?
   c. Timbre/Complexity?
2. A book falls off the desk while you're studying. What are the steps of the process that occur from the time the sound wave hits your outer ear until you identify the sound?
3. How do our two ears—and the separate parts of the brain to which they are connected—work separately and together to give us the information we need to identify what and where a sound is? And what is a "superior olive" anyway?
4. What is the function of the vestibular system and what are its important parts? How does it interact with the visual system?

The Chemical Senses: Smell and Taste

Smell and *taste* are different from vision and hearing. Rather than photons or pressure, we experience the chemicals in our world with smell and taste. We notice the smell of good food cooking, and we are attracted to where the smell is coming from. As this is happening, our digestive system prepares to process the food we are about to eat. However, if we open a container with rotten food, that is a different story. We are repulsed just by a quick experience of the odor. We have a long evolutionary history of protecting ourselves through the smells that we experience. The same is true with taste. Ask any 6-year-old. Humans generally seek sweet tastes and reject bitter ones. This makes sense in terms of evolution because, in nature, poisons are generally bitter rather than pleasant tasting.

Olfaction: The Smelling Sense

The wild pig's sense of smell is extremely well developed (much better than both their eyesight and hearing), and they rely strongly on it to detect danger and search out food (Estabrook, 2015). They are capable of sensing some odors 5 to 7 miles away and may be able to detect odors as much as 25 feet underground! (If you want to learn more about wild pigs, see https://feralhogs.tamu.edu/frequently-asked-questions/frequently-asked-questions-wild-pigs/).

Unlike other animals such as the wild pig or your cat, you do not see humans using their sense of smell to find their way. However, we can do so (Porter et al., 2007). In one study, humans tracked a scent outdoors, which they were able to do. Practice improved this ability. Also, the information received by each nostril helps to improve the tracking. By the way, the participants were tracking the smell of chocolate.

Since humans rely more on vision than smell as a major sense, you might think that there are fewer areas of our brain devoted to these discriminations. However, it is not that simple. It turns out that it is estimated that we still may be able to distinguish more than 10,000 different chemical smells (Buck & Bargman, 2013). Perfumers, food critics, and wine tasters can make even finer discriminations. Research shows that human mothers and their infants learn to detect the smell of each other.

Olfaction refers to your sense of smell. In your nose are sensory neurons that are responsive to *chemicals* that we experience as *odors* (see Buck & Bargman, 2013 for an overview). These sensory neurons are located in the *olfactory epithelium*, which is part of the *nasal cavity*. The cells in the olfactory epithelium are relatively short-lived and replaced by new cells every 30 to 60 days.

Surprising enough, mammalian species tend to have the relative same number of neurons in the olfactory bulb in relation to their overall brain size (McGann, 2017). As you see in the Myths and Misconceptions feature in this chapter, humans are actually excellent in terms of the ability to detect odors. When we perceive an odor, receptors produce electrical signals and send a pattern of activity to the *olfactory bulb* located below the frontal areas of the brain. The olfactory bulb processes the signal and serves as a relay station to other areas of the brain including the limbic area (see **Figure 5-33**). Thus, it is not surprising that we often have emotional reactions to odors. How about your grandmother's apple pie? Amusement parks such as Disney World use scents to enhance the park experience.

Does food smell different when you are hungry? As you know from experience, the answer is yes. Not only are there pathways going from the olfactory bulb to the brain areas related to detecting odors, but there are also pathways from the brain to the

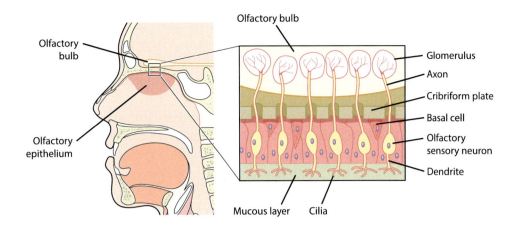

Figure 5-33 Smells stimulate the cells in your nose. Action potentials go from these to the olfactory bulb and then to other areas, especially those associated with emotionality.

olfactory bulb. This allows you to pay attention to important odors such as the smell of food when hungry. It also lets you do the opposite, that is, ignore odor sensations when not necessary. Thus, your physiological state can determine what and how you experience smells.

Across a number of animal species odors are able to bring forth specific innate behaviors. You may have heard of the chemicals called *pheromones*. Pheromones play an important role in mating and other behaviors. In some species, pheromones can signal when the female is receptive and able to conceive. They can also bring forth aggressive responses. Pheromones are excreted from the organism in sweat, urine, and other bodily fluids. This is how your dog, as well as other animals, marks his territory. In animals, pheromones (like odors) are detected by structures in the nasal passage but also by an additional tubular structure in the nasal area referred to as the *vomeronasal organ (VNO)*. Humans do not have the vomeronasal structure, which is why we are less affected by pheromones.

Myths and Misconceptions—Humans and the Ability to Smell

If asked, most of us would say that we humans do not have the same ability to smell odors as do other animals. Our dogs seem to spend the majority of their life smelling things, especially trees and other dogs. Well, the idea that we humans have a terrible sense of smell turns out to be a myth. New research shows that humans have an excellent sense of smell (McGann, 2017).

Much like the statement you should drink eight glasses of water a day, the idea that humans were inferior to other mammals in terms of olfaction had never been tested. It was just an idea that dated back to the 19th century and the work of Paul Broca. In a somewhat complicated interaction between the church and the scientists of the day, Broca had pointed out that the front lobes had increased in size over our evolutionary history. This was interpreted to support the idea of humans having free will.

He further pointed out that the olfactory bulb of humans had not increased in size. Further, it was reported that a number of animals have a larger olfactory bulb in relation to the size of other parts of their brain. As with many myths, the basic idea that humans had an inferior sense of smell was passed on without research from generation to generation.

In this century with better research techniques for identifying both chemical substances and neurons in different parts of the brain, a new picture of human abilities in terms of smell is appearing. For example, one study in the journal *Science* suggested that humans can discriminate more than one trillion different smells (Bushdid, Magnasco, Vosshall, & Keller, 2014). This is in comparison to being able to discriminate several million different colors, and half a million different tones. Even if the trillion number is high, our ability is clearly better than the 10,000 number often listed in textbooks.

Recent reviews support the idea that humans are strongly influenced by olfaction (McGann, 2017). Research has shown that environmental odors can prime specific memories and emotions, which can be related to post-traumatic stress disorder (PTSD) experiences. Odors can also influence autonomic nervous system activation, which can shape perceptions of stress and affect, which in turn results in approach and avoidance behaviors. Humans can even follow outdoor scent trails and exhibit dog-like behaviors when trails change direction. Also, humans are sensitive to the smell associated with other people. Of course, as with all of our senses, age, gender, and developmental stage can influence the ability to smell. Although humans may have a better sense of smell than many have suggested, dogs do have some advantages. These include more neurons in the brain structures associated with smell and noses that have the ability to breathe out without a decontamination of the scent trail. Dogs with their cold noses can also sense sources of heat (Bálint et al., 2020). Although dogs have important abilities, it is clear that the human sense of smell is much better and more important than previously thought.

Thought Question: How could our knowledge of smell be informed by a myth for such a long period of time? What are some other research studies that could be conducted based on this new knowledge of our sense of smell?

The Gustatory System: A Matter of Taste

Although smell is associated with a number of processes, taste is mainly related to food (see Buck & Bargman, 2013 for an overview). That is, the taste system determines the chemical makeup of foods and beverages in terms of nutrient content, agreeableness, and potential toxicity (Roper & Chaudhari, 2017). Previously we thought that humans and other mammals were sensitive to four qualities of taste. These were sweet, bitter, salty, and sour. We now know there is a fifth taste—umami. Umami is a Japanese word and can be translated as "pleasant savory taste." This is the taste associated with amino acids, which some experience as similar to monosodium glutamate (MSG). Both sweet and umami are found to be pleasant, whereas bitter brings forth aversive reactions. Salts are important to help organisms maintain electrolyte balance, and this taste typically adds flavor to foods. To complicate the story a little more, there is now a suggestion that some of the receptors on the tongue that were thought to be sensitive to sour are really sensitive to water (Zocchi, Wennemuth, & Oka, 2017).

By definition, *taste* refers to the five qualities processed by our **gustatory system**—*sweet, bitter, salty, sour,* and *umami*. *Flavor*—which is more complex—refers to the combination of sensory processes that we experience in terms of *taste, smell, and texture as well as our experience of chewing*. Not only do you smell food through your nose but also odors are transmitted through the back of your mouth. If your mouth is dry or you have a cold, the flavor of the food you eat is greatly changed. Further, genetic differences in alleles determines whether you experience foods such as brussels sprouts and broccoli as bitter or not (Roper & Chaudhari, 2017).

As seen in **Figure 5-34**, taste signals are produced in the mouth and go through the brain stem and the thalamus to the area of the brain related to taste. There is also a pathway from the thalamus to the hypothalamus that controls feeding behaviors. Most of our *taste buds* are located on the *tongue*, although there are some in other areas of the mouth and throat. The bumps on your tongue are not taste buds but *papillae*. Your taste buds lie buried around these. In order to taste something, it is dissolved in the saliva in your mouth. The combination of the food and your saliva makes its way to the taste buds, which are garlic-shaped structures.

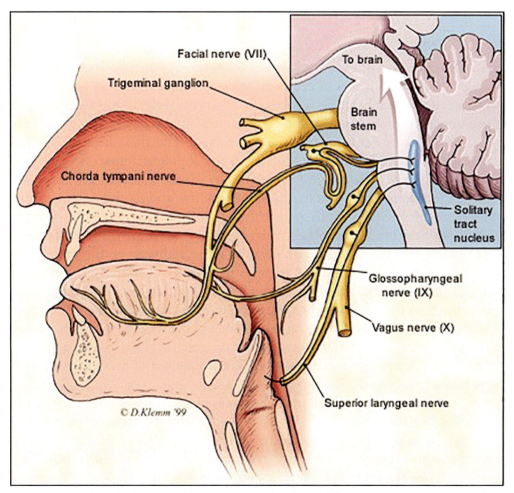

Figure 5-34 Taste signals begin with your taste buds and from there go to a number of pathways in the brain. These include those connected with eating. There are also facial muscles and those in the mouth that react to tastes we find repulsive.

CONCEPT CHECK

1. What evolutionary role do the sensory processes of smell and taste provide for humans?
2. What are pheromones, and what role do they play in many animal species? Why aren't they as relevant to humans?
3. What are the five qualities of taste that humans can detect?
4. Which three sensory processes combine to produce the human experience of flavor, and how is that different from taste?

Touch and Pain

We move through the world. We pick up a bottle of water. We write on our computer, text on a cell phone, and open a door without paying much attention to our sensation of touch. If we touch something that is hot, we feel pain. If we break a bone or have a headache, we also feel pain. Both touch and pain are critical to our ability to live our lives. This section describes the mechanisms involved and the experience of touch and pain.

The Sense of Touch

Touch plays a critical role in our lives. It helps us use tools. We use touch to tell us how much force is needed to pick up a cup of coffee or glass of water. If you are a cook, you might use touch to see if meat or bread or a cake is cooked correctly. If you work with wood or clay you use touch to measure smoothness. If you are blind you actually use touch to read using braille. Mothers of many species use touch to soothe their infants. In fact, infants of many species including humans show delayed developmental processes without touch. And, of course, individuals use touch to intensify romantic relationships.

Historically, a distinction has been made between active and passive touch. *Active touch* is when you move your body, generally your hands, against another object or person. *Passive touch* is when another person or object rubs against your skin. Both passive and active touch use the same receptors in the skin and the same pathways to the brain (Gardner & Johnson, 2013); however, the cognitive features may differ. If something rubs you as you walk through the woods, you initially react and seek to determine what it is. You may also pick up something in the woods and feel it actively to determine what it is. Although the question is the same—what is it?—in each case, the cognitive and emotional processes differ. There is also a close connection between active touch and the motor system. It is also the case that active and passive touch show different patterns of brain activation (Simões-Franklin, Whitaker, & Newell, 2011).

Think for a second as to what happens when you place an object between your fingers. Your skin conforms to the shape of the object. As your skin moves in relation to the object, information is sent to your brain. This information creates a tactile image, which includes the object's shape and texture as well as the amount of force needed to hold the object. Holding Jell-o is not the same as holding a pen.

Your hand has four types of receptors that supply information to your brain. As can be seen in **Figure 5-35**, the four types—Meissner corpuscles, Merkel cells, Pacinian corpuscles, and Ruffini endings or corpuscles—are shaped differently and are located at different depths

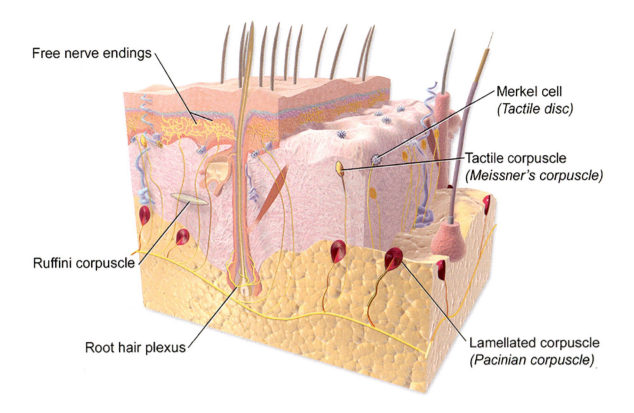

Tactile Receptors in the Skin

Figure 5-35 Your skin contains four types of cells that are sensitive to different aspects of touch—shape, texture, movement, and pressure.

of the skin. *Merkel receptors* are related to sensing fine details and fire constantly as long a stimulus is present. *Meissner corpuscles* fire when the stimulus is first applied and then again when it is removed. These are associated with controlling handgrips. Deeper in the skin are the *Ruffini endings*, which respond continuously when the stimulus is present and are related to the stretching of the skin. *Pacinian corpuscles* are also deeper and are sensitive to rapid vibrations and fine texture.

The four types of receptors work together to give you a sense of *shape, texture, movement, and pressure*. The receptors perform this task by being *sensitive to skin stretch, edges, lateral motion, and vibration* (**Figure 5-36**). Similar to receptor cells in the eye, touch cells have *receptive fields*. These receptive fields help you experience the tip of a sharp pencil differently from the blunt eraser end. Some of these receptors are quick-acting and respond to changes. For example, you notice when you initially put your smart watch or fitness tracker on, but after a time you no longer feel its pressure on your skin. Other longer-term receptors respond as long as the stimulus is present.

One way researchers study touch is to take two objects such as straight pins and place them at different distances on the skin. They then note when the pins are experienced as two pins versus one pin. The most sensitive areas of your body are your fingers and lower face (lips and cheek). Think of how you use your fingers and lips versus your back and legs. The least sensitive areas are your calf and thigh.

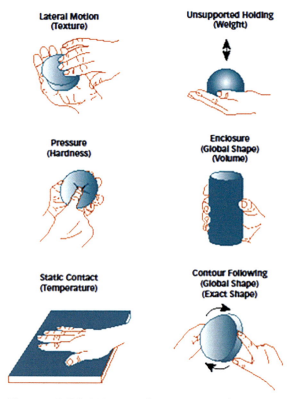

Figure 5-36 We use the receptors in our fingers to determine what an object is.

The information from the *touch receptors* goes through the *spinal cord* and then to the *brain stem* and the *thalamus*. As the information goes from the spinal cord to the brain, the fiber tracts cross to the other side so that information from your right hand goes to your left hemisphere and information from your left hand goes to your right hemisphere. From the thalamus, touch information goes to the *parietal lobe*.

The area of the parietal lobe involved in sensing touch is referred to as the **somatosensory cortex**. Touch information on the somatosensory cortex is organized in terms of locations on the body. More brain area is associated with greater sensitivity, as shown by the size of body parts in **Figure 5-37**. It should be noted that directly in front of the sensory cortex is the motor cortex. The *motor cortex* is organized similarly to the *sensory cortex*. This allows for an integration of the experience of touch with making actions.

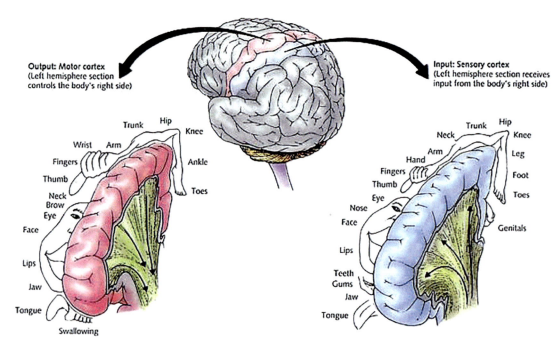

Figure 5-37 The sensory cortex receives information from our body, whereas the motor cortex controls movement.

Understanding Pain

Unlike blindness or deafness which is not uncommon in the population, few individuals are unable to experience pain. Those people who cannot experience pain typically have a genetic disorder associated with the inability to experience pain although they may experience touch. One such person was a 10-year-old boy found in Pakistan. He was a street entertainer who made money by putting knives through his arms or walking on burning coals. Unfortunately, he died at age 13 jumping off a roof.

(described in Cox et al., 2006).

As noted in the story of Tom at the beginning of Chapter 1, phantom limb is the global feeling that a body part still exists even after it was amputated. This experience is shown by the majority of people who have lost an arm or leg. Some group of these individuals not only have the experience of the limb being present but also experience pain in the limb. The nature of this pain varies from a constant pain to short lived episodes. It can vary in intensity.

(described in Flor et al., 2006)

Although most of us do not seek the experience of pain, historically it is critical for our survival (see Basbaum & Jessell, 2013 for an overview). *Pain* helps us know when we need to withdraw from a situation such as touching something hot. Pain also helps us know if there is a problem with our internal bodily systems such as a toothache or broken bone. Since pain tends to make us withdraw from a situation, it has the ability to help us minimize additional damage to our bodies.

The description of discomfort comes in many forms. We talk about shooting pain, dull pain, throbbing pain, burning pain, stinging pain, and cool pain to name a few. We also use the term soreness to reflect discomfort in our muscles. Pain can be short term, persistent, or even long term. As with other sensory processes, pain is the result of a complex sensory experience interpreted by the brain.

The simplest way we have to determine if pain is present in people is to ask them. The *verbal report* is the most common technique used in pain research. However, genetic factors make some individuals more sensitive to pain than others. Environmental conditions also play a role. Thus, there is an individual factor in all pain reports. Unfortunately for scientists, there is no direct measure of pain.

What if you were working on a project nailing some wood together and missed and hit your finger? Your first pain sensation would be a sharp sensation. This would be followed by a more prolonged pain that might have a burning sensation. The sharp sensation involves A delta (Aδ) pain fibers and the following dull sensation involves C fibers.

The cells related to the experience of pain outside of the brain are referred to as **nociceptors**. By the way, the brain itself cannot feel pain as it contains no nociceptors. So why do I get headaches you might ask. There are nociceptors in the tissues between your brain and skull. These tissues can be influenced by chemicals released from blood vessels, and blood flow itself can trigger migraine headaches. Outside the brain, nociceptors are located in the skin and the structures below the skin such as muscles and joints. Overall, these receptors convert thermal, mechanical, or chemical stimuli into action potentials.

These receptors connect to pathways that lead to the *spinal cord* and then the *thalamus* in the brain. The experience of pain is complex in that a number of areas of the brain are

220 Sensation and Perception

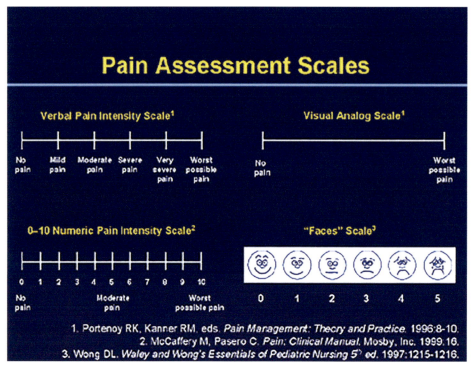

Figure 5-38 Examples of pain assessment scales.

involved. The areas involved depend on the context in which the pain is experienced as well as the person's previous experience of pain. As expected, the *limbic system* through the cingulate is involved in the emotional aspects of pain. The *insula*, which is associated with the internal state of the body, is also involved in processing pain. Damage to the insula results in the person being able to distinguish between different types of pain such as dull verses sharp, but not show emotional responses to the pain. This suggests that the insula is an area in which the sensory, affective, and cognitive components are integrated.

You may have noticed there is an exception to what has been said about pain so far. That exception is illustrated in the phenomenon of phantom limb pain. There is pain, but there are no receptors where we would expect them to be. Pain is this case originates from the central nervous system (brain and spinal cord). This is referred to as *neuropathic* pain. Generally, neuropathic pain is caused by damage to the central nervous system or damage to nerves in the periphery of our body.

CONCEPT CHECK

1. Define active touch and passive touch. In what ways are they the same, and in what ways are they different?
2. What are the four types of touch receptors that are in your hand? What is the role of each, and how do they work together for you to experience an object?
3. Trace the touch sensory pathway from the finger through to the somatosensory cortex.
4. What is unique about the organization of the motor cortex and the sensory cortex? What advantage does that organization provide?

5. What evolutionary role does the sensory process of pain provide for humans?
6. How can a phantom limb cause pain since there are no longer any nociceptors present?

Summary

Learning Objective 1: Describe how psychophysics relates to our understanding of how we experience the world.

The manner in which our brain and nervous system take energy that exists around us and turns it into an experience is a critical aspect of sensation and perception. *Sensation* refers to the manner in which our receptor system transforms energy into activity that can be interpreted by the brain. *Perception* is the manner in which the brain makes sense of this activity. Simple sensations are processed differently in each of our sensory systems. Each of the sensory systems uses different biological processes referred to as transducers to initiate the sensory process. Our brain begins with information from each of the sensory systems alone. Our nervous system then processes this information, which gives us an experience that we interpret as reality. Thus, our experience of reality is based on how our nervous system is constructed.

Psychophysics (established by Gustav Fechner in the 1800s) is the study of the relationship between the physical characteristics of a stimulus and the manner in which we experience it. The relationship between the increase in the physical intensity and the subjective experience is a logarithmic rather than a linear relationship. In each sensory system, there is a constant that reflects the ability to notice differences between two stimuli. This difference is referred to as the just-noticeable difference or JND. Fechner also noticed that the JND changes as the original weights change by a constant proportion—the difference threshold. When there is just one stimulus present, the concept is the absolute threshold.

Learning Objective 2: Describe the key processes in the visual system.

Vison is our most important sense. A least half of our brain is related directly or indirectly to the processing of visual information including areas involved in the recognition of faces.

Light is electromagnetic energy. The light we see is only a small part of the electromagnetic spectrum. In the visual spectrum, we refer to this light as waves, which can be described in terms of: (1) amplitude or how large it is; (2) frequency or how often it recurs; and (3) length or how much distance there is between two consecutive waves. When our eye transforms the visual spectrum, we see the lower frequencies (longer wavelengths) as red and orange and the higher frequencies (shorter wavelengths) as blue and violet. The greens and yellows are in between.

Light reaches the *cornea* where it is bent and the *lens* where it is focused. Both are located at the front of the eye. The object we see is focused on the *retina* at the back of the eye. The *pupil* is surrounded by muscles contained in the *iris*, which let the pupil allow in more or less light according to the intensity of the light energy. Within the eye there is a clear fluid referred to as the *vitreous*. Light passes through this fluid and reaches the back of the eye, which contains the receptors that change the electromagnetic energy of light into electrical energy. It is the job of this electrical energy to create information in the brain.

Rods permit nighttime vision and to see in dim light. *Cones* permit daytime vision and to see with high-spatial acuity, which gives you the ability to see detail. Rods and cones also differ in their location. There are many more rods in the peripheral parts of the retina, and more cones located in a more central region of the retina called the *fovea*. The cones in the retina are sensitive to different wavelengths of electromagnetic radiation that the brain is able to change into the experience of color. There are three different cone types in terms of frequency sensitivity: (1) blue, (2) green, and (3) red. Our ability to see colors requires that the signals from the different types of cones be compared in the brain. The idea that variations in three different light colors lies at the bottom of our experience of color came to be known as the Young–Helmholtz *trichromatic theory of color.*

Some individuals use only two of the three light sources to match colors. These individuals are commonly called *color blind;* some match colors to a standard color by using only green and blue light, while others use only blue and red light. Color blindness is found more often in males than females since it is caused by a recessive allele on the X chromosome.

The point at which axons leave the eye is referred to as the optic disk or *blind spot.* Although there are no receptors in this part of the eye to respond to light, the brain fills in the missing information by using information from the other eye and eye movement. Thus, you see a complete scene without a hole in the image.

As information leaves the eye, it travels by long axons—the optic nerve—to the lateral geniculate nucleus (LGN), part of the thalamus. Different types of information such as color and contrast go to different areas in the brain. Your visual field is what you see in front of you without moving your head or eyes. The visual information from each eye remains separate in the LGN and is conveyed to a variety of areas in the primary visual cortex in the occipital lobe. Each of the areas in the primary visual cortex is involved in different aspects of visual processing such as depth perception, color, movement, and form.

If the direct pathway from the eye to the LGN is lost through brain damage, the experience of vision is lost.

The pathway continues to the temporal lobe and has been referred to as the *what* pathway, which is involved with knowing what a given visual object is. The other type of ganglion cell is the M or large type cells. Information moves along a separate pathway to a different part of the primary visual cortex. It then goes to the parietal lobe and is referred to as the *where* pathway, which is involved with knowing where an object is in space. The *what* pathway helps an organism know what something is and its relation to space and time. The *where* pathway is involved in using vision for doing things in the world.

Our visual experience of motion is a combination of muscular and position feedback of the head and eyes and the visual stimuli on the retina. The illusion of apparent motion clearly shows that the perception of motion cannot be explained by the position of the image on the retina alone and that perceiving the position of an object is performed separately from determining motion.

There are two types of information that humans use to perceive depth. The first is a set of cues that can be determined from using only one eye or monocular cues: (1) our knowledge of the object: (2) occlusion, (3) linear perspective, (4) size perspective, (5) distribution of light and shadows, and (6) motion. The second type of information for perceiving depth comes from binocular cues related to the fact that humans have two eyes that are separated from one another by about 6 cm. Thus, for distances of less than about 100 feet, each eye receives slightly different information when looking at the same scene, called binocular disparity. The greatest differences or disparity between the images on the two retinas would come from objects that are close. When looking at a distant scene, your eyes are more parallel and there is almost no disparity between the images. Whether you focus close or focus far requires different eye-movement positions. The muscle movement of the eyes gives an additional channel of feedback to the brain for determining depth.

A variety of processes in our visual system are occurring at the same time. This parallel processing allows us to create an image quickly. However, at times this results in illusions, based both on a top-down process in which our expectations help to form what we see and on a bottom-up process by which our sensory system puts together the individual features into a coherent scene. Not only do we see things that are not there, but we are also able to see a world that cannot exist, such as in the etchings by the artist M. C. Escher. We can make a static figure move. In some ways, all of what we "see" is an illusion or construction of our nervous system. For example, we do not notice the edges of our visual field. Illusions are important since they help us understand how the visual system works.

Gestalt psychology was developed in Germany at the beginning of the 20th century and emphasized the manner in which our perceptual system organizes the visual world in a predetermined manner. The parts of a visual scene become organized in a manner such that a whole image emerges and include: (1) similarity, (2) proximity, (3) closure, (4) continuation, and (5) good figure.

Individuals who become blind early in life are shown to have increased auditory abilities. Likewise, individuals who become deaf early in life are shown to have superior visual abilities. The unused visual cortex in individuals who are blind is taken over by other sensory processes such as touch or hearing. This is also true with deaf individuals with the auditory cortex being taken over by other senses.

Learning Objective 3: Explain what happens in the auditory system that allows us to hear.
Mechanical activity in the environment, such as a tree falling, produces sound waves that enter the ear, and it is the pressure of these waves that influences our hearing of sound. The components of a sound wave include (1) frequency, which determines the pitch that we hear; (2) amplitude or intensity, which determines whether we experience it as loud or soft; and (3) complexity, which determines the richness or timbre of the experience of hearing. Sound waves are picked up by the ear and channeled down the ear canal to the ear drum, which they cause to vibrate. These sound pressure vibrations move the bones of the middle ear. The third bone, the stirrup, moves the oval window in relation to the frequency and amplitude of the sound waves. This moves the fluid of the inner ear, which in turn stimulates hair cells in the cochlea. The stimulated hair cells release neurotransmitters that result in the firing of neurons that send information to the auditory areas of the brain. Sound waves move through a number of physical structures before an action potential can be produced. Why so many transformations? From an evolutionary perspective, the auditory system is built on a very old system.

Three types of information come from the hair cells in the cochlea: (1) pitch or frequency; (2) amplitude or loudness; and (3) temporal nature or duration of the sound, or complexity. This information from each ear is initially kept separate as it goes to the left and right cochlear nuclei. Using both the time at which a sound arrived at the left and right ears and the loudness of the sound, the superior olive begins to create a map of where in the external world a sound may have originated. Pathways then go from the superior olive to the inferior colliculus and then to the medial geniculate nucleus and then to the primary auditory cortex. From the auditory cortex, there are two pathways that go to two different prefrontal areas of the cortex: (1) the *what* pathway, which is associated with determining what a sound is; and (2) the *where* pathway, which is involved with determining where in space an object is located.

The vestibular system, also located in the inner ear, contributes to your experience of movement, head position, and where you are in space in relation to gravity. There are three semicircular canals located near the cochlea, as well as two other structures called the saccule and the utricle. Like the cochlea, they contain hair cell receptors related to balance that work in the same way as those related to hearing. The canals are located in different orientations. As such, each is sensitive to movement in different directions. The saccule and utricle help you experience acceleration. As you move, information from the vestibular system is sent to the brain and in turn coordinates your movement to keep you balanced. The system is also able to stabilize your vision such that moving your head does not cause the object you are looking at to become blurred.

Learning Objective 4: Summarize the role that chemical processes play in smell and taste.
Smell and *taste* are different from vision and hearing. Rather than photons or pressure, we experience the chemicals in our world with smell and taste. We notice the smell of good food cooking, and we are attracted to where the smell is coming from. As this is happening, our digestive system prepares to process the food we are about to eat. However, if we open a container with rotten food, that is a different story. We are repulsed just by a quick experience of the odor.

Olfaction refers to your sense of smell. In your nose are sensory neurons that are responsive to chemicals that we experience as odors. These receptors produce electrical signals and send a pattern of activity to the olfactory bulb, which processes the signal and serves as a relay station to other areas of the brain including the limbic area. Your physiological state can determine what and how you experience smells. We have a long evolutionary history of protecting ourselves through the smells and tastes that we experience. It is estimated that we may be able to distinguish more than 10,000 different chemical smells.

Taste refers to the five qualities processed by our gustatory system: (1) sweet, (2) bitter, (3) salty, (4) sour, and (5) umami. Flavor, which is more complex, refers to the combination of sensory processes that we experience in terms of taste, smell, and texture as well as our experience of chewing. Taste signals are produced in the mouth—most of our taste buds are located on the tongue—and go through the brain stem and the thalamus to the area of the brain related to taste.

Learning Objective 5: Describe the different senses of touch and what happens when we experience pain.
Touch plays a critical role in our lives. Historically, a distinction has been made between active and passive touch: (1) active touch is when you move your body, generally your hands, against another object or person; and (2) passive touch is when another person or object rubs against your skin. Both use the same receptors in the skin and the same pathways to the brain; however, there are differences: (1) the cognitive features may differ; (2) there is a close connection between active touch and the motor system; and (3) active and passive touch show different patterns of brain activation. Your hand has four types of receptors that supply information to your brain: (1) Meissner corpuscles, (2) Merkel cells, (3) Pacinian corpuscles, and (4) Ruffini endings. The four types of receptors work together to give you a sense of shape, texture, movement, and pressure; they do this by being sensitive to skin stretch, edges, lateral motion, and vibration. The information from the touch receptors goes through the spinal cord and then to the brain stem, the thalamus, and the somatosensory cortex in the parietal lobe. Touch information on the somatosensory cortex is organized in terms of locations on the body. The

motor cortex is organized similarly to the sensory cortex, allowing for an integration of the experience of touch with making actions.

Pain is critical for our survival. As with other sensory processes, pain is the result of a complex sensory experience interpreted by the brain. Since there is no direct measure of pain, the verbal report is the most common technique used in pain research. Like other sensory processes, there are particular receptors in our body that are sensitive to pain. The cells related to the experience of pain outside of the brain are referred to as nociceptors. These receptors connect to pathways that lead to the spinal cord and then the thalamus in the brain. The experience of pain is complex in that a number of areas of the brain are involved depending on the context in which the pain is experienced as well as the person's previous experience of pain. The phenomenon of phantom limb pain is an exception—there is pain, but there are no receptors where we would expect them to be. Pain is this case originates from the central nervous system (brain and spinal cord) and is referred to as neuropathic pain.

Study Resources

Review Questions

1. The author states that "[we] do create the world we experience." How is this different from the idea that we experience the world directly as it really is? Use concepts presented in this chapter such as synesthesia, illusions, psychophysics, and signal detection theory in developing your response.
2. If you only had one type of cone, you would not be able to see the color associated with it or any color at all for that matter. Why?
3. You are sitting on a bench just looking at your visual field opening up in front of you. Suddenly, without turning your head, you see a change in the left part of your visual field. What are the multiple pathways that new information takes to your eyes and ultimately to your brain?
4. Do we live in a three-dimensional world? Of course we do, but since our visual perception starts with a two-dimensional image on the retina, what cues does our visual system use to add depth to that image and construct a three-dimensional world?
5. Before you read this chapter, it was easy moving around the world, taking in different sensory stimuli, identifying them, and responding appropriately. Now you know that each of these sensory systems is sensitive to very different types of stimuli that follow different and very complex paths through the nervous system and brain before you are able to identify what you are perceiving. How do all of these stimuli and processes work together to produce a stable and meaningful world in which we feel comfortable living? How does the story of S.B. whose sight was restored inform your understanding of how incredibly hard this all really is?
6. The author adopts an evolutionary perspective to answer the question of why sound goes through so many transformations. What does an evolutionary perspective have to offer in helping us understand our other sensory processes—vision, smell, taste, touch, and pain?
7. A chemical in the environment is detected by your nose. Describe the process that kicks into gear for you to experience that chemical as an odor and react to it.
8. A substance is placed on your tongue. Describe the process that enables you to identify the quality of the taste and then experience it as a flavor.
9. An object is placed in your hand. Describe the process that allows you to identify by touch what it is. What roles do the sensory cortex and the motor cortex play in that process?

10. Describe the pain process, focusing on the two main types of fibers/axons and the types of nociceptors that are located on them. What kinds of sensations activate each type?
11. You are reading this book to learn about psychology, so go back through each of the sensory processes covered in this chapter—vision, hearing, smell, taste, touch, and pain—and note instances in which these sensory processes interact with psychological processes.

For Further Reading

Cytowic, R., Eagleman, D., & Nabokov, D. (2011). *Wednesday Is Indigo Blue: Discovering the Brain of Synesthesia.* Cambridge, MA: MIT Press.

DeSalle, R. (2018). *Our Senses.* New Haven, CT: Yale University Press.

Frith, C. (2007). *Making up the Mind: How the Brain Creates Our Mental World.* Malden, MA: Blackwell Publishing.

Kandel, E. (2016). *Reductionism in Art and Brain Science.* New York: Columbia University Press.

Web Resources

Cochlear implant—http://www.nidcd.nih.gov/health/hearing/pages/coch.aspx

Key Terms and Concepts

color blind	networks	rods
cones	nociceptors	sensation
figure–ground relationship	olfaction	somatosensory cortex
gestalt psychology	opponent-process theory of color vision	synesthesia
gustatory system	optic disk or blind spot	transducers
hearing or audition	perception	vestibular system
illusions	photoreceptor	visual field
just-noticeable difference or JND	psychophysics	*Young–Helmholtz trichromatic theory of color*
	retina	

6 Consciousness

LEARNING OBJECTIVES
6.1 Discuss the different levels of consciousness, including attention and awareness.
6.2 Describe what happens when we sleep and dream.
6.3 Describe the techniques of hypnosis and meditation.
6.4 Discuss the three broad categories of psychoactive substances: depressants, stimulants, and hallucinogens

Alan Turing (1912–1954) was an English mathematician who was involved in developing forerunners to the modern computer and their algorithms. He was also involved in breaking the code of the German Enigma machine during World War II. In his work he confronted the question of artificial intelligence (AI) and human thinking. That is, can a machine think? One question that grew out of this work was how do you know if the voice you are talking with on your cell phone has consciousness? And, of course, what does it mean to be conscious? Turing's life was depicted in the 2014 movie The Imitation Game.

In Turing's 1950 paper, he developed a game called the imitation game (Turing, 1950). It is played with three people—a man, a woman, and an interrogator who may be of either gender. The interrogator stays in a room apart from the other two. The object of the game for the interrogator is to determine which of the other two is the man and which is the woman. He knows them by labels X and Y, and at the end of the game he says either, "X is a man and Y is a woman" or "X is a woman and Y is a man." The interrogator is allowed to put questions to the two. Since the responses are presented via a computer screen and the people are not required to tell the truth, it gave insight into the logic of decision making. What questions would you ask to determine gender?

Alan Turing modified this game to be a person and a computer, and the interrogator had to decide which is which. You could ask any questions you wished to decide which was human and which was computer. Neither had to tell the truth. How would you determine whether the messages you were getting on your computer were from a human or a machine? Are there distinct factors that would help you determine human consciousness from machine responses?

Consciousness

Most people think they understand what *consciousness* is, but few people can actually define it specifically. Some associate it with the continuous thoughts and feelings that we experience throughout the day. William James referred to this as the *stream of consciousness*. Like a stream, our ongoing experiences of what we think and feel continue with us always. Psychologists define consciousness as being aware and knowing that you are involved in a particular event.

We also seek ways to modify our consciousness. You listen to certain music because you like the feelings it gives you. You eat certain foods for the feeling of comfort and the memories associated with such meals. Reading a book or watching videos also can change our consciousness. Likewise, drinking coffee or alcohol changes our state of being. You may even seek to reduce your level of consciousness as when you take a nap. At times we may perform yoga or meditation as a way to better experience our internal processes.

A change in the scientific study of consciousness began with the advent of a scientific psychology. Individuals such as William James began to ask questions concerning the function of consciousness rather than its physical properties. James placed consciousness within an evolutionary perspective and sought to describe its function. As such, consciousness was seen as a process that developed as an adaptive mechanism over our evolutionary history that gave benefits to human functioning.

Freud described three types of consciousness, which we will discuss in greater detail in the chapter on personality. One type is what we are aware of, which is generally referred to as conscious awareness. There is also information such as your telephone number that at any moment you could bring into consciousness. Freud referred to this as latent consciousness or pre-consciousness. The third type of consciousness contains information we are not aware of and find difficult to bring into consciousness. However, this state, referred to as unconscious processes, according to Freud can still influence our thoughts, feelings, and behaviors. If, for example, you were in an automobile accident as a child, you might not remember this event but feel anxious or fearful when you ride in certain types of cars.

More recently, with the development of neuroscience techniques for understanding brain function, consciousness has become a more popular topic of scientific study. For example, Francis Crick (whom you met previously for his discovery of the structure of deoxyribonucleic acid (DNA)) and his colleague Christof Koch suggested that the way to understand consciousness is to study the neural correlates of consciousness (Crick & Koch, 2003). This has led to a variety of approaches (Dehaene, 2014; Hameroff & Penrose, 2014; Koch & Greenfield, 2007).

These approaches range from looking at particular types of cells in the brain to the manner in which neural networks can create emerging processes. The first approach seeks to find cells or areas in the brain that once activated lead to the experience of consciousness. This makes consciousness a discrete phenomenon related to specific brain areas. The second approach, as previously described by Hughlings Jackson in the 1800s, spoke of consciousness as a process that emerges from the activity of the brain. That is, consciousness is not the result of a specific brain cell being activated but the result of the entire brain working together. At this point, there is no definite answer as to the nature of consciousness. However, the neural correlates of consciousness continue to be studied (Demertzi et al., 2019; Hahn et al., 2021).

As noted, one aspect of consciousness from an evolutionary perspective is its functional nature. That is, what advantages does it give us? Not all organisms have the same experience of consciousness as do humans. However, like the Turing problem, it is difficult to know what consciousness in non-human animals is like. From an evolutionary perspective, William James saw consciousness as related to selective attention. Attention allows us to focus and prioritize our efforts. As such, there is survival value. We can know where it is safe and where it is dangerous. We can remember the foods that taste good to us as well as those that make us sick. This helps ensure our survival. Additionally, to be able to communicate this information to others helps them survive. This type of sociality also helps us establish a culture.

Consciousness and Attention

In considering consciousness and *attention*, we realize we are often not totally aware of what we are doing. As we drive on a long trip on the highway, we can get lost in our thoughts. Quite often on long trips, many people let their mind wander and daydream. We let some other part of ourselves take over and do the driving. Are we unconscious at that point? Of course not! If there is a problem, you quickly return to driving. It is almost as if you were unconscious but you were still able to drive the car successfully.

Often at a party we pay attention to those around us and ignore the conversations of others in the room. However, if you were to hear your name mentioned across the room, your attention would go directly to that area. This has been referred to as the *cocktail party effect*. What these experiences tell us is that we have different systems of consciousness and awareness for living life and making decisions. That is, whether at a party or driving, we are able to monitor other aspects of the environment without being aware of it.

Since having someone space out is not easy to accomplish in a research setting, scientists have sought other situations, mainly visual processes, to study. This allows for more careful scientific control over the setting. One example of such a stimulus is shown in **Figure 6-1**. If you focus on the "+" the pink dots will begin to disappear.

What this type of stimulus allows researchers to do is to ask what the underlying brain response is when the dots are in conscious awareness and when they are not. Many different researchers used visual awareness as a way to initially study consciousness in a scientific manner (Crick & Koch, 2003).

Another experimental approach is to use what is referred to as *backward masking*. The basic procedure is to show a stimulus such as a number on the computer screen quickly. This number could be followed by a blank screen. Generally, the person will say that she saw the number. However, if rather than a blank screen, a series of other stimuli such as letters are presented in the same area as the number, strange as it seems, the person will not report seeing the number.

A critical factor in determining whether the stimulus is seen is how soon after the number is presented the letters are presented. If the time between the number and the letters is over about one-quarter of a second, the person will report seeing the number. However, if the letters are presented before about one-quarter of a second, the person will not be aware of the number. Further, this is an all-or-none effect. Visual awareness does not increase slightly as the time between the number and the letters is increased. When the delay reaches a critical duration, the number is seen. When the delay is less than that, it is not seen.

Stanislas Dehaene and his colleagues at Collège de France in Paris have used the backward-masking approach to ask what happens in the brain when you see the number versus when you do not see it (Dehaene, 2014; Dehaene, Lau, & Kouider, 2017). Using EEG evoked potentials, these researchers showed that when the person is aware of the number, a particular EEG wave form, the P3, is seen. One important area of the brain that showed this EEG change was the prefrontal cortex. Thus, your brain shows a different EEG response with awareness of the stimulus.

Another type of task used to study conscious awareness is a stimulus in which the object seems to "pop

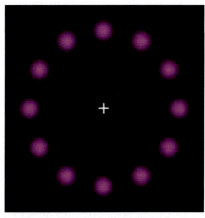

Figure 6-1 Troxler fading.

Figure 6-2 Dalmatian dog.

out" once it is seen. A number of researchers have become interested in this process (for example, Singer, 2009; Singer & Gray, 1995; Tallon-Baudry & Bertrand, 1999). For example, when you look at the image in **Figure 6-2**, you may not initially see the Dalmatian dog against the black and white background. When you do see it, there is a subjective experience of having the image "pop-out." Associated with this perception is a burst of EEG gamma activity. EEG gamma is associated with perception, and when that perception is experienced in conscious awareness, there is enhanced gamma band activity.

Overall, research shows sudden EEG changes in the brain to be associated with *conscious awareness*. These include evoked potential changes and EEG gamma band activity. In addition, during periods of conscious awareness, the brain forms connections or networks across more areas of the cortex than when conscious awareness is not present. That is, during conscious awareness, more areas of the brain are communicating with one another.

As you go through the day, your brain is solving problems, making expectations, and planning what to do next. In order to do this, different areas in our brain work on their own and in connection with other areas. Of course, our experience is that there is only one of us thinking and feeling. Somewhat amazing, isn't it. Further, there is no single brain area related to consciousness (Dehaene, 2014; Dehaene, Lau, & Kouider, 2017). As you will see in this chapter, consciousness is the result of the interactions among a number of neural networks in our brain.

Types of Awareness

In terms of attention, we can be aware of something. This is the basic level. We have sensations and create perceptions. For example, we can be aware of a cat. We can know it is raining. We can even be aware of images in our dreams. Sometimes we have a sense of how our self is involved while other times, like watching a movie, our self seems not to be part of our attention.

There is also another level of awareness that is important for humans, which is referred to as **meta-awareness**. That is, we can be aware of our awareness. I can experience myself watching something else. In conversations, meta-awareness lets us experience ourselves talking as well as having awareness of the other person at the same time. As such we use our awareness systems as a way to plan and direct our actions and cooperate with others. As you will see in this chapter, some individuals are even able to experience themselves having a dream and make changes to it.

As humans we not only have awareness of our awareness but also cognition about cognition or **metacognition** (Shea, Boldt, Bang, Yeung, Heyes, & Frith, 2014). Nicholas Shea and his colleagues suggest that metacognition is composed of two systems. The first metacognition system functions out of awareness, whereas the second system is able to accomplish a richer number of tasks. System one works quicker and in parallel, whereas system two performs action in a serial form. In playing a video game, system one tells us when we have made a mistake. System two, on the other hand, helps us learn to detect the feelings associated with these errors. It also helps us decide whether someone we are talking with is telling us the truth. We put together a number of clues in terms of their voice, posture, facial expressions, and so forth to make such a judgment. Researchers have shown that brain structure is related to individual differences in making these judgments before this information comes into awareness (Getov, Kanai, Bahrami, & Rees, 2015).

Levels of Consciousness

Not only has consciousness been discussed in terms of what we are aware of, but also our level of awareness. What a given individual is aware of is often seen as a local state, whereas sleep, coma, and wakefulness are seen as global states (Bayne, Hohwy, & Owen, 2016; Fazekas & Overgaard, 2016). Global states are typically measured in terms of cognitive, behavioral, and physiological measures such as eye movement and EEG during sleep. The basic question is how well a person is connected with his or her environment. From this perspective, we speak of **levels of consciousness**. These levels can be discussed in terms of coma, vegetative state, and wakefulness and awareness (Gosseries, Di, Laureys, & Boly, 2014). Coma typically is the result of stroke, loss of oxygen, or trauma to the head. Coma is characterized by a lack of wakefulness and awareness. A vegetative state is defined as wakefulness without signs of awareness (Laureys, 2005). From this perspective, consciousness can be described in terms of wakefulness and awareness. Between coma and normal consciousness, there is a continuum in which a person varies in terms of awareness and the ability to communicate.

A common procedure that is designed to change the level of a person's consciousness is the use of anesthesia. In fact, anesthesia changed the nature of medical care and operations in the 1900s. Both Sigmund Freud and William James experimented with different types of anesthesia. At times, they even tested the drugs on themselves.

Today, **anesthesia** allows for careful changes in a person's level of consciousness. This has allowed researchers to monitor the return to consciousness as anesthesia is withdrawn from the person. Typically, as the effects of anesthesia wear off, the person begins to respond to sensory processes such as hearing someone's voice and simple motor processes such as opening her eyes. Combining the ability to control anesthesia with current brain-imaging techniques has opened up new ways to study levels of consciousness.

One study in Finland examined young healthy adults who volunteered to be administered anesthesia (Långsjö et al., 2012). The particular anesthesia used creates a state similar to sleep in that the person can be aroused by touching or hearing someone's voice without changing the level induced by the drug. Brain activity in terms of blood flow was determined by PET (positron emission tomography).

What these researchers found was that the initial return to consciousness took place in the more evolutionarily primitive areas of the brain. That is, the brain stem, thalamus, hypothalamus, and anterior cingulate cortex (ACC) were the initial areas to respond. There were no changes in the neocortex.

CONCEPT CHECK

1. Most people think they understand what consciousness is, but few people can actually define it specifically. What are three different approaches historically that people have taken to try to study consciousness?
2. We talk about a basic level of awareness when we have sensations and create perceptions about an external or internal event. How do the concepts of meta-awareness and metacognition build on that basic level?
3. What are the three levels of awareness, and what are the distinctive differences between them?
4. What has the discovery of anesthesia taught us about how to describe the levels of consciousness and what happens as we move from one level to another?

Variations in Consciousness

As noted, when we look at an object, we become conscious of what it is. However, it generally takes about a half second before our brain gives us the experience of being aware of what is there. During this time, a large number of brain networks involving billons of neurons process the information. When we shift our attention to something else, the original object leaves our consciousness. In this manner, attention and consciousness are closely related in our everyday language. Although we think of consciousness being related to selective attention, some researchers have suggested that these are two separate brain processes (Koch & Tsuchiya, 2007). Part of their argument is that it is possible to attend to an object without its being consciously perceived. Let us now consider two different long-term conditions in which a person is able to process information without being aware of it—*blindsight* and being a *split-brain* individual.

Blindsight

Normal awareness depends on information being passed in both directions between a number of areas of the brain (Paller & Suzuki, 2014). Of course, if there is damage to any of these areas, normal awareness is disrupted. One example of this is referred to as *blindsight* (Weiskrantz, 1996). Blindsight occurs when there is damage to the primary visual cortex (V1). Although there is damage to the visual cortex, there are still visual pathways going to the subcortical areas. When individuals with this condition are asked what they see, they report seeing nothing.

However, if you were to ask them if they could detect movement from a cursor on a computer screen, for example, they will report seeing nothing but can correctly report the movement. They claim they just "guessed." Sometimes, they describe a sensation in a nonvisual realm such as a pinprick (Richards, 1973). Further, individuals who show blindsight are also able to discriminate different colors although they say they do not see them (Silvanto, Cowey, & Walsh, 2008). They also can detect emotions in another person's face (de Gelder, 2010). Thus, the person has no conscious awareness of his or her perceptions but can accurately describe motion, discriminate color, and react to emotions.

One amazing demonstration involving a person who experiences blindsight was created by Beatrice de Gelder and her colleagues (de Gelder, 2010). They studied a doctor who had a number of strokes that left his primary visual area (V1) not functioning correctly in both hemispheres. This person who is referred to in the scientific literature as T.N. is completely blind. What de Gelder did was to fill a corridor with a number of objects. However, T.N. was told that the hallway was empty and that he would not need his cane. T.N. then began to walk down the hallway. Surprisingly, as he walks, he avoids the objects and is able to walk down the hall without walking into them. This demonstration can be seen on YouTube (https://www.youtube.com/watch?v=4x0HXC59Huw). Visual information is still gathered and routed to other parts of the brain, allowing this person to see without seeing.

Split-brain Patients

Another situation in which an individual can process information outside of awareness was first noted in the middle of the last century. In the 1960s and 1970s, an operation was performed to reduce the frequency of uncontrollable epileptic seizures. These operations were performed on individuals who had had severe epilepsy for a number of years and were typically unable to work. The initial operations cut the fiber tract—the **corpus callosum**—that connects the left and right hemispheres of the brain. By performing this operation, epileptic seizures could not spread over the entire brain. These patients came to be referred to as **split-brain** patients. Overall, following the operation, these patients showed a drastic reduction in seizures. Surprisingly, cutting the corpus callosum (which contains some 200 million nerve fibers) did not appear to cause any changes in the everyday behavior or experience of these patients.

Before continuing with split-brain patients, let's consider some basics of brain function. These basics were originally described by Hughlings Jackson in the 1800s. He noted that the left and right hemispheres of the human brain are specialized for different tasks. The left hemisphere is involved in language processing and other serial processes. The right hemisphere processes spatial tasks and other global processes. This is referred to as **hemispheric specialization**.

Each of your eyes receives information in terms of what you see in front of you. If you imagine a line down the middle of what you see, your image could be divided into a left and a right image. If you don't move your eyes, what is in the left image (left visual field) goes to the right visual areas at the back of the brain. What is in the right visual field goes to left visual areas (see **Figure 6-5**). Since it takes a small amount of time to move your eyes, if visual information is presented in less than one-fifth of a second, it initially goes to just one hemisphere. This is faster than anyone's ability to make an eye movement, which could result in the information going to both hemispheres.

Normally, the left and right hemispheres are able to share information by transferring it through the corpus callosum. However, in the case of the split-brain patients the corpus callosum had been cut. Thus, information could not be transferred from one side to the other.

However, with more extensive experimental procedures, a different picture emerged with the split-brain patient. This work was initially performed by Roger Sperry and his colleagues (see Springer & Deutsch, 1998 for an overview).

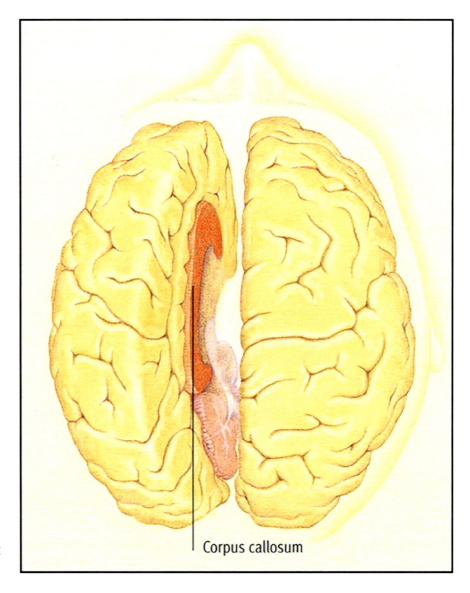

Figure 6-3 Brain cut in half front to back.

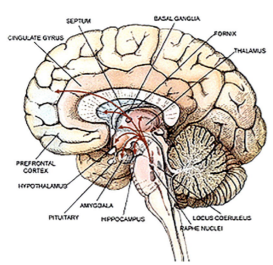

Figure 6-4 Parts of normal human brain.
Source: Washington University.

What Roger Sperry and his colleagues found was that when information was presented to the left hemisphere of the split-brain patients, they reported seeing it and could identify it verbally. If the information was presented to the right hemisphere, the patient would say he saw nothing. However, somewhat more amazing, if asked to point to a series of objects with the left hand, which is controlled by the right hemisphere, he was able to do it correctly. This led Sperry to suggest that split-brain patients contained the equivalent of two minds, each with its own separate consciousness. However, the experience of awareness was connected with the left hemisphere. Although when information was presented to the right hemisphere the person was able to point correctly, like the blindsight person, he did not experience it in his awareness.

A related difference between the two hemispheres is whether information is presented as a whole (as would be the case in visual scenes) or made up of parts (as would be the case with language where one word follows another). It is also possible to create images such as **Figure 6-6** in which one can focus on the details such as the "S" that makes up the "H" or the "H" itself as a whole. If this image is presented to the left hemisphere of a person with the corpus callosum split, she will say she saw "S." However, if it is presented to the right hemisphere, she will see the "H." Thus, the right hemisphere processed in terms of wholes, whereas the left hemisphere processed in terms of individual parts.

An intriguing example of the whole versus part dichotomy was performed by Michael Gazzaniga with a split-brain patient he had been following. The patient was shown art by the Italian artist Giuseppe Arcimboldo (c.1530–1593). What Arcimboldo did was to create faces by putting together images of fruit and vegetables (https://www.wikiart.org/en/Search/Giuseppe%20Arcimboldo). When the split-brain person was shown one of these pictures, the person would see a face if the picture was shown to the right hemisphere. However, he would see individual pieces of fruits or vegetables if the same picture was shown to the left hemisphere.

A particularly intriguing outcome of these two minds is the manner in which the conscious verbal left hemisphere appears to fill in gaps in information. That is, if the right hemisphere performed an action out of awareness of the left hemisphere, the person using his left hemisphere would create a story to explain the action. In this research, a snow scene was flashed to the right hemisphere of the patient and a chicken claw to the left hemisphere. The split-brain patient was then shown the pictures presented in **Figure 6-7**.

The person was then asked to point with each hand to an image that was related to what had been seen. The right hand, which is controlled by the left hemisphere, pointed to a chicken. The left hand, which is controlled by the right hemisphere, pointed to a shovel, which would be used to shovel snow. The person was able to observe where each hand pointed, although the verbal left side would not have been aware of seeing the snow scene since it went to the right hemisphere. When asked why he pointed to where he did, his verbal response from the left hemisphere was, "I saw a claw and I picked a chicken, and you have to clean out the chicken shed with a shovel" (Gazzaniga & LeDoux. 1978).

How should we understand this? Gazzaniga and LeDoux suggest that the left hemisphere acts as an interpreter of action and creates views of one's behavior that fits a consistent scheme. What is more is that these researchers suggest it is not just split-brain patients that do this but all humans. That is to say, it is part of our nature to fill in the gaps and create explanations for our actions. It is assumed that filling in the gaps is the resultant of neural network integration that integrates information from a variety of cortical areas.

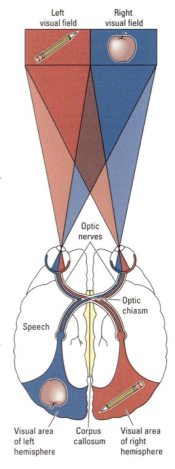

Figure 6-5 Left and right visual fields and visual areas.

Figure 6-6 Large H made up of small Ss.

Figure 6-7 Split-brain patient creates a story on what he sees.

Overall, in the case of humans, the resulting specialization is for spatial processing in the right hemisphere and language processing in the left. An intriguing question raised by the split-brain research is how language and awareness became associated with each other. One could also ask the opposite question of why spatial processing, at least in the split-brain patient, appears to exist independent of conscious awareness. We might also speculate that since language is associated with conscious awareness, it came at a later stage in our evolutionary process. As you will see throughout this book, all humans and not just those with the split-brain operation constantly process information outside of normal awareness.

Conscious Awareness

Although most of us have not experienced blindsight or the results of a split-brain operation, we have seen situations in which stimuli disappear from our experience. A simple one is the blind spot in our eye that you learned about in the chapter on perception. Our brain fills in what is missing. Also, when we focus on one aspect of a situation, we miss others. Numerous studies have shown that if you pay attention to texting on your phone, you lose awareness of what is going on around you. This is, of course, a problem if you are driving.

One of the most famous studies concerning environmental awareness was performed by Daniel Simons and his colleagues (see Chabris & Simons, 2010 for an overview). This phenomenon is referred to as the *invisible gorilla* (http://www.theinvisiblegorilla.com/gorilla_experiment.html). In the video you are asked to watch six people pass a basketball back and forth. Three of the people have white shirts and three have black shirts. Your job is to count the number of passes made by the people in the white shirts.

At one point in the video, a gorilla walks into the scene, faces the camera and thumps its chest, and then leaves. In all, the gorilla is in view for 9 seconds. Surprisingly, when this study was performed at Harvard University, about half of the participants reported not seeing the gorilla.

The World Is Your Laboratory—Out-of-Body Experiences

Throughout history individuals have described the feeling of being out of their body. This has been associated with spiritual experiences and other exceptional situations. Some individuals who experience trauma such as sexual assault also report out-of-body experiences in which they report watching the assault happen to them.

Often the description is one of the person being above the situation and looking down upon what is happening. Typically, three characteristics are present with out-of-body experiences. The first is the sense of self being outside of one's body. The second is the experience of seeing the world from above. And third, the experience of seeing one's own body.

Many people are skeptical and think that any talk of out-of-body experiences is crazy. They dismiss the idea that our sense of self can be experienced other than within our bodies (Blanke & Arzy, 2005). Although out-of-body experiences have been associated with clinical problems such as epilepsy, it has been reported by 10% of healthy populations. More recently, researchers have begun to explore the nature of this phenomenon scientifically (Blanke, Landis, Spinelli, & Seeck, 2004).

Our normal experience of our body is the result of an integration of information related to our position in space, our balance, what we view, and the internal feedback from our body. Normally, we have a sense of ourselves based on this information. In terms of our brain, the area between the frontal and temporal lobes, referred to as temporoparietal junction (TPJ) is associated with our location in space from a first-person perspective (Ionta, Martuzzi, Salomon, & Blanke, 2014). Current theory suggests that it is a lack of integration related to this information that produces the out-of-body experience.

One initial approach to understanding out-of-body experiences was to examine individuals with brain damage who reported having the experience of being outside of their body (Blanke & Arzy, 2005). Brain-imaging techniques showed that the location of the lesions or damage in these patients also was at the junction of the temporal and parietal lobes, or TPJ.

Amazingly, Olaf Blanke and his colleagues in Switzerland were able to produce out-of-the body experiences by electrical stimulation (Blanke, Landis, Spinelli, & Seeck, 2002). The person involved was a 43-year-old women who had epilepsy. During operations for epilepsy, the person remains conscious as the surgeon stimulates different areas of the brain to determine its relation to function so as not to operate in an area of critical importance such as language. As shown in the figure, stimulation of different areas of the brain results in different experiences. At one point, when the surgeon stimulated the areas shown in yellow, the woman said that she felt like she was falling or growing lighter. Then she said, "I see myself lying in bed, from above." All this, just from stimulating an area in the brain.

In what is the first of its kind, a 24-year-old reported that she could produce an out-of-body experience in herself. In fact, she thought everyone could. She first had these experiences as a child when required to take a nap that she did not want to do. At this time, she discovered that she could elicit the experience of moving above her body. She later used these out-of-body experiences to help her move into sleep. Andra Smith and Claude Messier at the University of Ottawa studied this person using fMRI. They found a number of brain areas activated during the self-induced out-of-body experiences (Smith & Messier, 2014). These included areas overlapping the TPJ, the cerebellum, which is consistent with the experience of movement reported, and other areas associated with action monitoring. Control tasks in which she imaged doing other movement activities resulted in different areas of the brain being activated than those seen in the out-of-body experience.

Modern brain-imaging techniques have given scientists new ways to study uncommon experiences whose existence has been denied.

Thought question: What three characteristics are normally present in people's descriptions of their out-of-body experiences? How have brain-imaging techniques given scientific support to these personal observations?

CONCEPT CHECK

1. What brain changes occur in an individual with blindsight? What specific evidence is presented that a person with blindsight is able to process information without being aware of it?
2. What brain changes occur in a split-brain individual? What specific evidence is presented that a person with a split-brain is able to process information without being aware of it?
3. What is meant by hemispheric specialization? What has research with split-brain individuals taught us about how everyone's brain hemispheres process information differently?
4. What is the "invisible gorilla" phenomenon? What other similar examples from everyday life can you offer?

Sleep and Dreams

What normal process involves one-third of your life? The answer of course is sleep. If you were asked to describe your state of consciousness during sleep, what would you say? You might initially say you were not aware of anything, yet some nights you experience lots of activity through dreams. Although asleep, we all have had the experience of incorporating sounds from around us during sleep into our dreams or waking up with a startle to an unfamiliar sound. Although sleep represents a stage of diminished consciousness, there is much going on in your brain.

We are just beginning to understand the various processes that go on during *sleep*. With sleep comes a change in muscle tone, hormonal levels, eye movement, and brain activation.

We know that after sleep we feel we have more energy. Sleep is also related to our body temperature, which goes down during the night. In terms of the brain, sleep is not the absence of cortical activity, just a different type of highly organized activity (Adamantidis, Gutierrez Herrera, & Gent, 2019; McCormick & Westbrook, 2013).

If sleep is prevented, then intrusions of sleep are seen in our waking day. Since our bodies seek to make up for lost sleep, this suggests that sleep plays an important role in our lives. Without sufficient sleep, performance on tasks is degraded. This has been shown in a number of cases of people who go without sleep. For example, pilots who fly emergency medicine helicopters with their immediate response to emergencies show signs of stress connected with lack of rest (Samel, Vejvoda, & Maass, 2004). Overall, sleep deprivation triggers a complex set of brain changes, which results in problems in attention, memory, and emotional processing (Krause, Simon, Mander, Greer, Saletin, Goldstein-Piekarski, & Walker, 2017). One event that happens during sleep is the removal of waste products in the brain (Nadergaard, 2013). With long-term lack of sleep, these waste products can lead to a number of disorders including Alzheimer's disorder.

As you can imagine, most human studies of sleep deprivation are of a short-term nature. However, there are a few examples of lack of sleep that lasts for more than a few days. One of these cases is that of Randy Gardner who sought to go without sleep as a science project when he was in high school in San Diego.

Randy sought to stay awake for 11 days to beat the Guinness world record as well as record cognitive activity for his science project. With the help of two friends, he went for 11 days without sleep. His experience was reported by sleep researchers including an EEG when he slept for the first time (Ross, 1965). By the second and third day without sleep, Randy had problems focusing his eyes and performing cognitive tasks and remembering new information. Also, his mood became more negative. Near the end of the 11 days, he had trouble finishing sentences and even experienced some hallucinations and delusions such as mistaking a street sign for a person. He also thought that he was a famous football player, although he weighed only 130 pounds at the time (http://www.esquire.com/lifestyle/a2527/esq0804-aug-awake/).

Randy described his experiences to the magazine *Gelf* as follows: "The only reason I got through it was because I was a kid. We got halfway through the damn thing and I thought 'Holy s***, this is tough. I don't want to do this anymore.' But everybody was looking at me at that point so I couldn't quit" (http://www.gelfmagazine.com/archives/sleeping_in.php). How did he do it? Gardner says he didn't even drink coffee. "It's mind over matter," Gardner said. "Your body will shut down. If you don't override it with your mind, you're f***ed. You're going to sleep. You're gone." So he kept his juices flowing by playing game after game of basketball with his friends and the sleep researcher William Dement. Dement also drove him and his friends around in a rented convertible. Randy performed several cognitive studies during the sleepless period that were the basis of a winning science-fair project.

Although Randy stayed awake to set a Guinness World Record, a number of individuals who perform various types of shift work experience sleep deprivation that results in fatigue and a reduction in performance. This has been referred to as sleep debt. A number of studies have sought to determine if it is possible to "bank sleep" prior to shift work, which would improve performance (Rupp et al., 2009). Banking sleep refers to extended time asleep prior to a period of anticipated sleep loss. Several studies have shown that banking sleep can improve performance as well as emotional mood (Patterson et al., 2019).

Although we all experience the need for sleep, you might be surprised to learn that we actually don't fully understand the function of sleep. As you will see in this chapter, sleep serves a number of functions. Our experience tells us that sleep is a strong drive and related to restoring our bodies in terms of energy and alertness. Thus, metabolic processes during sleep prepare us for the next day. As you will see later in this chapter, sleep also strengthens learning and memory. As you read in the chapter on development, the need for sleep is critical for the adolescent brain during a period of cortical development (Galván, 2020).

Evolutionary perspectives tell us that sleep may be protective and keep the organism out of danger. You will also learn in this chapter that animals that eat large amounts of plants sleep less than those who eat meat.

Sleep Patterns

Sleep patterns also evolved in terms of sensory systems. Humans and other animals that use vision as the primary way of finding food and interacting with the world sleep at night. On the other hand, animals such as rats that use nonvisual systems for dealing with the world tend to sleep in the day and look for food at night. As you will also see in the chapter, there are different types of sleep and that these different types of sleep involve different brain areas. One implication is that different types of sleep serve different purposes in the brain. We know, for example, that sleep is important for helping us remember information that we learned during the day.

Sleep became easier to study scientifically in the 1950s. Nathaniel Kleitman and his student Eugene Aserinsky at the University of Chicago published the first detailed account of the patterns of sleep (see Aserinsky & Kleitman, 2003 for a reprint of their 1953 research). What they documented was that during sleep there are periods in which the person's eyes were still. However, at some point during the night, the person's eyes—although closed—would move quickly. They referred to this as **rapid eye movement or REM sleep**. When individuals were wakened during REM sleep, they were more likely to report having a dream than if wakened during quiet sleep.

Another researcher in this University of Chicago lab, William Dement, was able to show that during REM sleep, the EEG looked very different than during quiet sleep. The EEG actually looked more like that seen in wakefulness. Because of this, REM sleep is also referred to as *paradoxical sleep*. EEG measures during sleep helped to establish that sleep is made up of a set of recurring patterns that we now call *stages* (Adamantidis, Gutierrez Herrera, & Gent, 2019).

In 2007 and 2016, the American Academy of Sleep Medicine modified the sleep scoring system based on research (see Berry et al., 2015). Their *American Academy of Sleep Medicine Manual for the Scoring of Sleep and Associated Events* describes non-REM (N) and REM (R) stages of sleep. Thus, stage 1 and stage 2 are referred to as N1 and N2. Stage 3 and 4 are combined and referred to as N3 or slow wave sleep. In the scientific literature, you may see either the older stages 1–4 and REM sleep system or the newer N1–N3 and REM designation.

What do these stages of sleep represent? As you begin to become sleepy, your EEG shows a pattern associated with relaxation, such as alpha waves. The transition from being awake to the onset of sleep varies in different people. Those who fall asleep easily move from being drowsy to the stage 1 of sleep in a few minutes. In stage 1 slower EEG patterns such as theta activity are seen. The move to stage 2, which is the first true stage of sleep, is characterized by sleep spindles and K complexes (see **Figure 6-8**). During this stage your mechanisms of arousal are reduced, including a real reduction of muscular activity. It is also during this stage that your breathing becomes slower and your body temperature begins to drop. In stage 3, the EEG shows high amplitude and slow frequency waves referred to as delta activity. These are increased in stage 4 sleep. Also, the long-range connections between

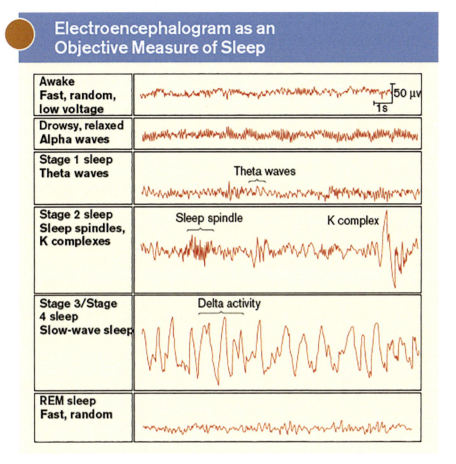

Figure 6-8 Stages of sleep.

SOURCE: Garrett (2010, Figure 15.5).

areas in the brain change to more local connections. The movement from stage 1 to the end of stage 4 takes about 45 minutes.

During the next 45 minutes, the sleep stages go in the opposite direction. That is, the stages go from stage 4 to stage 1 with most of this time being in stage 4. Although it may appear that the person is moving toward becoming awake, this is not the case. Following stage 4 and a quick movement through stages 3, 2, and 1 is a period of REM sleep. Not only are dreams seen during REM sleep, but there are also physiological changes. In particular, there is an increase in cortical activity but a decrease in the person's temperature

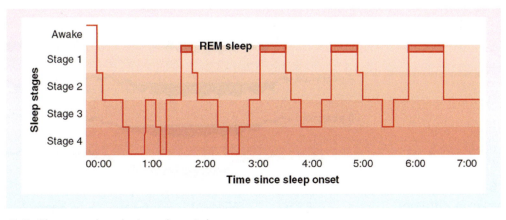

Figure 6-9 Sleep cycles during the night.

and metabolism. There is also a loss of muscle tone that inhibits movement during dreams. However, during REM, penile erections occur in men and in women clitoral engorgement is present. The purpose of these changes during REM is still a matter of debate. After a REM period, the person goes through another series of sleep cycles. These 90-minute cycles continue throughout the night although the deepest sleep is experienced in the early cycles. The first REM period tends to be of shorter duration than later REM periods. Overall, REM sleep in adults is present during about 25% of the night.

Sleep Changes Across the Lifespan

Human adults sleep for about 8 hours every 24 hours. This is a daily or **circadian** rhythm. Circadian comes from Latin and can be translated as "about a day." Thus, a circadian rhythm is a cycle that happens each day as with adult sleep patterns. However, it takes about 12 years for that to happen in humans. With newborn human infants, there is an irregular sleep/wake pattern of which some 50% is spent in REM sleep. By the time the infant is about 3 months old, he or she develops regular rhythms and sleep is seen more often at night. Later, at about one year of age, this changes to a nighttime sleep period and two naps during the day. About the age of two the two daytime naps change to one nap. During the first five years of life, sleep duration ranges from 10 to 16 hours a day, not counting the few months immediately after birth (Galland, Taylor, Elder, & Herbison, 2012). Even though REM sleep is seen in infancy (Hobson, 2009), the ability to recount dreams appears to develop after 5 years of age.

By school time, the afternoon nap has disappeared on a regular basis although children of this age will fall asleep when tired. At puberty, the sleep/wake cycle changes, as does brain development. Recent studies suggest that the sleep cycle of teenagers changes such that they go to sleep and wake up at a later time. In fact, when schools have started later to reflect this change, improvement is seen not only in schoolwork but also in other areas such as a drop in automobile accidents.

Young adults show a predictable pattern of sleep. This pattern, as described previously, occurs in terms of sleep cycles of 90 minutes. In young adults, the first period of REM sleep is usually the shortest of approximately 5 minutes (Raju & Radtke, 2012). Overall, a young adult spends 75% to 80% in non-REM and 20% to 25% in REM sleep. As one ages, the number of arousal and awaking events increase such that older adults may need to spend more time in bed to obtain the same amount of sleep as the young adult.

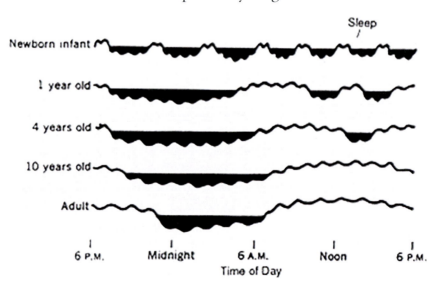

Figure 6-10 Sleep/wake cycles in different ages.

Stability of Sleep Cycles

Across species including humans and other animals, there is a sleep/wake cycle related to Earth's day/night cycle. With access to the sun, there is a stable sleep/wake cycle (see **Figure 6-11**). An environmental factor such as the sun, which influences a circadian rhythm, is referred to by the German word *zeitgeber*, roughly translated as time encoder or synchronizer. This circadian or 24-hour rhythm has been shown to be fairly stable even in species such as those that live in the Arctic with continuous daylight in part of the year (Golombek & Rosenstein, 2010). There are, of course, many clues to the change in seasons and the 24-hour rhythm as Earth rotates in its yearly movement around the sun. This suggests an evolutionary and genetic contribution to circadian rhythms controlled by a set of neurons in the brain.

Over the past 50 years, scientists have asked what would happen if humans had no access to environmental cues that determine sleep/

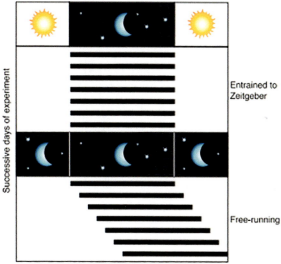

Figure 6-11 The sleep/wake cycle remains constant (top of figure) when environmental factors such as the sun are available. Without such environmental cues, the sleep/wake cycle increases by about 2 hours to a 26-hour day (bottom figure).

wake cycles. This was studied in what are called *cave studies* in which humans lived in caves or rooms without windows that would reflect whether it was day or night. Individuals lived alone in these rooms for a period of time, usually a few weeks, without clocks, radios, and other ways of knowing the time of day. These individuals were able to eat as they wished and to sleep and wake as they wished. As shown in **Figure 6-11** what happened without access to the sun was that the 24-hour sleep/wake cycle slowly increased by about two hours over a three-week period. What was originally a 24-hour day became a 26-hour day. As soon as these individuals returned to the normal day and night environment, their sleep/wake cycle returned to normal. These studies tell us that our bodies continue a similar sleep/wake cycle even without external cues such as the sun rising and setting.

Sleep Patterns Across Species

Humans are not the only species that sleeps. In fact, it is suggested that animals showed sleep patterns over evolutionary time related to metabolic functions (Anafi, Kayser, & Raizen, 2019). One characteristic across mammals is that sleep represents a quiet time that reduces energy expenditure. There are also postures associated with sleep across species. Humans lie down. Bats hang upside down. Some birds sleep standing up. Cows and horses can also sleep standing up, but they generally choose not to. Sleep is also a state that can be changed quickly. Loud sounds or physical contact will change the sleep state to a waking state.

As with humans, sleep can be determined in animals by using EEG along with observable measures such as posture. Some animals such as bats sleep almost 20 hours a day, whereas other species such as kangaroos sleep as little as an hour and a half a day (Campbell & Tobler, 1984).

Nonhuman primates tend to sleep the same amounts of time as humans. It is assumed that sleep patterns evolved in relation to body size and danger. That is, animals that cannot

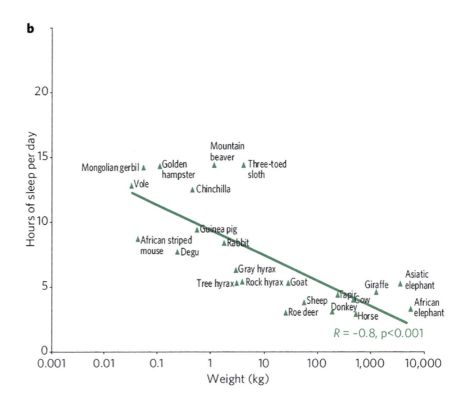

Figure 6-12 Length of sleep each day in relation to the weight of the animal.

Figure 6-13 EEG from beluga whale during sleep. Note that the hemispheres alternate sleep patterns.

hide, such as elephants, cattle, or giraffes, sleep less, whereas bats who can hide in dark caves sleep more. Other animals such as lions with fewer predators also sleep more. One study showed that body size and danger accounted for 80% of the variability in sleep time across species (Allison & Cicchetti, 1976). As shown in **Figure 6-12**, the more an animal weighs, the less it sleeps. It should be noted that this relationship is seen only in animals that do not eat meat. Meat eaters show little relationship between body weight and sleep duration.

In terms of insects and fish, there is less evidence that they meet the common definition of sleep (Siegel, 2008). Marine mammals such as dolphins, seals, and porpoises show sleep patterns that affect only half of their brain at a time. That's right, only one hemisphere at a time. This allows dolphins, for example, to stay awake for as long as 15 days at a time (Branstetter et al., 2012). This can increase the animals' survival skills. As shown in **Figure 6-13**, EEG is different in one hemisphere from the other during sleep.

One study examined human sleep patterns in some 20 countries (Walch, Cochran, & Forger, 2016). What these researchers found was that bedtime did differ by country, although these differences became less as a person aged from less than 30 years old to more than 55 years old. Sunrise and sunset also influenced bed and wake time. However, the actual duration of sleep was similar and averaged about 7.9 hours with a mean variation between 7.5 and 8.1 hours across the 20 countries. Thus, cultural factors can play a role in sleep patterns but not the actual amount of sleep one experiences.

Learning During Sleep

Although sleep is seen throughout the animal kingdom, its exact function is largely unknown. One role that is being explored is the manner in which sleep is involved in

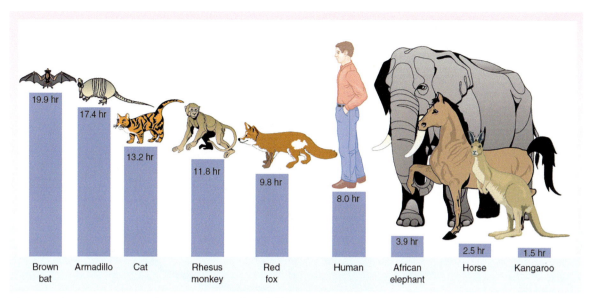

Figure 6-14 Average sleep amount for different species.

learning and memory (Paller, Creery, & Schechtman, 2021; Wamsley & Stickgold, 2011; Wamsley & Stickgold, 2018). In specific, sleep benefits memory in humans. In one study, college students who dreamed about a task they had just learned performed better on the task after sleep (Wamsley & Stickgold, 2019). It is also known that a good night's sleep before a test improves performance. Even trying to move up a level in a video game will be easier the next day compared with the previous night.

It is suggested that improved learning after sleep involves a reactivation of memory traces through changes in the connection of synapses (Frank & Cantera, 2014). That is, as noted previously, with new abilities and information come changes in the number of synapses and changes in their connections. Forgetting (or extinction) is associated with the elimination of existing connections. In sleep, neurons involved in activities during the day are reactivated, which strengthens the connections between neurons. Further, EEG slow wave activity during sleep has been shown to increase performance on cognitive tasks the next day. In this manner, sleep promotes learning. It has also been shown that depriving organisms of sleep will prevent or reduce the quality of memory consolidation and learning.

Using a state-of-the-art technique that allows researchers to view neurons in the mouse brain, Guang Yang and his colleagues examined the role of sleep in learning (Yang, Lai, Cichon, Ma, Li, & Gan, 2014; see also Euston, & Steenland, 2014). In this study the researchers trained mice to run on a spinning rod. This of course is not an easy task and takes practice. After this learning, changes in the neurons were examined. They found that after the mice learned to run on a spinning rod, changes in the spines on the dendrite were increased. Spines on the dendrite allow for enhanced connections with other neurons. If the mice also learned a different task, different new spines were found. This suggests that learning different skills produce changes in different parts of the dendrites of the neuron. If the animals were not allowed to sleep following the learning of the new task, then the number of new spines on the dendrites were reduced. However, with sleep, the newly formed spines were still present one day later.

As shown in **Figure 6–15**, there are three related processes involved in the manner in which sleep enhances learning. The first is slow-wave oscillations in the electrical activity

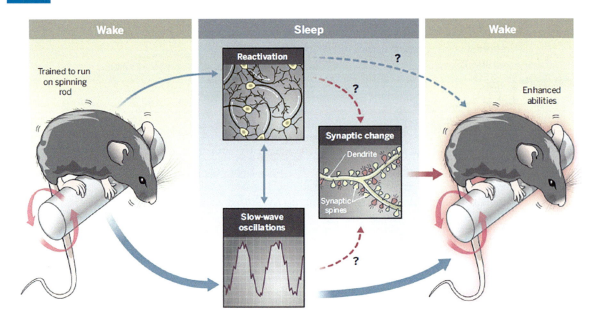

Figure 6-15 Sleep processes that increase performance. The three phenomena that increase memory enhancement are: slow-wave oscillations in brain electrical activity, reactivation of recent experiences, and changes in synaptic connectivity.

of the brain. EEG slow-wave activity has been shown to be important for learning new information. The second is reactivation during sleep of those neurons that were involved in the learning of the task during the day. In this way the brain repeats the patterns of activity associated with the task. And third, there is an increase in spines on the dendrite, which allows for connections with other neurons. Although this study taught the mice a new skill, other studies with humans have shown that sleep improves the learning of events and places as well. It is actually better for you to sleep before a test rather than do an all-nighter. Of course, you have to read the information first.

Neuroscience Studies of Sleep

Since sleep represents a special state of consciousness, some scientists suggest that it can give us a window into understanding consciousness (Hobson & Pace-Scott, 2002; Hobson, 2009). From this standpoint, the three processes of wakefulness, REM sleep, and non-REM sleep represent three different states of consciousness. Each of these states involves different brain and other physiological processes. Over the past 100 years, studies of sleep with humans and animals have painted a consistent picture of the physiological processes involved in sleep and wakefulness.

In the 1940s, Horace Magoun and Giuseppe Moruzzi found that stimulating neurons in the region of the pons and the adjacent midbrain in animals caused a state of wakefulness and arousal (Moruzzi & Magoun, 1949). We now know that this area is also active during REM sleep. This area of the brainstem has since been referred to as the *reticular activating system or RAS*. Thus, stimulation of the brainstem results in arousal of the forebrain. The opposite situation was found at about this time by Walter Hess in Switzerland. He showed that stimulating the thalamus with low-frequency electrical pulses in an awake animal produces slow-wave sleep. We now know that the basic sleep/wake cycles are under the control of the hypothalamus, the brain stem, and the lower part of the frontal brain.

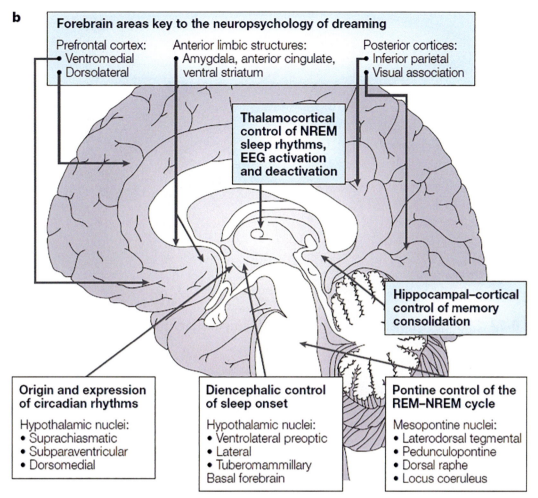

Figure 6-16 Brain regions of interest in the neurobiology of sleep. The blue boxes represent areas that are key to the generation of the EEG rhythms of sleep, the subjective experience of sleep mentation or dreaming, and sleep's effects on cognition. The subcortical regions (cream-colored boxes) constitute the loci of control for the regulation of sleep–wake transitions and the control of REM–NREM alternation.

The hypothalamus is involved in circadian rhythms and the onset of sleep. The pons, which is located below the thalamus on the brain stem, is related to changes in REM and non-REM sleep. In particular, neurons in the pons are active both during waking and REM sleep. Their activity is related to the type of EEG seen during the awake state. During non-REM sleep, these neurons are inactive. The subjective experience of sleep mentation or dreaming is related to the limbic areas, the visual areas, and the forebrain. Sleep's effects on cognition and memory are related to the hippocampus. During sleep the thalamus serves as the gatekeeper and prevents certain information going to the cortex. It also relays information from the RAS and influences EEG changes during sleep. Besides sleep, the thalamus also functions as a control switch in other states of consciousness such as coma and general anesthesia (Picchioni et al., 2014).

One part of the hypothalamus, the *suprachiasmatic nucleus* (SCN), works as a pacemaker to control the circadian rhythm. Part of the reason we know this is that if there is damage to the SCN, then an animal will still sleep, eat, drink, and exercise. However, there will no longer be a regular pattern to their activities. Thus, the suprachiasmatic nucleus is

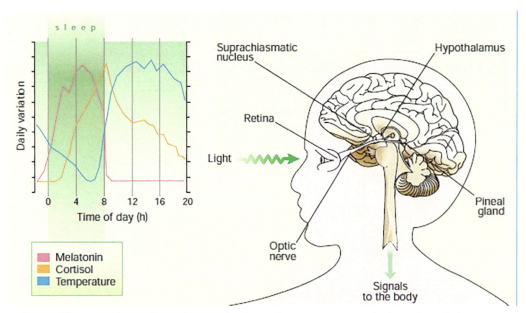

Figure 6-17 Changes in melatonin, cortisol, and temperature during the night.

important for making activities regular. In a number of animals, the SCN also is involved in determining which seasons mating takes place. Deer, for example, mate in the spring and fall of the year.

The name of the SCN refers to where it is located. Nucleus refers to a group of cells. In the case of humans there are about 48,000 neurons in the winter and 30,000 in the summer in the SCN (Hofmann & Swaab, 1992). The suprachiasmatic nucleus of the hypothalamus is located above (supra) the optic chiasm (chiasmatic). This is the place in the brain where the pathways from each eye cross to go to each hemisphere. Light influences the retina and then the SCN. Part of this process is to cause the pineal gland to decrease the production of melatonin in the morning and to increase it in the evening to induce sleep.

Your temperature falls during sleep and then increases as you wake up (Abbott, 2003). The two hormones, melatonin and cortisol, increase during sleep. Those individuals who produce less melatonin such as the elderly have more disturbed sleep. Some people also take melatonin medications to promote sleep on long-distance airline flights. Exposure to bright light during the day will also increase nighttime melatonin levels and promote better sleep.

Brain-imaging techniques such as fMRI show the manner in which cortical networks are involved in sleep (Picchioni, Duyn, & Horovitz, 2013). First, it is clear that the brain continues to be active in sleep even without external stimulation or self-control of our thoughts. Second, sleep is controlled by bottom-up processes involving the brain stem and the hypothalamus. Third, during sleep some of the same networks such as those involved in memory, arousal, and consciousness are active. In fact, different memory systems are seen to be active during different types of sleep. Fourth, during sleep the frontal areas of the brain are not connected to other areas of the default network (Horovitz et al., 2009). The loss of connection to the frontal areas is one reason our dreams can be irrational or even chaotic. Without logic, you can dream anything you want.

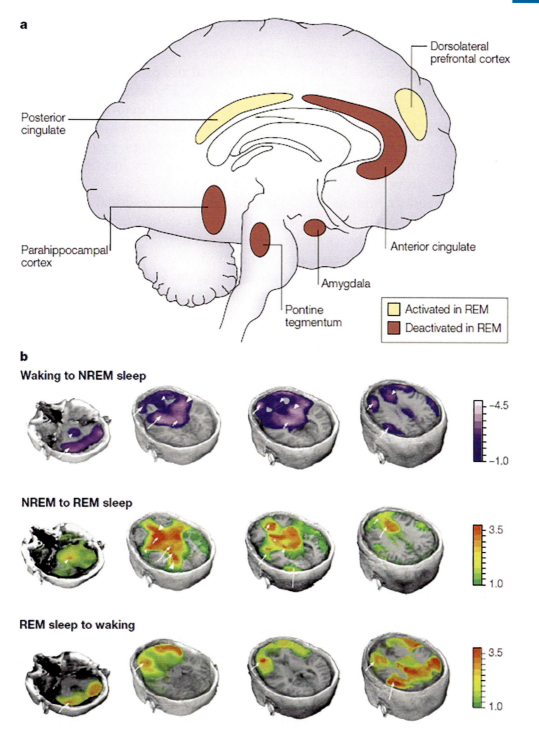

Figure 6-18 Brain regions of interest in the neurobiology of sleep. The top part of the figure shows areas of the brain that are activated (cream color) or deactivated (dark red) in REM sleep. The bottom part of the figure shows changes in the brain (from bottom to top) as sleep stages change from waking to REM sleep; from non-REM to REM sleep; and from REM sleep to waking.

Sleep Disorders

Complaints concerning sleep are second only to those concerning pain in terms of physician visits (Mahowald & Schenck, 2005). In the medical and psychological literature, more than 100 different sleep disorders have been described. However, most of these can be discussed in terms of four broad categories. These four are (1) **insomnia**, the difficulty to fall or stay asleep; (2) **hypersomnia**, that is, the experience of excessive daytime sleepiness without obvious explanation; (3) **circadian rhythm disorders**, that is, the inability to sleep during the desired time; and (4) **parasomnias**, which include sleepwalking, sleep talking, and night terrors.

Insomnia is the most common sleep disorder seen by professionals. It is described in terms of the inability to obtain enough sleep to leave one feeling rested. Historically, it was believed that insomnia was always the result of an underlying psychological or medical problem. That is, you took your problems to bed with you.

More recent research suggests that insomnia can be present without psychological or medical disorders. Although health disorders can contribute to insomnia, genetic factors also play a role. Further, those with insomnia may actually be more active during the day and have a higher metabolism, which influences their ability to fall asleep. Both behavioral treatment and medications have been shown to be effective. Surprisingly, if some sleep medications are taken for a long period of time, they will actually prevent sleep rather than make it possible. Melatonin is also useful in those individuals whose pineal gland does not produce enough of the hormone.

The second class of sleep disorders is referred to as *hypersomnia* or lack of sufficient sleep. There are a number of causes of these disorders. Working three jobs or not having time to obtain sufficient sleep leaves one feeling tired. The problem for society in relation to this condition is that a number of automobile, aircraft, and industrial accidents have been linked to lack of sleep on the part of the operators.

Some neurological disorders such as *narcolepsy* cause the individual to fall asleep at random times during the day. Narcolepsy affects about 1 in 2,000 individuals. Even when standing, the person may experience a sudden case of muscle weakness and fall to the ground in a state of apparent sleep. These individuals enter REM sleep from wakefulness without going through non-REM sleep. These attacks can last from less than a minute to some 30 minutes. When they awake, they may experience their body as paralyzed and be unable to move. This disorder has a strong genetic component and is not related to the amount of sleep obtained at night.

The third type of disorder is *circadian rhythm disorders*. These disorders result in the person being unable to sleep at the desired time. However, once the person falls asleep, they experience the normal sleeping pattern. A shift in one's circadian rhythm can be the result of situational factors. For example, flying to a different time zone can result in "jet lag" in which the person experiences sleep patterns that are not consistent with the day/night periods of that location. In general, it takes one day for each hour of time change for a person's body to adjust. Also, shift work in which a person works the day shift and then the night shift without time to adjust will also influence one's internal circadian rhythms. In addition to situational factors, there are those who find it difficult to fall asleep before 1 a.m. or 2 a.m. However, they sleep in a normal pattern and wake later in the day. Researchers have been interested in differences in those who are early risers as compared to late risers.

The fourth category of sleep disorders is *parasomnias*. These are a variety of conditions that may leave the person feeling distressed or bring distress to others. In general, these disorders are not related to one another from an underlying physiological or psychological standpoint. One type of distress occurs when a person experiences consciousness but is unable to move his muscles. This is referred to as *sleep paralysis*. Normally in sleep, you lose consciousness and then lose the ability to move your muscles. When awaking, the opposite happens. You regain the ability to move your muscles and then regain consciousness as you wake up. However, if you gain consciousness before you can move your muscles, you experience sleep paralysis. You find yourself unable to move and you are aware of that fact. Although this typically is a short-term event, it causes distress, especially on its first occurrence.

Another sleep disorder is called *night or sleep terrors* (Pavlova & Abdennadher, 2013). The peak prevalence of the disorder is 5 to 7 years of age. This is when the child sits up in bed and begins to scream. It usually occurs in stage 3 sleep and lasts for less than a few minutes. Once the episode is complete, the person returns to sleep and generally does not remember the event the next day. Individuals experiencing a night terror are difficult to arouse. Actually waking the person can prolong or intensify the episode. It is not limited to nighttime sleep but can also occur in daytime naps. The disorder is not related to dream content or other psychological factors. It can be seen in young children, which of course upsets their parents. Typically, the experience of sleep terrors begins before adulthood but can continue into adulthood.

Another parasomnia is *sleepwalking* (Ralls & Grigg-Damberger, 2013). Sleepwalking has been described in Shakespeare's plays and continues to be of interest to sleep researchers (Zadra & Pilon, 2011). Although sleepwalking was originally seen as a dissociative state without memory, current research suggests that at least half of the individuals can recall some events on occasion. The emotional experiences during sleepwalking can range from neutral emotionality to agitation. It typically occurs during non-REM sleep and lasts for about 15 minutes, although longer episodes have been reported. If the actions occur during REM sleep, it is referred to as REM sleep behavior disorder.

One example of sleepwalking occurred in a 31-year-old woman. She was found walking up the street in front of her home in her nightgown with a knife in one hand and an unopened package of deli ham in the other (Ralls & Grigg-Damberger, 2013). When examined, she was found to have a history of sleepwalking throughout her life. One confusing problem for those observing sleepwalking is that the person doing the walking may have her eyes open and not initially seem to be asleep. In adults, another problem with sleepwalking is the occurrence of accidents that lead to physical problems. Sleepwalking runs in families and appears to have a genetic component. Further, sleepwalking activity and the performance of complex behaviors during sleep has been linked to certain medications.

The comedian Mike Birbiglia was on tour in Washington State when he had a dream that a guided missile was heading toward his hotel room. In his dream he jumped out of his hotel room. Although asleep, he actually did jump out of his hotel room. Fortunately for him, he was on the second floor and lived to tell about the event, which he did in a book and movie called *Sleepwalk with Me*. After the hotel event, he saw sleep professionals and was diagnosed with REM sleep behavior disorder (http://www.npr.org/templates/story/story.php?storyId=130644070 and https://www.cnn.com/2012/10/02/health/sleepwalking-rem-behavior-disorder/index.html). Mike Birbiglia, while asleep, acted out a dream and jumped from his hotel window.

Two other common sleep phenomena are *sleep talking* and *sleep jerks or starts* (Weiss, 2013). Although these are not sleep disorders, they can be of concern especially to parents of young children. Sleep talking can range from just a few words or sounds to long speeches of understandable content. Although many young adults have had roommates who sleep talked, most do not remember what they said the next morning. Sleep talking does not occur at any particular stage of sleep. It also tends to decrease as one enters adulthood. Studies suggest that sleep talking is found worldwide and occurs in about one-quarter to one-half of all children at least once a year.

As you fall sleep, it is not uncommon to feel your body jerk for a second. Sleep starts or jerks are seen at the onset of sleep. These are brief contractions of the legs and arms and are experienced as body jerks that last for just a few seconds. These jerks are experienced by some 60 to 70% of the general population. Although they are seen in both children and adults and are normal occurrences, they may concern some parents who mistake them for some type of seizure. Sleep that starts with jerks may awaken the person.

CONCEPT CHECK

1. What is rapid eye movement (REM) sleep, and why is it important for sleep researchers?
2. In what ways does the pattern of sleep change throughout the lifecycle?
3. With access to the sun, there is a stable sleep/wake cycle related to Earth's day/night cycle. What happens when humans have no access to environmental cues in terms of sleep/wake cycles?
4. Humans are not the only species that sleeps. What factors account for similarities and differences across species?
5. Research has shown that sleep is involved in learning. List three results that support the importance of sleep for learning.
6. Briefly describe the four broad categories of sleep disorders and give an example of each.

Dreams

Another aspect of sleep is dreaming. **Dreams** that are experienced during sleep reflect mainly involuntary images, ideas, feelings, and sensations. How should we think about dreams? In dreams, we are aware of the unfolding situation in front of us. In dreams, we experience ourselves being part of the action unlike our *daydreams* or mind-wandering when we are awake. We participate in the experiences of the dream. During dreams we have emotional reactions and experience it as real. However, we would not say it was reality. On the other hand, some philosophers have asked which is more real—when we are dreaming or when we are not.

Research suggests that external events can play an important role in the experience of dreaming. For example, with the advent of COVID-19 worldwide in 2020, the pandemic influenced how individuals remembered their dreams and what they dreamt about (Nielsin, 2020). Overall, people reported more dreams related to the virus such as content about social distancing. One current perspective suggests that dreams present a story which allows the dreamer to explore and evaluate possible scenarios (Zadra & Stickgold, 2021). Thus, dreams allows a number of ideas to be put together in memory.

Since the beginning of recorded history dreams have played a role in the attempt of humans to make meaning of the world and ourselves (Ray, 2010). Dreams have represented the *other*, the aspects of ourselves and our world that stood outside of human knowledge. As illustrated in a variety of religious texts over the last few thousand years, dreams have been seen to foretell future events as well as allow for communication with the gods. Still, during this period others including the Roman poet Lucretius in 44 BC suggested that dreams are common in all animals. Charles Darwin echoed a similar theme in his *The Descent of Man* (1874) in which he suggests that all higher animals including birds have dreams.

Within the last 100 years, the understanding of dreams has been brought into a more theoretical perspective within dynamic and analytic psychology and more recently within the context of the neurosciences. Although a topic of heated debate, an initial contribution was Sigmund Freud's perspective that dreams could be understood within the context of instinctual functioning and neurology outlined in his *The Project for a Scientific Psychology* (1895).

As articulated in the Project, dreams offered an understanding of previously established networks of neurons and pointed to the manner in which ideas and events had come to be associated with one another in the brain. In this way dreams were reflective of an individual's psychology during the waking state. Freud also suggested that dreams were reflective of a reduction of logical or I (*ego*) processes. This in turn would allow for more instinctual processes such as sexuality to be present. Current brain-imaging research suggests that indeed the frontal lobe executive functions are inhibited during the dream state.

Carl Jung, who developed analytic psychology, had a more evolutionary perspective. For him, images in dreams had a particular meaning for a given person. Day-to-day events in our environment could be triggers for bringing forth ideas with a strong emotional component, or *complexes* as Jung called them. Jung suggested that to understand dreams it was important to examine a long series of dreams over time rather than just a single night's dream. Dreams in this context reflected patterns in a person's life. In this sense, what is *not* in a series of dreams, such as the lack of other people, would be as important as what is the content of the dream. Jung also visited different cultures around the world and reported a similarity of dream material worldwide.

Many view the scientific study of dreams as beginning in 1953 with the discovery by Aserinsky and Kleitman of an association between dreaming and rapid eye movement (REM) sleep. Sleep generally is characterized by four different stages as reflected in the EEG. In contrast to the higher voltage, more patterned EEG activity found in sleep, REM sleep appears to have an EEG pattern more like that of the waking state and is characterized by low voltage random appearing EEG activity. Dreams in the REM state are generally more emotional and vivid than the everyday content of dreams seen in the non-REM state (McCormick & Westbrook, 2013). Both REM and non-REM dreams are associated with decreases in low-frequency EEG activity in the posterior areas of the brain (Siclari et al., 2017).

Waking an individual during REM sleep is more likely than any other sleep stage to result in a dream report. Following the discovery of the association between REM sleep and dreams, a number of labs examined the dream state. The work included a variety of foci, including the nature of the dream itself, factors involved in dream recall, the influence of external factors on dreaming and other factors associated with dreaming. For example, following a natural disaster such as an earthquake, researchers have found an increase in nightmares suggesting that trauma can be related to dreaming. This could also be found during the COVID-19 pandemic in 2020 (Mota et al., 2020). Overall, REM dreams are heavy on emotions and light on logic. The main characteristics of dream processes include emotionally laden sensory processes and images without a sense of individual control.

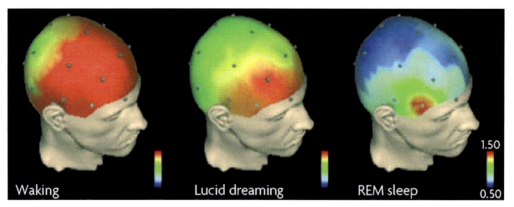

Figure 6-19 Brain activation during lucid dreaming appears more similar to being awake than during REM sleep.

Less well understood is the so-called *lucid dream* in which an individual, while dreaming, realizes that she is part of a dream and may even experience control of the dream. Lucid dreams are rare and occur in only 1% or 2% of all reported dreams. Physiological studies show the brains of those experiencing lucid dreaming to be more like an awake state than that seen in normal REM sleep (Voss, Holzmann, Tuin, & Hobson, 2009). In specific, gamma band EEG activity around 40 Hz is associated with the lucid dream experience, especially in the frontal and temporal areas of the brain (Voss et al., 2014). Researchers have asked if inducing gamma band could produce lucid dreams. This is described in the box: Applying Psychological Science—Producing Lucid Dreams with Gamma Activity.

Applying Psychological Science—Producing Lucid Dreams with Gamma Activity

What if you had never experienced a lucid dream, would you want to experience one? That is, would you want to experience thoughts and decisions normally associated with your waking hours, but during sleep? Ursula Voss and her colleagues gave 27 young adults at Göttingen University Medical Center in Germany that opportunity (Voss et al., 2014). Since gamma band EEG activity is associated with lucid dreams, these researchers asked if the opposite was also true. That is, could they induce gamma band activity in someone's brain that, in turn, would produce lucid dreams?

To induce gamma band EEG activity, they used a technique referred to as *transcranial alternating current stimulation* (tACS). This is a technique in which battery-produced alternating current is applied to the scalp through two electrodes positioned at the front and back of the brain. The level of the current is such that a person cannot detect its presence. Although lucid dreaming has been associated with 40 Hz EEG activity, these researchers tested seven different frequencies ranging from 2 Hz to 100 Hz. They also included a sham condition in which no alternating current was applied.

The participants spent four nights at the sleep laboratory. The researcher followed the people as they slept. The stimulation was applied for 30 seconds after REM sleep was detected. After the stimulation, the participants were wakened and asked to report their dreams and complete a scale that measured lucid dreaming.

Lucid dreams in terms of the experience of dream insight was experienced during 25 Hz and 40 Hz stimulation. Dream control was experienced with 25 Hz stimulation.

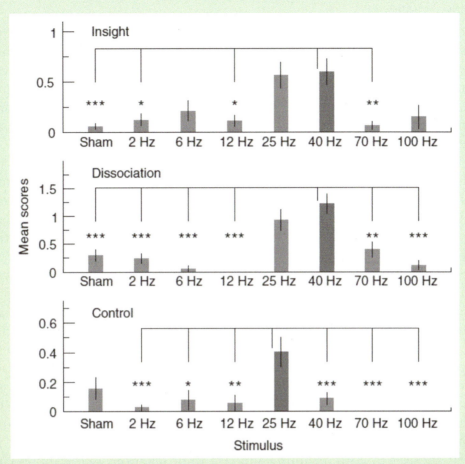

Figure 6-20 Rating of lucid dream measures for stimulation at each frequency.
Note: * reflects level of statistical significance.
Source: Voss, Holzmann, Tuin, and Hobson (2009).

Watching one's own dream (dissociation) was seen at both 25 and 40 Hz. The sham stimulation as well as stimulation at frequencies of 2, 6, 12, 70, and 100 Hz produced no lucid dream experiences. These results are shown in **Figure 6-20**.

One participant described a lucid dream as follows: "I was dreaming about lemon cake. It looked translucent, but then again, it didn't. It was a bit like in an animated movie, like *The Simpsons*. And then I started falling and the scenery changed and I was talking to Matthias Schweighöfer (a German actor) and two foreign exchange students. And I was wondering about the actor and they told me, 'Yes, you met him before,' so then I realized, 'Oops, you are dreaming.'"

This study suggests that 25 and 40 Hz stimulation can produce lucid dream experiences. The researchers further suggest that producing lucid dreams may be a technique for helping those with certain disorders to be able to make active changes to their dreams associated with negative experiences. For example, a person with PTSD might be able to redo a situation during a lucid dream that had previously been of concern to them.

Thought Question: Which of your dreams would you want to redo?

Dreams and Neuroscience

More recently, dream processes have been examined within the context of current neuroscience work. The goal of this research is to determine brain areas involved in dreaming. Also, they want to examine the manner in which dreaming and other cognitive processes (for example, visual imagery) are related. Early speculation suggested that dreams were related to brain-stem functioning especially the pons with its generators for rapid eye movement sleep. However, neuropsychological case studies have shown that damage to the pons does not stop dream reports, whereas damage to the forebrain area does.

Current brain-imaging studies suggest that a variety of brain areas are active during brain states associated with dreaming. These areas include the brain stem, which is responsible for basic arousal; the limbic system, which is highly involved in emotionality; and forebrain areas involved in sensory processing. Areas involved in higher level cognitive processes such as planning and logical thinking showed decreased activation during these dream periods.

Further explorations suggest that during dreaming, cortical pathways between areas involved in emotional processing and those involved in visual processing are active, whereas those between visual processing and higher-level logical thinking are not. In REM sleep, areas related to emotional processing such as the limbic and amygdala regions become activated. Thus, there is emotional processing without logical connections. This may help to explain the nature of dreams in which emotional and non-logical sequencing of imagery are accepted without reflective awareness or control. That is, we have no problem flying through the air or abruptly going from one place on earth to another in our dreams. The nature of dreams has led some researchers to ask if dreaming is like performing jazz music. Indeed, this is what was found. Similar activations in specific brain areas are seen in both dreaming and jazz improvisations (see Kahn & Gover, 2010 for an overview).

One implication that can be drawn from the brain-imaging work is that a variety of processes are involved in the creation of dreams. Such research helps to characterize the nature of the subjective experience of dreaming. However, even today, we often see a replay of the old debate (existing at least since the time of Plato and Aristotle) as to whether dreams reflect our hidden desires or are merely afterthoughts of our behaviors and experiences of the day (McCormick & Westbrook, 2013).

CONCEPT CHECK

1. Since the beginning of recorded history dreams have played a role in the attempt of humans to make meaning of the world and ourselves. What did the following people contribute to our historical understanding of dreams:
   a. Lucretius?
   b. Charles Darwin?
   c. Sigmund Freud?
   d. Carl Jung?
   e. Aserinsky and Kleitman?
2. What are the characteristics of a lucid dream? What significant results and possible applications came out of the research by Ursula Voss and her colleagues?

3. Brain-imaging studies suggest that a variety of brain areas show changes in activation during brain states associated with dreaming. Specifically, what happens in the different brain areas and how does this help explain the nature of dreams?

Hypnosis and Meditation

Hypnosis is considered by many psychologists to be an altered state of consciousness. Meditation is a technique that focuses one's consciousness away from the outer world and toward an inner sense of awareness. Although different processes, both hypnosis and meditation have been suggested to influence our consciousness as well as having numerous positive benefits. These positive benefits include reducing anxiety, depression, chronic pain, and stress.

Hypnosis

When we hear the word *hypnosis*, most of us have an image that comes to our mind. It may be the one from the old movies in which a strange-looking "doctor" moves a watch in front of someone's eyes. In these old movies, hypnotists can instruct the person to do anything they wish.

Although the old movies were dramatic, they were usually wrong in their presentation of hypnosis. People, for example, will not do anything under hypnosis that they would not do normally. People do report, however, that when experiencing hypnosis, they remain aware of what is being said to them. In this way, they can actively experience what is happening. When told, for example, that their hand is extremely light and will rise like a balloon, they report that they saw it happening by itself. They also report that no effort was involved.

Hypnosis is currently defined by researchers as *"an individual's ability to experience suggested alterations in physiology, sensations, emotions, thoughts, or behavior during hypnosis"* (Elkins, Barabasz, Council, & Spiegel, 2015). As can be seen from this definition, changes during the hypnotic experience can take place on different levels. Although the nature of hypnosis is not fully understood, with the advent of EEG and fMRI, researchers have been able to better describe the nature of the process (Ray, 2007; Hoeft et al., 2012; Oakley & Halligan, 2009).

In the 1800s, James Braid introduced the term "hypnosis," although practices similar to hypnosis had been described since ancient times. The term hypnosis comes from the Greek word for sleep. As such, much of the early work emphasized the nature of the hypnotic experience, especially its relationship to sleep. Ivan Pavlov (1937), for example, saw both hypnosis and sleep as processes that inhibited the brain. Later work began to differentiate hypnosis and sleep.

In the late 1940s, it was reported that EEG recorded during hypnosis was less like sleep and more similar to being awake (Gordon, 1949). Today, it appears that hypnosis allows the different types of information typically integrated in the brain to remain separate. For example, pain such as an electrical shock is composed of two experiences. One is the sensation of the shock and the other is the negative emotional reaction. When told they will not experience pain under hypnosis, individuals still report the sensation but not the negative emotionality. Further, the normal EEG reaction to the pain is not seen in those individuals who are hypnotized, whereas it is seen in those who are not (Ray, Keil, Mikuteit, Bongartz, & Elbert, 2002). Similar results were also seen with visual stimuli (Schmidt, Hecht, Naumann, & Miltner, 2017). Individuals during hypnosis were told to see a virtual wooden board in front of the computer display on which they were doing a counting task. Hypnosis not only reduced performance but also reduced EEG measures associated with attention in comparison to a control group.

Hypnotic Effects

Do you think you could experience hypnosis? It turns out some people experience the state quickly and easily. Those individuals typically enjoy the experience. However, about 25% of all people find it difficult to experience hypnosis. The rest fall somewhere in between. Your ability to experience hypnosis is fairly stable. It has been shown that after 10, 15, and even 25 years, a given person's ability to experience hypnosis remains constant. Monozygotic twins show a correlation of .5 to .6 in their ability to be hypnotized, whereas dizygotic twins show a correlation of less than .10.

When is hypnosis useful? Hypnosis has now been shown to be an important adjunct to a number of clinical treatments. It has been shown to be useful in controlling pain. The reduction of pain through the use of hypnosis is referred to as *hypnotic analgesia*. This can either be short-term pain from an operation, for example, or more long-term pain such as that seen in arthritis. Individuals can be taught self-hypnotic techniques, which allow them to reduce the pain on their own.

Hypnosis can also improve results found in traditional psychological treatments such as the treatment of anxiety (Kirsch, Montgomery, & Sapirstein, 1995). Hypnosis can even reduce stress and modify our immune systems in a positive manner (Kiecolt-Glaser, Marcha, Atkinson, & Glaser, 2001). In one study, medical and dental students who were hypnotically susceptible were given relaxation and hypnotic training compared to a control group who were also hypnotically susceptible but did not receive training. Taking a medical school exam is a stressful experience. As such, taking an exam influences the immune system. Those in the hypnosis group did not show the standard immune response to taking major exams. Other studies have shown that hypnosis is useful for helping patients recover more quickly from outpatient surgery.

During hypnosis, what if the person is told not to remember what they are currently doing? They will have difficulty remembering their experiences even after the hypnotic session is over. This is referred to as *posthypnotic amnesia*. That is, the person does not remember the events that he or she is instructed not to remember. This in turn can be reversed when so instructed.

However, hypnosis cannot improve your memory. Although the movies show a person in the courtroom remembering the license plate number with great certainty, it turns out that the person is often wrong. The thing that hypnosis does is to allow the person to present their answer with great certainty, even if wrong. For this reason, hypnosis is not allowed in court proceedings as a method of gaining accurate information from memory. There are a number of myths concerning hypnosis as described in the box: Myths and Misconceptions—The Myths of Hypnosis.

Myths and Misconceptions—The Myths of Hypnosis

People commonly learn about hypnosis from the movies or ideas that are repeated without scientific evidence. This leaves people believing that you can hypnotize someone and they will do what you tell them. By the way, that is not true. You will not commit crimes or hurt others under hypnosis unless that is what you do in your regular life. Hypnosis researchers at the University of Tennessee, Michael Nash and Grant Beham, have reviewed common myths of hypnosis in terms of what has been found in scientific research (Nash & Beham, 2005). Here is what they found:

Table 6-1 Hypnosis—myth versus reality

Myth	Reality
It's all a matter of having a good imagination.	Ability to imagine vividly is unrelated to hypnotizability.
Relaxation is an important feature of hypnosis.	It's not. Hypnosis has been induced during vigorous exercise.
It's mostly just compliance.	Many highly-motivated people fail to experience hypnosis.
It's a matter of willful faking.	Physiological responses indicate that people are not lying.
It is dangerous.	Standard procedures are no more distressing than lectures.
It has something to do with a sleeplike state.	It does not. Hypnotized individuals are fully awake.
Certain personality types are likely to be hypnotizable.	There are no substantial correlates with personality measures.
People who are hypnotized lose control of themselves.	Individuals are capable of saying no or terminating hypnosis.
Hypnosis can enable people to "relive" the past.	Age-regressed adults behave like adults play-acting as children.
A person's responsiveness to hypnosis depends on the technique used and who administers it.	Neither is important under laboratory conditions. It is the person's capacity that is important.
When hypnotized, people can remember more accurately.	Hypnosis may actually muddle the distinction between memory and fantasy and may artificially inflate confidence.
Hypnotized people can be led to do acts that conflict with their values.	Hypnotized people fully adhere to their usual moral standards.
People do not remember what happens during hypnosis.	Posthypnotic amnesia does not occur spontaneously.
Hypnosis can enable people to perform otherwise impossible feats of strength, endurance, learning, and sensory acuity.	Performance following hypnotic suggestions for increased muscle strength, learning, and sensory acuity does not exceed what can be accomplished by motivated individuals outside hypnosis.

Thought Question: Why do you think movies and other media portray hypnosis in a way that does not fit with scientific research?

In terms of brain function, research has suggested that the anterior cingulate (ACC) is involved in the type of executive function that allows one to drive down the street and ignore one set of signs while paying attention to another (Awh & Gehring, 1999). In terms of hypnotic modulation of experience, the anterior cingulate consistently is shown to be an area involved. In a series of polyethylene terephthalate (PET) studies, Rainville and his colleagues have shown that neural activity in the brainstem, thalamus, and ACC contribute to the experience of being hypnotized (Grant & Rainville, 2005; Rainville et al., 2019).

In particular, these authors report absorption-related changes to be seen in the more rostral regions of the ACC. In an earlier hypnotic study involving painful stimuli, Rainville and his colleagues (Rainville et al., 1997) found that activity in the ACC closely paralleled subjective experience, and that it reflected the emotional component (that is, unpleasantness) but not the sensory component of the painful stimuli. Another using high-density EEG showed that hypnosis reduced components of evoked potentials to painful stimulation (Ray, Keil, Mikuteit, Bongaartz, & Elbert, 2002).

In the introduction to neuroscience chapter, you learned that brain networks can be discussed in terms of the default mode network, the executive control network, and the salience network. Using fMRI, these networks were examined in 12 individuals who experienced hypnosis easily and 12 individuals who did not (Hoeft et al., 2012). Those individuals who were easier to hypnotize showed greater brain network connections between the executive network (prefrontal cortex) and the salience network (anterior cingulate) in comparison to low hypnotizable individuals. This suggested to the researchers that the prefrontal areas were able to inhibit the emotional responses through their connection with the anterior cingulate.

From an evolutionary perspective, you might think about whether hypnosis could help individuals adapt to their environment (Ray & Tucker, 2003). Clearly, the ability to modulate pain would be an important aspect of our history as humans. This is particularly true since the development of anesthesia is relatively recent.

Another question you could ask is whether processes similar to hypnosis appear in animals. In 1646, an Austrian monk published a detailed account describing how he had hypnotized a chicken by holding its head on the ground and forcing the animal to fixate on a line drawn away from its beak (Völgyesi, 1966). From that time to the present, there have been a number of stories of how alligators, rabbits, chickens, and other animals could be immobilized, generally by rubbing or stroking the animal, although eye-fatigue through fixation has also been used.

A variety of animal hypnosis studies suggest that in this condition the animals show an analgesia-like response to needle pricks and electric shock. Draper and Klemm (1967), using a learning procedure in rabbits, suggest that the dominant feature of animal hypnosis is a disconnection of overt motor functions without conspicuous inhibition of sensory functions.

Not unlike human hypnosis, immobilization in chickens has been characterized in three stages: (1) vocalizations and continuously open eyes; (2) suppressed vocal behavior and eye flutters; and (3) eyes closed, occasional body twitches, and lack of vocalizations (Rovee & Luciano, 1973). Yes, people have actually studied chickens. Research has shown that once tonic immobility is induced, it remains for anywhere from 10 minutes in chickens to more than 8 hours in lizards. One advantage of remaining still is in terms of survival. That is, predators tend to be sensitive to movement and without it they lose interest and become distracted, allowing the prey to escape. This suggests that animal hypnosis offers a method to tap into the systems related to remaining still.

Pavlov (1927) describes the manner in which inducing hypnosis in animals and humans utilize similar mechanisms and its relation to cortical inhibition. In the second half of the 20th century, a variety of studies examined the concept of animal hypnosis (Gallup, 1974) with some suggesting its value for understanding the hypnotic experience in humans (Draper & Klemm, 1967). However, at this point we do not know if hypnosis in humans and other species share similar underlying mechanisms.

Meditation

Historically, *meditation* has been a part of religious and spiritual traditions worldwide. Buddhist, Sufi, Zen, and Yogi traditions all have specific forms of meditation, which have been taught from one generation to another. Christian traditions also have used meditative techniques often in the form of prayer and contemplation. The emphasis in each tradition initially focused on how the meditative technique was to be practiced. From the outside each meditative technique appeared to be different. As such, it was difficult to have a single definition of meditation.

However, one can also examine the psychological experiences and internal states related to various forms of meditation. In the 1900s initial examinations of meditative processes sought to link meditation within a psychological perspective. Carl Jung at the beginning of the 1900s sought to see the connections between analytic psychology and meditation. With the influx of Eastern traditions to the United States in the 1960s, a number of psychologists began to research meditation and the meditative state. This has led to its use in treatments for psychological disorders.

In general, meditative techniques can be thought of in terms of three broad approaches (Naranjo & Ornstein, 1971). The first approach is an attempt to reduce awareness as normally experienced. One technique that uses this approach is to constantly repeat a mantra or single word while ignoring everything else. Other techniques have the person sit and pay attention to only their breathing. The second approach is more of an expressive experience as might be seen in free dancing. Freud's use of free association in which a person says whatever comes to his or her mind is not unlike these techniques. The third approach is located between these two approaches. That is, awareness of all activity is allowed without the attempt to reduce, modify, or react to what is being experienced. Such techniques were practiced in Theravada Buddhism and have come to be called *mindfulness* in current-day psychology.

Mindfulness has gained popularity and has been empirically shown to be effective in reducing stress and treating a number of psychological problems (Shapiro & Carlson, 2017). *Mindfulness* involves an increased focused purposeful awareness of the present moment. The idea is to relate to one's thoughts and experiences in an open, nonjudgmental, and accepting manner (Kabat-Zinn, 1990). The basic technique is to observe thoughts without reacting to them in the present. That is, you allow your thoughts and feelings to come without reacting to them. This increases sensitivity to important features of the environment and one's internal reactions. This in turn leads to better self-management and awareness as an alternative to ruminating about the past or worrying about the future. This reduces self-criticism.

Nonjudgmental observing allows for a reduction in stress, reduction in reactivity, and more time for interaction with others and the world. Also, feelings of compassion for another person become possible. This broadens attention and alternatives. Meta-analysis performed by Hofmann and his colleagues examined 39 studies of mindfulness (Hofmann, Sawyer, Witt, & Oh, 2010). He found significant reductions in anxiety and depression following mindfulness techniques. Paul Grossman and his colleagues examined 20 studies and found overall positive changes following mindfulness approaches (Grossman, Niemann, Schmidt, &, Walach, 2004; see also Hofmann, Grossman, & Hinton, 2011). Empirical evidence using mindfulness techniques has shown positive change with a number of disorders including anxiety, depression, chronic pain, and stress.

Overall, meditation has been shown to increase well-being. In relation to this, psychologists have asked if there is plasticity, that is, are brain changes associated with meditation. The answer appears to be yes. In one study, the increase in well-being was correlated with an increase in gray matter in areas of the brainstem (Singleton, Hölzel, Vangel, Brach, Carmody, & Lazar, 2014). Another study randomly assigned individuals to a six-week longitudinal trial of mindfulness meditation or to a control group that read about wellness (Allen et al., 2012). Although six weeks is a short period, those who learned mindfulness meditation were better able to inhibit negative emotionality. This was associated with changed brain areas associated with emotionality. Other studies have shown changes in EEG activity of long-term meditators (Richard, Lutz, & Davidson, 2014).

CONCEPT CHECK

1. What is the technical definition of hypnosis?
2. What individual differences are found in experiencing hypnosis?
3. What are some examples in which hypnosis has been used as part of a clinical treatment?

Are these statements about hypnosis true or false?

   a. Relaxation is an important feature of hypnosis.
   b. Hypnotized people cannot be led to do acts that conflict with their values.
   c. Hypnosis is something to do with a sleeplike state.
   d. Ability to imagine vividly is related to hypnotizability.

4. In general, meditative techniques can be thought of in terms of three broad approaches. Briefly describe each of these approaches.
5. What is mindfulness, and what are some of the benefits it can bring to the individual?

Psychoactive Substances

Throughout our evolutionary history, we discovered that there are some plants referred to as *psychoactive substances*, which change our brain in a manner that influences our consciousness, including thoughts and feelings. Betel nut has been chewed for its nicotine-like effects for at least 13,000 years in Timor, an island north of Australia (Saah, 2005). Cocaine is naturally available in coca leaves, and morphine is available from poppy plants. Archaeological evidence suggests that Peruvian foraging societies were chewing coca leaves some 8,000 years ago. Actual poppy seeds were recovered from a 4,500-year-old settlement in Switzerland. Other evidence shows that opium was available in the neolithic, copper, and bronze ages. We as humans thus discovered naturally occurring psychoactive substances.

Besides naturally occurring psychoactive substances, humans also learned to ferment and distill plants. With the beginning of farming about 10,000 years ago, humans discovered how to make alcoholic beverages such as beer and wine, although it may have happened even earlier. Evidence from Iran, the former soviet republic of Georgia, and China suggest humans were making wine 8,000 years ago, that is 2,000 years before we began to write (Estreicher, 2017; McGovern et al., 2017). Depending on the region, humans have used barley, wheat, grapes, rice, honey, and a variety of fruits to make alcoholic drinks. In fact, there is some suggestion that we made beer before we made bread (Hayden, Canuel, & Shanse, 2013).

Addiction

As noted, seeking psychoactive substances is part of human history. As humans, we like using these substances in a variety of situations. In comparison to liking a substance, wanting and seeking it uses a different pathway in the brain, which is related to *addiction*. Many researchers make a distinction between drug use, drug abuse such as binge drinking, and addiction.

In terms of addiction, there is a common pattern (see **Figure 6-21**). Initially, the positive experience of taking the drug leads to a compulsion to seek and take a given substance. It can be experienced as a rush or sense of well-being. This period of intoxication is also associated with impaired cognitive abilities. This is followed by a craving in which the individual loses control of the ability to limit intake of the drug. For example, even when the blood alcohol of a person with an alcohol addiction is high, he or she still drinks more. The next condition is the emergence of a negative emotional state when

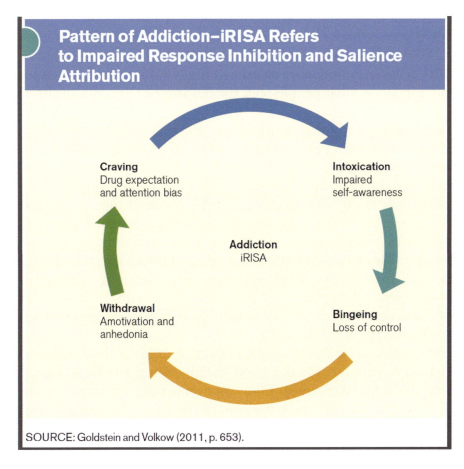

Figure 6-21 Pattern of addiction.

the substance is unavailable or access to it is limited. What once gave a positive feeling now does little. In fact, the person needs the drug to feel normal. There is a paradox in that by this last stage, people who are addicted *want* their psychoactive substance more than they *enjoy* it.

There is no one answer as to what causes addiction (see Volkow & Li, 2005 for an overview). One factor is related to timing of first use. With alcohol, those who began using alcohol before the age of 15 are four times more likely to become addicted in their lifetime in comparison to those who begin at age 20 or older. Our brain reorganizes itself beginning in adolescence. Current research suggests that drugs affect adolescents in a different manner than they do adults. Adolescence is clearly a time that the brain is reestablishing connections and networks and is sensitive to the use of addictive substances. During adolescence are brain changes that by the time you are in your 20s have led to the development of better impulse control and other executive functioning in the frontal lobes.

Another factor related to addiction is genetics. There is a strong genetic factor in that 40 to 60% of vulnerability to addiction can be attributed to genetic factors. These genetic factors and their relationship with the environment can be seen in the manner in which different drugs show different levels of reinforcing factors and influence metabolism. That is, some drugs are more addictive than others. Also, individuals show different sensitivities to particular drugs and thus some people can become addicted to some drugs more quickly than they can to other drugs. In addition, genetics can make one more addicted to a particular drug more quickly than other individuals with different genetic makeup.

Environmental factors such as stress and/or low socioeconomic level are also associated with greater drug use, which can lead to addiction. With adolescents, peer pressure can play an important role in deciding whether or not to try new types of drugs. Adolescence is also a time when individuals take risks and try new things. The environments in which both adults and adolescents live play a crucial role. This is compounded by research that shows that drugs may disrupt networks of the brain involved in making decisions. Drugs not only influence what people seek for rewards but also the ability to inhibit these desires.

With the advent of brain imaging and other neuroscience techniques, research has suggested that there is a common underlying process to a variety of disorders that share the desire to engage in certain activities. These disorders include drug addiction, binge eating, pathological gambling, and sexual addiction (see Goodman, 2007 for an overview).

Can drugs actually change your brain? The answer is yes. Drugs do change your brain. In fact, for someone addicted to a particular drug, just seeing the paraphernalia associated with it can produce physiological changes before the drug is actually ingested. It does not matter if it is heroin or whiskey. This works in a manner similar to how all learning changes your brain, although drug addiction seems to last longer than simple learning (see Nestler & Malenka, 2004 for an overview). Addiction can last for weeks, months, or even years after the last ingestion of the drug. This sets up the possibility of relapse since your body has a difficult time forgetting the effects of the drug.

On a neuroscience level, studies show the rewarding effect of drugs is their ability to increase **dopamine** (see Hyman, Malenka, & Nestler, 2006; Volkow, Wang, Fowler, & Tomasi, 2012; and Wise & Robble, 2020 for overviews). One important pathway begins in the *ventral tegmental area* (VTA), which is located near the base of the brain. Although a small population of neurons, the VTA has an impressive influence on reward and aversive behaviors (Morales & Margolis, 2017).

These pathways connect with the nucleus accumbens, prefrontal cortex, dorsal striatum, and the amygdala. Dopamine (DA) is released in these structures. Dopamine was initially thought to be the neurobiological correlate of reward or pleasure. However, more recent research has clarified dopamine's function. It is suggested that the presence of dopamine signals to the person that something good is about to happen. Thus, dopamine is not so much associated with pleasure as with the expectation of pleasure. In this sense, it is involved in motivating individuals to engage in certain behaviors that make them feel good. In this way, the presence of dopamine predicts a reward. In the process, the events associated with the reward become part of the person's memory. Thus, all of the events associated with using a drug come together to remind you of the pleasant experience. Overall, many drugs of addiction increase activity in the VTA and the nucleus accumbens.

Molecular mechanisms of many drugs leave excessive dopamine available in the brain (see **Figure 6-22**). This can work by different mechanisms. Cocaine either blocks dopamine uptake in the synapse or increases dopamine released by the terminals of VTA cells, which increases dopamine signaling in the nucleus accumbens. Alcohol and opiates such as opium and heroin enhance dopamine release by quieting neurons that would otherwise inhibit dopamine-secreting neurons. Nicotine induces VTA cells to release dopamine into the nucleus accumbens. Now, let us look at these and other psychoactive substances.

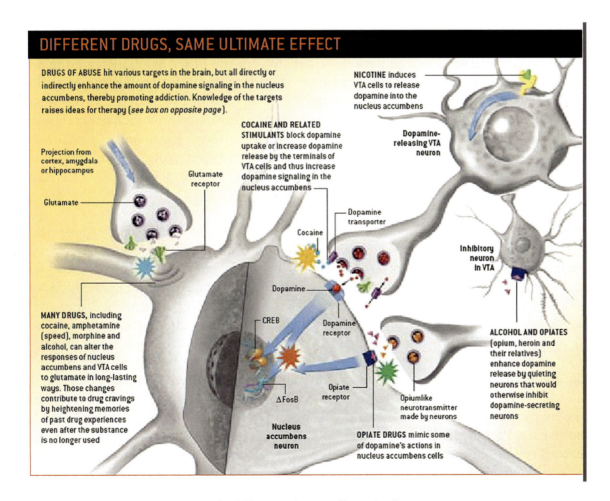

Figure 6-22 The manner in which different drugs affect the brain.

CONCEPT CHECK

1. Throughout our evolutionary history, humans have ingested psychoactive substances. Give a brief timeline of what we know about that history including dates, locations, and substances.
2. What can animal studies tell us about the power of psychoactive substances on the individual?
3. What are the steps in the pattern of addiction, and what drives the process from one step to the next?
4. There is no one answer to what causes addiction, but what are three important factors that should be considered?
5. How can drugs change your brain? What is the role of dopamine in the effect of psychoactive substances?

Major Psychoactive Substances

Traditionally, psychoactive substances are discussed in terms of their effects on the central nervous system. Three broad categories are depressants, stimulants, and hallucinogens. Depressants such as alcohol and barbiturates reduce the activity of the central nervous system. This reduction of activity can be seen overall as when a person falls asleep after drinking alcohol or more localized as when reduction in frontal lobe activity reduces the inhibitions experienced by the person. Stimulants, on the other hand, increase the activity of the central nervous system. Common stimulants include amphetamines, caffeine, nicotine, cocaine, and opiates such as morphine. The class of psychoactive drugs that has the most influence on the central nervous system is hallucinogens (Schartner, Carhart-Harris, Barrett, Seth, & Muthukumaraswamy, 2017). Although hallucinogens such as LSD, mescaline, and psilocybin have strong effects on the central nervous system, they tend to be the least addictive. Also, animals will not work for these drugs as they do for cocaine.

Alcohol

Alcohol has been available to humans for a large part of our history. For at least 10,000 years, humans have made wine, beer, and other drinks through a process of fermentation. During fermentation, yeast breaks down sugar found in grains, such as barley, and fruits, such as grapes, into ethanol (alcohol) and carbon dioxide. Once carbon dioxide is removed, the ethanol and water remain in the form of wine or beer. Higher alcohol drinks such as gin, vodka, rum, and whiskey are further heated after fermentation in the process of distilling to remove the water. The percentage of alcohol in a substance is measured in terms of proof, which is twice the percentage of alcohol (e.g., 20% alcohol equals 40 proof). The amount of alcohol in beer and wine can vary and is usually listed on the label. Researchers consider 12 oz. of beer, 5 oz. of wine, and 1.5 oz. of liquor to contain ½ oz. of pure alcohol.

In many cultures around the world, alcohol is used for celebrations such as weddings and parties. Part of the reason for alcohol's use in celebrations is its effect on our central nervous system. In most humans, the initial experience of alcohol intake includes pleasant subjective experiences that may lead to increased social interactions. This is partly related to the effects of alcohol on such neurotransmitters as serotonin, endorphins, and dopamine. Alcohol will also decrease inhibition by reducing the effects of the GABA system, which is associated with anxiety. However, if the amount of alcohol intake is increased, it will increase the effects of GABA, which can lead to sedation. This is why alcohol is generally listed as a depressant. As an addictive substance, it can also lead to social, legal, and medical problems.

Unlike most of the other foods you eat, alcohol is absorbed directly in the bloodstream without digestion. When you drink a beer or other alcoholic beverage, it goes to your stomach. In your stomach, only a small amount of alcohol is absorbed, as most alcohol is absorbed in the small intestine. However, if there is food in your stomach, it is absorbed more slowly. If the alcoholic drink contains food substances, as does beer, it is also absorbed more slowly. On the other hand, drinks with carbon dioxide such as champagne or a mixed drink with a carbonated beverage are moved from the stomach to the small intestine more rapidly where most alcohol is absorbed into the bloodstream. The experience of feeling the effects of alcohol takes place when alcohol is carried through the bloodstream to the brain. As a result, champagne will give you the experience of alcohol faster than beer since it gets to your brain faster.

Cannabis

Cannabis is a plant species also referred to as marijuana. Cannabis resin is referred to as *hashish*. The cannabis plant can easily be cultivated both indoors and outdoors. For this reason, it is grown and used throughout the world. In fact, cannabis has been used worldwide for at least 4,000 years for its psychoactive effects. During this period, it has been seen as an important medical compound and as a religious and recreational substance. The physician Galen in AD 200 wrote that it was customary to give cannabis to guests to promote hilarity and enjoyment (Stuart, 2004).

Cannabis has a history of use in China, India, Europe, and the Middle East. It came to the United States during the 1900s. In the United States during the 1960s, it became a recreational drug of choice for many individuals. Since the 1960s, there have been changing views as to whether the drug should be decriminalized for all adults, made available strictly for medical purposes such as pain relief, or banned completely. At this point about half of the states in the US have legalized some form of marijuana use. The United Nations estimates that 4% of the population of the world uses cannabis. The United States is one of the larger users of cannabis in the world.

Individuals who use cannabis report a wide variety of experiences. Small doses produce enjoyable positive feelings associated with a feeling of being "high." This can include states in which time stands still. The person often may see his or her own ideas as exceptionally creative and important. Cannabis can also influence appetite with short-term users reporting increasing hunger or "munchies." Larger doses can produce negative feelings such as anxiety and paranoia. Hallucinations and persecutory delusions have also been reported. Most of these experiences are short-lived but in some cases can last longer. More long-term use is also associated with cognitive impairment in executive functions (Crean, Crane, & Mason, 2011).

The main psychoactive ingredient in cannabis is THC (Δ9-tetrahydrocannabinol) and was first described in the 1960s. THC particularly affects receptors in the hippocampus, the cerebellum, the basal ganglia, and the neocortex. THC affects receptors in the brain that also release GABA, an inhibitory neurotransmitter related to anxiety. The brain also produces its own substances that are similar to cannabis. These are referred to as *cannabinoids*. These cannabinoids appear to be related to reducing the negative experiences associated with troubling past experiences, which is similar to the effects of cannabis.

Opioids

Opioids are substances derived from the opium poppy that have been used for thousands of years to control pain and bring on euphoric feelings. In fact, poppy seeds have been found at Neanderthal burial sites from 30,000 years ago (see Stuart, 2004, for an overview). About 3400 BC, Sumerians referred to the opium poppy as the "joy plant." From there, it spread throughout the world during the next 2,000 years. Opium was available in the street markets of ancient Rome. In 1860, Britain imported some 220,000 pounds of opium for medical and recreational use.

The more common opioids are heroin, opium, morphine, methadone, and oxycodone (trade names of OxyContin, Percocet). Variations of these drugs are currently used in medical settings primarily for reduction of pain following operations or pain experienced with some types of cancer. Opioids became popular in the United States after the Civil War for their ability to control pain; however, some individuals given these drugs became addicted to them. Abuse took the form of the opium den of the last century in which the drug was smoked. With the availability of the hypodermic needle, it was injected directly into the bloodstream. Before the early 1900s, opioids were available legally in the United States. In 2017, the United States Government declared opioid misuse and addiction related to pain relief a national emergency.

Cocaine

Cocaine comes from the naturally occurring coca plant. For thousands of years, individuals have chewed the leaves of the coca plant for its psychoactive experiences. It is largely grown in South America. Cocaine was even used to make Coca-Cola in about 1900. About this time, Sigmund Freud tried the drug and found it to be very pleasant. Its effects include a mental alertness including feelings of euphoria, energy, and a desire to talk. It also heightens the experience of sensory processes such as sound, touch, and sight, as well as producing physiological effects such as increased heart rate and blood pressure. The introduction of cocaine interferes with natural brain processes, resulting in an increase of dopamine. This increased dopamine is, in turn, involved in the effects experienced with cocaine.

Cocaine has been administered by smoking, snorting through the nose, or injecting directly into the bloodstream. The form of cocaine that is smoked is referred to as crack. Crack refers to the sounds made when the white cocaine crystals are heated to turn it into a form that can be smoked. Taking it through the nose results in a slower "high" than intravenously, which shows effects in 4 to 6 minutes. Cocaine has a shorter effect life in comparison with other drugs. That is, most of its effect is completed in 15 to 40 minutes. Like alcohol, individuals may use cocaine in binges.

Amphetamines

Like cocaine, **amphetamines** are stimulants that result in positive feelings, a burst of energy, and alertness. However, unlike cocaine, it is a substance produced in the laboratory rather than found in nature. Amphetamine was first developed in the 1880s. It was not until the 1930s that it was introduced as a medicine in the form of an inhaler for the treatment of a stopped-up nose. Also during this time it was introduced in the form of pills with the name Benzedrine, which were called "bennies" (see Iversen, 2006; Koob, Kandel, & Volkow, 2008, for overviews).

During the 1930s and 1940s, amphetamines were prescribed by health professionals for the treatment of more than 30 disorders, including epilepsy, Parkinson's disease, schizophrenia, migraine, and even behavioral problems in children. They were also prescribed to reduce addictions to other substances such as alcohol, morphine, and tobacco. During World War II, amphetamines were given to solders as *pep pills* to give them an edge in combat. The common ones were Benzedrine, Dexedrine, and Methedrine, the last one being methamphetamine. Although there are chemical differences in amphetamine and methamphetamine, they both function as stimulants.

As people experienced the stimulant effects, they began to abuse the use of amphetamines. In the 1950s, long-distance truck drivers would use them to drive farther. After they were publicized for use as a recreational drug from Hollywood to New York, the US government began to pay attention. Amphetamines were also making their way into teenage parties. In 1959, the US Food and Drug Administration (FDA) required that amphetamines only be available by prescription.

The main reason people take amphetamines is that they believe they enhance performance and help them feel good. The common experience is euphoria, increased vigilance, and hyperactivity. The reactions from amphetamines are also similar to other stimulant drugs. They are easy to take in the form of a pill, which can be conveniently purchased one pill at a time on the illegal market. Amphetamines are not considered to be harmful by many individuals. Taking these drugs through intravenous injection or smoking increases the feeling of a rush.

In their 2011 global assessment, the United Nations suggests that amphetamine-type drugs are the second most widely used drugs throughout the world (United Nations Office on Drugs and Crime, 2011). The first is cannabis. This makes amphetamine use greater than heroin or cocaine worldwide. Amphetamine-like drugs do not require the cultivation of plants. Instead, they can be manufactured almost anywhere without an advanced knowledge of chemistry.

As with other stimulant drugs, amphetamines affect the dopamine system to produce the initial euphoric experience. In addition to the short-term experience, there are also less positive long-term effects (see Marshall & O'Dell, 2012, for an overview). These long-term effects, especially from methamphetamine, create brain changes in three areas. The first is the development of compulsive patterns of use. The second produces negative brain changes consistent with brain injury. And third, methamphetamine produces changes in the individual's cognitive functioning.

People who use methamphetamine show problems with motor activities such as skill movements or perceptual speed. They also experience problems in the ability to shift attention. Finally, research also suggests memory, attention, and decision-making problems. These types of problems make it difficult for individuals to view their addiction objectively as well as be able to engage in therapy requiring cognitive responses. Methamphetamine also has a devastating effect on physical appearance, which can be seen in the before and after mug shots of the Oregon Multnomah County Detention Center (www.facesofmeth.us/main.htm).

Hallucinogens

Hallucinogens are drugs that alter perceptual experiences (see Nichols, 2004, for an overview). The word *hallucinate* actually comes from the Latin meaning to wander in the mind. Some of these drugs occur in nature and have been used by various cultures for thousands of years. These include mescaline, which comes from the peyote cactus and psilocybin, which comes from a variety of mushroom. Historians suggest they were often part of religious ceremonies to give experiences not part of everyday life. Other hallucinogens such as LSD (d-lysergic acid diethylamide) begin with a grain fungus, ergot. Although the fungus

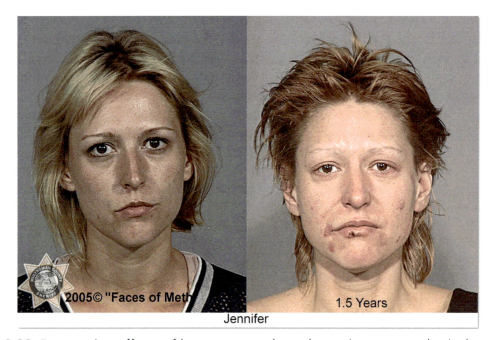

Figure 6-23 Devastating effects of long-term methamphetamine use on physical appearance.

is naturally occurring, LSD was first made in the laboratory. Other laboratory-made drugs include MDMA (3,4 Methylenedioxymethamphetamine), commonly known as ecstasy, MDA (3,4 Methylenedioxyamphetamine), sometimes referred to as the love drug, and PCP (Phencyclidine), also known as angel dust.

Hallucinogens are also called *psychedelics* and are able to alter perception, mood, and cognitive processes in often unpredictable ways (Hollister, 1984). These can be described in terms of somatic, perceptual, and psychic symptoms. Somatic symptoms include dizziness, weakness, tremors, nausea, drowsiness, and blurred vision. Perceptual symptoms include altered shapes and colors, difficulty in focusing on objects, sharpened sense of hearing, and at times synesthesia. Psychic symptoms include alterations in mood (happy, sad, or irritable at varying times), tension, distorted time sense, difficulty in expressing thoughts, depersonalization, dreamlike feelings, and visual hallucinations.

After about 50 years of ignoring psychedelic drugs for their possible use in the treatment of mental illness, new research has begun (Vollenweider & Preller, 2020). Although illegal in the United States, hallucinogens have been used in treating some mental disorders worldwide (Begola & Schillerstrom, 2019). Brain-imaging techniques are beginning to show the effects of psychedelics. At this point it is unclear which hallucinogens should be used in treatment such as LSD and which may be dangerous such as PCP. As with any process, abuse and dependence are possible, although the pattern is not the same. Drugs that are addictive typically affect the dopamine system and the experience of reward. It is also possible to train animals to self-administer addictive drugs, but this is not the case with hallucinogens. They also appear to lack the toxic effects on human organs seen in alcohol or tobacco, for example. However, not all experiences with hallucinogens are positive. A so-called *bad trip* can include extreme anxiety and fearful psychotic-like experiences.

Hallucinogens do not directly affect dopamine neurotransmission as do alcohol, cannabis, tobacco, and cocaine. Structurally, the chemical makeup of hallucinogens is similar to the neurotransmitter serotonin. In fact, early theories suggested that hallucinogens produced their effects by increasing serotonin in specific brain areas. It is now known that hallucinogens bind to the 5-HT serotonin receptor.

Drugs Found in the Brain

In the last century, a number of scientists began to wonder why our bodies seek various types of drugs. What became apparent was that our brains contain receptors that are sensitive to the actual drugs of addiction (see Bolles & Fanselow, 1982 for a historical overview). In particular, there are receptors in the brain that are sensitive to opiates such as morphine. What researchers then discovered is that our brains made a substance that is actually like morphine. These substances came to be called endorphins. **Endorphin** is a combination of the word for internally produced—endogenous—and the ending syllable of morphine. The particular endorphin of interest to psychologists is beta-endorphin or β-endorphin.

Research since that time has shown that *β-endorphin* (beta-endorphin) has an analgesia effect similar to drugs like morphine. Further, if a substance such as naloxone that blocks the effect of opiates is administered, the analgesia effects are reduced. Current research has shown that β-endorphin is also released during our body's response to stress (Charmandari, Tsigos, & Chrousos, 2005). This is seen by some as the explanation of how soldiers are able to fight or athletes to play under pain. The basis of positive experiences in running or eating have also been linked to β-endorphins.

CONCEPT CHECK

1. What are the three broad categories of psychoactive substances and what are their primary effects on the human central nervous system?
2. Describe the process of alcohol absorption to explain what causes the differences in how alcohol is experienced.
3. What is the primary psychoactive ingredient in cannabis? What are its impacts on an individual's body and brain?
4. What are some common opioids? What is it about opioids that makes them sought after as medicines as well as substances to abuse?
5. Describe the range of mental, sensory, and physiological effects related to cocaine?
6. What are some of the factors that promote the use and abuse of amphetamines?
7. What are three long-term negative impacts of methamphetamines?
8. Hallucinogens are not addictive, but in what other ways can they cause impairments to the individual using them?
9. What are endorphins, and how are they related to why our bodies seek various types of drugs?

Summary

Learning Objective 1: Discuss the different levels of consciousness, including attention and awareness.

Psychologists define consciousness as being aware and knowing that you are involved in a particular event. You listen to certain music because you like the feelings it gives you. You eat certain foods for the feeling of comfort and the memories associated with such meals. Reading a book or watching videos can also change our consciousness. You may even seek to reduce your level of consciousness as when you take a nap. At times, we may perform yoga or meditation as a way to experience our internal processes.

Experiences such as *spacing out* while driving suggest that there must be different processes that come together to give us the experience of consciousness. We have different systems of consciousness and awareness for living life and making decisions. That is, whether at a party or driving, we are able to monitor other aspects of the environment without being aware of it. Research shows sudden EEG changes in the brain to be associated with conscious awareness. That is, during conscious awareness, more areas of the brain are communicating with one another. Further, there is no single brain area related to consciousness; rather it is the result of the interactions among a number of neural networks in our brain.

In terms of attention, we can be aware of something. This is the basic level where we have sensations and create perceptions. Another level of awareness important for humans is referred to as meta-awareness. That is, we can be aware of our awareness. As humans, we not only have awareness of our awareness (meta-awareness) but also cognition about cognition or metacognition.

Levels of consciousness can be discussed in terms of (1) coma, (2) vegetative state, and (3) wakefulness and awareness. From this perspective, consciousness can be described in terms of wakefulness and awareness. Between coma and normal consciousness, there is a continuum in which a person varies in terms of awareness and the ability to communicate. A common procedure that is designed to change the level of a person's consciousness is the use of anesthesia. Combining the ability to control anesthesia with current brain-imaging techniques has opened up new ways to study levels of consciousness.

When we look at an object, we become conscious of what it is. However, it generally takes about half a second before our brain gives us the experience of being aware of what is there. When we shift our attention to something else, the original object leaves our consciousness. In this manner, attention and consciousness are closely related in our everyday language. This chapter considered two different long-term conditions in which a person is able to process information without being aware of it—*blindsight* and being a *split-brain* individual.

Learning Objective 2: Describe what happens when we sleep and dream.

We are just beginning to understand the various processes that go on during sleep. Sleep serves a number of functions. Our experience tells us that sleep is a strong drive and related to restoring our bodies in terms of energy and alertness. Evolutionary perspectives tell us that sleep may be protective and may keep the organism out of danger.

At some point during the night, the person's eyes—although closed—would move quickly. This is referred to as rapid eye movement or REM sleep. After a REM period, the person goes through another series of sleep cycles. These 90-minute cycles continue throughout the night, although the deepest sleep is experienced in the early cycles. Human adults sleep for about 8 hours every 24 hours. This is a daily or circadian rhythm, which takes about 12 years to develop in humans. Across species including humans and other animals, there is a sleep/wake cycle related to earth's day/night cycle. With access to the sun, there is a stable sleep/wake cycle. This circadian or 24-hour rhythm has been shown to be fairly stable even in species such as those that live in the Arctic with continuous daylight in part of the year.

Since sleep represents a special state of consciousness, some scientists suggest that it can give us a window into understanding consciousness. From this standpoint, the three processes of (1) wakefulness, (2) REM sleep, and (3) non-REM sleep represent three different states of consciousness. Each of these states involves different brain and other physiological processes. Over the past 100 years, studies of sleep with humans and animals have painted a consistent picture of the physiological processes involved in sleep and wakefulness. Brain-imaging techniques such as fMRI show the manner in which cortical networks are involved in sleep. (1) First, it is clear that the brain continues to be active in sleep even without external stimulation or self-control of our thoughts. (2) Second, sleep is controlled by bottom-up processes involving the brain stem and the hypothalamus. (3) Third, during sleep some of the same networks such as those involved in memory, arousal, and consciousness are active. In fact, different memory systems are seen to be active during different types of sleep. (4) Fourth, during sleep the frontal areas of the brain are not connected to other areas of the default network. The loss of connection to the frontal areas is one reason our dreams can be irrational or even chaotic. Without logic, you can dream anything you want.

Complaints concerning sleep are second only to those concerning pain in terms of physician visits. In the medical and psychological literature, more than 100 different sleep disorders have been described. However, most of these can be discussed in terms of four broad categories. These four are (1) insomnia, (2) hypersomnia, (3) circadian rhythm disorders, and (4) parasomnias.

Dreams are experienced during sleep and reflect mainly involuntary images, ideas, feelings, and sensations. In dreams, we (1) are aware of the unfolding situation in front of us; (2) experience ourselves being part of the action unlike our *daydreams* or mind-wandering when we are awake; (3) participate in the experiences of the dream; and (4) have emotional reactions and experience it as real although we would not say it was reality.

Learning Objective 3: Describe the techniques of hypnosis and meditation.
Although different processes, both hypnosis and meditation have been suggested to influence our consciousness as well as having numerous positive benefits. These positive benefits include reducing anxiety, depression, chronic pain, and stress.

Hypnosis is defined by researchers as *"an individual's ability to experience suggested alterations in physiology, sensations, emotions, thoughts, or behavior during hypnosis."* From this definition, changes during the hypnotic experience can take place on different levels. Although the nature of hypnosis is not fully understood, with the advent of EEG and fMRI researchers have been able to better describe the nature of the process. It appears that hypnosis allows the different types of information typically integrated in the brain to remain separate. For example, pain such as an electrical shock is composed of two experiences—the sensation of the shock and the negative emotional reaction. When told they will not experience pain under hypnosis, individuals still report the sensation but not the negative emotionality. Hypnosis has now been shown to be an important adjunct to a number of clinical treatments. It has been shown to be useful in controlling pain, in the treatment of anxiety, in reducing stress, and positively modifying our immune systems.

Meditation is a technique that focuses one's consciousness away from the outer world and towards an inner sense of awareness. Historically, meditation has been a part of religious and spiritual traditions worldwide. In general, meditative techniques can be thought of in terms of three broad approaches: (1) an attempt to reduce awareness as normally experienced; (2) an approach that is more of an expressive experience as might be seen in free dancing; and (3) an approach located between these two—awareness of all activity is allowed without the attempt to reduce, modify, or react to what is being experienced. This last approach has come to be called mindfulness in current-day psychology. Mindfulness involves an increased focused purposeful awareness of the present moment. The idea is to relate to one's thoughts and experiences in an open, nonjudgmental, and accepting manner.

Nonjudgmental observing allows for a reduction in stress, reduction in reactivity, more time for interaction with others and the world, a greater possibility of feelings of compassion for another person, and a broadening of attention and alternatives. Empirical evidence using mindfulness techniques has shown positive change with a number of disorders including anxiety, depression, chronic pain, and stress. Overall, meditation has been shown to increase well-being. In addition, there are brain changes associated with meditation.

Learning Objective 4: Discuss the three broad categories of psychoactive substances: depressants, stimulants, and hallucinogens.

Three broad categories of psychoactive substances are depressants, stimulants, and hallucinogens. Depressants such as alcohol and barbiturates reduce the activity of the central nervous system. This reduction of activity can be seen overall as when a person falls asleep after drinking alcohol or more localized as when reduction in frontal lobe activity reduces the inhibitions experienced by the person. Stimulants, on the other hand, increase the activity of the central nervous system. Common stimulants include amphetamines, caffeine, nicotine, cocaine, and opiates such as morphine. The class of psychoactive drugs that has the most influence on the central nervous system is hallucinogens. Although hallucinogens such as LSD, mescaline, and psilocybin have strong effects on the central nervous system, they tend to be the least addictive

In the United States, our attitude toward drug use has changed drastically over the past 200 years. Overall, drugs are rewarding to our body and give us experiences we seek, but drug use is a complex problem for a society to protect its citizens, especially those whose brains are still developing, from psychoactive substances that can be addictive, reduce productivity, and put the user and others at risk.

There is a common pattern to addiction: (1) craving characterized by drug expectation and attention bias; (2) intoxication and impaired self-awareness; (3) bingeing and the loss of control; and (4) withdrawal characterized by amotivation and anhedonia. There is no one answer as to what causes addiction, but a number of factors have been found to be involved. (1) One factor is related to timing of first use. (2) Another factor related to addiction is genetics. (3) Some drugs are more addictive than others. (4) Individuals show different sensitivities to particular drugs. (5) Environmental factors such as stress and/or low socioeconomic level are also associated with greater drug use, which can lead to addiction.

In the last century, a number of scientists began to wonder why our bodies seek various types of drugs. What became apparent was that our brains contain receptors that are sensitive to the actual drugs of addiction, in particular, to opiates such as morphine. Researchers discovered that our brains make a substance that is actually like morphine—substances that came to be called endorphins. The particular endorphin of interest to psychologists is beta-endorphin or β-endorphin, which has an analgesia effect similar to drugs like morphine and is also released during our body's response to stress.

Study Resources

Review Questions

1. Many people throughout history have taken different approaches to define consciousness. How would you weave what you've learned about awareness, attention, sleep, dreams, hypnosis, meditation, and psychoactive substances into a definition of consciousness?

2. This chapter begins by asking a question: *"How would you determine whether the messages you were getting on your computer were from a human or a machine? Are there distinct factors that would help you determine human consciousness from machine responses?"* Now it's your turn—what factors would you include in your response?
3. Plot out your cycle of sleep patterns throughout the night from the time you go to bed until you wake up in the morning—what happens at each stage?
4. Some philosophers have asked, which is more real—when we are dreaming or when we are not. Given everything you have read in this chapter as well as in the previous chapter on sensation and perception, how would you now answer this question?
5. The author states, "Today, it appears that hypnosis allows the different types of information typically integrated in the brain to remain separate." What types of information is he talking about, and what is the effect of separating them?
6. Looking back at the table on the myths of hypnosis, which three myths were most surprising to you? How has your view of hypnosis changed from examining these myths?
7. Historically, meditation has been a part of religious and spiritual traditions worldwide. Having read this chapter, do you think there is a place for meditative practice in the secular world? What evidence would you use to support your answer?
8. Your middle school heard you were taking a course in Introductory Psychology and has asked you to develop a lesson to present to middle school students—in terms they would pay attention to—including what you think they need to know about psychoactive substances, addiction, and naturally occurring drugs in the brain. What points would you include?
9. A number of the psychoactive substances covered in this chapter provide benefits as medicines—for example, opioids, cannabis, and amphetamines. On the other hand, it is clear that individuals can abuse or become addicted to these substances, which can lead to negative consequences. What principles would you use in developing a policy surrounding their use, including who could use them, what types of illnesses they should be used for, and who would regulate that use?

For Further Reading

Dehaene, S. (2014). *Consciousness and the Brain.* New York: Viking.

Feinberg, T., & Mallatt, J. (2016). *The Ancient Origins of Consciousness.* Cambridge, MA: MIT Press.

Leschziner, G. (2019). *The Nocturnal Brain: Nightmares, Neuroscience, and the Secret World of Sleep.* New York: St. Martin's Press.

Mendelson, W. (2017). *The Science of Sleep: What It Is, How It Works, and Why It Matters.* Chicago, IL: University of Chicago Press.

Ramachandran, V. (1998). *Phantoms in the Brain.* New York: William Morrow and Company.

Shapiro, S., & Carlson, L. (2017). *The Art and Science of Mindfulness, 2nd ed.* Washington, DC: American Psychological Association.

Zeman, A. (2002). *Consciousness: A User's Guide.* New Haven, CT: Yale University Press.

Web Resources

Blindsight—https://www.youtube.com/watch?v=4x0HXC59Huw
Invisible gorilla—http://www.theinvisiblegorilla.com/gorilla_experiment.html
Randy without sleep—http://www.esquire.com/lifestyle/a2527/esq0804-aug-awake/
Additional Randy-- http://www.gelfmagazine.com/archives/sleeping_in.php

Mike Birbiglia—http://www.npr.org/templates/story/story.php?storyId=130644070 and https://www.cnn.com/2012/10/02/health/sleepwalking-rem-behavior-disorder/index.html

Long-term meth use—www.facesofmeth.us/main.htm

Key Terms and Concepts

addiction
alcohol
amphetamines
anesthesia
attention
cannabis
circadian
circadian rhythm disorders
cocaine
consciousness
corpus callosum
dopamine
dreams
endorphin
hallucinogens
hemispheric specialization
hypersomnia
insomnia
levels of consciousness
meditation
meta-awareness
metacognition
opioids
parasomnias
psychoactive substances
rapid eye movement or REM sleep
sleep patterns
split-brain

7 Memory

LEARNING OBJECTIVES

7.1 Discuss memory and how information is stored and retrieved.
7.2 Describe how memories are organized and stored in the brain.
7.3 Describe how people differ in their memory abilities.
7.4 Discuss the key theories of how we create false memories and misinformation.

In March 1985, an English musician known for his knowledge of choral music of the 17th and 18th centuries reported experiencing a headache. The headache did not go away. Clive Wearing later collapsed and was rushed to a local hospital. It was determined that he had an infection in his brain, herpes encephalitis, which destroyed parts of his brain, including the hippocampus. Although he had no problem speaking or writing English, his memory was disrupted. Clive could recognize his wife and experienced delight at seeing her. However, he could not remember anything that occurred in the present time for longer than a few seconds. That is, within seconds after an event occurred, it was lost to his experience.

In her memoir, *Forever Today: A Memoir of Love and Amnesia,* his wife Deborah writes,

> *It was as if every waking moment was the first waking moment. Clive was under the constant impression that he had just emerged from unconsciousness because he had no evidence in his own mind of ever being awake before.... "I haven't heard anything, seen anything, touched anything, smelled anything," he would say. "It's like being dead."*
> (Wearing, 2005, p. 202-203)

Clive recorded in his journal in the hospital, "I am conscious for the first time…" and then noted the time. He made a number of such entries on the same day. Every event that Clive experienced was as if it were happening for the first time. Clive Wearing has been described as having the most devastating case of amnesia ever recorded.

(Sacks, 2007)

For more information see:

Sacks, Oliver (2007). The abyss. *The New Yorker* (24 September).
Wearing, Deborah (2005). *Forever Today: A Memoir of Love and Amnesia.* New York: Random House.

A Radiolab story told by Oliver Sacks and Clive's wife is available online (https://www.wnycstudios.org/podcasts/radiolab/segments/91578-clive).

A video presentation of Clive Wearing can be seen in the PBS series *The Mind* (Episode 1, 1988).

In thinking about Clive Wearing, it becomes apparent that memory is not a unitary process. Although Clive Wearing lost his memory for present events after some seconds, he could still recognize his wife, and speak, read, and understand English. He could also perform tasks such as playing the piano that he had previously learned. Think for a second what your life would be like if you could only remember things for a few seconds. Who would you be? Most of us think of ourselves in terms of experiences we have had in our life and our reactions to these experiences. It is our memories that give us an enduring picture of ourselves.

As you will see in this chapter, there are different types of memory. Where Clive had difficulty was in turning *short-term memories* into *long-term memories* that can be retrieved at a later time. In addition to short-term and long-term memory, other types of memory will be introduced in this chapter. These types of memory have to do with particular types of information, but that is getting ahead of our story.

As you will see, when we remember an experience, we actually recreate the experience in our minds. That helps us to understand why we remember the same event slightly differently each time. Depending on the nature of the memory, different parts of the brain can be involved. Some memories have to do with language, some with emotions, some with events, some with sensory experiences, and many with a combination of these.

There is, of course, great value in being able to have access to important parts of your experience and having some aspects be more important than others. From an evolutionary perspective, for instance, organisms that could remember which food was good for them and where it was located survived better than the ones that could not. Remembering and understanding our experiences protects us. Memory is a critical component of our lives.

Two thousand years ago, the Greek dramatist Aeschylus, in *Prometheus Bound*, said that memory is the mother of all wisdom. Think about what would happen if you lost your memory. Could you learn new things? Could you still ride a bicycle? Could you speak and understand others? Would your world look the same? Would you have a sense of identity? Would you still be you? As you answer these questions you may begin to see the critical role that memory plays in our lives.

Understanding Memory

Learning and *memory* are processes that go together. Traditionally, learning and memory have focused on different aspects of behavior and experience. In the next chapter, you will read about learning that has traditionally been measured in terms of changes in an individual's or organism's behavior based on experience. Historically, psychologists say learning has taken place when behavior changes. **Memory** traditionally has focused on how this information is stored and later retrieved. The current chapter focuses on memory, whereas the next chapter focuses on learning.

The manner in which you are asked to remember information can also influence your memory ability. For example, when you take a multiple-choice test, you use *recognition*.

That is, if you were asked which of these is the Spanish word for dog and were shown the words "pollo," "perro," "gato," and "cabra" you would only need to recognize that perro is the correct answer. However, if you were asked, "What is the Spanish word for dog?" you would need to *recall* the information. Essay tests are based on recall. In terms of information, individuals are better able to recognize than recall information.

Before information is stored, it is encoded. That is, certain aspects of your experiences are organized and stored in the brain. Thus, *encoding* includes how you store information in the brain. Although we use terms such as storing a memory, we now know that remembering an experience is more than just viewing an image of what happened. Memory is a dynamic process that can be changed depending on events (Lee, Nader, & Schiller, 2017). In fact, each time we remember information, our brain reconstructs the event or experience (Vaz, Wittig, Inati, & Zaghloul, 2020). Our brain also helps us to forget things that do not match our behavior and our goals (Anderson & Hulbert, 2021). Unlike a computer that gives you back exactly the information that is stored, our brain has a logic of its own based on our evolutionary history.

How our brains store information was studied in the last century by Wilder Penfield (1891–1976). Penfield was a physician at McGill Hospital in Montreal, Canada, who treated individuals with severe epilepsy. In the 1930s and 1940s, as today, this treatment included brain surgery to help reduce epileptic seizures. In order to protect critical cognitive functions, Penfield wanted to map critical functions in the brain. To do so, he stimulated different parts of the patient's brain. Since the brain has no pain receptors, these operations were conducted while the patient was conscious. Thus, Penfield would electrically stimulate a specific area of the brain and note the response.

Penfield reported that electrical stimulation to the temporal lobes, and not to other areas of the brain, resulted in the person's experiencing memories of a previous event or situation. With stimulation, a person might say that he has just had a flashback of his house in childhood or that he remembered a particular family event. One individual reported being at the corner of Jacob and Washington in South Bend, Indiana as a younger person (Penfield, 1952).

Today, in treating epilepsy, it is more common to place an array of electrodes on the person's cortex. These more recent procedures have also shown that electrical stimulation to the temporal lobe results in the experience of memories (Moriarity, Boatman, Krauss, Storm, & Lenz, 2001; Vignal, Maillard, McGonigal, & Chauvel, 2007). These memories could be recent or from longer ago. Depending on the area of the temporal lobe stimulation, one individual reported experiencing *The Flintstones* cartoons from childhood, hearing the rock band Pink Floyd, hearing a baseball announcer, or a female voice singing. Noninvasive techniques such as TMS (transcranial magnetic stimulation) are also being used to study memory (Kim, Ekstrom, & Tandon, 2016).

The Temporal Dimension of Memory

Overall, memory is described in terms of two dimensions. The first is the temporal or time dimension. The time dimension includes three domains: sensory memory, short-term memory, and long-term memory. The second dimension utilizes the type of information stored. As you will see, remembering how to ride a bicycle uses a different type of memory than learning information for a test. Let's first consider the temporal dimension.

Sensory Memory

If you were to listen to someone talk, you would retain the words said for just a few seconds as you processed the next words. This is referred to as **sensory memory**. *Sensory memory* lasts only a few seconds and takes place in all of our senses. If it involves the auditory system, it is referred to as *echoic memory*. If it involves the visual system, it is referred to as *iconic memory*. This is the first step of how we remember information.

Sensory memory lasts just long enough for the information to be processed by the brain. However, we can't possibly remember all of the information that is before us in this brief period. In 1859, Sir William Hamilton studied how much information we can process by throwing marbles onto the ground and then trying to instantly determine how many there were. More systematic research was performed by researchers at Bell Laboratories in the 1960s. One of these researchers was George Sperling (Sperling, 1960).

What Sperling did was to allow research participants to view a series of letters for a brief period of time and then asked the participants to repeat them (see **Figure 7-2**). You can try this yourself by looking at the letters and then quickly putting your hand on top of them. If you do this, you can probably remember a few letters but not more than four or five. They just disappear from your sensory memory. Sperling performed his experiments by presenting the letters for one-twentieth of a second. In another experiment, there were different tones that signaled whether the participant was to report the top row, the middle row, or the bottom row. The tones were presented after the display was no longer available. In this experiment, participants were able to report three of the four letters in the line. What is amazing is that this suggests that, on some level, participants had access to the entire array of letters. However, that access was very short-lived. When Sperling delayed the tone by more than half a second, participants recalled only about half as many letters. Thus, you initially have access to more information than you realize but it is very short-lived.

Short-Term Memory

The second step in remembering information is to transform the sensory information and work with it for a short period of time. This is referred to as **short-term memory**. As the name implies, short-term memory lasts for less than a minute. The concept of **working memory** evolved from short-term memory to reflect the systems required to keep things in mind while performing tasks (Baddeley, 2010). That is, working memory is all the information you keep in mind while you pay attention to the task you are doing. If you were ordering a pizza for your friends you might need to remember what toppings your friends liked as you look up the phone number of the pizza parlor. The term "working memory" is somewhat broader than "short-term memory" in that it also refers to your use of attention to influence short-term memory (Cowan, 2008). Both short-term memory and working memory would describe your looking up the number of a pizza place and retaining it briefly as you make the call. Research suggests that verbal short-term memory is stored differently than visual short-term memory in the brain (Schacter & Wagner, 2013).

Overall, short-term memory lasts for about 20 to 30 seconds without rehearsal. If you continue to repeat the phone number, for example, then rehearsal will lengthen the time the information is available to you. If you are not allowed to rehearse the

B C X Y

N F R W

T Z K D

Figure 7-2 Presentation of letters used by George Sperling.

information, then the initial information will be lost in 20 to 30 seconds. This was shown in the 1950s in research by Brown and Peterson (Brown, 1958; Peterson & Peterson, 1959). To ensure that the participants in the study did not rehearse the information presented they were asked to count backwards from a particular number after they were shown three letters that did not form a word. They also varied the amount of time between the presentation of the three letters and when the participants were asked to recall the letters. The shorter the time, the better the letters were remembered.

Overall, short-term memory is active and easy to access, and the contents are remembered in the order presented. However, there is a limit to the number of items that we can remember. Based on a 1956 study by George Miller, it was assumed that the number of items in short-term memory that could be remembered was seven, plus or minus two. That is, if I read you a set of numbers and then asked you to repeat them, most people would be able to repeat approximately seven of them. Some would do better and repeat nine and some people would do worse and repeat five.

It turns out that the limits on short-term memory are not totally straightforward. As you will learn later in the chapter, memory is influenced by many factors. The number of items we can remember may be influenced by how you feel, for instance (Hayes, Hirsch, & Mathews, 2008). It is also associated with how well you score on an intelligence test (Oberauer, Süß, Wilhelm, & Wittmann, 2008).

Are experts in a particular field able to remember more items? In order to answer this question, William Chase and Herbert Simon (1973) studied chess players who ranged from novice to master players. One question was how experts and novices differ in their approach to chess. Previous research had shown that they did not differ in the number of moves they considered, but the experts were better at choosing the right move. Chase and Simon then asked if the expert chess players differed in their ability to remember the board. In order to study this, they asked the chess players to reproduce where the pieces were located on a chess board from short-term memory.

They discovered that the expert chess players were better able than novices to reproduce the location of pieces in the middle of a game or at the end of a game. The experts did this by *chunking* the chess pieces into meaningful patterns. That is, they organized the chess pieces into groups. If the pieces were placed randomly on the chess board, the experts did no better than the novices at remembering their location. Thus, it was not the experts' memory ability that made the difference, but their ability to chunk the material into meaningful groups. With their expertise, the experts could have both more meaningful chunks and a larger number of items in each chunk. In any area of knowledge, if you have more expertise in that area, you can have more items in a single chunk.

Not only do experts use chunking, but we all do it every day. That is, if you place numbers or letters in meaningful groups, you can remember more items. For example, if I asked you to remember these letters—FBIYMCACBSNBCCIA—you may have a difficult time unless you group them. Once you chunk the letters into FBI—YMCA—CBS—NBC—CIA, then remembering 16 letters in five groups becomes easier. Similarly, you tend to chunk phone numbers. Thus, the phone number 9876543210 becomes 987–654–3210, which is easier to remember.

Chunking can take place on both a deliberate and an automatic level (Gobet, Lane, Croker, Cheng, Jones, Oliver, & Pine, 2001). That is, you can purposely chunk a telephone number to help you remember it. With other types of material, chunking is automatic. You will automatically chunk the letters FBIYMCACBSNBCCIA once you see FBI, YMCA, and so forth. In fact, it is hard to group the letters in other ways. This is not unlike the

Gestalt perceptual groupings you learned about in the chapter on perception. That is, the visual system also chunks information for efficient processing (Corbett, 2017).

Long-Term Memory

To have a memory available to us in the future, the information needs to be converted from short-term memory into **long-term memory**. Information available to us through long-term memory can be relatively permanent. Without much trouble, for instance, you can probably remember some of your elementary school teachers and friends, although you may not have seen or thought about them for a long time.

One important contribution to understanding long-term memory was the research related to Henry Molaison (known as H.M. in the research literature), which will be discussed in more detail later in the chapter. Molaison, who had damage to his temporal lobes, could not create long-term memories from short-term ones. Since he could perform short-term memory tasks, it became clear that there are different types of temporal memory and that these types involve different brain areas. It was also discovered that Molaison did possess certain types of long-term memory, such as the ability to increase his skills at specific puzzles. Thus, there are different memory systems. Long-term memory can thus be classified in terms of the type of information that is stored. We now turn to these distinctions.

Types of Long-Term Memory

When asked about the contents of our memory, many of us would think about what has happened to us. We remember being with friends, going to a foreign country, and aspects of our childhood. If you like music, you may remember a particular concert. If you like art, you may remember a particular museum. Sporting events for some people are particularly memorable. That is, we remember events that we have personally experienced. Technically, this type of memory is referred to as **episodic memory**. Episodic memory is also called *autobiographical memory*.

The production of episodic memory involves specific areas in the brain. Activity involving the hippocampus has been shown to be a core mechanism underlying episodic memory (Hanslmayr, Staresina, & Bowman, 2016). There are also connections between the hippocampus and the frontal lobe with episodic memory formation (Eichenbaum, 2017). It has also been shown that emotional memories are forgotten more slowly than neutral memories (Yonelinas & Ritchey, 2015). Moreover, it is the amygdala rather than the hippocampus that facilitates these emotional effects.

In addition to events we have personally experienced, we also remember facts. That is, we know information about people, places, and things. Every time you talk with someone about a particular set of facts, you recall information you know. Technically, this is referred to as **semantic memory**. Semantic memory has to do with impersonal facts and everyday knowledge.

One important characteristic of both episodic and semantic memory is that we can consciously bring forth this information from memory. That is, if someone asks us a question such as, "What is the capital of France?" or "Who was your favorite teacher in high school?"—we remember the answer. Thus, there are similarities between the two memory systems (Renoult, Irish, Moscovitch, & Rugg, 2019). Episodic memory and semantic memory are grouped under the larger heading of **explicit memory**. Explicit memory is also referred to as *declarative memory*.

As you will see, some individuals with brain damage can learn how to solve puzzles and develop skills such as tracing a star in a mirror, yet not know he or she had learned these skills.

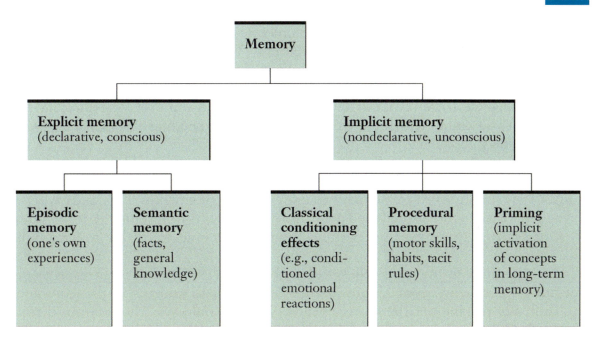

Figure 7-3 Organization of types of long-term memory.

This type of memory is referred to as **implicit memory**. Implicit memory has the ability to influence our behavior and experiences without our being aware of the learning taking place.

We also can perform a number of motor tasks without consciously remembering how to perform them. You ride a bicycle, drive a car, play a musical instrument, or type a text-message without consciously remembering every step. This type of memory is referred to as **procedural memory**. Procedural memory is a type of implicit memory.

Implicit memory also includes classical conditioning and priming. Classical conditioning, discussed previously and in more detail in the next chapter, occurs when an unconditioned stimulus is paired with a conditioned stimulus that, in turn, produces the conditioned response. This typically takes place outside of our awareness. For example, one of the physicians working with H.M. placed a tack in his hand so that when H.M. shook hands with him, he would feel a prick. When H.M. saw the group of physicians on a later occasion, as usual, he did not recognize them. However, H.M. was more hesitant to shake hands with one of the physicians—the one who had previously held the tack.

Priming is a situation in which previous experiences can influence present behavior. For example, suppose you were asked to learn a list of words, including *absent, income, filly,* and *discuss.* If you were then asked to complete the incomplete word inc___, you would more likely choose *income* rather than other words beginning with "inc," such as *incomplete, incense,* or *inchworm,* because you had been primed with *income.* **Figure 7-3** presents the different types of long-term memory.

Processes Involved in Learning and Long-Term Explicit Memories

At one time memory was thought to be a literal reproduction of what we experience, as if our brains were simply recorders. In the same way that our vision is not simply a photograph, memory is more than just information pulled out of a computer database. Remembering is a constructive process that allows each recall of information to be a constructive event.

Psychologists have described the long-term memory processes in terms of four separate steps: encoding, storage, consolidation, and retrieval. The first step, **encoding**, is the process by which information is attended to and connected with other information in memory. Craik and Lockhart (1972) noted that encoding can be "deep" if you pay close attention to the information. However, it can also be shallow, as when you read something and realize later that you cannot remember what you read. Thus, encoding can form a dimension going from deep to shallow.

Much of our encoding in the world is of a shallow nature. This was shown by Raymond Nickerson and Marilyn Adams in a series of studies (1979). In one of these studies, they simply asked participants to draw the face of a penny. This study was performed in a time before people used debit and credit cards for most purchases. Although all Americans at that time used pennies often, few people were able to accomplish this task.

In another study in the series, Nickerson and Adams (1979) asked participants to pick out the correct penny from 15 possibilities. Most college students in the experiment had difficulty picking out the correct penny. Which would you choose from those in **Figure 7-4**? The authors concluded that frequent exposure to an object does not result in accurate memory of the object.

For information to be retained in memory, the information must move past the sensory memory stage. A number of factors can influence encoding, including your level of motivation and emotional state. For example, most people only look at pennies to differentiate them from other coins such as nickels or dimes. Our motivation in this case is not to know the image on a penny. In learning information, it is important to do more than just look or read. It is critical to use a deeper structure approach such as considering the different aspects of the material and the manner in which they relate to each other. Overall, the level of encoding is critical for memory retrieval. One practical implication is that if you want to learn information for a class, the more you can connect one type of information with other information in a deep structure manner, the more likely you will be able to remember it on an essay test, for example.

Following encoding, the information must be stored. **Storage** involves those areas of the brain and neural mechanisms by which memories are retained over time. These mechanisms are different from those of sensory memory and short-term memory. Additionally,

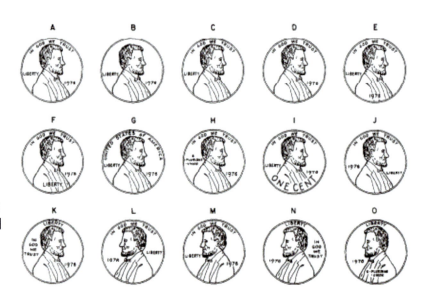

Figure 7-4 Examples of the top side of the pennies used in the Nickerson and Adam (1979) study. Only one is correct.

the capacity limitations are different. Whereas sensory memory disappears quickly, and short-term memory can contain only a limited amount of information, long-term memory appears almost limitless.

The third step, **consolidation**, is the process by which the information stored becomes more stable. Consolidation takes place in the brain on two levels (Sandrini, Cohen, & Censor, 2015). The first level involves structural changes at the synapse that take place as noted with the work of Kandel in Chapter 3. The second level involves a reorganization of long-term memories over brain networks. Sleep improves memory consolidation (Genzel, Kroes, Dresler, & Battaglia, 2013; Paller, Creery, & Schechtman, 2021), and lack of sleep interferes with memory consolidation. This has been shown to be true for humans as well as other species. Taking breaks and obtaining sleep will enhance learning of any type including course material.

The fourth step is **retrieval**. This stage is what we think of when we say we recalled something. Typically, retrieval involves different types of information stored in different places throughout the brain. This information can include sensory, emotional, and cognitive information. Memories can also be updated with the addition of new information, a process referred to as *reconsolidation*. In terms of course material, the retrieval required in a practice test will actually improve future performance.

The Role of Meaning in Memory

What if you were to learn information that had no meaning? How well would you remember this information? This question was posed by a German researcher in the 1880s, Hermann Ebbinghaus (1850–1909). Ebbinghaus wanted to make things very simple. He became the only participant in his research. He introduced strict controls in terms of timing and number of study trials. He also wanted to remove any meaning of the information that needed to be learned. In order to do this he invented the *nonsense syllable*. A nonsense syllable is composed of a consonant–vowel–consonant. Some examples would be MEQ, CAZ, and QON. He created more than 2,300 nonsense syllables and put them into random lists.

Ebbinghaus learned sequences of these nonsense syllables by repeating them out loud to himself. He kept careful records of the number of recitations required to learn each list. He did this for more than six years. Generally, he found that delay between memorization and recall resulted in the forgetting of a large portion of the material. This relationship is shown in **Figure 7-5**.

As Ebbinghaus showed, we forget information over time. It is also the case that learning new information may be influenced by what we had learned previously. That is, we have a harder time remembering certain information. For example, if your favorite pizza parlor changes its phone number from 973–555–0175 to 973–555–0172, you may have more difficulty remembering the new number since the old one may interfere as you try to call. Technically, this is called **proactive interference**. Proactive interference is the case in which old information inhibits your ability to remember new information. You may also find that when you try to input a new password, the old one inhibits your ability to remember the new one. The opposite can also be the case. This is referred to as **retroactive interference**. This is the case in which new information inhibits your ability to remember old information. For example, you might have a new combination lock on your bicycle that you learn the combination to. Then you need to open the combination lock on a storage shed. Since you have had this lock for a number of years, the new bicycle combination lock could inhibit your ability to remember the old numbers.

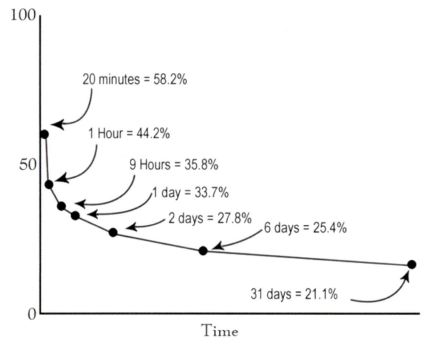

Figure 7-5 Ebbinghaus's forgetting curve. Percent of the original information learned by Ebbinghaus in terms of time. Immediate recall was 100%.

From an evolutionary perspective, most of what we remember has significance for our lives, not nonsense syllables. We learn information that helps us to adapt, that protects us, that feeds us, that involves our friends, and helps us to find mates. That is, we remember things that have meaning to us. As noted previously, remembering is a constructive process that allows each recall of information to be a constructive event. We actually recreate each memory as we recall this. This is referred to as **reconstructive memory**.

In the 1930s Frederic Bartlett demonstrated the nature of reconstructive memory (Bartlett, 1932). He had British college students read a story about Native Americans called "The War of the Ghosts." Bartlett had the students recall the story at different intervals after the first reading. He discovered that the memory of the story changed with each recalling. At times, new events were added, or the order of events was changed. One person remembered that the characters were hunting whales, an event that was not part of the story.

Bartlett suggested that when we remember something, we store the key facts. Later we reconstruct the memory and fill in the missing parts. This reconstruction generally involves our own perspective or point of view. In the process of reconstruction, there is the possibility for errors as seen in eyewitness testimony.

Bartlett's work helped to establish a current view of memory. This perspective is to see memory as constructive rather than reproductive (see Schacter, Addis, & Bucknew, 2007; Schacter, 2012 for overviews). That is, we construct what we remember in our brain rather than just reproducing an exact copy of the information.

The importance of our understanding of information and how it relates to memory was studied in a classic experiment by John Bransford and Marcia Johnson (1972). Bransford and Johnson focused on the factors that influence how we remember and encode what we hear. They asked, do we remember information differently if we can put it in a particular context or frame of reference? Imagine that you are a participant in that experiment and you are asked to listen to and later recall the following passage:

> If the balloons popped, the sound wouldn't be able to carry since everything would be too far away from the correct floor. A closed window would also prevent the sound from carrying, since most buildings tend to be well insulated. Since the whole operation depends on a steady flow of electricity, a break in the middle of the wire would also cause problems. Of course, the fellow could shout, but the human voice is not loud enough to carry that far. An additional problem is that a string could break on the instrument. Then there could be no accompaniment to the message. It is clear that the best situation would involve less distance. Then there would be fewer potential problems. With face-to-face contact, the least number of things could go wrong.

After the passage was read, the participants were asked to rate how well they understood the passage, with a rating of 7 meaning it was highly comprehensible. You might try this yourself. If you are like the participants in the experiment, you will rate the material as incomprehensible. Their actual average rating was 2.3 on the 7-point scale. The next task for the participants was to recall what they had read. Here they were instructed to write the main ideas that they remembered from the passage. How many ideas did you remember? The research participants in the experiment recalled, on average, 3.6 ideas out of a possible 14.

A second group of participants was shown **Figure 7-6** before they heard the passage. The participants in the group that saw the picture rated comprehensibility more than twice as high as those in the group who did not see the picture; they gave it a mean rating of 6.1 (versus 2.3 for the first group) on the 7-point scale. The second group also recalled many more ideas than the first group (8 versus 3.6 ideas). It is clear that having a context or schema in which to understand the information changes our ability to remember information. That is, we remember information best when we can make it part of a coherent story.

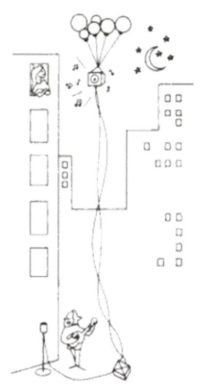

Figure 7-6 How does this help you understand and remember the passage?
Source: Bransford and Johnson (1972).

CONCEPT CHECK

1. What did Penfield's treatment of people with epilepsy add to our understanding of memory and the brain?
2. Describe the important characteristics of each of these aspects of the temporal dimension of memory:
   a. Sensory memory
   b. Short-term memory
   c. Long-term memory

3. How is chunking used in improving short-term memory? Give an example of how you could use it in your daily life.
4. Describe the important characteristics of each of these types of long-term memory:
   a. Episodic memory
   b. Semantic memory
   c. Explicit memory
   d. Implicit memory
5. Describe the important characteristics of each of the steps in learning and the long-term memory processes:
   a. Encoding
   b. Storage
   c. Consolidation
   d. Retrieval
   e. Reconsolidation
6. What do the studies of Ebbinghaus, Bartlett, and Bransford and Johnson contribute to our understanding of the role of meaning in memory?

Memory and the Brain

For at least 2,000 years following the ideas of Aristotle, the brain was seen as a blank slate on which experiences and information was stored. Like a computer disk, new information is added and retrieved as needed. We now know that memory is not a passive process. Rather, our brain recreates experiences as we remember events. That is, remembering is an active process.

The German scientist Richard Semon (1859–1918) sought to describe memory in precise scientific terms. One of the terms he introduced was the *engram* or memory trace. During the last century, researchers such as Karl Lashley (1890–1958) sought to find the location of memory in the brain. His three-decades-long search for the engram led to a large number of studies, but he was unable to find a specific location in the brain in which memory resides.

In the middle of the 20th century, Donald Hebb (1904–1985), who was a student of Lashley's, proposed a model of learning and memory. Hebb suggested that the experience of an object would be reflected in the neurons that are activated. That is, with each experience of an object, certain neurons in your brain would become active. Different experiences would result in different sets of neurons being active. That is, each experience would consist of a different internal representation of cells. Hebb referred to these cells that are activated as a **cell assembly**. Through repetition or other processes, the cell assembly could be strengthened and form a memory trace. That is, memory consolidation would occur as these cell assemblies became more efficient.

The basic model suggests that when one neuron in the brain excites another one nearby repeatedly, then the connection between the two is strengthened. This came to be described as "cells that fire together wire together." One implication of this is that even if only a few cells of a well-established cell assembly are activated, this has the potential to activate the other neurons in the entire cell assembly. Thus, being able to remember one aspect of an event may lead to your remembering of the entire event.

One implication of Donald Hebb's work is that memories of related items are associated with one another. If you enjoy long bike races, then all of the items related to the bicycle, the experiences of riding as well as methods of training could be seen as part of a larger network. One example of a network model as depicted by Allan Collins and Elizabeth Loftus (1975) is shown in **Figure 7-7**. This diagram shows the relationships between items. The shorter the path between items the stronger the connection. If you were talking about apples, then you could activate memories of other fruits or the perception of red more quickly than the items that make up your bicycle. Research has shown that if you were shown the word "red" and then asked to name a vehicle, you would more likely name a fire engine than a garbage truck. Likewise, if you were shown the word "cough," and asked to name an experience, you would more likely say having a cold than having a sunburn. Although not shown in **Figure 7-7**, items can also be organized in terms of concepts such as colors or fruits. Further, there can be overlapping networks. For example, "comfort foods" may include not only specific types of food but also the places where you consume these foods.

As suggested by Hebb, these associations between items appear not only in our cognitions but also in our brain. That is, neurons in our temporal lobe are seen to respond to concepts that are related to one another (Ison, Quiroga, & Fried, 2015). In this study, it was shown that neuronal changes to new associations could be established in a few presentations of the new material. Neurons in other areas such as the hippocampus respond when the organism is moving through space. As you learned previously in Chapter 3, it has been shown that neurons in the hippocampus increase connections when London taxi drivers learned new routes. Although it is assumed that each memory has a unique representation in the brain in terms of neural connections, the exact nature of these connections is still being worked out (Guan, Jiang, Xie, & Liu, 2016; Josselyn & Tonegawa, 2020).

H.M. and Memory

We now know that one critical area involved in memory processes is the hippocampus, which is located in the temporal lobe (see **Figure 7-1**). In the 1950s, a patient known as H.M. had his hippocampus and nearby structures removed in order to treat his severe epileptic seizures. After the surgery, his seizures were greatly improved, but there was an unexpected event. He lost the capacity to form new memories. That is, he forgot daily events nearly as fast as they occurred. However, he did not have problems with language, attention, cognitions, or perceptual tasks.

In a series of studies, the psychologist Brenda Milner detailed the nature of the memory problems seen in H.M. (Milner, Corkin, & Teuber, 1968). H.M., whose identity as Henry Molaison was revealed after his death in 2008, showed some memory abilities but not others. Molaison could remember events that took place before his surgery. He remembered his name, his occupation, and events from his childhood. He still could use English as well as he did previously, and his IQ was unchanged. However, he did not know words that appeared in English since the time of the operation, such as "jacuzzi," "frisbee," and "slamdunk."

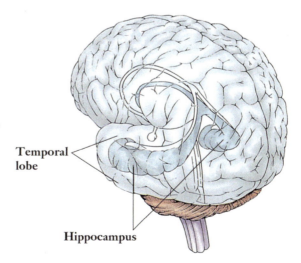

Figure 7-1 Hippocampus is part of the temporal lobe of the human brain.

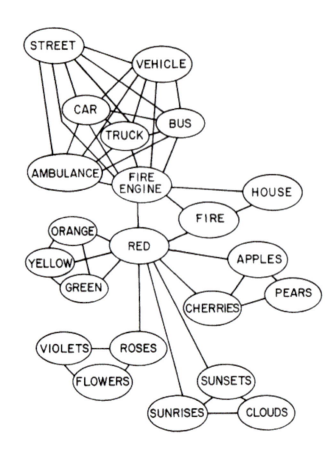

Figure 7-7 A model of how information is stored in the brain. Shorter lines suggest that one item is more related to another.
Source: Collins and Loftus (1975).

One important ability that Molaison did not have after the operation was to recall information regarding what he had just experienced. Said in more technical terms, he could not move information from *short-term memory* to *long-term memory*. Short-term memory as noted is the type of memory we use to accomplish tasks in the present, usually spanning less than a minute in time. We look up a phone number and make the call. We check an address when we arrive to see if we are at the correct location. If we need to use this information in the more distant future, we need to move it to long-term memory. After the operation, then, Molaison could not move information from short-term memory to long-term memory. He could not remember new people he met. Because Dr. Milner began to study Molaison after the operation, he reacted to her as if she were a new person each time they got together. He could not remember simple events that most of us take for granted, as shown in the following conversation:

> Dr. MILNER: Do you know what you did yesterday?
> H.M.: No, I don't.
> Dr. MILNER: How about this morning?
> H.M.: I don't even remember that.
> Dr. MILNER: Could you tell me what you had for lunch today?
> H.M.: I don't know, to tell you the truth.
> More information is available online (http://www.npr.org/templates/story/story.php?storyId=7584970).

Although he didn't remember doing it, Molaison was also able to learn new tasks. As noted this is an example of implicit memory, which is the ability of information to influence our behavior and experiences without our being aware of the learning taking place

Figure 7-8 Tower of Hanoi puzzle.

One of these tasks was the Tower of Hanoi puzzle (see **Figure 7-8**). As seen in the figure, you begin the task with all the disks on one peg. The task is to transfer all the disks to another peg. You are allowed to move only one disk at a time and may never place a larger disk on top of a smaller disk. Basically, you use the other two pegs to move the disks back and forth until they are all on one peg. After doing the task a number of times, you learn the best strategy to solve the puzzle.

Molaison was able to learn the task, but each time he was shown the puzzle, he would respond that he had not seen it before. He showed similar abilities in learning to draw a star in a mirror. This required that he move his hands in the opposite direction from what he saw visually. After some days, he learned to do this as well as individuals without temporal lobe damage. However, he could not consciously remember ever having performed the task. This suggests that learning a task involves a different type of memory than recognizing the task or remembering your experience with it.

Although a tragic event, the operation that removed Molaison's hippocampus helped to change the way we view memory. From her studies, Brenda Milner came to four critical conclusions regarding memory.

- The first is that the ability to acquire new memories is a distinct function of the brain located in the temporal lobes.
- The second is that the temporal lobes are not required for short-term memory.
- The third is that the temporal lobes and hippocampus cannot be the storage sites for long-term memories.
- And the fourth is that the temporal lobes are not the site for the memory of tasks such as the Tower of Hanoi puzzle.

Research involving Henry Molaison and others helped to develop a way to organize the different types of memory systems (Corkin, 2002; Squire, 2009).

Brain Areas Involved in Memory

We now know that different types of memory involve different brain regions that are connected together by cortical networks. We also know that some types of memory include conscious experiences and others do not (Squire, 2004). On the level of the neuron, we know that learning can influence connections of synapses with one another, as described previously in Chapter 3 with the research of Eric Kandel. The increase in connections can take place in all parts of the brain, which allows for greater activation in the future. Further, different brain areas connect with one another to allow for memories to involve any of the senses such as vision, hearing, and touch.

Working memory is a memory process in which a limited amount of information is retained for a short time. It is the information you need to accomplish your immediate task. MEG, EEG, and fMRI studies show brain changes, especially an increase in high-frequency cortical activity during working memory tasks (Constantinidis & Klingberg, 2016). Working memory involves the frontal lobes and their connections with parietal areas. The neurotransmitter dopamine in the striatum also plays a critical role in working memory (D'Esposito & Postle, 2015).

In essence, when we remember past events (long-term memory) our brain shows a pattern of activation that is very similar to how our brain responded to the initial event (Davachi & Preston, 2014). That is, it is as if every memory is a reenactment of the original event. You see your keys on the table, which allows you to later remember where you put them by reactivating this image in your brain. You may also have the bodily memory of throwing them on the table. Of course, how you seek to remember where your keys are could determine which brain areas are involved. If you logically ask, are the keys in my coat, in my car, in my house, you will use different parts of your brain than if you imagine driving home, getting out of your car, going into your house, and so forth (Sheldon & Levine, 2016).

As shown in the case of H.M., damage to parts of the medial temporal lobe impairs the ability to move events occurring in the present into long-term memory. In this way, it is critical to memory consolidation. Two specific areas that are parts of the medial temporal lobes are critically involved in memory networks; they are the hippocampus and the amygdala. The first area is the hippocampus, which is important to memory, especially spatial memory, as with the London taxi drivers. In fact, you saw that with the learning of the taxi routes of London, these taxi drivers showed changes in the size of their hippocampus. Earlier research with animals has also shown that different neurons in the hippocampus respond differently in terms of specific locations in space (O'Keefe, 1978). From this it has been suggested that the hippocampus is important for a spatial map of one's world.

Overall, the hippocampus is involved in four aspects of memory. The first is spatial memory, as discussed. The second is the timing of events, such as would be seen in autobiographical memory. That is, we know events happened in a specific order in our life and the hippocampus works with other areas of the brain to determine which events are encoded with which other events. The third memory aspect is related to putting together sensory information—how did it smell and what did it look like and how did it feel—with other aspects of the task—such as did I like it and where did it take place. Fourth, as shown by the experience of H.M., the hippocampus is important in the consolidation of memories from short-term to long-term memory.

If we experience an event that is emotionally arousing, we remember it better. This was shown in early studies by James McGaugh (see McGaugh, 2015 for an overview). When we see a bear in the woods, our body reacts with a release of adrenaline (epinephrine) that excites our bodies and prepares us to protect ourself by running or fighting. If immediately after an animal learns a task, it is given an injection of epinephrine, then its ability to remember the task is enhanced. It is critical that the epinephrine be administered immediately after the learning has taken place. Further, this works with many different kinds of tasks. From an evolutionary perspective, it would be important to remember events that produce emotional arousal, as these usually are associated with pleasure or pain.

Specific emotionally arousing public events have come to be called *flashbulb memories*. Most generations of people have particular events that they feel they can remember vividly, such as the attack on Pearl Harbor, the assassination of John F. Kennedy, the Challenger explosion, the killing of Martin Luther King, the attack of September 11, 2001, the Boston Marathon bombing, the killing of Osama Bin Laden, the Sandy Hook Elementary School shooting, and the death of Prince. People will report that they remember exactly where they were when they heard the news and give vivid and elaborate descriptions with great certainty. Flashbulb memories typically refer to those events that a person heard about rather than being directly involved in. Although, in the past, flashbulb memories were thought to involve special memory systems, current research suggests they are part of normal memory mechanisms (Hirst & Phelps, 2016). Further, although remembered with confidence, they are subject to the same types of distortions as are other memory processes (Talarico & Rubin, 2003, 2007).

The region of the medial temporal lobe that is important for emotional processing is the amygdala. As you will learn in the chapter on stress, the amygdala is influenced in response to arousing material. Overall, experiences that are emotionally arousing are remembered better than routine events (see McGaugh, 2004, 2013 for overviews). We all remember specific birthdays, holidays, or other such events and can recall them easily. In one study using PET (positron emission tomography) to measure blood flow in the brain, it was shown that initial changes in the amygdala after individuals watched emotionally arousing videos correlated with how well they remembered the videos a few weeks later (Cahill et al., 1996). Another role of the amygdala in memory appears to be memory consolidation.

The frontal lobes of the brain are also involved in memory (Eichenbaum, 2017a, 2017b). When you ask where you left your keys, you want to remember information about your keys, not the material you learned for the test. In an amazing manner, we are able to recall the information we need from memory without being bothered with all the other information our mind contains. Thus, the frontal lobes help to coordinate information from memory for the task you are currently trying to execute. **Figure 7-9** shows the types of long-term memory and the brain areas involved with each.

It is also important to understand that memory can be influenced by brain areas involved in other cognitive processes such as language production. If I were to ask you for an answer as to who was the singer and actress in *The Wizard of Oz*, how would you answer? You may

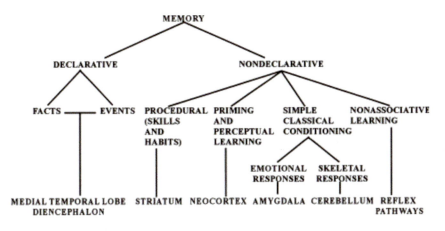

Figure 7-9 Are different areas involved with different types of memory? Yes.

Source: Squire (2004).

immediately know the answer or not know it at all. If you know the answer, brain activity in the frontal and temporal regions will be seen. However, if you were shown a photo of Dorothy, you may say I recognize that actress, I know her name, but can't produce it—it is as if it is on the tip of my tongue.

The *tip of the tongue* phenomenon is the inability to recall total information while having the feeling that you will be able to remember it at any moment. The tip of the tongue experience activates brain areas that involve both memory and language production as well as cognitive control (Shafto & Tyler, 2014). Brain activity continues for a longer period when the tip of the tongue is experienced than when the answer comes quickly, which suggests that brain networks continue to be active and complete the task of remembering the name. Brain areas involved in memory and language production include parts of the frontal, temporal, and parietal lobes, whereas cognitive control includes the insula, frontal areas and the anterior cingulate area. Brain activities in these areas is weaker than if a person is able to easily recall the name Judy Garland.

CONCEPT CHECK

1. How are memories stored in the brain? What has the research of Hebb and Collins and Loftus contributed to our understanding of memory networks?
2. How is the hippocampus critically involved in four different aspects of memory?
3. What four important conclusions about learning, memory, and the temporal lobes are illustrated by H.M.'s ability to successfully solve the Tower of Hanoi puzzle?
4. If we experience an event that is emotionally arousing, we remember it better. What is happening in the brain to facilitate this?
5. How is the frontal lobe involved in memory?

Individual Differences in Memory Abilities

Most of us have gone out to a restaurant with a number of our friends. Occasionally, you might have been surprised that even when there were ten or more people at the table, the server was able to take everyone's order without writing it down. And even better, when the food arrived, everyone received what they ordered without the server asking who ordered which food.

There are even contests such as the National Memory Championships in which contestants learn names, spoken words, random numbers, and other such lists. Many of these individuals are successful by using some type of system to improve memory. For example, if you have a list of words to learn, you could imagine you were walking through your house or other familiar place. Each word in the list would then be associated with a particular place in the house. To do recall, you would simply imagine you are walking through your house and recall the word associated with each location. Psychologists are interested in how people achieve what appears to be exceptional memory performance.

Clearly people differ in their memory abilities. In this section, you will be introduced to some individuals who are able to display exceptional abilities in memory as well as those who have problems with different types of memory. In the feature The World Is Your Laboratory, you will read about individuals who can remember every day of their life.

The World Is Your Laboratory: Exceptional Memory Ability

We all remember important events in our life. However, on the days in between these events, we typically remember very little. That is the typical nature of our memory. However, what if you could remember every day? What would your life be like? One individual who could do this wrote an email to the memory researcher James McGaugh in the spring of 2000 that began a line of research on individuals with exceptional autobiographical memory, which is formally known as Highly Superior Autobiographical Memory (HSAM). The email stated:

> I am thirty-four years old and since I was eleven I have had this unbelievable ability to recall my past, but not just recollections. My first memories are of being a toddler in the crib (circa 1967) however I can take a date, between 1974 and today, and tell you what day it falls on, what I was doing that day and if anything of great importance (i.e.: The Challenger Explosion, Tuesday, January 28, 1986) occurred on that day I can describe that to you as well. I do not look at calendars beforehand and I do not read twenty-four years of my journals either. Whenever I see a date flash on the television (or anywhere else for that matter) I automatically go back to that day and remember where I was, what I was doing, what day it fell on and on and on and on and on. It is non-stop, uncontrollable and totally exhausting.
>
> (Parker, Cahill, & McGaugh, 2006, p. 35)

Although James McGaugh and his colleagues were initially skeptical about this person's memory abilities, Jill Price was also able to remember events from her life (McGaugh & LePort, 2014). Since she has kept diaries from the age of 10, it was possible to check her memory with information in the diary. Public events going on at the same time could also be checked from public sources. Ms. Price says her personal memories are vivid and full of emotion. She also said that her remembering is automatic. This was demonstrated to the researchers as she gave quick, immediate answers to their questions concerning what she did on a certain day in her past. She could also remember what happened in the world on a given day. When asked what happened on August 16, 1977, she quickly replied that this was the day Elvis Presley died.

Although Jill Price could remember every day of her life since age 11, there were other types of memory in which she was not exceptional. She did not remember which of the five keys on her key ring went to which lock. In neuropsychological testing, she did not excel in the ability to remember complex figures or recognize faces. She also did not show any exceptional ability to remember the story "The War of the Ghosts," which Bartlett had used in his memory research discussed previously. Thus, she had exceptional memory abilities in autobiographical memory but not in some other types of memory.

After attention to Jill Price's ability was brought to the public on a National Public Radio show in 2006, a number of other individuals wrote to James McGaugh to describe similar abilities (http://www.npr.org/templates/story/story.php?storyId=90596530). A later *60 Minutes* show brought forth even more individuals (http://www.scientific

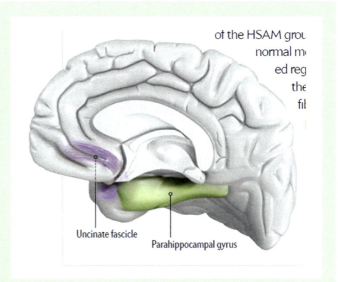

Figure 7-10 What brain areas are different in those with exceptional autobiographical memory? Two memory-related regions stood out in brain scans: the uncinate fascicle, a nerve fiber tract that links the temporal and frontal cortices, and the parahippocampal gyrus, which are better connected to other brain areas.
Source: McGuagh and LePort (2014).

american.com/article/remember-what-it-means-to-have-an-extraordinary-memory/). From these, McGaugh and his colleagues studied 11 individuals who clearly had exceptional autobiographical memory abilities. Like Jill Price, these 11 individuals showed exceptional autobiographical memory but performed similar to a control group on other types of memory. By about age 11 and a half, these individuals realized they had a highly developed knowledge of dates.

Brain-imaging studies of individuals with exceptional autobiographical memory showed differences from a control group in both white and gray matter in different areas of the brain (LePort et al., 2012). Further, the connection between those brain areas associated with autobiographical memory were stronger in the HSAM group (see **Figure 7-10**).

Thought Question: What might be an advantage of having exceptional autobiographical memory? What might be a disadvantage?

Mnemonists

A *mnemonist* is a person who can remember and recall long lists of information such as numbers, words, or names. Interestingly, these individuals do not show superior autobiographical memory. Similarly, individuals with exceptional autobiographical memory do not display other superior memory abilities.

In the 1920s, a newspaper editor sent one of his reporters named Sherashevsky to the famous Russian psychologist A. R. Luria. The editor of the newspaper noted the reporter's lack of notetaking and his ability to remember all of the information that was needed. Luria studied this individual who he referred to as S and wrote a book describing his abilities, *The Mind of a Mnemonist* (Luria, 1987). In essence, S was able to remember long lists. In fact, Luria could not find a memory test that S did not do well on.

However, this ability was not accomplished with ease. S had developed techniques for remembering information. One of his techniques, which has also been used by others with this ability, is to take a mental walk through a familiar route and to pair each item with a specific place on this walk. Using such a technique, S could remember information in either a forward or backward manner by imagining his walk beginning at different locations.

Another individual who demonstrated superior memory abilities was Rajan Mahadevan (Ericsson et al., 2004). As a child, he would surprise his friends by reciting the complete railway timetable for the Calcutta railway system. Later, to establish a place in the Guinness Book of World Records, he reproduced more than 30,000 numbers in the derivation of pi (3.141592 and so forth). Not only could he do this with pi but also with any string of digits that were presented to him. As with Luria's description of S, Rajan Mahadevan had developed a technique based on a matrix approach that allowed him to remember numbers. However, this ability did not generalize to other types of memory.

Photographic Memory

It should be noted that the memory abilities shown by Sherashevsky and Mahadevan, impressive as they are, were based on techniques that required some effort to achieve. Although these are sometimes referred to as photographic memory, this was not the case. True photographic memory would suggest that the person could retrieve the image perfectly. However, research suggests that *photographic or eidetic memory* exists in only a small number of individuals, if at all (MacLeod, Jonker, & James, 2014).

Those who are able to reproduce an image with great accuracy are mainly children. In general, less than 10% of children are able to show signs of eidetic memory. By about age 10, this ability almost completely disappears. There are, from time to time, examples of individuals with exceptional long-term visual memory. The late neurologist Oliver Sacks (1995) describes two artists who were able to draw near perfect images from memory.

The artist Franco Magnani came to America from Italy in 1965. Although he did not go back to his home town of Pontito, he was able to able to draw in great detail his home town even after 30 years. Although he was able to remember his hometown, his drawing added some detail that was not be present in an actual photo. Still it is amazing that he was able to retain the visual information.

The second person Oliver Sacks wrote about was Stephen Wiltshire. Sacks wrote about Wiltshire when he was a teenager and was impressed that he could reproduce a drawing of Sacks's house by just quickly looking at it. Since that time, Stephen Wiltshire has been profiled on the BBC in the UK and *60 Minutes* in the United States. He has been able to take a helicopter flight of a major city such as Mexico City, Rome, New York City, or Singapore and then reproduce his view of it. A description of his work can be seen on YouTube (https://www.youtube.com/watch?v=g2EpmFzG2AM). In addition to being able to recognize cities, other individuals are able to recognize faces over a period of time. This situation is presented in the Applying Psychological Science: Super-Recognizers and Never Forgetting a Face box.

Applying Psychological Science: Super-Recognizers and Never Forgetting a Face

We recognize one another in a number of ways. We recognize how the other person walks, or the sound of their voice, or the shape of their face. In fact, humans are considered experts at processing faces. However, about 2% of the general population have difficulty recognizing faces even though they have normal vision. The inability to recognize faces is referred to as *developmental prosopagnosia*.

Not only do some people have problems recognizing faces, but others claim they never forget a face. Some say they can recognize a person seen in one movie or TV show, even if they play a small part in another. To test these claims, Richard Russell and his colleagues studied these individuals with face-recognition tasks that required both the recognition of familiar and unfamiliar faces (Russell, Duchaine, & Nakayama, 2009). What these researchers found was that the four *super-recognizers* as they were called were much better than 25 control subjects at the face-recognition tasks. More recent research has shown that the ability to memorize words and faces is not the same as the ability to recognize faces (Ramon, Miellet, Dzieciol, Konrad, Dresler, & Caldara, 2016).

Many people could use the ability to recognize faces in their occupation. This would be an advantage for salespeople in large stores. They could recognize the frequent shoppers and acknowledge this to the customer. However, stores do not typically actively search for individuals who are super-recognizers.

One organization that does actively seek super-recognizers is the London England Metropolitan Police. London has many closed-circuit cameras (CCTV) installed around the city of some eight million residents. What started as cameras being installed around government buildings and embassies has grown to one estimate of more than a million cameras, including those installed by businesses (O'Keefe, 2016). With this much information, the ability to recognize faces would give the police an advantage to be able to recognize individuals who are present during the time a number of different crimes were committed. Thus, the London police created a unit that is made up of individuals who share the ability to recognize and remember faces. In fact, the police called upon scientists to help them identify individuals for this unit.

In one situation, women reported being groped on London transit. By examining video, it was possible to note if anyone was present at each occurrence. This led to the man being identified in live video as he left a railroad station. In another situation, stores reported that a handsome man of about 40 years of age would come into a jewelry store or boutique. He would begin talking to the salesperson posing as a wealthy person seeking a gift for his girlfriend. The salesperson would show him an expensive gift. If the salesperson turned away, the man would take the expensive item and hide it in his clothes. After some forty acts of robbery involving more than $100,000, the police realized that they had a number of pictures of the man and were able to arrest him.

Of course, as with any good criminal investigation, other clues besides facial recognition are also employed. For example, some criminals wear the same clothes at each crime they commit. Others can be traced using transit cards they used. However, in many cases facial recognition is critical.

The unit was started in 2008 by Detective Chief Inspector Mick Neville. Patrick Keefe, a writer for *The New Yorker* magazine, spoke with the London Metropolitan Police and wrote an article, dated August 22, 2016, describing the super-recognizers unit.

Thought Question: What are some other occupations in which being a super-recognizer would be beneficial? What would be the benefit? What common aspects do these occupations share?

Memory Disorders

Memory problems can be seen after a variety of traumas. Many people who have a concussion, for example, will not be able to remember the period during which their head was hit. This is an example of a memory problem of only a few minutes. However, those who have had a stroke in which blood is not available to specific brain areas may be unable to recall specific information that they once knew. The inability to recall information is referred to as *amnesia*.

A distinction is often made between ***retrograde amnesia*** and ***anterograde amnesia***. Retrograde amnesia refers to the situation in which a person cannot remember events prior to the trauma to the brain. Such a person may not be able to remember events, facts, or people that were known before the trauma. It is interesting that in some cases, memories from a few years prior to the trauma are not remembered, but memories from 20 or 30 years earlier are remembered. Depending on the location of the trauma to the brain, different people may show different types of memory deficits. The movie *The Majestic* (2001) shows a person with retrograde amnesia who has lost the memories of his personal past while still knowing language, and ways of human social interaction.

Anterograde amnesia, on the other hand, is the situation in which the person is not able to form new memories, as was the case with H.M. The movie *Memento* (2000) describes a person named Lenny who cannot form new memories. Likewise, the movie *50 First Dates* (2004) describes a woman who could not form new memories and the man who romantically seeks to win her affections each new day. There can also be less severe cases in which it takes more practice for the person to form new long-term memories. In general, those with brain damage show signs of both retrograde and anterograde amnesia.

CONCEPT CHECK

1. Define each of the following superior memory abilities:
    a. Highly Superior Autobiographical Memory (HSAM)
    b. Mnemonists
    c. Photographic or eidetic memory
    d. Super-recognizers
2. What are anterograde amnesia and retrograde amnesia, and how are they different?

False Memories

False memory research has focused on the factors that cause us to remember an event in a manner that does not reflect that particular event accurately. If indeed when we remember an event we reconstruct it in our brains, can we be led to perform inaccurate reconstructions? The answer to this question turns out to be *yes*. This has important implications for eye-witness testimony in court, how information-gathering techniques of governments are to be evaluated, and the factors that influence our memory.

A *false memory* is one that is experienced as any other memory and you believe it to be true. One researcher who has focused her career on the nature of false memories and how to create them is Elizabeth Loftus who began her research at the University of Washington.

She initially referred to false memories as the *misinformation effect*. Loftus describes her work in a Ted Talk (https://www.ted.com/speakers/elizabeth_loftus) and a segment of Radiolab (https://www.wnycstudios.org/story/91573-adding-memory).

The misinformation effect is based on the fact that we continue to reconstruct memories even after the experience has happened. In some of her early work, Elizabeth Loftus and her colleagues had participants watch videos of automobile accidents and then answer questions about the event (Loftus & Palmer, 1974). The nature of these questions was an important part of the study. For example, one group was asked, "About how fast were these cars going when they hit each other?" Another group was asked, "About how fast were these cars going when they smashed into each other?" A final group was not asked any questions about the one-minute accident video they saw.

The three groups then returned a week later and answered ten questions about the video they had seen. One question, for example, asked if the participant saw any broken glass during the accident—there was none. The group that heard the verb "hit" and the group that were not asked any questions both said there was not any broken glass. However, twice as many people in the group that heard the question with the verb "smashed" reported broken glass than those who did not. Thus, a false memory could be induced just by the manner in which a person is asked a question after an event.

Another procedure for inducing false memories is referred to as the Deese–Roediger–McDermott (DRM) procedure. Read the words presented in **Table 7-1**. Once you do this, close the book and write down all the words you can remember (based on Roediger & McDermott, 1995).

How many words did you remember? But, more important for the false memory situation, did you remember a word that was not there? If you are like many people, you included the word *sleep*, which was not on the list. The point is that we remember things in terms of their meaning to us. Each of the words in the list is related to sleep, so we assume it was there. Thus, what something means to us is critical for how we remember information. Further, as noted previously, we remember information in terms of networks or interconnection between different pieces of information. Remembering the words *dream*, *nap*, and *drowsy* activates the network that would also contain the word *sleep*.

Another way you can create false memories is through the use of imagination. Giuliana Mazzoni and Amina Memon asked college students at the University of Aberdeen in Scotland to imagine either a frequent or an impossible event (Mazzoni & Memon, 2004). The frequent event was having a tooth pulled by a dentist. The impossible event was having a school nurse remove a skin sample from their little finger. This is an impossible event since school nurses in the UK are not allowed to take skin samples. A week previously, all of the participants had filled out a 20-item questionnaire on which they rated the

Table 7-1 Deese–Roediger–McDermott (DRM) procedure.

Bed	Dream	Slumber
Drowsy	Awake	Snore
Rest	Tired	Wake
Yawn	Doze	Snooze
Peace	Nap	Blanket

Source: Based on Roediger and McDermott (1995).

possibility that an event had happened to them before the age of 6. This included such items as finding money in a parking garage, feeling an earthquake, and becoming ill and going to the hospital.

In the experiment a week later, one group of students imagined having a tooth pulled by a dentist and read a one-page passage about the skin sample. A second group of students imagined having a skin sample taken and read a passage about having a tooth pulled. A week later all participants repeated the 20-item questionnaire of which event happened to them as well as report any memories they have of the tooth and skin event and three other noncritical events. At no point during the experiment did the researchers try to convince the participants that any particular event had happened to them.

As expected, those who imagined or read about a tooth being pulled reported more memories about that event. However, in relation to the event that did not happen, a school nurse taking a skin sample, imagining the event increased the number of individuals who reported that the event had happened to them. They also reported more memories about this event. Thus, individuals can develop a memory of an event that did not happen simply by imagining its occurrence.

Imagination has also been shown to influence students in the United States. What if someone took you on a walk around a familiar college campus, and asked you later what you saw or did? What if the researchers asked if you saw someone shake hands with a fire hydrant or propose to a Pepsi machine? Most of us would say we would know if we saw such events. We would also assume that we would accurately remember what we did or saw. However, that turns out not to be the case.

In a creative study, each student in the experiment was asked to walk around his or her campus with a researcher and a confederate of the researcher (Seamon et al., 2009). On the first day, the student went on a walk on which they stopped at 48 locations. At each location, the experimenter read an action statement and either performed that action or asked the participant to imagine themselves performing that action. Half of the actions were familiar and half were bizarre, such as proposing to a Pepsi machine. A day later, the participant was taken on another walk. On this walk they stopped at 36 locations. These stops included 24 locations they had stopped at previously and 12 new locations. On this walk, the participant was asked to imagine the experimenter performing each action. Again, half of the actions were familiar and half bizarre.

Two weeks later, the participant and the confederate were asked about certain actions and whether they happened or were imagined on the day one walk. The confederate and the participant alternated their responses to an event. On some events, the confederate was accurate, on some inaccurate, and on others, said that he or she did not remember. Following this, the experimenter said that they were to be tested alone for additional information. Then, the participant was tested alone and asked if a particular action was presented on a particular day and, if so, was it performed or imagined. The participant was also asked to rate how confident they were in their answer.

Overall, participants had trouble remembering and distinguishing events that were experienced or viewed in comparison to imagined events. For example, both familiar and bizarre events were remembered as happening on the first walk if they were merely imagined on the second walk.

As human beings, we fill in the gaps of our memory to make things work. We also tend to remember events in a way that fits into our own conception of the world. Politics is one area of life in which many people have strong feelings. In May 2010, Slate.com invited its readers to complete a survey about their perspectives on various political events. Those

Figure 7-11 Example of real (on the left) and altered photo (on the right). The real photo was taken on President Bush's ranch with the baseball player Roger Clemmons at the same time Hurricane Katrina was hitting the coast.
Source: Frenda, Knowles, Saletan, & Loftus (2013).

who volunteered read about five unrelated news events with accompanying photographs and were asked about their memories for them. The five events from 2010 were a Hillary Clinton attack ad, Cheney/Edwards debate, an Obama handshake, the Lieberman vote, and the Bush vacation. Unbeknownst to the respondents, one of the five events they were asked about was a complete fabrication; it never happened at all. More than 5,000 respondents completed the study (Frenda, Knowles, Saletan, & Loftus, 2013).

The initial part of the survey ensured that the participants were familiar with the events. A total of 82% of the participants reported knowing of all three true events and 98% said they knew of two of the three. In terms of the false events for which each person only saw one example, 50% reported that they remember that particular event as having taken place. The other participants said that they did not remember the event (44%) or that they remembered it differently (6%). Participants in the Hillary attack ad condition showed the highest rate of false memory (68%), followed by the Cheney/Edwards debate (65%), the Obama handshake (47%), the Lieberman vote (40%), and the Bush vacation (31%). A follow-up study showed that false events are more easily accepted if they are similar to the person's previously existing attitudes.

False memory research has led to changes in legal procedures (Loftus, 2003; Schacter & Loftus, 2013). Schacter and Loftus described a crime that happened in Camden, New Jersey, on New Year's Day 2003. Larry Henderson was accused of holding a gun on James Womble while another man shot Rodney Harper to death. Larry Henderson was not involved in the crime. Almost 2 weeks after the murder, Womble identified Henderson from a photograph. Womble again identified Henderson at trial, and Henderson was easily convicted of reckless manslaughter and aggravated assault, among other charges.

The case was appealed to the New Jersey Supreme Court, which resulted in the court issuing a new set of guidelines that reflected the reconstructive nature of memory and the various factors that can influence it. Specifically, jurors are now to be told that memory is not like a video recording, and it is not foolproof but can be influenced. Research has also shown that those in authority such police officers, military personnel, and emergency responders are susceptible to memory errors during challenging incidents (Hope et al., 2016).

In addition to problems with eye-witness testimony, police investigations at times ask leading questions, suggest events that did not happen, or pressure the person to report details that may be inaccurate. In fact, individuals may come to believe that they participated in or committed a crime that they did not. Research related to this is discussed in the following Myths and Misconceptions box.

Overall, false memory research has focused on the factors that cause us to remember an event in a manner that does not reflect that particular event accurately. As you have seen, there are a variety of ways that we remember events in a different manner than which they initially occurred. If indeed when we remember an event, we reconstruct it in our brains, we can be led to perform inaccurate reconstructions. This has important implications for eye-witness testimony in court, how information-gathering techniques of governments are to be evaluated, and the factors that influence our memory.

Myths and Misconceptions: What You Remember is True

In 2015, Julia Shaw and Stephen Porter sought to determine if completely false memories of committing crimes involving police contact could be created in a laboratory setting. The study asked if college students could be convinced that they had committed a crime when they were between the ages of 11 and 14 years of age. To begin with, the researchers sent questionnaires to the parents and caregivers of the participants. They were asked to report at least one highly emotional event that happened during their child's adolescence. Individuals were ineligible if their caregivers mentioned any kind of police contact or reported events that resembled the target events at any point during adolescence. On the questionnaire, caregivers were asked whether their child had experienced any of six negative emotional events, three of which were criminal (assault, assault with a weapon, and theft) and three of which were noncriminal (an accident, an animal attack, and losing a large amount of money). For each recalled event, caregivers were asked to write a description of what they could remember, including the location, people present, time of year, age of the participant, and how confident they were that the event had occurred.

The participants in the study completed three interviews, about one week apart. In the interviews, the participants were presented verbally a true event that happened to them and a false one that they did not experience. Participants were then asked to add any information about the true and false memory. The interviewer added accurate information such as the city the person lived in, the name of a friend who was said to be part of the event, the season the event took place in, and other such information. When the participants had difficulty recalling the false event, the interviewer encouraged them to try to remember it. They were also told to try to visualize the event during the period between the interviews. The interviewers also suggested that they had additional information from the parents but did not give it as the memories needed to come from the participant.

The false memories during the interviews were based on six types. That is, participants were assigned to one of six false memory groups. The individuals in the first three groups were told that they had committed a crime in adolescence that was either an assault, an assault with a weapon, or a theft. The next three groups were told they had experienced a non-criminal emotional event during which they injured themselves, had been attacked by a dog, or got in trouble with their parents about losing money.

Overall, participants in the study reported more confidence in remembering the true memory events. However, they still reported specific details in the false memory condition. The results of this study showed that over 71% of those in the criminal false memory groups indeed reported false memories. Specifically, 75.6% reported details in the assault group, 71.3% reported details in the assault with a weapon group, and 67.2% reported details in the theft group. In the non-criminal conditions, some 76.7% reported false memories. The percentages in each of the three non-criminal groups were similar.

The Shaw and Porter study points to the ability of researchers in a laboratory setting to have individuals come to visualize and recall detailed false memories of both criminal and non-criminal behavior. In fact, these false memories were richly detailed. If this can be accomplished in a relatively benign laboratory setting, one can wonder the degree to which police or other government settings are able to induce false information. The Innocence Project (http://www.innocenceproject.org), which seeks to free those who have been wrongfully convicted, suggests that about 25% of false convictions are related to faulty confession information. Thus, both faulty eye-witness testimony and questionable interrogation tactics leading to false memories set the stage for miscarriages of justice.

Thought Question: What information do you think it would be helpful for all individuals to have to minimize the effects of false memories in areas of criminal and civil justice?

CONCEPT CHECK

1. What are three different ways for inducing false memories? How does each of them work?

Summary

Learning Objective 1: Discuss memory and how information is encoded, stored, and retrieved.

Memory is focused on how information is encoded, stored, and later retrieved. Before information is stored, it is encoded. That is, certain aspects of your experiences are organized and stored in the brain. Encoding includes how you store information in the brain. Although we use terms such as storing a memory, we now know that remembering an experience is more than just viewing an image of what happened. Unlike a computer that gives you back exactly the information that is stored, our brain has a logic of its own based on our evolutionary history. When we remember, we actually recreate the experience in our minds. Depending on the nature of the memory, different parts of your brain can be involved. Some memories have to do with language, some with emotions, some with events, some with sensory experiences, and many with a combination of these. Overall, memory is described in terms of two different dimensions: (1) the temporal dimension which includes short-term and long-term memory; and (2) the type of information stored.

Sensory memory lasts only a few seconds and takes place in all of our senses. If it involves the auditory system, it is referred to as echoic memory. If it involves our visual system, it is referred to as iconic memory. This is the first step of how we remember information. Sensory memory lasts just long enough for the information to be processed by our brain. However, we can't possibly remember all of the information that is before us in this brief period.

The second step in remembering information is to transform the sensory information and work with it for a short period of time. This is referred to as short-term memory or working memory. As the name implies, short-term memory lasts for less than a minute. The concept of working memory evolved from short-term memory to reflect the systems required to keep things in mind while performing tasks. Short-term memory lasts for about 20 to 30 seconds without rehearsal. To have a memory available to us in the future, the information needs to be converted from short-term memory into long-term memory. Information available to us through long-term memory can be relatively permanent. Long-term memory can be classified in terms of the type of information that is stored.

We now know that one critical area involved in memory processes is the hippocampus, located in the temporal lobe. In the 1950s, a patient known as H.M. had his hippocampus on both sides of the brain and nearby structures removed in order to treat his severe epileptic seizures. After the surgery, his seizures were greatly improved, but there was an unexpected event. He lost the capacity to form new memories. Although a tragic event, the operation that removed H.M.'s hippocampi helped to change the way we view memory. From her studies with H.M., Brenda Milner came to four critical conclusions regarding memory: (1) the ability to acquire new memories is a distinct function of the brain located in the temporal lobes; (2) temporal lobes are not required for short-term memory; (3) the temporal lobes and hippocampus cannot be the storage sites for long-term memories; and (4) the temporal lobes are not the site for the memory of tasks. Overall, memory is described in terms of two different dimensions: (1) the temporal dimension, which includes short-term and long-term memory; and (2) the type of information stored.

Episodic memory is a collection of events that we personally experienced. *Semantic memory* has to do with impersonal facts and everyday knowledge. *Implicit memory* has the ability to influence our behavior and experiences without an awareness of the learning taking place. We also can do a number of motor tasks without consciously remembering how to do it. This type of memory is referred to as procedural memory. Other types of implicit memory include classical conditioning and priming. Priming is the situation in which previous experiences can influence present behavior.

Psychologists have described the long-term memory processes in terms of four separate steps.

1. The first step is encoding. Encoding is the process by which information is attended to and connected with other information in your memory. Following encoding, the information must be stored.
2. The second step, storage, involves those areas of the brain and neural mechanisms by which memories are retained over time.
3. The third step is consolidation. Consolidation is the process by which the information stored becomes even more stable. Consolidation takes place in the brain on two levels. The first level is structural changes at the synapse; the second level involves a reorganization of long-term memories over brain networks.

4. The fourth step is retrieval. This stage is what we think of when we say we recalled something. Typically, retrieval involves different types of information stored in different places throughout the brain.

Learning Objective 2: Describe how memories are organized and stored in the brain.

We now know that different types of memory involve different brain regions, which are connected together by cortical networks. We also know that some types of memory include conscious experiences and others do not. On the level of the neuron, we know that learning can influence connections of synapses with one another. The increase in connections can take place in all parts of the brain, which allows for greater activation in the future. Further, different brain areas connect with one another to allow for memories to involve any of the senses such as vision, hearing, and touch.

Working memory (short-term memory) is a memory process in which a limited amount of information is retained for a short time. MEG, EEG, and fMRI studies show an increase in high-frequency activity during working memory tasks. Working memory involves the frontal lobes and their connections with parietal areas. The neurotransmitter dopamine in the striatum also plays a critical role in working memory.

In essence when we remember past events (long-term memory), our brain shows a pattern of activation that is very similar to how our brain responded to the initial event. That is, it is as if every memory is a reenactment in the original event. Damage to parts of the medial temporal lobe impairs the ability to move events occurring in the present into long-term memory. In this way, it is critical to memory consolidation. Two specific areas that are parts of the medial temporal lobes are critically involved in memory networks—the hippocampus and the amygdala.

The first area is the hippocampus, which is important to memory, especially spatial memory. In fact, it has been suggested that the hippocampus is important for a spatial map of one's world. The hippocampus is involved in four aspects of memory: (1) spatial memory; (2) the timing of events such as would be seen in autobiographical memory (that is, we know events happened in a specific order in our life and the hippocampus works with other areas of the brain to determine which events are encoded with which other events); (3) putting together sensory information—how did it smell? what did it look like? how did it feel?—with other aspects of the task—did I like it? where did it take place? and so forth; (4) as shown by the experience of H.M., the hippocampus is important in the consolidation of memories from short-term to long-term memory.

Specific emotionally arousing public events have come to be called *flashbulb memories*. People will report that they remember exactly where they were when they heard the news and give vivid and elaborate descriptions with great certainty. Flashbulb memories typically refer to those events that a person heard about rather than being directly involved in. Although, in the past, flashbulb memories were thought to involve special memory systems, current research suggests they are part of normal memory mechanisms. Further, although remembered with confidence, they are subject to the same types of distortions as are other memory processes.

Learning Objective 3: Describe how people differ in their memory abilities.

Clearly people differ in their memory abilities. You might have been surprised in a restaurant that even when there were ten or more people at the table, the server was able to take everyone's order without writing it down.

Memory problems can be seen after a variety of traumas. Many people who have a concussion, for example, will not be able to remember the period during which their head was hit. This is an example of a memory problem of only a few minutes. However, those who have had a stroke in which blood is not available to specific brain areas may be unable to recall specific information that they once knew. The inability to recall information is referred to as amnesia. *Retrograde amnesia* refers to the situation in which a person cannot remember events prior to the trauma to the brain. Depending on the location of the trauma to the brain, different people may show different types of memory deficits. *Anterograde amnesia*, on the other hand, is the situation in which the person is not able to form new memories.

Learning Objective 4: Discuss the key theories of how we create false memories and misinformation.
A false memory is one that is experienced as any other memory and you believe to be true. False memory research has focused on the factors that cause us to remember an event in a manner that does not reflect a particular event accurately. If indeed when we remember an event, we reconstruct it in our brains, can we be led to perform inaccurate reconstructions? The answer to this question turns out to be *yes*. This has important implications for eye-witness testimony in court, how information-gathering techniques of governments are to be evaluated, and the factors that influence our memory.

Research has shown that a false memory could be induced in several ways, including (1) just by the manner in which a person is asked a question after an event; (2) by using the Deese–Roediger–McDermott (DRM) procedure. We remember things in terms of their meaning to us and each of the words in the list in the example is related to sleep, so we assume it was there. Further, we remember information in terms of networks or interconnection between different pieces of information. Remembering the words *dream*, *nap*, and *drowsy* activates the network that would also contain the word *sleep*. (3) By the use of imagination: imagining the event increases the number of individuals who reported that the event had actually happened to them. They also report more memories about this event. Thus, individuals can develop a memory of an event that did not happen simply by imagining its occurrence.

False-memory research has led to changes in legal procedures. A case was appealed to the New Jersey Supreme Court, which resulted in the court issuing a new set of guidelines that reflected the reconstructive nature of memory and the various factors that can influence it. Specifically, jurors are now to be told that memory is not like a video recording, and it is not foolproof but can be influenced. Research has also shown that those in authority such as police officers, military personnel, and emergency responders are susceptible to memory errors during challenging incidents. In addition to problems with eye-witness testimony, police investigations at times ask leading questions, suggest events that did not happen, or pressure the person to report details that may be inaccurate. In fact, individuals may come to believe that they participated in or committed a crime that they did not.

Study Resources

Review Questions

1. What does it mean when we say that memory is a constructive process rather than a reproductive process? What are the implications of describing memory in that way?

2. Identify the four types of exceptional memory abilities that were described in this chapter. How is each of them unique? What do they have in common?
3. What are false memories? How are they different from real memories? How can we know that we ever reconstruct an event accurately?

For Further Reading

Foer, J. (2011). *Moonwalking with Einstein.* New York: Penguin Press.
Kandel, E. (2006). *In Search of Memory.* New York: Norton.

Web Resources

Clive—https://www.wnycstudios.org/podcasts/radiolab/segments/91578-clive
H.M.—http://www.npr.org/templates/story/story.php?storyId=7584970
Extraordinary memory—https://www.npr.org/templates/story/story.php?storyId=90596530
Extraordinary memory—https://www.scientificamerican.com/article/remember-what-it-means-to-have-an-extraordinary-memory/
Stephen Wiltshire—https://www.youtube.com/watch?v=g2EpmFzG2AM
Elizabeth Loftus—https://www.ted.com/speakers/elizabeth_loftus) and (https://www.wnycstudios.org/podcasts/radiolab/segments/91573-adding-memory)
Innocence Project—http://www.innocenceproject.org

Key Terms and Concepts

amnesia	false memory	retroactive interference
anterograde amnesia	implicit memory	retrograde amnesia
cell assembly	long-term memory	semantic memory
chunking	memory	sensory memory
consolidation	proactive interference	short-term memory
encoding	procedural memory	storage
episodic memory	reconstructive memory	working memory
explicit memory	retrieval	

8 Learning, Ethology, and Language Processes

LEARNING OBJECTIVES
8.1 Describe the basic processes of classical conditioning.
8.2 Describe the basic processes of operant conditioning.
8.3 Summarize the types of learning that occur during imprinting, play, observational learning, and imitation learning.
8.4 Describe how we learn languages.
8.5 Identify the parts of the brain that are active in language processes.

One classic study in fear learning is that of Susan Mineka and her colleagues (see Öhman & Mineka, 2001, for an overview). It had been observed that primates in the wild show a fear of snakes. Since a similar fear is seen in lab monkeys, it was assumed that the fear was somehow innate. However, Mineka asked the question of whether early experience could influence this. In particular, she wanted to know if learning could play a role.

What she and her colleagues did was to compare wild-reared rhesus monkeys with those that had been reared in the lab. The wild-reared monkeys that had been brought to the lab some 24 years earlier showed a fear of snakes. This fear existed even though they would have had no experience with snakes during their time in the lab. The lab-reared monkeys, on the other hand, did not show any fear of snakes. In fact, they would reach over the snake to grab food.

How did monkeys develop the fear of snakes? What Mineka did next was to pair a wild-reared monkey with a young lab-reared one. A snake was then presented, and a wild-reared monkey showed fear. The young lab-reared monkey was able to observe this. After this, the lab-reared monkey also showed fear. Clearly, the lab-reared monkey had the ability to quickly learn the fear but required an experience in which another monkey showed fear for it to happen. The next question Mineka and her colleagues asked was the importance of the feared object itself.

In a very clever study, she showed some of the young monkeys a videotape of a wild monkey showing fear toward a snake. As expected, they learned the fear of snakes. However, with another group of young monkeys, she edited the tape so what the young monkey saw was the original fear reaction of the older monkey but this time to a flower. If fear was acquired by a simple learning process in which the stimulus did not matter, then you would expect the young monkeys to learn a fear of flowers. However, the monkeys did not learn to fear flowers. Thus, the nature of what the monkey sees is important. In the real world, snakes but not flowers can be dangerous.

Although most of us have an idea of what it means to learn something, learning is actually a difficult and complex concept to define. In fact, it has been pointed out that the definition of learning differs across different areas of study including psychology (Barron et al., 2015).

B. F. Skinner, who supported a behaviorist view of psychology in the last century, suggested that learning should be defined as behavior change, that is, a change that can be seen.

Skinner emphasized the modification of behavior in which a response followed by a reward will be increased. This came to be called operant conditioning, which is a special type of learning. Skinner saw almost all human behavior, including the learning of language and the development of mental disorders, as controlled by the laws of learning based on external rewards. Today, we know that conditioning is only one type of learning. Overall, learning is influenced by both external processes such as rewards and internal processes such as previous memories or preparedness. The stages of language learning in children is an example of learning that takes place as the brain develops or is prepared for its occurrence.

Almost every chapter in this book describes changes in behavior. These changes in behavior can come about by being with others, changes in motivation, feeling tired, or experiencing mental disorders. Thus, not every change in behavior involves learning. We need to remind ourselves that learning is not a simple process that just changes behavior. We can define *learning* as the acquisition of knowledge or skills through experience, study, or by being taught.

So far in this book, you have seen how learning to play a musical instrument or learning the taxi routes of London can change your brain. You have also seen the research of Eric Kandel, who showed that learning affects neural connections in the brains of sea slugs. Piaget showed that learning takes place in an interaction with the environment. However, a child must be in a specific stage of development before this learning can take place. Likewise, leaning language is easier at some stages of development than others. Whereas language learning is what every child does, learning to read or write takes more effort. Learning math is also a more difficult task. As you will see, ease of learning is related to our evolutionary history.

Since the time of Darwin, learning has been considered an important mechanism by which an organism adapts to changing environmental conditions. In this sense, learning is part of the human processes that use our past experiences to predict what will happen in the future (Bar, 2011). You just read that young monkeys who were not afraid of snakes learned this fear just by watching another monkey show fearful behavior. However, the monkeys did not learn to be afraid of flowers. This suggests that learning takes place in a context related to our evolutionary history. That is, some information is more important to us than other information. This is especially true of information that can help us survive. Snakes are more likely to harm us than flowers. Thus, our evolutionary history influences what and how we learn.

This chapter will introduce you to some of the ways that learning has been studied. In the beginning and middle of the last century, learning studies were strongly influenced by behaviorism. Behaviorism stressed external factors and ignored internal processes. This led to a view of humans as passive and basically the result of rewards in their lives. This chapter will include historical views of conditioning as well as the manner in which research has expanded our view of learning. The development of cognitive psychology in the 1960s greatly expanded the behaviorist view.

Not only can learning be rapid, but it can also be part of a normal pattern of development. As you will see, naturalistic research emphasizes the natural environment of the organism, whereas Skinner had created an artificial one. Both humans and other animals can learn simply by observing the action of others. We as humans are actively involved in perceiving, acting, and increasing our understanding of new information. This chapter will end with a discussion of the most natural learning of all, that of language. Language is critical for humans as it allows us to reason, solve problems, and have social relations with others. These aspects of our cognitive processes will be discussed in later chapters.

In this chapter, you will see that some learning can happen quickly, whereas other learning can take a long time. You will also see that some learning can happen naturally, as with the case of learning a language as a child. Other learning, such as memorizing the names of chemical elements or stars, requires more effort and practice. We can also learn just by watching someone perform an action. We know that many animals learn by just watching other animals. By the way, humans are the only species that has developed institutions that are specifically designed to teach and transfer information. In order to understand one aspect of learning, that of conditioning, let's begin with two basic learning mechanisms—*classical conditioning* and **operant conditioning**.

Classical Conditioning

Perhaps you have started to open a pet food can to feed your pet, and all of a sudden your pet is there. Waiting to be fed. How did this happen? Of course, your pet may have smelled the food even if you could not. However, often your pet is there before the can is opened. As a psychologist, you might want to know what mechanisms are at play to bring your pet to you as you open the can. How did your pet learn this? It is through the mechanism of classical conditioning.

Classical conditioning was first described at the turn of the last century by the Russian physiologist Ivan Pavlov. After studying physiology and medicine in St. Petersburg, Russia, Pavlov became the director of a new laboratory for animal experiments in 1879. Pavlov was particularly interested in the body as a whole and the manner in which all of the parts worked together (Paré, 1990). As such, his was an early emphasis on homeostasis, the manner in which the body stays in equilibrium. Pavlov was also influenced by Darwin and sought to understand the mechanisms by which animals adapt to their environment. His early research focused on the heart and digestive system. He was awarded the Nobel Prize in 1904 for his work.

Pavlov believed that the nervous system controlled all body systems, and he sought to determine how the secretion of gastric juices was controlled by neural reflexes. This led him to show that food will produce gastric juices even if the food never enters the stomach. In fact, working with dogs, he was able to show that just the sight of food would produce saliva in the mouth.

Pavlov referred to these as *psychic secretions*, since there was no physical connection between the food and the salivation. Pavlov saw the salivation as the result of a reflex that involved the brain and referred to the process as a *conditional reflex*. The term was mistranslated into English as **conditioned reflex**, a mistake that helped create the terminology we currently use to describe classical conditioning. His lab began to systematically study this process.

Classical conditioning is the process in which two stimuli become associated with each other (see Gottlieb & Begej, 2014 for an overview). One of these stimuli, such as food, will produce a natural response, such as salivation. That is, animals consistently respond to food with salivation. In this case, salivation is referred to as the **unconditioned response** (UCR). Because the food stimulus will consistently produce a response, it is technically referred to as an **unconditioned stimulus (UCS)**.

In the studies of classical conditioning, it was noted that events that happened at about the same time as an unconditioned stimulus could themselves produce a response. For example, the dogs in Pavlov's lab might hear the door opening or the footsteps of the person who fed them. In themselves, neither the sound of a door opening nor the sound of footsteps would produce salivation. However, when the sounds were paired with the

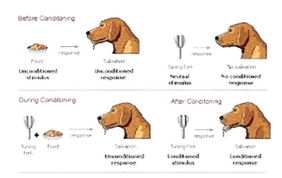

Figure 8-1 Graphic of conditioning process.

food given to the dogs, after a time, the sounds alone produced salivation. These types of events are referred to as *conditioned stimuli (CS)*. Technically, we say that if the unconditioned stimulus is paired with the conditioned stimulus, then after a number of times of pairing, the conditioned stimulus alone will produce the natural response. This response is referred to as a *conditioned response (CR)*.

The process of pairing a UCS and a CS is referred to as *acquisition*. As you can imagine, the strength of the CR will be less if it has been paired with the UCS only a few times as opposed to many times. Thus, if you were to ring a bell just before you introduce food to the dog only once, the bell alone would probably not produce much in the way of salivation. However, if you were to pair the ringing of the bell with the food a large number of times, then the bell alone would produce salivation (see **Figure 8-1**).

Once the bell alone would produce salivation, what do you think would happen if you rang the bell a number of separate times without the presentation of food? That's right, although initially the bell would produce the salivation, this response would change over time. As one continued to ring the bell without the pairing with food, the salivation response would decrease and eventually disappear. The process is referred to as *extinction*. Extinction happens when the CS is presented alone. What if you waited a day or two and rang the bell again? A surprising thing will happen. Salivation will again appear. This is referred to as *spontaneous recovery*.

Classical conditioning can work with any naturally occurring physiological process. Food is a classic example. However, in adapting to changing environments, you would not only want to learn about things that were positive for you, but also those that you might want to avoid. For some people just hearing the sound of the drill in a dentist's office will produce a response. Likewise, if a puff of air is released near your eye, you blink. Researchers have used such unconditioned stimuli as a small shock or puff of air to study classical conditioning. Thus, the principles of classical conditioning work equally well both with emotionally positive and negative stimuli.

Conditioning in Your Daily Life

You might think that classical conditioning is just an academic topic. However, if you look at the advertisements you see every day, it becomes apparent that it is all around. You begin by asking the question what has emotional positive connotations for humans. Food, sexuality, and friends are three such unconditioned stimuli. Many beer ads will feature a sexually suggestive scene (the unconditioned stimulus) paired with a particular brand of beer (the conditioned stimulus). Other ads may show a dog or other animal that provokes an emotional response (unconditioned stimulus), which is paired with a particular brand of car or other product (conditioned stimulus). For many of us, these pairings take place completely out of our awareness. Typically, advertisers seek to find images that produce instinctual responses in their targeted consumer such as an attractive person. Another everyday example of conditioning involves drug reactions as described in the box: The World Is Your Laboratory: Reactions to Addictive Drugs.

Drug Reactions

The World Is Your Laboratory: Reactions to Addictive Drugs

Initially, professionals who worked with those addicted to drugs were surprised to see physiological changes as the person was only preparing to take the drug. That is, as a person prepares his heroin dose, his body showed a physiological reaction. Even stranger was that the person showed reactions that were opposite to the normal effects of the drug. What we now know is that these opposite responses were the body's way to prepare for the negative effects of the drug.

One important way of understanding the factors associated with drug use is through the principle of *classical conditioning* (Siegel, 2008; Siegel & Allen, 1998). From this standpoint, the direct effects of the drug would be considered the *unconditioned stimulus (US)*. The cues associated with the primary effects would be the *conditioned stimuli (CS)*. Over time, making a cup of coffee, opening a bottle of wine, rolling a joint, or preparing cocaine can, through classical conditioning, bring forth a reaction before the drug is actually consumed.

Further, the effects of many drugs decrease as one uses the drug more frequently. This is referred to as *drug tolerance*. For example, those who smoke or use alcohol frequently will not experience the same effects that they initially did. This phenomenon also has a learning effect. This is particularly true if the person takes the drug in the same environment under the same conditions.

What would happen if the person took the drug in a totally different situation? It is almost like the person is taking the drug for the first time. In novel environments, the effect of the drug becomes stronger. It is suggested that this results from the fact that cues traditionally associated with the administration of the drug are not there. In fact, it has been shown that if an opiate is given through an intravenous infusion in which the subject cannot know whether administration is taking place or not, the tolerance effect will not be seen. Giving the opiate through an injection would produce tolerance effects. Likewise, college students who drink will show greater tolerance to the intoxicating effects of alcohol when consumed in beer than if the same amount of alcohol is consumed in a blue, peppermint-flavored beverage (Siegel, 2005). That is, the traditional consumption of alcohol in beer is well known. Consuming alcohol in a blue, peppermint-flavored beverage is novel and strange and the traditional learning effects are not experienced.

Using these learning principles can help us understand a number of factors related to drug use. One of these is why individuals who have given up an addictive substance such as alcohol or tobacco will experience craving when placed in situations in which these drugs were previously used. Just seeing the items associated with drug use can bring forth these cravings. Further, in certain novel situations, the effects of the drug can be stronger than normal (Siegel, 2001). Thus, someone can experience an overdose by first developing tolerance to a drug in a familiar situation. This tolerance may be associated with an increase in the amount of the drug to counter the effects of tolerance. However, if the person is to use the same amount of the drug in a novel situation, an overdose can be experienced. The result is that the overdose is more associated with

314 Learning, Ethology, and Language Processes

the external and internal cues of the situation than the actual amount of the drug used. Thus, to be effective, drug treatments need to consider both the external and internal cues associated with the use of the drug by extinguishing these associations.

Thought Question: What are three specific take-aways from this feature that help you understand drug addiction and its treatment better?

Emotional Conditioning

John Watson, whom you met in Chapter 1, emphasized psychology as the study of behavior. He further emphasized behavior as the result of learning. That is, Watson wanted to show that seemingly complex behaviors such as phobias could be the result of simple conditioning. In order to do this Watson worked with a normal 9-month-old child named Little Albert. The child initially played with whatever animals he was shown—a rabbit, a white rat, a dog, and so forth (as shown in **Figure 8-2**). In the classic case study of Little Albert, John Watson, in the 1920s, showed that animals that the child had previously played with happily could, through classical conditioning, come to be feared (Watson & Rayner, 1920).

The conditioning procedure was to pair a loud noise with the animal. The loud noise itself (produced without warning by hitting a steel bar with a hammer) would produce a fear response. This loud sound was made when the animal, such as a rabbit or white rat, was with the child. After the pairing the animal with a loud sound, the child would withdraw. As a result, Little Albert showed fear when in the presence of these animals, even without the loud sound.

Initially, Little Albert was conditioned by pairing a white rat and a loud noise. After this, any furry animal such as a rabbit would produce the same fear response. This is referred to as *generalization*, first noted by Pavlov in his work with dogs. It should be noted that the less the stimulus is like the original conditioned one, the less intense the conditioned response will be. That is, if the original stimulus was a 10,000 hertz tone, for example, then tones of 8,000 hertz and 12,000 hertz would produce larger responses than those of 4,000

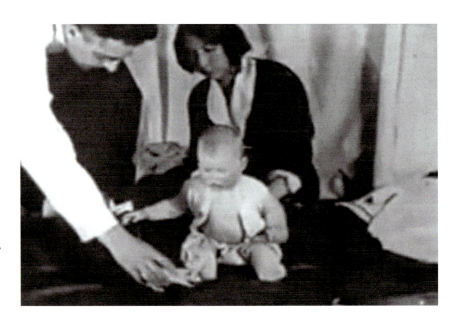

Figure 8-2 Nine-month-old Little Albert, John Watson, and Rosalie Rayner initially playing with animals.

hertz or 16,000 hertz. The more similar the new stimulus is to the original conditioned one, the stronger the response. In Little Albert's case, a furry bunny is more like a white rat than is a ball of yarn. However, we now know that learning takes place in relation to our evolutionary history.

Watson's demonstrations with Little Albert appear in many introductory psychology textbooks. However, what is often left out is the finding that fear conditioning worked better with evolutionarily relevant objects such as animals but less so with a bag of wool or with person-made objects such as a wooden toy (cf. English, 1929; Watson & Rayner, 1920). In short, we are biologically "primed" to learn to fear animals or situations that could truly threaten us, and not "primed" to be conditioned to fear inanimate objects.

Fear conditioning in both humans and other animals serves a critical role in helping organisms detect and respond to threat. Learning which situations are dangerous and which are not is critical to survival. However, the fear response can be generalized to situations that are not dangerous. Often children who are stung by a bee will try to avoid any insect with a similar buzzing sound. Freud discussed how being in an automobile accident could result in a person being afraid of future car rides or even situations associated with the previous accident. If this type of generalization to other similar situations continues for a long time, then this can cause problems in human functioning that limit one's response by making safe situations seem dangerous. Since humans also make cognitive inferences concerning their behavior, the interpretation of fearful events can go beyond the principles of classical conditioning (Dunsmoor & Murphy, 2015).

Garcia Effect and Food Aversion

Another type of learning that does not follow simple conditioning procedures is food aversion. Have you ever eaten something that made you sick, and for the next few years you couldn't stand the sight of that food? For some, it is fish, for others it is chicken salad, or for some it can even be green Jell-o. From an evolutionary perspective, this is a critical mechanism. To learn quickly that a food is bad for you could prevent you from experiencing a number of trials until you learned that a certain food was bad for your health. Over evolutionary time, this mechanism would have allowed all types of species to adapt to their environment.

What is amazing about this type of learning is that it is so quick. It only takes one pairing of the food and nausea. What is also different than traditional conditioning procedures is that the response of feeling sick may come some hours after actually eating the food. Future situations with the food only require that you see or smell the food. You do not actually have to taste it. In fact, the aversion is so strong for most people that they will refuse to be around the food.

The nature of learning food aversion may initially seem like classical conditioning, but it does not follow normal conditioning procedures. With Pavlov's techniques, it would take a number of trials for the bell or other conditioned stimulus to be associated with the food. Food aversion takes only a single trial to be learned. With traditional classical conditioning techniques, the pairing of the UCS and the CS must be close to each other in time. Otherwise, classical conditioning will not take effect. This was an upsetting fact to many researchers when taste aversion was initially studied in animals since ideas concerning *evolutionary preparedness* were rarely considered.

One of the early researchers in the 1950s to study taste aversion was John Garcia (1917–2012). In fact, the phenomenon of taste aversion is often referred to as the Garcia effect. In an important paper that appeared in the journal *Science*, Garcia and his colleagues showed that rats, when given a saccharin solution paired with a radiation procedure that would make them sick, would avoid saccharin water some days later (Garcia, Kimeldorf, & Koelling, 1955). The actual study paired a procedure with no radiation or different levels of radiation with the saccharin tasting water. Three days later a regular bottle of water and a bottle of saccharin water were put in their home cage and the amount consumed daily was measured for two months. It was found that the rats who received the radiation avoided the saccharin water relative to how much radiation they received.

Today, health care professionals are paying attention to those receiving radiation and other treatments for cancer (Kusnecov, 2014). That is, they are seeking to condition a non-normal taste to the radiation rather than the foods that the person likes the best. In this way, the cancer treatment will not negatively influence through conditioning the pleasant aspects of a person's life.

Conditioning and the Brain

Eric Kandel, to whom you were introduced in the introductory neuroscience chapter, set out to understand how learning and memory were represented in the brain. As you remember, he chose the California sea slug *Aplysia* to study. Although this sea slug is complicated in many ways (for example, they can be both male and female as needed), it does have a simple reflexive behavior—the withdrawal of its gill. The gill is an external organ that the sea slug uses to breathe. Touching the gill causes it to withdraw.

It turns out that this gill reflex is similar to a number of responses in humans. For example, the first time you hear a clock tower chiming or a train going by your house, it seems loud. However, after a time, your response decreases as the sound is repeated. Technically, this process is referred to as **habituation**. Habituation is the situation in which a reflexive action decreases with repeated presentation of the stimulus. Why would we want to habituate to a repeated stimulus? Exactly, because its repeated occurrence carries with it no new information. The first time we experience it, it could be signaling danger or other information important to our existence. We may need to adapt to protect ourselves. However, once we know we are not receiving new information, there is no need to respond. This is part of our evolutionary history in which organisms use their energy for events that are important and reduce their energy expenditure for those that are not. Habituation is thus a natural response for regulating our cognitive and emotional energy.

What Kandel and his colleagues did was to focus on a critical synapse. This synapse was located between the neuron that brought sensory information related to being touched and the motor neuron that caused the gill to withdraw. What they discovered was that with repeated stimulation, habituation took place, and the sensory neuron released less neurotransmitter. The neurotransmitter involved was glutamate—the major excitatory neurotransmitter in our brain. Less of the neurotransmitter glutamate reduces the chance that an action potential will be produced.

The opposite of habituation is **sensitization**. For example, if you receive a painful shock, then the next shock would result in a greater response in a number of different systems. The shock could, for example, make a noise seem louder. Kandel and his colleagues found that sensitization results in a greater level of glutamate at the synapse. Thus, this increases the chance that an action potential will be produced. In other studies, Kandel showed that when experiences become part of long-term learning and memory, the connections at the synapse are increased. This shows that with learning the brain changes (see Kandel, 2006 for an overview).

After nearly a century of research using classical conditioning, the manner in which the brain is involved in conditioning, particularly fear conditioning, has been determined (Pellman & Kim, 2016). The general picture is that information related to the conditioned stimulus is processed in the amygdala. This information is then connected with the unconditioned stimulus to create a relationship. The amygdala also has strong connections to the hippocampus, which plays an important role in *episodic memory*. The hippocampus not only is related to memory but also the location in which an event took place, referred to as *spatial memory*. Cognitive processes along with habituation can be used to treat learned aversions, as shown in the box: Applying Psychological Science: Fear of Flying.

Applying Psychological Science: Fear of Flying

More than one in ten people have a fear of flying (Oakes & Bor, 2010). As would be expected, the initial increase in cases of reluctance to fly began to develop in World War I with the development and use of airplanes for observation and warfare (Laker, 2012). This is reasonable on a risk basis since warfare includes destruction and death. Also, stress factors on materials used to make airplanes were not well understood during the early part of the 20th century, resulting in a number of accidents. Today, the factors that increase airline safety are better understood. In fact, today it is riskier to take a trip in an automobile than one in an airplane.

Since flying in an airplane is a relatively new experience for humans, there is little reason to suggest a direct evolutionary link to the fear of flying. Of course, indirect relationships to self-preservation can play a role. However, fear of flying is not associated with other phobias such as a fear of elevators. It is assumed that fear of flying is learned. Further, the fear can be related to observation learning or other learning mechanisms if the person has experienced others around her showing fear in the presence of taking an airplane trip. This suggests that learning procedures centered on the extinction of responses could play a role in reducing the fear of flying.

One treatment approach that you will learn more about in the chapter on treatment of psychological disorders is *systematic desensitization*, which is based on classical conditioning procedures (Wolpe, 1958). The basic idea is that fear responses have become connected with events that are not fear-producing in themselves. For example, for some people seeing a physician in a white coat will result in increased emotional reactions associated with anxiety. Classical conditioning works in a similar manner to that of Pavlov's dogs in that the white coat becomes associated with other events that lead to emotional arousal.

Systematic desensitization works by pairing the emotionally arousing object or event with relaxation. Wolpe suggested that you cannot be relaxed and afraid at the same time. Thus, the procedure was to teach someone relaxation and then to pair the relaxed state with that of an anxiety-arousing situation. In the case of fear of flying, a person would construct a hierarchy of fear beginning with the least arousing situation and ending with the most arousing one. As illustrated in the list below, the person would enter a relaxed state and then imagine seeing an airplane in the sky. If she was able to remain relaxed as they considered that situation, she would then move on to the next situation. If she became anxious, then she would move back in the hierarchy until she could achieve a relaxed state.

- Fear of flying:
  - Seeing an airplane overhead
  - Driving to an airport
  - Walking into the terminal
  - Waiting for an airplane
  - Entering the airplane
  - Sitting down
  - Buckling the seatbelt
  - Feeling the airplane move
  - Taking off

Since the time of Wolpe, a number of modifications have been made to these procedures. One is the use of virtual reality as well as airplane sounds to give the person a heightened experience of the anxiety-producing situation (Brinkman, van der Mast, Sandino, Gunawan, & Emmelkamp, 2010). Currently, a number of airlines around the world offer courses in which the anxious individual goes through actual situations similar to the previous hierarchy. Using classical conditioning techniques, these airlines will pair pleasant situations such as eating food or candy with the airport and flying experience. Additionally, many of these programs add a cognitive component to help the person reinterpret the anxiety-arousing event. For example, when an airplane initially takes off, power to the engines is increased. About ten seconds after takeoff, the power to the engines is decreased. This is experienced initially as if the plane is standing still. Without this knowledge, the person may think the plane will fall and become anxious. Knowing this, the person can reinterpret her initial fear and see it as a normal part of flying. Overall, techniques based on learning and extinction principles have been shown to be effective in reducing a person's fear of flying (Laker, 2012).

Thought Question: Suppose you have a fear of public speaking. Construct for yourself a hierarchy of fear beginning with the least arousing situation related to public speaking and ending with the most arousing one.

CONCEPT CHECK

1. Define and describe the relationships between the following concepts in classical conditioning:
   a. Unconditioned stimulus (UCS) and unconditioned response (UCR)
   b. Unconditioned stimulus (UCS) and conditioned stimulus (CS)
   c. Conditioned stimulus (CS) and conditioned response (CR)
2. What is the role of the following processes in classical conditioning:
   a. Extinction
   b. Spontaneous recovery
   c. Generalization
3. What do Watson's experiments with Little Albert illustrate about the role of evolution in classical conditioning of fear? What types of experiences are we

"primed" to fear? How can the concept of generalization lead to problems in human functioning?
4. What is the process of learning a food aversion? How is it different from classical conditioning? How is the process beneficial in an evolutionary sense?
5. How was it discovered that the immune system itself could be conditioned? What is an example of when that conditioning would have a negative effect? What is an example of when that conditioning would have a positive effect?
6. What roles do habituation and sensitization play in learning from an evolutionary perspective? What specifically happens in the brain as a result of these two processes?

Operant Conditioning

What if you wanted to teach your dog to perform a certain trick? Perhaps you wanted your dog to roll over or jump over a small fence. How would you do that? One approach is to give your dog a treat after it performed the behavior. In this case, your dog would be producing a behavior for a reward. Formally, this type of learning is referred to as operant conditioning.

Operant conditioning, also called *instrumental conditioning*, is the type of learning in which the frequency of the behavior is controlled by its consequences (see Murphy & Lupfer, 2014 for an overview). The behaviors that an organism performs are referred to as *operant responses*. The term "operant" is the combination of two terms, "operate" and "environment." Thus, they are behaviors that operate on the environment to produce consequences. In the case of your dog, the consequence was receiving food.

Thorndike and the Puzzle Box

Before operant conditioning received its name, Edward Thorndike (1874–1949) began studies of how animals solve problems and learn. This was about the same time as Pavlov's work. What Thorndike did was to place an animal such as a cat in what came to be called a *puzzle box*. The box was designed so that the cat could open the box by performing a particular action such as stepping on a lever or pulling a rope that would open the door. Outside the box was a bowl of food. Since the animals had not been fed before they were put in the box, the hungry animals sought ways to get to the food.

As you can imagine, the cat would initially engage in behaviors such as pushing on the bars, allowing them to eat the food. After trying a large number of behaviors that did not result in opening the door, the animal would finally engage in the behavior that did result in the door being opened. At this point the animal had access to the food. Thorndike repeated this procedure a number of times to determine how the animals learned. In the first few trials, the animals would engage in different series of behaviors until they were able to open the door and get to the food. By 20 or 30 trials, the animal was able to open the door as soon as it was placed in the puzzle box.

Based on his research Thorndike was able to influence the study of learning in two ways. First, he formulated his **law of effect**. The law of effect says:

> *Of several responses made to the same situation, those which are accompanied or closely followed by satisfaction to the animal will, other things being equal, be more firmly connected with the situation, so that, when it recurs, they will be more likely to recur; those which are accompanied or closely followed by discomfort to the animal will, other things*

being equal, have their connections with that situation weakened, so that, when it recurs, they will be less likely to occur. The greater the satisfaction or discomfort, the greater the strengthening or weakening of the bond.

(Thorndike, 2011, p. 244)

That is, when the cat made a response that led to the opening of the door and food (the satisfying effect), then the cat would be more likely to perform that same response again. The opposite is also true. If the response produces discomfort, then those responses will be reduced. The second way Thorndike influenced the study of learning was to graph the animal's response, which is referred to as a *learning curve*. Learning will be described in the next section with the work of B. F. Skinner.

B. F. Skinner and Operant Conditioning

B. F. Skinner (1904–1990) was the person who most influenced the study of learning in psychology during the middle of the last century. Like Watson, Skinner believed that psychology should only study behaviors that could be observed. In particular, the goal of psychology should be the prediction and control of behavior. As such the emphasis was on data rather than theory.

Skinner coined the term **operant behavior** to refer to the behavior that an organism produces that influences its environment. He also suggested the term **reinforcer** or **reinforcement** be used rather than satisfaction as with Thorndike's law of effect. This was to avoid any reference to the inner processes of the organism. Thus, an organism emits behaviors that influence the environment. If the behavior (for example, pressing a bar) is reinforced (for example, receiving food), then its occurrence will increase.

In order to study learning, Skinner developed a simplified version of Thorndike's puzzle box. This came to be known as a *Skinner box* (see **Figure 8-3**). The animal, usually a

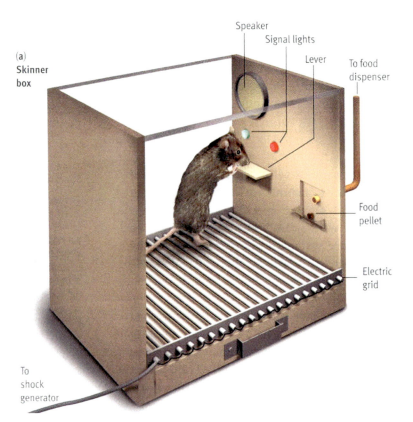

Figure 8-3 Skinner box—the animal presses a lever to receive food.

rat or pigeon, is placed in the box. As with Thorndike's animals, Skinner kept his animals hungry during the learning experiments. Initially, the animal would move around the cage until it pressed the lever and food would be released into the Skinner box. One advantage of the Skinner box over the puzzle box was that the animal stayed in the box and could continue learning the response.

Shaping

The first time the animal is placed in a Skinner box, it will typically move all around the box. To help it learn the relationship between pressing the lever and obtaining food, a technique referred to as **shaping** is used. Shaping is a process by which the animal is led to make the desired response in small steps. For example, you could initially give the animal food just by facing the lever in the Skinner box. Next, give the animal food as it moves toward the lever. Then, give it food as it touches the lever. Finally, it will press the lever and receive food.

Shaping is a common procedure used to train animals to perform any new task. Animal performances in a circus are largely the result of shaping. Even a complex performance can be broken down into discrete steps that can be learned through reinforcement. If you want to teach your dog to stand on its hind legs and turn around in a circle, you would start with teaching it to stand. You would give it a treat each time it stood until it was able to adopt this posture. You would then give it a reward for initially turning slightly. Then a reward as it turned more. In this way you can use shaping to train your dog to do new tricks. However, for shaping to be effective the reinforcement must quickly follow the desired response.

Reinforcement and Punishment

Giving a reinforcement following a particular behavior increases the likelihood that the behavior just produced will reoccur. Technically, this is referred to as **positive reinforcement**. In Skinner's research, the rat presses a lever and receives a pellet of food. Following this the rat will continue to press the bar and receive food.

What if at this point you wanted the rat not to press the bar, what would you do? One thing you could do is to pair the bar pressing with something the rat did not find reinforcing. For example, if the bar press is followed by a shock, then the animal is less likely to continue pressing the bar. Technically, this procedure is referred to as **positive punishment**. Positive punishment decreases the likelihood that a particular response will be repeated.

The meaning of *positive* in the case of both positive reinforcement and positive punishment refers to something being added that changes the likelihood of a response. Positive reinforcement increases the likelihood that the response will increase. Positive punishment increases the likelihood that the response will decrease.

In Skinner's terminology, there is also *negative* reinforcement and punishment. Negative reinforcement occurs when the likelihood of a behavior is increased by the removal of an event. Typically, the event is aversive to the organism. In this case removing an event changes the likelihood that it will occur. What if there was a loud noise and performing an act would stop it. All of us, including rats, would perform an act if it turned off the loud noise. The removal of the loud noise following such an act would be an example of a negative reinforcer.

Negative punishment occurs when the likelihood of a behavior is decreased by the removal of an event. What would happen, for example, if your employer quit paying you each time you did a job? Of course, you would quit doing the job. Hungry rats do the same thing in the Skinner box although it is food and not money they seek. Thus, reinforcement

Table 8-1 Table of positive and negative reinforcement and punishment.

	Positive	Negative
Reinforcement	Increases the likelihood that the response will be repeated by adding something the organism desires.	Increases the likelihood that the response will be repeated by removing something the organism does not desire.
Punishment	Decreases the likelihood that the response will be repeated by adding something the organism does not desire.	Decreases the likelihood that the response will be repeated by removing something the organism desires.

and punishment influence the likelihood that behaviors will be performed. As you can see in **Table 8-1**, positive and negative reinforcement increase the likelihood of the behavior; positive and negative punishment decrease the likelihood of the behavior. In the next section, the manner in which they are delivered will also influence an organism's responses.

Schedules of Reinforcement

When you play a slot machine in a casino, you don't receive money each time you play. It would be great if you did. However, if you won each time you played you would act very differently. Most likely, you would play the slot machine as fast as you could. What if the opposite happened? What if word got out that no one ever wins on a certain machine? What would you do? You would quit playing that machine. Skinner realized the same was true with his rats and pigeons. That is, Skinner realized that how reinforcers are administered can determine how behaviors are emitted.

If the reinforcement follows every operant response, it is referred to as **continuous reinforcement**. If the reinforcement only sometimes follows the operant response, it is referred to as **partial reinforcement**. Typically, continuous reinforcement is used to shape and train the animal to perform the desired response. That is, when teaching the animal to approach the lever, you give a reinforcement for each desired response. Once it has learned to press the lever for food, the animal will continue to press the bar even if food is not given for each bar press. This is a partial reinforcement schedule. Once the animal has learned the response such as bar pressing in the Skinner box, stopping all reinforcement will result in the animal no longer pressing the lever. Technically, this is referred to as **extinction**.

Partial reinforcement can be programmed in relation to the number of responses (ratio) the animal makes or the amount of time (interval) between responses. Skinner examined a number of these patterns, which came to be called **schedules of reinforcement**. The ratio and interval schedules of reinforcement can be either fixed or variable resulting in four major categories.

Using a *fixed ratio schedule*, the animal receives a reinforcement every certain number of times. For example, the animal could receive a reinforcement every fourth time it presses the bar. Humans who work in a factory that pays them a certain amount after producing five widgets would be paid in terms of a fixed ratio schedule. Using a *variable ratio schedule*, the animal receives a reinforcement in a manner that averages out to a certain number. For example, if the average was five, then the reinforcement could come after two responses and then seven responses and then after one response and then after nine responses.

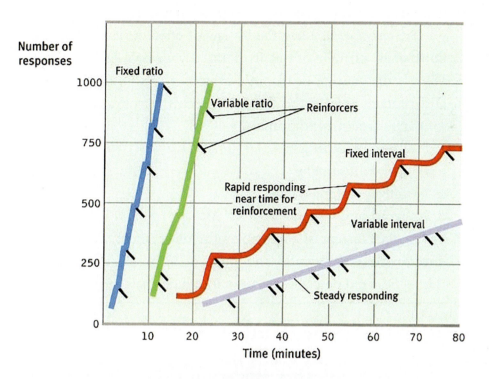

Figure 8-4 Graphic of different schedules of reinforcement.

Using a *fixed interval schedule*, the animal receives a reinforcement after a certain amount of time. For example, you could wait 30 seconds after the last reinforcement before the next reinforcement would follow a bar press. During this time, the animal could press the bar, but there would be no food given. Pain medication in hospitals is often set up to be administered only after a certain amount of time no matter how often the patient asks for it. Using a *variable interval schedule*, each reinforcement would vary such that the average amount of time would be constant. That is, if the average amount of time was 30 seconds, then some of the intervals would be shorter than 30 seconds and some longer (**Figure 8-4**).

How do you think that these four different schedules of reinforcement would influence the rate of responding of the animal? To answer this question, imagine yourself sitting at a slot machine. How would you respond if you won every fifth time or every five seconds? You would of course pull the handle (or push the button) faster if it was a fixed ratio schedule. On an interval schedule, you would learn to wait some amount of time before you pressed the button. There are slight differences in responding as to whether the schedule is fixed or variable. However, ratio schedules produce faster and more responses than interval ones. This, of course, is known by every casino, which is why slot machines are set to variable ratio schedules of reinforcement. Assume you are reinforced when you check your social media or text messages. What schedule of reinforcement most matches your pattern of checking your iPhone or iPad?

CONCEPT CHECK

1. What roles do the terms *operate*, *environment*, and *consequence* play in the definition of operant conditioning?

2. One of Edward Thorndike's two major contributions to the study of learning was the *law of effect*. Describe his law of effect in your own terms. Can you think of an example of this working in your own life?
3. What is the concept of shaping? How is it used in learning?
4. Differentiate among the following terms introduced by B. F. Skinner in studying operant conditioning:
   a. Positive reinforcement
   b. Positive punishment
   c. Negative reinforcement
   d. Negative punishment
5. Define the concept of a schedule of reinforcement. Why did Skinner introduce the concept? Identify the four schedules of reinforcement described in this section and describe the ways in which they are different.

Learning as Viewed through Ethology

Ethology, simply said, is the study of animals and what they do. The word itself is derived from the Greek and means manner, trait, or character. At the heart of ethology is the naturalistic observation of behavior within an organism's natural environment. Within this field, it is assumed that behavioral processes have been shaped through evolution to be sensitive to environmental conditions. Thus, behavior can be understood only within the context of a particular environment.

One of the pioneers in the field of ethology was Konrad Lorenz (1903–1989). Since his early childhood on the outskirts of Vienna, Lorenz was interested in observing animals. After receiving a medical degree and continuing studies in zoology, Lorenz more formally studied behavioral patterns. He focused on those patterns that he considered characteristic of a species.

One of the important contributions of Lorenz to psychology was the study of imprinting. **Imprinting** is a built-in pattern in which birds such as ducks and geese follow an object, usually their mother, which moves in front of them during the first 18 to 36 hours after birth. In a series of now classic studies, Lorenz showed that orphaned baby birds would follow any moving organism, including Lorenz, as if it were their mother. Not only would they follow Lorenz but they would also ignore members of their own species and still later in life attempt to court humans rather than other geese. If the baby birds did not encounter a suitable object during this critical period of 18 to 36 hours, the birds would not imprint and would even show terror.

How did Lorenz understand imprinting? He suggested that imprinting and other similar phenomena worked like a lock and key. The key in this case would be the characteristics of the mother, including the manner in which the mother moved in front of the babies. The lock would be an innate brain pattern or template in which knowledge concerning the key would be encoded. Further, the lock and key would only work together for a critical period, in this case the first two days of life. More intriguing is the fact that once the imprinting has taken place, it is almost irreversible and cannot be changed.

Play as Learning

If you ask kids what they want to do, they usually answer "play." Play is seen in all human cultures and across a variety of animal species (Burghardt, 2005; Göncü & Gaskins, 2007;

Panksepp & Biven, 2012; Smith, 2005). **Play**, like babbling, appears to be preparation for future developmental stages, although the participants remain unaware of its future potential. They enjoy it for what it is. Play can be simple or it can be extremely complex, as when individuals take on roles and play them out. Even animals will sometimes shift roles, as when a dominant individual "loses" in order to keep the game going. Given its ubiquitous nature, especially in mammals, play is thought to be important and have profound value for the individual. That is, play helps the child learn relationship roles that will be needed in adulthood. In all species, play also is important for learning physical skills (Panksepp & Biven, 2012).

Burghardt (2005) suggests five criteria for characterizing play. The first is that engaging in play does not contribute to an organism's survival at that moment. The second is that play is spontaneous, and something individuals engaged in voluntarily. Also, it is pleasurable and done for its own sake. The third factor is that play tends to be characterized by incomplete, exaggerated, and sometimes awkward movements. In this sense, it differs from behaviors performed in the service of more serious processes seen in adults related to survival and sexuality. Further, in some species, play is only seen in juveniles. Fourth, play occurs repeatedly in a similar form. This repetition of patterns is seen in play and games in both humans and other animals. Fifth and finally, play tends to take place when organisms are well-fed, healthy, and free from stress. It has been observed that play is one of the first types of behavior to drop out when animals are hungry, threatened, or in a difficult environment. Overall, organisms appear to have fun during play and do not engage in it if a positive emotional experience is not possible.

Play has been grouped by researchers into three types. These are rough-and-tumble play, object play, and pretend or role play. Rough-and-tumble play may look like real fighting or conflict, but it can be differentiated from these in a number of ways (Smith, 2005). First, rough-and-tumble play is usually engaged in by friends. Second, it does not begin with a threat and usually ends with other social activity. Third, the participants usually appear to be enjoying themselves. And fourth, the roles played appear to be flexible and there is sensitivity to environmental restraints.

Developmentally, rough-and-tumble play changes in focus from the elementary to high school years. In elementary school, rough-and-tumble play is centered on friendship themes. By adolescence, dominance becomes a more common theme. Strong gender differences in rough-and-tumble play are found across all cultures. It is always more males than females who engage in rough-and-tumble play. One common theory of rough-and-tumble play suggests it is preparation for later dominance challenges.

A modern example of object play is children playing with toys. Both anthropological and archeological studies suggest that object play is found in a variety of cultures across time. Unlike rough-and-tumble play, object play is engaged in equally by both males and females.

Table 8-2 Burghardt's five characteristics of play.

1. Not related to survival	At that moment
2. Spontaneous	Pleasurable and done for its own sake
3. Incomplete and exaggerated movements	Not part of more serious processes—often seen in juveniles
4. Seen repeatedly in a similar form	Such as games
5. Organism healthy and free from stress	Drops out with hungry animals

Pretend or role play is seen across cultures and often reflects tasks that the children observe their parents or elders engaging in. Since the peak period of pretend play occurs in children between 3 and 6 years of age, there is some suggestion that pretend play is related to understanding the intentions of others or theory of mind. That is to say, pretend play helps children understand what can happen and how others may react to these changes. Watching children of this age, you can observe how often these children refer to other people and how they might feel.

Observational Learning

At the beginning of this chapter, you read descriptions of how lab-reared chimps, who were not afraid of snakes initially, became fearful of snakes just by watching another chimp react with fear to a snake. This is referred to as *observational learning*.

Jane Goodall reported that chimps will take a stick and remove the leaves (https://www.youtube.com/watch?v=inFkERO30oM). They will then put this stick into a mound of termites, which looks like a big ant hill. The termites, which the chimps like to eat, will be attached to the stick when it is pulled out of the ground (like a termite popsicle). How do the young chimps learn to do this? They just watch the older chimps fish for termites.

Observational learning is seen across a variety of species including humans. Bottlenose dolphins learn from their mothers how to find sponges. Sponges are used to protect their snout while searching for food on the sea floor. Besides termite hunting with a stick, chimps also learn how to groom. Grooming produces both a social bond and removes bugs from the other chimps' fur. What is interesting is that the manner of grooming learned in early life remains stable throughout their lifetime even when living in a different community (Wrangham et al., 2016).

Overall, **observational learning** is when an organism watches another organism perform an activity and copies it. In this sense, it is different from other types of learning. With classical or operant conditioning, the individual organism directly experiences the events. Observational learning, on the other hand, does not involve the person doing anything but watching. Observational learning is also referred to as social learning. It is seen across a number of species as an efficient way of acquiring new information including cultural transmission (Sapolsky & Share, 2004).

In psychology, observational learning was described in 1941 by Neal Miller and John Dollard (Miller & Dollard, 1941). Rather than reinforcement, the important component of observational learning is motivation. That is, if a person is motivated to learn a set of behaviors, then this can occur through observation.

One famous set of observational learning studies was performed by Albert Bandura and his colleagues in the 1960s. These came to be called the "Bobo doll" studies (Bandura, Ross, & Ross, 1961). The Bobo doll was an inflated clown. When hit, the clown would fall over and then come back to an upright position.

What Bandura did in his experiment was to bring 3- to 6-year-old children, one at a time, into the lab. The lab room contained a number of toys including the Bobo doll. In the lab was an adult who initially played with some of the toys but then began to hit the Bobo doll, kick the doll, and even hit it with a mallet. After 10 minutes, the child was taken to another room where he or she talked with an experimenter. After this, the child was taken to another room full of toys including a Bobo doll where the child could play. A control condition of the experiment was the same except that the adult did not hit the Bobo doll.

What do you think the child did on his or her own? Yes, if the adult hit the doll, the child did also. The children in the control condition showed much less aggression toward the Bobo doll. In the experimental condition, boys showed more aggression than girls. Also, children who were with an adult male showed more aggression than those with an adult female. Not only did this research show the importance of observational learning but also called into question the role of violence in the media.

Imitation Learning and Mirror Neurons

Observational learning is also referred to as **imitation learning**. What makes it so easy for humans and other animals to copy what is seen in front of them? At the end of the last century, Giacomo Rizzolatti and his colleagues made an important discovery that has helped to answer this question. The answer, which was found by accident, is related to neurons in your brain referred to as *mirror neurons*, which were described in the chapter on developmental processes.

As noted in this chapter, the basic idea for imitation learning is simple. Each time an individual sees an action done by another, the neurons in the observing person that would be involved in that action are activated. This activation in brain circuits in turn creates a motor representation of the observed action. That is, we see an action and our brain considers how we might make it ourselves, although we don't do this consciously.

This process can explain one aspect of how imitation learning can take place. That is, by seeing something, your brain also comes to know how you can do it. Since the same neurons fire in your brain as you watch another do a task, your brain is able to create an action plan when you wish to produce the motor response. Even more important for Rizzolatti and Fogassi (2007) is that such a network puts the organism at an advantage. The advantage is not only do I understand "what" others are doing, but also "why" they are doing it. I am able to make guesses at their motivation and their plan of action. Thus, by having my brain work similarly to another's brain, I have some understanding of what he or she is experiencing. Thus, I learn what someone is doing and how they are experiencing it. However, there are times when new learning may not take place such as when you are asleep. This is described in the box: Myths and Misconceptions: You Can Learn in Your Sleep.

Myths and Misconceptions: You Can Learn in Your Sleep

If you look on the Internet or at the ads in some magazines, you will find products that claim you can learn in your sleep. One ad suggests that we should start using our brain's full potential and buy their products for learning while we sleep. Sleep learning has been a theme seen in television shows and in films for at least the last 50 years. Even an article on the *Smithsonian* magazine website (June 26, 2012) had the title "Experiments show we really can learn while we sleep." It would be wonderful if you could learn a foreign language while you slept without effort!

Even with all the claims in the ads, research since at least the early 1900s has shown little evidence to support the idea you can learn new material in your sleep (Simon & Emmons, 1955). Often, the early studies did not actually ensure that their participants were asleep by using objective measures such as EEG. Thus, it was not possible to know if the person was really awake or asleep when the new material was played.

Possibly, one of the reasons that sleep and learning is thought of as a possibility is that there is a connection. A number of studies have shown that if you learn new material while you are awake, and then sleep, sleep will make the connections stronger. Material that was learned and then followed by sleep immediately was remembered better than that learned ten hours prior to sleep (Diekelmann & Born, 2010). Studies have also shown that allowing participants to sleep after learning new information resulted in better performance than if the participants were not allowed to sleep.

The brain is active during sleep. This activity allows a person to hear a sound or smell an odor and incorporate it into their consciousness, as seen in dreams. Playing foreign-language sounds previously learned during sleep also improved later recall (Schreiner & Rasch, 2014). However, material has to be presented outside of sleep for learning to take place. Overall, brain activity during sleep allows for material learned during the day to be incorporated and consolidated but it is a myth that totally new material can be learned during sleep.

Thought Question: What are some specific ways you can use the information in this feature to change how you study for your classes?

Learning Takes Place as Part of Life

The study of learning for much of the 20th century was about more basic forms of learning such as classical and operant conditioning. As we look across evolutionary history, it is easy to see how the mechanisms of learning are critical for life. We need to know which foods are important for us. We need to know where there is danger. We need to know which people are safe to be with and which are not. As you will see next, we come into the world ready and willing to learn a language. All children repeat what they hear and become able to create new sentences on their own. Not only humans, but also song birds repeat the songs they hear.

Although the basic principles of classical and operant conditioning are seen throughout nature, not every species can be conditioned in the same way. Some species of mice, for example, can be conditioned by pairing a sound or light with an electrical shock. However, the same is not true if the shock is paired with a taste. With humans, Little Albert could be conditioned by pairing a loud sound with an animal but not if the sound was paired with a toy. Thus, the evolutionary history of a specific species plays an important role in determining the nature of conditioning. We need to know where there is danger. We need to know which people are safe to be with and which are not. We also need to learn how to communicate with others and for that we use language.

CONCEPT CHECK

1. What is ethology? How is learning understood from the perspective of ethology?
2. Describe Lorenz's pattern of imprinting. How is it like a lock-and-key? How is it different?

3. Why do animals and humans play? What are some ways we can know that play is happening? What are three different types of play?
4. How is observational learning different from learning through classical and operant conditioning?
5. What are some of the ways the discovery of mirror neurons by Rizzolatti and colleagues extends our understanding of learning through observation?

Language

Learning a language is something that is available to humans everywhere. In an amazing manner, a human infant can acquire any of the more than 6,000 languages present on earth. Environmental factors of course determine which languages any of us learns. Like imprinting, language learning is something that unfolds as the child develops. Skinner developed a theory of language acquisition based on reinforcement principles (Skinner, 1957). That is, a child would learn each word and its meaning and then how to create sentences. This view was criticized by Noam Chomsky who pointed out in his review of Skinner's book *Verbal Behavior* that children can create sentences they have never heard as well as understand sentences they have not been exposed to (Chomsky, 1959). Thus, language could not be acquired in a response and reinforcement manner.

Knowing the mechanism of human language has been a great challenge. Speaking and understanding a language is something we all do. In fact, children around the world are able to understand and speak a language by the age of 3, and it only gets better from there. Children also know what words refer to and are able to use language to ask for what they want. It is somewhat miraculous that we speak to others without thinking about it. Unless we are going to give a public talk or are to be involved in an important interaction, we don't prepare what we are going to say. We just say it. As humans, we understand and speak without effort. Further, speech is more than just reflecting language; it also plays an important role in our social life (Scott, 2019). In fact, people with similar linguist styles are likely to become friends (Kovacs & Kleinbaum, 2020).

Speech Processing and Vocalization in Infants

One approach to understanding human speech processing and vocalization has come through the study of the development of speech in human infants and young children (Gervain & Mehler, 2010; Skeide & Friederici, 2016). Surprisingly, the human embryo can distinguish vowels in utero although grammatical complexity is not fully mastered until at least 7 years of age. It should be noted that hearing is the first sense to be fully developed before birth. As you learned in the chapter on development, newborns were able to recognize stories such as *The Cat in the Hat* that were read to them in utero.

Newborn infants show surprising speech-processing abilities from birth (Gervain & Mehler, 2010). These include a preference for natural speech as opposed to non-speech sounds. Infants prefer their mother's voice over that of other females and their native language over other languages. They are also able to distinguish function words such as *it, this, in, of,* and *some* from content words such as *baby, table, eat,* and *happy*. Further, they are able to detect acoustic cues that note the beginning and end of a word. Overall, infants by the sixth month of life are able to distinguish any sound (phoneme) in any language on earth. By 12 months of age, with changes in brain connections and networks, infants have more difficulty making these same distinctions in languages that are not their own (Kuhl, 2004).

In terms of vocalization, during the first month of life, the human infant produces a wide variety of sounds that are assumed to be precursors to speech. These sounds may be uttered in any context, when the infant is alone, when he or she is with caregivers, and so forth. By the second month, the infant produces "cooing" like sounds, especially in the context of interactions with others. Of course, throughout these periods, caregivers spend considerable time talking to the infant.

During the next three months, children expand their range of sounds to include squeals, growls, and more vowel-like sounds as their vocal cords begin to change. These "babbling" like sounds contain both consonant and vowel sounds. What is interesting is that deaf and hearing infants coo and babble at the same ages. By about 10 months of age, however, the babbling of hearing infants becomes more like their native language. Deaf infants begin to babble with their hands if they have been exposed to sign language. Finally, at about a year of age, words begin to appear in the speech of hearing infants. It has been estimated that infants understand about 50 words in their native language by year one. They also begin to lose the ability to recognize phonemes from any language other than their own. By a year and a half, children can understand about 150 words and produce about 50 words. The timeline of human speech production and perception is shown in **Figure 8-5**.

By 2 years of age, most infants have combined simple words and continue during the next year to reflect the grammatical rules of their language. Thus, they might say something like "mama eat." By age 3, children have demonstrated implicit rules of grammar. For example, they say "cats" for more than one cat and "dogs" for more than one dog. They also apply the rule to irregular nouns and say "mouses" and "sheeps." They use the past

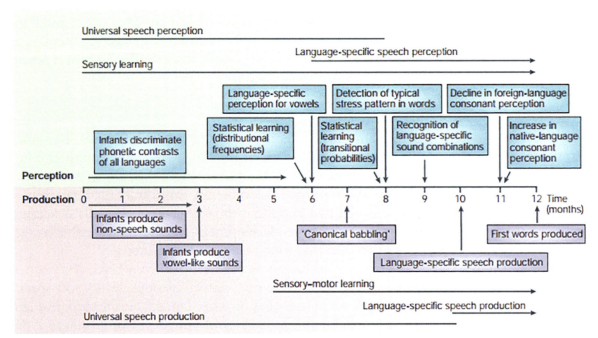

Figure 8-5 During the first year of human life, infants go through a series of changes in terms of speech production, which includes babbling and simple words such as "mama." Likewise, speech perception changes from a recognition of all language sounds to those of one's native language.

tense such as "kicked" and "played." However, they also apply the "ed" rule to irregular verbs and say "goed" and "thinked." This suggests that children acquire language in terms of rules rather than learning each specific word.

By age 4, a child is able to have conversations and demonstrate an implicit understanding of grammar. Over time, the child's vocabulary increases such that he or she knows about 10,000 words in the first grade and 50,000 in the fifth grade. Children of about 3 years of age when listening to sentences activate brain areas in the left temporal cortex and the frontal cortex. The activation of the frontal cortex suggests that language learning by this age begins to involve top-down or more executive functioning.

Structure of Language

Language is a system of communicating with others using words that convey meaning and are combined according to the rules of grammar. When we think about **language**, there are at least five factors that should be considered. First, a language is regular and has rules, which we call a grammar. Second, language is productive. That is to say, there are an almost infinite number of combinations of words that a language can use to express thoughts. Third, language is arbitrary in that across languages any word can refer to anything. For example, the words "dog," "chien," "perro," and "hund" all refer to the same animal but in different languages. As far as anyone can tell, there is an arbitrary relationship between words and their meanings. Fourth, languages are discrete in that sentences can be divided into words and words into sounds. And fifth, languages are linear in that words are presented one after the other. Further, for psychologists, language is special in that it can help us to describe both the internal world that we experience personally and the external world that we experience around us.

The basic sound of a language is the *phoneme*. If you say, "Hey, Bill" you produce five different phonemes. The sounds of "Hey Bill" are composed of two vowels and three consonants: /h/, /eI/, /b/, /I/, and /l/. When you read "Hey Bill" you know there are different words since there is a space between them. However, when you hear "Hey Bill" your brain must quickly make the distinction between sounds.

There are approximately 100 different phonemes used in all of the languages around the world. English uses approximately 40 of these phonemes. These 40 phonemes in English create about a half million words. The phoneme "ba" associated with the letter "b" is an element unto itself. As it is, it has no meaning other than the sound we process. Every infant can detect all of the 100-plus phonemes found in languages around the world. However, as we grow older, connections between neurons change with use and we lose this ability. At this point, we are limited to the phonemes in the languages we learned early in our lives. For example, languages such as Hebrew, Czech, and German do not have the "w" sound and often produce "w" and "v" as the same. In these cases, "wine" and "vine" may sound the same. Japanese does not have the phoneme associated with the "q" sound in English, and Japanese speakers find it almost impossible to make the sound of a duck in English—"quack." Single-language Japanese speakers also have problems telling the difference between the /r/ and /l/ sounds found in "lock" and "rock" as both sounds are part of the same phoneme in Japanese. Thus, they may call a person named "Lynn" as "Rynn." Of course, English speakers have similar problems when other languages use phonemes not found or differentiated in English.

The study of the ways phonemes can be combined in a language is called *phonology*. There are rules in every language for how phonemes can be put together. Even

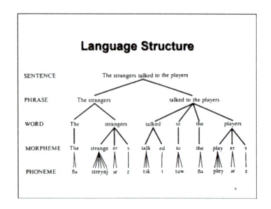

Figure 8-6 The structure of language.

in languages that have the same phonemes, their combination may be different. For example, the phonemes /z/ and /b/ are found in both English and Polish. However, zb is allowed in Polish and not in English. For example, Zbigniew Brzezinski was a Polish American and national security advisor to President Jimmy Carter. A similar name would not be found in English.

The next level of analysis is a **morpheme**—the smallest meaningful unit of a language. A common example would be "ed," which would signal past tense as in *talked*, or "s," which would signal plural, as in *books*, or "un," which would signal not, as in *unbelievable*. A word can contain a single morpheme, such as "cow," or can be made up of multiple morphemes. For example, the word "un-believ-able" would have three morphemes, whereas the word "antidisestablishmentarianism" would contain six morphemes—anti-dis-establish-ment-arian-ism. Another morpheme such as "er" can change the meaning of the word such as *farm* (a place to grow food) to *farmer* (the one who grows food).

The next level of analysis is **syntax**—the structure of a sentence and the rules that govern it. Syntax describes the way we string words together. For example, one rule is that sentences must have both a noun and a verb. Different languages may differ in what these rules are. English tends to have the subject followed by a verb and then an object such as "Jim flew the airplane." German and Japanese, on the other hand, tend to place the verb at the end of the sentence. English also tends to place the adjective before the noun, as in "white wine," whereas Spanish and French tend to place it afterwards, as in "vino blanco" or "vin blanc."

Finally, **semantics** is the study of meaning. That is, how do we understand what is being said? One important line of research has sought to determine how individuals mentally represent the meaning of what they hear and read. A critical question in the study of language has been the way in which humans are able to move between the levels of meaning and syntax. The overall structure of language is shown in **Figure 8-6**.

Evolutionary Roots of Language across Species

We appear to be the only species that speaks. However, a variety of species, including certain marine mammals, parrots, hummingbirds, and songbirds have the ability to imitate sounds, which is necessary for the evolution of language (see Bolhuis, Okanoya, & Scharff, 2010). Other animals have distress calls to inform others of danger. Bees communicate through a dance to tell other bees the location of flowers. Further, Darwin noted the parallels between language learning in infants and song learning in birds.

At least since the writing of the French philosopher Condillac in the 1700s until the present day, scientists have noted the large gap between the types of communication patterns seen in humans as compared to those of any other species. In terms of complexity, including vocabulary, grammar, and the range of ideas that can be expressed, there is nothing like human language in other species. Humans communicate with language in a way that is different from every other species. In other species, communication systems tend to be mapped in a one-to-one manner. For example, a chickadee makes a sound directly related to the size and location of a predator. There is only one way of saying what was said. With human language, on the other hand, there are a variety of ways of conveying the same information. If there is a dangerous fire, you can say "leave," "run," "get out of here," "there is a fire," "there is danger," and so forth.

What do other primates do to bond in social groups? The answer is grooming. By analogy, Dunbar (1996, 2003, 2004) suggested that language is to humans as grooming is to other primates. Actually, he suggests that language evolved in a series of stages with grooming at the earliest stage followed by vocal chorusing by way of bonding in a group followed by a socially focused language and finally the metaphoric and technical language we use today (Dunbar, 2003). Although we don't pick small insects from the hairs of one another, we do gossip. It is clearly a way we bond with one another. Walk across a college campus and notice what most people are saying to one another on their cell phones. It is usually about other people and, of course, themselves.

The idea of language as grooming might also support the idea that language evolved from basic motor processes (Lieberman, 2000, 2006). This might help us think about the importance of using our hands as we talk to others. It might also suggest that language is an extension of the basic mating dances seen in a variety of species. Rather than a mating dance, we "chat someone up" as the British say. Further, language is used to convey a variety of underlying processes. For example, if we are teenagers, we may use "like" to plug gaps in our speech.

We use language to describe empathetic reasoning in which we understand another person's experience. We also describe very abstract ideas such as freedom or democracy or even a multidimensional universe. If we are scientists we use more formal logic to rule out alternative hypotheses. The point is that language can describe a variety of both internal and external processes. It is this cumulative process that allows languages and their derivatives in terms of spoken and written forms to set the stage for culture to play a role in human history very different from that of other species. We can even be influenced by what was written thousands of years ago.

Language Learning in Animals

In the 1960s, Allen and Beatrix Gardner raised a chimp named Washoe in their home (Gardner, Gardner, & van Cantfort, 1989)—their single-story, brick home in the suburbs of Reno, Nevada with a fairly large backyard. Washoe was named for the county in which Reno is located. She was born in Africa and brought to the United States when she was about 10 months old. Washoe was raised as if she were a deaf child and used the American Sign Language. She actually wore clothes and shoes as well as learned to use a spoon and a cup. She learned to dress and undress herself and even use the toilet. Washoe had children's toys and was fond of dolls. She was very interested in household tools and learned to use a hammer and screwdriver. She also liked to look at magazines. Her home was a used house trailer parked behind the house. The trailer itself contained the same furniture used by the previous owners. Someone checked on Washoe every night and an intercom allowed others to know what was happening in the trailer.

She was with adults who both used sign language with one another and with her. By the end of her first year with the Gardners, she knew about 50 words in sign language. Her level of sign language equaled human infants who lived in a household in which sign language was used. Additionally, she began to construct phrases of two or more signs. After about five years, Washoe's vocabulary was about 140 words. She continued to combine these into meaningful phrases. She would sign, "YOU ME GO OUT." She called her doll "BABY MINE" and the sound of a barking dog "LISTEN DOG." The refrigerator was signed "OPEN EAT

DRINK." And like human children she would say, "COOKIE MORE." At one point, she dropped a toy down a space in her trailer when another assistant was taking care of her. When Allen Gardner came to the trailer, she signed "OPEN" at the place where the toy had fallen behind the wall. She also signed "WATER BIRD" when seeing ducks on a pond. This suggests that Washoe was doing more than just repeating signs she had learned.

The work with Washoe and other primates has raised many questions about the nature of language, which are still being debated. However, there exist some common traits across many species (Jarvis, 2019). For example, a number of species can learn specific sounds, such as the ability of your dog to respond to commands or songbirds to seek mates. One suggestion is that there is a similarity in terms of genes and brain connections across many species (Jarvis, 2019). Across all primates, humans show greater linguistic abilities than any other species. At about age 2, human infants show an increased learning of language not seen in Washoe. In comparison, a human first grader would know about 10,000 words, which would increase to 50,000 by the fifth grade. As an adult, you will have about 75,000 words in your vocabulary.

What Is Language?

What is the function of language and how did it evolve? Darwin viewed language as the result of an evolution that began with inarticulate cries, gestures, and expressions, as seen across a variety of species followed by a series of steps in which humans moved to an articulated language. Indeed, one hypothesis suggests that a common origin for vocalization evolved more than 400 million years ago in fish. We usually do not think of fish vocalizing, but some are able to do so with the aid of an air sac that is used for buoyancy. Using muscles associated with the air sac, these fish are able to vibrate it in such a way that it functions as a resonance chamber and amplifies sound. These vocalizations are related to mating and defense of their territory.

Researchers have been able to examine the brain circuits related to these sounds in fish (Bass, Gilland, & Baker, 2008). What is intriguing is that the organization of these circuits is consistent with vocal systems in frogs, birds, and mammals, suggesting a common body plan for vocalization. The relation of this type of social vocalizations to speech in humans is still being determined.

In the 1960s, Noam Chomsky helped to establish many of the ideas and debates that today influence how we think about language. He suggested that all humans have a set of innate principles and parameters, which he called "Universal Grammar." *Universal grammar* describes the total range of morphological and syntactic rules that can occur in any language. The original goal for Chomsky was to describe the manner in which spoken language is mapped onto meaning. The actual spoken words with their grammatical structure is called *surface structure*, whereas the meaning of the speech is called *deep structure*. As illustrated previously with the example of there being a dangerous fire, there are a variety of ways (surface structure) of saying this that would convey the same meaning (deep structure). An extension of this idea is shown with bilingual individuals who often will remember an event or idea but cannot remember in which language they learned about the event. Thus, Chomsky was interested in describing the rules in which deep structure meaning is transformed to language and vice versa.

One important idea is that language is *generative*. The basic observation is that we can generate sentences we have never uttered before as well as understand sentences we have never heard before. Children by the age of 3 are fluent speakers of their language without any formal instruction in the nature of grammar. Even more impressive is their ability to invent languages that are more systematic than the ones they hear and to follow subtle grammatical principles for which there are no examples in their environment (Pinker & Bloom, 1990).

Stop for a second and listen to what you say to your friends. Each time you speak, you generally use a sentence you have never used before. Sure, the meaning is similar to other times you have spoken, but the exact wording is different. Without thinking, you produce the sentences and you understand the sentences. What is more, you extract meaning even when there is ambiguity. "Flying planes are dangerous" is simple for humans to understand but difficult for a computer given the ambiguous nature of the sentence. This is not unlike, "Time flies like an arrow; fruit flies like a banana." There is also the REO Speedwagon album *You Can Tune a Piano but You Can't Tuna Fish*. Ambiguity is something humans do well given the context of the interaction in which the statement is made. Further, we extract meaning from language in a way that is not always logical, as in the famous, "We park in a driveway and drive on a parkway."

It has been suggested by a variety of authors that the expanded childhood of humans sets the stage for language learning. That is to say, the longer contact of the human infant with its family and the need for complex communication would support the development of language. In fact, brain-imaging studies show that before infants have produced their first words, they have already learned critical sound patterns of the language they will speak. From there, language learning explodes. Children in elementary school talk to one another and share their needs and moods with others. This in turn is followed by a period of adolescence with the pressures of social interactions (Locke & Bogin, 2006). Surprisingly, a variety of research studies from numerous cultures suggests that one main topic of language is social relationships—generally referred to as gossip. What do you talk to your friends about? The answer is usually other people. In this sense, one function of language is to keep the connection in social relationships.

Although children learn to speak a language and use the rules of grammar so quickly, Chomsky was not convinced that language could be explained by Darwin's understanding of evolution. For Chomsky, language may have appeared as our brains became larger and more complex. Thus, language learning was not a product of natural selection but an emergent property of brain complexity. Chomsky rejected language being influenced by natural selection and suggested it has not evolved in any significant way in the last 100,000 years (Berwick, Friederici, Chomsky, & Bolhuis, 2013). Overall, Chomsky sees language facility as an inborn ability and refers to language learning in humans as the innate *Language Acquisition Device* or *LAD*.

One language researcher who does see language as shaped by natural selection is Steven Pinker. Pinker (1994) begins with the suggestion that the process of language learning must be innate. In this way, language can be considered as any sensory process or instinct whose development can be viewed from an evolutionary perspective. In fact, Pinker suggests that language reflects the same type of design features as physical structures such as the eye. Since it is difficult to compare the development of language in humans with other species, one alternative is to compare typical language development in humans with impaired language development (van der Lely & Pinker, 2014).

What is especially intriguing to Pinker is that in learning a language, parents give children examples of language through their speech, but do not teach rules per se. However, children are able to infer the rules and apply them automatically. One example of this in English is when children say "he run-ed" or "she go-ed" rather than "he ran" or "she went." Clearly the child is applying a past-tense rule rather than just repeating what his or her parents said.

The fact that children apply such language rules suggests innate mechanisms for language learning based on universal principles rather than just copying what a parent says. In this sense Pinker asks us to look to biological predispositions rather than culture in order to understand language learning.

Over the years, it has been argued by such researchers as Alvin Liberman that speech is special. That is to say, humans are able to recognize certain sounds used in human speech in ways that other species cannot. However, other research has suggested that certain other species are able to make these discriminations. This would suggest that the ability to perceive speech-like sounds predates the evolution of language in humans. The picture is complicated by the fact that humans use different areas of their brains for perceiving speech versus other auditory sounds. In fact, there is a certain type of brain damage called *pure word deafness* in which a person can hear environmental sounds but not analyze speech (Maffel et al., 2017). There is also the opposite condition in which a person can analyze speech but not recognize environmental sounds.

If language is special for humans, what aspects of language represent this specialness? We know that human infants raised in an environment in which they are introduced to language will begin to communicate and show all the aspects of language generally before age 3. We also know from some tragic situations that human children raised without exposure to language will never develop normal language abilities. It is also clear that other species do not develop the major aspects of human language in the wild. The question arose as to what would happen if a chimpanzee—who is our closest genetic relative—was reared in an environment in which language was present.

As described previously, Allen and Beatrix Gardner raised a chimp named Washoe in their home. She was raised as if she were a deaf child using American Sign Language. By the end of her first year with the Gardners, she knew about 50 words in sign language. After about five years, Washoe's vocabulary was about 140 words. In the 1980s, Sue Savage-Rumbaugh took a somewhat different approach to teaching communication to a bonobo, also referred to as a pygmy chimpanzee. This bonobo was named Kanzi. What was really interesting was that Kanzi learned his first words by watching the researchers try to teach his mother language. He actually displayed knowledge of words without ever being asked. The idea with Kanzi was to teach him to communicate. Like Washoe, Kanzi played with toys and was involved in conversations taking place around him. He was also taken on walks around the research center on which he was spoken to. However, this time the conversations were in spoken English and not sign language. There are a number of videos showing Kanzi responding to such English sentences as "Take off Sue's shoe" by performing the requested action. Also, Kanzi could respond by pointing to symbols. Each symbol represented an English word. Given Kanzi's ability to perform acts and respond to English questions, many researchers suggest he was able to understand sentence structure. For example, he was correct 75% of the time when given sentences like "place the book on the rock" as opposed to "place the rock on the book." However, he had more of a problem when asked to do two activities such as "give Sue the bottle and the cup." He could do one but not both. Like Washoe, Kanzi's comprehension of language appears to be fixated to that of a child aged 2 and a half. If you want to see pictures of Kanzi as an adult, you can go to the Internet (http://www.npr.org/templates/story/story.php?storyId=5503685). If you would like to hear a TED Talk by Dr. Savage-Rumbaugh about primate language, you can go to the Internet (https://www.ted.com/talks/susan_savage_rumbaugh_the_gentle_genius_of_bonobos and http://www.ted.com/talks/susan_savage_rumbaugh_on_apes_that_write.html). The research involving primate language suggests that basic linguistic abilities of some form existed before the evolution of human speech. What allowed humans to develop speech and move beyond the level of a 2-year-old child is still a hotly debated question (see Deacon, 1997; Lieberman, 2000 for overviews). You can also think about what your dog hears in the box: Real World Psychology: Do Dogs Know Words?

Real World Psychology: Do Dogs Know Words?

Anyone who knows someone with a dog has observed that person speaking to the dog, often in complete sentences. You may have even observed the dog respond to commands. In fact, research suggests that dogs can respond to at least 1,000 words. That is, they can bring back a ball rather than a stick if commanded. But what does the dog hear? Does it know that words are being spoken or just wag its tail when its owner smiles and pets it? For years we could have our opinion, but there was little research as to what was actually going on in the brain of a dog when it hears human speech.

Attila Andics and his colleagues sought to answer this question (Andics, Gábor, Gácsi, Faragó, Szabó, & Miklósi, 2016). First, the dogs were trained to lie still in a brain-imaging fMRI machine. Although the dogs could move and leave whenever they wanted, they tended to lie still in the fMRI as they do in their homes on their bed or rug. Prior to the experiment, voice commands from a trainer were recorded. This trainer had worked with each of the dogs in the experiment. The experiment manipulated the meaning of the word presented and the emotional intonation in which it was presented. That is, a word could be presented that either had meaning as a praise word or not. The word could also be presented in a neutral manner or one with emotional feeling.

What these researchers found was that praise words presented in both a neutral and emotional manner activated the dog's left hemisphere. Neutral words did not activate the left hemisphere in the same manner. This suggests that the dogs can distinguish words related to praise from those that are not. When looking at the emotional intonation of the praise and neutral words, fMRI results showed that it was processed in a different part of the brain. Thus, meaning and emotion are processed independently in different parts of the dog's brain. From a complete analysis of the data, the research concludes that dogs rely on both word meaning and emotional intonation when determining the reward value of the phrase. Overall, dogs are able to link the sounds of human speech to basic meaning. On a research level, the study also shows that it is possible to study brain activation in awake animals.

Thought Question: What do you think the results would be if you could repeat this experiment with a chimpanzee or a bonobo or other animal? What about with a human infant?

Structure of Vocal Cords

The structure of our vocal cords is one important aspect of our ability to speak. How do humans make sounds that we hear as speech? We do it with our *larynx*, which also contains a cartilage we call our *Adam's apple*. If you feel your Adam's apple, you realize it is in your neck well below your mouth. By having your larynx low in your throat, you are able to make a wider range of sounds than other species can produce. To make a sound, the *vocal cords* in our larynx move in and out, modifying the continuous flow of air from our lungs into puffs of air. We also use our tongue to modify speech sounds. Notice how your tongue is in different places when you say "to" as opposed to "shoe." Although we will not go into details here, what we hear is also related to spacing between the basic sounds we produce (Lieberman, 2006).

Most other primate species have the larynx higher in the throat. This allows them to breathe and drink at the same time but not to make speech sounds. The human infant actually begins life with the larynx high in the throat. This also allows for breathing and drinking at the same time. That is, human infants like other mammals are able to ingest air and liquid at the same time. In about the third month of life as human infants develop, their vocal tract begins to descend so they can begin to produce a unique set of vowels. Such vowels allow us to make differential sounds as would be found in words such as *see*, *saw*, and *sue*. Also, humans have a larger area of the spinal cord necessary for breath control in producing speech compared to other primates as well as an auditory system tuned to the predominant frequencies found in speech. It has also been noted that during the first year of life, the human face changes from one with the features found in Homo erectus and Neanderthals to that of modern humans (Lieberman, 2006). From the first year to about 6 years of life, our tongues gradually descend into the pharynx. This change allows us to make a wider variety of sounds that make up our languages. But also, as Darwin noted, this increases the likelihood of choking in humans as compared to other primates.

CONCEPT CHECK

1. What evidence can you point to to conclude that the chimpanzee Washoe was capable of going beyond just repeating signs she had learned?
2. What are the evolutionary stages Dunbar and Lieberman suggest language went through, beginning with grooming and basic motor processes respectively?
3. What are some critical factors to consider in defining what language is?
4. Define the following terms that are important aspects of the structure of language:
   a. Phoneme
   b. Phonology
   c. Morpheme
   d. Syntax
   e. Semantics
5. What did language researcher Noam Chomsky mean by the following terms: universal grammar, surface structure, and deep structure? How were these concepts related?
6. What does it mean when we say that language is generative? Give an example.
7. If language is special for humans, what aspects of language represent this specialness? How does the research with the chimpanzee Washoe and the bonobo Kanzi relate to this question?

8. What are the parts of the structure of the vocal tract that are important to human vocalizing? What benefit does that provide humans versus other primate species in the development of language?

Language, Genes, and the Brain

The traditional model of language processing in the brain dates back to the 1800s. The French neurologist Paul Broca had a patient who had a stroke. The damage to the brain resulted in the patient having difficulty in producing speech, but not in understanding it. This type of language disorder has come to be called *Broca's aphasia*, and the left frontal area of the brain affected, *Broca's area*. In 1887, about 25 years after Broca described his patient, the German neurologist Carl Wernicke described the opposite condition in which a person could produce speech, but it lacked coherent meaning. This disorder came to be called *Wernicke's aphasia* and the left posterior area generally affected in the brain as *Wernicke's area* (**Figure 8-7**). The term **aphasia** refers to the loss of ability to understand or express certain aspects of speech related to damage in the brain.

The basic idea is that spoken language is first perceived in Wernicke's area, which is related to the processing of auditory information. This information is then transmitted by

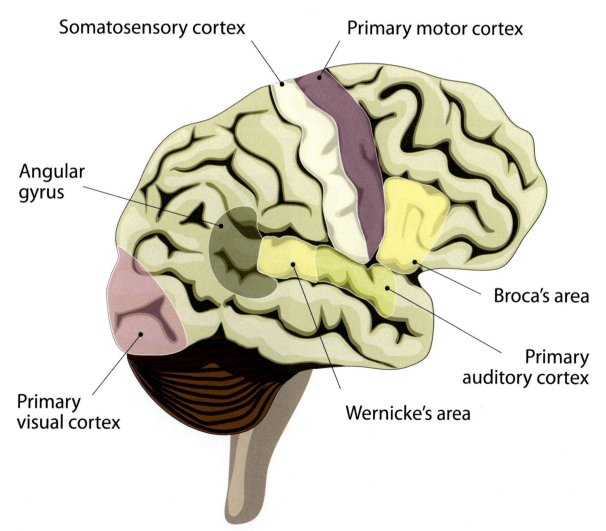

Figure 8-7 Brain areas involved in language.

pathways to Broca's area. Broca's area is related to speech production. Studies from individuals with some form of brain damage suggest that Broca's area is involved in not only the production of speech but also syntax, which includes grammatical formations involving verbs. Individuals with damage in Wernicke's area do not have similar problems producing speech, but with those aspects related to the meaning of the words, especially nouns.

More recent brain-imaging studies have asked individuals either to read or to repeat spoken words. These studies show brain activation in the individual's left hemisphere in those areas associated with motor responses, such as the primary motor cortex, the premotor cortex, and the supplementary motor cortex as well as areas in both hemispheres around Broca's area.

Philip Lieberman (2000, 2006) cautions against seeing language as encapsulated in just Broca's and Wenrnicke's areas. He has described the evolution of language in terms of its connections with early motor processes, especially subcortical structures such as the basal ganglia. Lieberman further notes that most language disorders include these subcortical structures along with Broca's and Wenrnicke's areas. In addition to specific brain areas that are activated during language tasks, there are extensive networks of brain connections (Fedorenko & Thompson-Schill, 2014; Hagoort, 2019; Pylkkänen, 2019). **Figure 8-8** shows the areas of the brain activated during different types of language tasks.

If you think about understanding and speaking language, you quickly realize there are a large number of separate tasks that add to the complexity of language. A number of these take place out of our awareness as we put together the information available to us. What we see can actually influence what we hear. One simple example is referred to as the *McGurk effect*. You can see this on the Internet (https://www.youtube.com/watch?v=G-lN8vWm3m0). Just changing the way someone moves his lips determines which sound we hear. All of this takes place out of our awareness.

During the decades of brain-imaging studies examining the nature of language, consistent findings have emerged. For example, there is a group of regions in the brain that

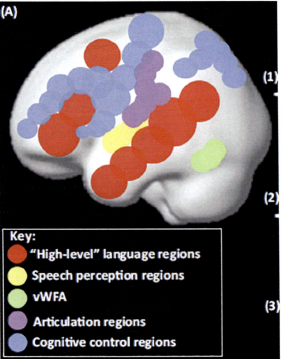

Figure 8-8 Specific brain areas seen to be activated during language-related tasks. These areas include those involved in understanding meaning (red—high-level language regions), speech perception areas (yellow), reading areas (vWFA—green), speaking areas (purple—articulation regions), and those areas involved in problem solving (blue—cognitive control regions).

represents information about the meaning of language (Huth et al., 2016). These regions are referred to as the *semantic system* and are sensitive to natural speech and its meaning. The overall semantic system involves brain areas in the temporal, parietal, and prefrontal areas. Within the larger systems more specific areas are sensitive to language features, such as nouns, action verbs, and social narratives. Other areas are utilized in the understanding of related concepts such as living things, tools, food, or shelter. This suggests that language information is organized in terms of *categories*. Most of the research involves one's first language but more recent studies involved a second language as described in the box: Applying Psychological Science: Learning a Second Language.

Applying Psychological Science: Learning a Second Language

There are some 6,000 languages in the world. Some of us spend our lives speaking only one, whereas others can speak a number of languages. In fact, it has been estimated that more than half of the world's population can speak more than one language (Grosjean, 2010). Knowing more than one language can often be an accident of location. For example, citizens of Europe often speak the language of their country, as well as those of neighboring countries. English may also be present as it represents both the language of science and a common language across European countries. In fact, more than half of the population of Europe is bilingual. In the United States, about 20% of people speak a language other than English at home. This percentage increases in major cities.

Learning two or more languages can occur in a number of different situations. Some individuals learn two languages from birth. It is somewhat surprising that infants are able to learn two languages with apparent ease. For example, infants learning Japanese have to learn that articles and prepositions come after nouns, whereas in English they come before. Thus, if the same infant were to learn both Japanese and English, then he or she would need to know two sets of phonemes, two sets of words, and two grammatical systems. Even before the first 6 months of life, infants are able to differentiate two different languages (Costa & Sebastián-Gallés, 2014). Infants are also able to differentiate languages by the gestures that native speakers make.

Others learn a second language at a later time as with people who were brought to another country as children. Both learning a second language from birth and or as a young child appears not to be a difficult task. Although still under some debate, learning a second language after puberty requires more effort. However, those who learn a second language later in life still show brain changes.

As with learning any new task, we can expect brain changes in learning a new language. Unlike learning to juggle or navigate the roads of London, learning a second language results in different areas of your brain being changed (Li, Legault, & Litcofsky, 2014). Additionally, the age of the second language acquisition is related to cortical activation (Wei et al., 2015). Both those who learn a second language early and later in life show changes in different brain activations than those who learn only one language. However, there is more variability in the results of those who learn the second language later in life.

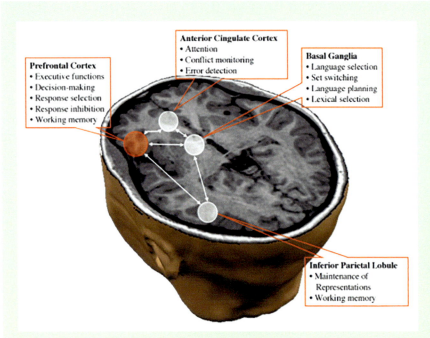

Figure 8-9 Areas of the brain related to cognitive control and language.
Source: Abutalebi and Green (2007).

One task for a person who is bilingual is to choose which word to use. If you see a piece of fruit do you say "apple" or "manzana" (Spanish). Although similar brain structures may be involved in processing both languages, it is not surprising that those areas of the brain related to cognitive control would show different activation in those who speak one versus two languages (Sulpizio, Del Maschlo, Fedeli, & Abutelebi, 2020). Specifically, bilingual individuals show more activation of the left frontal areas of the brain during comprehension tasks than those who speak one language. Bilingual individuals also show more activity in left hemisphere language related brain areas. Further, bilingual individuals also show more white matter in brain areas associated with verbal speech production. Additionally, greater volume in the corpus callosum, an area involved in transferring information between the hemispheres of the brain, is seen in bilingual individuals (Felton et al., 2017). Interestingly, bilingual individuals also show more of an ability to switch between tasks, even nonlinguistic ones, than those who speak only one language. **Figure 8-9** shows areas of the brain related to language and cognitive control. It should be noted that at one time school administrators in the US discouraged teaching a second language in elementary schools because of interference between the two languages. We now know that bilingual individuals can switch between languages with ease (Kleinman & Gollan, 2016).

If learning a second language changes brain activation and increases cognitive control throughout one's life, is this related to cognitive changes in aging? Some studies are beginning to suggest the answer is *yes*. It is suggested that those who know two languages have an advantage in switching tasks, sustaining attention, and memory processes (Bialystok, 2017; Bialystok, Craik, & Luk, 2012). Additionally, bilingual individuals who develop cognitive and memory problems associated with aging such as Alzheimer's do so three to four years later than those who speak a single language.

Thought Question: You have just been asked to develop a new language curriculum for your home school district. Given what you have just read about learning more than one language, what suggestions would you make in your initial proposal?

Reading

Although language is something that we as humans do naturally, we have to actively learn to read (Dehaene & Dehaene-Lambertz, 2016). As humans, we have only been reading for about 5,000 years. It would take another 1,000 years for us to develop a formal alphabet. One important brain area related to reading is referred to as the *visual word form area (VWFA)*. This area is located near the bottom of the brain where the temporal lobe and occipital lobe come together. This area activates whenever we see a written word. It does not show activation in those individuals who cannot read or in response to objects or faces. The VWFA is also located close to the area that responds to faces (*fusiform face area—FFA*) and the area that responds to places. Activation of the visual word area is only seen after a child learns to read.

Evolution of Language

In terms of evolution of language, there has been a debate as to whether it arose gradually over time or arose very quickly with the anatomical changes that give humans linguistic abilities (see Corballis, 2017; Ghazanfar, 2008 for overviews). In a variety of human traits such as color vision, there is clear evidence for a gradual evolution. However, others have argued that language is totally human and happened quickly.

Although the question is not completely settled, brain-imaging studies are beginning to suggest a gradual development of language. For example, James Rilling and his colleagues examined the differences in the way fiber tracts go between the frontal and temporal lobes in humans and other primates (Rilling et al., 2008). This is an important pathway in the brain for language. Damage to this pathway in humans leaves the person with the ability to understand speech but not to be able to repeat what was said.

Language and Genes

Since the writings of Darwin, the evolution of language has been a topic of debate. However, understanding the relationship of genes and language has been difficult (Fisher & Marcus, 2005). One approach has been to study those individuals who show language disorders from a genetic perspective. There is a rare language disorder that is inherited and has been linked to an allele of the FoxP2 gene on chromosome 7. Humans with this allele show problems in articulation, production, comprehension, and judgments related to grammar. The normal version of the gene is found universally in humans, but not in other primates. However, the gene is found in songbirds and has been related to song production. In humans, the gene is related to vocal learning and the integration of auditory and motor processes. Some estimates suggest that this gene appeared within the last 200,000 years. At present this research is in the early stages and there is controversy concerning the exact genetic basis of language.

CONCEPT CHECK

1. What are the primary contributions of the following researchers to our understanding of language processing in the brain:
   a. Pierre-Paul Broca?
   b. Carl Wernicke?
   c. Philip Lieberman?

d. Skeide and Friederici?
e. Alexander Huth?
2. What evidence would you cite to show that reading (processing visual language) is different from processing verbal language in the brain?
3. Did human language evolve gradually over time or very quickly? What evidence can you cite to support your answer?
4. At this point in time, what can we say about the genetic basis of language using the example of the FoxP2 gene on chromosome 7?

Summary

Learning Objective 1: Describe the basic processes of classical conditioning

Classical conditioning was first described at the turn of the last century by the Russian physiologist Ivan Pavlov. Classical conditioning is the process in which two stimuli become associated with each other. One of these stimuli, such as food, will produce a natural response, such as salivation. In this case, salivation is referred to as the unconditioned response (UCR). Because the food stimulus will consistently produce a response, it is referred to as an unconditioned stimulus (UCS). Classical conditioning can work with any naturally occurring physiological process. The principles of classical conditioning work equally well both with emotionally positive and negative stimuli.

In studies of classical conditioning, it was noted that events that happened at about the same time as an unconditioned stimulus could themselves produce a response. After a time, the events alone will produce salivation. These types of events are referred to as conditioned stimuli (CS). Technically, we say that if the unconditioned stimulus is paired with another stimulus, the conditioned stimulus, then after a number of times of pairing, the conditioned stimulus alone will produce the natural response. This response is referred to as a conditioned response (CR). The process of pairing a UCS and a CS is referred to as acquisition. Extinction (absence of the CR) happens when the CS is repeatedly presented alone without the UCS. Spontaneous recovery (of the CR) can happen after the CS is again presented after a time delay.

Scientists have used the principles of classical conditioning to understand the experiences of those who use drugs. Initially, professionals were surprised to see physiological changes as the person was only preparing to take the drug. Even stranger was that the person showed reactions that were opposite to the normal effects of the drug. We now know that these opposite responses were the body's way to prepare for the negative effects of the drug.

Phobias can be the result of simple conditioning. John Watson worked with a normal 9-month-old child named Little Albert. Initially, Little Albert was conditioned by pairing a white rat and a loud noise. After this, any furry animal such as a rabbit would produce the same fear response. This is referred to as generalization.

A type of learning that does not follow simple conditioning procedures is food aversion. One of the early researchers in the 1950s to study taste aversion was John Garcia. In fact, the phenomenon of taste aversion is often referred to as the Garcia effect. From an evolutionary perspective, this is a critical mechanism. To learn quickly that a food is bad for you could prevent you from experiencing a number of trials until you learned that a certain food was bad for your health.

Robert Ader was able to show that the immune system, like other physiological systems, could be classically conditioned. Dating back to Russian studies in the 1920s, it has been shown that immune system responses such as antibody production could be conditioned. That is, if a drug that produced these responses was paired with a neutral stimulus as in normal classical conditioning, the neutral stimulus alone could produce the immune system response.

We habituate to a repeated stimulus because its repeated occurrence carries with it no new information. The first time we experience it, it could be signaling danger or other information important to our existence. We may need to adapt to protect ourselves. However, once we know we are not receiving new information, there is no need to respond. This is part of our evolutionary history in which organisms use their energy for events that are important and reduce their energy expenditure for those that are not. Habituation is thus a natural response for regulating our cognitive and emotional energy. The opposite of habituation is sensitization.

Learning Objective 2: Describe the basic processes of operant conditioning.

Operant conditioning, also called instrumental conditioning, is the type of learning in which the frequency of the behavior is controlled by its consequences. The behaviors that an organism performs is referred to as operant responses. The term operant is the combination of two terms, operate and environment. Thus, they are behaviors that operate on the environment to produce consequences. In the case of your dog, the behavior may be a trick and the consequence may be receiving food.

Thorndike formulated his *law of effect*. That is, when the cat made a response that led to the opening of the door and food (the satisfying effect), then the cat would be more likely to perform that same response again. The opposite is also true. If the response produces discomfort, then those responses will be reduced. The second way Thorndike influenced the study of learning was to graph the animal's response, which is referred to as a learning curve.

B. F. Skinner was the person who most influenced the study of learning in psychology during the middle of the last century. Skinner coined the term operant behavior to refer to the behavior that an organism produces that influences its environment. If the behavior (for example, pressing the bar) is reinforced (for example, receiving food), then its occurrence will increase. In order to study learning, Skinner developed a simplified version of Thorndike's puzzle box. This came to be known as a Skinner box. One advantage of the Skinner box over the puzzle box was that the animal stayed in the box and could continue learning the response.

Reinforcement and punishment influence the likelihood that behaviors will be performed. The meaning of positive in the case of both positive reinforcement and positive punishment refers to something being added, which changes the likelihood of a response. Positive reinforcement increases the likelihood that the response will increase. Positive punishment increases the likelihood that the response will decrease. In Skinner's terminology, there is also negative reinforcement and punishment. In this case removing an event changes the likelihood that it will occur. Negative reinforcement occurs when the likelihood of a behavior is increased by the removal of an event. Typically, the event is aversive to the organism. Negative punishment occurs when the likelihood of a behavior is decreased by the removal of an event.

Skinner realized that how reinforcers are administered can determine how behaviors are emitted. If the reinforcement follows every operant response, it is referred to as continuous reinforcement. If the reinforcement only sometimes follows the operant response, it is referred to as partial reinforcement. Typically, continuous reinforcement is used to shape and train the animal to perform the desired response.

Learning Objective 3: Summarize the types of learning that occur during imprinting, play, observational learning, and imitation learning.

Ethology is the study of animals and what they do. At the heart of ethology is the naturalistic observation of behavior within an organism's natural environment. Ethology assumes that behavioral processes have been shaped through evolution to be sensitive to environmental conditions. Thus, behavior can be understood only within the context of a particular environment. One of the pioneers in the field of ethology was Konrad Lorenz. One of the important contributions of Lorenz to psychology was the study of imprinting. Imprinting is a built-in pattern in which birds such as ducks and geese follow an object, usually their mother, which moves in front of them during the first 18 to 36 hours after birth.

Play is seen in all human cultures and across a variety of animal species. Play appears to be preparation for future developmental stages, although the participants remain unaware of its future potential. They enjoy it for what it is. Play is thought to be important and to have profound value for the individual. That is, play helps the child learn relationship roles that will be needed in adulthood. In all species, play also is important for learning physical skills.

Observational learning is when an organism watches another organism perform an activity and copies it. In this sense, it is different from other types of learning. With classical or operant conditioning, the individual organism directly experiences the events. Observational learning, on the other hand, does not involve the person doing anything but watching. Observational learning is also referred to as social learning. It is seen across a number of species as an efficient way of acquiring new information. Observational learning is also referred to as *imitation learning*. That is, we see an action and our brain considers how we might make it ourselves, although we don't do this consciously.

Although the basic principles of classical and operant conditioning are seen throughout nature, not every species can be conditioned in the same way. The evolutionary history of a specific species plays an important role in determining the nature of conditioning. As we look across our own evolutionary history, we can see how the mechanisms of learning are critical for our lives. We need to know which foods are important for us. We need to know where there is danger. We need to know which people are safe to be with and which are not. We come into the world ready and willing to learn a language.

Learning Objective 4: Describe the process of how we learn a language.

Learning a language is something that is available to humans everywhere. In an amazing manner, a human infant can acquire any of the more than 6,000 languages present on earth. Environmental factors of course determine which languages any of us learns.

The human embryo can distinguish vowels in utero although grammatical complexity is not fully mastered until at least 7 years of age. Infants prefer their mother's voice over that of other females and their native language over other languages. By the sixth month of life, infants are able to distinguish any sound (phoneme) in any language on earth. By 12 months of age, infants have more difficulty making these same distinctions in languages that are not their own (Kuhl, 2004). In terms of vocalization, during the first month of life, the human infant produces a wide variety of sounds that are assumed to be precursors to speech. By the second month, the infant produces "cooing" like sounds, especially in the context of interactions with others. It has been estimated that infants understand about 50 words in their native language by year one. They also begin to lose the ability to recognize phonemes from any language other than their own. By a year and a half, children can understand about 150 words and produce about 50 words. By two years of age, most infants have combined simple words and continue during the next year to reflect the grammatical rules of their language. By age 3, children have demonstrated implicit rules of grammar. By age 4, a child is able to have conversations and demonstrate an implicit understanding of grammar. Over time, the child's vocabulary increases such that he or she knows about 10,000 words in the first grade and 50,000 in the fifth grade.

Language is a system of communicating with others using words that convey meaning and are combined according to the rules of grammar. When we think about *language*, there are at least five factors that should be considered. First, a language is regular and has rules that we call a grammar. Second, language is productive. That is to say, there are an almost infinite number of combinations of words that a language can use to express thoughts. Third, language is arbitrary in that across languages any word can refer to anything. Fourth, languages are discrete in that sentences can be divided into words and words into sounds. And fifth, languages are linear in that words are presented one after the other. Further, for psychologists, language is special in that it can help us to describe both the internal world that we experience personally and the external work that we experience around us.

The basic sound of a language is the *phoneme*. The study of the ways phonemes can be combined in a language is called *phonology*. The next level of analysis is a morpheme—the smallest meaningful unit of a language. The next level of analysis is *syntax*—the structure of a sentence and the rules that govern it. Syntax describes the way we string words together. Finally, *semantics* is the study of meaning. That is, how do we understand what is being said?

Learning Objective 5: Identify the parts of the brain that are active in language. Spoken language is first perceived in Wernicke's area, which is related to the processing of auditory information. This information is then transmitted by pathways to Broca's area. Broca's area is related to speech production. Studies from individuals with some form of brain damage suggest that Broca's area is involved in not only the production of speech but also syntax, which includes grammatical formations involving verbs. Individuals with damage in Wernicke's area do not have similar problems producing speech, but with those aspects related to the meaning of the words, especially nouns.

Recent brain-imaging studies have shown brain activation in the individual's left hemisphere in those areas associated with motor responses, such as the primary motor cortex, the premotor cortex, and the supplementary motor cortex as well as areas in both hemispheres around Broca's area.

Study Resources

Review Questions

1. This chapter starts out by saying, "Although most of us have an idea of what it means to learn something, it is actually a difficult and complex concept to define. In fact, it has been pointed out that the definition of learning differs across different areas of study including psychology." Now that you've finished the chapter, how would you define learning?
2. What contributions have the following researchers made to their specific types of learning as well as to our understanding of learning as a whole:

a. Classical conditioning: Ivan Pavlov, John Watson, John Garcia, Robert Ader, Eric Kandel, Joseph Wolpe
b. Operant conditioning: Edward Thorndike, B. F. Skinner
c. Learning from the perspective of ethology including play: Konrad Lorenz, Gordon Burghardt, Neal Miller and John Dollard
d. Observational learning—Albert Bandura, Giacomo Rizzolatti, and Leonardo Fogassi

3. In this chapter we have seen many examples of research into all types of learning with both animals and humans. Considering each of these types of learning—classical conditioning, operant conditioning, play, and observational learning—identify how you have used each of them in the past in your own learning. How might you use each of them in the future?
4. Describe the structure of language.

For Further Reading

Eibl-Eibesfeldt, I. (1989). *Human Ethology*. New York: Aldine de Gruyter.
Lorenz, K. (1981). *The Foundations of Ethology*. New York: Springer-Verlag.
Pinker, S. (1994). *The Language Instinct*. New York: William Morrow & Co.
Pinker, S. (2007). *The Stuff of Thought: Language as a Window into Human Nature*. New York: Viking.

Web Resources

Jane Goodall—https://www.youtube.com/watch?v=inFkERO3ooM
Kanzi—http://www.npr.org/templates/story/story.php?storyId=5503685
Primate language—https://www.ted.com/speakers/susan_savage_rumbaugh and http://www.ted.com/talks/susan_savage_rumbaugh_on_apes_that_write.html

Key Terms and Concepts

acquisition
aphasia
classical conditioning
conditioned response (CR)
conditioned stimuli (CS)
continuous reinforcement
deep structure
extinction
fixed-interval schedule
fixed-ratio schedule
generalization
generative
habituation
imitation learning
imprinting
law of effect
morpheme
negative punishment
negative reinforcement
observational learning
operant behavior
operant conditioning
partial reinforcement
phoneme
phonology
positive punishment
positive reinforcement
reinforcement
schedules of reinforcement
semantics
sensitization
shaping
spontaneous recovery
stimulus generalization
surface structure
syntax
unconditioned response (UCR)
unconditioned stimulus (UCS)
universal grammar
variable-interval schedule
variable-ratio schedule

9 Cognition, Problem-Solving, and Intelligence

LEARNING OBJECTIVES

9.1 Describe the research on thinking processes, including decision making and behavioral economics.

9.2 Discuss the processes involved in solving problems.

9.3 Describe the different ways that intelligence is measured.

9.4 Identify five cognitive domains that are associated with general intelligence.

9.5 Discuss the genetic factors associated with intelligence.

Many of you have heard about the flock of Canadian geese hitting the US Airways airplane three minutes after takeoff from a New York airport on January 15, 2009. The plane lost power. As the plane lost altitude, the pilots considered flying to another airport, but without power that was not possible. The pilots looked for a place to land that would minimize the loss of life. The captain Chesley Sullenberger (Sully) was able to land the plane without its engines working. He landed the plane on the Hudson River and everyone on board escaped. This event came to be known as the "Miracle on the Hudson" and was made into a movie (*Sully*) in 2016.

You may not know the story of another flight that ended in a very different way. Air France Flight 447 left Rio de Janeiro, Brazil for Paris on June 1, 2009. At some point when the flight was over the Atlantic Ocean, the airspeed indicators, which are small tubes, began to collect ice crystals. This gave the pilots incorrect readings. Without accurate readings to run the equipment, the pilots disengaged the autopilot and began to fly the plane manually. Without autopilot, the plane rolled during turbulence and the cockpit recorders later suggested that the pilots overcompensated. The plane began to lose altitude.

One of the pilots sought to correct for this by pulling the nose of the plane upward. This placed the plane into a stall. The necessary reaction for a stall is to place the nose of the plane down to increase its speed and regain control. The pilot, on the other hand, kept the plane pointed upward in an attempt to regain altitude. After three and a half minutes, the plane hit the Atlantic Ocean and everyone on board was killed.

How we make decisions is complicated. Sometimes we carefully consider our choices and make a decision. Other times, we quickly make a decision. Some of our responses, as in the two airline crises above, are made under great pressure. Feeling under pressure or fatigued causes us to consider fewer alternatives or solutions to a problem. Sometimes, we have a hard time deciding. In these times, we go back and forth trying to decide. This chapter will focus on how we solve problems and make decisions and the individual differences in these abilities, which we refer to as intelligence.

Cognition, Problem-Solving, and Intelligence

How We Think

Although we tend to use the word "thinking" to represent a single process, that is not the case. In this chapter, you will come to understand different types of thinking and different ways we approach problem solving and decision making. This is commonly referred to as reasoning or creating explanations. In later chapters, you will learn about problems in decision making as seen as those with schizophrenia and other disorders.

Fast and Slow Thinking

Psychologists have noted that some decisions we make are performed quickly and some require more time and effort. These different types of thinking have been described by different terms such as automatic versus controlled, unconscious versus conscious, implicit versus explicit, or System 1 versus System 2 (Stanovich & Toplak, 2012). The psychologist Daniel Kahneman, who won the Nobel Prize in 2002 for his decision-making research in behavioral economics, refers to these two systems as "fast" and "slow" thinking. His ideas were brought to the general public in his 2011 book, *Thinking, Fast and Slow*.

Fast thinking or decision-making occurs quickly with little or no effort, and little sense of you being actively involved in the process. When you speak with a person you know or walk or drive home, you just do it. There is no feeling of effort or constantly thinking about what to do next. Much of our daily life involves this type of processing. We read words on a sign, judge the emotion in someone's face, recall the phone number we've had for years, turn when we hear an unexpected sound, and interact with our friends. All the time we are (or rather our brain is) constantly making decisions.

Slow thinking requires more effort, and we experience ourselves as a part of the thinking process. Its characteristics include the feeling of making a choice, of being involved in the decision-making process, and requiring concentration and effort. A hallmark of the slow system is attention. If you don't pay attention it is hard to make a decision or solve a problem. When considering which of two trips you should go on during Spring Break, you typically use the slow way of thinking. You also use the slow system when you fill out an application for a job and decide how to describe yourself. And, of course, when you take an essay test, you must make a number of decisions about what to say.

As you will see throughout this book, the fast system is seen in a number of contexts. Walking in the woods and jumping when you mistake a stick for a snake is one such context. Recognizing the emotional expression on a face is another. Experiencing an optical illusion as you saw in the chapter on sensation and perception is also part of the fast system. Having a conversation or reading signs on the road are other contexts.

For years economists suggested that humans were rational and used logic for making decisions. However, as psychologists became involved in determining how people make decisions, it became clear that we as humans are not rational (Evans & Over, 2013). We make predictions about what to expect. In making a prediction, we rely on some types of information differently than other types of information. This results in our judgments being biased. In fact, there are a number of biases that we employ when making a choice. One of these is to rely on fast thinking.

Solve this problem as quickly as you can:

> A ball and bat together cost $1.10.
> A bat costs one dollar more than the ball.
> How much does the ball cost?

Many people found that their first thought was that the ball costs 10¢. In fact, many thought this was the correct answer (Frederick, 2005). You mean 10¢ is not the correct answer? Think about it: if 10¢ was the correct answer, then the bat would cost $1.10 plus the 10¢ for the ball or $1.20. The correct answer is the ball costs 5¢ and the bat $1.05. Shane Frederick (2005) suggests that because the problem seems easy at first, it is System I or fast thinking that we use to save effort. Slow thinking, which requires attention and effort, would have probably given you the correct answer.

> Want to try another problem?
> If it takes 5 machines 5 minutes to make 5 widgets, how long would it take 100 machines to make 100 widgets?

Again, if you let the fast system answer this problem, you probably said 100 minutes. However, if you were to reason with System 2 or slow thinking, you would realize that 1 machine can make 1 widget in 5 minutes. Thus, 100 machines can make 100 widgets in 5 minutes. Having realized your error, if you had one, in the first problem, you probably changed to slow thinking for solving the second problem.

Concepts and Categories

A *concept* is an abstract idea or representation. We tend to use *categories* to organize concepts that have shared features. Although there are a number of types of *cats*, for example, we know the features of the general category, such as four legs, a tail, a certain shaped face and ears, makes a meowing sound, and so forth. Although the category of *dogs* shares some of these features, we make a distinction between dogs and cats, but we also consider them both in the category of animals. We also make distinctions between nonliving objects such as chairs, bicycles, cars, and other such objects. Further, we distinguish between nouns and verbs as parts of speech. Overall, we use our concepts and categories to help us make decisions. Our language influences how we consider and talk about what we perceive and experience in terms of concepts and categories (Goldstone, Kersten, & Carvalho, 2012).

If you try to define a concept or category, you will discover that it is not easy. You could define the category of *birds* but then a penguin would probably upset your definition. The philosopher Ludwig Wittgenstein (1953) pointed out the difficulty of finding an exact definition for concepts. As an alternative he introduced the idea of *family resemblance*. As the name implies, a family resemblance points to features that appear to be characteristic of a category. However, as in a family photo, the family members may look alike but not every member of the family has every characteristic.

In psychological research, the family resemblance approach was developed by Eleanor Rosch (1975; Rosch & Mervis, 1975). Rosch suggested the categories that form naturally are based on a *prototype*. A prototype is generally the best example of a category. You can image what you think of when you hear the category "dog," "bird," "chair," or "game." Of course, where you grew up would influence your concept of a "bird." Penguins and toucans would not be included in most of our prototypes of a bird.

An alternative model for understanding how we place items in a category is referred to as the *exemplar approach* (Medin & Schaffer, 1978). This approach suggests that you categorize an object by comparing it to similar items in your memory. If you are walking in the woods and see something move, you would compare it to your memory of other animals. Is it a house cat, a fox, a weasel, or some other animal? You would compare the actual animal to those in your memory, and realize that it is a fox. Although at first the exemplar may seem like the prototype approach, the difference is that the exemplar approach is a comparison with your memories, whereas the prototype approach is an abstraction of your experiences.

Brain research suggests that we use both the exemplar and the prototype approach, depending on the condition. As would be expected, the exemplar approach involves those areas of the brain involved in vision, whereas the prototype approach uses areas more involved in conceptualization such as the frontal lobes. In addition, individuals with brain damage have shown specific types of problems with certain categories. For example, with one type of damage, people were able to describe living things and foods but were unable to recognize human-made objects. Other individuals with different types of brain damage were able to recognize human-made objects but were unable to recognize living things and foods (Martin & Caramazza, 2003). This suggests that various brain networks at particular locations in the brain are involved in organizing different types of categorizations.

Making Decisions

In watching humans make decisions, researchers often use the term *bounded rationality* (Simon, 1982). What this means is that our decisions as humans are limited or bounded by a number of factors, as seen in the two airplane situations at the beginning of the chapter. Three information-limiting factors are the amount of information we have, our cognitive abilities, and the amount of time available to make the decision or judgment. For example, if we saw someone driving fast, we might come to a different conclusion if we did not know the person was taking someone to the hospital. This section will examine some of the ways that psychologists have come to view our cognitions and decision-making processes. As you will see, we as humans are often not logical in how we reason and make our decisions. In fact, we are often biased when we reason. Let's see how.

Analogies

Napoleon is to brandy as Caesar is to _____? How would you answer this question, which is an analogy? You might begin by saying what is common to Napoleon and Caesar? One answer is that they were both military leaders. What is the relationship of Napoleon with brandy, which is something people consume? It is simply a name or descriptor. What is consumed that uses the descriptor Caesar? One answer is salad. Thus, Napoleon is to brandy as Caesar is to salad.

An *analogy* is nothing more than a comparison of one item with another. The item can be a behavior, an experience, a function, or a relationship. When you learned that imprinting in ducks worked like a lock and key, you were given an analogy. In this way an analogy is a way to understand a process. Often, scientists, when they initially study a process, use analogies to help others understand how something works. Usually, the unknown process, such as genetic replication or the functioning of the brain, is compared to something that is known. At one time people said the brain was like a telephone switchboard or that deoxyribonucleic acid (DNA) worked like a blueprint. As such, analogies give a general understanding of one process in terms of another. Although useful in many cases, analogies are limited in terms of psychological definitions.

Logic

As you learned in the chapter on research methods, science is based on logic and observation. When we begin with a statement and arrive at its logical consequences, this is called *deductive reasoning*. For example, we use deductive reasoning when saying, "If it is true that schizophrenia is genetically determined, then we should find greater similarity in the presence or absence of the disorder between twins than between strangers." On the other hand, when we begin with an observation and figure out a general rule that covers it, this is called *inductive reasoning*. For example, inductive reasoning might be of the form, "I just saw a monkey use sign language to ask me for food; therefore, it is true that monkeys can communicate with humans." In summary, deductive reasoning goes from theory (the premise) to data (the conclusion), whereas inductive reasoning goes from data to theory.

Suppose a friend said to you, "You know, all textbooks are really dull." You might respond, "That's not true; I am reading one right now that is really interesting." (Well, what did you expect a textbook author would have you say?) This is a logical way to disprove the statement, "All textbooks are really dull." By finding an exception to a statement, you can show it to be false. This is an important use of logic where we look for an exception to disprove the rule. Thus, if you suggest that all swans are white, then a black swan will disprove the rule.

However, humans, especially those trying to sell you something on late night TV, use an invalid type of propositional logic. For example, you may be told that your brain changes as you age and that some people who take certain pills do not age as fast. Therefore, it is the pill that prevents aging. Is this proposition valid?

> All roses are flowers.
> Some flowers fade quickly.
> Therefore, some roses fade quickly.

Even college students will see this as valid. However, it is not, since logically being a flower does not lead to the conclusion that roses fade quickly. There could be no roses that fade quickly.

Better yet, remember the story of our friend from Boston in the research methods chapter who got up every morning, went outside his house, walked around in a circle three times, and yelled at the top of his voice. His neighbor, being somewhat curious after days of this ritual, asked for the purpose behind his strange behavior. The man answered that the purpose was to keep away tigers. "But," the neighbor replied, "there are no tigers within thousands of miles of here." To which our friend replied, "Works quite well, doesn't it?"

> Formally, the logic would be as follows:
> Yelling keeps away tigers.
> There are no tigers in Boston.
> Therefore, yelling was the factor that kept the tigers away.

How could we demonstrate to our friend that his yelling is not causally related to the absence of tigers? One strategy might be to point out that the absence of tigers might have come about for other reasons, including the fact that there are no tigers roaming in the greater Boston area. In technical terms, we would say that yelling could be a *necessary* condition but not a *sufficient* condition for the absence of tigers. Our friend's reasoning was incorrect because it overlooked many other plausible explanations for the obvious absence of tigers. Although our friend sought to infer a relationship between his yelling and the absence of tigers, his inference was weak.

Heuristics

Here is a problem. A father and his son were riding in a car that was involved in a terrible accident. The father was killed, and the son was immediately taken to the hospital. The surgeon looked at the boy and said, "I cannot operate on this boy. He is my son." How could this be?

When you first hear the question—you might say to yourself, is there a way the boy could have two fathers? Did the surgeon remarry? The answer of course is that the surgeon was his mother. If you initially did not consider this possibility, it is because we tend to reason and solve problems in ways that do not consider all the logical possibilities. We look for ways to make problem solving easy on ourselves.

In solving problems, we as humans tend to make decisions in a manner that requires less effort rather than more. One of the ways we do this is to adopt strategies that guide our thinking. These approaches are referred to as a **heuristic** or *bias*. Heuristics have been extensively studied by Daniel Kahneman and Amos Tversky (e.g., Tversky & Kahneman, 1973, 1974; Kahneman, 2011). *Heuristics* place more value on some types of information than on other types. In order to speed up our processing, we actually ignore some types of information.

It is assumed that these heuristics developed over our long evolutionary history. It is also not surprising that humans are not the only species to use heuristics (Gigerenzer, 2008). An important area of study for biologists has been the rules of thumb that animals use for choosing mates, finding food, and choosing where to nest. As noted, the female peahen looks at the male peacock's tail for choosing a mate. Those heuristics that involve relationships with other people will be discussed in Chapter 12 on social psychology.

From the evolutionary perspective, there is an adaptive value to using heuristics that helped us to live our lives. We also know we use different types of heuristics in different domains. We make decisions about social relationships differently than decisions about buying a computer. Further, different areas of our brain influence different types of heuristics. Overall, these heuristics allow us to use fast thinking with less effort, although we also use the slower form of thinking once we have our "facts" and decide what to focus on.

One of the common heuristics we use is referred to as the ***availability heuristic*** or availability bias. As the name implies, this bias is simply our tendency to use information that we can quickly access in our minds. Do you think it is more common for words to begin with the letter L or to have L as the third letter of the word? Most of us will say it is more common for words to begin with L since those are easiest to remember. Actually, there are more words that have an L as the third letter. You can try this same question with the letters R, N, and V. All of these letters appear in the third space of words more often than the first. It is just easier to remember words in which they appear in the first position of a word.

Let's try another example. Do you think more humans are killed by sharks or cows? Since you hear on TV or on the Internet that sharks harm people, you would probably say sharks. You rarely hear about cows harming people unless perhaps you are a bull rider. However, it is cows that actually kill more people according to the US Centers for Disease Control (https://www.cdc.gov/mmwr/preview/mmwrhtml/mm5829a2.htm). Again, the availability bias influences our reasoning.

Those ideas that come easiest to mind are the ones we are more likely to initially consider as the correct answer. For example, one study showed that medical students in training are more likely to diagnose new cases with a similar diagnosis to that of cases they have recently seen (Mamede et al., 2010). On a personal level, seeing airplane crashes in the news will result in a perception that airline travel is more dangerous than car travel, which it is not. Since we can never consider all the information available for solving a problem, we use that which is available to us first.

Another common bias is the ***confirmation bias***. This was demonstrated by our friend from Boston who yelled to keep tigers away. That is, he only searched for evidence that supported his hypothesis. If we have a strongly held belief, we are more likely to see information that supports our views. Lawyers in a court trial will only present evidence that supports their hypothesis to help the jury not engage in the slower process of looking for contradictions to the evidence. Research has shown that we engage in the confirmation bias even when we perform a simple search task to find certain letters or colors (Rajsic, Wilson, & Pratt, 2015).

Most of the times when we make a decision, we are just going about our normal day-to-day activities. However, as Paul Slovic and his colleagues have shown in a number of studies, decision-making can be greatly influenced by our emotional feelings at that moment (Slovic & Peters, 2006). In these studies, Slovic was not interested in extreme emotions such as anger or fear, but everyday feelings. This is referred to as the ***affect heuristic***. The basic idea is that people make a decision based not only on what they think but also on what they feel. Your emotional reaction to the use of pesticides, nuclear energy, and genetically modified foods will influence how you reason about their use.

One of the clear examples of the affect heuristic involves *risk*. In one of his early studies, Slovic and his colleagues asked participants in a survey to estimate which events would more likely result in death and by what proportion. This type of study illustrates both the availability bias since floods, lightning, tornadoes, and diseases are often carried on the local news, and the affect bias since we all have an affective reaction to the risk of death. Some 80% of the people in the survey judged accidental death to be more likely than strokes, although the health data at that time showed the opposite to be true. Likewise, tornadoes were seen as more likely to kill you than asthma, although the data show a 20-to-1 ratio in favor of asthma. In addition, death by disease is 18 times more likely than accidental death, but the individuals in the survey thought the two were equal.

If you ask one group of people to quickly tell you the answer to this multiplication problem in five seconds—8 × 7 × 6 × 5 × 4 × 3 × 2 × 1—they will give you a larger answer than if asked to guess the answer to the same problem presented in the opposite order—1 × 2 × 3 × 4 × 5 × 6 × 7 × 8. In fact, when these problems were given to high-school students, they guessed the answer to the first problem would be 2,250, whereas the answer to the second problem was only 512. Kahneman and Tversky referred to this heuristic as *anchoring* (Tversky & Kahneman, 1974). That is, if you need to answer a question quickly, what you see first can influence your judgment. By the way, 40,320 is the actual answer to the multiplication problem.

Another critical factor in terms of how we make decisions is the way it is presented or ***framed***. Let's begin with this problem:

New York faces an outbreak of an unusual disease that is expected to kill 600 people. Two programs have been suggested.

1. Program A: 200 people will be saved.
2. Program B: 33% probability that 600 people will be saved and 66% probability that no one will be saved.

Which would you recommend?
Let us now look at two more programs:

1. Program C: 400 people will die.
2. Program D: 33% that no one will die and 66% that 600 will die.

Which of these two would you recommend?

In one study, the participants in the first choice condition chose A by 72% (Tversky & Kahneman, 1981). In the second condition, 78% chose D. What is interesting is that program A and program C are the same and programs B and D are the same. How the problem is presented makes all the difference. In these examples, they chose the programs that initially sounded more positive.

Behavioral Economics

Based on a psychological understanding of how humans make decisions, a new field of study has developed referred to as **behavioral economics** (or *neuroeconomics* when brain-imaging techniques are used) (Bossaerts & Murawski, 2015; Camerer, 2014; Loewenstein, Rick, & Cohen, 2008; Thaler, 2015). A primary focus of economics is the consideration of decision and choice. Unlike traditional economics, which suggests that humans optimize their choice in a rational manner, behavioral economics uses behavioral and neuroscience research to understand the factors involved. That is, people do not make decisions in isolation, but in relation to other choices as well how these choices are framed and the effort required. For example, more people accept deductions from their pay checks if they do not have to make a decision about them. That is, if given a choice to *opt-in* (agree to a deduction) or *opt-out* (agree to not take the deduction), most people will go with the alternative that does not require them to decide. Behavioral economics approaches would also include the heuristics just described.

Let's look at one example:

When you arrive at the movie theater, you get out your wallet to pay for the $10 ticket. Although you have enough money to pay for the ticket, you realize you are missing a $10 bill. Would you still buy the ticket?

Most people say they would (Tversky & Kahneman, 1981). What if the story is changed by a few details?

You get to the theater and buy a ticket for $10. You then go back to your car to make sure it is locked. When you return to the theater, you realize you have lost your movie ticket. Would you buy a new ticket?

Figure 9-1 Probability pie chart shown in the study.

In this second case, just over half of the people say they would not buy a second ticket. However, in both cases you would have $20 less than when you began the story. What Tversky and Kahneman discovered is that individuals frame the second story differently. That is, they see the cost of the movie as $20 in the second situation and $10 in the first. Thus, they felt that $20 was too much to pay for a movie.

Following the behavioral framing effect described by Kahneman and Tversky, other researchers have asked how the brain is involved in making these decisions (DeMartino, Kumaran, Seymour, & Dolan, 2006). Benedetto De Martino and his colleagues used a framing situation that offered participants to receive money for sure or to gamble for additional money. The participants were

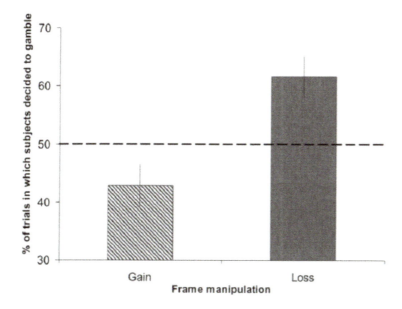

Figure 9-2 Behavioral data in framing.

initially given $50. The sure condition was framed as either they would keep $20 of the initial $50 or lose $30 of the original $50. As can be seen, both frames left the person with the same amount of money, but one presented it as a gain and the other as a loss. Following this, the participants were given the opportunity to gamble their original $50. The gamble option was the same for both of the frames and the probability presented as a pie chart (see **Figure 9-1**). As can be seen in the chart, there was a slightly larger chance to lose all the money but exact numbers were not given.

In looking at the behavioral data, framing played an important role. If told they could keep $20 of the $50, participants were less likely to choose the gamble option. However, when presented as they would lose $30 of the original $50, they were more likely to gamble. These data are presented in **Figure 9-2**.

Does your brain respond differently to the gain and loss framing? The answer is *yes*. Overall, activity in the amygdala was related to how the information was framed. In the gain frame, amygdala activity increased if the person did not gamble, but decreased if they did. In the loss frame, amygdala activity increased if the participants gambled, and decreased if they did not. Since the amygdala is associated with personal emotional material including threat, its activity reflects the behavioral patterns in terms of choice. That is, stay conservative in the sure condition and take a risk in the loss condition. This is shown in **Figure 9-3**.

Humans are more concerned with losing money than gaining money. Amygdala activity is more associated with loss than gain (Charpentier, DeMartino, Sim, Sharot, & Roiser, 2015). Other research has shown that individuals who have damage to the amygdala show a dramatic reduction in loss aversion (DeMartino, Camerer, & Adolphs, 2010). Although these individuals understood risk, they no longer had the same emotional reaction to loss. The amygdala also has connections with areas of the prefrontal cortex. If the prefrontal cortex is damaged, then people show problems with making decisions. Areas

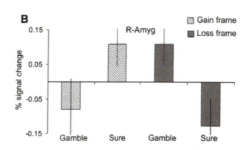

Figure 9-3 Gain and loss framing and its influence on amygdala activity.

of the prefrontal cortex also are involved when we compare items in terms of value and our confidence in our decision (DeMartino, Fleming, Garrett, & Dolan, 2013). Overall, this suggests that the amygdala is involved in the affect heuristic that emotionally influences our decisions related to gains and losses. Perfect logic is not the nature of humans as described in the box: Myths and Misconceptions: Human Beings Are Rational and Logical.

Myths and Misconceptions: Human Beings Are Rational and Logical

If you read one of the early issues of *Scientific American* in 1846, you would read about the rationality of men, especially those in business. The rationality of humans continued to be emphasized over the next 150 years. Economists and even some cognitive psychologists suggested for years that humans were rational and made decisions always in their own self-interest. At many economic and scientific meetings, there would be big debates concerning whether humans were rational or irrational. However, by the beginning of the 21st century it became clear that to view humans as logical and rational was a myth (Ariely, 2009; Thaler, 2015; Ubel, 2009). This is also described in a TED Talk (https://www.ted.com/talks/dan_ariely_asks_are_we_in_control_of_our_own_decisions?language=en). Further, as you have read in this chapter, this is a myth that no longer can be supported scientifically.

However, our manner of reasoning has benefited us in many situations. To understand this and how we reason, we need to remind ourselves that we as humans have a long history of interacting with our environment, others, and ourselves. The manner in which we make judgments and decisions has developed during this period and reflects decisions that are adaptive in specific situations. For example, as you learned previously, if you eat a food that makes you sick, you will avoid that food, sometimes even for years. Given the care and handling of foods today, it may not seem logical to not eat a particular food just because a one-time consumption made you sick. However, it does make sense if you obtain all of your food from unknown sources in the environment.

From this evolutionary perspective, we can also understand there is not just one type of reasoning. Over time, we have developed different heuristics for different situations. Protecting ourselves, choosing a mate, and having social relationships all require different types of decisions. Thus, it is not surprising that our decision-making processes are influenced by cognitive, emotional, and bodily experiences that are going on within us at the moment. We buy more food at the grocery store when we are hungry and buy things we do not need when we feel emotional, especially if we think there are only a few of the item.

There are ways we can use our knowledge of how we make decisions to help us make smarter decisions. For example, if people are asked to be part of a retirement system in their workplace, not everyone will join even though it is in their best interest. However, if you automatically sign everyone up for the plan with an option to opt out, fewer people will opt out. Another example is organ donation (Johnson & Goldstein, 2003). France and some other European countries require people to opt out and they have a larger percentage of people who are organ donors than does the US where people must opt in. **Figure 9-4** shows the differences in Europe of those countries that require an opt in for organ donation and those that require an opt out.

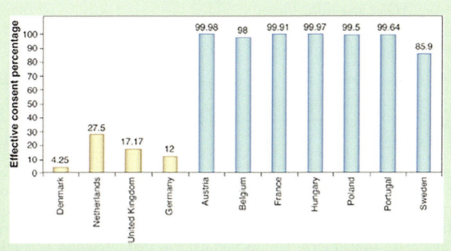

Figure 9-4 The differences in Europe of those countries that require an opt-in for organ donation and those that require an opt-out.
Source: Johnson and Goldstein (2003).

The US has a rate of 28% even though some states offer the ability to sign up for organ donation when one's driver's license is obtained or renewed (Gigerenzer, 2008).

Part of the task for psychologists is to understand the nature of our irrationality. This includes both situations in which our decision-making processes are helpful to us as well as those that are hurtful to us. We can then construct environments such as an automatic opt in for retirement or organ donation that benefit society as a whole.

Thought Question: How has evolution impacted human decision-making processes?

CONCEPT CHECK

1. What are *fast thinking* and *slow thinking* and what are the conditions when you would use each of them?
2. How are the following terms, which help us think about and talk about what we perceive and experience, related to one another?
   a. Concept
   b. Categories
   c. Family resemblance
   d. Prototype
   e. Exemplar
3. What is an *analogy* and what are the conditions in which you would use it?
4. What are *deductive reasoning* and *inductive reasoning* and what are the conditions when you would use each of them?
5. We use heuristics all of the time in our thinking. What is the definition of each of these heuristics and when are they likely to occur?
   a. Availability heuristic
   b. Confirmation bias

360 Cognition, Problem-Solving, and Intelligence

   c. Affect heuristic
   d. Anchoring
   e. Framing
6. How are traditional economics and behavioral economics different in terms of gain and loss framing?

Solving Problems

In the last section, you learn about how we reason and make decisions. In doing this, a number of factors were considered, including the effort involved in coming to a conclusion, the types of heuristics that can influence our decisions, and the way in which fast and slow thinking can influence our conclusions. Much of this discussion emphasized how we reason and make conclusions. This section extends that discussion to another type of problem—those that have a possible or correct solution. Many people do crossword puzzles or Sudoku each day. These are referred to as ***well-defined problems*** since a solution can be determined given that there are known constraints with a specific outcome. This type of problem became the basis for measuring differences between humans, historically referred to as *intelligence*.

Figure 9-5 Nine-dot problem.

Figure 9-6 Hanging strings of lights problem.

Insight Problems

Let's begin with a simple-looking problem, as shown in **Figure 9-5**:

Your task is to connect all nine dots using four straight lines. That is, you are to take your pencil and draw four lines that will connect all the dots without taking your pencil off the paper. Can you do it? One reason the task is difficult for many of us is based on the Gestalt principle discussed in the chapter 5 on perception. That is, we see the nine dots as if they form a box. Further, we want our solution to stay within the box. Of course, with this constraint, it cannot be done. To solve the problem, we literally must think outside the box. You will see one solution to the problem later in this chapter.

There are other similar problems. For example, imagine you are hanging strings of lights on your back porch. You have a tack hammer and some tacks to attach them to the ceiling. Once you finish, you see the ends of the strings hanging down (**Figure 9-6**). However, they are too far apart for you to reach them at the same time and plug one into the other. What do you do?

To solve the problem, you must use your tools in a different way. That is, you must tie the tack hammer to the end of one of the light strings and swing it back and forth. In that way, you will be able to reach both of the light strings (see **Figure 9-7**).

This type of problem was originally studied by Norman Maier in the 1930s (Maier, 1930, 1931). Maier placed subjects in a room with two strings hanging down and told them their task was to tie the two strings together. In the room were tables, chairs, poles, clamps, extension cords, and pliers. Without any help almost 40% solved the problem, but 60% did not. If they didn't solve problem, then the experimenter would accidentally walk by one of the strings so that it began to swing. With this help another 38% of the people solved the problem. At the conclusion of the experiment Maier asked those who solved the problem how they did it. What he reported was that usually the solution appeared suddenly and as a complete idea (Maier, 1931). That is, they had an insight.

Figure 9-7 Hanging strings of lights solution.

Another common insight problem is the candle problem (Duncker, 1945). On the table in front of you is a book of matches, a box of tacks, and a candle. On the wall is a bulletin board. You task is to attach the candle to the bulletin board in a manner that allows it to be lit and burn normally. How would you do this?

To solve the candle problem, you must use the objects you have in a different way. That is, you must first use the tacks to hold the box on the bulletin board (see **Figure 9-8**). By attaching the box horizontally to the floor, the candle can be placed inside of the box and burn normally. This can be a difficult problem to solve. If the problem is presented with the tacks being on the table and the box empty, individuals find it easier to solve (Glucksberg, 1962). **Figure 9-9** shows the answer to the nine-dot problem.

Nature of Insight

The types of problems you have just attempted are referred to as ***insight problems*** since the solution often comes suddenly. An insight problem is a problem that requires a person to shift his or her perspective and view the problem in a different way. This has been referred to as the "aha" or "eureka" moment (Knoblich & Oellinger, 2006; Kounios & Beeman, 2009, 2015; Sprugnoli et al., 2017). Suddenly, you know the answer. The answer is often a reorganization of the information available and seeing the situation in a new light. Although

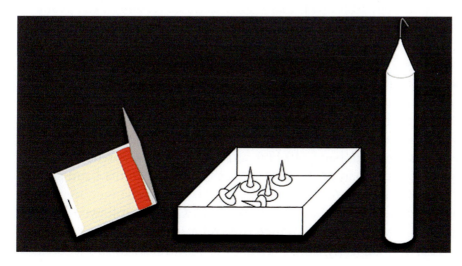

Figure 9-8 Candle problem.

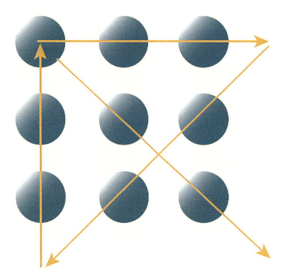

Begin at top left dot and follow the arrows.

Figure 9-9 Answer to nine-dot problem.

not necessary, the realization of the answer to an insight problem may come with an emotional feeling. The solution of insight problems is not unlike seeing a hidden image in a perceptual scene that all of a sudden pops out at you. From the last century, insight problems have been studied from a psychological perspective and, with the advent of brain imaging, from a cognitive neuroscience perspective (Kounios & Beeman, 2014; Sprugnoli et al., 2017).

Another aspect is that the insight breaks an impasse since the person is fixated on an incorrect solution to the problem. Karl Duncker (1945) devised the candle problem and noticed that individuals would want to use the tacks to fix the candle to the bulletin board. Others tried to use the wax from the burning candle to fix it to the board. As with the nine-dot problem, they had a hard time seeing that the box that held the tacks could be used to hold the candle. They could not break their mental set that the box was to hold tacks but not the candle. To be fixed on a limited view of how an object is used is referred to as *functional fixedness*.

Although functional fixedness may hurt our ability to solve insight problems, it does have the evolutionary value of helping us limit our alternatives. This saves us valuable energy and time. If you were planning to build a house, it would not be useful to consider every possible building material such as mud, cork, straw, and even ice. It is our frontal lobes that help limit our considerations and make traditional problem-solving more efficient. What if there is damage to someone's frontal lobes, would it make solving insight problems easier? The surprising answer is *yes*.

Carlo Reverberi and his colleagues gave insight problems to a group of individuals who had damage to their lateral frontal cortex and to a group without any frontal damage (Reverberi, Toraldo, D'Aostini, & Skrap, 2005). They used the matchstick problem, which will be described shortly. What they found was that with a difficult version of the problem, only 43% of the normal controls could solve the problems, whereas 82% of those with frontal lobe damage could. The finding that brain damage could actually help you solve insight problems is surprising. This suggests that executive control may limit our consideration of alternative solutions. It also suggests that solving insight problems uses areas of the brain different from the frontal lobes.

One of these areas is the right hemisphere, especially the temporal lobes. Previously, you learned that when you recognize an image that pops out at you (the dalmatian dog), your brain produces a burst of EEG gamma band (40 Hz) activity. The same is true when you solve an insight problem (Jung-Beeman et al., 2004). Also, the EEG gamma band activity is preceded by a burst of EEG alpha band (8–13 Hz) activity. These changes are seen in the right temporal lobe. Some researchers see this burst of EEG alpha followed by EEG gamma activity as like the brain resetting itself, which they refer to as a *brain blink* (Kounios & Beeman, 2009). Likewise, fMRI activity shows changes in blood flow in similar areas of the brain when solving similar types of problems. The EEG changes were not seen when the participants solved normal problems that did not require an insight to solve.

Another way to approach problem-solving is to ask whether it is unique to humans or also found in other species. At this point, you know it has an evolutionary history in that it is seen in other species such as Thorndike's cats solving their way out of the box to gain food. Another one of the early set of studies to examine *insight problems* was performed by the Gestalt psychologist, Wolfgang Köhler (1887–1967). Köhler (1925) studied chimpanzees on the Canary Island of Tenerife off the coast of Africa. In one study, a banana was placed just outside the chimp's cage but beyond the reach of the chimp. If a stick was placed near the banana, the chimp would use the stick to pull the banana into reach. However, if the stick was placed in the cage behind the chimp, the chimp would not solve the problem as quickly. Köhler suggested that the perceptual field as seen by the chimp was critical to solving the problem.

Another version of the banana problem was to place two bamboo sticks in the cage, neither of which was long enough to reach the banana. To solve this problem, the chimp needed to realize that one stick could be inserted into the other in order to reach the banana. Other studies required that the animals place one box on top of another to reach the food. In his report of these studies, there was a focus on the insight that took place and allowed the animal to solve the problem (Köhler, 1925). Köhler also noted which of the chimpanzees were better able to solve the problems, which he referred to as *clever*. Ways in which insight can be improved is described in the box: Applying Psychological Science: Improving Insight.

Applying Psychological Science: Improving Insight

What can you do to improve solving insight problems? A number of studies have shown that inducing positive emotions, letting one's mind wander, and mindfulness meditation help to improve the solving of insight problems (Kounios & Beeman, 2009; Ostafin & Kassman, 2012). Although the solving of insight problems was helped, these procedures did not improve the solving of traditional types of problems.

Researchers have asked if you stimulate or inhibit different parts of the brain, would that also improve solving insight problems? That is, could you create a *brain blink* that would allow for information to be organized in a different way? To answer this question, researchers used a technique that places a battery-powered low-level current across one's scalp. This is referred to as *transcranial direct current stimulation* (tDCS). tDCS has been shown to be able to increase or decrease cortical excitability as well as change blood flow in areas of the brain below the electrodes.

Richard Chi and Allan Snyder used tDCS to stimulate the right temporal lobe and inhibit the left temporal lobe (Chi & Snyder, 2011, 2012). As you learned previously, the left hemisphere processes information in a more serial manner, whereas the right hemisphere organizes information in a more holistic manner. The idea was that by inhibiting the left hemisphere and stimulating the right, it would be easier for the person to reorganize the information and solve the insight problem. The right temporal area of the brain is also associated with making connections with other parts of the brain during problem-solving.

In the first study, they used the matchstick task that required participants to rearrange matchsticks such that the Roman numeral equations would be correct. Examples of this problem are presented in **Figure 9-10**.

364 Cognition, Problem-Solving, and Intelligence

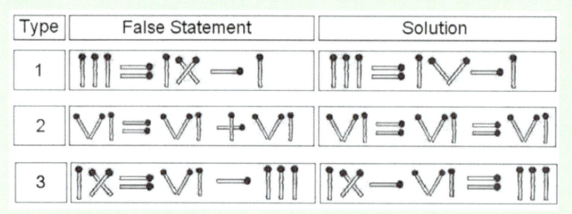

Figure 9-10 Roman numeral insight problem used by Chi and Snyder (2011). The first false statement shows III = IX − I (3 = 9−1). To make a correct solution, the X needs to be changed to a V, thus III = IV - I (3 = 4−1).

They found that, in a control condition, 20% of the participants could solve the problem. With tDCS stimulation, three times as many participants could solve the problem. In the second study, they used the nine-dot task. In this case, the results were even more dramatic. Whereas in the control condition no one was able to solve the nine-dot problem, in the tDCS condition, more than 40% of the participants were able to solve the problem.

Overall, activities that help us think in different ways help to solve insight problems. Some of the ways of doing this are to use humor, to relax, to meditate, or to use brain stimulation. These techniques can help us see the world in a new way and thus solve insight problems.

Thought Question: Being in school is all about problem-solving. In your schoolwork have you been given any insight problems to solve? If so, what approaches did you use to solve them? What might you try in the future after reading the information in this feature?

CONCEPT CHECK

1. What is an insight problem and how is it different from traditional problem-solving?
2. What is functional fixedness?
   a. What role does it play in solving insight problems?
   b. What role does it play in traditional problem-solving?
3. Which areas of the brain are involved in solving insight problems?
4. What techniques can you use to improve your ability to solve insight problems?

From Problem-Solving to Measuring Intelligence

It has been noted that some people seem able to solve problems better than other people (Deary, 2014). Some people are also able to work faster or come up with just the right thing to say. Others seem to learn new information quickly and understand how to apply it in very different situations. How might we understand these differences? Is it a general ability associated with the individual, or are certain people better at some particular tasks than others? Of course, you can think of examples of both.

In the 1800s, Sir Francis Galton (1822–1911) in London became interested in the question of individual differences. Partly influenced by his cousin, Charles Darwin, Galton began to study heredity. Like Darwin, one of Galton's ideas was that there is variation among members of a species and that inheritance plays a role in this variation. Galton published his book *Hereditary Genius* in 1869.

Based on following the lineage of well-known individuals in Europe, Galton came to the conclusion that mental ability was inherited in a way similar to the physical characteristics of plants and animals described by Darwin. As such, natural abilities according to Galton would center on a mean on a normal distribution. Galton's main data for assuming a genetic basis of natural abilities was that these abilities appeared to run in families. Of course, at that time in history, one prediction of what children would become later in life was related to the occupations of the family into which they were born. Children of bread makers tended to become bread makers and children of lawyers and doctors tended to follow the occupations of their families.

Galton had been trained in mathematics at Trinity University and invented the correlation and regression procedures as a means of understanding the relationships between human abilities. In 1884 at an international exhibition in London and for a few years thereafter, he measured some 17 different aspects of more than 9,000 people. Actually, he managed to have these people pay to take his tests. These tests included physical measures such as height and mental abilities such as speed of response and memory. He found little relationship between the different measures, although he did suggest that such measures would form a normal distribution.

Understanding the differential abilities of others and the nature of these differences is an important part of the study of intelligence (Mackintosh, 2011). Intelligence is one of the best predictors of such important life outcomes as education, occupation, mental and physical health, illness, and mortality (Plomin & Deary, 2014; Plomin, 2018). However, these are correlational relationships. That is, such factors as bad nutrition or difficult early life experiences could influence both IQ and later health.

How Do We Measure Intelligence?

Overall, **intelligence** is defined as the ability to learn from and adapt to our environment by solving problems and predicting what might happen next. This is a broad understanding of intelligence. There is also a narrower definition that refers to how we perform on tests of intelligence and compare to others. By using the larger definition, we consider a number of different ways humans adapt and interact with one another. When we use the narrower definition, we tend to define intelligence as a single term with only a few subcategories.

The study of intelligence is in some ways different from other psychological concepts, such as memory or learning, which you have studied thus far. Traditionally, scientists seek to understand a concept by dividing it into its component parts. Memory, for example, is divided into short-term memory, long-term memory, and so forth. Also, you learned about particular areas of the brain involved with each type of memory. The concept of intelligence is in some ways the opposite of this. In fact, the history of the study of intelligence has emphasized the concept as a whole. Further, there is no one brain area that is associated with differences in intelligence.

Scientists have studied what this larger concept of intelligence is related to, and what factors are involved in its expression. As you will see, a historical question has been the manner in which genetic makeup is important and the manner in which the environment in which you live contributes to a person's intelligence level. Environmental factors have included your schooling, the nutrition that was available to you, the stress you experienced, and other such factors. Lead levels in water, paint, and leaded gasoline in a person's environment have been shown to reduce cognitive functioning and IQ over a long period of time (Reuben et al., 2017). Thus, it is not surprising that each underlying factor that contributes to intelligence can be influenced by a number of variables. What is somewhat amazing is that intelligence as measured on tests is a relatively stable individual difference that remains stable over a number of years.

The study of intelligence also has, at its core, prediction. The Han dynasty of China in 206 BC gave tests to determine who would make the best administrators. Civil servants in a number of countries have been selected by intelligence tests. In the United States, college students are partly selected by the SAT (Scholastic Achievement Test), ACT (American College Testing), and the GRE (Graduate Record Examinations) for graduate study, which show a positive correlation with standard intelligence tests. But we are getting ahead of the story.

At the beginning of the 1900s, the French government sought to solve a practical problem in terms of which children would benefit from normal schooling. As they began to expand public schooling, the French Government needed to know who would and would not benefit from normal schooling. To answer this question, they needed a way to measure mental abilities. Alfred Binet (1857–1911) and his associate Théodore Simon developed a measure of mental abilities, the *Binet–Simon Intelligence Scale*, in 1905. In choosing items for the scale, Binet began by asking teachers what types of tasks children of different ages could perform. The tasks were largely related to practical tasks such as telling time from a clock, naming parts of their body, knowing the definition of words, repeating a series of numbers, and copying geometric figures. In doing this, Binet helped establish the modern tradition of viewing intelligence as a composite of different abilities that relate to learning about and solving problems related to one's environment.

In developing the scale and his measure of intelligence, Binet made two assumptions. The first assumption was that one's abilities improve with age. This is the assumption that a child can perform better in different tasks in the sixth grade than in the first grade. What this means is that a child can be compared to other children at a given age. That is, Binet could say that a 10-year-old child should be able to perform a specific set of tasks. This allowed for the concept of *mental age*. Mental age is based on the set of tasks that children of a certain age can perform. However, if an 8-year-old child could successfully perform tasks that 10-year-olds usually perform, then this child would have a mental age of 10 years.

Binet's second assumption was that the child's ability in comparison to other children remains constant. That is, if one had a mental age of 10 when he was 8 years old, then it was assumed he would have a mental age of 12 when he was 10 years old. This second assumption has been supported by research over the last 100 years. That is, after the teenage years, scores on intelligence measures remain relatively stable for the rest of the person's life in comparison to his or her peers. In addition to the two assumptions about a child's intelligence level, an additional assumption was that a test could be constructed and given in a relatively short period of a few hours that would measure mental age. Binet's test and basic ideas were brought to the United States. It was modified by Lewis Terman at Stanford University in 1916 and became known as the *Stanford–Binet Intelligence Scales*.

Whereas Binet used the concept of mental age, William Stern (1871–1938) turned it into a ratio by dividing mental age by chronological age. The concept of **IQ or intelligence quotient** is calculated by the following:

Intelligence Quotient (IQ) = mental age divided by chronological age times 100

Thus, a 12-year-old with a mental age of 16 would have an IQ of 125 (16/12 × 100 = 125). With this formula, a child whose mental age and chronological age are the same would have an IQ score of 100. An IQ score above 100 would be above average and one below 100 would be below average.

By the 1920s, intelligence tests were being administered in the United States, England, France, and other European countries. They were not only administered in schools but also in the armed services as a way to classify individuals and assign them to jobs. When the United States entered World War I, the army asked psychologists to help determine which men should be officers. This test was known as the *Army Alpha*. Another version of the test, the *Army Beta*, was designed for individuals who could not read.

Today, the most common intelligence measures are the *Wechsler Adult Intelligence Scale (WAIS)* and the *Wechsler Intelligence Scale for Children (WISC)*. The initial *WAIS* was released in 1939 and the current version, referred to as *WAIS-IV*, was released in 2008. The 2008 version of the test was initially given to 2,200 individuals who were chosen in terms of age,

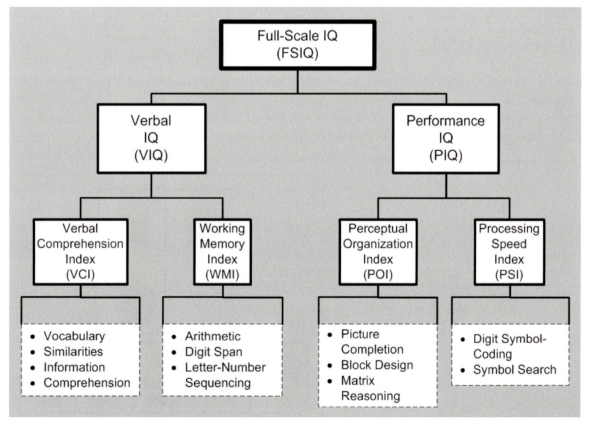

Figure 9-11 The structure of the WAIS.

sex, education level, ethnicity, and region. The test structure of the *WAIS* is directed at four major abilities. These are verbal comprehension, perceptual reasoning, working memory, and processing speed. The structure of the WAIS can be seen in **Figure 9-11**.

Verbal comprehension includes subtests in terms of:

Similarities: How are a hammer and a screwdriver alike?
Vocabulary: What does *ambivalent* mean?
Information: What is the capital of France?

Perceptual reasoning includes:

Block design: Using nine blocks (each block had two sides all red, two sides all white, while the other two sides had diagonals of red and white) copy a design such as **Figure 9-12**.
Matrix reasoning: The person is shown a number of figures and determines what would be the shape of the missing one from a list. A matrix problem is shown in **Figure 9-13**.
Visual puzzles: Choose which three of six pieces go together to make a single figure (which is shown in the test).

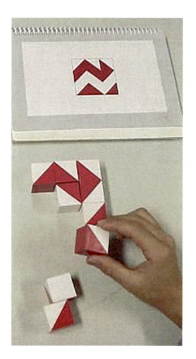

Figure 9-12 Block design.

Working memory includes:

Arithmetic: If 2 people can do a job in 1 hour, how long would it take 8 people to do the job?
Digit span: Repeat the digits read to you (for example, 8, 2, 4, 7, 9, 3, 1).

Processing speed includes:

Symbol search: Determine as fast as possible whether a particular symbol appeared in a previous list.
Coding: Symbols are paired with numbers. A list of numbers is shown and the task is to add the symbol that was associated with that number as fast as possible.

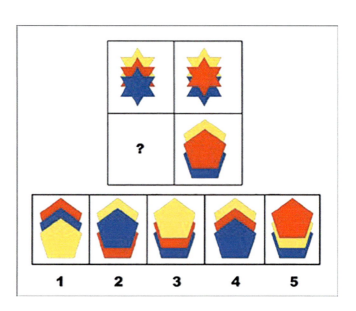

Figure 9-13 This is an example of a matrices test.

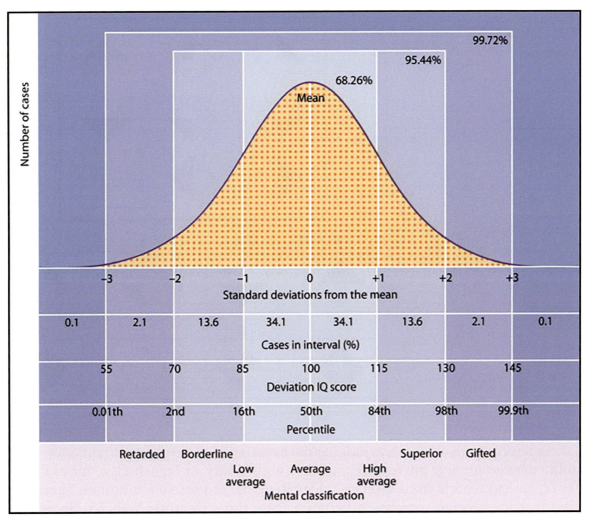

Figure 9-14 WAIS IQ normal curve.

The items in each subscale range from easy to difficult so that the same test can be given to individuals who vary in mental abilities. One problem with measuring intelligence in terms of mental and chronological age is that chronological age continues to change, whereas mental age does not. Thus, if you wanted to compare adults, a different measure was needed. Rather than using mental and chronological age, the Wechsler test determined intelligence level by comparing a person's score to others in his or her age group. To do this a normal curve was used. Initially, the scores on the test and their standard deviation were determined. Using a normal curve (see **Figure 9-14**) the mean score of the group on the test was set at 100. The vertical lines in the graph represent a standard deviation and the percentage shown would be the number of individuals who fall within that deviation. For example, 98% of all individuals have an IQ of 130 or less.

Since IQ is determined by comparing a person's performance with his or her peers, the same number of items correctly answered would result in a different IQ for different age groups.

Psychometric Theories of Intelligence

During the 1900s when intelligence tests were being developed, Charles Spearman began to explore the structure of intelligence. One of his early studies was to ask teachers and older students about the *cleverness* of a particular student. He also measured performance

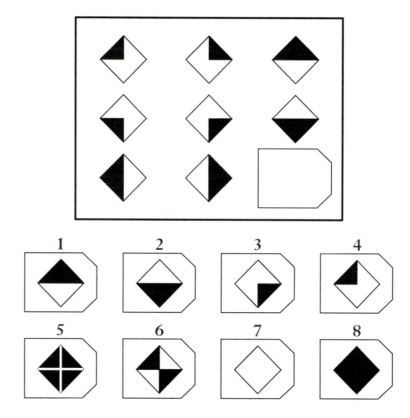

Figure 9-15 Raven Matrices Test.

on three sensory measures such as judging the experience of weight, light, and sound. He would compare musical pitch discrimination with ability in French class, for example. Overall, he had reports from teachers, older students, and sensory measures. Spearman found that the average correlation between these three measures was .55 (Spearman, 1904). He also found a strong relationship between academic subjects such as Latin and other areas such as music. This suggested to him that there must be an overall factor in intelligence.

Spearman's research led to his development of a two-factor theory of intelligence. The first factor is related to the specific test itself, such as the ability to do math or language. The second factor, based on the correlation between measures, is a global factor. Spearman referred to this general cognitive ability as **"g" or general intelligence**. Spearman actually saw "g" as an energy or power that was available to the entire brain (Spearman, 1923). In essence, "g" refers to the situation in which someone who does well in one domain tends to perform well in others.

Raymond Cattell suggested that general intelligence is made up of two separate factors (Cattell, 1971). The first factor is referred to as *fluid intelligence*. Fluid intelligence reflects the ability to perceive relationships with previous specific experience. One early idea was that fluid intelligence reflects one's native abilities. Such measures as the *Raven Matrices Test* (see **Figure 9-15**) are seen to reflect this ability. The Raven Matrices Test shows a person eight figures and he or she needs to determine what would be the shape of the ninth. The first two shapes in each row, if combined, result in the third shape. Likewise, the first two shapes from the top in each column result in the bottom one.

The second factor of intelligence for Cattell was referred to as **crystallized intelligence**. This type of intelligence reflects the ability of a person to acquire knowledge available in his or her culture. For example, the ability to use tools, know the meaning of words, or understand cultural practices such as having a driver's license all reflect what one has learned from the culture. An interesting question is whether a group of people can be more correct than one individual. This question is described in the box: The World Is Your Laboratory: Wisdom of the Crowd.

The World Is Your Laboratory: Wisdom of the Crowd

In 1907 Francis Galton published a paper in the journal *Nature* examining the wisdom of crowds. He described a contest he created at a local fair to guess the weight of an ox. What he found was that based on the guesses of more than 700 people, the collective estimate of the group was correct within 1% of the actual weight. Since that time, *prediction markets*, as they are currently called, have been able to predict a variety of topics including election outcomes and the use of health care.

A more recent version of Galton's demonstration was performed at a state-owned casino in the Netherlands (van Dolder & van den Assem, 2018). On three separate occasions, individuals guessed via computer the number of pearls, diamonds, or casino chips in large glass containers. The winner received € 100,000. Using more than 1.2 million guesses, it was shown that the collective estimate was indeed an accurate representation of the true value.

Psychologists define intelligence in terms of a number of subtests that measure different abilities. For some, there is a global ability referred to as general intelligence or "g," which is seen to be measured by intelligence tests. Recently, psychologists have asked if you could measure the global intelligence of a number of people (Woolley, Chabris, Pentland, Hashmi, & Malone, 2010). That is, is there a *wisdom of the crowd* and can it be measured? In order to answer this question, Anita Woolley and her colleagues randomly assigned individuals to three-person groups and asked them to perform a variety of tasks. The tasks included visual puzzles, brainstorming, making collective moral judgments, and negotiating over limited resources. Before the group session, the ability of each individual was determined. In a second experiment, 152 groups of two to five members were given a broader range of tasks. Overall, these researchers found

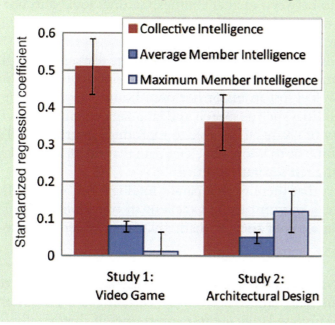

Figure 9-16 Scores of the group as a whole compared to that of individual measures.

Source: Woolley, Chabris, Pentland, Hashmi, and Malone (2010).

that there was a collective performance measure that could not be explained by the individual intelligence of the group members alone. Further, two factors were related to the overall group score. The first was *social sensitivity*. The more a person was able to understand others in his or her group, the higher the group score was. And, second, in groups where a few people dominated the problem-solving, the overall group score was lower. Using this information, these authors suggest that for problem-solving it would be easier to raise the intelligence level of the group than the intelligence level of the individual (see **Figure 11-21**).

Thought Question: From what you've read here, what measures might you take to improve the intelligence level and performance of your next project team?

Multiple Intelligences

Most of the items seen on intelligence measures lack one aspect—context. In our daily lives, we solve problems and understand others that reflect abilities not seen in traditional intelligence tests. Even when we need to know the definition of a particular word, it is often clarified for us in reading or in our discussions with others. In fact, it is suggested that development of intelligence as a species came from our interactions with others over evolutionary time. It is in these interactions with others that our ability to think abstractly and manipulate symbols becomes critical.

Thinking of mental abilities in a broader sense leads one to conceptualize intelligence in a different way than that of an intelligence test. That is to say, intelligence can be understood in relation to solving problems in the context of our culture (Gardner, Kornhaber, & Wake, 1996; Davis, Christodoulou, Seider, & Gardner, 2011). Our experience in culture also shows that a particular person may be very successful in one domain such as sports and not in another such as language skills. This would suggest that abilities can be separate from one another.

Howard Gardner sought to define intelligence within the context of different domains with his ***theory of multiple intelligences*** (Gardner, 1993). Unlike the psychometric approach that examined the statistical relationship between mental abilities, Gardner looked to normal individuals who were particularly talented in a particular ability such as playing chess, music, politics, athletics, and entrepreneurship.

He also examined individuals who had suffered some type of brain damage through accidents or disorders. Following the brain damage, an individual who once could find his or her way through any city may now feel lost in his or her own home. However, even with problems in spatial ability, other abilities such as speech and language remained intact. Likewise, as noted previously, the ability of savants to be able to reproduce in great detail a drawing of a city seen for only a short time or to know the exact date that the first Monday in November will fall on in 20 years suggest separate abilities.

This led Howard Gardner to the idea that there exist separate intelligences. Unlike the concept of "g" or general intelligence, a person can be excellent in one ability such as dancing or music and less proficient in another such as mathematics. Gardner suggested there are eight separate intelligences:

Linguistic intelligence involves sensitivity to spoken and written language, the ability to learn languages, and the capacity to use language to accomplish certain goals. This intelligence includes the ability to effectively use language to express oneself rhetorically or poetically as well as using language as a means to remember information. Writers, poets, lawyers, and speakers are among those whom Howard Gardner sees as having high linguistic intelligence.

Logical-mathematical intelligence consists of the capacity to analyze problems logically, carry out mathematical operations, and investigate issues scientifically. In Howard Gardner's terms, it entails the ability to detect patterns, reason deductively, and think logically. This intelligence is most often associated with scientific and mathematical thinking.

Musical intelligence involves skill in the performance, composition, and appreciation of musical patterns. It encompasses the capacity to recognize and compose musical pitches, tones, and rhythms. According to Howard Gardner, musical intelligence runs in an almost structural parallel to *linguistic intelligence*.

Bodily kinesthetic intelligence entails the potential of using one's whole body or parts of the body to solve problems. It is the ability to use mental abilities to coordinate bodily movements. Howard Gardner considers mental and physical activity to be related.

Spatial intelligence involves the potential to recognize and use the patterns of wide space as well as more confined areas. Some people can drive through a city once and be able to navigate the same city at a later time.

Interpersonal intelligence is concerned with the capacity to understand the intentions, motivations, and desires of other people. It allows people to work effectively with others. Educators, salespeople, religious and political leaders, and counselors all need a well-developed interpersonal intelligence.

Intrapersonal intelligence entails the capacity to understand oneself and to appreciate one's feelings, fears, and motivations. In Howard Gardner's view, it involves having an effective working model of ourselves and to be able to use such information to regulate our lives.

Naturalistic intelligence entails the ability to identify and distinguish aspects of the natural world. This would include weather patterns, types of plants, animals, or rock structure. Experts in meteorology, botany, and zoology are professionals who demonstrate high levels of naturalistic intelligence.

CONCEPT CHECK

1. What is the broad definition of intelligence? What is the narrow definition of intelligence?
2. What contribution did Alfred Binet and his associate Théodore Simon make to the measurement of mental abilities? What are three assumptions they adopted in developing their measurements?
3. Define the concept of mental age. How is it related to IQ (intelligence quotient)?
4. What are the four major abilities covered by the Wechsler Adult Intelligence Scale (WAIS)? What is an example of each of those abilities?
5. One problem with measuring intelligence in terms of mental and chronological age is that chronological age continues to change, whereas mental age does not. How did Wechsler solve this problem in comparing adults?
6. Describe the theories of intelligence proposed by the following researchers: Charles Spearman, Raymond Cattell, and Howard Gardner. What unique contribution did each make to our overall understanding of intelligence?

Relationship of "g" to Cognitive Factors

A number of studies have sought to determine the relationship of a person's performance on different cognitive domains. Timothy Salthouse combined the data from 33 separate studies involving 6,832 people ranging in age from 18 to 95 (Salthouse, 2004). He found that a number of domains could be combined into five larger categories based on their relationship with one another. These five domains are *reasoning* (such as the Raven Matrices Test), *spatial ability*, *memory*, *processing speed*, and *vocabulary*. **Figure 9-17** shows the relationship of each of these domains with a general factor of intelligence. This figure shows it is possible to find different measures of a particular domain such as reasoning, which are highly correlated with one another. In turn, the five domains are correlated with the general intelligence factor called "g."

Cognitive abilities do change as one ages. Timothy Salthouse not only looked at the relationship of specific domains with "g" but also how these change with age (Salthouse, 2004, 2011). As can be seen in **Figure 9-18**, as one grows older, there is a decrease in processing speed (digit symbol coding) and memory (digit span). Reasoning and spatial ability tend not to change, whereas one's vocabulary improves. It is also the case that language comprehension remains stable although language production such as finding the right word becomes more difficult (Shafto & Tyler, 2014).

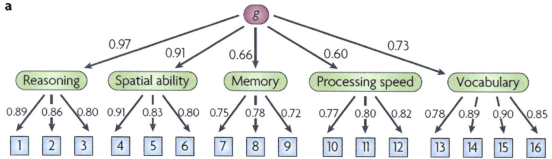

Figure 9-17 This figure shows the correlation between the general measure of intelligence (g) and five domains. Specific tests of each domain are numbered 1 to 12.

Source: Deary, Penke, and Johnson (2010).

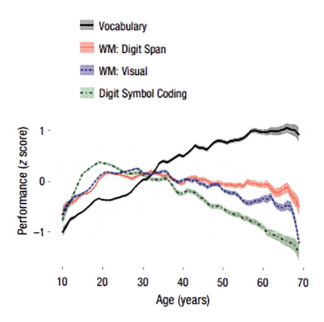

Figure 9-18 Changes in cognitive abilities with age.

One implication of this is that any intelligence measure such as digit symbol coding that emphasizes speed will show decline over time, whereas those that emphasize vocabulary will not. That is, measures of crystallized intelligence with its emphasis on knowledge and vocabulary will not show the decreases that would be seen in fluid intelligence with its emphasis on speeded reasoning. However, since IQ is based on how a person compares with his or her peers, their IQ would not change as they age.

Although memory is often seen as a problem of aging, other abilities are also affected. As can be seen in the graphs, there is a consistent picture of change over the lifespan for each category with the exceptions of vocabulary ability, which does not decrease over the lifespan, and perceptual speed, which shows a consistent decrease over the lifespan (Salthouse, 2011). Overall, except for vocabulary and perceptual speed, cognitive processing remains constant until the person is in his or her 60s. After that age, there is a decrease in certain cognitive abilities, but decision-making competences can be retained (Bruine de Bruin, Parker, & Fischhoff, 2007.

Brain Change with Age

Two consistent findings are that older adults show changes in brain structure and that they use their brains in different ways from younger adults (see Park & Reuter-Lorenz, 2009; Reuter-Lorenz & Park, 2010 for overviews). In terms of brain volume, volume reduction is seen in the hippocampus, cerebellum, prefrontal cortex, and caudate nucleus, which are areas related to executive control and memory. Problems with the hippocampus are associated with a reduction in declarative memory, whereas problems in the prefrontal cortex are related to working memory (Morrison & Baxter, 2012). However, volume reduction alone cannot explain the decline of cognitive functioning (Salthouse, 2011). On the other hand, the visual cortex and the entorhinal cortex show little reduction in volume with age. The entorhinal cortex is located in the temporal lobe and serves as a hub that connects the hippocampus and the neocortex. It is involved in memory and spatial navigation. It is one of the first areas affected in Alzheimer's.

In order to solve problems, older individuals use their brains differently. Even when younger and older adults both perform a memory task successfully, older adults recruit more brain regions than do younger adults. One interpretation is that older adults need additional executive resources to perform the same task. This is referred to as **compensation**. That is, in order to optimize their performance, older adults perform the same task using additional neural circuitry. When older adults use just the brain areas that are activated in younger individuals, they do not perform the tasks as well as younger adults. If younger adults are given more difficult tasks, then they also recruit additional areas.

When you are sitting and doing nothing, the default network in your brain turns on. When you start performing a task, more task-related networks are activated, and the default network is inhibited. In younger individuals, the same pattern of activity in the frontal lobes, the parietal lobes, the temporal lobes, and the cingulate is seen across a variety of tasks in numerous studies (see Beason-Held, Hohman, Venkatraman, An, & Resneck, 2017 for an overview). In older individuals, the number of brain areas involved in the default network is larger, especially in the frontal lobes. Older adults also have a more difficult time turning off the default network. It is assumed that this is related to the problems some older adults have in shifting cortical resources to new tasks. However, it should also be noted some older individuals show the same levels of performance as younger individuals.

The Scottish Mental Survey Study

On June 4, 1947, more than 70,000 11-year-olds across Scotland were given an intelligence test that sought to determine who would benefit from school (Deary, Whalley,

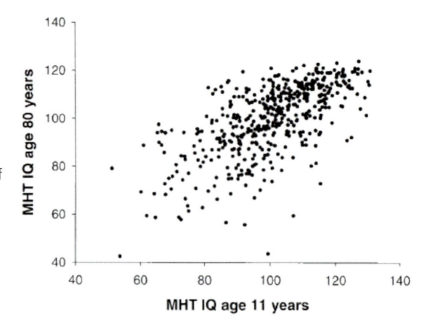

Figure 9-19 Scattergram of age corrected Moray House Test (MHT) scores at age 11 and age 80. Note: each dot represents one person.

Source: Deary, Whiteman, Starr, Whalley, and Fox (2004).

& Starr, 2009; Underwood, 2014). This was known as the Scottish Mental Survey and was a follow-up to an earlier 1932 testing session. What was unique about the 1932 and 1947 test sessions was that they included almost everyone born in Scotland in 1921 and 1936. Some years later, Ian Deary and his colleagues at the University of Edinburgh were able to have 1,000 individuals in the Lothian region of Scotland near Edinburgh who were in the 1932 testing session retake the test as well as be part of brain-imaging studies with an MRI.

This interesting study followed this group of individuals who took the IQ test at age 11 and then again at age 79 (www.lothianbirthcohort.ed.ac.uk/). Beginning at age 79, they were also followed until they were 87 using a logical memory task. The website lists more than 250 publications that have resulted from these data. One general conclusion from this program of research is that an individual's score on the test at age 11 can predict about 50% of the variance in their IQ at age 77 (Deary, 2014; Deary, Whiteman, Starr, Whalley, & Fox, 2004). **Figure 9-19** shows a scatter plot of these data. Each dot in the figure represents a person and shows his or her score at age 11 and at age 80 on an intelligence measure. It was also shown that intelligence level at age 11 was a predictor for health and longevity (Gottfredson & Deary, 2004). This study strongly supports the idea that intelligence can remain constant across one's life. Further, these authors suggested that intelligence enhances individuals' care of their own health because it represents learning, reasoning, and problem-solving skills useful in preventing chronic disease and accidental injury and in adhering to complex treatment regimens.

Genetic Factors Associated with Intelligence

By this point, you have realized that genes and the environment work together in very complicated ways. For example, having genes associated with seeking excitement and adventure may put you in different environments such as climbing mountains than those who do not show the expression of these genes. These environments in turn can affect one's experiences.

Other environments, such as those without hygiene or sufficient food, may result in psychological or physical conditions separate from one's genetics. One common analogy is to point out that seeds with the same genetic components when planted in poor soil with insufficient water develop very differently than when planted in good soil with sufficient sun and water (Lewontin, 1976). However, if there were differences in the seeds planted in the same container that received the same environmental conditions, then one should consider genetic differences.

Those who grow up in impoverished areas may not show the same physical and mental achievement as those who have their needs met. Safe neighborhoods with friends and challenges offer greater physical and mental development opportunities.

Human height is considered to be 80% heritable. However, like intelligence, height has increased over the past 150 years. Clearly, environmental factors such as nutrition, health care, and sanitation have increased during this period and play a part in the increase in height. How could genes play a role in height and intelligence if it has changed over time?

The answer is that heritability is about individual differences not group means. That is, in each generation, genetic factors would result in some individuals being taller than others, and these individuals would have come from the same family. In the next generation, that family would also have even taller children as compared to others.

The technical estimate of **heritability** is a statistic that describes the proportion of a given trait's variation within a group of people that is attributable to variations in the genes. If the trait or phenotype is completely determined by genetic variation, then the heritability factor would be 1.0. If genes have no influence, then the heritability would be 0.0. Some physical traits such as hair color or blood type have very high heritability. Most psychological traits show heritability of .4 to .6, which would suggest both genes and environment contribute to the trait.

Overall, genetic factors are related to how one individual compares with another based on a specific trait. In this manner, environmental factors can increase the IQ of all individuals, whereas genetic factors influence the rank order of where the person falls in the group. Further, epigenetic factors based on the environment may result in behaviors seen in some individuals that is different from the behaviors of others. When we turn to an understanding of intelligence, there is a great opportunity for numerous factors to have an impact. For example, in one study of 11,000 pairs of twins from both the US and Europe, individuals with a high IQ show that environmental factors influence IQ into adolescence, whereas individuals with a low IQ show that heritability factors influence IQ in adolescence (Brant et al., 2013).

To remind you of what you learned previously in terms of behavioral genetics, there are three types of *twin studies*. The first was based on the study of how one individual was related to another. Monozygotic (MZ) twins are identical twins resulting from the zygote (fertilized egg) dividing during the first two weeks of gestation; they share 100% of their genes. Dizygotic (DZ) twins, on the other hand, result from the situation in which two different eggs are fertilized by two different spermatozoa, and they share on average 50% of their genes. In terms of genes, MZ twins are more alike than DZ twins. These individuals are called fraternal twins since their shared genes are approximately 50%, which is the same as that between any two siblings. DZ twins can be either same sex or opposite sex, whereas MZ twins must always be the same sex. The basic idea is that if genes influence cognitive abilities, then you would see a higher correlation between IQ scores, for example, in MZ twins as compared to DZ twins.

Research over the past 50 years has consistently shown that genes influence cognitive abilities. In terms of IQ, MZ twins show a higher correlation of IQ scores between the two twins (.86) than DZ twins do (.60). In one study, both types of twins were reared in the same household (Segal & Johnson (2009). **Figure 9-20** shows these data. Like DZ twins, parents and their children as well as siblings show the same amount of genetic similarity, which is .5. If raised in the same home, they show a correlation between IQ scores of about .42.

The second type of twin study is the *adoption study*. This is the situation where DZ and MZ twin pairs were split up and have been raised apart by different parents. Since the children were raised in different environments, this made it possible to better determine the environmental and genetic influences. However, genetic factors may have led each twin to seek similar experiences although in different environments. In this way, genetic factors could make different environments more similar.

As seen in **Figure 9-21**, MZ twins who were adopted and raised in different environments show less correlation in their IQ scores than those who were raised together in the same environment.

A third type of study emphasizes molecular genetics. This examines generations of families and looks for the association between particular DNA marker alleles and particular traits. Although individual differences in intelligence are highly heritable, it has been difficult to find single genes involved, even in the small percentage of individuals with very high intelligence (Spain et al., 2016). This has led researchers to suggest that a large number of genes make small contributions to the overall intelligence score. What has been suggested is that individual genes are more likely to result in problems in intellectual functioning such as the identification of genes associated with disorders of cognitive abilities such as dyslexia (Mascheretti et al., 2015).

Overall, genetic factors have been associated with intelligence. In fact, intelligence is one of the most heritable behavioral traits (Plomin & Deary, 2014; Plomin, 2018). Physical traits such as height will show a higher correlation, but behavioral traits do not show relationships much over .50. In terms of fluid intelligence, such as the Raven Matrices Test, heritability has been estimated at 51% (Deary, 2012). For crystallized intelligence, which includes what one learns in life, heritability is associated at 40%. Both of these estimates suggest that intelligence is influenced by environmental factors at least as much as by genetic factors. These environmental factors can include the quality of the foods you eat, the availability of health care, whether you exercise, your educational experiences, and other such factors.

As discussed, much of the research on intelligence has come from studies of MZ and DZ twins who vary in genetic similarity. One general finding suggests that there are genetic components that are related to "g" (Plomin & Spinath, 2002; Knopik, Neiderhiser, DeFries, & Plomin, 2017). Robert Plomin and

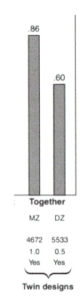

Figure 9-20 The figure shows similarity of MZ and DZ twins reared together.

Source: Segal and Johnson (2009).

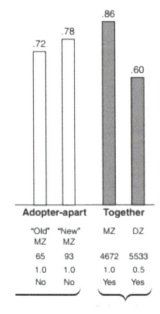

Figure 9-21 IQ correlations for twins varying in genetic and environmental relatedness. Old and new MZ twins represent different samples.

Source: Segal and Johnson (2009).

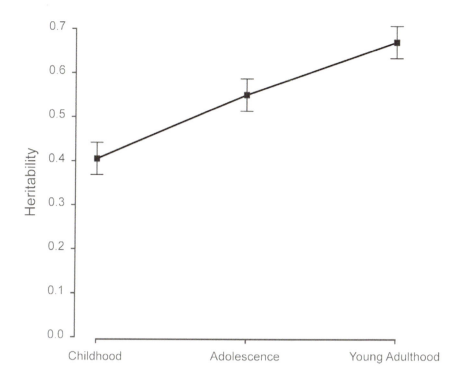

Figure 9-22 A meta-analysis of 11,000 pairs of twins shows that the heritability of intelligence increases significantly from childhood (age 9) to adolescence (age 12) and to young adulthood (age 17).

Ian Deary have summarized this research in terms of five critical findings (Plomin & Deary, 2014).

1. **Heritability increases dramatically from infancy through adulthood:** The effect of genes on intelligence is about 20% in infancy, about 40% in adolescence, and about 60% in adulthood. There is some evidence to suggest that this increases to 80% in later life. It is likely that different genes play a role in intelligence at different times of life.
2. **Intelligence reflects genetic effects on diverse cognitive and learning abilities:** In essence what this suggests is that genetic effects are general rather specific. That is, there is not a set of genes for each ability but rather a number of genes affect general intellectual ability.
3. **Assortative mating is greater for intelligence in comparison to personality and psychopathology:** Assortative mating suggests that humans do not randomly choose partners but choose partners who are like themselves on some selected trait. Intelligence level is a critical behavioral factor for choosing a mate. This means that spouses are more genetically similar than that found in two individuals chosen at random.
4. **Intelligence is normally distributed:** Research has shown that the top section of the distribution is just as heritable as the other parts of the distribution.
5. **Intelligence is associated with education and social class:** This suggests that the genes that influence intelligence also influence education level and social class, and in turn influence health outcomes and mortality.

APOE Gene and Intelligence

Each of your parents contributes to your genetic makeup, which means you can have one variant (allele) of a gene you receive from your father and the same or a different one from your mother. A particular gene related to brain processes is the APOE gene named after the protein it produces. The APOE 4 variant is associated with dementia and Alzheimer's disease. The risk of dementia is increased in those who have one APOE 4 allele and even more for those who have two APOE 4 alleles (Glorioso et al., 2019).

The Scottish Mental Study of intelligence discovered that those individuals with the APOE 4 allele showed more cognitive decline even in the absence of a neurocognitive disorder (Harris & Deary, 2011). **Figure 9-23** shows that at age 11, there was little difference in the IQ scores of those with and without the APOE4 allele. However, by age 79 those with the APOE 4 allele showed a lower IQ score, whereas those without this allele showed a similar IQ score to that seen when they were age 11. On the logical memory task, those with the APOE4 allele showed a decline over the next eight years.

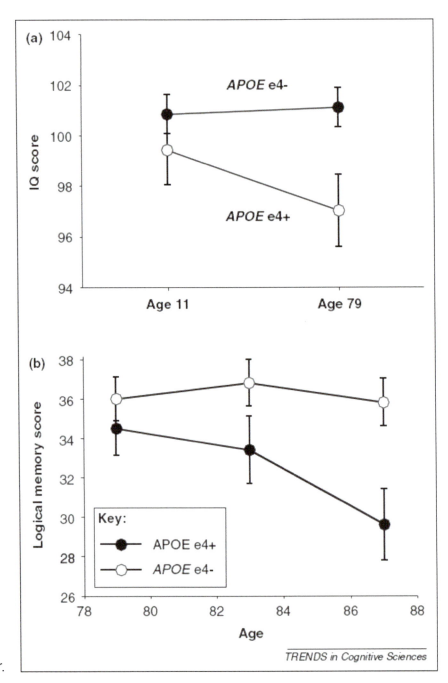

Figure 9-23 Presence of the APOE 4 allele is associated with cognitive decline in individuals without a neurocognitive disorder.

Maintaining Intelligence throughout Life

Maintaining intellectual functioning throughout life has become a popular topic in the media. Numerous brain game systems are available that claim to improve performance and prevent cognitive decline with age. However, the data to support these claims are not definitive (Slagter, 2012). Other techniques that include increased effort may be effective (Tang & Posner, 2014).

What is known is that physical exercise has a profound effect on brain function in both humans and animals (Voss, Vivar, Kramer, & van Praag, 2013). Even more, physical exercise of an hour a day reduced the negative effects of APOE 4 (Schuit et al., 2001). Exercise protects and restores the brain through increased blood flow and other mechanisms. This results in functional and structural changes throughout the brain. The hippocampus, involved in learning and memory, is one specific structure that benefits from exercise. In fact, exercise increases the production of new neurons in the hippocampus. Exercise also plays an important role in aging by promoting healthy cardiovascular function. That is, exercise increases blood flow to the entire brain.

In a review of literature from different areas, Kramer and Erickson (2007) suggest that exercise provides multiple routes to enhancing cognitive vitality across the lifespan. These include both the reduction of disease risk as well as improvement in molecular and cellular structures of the brain. This in turn increases brain function. Further, it is suggested that aerobic exercise affects executive function more than other cognitive processes. Exercise has also been shown to slow the expression of Alzheimer's-like disorders in a mouse model.

It was first noticed that not all individuals showed the same cognitive changes to aging, neurocognitive disorders, or brain injury. From this observation, the concept of *reserve* was developed. That is, high-functioning individuals tend to show less loss of cognitive abilities in relation to aging and neurocognitive disorders. Being able to speak more than one language has also been shown to protect against cognitive decline in older adults and seen to be related to reserve (Bialystok, Craik, & Luk, 2012). The concept of reserve suggests that the brain can compensate for problems in neural functioning. This is illustrated by the case in which the brains of older individuals use larger areas of the brain to solve problems than younger individuals. High-functioning or intelligence is often associated with greater reserve.

Following more than 700 older individuals without neurocognitive disorders for several years, Aron Buchman and his colleagues found that daily physical activity slowed cognitive decline (Buchman et al., 2012). Exercise was also associated with a lower risk for developing Alzheimer's disease. Although performing various types of cognitive tasks such as crossword puzzles or speaking a second language are also associated with successful aging, these brain effects appear to be more localized in those areas of the brain related to the specific task.

In order to better help articulate the causal role of exercise, Lindsay Nagamatsu and her colleagues randomly assigned older individuals who were beginning to show mild cognitive impairment to one of three groups (Nagamatsu et al., 2013). The first group received resistance training and lifted weights. The second group received aerobic training and walked outdoors at a level that increased their heart rate. The third group received balance and stretching exercises. The third group served as the control group. After six months of twice-weekly exercise, the first two groups showed improvement in memory functions. This was seen more strongly on a difficult spatial memory test. The aerobic group also improved performance on the verbal memory test. The important point of this study is that six months of exercise can improve memory in 70-year-olds.

Social support has also been associated with a reduced risk for neurocognitive disorders. Two of these factors are the size of one's network of friends and whether one is married or not. As suggested in studies of the social brain, understanding and maintaining networks of friends requires a variety of cognitive resources that, in turn, offer a reserve for dealing with brain pathologies. One study followed 16,638 individuals over the age of 50 for six years. Those individuals who were more socially integrated and active showed less memory loss during the six-year period (Ertel, Glymour, & Berkman, 2008). With greater conceptualization of intelligence, we begin to see it as a complex measure, as noted in the box: Myths and Misconceptions: IQ Is a Single Measure, Stable, and Caused by a Single Factor and Can Be Applied to Education.

Myths and Misconceptions: IQ Is a Single Measure, Stable, and Caused by a Single Factor and Can Be Applied to Education

While it is true that intelligence has a strong genetic influence, this can lead to erroneous conclusions and myths about genetic influences. For example, it is a myth that genetic influences on intelligence represent a simple relationship and can be applied directly in schools. In fact, if the environment of the school is changed, the genetic effects that normally result in performance differences can be reduced (Thomas, Kovas, Meaburn, & Tolmie, 2015). In a similar way, being involved in team sports protects teenagers from becoming regular smokers, even if they have genes associated with smoking. However, the opposite is also the case. If the environment remains stable for all, genetic effects will be more apparent. In the United Kingdom, where classrooms and content are similar across the country, genetic influences on exam performance were shown to be highly heritable across 13,306 16-year-old twins (Krapohl et al., 2014).

Adding results from psychological domains with a genetic influence including self-efficacy, personality, well-being, and behavior problems increased the effect of heritability on the results. It should also be noted that gender differences accounted for less than 1% of the variance. Students may create their own educational environments even in structured environments by approaching the school material in different ways.

Another myth is that IQ or "g" is stable across one's lifetime. If you were to examine preschool children, you would not find the 60% differences in terms of genetic influence on performance that is found in later school years. What you would find is that genes can only explain about 20 to 30% of the differences between preschool children. In fact, the environment, typically the home at this point, can account for about 60% of the individual differences in cognitive abilities (Asbury & Plomin, 2013). The children who are being read to, talked to, shown how to play with age-appropriate toys, and introduced to the world in an interesting manner do better than those who are not treated in this way.

As you think about what has been presented thus far, it becomes clear that it is a myth to see genetic influence on intelligence as deterministic. However, this myth has been stressed throughout history. In the 1930s there were Nazi programs in Germany to increase what was seen as desirable traits, including intelligence, by controlling mating patterns and availability of partners. The idea that large groups of people, often described in terms of race, differ in intellectual ability continued in a number of countries including the United States and at times included forced sterilization.

In 1969 Arthur Jensen published a paper in the *Harvard Education Review* that stated that programs such as Head Start, which were designed to improve performance in children failed because intelligence has a strong genetic component. Jensen estimated that about 80% of the variance in intelligence was genetic. This set off a debate in terms of racial differences in IQ. Some 25 years later, a book was published, *The Bell Curve*, which continued this debate. The authors, Richard Herrnstein and Charles Murray, said that historically there has been a difference in the intelligence scores of black and white individuals of about 15 IQ points. Further, they suggested that these results were not the result of test bias, but reflected differences in cognitive functioning. As you can imagine, these conclusions created great debate.

What was missed in these debates was that IQ and achievement are not the same thing, although they may be related. In one study performed in the 1960s, 3-year-old and 4-year-old African American children considered to be at risk for school failure went through a special two-year program (Heckman, 2006). By age 10 the IQ scores of these children were no higher than a control group. However, their achievement scores in school were significantly higher. Further, these children at age 40 were shown to have higher rates of high-school graduation, higher salaries, more home ownership, as well as receiving less welfare and having fewer criminal charges than controls (Schweinhart et al., 2005). Clearly, society benefited from the initial money spent on the program. Thus, although related, IQ and achievement do not always go together.

How might society use genetic research on IQ to improve school achievement? Some researchers suggest that one way to improve the educational experience is by an emphasis on individualized learning procedures (Asbury & Plomin, 2013). Specifically, three types of proposals for educators and policymakers can be emphasized: (1) embrace genetic variation in abilities; (2) tailor educational curricula to allow maximization of children's different genetic potential and encourage children to play a role in this process; and (3) invest in alleviating the limiting effects of deprived backgrounds early in development.

Thought Question: The title of this feature is "IQ Is a Single Measure, Stable, and Caused by a Single Factor and Can Be Applied to Education." If this sentence is a myth, or at least a concept that needs to be reconsidered, how would you finish the sentence "IQ is…"?

CONCEPT CHECK

1. Timothy Salthouse identified five different cognitive domains that are associated with general intelligence. For each of these domains:
    a. Give a brief description of the domain and an example.
    b. Trace the typical change in an individual's ability level across the lifespan.

2. What are the two primary ways in which the brains of older adults are different from the brains of younger adults?
3. Describe the Scottish Mental Survey. What were two major conclusions it made about intelligence over the individual's lifespan?
4. What conclusions can we draw from the following types of research studies about the roles of genetics and environment in developing cognitive ability:
    a. Twin studies comparing monozygotic (MZ) and dizygotic (DZ) twins?
    b. Twin adoption studies comparing MZ and DZ twins who were raised apart in different environments?
    c. Molecular genetics studies examining generations of families?
5. What are the five critical findings identified by Robert Plomin and colleagues in the genetic components related to general intelligence?
6. What are three strategies that have been shown to be important in maintaining intellectual functioning throughout life? What kinds of benefits does each of these strategies provide?

Flynn Effect

One advantage of using a normal distribution for determining IQ is that an individual can be compared with other people of the same age range. In fact, IQ is currently determined by comparing one individual with others of a similar age. If we did not do this, we would have to confront some surprising results. For example, IQ has changed in different groups of individuals over time. If you were to look at just the score that a group of people received on IQ tests across generations, you would see an increase in IQ. That is, people today perform much better on IQ tests than did those of earlier generations. Soldiers, for example, showed increases in intelligence measures between World War I and World War II. This effect has been found across the world and in all ethnic/racial groups. This has been referred to as the *Flynn Effect* after James Flynn who studied this effect using the major IQ tests in the United States (Flynn, 2011). **Figure 9-24** shows this effect for the years 1909 to 2013. This research report looked at a number of individual studies involving 31 countries and almost 4 million individuals (Pietschnig & Voracek, 2015). As can be seen in the graph, IQ changes using a variety of IQ tests show changes over the past 100 years.

Why might this have happened? A number of factors have been suggested. Our health and public hygiene have changed greatly during this time. Water supplies and food sources are safer and more available. Health agencies also are more available. It is also true that individuals today are more involved in technology, which requires a different type of interaction with the world. However, this alone would not explain the changes seen between World War I and World War II. At this point no single answer to the Flynn Effect has been demonstrated. There is some debate as to whether it could still be demonstrated. For example, a study of 10,000 adolescents from 1989 and 2003 did not show the effect (Platt, Keyes, McLaughlin, & Kaufman, 2019).

Group Differences in Intellectual Ability

One of the most debated topics in relation to IQ is group differences. These groups include differences in socioeconomic level (SES), race, and gender. These debates are usually caught

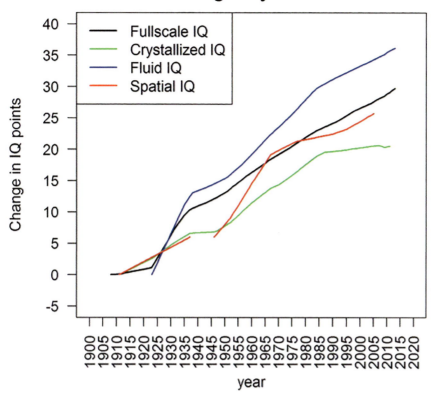

Figure 9-24 IQ gain over time for 31 different countries and almost 4 million individuals. The positive change is referred to as the Flynn Effect.
Source: Pietschnig and Voracek (2015).

up in political and societal debates concerning how education should work, who should receive special opportunities, what is the role of national and local government, and how should cultural differences be understood. For most countries, education is the second-largest cost to society following health care.

For the individual, assumptions about factors related to IQ and achievement can follow throughout one's life and determine future possibilities. However, it is important to remember that genetic research related to human abilities is about correlations and the relationship of one person with another (Turkheimer, 2016). At this point there is very little that can be said about causation of intellectual abilities in groups. However, it is important to consider possible relationships between variables.

One intriguing psychological factor related to group differences in cognitive performance is stereotype bias. **Stereotype bias** reflects negative stereotypes about one's group (Steele & Aronson, 1995). Claude Steele studied stereotype bias experienced by both females and African Americans as a faculty member at the University of Michigan and Stanford University. Although initially his focus was on why certain groups were underrepresented in certain areas of college, stereotype bias can have an impact on any group—from white males, to liberals, to hillbillies. The basic idea is that a negative stereotype can influence one's performance, as he describes in a Radiolab broadcast (https://www.wnycstudios.org/story/stereothreat).

One study had black and white college students take a 30-minute test composed of difficult items from the Graduate Record Exam (GRE) (Steele, 1997). In the stereotype threat condition, the test was described as being diagnostic of intellectual ability. In the other condition, the test was described as a laboratory problem-solving task that did not reflect ability. A third condition described the test as a challenge. Thus, everyone took the same test with the only difference being how it was described.

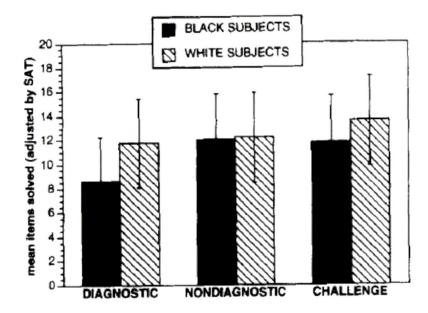

Figure 9-25 Mean scores on the GRE test by group.
Source: Steele and Aronson (1995).

As can be seen in **Figure 9-25**, just telling the black college students that it was an IQ test resulted in a lower score. Clearly, it was not the student's ability since the only difference was what the students were told.

Another stereotype exists that suggests that females do not do as well as males in topics requiring mathematical abilities. Similar to the earlier study, one group of college students was told that the difficult math problems that they were to solve had been chosen to reflect gender differences (Aronson, Quinn, & Spencer, 1998; Spencer, Steele, & Quinn, 1999). The second group was told these problems were just being tested in the lab. To ensure that the male and female participants in the study were indeed good at math, they were required to have scored above the 85th percentile on the math subsection of the SAT or ACT when they applied to college. Also, all participants had taken at least one semester of calculus. Again, just describing the test as reflecting gender differences resulted in the female students not performing as well.

These studies of stereotype threat point to the complexity of understanding group differences in IQ. Stereotype threat by itself cannot explain all of the group differences found in IQ (Sackett, Hardison, & Cullen, 2005). However, it is important to understand that as one is learning to solve verbal, spatial, and mathematical problems as found on IQ tests,

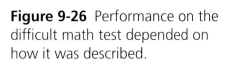

Figure 9-26 Performance on the difficult math test depended on how it was described.
Source: Spencer, Steele, and Quinn (1999).

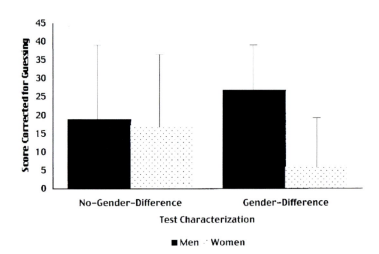

the individual is also learning about his or her culture and the abilities attributed to him or her by stereotype bias.

SES and Achievement and IQ

Socioeconomic level (SES) in educational settings is typically defined in terms of the educational level of a child's parents and the type of work that the parents perform. As such, SES is an environmental factor that can influence the development of a child. It is a factor that has been found to predict reading ability and vocabulary size in children in Head Start programs (Scheffner-Hammer, Farkas, & Maczuga, 2010).

On the surface, it is easy to suggest that low-income parents may be working a number of jobs and not have the time to interact with their children in activities such as reading. The home environment may also contain fewer books or media devices. The family may also lack the money for music lessons, educational trips, and sports equipment. Overcrowded homes may also lead to stress throughout the family and the lack of quiet space to do homework or reading. As noted in the previous Box, *Myths and Misconceptions*, programs such as Head Start can influence future achievement while still not influencing IQ levels.

Interestingly, SES itself can be influenced by genetic factors (Asbuty & Plomin, 2013). In one study of more than 500 mother–child pairs, the IQ of the mother was related to SES (Ronfani et al., 2015). The IQ of the mother was also related to the child's development at 18 months and this was influenced by the home environment. This suggests that parent IQ factors and home environment contribute to a child's development. What is not known is how SES is influenced by genetic factors and how this in turn influences the child. Clearly, some children from low SES conditions show high IQs and achievement, which would suggest a number of factors are involved and it is not a simple relationship.

Racial Differences in IQ

The question of race in IQ is a difficult one. From a technical standpoint, race does not exist. That is, there is no single factor or set of factors that distinguishes one race from another. Most of what we consider to be race involves particular physical factors of the face and body and the groups that one identifies with. Although there are genetic differences that reflect where in the world your ancestors came from, in most cultures, especially in the United States, there is a genetic combining of cultural origin. Racial differences are also connected with cultural differences, which makes it difficult to distinguish environmental practices such as parental expectations and SES from those related to genetics.

The question that has intrigued researchers is why IQ differences exist around the world (Burhan et al., 2017). In one measure of cognitive development given around the world (the Programme for International Student Assessment (PISA)), people in Asian countries such as South Korea and Japan show the highest scores. Next are countries in Europe and the United States and then the countries of South America. In this study, the educational level of the parents did not have a direct impact on the children's scores. In the United States, IQ measures show higher mean scores for whites, then Hispanic individuals, and then African Americans. However, the distributions of IQ measures of these groups overlap. Further, over the 30 years from 1972 to 2002, the gap between the IQ scores of whites and African Americans in the US was cut by 4 to 7 IQ points (Dickens & Flynn, 2006). Since this was little changed in who is included in the population of African-American individuals, this suggests an important role for the environment.

Gender Differences in IQ and Achievement

Gender differences in intellectual abilities has been a source of debate throughout history often along very simple lines. Today, the study of gender differences in intellectual abilities has been shown to be much more complex (Miller & Halpern, 2014). In particular, better research in terms of infant abilities, sex hormones, brain differences, culture, and stereotyping lead to different conclusions than those suggested in the last century.

One summary of the literature suggests little differences on IQ tests between the genders (Halpern, Beninger, & Straight, 2011). Also, it should be noted that items on IQ tests are chosen to minimize differences between males and females. However, the opposite is the case in terms of researchers who study differences outside of the context of intelligence. That is, these researchers seek to find tasks such as rotating an image in your mind in which one gender performs better than the other. Gender differences have been reported in specific types of tasks. Males, for example, show better performance on tasks that require mental rotation of geometric objects. Females, on the other hand, show better performance on tasks requiring writing and language abilities. Males and females show similar levels of abilities on tests assessing subjects learned in high school.

Some of the studies that have found gender differences in intelligence have not been based on complete populations. For example, one longitudinal study found that higher IQ females who took the test at age 10 were more likely to return for future testing at 26 and 30 years of age than males (Dykiert, Gale, & Deary, 2009). Another possible problem with group differences in IQ is that large groups of individuals may be missing. For example, not everyone applies to college and thus SAT or ACT scores could be biased in terms of who did not apply to college.

One study that did include an entire population was the Scottish Mental Survey of 1932 described previously (Deary, Thorpe, Wilson, Starr, & Whalley, 2003). As you remember, this test was given to almost everyone in Scotland born in 1921. The total IQ score was 100.64 for girls and 100.48 for boys, which clearly represents no difference. However, what they did find were real differences in males and females at the extreme low and extreme high end of the IQ scale. As can be seen in **Figure 9-27**, there is an increase in

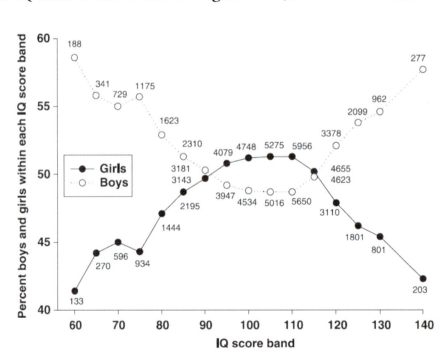

Figure 9-27 Number and percentage of boys and girls found within each IQ score band of the age 11 students.

Source: Deary, Thorpe, Wilson, Starr, and Whalley (2003).

the number of males who score below an IQ of 90 and above that of 120. Other studies have also reported that males show a greater variation in IQ scores at the lower and higher end of the IQ range (Halpern, Beninger, & Straight, 2011).

Another large-scale longitudinal study in the United Kingdom showed that girls at 7 and 11 years of age show IQ differences of about 1 point over boys (Lynn & Kanazawa, 2011). At age 16, this finding was reversed, with boys showing a slight advantage of less than 2 IQ points. The authors considered this to be related to the timing of maturity in boys and girls. Other studies have also reported changes in verbal and non-verbal IQ in the teenage years (Ramsden et al., 2011). A combination of structural and functional imaging showed that verbal IQ changed with gray matter in a region that was activated by speech, whereas non-verbal IQ changed with gray matter in a region that was activated by finger movements. This suggests that a teen's IQ can increase or decrease during the teenage years.

As noted with the work of Claude Steele and others, stereotyping both by society and individuals themselves can influence the intellectual abilities of males and females. One study published in the journal *Science* suggests that these gender stereotypes emerge early in a girl's life (Bian, Leslie, & Cimpian, 2017). In this study, both boys and girls at age 5 associated brilliance with their own gender. By age 7, girls compared to boys were less likely to associate their own gender with brilliance. Even more troubling was that girls at this age began to avoid activities said to be for children who were "really, really smart." This, in turn, would limit their exposure to experiences that would increase their abilities.

Every society also has stereotypes related to gender differences. At one point the debate concerning gender and ability centered on what was observed in society. For example, in 1970 no female had held these occupations in America:

- Astronaut
- Rabbi
- Episcopalian minister
- Attorney general
- Armed forces general
- Secretary of state
- Supreme Court justice
- "Fireman"

Of course, today all of these occupations have been held by both females and males. However, our stereotypes can be out of awareness. For example, many museums have shown murals of hunter gatherers who lived before farming developed some 10,000 years ago. In these depictions, only males are shown being hunters. However, anthropological research suggests that females were also respected hunters, and their burials reflect this (Haas et al., 2020).

Today, it has also been noted that fewer women are involved in fields related to STEM (science, technology, engineering, and math) than men. This has led to a number of initiatives to try to understand these differences and support women who seek to go into these fields. In 2003, 41% of those employed as a "biological or life scientist" were female. The percentage increased to 46.9% in 2011. In engineering, these numbers were lower with 10.4% being female in 2003 and 11.7% in 2011. These and other differences related to gender differences can be found at the National Academy of Sciences website (https://www.nationalacademies.org/cwsem/women-in-science-and-engineering-statistics). Although a number of factors are involved in gender differences, the current consensus is that IQ is not directly related to being a male or female.

390 Cognition, Problem-Solving, and Intelligence

CONCEPT CHECK
1. What is the Flynn Effect?
2. What evidence can you cite to show that stereotype bias impacts cognitive performance?
3. What can we say about group differences related to achievement and IQ for each of the following groups:
   a. Socioeconomic level (SES)?
   b. Race?
   c. Gender?

Summary

Learning Objective 1: Describe the concepts and categories involved in making decisions.

We commonly use our concepts and categories to help us make decisions. A *concept* is an abstract idea or representation. We tend to use *categories* to organize concepts that have shared features.

Researchers often use the term *bounded rationality* in watching humans make decisions. What this means is that our decisions are limited or bounded by a number of factors. Three information-limiting factors are (1) the amount of information we have, (2) our cognitive abilities, and (3) the amount of time available to make the decision. *Fast thinking or decision-making* occurs quickly with little or no effort, and little sense of you being actively involved in the process. *Slow thinking* requires more effort, and we experience ourselves as a part of the thinking process.

Behavioral economics uses behavioral and neuroscience research to understand how humans make decisions. People do not make decisions in isolation, but in relation to other choices as well as how these choices are framed and the effort required. For example, more people accept deductions from their pay checks if they do not have to make a decision about them. That is, if given a choice to *opt-in* (agree to a deduction) or *opt-out* (agree to not take the deduction), most people will go with the alternative that does not require them to make a decision.

Learning Objective 2: Discuss the processes involved in solving problems.

An *insight problem* is a problem that requires a person to shift her perspective and view the problem in a different way. The solution often comes suddenly. This has been referred to as the "aha" or "eureka" moment. Suddenly, you know the answer. The answer is often a reorganization of the information available and seeing the situation in a new light.

To be fixed on a limited view of how an object is used is referred to as *functional fixedness*. Although functional fixedness may hurt our ability to solve insight problems, it does have the evolutionary value of helping us limit our alternatives. This saves us valuable energy and time.

Learning Objective 3: Describe the different ways that intelligence is measured.
Intelligence is defined as the ability to learn from and adapt to our environment by solving problems and predicting what might happen next. This is a broad understanding of

intelligence. There is also a narrower definition that refers to how we perform on tests of intelligence and compare to others.

Alfred Binet (1857–1911) and his associate Théodore Simon developed a measure of mental abilities, the *Binet–Simon Intelligence Scale*, in 1905. In choosing items for the scale, Binet selected tasks such as telling time from a clock, naming parts of their body, knowing the definition of words, repeating a series of numbers, and copying geometric figures. Binet helped establish the modern tradition of viewing intelligence as a composite of different abilities that relate to learning about and solving problems related to one's environment. Binet's test and basic ideas were brought to the United States. It was modified by Lewis Terman at Stanford University in 1916 and became known as the *Stanford–Binet Intelligence Scales*.

William Stern (1871–1938) turned the concept of mental age into a ratio by dividing mental age by chronological age. The concept of *IQ or intelligence quotient* is calculated by the following: Intelligence Quotient (IQ) = mental age divided by chronological age times 10.

Today, the most common intelligence measures are the *Wechsler Adult Intelligence Scale (WAIS)* and the *Wechsler Intelligence Scale for Children (WISC)*. The test structure of the *WAIS* is directed at four major abilities. These are verbal comprehension, perceptual reasoning, working memory, and processing speed.

Charles Spearman's research led to his development of a two-factor theory of intelligence. He suggested that each measure of intelligence is composed of two factors. The first factor is related to the specific test itself, such as the ability to do math or language. The second factor, based on the correlation between measures, is a global factor. Spearman referred to this general cognitive ability as *"g" or general intelligence.*

Howard Gardner sought to define intelligence within the context of different domains with his *theory of multiple intelligences*. Gardner suggested there are eight separate intelligences: *linguistic, logical-mathematical, musical, bodily kinesthetic, spatial, interpersonal, intrapersonal, and naturalistic.*

Learning Objective 4: Identify five cognitive domains that are associated with general intelligence.
Timothy Salthouse identified five different cognitive domains that are associated with general intelligence. These five domains are *reasoning, spatial ability, memory, processing speed*, and *vocabulary*. Salthouse proposed that it is possible to find different measures of a particular domain such as reasoning that are highly correlated with one another. In turn, the five domains are correlated with the general intelligence factor called "g."

Salthouse not only looked at the relationship of specific domains with "g" but also how these change with age. As one grows older, there is a decrease in processing speed (digit symbol coding) and memory (digit span). Reasoning and spatial ability tend not to change, whereas one's vocabulary improves. It is also the case that language comprehension remains stable although language production, such as finding the right word, becomes more difficult.

Learning Objective 5: Discuss the genetic factors associated with intelligence.
Genetic factors have been associated with intelligence. In fact, intelligence is one of the most heritable behavioral traits. Research over the past 50 years has consistently shown that genes influence cognitive abilities. In terms of IQ, MZ twins show a higher correlation of IQ scores between the two twins (.86) than DZ twins do (.60). In this study, both types of twins were reared in the same household. Like DZ twins, parents and their children, as

well as siblings, show the same amount of genetic similarity, which is .5. If raised in the same home, they show a correlation between IQ scores of about .42.

One particular genetic factor found in the Scottish Study of intelligence was the APOE gene. The researchers discovered that those individuals with a variant of the APOE gene, referred to as the APOE 4 allele, showed more cognitive decline even in the absence of a neurocognitive disorder.

Maintaining intellectual functioning throughout life has become a popular topic in the media. What is known is that physical exercise has a profound effect on brain function in both humans and animals. Exercise protects and restores the brain through increased blood flow and other mechanisms. This results in functional and structural changes throughout the brain.

People today perform much better on IQ tests than did those of earlier generations. Soldiers, for example, showed increases in intelligence measures between World War I and World War II. This effect has been found across the world and in all ethnic/racial groups. This has been referred to as the *Flynn Effect* after James Flynn who studied this effect using the major IQ tests in the United States. One of the most debated topics in relation to IQ is group differences. These groups include differences in socioeconomic level (SES), race, and gender.

Study Resources

Review Questions

1. Make the evolutionary argument that having the ability to solve well-defined problems as well as the ability to solve insight problems provides benefit to individuals and species. What characteristics of different environments will favor one type of problem-solving over another?
2. This chapter has presented a number of scientists who have developed methods for measuring intelligence, for example, Alfred Binet and Théodore Simon, and David Wechsler. For each of these researchers, from looking at what and how they tested, how would you describe their underlying theory of intelligence?
3. This chapter has presented a number of scientists who have proposed theories of intelligence, for example, Charles Spearman, Raymond Cattell, and Howard Gardner. For each of these researchers, from looking at their theories of intelligence, what methods would they develop for measuring intelligence?
4. Research on intelligence typically focuses on the individual. Is there such a thing as a "collective intelligence"? If so, how would you characterize it? What kinds of research questions would you propose to increase our understanding of the phenomenon?
5. Genetics and the environment both play important roles in determining intelligence. How would you plot the changing impact of these two factors over an individual's lifespan?
6. Historically, focusing on group differences in intelligence on the basis of groups such as socioeconomic level (SES), race, and gender has sometimes been used to negatively stereotype members of certain groups. What benefits are gained from studying group differences? What limitations do we need to keep in mind when extending group results to individual group members?

For Further Reading

Kahneman, D. (2011). *Thinking, Fast and Slow.* New York: Farrar, Straus and Giroux.

Kounios, J., & Beeman, M. (2015). *The Eureka Factor: AHA Moments, Creative, and the Brain.* New York: Random House.

Lewis, M. (2017). *The Undoing Project.* New York: W.W. Norton.

Web Resources

Humans are not rational—https://www.ted.com/talks/dan_ariely_are_we_in_control_of_our_own_decisions

Scottish Mental Study—https://www.ed.ac.uk/lothian-birth-cohorts

Claude Steele—https://www.wnycstudios.org/story/stereothreat

NAS gender differences—(https://www.nationalacademies.org/cwsem/women-in-science-and-engineering-statistics).

Key Terms and Concepts

affect heuristic
availability heuristic
behavioral economics
bodily kinesthetic intelligence
compensation
confirmation bias
crystallized intelligence
framed
fluid intelligence

Flynn Effect
functional fixedness
"g" or general intelligence
heritability
heuristic
insight problems
intelligence
interpersonal intelligence
intrapersonal intelligence
linguistic intelligence

logical-mathematical intelligence
musical intelligence
naturalistic intelligence
reserve
spatial intelligence
stereotype bias
theory of multiple intelligences
well-defined problems

10 Motivation and Emotion

LEARNING OBJECTIVES

10.1 Discuss the processes that influence how people are motivated.
10.2 Summarize the mechanisms that affect our levels of hunger and our eating behavior.
10.3 Explain the factors that affect our sexual motivation and behavior.
10.4 Discuss the scientific understanding of emotionality.
10.5 Discuss the major theories of emotion.

Imagine that as you walk across campus, a person of the opposite sex walks up to you and says, "I have been noticing you around campus. I find you to be very attractive." She or he then says to you, "Would you go out with me tonight?" What would you do? If you were similar to the students who actually participated in this study, about half of you would say "yes," which also means that about half of you would say "no."

Would it matter if you were a male or a female? No, men and women both equally agreed to (or turned down) the request for a date.

Now, what if the person who found you attractive asked you to come over to their apartment that night?

Would you agree? What if they directly asked you to go to bed with them that night? What would be your response then?

Would you expect males and females to answer these last two propositions differently?

The answer is, of course, yes. In two original studies, about 70 percent of the males agreed to either go to the female's apartment or to go to bed with her (Clark & Hatfield, 1989). No female, on the other hand, agreed to go to bed with the male who told her she was attractive. A few women (6% in one study and 0% in the other) agreed to go to his apartment that night.

We all have needs, but how we experience and express them is an important question for psychologists. This chapter focuses on basic motivations and emotions as well as factors that influence how individuals and groups differ in their expression.

Motivation

All of us come into the world with needs. We need food, water, and oxygen to create energy and live life. We need stimulation to help our nervous systems develop. Part of being human is to experience these needs. Swimming under water will at some point compel us to seek air. We also feel hungry and thirsty. Such needs are very basic. Some of these experiences follow a predictive pattern, such as feeling sleepy every night or hungry after not eating. These processes are built into us as humans and other multi-cell organisms. In fact, we even come into the world with preferences. Three-day-old babies show preferences for certain flavors (Mennella & Beauchamp, 1998).

Darwin initially spoke of two basic needs that motivate all organisms. These are self-preservation and sexuality. The common term used at that time was *instinct*. For Darwin, an *instinct* was a set of behaviors that was present in the organism and did not need to be learned (Darwin, 1859). In his *Principles of Psychology*, William James used a similar definition of instinct as "the faculty of acting in such a way as to produce certain ends, without foresight of the ends, and without previous education in the performance" (James, 1890: Chapter 24: 1,004). James further suggested that every instinct is an impulse. As such, instincts were critical processes that were part of the organism, which involved internal processes that can lead to action.

The subjective experience of a need is a stirring or desire to *move*. Actually, this is the Latin etymology of the English word *motivation* as well as of the English word *emotion*. Thus, **motivations** and **emotions** are processes that cause us to move and potentially engage in an action. Psychology has traditionally conceptualized motivation in terms of *needs* and *drives*, although these terms are rarely used today. Today, motivation is defined as the process that makes a person move toward a goal-directed behavior. Emotion is defined as a subjective or internal experience that is accompanied by physiological changes. Psychologists focus more on the mechanisms that create the states traditionally referred to as needs and drives as well as the underlying states accompanied with emotions.

One characteristic of needs or drives is that there is a goal state that is sought. We can think of experiences such as being hungry as having the goal of finding food. We can also describe the subjective experience of feeling satisfied after eating. On a physiological level we can consider the changes that take place in the gastrointestinal system and the brain structures that interact. One term used to describe this process is **homeostasis**.

Homeostasis was initially described by the French physiologist Claude Bernard. The term comes from the Greek meaning same and steady. The concept was further expanded by the Harvard physiologist Walter Cannon in his 1930s book *The Wisdom of the Body*. The basic idea is that a number of systems in our body seek to maintain the body's stability. If our body becomes too hot, we begin to sweat to decrease our body's temperature. Likewise, if we become cold, we shiver in order to increase our body's heat. In this way homeostasis works like a thermostat in your house that keeps the temperature at a certain level. Besides temperature, hunger can also be seen as a homeostatic process in that when we feel hungry, we eat to create energy and return to a normal state. Overall, our search for a certain level of energy can be seen as homeostatic.

Basic Motivations

The humanistic psychologist Abraham Maslow (1908–1970) suggested that beyond basic needs humans also have the need to be recognized by others as well as to acknowledge their own self. Maslow referred to the desire to express one's self in the context of humanity as **self-actualization**. However, he suggested that self-actualization would only come after basic needs were satisfied. For Abraham Maslow, these different needs can be organized in the form of a hierarchy.

This hierarchy is often portrayed as a pyramid (see **Figure 10-1**). The pyramid describes five basic sets of needs.

1. Physiological needs such as hunger, thirst, sleep, breathing, and sexuality.
2. Safety needs, which include the need for security, stability, protection, and order.
3. Belongingness and love needs, which include the desire to be part of a family or group.
4. Esteem needs, which include the desire for achievement, mastery, competence, and independence. Maslow also describes a subset of esteem needs, which include the desire for reputation, prestige, status, and appreciation.
5. The need for self-actualization represents a person's desire for self-fulfillment.

Figure 10-1 Maslow's hierarchy of needs.

The base of the pyramid is composed of physiological needs such as hunger and thirst. One basic idea is that the needs portrayed at the bottom of the pyramid must be satisfied before a person will seek higher needs. If you're hungry, you will eat before you look for someone to become friends with. Likewise, you don't seek status if you feel unsafe in your environment.

In describing the basic physiological needs, Maslow (1970) echoes Walter Cannon by emphasizing the role of homeostasis and the manner in which these needs reflect the wisdom of the body. This suggests that the physiological needs of a human are in constant flux and vary around a number of physiological parameters such as oxygen or blood sugar level. There are also a variety of unconscious mechanisms that motivate individuals in particular directions. For example, various studies have shown that children with nutritional deficits will seek foods that will correct these deficits. It is the physiological needs that are emphasized in the first part of the chapter.

Intrinsic and Extrinsic Motivation

Maslow initially developed his theory of needs in reaction to the strong learning through reinforcement view of human behavior. This view, as described by B. F. Skinner and others, suggested that humans do what they do to receive reinforcements with little emphasis on internal thoughts or feelings. Today, we know that ideas themselves can influence and direct our behavior. One focus in the history of motivation research in psychology was an emphasis on external factors. In our own lives there are numerous examples of external rewards. We study to make good grades, we work for money, and we sometimes do things to obtain praise from others. To perform behaviors for the seeking of rewards is referred to as ***extrinsic motivation***.

Maslow suggested that there was more to life than just seeking rewards. We perform behaviors because we enjoy it. We play video games, listen to music, read books, or exercise for the experience itself. This is referred to as ***intrinsic motivation***. Clearly, Maslow was using the concept of intrinsic motivation when he described self-actualized individuals. These are people who need to write or play music, create literature or science, or perform physical feats to be who they are.

The concepts of intrinsic and extrinsic motivation are person and situation specific. That is, you can see one individual displaying extrinsic motivation when they study for an exam while another person may genuinely love the material and want to learn everything they can. Given different material, you could see the opposite situation for these same two people.

CONCEPT CHECK

1. How does having a need or drive lead to motivation?
2. What is the meaning of homeostasis? What role does it play in our functioning as humans?
3. What are the five levels of Maslow's hierarchy of needs? Give an example of each.
4. What is the difference between extrinsic and intrinsic motivation? Give an example of each.

Motivation for Food

Food plays an important role in the life of humans. On a basic level, we need food to supply energy to support our daily functioning. Unlike our need for oxygen, which must be satisfied in the moment, we are able to store the components of food for later use. The desire for food can be seen on a number of levels going from culture to genes.

Food also plays an important role in our social and cultural life. For example, food plays a critical role during the celebration of holidays such as Thanksgiving. Religious holidays also give food a critical role. In our everyday life, there are television channels dedicated to preparing and cooking food as well as eating foods from around the world. On an individual level, many of us look for "comfort foods" to change our feeling states. Likewise, there are also a number of individuals who eat when they experience stress, although some people eat less when stressed (Dallman, 2009). However, both those who eat more and those who eat less during stress increase the amount of comfort foods such as chocolate and sweets they eat. Further, feeling sad favors eating foods that are high in fat and sweetness.

Everyone has certain foods that they love and foods that they don't like. Some of our choices are cultural and related to the foods that we grew up with. Some of our choices are genetic, such as the ability to drink milk into adulthood described previously. At times our evolutionary history may have us seeking substances that do not lead to a healthy lifestyle. For example, in our early history, sugar was not easy to come by. It was only found in foods that were not constantly available, such as fruits.

Since sugar gives us a pleasant feeling, we came to seek it. In fact, we consume sugars even when full. We think of drugs as being highly reinforcing for humans and other animals. However, one study showed that rodents are more likely to work for sweet rewards, even when not hungry, than to work for cocaine (Lenoir, Serre, Cantin, & Ahmed, 2007). The constant availability of sugars and other such substances today plays a critical role in obesity and some eating disorders, although other factors also play a role (Drewnowski, 1997).

What foods do you crave and when do you crave them? In terms of particular foods, chocolate is one of the most heavily craved foods. Why is this so? At this point it appears to be more than its physiological effects including the effects of sugar. These other factors also include aroma, caloric content, and texture. Further, the craving of chocolate is seen to be stronger in those who engage in binge eating than in those who do not (Wolf et al., 2017).

Feeling hungry and feeling full is also a homeostatic system that balances the intake of calories and their expenditure to perform the functions of our body. This is a complex system that monitors energy available and that involves both our gastrointestinal (GI) system and the brain. In fact, our brain is a major component of metabolism that is involved in the creation of energy. Over the past three decades, research involving appetite regulation has identified numerous hormones that influence feeling hungry and feeling full (Sandoval, Cota, & Seeley, 2008; Kaviani & Cooper, 2017). It is also these mechanisms that keep our weight fairly stable.

Experiences of Hunger and Satiety

Our experience around food ranges from feeling hungry to feeling full. Most of us have felt hungry between meals and gone looking for a snack. What are the mechanisms that underlie these experiences? Although the mechanisms that relate to food intake and metabolism are complicated in terms of the brain, the hypothalamus has been shown to play an important role (De Araujo, Schatzker, & Small, 2020; Koch & Horvath, 2014). Further, the hypothalamus can adapt quickly to changes in the environment in terms of particular hormones.

It is the hypothalamus that monitors the body's energy supplies (Dietrich & Horvath, 2013). One of the ways it does this is to detect how much long-term energy is stored in fat. This is accomplished by detecting levels of the hormone *leptin*, which is secreted by fat and produced by a certain gene. With increased fat levels, more leptin is produced and can be monitored by the brain. In this way leptin reduces appetite and stimulates energy usage. Leptin is also seen to reduce the experience of reward associated with eating (Monteleone & Maj, 2013). If an individual lacks the gene that produces leptin, he or she will become obese. However, most people who are obese do not lack this gene.

Neurons in the hypothalamus are also sensitive to the body's level of blood glucose. Because the brain needs energy, it is not surprising that there are neurons in the hypothalamus that are very sensitive to blood glucose levels. Specifically, there is a small area of the hypothalamus referred to as the *arcuate nucleus* that accomplishes the regulation of energy balance (Dietrich & Horvath, 2013).

The hypothalamus in terms of eating is often seen to work in a homeostatic manner. As described previously, homeostasis is the process by which the body keeps itself in balance. Like a thermostat that turns on heat when the air is cold and turns off heat when the air is warm, neurons in the hypothalamus are able to stimulate the appetite when energy levels are low. In one part of the hypothalamus, there are two different sets of neurons. One set stimulates food consumption, and the other set of neurons inhibits food intake.

Motivation for eating takes place on number of levels, including craving food, paying attention to food, and increased experiencing of foods. This is illustrated by the situation in which you go to the grocery store hungry and buy more food than normal (de-Magistris & Gracia, 2017). Neurons in the hypothalamus also perform the opposite function when you do not need food. That is, when you've had your snack, the hypothalamus sends out messages that make you feel less hungry. Specifically, eating a snack that results in an increase in leptin and glucose levels in your blood will reduce your desire to eat more food.

Eating a snack with another form of sugar, fructose, will actually increase your desire to eat (Lane & Cha, 2009). Eating foods with a fructose component, as compared to a glucose component, shows a smaller increase in the hormones that signal the experience of feeling full, or **satiety**. In one brain-imaging study, individuals were given drinks with either fructose or glucose (Page et al., 2013). The results showed that glucose, but not fructose, influenced the brain regions associated with appetite regulation and reward

Motivation and Emotion

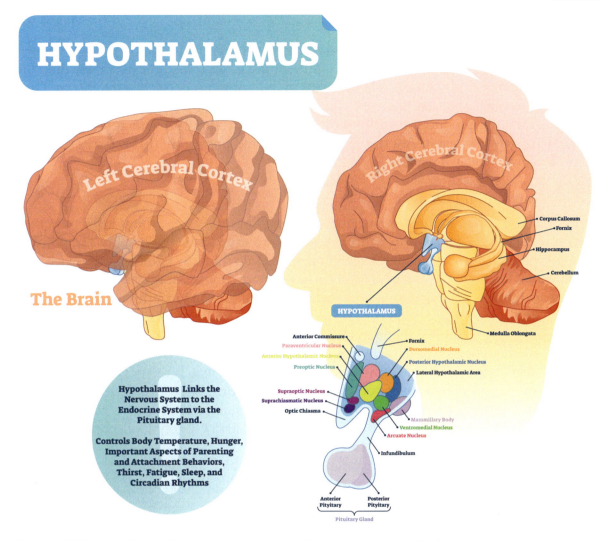

Figure 10-2 Location of hypothalamus and other structures in the brain.

processing. Since fructose is often added to soft drinks, this can result in increased intake and obesity.

Overall, researchers suggest there are three pillars for understanding how the brain controls appetite (Sternson & Eiselt, 2017).

1. The first pillar is neurons in the hypothalamus that, when activated, make us feel hungry. These are referred to as AGRP (agouti-related protein) neurons in that they produce a protein that acts to increase appetite. The activity of these neurons is more involved with food seeking rather than its consumption.
2. The second pillar is circuits of neurons involving the lateral hypothalamus. These circuits are related to the consumption of food and the positive effects of eating.
3. The third pillar is neurons in the hypothalamus that suppress eating when activated. They produce a protein referred to as CGRP (calcitonin gene-related peptide).

Thus, in separate parts of the hypothalamus are neurons whose activity make us seek food, feel good from eating food, and feel full, which is related to a cessation of eating. It is assumed that the circuits interact to maintain a homeostatic pattern.

Hormones in the Gastrointestinal System

After we eat food, hormones are released in the gastrointestinal system. These hormones signal a number of factors including the nature of the foods eaten. For examples, diets low in proteins increase food intake, whereas diets high in proteins decrease food intake. These hormones in turn go to our brain, especially the hypothalamus. One of these hormones is ghrelin. Ghrelin is produced by cells in the stomach that stimulate your appetite as well as promote gastric emptying. Another hormone as noted previously that reduces the desire to eat is leptin, which is released from fat cells.

Eating Pattern and Obesity

Motivation for eating has a longer-term evolutionary history. Over evolutionary time, there were environmental demands in which we needed to expend energy quickly and others in which little energy was required. One way our bodies do this is by reducing our metabolism when we eat less food. We also have mechanisms to store fat when foods are plentiful. In fact, all animals, including humans, tend to favor the intake of foods and fat storage in comparison to using available energy resources. This was reasonable since in our long past there were periods of famine. Although useful in highly unpredictable times, today with freely available foods in the developed world, there can be a mismatch between our evolutionary history and our current demands. For many people, a sedentary lifestyle is the norm. As such, these mechanisms make the balance of energy storage in the form of fat from eating and energy expenditure a difficult one for many people today. In fact, since 1980, the prevalence of obesity has doubled in more than 70 countries (The GBD 2015 Obesity Collaborators, 2017).

It is not only the amount of food eaten that is important but also the types of foods that one eats. One study showed that eating fruits, vegetables, and legumes reduced disease and death (Miller et al., 2017). This study examined 135,335 individuals aged 35 to 70 in 18 countries around the world. From a review of a number of studies, it is possible to make recommendations in terms of foods that one eats (Willett & Stampfer, 2013).

Good data now support the benefits of diets that are rich in plant sources of fats and protein, fish, nuts, whole grains, and fruits and vegetables. It is also suggested that you eat red meat in moderation and that you avoid excess sugar and processed foods, which often contain excessive sugars and salt. Many fad diets have not been shown to have exceptional health benefits. Also, the Centers for Disease Control and Prevention (CDC) has a number of resources to help individuals eat well (https://www.cdc.gov/nccdphp/dnpao/features/nutrition-month/ and https://www.cdc.gov/healthyweight/healthy_eating/index.html). Likewise, the US Department of Health and Human Services has a series of dietary guidelines for healthy eating (http://health.gov/dietaryguidelines/). In spite of this, Americans consume more calories than many other places in the world. Daily calorie intake for various countries in the world is shown in **Figure 10-3**.

Gender Differences in Weight

The effects of food intake influences body changes differently in males and females (Berthoud & Morrison, 2008). One major difference is where in the body excess food deposits fat (Blaak, 2001). In females, fat tends to be deposited in the hips and thigh regions. Excessive fat deposits result in a pear shape in females. Males, on the other hand, tend to store fat around the abdominal area. This results in more of an apple shape or "beer belly." Also, as seen in **Figure 10-4**, women have more overall body fat than men, even when they are not overweight. From an evolutionary perspective, this would be adaptive for females as they require a greater access to nutrition during reproductive experiences (Power & Schulkin, 2007). Levels of body fat are lower in athletes and higher in obese individuals (see **Table 10-1**).

■ **FIGURE 10.3** Daily Calorie Intake, 2004–2013

Source: Reuters Staff. "Future of Food: Daily calorie intake." Reuters. November 9, 2009.
http://blogs.reuters.com/commodity-corner/2009/11/09/future-of-food-daily-calorie-intake/

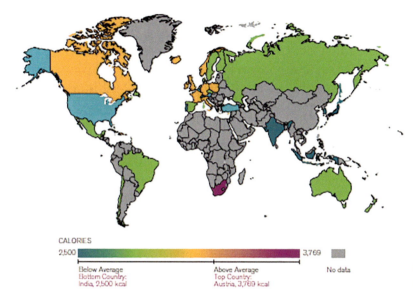

Figure 10-3 Daily calorie intake worldwide.

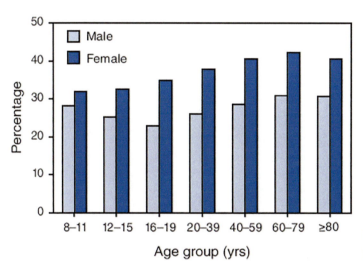

Figure 10-4 Percentage of body fat for males and females by age.

Table 10-1 Percentage of body fat and males and females in terms of activity levels.

Description	Women	Men
Essential fat	10–13%	2–5%
Athletes	14–20%	6–13%
Fitness	21–24%	14–17%
Average	25–31%	18–24%
Obese	32%+	25%+

Body Mass Index (BMI)

Weight and weight gain have become common topics in the popular press, including a large number of books on dieting. Part of this is an estimation of whether you are underweight or overweight. A common measure of weight in relation to obesity is **body mass index** or BMI. This is an indirect measure of body fat based on a person's height and weight (see **Figure 10-5**). There are a variety of BMI calculators on the web as well as cell phone apps.

In general, a BMI score below 18.5 is considered underweight; 18.5–24.9 is considered normal; 25–29.9 is considered overweight; and 30 and above obese. A BMI greater than 30 is associated with increased mortality from cardiovascular diseases, diabetes, cancer, and other diseases. Further, weight gain in adulthood was associated with increased risk of developing chronic diseases in later life (Zheng et al., 2017).

CDC data suggest that 33.9% of Americans over the age of 20 are obese and 34.4% are overweight (http://www.cdc.gov/nchs/fastats/overwt.htm). There is a difference in these statistics by state. All states show an increase in obesity over the past 20 years. There has also been an increase in obesity for both adolescent boys and girls in the latest data over 20 years.

According to the CDC, overweight and obese individuals are at higher risk for the following disorders:

- Hypertension
- Dyslipidemia (for example, high low-density lipoprotein (LDL) cholesterol, low high-density lipoprotein (HDL) cholesterol, or high levels of triglycerides)
- Type 2 diabetes
- Coronary heart disease

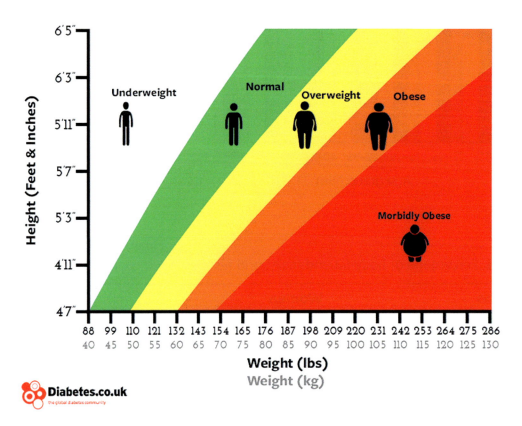

Figure 10-5 BMI is determined by comparing height and weight.

- Stroke
- Gallbladder disease
- Osteoarthritis
- Sleep apnea and respiratory problems
- Some cancers (endometrial, breast, and colon)

In addition to an individual's actual weight, there is also the person's attitude toward their weight. In some cultures, being heavier in weight is seen as positive, whereas in others, it is thinness that is sought. Currently, in the US as shown by the popular press including books, dieting is a topic of great interest. However, there are times in which attitudes and behaviors related to eating go to the extreme. These situations may involve eating disorders.

Eating Disorders

The three major eating disorders are *anorexia nervosa*, *bulimia nervosa*, and *binge-eating disorder* (Brownley et al., 2016; Keel, Brown, Holland, & Bodell, 2012). Anorexia nervosa and bulimia nervosa are the most commonly discussed eating disorders. They tend to have an onset before puberty and mainly influence women. However, the issue of eating disorders in men is beginning to gain more attention, especially in such situations as male athletes attempting to achieve a certain weight to participate in a sporting event.

Anorexia Nervosa

Since the 1600s, **anorexia nervosa** has been described in terms of three characteristics. These are:

1. Food refusal
2. Onset in adolescence
3. Lack of concern of the consequences of not eating

There is a consistency in the way individuals with anorexia nervosa display the symptoms. These include a preoccupation with food while at the same time showing a resistance to eating. Body image is also distorted. That is, in addition to the outward signs of anorexia nervosa, there are also distortions in body image (Gaudio & Quattrocchi, 2012; McLean & Paxton, 2019).

One common characteristic is for the person to see both specific body parts and overall weight as being heavier than they are. The body image distortion has been described as having a perceptual, an emotional, and a cognitive component. The perception consists of whether one's self or others are underweight, normal, or overweight. The emotional, or affective, component involves whether the person is satisfied or dissatisfied with one's own body. The cognitive component consists of beliefs concerning one's body image as well as the mental representation of one's body. These beliefs exist separately without actually viewing body types.

Both cultural and biological factors play an important role. Twin studies suggest that 50% to 80% of the variance in both anorexia nervosa and bulimia can be accounted for by genetics. Overall, these genetic influences appear to show heritability of global attitudes toward food and dieting including the restriction of eating, binge eating, and self-induced vomiting. Genetic influences may keep those with anorexia nervosa from experiencing normal feelings of hunger (Couzin-Frankel, 2020; Zeltser, 2018).

In terms of cultural factors, anorexia is seen more in developed economies. Paradoxically, anorexia nervosa is higher in cultures where food is abundant. As a country develops, there is an increase in the occurrence of anorexia. It has been suggested that with economic development come changing roles for women, a shift in eating patterns, and an emphasis on thinness (Nasser, Katzman, & Gordon, 2001).

Bulimia Nervosa

Although overeating followed by purging has been described since Roman times 2,000 years ago, the eating disorder **bulimia nervosa** was not introduced into the medical literature until 1979 (Russell, 1979). The main characteristics are periods of overeating, in which the person feels out of control, followed by purging. This disorder is generally reported in women and associated with an over concern related to weight and appearance.

Overall, there are three major aspects of bulimia. The first is binge eating in which the person consumes large amounts of food. Typically, the individual consumes 2,000 calories in one sitting, which is equal to the number of calories recommended for a female's daily intake for a healthy lifestyle. The second aspect is the purging. **Purging** is where a person eliminates food from the body by such means as vomiting, taking laxatives, diuretics, or enemas. The third aspect is a psychological one in which one's self-worth is seen in relation to one's weight or body shape.

Binge-Eating Disorder

Binge-eating disorder is characterized by the consumption of large amounts of food and the sense that one cannot control her eating behavior. Although the amount of food varies from person to person, it can go as high as 10,000 calories. Binge-eating is higher in those who are overweight than those who are normal weight. The prevalence is 2.9% in overweight individuals and 1.5% in normal weight individuals. Also, obese individuals take in a larger number of calories during binge eating and non-binge eating episodes. There is evidence to suggest that binge eating runs in families and is not related to obesity per se. Thus, it should be considered to be different from familial obesity. In terms of all eating disorders, it is a myth that eating disorders are only seen in females, as described in the box: Myths and Misconceptions: Eating Problems Are Only Seen in Females.

Myths and Misconceptions: Eating Problems Are Only Seen in Females

For many people when they hear about eating disorders, the image that comes to mind is that of a female. It may be a female who is underweight or someone we know who binges and purges. Although it is true that more females than males report eating disorders, it is not true that males do not also show any of these disorders. In fact, in cases of severe anorexia nervosa, both males and females show similar rates of death.

One review of the literature suggests that eating disorders in males are under-recognized and under-reported (Raevuori, Keski-Rahkonen, & Hoek, 2014). Health care professionals are also beginning to recognize that males differ from females in how they display problems in eating. For example, issues with eating may also occur with issues with exercise and being muscular in men. That is, males may engage in extreme exercise at the same time they engage in problematic eating. Also, certain groups such as gay males show problems in eating patterns and exercise.

Another area in which male eating disorders are seen is that of sports. It may be surprising that eating disorders have been found to be more common among elite athletes than among the general population (Sundgot-Borgen & Tortstviet, 2004). Eating disorders are seen in both male and female athletes, although they are more common for females than males. For men, the most common disorder was bulimia, found especially in the weight category sports such as wrestling (9%). In sports such as wrestling, an athlete must "make weight." That is, to compete in a certain weight category, the individuals must show their weight to be at certain level. For some, this puts pressure on them as they consider ways to make their required weights. One way to do this follows the purging pattern seen in bulimia.

Student athletes are influenced by a number of individuals, including their coach. In one case study of a 12-year-old runner, his coach suggested he might do better competing in a different track and field event such as shot put (Dosil, 2008). Since this student had wanted to be a lean runner as he had seen on TV, he became upset at this advice. Rather than discuss it, he went home and said to himself that he should stop eating so he could become lean. This upset his parents as he refused to eat and began to lose weight. Fortunately, in this case a psychologist was able to work with the adolescent, his parents, and his coach to reduce the problematic eating behaviors.

Another case involved a 22-year-old taekwondo national champion competing to go to the Olympics (Dosil, 2008). He was at a higher weight level than he liked and argued with his coach about his weight. The coach thought the athlete was letting himself go and putting on weight. With the competition coming soon, he considered a number of ways to lose weight and be allowed to compete in a lower weight-class category. These included taking laxatives and diuretics, going to a sauna, and training in plastic clothing. Feeling the athlete was not working at his potential, the coach consulted a sports psychologist who was able to work with the athlete and his coach in terms of the advantages and disadvantages of remaining in the current weight class. This turned into a more long-term collaboration, which resulted in adequate food intake with the athlete performing well.

At this point health care workers and researchers are beginning to identify assessment techniques that identify males with eating problems as well as groups that may be at risk. This includes understanding how eating disorders differ in males and females.

Thought Question: What factors do you think are important in characterizing the differences in eating disorders in males and females?

CONCEPT CHECK

1 Food clearly represents a basic human need. What are some ways it goes beyond that basic level to become a motivation?

2. What are the three critical pieces in understanding how the brain, particularly the hypothalamus, controls appetite?

3. How does our evolutionary history in terms of eating pattern play a role in obesity today?

4. What are the three major eating disorders described in this chapter? What are the defining characteristics of each?

Sexuality

Sexuality is a driving force in many species including humans. The creation of offspring is different in different species. In some species such as frogs a single sexual encounter can produce a hundred offspring. In other species such as humans, sexuality generally leads to a single infant. Also, timing of sexual activity varies. Most primates only engage in sexual activity when there is a high probability of producing offspring. Humans, on the other hand, may engage in sexual activity at any time. In fact, the World Health Organization estimates that more than 100 million acts of sexual intercourse between humans take place each day. However, only 1 in a 100 will result in conception.

Humans use the internal experience of sexual arousal and the external experience of sexual activity for a variety of purposes (see LeVay & Baldwin, 2012, for an overview). Humans spend more time in the sex act itself than do other species. For example, unlike male chimpanzees who go from penile penetration to ejaculation in only 90 seconds, seven out of ten American adults questioned reported spending 15 minutes to 1 hour making love. Further, unlike many species, humans are one of the few species that has sex face to face. This suggests that sexual activity for humans goes beyond basic motivation and has an important pair bonding and social component.

Historical Perspectives

Humans have depicted sexual activities in paintings and carvings for thousands of years. Some of the more famous are Etruscan ceramic plates showing a variety of sexual positions dating from some 2,500 years ago in Italy. With the excavation of Pompeii and Herculaneum near Naples, Italy, a variety of scenes were discovered on the walls in the cities that graphically depicted sexual activities. These towns were covered by volcanic ash when Mount Vesuvius erupted in 79 AD. Similar sexual illustrations have been found throughout the world.

However, at certain times, some cultures have seen sexual activity as a negative force in human life. In the 18th and 19th centuries in Europe and the United States, there were those in the medical profession who suggested that sexual stimulation, especially masturbation, could lead to mental illness. In the late 1800s, John Kellogg was a physician who ran the Battle Creek Sanitarium in Michigan and crusaded against masturbation. Both graham crackers and unsweetened cornflakes were introduced as an aid for reducing sexual desire. His brother added sugar to the cornflakes and sold them through his Kellogg's company.

Also in the 1800s, a number of scientists began to approach sexuality from a scientific perspective. Charles Darwin presented the manner in which sexual selection and self-preservation were important instincts seen across many species. Sigmund Freud emphasized the manner in which sexuality was an important driving force in humans. Havelock Ellis in England was one of the first to study human sexuality itself.

From 1897 to 1910, Ellis published a series of books entitled *Studies in the Psychology of Sex*. In these books he suggested variations in sexuality should be viewed statistically in terms of frequency. He also suggested that variations in sexual practices had their roots in normal sexual practices. Ellis also went against a common notion at that time and suggested that females like males have sexual desires and seek and enjoy sex. Further, he suggested that a gay or lesbian orientation was a normal variation of human sexuality and should not be viewed as a disorder. He also suggested that homosexual tendencies were present at birth.

In the 1930s, Alfred Kinsey, a zoologist, was asked to teach a course on marriage. In preparing for the course, Kinsey realized that little was known about the sexual behavior of Americans. Further, students found it difficult to obtain factual information free of moral or social perspectives. This led Kinsey to conduct a large-scale survey of some 12,000 individuals across the United States. The results of these surveys were published in two books: *Sexual Behavior in the Human Male* (1948) and *Sexual Behavior in the Human Female* (1953). In 1947, the Institute for Sex Research was established at Indiana University with Alfred Kinsey as director. This was later renamed the Kinsey Institute and continues performing research related to sexuality (https://kinseyinstitute.org/).

The original Kinsey survey focused on sexual experiences in terms of various socioeconomic variables such as age, education, marital status, occupation, and religious identification. The prevailing cultural myth of the middle of the last century was that females merely engaged in sex for procreative purposes or to please their male partners.

Many Americans in the 1950s were shocked to learn that females are as capable as males of sexual response. Further, 50% of the females interviewed had engaged in premarital coitus and 25% had engaged in extramarital sex. In addition, 84% of the males and 69% of the females reported being aroused by sexual fantasies. Also, 89% of the males and 64% of the females used fantasy as part of masturbation. Even more shocking to some was the number of males and females who reported they had masturbated (92% for males and 62% for females). Some newspapers and magazines refused to publish stories about this survey and its data. Some lawmakers even suggested it undermined the moral fiber of the nation.

Sexual Activities of Americans

In 2016 the Centers for Disease Control and Prevention (CDC) reported a survey that included face-to-face interviews with a national sample of 10,416 males and females in the US (https://www.cdc.gov/nchs/data/nhsr/nhsr088.pdf). In order to obtain more accurate information, the information in the survey that was related to sexuality was collected using a laptop computer instead of communicating it directly to the interviewer. As can be seen in **Figure 10-6**, among males and females 15–44 years of age, 92% of males and 94.2% of females have had vaginal intercourse. Further, 87.4% of males and 86.2% of females have had oral sex with a member of the opposite sex. Anal sex with the opposite sex was lower: 42.3% for males and 35.9% for females. In this survey, any reported same-sex contact was 6.2% for males and 17.4% for females. This included people who saw themselves as bisexual and homosexual/lesbian. This survey was updated from 2002 and 2011 surveys, which showed similar results.

In 2010, the Center for Sexual Health Promotion at Indiana University's School of Health, Physical Education and Recreation published a comprehensive study on sexual attitudes and behaviors (http://www.nationalsexstudy.indiana.edu/). The survey included description of more than 40 combinations of sexual acts that people perform during sexual events, the use of condoms, and the percentage of Americans participating in same-sex encounters. The survey gathered information from 5,865 adolescents and adults aged 14 to 94. This survey (see **Table 10-2**) shows that sexual activity continues across the lifespan and that there is a variety in the types of sexual acts that humans engage in. It should be noted that the CDC study asked if a person had performed a specific sexual act, whereas the Center for Sexual Health Promotion study asked if the sexual act had been performed in the last 12 months.

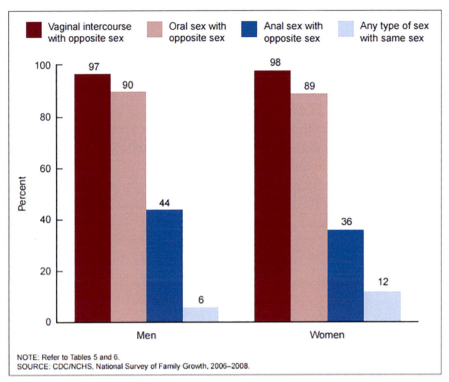

Figure 10-6 Percentage of males and females 15–44 years of age who have had each type of sexual contact: United States, 2011–2013.

Understanding Human Sexuality

Like many human processes, sexual arousal and desire take place on a number of levels in a complex manner. There are cognitive considerations through which an individual may increase desire or choose to inhibit sexual activity. Thoughts, images, and other human cognitive processes can both increase and decrease desire. This level of functioning is only beginning to be understood in terms of sexual disorders. There are also emotional experiences contained within the sexual experience that may include joy and love. Finally, there is the physical level of functioning that includes the activities included in sexual encounters. Across all three levels, one important research question has been the manner in which measurements can be made.

With the advent of psychophysiological techniques to measure blood flow in the sexual organs of males and females, a different type of precision is possible. However, as with a number of psychophysiological measures, the relationship between changes in physiology and the experienced cognitions and feelings may not be exact. More recently, measures of brain activity using such brain-imaging techniques as EEG or fMRI allow for an understanding of cortical involvement. Sexual responding in a variety of species is related to specific external signals that are related to the possibility of conception. Humans, on the other hand, can also respond to internal thoughts and continued sexual arousal even without external stimuli.

In the popular press, men are often portrayed as thinking about sex much more often than women. However, clear research has not been available. In order to study the differences between men and women in cognitions, college students were asked to click a small counter every time they thought about sex, food, and sleep (Fisher, Moore, & Pittenger, 2012). These data show that men did indeed think more about sex than women. However, they also thought more about food and about sleep than women did. Statistical analyses did not show

Table 10-2 Percentage of Americans performing certain sexual behaviors.

Percentage of Americans Performing Certain Sexual Behaviors in the Past Year (N=5865)

Sexual Behaviors	14–15 Men	14–15 Women	16–17 Men	16–17 Women	18–19 Men	18–19 Women	20–24 Men	20–24 Women	25–29 Men	25–29 Women	30–39 Men	30–39 Women	40–49 Men	40–49 Women	50–59 Men	50–59 Women	60–69 Men	60–69 Women	70+ Men	70+ Women
Masturbated Alone	62%	40%	75%	45%	81%	60%	83%	64%	84%	72%	80%	63%	76%	65%	72%	54%	61%	47%	46%	33%
Masturbated with Partner	5%	8%	16%	19%	42%	36%	44%	36%	49%	48%	45%	43%	38%	35%	28%	18%	17%	13%	13%	5%
Received Oral from Women	12%	1%	31%	5%	54%	4%	63%	9%	77%	3%	78%	5%	62%	2%	49%	1%	38%	1%	19%	2%
Received Oral from Men	1%	10%	3%	24%	6%	58%	6%	70%	5%	72%	6%	59%	6%	52%	8%	34%	3%	25%	2%	8%
Gave Oral to Women	8%	2%	18%	7%	51%	2%	55%	9%	74%	3%	69%	4%	57%	3%	44%	1%	34%	1%	24%	2%
Gave Oral to Men	1%	12%	2%	22%	4%	59%	7%	74%	5%	76%	5%	59%	7%	53%	8%	36%	3%	23%	3%	7%
Vaginal Intercourse	9%	11%	30%	30%	53%	62%	63%	80%	86%	87%	85%	74%	74%	70%	58%	51%	54%	42%	43%	22%
Received Penis in Anus	1%	4%	1%	5%	4%	18%	5%	23%	4%	21%	3%	22%	4%	12%	5%	6%	1%	4%	2%	1%
Inserted Penis into Anus	3%		6%		6%		11%		27%		24%		21%		11%		6%		2%	

that males and females had different patterns of thought in relation to food, sex, and sleep. Thus, the gender differences relate to appetites in general rather than in a specific domain.

In studies of sexual orientation including heterosexual, homosexual, and bisexual individuals, it has been shown that these different groups are aroused by different types of stimuli. One study examined self-reported arousal in males as well as changes in penis size in relation to videos of explicit sexual interactions (Cerny & Janssen, 2011). Males who identified themselves as heterosexual, homosexual, or bisexual were asked to watch videos of males and females engaging in sex, males engaging in sex, and scenes including both males and females in a bisexual situation. As in previous research, heterosexual males showed the most changes in erections and self-report arousal to the heterosexual videos. They also showed the least changes to the homosexual videos. Both bisexual and homosexual men showed similar changes to the homosexual videos. However, the bisexual males showed the greatest changes to the bisexual videos. Overall, this research suggests that males show both subjective and physiological arousal in a manner that is consistent with their sexual orientation.

Brain Activity and Sexuality

Brain-imaging studies allow for cortical measures of arousal in addition to self-report and blood flow changes in sexual organs. Overall, when both males and females achieve orgasm, there are changes in the brain. In males, areas involved in vigilance shut down. When males experience an ejaculation, the same areas of the brain are active as when the person takes heroin. As seen using positron emission tomography (PET) these areas are the midbrain and the ventral tegmental area (VTA). In females, areas involved in controlling thoughts and emotions become silent (see Portner, 2008 for an overview).

Do men and women look at different aspects of a picture depicting sexual activity? One way to answer this question is to use eye tracking, which measures where a person looks when viewing stimuli in real time. One study suggests that both males and females look at the bodies of opposite sex nudes rather than the faces (Lykins et al., 2006). In another study, while viewing sexually explicit photographs of heterosexual couples engaged in intercourse or oral sex, males spent more time looking at the face of the female, whereas females spent more time looking at genitals (Rupp & Wallen, 2007). Females who were on birth control pills spent less time looking at the sexual characteristics of the picture.

Sexual Arousal

Since the term *sexual arousal* was introduced to the scientific literature in the 1930s, it has referred to a number of distinct processes (see Janssen, 2011; Sachs, 2007 for overviews). The term has been used in a psychological sense to refer to the internal experience of both cognitive and emotional processes. It has also been used in a physiological sense to refer to hormonal changes, brain changes, and changes in sexual organs related to blood flow. It is also the case that the subjective experience of arousal and genital physiological responses and arousal may not go together. In terms of gender differences, males show a higher correlation between genital responses and subjective sexual arousal than women (Chivers et al., 2010). This has led some researchers to suggest that females are more sensitive to the situational context in which sexual activity takes place than are males.

Sexual Functioning

In the 1960s, William Masters and Virginia Johnson began laboratory studies of the human sexual response by observing couples engaging in sexual activities. Although sexual activity had been studied in animals for at least 200 years, human laboratory studies were first reported in the 1960s. Before this time, little was known concerning what happens to our bodies as we become aroused and engage in sexual activity. In order to understand these processes, Masters and Johnson created instruments that were able to film and measure changes in male and female sexual responsiveness during arousal and sex. Masters and Johnson also studied clinical populations to help treat sexual and reproductive problems. Their major books include: *Human Sexual Response* (1966), *Human Sexual Inadequacy* (1970), and *Homosexuality in Perspective* (1979).

In studying the sexual responses of males and females, Masters and Johnson realized that there was a similarity in how men and women experienced the sexual experience (Masters & Johnson, 1966). They identified four phases of the human sexual response, which are (1) excitement, (2) plateau, (3) orgasm, and (4) resolution (see Figure 10-7). It should be noted that Masters and Johnson saw dividing the sexual experience into four parts as arbitrary and other researchers have used slightly different categories. Also, outside the laboratory, sexual activity begins with desire and this should be considered as an initial step

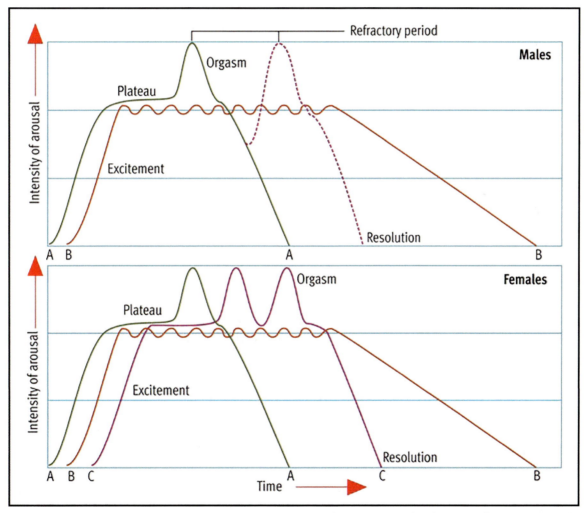

Figure 10-7 The human sexual response in terms of Masters and Johnson's four stages. The letters A, B, and C show different patterns of sexual responses seen in the study. Pattern A in males and females shows an orgasm. Pattern B shows a pattern that does not lead to orgasm. Pattern C shows multiple orgasms.

preceding Masters and Johnson's four phases (see Wincze & Carey, 2001 for an overview). The four phases of sexual response can be described on a variety of levels. The two main ones are blood flow, which is referred to as *vasocongestion*, and muscular tension, which is referred to as *myotonia*.

In the excitement phase, blood flow is increased in the genital region in both males and females. This is both a physiological and a psychological state. In males, this results in an erection of the penis and the testes becoming elevated. In females, blood flow swells the clitoris and enlarges the labia. Also, the vagina begins to moisten. Excitement is felt throughout the body with increased muscle tension. Both the penis and the clitoris are richly endowed with nerve endings, which make them highly sensitive to touch, pressure, and temperature, which leads to the sensation of pleasure.

The experiences begun in the excitement phase continue during the second of Masters and Johnson's phases, the plateau phase. During this phase, most individuals pay little attention to external stimuli as the pleasurable internal experiences continue. In the male, the Cowper's gland releases a substance that changes the pH of the urethra from the acidity of urine to protect the sperm that will be released during orgasm. There is also an increase in heart rate and breathing. Some individuals also show a flush throughout their body.

The tension of the plateau stage climaxes in the third phase: orgasm. Muscular contractions in the male cause the sperm from the testes to be released, become part of the seminal fluid from the prostate, and be expelled. This experience lasts only a few seconds. In the process of ejaculation, the internal sphincter of the bladder closes in a manner that both prevents semen under pressure from entering the bladder and urine from the bladder from becoming part of the seminal fluid. In females, pelvic muscles also contract in a somewhat rhythmical manner, which may lead to the experience of a climax. Both men and women show muscular spasms throughout their bodies.

The fourth phase is the resolution phase following orgasm. Both males and females return to pre-arousal levels during the resolution phase. This includes a decrease in blood flow and muscle tension. During resolution, males, unlike females, experience a time period in which they cannot achieve another orgasm. This time period generally increases with age.

Gender and Sexuality

The beginning of this chapter asked you to imagine that as you walk across campus, a person of the opposite sex walks up to you and says, "I have been noticing you around campus. I find you to be very attractive." She or he then offers you a number of alternatives. These range from going out on a date to having a sexual affair. Clearly, there could be individual differences for why one gave the answer he or she did. They could have been busy, not felt comfortable, responded in terms of a cultural or religious norm, and so forth. However, there were clear gender differences in our willingness to make ourselves available to another, especially for sexual activity. Why is this?

One answer is related to our human history. In thinking about sex differences from this perspective, we would expect to see the greatest differences in areas in which males and females have faced different adaptive problems. Conversely, with challenges that both males and females alike faced, we would expect to see fewer sex differences. The basic idea is that males and females have experienced different roles in reproduction and parenting throughout our long human history. In turn, males and females have faced different challenges, which have led to different processes in structure and function. This may have also led to different priorities in accomplishing these goals. In many ways scientists are just beginning this exploration and thus many important factors have yet to be articulated.

Let's begin with the realization that the mechanisms of reproduction differ in males and females. In mammals, males produce small mobile sperm in large numbers, whereas females produce a relatively limited number of large eggs. One important pressure of the female is that she carries the fertilized egg to the birth of the offspring. The male, on the other hand, is not required to be temporally and spatially involved in the development of the fetus in the same way as the female. Thus, it is potentially possible for a given male to be involved in the production of many more offspring than a given female. Further, during both the time in which the female carries the fetus and after birth, the female must find resources such as food to supply the energy requirements of both herself and her offspring. Traditionally, the consequences of having a sexual relationship differ for a male and female in terms of pregnancy. Culturally, the burden of pregnancy has been on the female worldwide. Sexual practices have changed in the last 50 years with the advent of more successful forms of birth control.

The differences in terms of reproduction requirements between men and women have also led evolutionary psychologists to suggest jealousy would be expressed differently (Buss, Larsen, & Semmelroth, 1992; Buss, 2018). The basic idea is that since a male cannot know for certain who was the father of a child, this will lead to greater jealousy in relation to a female having sexual relations with another man. A female, on the other hand, desires that her mate be invested with her child and thus would show more jealously in terms of emotional infidelity. One review looking at 25 years of research in this area suggests support for the gender differences in jealousy, although a debate still exists (Edlund & Sagarin, 2017). It should also be noted that jealousy is not experienced in the same way with same-sex couples.

Other related answers to the gender differences can be seen in four major areas. These are sexual desire, commitment, aggression, and flexibility.

The first gender difference in sexuality is sexual desire. Overall, men show more interest in sex than do women, and this can be seen in a variety of ways. For example, males report thinking about sex more than females, including more sexual fantasies and feelings of desire. Males are also more interested in visual sexual stimuli. They like looking at sexually orientated magazines or Internet sites and are also more willing to spend money to obtain such stimuli. This is less true with females. Recent brain-imaging research has shown that males produce greater activation of the amygdala and hypothalamus than do females in response to viewing sexual stimuli, although both males and females showed similar responses in areas of the brain associated with reward, and both rated the material as equally arousing (Hamann, Herman, Nolan, & Wallen, 2004). In actual sexual behavior, there are also gender differences, with males seeking sex more often than females. This is also true with same-sex orientation, as seen in comparisons of gay and lesbian couples. That is, homosexual gay couples report having sex more often than lesbian couples. In one meta-analysis of 177 studies examining gender differences in a variety of sexual behaviors and attitudes, incidence of masturbation showed the largest difference (Oliver & Hyde, 1993). The gender differences found in sexual desire or behavior cannot be related to satisfaction of experience since this meta-analysis also found no differences in level of sexual satisfaction between males and females.

The second gender difference in sexuality is commitment. This is true for both attitudes and behavior. When asked about sexual desire, males are more likely to emphasize physical desire and intercourse, whereas females are more likely to describe relationship elements.

Likewise in fantasies, females tend to include familiar partners and commitment, whereas males are more willing to include strangers and emphasize specific sexual acts. Males are also more willing to engage in premarital and extramarital sexual behaviors than females.

The third gender difference in sexuality relates to aggression and sexuality (see Campbell, 1999 for an overview). Human males have been shown to engage in aggression more often than human females from about age 2 onward. Such data as police records from across a variety of cultures universally show males to be more aggressive than females. Not only are males more aggressive, but they commit more serious crimes, including almost 90% of the murders reported in the United States. When asked to describe their own sexuality, males are more likely than females to include a dimension involving aggression, power, and dominance (Andersen, Cyranowski, & Espindle, 1999). Men are also seen as taking the lead in early stages of dating relationships, and although females do initiate sexual behaviors, they do so less frequently than their male partners (Impett & Peplau, 2003). Finally, using physical force to initiate sexual intercourse is primarily a male behavior (Felson, 2002).

The fourth gender difference in sexuality relates to the manner in which external factors can influence attitudes and behaviors (see Baumeister, 2000 for a review). The research suggests that males are less sensitive to situational factors than are females in terms of sexual behaviors. In reviewing this research, Baumeister (2000) describes three basic themes that emerge. One theme is that once a male's sexual predispositions or tastes emerge, they will remain stable. Another theme is that a female's predispositions will be more influenced by her culture and society than will a male's. From this one would predict that females would vary from one culture to another in terms of sexual predispositions. The final theme is that the relationship between one's attitudes toward sexuality and one's behavior will be different for males and females. That is to say, females should show higher correlations between cultural attitudes and sexual behavior than males, whereas males should show higher correlations between their own sexual attitudes and behaviors.

CONCEPT CHECK

1. Sexuality clearly represents a basic human drive. What are some ways it goes beyond that basic level to become a motivation?
2. What are the unique contributions of the following people to our understanding of the historical perspectives of human sexuality:
   a. John Kellogg?
   b. Charles Darwin?
   c. Sigmund Freud?
   d. Havelock Ellis?
   e. Alfred Kinsey?
3. What did the Centers for Disease Control and Prevention (CDC) survey in 2016 and the Center for Sexual Health Promotion at Indiana University's School of Health, Physical Education and Recreation study in 2010 contribute to our understanding of the sexual activities of Americans?
4. What are the three levels on which human sexual arousal and desire take place?

5. Describe human sexual arousal from the following perspectives:
   a. Physiological
   b. Psychological
   c. Subjective experience
   d. Gender
6. What are the four phases of Masters and Johnson's model of human sexual response? How is it different for males and females?
7. Research has shown clear gender differences in our willingness to make ourselves available to another, especially for sexual activity. What five explanations were presented as to why this might be so?

Emotion

William James published an article in 1884 with the title "What is an emotion?" More than 130 years later we still do not have a definitive answer to his question. As noted by many authors, emotionality is a difficult concept to define. Everyone seems to know what it is until asked. To complicate matters, everyday English does not clearly distinguish between feelings, moods, emotions, passions, affects, and motivations. Further, emotional experience and expression are related to your culture and situation (Barrett, Adolphs, Marsella, Martinez, & Pollak, 2019).

One neuroscientist, Antonio Damasio, suggests that emotions are our instinctual bodily reactions to specific situations such as seeing a bear in the woods (https://www.scientificamerican.com/article/feeling-our-emotions/). That is, when we see the bear, our heart races, our breathing changes, our mouth becomes dry, and our muscles prepare to run. Feelings, on the other hand, occur when we become aware of these bodily changes. As such, feelings can be influenced by our expectations and previous experiences. That is, if we believe that where we are walking is a dangerous place, then we may experience changes in our bodily processes in a stronger fashion. Likewise, we can experience the feelings a sick person is going through as we have memories of ourselves being sick.

We can also have mixed emotions at the same time (Russell, 2017). However, most of us are able to describe the emotions that we are experiencing and are able to distinguish between feeling states. An emotion is a positive or negative reaction that is in response to a particular behavior or physiological activity. Most psychologists see emotions as part of our human history as adaptations and communications. Mammal mothers, including humans, have a brain circuit that goes from the hypothalamus to the ventral tegmental area (VTA). This pleasure area in the brain shows an increase in the neurotransmitter oxytocin, which is associated with a feeling of caring (Asma & Gabriel, 2019). Emotions are not only expressed in our faces, but also in our voice and touch, as when we hug one another (Schirmer & Adolphs, 2017). Seeing a mother kiss her son in an MRI (magnetic resonance imaging) can help us to realize the universality of feelings. We experience the image without regards to culture, race, or socio-economic factors.

How to understand and define emotionality is a topic of current debate (see Adolphs, 2017; Adolphs & Anderson, 2018; Asma & Gabriel, 2019; Barrett, 2017; Keltner, Sauter, Tracy, & Cowen, 2019; Ortony & Turner, 1990; Russell, 2003). Carroll Izard asked more than 30 experts in the field of emotion research to give a definition of emotion. He found no consensus and some even said it was not possible to define the term emotion (Izard,

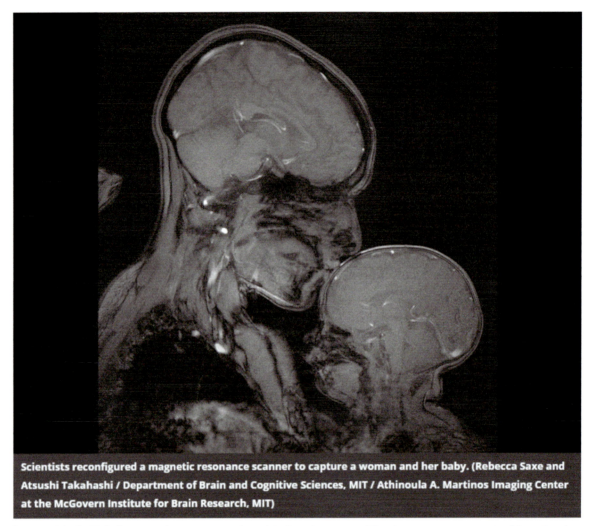

Scientists reconfigured a magnetic resonance scanner to capture a woman and her baby. (Rebecca Saxe and Atsushi Takahashi / Department of Brain and Cognitive Sciences, MIT / Athinoula A. Martinos Imaging Center at the McGovern Institute for Brain Research, MIT)

Figure 10-8 This image shows a mother kissing her son. The image was created in a brain-imaging scanner and shows the brains of both the mother and son as well as the act of kissing. People from around the world experience this as a mother loving her son.

2007). However, current research suggests that emotional information is important and influences all of our decisions, including what we pay attention to, how we learn, as well as what we remember (Todd, Miskovic, Chikazoe, & Anderson, 2020).

One debate centered on the number of specific emotions. Darwin suggested that a number of specific emotions were part of the patterned reaction of the organism to specific situations. He basically saw emotions as an action pattern. You see a bear and experience fear. These basic emotions include surprise, fear, disgust, sadness, anger, and fear. But he also considered what are called social emotions in that they are often seen in a social context. These include guilt, love, shame, and blushing. In the same way that we see a multitude of colors based on the processing of three types of receptors, our emotional processes can be based on a few primary ones. Other researchers have noted the close connection between motivational states and emotions, as would be seen in sexuality, play, helplessness, and anger, as well as caring and attachment (Panksepp, 1998, 2004, 2017).

Current research is seeking to combine the basic emotion approach of examining six or so emotions with social and motivational emotions to examine some 20 or 30 different states (Cowen & Keltner, 2017, 2020; Cowen, Sauter, Tracy, & Keltner, 2019). Most examples of emotional expression or experience are blends of different states. Some emotions such as sadness, anger, or fear show more cross-cultural consistency than others. Overall, current researchers not only note the manner in which emotions can be evoked in specific situations but are also influenced by expectations as well as one's culture (Barrett, Lewis, & Haviland-Jones, 2016). Further, with the advent of digital media, we can share emotional experiences with a large number of people (Goldenberg & Gross, 2020).

Research examining how emotional terms in different languages are related to one another suggest that emotionality has both a cultural and universal basis (Jackson et al., 2019). That is, although happy is very different from fear or anxiety in most cultures, cultural factors can influence how happy or anxiety is related to which other emotional states. Individuals are also able to experience emotional differences from another's voice cross-culturally (Laukka & Elfenbein, 2020). Further, physiological activation is an important aspect of understanding emotional terms.

Research suggests that our brain uses a range of pre-programed solutions for solving problems of daily living (Bach & Dayan, 2017). Emotions are a critical part of these programs. However, with humans in comparison to some other animals, the brain plays an active role in predicting what happens next and, in this way, emotional expression and regulation varies by situational factors as well as our expectations. Further, our sensory system plays an important role in how we create and experience emotional processes (Kryklywy, Ehlers, Anderson, & Todd, 2020). Thus, more sophisticated pattern analyses of neuroimaging data show that affective dimensions and emotion categories are uniquely represented in the activity of distributed neural systems that span cortical and subcortical regions (Kragel & LaBar, 2016).

What is troubling for some authors is that research has not found exact brain patterns that completely differentiate one specific emotion from another. However, it is clear that some parts of the brain and the networks connected with them are involved in different specific emotions (Gu et al., 2019). In specific, the amygdala has been associated with fear, the insula with disgust, the anterior cingulate cortex with sadness, and the orbitofrontal cortex with anger.

This part of the chapter will present a scientific understanding of emotionality. As a scientific topic, emotions have been studied from the standpoint of watching humans and other animals experience different states. Human facial expressions have been a large part of this approach. This was the classic approach of Darwin in the 1800s, which will be discussed in some detail. Emotions have also been studied from the standpoint of human experiences in terms of self-reports, often using rating scales. This approach was used by Wilhelm Wundt in the 1800s. For more than 100 years, the physiological responses such as changes in heart rate and electrodermal responses such as sweating have also been used. More recently, emotions have been studied in terms of brain networks and particular brain structures involved. From an early age, humans also learn to regulate their emotions (Tottenham, 2017).

Historically, emotionality has been studied in terms of specific emotions such as anger, fear, and happiness. As you will see, Darwin saw these emotional states as helping the person or animal to better function in his or her environment. Emotional states also function as a way in which we communicate important information with one another. Whereas Darwin sought to use emotionality to describe the sum of a set of experiences and reactions to the environment, Wundt (1912) sought to break down the emotional experience into its component parts. Wundt emphasized two properties. The first was *valence*, which ranged from feeling pleasant to unpleasant. The second property was *arousal*, which ranged from low to high arousal. Thus, any emotion could be described in terms of these two dimensions.

There has been considerable debate concerning these two approaches. That is, should we use a categorical approach of describing specific emotions such as anger, fear, or happiness or should we use a dimensional approach of noting where an emotional experience falls on the pleasantness/arousal dimensions. The answer appears to be both. It may be the case, as in many debates in science, that we discover that both positions are useful but under different conditions. For example, in science, ice and steam are categorical states. However, they can also be understood by their relation to an underlying dimension, that of temperature or the kinetic theory of heat to be specific. Likewise, our visual system transforms a continuous electromagnetic spectrum into discrete experiences. Receptors in our nervous system are tuned to three major frequencies that result in our experience of specific colors related to red, green, and blue. If our experience of emotionality is similar, this would suggest that it is quite possible to have both a dimensional approach and a categorical approach to emotionality.

We can further consider emotions as experiences created by our brain. Although we speak of emotions in the same way we speak of colors, different emotions like different colors may have evolved at different times in our human history. Öhman (1999), for example, has suggested that different emotions should be viewed as independent from one another in that they may have evolved at different times in our human history.

Darwin suggests that certain of our emotions such as joy or fear occurred early in our evolutionary history while others such as contempt or disdain would have come later. Darwin also speculates that early emotions such as disgust share the same facial expression as that seen in the motor action of vomiting. What could this mean? For Darwin it meant that emotional expressions such as disgust accompanied previous acts such as vomiting. Over evolutionary time, the expression of disgust came to be a response of its own. In this sense, our emotional expressions can be seen as coming from primitive motor processes and in this way represent the beginning of an action that is not completed. However, humans have developed means of regulating emotions and their expression. As such human emotional systems have rich interconnections with cognitive processes in the brain.

Different emotions also influence our bodies in different ways. If you make the facial expression of fear, for example, you will be able to view a larger part of the environment around you and find a particular object in your vision than if you experience disgust (Susskind et al. 2008). Disgust shows just the opposite pattern. Not showing emotions can also disrupt our relationships with others (Niedenthal & Brauer, 2012). Some expressions such as a smile can be used for different purposes. These different social functions are reinforcing desired behaviors in others, affiliation and maintaining social bonds, and reflecting social hierarchies and dominance (Martin, Rychlowska, Wood, & Niedenthal, 2017). However, each of these smiles use a different set of facial muscles.

From a human origins perspective, we want to ask the functional question of the role of emotionality in our human history. In doing this, we can break up the concept of emotion into emotional recognition, emotional production, and even the nature of emotions themselves. We can also describe the external aspects of emotions and consider the situations that bring forth particular emotional processing. Some films make us cry while others make us laugh. Of course, the emotion is not in the film but in us and in our interaction with the plot of the film. We can also consider the internal aspects of emotions and describe the internal recognition and experience of emotionality. Current research also suggests that our ability to quickly make trait characterizations of other people in social situations, such as their trustworthiness, may have evolved from our ability to analyze emotional expressions (Todorov, 2008).

Darwin and The Expression of Emotions

One critical scientist in the study of emotions is Charles Darwin. In *The Expression of the Emotions in Man and Animals,* Darwin portrays a careful observation of emotionality. Throughout his book, Darwin presents drawings and photographs of people and animals as they express different emotions. The common theme is that emotions are universal and represent an example of evolution through natural selection.

Paul Ekman (2009) suggests Darwin made a number of important contributions to our study of emotions.

1. Darwin saw emotions as discrete. That is to say we experience fear, anger, disgust and so forth as distinct entities.
2. Darwin emphasized the human face in the expression of emotions, as illustrated by the photographs of human faces he used in his book.
3. One of Darwin's main ideas is that emotional processes are innate and found across a variety of species including humans. Darwin clarified this idea by suggesting that while facial expressions are universal, gestures may be specific to a given culture.
4. Emotions are not unique to humans and may be found in a variety of species.
5. Particular muscle movements may signal a particular emotion.

Let's begin by considering the muscles in our faces. There are more than 50 muscles in the human face, far more than are needed for eating, language, or closing the eyes alone. Why do we have these muscles in the face? One answer for psychologists is that these muscles have evolved for the expression of emotion. In fact, the ability to quickly express and to recognize these expressions gave humans an important means of communication. Darwin suggests that these expressions are displayed involuntarily and also exist in non-human animals for purposes other than social communication. Darwin emphasized that facial expressions play an important role in preparing an organism for taking in information from the environment and acting on that information. Thus, facial expressions of emotions have a long evolutionary history that predates social communication.

Darwin also saw patterns related to approach or withdrawal, which is described as *valence* in current emotional theories. Overall, for Darwin, opposite internal states produce the opposite external movements from those of the principle one. That is to say, we shrug our shoulders when we feel helpless because it is the opposite set of movements from when we feel aggressive.

As can be seen in the illustration (see **Figure 10-9**) from *The Expression of Emotion*, a hostile dog has its ears up, its tail up, its eyes fixed, its back elevated, and so forth. The opposite internal state according to Darwin would result in the opposite external manifestation with its ears down, its tail down, its back down, and so forth. However, as Darwin noted, these responses may be species specific. For example, although dogs and cats have different postures for fear and aggression, each species displays the opposite response for the opposite emotion.

With emotions also come physiological reactions. For example, in rage, the face becomes red with the veins on the forehead and neck distended. Monkeys also redden from passion. Various species of animals, including humans, when frightened experience the hairs of their arms standing upright. Darwin also notes that with different emotions, the heart rate speeds up, which in turn influences the brain, which in turn influences the heart.

The idea that there are specific physiological reactions for different emotions and that the cardiovascular and cortical system mutually interact with each other are two of Darwin's

Figure 10-9 Figures from Darwin showing opposite external movements with opposite emotions.

ideas from this book that were considerably ahead of their time. Darwin further notes that anger, rage, and indignation are displayed in a common manner throughout the world. In this way, it is not voluntary action or previous learning or habit that influences the expression of emotion but the organization of the nervous system.

These ideas today continue to drive research in the neurosciences (for example, Susskind et al., 2008). Susskind and his colleagues examined two emotional expressions—fear and disgust. Fear is an emotional response that has been associated with greater perceptual attention, whereas disgust has been associated with sensory rejection. Given that these emotional responses reflect opposite types of sensory processing, Darwin's ideas would suggest that their expression would involve opposite responses. Indeed, when Susskind and his colleagues examined how the skin of the face changes in fear and disgust, they found the skin to deform in the opposite ways in these two emotional expressions, as shown in **Figure 10-10**.

These researchers next looked at three different physiological measures during the expression of fear and disgust. These were: (1) how much air an individual was able to breathe in during each of these emotions, (2) how fast the eye was able to move, and (3) how large a visual area were individuals able to see. Again, fear and disgust resulted in the opposite with individuals able to take in more air, move their eyes faster, and see a larger visual area during fear and less during disgust. These authors see their research supporting Darwin's

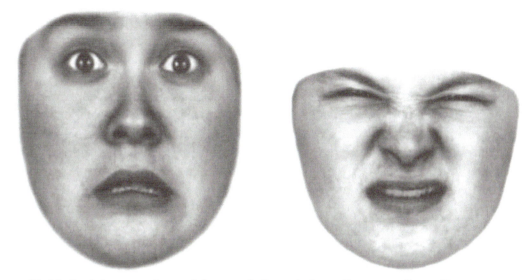

Figure 10-10 Facial expressions of fear and disgust show the opposite patterns.

idea that not only does emotional expression allow for social communication but that it also modifies our ability to prepare for perception and action. The connection between facial expressions and physiological changes suggests that facial expressions are more than just social signaling, important as that is, but also offer biological advantages in terms of potential perception and action.

Throughout *The Expression of the Emotions in Man and Animals* Darwin saw emotional expression to be universal, shaped by natural selection, having survival value, and found in humans and a variety of animal species. Darwin also helps us to think about larger "why" questions such as why do a number of species, including humans, touch one another when being affectionate, or weep when feeling grief, or show their teeth when angry. Using careful observation, Darwin sought to articulate the specific muscles involved in many facial expressions including surprise, fear, helplessness, disgust, guilt, love, suffering, shame, and blushing. Current neuroscience research shows that specific facial expression in mice in response to emotional stimuli can be classified in distinct categories and related to specific brain activity (Dolensek, Gehrlach, Klein, & Goglla, 2020).

Darwin also sought to demonstrate the universality of emotion recognition by showing different emotions to people. For example, he showed pictures displaying surprise to some 24 people and reported that all but two reported some variation of surprise or astonishment (p. 279). Darwin was clearly using his work to forward his argument of universal expression of emotion, as he said in the concluding chapter, "I have endeavored to show in considerable detail that all the chief expressions exhibited by man are the same throughout the world" (p. 355).

Universal Emotionality

By the end of the 20th century, researchers such as Paul Ekman had followed Darwin's tradition by studying facial expressions cross-culturally and demonstrating the universality of emotional expression (Ekman, 1973). For example, Ekman performed interesting research in New Guinea by showing individuals different emotional facial expressions and asking them to tell a story that causes the person to look the way they were in the picture (Ekman & Friesen, 1971). He also performed the research in reverse manner in which a story was told without using emotional terms. The person was then asked which of a series of emotional faces would best represent the person in the story. This type of research supported the idea that both emotional recognition and emotional expression were universal.

Let's think about the task. How did you come to recognize the facial expressions that you see? It has been estimated that human faces can produce more than 10,000 different expressions (Ekman, 2003). Clearly one aspect of it is experience. You hear others commenting on someone's expression and giving it a label. However, if your recognition of emotions was totally through your culture, as some researchers thought, then we might expect to see different cultures having different expressions even for such basic emotions as fear or disgust or surprise. Popular culture has taken these basic facial expressions and turned them sideways to create emoticons. Thus, a happy face becomes :-) or ☺ and a sad one :-(or ☹

Like many in psychology in the 1950s, Paul Ekman assumed facial expressions to be socially learned and largely influenced by culture (Ekman, 1957). However, his own cross-cultural work and that of others forced Ekman to adopt the opposite position. Ekman asked if emotional expression differed across cultures (see Ekman, 1999b for an overview). He presented a series of emotional faces to people in five different countries: Chile, Argentina, Brazil, Japan, and the United States.

What Ekman found echoed what Darwin had suggested years earlier: Facial expressions can be seen as universal. As noted previously, Ekman later confirmed this by observing facial expressions displayed by isolated tribes in New Guinea who had no contact with Western culture or seen television, movies, or photographs. Facial expressions research is described in the box: Applying Psychological Science: An Ingenious Way to Look at Facial Expressions.

Applying Psychological Science: An Ingenious Way to Look at Facial Expressions

If you were asked to create experiments to understand the role of innate patterns of reaction and the role of culture in facial expressions, how might you do that? You could of course do what Paul Ekman did and study how emotional expressions are understood in different cultures around the world. You would have even stronger support for your conclusions if the cultures you studied did not have much contact with other cultures through media and television. If people in each culture displayed different facial expressions for a particular emotion, then you could conclude that an individual would have learned their facial expressions from their own culture. If, on the other hand, the facial expressions were more similar around the world, then you would have more support for the idea that emotional expression was universal. How else might you answer this question?

One ingenious set of studies used a group of individuals who could not have seen the facial expressions of others. They studied individuals who had been blind all their life (Galati et al., 1997). In performing the study, they created a number of stories designed to produce specific emotions. In particular these stories elicited joy, disgust, anger, fear, sadness, and surprise. These stories were read to both blind and sighted individuals. In addition, both the sighted and blind individuals were asked to pose the facial expressions associated with these emotions.

In order to rate the emotional expressions they had experts use a coding system for describing facial expressions. These researchers found that both sighted and blind individuals produced similar facial expressions. However, the blind participants used a smaller set of facial muscles. In both groups, emotions such as joy were more adequately produced. These researchers concluded that blind individuals were capable of performing emotional expressions voluntarily. Clearly, internal emotions are expressed in facial expressions whether one has seen facial expressions or not.

Thought Question: What other kinds of questions concerning whether a particular human experience or behavior is universal or culturally determined could you study using this approach?

Display Rules Across Cultures

If facial expressions are universal, how are cultural factors involved? That is, are there rules for how emotions are displayed? For example, smiles appear to be seen all over the world in humans. However, there are cross-cultural differences in terms of when and how to display smiles. In a clever series of studies, Ekman and others have shown that, although the ability to recognize an emotional expression may be universal, people do not always allow themselves to make the expression. That is, one characteristic of humans is that we are able to regulate our emotions and their expression (Tottenham, 2017).

To examine emotional expression cross-culturally, Paul Ekman showed films of surgery and accidents to Americans and Japanese individually (see Ekman, 1999b). When they were viewing the films alone, people from both cultures showed the same facial expression to the films. However, if there was an experimenter in the room with the person while they were watching the films, the Japanese more than the Americans would not fully display their emotional reactions. Thus, situational and cultural factors can influence emotional expression. These are called *"display rules."*

In order to better understand display rules, David Matsumoto and his colleagues examined emotional expression in some 32 countries (Matsumoto et al., 2008). As would be expected, across the world, people are more willing to express their emotions in groups they are a part of as compared to strangers.

Another distinction that was made by these researchers was whether the culture emphasized individualism versus a collective approach. For example, the United States emphasizes the individual and his or her achievement. On the other hand, some countries such as China define people in terms of the group they are a part of. **Figure 10-11** shows the relationship between emotional expression and individualism in the countries studied. As you can see, there is a positive correlation between the amount of emotional expression and the degree of individualism across countries. That is, those whose culture stresses individualism are more likely to show their emotions than those whose culture emphasizes the group.

Evolutionary Perspectives of Emotionality

The basic perspective from the standpoint of evolutionary psychology is that emotions evolved for their adaptive value in dealing with *fundamental life tasks* (Ekman, 1999a; Al-Shawaf, Conroy-Beam, Asao, & Buss, 2016). Fundamental life tasks are universal human predicaments such as losses, frustrations, and achievements. Specially, these events can include fighting, falling in love, escaping predators, and so forth (Tooby & Cosmides, 1990). The important implication is that our current emotional expression and experience is directly influenced by our ancestral past. In general, similar cortical and neurochemical

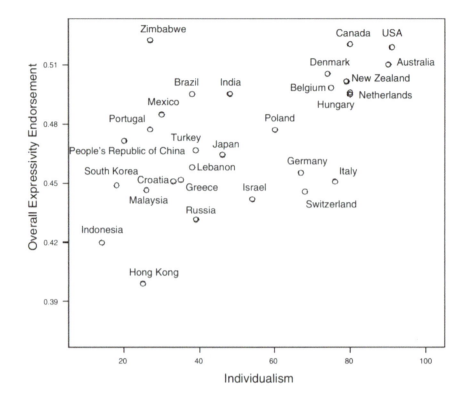

Figure 10-11 The relationship between emotional expression and individualism.

Source: Matsumoto, Yoo, and Fontaine (2008).

mechanisms involved in emotional experience and expression can be found across a variety of species. For example, current research suggests that facial expressions seen in primates during play and during submission map onto the human expressions of laughter and smiling, respectively (Ekman, Campos, & de Waal, 2003).

One researcher who has connected emotionality with basic life tasks is Jaak Panksepp. Panksepp (1998, 2004, 2017) suggested that there are basic systems from which emotions develop. These systems are anger, fear, sexual lust, maternal care, separation distress, and social bonding, as well as playfulness and a resource acquisition system. He further suggests that these can also be seen to be related to particular psychopathologies. Below are the emotional systems and the psychopathologies that develop from them.

1. Anger or rage is evoked when there is stiff competition for resources. This system can also be aroused by restraint, frustration, and other irritations. Out of this system can emerge irritability, contempt, and hatred. Psychopathologies associated with this system would be those involving aggression, such as conduct disorders in children, psychopathic tendencies, and personality disorders.
2. Fear is evoked when the organism is in the presence of danger. This system will evoke freezing at low levels of arousal and flight at higher levels. Research suggests that external stimuli may be processed at fast, but less-conscious, levels through low-level brain circuits or slower, but more accurately, at high cognitive levels. Out of this system can emerge simple anxiety, worry, and psychic trauma. Psychopathologies associated with this system include generalized anxiety disorder (GAD), phobias, and various forms of post-traumatic stress disorder (PTSD).
3. Sexual lust becomes manifest during puberty, although the basic components of the system exist early in the development of the organism. Out of this system can emerge

erotic feelings, as well as jealousy. Psychopathologies associated with this system include fetishes and sexual addictions.

4. Care systems are designed to allow us to nurture one another. Out of this system can emerge nurturance, love, and attraction. Psychopathologies associated with this system include dependency disorders, attachment disorders, and aloofness.

5. Separation distress is seen when a young organism is separated from its mother. In a variety of species, the infant will cry out in these situations. Extreme cases become more of a panic situation. Panksepp suggests that these feelings of abandonment may build on early pain circuits. Out of this system can emerge sadness, guilt, shame, and shyness. Psychopathologies associated with this system include panic attacks, pathological grief, depression, agoraphobia, and social phobia.

6. Play is seen in a variety of species and is often accompanied by the expression of joy and laughter. As we saw earlier, play is considered an important preparation for later social life. Out of this system can emerge joy and happy playfulness. Psychopathologies associated with this system include mania and disorders of hyperactivity, such as attention deficit hyperactivity disorder (ADHD).

7. The seeking system controls our desire to find and harvest the resources of the world. Across species, it is related to the motivation to obtain resources from the environment. In humans, it is connected with goal-directed urges and positive expectations concerning the world, as well as with awareness and appraisals of the world. Out of this system can emerge interest, frustration, and caring. Psychopathologies associated with this system include obsessive compulsive disorders (OCD), paranoid schizophrenia, and addictive disorders.

CONCEPT CHECK

1. Explain why it has been difficult for researchers to settle on a single definition for *emotion*.
2. Describe four methods that have been used to study emotions scientifically.
3. Charles Darwin used a categorical approach to studying emotions, while Wundt emphasized the dimensions of emotions. How can we understand emotions as both categories and dimensions?
4. What important contributions did Charles Darwin make to our study of emotions?
5. Describe Paul Ekman's research to determine whether emotional expression is universal or culturally determined. What was his conclusion?
6. In what ways do "display rules" impact emotional expression?
7. What are the seven basic systems that Jaak Panksepp proposed for understanding how emotions evolved because of their adaptive value in dealing with fundamental life tasks?

Nature of Basic Emotions

What is a basic emotion? One way to answer this question is to consider what criteria are common to all emotions. Ekman suggested a set of characteristics common to all emotions (Ekman, 1999a). They are:

1. distinctive universal signals—By this Ekman is referring to a distinctive facial expression that goes with each of the basic emotions. As illustrated by the facial expressions presented by Darwin or the experimental procedure described by Ekman, a specific facial expression is associated with each of the basic emotions.
2. emotion-specific physiology—This means that underlying emotional states are distinctive patterns of physiological activity expressed in the central and autonomic nervous systems. Indeed, in a variety of studies it has been shown that autonomic nervous system activity displays different patterns for anger, fear, disgust, and sadness.
3. automatic appraisal mechanism—The basic idea is that there is a very fast—usually out-of-awareness—process that allows for appraisal of both internal and external stimuli.
4. universal antecedent events—In sadness, for example, there is a loss of someone or something significant to the person.
5. distinctive appearance developmentally—This suggests that each emotion may appear developmentally across individuals in the same order.
6. present in non-human primates—Current research, as well as Darwin's observations, suggests that non-human primates share most if not all emotional expressions with humans.
7. quick onset—The basic idea is that emotions are quick and that is their survival value. You see something disgusting, have a reaction, and move away.
8. brief duration—The basic idea is that emotions are short term.
9. unbidden occurrence—The basic idea is that emotions are spontaneous. This simply means that individuals do not plan to have an emotional reaction.

One current example of these characteristics of emotions is that of LeDoux's (1994) research. He describes the presence of a second visual system that runs through the midbrain, allowing for quick responses without the visual clarity of our normal visual system. Such a system might cause you to jump as you walk through the woods if you see a snake-like structure on the ground in front of you. It is only through the slower normal visual system that you can make a distinction of whether what you saw was a snake or a stick. From an evolutionary self-preservation perspective, it is better to be wrong and think a stick is a snake than vice versa. The basic idea is that emotions are quick and that is their survival value. You see something disgusting, for example, have a reaction, and move away.

For clarity, it is important to distinguish emotions from moods, which are more long-lasting. It is also possible to turn an emotion into a mood by the continued presence of the stimuli or by talking to yourself about the situation. Neuroscience research involving emotions are sometimes referred to as affective neuroscience.

A number of researchers including Ekman followed Darwin's lead to suggest there is a finite number of basic emotions (Tomkins, 1965). In the 1980s Silvan Tomkins articulated the basic theoretical ideas that directed emotion research during the last quarter of the 20th century. One idea is that affect is a separate system and works as an amplified response, which gives a sense of urgency to basic cognitive processes as memory, perception, thought, and action (Tomkins, 1984). Another one of Tomkins's ideas was that the body response produced by emotions is centered on the face.

Various researchers have described these in slightly different terms, although most include anger, disgust, fear, happiness, sadness, and surprise. Sometimes contempt is included, although this shows less universality across studies (Elfenbein & Ambady, 2002). The analogy to this approach is similar to seeing colors. With colors, there are basic primary colors recognized by all people from which combinations may be made. Similarly, basic emotions can combine to have complex blends or combinations.

Classic studies in facial recognition have been conducted by Paul Ekman and Carroll Izard and others over the past 40 years, suggesting universality in emotional facial recognition in both literate and preliterate cultures. A meta-analysis describing almost 100 separate studies with over 20,000 participants further supports the existence of these emotional universals (Elfenbein & Ambady, 2002). As would be expected, emotions are most accurately rated if they are judged by the same national, ethnic, or regional groups that expressed the emotion. As with language, environment plays a role in shaping the expression and recognition of basic emotions.

Underlying Dimensions of Emotionality

In the late 1800s, Wundt sought to find the elements that underlie emotionality (Wundt, 1896). He constructed three-dimensional variables. The first was a dimensional scale ranging from pleasure to displeasure, which is referred to as valence. The second was a scale ranging from tension to relief referred to as arousal, and the third was a scale ranging from excitation to calm referred to as power. Over the years these dimensions have come to be described as valence, arousal, and power. Most recent utilizations of this approach have emphasized valence (positive–negative) and arousal (activation–deactivation) as underlying the experience of emotionality (Russell, 1980, 2003, 2009). Power is typically not included in this conceptualization.

In order to test this, James Russell asked individuals to rate a variety of emotional words. Russell's model suggests the experience of any emotion can be seen as reflecting a point related to the degree of arousal and the degree of pleasure (Russell, 1980). This can be diagramed, as shown in **Figure 10-12**.

The dimensional approach emphasizes the experience of emotionality and sees pleasure and displeasure as core concepts (Barrett, Mesquita, Ochsner, & Gross, 2007). It also emphasizes the situational and cultural variants in emotional experiences. However, brain-imaging studies have shown that different arousal and valence states are reflected in different patterns of brain activation (Baucom, Wedell, Wang, Blitzer, & Shinkareva, 2012).

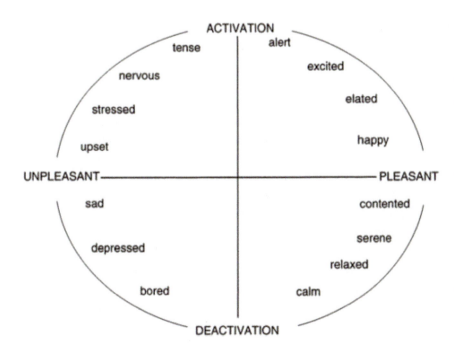

Figure 10-12 A graphical representation of the circumplex model of affect with the horizontal axis representing the valence dimension and the vertical axis representing the arousal or activation dimension.

Source: Posner, Russell, and Peterson (2005).

In another series of studies, Peter Kuppens and his colleagues examined the relationship between valence and arousal (Kuppens, Tuerlinckx, Russell, & Barrett, 2013). What they found was that arousal increases as one approaches the extreme stages of valence. That is, high arousal is associated with feeling miserable as well as feeling happy. There is less arousal with feeling states found in the middle of the valence continuum. They also found that when reporting similar feelings, there are great individual differences in terms of valence and arousal. This suggests that the valence–arousal dimensions are not universal for every person. Further, it is possible for a person to have mixed emotions and actually feel happy and sad at the same time (Russell, 2017).

Historical Theories of Emotionality

Historically, emotions have been described in terms of three separate components. These are the physiological response, the behavioral response, and the emotional experience or feeling. Further the physiological response has been divided into that of the brain and that of the bodily response, such as heart rate and blood pressure changes. At the end of the 19th century and throughout the 20th century, three major approaches were suggested to describe the nature of emotion generation. These were the James–Lange theory developed in the 1880s, the Cannon–Bard theory developed in the 1920s, and the Schachter–Singer theory developed in the 1960s. One key element in these theories was the role of the brain and the role of the peripheral physiological activity.

James-Lange Theory

William James's theory of emotions evolved out of his understanding of the research of his day (James, 1884). At that time, sensory processing and movement processes were well studied in terms of their relationship to the brain. James, who thought that humans have more instincts than other animals, places the creation of emotions within this context. That is, we see a bear and react in an automatic manner. Our heart rate increases and we may tremble. For James, our experience of these bodily manifestations is the emotion. That is, we see a bear, our body reacts, and we call the experience of this reaction an emotion. In this way he turned the common sense sequence of events backwards. Carl Lange developed a similar theory independently and thus today we refer to the James–Lange theory of emotion. Overall, the James–Lange theory of emotion suggests our experience of emotion occurs from peripheral activity in our body rather than from the brain's initial reaction.

Cannon-Bard Theory

Walter Cannon, who was a physiologist at Harvard and a former student of James, suggested that the peripheral physiological responses to seeing a bear, for example, were too slow to precede the experience of an emotion (Cannon, 1927). Further, he suggested that we see similar reactions, such as increased heart rate, to a number of environmental stimuli, making it difficult to experience different emotions from non-brain physiology alone. Working with a doctoral student of his, Philip Bard, Cannon and Bard offered an alternative to the James–Lange theory of emotion some 40 years later. Unlike the James–Lange theory in which one step is followed by another, Cannon and Bard suggested that brain and body physiological reactions could occur at the same time. Thus, you can experience an emotion as created by your brain and a bodily reaction produced separately.

Schachter-Singer Theory

Some 40 years after the Cannon–Bard theory was published, the social psychologists Stanley Schachter and Jerome Singer suggested a combination of the James–Lang and Cannon–Bard theories (Schachter & Singer, 1962). This came to be referred to as a two-factor theory of emotion and the cognitive-arousal theory of emotion. The first factor was the suggestion that the physiological response to many emotional events was basically the same. That is, there is physiological arousal associated with many emotional events involving happiness, surprise, fear and anger. This arousal was then interpreted according to the situation and thus received a label. In this way, you experience arousal and then seek an explanation to understand this arousal.

They tested this idea by giving adrenaline, which produces arousal, to groups of participants (Schachter & Singer, 1962). One group was told they would experience the symptoms associated with adrenaline such as a higher heart rate. The other group was told that they were injected with vitamins and would not experience anything. After the injection, they met a confederate of the experimenters who either acted in a manner that would provoke a happy or angry response. In response to the experience of arousal, the second group reported that they were feeling either happy or angry, whereas the first group attributed their reactions to the adrenaline. Thus, the Schachter–Singer theory suggests that your experience of an emotion is based on both basic internal reactions as well as your interpretation of these experiences.

Physiological Systems Involved in Emotion

Which parts of the brain are important for the processing of emotional information? A number of studies in a variety of species including humans are beginning to answer this question (Bennett & Hacker, 2005). Although various brain areas are involved with different emotions, it is not the case that one brain area is only involved with one emotion. Rather a number of networks involving different brain areas are involved with different emotions (Kragel & LaBar, 2016). Using statistical techniques, it is possible to show which brain areas show activation during particular emotions, such as surprise, fear, anger, and sadness (Kragel, Knodt, Hariri, & LaBar, 2016). **Figure 10-13** shows the results from one such network analysis.

It is important to realize that the neural organization involved in emotionality can span multiple levels of the brain depending on the nature of the emotional response (see Tucker, Derryberry, & Luu, 2000, for an overview). For example, at the brain stem level including

Figure 10-13 Areas of the brain associated with the experience of discrete emotions. Notice that different areas of the brain are involved with different emotions.

Source: Kragel, Knodt, Hariri, and LaBar (2016).

the pons, one can see basic representations of laughing and crying. The basic brain stem level controls many of the basic physiological processes involved in movement, chewing, eye movement, and facial expression as well as levels of arousal involving the sympathetic and parasympathetic nervous systems. Even in rare cases when an infant is born with only a brain stem, he or she is still able to show facial displays of pleasure and distress. When this occurs, it is difficult to distinguish emotional responses from those involved in motivational processes. In fact, some researchers have suggested that emotion is always involved in motivation to action or its inhibition.

Emotionality involves our total body (de Gelder, 2016). When we are walking in the woods or on a dark street in the city at night, a slight sound can quickly give us an emotional reaction of surprise or fear. In this case our sensory systems play an important role. The *autonomic nervous system*, which will be discussed in detail in the next chapter, can increase our heart rate and blood flow in relation to an unexpected event. Overall, this gives us the experience of arousal. The autonomic nervous system is regulated by the hypothalamus, which is also important for motivation. Thus, the brain is crucial for both motivation and emotion.

As you read previously, the hypothalamus is part of a system referred to as the limbic system. Other areas, as shown in **Figure 10-14** of the limbic system, are parts of the thalamus, the amygdala, the hippocampus, and the cingulate gyrus. The limbic system is sometimes referred to as the *emotional brain* in the same way that the occipital lobe is referred to as the *visual brain*. Of course, emotional processing does not take place totally in only one area of the brain without connections to other cortical networks.

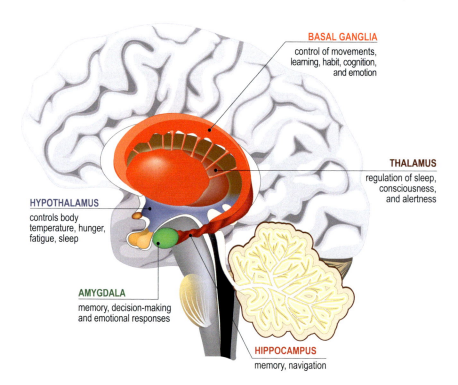

Figure 10-14
Structures and areas in the limbic system. The limbic system is associated with emotional processing.

One of the first reviews of the brain-imaging literature suggested that particular brain areas are involved with different tasks that reflect different emotions (Phan, Wager, Taylor, & Liberzon, 2002). They found six specific relationships. First, the medial prefrontal cortex has a general role in many emotional tasks. Second, fear specifically engages the amygdala. Third, sadness was associated with activity in the subcallosal cingulate. Fourth, if the person viewed emotional material, then the occipital lobe was activated along with the amygdala. Fifth, if memory or imagery was used to create the emotional experience, then the insula and anterior cingulate was activated. The insula, which is involved in our sense of self, is also involved in our experience of emotion (Craig, 2016). And sixth, in emotional tasks that required cognitive effort, activation was seen in the anterior cingulate and the insula. Let us now turn to specific brain areas involved in emotion.

The type of task is critical. Emotional memory tasks involve the hippocampus to a greater extent than some other structures. Fear processing includes the amygdala. Seeing emotional faces includes the fusiform face area (FFA) of the temporal lobe. Overall, in research utilizing emotional stimuli and emotional responses, the limbic system has been shown to be critical.

One prime brain structure for involvement in emotion is the amygdala (see Adolphs, Tranel, Damasio, & Damasio, 1994; Méndez-Bértolo et al., 2016). The amygdala, as the name implies in Latin, is an almond-shaped structure found on each side of the brain. It is a subcortical area found in the frontal part of the temporal lobe. The amygdala receives processed sensory information and also has a direct connection to the olfactory bulb. Structures involved in memory and attention such as the hippocampus, basal ganglia, and basal forebrain connect to the amygdala. The amygdala also has direct connections with the frontal lobes, which are involved in planning and decision-making. Given these connections, the amygdala sits between external information brought in through our sensory systems and the necessary attentional, memory, and emotional responses.

The amygdala shows faster responses when confronted with threating stimuli as opposed to pleasant ones (Méndez-Bértolo et al., 2016). In electrophysiological studies with primates, the amygdala shows the highest levels of responding to threatening face displays. On the other hand, scenes of grooming or huddling show less responding. There are actually two amygdala, one on each side of the limbic system. With humans, brain-imaging studies show greater left amygdala activity when viewing fearful faces as opposed to happy ones. The level of change in amygdala activity correlates with the intensity of the expression. There is also data to show that you make a larger amygdala response when seeing fear faces in individuals of your own culture than in individuals of another culture (Chiao, 2018).

Both humans and monkeys who have had damage to this area do not respond appropriately to fearful faces, as was the case of SM described in the feature Real World Psychology later in this chapter. Lack of sleep can also influence the connection between the amygdala and the frontal cortex, which results in problems in emotional recognition and expression (Goldstein & Walker, 2014).

Humans normally remember emotional material better than non-emotional material and this can even influence future learning (Tambini, Rimmele, Phelps, & Davachi, 2017). With damage to the amygdala, this is not the case. Most recent research with the amygdala extends the view of the amygdala processing negative emotions to a structure involved in any event that may have major negative significance for an individual. In non-human primates, there is a long tradition showing the role of the amygdala in social processes, especially those related to dominance. Monkeys normally establish dominance hierarchies with the alpha male being the one in charge. Following damage to the amygdala, the monkey would no longer display any aggressive behavior. Overall, the amygdala is seen to play an important role in the evaluation of both emotional and social processes.

The amygdala has projections that go to the temporal lobe. This allows it to be involved in emotional recognition involving both emotional face perception and emotional memories. The area of the right temporal lobe, the fusiform gyrus, appears to respond selectively to faces as compared to other types of complex visual stimuli, and networks with the amygdala are thought to process the emotional content of the face. In terms of memories, scientists make the distinction between explicit memories and implicit memories. In relation to emotionality, implicit memories would involve the internal feeling or how one felt in a particular situation and explicit memories would involve details of the external situation. These two aspects of emotional memory are influenced differently by damage to the amygdala and areas of the temporal lobes (Bennett & Hacker, 2005). Damage to the amygdala interferes with emotional memories that are implicit but not explicit. Damage to areas of the temporal lobe on the other hand do the opposite. It interferes with explicit memories but not the implicit ones. Thus, with temporal lobe damage you could remember feeling a certain way but not the situation in which it occurred.

Another part of the brain involved in emotional processes is the prefrontal cortex, especially the bottom third of it, which is called the orbitofrontal cortex (see Berridge, 2003 for an overview). In a variety of studies, the left frontal area has been seen to mediate positive affect, whereas the right is related to negative affect. Neurons in the prefrontal cortex have been shown to fire when the organism sees foods it likes. However, unlike the amygdala, damage to the prefrontal cortex does not result in a loss of emotional reactions. The involvement of this area in emotionality appears to be of a higher level. For example, individuals with damage to this area appear not to incorporate the emotional consequences of their own actions into their everyday behaviors. It has also been suggested that this area is related to our ability to induce an emotion in ourselves through cognitive means or to reduce an emotional reaction.

As we saw in the chapter on brain evolution, the complexity of the human brain has allowed for a type of emotional functioning different from that of other animals. We can think about our emotions. We can inhibit them. We can voluntarily create them. They also influence our cognitions (Phelps, 2006). Difficulties in emotional control and regulation are associated with a number of mental disorders including schizophrenia (Sheppes, Suri, & Gross, 2015; Kring & Elis, 2013). As Hughlings Jackson noted, our higher level cognitive processes can re-represent and thus transform the lower level emotional processes. In such a process we can add new features to an emotional reaction. We can also experience emotional responses to symbolic objects such as the flag of one's country or religious symbols as well as music and art. At times, an individual has a disorder that makes emotional recognition difficult. One such example is described in the box: The World Is Your Laboratory: What If You Couldn't Feel Fear?

The World Is Your Laboratory: What If You Couldn't Feel Fear?

In 1994, a case study was published in the journal *Nature* concerning a woman who had a rare genetic disorder (Adophs, Tranel, Damasio, & Damasio, 1994). This genetic disorder called Urbach–Wiethe disease resulted in almost complete destruction of the amygdala on both sides while sparing other brain structures. The destruction of the amygdala in individuals with this disorder begins at about 10 years of age. At the time of this first report, SM, as she was referred to, was 30 years old. She was cheerful and showed no problems as she completed personality and IQ tests. In fact, her social behavior was indiscriminately trusting and friendly.

Since the amygdala is associated with the experience of emotions, the researchers sought to determine her experience of emotions. To do this they showed her pictures of faces, each with a different emotional expression. These facial expressions included happiness, surprise, fear, anger, disgust, sadness, and a neutral expression. Her results were compared to others who showed brain damage but not of the amygdala. Although she could recognize and remember faces without any problem, emotional expression was more difficult for her. She rated the faces of fear, anger, and surprise less intense than did the other participants. She also had difficulty when a single face portrayed complex emotions.

During the years that followed this initial report, SM participated in a number of studies (Adolphs, Gosselin, Buchanan, Tranel, Schyns, & Damasio, 2005; Feinstein, Adolphs, & Tranel, 2016). Consistently, she has shown the inability to recognize fear from facial expressions. However, she can recognize fearful natural scenes or fear from a person's tone of voice. The question that arose was where did she look when she saw a face? To answer this question, the researchers showed her, and a set of control participants, more than 3,000

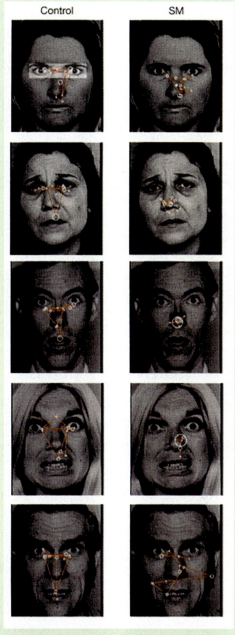

Figure 10-15 The location of where individuals look when viewing emotional faces. SM does not look at the eyes.

faces that varied in gender and were either happy or fearful. Through a series of studies, it became clear that when SM looked at faces, she did not look at the eyes. The eyes are important in the display of fear as they are opened wide with the upper eyelids raised. As can be seen in **Figure 10-15**, SM looked in the area of the nose and did not look at the eyes. Looking at the mouth makes it easier to perceive happiness but not fear. However, if instructed to look at the eyes, SM still did not recognize fear.

Even more interesting was that SM showed no reaction to experiences in which she was directly involved (Feinstein, Adolphs, Damasio, & Tranel, 2011). Although she reported not liking snakes, when the researchers took her to a pet store, she walked over and picked up one of the snakes without showing any fear. Likewise taking her to a "haunted house" or showing her emotionally evocative films did not elicit fear in SM as it did in control participants.

Where other individuals show fear, SM showed interest and arousal. In fact, in everyday situations that are dangerous, SM did not avoid danger. This resulted in her being held up at gun point as well as nearly killed in an act of domestic violence. Without the amygdala as part of larger networks, different aspects of the evolutionary value of emotional experiences are lost. However, the psychologists who work with SM see her as a survivor (Feinstein, Adolphs, & Tranel, 2016). In 2015, she celebrated her 50th birthday.

Thought Question: What if, like SM, you couldn't feel fear? How would your everyday life be affected?

CONCEPT CHECK

1. What are the nine characteristics that Paul Ekman suggests are common to all emotions?
2. Various researchers have slightly different lists of basic emotions. What is your list of basic emotions?
3. Wilhelm Wundt introduced the concept of looking at the underlying dimensions of emotionality by specifying three dimensions: valence, arousal, and power. Over time, how have these three dimensions changed in meaning and in our understanding of how they are related?
4. Three major approaches have been suggested to describe how emotions are generated. What are they? What is the unique contribution of each of them?
5. How would you describe how different brain areas are involved with different emotions, for example, is it a one-to-one matching, all brain areas are involved with all emotions, or something else?
6. In what ways does emotionality involve our total body?
7. What system is referred to as the *emotional brain*? What structures are part of that system?
8. The amygdala is a central player in emotionality. List at least five processes or tasks in which it plays an important role.
9. "The complexity of the human brain has allowed for a type of emotional functioning different from that of other animals." List at least four ways in which this is true.

Summary

Leaning Objective 1: Discuss the processes that influence how people are motivated.

Motivation is defined as the process that makes a person move toward a goal-directed behavior. Psychologists focus more on the mechanisms that create the states traditionally referred to as needs and drives. One characteristic of needs or drives is that there is a goal state that is sought. We can think of experiences such as being hungry as having the goal of finding food. We can also describe the subjective experience of feeling satisfied after eating. On a physiological level, we can consider the changes that take place in the gastrointestinal system and the brain structures that interact. One term used to describe this process is *homeostasis*.

Maslow's Hierarchy of Needs pyramid describes five basic sets of needs: (1) physiological needs such as hunger, thirst, sleep, breathing, and sexuality; (2) safety needs, which include the need for security, stability, protection, and order; (3) belongingness and love needs, which include the desire to be part of a family or group; (4) esteem needs, which include the desire for achievement, mastery, competence, and independence; (4b) a subset of esteem needs, which include the desire for reputation, prestige, status, and appreciation; and (5) the need for self-actualization, representing a person's desire for self-fulfillment.

To perform behaviors for the seeking of rewards is referred to as *extrinsic motivation*. We perform behaviors because we enjoy it. We play video games, listen to music, read books, or exercise for the experience itself. This is referred to as *intrinsic motivation*.

Learning Objective 2: Summarize the mechanisms that affect our motivation for food.

Food plays an important role in the life of humans. On a basic level, we need food to supply energy to support our daily functioning. The desire for food can be seen on a number of levels going from culture to genes. Food also plays an important role in our social and cultural life.

Feeling hungry and feeling full is also a homeostatic system that balances the intake of calories and their expenditure to perform the functions of our body. This is a complex system that monitors energy available and that involves both our gastrointestinal (GI) system and the brain. In fact, our brain is a major component of metabolism that is involved in the creation of energy. Over the past three decades, research involving appetite regulation has identified numerous hormones that influence feeling hungry and feeling full. It is also these mechanisms that keep our weight fairly stable

There are three pillars for understanding how the brain controls appetite. The first pillar is neurons in the hypothalamus that, when activated, make us feel hungry. These are referred to as AGRP (agouti-related protein) neurons in that they produce a protein which acts to increase appetite. The activity of these neurons is more involved with food seeking rather than its consumption. The second pillar is circuits of neurons involving the lateral hypothalamus. These circuits are related to the consumption of food and the positive effects of eating. The third pillar is neurons in the hypothalamus that suppress eating when activated. They produce a protein referred to as CGRP (calcitonin gene-related peptide). After we eat food, hormones are released in the gastrointestinal system. These hormones signal a number of factors including the nature of the foods eaten, and, in turn, go to our brain, especially the hypothalamus. In one part of the hypothalamus, there are two different sets of neurons.

CDC data suggest that 33.9% of Americans over the age of 20 are obese and 34.4% are overweight. There is a difference in these statistics by state. All states show an increase in obesity over the past 20 years. In terms of adolescents, there has also been an increase in obesity for both boys and girls in the latest data over 20 years. The three major eating disorders are *anorexia nervosa*, *bulimia nervosa*, and *binge-eating disorder.*

Learning Objective 3: Explain the factors that affect our sexual motivation.
Sexuality is a driving force in many species including humans. Most primates only engage in sexual activity when there is a high probability of producing offspring. Humans, on the other hand, may engage in sexual activity at any time. Humans use the internal experience of sexual arousal and the external experience of sexual activity for a variety of purposes. This suggests that sexual activity for humans goes beyond basic motivation and has an important pair bonding and social component.

Humans have depicted sexual activities in paintings and carvings for thousands of years. Some of the more famous are Etruscan ceramic plates, showing a variety of sexual positions dating from some 2,500 years ago in Italy. However, in the 18th and 19th centuries in Europe and the United States, some cultures have seen sexual activity as a negative force in human life. Also, in the 1800s, Charles Darwin, Sigmund Freud, and Havelock Ellis began to approach sexuality from a scientific perspective. In the 1930s, Alfred Kinsey conducted a large-scale survey of some 12,000 individuals across the United States. The results of these surveys were published in two books: *Sexual Behavior in the Human Male* (1948) and *Sexual Behavior in the Human Female* (1953). In 1947, the Institute for Sex Research was established at Indiana University with Alfred Kinsey as director. This was later renamed the Kinsey Institute and continues performing research related to sexuality.

In 2016, the Centers for Disease Control and Prevention (CDC) surveyed a national sample of 10,416 males and females in the United States. Among males and females 15–44 years of age, 92% of males and 94.2% of females have had vaginal intercourse. Further, 87.4% of males and 86.2% of females have had oral sex with a member of the opposite sex. Anal sex with the opposite sex was lower: 42.3% for males and 35.9% for females. In this survey, any reported same-sex contact was 6.2% for males and 17.4% for females. This included people who saw themselves as bisexual and homosexual/lesbian. This survey was updated from 2002 and 2011 surveys, which showed similar results.

In studying the sexual responses of males and females, Masters and Johnson realized that there was a similarity in how men and women experienced the sexual experience (Masters & Johnson, 1966). They identified four phases of the human sexual response, which are (1) excitement; (2) plateau; (3) orgasm; and (4) resolution.

Learning Objective 4: Discuss the scientific understanding of emotionality.
An emotion is a positive or negative feeling that is in response to a particular behavior or physiological activity. Also, emotions are not only expressed in our faces, but also in our voice and touch as when we hug one another.

One critical scientist in the study of emotions is Charles Darwin. In *The Expression of the Emotions in Man and Animals,* Darwin portrays a careful observation of emotionality. Throughout his book, Darwin presents drawings and photographs of people and animals as they express different emotions. The common theme is that emotions are universal and represent an example of evolution through natural selection.

By the end of the 20th century, researchers such as Paul Ekman had followed Darwin's tradition by studying facial expressions cross-culturally and demonstrating the universality of emotional expression. For example, Ekman performed interesting research in New Guinea by showing individuals different emotional facial expressions and asking them to tell a story that causes the person to look the way they were in the picture. He also performed the research in reverse manner, in which a story was told without using emotional terms. The person was then asked which of a series of emotional faces would best represent the person in the story. This type of research supported the idea that both emotional recognition and emotional expression were universal.

Learning Objective 5: Discuss the major theories of emotion.
Historically, emotions have been described in terms of three separate components. These are the physiological response, the behavioral response, and the emotional experience or feeling. Throughout the 20th century, three major approaches were suggested to describe the nature of emotion generation. These were the James–Lange theory developed in the 1880s, the Cannon–Bard theory developed in the 1920s, and the Schachter–Singer theory developed in the 1960s. One key element in these theories was the role of the brain and the role of the peripheral physiological activity.

Several brain areas play key roles in the experience of emotion. First, the medial prefrontal cortex has a general role in many emotional tasks. Second, fear specifically engages the amygdala. Third, sadness was associated with activity in the subcallosal cingulate. Fourth, if the person viewed emotional material, then the occipital lobe was activated along with the amygdala. Fifth, if memory or imagery was used to create the emotional experience, then the insula and anterior cingulate was activated. And sixth, in emotional tasks that required cognitive effort, activation was seen in the anterior cingulate and the insula. Emotional memory tasks involve the hippocampus to a greater extent than some other structures. Fear processing includes the amygdala. Seeing emotional faces includes the fusiform face area (FFA) of the temporal lobe. Overall, in research utilizing emotional stimuli and emotional responses, the limbic system has been shown to be critical.

Study Resources

Review Questions

1. How is motivation related to learning in humans? Describe and develop a comprehensive learning environment for young children using Maslow's hierarchy of needs.
2. From an evolutionary perspective, what is the functional role of motivation in our human history?
3. What roles do motivation and emotion play in the development and treatment of eating disorders?
4. What are the relationships between motivation and sexuality in humans?
5. What are the relationships between emotions and sexuality in humans?
6. Construct a comprehensive model of human sexuality beginning with Masters and Johnson's model of human sexual response and incorporating other contextual factors covered in this chapter, for example, gender differences and role of culture.
7. What is an emotion? How have various researchers from different time periods answered this question? What research questions did they ask? What is your answer to the question of what is an emotion? What research questions would you like to ask?
8. From an evolutionary perspective, what is the functional role of emotionality in our human history?
9. In what ways are emotions similar across animals and humans?

For Further Reading

Asma, S., & Gabriel, R. (2019). *The Emotional Mind: The Affective Roots of Culture and Cognition.* Cambridge, MA: Harvard University Press.

Ekman, P., Campos, J., Davidson, R., & de Waal, F. (2003). *Emotions Inside Out: 130 Years after Darwin's The Expression of Emotions in Man and Animals.* New York: New York Academy of Sciences.

Johnston, E., & Olson, L. (2015). *The Feeling Brain: The Biology and Psychology of Emotions.* New York: W.W. Norton & Co.

Web Resources

CDC eating guideline—https://www.cdc.gov/nccdphp/dnpao/features/healthy-eating-tips/ and https://www.cdc.gov/healthyweight/healthy_eating/index.html
HHS dietary guidelines—http://health.gov/dietaryguidelines/
CDC weight—https://www.cdc.gov/nchs/fastats/obesity-overweight.htm
Kinsey Institute—https://kinseyinstitute.org/
CDC sexual activity—https://www.cdc.gov/nchs/data/nhsr/nhsr088.pdf
Sexual attitudes—http://www.nationalsexstudy.indiana.edu/
Reactions to fear—https://www.scientificamerican.com/article/feeling-our-emotions/

Key Terms and Concepts

anorexia nervosa	extrinsic motivation	satiety
binge-eating disorder	homeostasis	self-actualization
body mass index	intrinsic motivation	sexuality
bulimia nervosa	motivations	
emotions	purging	

11 Stress and Health

LEARNING OBJECTIVES

11.1 Define stress and the ways people experience and respond to stress.

11.2 Discuss the early approaches to the study of stress.

11.3 Describe the autonomic nervous system (ANS).

11.4 Discuss the research that suggests that social relationships provide a protective mechanism in improving health and managing stress.

11.5 Explain the role of behavioral and emotional processes in the expectation of health outcomes.

Imagine you work in a large corporation. Everything seems to be going fine and then you hear that a number of people in your organization are losing their jobs. All of a sudden, your boss calls you into her office. How do you react? If you are like most people, you probably feel apprehensive. As you walk into her office, you may notice your heart beating a little faster and subjectively feeling anxious. Your boss then says sit down. As you wait for the worst, she says that she appreciates your hard work and would like to take you to lunch to hear more of your ideas. Although you clearly feel relieved, your body still continues to have an anxious feeling.

What Is Stress?

This chapter focuses on stress and health. As you can see in the scenario just presented, psychological factors play a critical role in how we experience stress. We can experience stress both from real situations and from our expectations of what might happen. Even after the event has passed, our body can continue to display characteristics of stress. Further, stress plays an important role in determining our health (O'Connor, Thayer, & Vedhara, 2021). How our body works in reaction to stress is an important aspect of this chapter.

Think about this. If you were to discover a wild animal in your path, as might have happened to our ancestors, what would you do? Your first instinct would be to leave the situation. In order to leave, you would need the ability to supply your body with the energy needed to move your legs as fast as possible, which includes your heart beating faster and your lungs obtaining more oxygen. Indeed, as you will see in this chapter, our body has such a system for dealing with threat. It is generally referred to as the *stress response*. It is also referred to as the *fight or flight response*.

Animals know who their predators are. They know when to run. As humans, we are different in that we don't have predators who view us as their food. Of course, there are a number of ways that we humans can get into trouble. Unlike other animals, humans have no single predator. However, we do assess whether there is danger.

Stress responses have developed over our evolutionary history. The evolutionary logic of survival is one of the easiest to comprehend. If an organism is not able to successfully respond to threat, it can be hurt or killed. If it is killed, its genes can no longer be passed on. If it is hurt, this may make it a less appealing mate or less able to seek mates. Thus, it is expected that organisms will have evolved sophisticated mechanisms that benefit survival.

Over evolutionary time, organisms, including humans, have developed processes that protect them in dangerous situations. Animals never know when they could be attacked and eaten. This is the world of nature. However, as humans, we live more in culture than in nature and the chance of us seeing a bear is not a common experience. What we experience as stressful situations may not be life-threatening at all. For many people, flying on an airplane or giving a speech are stressful tasks.

Scientifically, stress is a difficult concept to define. The term is used in everyday language and in scientific research in a number of different ways. **Stress** is commonly defined as a response that is brought on by any situation that threatens a person's ability to cope. Scientists speak of the **stress response** as a response to a critical situation that allows an organism to avoid danger or reduce other types of threat.

Stress is actually a complicated process that takes place on a number of levels. The cognitive level, that is, what we tell ourselves, is an important level. Physiologically, our body reacts without consciousness awareness. For example, some people show a higher blood pressure reading just by going to see a doctor. The *white coat syndrome* is so well known to medical professionals that they commonly take a second blood pressure measurement at the end of the examination. This second measurement typically shows a lower blood pressure reading.

Our bodies have a number of responses related to stress. For example, all individuals show a startle response when hearing an unexpected loud noise. Babies bring their arms and legs toward their chest. Adults typically blink their eyes and show flinching in their muscles. Some people also show unlearned reactions to looking down from a high place. Charles Darwin spoke of visiting the zoo in London and watching the snakes behind glass. He couldn't help himself from jumping back when a snake attacked his image even though he was protected by the glass.

Culturally and socially, we may fear doing something at odds with our group and looking foolish to others. As seen previously, epigenetic changes also take place in reaction to stress. As you will see throughout this chapter, the different levels discussed in the first chapter of the book play an important role in stress. These different levels include cultural, social, individual, cognitive/emotional, physiological, brain, and genetic. As you will see, each of these levels are directly related to our responses to stress. For example, what we tell ourselves on a cultural, social, or individual level helps to identify situations in which we experience stress. Our experiences of stress involve our cognitive/emotional systems, which are determined in terms of physiological, brain, and genetic responses.

As humans, we share stress responses to similar situations. However, different individuals may respond to the same situation in very different ways. What we tell ourselves plays an important role. We as humans can talk to ourselves and characterize our world in positive and negative ways. This makes our emotional expectations and reactions an important aspect of what we consider stressful.

What if we just think there is a danger? This is part of the other side to the story. This is our ability to create our view of threat. As shown in the scenario of meeting with your boss, humans can anticipate that there is danger before actually knowing that there is a threat. Such threats can be losing a job, getting a disease, doing badly on a test, or having an accident. Unlike actually experiencing a dangerous situation, our anticipations can be totally wrong; however, our body may still show the stress response. Further, what is experienced as stressful may be different to different people.

Which of the following would be stressful to you?

- Being caught in traffic
- Being late for a meeting
- Seeing a bear
- Having two tests on the same day
- Seeing a physician
- Living with a roommate or partner you don't get along with

As you think about each of these potentially stressful events, you realize they are very different. Seeing a bear in the wild could actually place you in danger. However, being late for a meeting is stressful for how you imagine others will think of you, but it is rarely a life-or-death situation. Seeing a doctor creates stress for some people since the possibility exists that the physician may discover that they may have a serious disorder. Being caught in traffic may evoke stress differently for each person. One person might find the loss of control difficult to experience, whereas another might feel she cannot accomplish what she set out to do that day.

Historical Approaches to the Study of Stress

In the early 1900s, the French physiologist Claude Bernard (1927) realized that the brain had circuits that were specialized for monitoring and controlling internal events, which he referred to as the *internal milieu*. These internal states included physiological processes such as thirst, temperature, and metabolism. This idea of an internal monitoring of bodily states underlies the development of the concept of *homeostasis* as described previously.

In 1915, Walter Cannon at Harvard developed the concept of homeostasis to reflect the manner in which a physiological system tended to center on a set point. Homeostasis is the process in which the body keeps itself in balance. Like a thermostat, if you become too hot, your body sweats to reduce heat by processes such as sweating and if you become cold, your metabolism is increased. In this view, the body's reaction to stress was largely a passive and mechanical one. *Stress* for Cannon reflected the situation in which these systems deviated away from this set point. Thus, the concept of stress points to events that move your physiology out of balance. Cannon referred to homeostasis as the *wisdom of the body* that was controlled by the autonomic nervous system (ANS), which will be described later in this chapter (Cannon, 1932).

Another major figure in the history of stress research was the Hungarian endocrinologist Hans Selye who worked at the University of Montreal. His work in the 1930s helped to set up the connection between stress and the development of diseases. It was Selye that borrowed the term "stress" from physics. In physics, stress refers to the strain placed on a physical material. Selye used the term as a way of organizing physiological responses to a variety of challenges including heat, cold, pain, noise, hard work, and so forth. In general, in response to different stressors, Selye's laboratory animals showed peptic ulcers, enlarged adrenal glands, and negative immune system changes. One of Selye's early findings was that the body reacts similarly to a variety of different stressors. Selye called this response the **General Adaptation Syndrome (GAS)**.

The GAS involved three stages. The first was the *alarm stage*. The alarm stage was an initial reaction to the stress, which involved an increase in adrenal activity in terms of producing stress hormones and sympathetic nervous system reactions such as increased heart rate. The second stage was the *resistance stage*. This stage represents an adjustment to the stress, which includes the availability of additional energy resources and mechanisms for fighting infection and tissue damage. The third stage was the *exhaustion stage* in which bodily resources are depleted.

One paradox that Selye (1956) recognized was that the physiological stress responses that protect and restore the body can also damage it if allowed to continue over time (Selye, 1956). However, Selye also reported that repeated exposure to a particular stress situation could also increase the organism's ability to withstand that same stress in greater amounts.

More recently, Bruce McEwen has begun to suggest a more flexible set of processes that involve the brain in the regulation of the body's reaction to stress (McEwen, 2013; McEwen et al., 2015). McEwen begins by suggesting that part of the problem in understanding stress is the ambiguous meaning of the term *stress*. He suggests that the term stress be replaced with the term **allostasis**. Allostasis refers to the body's ability to achieve stability through change. His view emphasizes the brain as the means of stability, which can be accomplished in a number of different ways. That is, there is not just one single response to stress according to McEwen.

Allostatic systems are designed to adapt to change. Change traditionally related to stress for humans takes on a broad range of possibilities including dangerous situations, crowded and unpleasant environments, infection, and performing in front of others. Some researchers even suggest that stress may be greater for humans than other animals since we are also able to use our cognitive abilities to increase the experience of stress through imagination.

The overall stress response involves two tasks for the body. The first is to turn on the allostatic response that initiates a complex adaptive pathway. Once the danger has passed, the second task needs to be initiated—turning off these responses. Research suggests that prolonged exposure to stress may not allow these two mechanisms to function correctly and in turn leads to a variety of physiological problems. This cumulative wear and tear on the body by responding to stressful conditions is called **allostatic load**.

Allostatic load has been discussed by McEwen in terms of four particular situations (McEwen, 1998).

1. The first situation reflects the fact that allostatic load can be increased by frequent exposure to stressors. These stressors can be both physical and psychological in nature. A variety of psychological studies have shown an association between worry, daily hassles, and negative health outcomes. One of the most studied areas is cardiovascular risk factors with stress showing a strong association with heart attacks and the development of atherosclerosis.
2. The second condition for the increase in allostatic load is where an individual does not adapt or habituate to the repeated occurrence of a particular stressor. For example, some people continue to show larger physiological responses to everyday situations like driving a long distance or taking an airline flight even though the data suggest there is limited risk in these situations. Asking individuals to talk before a group also induces stress-like responses in many individuals.
3. The third situation reflects the fact that not all individuals respond the same to changing situations. Some individuals show a slower return to a non-challenge physiological condition once the initial threat is removed. These individuals appear to be more at

Stress and Health 443

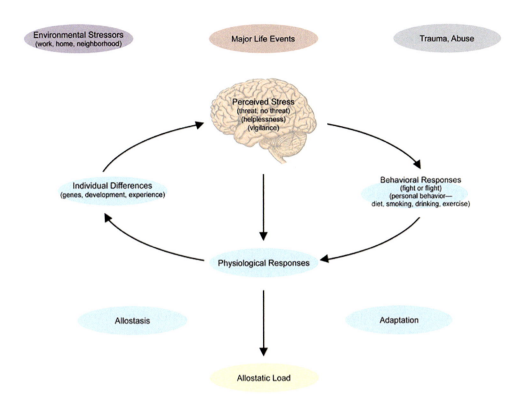

Figure 11-1 The brain interprets experience and determines what is threatening and therefore stressful.

risk for developing health-related conditions. Some researchers suggest that high blood pressure is associated with a normal stress response not being turned off.

4. The fourth and final condition discussed by McEwen reflects the situation in which a non-response to stress produces an overreaction in another system. That is, if one system does not respond adequately to stress then activation of another system would be required to provide the necessary counter-regulation and return the system to homeostasis.

Overall, McEwen emphasized the important question of individual differences and the variety of ways in which perceived stress can influence future health. His graphic depiction of the allostatic system is seen in **Figure 11-1**. Following McEwen, others have also emphasized the role of the brain in making predictions about what physiological responses are needed to ensure evolutionary fitness (Schulkin & Sterling, 2019). Research has also shown that individuals who consume a high intake of fruits, vegetables, whole grains, fish, and poultry, and who engage in physical activities have lower allostatic load in comparison to those who do not (Suvarna, Suvarna, Phillips, Juster, McDermott, & Sarnyai, 2020). This reduction in allostatic load is associated with a reduction in chronic disease.

CONCEPT CHECK

1. In what ways are the following seven levels directly related to our responses to stress: cultural, social, individual, cognitive/emotional, physiological, brain, and genetic?

2. Why is *stress* a difficult concept to define scientifically?
3. How did each of the following researchers define the term *stress* and our responses to it: Claude Bernard, Walter Cannon, Hans Selye, and Bruce McEwen?
4. Describe the three stages of Selye's *General Adaptation Syndrome (GAS)*.
5. What four particular situations or conditions does McEwen present in characterizing his concept of *allostatic load*?

Autonomic Nervous System (ANS)

We look over at the table and reach for a glass of something to drink. We put the glass back and pick up a book. These actions are voluntary, and we experience ourselves making them. Our brain sends signals through the spinal cord to the muscles involved.

Our brain also sends signals through what we experience as an involuntary system. We experience our body sweating as if someone else had made it happen. Our mouth becomes dry as we are about to give an important talk. We experience sexual arousal in a different way than reaching for a book. Sweating, dry mouth, and sexual arousal are all actions of the *autonomic nervous system (ANS)*. There is an evolutionary logic to the ANS. In a time of danger such as seeing a bear, you want to be able efficiently to do what would protect you such as run. You would need increased blood flow and thus energy to help your legs run. You would also want to shut down any process such as digestion that could interfere with your running. These responses to danger and stress are controlled by the ANS.

The **autonomic nervous system (ANS)** consists of the neural circuitry that controls the body's physiology (Wehrwein, Orer, & Barman, 2016)). This physiology involves organs such as the heart, gastrointestinal, genital, and lung systems (see **Figure 11-2**). Along with the endocrine system, the ANS manages continuous changes in blood chemistry, respiration, circulation, digestion, reproductive status, and immune responses. Two branches of the ANS are the **sympathetic nervous system** and the **parasympathetic nervous system**.

The sympathetic division of the ANS is involved in intense activity, seen in the *fight-or-flight response*. It is the purpose of the sympathetic nervous system to increase arousal and allow for a behavioral response. If we think there is danger or an emergency, it is the sympathetic branch of the ANS that is activated. Cannon (1929) suggested this happened in a diffuse, nonspecific manner. For example, if you are surprised by a bear as you walk in the woods, you run. Running requires blood, oxygen, and glucose to go to the periphery of your body to fuel your leg muscles.

As shown in **Figure 11-2**, this situation quickly turns on the sympathetic division of the ANS to ensure the ability to quickly leave the situation. Your heart speeds up and your blood vessels in the skeletal muscles enlarge. This ensures your muscles receive the energy they need to function properly. Since digestion is not needed and would use valuable blood supply, those processes are inhibited. However, glucose from the liver is increased. Also, as can be noted from **Figure 11-2**, the sympathetic division is activated at the middle (thoracic and lumbar) divisions of the spinal cord.

If you're able to escape the bear, what happens next? You need to calm down and rest! The system involved in the *rest and digest response* is the parasympathetic division of the ANS. It is the function of the parasympathetic division to return the system to homeostasis and to store energy. As can be seen in **Figure 11-2**, the parasympathetic system performs operations opposite to the sympathetic division. It shuts off what the

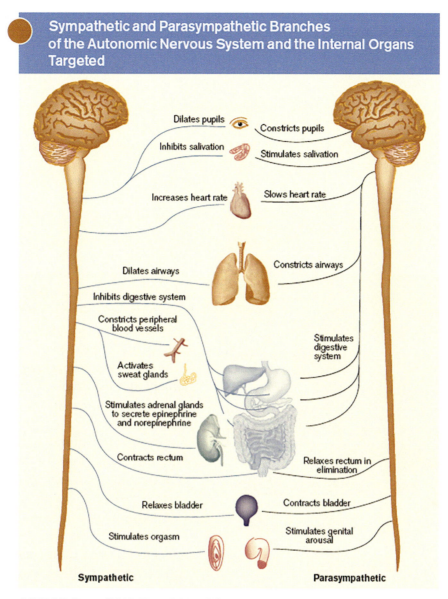

Figure 11-2 Sympathetic and parasympathetic branches of the ANS.

sympathetic division turns on and turns on those systems involved in digestion and energy storing. As noted in **Figure 11-2**, the parasympathetic division is activated through the top (cervical) and bottom (sacral) parts of the spinal cord. Although it was historically thought that the sympathetic and parasympathetic divisions worked in opposing ways, this is not always the case. We now know that they both can increase or decrease together (Berntson, Cacioppo, & Quigley, 1991; Christensen, Wild, Kenzie, Wakeland, Budding, & Lillas, 2020).

Initially, many of the systems described in this chapter, such as the autonomic nervous system, the endocrine system, and the immune system were considered to function independently. However, we now know that not only do internal pathways exist allowing for communication among the systems, but also external psychological and cultural influences can play a role. There is also recent research to suggest that a hormone released by our

446 Stress and Health

skeletal structure may also play a role in the stress response (Berger et al., 2019). Overall, our response to stress involves a number of integrated systems including our brain's ability to predict what is needed.

Physiology of Stress

One critical mechanism involved in response to stress includes the autonomic nervous system, which we just discussed, and a network of hypothalamic, pituitary, and adrenal responses shown in **Figure 11-3** as well as the cardiovascular system, metabolism, and the immune system.

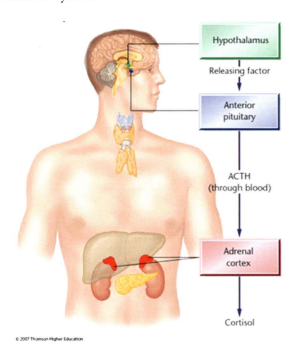

Figure 11-3 Basic mechanisms involved in response to stress.

The brain has two major pathways in which it influences peripheral physiology. These pathways are distinct but interrelated (see Gunnar & Quevedo, 2007 for an overview). The first is more fast acting and is referred to as SAM (*sympathetic adrenal medullary* system). The second pathway is slower and referred to as the HPA (hypothalamic pituitary adrenal) axis.

The **SAM (sympathetic adrenal medullary) system** involves the sympathetic division of the autonomic nervous system. As shown in **Figure 11-4**, stress can be seen to influence the body in two different ways. First, the adrenal medulla is activated, and adrenaline (epinephrine) is released. Second, nerves of the sympathetic nervous system stimulate organs of the body such as the heart and lungs to increase their output. The basic consequence of this action is to prepare the body for action.

In humans, the **HPA (hypothalamic pituitary adrenal) pathway** (**Figure 11-5**) involves the hypothalamus, which releases cortisol into the bloodstream, which goes to the pituitary gland in the brain. Cortisol is a major stress hormone, which increases glucose in your blood and thus increases energy both in your body and brain. Release of cortisol causes the pituitary to release hormones that influence other hormones, which in turn influence peripheral organs such as the adrenals and cells in the immune system. This system helps to convert stored fats and carbohydrates

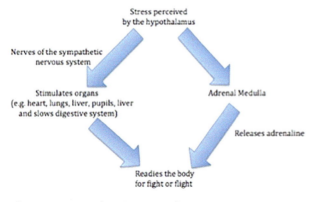

Figure 11-4 The SAM pathway.

into energy sources that can be used immediately. Over our human history, survival processes that activated this system would have involved conflict and fights, so it was important that the immune system also be activated to protect the organism from wounds.

The SAM and HPA systems have been studied as part of stress. The SAM stress response was initially described by Walter Cannon as a bodily response to danger. Although Cannon originally studied animals, since his time, research has shown the basic stress response also applies to humans.

Previously, you learned that the neuron can secrete a chemical, a *neurotransmitter*, which influences how the signal is passed to the next neuron it connects with. However, if the chemical is secreted into your bloodstream and influences different processes in your body, that chemical is referred to as a *hormone*. Thus, depending on the situation, norepinephrine, for example, can function as either a neurotransmitter or a hormone.

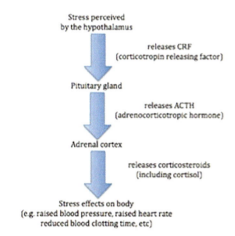

Figure 11-5 The HPA pathway.

What happens when you are faced with a potential threat? According to Cannon, your body prepares you either to fight or to leave the scene. How does it do that? Since Cannon's time, we have come to see that the stress response is accomplished by a variety of interacting systems, which include the amygdala and other cortical systems, resulting in the hypothalamus activating the sympathetic nervous system and the HPA axis. The hypothalamus is able to release hormones that increase certain processes as well as inhibit others.

Basically, the hypothalamus in your brain produces a substance referred to as CRF (corticotropin-releasing factor, also called CRH (corticotropin-releasing hormone)), which in turn produces ACTH (adrenocorticotropic hormone) in the pituitary. It is the pituitary that is able to influence glands in your body. Thus, ACTH in your blood in turn results in the adrenal glands producing cortisol. Research studies will often take a measure of cortisol to reflect the stressfulness of the situation. Cortisol can be measured by swabbing a Q-tip in your mouth.

During stress, the sympathetic nervous system releases norepinephrine and epinephrine (noradrenaline and adrenaline) into your blood stream. During this activation, your heart rate is increased, sending blood to your legs and arms so you can be ready to fight or flee. Other sympathetic responses include the dilation of the pupils, which allow you to see better in shadows and darkness, increased breathing rate, and the reduction of blood flow into organs not involved in action.

Does "Fight and Flight" Apply Equally to Males and Females?

After examining a variety of studies, Shelley Taylor and her colleagues (Taylor et al., 2000) suggest that the fight or flight response better describes a human male's response to stress and not a female's. For females, they suggest a better descriptor is the **tend and befriend response**. What do they mean by this? They make three major points.

1. They suggest that over evolutionary time, females have evolved behaviors that maximize the survival of both themselves and their offspring.
2. When stressed, females respond by nurturing offspring as well as displaying behaviors that protect them from harm. These tending behaviors have also been shown to reduce the presence of stress hormones in the infants.
3. Like fight or flight, these behaviors are associated with particular neuroendocrine responses, although different hormones are involved. One of these hormones is oxytocin.

Oxytocin is rapidly released in response to stress in females. When released, oxytocin increases affiliative behaviors. Associated with this is an increase in feeling relaxed and calm. Females under stress seek contact with their social group, which is also protective in survival terms. In many ways, this is the opposite response seen with the fight or flight response. The tend and befriend response is seen across females of a variety of species and not just human females.

These responses make up the tending response. The tending response activated by stress is seen as part of the larger attachment process that was discussed previously. The befriending response involves a large social group.

What is intriguing is that the basic neuroendocrine responses to stress appear to be similar in both males and females (Kudielka & Kirschbaum, 2005). It is an initial sympathetic response as described previously. What is different is that these hormones affect males and females differently. Human males show the sympathetic response of activation and increased arousal, which can lead to aggression—the fight part of fight or flight. The male brain appears to be organized to give aggressive responses in the presence of such substances as testosterone that are less present in the female brain.

What is present in the female brain is the hormone oxytocin, which is released in larger amounts in females compared to males. Oxytocin has been found in a variety of animal studies to reduce anxiety and calm the organism. According to Shelly Taylor and her colleagues, oxytocin leads females to quiet and calm down offspring in response to stress. Thus, whereas males are seen to produce more sympathetic-like responses to stress, females show more parasympathetic-like responses. Oxytocin is considered to lie at the basis of these responses for females—the tend and befriend response.

Additional support for the presence of gender differences in response to stress has come from the work of Repetti (1989). She examined the behaviors of fathers and mothers following a stressful workday. Whereas fathers tended to isolate themselves at home following stress, mothers tended to be more nurturing and caring toward their children. Further, similar differences also are found in the larger social networks. That is, when stressed, females tend to seek out other women for comfort and support. Compared to females, males seek support from same-sex friends less often. A variety of anthropological studies suggest that males and females form groups for different purposes. Male groups tend to be larger and directed at well-defined tasks such as defense. Female groups tend to be smaller and carry with them social and emotional connections to a greater degree.

Why did researchers initially not see differences in male and female responses to stress? The answer is simple. During most of the 20th century, females were not studied in this research. Even the animal studies typically used males. Once females were studied more intensely, then these differences were observed for the first time. If you think about it, you can see that these stress-response differences are consistent with mating differences and investment in the care of offspring. That is, given that females typically have a greater role in caring for offspring, then her response to stress should not jeopardize herself or her offspring as might be the case with fleeing or fighting.

Immune System

Our immune system is there to protect us from various germs, also called *pathogens*, that make us sick. Our immune system also produces inflammation such as that you may experience with an insect bite. As you will see, at birth our immune system already knows how to recognize and destroy some pathogens. However, our immune system can also learn to recognize new pathogens through experience. Day care and nursery school are often places children trade their sicknesses with one another. Basically, the immune system learns to recognize the presence of specific pathogens. Today, measles, chickenpox, mumps, diphtheria, whooping cough, yellow fever, and polio can be prevented through vaccines that activate the immune system. However, novel pathogens that are unknown to our immune system have caused real problems throughout human history. The COVID-19 pandemic seen in 2020 is the most recent example.

What is less well known is that stressful events activate the same immune and brain circuits as do infections (Watkins & Maier, 2002). Why is this so? Maier and Watkins suggest that the immune system first evolved to be sensitive to pathogens such as those associated with disease—for example, the common cold. It then began to use the same systems to respond to stress. In evolutionary time, the immune system is thought to have evolved before such responses as fight or flight since all organisms have mechanisms for dealing with pathogens.

Psychological factors can also affect the immune system. At one time, the immune system was viewed as a separate system that functioned independently. However, since the 1970s a variety of studies have demonstrated that the immune system is influenced by the brain and vice versa. In the 1980s, Robert Ader was able to show that the immune system could be changed through learning (see Ader, 2003 for an overview). In particular, they showed that animals could learn to associate specific experiences with changes in their immune system.

It has also been shown that stress can influence the immune system such that the organism is more likely to become ill following stress. Some early research studied medical students taking their exams, which they experienced as stressful. Yes, even taking an exam can influence your immune system. Thus, the immune system comes into play in terms of both stress and specific pathogens.

Understanding how an event was perceived could influence your immune system and how this involved brain processes created the new field of psychoneuroimmunology. One meta-analysis of more than 300 studies suggests that stress in the form of loss or trauma will suppress the immune system (Kiecolt-Glaser, McGuire, Robles, & Glaser, 2002). This review shows that negative emotions can change immune responses and delay healing. Some of the psychological factors that can influence the immune system include loneliness, poor social support, negative mood, disruption of marital relationships, bereavement, and natural disasters.

These same negative factors can also lead to psychological disorders such as anxiety and depression. It is suggested that inflammation produced by the immune system is how this comes about (Bullmore, 2019; Dooley et al., 2018). In particular, it is suggested that environmental and social stress produces an elevation in inflammation (Slavich & Irwin, 2014). This inflammation may in turn be related to the development of depression in both young adults and old age (Bell et al., 2017). One longitudinal study measured inflammation markers at age 9 and again at age 18 (Khandaker, Pearson, Zammit, Lewis, & Jones,

2014). Those participants who showed higher levels of inflammation markers at age 9 were more likely to experience depression at age 18 compared with those with low levels of the markers.

If negative emotions can suppress the immune system, is the opposite also true? The answer is *yes*. Positive affect or the experience of pleasurable emotions is associated with better health outcomes (Pressman, Jenkins, & Moskowitz, 2019). Factors such as close friendships, which reduce negative emotions, also enhance immune-system functioning. It has also been shown that positive affect can reduce the effects of stress and reduce the chance of developing anxiety and depression (Sewart et al., 2019). Additionally, it has become apparent that not only does experience influence the immune system but that the immune system can influence the brain and thus behavior (Kipnis, 2018). Let's now look at the nature of the immune system.

Overall, our body needs a way to protect itself from toxins from the outside. Over evolutionary time, organisms developed various types of skin to initially accomplish this goal. Basic reflexes such as sneezing, coughing, and crying are additional mechanisms for removing pathogens before they can enter the body. However, if a pathogen does get inside our body, the immune system is called into action. It is the task of the immune system to recognize foreign agents in the body and destroy them. There are a number of layers of immune function.

The defense mechanisms of the immune system appear to be some of the earliest to have evolved. One important task of the immune system is to determine what is foreign and what cells are part of the self. These foreign substances include bacteria, viruses, and parasites, which enter our system and are detected by the immune system. Antibodies that are produced by our immune system can detect literally millions of different foreign substances and engage in a process that—in the best case—leads to their destruction. Our immune system has evolved to recognize a variety of pathogens. It is also capable of learning the characteristics of new pathogens and attacking them upon later exposure. This, of course, is the basic mechanism through which immunizations work.

There are two major types of immunity that protect the organism (see Brodin & Davis, 2017; Rouse & Sehrawat, 2010 for overviews).

1. The first system is general. It involves those processes of the immune system that are present at birth, and it responds to a variety of pathogens including bacteria and other toxic organisms. It tends to be fast-acting, nonspecific, and usually of short duration.
2. The second type of immunity develops after birth. This type of immunity is involved in recognizing specific pathogens, such as bacteria, viruses, or toxins, after initial contact. This system is more long-lasting and is able to contain a memory of a specific pathogen. This system is also the basis of immunizations for preventing specific diseases.

Overall, the two immune processes—both innate prevention at birth and learned recognition after birth—are what we usually focus on in discussions of the immune system in fighting infections. However, it is even broader than that. The immune system is designed to attack *whatever is not you*. That is why you have allergies. Allergies are simply your immune system attacking what it considers a pathogen. It is also why so much care must be taken in organ transplants. The immune system realizes that the transplanted organ is not yours and may even attack it. Although we experience the effects of the immune system, especially with allergies, most of what it does takes place outside of awareness. Let's look at the immune system itself (see Parkin & Cohen, 2001 for an overview).

There are a variety of types of immune cells. In general, immune cells originate in the bone marrow. Some of these cells migrate to the thymus and develop into T cells. T cells circulate through the blood and lymph systems as well as exist in the lymph nodes. There are also other types of cells such as B cells that produce antibodies. Both B and T cells require prior exposure to the pathogen to produce an immune response. Other natural killer (NK) cells do not require prior exposure and form a first line of defense against pathogens. Additionally, the spleen contains white blood cells created in bone marrow that fight infections and disease.

In addition to attacking pathogens, immune-system responses are also associated with the experience of feeling ill. From an evolutionary perspective, feeling ill would be protective as it would result in withdrawal from dangerous situations as well as allow for rest. Also, from an evolutionary perspective, interacting with our environment can actually educate your immune system, as described in the box: Myths and Misconceptions: Keep Your House Clean—Dirt Is Bad for You.

Myths and Misconceptions: Keep Your House Clean—Dirt Is Bad for You

Although television and media commercials suggest that we should keep our houses immaculately clean and our children out of the dirt, current research suggests that this may be actually hurting our health.

One study compared children from two Christian religious rural groups—the Amish and the Hutterites (Stein et al., 2016). Both of these groups eschew much of modern technology and make their living by farming. The Amish typically have houses without electricity and use horses and buggies instead of trucks and cars. Amish farming uses farm animals to pull plows and move crops. Likewise, their tools are those seen at the end of the 1800s. The Hutterites, on the other hand, live on highly industrialized communal farms with modern equipment.

The question asked was did these different lifestyles influence their health. Previous researchers found that the prevalence of asthma in Amish children was 5.2%, whereas it was 21.3% in the Hutterite children. Further, the sensitivity to allergies was also lower (7.2%) in the Amish as compared to the Hutterite children (33.3%). The current study found no asthma in the Amish children and 20% in the Hutterite children.

Why did this happen? The basic idea is that dirt and common allergens found in the Amish communities protected the children from later disorders. These allergens educated the child's immune system to know that it did not need to react at a later time. The Hutterite children, on the other hand, had an immune system without this information and later encounters with allergens produced a stronger reaction. Of course, you might think that the Amish and Hutterites had a different genetic makeup and this produced the differences. However, both of these groups originally came from nearby areas in Europe and are genetically similar.

In order to test the hypothesis that it was the levels of natural substances that educate the immune system, the researcher first tested the levels of dust and animal substances that can cause allergic reactions in the households. These are referred to as *endotoxin levels*. Indeed, the endotoxin levels were much higher in the Amish homes as compared to the Hutterite homes.

> To further test the idea that the dust and other substances found in the home were involved in the prevention of asthma, the researchers exposed young mice to these substances over time. The mice that were exposed to the dust from the Amish houses showed less of a response to asthma-producing agents than did control animals. The mice that were exposed to dust from Hutterite houses showed a larger asthma response. Other studies have also shown that mice exposed to microbes during early childhood show more protection from immune-system-related disorders such as inflammatory bowel disease and asthma (Olszak et al., 2012).
>
> Thus, for their own good, we might want to give children a chance to play in the dirt and visit farms as they are growing up and their immune systems are developing.
>
> **Thought Question**: If you were running a daycare for young children, how might you change your approach to planning activities for the children based on these findings? How would you explain your approach to the parents?

CONCEPT CHECK

1. What is the autonomic nervous system (ANS)? Describe the steps it goes through when you unexpectedly run into a bear in the woods. What steps does it go through when the bear runs away and you make it safely back to your car?
2. Describe how the SAM and HPA pathways work as part of the human stress response. What is the unique contribution of each pathway to that response?
3. Describe the three important characteristics of Shelley Taylor's concept of *tend and befriend*, the female response to stress.
4. What is the same and what is different in the male (fight or flight) and female (tend and befriend) responses to stress on the physiological level?
5. What are three ways in which psychological factors, stress, and our immune system are interrelated?
6. Describe the two major types of immunity. What is the primary contribution of each type?

Social Support Research and Stress

Do you ever take a friend with you when you are about to do something that you imagine will be stressful? If the answer is *yes*, then you may be preventing or reducing the normal stress response. A variety of studies show that if a friend is present, you experience less stress than when you perform the task alone (see Knox & Uvnäs-Moberg, 1998; Taylor & Stanton, 2007 for an overview). After school shootings, individuals comfort one another. Other people find animals supportive and find them to bring comfort. Various studies have shown that following disasters and other negative events such as terrorist attacks, humans turn to others for comfort.

What this suggests to a number of researchers is that we should view social relationships and bonds as a protective mechanism. That is to say, whereas different organisms have a variety of protective mechanisms, including camouflage, thick skin, sharp teeth, and quick reflexes, in humans, social relationships serve a similar function (Taylor et al., 2006). The opposite has also been shown to be the case. Social isolation is shown to be unhealthy and associated with a risk for disease and early mortality.

One of the first forms of the social bond that humans experience is attachment. Attachment is the relationship infants have with their caregivers. Although you learned about attachment in the chapter on development, attachment is usually not discussed in terms of its health benefits. However, a variety of studies suggest that early attachment relationships help to influence later reactions to stress (Taylor et al., 2006). For example, rat pups who received positive maternal care showed less negative hormonal response to stress. These animals also showed more open field exploration, suggesting less anxiety.

In another study, monkeys were raised in one of three environments (Rosenblum & Andrews, 1994). In the first environment, food was readily available, and the mothers were attentive to their young. In the second environment, food was less readily available, but the mothers were still attentive to their offspring. In the third environment, food was sometimes available and sometimes not. This condition resulted in the mothers being harsher and inconsistent in their mothering. The offspring in this third condition displayed more clinging behaviors to their mothers and lower levels of exploration and social play.

As adults, these monkeys displayed more extreme HPA axis responses to stress. They also appeared more fearful and lacked the normal social responses. With humans, similar responses are seen in response to difficult rearing environments. For example, in a study of 13,494 adults, a relationship was found between exposure to abuse and household dysfunction and later adult negative health outcomes (Felitti et al., 1998).

The evolutionary link that connected social challenges with the stress system for life-and-death situations is less well understood. One would assume that, as with many other evolutionary processes, nature used systems already available. Flinn (2007) reviews the idea that the adaptive value of the social stress response begins in childhood. A variety of studies across a variety of species has shown that early exposure to stress will modify how the stress response is expressed in later life and how early stress influences the brain (Murthy & Gould, 2020). It appears that children who experience trauma in the form of abuse, death of a parent, or divorce, show larger stress responses to social stress later in life. It is the not the case, however, that early physical stress such as experiencing hurricanes or political upheaval in one's country results in a differential stress response.

A number of studies in animals, particularly rats, has shown that early life stress can make a number of changes in the stress response throughout the animal's life (Maras & Baram, 2012). In particular, early stress increases CRF expression throughout life in response to stress. Early stress also changes the nature of neuronal connections. Pyramidal cells of adult rats that have experienced chronic early life stress do not grow as well compared to those without stress. Those with early life stress have less well-developed dendrites. Since stress influences the hippocampus, this can in turn influence later life learning and memory. Research also shows less synaptic density in humans in relation to long-term stress (Holmes et. al., 2019).

Childhood stress also results in brain differences in humans (Teicher, Anderson, Ohashi, & Polcari, 2014). When these authors examined 142 men and women who had experienced childhood abuse in comparison to 123 men and women who had not, they found differences in those areas of the brain related to emotional regulation and perception as well

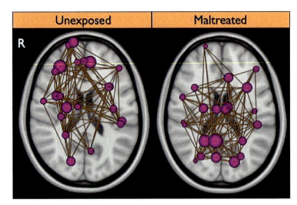

Figure 11-6 Brain connections in those who were maltreated as children and those who were not.

as areas related to self- and other-awareness. These areas were the anterior cingulate, the insula, and the precuneus. The anterior cingulate plays an important role in attention and the regulation of emotions. The insula is involved in experiences of the self and the importance of those experiences as reflected in the salience network. The precuneus is involved in the default network and internal thoughts and images. As you will see at the end of this chapter, these areas are also related to stress reduction through meditation. **Figure 11-6** shows that brain connections differ between those who were maltreated in childhood and those who were not.

Social Shaping

Based on the studies examining social relationships and health, Taylor and Gonzaga (2006) developed a *social shaping hypothesis*. Overall, this hypothesis suggests that early social relationships can shape the manner in which a person's biological, social, and behavioral processes respond to a variety of situations including stressful ones. For these researchers, social shaping has three functions.

1. Early relationships can calibrate how those systems involved in stress responses will develop.
2. Social relationships help to regulate the stress response in terms of day-to-day experiences. Social relationships tend to buffer stress responses, whereas the lack of social relationships tends to exaggerate the responses.
3. Social relationships can serve as a source of information as to the nature of the present environment. The information can be presented directly or indirectly.

The research suggests that people with social support live longer. On the other hand, those who are isolated display more detrimental health problems. For example, there is a variety of studies that show a strong relationship between social isolation and subsequent cardiovascular morbidity. Overall, social support reduces cardiovascular reactivity to acute stress, and lack of social support is associated with increased resting levels of sympathetic activation. Thus, lack of social support may itself be a stressor.

Individual Differences

Not everyone responds to the same stressor in the same way. Some individuals like to eat foods, especially sweets, after stress. Some people have comfort foods that they eat during chronic stress. It turns out that for some individuals comfort food does indeed reduce stress (Dallman et al., 2003). To eat during or after stress is referred to as *stress eating*. However, some individuals show the opposite reaction to stress and do not crave foods. The reason for this is both psychological and related in a complex way to the amount and types of hormones you secrete. In a group of 131 medical students (55% were female), weight gain during an exam period was about 5 pounds for the stress-eating group. There was also an increase in cortisol and insulin secreted during the night (Epel, Jimenez, Brownell, Stroud, Stoney, & Niaura, 2004).

Individual differences in stress are also shown in our cardiovascular system. More than 50 years ago, two cardiologists, Meyer Friedman and Ray Rosenman, were trying to study factors such as diet related to heart disease. The story goes that the wives of the men with heart disease helped these cardiologists understand it was stress that was influencing their husbands. Specifically, these cardiologists began to understand that how these men approached the world was a factor in their disease. This pattern of behavior became known as the *Type A* pattern of behavior. Individuals with Type A showed four major characteristics:

1. Competitiveness—Type A individuals take most tasks, such as driving in traffic, as a form of competition. This need for competition often takes the joy out of doing the task.
2. Time urgency—Type A individuals are impatient and constantly performing tasks as if they are fighting the clock. This may lead to trying to perform a number of tasks at the same time.
3. Anger and hostility—Type A individuals often react to others in an angry and hostile manner although they may not show the anger.
4. Forced speech—Type A individuals may talk over others and display a pressured style of speech.

Individuals who show the opposite pattern with low levels of competitiveness, time urgency, anger, and forced speech are referred to as *Type B* individuals. Consistent research has shown that those with a Type A pattern of behavior are at greater risk for coronary heart disease (CHD). This can result in symptoms of angina, which is experienced as chest pains. CHD is also associated with heart attacks. Overall, it is suggested that Type A individuals are twice as likely to develop CHD and die of heart disease than non-Type A individuals. Later research suggests that the critical factor that connects Type A behavior to disease is hostility. Hostility may also influence other factors such as making it difficult for the person to experience social support or respond to stress in a productive manner.

Uncontrollable Stress

Another critical factor in how we experience a situation is whether we feel that we are in control or not. Over the past 50 years, a variety of studies have shown that individuals who experience high demands in their jobs but have little control over how and when they perform their work have been shown to display more symptoms of a variety of disorders including heart disease. Those individuals who felt that they had control even though they may have had demanding jobs displayed fewer disorders.

Jay Weiss examined the results of **uncontrollable stress** (see Weiss, 1972). Uncontrollable stress is a negative experience that the organism cannot influence or control. In experimental animals, such procedures as shock will produce stress. To examine the effects of control, researchers used a procedure referred to as *yoked-control*. The control animal is in the same experimental procedure but does not receive any shocks. Another animal can perform a task to turn off the shock once it begins. The other rat receives the same shocks but does not have the ability to turn it off. What became apparent in this research was that uncontrollability produced both health problems (for example, gastric ulcers) and depressive symptoms.

What was intriguing was that the depressive symptoms in animals were very similar to clinical definitions of human depression. According to the *Diagnostic and Statistical*

Manual of Mental Disorders (DSM), which is used by psychologists and psychiatrists in the United States and other parts of the world, depression includes such symptoms as loss of appetite, psychomotor retardation, fatigue, disrupted motivation, sleep disturbances, and reduced capacity for attention. These were exactly the symptoms that Jay Weiss and his colleagues found in the organisms they studied (Weiss et al., 1981). This has led some researchers to examine the role of stress in experiencing depression. An interesting Radiolab presentation by Robert Sapolsky describes our reactions to stress (https://www.wnycstudios.org/story/91580-stress).

CONCEPT CHECK

1. Describe three studies from this chapter that show how social relationships and bonds serve as a protective mechanism in terms of stress.
2. What brain changes have been observed in adults as a result of their exposure to early childhood stress?
3. Describe Taylor and Gonzaga's social shaping hypothesis. What are its implications for both social support and social isolation?
4. Not everyone responds to stress in the same way. How is the fact of individual differences evidenced in the two examples given here: (1) eating and (2) our cardiovascular system?
5. What do Jay Weiss's experiments with rats and other researchers' studies with humans reveal about the role of individual control in how they experienced stress?

Trauma and PTSD

Psychological stress and trauma are experienced when something happens to us that we do not expect. Generally, these situations put us in a position where we have little control over what is happening to us. Besides the initial stress response, these types of experiences can lead to a particular long-term problem referred to as ***post-traumatic stress disorder (PTSD)***. PTSD can result both from experiencing trauma, such as sexual assault, serious injury, or a death-threatening situation as the victim, or from seeing others in these sorts of situations. PTSD can result from one traumatic event or a series of traumatic events, as would be seen by solders in combat.

Those who experience PTSD will have memories of the traumatic event break into their consciousness without warning. It is also the case that physical events associated with the traumatic event can bring forth a flashback or re-experiencing of the event. This re-experiencing can include bodily and emotional responses associated with stress. This leads some individuals to avoid situations that could remind them of the previous trauma.

PTSD can also lead individuals to having distorted ideas and emotions, including blaming themselves for the event. This is especially true in cases of sexual assault in which the person feels shame and sees herself or himself in negative terms. They may also be irritable and sensitive to others and their surroundings. It is common for those with PTSD to have sleep problems and intense dreams. Those with PTSD may also seek to self-medicate with alcohol or drugs. PTSD is a complicated disorder in that not everyone who experiences

Table 11-1 Stressors that can lead to PTSD.

TYPE OF STRESSOR	EXAMPLE
Serious accident	Car, plane, boating, or industrial accident
Natural disaster	Tornado, hurricane, flood, or earthquake
Criminal assault	Being physically attacked, mugged, shot, stabbed, or held at gunpoint
Military	Serving in an active combat theater
Sexual assault	Rape or attempted rape
Child sexual abuse	Incest, rape, or sexual contact with an adult or much older child
Child physical abuse or severe neglect	Beating, burning, restraints, starvation
Hostage/imprisonment or torture	Being kidnapped or taken hostage, terrorist attack, torture, incarceration as a prisoner of war or in a concentration camp, displacement as a refugee
Witnessing or learning about traumatic events	Witnessing a shooting or devastating accident, sudden unexpected death of a loved one

Source: Vermetten and Lanius (2012, p. 293).

similar stressful conditions develops PTSD. **Table 11-1** shows some of the stressors that can lead to PTSD.

PTSD has been an important focus of the US Department of Veterans Affairs, since PTSD shows up in greater numbers in the military than in the general population. Part of this results from the nature of current military actions in wars in which small groups of soldiers go out from the base and cannot predict when there will be an attack. In this situation, there is not a traditional front line. Further, roadside bombs and suicide bombers present additional dangers. Thus, soldiers find their lives under constant threat.

Among Vietnam veterans, lifetime prevalence of PTSD is estimated to be 30.9% for men and 26.9% for women (https://www.ptsd.va.gov/index.asp). For Gulf War veterans, lifetime prevalence is lower and estimated to be about 10% to 12%. The Iraq War estimates are about 13.8%. Soldiers who were in recent war zones have not only experienced PTSD but also mild traumatic brain injuries (TBIs) usually in the form of concussions. Additionally, sexual assault was reported by 23% of the female veterans who use VA health care facilities.

One way to consider the physiological changes associated with trauma is to consider the networks involved on both an associative level and on a cortical level. On an associative level, it has been suggested that some associations become more potent or "hot" than others that remain "cold." A hot association is one that, when we consider it, we react strongly and emotionally. If we were afraid of walking in a certain part of town, this would be a hot association when someone mentioned that possibility. A cold association is one we have little reaction to, such as remembering that a grocery store is on 3rd Avenue. The same set of facts can be either hot or cold depending on the experiences

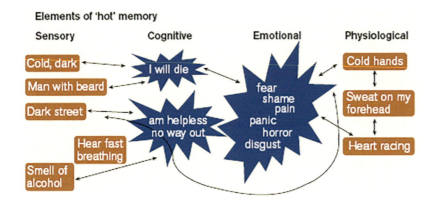

Figure 11-7 Elements of "hot" memory.

associated with it. It has been shown that repeated experiences of trauma will make it more difficult to integrate the experiences into less emotional, or cold, autobiographical memories. **Figure 11-7** illustrates such a network in which being on a dark street results in a cognitive proposition such as "there is no way out" and the following emotional and physiological responses.

One goal of therapy is to help the individual move the hot trauma associations to a cold, or nonreactive, memory process. PTSD is frequently comorbid with other disorders such as depression, substance abuse, and anxiety disorders such as obsessive-compulsive disorder (OCD), panic disorder, agoraphobia, and social anxiety. For example, the National Vietnam Veterans Readjustment Study shows that 98% of individuals with combat-related PTSD have a comorbid lifetime mental disorder (Kulka et al., 1990). They also reported more physical health problems. This suggests that the treatment of PTSD requires more than a single strategy.

In terms of brain structures, animal models of stress and trauma have shown that exposure to severe and chronic stress can damage hippocampal formation. This is seen to be mediated by elevated corticosteroids, which are thought to damage cells, diminish neuronal regeneration, and reduce dendritic branching. This has resulted in a variety of human studies examining the hippocampus in individuals with PTSD.

In addition, an improved understanding of the cortical networks involved in emotional regulation, threat detection, and the acquisition and extinction of fear have pinpointed specific brain regions connected with PTSD (Shalev, Liberzon, & Marmar, 2017). These include the hippocampus, the amygdala, and medial prefrontal cortex (PFC). The hippocampus is important because of its role in the encoding of memories including emotional ones. The amygdala is involved in the assessment of threat and plays a role in fear conditioning. The medial PFC, including the anterior cingulate cortex (ACC), is involved in the inhibition of emotional information during task performance. The brain regions involved in PTSD are shown in **Figure 11-8**.

In general, there is clear support that individuals with PTSD have smaller hippocampal volume than those without PTSD. In one meta-analysis, individuals with PTSD had, on average, a 6.9% smaller left hippocampus and a 6.6% smaller right hippocampus by volume. An intriguing idea is that stress limits the normal regeneration of new neurons in the hippocampus. ACC differences have also been noted in PTSD as well as reduced connectivity between the ACC and the amygdala.

The amygdala also can take in information that bypasses the frontal lobes (see Sapolsky, 2003 for an overview). This may be part of the experience of vivid flashbacks in PTSD. In

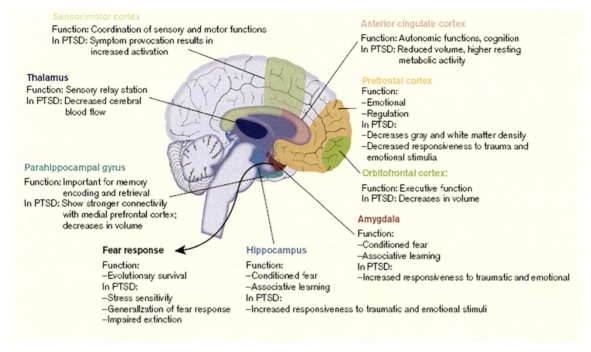

SOURCE: Mahan and Ressler (2012).

Figure 11-8 Cortical networks involved in the acquisition and extinction of fear.

turn, this hyper-responsiveness of the amygdala is related to an exaggerated fear response. This may result from a lack of inhibition from the frontal areas to the amygdala. This would also be associated with the inability to inhibit or extinguish fear-related stimuli.

CONCEPT CHECK

1. How is post-traumatic stress disorder (PTSD) different from a typical stress response?
2. What are some examples of events that can bring forth PTSD?
3. What are some common symptoms of PTSD?
4. How does PTSD play out on the memory and emotional levels?
5. Describe three changes seen in the brains of individuals with PTSD?

Health

We usually only think about health when we experience its opposite, that of a disease or a disorder. We also tend to look for biological reasons such as viruses or bacteria as the cause of the problem. We now know that psychological factors play a critical role in health and disease. What we choose to eat, how we exercise, and even how we think and feel are critical factors in our health. This has been a change over the past 100 years, which is found in the field of behavioral medicine and health psychology.

One part of this has been the study of resilience. **Resilience** research seeks to understand how some individuals are able to encounter severe psychological or physical adversity

460 Stress and Health

Number of deaths for leading causes of death

- Heart disease: 647,457
- Cancer: 599,108
- Accidents (unintentional injuries): 169,936
- Chronic lower respiratory diseases: 160,201
- Stroke (cerebrovascular diseases): 146,383
- Alzheimer's disease: 121,404
- Diabetes: 83,564
- Influenza and pneumonia: 55,672
- Nephritis, nephrotic syndrome, and nephrosis: 50,633
- Intentional self-harm (suicide): 47,173

Source: Deaths: Leading Causes for 2017, table 1 [PDF- 2 MB]

Figure 11-9 Cause of death in the United States for 2017. US population was approximately 325 million.

without showing traditional stress effects (Kalisch, Müller, & Tüscher, 2015). One key finding suggests that resilience is associated with the ability to reinterpret both internal and external events in a more positive manner. This is similar to some of the factors associated with mindfulness meditation.

Since the beginning of the 20th century, health statistics have shown a change in terms of both types of diseases encountered and the role of behavioral processes. The top three leading causes of death in 1900 were related to infectious diseases. With the advent of public water supplies and sewage treatment plants, the death rate percentages of these disorders were greatly reduced, as shown in the 1997 figure. **Figure 11-9** shows the exact number of deaths by disorder from 2017—more than 100 years later. One important change is that current causes of death can have a behavioral component, such as the types of foods eaten or drugs used.

These behavioral factors can have both direct and indirect effects. Accidents and suicide have strong behavioral components. For example, not sleeping enough or using drugs and alcohol can lead to highway accidents. Other disorders have related behavioral components. Using tobacco can also lead to various cancers. Being overweight has a direct relationship with diabetes. Heart disease, which is the number one cause of death in the US currently, is associated with behavioral factors such as the foods one eats, exercise, smoking, and alcohol use. The top four major causes of death today result from a slow accumulation of damage that involves behavioral components.

During the 20th century, psychologists became health care professionals. This represents an understanding that treatment of most disorders involves a strong behavioral and emotional component. In fact, different individuals recover differently from the same disorder. This has led to both research and treatment studies involving psychological factors and health. As described in Chapter 1, the biopsychosocial model of health continues to be important. Overall, it became clear that culture, lifestyle, and physical components such as genetics needed to be considered to understand health and disease.

With the development of better public works systems and sanitation and medical treatments including vaccinations, life expectancy began to increase. The World Health Organization (WHO) has collected statistics regarding health and disease from around the world. **Figure 11-10** shows a map of healthy life expectancy from around the world in 2016.

In 2016, healthy life expectancy was 63.1 years globally. However, many individuals end their lives with a disorder such as cancer or Alzheimer's disease that leads to a disability. Life expectancy including those in both healthy and disabled states was 62 years worldwide in 2015. The United States had an overall life expectancy for 79.3 in 2015. It was 76.9 years for males and 81.6 years for females. By the way, the United States is 31st in the world in terms of life expectancy. Japan is number one with an overall life expectancy of 83.7 years. Compare this to 1889 in Germany when the first social security pension was established by Chancellor Otto von Bismarck. At that time, life expectancy was 45 years of age.

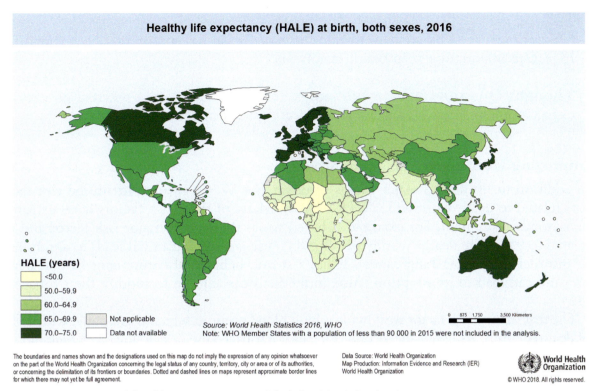

Figure 11-10 Healthy life expectancy at birth in 2016 for both sexes.

Applying Psychological Science: The Role of Expectation in Health Outcomes

Giving a drug to treat a disorder seems fairly straightforward. One might even think that psychological factors would not be involved. Take Parkinson's disease, for example. Parkinson's disease is a motor disorder that affects about 1% of the population more than age 60. People with the disorder may show tremors, particularly involving the hands, and a slowness of movement when walking. The disorder is associated with the loss of neurons that produce the neurotransmitter dopamine in one particular part of the brain, the *substantia nigra*. Treatment for the disorder is to give a medication that increases dopamine in the brain.

Researchers told 12 individuals with Parkinson's disease that they were testing a new injectable drug that increased dopamine along with a lower priced drug of similar efficacy (Espay et al., 2015). The new drug cost $1,500, whereas the lower cost one was $100. Both drugs were actually a normal saline solution, which does not influence dopamine, that is, a *placebo*. Following administration of the drugs, the individuals with Parkinson's disease were given motor tests and an fMRI task.

Both placebo drugs improved motor function, and the expensive placebo drug worked better than the cheap one! It not only improved motor function but also showed brain-imaging changes consistent with an increase in dopamine. These researchers suggest that an expensive medication increases the expectation of change and this in turn increases dopamine. Positive expectations in all individuals, not just those with Parkinson's disease, are associated with an increase in dopamine. The Parkinson's disease placebo study shows how expectations can influence health outcomes including brain changes. The psychological factor of expectation has consistently been shown to play an important role in health treatments.

Thought Question: What is an example from your experience where a positive expectation of change has made a difference in your health or life?

Improving Health and Managing Stress

In addition to listing the major causes of death, the WHO also has identified risk factors related to death worldwide (WHO, 2010). Many of these risk factors have a strong behavioral component. For example, tobacco use is the second major risk factor and is related to 9% of the deaths worldwide. Tobacco use is a risk because it leads to a number of disorders including lung cancer. It has a strong behavioral component in that peer pressure can lead to its adoption. Also, individuals can choose to modify their tobacco use.

The first leading risk factor worldwide is high blood pressure, which is associated with 13% of deaths globally. As noted, the second risk factor is tobacco use (9%) followed by high blood glucose (6%), which is associated with diabetes and other disorders. The fourth risk factor is physical inactivity, which is associated with 6% of deaths worldwide. The fifth risk factor is being overweight and obese, which is associated with 5% of deaths worldwide.

These five risk factors are interrelated such that inactivity can be associated with being overweight and developing diabetes. In this manner, inactivity is estimated to be a 30% cause of heart disease. Unlike the patterns of communicable disease seen in the early part of the 1900s, which were reduced through public works projects such as better water system and sewage treatment, these five risk factors involve behavioral factors.

Physical activity is one of the easiest stress reduction and life-increasing activities that we as humans engage in. Physical activity comes in so many forms. You can run, canoe, swim, dance, as well as walk, or work in the garden to name a few. Most of the time physical activity makes us feel better and improves our mood. Given the right amount of exercise, our bodies produce endorphins, the brain-made, opiate-like biochemicals that leave us feeling good.

In 1979, researchers began to study 2,235 men from 45 to 59 years of age in South Wales of the United Kingdom (Elwood et al., 2013). They followed these men for the next 30 years, including cognitive performance tests in 2004. This study examined the effects of a healthy lifestyle on disease and cognitive functioning. Five items were studied in terms of a healthy lifestyle. These healthy activities included not smoking, eating fruits and vegetables, engaging in physical activity, not being overweight, and a low to moderate intake of alcohol. The results showed that a healthy lifestyle is associated with a 50% reduction in diabetes, 50% reduction in vascular disease, and a 60% reduction overall in all causes of mortality. Further, there was a 60% reduction in cognitive decline with aging. These results are similar to previous studies in the US with both males and females.

In their review of the literature, WHO found strong evidence that compared to less active adult men and women, individuals who are more active have lower rates of all causes of mortality, including coronary heart disease, high blood pressure, stroke, diabetes, metabolic syndrome, colon cancer, breast cancer, and depression. Strong evidence also exists to support the conclusion that, compared to less active people, physically active

Table 11-2 Weekly minutes of moderate intensity aerobic physical activity and level of health benefits (from Powell, Paluch, & Blair, 2011, p. 350)

Volume of Activity	Health Benefits	Comment
Baseline	None	Being inactive is unhealthy
Above baseline but <150 min/week of moderate intensity activity	Some	Low levels of activity are preferable to inactivity
150–300 min/week of moderate intensity activity	Substantial	Activity at the high end provides more benefits than at the low end
>300 min/week of moderate intensity activity	Additional	Current scientific information does not indicate an upper limit for benefits nor an amount that appears to be hazardous.

One minute of vigorous intensity activity provides benefits roughly equal to two minutes of moderate intensity activity. The two intensities can be mixed.

adults and older adults exhibit a higher level of cardiorespiratory and muscular fitness, have a healthier body mass and composition, and a biomarker profile that is more favorable for preventing cardiovascular disease and type 2 diabetes and for enhancing bone health.

Based on their review of the literature, the WHO made specific activity recommendations for three age levels. For those from 5 to 17 years of age, they recommend 60 minutes of physical activity daily. This can be playing sports, hiking, and other activities with family, friends, and school. They further conclude that more than 60 minutes of physical activity will provide additional health benefits. In order to strengthen muscle and bone, vigorous intensive exercise should be performed three times a week.

For those in the 18- to 64-year age range, they recommend at least 150 minutes of activity each week. Likewise, increasing this amount has additional health benefits. From their review, the WHO concludes that an increase in physical activity is correlated with a reduction in cardiovascular health problems, including heart attack and stroke. Physical activity also reduces the risk of diabetes and helps with weight control. Exercise has also been shown to improve brain function and performance on cognitive tests (Raichlen & Alexander, 2017; Voss, Vivar, Kramer, & van Praag, 2013).

As people enter the age of 65 and over, the results of previous inactivity become more apparent including cardiovascular problems, obesity, and diabetes. For those more than 65 who are healthy, the same recommendations hold as for the 18–64 age group. Actually, WHO suggests that for those more than 65, the benefits of physical activity are greater since inactivity can be more detrimental at this age. For those more than 65 with problems in exercising, the emphasis should be on enhancing balance and preventing falls.

In summary, a number of studies have sought to determine what simple things you can do to promote psychological and physical health throughout your life. Some of these are not complicated, such as exercise, eating good food, and having good social relationships. Working at a job you feel good about is also an important contributor to a healthy life. Combining these factors such as eating well and exercising show synergistic positive effects on the brain (van Praag, 2009).

Table 11-3 Column 1 shows examples of physical activities. Column 2 shows overall physiological changes associated with any of these. Column 3 shows the health benefits from engaging in any of these activities on a consistent basis (from Powell, Paluch, & Blair, 2011)

Examples of Physical Activities	Examples of Physiologic Changes	Examples of Health Outcomes
Gardening	↑ Autonomic balance	↓ Breast cancer
Home repair	↑ Bone density	↓ Colon cancer
Painting	↑ Capillary density	↓ Coronary heart disease
Raking	↑ Coronary artery size	↓ Depression
Shoveling	↑ Endothelial function	↓ Excess weight gain
Sweeping	↑ High density lipoprotein	↓ Fractures
Vacuuming	↑ Immune function	↓ Injurious falls
Basketball	↑ Insulin sensitivity	↓ Osteoporosis
Cycling	↑ Lean body mass	↓ Risk of death
Dancing	↑ Mitochondrial volume	↓ Stroke
Running	↑ Motor unit recruitment	↓ Type 2 diabetes
Skiing	↑ Muscle fiber size	↑ Cognitive function
Soccer	↑ Neuromuscular coordination	↑ Physical function
Swimming	↑ Stroke volume	↑ Weight management
Tennis	↓ Blood coagulation	
Walking	↓ Inflammation	

Meditation

Over the past 50 years, relaxation and meditation have been shown to play a role in stress reduction and health promotion. Relaxation training has been shown to be an important component for promoting both mental and physical health. Likewise, meditation is becoming an important component in treatment. The most widely studied form of meditation is *mindfulness* (Wielgosz, Goldberg, Kral, Dunne, & Davidson, 2019). Although mindfulness has many different meanings in psychological and spiritual literature, it is commonly referred to as both a practice and a state of mind. The basic procedure is that during meditation one simply watches one's thoughts or bodily experiences. The task is not to be distracted by one's reactions to these but to allow both the perceptions and the reactions to come and go. The focus is on viewing the present in a nonjudgmental manner without being distracted by what one is observing.

One review of the meditation research examined the effects of mindfulness meditation on psychological health (Keng, Smoski, & Robins, 2011). Most of this research was conducted with individuals who were not seeking psychological treatment for specific problems. The overall general finding was that mindfulness meditation was associated with positive psychological health. Positive psychological health included the person feeling better, showing less psychological distress, and a greater ability to experience and regulate his or her emotional life.

In addition to mindfulness, which involves *nonreactive monitoring* of the contents of experience, there are *focused meditations* that has the individual voluntarily focus on a particular object or process. The object of attention can be a visual image, a repeated sound, or even your own breath. Using both types of meditation, researchers have sought to determine how meditation affects the brain (Lutz, Slagter, Dunne, & Davidson, 2008). Using fMRI, experts in a focused meditation showed less activation of the amygdala during the meditation than did novice meditators, which is associated with less negative emotionality. In terms of nonreactive meditation, those who had been meditating for more than ten years showed EEG differences from those who were less experienced. These differences included greater synchrony in different areas of the brain. Several studies have also shown that the anterior cingulate cortex and the insula are involved in meditation. These areas of the brain are involved in emotional regulation and our sense of self. The current perspective is described in the box: The World Is Your Laboratory: Complementary and Alternative Medicine.

The World Is Your Laboratory: Complementary and Alternative Medicine

Initially, the terms *complementary medicine* and *alternative medicine* referred to those treatments that were not taught in medical school. These techniques could include procedures such as acupuncture, meditation, hypnosis, diet, biofeedback, yoga, relaxation, and exercise. In 1993, an article was published in the *New England Journal of Medicine* showing that one in three people in the United States used some form of alternative treatment during the past year (Eisenberg et al., 1993).

At about the same time, the United States National Institutes of Health (NIH) established a center for the study of complementary and alternative medicine. The National Center for Complementary and Alternative Medicine (NCCAM) developed research to understand the safety and effectiveness of these approaches. Reflecting the continued use of these procedures alongside traditional approaches, NCCAM changed its name to the National Center for Complementary and Integrative Health (NCCIH) in 2015. Today, many major medical centers around the country offer integrative medicine.

One research study examined how acupuncture can reduce pain in carpal tunnel syndrome. Acupuncture to the correct site for 16 sessions compared with sham procedures showed a reduction in pain. With actual acupuncture, there were changes in the brain areas related to sensory processing (Maeda et al. 2017). Acupuncture has also been shown to reduce hot flashes during menopause (Avis et al., 2016). Overall, acupuncture has been effective with a number of disorders.

Cardiovascular disease is the leading cause of death in the United States. Various forms of stress can also contribute to this disorder. In addition, African Americans are at greater risk for cardiovascular problems than other groups. In one study, African Americans who had cardiovascular disease were taught a meditation technique or offered health education (Schneider et al., 2012). The participants in these two groups were followed at various intervals. During a five-year period, those who practiced the meditation procedure showed a 48% risk reduction in deaths, and lower blood pressure as well as a reduction in anger expression. Meditation has also been shown to be effective in the treatment of insomnia (Ong et al., 2014).

At this point, it is critical that integrative health procedures, like all treatment procedures, receive careful research to determine their effectiveness and which individuals they work with. The evidence thus far is that a number of procedures that use psychological principles can affect and improve our health.

Thought Question: What is the significance of changing the terminology from "complementary and alternative medicine" to "integrative health"? Think about a disorder you or a friend or family member has had and what kinds of treatment you would include under the umbrella of "integrative health."

CONCEPT CHECK

1. What is the role of psychological and behavioral components in the major causes of death today?
   a. How has that changed over the last 100 years?
   b. Currently, what are the leading health risks worldwide?
   c. What are four steps you can start taking now to improve your health and manage stress?
2. What is the placebo response? How is expectation related to it?
   a. Expectation?
3. What is mindfulness meditation? What role can it play in improving health and managing stress?

Summary

Learning Objective 1. Define stress and the ways people experience and respond to stress.
Stress is commonly defined as a response that is brought on by any situation that threatens a person's ability to cope. Scientists speak of the *stress response* as a response to a critical situation that allows an organism to avoid danger or reduce other types of threat.

Psychological factors play a critical role in how we experience stress. We can experience stress both from real situations and from our expectations of what might happen. Even after the event has passed, our body can continue to display characteristics of stress. If you perceive there is danger, your body immediately reacts. Adrenalin is released and blood is sent to your legs to supply biochemical substances so that you can run. To help in the process, your heart rate and lung capacity is increased. Processes that you don't need such as the digestion of food or your sexual responses are inhibited. This has been referred to as the fight or flight response.

Learning Objective 2. Discuss the early approaches to the study of stress.
In the early 1900s, the French physiologist Claude Bernard realized that the brain had circuits that were specialized for monitoring and controlling internal events that he referred to as the *internal milieu*. These internal states included physiological processes such as thirst, temperature, and metabolism. This idea of an internal monitoring of bodily states underlies the development of the concept of *homeostasis* as described previously.

In 1915, Walter Cannon at Harvard developed the concept of homeostasis to reflect the manner in which a physiological system tended to center on a set point. Homeostasis is the process in which the body keeps itself in balance. Like a thermostat, if you become too hot, your body sweats to reduce heat by processes such as sweating and if you become cold, your metabolism is increased.

Another major figure in the history of stress research was the Hungarian endocrinologist Hans Selye who worked at the University of Montreal. His work in the 1930s helped to set up the connection between stress and the development of diseases. One of Selye's early findings was that the body reacts similarly to a variety of different stressors. Selye called this response the General Adaptation Syndrome (GAS).

Bruce McEwen has begun to suggest a more flexible set of processes that involve the brain in the regulation of the body's reaction to stress. McEwen begins by suggesting that part of the problem in understanding stress is the ambiguous meaning of the term *stress*. He suggests that the term stress be replaced with the term allostasis. Allostasis refers to the body's ability to achieve stability through change. His view emphasizes the brain as the means of stability, which can be accomplished in a number of different ways. That is, there is not just one single response to stress according to McEwen.

Learning Objective 3. Describe the autonomic nervous system (ANS).
The *autonomic nervous system (ANS)* consists of the neural circuitry that controls the body's physiology. This physiology involves the smooth muscle organs and tissues as well as the other organs such as the heart, gastrointestinal, genital, and lung systems (see **Figure 11-2**). Along with the endocrine system, the ANS manages continuous changes in blood chemistry, respiration, circulation, digestion, reproductive status, and immune responses. Two branches of the ANS are the *sympathetic nervous system* and the *parasympathetic nervous system*.

Learning Objective 4. Discuss the research that suggests that social relationships provide a protective mechanism in improving health and managing stress.
Research suggests that people with social support live longer, whereas those who are isolated display more detrimental health problems. For example, there are a variety of studies that show a strong relationship between social isolation and subsequent cardiovascular morbidity. Overall, social support reduces cardiovascular reactivity to acute stress, and lack of social support is associated with increased resting levels of sympathetic activation. Thus, lack of social support may itself be a stressor.

Based on the studies examining social relationships and health, Taylor and Gonzaga (2006) developed a *social shaping hypothesis*. This hypothesis suggests that early social relationships can shape the manner in which a person's biological, social, and behavioral processes respond to a variety of situations including stressful ones. For these researchers, social shaping has three functions.

1. Early relationships can calibrate how those systems involved in stress responses will develop.
2. Social relationships help to regulate the stress response in terms of day-to-day experiences. Social relationships tend to buffer stress responses, whereas the lack of social relationships tends to exaggerate the responses.
3. Social relationships can serve as a source of information as to the nature of the present environment. The information can be presented directly or indirectly.

Learning Objective 5. Explain the role of behavioral and emotional processes in the expectation of health outcomes.
During the 20th century, psychologists became health care professionals. This represents an understanding that treatment of most disorders involves a strong behavioral and emotional component. In fact, different individuals recover differently from the same disorder. This has led to both research and treatment studies involving psychological factors and health. Overall, it became clear that culture, lifestyle, as well as physical components such as genetics needed to be considered to understand health and disease.

Study Resources

Review Questions

1. In the study of stress, researchers Selye and McEwen both referred to the paradox that the same physiological and stress responses that protect and restore the body can also damage it. In terms of that paradox, please answer the following questions:
   a. How did our stress responses evolve, and what led to the paradox?
   b. How do our stress responses protect and restore our body and mind?
   c. How can our stress responses damage our body and mind?
2. A description of physiology—both human and animal—and its response to stress makes up a large portion of this chapter in an introductory psychology book. How would you characterize the overall relationship among our physiology, psychology, and responses to stress? What are some specific examples of the interrelationships?
3. This chapter has described a number of concepts that are related to adapting to and managing stress successfully. These concepts include control, positive expectations, and being exposed to stressors early and gradually. What other concepts from the chapter and your experience would you include in this list? What overall label and description would you give to this category of concepts?
4. From what you have read in this chapter and learned in your course about PTSD, develop a statement of your understanding of PTSD including causes; psychological, neurological, emotional, and behavioral symptoms; individual differences; and treatment approaches. What questions do you still want answers to about PTSD?
5. Health is something we think about every day in one way or another. Is health only the absence of disease? From what you have read in this chapter, how would you define health from the following seven perspectives: cultural, social, individual, cognitive/emotional, physiological, brain, and genetic?

For Further Reading

McEwen, B. (2002). *The End of Stress as We Know It.* New York: Dana Foundation Press.
Sapolsky, R. (2004). *Why Zebras Don't Get Ulcers, 3rd edition.* New York: Henry Holt & Co.

Web Resources

Human stress—https://www.wnycstudios.org/podcasts/radiolab/episodes/91580-stress
Veteran PTSD—https://www.ptsd.va.gov/index.asp

Key Terms and Concepts

- allostasis
- allostatic load
- allostatic systems
- autonomic nervous system (ANS)
- fight or flight response
- General Adaptation Syndrome (GAS)
- HPA (hypothalamic pituitary adrenal) pathway
- mindfulness
- parasympathetic nervous system
- post-traumatic stress disorder (PTSD)
- SAM (sympathetic adrenal medullary) system
- social shaping hypothesis
- stress
- stress response
- sympathetic nervous system
- tend and befriend response
- uncontrollable stress
- resilience

12 Social Psychology

LEARNING OBJECTIVES

12.1 Define what it means to be social and how we evaluate our social relationships.

12.2 Discuss the role that social cognition plays in understanding how we form opinions and make decisions about ourselves and others.

12.3 Discuss the role that social emotion plays in prosocial and helping behaviors.

12.4 Explain how social influences affect behavior.

12.5 Describe our understanding of the distinctive characteristics of a moral judgment.

The story begins on March 13, 1964. It was about 3 a.m. when a woman named Kitty Genovese arrived home. She parked her car in a parking lot across from her home. She then walked across the street from the parking lot in the direction of her home. She became uneasy, as she was walking since someone was walking toward her and she didn't like the way he looked. She became extremely uneasy and turned around and started to walk toward a police telephone. She never reached the police call box. He overtook her and stabbed her. She screamed, "OH MY GOD, I HAVE BEEN STABBED. PLEASE HELP ME! PLEASE HELP ME!" With that scream, windows were opened, people's heads came out, and lights came on. The people shouted. With that, the man got scared and left. A bus then came by and people got out of the bus. People in the houses then closed their windows and went back to sleep. She apparently was not helped by anybody. She managed to crawl to another building and the man came back and overtook her and stabbed again. Again, she screamed. She shrieked, "I'm DYING!" Again, windows opened and lights came on. The people shouted and the man again ran off and got into his car. The third time, he came back again, and this time he killed her. The entire event took more than half an hour. It was not until 3:50 a.m. that the police received the first call.

Based on Martin Greenberg *The New York Times* article March 27, 1964 and Latané and Darley (1969).

Social Psychology

As humans, we are social creatures. There has never been a time in our history where we humans have lived alone. From the earliest times as hunter-gatherers, we have lived in social groups with strong social bonds. It is these groups that have shaped our social skills and abilities. For example, we need to know who our friends are as opposed to who might want to hurt us. We also need to be able to select mates. Further, we need to understand the dynamics of our larger group. These abilities have been passed down over evolutionary time and are part of our human social interactions today.

As part of our interest in social interactions, we seek information about others. It has been estimated that more than half of our conversations with others are about social topics (Dunbar, Marriott, & Duncan, 1997). In social situations, we are quick to make judgments concerning other individuals (Zebrowitz, 2017). Shortly after meeting someone, we make a judgment about them, including whether we like them or not, as well as our overall impression of them.

More than 70 years ago, the social psychologist Solomon Asch noted that not only do we develop quick impressions of others, but that it is also involuntary (Asch, 1946). All of this takes place out of our awareness through a complex set of determinations in our brain (see Kang & Bodenhausen, 2015 for an overview). Not only does our brain influence social interactions, but our social relations influence how our brain develops (Falk & Bassett, 2017).

Given the long history of humans interacting with other humans, it is not surprising that there is great complexity in the manner in which we interact with one another. We treat relatives differently than others. We treat those who look like us differently than those who do not. We would choose to save a child in a burning building as opposed to an older adult. Overall, what this means is that there is no simple way of describing our social relationships with one another. However, we can view this complexity within larger categories of behavior and experience.

This chapter emphasizes social relationships, especially those such as cooperation and competition, and the rules that underlie our social relationships. Not only do we make social evaluations, but we also make decisions concerning when not to act or share information with others. This requires a type of inhibition on our part. Further, in the chapter you will learn about what factors lead us to do what others tell us as well as how we evaluate others in potential social roles. This is one hallmark of social psychology. That is, social psychology has traditionally focused on the situation and the way in which changing the situation influences how we form attitudes and interact with others.

It is clear that a variety of abilities and developmental processes of humans support a high level of social interaction for an extended period of time. We remember relationships we grew up with and this influences our adult relationships. We tend to use attachment styles similar to those we experienced as children. Additionally, humans have the ability to use language with ease, which fosters social interactions even at long distances. We are particularly sensitive to emotional cues that deepen social interactions such as emotional faces. We even include emotional symbols in our text messages to one another (☺).

As you can imagine, the human brain has evolved to reflect the complexity of our social interactions. We interact with others individually, in groups, and in larger society and cultural functions. In fact, the activation of certain parts of our brain is related to how complex our social relationships are (Dziura & Thompson, 2014).

What it means to be social and how we evaluate our social relationships will be important questions to consider in this chapter. Many things we do as humans are done in the service of social interactions. As infants, we not only pay attention to others but we are eager to connect with them. This continues throughout our lives. We can note the manner in which humans have taken modern technology, such as the cell phone or the Internet, and placed the technology in the service of social interactions. Text messaging is one clear example of using technology to keep connected socially.

Social processes may have also influenced the evolution of our higher-level cognitive abilities, including mathematics. The pressures of living in close social groups are seen by some psychologists to have not only driven the increasing complexity of social facilitation but also an increase in our cognitive abilities (Dunbar, 2003; Adolphs, 2003). In fact, across non-human primate species, brain size is related to the size of the social group each individual interacts with in these species (Dunbar, 2014). In a complex fashion, this increase in cognitive abilities and social facilitation in humans also lies at the base of our development of culture.

As humans, we often want to conserve our energy. You might ask a teacher whether certain information will be on the test. If the answer is *no*, most people typically do not put in the effort to learn that information. The same is true with social relationships. As humans, we have developed strategies to make social decisions with minimal effort. We have also developed strategies that allow for more cohesion in social relationships. As you watch yourself interact with others during the day, you can notice the ways you both reduce effort and support positive relationships.

The report of Kitty Genovese at the beginning of this chapter raises a number of important questions concerning how humans interact with one another. We all tend to think we would have helped. However, what we say we would do in a particular situation is often not what social psychology research has shown that we actually do. Part of our social interactions relate to different conditions. Think of situations in which you would have helped and those in which you would not.

Previously, *heuristics* were described in terms of cognitive decisions. We also use heuristics in our social relationships. Most of our social decisions are made in real time, which does not allow for lengthy considerations. Since we are unable to rationally determine our social interactions, we use heuristics—the rules or strategies by which we make decisions and actions, although these rules are often not in awareness. These heuristics also influence how we make attributions—that is, how we make inferences about the behavior of others.

Social Cognition

Social cognition refers to the manner in which we understand others. Social cognition is a broad term, which can include our attributions about others, how we stereotype others, as well as our prejudice of others. One example of social cognition is the fundamental attribution error, as was introduced earlier in the book.

Here is the situation in which it takes place. What would happen if you were walking to class and almost got hit by a car? What would you say? If you are like most people, you would say the driver is "stupid" or some other similar term. However, if you are driving and almost hit someone, what would you say then? Typically, most people say something like "the sun was in my eyes" or "he ran in front of me" or another situational explanation.

Humans tend to attribute *trait characteristics* such as being stupid to others while using *situational explanations* such as having the sun in our eyes for ourselves. In essence, trait characteristics are internal characteristics, whereas situational ones happen outside of the person. To explain others in terms of internal characteristics and ourselves in terms of external characteristics is referred to as the fundamental attribution error or person bias and will be discussed in this section. It is also another example of how humans conserve cognitive effort by ignoring situational information when making sense of others' actions.

Attribution

As humans, we are always trying to explain to ourselves why people do what they do or why events happen in a certain way. This tendency has been studied by social psychologists as attribution theory. One of the early researchers to examine attribution was Fritz Heider (1958). Heider suggested that humans are motivated by two primary needs. The first is the need to form a coherent view of the world. That is, we want our world to make sense. And the second need is the desire to gain control over our environment. **Attributions** are one way we create a world view that makes sense to us. Technically, an attribution is how we explain events in the world. In this way, we create causal explanations for what we experience and do.

Heider discussed two types of attributions. The first is **internal or dispositional attribution**. This is the situation in which observed behaviors are attributed to the internal state of the person. Saying someone is lazy when they do not get a job would be an example of internal attributions. The second type of attribution is **external or situational attribution**. As the name implies, this is the case where a person's behavior is attributed to external factors. If you said your grade on a test was low because you were not given enough time, you would be attributing your behavior to an external or situational factor.

If you know the person well, you might use your previous experiences with this person to make these inferences. You might know that the person looks a certain way when they are tired. What if you don't know the person well? It turns out that we make guesses or predictions about what is going on. It also turns out that the manner in which we make these predictions follows a set of psychological rules that can be studied and described.

Humans make inferences in terms of the person, the situation, and the behavior observed. What has been discovered is that humans are consistent in the way we use observations of the person, the situation, and behaviors. These consistencies have been referred to as *bias*, *error*, or *heuristic*. Not only are heuristics used to solve cognitive problems, but they are also important in determining social relationships. As such, social attributions reflect our psychological tendencies to perform *person perception* in similar ways.

As research in social psychology progressed, it was suggested that individuals tend to see the behavior of others as internally directed even when there might be evidence for external influences. In fact, one of the earlier studies in this area showed that individuals still saw behaviors as internally directed even if they were told the experimenters had instructed the person to act a certain way (Napolitan & Goethals, 1979). As noted, this was referred to as the ***fundamental attribution error***. It is also known as **correspondence bias** since there is a tendency for individuals to see that how another person acts reflects their internal thoughts and feelings. Movie stars, for example, will tell you that people come up to them and expect them to behave as they have in their movies. Lab research suggests that people become associated with positions they take even if the position such as having liberal or conservative ideas was randomly assigned to them.

It was initially suggested that the fundamental attribution error or *actor–observer hypothesis*, as it was also called, was a general principle (Jones & Nisbett, 1971). This suggested that people tend to explain their own behavior with situational causes and other people's behavior with internal or personality causes. Later research has shown that there is an outcome dimension to this distinction. That is, humans tend to present themselves in ways that are most favorable to themselves (Malle, 2006). When events are negative, we are more likely to attribute our behavior to situational events. If, on the other hand, the events are positive, we are more likely to see the outcome as an expression of who we are and our abilities. We do well in a job because we are really smart and have a number of skills. If something did not work out, it is because of the people we had to work with or the limitations of the situation. This tendency to see positive events as our making and negative events as situational is referred to as the ***self-serving bias***.

The fundamental attribution error was referred to as fundamental, as it was assumed to be a common process in all cultures. However, this has not been shown to be the case (Ma-Kellams, 2020). Non-Western especially Asian cultures do not show the attribution bias in all situations. It is suggested that even in simple perceptual tasks, Western and non-Western groups attend to different cues in the environment. In general, Western individuals attend less to contextual stimuli. Contextual stimuli can be the sound of the voice rather than specific words or background information rather than the focus of the image (Masuda & Nisbett, 2001). Overall, the emphasis of conceptual cues would reduce the attribution error. Further, the attribution error is seen less in collective versus individualistic cultures. Collective cultures emphasize the manner in which each person is related to the group. China and some South American countries emphasize the collective aspects of their culture. Individual cultures, on the other hand, place more emphasis on the individual and his or her achievements. The United States, Australia, and part of Western Europe emphasize individualism.

Brain Functioning in Attribution

With the development of brain-imaging techniques, it became possible to better understand brain processes involved in attribution. Using fMRI studies, it has been shown that thinking about people tends to activate the medial prefrontal cortex (MPFC) (see Harris, Todorov, & Fiske, 2005, for an overview). Further, research tasks that emphasize internal attribution show activation in the superior temporal sulcus. This suggests that different networks of our brain are involved in just thinking about social processes as opposed to making an internal attribution.

Brain differences have also been shown when cognitive conflict is present, a condition referred to as *dissonance* (Kitayama, Chua, Tompson, & Han, 2013). Cognitive dissonance was initially studied by Leon Festinger in the 1950s. According to Festinger, ***cognitive dissonance*** is an unpleasant state that occurs when a person realizes that attitudes, actions, or beliefs are inconsistent (Festinger, 1957). For example, what do people do when asked to do or say something that was contrary to their opinion?

One classic study asked individuals to simply turn knobs in one direction and then in another (Festinger & Carlsmith, 1959). As you can imagine this was one boring task to do for a length of time. After a time, the experimenter said that additional participants were needed. The current participant was offered money to tell others that the task was fun. One group was given $1 to do this, whereas another group was given $20 to make this statement. All participants agreed to do this and did indeed make the statement that the task was fun to another person. At the end of the session, the participants were asked to rate their enjoyment of the knob-turning session. It turns out that those who were paid the $1 rated the enjoyment of the dull task higher than those who were paid $20. Why is this? According to cognitive dissonance theory, those paid $1 to say the experience was fun experienced more dissonance and thus needed to change their perspective to match the lie that they told than those paid $20.

The overall theory that has been supported in numerous studies around the world shows that we will change our attitudes and memories of events to be consistent and this is reflected in the brain. Although it has been assumed that cognitive dissonance requires conscious awareness, this may not be the case. One study examined individuals who had experienced brain damage and could not form new memories. These people could not remember they had performed a boring task. However, they showed the same attitude changes to dissonance tasks as was shown with individuals without this memory disorder (Liberman, 2007). Thus, cognitive dissonance may reflect a basic human characteristic.

Categorization and Stereotyping

A large number of social psychology studies have shown that there is a consistent tendency for individuals to view themselves, their worlds, their friends, and other aspects of themselves in an overly positive manner. Not only do we categorize whether another individual is like us (our *in-group*), we also determine who is not like us (our *out-group*). If someone is seen to be in our out-group, we tend to see them in more negative terms, as less deserving, and as more responsible for any negative event in their life. If indeed they were able to accomplish something positive, we would call it *luck*. However, if you happen to be in our in-group, then the opposite attributions are made. It is you who are responsible for your successes and situations that are responsible for your failures.

Traditional categories of **person perception** include age, gender, and race. Person perception is simply how we categorize others. These categories are processed spontaneously and effortlessly (see Devos, 2014; Liberman, Woodward, & Kinzler, 2017 for overviews). Categorization is also a type of heuristic. We use categories to simplify our social relations. Just by seeing someone, we have ideas about who they are. These categories have also been referred to as schemas. We make inferences about individuals who ride motorcycles, are obese, have tattoos, and other such features, although the processing for groups of such individuals requires more cognitive effort. When we make inferences about a group of individuals that share similar characteristics, it is referred to as **stereotyping**.

In the 1990s there was a film named *White Men Can't Jump*, which reflected the stereotype that white men were not able to play basketball as well as African American men. Older films may also reflect the stereotype that women are bad drivers. Rich people are often portrayed as uncaring. Asian students are at times seen to be good at math. Various stereotypes go with perceptions of age, gender, and race as to whether the person is lazy, dangerous, smart, a good automobile driver, outgoing, and so forth. Often comics in the newspaper play on these stereotypes.

Many corporations have sought to reduce stereotyping through employee training as well as their interaction with the public. In 2015 Airbnb permanently banned a host after she canceled a guest's reservation minutes before her arrival because the guest was Asian. In 2017, a conservative activist was banned from both ride sharing companies Uber and Lyft after she said that she didn't want a Muslim driver. Media has also sought to bring stereotyping to their readers' attention. In 2020, *The New York Times* (March 29) reported that Asian Americans were yelled at, attacked, and blamed for the COVID-19 epidemic even though they were second- or third-generation Americans who had lived in no other country than the US.

Research suggests that these stereotypes are acquired in early childhood and are difficult to change. One study looked at 6-year-olds, 10-year-olds, and adult white Americans (Baron & Banaji, 2006). These individuals were asked to complete a measure that reflects automatic associations. The basic idea is that if you view the person of one race in a negative manner, then you should be able to react faster if you are asked to identify that person's face with a negative word. Your reaction time would be slower if the opposite was the case. Using this measure, it was shown that implicit race attitudes are acquired early in life and remain relatively stable into adulthood. What does change is one's explicit attitudes. Explicit attitudes are what you tell yourself and others about your views of race and other aspects you believe are critical to your identity (Howe & Krosnick, 2017). A number of studies show that familiarity with a person of a different race or ethnic group will lead to less stereotyping.

Social psychology research has sought to describe the mechanisms that support social stereotyping. In the study of stereotyping, three aspects have been identified (Macrae & Quadflieg, 2010).

1. The first is *social categorizing*. We may say that the person is female, or Latina, or an older adult. That is, we place the person in a certain group.
2. The second aspect is *stereotype activation*. That is, once we have stereotyped another person, then a series of opinions about the person come into our mind. Numerous studies have shown that we can quickly create a series of adjectives concerning any social category.
3. The third aspect is *stereotype application*. That is, we use the information to understand the situation we have observed or what to expect in an interaction. If we saw an older person not understand someone, we might say he or she is getting senile.

It is not necessary that all three steps happen. If the person is doing a number of other tasks at the time, he or she may not make it to the stage of stereotype application (see Devos, 2014 for an overview).

Brain Aspects of Stereotyping and Prejudice

Stereotyping refers to perceptions, beliefs, and expectations we have about a group of individuals. Stereotyping is seen as a cognitive assessment of a particular group typically defined by society or culture. These cognitive assessments can be either positive or negative. They can be either accurate or inaccurate. Stereotyping reduces cognitive effort. If we assume that all members of a certain class of individuals share the same characteristics, then we do not need to consider the complex situation we see in front of us.

When a person makes a negative assessment of another person on the basis of group membership such as race, age, or gender, it involves brain areas related to cognition and memory. These areas would include the medial prefrontal areas of the brain and the temporal areas related to memory (Amodio, 2014).

Whereas stereotyping involves more of a cognitive assessment, prejudice, on the other hand, reflects a more emotional evaluation (Amodio, 2014). Prejudice is considered to precede cognitive evaluations. One common example is to see one's own group as more favorable than those who are not part of one's own group. Prejudice represents the emotional reaction, often negative, to those who are not like ourselves on what we see as critical aspects.

Prejudice is considered to involve those brain areas related to emotion and motivation (Amodio & Cikara, 2021). These areas include the amygdala, insula, striatum, prefrontal cortex, and orbital frontal cortex. As noted previously, the amygdala responds quickly to threat, including perceived social threat, which includes responses to those who are not part of our cultural group. What is interesting is that if the person sees a different face quickly, then amygdala activation is seen. However, if the face is seen for a longer period, prefrontal cortex and anterior cingulate will inhibit the amygdala (Kutson, Mah, Manly, & Grafman, 2007; Richeson et al., 2003).

The insula is related to internal feeling states, which gives us a sense of self (Namkung, Kim, & Sawa, 2017). Insula activity has also been seen to be active in terms of racial bias. The striatum is part of the basal ganglia and is involved in goal-directed responses as well as habits. This area is also active in terms of same-race responses (Amodio, 2014). Overall, research has shown the prefrontal cortex to be related to the processing of social information. As with many emotional and cognitive processes, there is a close connection between prejudice and stereotyping. Additional brain areas, such as the medial prefrontal cortex, are involved in both prejudice and stereotyping. We cannot avoid stereotyping and prejudice, as described in the box: Myths and Misconceptions—You Can Be Bias Free.

Myths and Misconceptions—You Can Be Bias Free

As humans, we often see ourselves as bias free. That is, we can take a perspective and understand people as individuals. However, most of our perception of others does not happen with careful thought. We make quick decisions, particularly at times when we are tired or busy. Research suggests that this is the very time that bias can happen. In this case, bias is the process of having a set of attributes associated with a category of objects or people.

Early research showed that people could sort pairs of words more quickly when they followed the person's existing categories. In this study, participants responded more quickly when pairing flower names, such as rose or tulip, with good words such as peach, glory, or laughter and when pairing insect names, such as fly, wasp, or beetle, with negative words such as war, failure, or sadness (Greenwald et al., 1998). It took longer to pair the flower names with the negative words and the insect names with the positive words. The basic idea is that you have a set of attitudes or associations with different categories of people or objects.

At this point, more than 500 studies have used this basic idea to study implicit attitudes. The ***Implicit Association Test (IAT)*** measures attitudes and beliefs that people may be unwilling or unable to report. The IAT may be especially interesting if it shows that you have an implicit attitude that you do not know about. For example, you may believe that women and men should be equally associated with science, but your automatic associations could show that you (like many others) associate men with science more than you associate women with science. A recent study showed that hiring managers whose scores on the IAT indicated gender bias tended to favor men over women in their hiring decisions (see Sleek, 2018 and Vianello & Bar-Anan, 2020 for overviews).

One meta-analysis of the IAT incorporated more than 100 research studies with more than 14,000 participants (Greenwald, Poehlman, Uhlmann, & Banaji, 2009). This research compared what a person would say they believed or would do as opposed to their responses on the IAT. The self-report predictions were worst for sensitive topics, such as those that involved inter-racial behaviors and best for those that involved close relationships, political preferences, or use of alcohol and drugs. The IAT predictions were best for sensitive topics such as intergroup relationships. Thus, in those areas that involve sensitive topics, people are not aware of their own biases.

You can take this test online (https://implicit.harvard.edu/implicit/education.html). There is also an NPR Invisibilia show about several types of bias including the IAT (https://www.npr.org/programs/invisibilia/532950995/the-culture-inside).

Thought Question: Take the Implicit Association Test (IAT) for yourself at the link above. Are you surprised at the results? What specific steps can you take to examine and reduce bias in your daily life?

CONCEPT CHECK

1. This chapter begins with a long list of the ways in which we humans are social creatures. Which are most central to understanding our human psychology?
2. What are the definitions and interrelationships among the following concepts related to *attribution*:
   a. Fundamental attribution error?
   b. Internal or dispositional attribution?
   c. External or situational attribution?
   d. Self-serving bias?
3. Identify and describe the three rules by which we make internal or external attributions.
   a. How do the three rules combine to form the condition for an internal attribution?
   b. How do the three rules combine to form the condition for an external attribution?
4. What are the three categories traditionally included as part of person perception? What is the relationship between stereotyping and person perception?
5. Identify and describe the three stages that support the process of stereotyping.
6. What is the difference between stereotyping and prejudice? What evidence does the brain provide in describing their differences?

Looking at Others and the Face

In *Macbeth*, Shakespeare described the face "as a book where men may read strange matters" (Act 1, Scene 5). Faces are extremely important social stimuli. Looking at someone's face tells us whether we recognize them. They also tell us about a person's identity such as gender, age, and ethnicity. In our interactions with others, the face gives us clues to the other person's mood. The gaze of the eyes also tells us about how the person is interacting with us. Even infants would rather look at a face than other stimuli. Given that the face plays such an important role in our social interactions, it is not surprising that we have cognitive and neural mechanisms associated with face processing (see Adolphs & Tusche, 2017; Kanwisher & Yovel, 2006 for overviews).

Across a number of species, infants evoke a special type of social interaction. Babies receive more gentle and loving care than older children. Humans will often smile and begin a type of "baby talk" whenever they see an infant. Baby talk generally includes a higher pitched voice with very simple language structure. We also like cartoon characters or stuffed animals that have baby face characteristics.

Interestingly, social psychology research has also shown that humans treat other humans with baby-like faces in a more positive way (Zebrowitz & Montepare, 2008). Judges actually give lighter sentences to those convicted of a crime whose faces have more baby-like face characteristics. On the other hand, those without a baby face were judged to be better at demanding occupations that involve less social interaction.

As a social appraisal characteristic, we tend to overgeneralize from someone's facial features to other characteristics of the person. People with attractive faces are seen to be more outgoing, socially competent, sexually responsive, intelligent, and healthy (see Zebrowitz & Montepare, 2008 for an overview). Popular magazines, websites, and videos feature people with attractive faces. Further, not only do we judge those with attractive traits to have more positive traits, we also treat them in a more positive way. Attractive people are more likely to be hired. The opposite is also true in that those with less attractive faces are viewed and dealt with in a more negative manner. These positive and negative tendencies are not limited to American culture but are seen across the world. Whereas different cultures may evaluate body size or skin color in different ways, facial attractiveness is evaluated in a more universal manner (Little, Jones, & DeBruine, 2011).

Historically, in most cultures it has been assumed that the human face can reveal a person's true nature and intentions (see Jack & Schyns, 2017; Todorov, Olivola, Dotsch, & Mende-Siedlecki, 2015 for a review). Research has also shown that facial appearance predicts social outcomes in areas such as politics, law, business, and the military.

In one study (Willis & Todorov, 2006), college students were asked to look at photos of unfamiliar faces for as little as a one-tenth of a second. Their judgments concerning such characteristics as attractiveness, competency, trustworthiness, likeability, and aggression were similar to other students who could view the faces for a long period of time. Everyone was able to make judgments in a tenth of a second. However, with a longer viewing time, individuals became more confident in their judgments. Overall, individuals can create impressions of others effortlessly in a quick glance.

We not only make appraisals of appearance but also of intention. We are able to make quick estimates of someone's intentions and prepare to respond appropriately. From an evolutionary standpoint, we can begin to understand what types of tasks were required from our earliest history. One important task is decrypting information from another's face. As we have seen, we can identify emotions in someone's face without problem—unless, of course, it is upside down, as we saw earlier in this book!

We have come to understand that certain types of processing are given priority over other types. Things that represent a danger are processed faster and receive a high priority of action. What we pay attention to is clearly part of evolutionary history. An important part of this history is what aspects of our culture we incorporate into our world view. Like children's ability to efficiently absorb the language around them, we humans absorb the social norms of our culture and the ability to use this effectively puts one at an advantage (Simon, 1990). The inability to understand and respond in terms of social norms is often seen at the heart of disorders such as autism spectrum disorder (Happé, Cook, & Bird, 2017).

Also, as discussed in terms of developmental processes, humans can infer intentions and behaviors of others from limited information. Human infants, children, and adolescents remain dependent in a variety of ways that encourage social interactions. Not only do we enjoy and seek social contact, but the denial of this contact leads to pain. Historically, we felt isolation when away from our group. Today, with modern technology social networking can take place at great distances. Being part of a group is typically associated with well-being. However, it is also possible to feel left out with digital social networking. This has led some individuals to constantly check their social networking platforms such as Facebook or Twitter to remain in contact. When not connected, some individuals experience the *fear of missing out* (FOMO). That is, they are concerned that an event is happening without being a part of it. This fear has been seen in adolescents and young adults around the world (Alt, 2015; Buglass, Binder, Betts, & Underwood, 2017; Oberst, Wegmann, Stodt, Brand, & Chamarro, 2017).

In terms of feeling left out, our brain uses similar pathways that are active during physical pain. That is, when people experience social pain such as being socially excluded, the same areas are active as during physical pain (Eisenberger, Lieberman, & Williams, 2003; Eisenberger & Muscatell, 2014; Eisenberger, 2015). Further, EEG differences are also seen in those with a high fear of missing out (Lai, Altavilla, Ronconi, & Aceto, 2016).

Figure 12-1 shows the brain areas involved in social and physical pain, which are activated by such social experiences as feeling excluded, bereavement, being treated unfairly, and negative social comparisons as well as positive experiences. On the right side of the figure, you can see the reward network that responds to a variety of physical and social pleasures. Some of these social experiences include having a good reputation, being treated fairly, cooperating, and giving to charity. This reward network activates the same brain areas

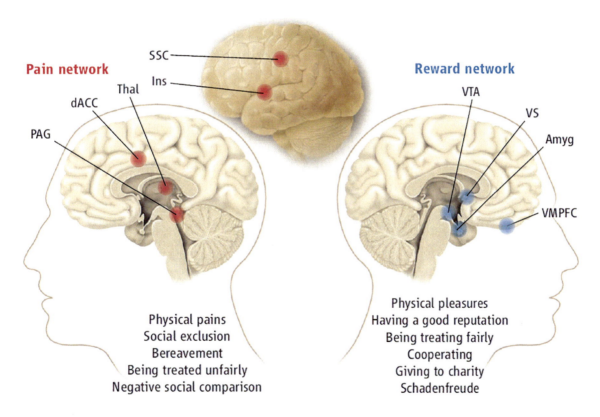

The pain and pleasure systems. The pain network consists of the dorsal anterior cingulate cortex (dACC), insula (Ins), somatosensory cortex (SSC), thalamus (Thal), and periaqueductal gray (PAG). This network is implicated in physical and social pain processes. The reward or pleasure network consists of the ventral tegmental area (VTA), ventral striatum (VS), ventromedial prefrontal cortex (VMPFC), and the amygdala (Amyg). This network is implicated in physical and social rewards.

Figure 12-1 Pain and pleasure system.
Source: Lieberman and Eisenberger (2009).

as seen in the rewarding effects of drugs and sex (Volkow et al., 2012). One critical part of this network is the *ventral tegmental area* (VTA), which is involved in the positive experience during social contact. In particular, it has been shown that the hormone oxytocin influences the VTA and is involved in prosocial behaviors such as making connections with others (Hung et al., 2017; Preston, 2017). This suggests that our brain is motivated for human interactions in the same way we want sex, drugs, and even chocolate.

Face Processing and the Brain

Two areas of the brain that play important roles in face processing are known as the *occipital face area (OFA)* and the *fusiform face area (FFA)*, which are located relatively close to each other. As you learned in the chapter discussing vision, information from the retina goes to the occipital lobe for low-level processing. Information then goes to a variety of areas for specific types of processing, such as color, motion, and line features. One area in the occipital lobe is the occipital face area. Given that the OFA shows activity to both inverted and upright faces, it is assumed that facial feature analysis takes place there (see Macrae & Quadflieg, 2010 for an overview).

Research suggests that the FFA is involved in more total face recognition rather than low-level feature detection (Kanwisher & Yovel, 2006). The FFA is sensitive to how the face is presented (upright or inverted), which suggests a more holistic level of analysis. The FFA has also been found to play a role in analyzing features related to determining the gender and racial characteristics of the face. This suggests that these facial features can be evaluated quickly in an interaction with another person.

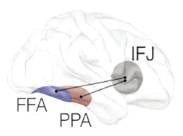

Figure 12-2 Attention to faces involves different areas of the brain.

From Baldauf & Desimone, 2014 Science 344, p. 426

Pictures of faces are processed in the brain differently than pictures of houses. As shown in **Figure 12-2**, attention to faces enhances cortical activity in the FFA, whereas attention to houses increases activity in the parahippocampal place area (PPA) (Baldauf & Desimone, 2014). Further, MEG activity and synchrony were seen between the inferior frontal junction (IFJ) and the FFA when looking at faces. When looking at houses, greater MEG synchrony was seen between the IFJ and PPA. What information we derive from seeing a face can also influence our actions, as described in the box: The World Is Your Laboratory—Are Police More Likely to Shoot Black Suspects?

The World Is Your Laboratory—Are Police More Likely to Shoot Black Suspects?

In the early hours of February 4, 1999, in a notorious neighborhood in the South Bronx, four white plain clothes police officers spotted Amadou Diallo, a 22-year-old Black man, in front of his apartment. The officers approached, Diallo turned to enter his building, and the officers pursued. In the vestibule, they ordered Diallo to show his hands and freeze (Flynn, 1999; Fritsch, 2000). Diallo reportedly reached into his pocket. One of the officers identified the object Diallo pulled out as a gun and yelled that he had a gun (Fritsch, 2000). The officers opened fire, ultimately discharging 41 rounds and fatally wounding Diallo. A wallet – not a gun – was found at the scene.

In 1994, 13-year-old Nicholas Heyward, Jr., was shot and killed by an officer while playing with a toy gun in the stairwell of his apartment building. In 2003, Orlando Barlow was shot while surrendering on his knees. The officer stated that he feared Barlow was feigning surrender and was going to reach for a gun. In 2010, Aaron Campbell was walking backward toward police with his hands behind his head (presumably to surrender) and was shot by an officer who believed he was going to reach for a gun. In 2014, Michael Brown was shot in Ferguson, MO. In 2018, Sacramento police shot Stephon Clark holding a cellphone in his grandmother's yard because they believed he was holding a gun.

Although each of these cases involves different circumstances, in each case, the suspect was a Black man, and in each case, officers stated that they believed their lives were in immediate danger because the suspect was reaching for, or had, a gun.

What does research suggest? Overall, research suggests that *race* is a socially constructed construct that can be changed (Richeson & Sommers, 2016). That is, we come to view race through a cultural lens of who is like us and who is not. As shown in the media, contact across racial lines is disquieting and difficult for some people. Stereotype application and activation may lead us to predict we could experience a difficult situation.

One group of individuals who are often forced to make a quick decision about risk is the police. Using a video game format, participants were asked to "shoot" armed individuals and "not shoot" unarmed individuals who appeared quickly on the screen (Correll, Park, Judd, & Wittenbrink, 2002). White college students were quicker to shoot an armed individual if he was Black than if he was White. Likewise, they were quicker to not-shoot an unarmed person if he was White. In terms of making an error, participants erroneously shot unarmed Black individuals more often than unarmed Whites. These same results were found when the participants were from the local community.

Is this also true for the police who receive extensive training including similar video game shooter/non-shooter experiences? Using a large city police force in a video game situation, differences were found from results with college students and community groups (see Correll, Hudson, Guillermo, & Ma, 2014, for an overview). First, the police were more often correct. They were better able to pick out who had a gun and who did not. Second, the police made the correct decision faster. Third, the police did not show racial bias when they shot an unarmed person. If they made a mistake, it was just as likely to be a White as a Black person. However, they did show bias in their reaction times. That is, police officers were faster to shoot individuals with guns if they were Black and faster to not shoot unarmed individuals if they were White. Overall, this suggests that police, as well as other individuals through practice, can learn that race is not an important characteristic for determining whether a gun is present. However, when they are tired, overworked, or lack energy for other reasons, then stereotypical reactions may be more frequent.

Research also suggests that interracial interactions require more energy to conduct and may actually impair cognitive functioning (Richeson & Trawalter, 2005). These authors note that direct interpersonal contact with a member of a racial minority

BLUE	GREEN	YELLOW
PINK	RED	ORANGE
GREY	BLACK	PURPLE
TAN	WHITE	BROWN

Figure 12-3 Read out loud the color of the ink used. This is the Stroop effect; individuals are slower when asked to name the color of the ink.

group may encourage the person to actively suppress any stereotypical feelings. In a series of studies, these researchers varied the effort needed to interact with another person of either the same race or a different race.

Following the interaction, the participant performed the Stroop Color Interference Task, as shown in **Figure 12-3**. The traditional Stroop test has color names in ink of a different color. For example, the word green would be shown in red ink. When asked to name the color of the ink, individuals are slower when the name and color do not match as compared with when the ink and color name are the same.

In low-effort conditions or with a member of the same racial group, there was better performance on the Stroop than in interracial interactions. That is, individuals could read the color of the ink faster with members of their same race. With members of different races, the suggestion is that there is also unconscious processing related to race. This, in turn, would interfere with the Stroop task. The researchers suggest that effortful interracial interactions can actually limit executive functioning. Given that executive functions are associated with the inhibition of actions, these findings help us understand how some interracial interactions turn negative as if the person was not thinking or considering what was happening.

Data from the Department of Justice (DOJ, 2001) indicate that, per capita, police are roughly five times more likely to shoot a Black person than a White person (Correll, Hudson, Guillermo, & Ma, 2014).

Thought Question: You are a psychologist hired by a big city police department to develop a training program to reduce the impact of racial bias in day-to-day policing. From what you have read, what are three major components of the training program you would recommend?

The Social Brain Hypothesis

The ***social brain hypothesis*** developed in the 1980s suggests that humans and other primates differed from non-primates principally in the size of their brain as compared to their body size. The basic idea is that complexity of social skills requires a large brain. In our social reactions, we need to be able to interact with a number of individuals. With some of these people we have close relationships, and with others we need to pay attention to what they want or expect of us. All of this requires cognitive and emotional effort.

Prior to the social brain hypothesis, it was generally assumed that human intellectual abilities were the result of the skills required for hunting and other tool use. It is now

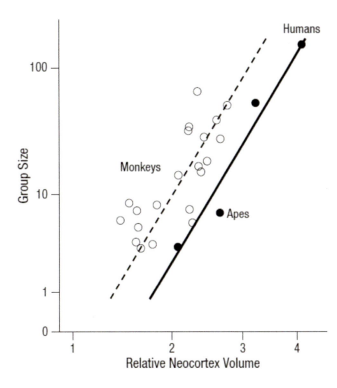

Figure 12-4 There is a relationship between the group size of a species and brain volume.
Source: Dunbar (2014).

known that the brain size of areas involved in social processing does correlate with social skills in humans (see Dunbar, 2011, 2014, for an overview).

In reviewing the literature, Dunbar (2003, 2014) points out that at least five separate measures of social complexity have been shown to correlate with neocortex volume in primates (see **Figure 12-4**). These five measures are:

1. social group size
2. grooming clique size
3. extent to which social skills are used in male mating strategies
4. frequency of tactical deception
5. frequency of social play

Are there any particular areas of the brain that show higher correlations to social group size? Yes, it is the frontal lobes and the part of the amygdala that has direct neural connections to the frontal lobe as well as the area of the temporal lobe. As you remember, the frontal lobes are concerned with planning and executive function and the amygdala is involved in emotional processing. The temporal lobe is involved in sensory processing including face recognition.

As you can see from the graph (**Figure 12-4**), the social group size of humans is shown to be 150. This number is seen by scientists as the number of individuals that humans have lived with throughout our evolutionary history. This is roughly the number of people that you have a personal connection with or the number of people you could ask a favor and expect it to be granted. There are, of course, more people than this that you interact with in various ways, such as the person who sells you coffee in the morning. You can probably recognize and name at least 1,000 individuals and some individuals have even more "friends" on Facebook.

Brain Systems Involved in Social Relations

Our present-day emotionality has largely evolved within a social context. In terms of brain structure, many of the structures involved in the processing of emotion are also important for social behavior. Brain structures involved in social interactions can be organized in terms of three processes (Brothers, 1990; Adolphs, 2003). The first process involves higher-level neocortical regions in the processing of sensory information. This is how we know who we experience through vision, hearing, touch, and other sensory processes. Research suggests when looking at a face, we process broad categorizations related to gender and to the emotion expressed before we complete the detailed construction of the entire face and determine who we are seeing.

Second, our sensory system also helps us predict what people will do socially, based on their physical movements. As we experience a social interaction, what happens on the level of the brain? What happens first involves the amygdala, striatum, and orbitofrontal cortex. The amygdala is involved in processing the emotional significance of an event. This includes both positive emotions such as a person you care about smiling at you, as well as negative emotions such as seeing someone angry or fearful. Activation also takes place if a person looks untrustworthy. This determination occurs independent of gender, race, eye gaze, or emotionality expressed. Through its connections to other areas, the amygdala also can influence memory, attention, and decision-making. Overall, these areas help us know the emotional context of our perceptions and what we need to do about them.

The third process involves the higher cortical regions of the neocortex including the prefrontal cortex, as shown previously in this chapter. These are the regions that let us construct an inner model of our social world. Included in this model would be some social understanding of others, their relationship with us, and the meaning of our actions for the social group. It is these areas that are most likely associated with *theory of mind*, our ability to attribute mental states to other people. Indeed, damage to the orbitofrontal cortex does reduce our ability to detect a faux pas in a given situation.

The prefrontal cortex has also been shown to be activated during humor, social-norm transgressions resulting in embarrassment, and so-called moral emotions. With damage to this area, individuals have difficulty knowing that another person is being deceptive. Although there is limited research to date directed at the topic, it may turn out that we have not only evolved systems for determining the basic emotions, such as fear, joy, or anger, but also for the more socially related ones, such as guilt, shame, embarrassment, jealousy, and pride.

The prefrontal cortex also appears to be involved in various aspects of social relationships, social cooperation, moral behavior, and social aggression. Using fMRI research, brain processes involved in the variety of tasks required for social interactions have been identified (see Burnett, Sebastian, Kadosh, & Blakemore, 2011; Frith & Frith, 2010; Nelson et al., 2005 for overviews). As can be seen in **Figure 12-5**, the social brain can be seen as composed of areas involved in the detection of social processes including face recognition (the fusiform face area—FFA) including emotional recognition (the amygdala, insula, and the anterior cingulate cortex—ACC), and regulating cognitive processes involving the frontal areas of the brain.

Preference for human faces begins shortly after birth in humans. As the child matures, cortical areas such as the fusiform face area in the temporal lobe show greater differentiation. Through its connections comes the ability to recognize and remember faces—an ability that continues into adulthood. This includes increased differentiation of emotional

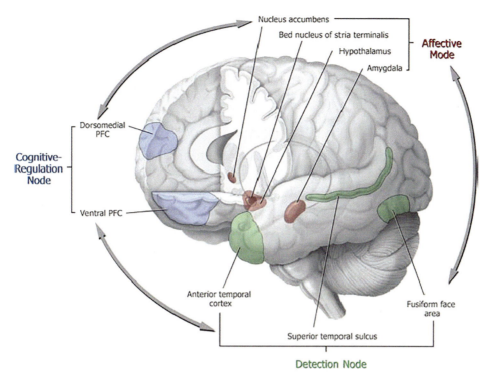

Figure 12-5 The social brain can be seen as composed of areas involved in the detection of social processes including face recognition (the fusiform face area—FFA) and emotional recognition (the amygdala, insula, and the anterior cingulate cortex—ACC), and regulating cognitive processes involving the frontal areas of the brain.
Source: Nelson, Leibenluft, McClure, and Pine (2005).

facial expression, which involves the amygdala. Interestingly enough, adolescents show greater reactivity to emotional faces than do adults.

One area of the brain that is gaining interest from researchers is the bottom part of the frontal lobe, referred to as the ventromedial prefrontal cortex (vmPFC) (see Roy, Shohamy, & Wager, 2012, for an overview). The vmPFC appears to be important when affective responses are influenced by conceptual information about specific outcomes. In this way, it serves as a hub that links this affective-conceptual information with the brainstem that is involved in emotional responses of the entire organism through autonomic and endocrine regulation. This includes emotion, emotion regulation, fear conditioning and extinction, episodic and semantic memory, prospection, economic valuation, self-directed cognition, and understanding the feelings and intentions of others. As such, it is an evolutionarily important structure that coordinates information important for survival. The disruption of this system is associated with PTSD, depression, and chronic stress and pain.

Brain Activity in Playing Games

You may think that playing games is not part of the real world, but our brain doesn't know this (van Dijk & De Dreu, 2021). Recent research has begun to examine how our brains respond when we are playing the *prisoners' dilemma* or *ultimatum* game. In the ultimatum game, two players are given the opportunity to split a sum of money. One player makes an offer as to how the money should be split between the two of them. The other player can either accept or reject the offer. If the offer is accepted, the money is split as suggested. However, if the offer is rejected, neither receives any money. What would you do? If you were trying to maximize your gain, you would offer as little as possible. Likewise, if given a choice, you might assume that the other person would take whatever was offered because, otherwise, he or she would receive nothing. This is what economists claim is the rational thing to do.

What do you think people really do? It turns out when you look across a wide variety of studies in various countries that the most frequent offer made is about 50% of the money. If the offer is much lower than this, say approximately 20% of the total, it has about a 50% chance of being rejected. Why are such offers rejected? Because the offer is believed to be unfair. It is suggested that this is an emotional response in which the person feels angry and seeks to punish the other person because of the low offer.

In one brain-imaging study, fair (split 50% of the money) and unfair offers (split 10% or 20% of the money) showed differential brain activation (Sanfey et al., 2003). Unfair offers in comparison to fair offers showed greater activation of the bilateral anterior insula, dorsolateral prefrontal cortex, and the anterior cingulate cortex. As you remember, these are brain areas involved in the processing of emotional information. Further, that these findings were the result of a *human* social reaction was demonstrated by the fact that the insula showed greater activation when the participants thought they were playing against real people as opposed to a computer. Overall, these data suggest that emotionality lies at the basis of our social interactions.

CONCEPT CHECK

1. "The face is a critical part of social appraisal across all ages." Describe three situations that provide evidence of the importance of the face in humans' relations with others.
2. How is face processing represented in the structures and processes of the brain?
3. Describe the social brain hypothesis including the following aspects identified by Dunbar:
    a. What are the five measures of social complexity that are related to neocortex volume in primates?
    b. Which particular areas of the brain are related to group size?
4. Three processes are considered to be involved in social interactions:
    a. Describe these three processes.
    b. Where in the brain do these processes occur, and specifically what does each brain structure contribute to our experience of social interactions?
    c. According to the results in the ultimatum game study, what lies at the basis of our social interactions? How is this reflected in the brain?

Social Emotions

As researchers studied social and emotional processes, it became clear that there was an additional type of emotional processing. These emotions generally appeared within the context of social interactions. What happens if you say something stupid, or call your current boyfriend by the name of your previous boyfriend? You feel embarrassed. Just like basic emotions, your body reacts with physiological responses, such as your face turning red and your body moving in a characteristic way, such as averting your eyes and touching your face. It feels like a basic emotion. However, it is different in that it requires the presence, or the imagined presence, of another person. In this sense, embarrassment is a ***social emotion***. Social emotions are those emotions that involve our interactions with other people in a social context. Examples of these emotions are embarrassment, shame, guilt, jealousy, envy, and pride.

From an evolutionary perspective, this allows us to think about emotions such as fear that satisfy a self-preservation function and emotions such as embarrassment, guilt, or shame that serve a more social function. Since these social emotions also require a more developed sense of self, we would also predict that they appeared later in our evolutionary development. Let us look at these social emotions.

Embarrassment is a social emotion easily understood by people, and it has been observed in a variety of cultures (see Keltner & Buswell, 1997 for an overview). In terms of understanding the situational nature of embarrassment, Iranian and Japanese children classified the causes of embarrassment in similar ways. Embarrassment is commonly reported in response to physical mishaps such as spilling something on someone, cognitive mistakes such as forgetting someone's name, loss of body control such as belching, or finding oneself the center of undesired attention as with teasing.

Surprisingly, embarrassment has been less well-studied by researchers interested in basic emotions, although Darwin did describe blushing in relation to a violation of etiquette, which he saw as a type of shame (Darwin, 1872). However, patterns of embarrassment satisfy the nine requirements of a basic emotion as suggested by Paul Ekman in the chapter on emotions. These include being automatic, of quick onset, with a specific physiology, and found across cultures. Another of these requirements was that the emotion be seen in non-human species. Where embarrassment-like body movements, including gaze aversion, smiling, head movement, self-touching, and grooming are seen in nonhuman primates, they are in appeasement displays in which one individual seeks to pacify the other and keep the social bond intact. Thus, embarrassment may have had its origins in terms of appeasement.

Besides embarrassment, which is usually short-lived with minor consequences, other social emotions may be more long lasting. Guilt and shame are two examples. Although similar, social psychologists see these as two separate emotions (Eisenberg, 2000). *Guilt* is described as an emotional state associated with other people objecting to your actions, inactions, or intentions and may be preceded by lying, cheating, stealing, infidelity, and neglecting duties (Keltner & Buswell, 1997; McCullough et al., 2001). *Shame* also involves the opinion of others to a greater extent. Overall, shame appears to involve our entire concept of ourselves, whereas guilt is more distinct from the self. Guilt involves feelings of tension, remorse, and regret without involving our core identity. One distinction that has been made is that shame is associated with the desire to undo aspects of the self, whereas guilt involves the desire to undo aspects of behavior. Research suggests that individuals' shame experiences are more painful and intense than guilt experiences (Eisenberg, 2000). Since guilt and shame involve transgression against the conventions of the group, these have been called ***moral emotions***. Feelings of sympathy and guilt have been seen to motivate cooperative behavior and altruism (Trivers, 1971). Additionally, guilt appears to help individuals keep commitments and thus maintain relationships.

Besides social emotions that we experience ourselves, we also experience social emotions when we see events happening to other people. One of these is *envy* when we observe positive events happening to another person. Another situation is when something negative happens to someone who we envy, and he or she falls from grace. When negative things happen to such a person, we may find ourselves feeling positive about the events. Delight in the misfortune of others is referred to by the German word *schadenfreude*. Brain-imaging studies show that when we experience envy, pain-related neural networks, as described previously (**Figure 12-1**), are activated. On the other hand, *schadenfreude* or the delight in someone else's misfortune activates the reward network (Takahashi et al., 2009).

Prosocial Behavior and Helping

What would you have done if you were in the apartment building and saw what was happening to Kitty Genovese in the story that begins this chapter? Most of us believe we would have helped. Yet, none of the individuals there did. Why not? One person who was the first to call the police said, "I didn't want to get involved." Actually, he first called a friend to ask what to do and then had another neighbor make the call to the police. Other neighbors said they were tired and just wanted to go back to bed. Others, when asked why they did not call the police, just said, "I do not know."

The Kitty Genovese story was portrayed in the popular press as showing the indifference, moral callousness, and loss of concern on the part of humans (Latané & Darley, 1969). Two social psychologists, Bibb Latané and John Darley, viewed the media reaction to the Kitty Genovese event as missing the complexity of human psychology and ignoring the situational conditions involved. For example, Latané and Darley noted that the people who watched the Kitty Genovese event did not just ignore it. Rather, the people continued to stare out their window. They were tentative about what was happening in the street below them. As suggested by Latané and Darley, the people watching could be seen as unwilling to act but unable to turn away.

In this sense, it was neither helpful nor heroic. However, these individuals were not indifferent, as suggested by the popular press. It should also be noted that the documentary *The Witness* released in 2016 by Kitty Genovese's brother, Bill Genovese, suggested that *The New York Times* may have gotten some of its facts wrong in the initial story. However, the original report did motivate social psychologists to better understand helping behavior.

It is a characteristic of people to help one another. If you are walking across campus and someone asks for help moving a box, you will probably say *yes*. If your neighbor needs to borrow some food, you generally say *yes*. We collect money for others who are in need. We give blood for use by those we don't know. We give our own labor to help a friend move or offer a ride to someone. None of these situations would be considered an emergency or perhaps put us at risk of harm as did the Kitty Genovese situation.

An emergency has different characteristics. It is a relatively rare event that we don't encounter every day. An emergency is also an event that can put us in harm's way. These two events tend to lead us into not being able to accurately estimate the potential harm that can occur and to distort our view of the situation. Not only is there confusion concerning the nature of the situation but also concerning our responsibility to become involved. Understanding the factors involved in helping led to a series of studies examining bystander intervention. **Bystander intervention** research predicts the likelihood that someone will actively address a situation they view as problematic. In general, it has focus on the situational factors that influence whether a person will intervene or not.

Bibb Latané and John Darley decided to examine emergency situations in the laboratory (Latané & Darley, 1969). The first question they asked was whether the number of people involved matters. They asked college students in New York to discuss some of the problems encountered in a big city university. Initially, each participant was asked to fill out a questionnaire in a small room. In one condition, a student filled out the questionnaire alone. In a second condition, there were three individuals in the room each filling out a questionnaire. In the final condition, there were also three individuals but two of them were part of the experiment. That is, the two who were part of the experiment were confederates who had been instructed to remain passive.

At some point, smoke began to come into the room through a wall vent. The volume of smoke was such that, after six minutes, vision would be obscured. If the participant was the only one in the room, the participant would investigate the smoke and then go out of the room to find someone to tell. Three-quarters of the participants reported the smoke within 6 minutes, although the average participant did it within 2 minutes. In the condition with two confederates who were instructed to do nothing, the participant largely did not report the smoke. In fact, only 10% reported the smoke compared with the 75% in the alone condition who reported the smoke. When all three individuals were naïve to the experiment, there was a greater number of reports (38%) than in the confederate condition, but less than in the individual-alone condition. This research suggests that having others around us who are not reacting to the situation leads us also to not react.

Social psychologists understand *social inhibition* in which a person does not act to be a general phenomenon that can be observed across a number of situations even outside the laboratory. In October 2011, a 2-year-old girl was run over in Beijing and left lying on the street ignored by bystanders. At least 18 people passed by the bleeding toddler alone in the road without offering to help. Some even had to steer their motorcycles around the toddler. Finally, a 58-year-old person who was scavenging for garbage pulled the toddler to the side of the road and sought help. Sadly, the toddler died in a hospital a week later. Similarly, in 2014 a man on a subway in Shanghai fainted. Surveillance video shows that within 10 seconds all of the people on the train had left and he was lying on the floor of the car. In terms of helping, safety in numbers does not apply.

Even if a person is alone, the context of the situation can play a role. What would you do if you saw a man and a woman fighting with each other? Would it be different if the woman said to the man, "Get away from me; I don't know you," than if she said, "I don't know why I ever married you." Lance Shotland and Margaret Straw demonstrated that 65% of the time people would help the woman if they thought she did not know the man, but only 19% of the time if they were thought to be married (Shotland & Straw, 1976).

CONCEPT CHECK

1. What is a social emotion? Describe some examples of social emotions.
2. What is a moral emotion? Describe some examples of moral emotions.
3. This section states, "Besides social emotions which we experience ourselves, we also experience social emotions when we see events happening to other people." Describe two examples of this.
4. How does the research of social psychologists Bibb Latané and John Darley give us a more comprehensive understanding of the context of helping behavior? Give two specific conditions they reported in determining who would help and when.

Human Origins Perspectives on Helping Others and Altruism

As humans, we ask one another for help often. We may be walking across campus and someone says can you help me move this box. We probably say yes, even though we will never see that person again and they will never be able to help us in times of need. Although moving a box is a simple task that does not cost us anything, humans also help one another when risks are high. For example, in the COVID-19 virus epidemic that began in 2020, a number of health care workers volunteered in other cities, which literally put their lives at risk. Helping others is referred to as altruism.

Altruism is defined as helping another person when it does not directly benefit ourselves. If someone stops you on campus and asks you to help them do something, what do you do? "Depends upon what I am asked to do," is probably your first answer. If it really does not cost you anything, then you will most likely say *yes*. This is what Donald Campbell (1983) called **weak altruism**. Weak altruism refers to helping others without any sacrifice on your part. If it costs you something, then he referred to it as **strong altruism**. For example, a honeybee worker will sting an intruder to save the group even if this results in death for the bee. How do we figure out whether helping is going to cost us something or not? One answer is whether it benefits our family. If the person who asks you is related to you, then we are more likely to help, even if it costs us something.

The theory of **kin selection** or **inclusive fitness** was developed by William Hamilton in the 1960s. The basic theory suggests that we help relatives because it increases the chances that genes similar to our own will be passed on. The outcome of the theory is that the more related we are genetically, the more we will help. As noted, altruistic behavior is seen across all species. The existence of altruism was a problem for Darwin's theory of evolution, which Hamilton helped to solve. Darwin was concerned that altruistic behavior could not be explained by natural selection since altruism did not appear to aid a given organism's fitness. That is, helping someone you will never see again doesn't increase your offspring in any way.

Hamilton realized that altruism could evolve if it aided the organism's genetic kin to pass on their genes. Included in these genes would be the mechanism for altruism among kin. By acting altruistically, Hamilton suggests that the organism ensures that genetic material more similar to its own is passed on. That is to say, if a behavior helps to ensure the passing on of genes similar to one's own, then this behavior would be favored. Inclusive fitness as a property can be measured by considering the reproductive success of the individual plus the effects of an individual's actions on the reproductive success of one's relatives.

How about unrelated individuals? Do we help them? We help unrelated individuals if we can reasonably expect them to help us in turn. This is the theory of **reciprocal altruism**, which was developed by Robert Trivers in the 1970s. The basic idea is that our own fitness in an evolutionary sense can be increased if we can expect others to help us sometime in the future. Trivers saw this tendency growing out of the evolutionary past when humans lived in small groups and it was possible to note who helped whom or not. Those who helped were helped in return and thus had a greater chance of surviving and passing on the genes related to these processes. Since one condition of this theory is that the individual is able to recognize and remember who had helped in the past, then reciprocal altruism should be limited to species with these abilities. Primates, including humans, would fit this qualification for *weak altruism*. *Strong altruism* or *kin selection* relationships on the other hand can be found across a wide variety of species.

Understanding **cooperation**, which is helping others even when it does not help ourselves, was initially a daunting task for evolutionary psychology (Henrich & Muthukrishna,

2021). If we just pay attention to natural selection and sexual selection, where does cooperation fit in? One answer to this question was found in the 20th century as scientists began to examine a variety of species. In this examination, it became clear that a number of species displayed clear examples of cooperation. This was seen in bees that collect pollen for the whole hive, or mole rats that build elaborate tunnels for the whole community, or meerkats that risk their lives to guard a common nest, or vampire bats that feed other bats when there is need. There are even cases of altruism in which whales and dolphins have been seen to help members of another species (Trivers, 1985). Young children have also been shown to be naturally cooperative and helpful in many situations (Tomasello, 2014). With the extensive research on bees, ants, and humans, it became clear that, in addition to self-preservation and sexuality, there were also instinctual programs for social processes related to cooperation. The task was then to understand the details of these programs.

Using Games to Study Cooperation

How can we study our tendencies to cooperate with another person in a more experimental manner? One answer to this question is through games. One of the best studied games is known as the *prisoners' dilemma*. Imagine the situation in which two individuals are imprisoned and accused of performing some crime together. The police hold the two suspects in separate cells. In their dealings with the prisoners, the police attempt to have one individual give evidence about the other's involvement in the crime. The police say, "If you implicate the other person, you can not only go free but also receive a reward." In this case, the other individual would go to jail. If both individuals implicated each other, then both would go to jail, but the sentence would not be as great as if one had refused to testify. However, if neither person implicated the other, both would go free.

What would you do if you were one of these individuals? Of course, if you could talk to your acquaintance, then you both would agree to cooperate with each other and not talk to the police. In that way, both of you would go free. However, you are not allowed to have this conversation. What to do? If you just said, "I will take care of myself," you would implicate the other and perhaps you would receive a reward and go free. Traditionally, some economists said that is the rational thing to do since it potentially maximizes gain for a given individual. However, reciprocal altruism, in which you both cooperate with each other, would allow you both to gain. The game can be diagramed as shown in **Table 12-1**.

If you were to play the game only once, then it would be difficult to know what to do. However, in real life, our dealings are usually not just about one-time encounters, but repeated interactions with people we know on at least some level. On a cultural level, countries around the world interact in terms of trade and diplomacy. Over evolutionary

Table 12-1 Diagram of the prisoners' dilemma (after Axelrod & Hamilton, 1981).

		The Other Person	
		Cooperation	**Implicate the Other**
You	**Cooperation**	It was neither of us Reward for mutual cooperation (3 points)	It was her Sucker's payoff (0 points)
	Defection	Temptation (reward for turning the other person in) (5 points)	Punishment for mutual defection (1 point)

time in which we lived in groups, it is assumed that the social dealings we had with one another were with those we knew by acquaintance. Thus, the most realistic way of playing the game would be to repeat it a number of times. We assume that playing the game a large number of times in the laboratory would model the solution that humans evolved. That is to say, there would have been a variety of situations in which we needed to know whether to cooperate with one another or not. The prisoners' dilemma models these situations.

Using the prisoners' dilemma game, Axelrod and Hamilton (1981) looked at the evolution of cooperation. That is, how did cooperation evolve over evolutionary time. They suggested that the **evolution of cooperation** can be conceptualized in terms of three separate questions. These questions are related to robustness, stability, and initial viability. The first question of *robustness* asks what type of cooperative strategy can best survive given the wide variety of alternative strategies. The second question of *stability* asks under what conditions can such a strategy, after it has been established, resist invasion by mutant strategies. And finally, the question of *initial viability* asks how can cooperative strategies come to play a role in environments that are predominantly non-cooperative?

What is the best strategy for playing the prisoners' dilemma game? To help answer this question, in 1980 various academics from around the world were asked to submit procedures for playing the game, which could be computer-tested against one another. Although many of these were very complicated, in the end a simple procedure worked best. The answer is what has been called *tit-for-tat* and was submitted by a Canadian named Anatol Rapoport (see Kopelman, 2020).

Tit-for-tat has only two rules. The first rule is that on your first move you should cooperate. The second rule is that on every move after that, do what the other person did on the last trial. Embedded in this second rule is a flexibility that ensures that if the other person changes from being retaliatory to being cooperative, then you would also. In terms of Axelrod and Travis's other questions, it was found that tit-for-tat is an extremely stable strategy once it is established, and that it is possible for it to be started even in non-cooperative environments. Trivers (1985) has restated the rules to read—*first do unto others as you wish them to do unto you, but then do unto them as they have just done unto you.*

Does tit-for-tat work in the real world? One answer to this question can come from places we would not expect cooperation to be expected: war. Axelrod (1984) has argued that in the trench warfare of World War I, the soldiers on each side acted as if they were playing the prisoners' dilemma game. The soldiers, who could literally see one another across the battle lines, adopted a "live and let live" strategy, which is another way of saying "tit-for-tat." It was reported that soldiers shot at the other side but purposely missed. If soldiers on one side were killed, then an equal number on the other side would be killed. In actuality the strategy was broken only when the officers ordered raids behind enemy lines.

Another place we might not expect cooperation is with birds. Using blue jays, Stephens, McLinn, and Stevens (2002) created a simplified version of the prisoners' dilemma game. Two blue jays were placed side by side in two separate parts of a V-shaped apparatus. They created a series of levers and chutes such that a blue jay could either put a small piece of food in its own dish or a larger piece in the other's dish. If performed as a single-trial event, blue jays, like humans, are more likely to take the immediate reward. To make it more than a single-trial event, the food was dispensed into a transparent tray so that the bird could see food accumulate. In this study, the bird could eat the food after playing the game four times.

To gain experimental control, one of the blue jays responded freely while the other's response was programmed to be either all cooperative (put food in the other's dish) or all defecting (put food in its own dish). Experimentally, this was an experimental design in which the bird could eat the food immediately or had to wait four trials and experienced either all cooperation or all defecting. What did they find? When the other bird always defected, cooperation declined toward zero. It did not matter if the food could be eaten on each trial or if it accumulated. When the other bird always cooperated, the experimental bird showed high levels of cooperation also. However, in this situation, the cooperation was highest when the food was allowed to accumulate, somewhere between 60 and 70 percent. This suggests that the timing of when one receives benefits makes a crucial difference as to the level of cooperation, at least with birds. Further, these researchers noted that these birds were extremely forgiving and would continue cooperating at rates near 50% even after they had been "suckered."

Would you help someone you would never see again? If so, why would you? To help us understand why one person helps another, we can look at another game. This game is called the *trust game*. In this game, one of two anonymous players is given a sum of money. The player with the money has the choice. He or she can give the other player nothing or any percentage they wish. The other player then receives twice the amount suggested by the first player and has the opportunity to return some of the money. How much would you return given that you will never see this person again? It turns out that more than half of the people involved returned some of the money. In order to understand the motivations to give some of the money back, researchers modified the game so that the players are no longer anonymous or, in other cases, play a series of these games. With these modifications, the number of individuals who will give some money back increases. This has led some researchers to suggest that *reputation*, that is, to be known as a charitable person—someone who will help—is a key motivation for cooperation (Nowak & Sigmund, 1998; Milinski, 2016).

One model based on reputation is **indirect reciprocity** (Alexander, 1987). Indirect reciprocity is a form of reciprocity where help is given to individuals based on their reputation. The advantage of this model is that it helps to account for helping behavior even in situations in which individuals may not see one another again. Underlying the model is still the desire to increase one's own fitness. That is, if I act in such a way as to be seen as charitable, another person will at some time in the future be more likely to help me out and thus increase my evolutionary fitness. If this is the case, then what these experimental games do is help us see a link between action as a means of increasing fitness and manipulating our image of ourselves. We will return to images and attitudes later. Now, let's turn to look at the *dark side* of cooperation—non-cooperation in the social milieu.

Non-Cooperation

Humans do not always help one another. There are situations in which we seek to punish others, compete with others, and even hurt others. This section will describe some of the social psychology research related to social punishing, intergroup conflict and cooperation, and aggression.

Social Punishing

What if someone offers to paint your neighbor's house for a low price, which, of course, would be to your neighbor's benefit. However, while they are painting they are also stealing items from inside the house. What do you do? Let's go back to playing games for an answer. We know that people will give others money just to be known as cooperative, will they also spend some of their money to punish those who cheat? The answer is *yes*. This came to be called **altruistic punishment**. Altruistic punishment is when an individual forgoes a personal gain to punish another.

In one study, Fehr and Gächter (2002) tested this using a *public goods game*. They created groups with four individuals in each. Each member of the group received 20 money units of which they could contribute from nothing to 20 to a group project. Whatever a given individual did not contribute, they could keep. Thus, if you gave nothing, you would have 20 money units for yourself. However, if you contributed one money unit, then you and everyone else in the group would receive four money units. As part of the game, each person could earn more than they began with since each money unit was multiplied by four. Let's consider for a moment what would happen if no one gave anything. Then, everyone would keep their 20 money units. However, if everyone gave everything (20 money units), then each person could earn more than they began with. In the game, everyone is free to give what they wish and everyone must make their decision at the same time. What this sets up is the possibility that someone who gave nothing could receive money from those who did contribute. In one condition of the game, once the individuals knew what the others in their group had contributed, they had the opportunity to punish them by taking away some of their money. However, in order to take away three money units from the other person, you would also have to give up one money unit of your own. Thus, it costs you to punish another. What would you do?

Of the 240 individuals who played the game six different times, more than 84% punished at least once, and 34.3% punished more than five times in the six games. There was also a clear pattern in the way punishment was carried out. It was generally enacted by those who had contributed more than the average amount of the money units on those who had contributed less than the average. Also, the less someone gave, the more they were punished.

Another study asked what factors influence who you punish, and how. Helen Bernhard and her colleagues studied two small groups who lived in the Western Highlands of Papua, New Guinea (Bernhard, Fischbacher, & Fehr, 2006). These two distinct small groups lack traditional police forces and thus use social norms to regulate their social life. Playing similar punishment games, this study showed that individuals tend to protect those who are part of their own social group and give more punishment to those who belong to a different tribal group. Thus, your relationship to others influences how you protect, as well as punish, others.

Although we don't usually think of cheating as being pervasive, Robert Trivers (1985) suggests that **deception** is a wide-spread feature of communication within many social species. Deception in this case is to make things seem as they not. Trivers further suggests that since being deceived has real consequences for the victim, there is evolutionary pressure to develop better means of detecting deception. He further suggests that over evolutionary time, selection to spot deception may also have improved cognitive capacity including simple abilities to count. Clearly, we pay closer attention to someone if we are not sure of the transaction that is taking place. We also assume that deceiving another requires a greater amount of effort than just engaging in normal social interaction. For this reason, deception may evoke changes in the voice, facial expressions, and body movements in the person trying to deceive another.

Some of the changes associated with deception are intentional. For example, a salesperson may smile at you and touch you to portray a social connection with you. However, in social interactions, people often show cues that are not intentional (see Puce, 2014, for an overview). Some of these cues, such as changes in facial expressions, may be very quick.

Humans also will mask their true feelings by trying to keep a neutral facial expression. Likewise, changes in one's voice and forced laughter can be used to mask real emotions. Interestingly, brain-imaging studies have shown that different types of laughter are processed in different areas of the brain.

Intergroup Conflict and Cooperation

A very clever classic study of group process was conducted in the 1950s by Muzafer Sherif, Carolyn Sherif, and their colleagues (Sherif, Harvey, White, Hood, & Sherif, 1961). The initial hypothesis was that normal, healthy people would develop all of the earmarks of prejudice when (1) they found themselves in situations of strong group identification, and (2) their group was placed in circumstances such that it had to destroy the aspirations of another group in order to reach its most cherished goals. To test such a hypothesis, it was necessary to set up a situation involving groups in which only one group could win. Many alternatives might come to mind, such as a college sports event or a business competition between companies. In order to have experimental control, these researchers chose a summer camp. To better understand what naturally happens in a summer camp, one of the researchers, Muzafer Sherif, spent the summer of 1948 visiting camps and watching daily activities. Unlike other group environments such as businesses or universities, a summer camp at that time offered the potential for few outside influences except letters from home or visits from parents and thus extended to the researchers the possibility of a high degree of control in a naturalistic setting.

Once a camp was chosen for the experiment, the staff of the camp was trained in observational techniques so that they could note the interactions without being noticed by the boys involved. To allow for access and observation, some of the researchers became part of the staff. For example, one became a handyman and thus was able to wander around camp without being noticed. The counselors recorded observations twice a day. For ethical purposes, the parents were told of the experiment before they chose that particular camp, which was held at Robbers Cave State Park in Oklahoma. Jesse James was said to have hidden out there and thus the name.

In the camp experiments that have come to be called the Robbers Cave Experiment (Sherif et al., 1961), the researchers observed the formation of group leadership structures. As the researchers had postulated, a group culture formed even when participants had no idea of the existence of another group. After about a week, each group learned of another group of campers who were in a separate part of the camp. They also wanted to compete with them. The staff arranged a sports competition between the two groups, which lasted for a few days. What the researchers were most interested in was whether prejudice would develop between the groups and, if so, how it would develop.

Carolyn Sherif reported that the boys initially were competitive in a friendly way but that this started to evaporate very quickly (Ray, 2022). The extent of the rivalry began to appear very quickly with one group saying the other was not playing fair, and so forth. When those things would happen, the boys would then start to behave more aggressively toward the other group. These sorts of aggressive actions, in turn, would increase the negative images each group had of the other. In a short period, rather clear-cut stereotypical views of the other group developed. The other group are cheats and stinkers, whereas our group is brave, honorable, and true. After the tournament, each group said they would just as soon never see those other guys again.

The question then arose for the researchers as to how to reduce the intergroup conflict. Their initial hypothesis was that in order to reduce intergroup conflict and prejudice once it was generated, it would be necessary to have conditions in which there were goals strongly desired by members of both groups, but absolutely not obtainable without the resources and efforts of both groups together. That is, if they could get the two groups to work together, then conflict would decrease. Those were called *superordinate goals*.

In one study, the researchers used a sporting event with another camp to bring the two groups together. That is, the two groups would need to work together to compete with the other camp. In another study, they used a water shortage for the same purpose. The two groups were told that there was something wrong with the camp's water system but no one knew what the problem was. This required that the two groups work together to find a leak in the water system for the camp. The problem could either be at the water tank or with the pipes leading from the tank to the camp. Both groups worked together and were happy when the problem was found to be the faucet on the tank.

Overall, this series of studies showed that boys from similar backgrounds would form in-groups and compete with those in an out-group. Once established, their attitudes remained stable. However, with the presence of a common source of distress, the competitiveness toward the other group was reduced and the boys worked together. In this manner superordinate goals were able to alter the significance of other influences. An audio description of the Robbers Cave study is online (https://www.abc.net.au/radionational/programs/archived/hindsight/inside-robbers-cave/4515060).

Inter-Personal and Inter-Group Violence and Aggression

As we look over recorded human history, there appears not to be a time when wars or conflict were not taking place somewhere on earth. Even limiting our observations to the last 100 years, we still find a world in which war is common—not a unique event. Initially, it was assumed that war was somehow unique to humans and perhaps resulted from the development of weapons or to density of the population. However, with the observation that chimpanzees also engage in lethal attacks on one another, this view changed. The question then arises as to how to understand warfare from both a comparative standpoint and an evolutionary one (see Wilson & Wrangham, 2003; Jones, 2008, for overviews).

Since the 1960s, some 11 different communities of chimps and bonobos have been studied by Wilson and Wrangham (2003). As noted previously, chimps live in communities of about 150 individuals following a fission-fusion pattern in which smaller subgroups are constructed and then disbanded. Chimps will show hostility when they detect other chimps who are not part of their community. Initially, this hostility is of a vocal nature, which may lead to more physical encounters. The level of hostility appears to be different between females and males of the same community. Females, especially if they have infants, tend to avoid encounters with neighboring groups. Other females have been seen to be more aggressive. Males, however, are the most aggressive. They typically show hostility to stranger males, but will retreat if they are outnumbered. If the males from each community are evenly matched, the attacks tend to be more vocal with some charging. These situations typically end with less than severe injuries. If, however, a group of males finds a lone male from the other community, this results in severe injuries, including death. If males encounter other females, they will often attack them and may kill their infants. Male chimps generally do not attack females who show signs that they are in estrous such as sexual swelling, but rather attempt to mate with them.

Wilson and Wrangham (2003) complete their review of chimpanzee aggression by asking how this might relate to humans. In terms of humans, it should be noted that aggression between present-day hunter-gatherer groups has existed within a fairly stable pattern. The most common pattern was for a party of men from one group to launch a surprise attack on the other group. These attacks were typically set up in a manner such that the attackers were less likely to be harmed. In comparing hunter-gatherers to chimps, Wilson and Wrangham suggest that both share three tendencies.

- First, they both show a tendency to respond aggressively in encounters with members of other social groups.
- Second, they both avoid intensive aggressive confrontation by retreating.
- Third, they both take advantage of imbalances of power for males to kill members of neighboring groups. Interestingly, bonobos do not appear to conduct any type of lethal violence although they defend their territories.

Today, there is continuing debate as to whether humans evolved an inclination to kill. However, even if this were true, there is also evidence to suggest that humans have evolved an ability to live without killing given certain circumstances (Jones, 2008). It has been suggested by a variety of researchers that the availability of resources is one set of circumstances that reduces the killing of one human by another. Correlational research suggests that over time, as opportunities become more available for acquiring necessary resources within a population, killing is decreased. For example, from the Middle Ages (characterized by greater inequality) until today where there is more availability of resources, the murder rate in Europe has dropped. It has gone from 32 killings per 100,000 people in the 1200s to 1.4 killings per 100,000 in the 20th century (Eisner, 2001).

Using a life-span perspective with humans, **aggression** has been studied from infancy to adulthood. Aggression is composed of hostile behavior or attitudes toward another. This includes the aggressive biting seen in children to the aggressive behaviors seen in adults (Tremblay, Vitaro, & Côté, 2018). Physical aggression is often seen during the first year of life and then increases until 3 or 4 years of age. Beginning at about 3 or 4 years of age, physical aggression begins to decline. Longitudinal studies in North Carolina and in Canada have also shown an overall decrease in physical aggression from the beginning of elementary school to adolescence. Studies from around the world have shown that those who do display physical aggression in adolescence also displayed physical aggression as a child. There are few studies that have examined aggression from adolescence to old age, but court records show a decline in arrests for violent crimes from young adulthood to old age.

A common finding is that human males are more aggressive than human females. Human males have been shown to engage in aggression more often than human females from about age 2 onward. Such data as police records from across a variety of cultures universally show males to be more aggressive than females. Not only are males more aggressive, but they commit more serious crimes, including almost 90% of the murders reported in the United States. When asked to describe their own sexuality, males are more likely than females to include a dimension involving aggression, power, and dominance (Andersen, Cyrnaowski, & Espndle, 1999). However, where males tend to display physical aggression, females more often display social or psychological forms of aggression. One example of social aggression is having others dislike a person rather than physically attacking that person.

Since aggression follows developmental patterns and appears at an early age, researchers have sought to understand the relationship between genes and the environment in terms of physical aggression. At this point, twin studies involving elementary school age children, adolescents, and adults suggest that there is a relatively strong genetic component to the use of physical aggression (Tremblay, Vitaro, & Côté, 2018). Another study followed twins in terms of two characteristics, that of physical aggression and that of expressive vocabulary (Dionne, Tremblay, Boivin, Laplante, & Pérusse, 2003). Data were reported at 20, 36, and 50 months. At 20 months, the strength of the genetic influences on individual differences was higher for physical aggression (58%) than for expressive vocabulary (39%), whereas the strength of the shared environmental influence was high for expressive vocabulary (51%) but zero (0%) for physical aggression. Environmental influences on epigenetic mechanisms are also showing a link to physical aggression, especially in terms of brain development (Tremblay, Vitaro, & Côté, 2018).

CONCEPT CHECK

1. There are a number of terms presented in this section concerning different aspects of *altruism*, including *weak altruism*, *strong altruism*, *reciprocal altruism*, and *altruistic punishment*. What does each of these terms mean, and how are they related?

2. Several games have been used in research for examining the nature of cooperation—and non-cooperation. Describe each of the following games and what the research results contribute to our understanding of who cooperates, or doesn't, and under what conditions:
   a. Prisoners' dilemma
   b. Tit-for-tat
   c. Trust game
   d. Public goods game

3. This section states, "[T]here is evolutionary pressure to develop better means of detecting deception." What cues has research shown to be available for detecting deception?

4. How did the camp experiments, known as the Robbers Cave Experiment, help us understand about the development, maintenance, and reduction of prejudice and conflict in intergroup situations?

5. This section states, "[T]here is continuing debate as to whether humans evolved an inclination to kill." What evidence is presented to support the opposite point of view?

Social Influences on Behavior

We all have ideas of what to expect in different relationships. If you are going out on a first date, you would expect a different sequence of events than if you were going out with someone for the 50th time. Likewise, when you first meet someone, the types of conversations you have are typically different than if it is a close friend. When the person who delivers the mail or packages asks, "How are you doing?" most of us will respond, "Fine." In social interactions, there are scripts for what we say to one another.

These *scripts* have both a cultural and a universal level. In some countries, it is rude not to eat all the food on your plate when you are invited to dinner, while in others you should never eat everything presented (Axtell, 1993). Likewise, it is important to remove one's shoes when entering a home in some cultures, but not others. In some Asian cultures, you bow when you meet someone of higher rank in the company you work for. Nonverbal gestures also vary greatly. The same gesture can mean "OK" or something vulgar depending on where you are in the world. How men and women initially great each other can vary greatly in terms of culture. Overall, cultures have developed rules for allowing individuals to be part of the culture with minimal effort and conflict.

There are also some more universal ways of interacting depending on the type of relationship involved. These are related to the domains of social living (Fiske, 1992). Alan Fiske begins with the assumption that humans are fundamentally sociable and that societies throughout the world can be understood in terms of how people organize their relations with other people. That is to say, as humans we seek to relate to others in some basic and fundamental ways. These fundamental ways of relating have basic rules in the same way that language has a grammar to guide its construction. Based on a variety of research studies, Fiske suggests that everyday life can be seen as involving four basic social-cognitive processes. These processes are:

1. communal sharing
2. authority ranking
3. equality matching
4. market pricing

Communal sharing is the type of relationship in which a community treats material objects as something that belongs to all. This type of relationship is seen with family members who share holiday meals or religious groups where everyone is seen as equal. In these relationships, people take what they need and contribute as they can. As with a party punch bowl or a shared meal, there are no predefined allotted shares and no one monitors who takes what. Decisions in these types of groups are often made by consensus with collective discussions but no vote on the matter at hand.

Historically, this type of relationship has been seen with people genetically related either in terms of family or culture. Those outside of the kin are seen as the other or "they," and collectively viewed as different from "we." This type of relationship is often seen at sporting events where everyone for our team is viewed as "one of us" and everyone for the other team is viewed as "not one of us" or "the enemy."

Authority ranking is the type of relationship where people are ranked according to some linear hierarchy. The military presents the prototypical example of this type of relationship. Everyone has a rank and thus a place in the hierarchy. Typically, in authority ranking relationships, individuals higher in the rankings have more prestige, prerogatives, and privileges than those lower down the hierarchy.

In describing the hierarchy, spatial metaphors are often used with individuals being described as "higher up" or "lower down." As in the case of tribal leaders or kings and queens, those in charge are seen to make decisions or rules that influence those lower in the hierarchy. However, in many cultures those higher up are also expected to take care of, and look out for, others lower down. Psychologically, Sackeim and Gur (1979) reported that humans expand their view of themselves when they are succeeding and shrink their view of themselves when they are failing. Further, brain-imaging studies conducted on individuals in stable social hierarchy relationships showed activity in the dorsolateral prefrontal cortex when viewing other individuals of different status (Zink, Tong, Chen, Bassett, Stein, & Meyer-Linderberg, 2012).

Equality matching can be thought of as "tit-for-tat" relationships. That is, you do something for me and I do something for you. The basic idea is that each person is entitled to an equal amount in the relationship. "If you invite me to your house, then I should invite you to mine" would be one common manifestation of this type of relationship. Part of the consideration of this type of relationship is determining what is equal to what. "If you give me a ride to school every day, then I should buy you gas" could be one typical outcome. Competitive sports display this type of relationship in that each team has a turn to score, equal opportunity in terms of equal team size, and other structures that place neither team at a disadvantage. Thus, the structure of equality matching relationships is *balancing*.

Market pricing attempts to determine through ratios and rates the value of some aspect of the relationship. For example, if I own 75% of a business, then I would expect to receive 75% of the profits. The most common examples of market pricing relationships involve money and typically require some detailed analysis of the situation. This type of relationship is often referred to as cost–benefit analysis. For example, if you decide to buy a car with payments of $540 a month, then you determine that you cannot go to Europe for a vacation based on your current salary. As we saw previously, a new field has developed called behavioral economics, which studies the manner in which humans calculate market pricing relationships. Market pricing relationships have not been reported in other species.

Although these four types of relationships have been discussed in terms of scripts, they can also be understood in terms of competition and dominance. That is, what type of social environments bring forth different brain functions and hormone reactions. This has allowed for a broader neuroscience perspective that is just beginning to be developed (Qu, Ligneul, Van der Henst, & Dreher, 2017).

How We Act in Groups

Often as part of college or companies, you may have been placed in a group to perform a task. You may have noticed that some individuals do less work than others. This phenomenon has been referred to as **social loafing** (Latané, Williams, & Harkins, 1979). Some of the early studies had blindfolded individuals do a tug-of-war task. What was seen was that individuals would pull harder if they thought they were the only one pulling on the rope than if they thought there were others helping. Thus, people tended to let others do the work in a group.

When in a group we can also work harder if we think others are watching us. This is referred to as **social facilitation**. Social facilitation is defined as an improvement in performance when working with or being accompanied by others as opposed to being alone. A number of studies have shown that there is a home team advantage in a number of sports (Jamieson, 2010). That is, there are more wins in front of a home audience than those from the other team. Good performers such as actors know that a full house is associated with a better performance. However, if you are not experienced at a task, having others watch you can lead to mistakes and a poor performance.

Social Influences on the Level of the Self

One critical part of our social interactions involves our sense of self. The study of the *self* has a long history in psychology. For thousands of years, there have been invocations that you should "know thyself." Today, most people think that they do know themselves and can accurately predict how they would act in a given situation using their *self-scripts*. However, research in social psychology suggests that that may not be the case. There is clearly some information that is available to us that we refer to as *explicit*. However, as you have seen, there are other attitudes and stereotypes that are formed outside of awareness, which are referred to as *implicit*.

In terms of the *self*, a number of distinctions have been made. William James (1890/1983) made a distinction between the self that knows things, which he referred to as "I," and the self that is known about, which James referred to as "me." In this sense it is "I" who thinks, feels, and acts in the world. What I know about myself is "me." The self is what gives us a sense of continuity in that we remember our lives as an unbroken history of experiences. However, James recognized the complexity of the self by suggesting that we have many different selves depending on who we are with and the topic under discussion.

One traditional view of the *self* in social psychology is that it is made up of **schemas** or beliefs about oneself (Markus, 1977). These schemas help us define who we are and how we see ourselves. These schemas differ for different people. As you saw in the chapter on eating behaviors, males and females differ in the schemas they use to define themselves as over- or under-weight. Individuals can also have schemas for skills they are particularly good at or find difficult.

As noted in the chapter on memory, we treat memories related to ourselves different from factual knowledge. In the brain, memory about myself, in comparison to memory about others, shows heightened activity in the prefrontal cortex, cingulate cortex, and the precuneus (see Gilboa & Marlatte, 2017; Moran, Kelley, & Heatherton, 2014, for overviews). As we develop, we develop this type of memory and come to understand that as an individual we are separate from others. That is to say, your memories and my memories are different. We further come to compare ourselves to others and understand how we are different and how we are similar.

Our self-concept is also influenced by cultural factors. As noted previously, some cultures, such as the United States, emphasize individualism. That leads you to define yourself in terms of your individual abilities. Other cultures, such as China and some South American countries, emphasize collectivism—the idea that individuals are part of a group. In these cultures, the self is defined as it relates to a larger group.

As humans, we have the ability to reflect on our internal processes (see Bauer & Baumeister, 2011, for an overview). At times, this allows individuals to self-regulate their behaviors or to have their behavior remain consistent with an external set of values. Research has also shown that humans are better at accurately describing their thoughts and feelings, but less accurate in their ability to name the conditions that led to these underlying thoughts and emotions. However, we will always make sense of our world and create a reason why we think or feel in certain ways.

Social Influence and Compliance

How would you go about getting another person to support a cause you thought was important or vote for a political candidate you wanted to win? If you know them well, you might use your personal relationship to influence them. However, if you did not know the person, what techniques might you use to bring about compliance? Social psychologists have examined a number of the techniques and the factors that lead to compliance.

One common technique used by salespeople and others wishing for you to agree to their requests is the ***foot-in-the-door technique***. This technique is based on the fact that if you can get someone to agree to a small request, then that person is more likely to agree to a larger request. The name came from the early days of door-to-door salespeople, who learned that any request that would allow them to "get their foot in the door" would lead to a longer conversation and possibly a sale. A car salesperson may ask you what color car you would like and request you sit in a car of that color before discussing the price. Likewise, a salesperson in a store may ask how a piece of clothing feels to you and hold it in front on you.

One of the early studies of the foot-in-the-door technique asked the experimental participants to either put a small sign in the window of their house promoting safe driving or sign a petition in terms of safe driving (Freedman & Fraser, 1966). About two weeks later, the experimenters returned to the homes and asked the participants to place a much larger sign in their yards. The control group was only asked to place the larger sign in their yards. Whereas fewer than 20% of the control group agreed to put a large sign on their lawn, more than 55% of the experimental group did. Thus, a simple small request followed by a larger request is more likely to be agreed to than a large request alone.

Another technique that has been studied in terms of compliance is just the opposite of the foot-in-the-door technique. This technique involves making a large request that tends to be rejected, and then followed by a smaller one that tends to be accepted. This is referred to as **door-in-the-face technique**. It is also called *reciprocal concessions*. Imagine a Boy Scout or Girl Scout coming to your house and asking if you would give $100 to their troop. When you say no, as most people would, they then ask if you buy the $1 candy bar they are selling for the troop. After saying no to the $100, you are more likely to say yes to the $1. An early study in this area asked college students if they would support the "County Youth Counseling Program" and be part of a group taking juvenile delinquents on a day trip to the zoo (Cialdini et al., 1975). As you can imagine, 17% of the college students said yes. However, another group of college students were initially asked if they would counsel juvenile delinquents two hours a week for the next two years. Although all of the students declined to counsel the youth, 50% said they would take them to the zoo. Thus, a small request is more likely to be accepted if it follows a larger one that has been rejected.

A common technique that you will often see on television or in mailings from organizations is the *free-gift technique*. This is a situation in which you are given a small gift from an organization, such as a calendar, address labels, or even a dollar in the solicitation, requesting that you give money to the organization. Salespeople on TV often say, "But wait, there is more. Buy this and you will get this for free." Research has also shown that if you do an unexpected favor for someone, they are more likely to comply with your requests.

Social Influence and Conformity

Our desire to be part of the group is strong. We conform with the group even when we believe that our response is actually not correct. At times, people may think they would appear foolish if they gave a different answer. Other times, people may think that the other members of the group would be angry with them for being different. Clearly being part of a group is an important aspect of our human nature. Further, we process information differently in our brain when we conform to peer pressure than when we do not.

As you look at **Figure 12-6**, what do you see? Clearly, all three people are looking at something. However, the person in the middle is working harder to understand what he is seeing. The people in this room were part of a social psychology experiment performed in the 1950s (Asch, 1956). Psychologist Solomon Asch (1956) performed a famous series of experiments illustrating the power of social influence.

Figure 12-6 What do you see?

In the study, the participants were simply asked to pick which of three comparison lines matched the standard line (see **Figure 12-6**). You are person number six in the room and on the first few trials everyone picks the line you would pick, number two in **Figure 12-6**. However, after a few trials with similar comparisons, the first person chooses a line that does not appear to match. Then, the second person chooses the same line. By the time it is your turn everyone before you has chosen a different line than you thought was the correct answer. Which line would you choose now? When confronted with six people who gave a wrong answer, three-fourths of the individuals conformed to the other individuals at least once during the experimental session.

All of the individuals in the Asch experiment except one were confederates and answered as instructed. The task is not a difficult one since when there is only one person doing the task he gets it correct 99% of the time. Overall, more than one-third of the naïve participants conformed to the answers given by the others. However, when the naïve participant was allowed to write down his response rather than say it aloud after hearing the others verbally respond, the rate of conformity was reduced.

What goes on in our brain when we are experiencing the pressure to conform, even if it is internal pressure? It took more than 50 years from the time Asch performed his experiments to be able to answer this question with brain imaging. Gregory Berns and his colleagues asked individuals to perform a mental rotation task in an fMRI (Berns, Chappelow, Zink, Pagnoni, Martin-Skurski, & Richards, 2005). The mental rotation task has been studied intensively by cognitive psychologists and was originally developed by Shepard and Metzler (1971). This task is shown in **Figure 12-7**. In the fMRI experiment, participants were asked if the object shown when rotated was the same as the original object.

As with the original Asch task, the subject was led to believe that the other four people in the experiment were giving their own answers. However, the other people were all confederates who gave the incorrect answer half of the time. Initially, practice responses were given in a group setting via computer without feedback. This allowed the experimenter

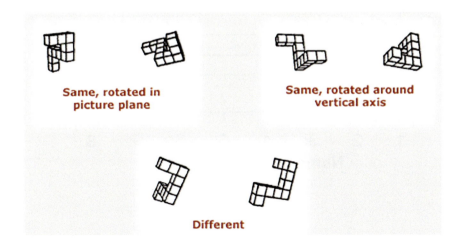

Figure 12-7 Mental rotation task.

to know that the person could perform the visual rotation task since it is more difficult than Asch's task of comparing lines. Following this, the person was placed in the fMRI and the responses of the others were presented via a computer display. The participant saw the other responses before they made their own response.

On trials when the confederates responded with the correct response, the subjects showed the same level of error rates as they did in the initial group session with no group feedback. However, when the confederates gave the incorrect response, the participants were more likely to also give the incorrect response. Thus, as in the Asch experiment, group influence led to conformity. In the baseline condition there was about a 14% error rate. However, when the confederates gave the incorrect answer, the participant's error rate went up to 41%.

Since mental rotation is a spatial task, it is not surprising that the brain activity seen when there was no peer pressure was consistent with performing spatial tasks. That is, greater cortical activity was seen in the occipital areas, which are associated with vision; the parietal areas, which are associated with spatial activity; and the frontal lobes associated with executive functioning. When the researchers examined those trials where the person gave incorrect answers related to group pressure versus gave the correct answer in spite of group pressure, there was a difference. When there was conformity, there was greater activity in those areas such as the occipital and parietal areas related to spatial processing. However, when the person went against the group, areas related to emotional processing and social processing were activated. Nonconformity was associated with greater activation in the amygdala and the right caudate nucleus. These areas have been associated with understanding the meaning of emotional and social information.

Follow-up studies suggest two important factors in social conformity. The first is the size of the group. As shown in **Figure 12-8**, once the size of the group reaches three or four individuals you are more likely to conform than when there are fewer than three people in the group. The second factor is whether there is unanimous agreement or not. If only

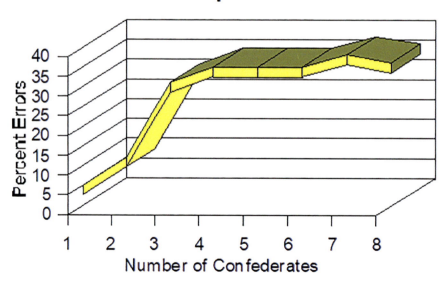

Figure 12-8 Social influence is related to number of other individuals presenting the incorrect answer.

one person disagrees with the group, even if it is the wrong answer, a participant is more willing to express a nonconforming view.

Social Influence and Persuasion

In the Asch line-judging experiment, conformity was induced by being with other people you thought were similar to you. What do you think would happen if the relationship is a more hierarchical one? That is, the experimenter is instructing you what to do. This was the question asked by Stanley Milgram in his set of obedience experiments. These experiments are classics in the history of psychology, although some have questioned whether this research was ethical.

Milgram begins his discussion of *obedience* with noting how important it is as well as how it can lead to crimes against humanity (Milgram, 1963). When you go to concerts or sporting events, it is important for everyone to follow directions. Likewise in an emergency situation, obedience is critical to preventing undue harm. However, during World War II, millions of innocent people were killed by Nazi soldiers who said they were just following orders. Questions were asked as to whether some cultures produced individuals who were more independent and thus less likely to follow orders than others. Studies examined French and Norwegian students in an Asch-like experiment (Milgram, 1961). In these studies, the French showed themselves to be more resistant to group pressure. However, group pressure to make a response is different than actually harming another person.

In World War II, a great number of people were harmed and killed in concentration camps. Some suggested that, because of their culture, Germans would be more likely to obey authority than would Americans. The basic idea was that Americans were taught to be independent, whereas the Germans were taught to follow authority. Also, during the 1960s there were war crimes trials in Israel of Adolf Eichmann and others who carried out the Holocaust. Although many saw Eichmann as evil, the question arose as to why so many others went along with his orders. Some even suggested that Eichmann was just a bureaucrat doing his job (Arendt, 1958). With this as a background, Stanley Milgram began a simple experiment to study obedience.

Milgram created an experimental procedure that required that a naïve subject would administer electrical shocks to another person (Milgram, 1963, 1974). The shock generator was clearly marked with voltage levels that ranged from 15 to 450 volts. Approximately every four levels were labeled with descriptions such as slight shock, very strong shock, danger: severe shock, and, at the 435 and 450 volts levels, XXX.

The purpose of the initial experiment was just to collect baseline data. When mental health professionals were asked what percentage of individuals would significantly shock another person, most professionals responded that they expected only 1% or 2% of the people would do so. College students at Yale also estimated that less than 2% of the participants would administer high shock levels. Thus, Milgram began his research expecting that he was only collecting baseline data that could be used in future research. However, what he found was not what he expected.

Before looking at the results, let's examine the basic procedures of the study. An ad was placed in the local paper where Yale University is located. People of all ages and occupations responded to the ad. When they arrived at the laboratory, they were told that this was an experiment concerning learning. There was also a middle-aged likable man who also appeared to be a participant in the experiment. A drawing was held to determine who would be the "teacher" and who would be the "learner." In fact, the drawing was rigged and the naïve participant would always be the teacher. The teacher was given a list of word pairs (for example, clean–air) to be taught to the learner. The learner was actually a confederate. The experimenter and the naïve subject took the learner into another room and attached shock electrodes and a strap to hold his arm in place. The experimenter was a 31-year-old high-school teacher of biology who portrayed an impassive and stern manner throughout the experiment.

Before the experiment began each "teacher" was given a shock at the 45-volt level so he would have the experience of receiving a shock. He was also told that the shocks would be painful but not cause permanent damage. When the experiment began the teacher was instructed to move up one level of shock with each wrong answer. He was also instructed to announce the shock level aloud before he administered the shock. The number and sequence of incorrect answers by the learner were predetermined.

After this, the teacher was taken to another room with the shock generator. It was the teacher's job to administer a shock every time the learner made a mistake in repeating a series of words he was to learn. With each mistake, the shock level was increased. Of course, no shock was actually delivered to the learner in the other room. In the initial version of the study reported in 1963, the teacher did not hear the learner as he responded by a keypad.

At the 300-volt level, the teacher heard the learner pound on the walls. After this, the teacher saw no answers from the learner. At this point, the participant tended to look to the experimenter for guidance. The experimenter told the teacher to consider the lack of an answer as a wrong answer and continue with the shocks. At this point, some of the participants looked to the experimenter with concern.

If the subject showed an unwillingness to go on, the experimenter responded with the first of the following statements and then continued with the next until the subject continued or withdrew from the experiment. In this way, the experimenter prodded the subject to continue.

Prod 1: Please continue, or Please go on.
Prod 2: The experiment requires that you continue.
Prod 3: It is absolutely essential that you continue.
Prod 4: You have no other choice, you must go on.

Milgram kept careful notes of the reactions of the subjects as they progressed through the experiment. Many of the subjects showed distress and discomfort at their task. They would sweat, tremble, stutter, bite their lips, groan, and dig their fingernails into their flesh. About a quarter of the subjects displayed nervous laughter and smiling. Even those who went to the highest shock level showed signs of relief when the experiment was over.

What would you expect in terms of level of shocks administered? The actual results were unexpected and surprising. No subject stopped before the 300-volt level, which was when the learner pounded on the wall. A total of 5 of 40 subjects refused to go beyond this point. Four more subjects administered the next level of shock and then refused to go on. Five more subjects stopped at various levels beyond the 300 volt level. Overall, this meant that 14 subjects stopped at some point in the experiment, and 26 subjects went to the final level of shock (450 volts).

In a second study with similar procedures, the teacher could hear the learner protest from the other room earlier in the procedure. This resulted in some eight participants withdrawing from the experiment at an earlier point than in the first experiment. However, 25 participants in the second experiment, as compared to 26 in the first experiment, went to the highest level of shock administration.

Once the study was completed, the participant (teacher) was reunited with the learner. It was explained to the participant that the learner had not been shocked and was not upset with the subject. As a further part of the debriefing, every attempt was made so that the participant would leave the experiment in a state of well-being.

Following this study in which about 65% of the participants continued to administer shocks until the highest level was reached, other factors were considered. Since Yale was a well-known institution, the experiment was moved to a nondescript building in the downtown. This reduced obedience to under 50%. If the teacher was in the same room as the learner, the obedience declined to about 40%. If the teacher was required to hold the learner's hand on the shock plate, then obedience declined to 30%. Likewise, giving the orders to shock the learner by phone or having an ordinary person not wearing a lab coat be the experimenter also reduced the level of obedience. These different conditions are shown in **Figure 12-9**.

To return to one of the original questions as to whether the nature of a society can influence obedience, Stanley Milgram suggested the following:

> The results are . . . disturbing. They raise the possibility that human nature, or—more specifically—the kind of character produced in American democratic society, cannot be counted on to insulate its citizens from brutality and inhumane treatment at the direction of malevolent authority.
>
> (Milgram, 1965, p. 75)

Since the Milgram study was conducted more than 50 years ago, there has been some criticism of the manner in which the Milgram study was conducted and the manner in which the results were reported (Griggs, 2017). These criticisms have also been extended to the film *Obedience* that Milgram produced to summarize his experiments. One interpretation of the Milgram results based on an examination of the original Milgram notes in the Yale University archives suggests that the results were based on the participants' desire to be part of scientific research rather than obedience to authority per se (Haslam, Reicher, & Birney, 2016). That is, participants wanted to be part of an in-group even if an out-group was harmed.

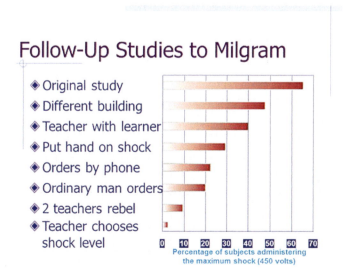

Figure 12-9 Follow-up studies and the level of obedience by condition.

Would similar results be found if Milgram's study was replicated today? To answer that question, Jerry Burger performed a similar study taking into account today's ethical standards (Burger, 2009). What he found was that rates of delivering shocks were only slightly lower than those seen in the Milgram study 45 years earlier. Despite the exact mechanism, people can be put into situations in which they will deliver harm to others. Outside of research, every few years a media story reminds us of our disposition to follow orders that lead to negative consequences, even for ourselves. For example, in the Vietnam War, American solders followed orders at My Lai and killed innocent unarmed civilians. In 1978, 900 people who were followers of a cult leader, Jim Jones, followed his orders and committed mass suicide.

About ten years after the Milgram studies, another study looked at the willingness of ordinary people to assume roles that would oppress others. The Stanford Prison Study, which was conducted in 1971, had male undergraduates at Stanford University play the role of either prisoners or guards (Haney, Banks, & Zimbardo, 1973). The basic claim of the study is that individuals are strongly influenced by the situation they find themselves in, which can include taking power over others. This study is included in this book since it is well known in the popular press and even a movie is based on the study. However, it should be recognized that scholars in both psychology and criminology suggest that the findings of the study should be carefully evaluated and not accepted without consideration (Griggs, 2014; Kulig, Pratt, & Cullen, 2016).

The leader of the study was Stanford faculty member, Philip Zimbardo. Before the study began, the students were given a series of tests and determined to be psychologically stable. Information given to the participants suggested that the purpose of the experiment was to see how individuals react in novel situations and take on the role they are given.

The students were randomly assigned to being a "prisoner" or a "guard." The guards were given uniforms and told not to hurt the prisoners. The prisoners were picked up at their homes, taken to the local police station, and then "booked" and fingerprinted. They were then taken to the prison, which was in the basement of the psychology department at Stanford University. Nothing out of the ordinary happened on the first day. However, a day or two later the prisoners revolted, and the guards reacted.

According to Zimbardo, at a time the prisoners were to be taken to the toilet, "The prisoners come out, and the guards put bags over their heads, chain their feet together and make them put their hands on each other's shoulders, like a chain gang. They're yelling and cursing at them" (https://stanfordmag.org/contents/the-menace-within). Although the study was designed to last for two weeks, it was stopped after only six days when some prisoners showed psychological distress and some guards were abusive.

Why did normal college students assume the roles they were given, even being sadistic? Although people do accept roles they are given, careful analysis of the study suggests that the participants were led to behave in certain ways. Zimbardo, himself, rather than being an outside observer, assumed the role of prison warden, which influenced the participants' behaviors. One of the consultants to the study, himself an ex-convict, reported that he had told the experimenters about abusive and humiliating behaviors that guards could express (Griggs, 2014). Thus, rather than show what individuals do in novel situations, the participants in the experiment responded to demand characteristics unique to this experiment (Banuazizi & Movahedi, 1975). Knowing you are in an experiment does influence your behavior. Further, a similar study performed in the United Kingdom known as the BBC prison study found very different results (Reicher & Haslam, 2006).

If you are interested in what it was like to be a part of this study, you can read interviews with Zimbardo and participants in the study some 40 years later in the *Stanford Magazine* (https://stanfordmag.org/contents/the-menace-within) and Stanford Library Special Collections (https://searchworks.stanford.edu/view/vx097ry2810).

Making Moral Judgments

How we perform in relation to others is often studied in terms of moral decisions (Malle, 2021). How do you make a moral judgment? That is to say, how do you decide if something you observe is wrong? If you watch someone hurt a helpless animal, how do you respond? Likewise, if you see someone help someone who is helpless, what is the difference in your response? Where does this response come from? Is it like a preference? That is, do we have some sort of code in our heads that says helping is good and when we see someone help, we say that is good? Or perhaps do we have an internal feeling such as the feeling that makes us feel satisfied? The origin of moral judgment has been a topic that has recently become of interest to evolutionary psychologists as well as those interested in the underlying brain states (Decety & Yoder, 2016).

How do you make a moral judgment? **Moral judgments** are judgments that involve values related to human functioning such as life and death. A variety of studies suggest that moral judgments happen quickly (see Miller, 2008, for an overview). It is more of an emotional or gut reaction to the situation. If asked why you made that decision, most individuals will either say, "I don't know," or "It just felt right," or try to create a cognitive reason to justify the decision. There is also research to suggest that creating a feeling of disgust in a person will increase the sense of moral outrage or immorality.

Steven Pinker (2014) suggests that the nature of moral judgments is different from other types of thinking. Think of a food you dislike. Do you care if someone else eats that food? No! We may like chocolate ice cream, but would not be upset if someone else had strawberry. However, you don't say it is fine with me if you want to hurt someone. Thus, moral judgments are not like preferences. Pinker also suggests moral judgments are not like what is in fashion. You may think that bell-bottoms are out of style but we don't consider doing harm to another to go in and out of style. Pinker also makes a distinction between moral judgments and what is imprudent. We tell others not to scratch mosquito bites, but this is different from saying you should not randomly kill others.

Pinker further suggests that there are two important hallmarks of moral judgments. The first is that these judgments are felt to be universal. Someone who thinks that rape or killing is wrong does not think that this only applies to their hometown, but to the entire world. In this sense, moral judgments are experienced differently from cultural ones. The second hallmark is the belief that committing immoral acts should be followed by punishment. People often say it is wrong to let someone "get away with it." Thus, according to Pinker, humans not only make moral judgments, but also believe that immoral behavior should be punished.

There are a variety of ways to study moral judgment in the lab. Most use hypothetical scenarios such as if you could only save one person from a burning building, who would you save—a young child or an old man? Almost everyone would say the young child without a second thought. Another scenario is referred to as the trolley problem (see **Figure 12-10**). In this case, you are a trolley driver. You lose your brakes and are headed for five workers on the tracks in front of you. The only way to save the lives of these workers would be for you to hit a switch on the control panel that would send

Figure 12-10 The Trolley Problem.
Source: Miller (2008). ©Peter Hoey.

the trolley down another set of tracks. If you did this you would kill a single worker on these tracks. What would you do? Again, most individuals would say it was OK to kill the one person if that meant five people would be saved. This type of scenario is generally classified as *low conflict* since most individuals agree with the moral decision.

Now let's consider a *high conflict* situation (see **Figure 12-11**). What if you were on a bridge above the trolley and you saw the runaway trolley coming. The only way you could stop the trolley was to push a large person off the bridge and stop the trolley. What would you do in this case? This scenario produces much less agreement that it is OK to push the man off the bridge, even though the result is the same as in the previous scenario—that is, saving the lives of five people. The act of hurting another for the greater good is experienced by most people as more morally ambiguous than throwing a switch.

Figure 12-11 What would you do in this case?
Source: Miller (2008). ©Peter Hoey.

To understand how high and low conflict situations involve emotional circuits in the brain, Michael Koenigs and his colleagues presented these problems to individuals who had damage to an area of the brain involved in emotional action (Koenigs et al., 2008). This area is the ventromedial prefrontal cortex (vmPFC)—an area in the front of the brain involved in encoding the emotional value of sensory information as well as emotional components of human actions. These researchers found that individuals with damage to these frontal areas of the brain were less likely to show differences between high and low conflict scenarios. That is to say, they made their decision on the utilitarian premise that, in each case, five individuals would be saved. Overall, this suggests that moral judgments rely on emotional processing in the brain. In other research, the vmPFC has also been shown to be activated when someone chooses to give money to charity or views pictures of hungry children.

A variety of studies have asked whether children below the age of six differentiate between a moral judgment and a conventional one. An event that requires a moral judgment would involve aggression, such as hitting or biting another; stealing, such as taking another child's possession; or psychological harm, such as teasing. Events related to conventional judgments would include not being neat or making a mess and breaking school rules, such as playing in an area off-limits. In a classic study, preschool children were asked to evaluate naturally occurring and hypothetical events involving moral and conventional transgressions (Smetana, Schlagman, & Adams, 1993). These researchers found that preschool children did make a distinction between the moral events and the conventional ones. The moral events were seen as more serious, wrong, and more deserving of punishment than the conventional events. Evolutionary psychologists view these types of results as suggesting that cultural and moral judgments rely on different systems of judgment and that moral transgressions are seen as more serious an offense than cultural ones. With development of self-driving vehicles, rules for moral judgments must be developed, as described in the box: Applying Psychological Science: Letting Self-Driving Cars Make Decisions for You.

Applying Psychological Science: Letting Self-Driving Cars Make Decisions for You

With the advances in the electronics and computing capacity available, there has been a desire to develop cars that drive themselves. Those who support this suggest that a self-driving car can benefit society as the population ages. These cars can be better aware of the surrounding environment and thus reduce traffic accidents. However, not all traffic accidents can be prevented. There could be situations in which the car must make a decision as to the type of accident it allows to happen.

This has raised critical questions. What if the car has to choose between hitting a pedestrian or another car? Or, what if the car needs to sacrifice its own passenger to save hitting two or more pedestrians? For self-driving cars to be accepted, it is important that their decision rules be acceptable to the people who use them.

In order to determine what decision rules should be used, researchers presented a number of scenarios to people (Bonnefon, Shariff, & Rahwan, 2016). Over a series of studies, participants strongly agreed that it would be more moral for self-driving cars to sacrifice their own passenger when this sacrifice would save a greater number of lives. In one of these studies, 76% of participants thought that it would be more moral for the car to sacrifice one passenger rather than kill ten pedestrians. In another study in which the number of pedestrians saved ranged from 1 to 100, more saved lives was the most acceptable outcome, even if the passenger was killed. If the event involved only one pedestrian, then people were not willing to sacrifice the life of the passenger. People were also less willing to sacrifice the life of the passenger if they imagined the person to be a family member of theirs.

The researchers then asked participants if they would rather buy the car that minimizes death in general or one that minimizes their own death or that of their family members. Although people valued the global saving of life, they were less likely to buy such a car for themselves. This leaves society in an ethical dilemma. Should we have self-driving cars that are programmed in a number of different ways? Should the government be able to set which way the self-driving car is programmed? This could result in different countries having different rules depending on the cultural values of that society. The authors of these studies see the ethics concerning self-driving cars as a difficult issue. They further suggest the value of research into humans' moral values as a way to help inform the manner in which self-driving cars are programmed. A Radiolab podcast concerning these types of situations is available (https://www.wnycstudios.org/podcasts/radiolab/articles/driverless-dilemma).

Thought Question: You knew that self-driving cars were programmed to operate, but is it a new idea to you that they make moral judgments? What about other technology or apps that you use? What are some examples of moral judgments or other decisions they make that you're not aware of?

CONCEPT CHECK

1. Identify and describe the four basic social-cognitive processes that Fiske proposes as the "grammar" of social relationships. Give an example of each from your own experience.
2. What is a script? How does its nature change as you change your focus from the universal level, to the cultural level, to the interpersonal level, and to the individual level?
3. Briefly describe the two experiments (Asch; Berns and colleagues) studying the impact of social influence. Why do individuals conform—even when they know the answer is wrong? What factors are suggested by follow-up studies to reduce the level of conformity?
4. Briefly describe Stanley Milgram's obedience experiment. What was the larger cultural question Milgram was trying to answer when he undertook this study? In what ways was he surprised at the results? Were you shocked? How could this question be studied experimentally today?
5. What unique contributions did the following researchers add to our understanding of the distinctive characteristics of a moral judgment:
   a. Stephen Pinker?
   b. Michael Koenigs and his colleagues?
   c. Smetana, Schlagman, and Adams?

Summary

Learning Objective 1: Define what it means to be social.
As humans, we are social creatures. There has never been a time in our history where we humans have lived alone. From the earliest times as hunter-gatherers, we have lived in social groups with strong social bonds. It is these groups that have shaped our social skills and abilities. For example, we need to know who our friends are as opposed to who might want to hurt us. We also need to be able to select mates. Further, we need to understand the dynamics of our larger group. These abilities have been passed down over evolutionary time and are part of our human social interactions today.

Learning Objective 2: Discuss the role that social cognition plays in understanding how we form opinions and make decisions.
Social cognition refers to the manner in which we understand others. Social cognition is a broad term that can include our attributions about others, how we stereotype others, as well as our prejudice of others. Humans tend to attribute *trait characteristics*, such as being stupid, to others while using *situational explanations*, such as having the sun in our eyes, for ourselves. This is referred to as the *fundamental attribution error or person bias*. It is also another example of how humans conserve cognitive effort by ignoring situational information when making sense of others' actions.

Humans are motivated by two primary needs: (1) to form a coherent view of the world and (2) to gain control over our environment. *Attributions* are one way we create a world view that makes sense to us. There are two types of attributions. The first is *internal or dispositional attribution*. This is the situation in which observed behaviors are attributed to the internal state of the person. Saying someone is lazy when they do not get a job would be an example of internal attributions. The second type of attribution is *external or situational attribution*. As the name implies, this is the case where a person's behavior is attributed to external factors. If you said your grade on a test was low because you were not given enough time, you would be attributing your behavior to an external or situational factor.

We make internal or external attributions based on three types of information: *consensus, consistency*, and *distinctiveness*.

There is a tendency for individuals to view themselves, their worlds, their friends, and other aspects of themselves in an overly positive manner. Not only do we categorize whether another individual is like us (our *in-group*), we also determine who is not like us (our *out-group*). If someone is seen to be in our out-group we tend to see them in more negative terms, as less deserving, and as more responsible for any negative event in their life. Traditional categories of *person perception* include age, gender, and race. When we make inferences about a group of individuals that share similar characteristics, it is referred to as *stereotyping*.

Three aspects describe the mechanisms that support social stereotyping: *social categorizing, stereotype activation, stereotype application*. Whereas stereotyping involves more of a cognitive assessment, prejudice, on the other hand, reflects a more emotional evaluation.

Learning Objective 3: Discuss the role that social emotion plays in prosocial and helping behaviors.

Social emotions are those emotions that involve our interactions with other people in a social context. Examples of these emotions are embarrassment, jealousy, envy, and pride.

Since guilt and shame involve transgression against the conventions of the group, these have been called *moral emotions*. Research suggests that individuals' shame experiences are more painful and intense than guilt experiences. Feelings of sympathy and guilt have been seen to motivate cooperative behavior and altruism. Additionally, guilt appears to help individuals keep commitments and thus maintain relationships.

Altruism is defined as helping another person when it does not directly benefit ourselves.

Learning Objective 4: Explain how social influences affect behavior.

We all have ideas of what to expect in different relationships. If you are going out on a first date, you would expect a different sequence of events than if you were going out with someone for the 50th time. Likewise, when you first meet someone, the types of conversations you have are typically different than if it is a close friend. In social interactions, there are scripts for what we say to one another. These *scripts* have both a cultural and a universal level. Overall, cultures have developed rules for allowing individuals to be part of the culture with minimal effort and conflict.

One traditional view of the *self* in social psychology is that it is made up of *schemas* or beliefs about oneself. These schemas help us define who we are and how we see ourselves. These schemas differ for different people. As humans, we have the ability to reflect on our internal processes. This allows individuals to self-regulate their behaviors or to have their behavior remain consistent with an external set of values. Our self-concept is also influenced by cultural factors. As noted previously, some cultures, such as the United States, emphasize individualism. That leads you to define yourself in terms of your individual abilities.

Our desire to be part of the group is a strong one. We conform even when we believe that our response is actually not correct. At times, people may think they would appear foolish if they gave a different answer. Other times, people may think that the other members of the group would be angry with them for being different. Clearly being part of a group is an important aspect of our human nature. Further, we process information differently in our brain when we conform to peer pressure than when we do not.

Learning Objective 5: Describe our understanding of the distinctive characteristics of moral judgment.

Steven Pinker suggests that there are two important hallmarks of moral judgments. The first is that these judgments are felt to be universal. Someone who thinks that rape or killing is wrong does not think that this only applies to their hometown, but to the entire world. In this sense, moral judgments are experienced differently from cultural ones. The second hallmark is the belief that committing immoral acts should be followed by punishment. People often say it is wrong to let someone "get away with it." Thus, according to Pinker, humans not only make moral judgments, but also believe that immoral behavior should be punished

Study Resources

Review Questions

1. The beginning of this chapter focuses on concepts that are under the heading of social cognition, while the end focuses on concepts that are under the heading of social groups. But clearly, concepts in each of the two sections are closely related to concepts in the other. So…
   a. Review the section on social cognition to identify how specific concepts of social groups impact the social cognition concepts of attribution, categorization, stereotyping, and prejudice.
   b. Review the section on social groups to identify how specific aspects of social cognition impact the social groups concepts of social emotions, cooperation, conflict, scripts, influence and persuasion, conformity, and moral judgments.
2. This chapter states, "The existence of altruism was a problem for Darwin's theory of evolution." What was the problem? What unique contributions were made by the following researchers in resolving the problem:
   a. William Hamilton?
   b. Robert Trivers?
   c. Axelrod and Travis?
   d. Anatol Rapoport?
   e. Stephens, McLinn, and Stevens?
   f. Martin Nowak and Karl Sigmund; Manfred Milinski et al; Alexander?
   g. Ernst Fehr and his colleagues?
3. What do the following perspectives contribute to our understanding of the concept of the *self*:
   a. Explicit versus implicit knowledge?
   b. William James's distinction between "I" and "me"?
   c. Markus's concept of self-schema?
   d. Memory?
   e. Social and cultural influences?
4. Smetana, Schlagman, and Adams developed a study to determine whether children below the age of 6 differentiate between a *moral judgment* and a conventional one (yes,

they do). Design a research study to look at each of the following two concepts: (1) the impact of *social influence* on young children; and (2) the impact of *social persuasion* on young children. Answer the following questions:
   a. What is your research hypothesis?
   b. What is your independent variable (IV)? What is your dependent variable (DV)?
   c. Who will your participants be? Will you have a control group?
   d. How will you perform the study? What methods will you use?
   e. What do you expect the results to be?
5. A wide variety of research techniques have been featured in this chapter in studying concepts within social psychology.
   a. Make a list of the research techniques that were mentioned and a study in which each was used. For example, brain imaging (fMRI) was used in a study that showed that brain areas activated when experiencing physical pain are also activated when experiencing social pain.
   b. Given the pervasiveness of social media use today, particularly among young people, select one of the studies from the list above—or come up with one of your own—and redesign it to use some aspect of social media as a research technique.

For Further Reading

Cacioppo, J., & Berntson, G. (2005). *Social Neuroscience.* New York: Psychology Press.
Sapolsky, R. (2017). *Behave: The Biology of Humans at Our Best and Worst.* New York: Penguin.
Trivers, R. (2011). *The Folly of Fools.* New York: Basic Books.
Ware, J. (2012). *The Student's Guide to Social Neuroscience.* New York: Psychology Press.

Web Resources

IAT Test—https://implicit.harvard.edu/implicit/education.html
IAT—https://www.npr.org/programs/invisibilia/532950995/the-culture-inside.
Robbers Cave—https://www.youtube.com/watch?v=8PRuxMprSDQ and https://www.simplypsychology.org/robbers-cave.html
Ethics of self-driving cars—https://www.nature.com/articles/d41586-018-07135-0

Key Terms and Concepts

aggression
altruism
altruistic punishment
attributions
bystander intervention
cognitive dissonance
cooperation
correspondence bias
deception
door-in-the-face technique
evolution of cooperation
external or situational attribution
fear of missing out
foot-in-the-door technique

free-gift technique
fundamental attribution error or person bias
Implicit Association Test (IAT)
indirect reciprocity
internal or dispositional attribution
kin selection or inclusive fitness
moral emotions
moral judgments
obedience
person perception
reciprocal altruism
schemas
scripts

self-scripts
self-serving bias
social brain hypothesis
social categorizing
social emotion
social facilitation
social inhibition
social loafing
stereotype activation
stereotype application
stereotyping
strong altruism
superordinate goals
theory of mind
weak altruism

13 Personality

LEARNING OBJECTIVES

15.1 Describe the historical influences on the early study of personality.

15.2 Summarize the main ideas of the psychodynamic perspective on the development of personality.

15.3 Summarize the main ideas of the existential-humanistic approach to personality.

15.4 Summarize the main ideas of the social cognitive theories of personality.

15.5 Summarize the main ideas of the current perspectives on personality.

15.6 Define the concept of self.

Niccolò di Bernardo dei Machiavelli (1469–1527) was an Italian diplomat who lived in Florence. As he watched the comings and goings of rulers, he begins to develop a sense of how to achieve and retain power. These observations were written in a small book titled The Prince *(Machiavelli, 1513/1947).* The Prince *describes how to obtain and maintain power with examples from both ancient and times current to Machiavelli.*

He wrote of a previous king of Syracuse: "When he was secure in this rank, he made up his mind to become a prince and to hold by force and without obligation to others what had been given him by agreement" (Machiavelli, 1513/1947, p. 23). He also wrote of some more current rulers: "Nonetheless we have in our times seen great things accomplished by many princes who thought little of keeping their promises and have known the art of mystifying the minds of men" (Machiavelli, 1513/1947, p. 50). It looks like politicians for a long time have broken agreements and told us what we want to hear.

Machiavelli also suggested, "Men are so simple and so much inclined to obey immediate needs that a deceiver will never lack victims for his deceptions." It is the idea of manipulation to which Machiavelli's name has been attached. In the 1970s, two psychologists, Richard Christie and Florence Geis, developed a questionnaire designed to measure the degree to which an individual followed Machiavellian principles (Christie & Geis, 1970). It included such items as "The best way to handle people is to tell them what they want to hear." "Never tell anyone the real reason you did something unless it is useful to do so." The scale also contained items portraying the opposite characteristics such as "Honesty is the best policy in all cases." Overall, the measure of Machiavellianism is composed of four factors: distrust of others, amoral manipulation, desire for control, and desire for status. This personality factor has been used to classify people in terms of business success, an understanding of others, social relationships, and psychological reactions from others. Personality psychologists seek to find enduring individual differences that have existed in our human history and scientifically study these personality factors.

Personality

Generally, we think of personality as that which gives individuals a particular "flavor"—is the person more outgoing, more shy, more concerned with others, more concerned with their own image, seeking excitement, liking detail, and so forth. On a basic level, personality refers to these behaviors, thoughts, feelings, and approaches to life that are more enduring over time on the part of the person.

Two important researchers in the study of personality—Paul Costa and Robert McCrae—define personality in terms of individual differences between people in characteristic thoughts, feelings, and behaviors (McCrae & Costa, 1995). As such, the study of *personality* is the study of internal dispositions or ways of being. Another way of thinking about personality is to consider what we value. Do you value good design, logic, accomplishing things, and so forth? For example, what do you notice when you walk into a room or meet with new people? These are some of our predispositions to see the world in a certain way. Of course, all of us are influenced by situational factors, as we saw in the last chapter on social psychology. In certain situations, we may even act very differently than we generally do. However, personality psychologists focus more on those aspects of ourselves that can be seen across a number of different situations.

Historical Aspects of the Study of Personality

Historical characteristics of personality and temperament have been described in early Indian, Babylonian, and Egyptian cultures. These ideas were systematized by the Greeks (Millon, 2012; Dumont, 2010). Hippocrates (*c.*460–*c.*375 BC) suggested that the four *humors*—choleric, sanguine, phlegmatic, and melancholic—influenced an individual's personality and temperament. These four humors were connected to four elements. The Greeks believed, as most scientists do today, that complex processes can be understood by breaking them down into their parts. The Greeks suggested that all things in the world, including personality and temperament, can be understood in terms of just four elements—earth, air, fire, and water. In the body, they thought that these four elements were connected with the humors—yellow bile (fire), blood (air), phlegm (water), and black bile (earth) (see **Figure 13-1**). Blood was associated with the heart, black bile with the spleen, yellow bile with the liver, and phlegm with the brain.

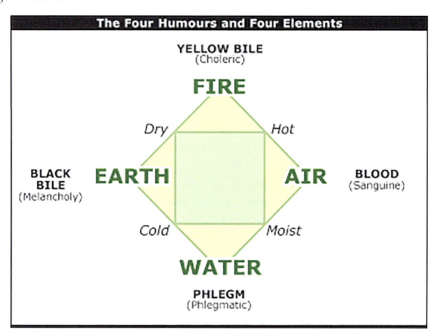

Figure 13-1 Four humors and their connection with body fluid (blood, phlegm, black bile, and yellow bile) and the four elements (earth, fire, air, and water).

Those individuals quickly aroused defined the choleric personality, which was associated with the circulatory system and blood. Easygoing and sociable individuals are sanguine and associated with yellow bile. Calm, controlled individuals are referred to as phlegmatic and associated with phlegm in the body. Melancholic individuals are those who are serious and worried and represented by black bile.

About 100 years after Hippocrates, Theophrastus (c.371–c.387 BC) wrote a series of personality sketches he referred to as "characters." Each of the characters described one or more psychological traits. These included the flatterers, the garrulous, the penurious, the tactless, the boors, and the surly (Millon, 2012).

In the early part of the 20th century, Carl Jung invented the terms *introversion* and *extraversion* to describe a person's approach to the world. Extraversion was seen as a flow of energy outward to the world, whereas introversion was seen as a flow inward toward a person's inner world (Jung, 1989). In this way, extraverts are more concerned with the external world. That is, they focus on their actions that involve other people and things. On the other hand, introverts focus on their internal thoughts and feelings.

Jung further talked about personality in terms of a particular sensitivity that an individual had. If you went into a roomful of people, what would you pay attention to? Who was there? What they wore? The purpose of the event? The way the room was designed or decorated? Or what the event meant to you? These are all different perspectives that, for Jung, represented a sensitivity that directs one's values in the world.

Jung described personality in terms of a sensitivity in four different realms—intellect, feeling, sensation, and intuition. *Intellect* sees the world through analysis and asks what something is. *Feeling* asks the question of whether something is agreeable. *Sensation* asks the question of how it works. And *intuition* asks the question of what pattern is represented in a series of events. Each of these four represents a different way of understanding ourselves and the world. Jung further suggests that these four sensitivities can refer to the external world or the internal world, that is, extraversion and introversion. The four realms combined can be expressed in an extroverted or introverted way to form eight different personality styles. For example, a person who is sensitive to the way the external world appears (feeling) would be interested in design or decorating. An introverted feeling type might find poetry or musical composition important to them.

Also in the 20th century, Ernst Kretschmer in Germany and later William Sheldon in the United States sought to develop a personality system that combined physical body type with temperament. Sheldon suggested that an individual could be described in terms of three types. The *endomorph* body type is soft and round with a relaxed and sociable temperament. The *mesomorph* body type is muscular, strong, and low fat with an energetic and assertive temperament. The *ectomorph* body type is long and thin with more of a cerebral and introverted temperament. Although body type approaches have endured, research relating it to personality and psychopathology has produced mixed results (Ikeda et al., 2018).

Later in the 20th century, Hans Eysenck translated the idea of Greek humors into modern psychological language in terms of two dimensions. He was also influenced by Jung, Kretschmer, and Pavlov (Millon, 2012). Eysenck factor-analyzed the responses of participants on personality measures and identified two larger dimensions that were not correlated with each other. The first dimension ranged from *extroversion* on one end to introversion on the other. The second dimension was *stability*, which ranged from stable to unstable. This second dimension also included the idea of emotionality in that unstable was seen as including negative emotionality and neuroticism. Eysenck's perspective can be seen in **Figure 13-2**. A variety of factor analytic studies consistently demonstrated the dimensions of extroversion and stability to exist across a variety of cultures.

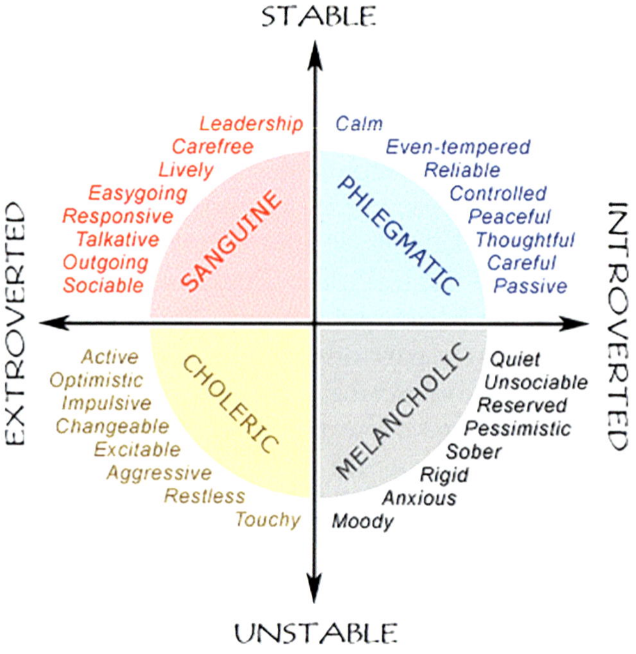

Figure 13-2 Personality factors seen in terms of two dimensions (stability and extroversion), as developed by Hans Eysenck.

Note: extroversion and extraversion are different spellings of the same concept.

CONCEPT CHECK

1. The definition of personality has been conceptualized differently across human history. Describe the following historical conceptions of personality:
   a. The ancient Greeks' *humors* and *elements*
   b. Theophrastus' *characters*
   c. Jung's *sensitivity* in four different realms
   d. Kretschmer's and Sheldon's *body types*
   e. Eysenck's *dimensions*
2. What unique contribution does each of the historical perspectives above make to our understanding of personality today?

Myths and Misconceptions: Astrology

We learned in school that the moon influences the tides. It is a scientific fact, and this relationship has been demonstrated. For many, the moon, sun, and planets are also thought to influence human personality and behavior. This approach is referred to as *astrology*. The approach most commonly used is to refer to the placement of the solar system at the time of your birth. This is generally presented in the form of an astrologer's horoscope, which uses the relative positions of planets and signs of the zodiac at a specific time in inferring an individual's character and personality traits and in foretelling the events of a person's life. Today, many people look to horoscopes in newspapers and online. Further, people from around the world have used horoscopes to make business deals, buy stocks, and even choose dates or marriage partners. Numerous books and websites can be found related to astrology.

How do people understand astrology? In one large-scale European study, more people thought that astrology was scientific than thought that economics was based on science (Allum, 2011). However, this same group of people thought that horoscopes were even less scientific than both astrology and economics.

In some ways, personality traits and astrological traits are similar in that both are considered to be relatively stable. If we know how someone scores on a personality test or what their astrological sign is, we tend to see them in those terms. However, could you recognize your own personality profile or astrological characteristics? This question was approached by Alyssa Wyman and Stuart Vyse (Wyman & Vyse, 2008). They asked 52 college students to identify their personality based on computer-generated astrology reports and traditional personality tests (Five-Factor Model). In this study, the participant had to choose between an accurate report and a false report as reflecting their personality. The participants were able to choose their accurate five-factor personality report better than by chance, whereas this was not the case with the astrological report. Overall, when asked to choose the most accurate five-factor personality report, 55% chose the real report and only 10% chose the bogus report. On the other hand, the true and bogus astrological reports were chosen as most accurate at about the same rate (20% and 16%).

Why individuals accept astrological reports has been a topic of psychological interest and research. A number of factors come into play. First, astrological statements are typically general in nature. Second, humans seek to make sense of whatever information they are presented even when it is not complete. And third, astrological reports are described as specific to your birthday.

To study this last point, three conditions were used in which each person was interacted with individually (Snyder, 1974). In the first condition, the participants were told that the purpose of the study was to examine people's feeling about horoscopes. In the second condition, each participant was asked the year and month in which they were born. And in the third condition, participants were asked the year, month, and day on which they were born. In each condition, the experimenter left the room for 10 minutes to suggest that the horoscope presented was constructed individually for the person. After 10 minutes, the person was given the following:

> *You have a very practical bent and enjoy earning money, but sometimes your deep desire to be a creative person triumphs over your practicality. You lead other people with your innovative ideas, or could do this if you felt more sure of yourself. Insecurity is your greatest weakness, and you would be wise to try to overcome this. Your deep sense of humor and warm, understanding nature wins you true friends, and although they may not be numerous, you share a rather intense loyalty to each other. With your innovative mind, you rebel against authority, either inwardly or openly. Even though you could make a stable businessman, you would be a very idealistic one, finding it hard not to defend the underdog or try to settle arguments that arise. You like to think of yourself as unprejudiced, but periodically examine yourself to make sure you aren't overlooking some harmful judgments. You will live a long, full life if you take care of yourself. You love to have freedom in whatever you're doing, and this makes you dislike monotonous tasks and being in large crowds where you can't seem to move freely. If someone pays you a well-deserved*

> *compliment, you enjoy hearing it, but you may not show that you do. Sometimes you find that the actions you take do not accomplish as much as you'd like them to, especially in dealing with people. You have a real grasp on how people are feeling or what they are thinking without their necessarily telling you.*
>
> Does this sound like you? If you say *yes*, then you are like the people in the study who saw the personality description as "fairly accurate." Further, the more that the participants believed that the report was based on their specific information in groups two and three, the higher they rated the astrological report.
>
> At this point, reviews of more than 100 controlled studies involving various aspects of astrology suggest that there are trivial results to support any aspect of astrology scientifically (Kelly, Janzen, & Saklofske, 2012). There is, of course, lots of evidence to suggest that we as humans accept self-description from external sources as accurate (Snyder & Larson, 1972). We also make sense of our world and fill in gaps. As Shakespeare reminds us, it is truly not in our stars but in ourselves.
>
> **Thought Question**: What are three characteristics about the horoscope presented above that make it seem applicable to so many people? What can you do, as an educated consumer, to read such horoscopes more critically?

Psychodynamic Perspectives on the Development of Personality

Sigmund Freud (1856–1939) was initially trained as a zoologist before he completed medical school. The nature of the neuron was just being discovered, and Freud based his early theories on the neuroscience of his day. One of Freud's important ideas for his time was that humans can be influenced by unconscious processes. One of his early books focused on understanding the meaning of dreams and how dreams reflect a person's psyche (Freud, 1900). Freud was very influential by creating a system for understanding human behavior and experience that has been applied to a number of different disciplines ranging from psychology to literature.

Freud was an enthusiastic reader of Darwin and credited his interest in science to an early reading of Darwin. A number of Freud's ideas can be seen as coming from Darwin (Ellenberger, 1970; Sulloway, 1979). In fact, Freud quotes Darwin in many of his written works (Sulloway, 1979). With some topics, such as the development of emotions, including fears, in children, Darwin and Freud followed parallel tracks. One important theme in both of their work was the role of instinctual processes in child development. Darwin emphasized two main instinctual processes—self-preservation and sexual selection. Similarly, Freud said that he began his studies with the idea that hunger and love are what move the world. However, in his writings Freud emphasized sexual processes over those of self-preservation. In fact, in later writing, Freud combined the sexual and self-preservation instincts into a life-force instinct.

For Freud, the sexual instinct becomes the major driving force for human life and interaction. He was also influenced by the suggestion of the neurologist Hughlings Jackson that in our brains we find more primitive brain areas underlying more advanced ones. Thus, it is quite possible for the psyche to be in conflict with itself or at least to have different layers representing different processes.

The Structure of Personality

Freud divides the mind into three parts. Although Freud used the German equivalents of the English "I" and "it," when his work was translated into English, the translators used the Latin terms, *id*, *ego*, and *superego*.

The id is present at birth. It represents those instinctual processes that help us to obtain our basic needs. From a developmental perspective, the life of an infant for Freud was governed by the *pleasure principle*. That is, the infant seeks those things that are pleasurable and avoids those that are not. It is the *"id"* or "it" that directs this instinctual period.

Beginning at about 3 years of age, the child learns to mediate his or her desires and the rules of the external reality. This is referred to as the *reality principle* by Freud. This reflects the development of an "I" or *"ego"* that helps the child to live in the world. The ego is seen to be part of personality that helps us navigate the demands between external requirements and our internal experiences.

At a later point, an individual develops a moral sense, which directs our behaviors with one another. The structure is referred to as the *"superego"* and reflects perspectives we learn from our parents and our culture as well as our own moral development.

The three parts of the psyche, the id, ego, and superego, can direct a person in very different directions. That is, your ego may know that you need to be in class, but you feel hungry and have the desire to eat something immediately. Often, you come up with a strategy that allows you to put off eating until after class or buy something on the way to class. From a superego perspective, you know that stealing someone else's food is not the way to go. Freud suggested that many of the id impulses are working outside of our awareness. Further, many of these impulses may not be acceptable to society. Freud's imagery is also shown as an iceberg with only the ego shown above water, suggesting we are not aware of our id impulses.

Freud described three types of consciousness. One type is what we are aware of, which is generally referred to as conscious awareness. There is also information such as your telephone number, which at any moment you could bring into consciousness. Freud referred to this as latent consciousness or pre-consciousness. The third type of consciousness contains information we are not aware of and find difficult to bring into consciousness. However, this state, referred to as unconscious processes, according to Freud can still influence our thoughts, feelings, and behaviors. If, for example, you were bitten by a dog as a child, you might not remember this event but feel anxious or fearful when you see dogs as an adult.

Psychosexual Development

In addition to the internal structures of the psyche, Freud also suggested there are stages of development that are often referred to as *psychosexual development*. At each of these stages there is a physical focus and a psychological theme. The first stage is referred to as the *oral* stage. During the first 18 months of life, the physical focus for an infant is the mouth, lips, and tongue. Psychologically, the infant is dependent on those around him or her. From 18 months to about 3 and a half years of age, the child begins to walk and learn self-control. It is during this period that toilet training begins. Freud suggests that parental interactions around learning bodily self-control can influence future interactions. This stage is referred to as the *anal* stage of development. The next stage is referred to as the *phallic* stage, which lasts from 3 and a half to 7 years of age. This is a period of initial development of the sexual organs and the beginning of gender identity. This is also the period when emotions such as love, fear, and jealously develop. This is followed by the *latency* phase, which last from 7 years of age to puberty. The final stage is the *genital* phase and represents an understanding of one's sexuality and the development of mature relationships.

Not everyone passes through these stages in a successful manner. Freud suggested that if someone does not resolve the psychological issues associated with a particular stage, then he or she will continue to have problems related to that stage even as an adult. Individuals with problems in the oral stage will have problems related to dependency. The adult anal character will remain overly concerned with order and detail. Problems during the phallic stage are seen to result in either a rigid moral code or the opposite. Although these character descriptions have been used in a variety of areas, they have never been examined with strong research studies.

To understand the nature of our more primitive processes, Freud looked to the description of dreams and wish fulfillment. During dreams, we have less rational considerations and more emotional considerations. Likewise, our daydreams or wish fulfillment reflects our desires and instinctual processes. Freud referred to these as *primitive processes* in that they reflect basic needs and desires.

The Project for a Scientific Psychology

One of his works, *The Project for a Scientific Psychology*, utilized these ideas and sought to place psychology on a firm scientific basis. The *Project* was based on three separate ideas. The first was *reflex processes*. For example, organisms physically withdraw when confronted with unpleasant stimuli. Freud extended this idea to cognitive and emotional processes to suggest that, mentally, humans avoid ideas or feelings that are unpleasant to them. The second principle Freud used was *associationism*. That is to say, ideas that are presented together in time will be mentally called forth together. Freud suggested that if as a child you experience a fearful situation such as falling out of a car, then riding in a car could make you feel fearful or anxious, even if you did not know why. The third idea is that the nervous system is capable of retaining and discharging energy. This energy was initially called "Q," but Freud later identified it as *libido or sexual energy*.

As Freud described in his early work, he viewed libido as a form of biological energy that could build up unless it was in some way expressed. The lack of expression of sexual energy, for example, was seen to be the basis of various types of psychopathology. Likewise, the experience of sexual and self-preservation instincts, when met with restrictive rules of a particular society, were seen to lead to anxiety. Overall, Freud saw *neurosis* as an attempt by individuals to treat the problem they were experiencing. For example, anxious individuals often worry too much about problems or events that could happen in the future. Although consideration of future problems may be helpful in problem-solving, constant consideration or worry is not.

The *Project* sees the brain as basically a blank slate upon which experiences become connected with one another driven by instinctual processes of sexuality and self-preservation.

Some see Freud's ideas in the *Project* as anticipating Donald Hebb's concept that use modifies neuronal connection in the brain (Schott, 2011). The human, for Freud, becomes the real-life laboratory in which nature and nurture struggle. The *Project* was finished in 1895. After this period, Freud mainly spoke of mental illness in terms of psychological processes and did not return to brain-based ideas.

Although many people think of Freud as being outdated, there is currently a resurgence of interest in the interface between dynamic approaches and neuroscience. Eric Kandel, who won the Nobel Prize for his work on learning and memory, described his interest in Freud and the manner in which dynamic principles can be viewed in terms of brain functioning (Kandel, 1998, 1999, 2005). Freud's ideas have also been updated in terms of the brain networks discovered using current brain-imaging techniques (Carhart-Harris & Friston, 2010; Rizzolatti, Alberto Semi, & Fabbri-Destro, 2014). One important concept in both Freud's *Project* and current neuroscience research is the manner in which the brain conserves and uses energy to perform psychological functions including the development of mental illness.

Defense Mechanisms

In the same way that any animal, including humans, will pull away from a painful stimulus, Freud suggested that we also pull away from, or repress, painful ideas or thoughts. We also seek to pull away from external stresses. Freud suggested there were patterns of avoidance that are defense mechanisms. Defense mechanisms not only minimize anxiety, but they also protect the ego. That is, they seek to keep intact our image of our self.

This psychic manipulation of energy allowed for the possibility that higher cortical processes could inhibit the experience of lower ones, a process that would come to be called *repression*. Anxiety for Freud is the result of society and culture having inconsistent rules for the expression of sexuality and aggression. This anxiety and our inability to acknowledge these instinctual experiences lead to **defense mechanisms** to reduce neurotic anxiety. Thus, repression, or the process of inhibiting anxiety-producing ideas, underlies all defense mechanisms.

One common defense mechanism is *rationalization*. Rationalization is the use of a plausible but false excuse. If you forgot to do something that was important, you might rationalize that you had a headache that made you forget. In another situation, someone might remind you of a time you broke something important to another person. If you avoid the anxiety associated with remembering the event by saying "that never happened" you are using the defense mechanism of *denial*. With the defense mechanism of *projection*, you take characteristics of yourself that you do not like and attribute them to others. Sometimes you might hear a leader in an organization who is experiencing difficulties say, "I am surrounded by stupid fools." *Reaction formation* is the converting of a socially unacceptable impulse into its opposite. For example, an angry person might show an exaggerated effort to show how peaceful and tolerant they are. *Sublimation* is the converting of basic impulses such as anger or sexuality into more acceptable choices such as art, playing music, playing sports, or physical exercise. The use of defense mechanisms is a normal process seen in all humans. However, it would be a problem if a person uses the same defense mechanism in every situation. Several common defense mechanisms are listed in **Table 13-1**.

Table 13-1 Table of defense mechanisms.

Defense Mechanism	Definition	Example
Rationalization	Explaining or creating an explanation for impulsive behaviors	A student cheats on a test because everyone does it
Denial	The failure to acknowledge information that can cause anxiety	Person says their lack of exercise or smoking will not affect them
Projection	Assigning unacceptable urges of one's self to another person	Seeing other people as arrogant and pushing to get ahead
Sublimation	Channeling unacceptable impulses into productive activities	Using your anger or sexual urges to produce art or engage in physical exercise
Reaction formation	Behaving or thinking in a way that is the opposite of one's unacceptable urges	An angry person might show an exaggerated effort to show how peaceful and tolerant they are
Displacement	Shifting an emotional experience to a safer person or object	Getting angry at a partner after a difficult meeting at work or school

Other Psychodynamic Approaches Influenced by Freud

During Freud's time, there were a number of professionals who took a *psychodynamic approach.* Psychodynamic psychology is based on the idea that thoughts and emotions basically learned in childhood can influence your behavior and experiences. Others adopted or modified Freud's ideas in their theories and the treatment of their patients. For example, Alfred Adler emphasized social processes, especially in childhood, as important for personality development (Adler, 1924). Adler further suggested that part of feeling that one's life is worthwhile is having the experience that you are useful to others. Adler also created the concept of an *inferiority complex.*

Overall, a number of individuals believed that Freud overemphasized the role of instincts and our reaction to them. One group emphasized *ego psychology*. This group, which included Freud's daughter, Anna Freud, placed more emphasis on the ability of the ego to live life and adapt to the demands of life. Another group emphasized *object relations*. The common term for object relations is attachment, which you learned about in the developmental chapter. Their view, which is similar to John Bowlby's, is that early relationships with significant people in one's life constitute a powerful role in relation to many personality factors. Two others who expanded the psychodynamic perspective were Carl Jung, who emphasized the evolutionary aspects of development, and Karen Horney, who emphasized social aspects of personality development. Both of these individuals made contributions that were later incorporated into the *existential-humanistic perspective*, which will be discussed later in this chapter.

Whereas Freud emphasized the drives of the sexual and self-preservation instincts within the context of experience, Carl Jung, a Swiss psychiatrist and a colleague of Freud, viewed human behavior and experience in much broader terms. Jung asked this question: In the same way that there is an evolutionary history of the body, is there also an evolutionary history of consciousness? He spent a great amount of time examining old myths, stories, and artifacts in an attempt to reconstruct a history of the psyche. Jung was particularly interested in the close connection between instinctual processes and the environmental factors that influence them.

Like Darwin, Jung examined human universals. He spent time in Africa, the American Southwest, and other non-European areas to determine whether the psychic structure of all humans was similar. For example, one question that Jung asked was the following: Do individuals throughout the world have similar dream patterns? He answered this question in the affirmative and suggested that humans worldwide showed similar cognitive, emotional, and reflexive patterns. One important aspect of therapy for Jung was to bring together discrepant aspects of one's personality to create a unified self, which would give meaning to one's life. Jung also introduced the terms *introversion* and *extraversion* to reflect a person's tendency to value internal or external information. By noting that introversion in itself is not a sign of mental illness, Jung helped to set up the valuing of internal experience that existential-humanistic therapy focuses on.

Karen Horney, a German-born psychoanalyst, felt that Freud's approach did not fully present a psychology that applied to women as well as men. Overall, for both men and women she differentiated between healthy growth in which a person developed to her full potential and neurotic growth in which a person limited her development by unrealistic ideas and feelings. These ideas would include ideas such as "everyone should love me," "I should never make mistakes," or "the world should always give me what I want."

Horney's (1950) final book, *Neurosis and Human Growth*, described how these types of unrealistic ideas along with an idealized self-image leave the person feeling out of touch with herself and others. In contrast to an idealized self-image in which one is always perfect and loved by everyone, Karen Horney created the concepts of **self-realization** and a **real self**. A real self includes who one is and what one appreciates. It is this real self that should be the focus of development referred to as self-realization. It is the alienation from the real self that is seen to constitute a key process of neurotic development. It also requires energy to present a false self. That is, if you are always trying to make yourself look good, you will pay less attention to other parts of yourself, and you will have fewer resources for developing healthy human growth. Her ideas were echoed later in the 20th century by Abraham Maslow and more recently in the concept of a true self in social psychology (Strohminger, Knobe, & Newman, 2017).

Using Internal Processes to Understand Personality

If we see personality as a way of thinking and feeling, then it could be assumed that a person would approach different ambiguous situations in a similar unconsciousness manner. One method for studying this in the history of psychology is the **projective technique**. It is called projective since the person projects onto an image certain ideas and emotions. *Projective instruments* are assessment tests composed of ambiguous stimuli. They can range from seemingly random patterns such as an inkblot to ambiguous drawings or photos of individuals or objects. The individual is asked to describe what the patterns look like, what they remind him or her of, or what is being depicted in the drawing.

The basic idea of projective testing is based on the theoretical ideas of Sigmund Freud and others who sought to understand the dynamics of the mind. One important distinction Freud made was between types of thinking (see Erdelyi, 1985; Westen, 1998, for overviews). *Primary process thought*, which is seen in dreams or letting your mind wander, is not organized logically but in terms of associations between thoughts and feelings. On the other hand, *secondary process thought* is logically organized. Freud suggested that it was possible to understand the cognitive and emotional connections of a person's mind in terms of primary process. His techniques for exploring these connections were *free association* and *dream analysis*.

Projective techniques were formally introduced in the first half of the 1900s as a means of detecting primary process types of thinking and feeling, including instinctual and motivational processes. Since there were few techniques for understanding the connections in one's mind at this time, professionals saw projective techniques as having potential for understanding how thoughts and feelings formed a cognitive network. It was assumed that projective techniques would give a window into the thought processes of those with mental disorders and how they differ from the thought processes of healthy individuals. It was also assumed that projective techniques would give insight into one's personality.

Two of the most well-known projective techniques are the *Rorschach inkblot* and the *Thematic Apperception Test (TAT)*. Both of these tests have a long history of use, although various researchers have been critical of the Rorschach and other projective techniques and suggest clinical situations in which these types of techniques are not useful (Garb, Wood, Lilienfeld, & Nezworski, 2005).

Rorschach Inkblots

During the early part of the 1900s, Herman Rorschach, a Swiss psychiatrist, experimented with using inkblots. The **Rorschach inkblots** were made by simply dripping ink on a piece of paper and then folding it in half to create a symmetrical design. Some of the inkblots were in black-and-white and others were in color (see **Figure 13-3**). He initially gave his inkblots to a large number of schoolchildren (Ellenberger, 1970). Rorschach was interested in the sensory processing of these images, which he connected with Carl Jung's idea of introversion and extraversion.

Rorschach saw introversion as focusing on the inner world of kinesthetic images and creative activity. Extraversion, on the other hand, was a focus on color, emotion, and adjustment to reality. For Rorschach, the content of what was seen in the inkblot was less the focus of the interpretation than the elements used, such as whether the person saw whole images or focused on small details of the blot. Viewing the image as containing movement and the use of the colors was also seen as important. A limited number of ten plates was selected, and Rorschach published a book in German, *Psychodiagnostics*, in 1921. He died some months later at age 37. His book was translated into English in 1942 (Rorschach, 1942).

Following his death, various clinicians used the Rorschach in their clinical practice. For a number of years, there was little scientific data concerning the reliability and validity of the measure. Since the late 20th century, there has been a movement to standardize the presentation of the test and the manner in which it is scored. Exner (1993) offered one such system. Various studies have examined the reliability and validity of the measure with specific diagnostic groups and theoretical constructs (see Hunsley & Mash, 2007; Meyer, 2001; Meyer & Archer, 2001, for overviews). In 2001, a special issue of the journal *Psychological Assessment* was devoted to clarifying the utility of the Rorschach, along with its problems, from an evidence-based position. In order to address questions of reliability and validity, a series of norms using the Exner system based on more than 5,800 people from 17 countries has been published (Meyer, Erdberg, & Shaffer, 2007). This review showed consistency across samples for adult Rorschach responses but problems with data from

Figure 13-3 When you look at this, what do you see? An example of a color Rorschach inkblot.

children. Overall, the Rorschach and its scoring is a complicated process that continues to be the focus of scientific debate.

Other researchers have begun to use neuroscience techniques such as brain imaging and electrophysiology to understand physiological processes underlying Rorschach responses. For example, Giromini and his colleagues examined movement responses on the Rorschach and how these were reflected in the EEG (Giromini, Porcelli, Viglione, Parolin, & Pineda, 2010).

Thematic Apperception Test (TAT)

The **Thematic Apperception Test (TAT)** is composed of 30 black-and-white drawings of various scenes and people (see **Figure 13-4** for an example). The instrument was developed by Christiana Morgan and Henry Murray in the 1930s. Typically, an individual is shown 20 of the cards, one at a time, and asked to create a story about what is being depicted on the card. The basic idea is that by noting the content and emotionality of the individual's responses, it is possible to gain insight into his or her thoughts, emotions, and motivations including areas of conflict. For example, if an individual described many of the cards in terms of someone leaving another person, the clinician might ask if abandonment was an important issue for the person. Although the TAT technique may be useful to gain additional information concerning a person such as suicidal thoughts, it lacks scientific

Figure 13-4 What is happening in this picture? Example of a TAT drawing. The person being evaluated is asked to create a story about the picture.

Source: Murray et al. (1938, p. 622). By permission of Oxford University Press, USA.

evidence to make it useful in obtaining a formal diagnosis. Similar problems of reliability and validity exist with the TAT as with the Rorschach.

Overall, projective techniques have been the subject of great debate and controversy. Frick, Barry, and Kamphaus (2010) presented some of the major pros and cons concerning the use of projective techniques. Some professionals see their value not in terms of giving exact diagnoses but in their ability to allow a professional to see how an individual responds to ambiguous stimuli—especially in terms of suicidal ideation as well as disorganized thought processes. This may lead to further discussions of areas that a professional would not normally discuss. The major disadvantage of projective techniques centers on questions of validity in terms of both the tests' ability to identify specific mental disorders and personality processes.

CONCEPT CHECK

1. How were Sigmund Freud's ideas influenced by Charles Darwin and Hughlings Jackson?
2. Freud divides the mind into three parts: *ego*, *id*, and *superego*. Describe the role each of these parts plays in the psyche. How do the parts work together? How do they conflict?
3. Freud was interested in an individual's psychological development.

    a. He developed the *pleasure principle* and the *reality principle* to talk about an individual's development. Describe the two principles.
    b. He proposed stages of psychosexual development. Identify the stages and describe what is happening in each of them.
4. Freud describes three types of consciousness. Describe them and give an example of each.
5. In his book *The Project for a Scientific Psychology*, Freud introduced three ideas. What are these ideas, and, from Freud's perspective, what role do they play in psychological health and psychological problems?
6. Other researchers have expanded on Freud's psychodynamic perspective. What contributions have the following researchers made to our understanding of personality?
    a. Alfred Adler?
    b. Anna Freud?
    c. The "object relations" group?
    d. Carl Jung?
    e. Karen Horney?
7. Describe projective techniques in the study of personality including the following questions:
    a. What is their focus?
    b. How do they work?
    c. What are two well-known projective techniques?
    d. What can we learn from them?
    e. What are some pros and cons in using projective techniques?

The Existential-Humanistic Approach to Personality

In the middle of the last century, a group of psychologists began to explore alternatives to the Freudian emphasis on unconscious motivations, as well as to the Skinnerian emphasis on learning as the basis of all human processes. Both Freud and Skinner deemphasized the role of choice in a person's life. One alternative approach was based on existential and humanistic concerns.

The existential movement began in Europe in the 1800s and gained followers after World War II. The major focus of **existentialism** was the nature of human nature and the meaning of life. One critical question of existentialism focused on the basic experience of being alive and living life. This movement was combined with humanistic psychology in the United States in the 1950s and 19060s.

One important aspect of the **humanistic** tradition was an emphasis on choice. Throughout our lives, we all make critical choices that determine who we are and how we live our lives. In this way, we express our personality by the choices we make. For the humanistic psychologists, these choices can lead to positive as well as negative outcomes. One critical aspect of these choices according to the **existential-humanistic approach** is our ability to be true to one's self. One emphasis was how to live in the present and consider one's choices.

This is sometimes contrasted with being a "company person" who just does what they are told in their job without thinking about themselves or their own values. Other psychologists such as Rollo May spoke of the courage required to live life to the fullest.

What makes life worth living? One researcher who has focused on moment-to-moment experience is Mihalyi Csikszentmihalyi (1990) (https://www.ted.com/talks/mihaly_csikszentmihalyi_on_flow). One of his questions was what makes life worth living? In order to answer this, Csikszentmihalyi examined the experiences of artists, writers, athletes, and others to see what they enjoyed the most. What he found was that many of the experiences they enjoyed, they performed for their own sake. The subjective experience of these activities he referred to as being in the *flow*. When one is in a flow state, there is no problem with concentration, that is, a lack of distraction, and little notice of the passing of time. Playing music, playing tennis, or even playing video games can produce the flow state in some individuals.

Your experience takes place on a number of levels, including your biology, your culture, and your psychology. Maslow, as you learned previously, suggested that certain needs must be met before one can make psychological decisions. Maslow emphasized the possibility of self-actualization or fully being who one really is. Within this view is the possibility of growth. For Maslow, this growth does not come from a deficit or lack as suggested by Freud and Skinner. Rather, growth is an important human motivation in itself.

Carl Rogers also emphasized that each of us has the basic tendency to *actualize* (Rogers, 1951). Although different in specifics, this tendency to actualize is a motivating factor similar to Freud's suggestion of a *life drive*. This drive for Rogers was toward becoming a fully functioning person who is authentic in relation to their internal and external environment.

Social Cognitive Theories of Personality

Social cognitive theories of personality are also referred to *social learning theories*. These theories emphasize a person's view of the world, that is, the person's cognitive understanding of their environment. The social aspect is that many of these beliefs are the result of our interactions with others. In this sense, they are learned through our interactions. The research related to the social cognitive theory of personality typically focuses on how a person's cognitive views of the world interact with situational variables to produce different behaviors.

One researcher associated with the social cognitive approach is Julian Rotter. Rotter also wrote the first book that described a social cognitive approach to personality, *Social Learning and Clinical Psychology* (Rotter, 1954). For example, would you more likely buy a lottery ticket if there was a 2-to-1 chance of winning $10 or a 100-to-1 chance of winning $1,000. Most people would choose the $10 since your odds are better. In this way, our expectations are more a factor of our choices than the actual reward. Thus, what we expect to happen is a critical factor.

Following this line of reasoning, Rotter was able to show that a person's behavior in solving a problem depended on whether they believed that it was based on skill or on luck. If the person thought it was based on skill, they would work harder at the task than if they thought it was based on luck. Rotter referred to this tendency as *locus of control*. Those with an internal locus of control believe that their environment is more in their control. Those with an external locus of control see events as more outside of their efforts and more the result of chance. Rotter saw locus of control as an enduring perspective or personality trait on the part of the person.

A related concept referred to as *self-efficacy* was developed by Albert Bandura at Stanford University (Bandura, 1977). If you believe that you can perform a certain task, then you have high self-efficacy, whereas if you do not believe you can do the task, you have low self-efficacy. Bandura performed a number of studies showing that by increasing self-efficacy, actual performance on a task would improve. In terms of therapy, Bandura was able to show that if someone who was afraid of snakes could come to believe that it is possible to reduce this fear, then actual change could be seen with an actual snake (Bandura, 2019; Bandura et al., 1980). Just coming to believe that you could be chosen for a job will actually increase your interview performance.

Although self-efficacy and locus of control may seem similar, there are theoretical differences. Rotter emphasized the general expectation that it is possible to accomplish a goal through your efforts. Bandura, on the other hand, emphasized whether you actually had the ability to accomplish the task. At times, one may show both an internal locus of control and high self-efficacy. However, it is also possible that you believe that you have the ability but that the situation prevents you from succeeding. That is, you believe you can accomplish a task at work but your boss will not follow your suggestions. In this case you would have high self-efficacy but an external locus of control. Further, Bandura's research suggested that it was possible to change one's level of self-efficacy in a given situation, whereas Rotter tended to see locus of control as a global personality trait.

Current Perspectives on Personality

Current perspectives on personality have tended to focus on the stability of personality traits. This is not to suggest that we do not act differently in very different situations. What personality does focus on is our long-term ways of relating to the world. As individuals move into adulthood and become employed, for example, there are changes in approaches to one's environment. However, like intelligence, we can note differences between individuals as these changes take place. This section will focus on how psychologists currently approach the topic of personality.

Typical Personality Traits

In the early part of the 20th century, most psychologists who discussed personality used a theoretical perspective that emphasized the descriptive nature of specific traits. One of the first psychologists to study personality was the Harvard University professor Gordon Allport (1897–1967). Allport emphasized **traits** as the basic units of personality. He saw traits as "generalized and personalized determining tendencies—consistent and stable modes of an individual's adjustment to his environment" (Allport & Odbert, 1936). He further suggested that traits are based in the nervous system. Although Allport studied personality traits, he also emphasized the uniqueness of the individual.

Allport asked his assistant, Henry Odbert, to count all of the words in an English dictionary that could be used to describe characteristics of personality. Sometime later in 1936 Odbert returned with some 17,953 words. These included words such as *shy, arrogant, warm, reliable, manipulative,* and *conscientious*. These terms were analyzed to determine more basic traits and the components that underlay these.

Researchers during the first half of the 20th century tended to focus on only a few traits. Outgoing individuals were described in terms of *extraversion*, for example. Those who frequently took risks in activities such as skydiving were referred to as *sensation seekers*. The problem was that there were far too many personality terms to describe a person's behavior and experience. This made it difficult to create a coherent theory of personality.

Using mathematical techniques that compared the similarity of responses between the different measures offered an alternative to a purely descriptive approach. This was the approach chosen by Raymond Cattell (1905–1998). He used factor analysis, which seeks to find similarities among a large number of individual terms. He began with the 17,953 words that Allport and Odbert had used. From this Cattell created 170 personality descriptions, which he then reduced to 16 personality factors. These are shown in **Table 13-2**.

The next development continued the factor analytic approach and was directed by Robert McCrae and Paul Costa (1987; see also McCrae, Gaines, & Wellington, 2013, for an overview). They used a factor analytic approach to personality, which suggested five major personality dimensions. This is referred to as the *five-factor model (FFM), often called the Big 5*. These five dimensions include *extraversion, neuroticism, openness, agreeableness*, and *conscientiousness*.

Extraversion is associated with sociability, cheerfulness, energy, and a sense of fun. This dimension ranges from being passive, quiet, and inner-directed to being active, talkative, and outer-directed. ***Neuroticism*** is associated with a tendency to express distressing emotions and difficulty experiencing stressful situations. This dimension ranges from being calm, even-tempered, and comfortable to being worried, temperamental, and self-conscious. ***Openness*** as a personality trait is associated with curiosity, flexibility, and an artistic sensitivity, including imaginativeness and the ability to create a fantasy world. This dimension ranges from inventive and curious to cautious and conservative. ***Agreeableness*** is associated with being sympathetic, trusting, cooperative, modest, and straightforward. This dimension ranges from being friendly and compassionate to being competitive and outspoken. ***Conscientiousness*** as a personality trait is associated with being diligent, disciplined, well-organized, punctual, and dependable. This dimension ranges from being efficient and organized to being easygoing and careless. These five dimensions are shown in **Table 13-3**.

Scores are determined by asking individuals a number of questions about what they like to do and how they experience the world. If someone says they worry a lot, then he or she would score higher on the factor of neuroticism. Are personality scores of any value? It turns out from a number of studies that how people score on personality dimensions can predict how they will behave, especially if the behavior is sampled across a number of different situations over time (McAdams & Olson, 2010; Soto, 2019).

A meta-analysis of studies examining agreeableness, conscientiousness, and emotional stability (opposite pole of neuroticism) found these variables to be related to a positive investment in work and family (Lodi-Smith & Roberts, 2008). Another review reported that longevity was related to extraversion and consciousness. Overall, factors of the five-factor model were also related to family relationships and occupational satisfaction and performance (Ozer & Benet-Martinez, 2008). Further, meta-analyses link optimism, extraversion, conscientiousness, and openness to better coping and neuroticism to poorer types of coping (Carver & Connor-Smith, 2010).

Solid research on the FFM has also demonstrated that there is a consistency of results across a variety of cultures (McCrae, 2009). However, there are changes across the lifespan. In one study, McCrae and colleagues (1999) gave personality measures to individuals in five countries. They found that there were some changes in the levels of the five factors over the lifespan. These differences were found in all of the cultures studied (McCrae et al., 1999). Overall, lifespan data suggest that from age 18 to 30, individuals show declines in neuroticism, extraversion, and openness to experience and increases

Table 13-2 Cattell's 16 personality factors (based on Conn & Rieke, 1994)

Descriptors of Low Range	Primary Factor	Descriptors of High Range
Reserve, impersonal, distant, cool	Warmth	Warm, outgoing, attentive to others, kindly, easy going
Concrete thinking, lower general mental capacity	Reasoning	Abstract-thinking, more intelligent, bright, higher general mental capacity
Reactive emotionally, changeable, affected by feelings, easily upset	Emotional Stability	Emotionally stable, adaptive, mature, faces reality calm
Deferential, cooperative, avoids conflict, submissive, humble	Dominance	Dominant, forceful, assertive, aggressive, competitive, stubborn
Serious, restrained, prudent, introspective	Liveliness	Lively, animated, spontaneous, enthusiastic, cheerful, expressive
Expedient, nonconforming, disregards rules, self-indulgent	Rule-consciousness	Rule-conscious, dutiful, conscientious, conforming
Shy, threat-sensitive, timid, hesitant, intimidated	Social Boldness	Socially bold, venturesome, thick skinned, uninhibited
Utilitarian, objective, unsentimental, tough minded, self-reliant	Sensitivity	Sensitive, aesthetic, sentimental, tender minded, intuitive, refined
Trusting, unsuspecting, accepting, unconditional, easy	Vigilance	Vigilant, suspicious, skeptical, distrustful, oppositional
Grounded, practical, solution orientated, steady, conventional	Abstractedness	Abstract, imaginative, absent minded, impractical, absorbed in ideas
Forthright, genuine, artless, open, guileless, naïve, unpretentious	Privateness	Private, discreet, nondisclosing, shrewd, polished, worldly, astute
Self-assured, unworried, complacent, secure, free of guilt	Apprehension	Apprehensive, self-doubting, worried, guilt prone, insecure, worrying
Traditional, attached to familiar, conservative	Openness to Change	Open to change, experimental, analytical, free thinking, flexibility
Group-oriented, affiliative, a joiner and follower dependent	Self-reliance	Self-reliant, solitary, resourceful, individualistic, self-sufficient
Tolerated disorder, unexacting, flexible, undisciplined, lax, self-conflict, impulsive	Perfectionism	Perfectionistic, organized, compulsive, self-disciplined, socially precise
Relaxed, placid, tranquil, torpid, patient, composed low drive	Tension	Tense, high energy, impatient, driven, frustrated, over wrought

Table 13-3 Five-factor model

Factor	Low Scorers	High Scorers
Extraversion (positive emotionality)	Passive Quiet Inward directed	Active Talkative Outwardly directed
Neuroticism (negative emotionality)	Calm Even-tempered Comfortable	Worried Temperamental Self-conscious
Openness	Not curious Less flexibility Down-to-earth	Curiosity Flexibility Imaginativeness
Agreeableness	Suspicious Aggressive Antagonistic	Trusting Sympathetic Cooperative
Conscientiousness	Less dependable Undisciplined Disorganized	Dependable Disciplined Well-organized

Source: From Thomas A. Widiger and Stephanie N. Mullins-Sweatt (2009). "Five-Factor Model of Personality Disorder: A Proposal for DSM-V." *Annual Review of Clinical Psychology,* Vol. 5: 197–220.

in agreeableness and conscientiousness. McCrae and Costa (1996, 1999) suggested that the five factors of personality be considered as biologically based tendencies, as opposed to culturally conditioned characteristic adaptations. Genetic research has supported this perspective. Additional research from around the world shows that individuals become more agreeable, more conscientious, and less neurotic during early adulthood (Bleidorn et al., 2013). These authors suggest that these changes in personality traits are the result of making the transition to adult roles.

Evolutionary Perspectives on Personality

Darwin set the stage for looking at personality traits in his discussion of the traits of animals and the manner in which they can be modified by selective breeding. Evolutionary researchers have also noted the way in which dogs became domesticated over the past 100,000 years. The value of looking at personality traits in animals is that it helps to better understand the role of genes and adaptations seen in human processes. Since many human processes have been shown to be built upon earlier ones seen in a number of different animals, it is possible to ask the same question concerning personality. The feature "Applying Psychological Science: Personality in Animals" focuses on this aspect of personality research.

Focusing on humans, Daniel Nettle (2006) has examined the McCrae and Costa dimensions of five factors in relation to an evolutionary perspective. He suggests that each of the dimensions has a particular advantage given certain environmental conditions. Extraversion, for example, is associated with success in mating, having social allies, and exploration of the environment. Neuroticism, on the other hand, is associated with greater vigilance and labeling situations as dangerous. In times of little stress, extraversion would be a successful strategy. However, in dangerous times, it may not afford the necessary caution as would be found with neuroticism. Nettle's summary of the costs and benefits of each of the Big 5 factors is presented in **Table 13-4**.

Some individuals form routines and display consistent behavior even when changes to the task are made. We all know humans who develop routines and rarely change their behaviors even when the world around them is changing. A critical question for an evolutionary psychology is why do responsive and unresponsive individuals coexist within a population. A second related question is why do some individuals show this consistency over time and situations. If we think about being responsive to the environment, we realize that this involves some costs in the form of effort and the inability to spend the energy in other ways. However, we can also imagine that paying attention to, and being influenced by, the environment could bring us some benefits.

Wolf and his colleagues suggest that for responsiveness to spread throughout a population, the benefit of the behavior must be greater than the cost. Otherwise, unresponsiveness would spread. Further, responsiveness appears to spread when it is rare but not when it is common. One example of this is a store having a sale. If only a few individuals pay attention to the sale, then their effort pays off. Indeed, this would support future efforts to pay attention to sales. However, if everyone in a population pays attention to the store's announcement of a sale, then the effort would not pay off in terms of long lines and limited goods. These individuals would be discouraged from going to future sales.

Another question is what leads to the stability of personality traits across generations. One possible mechanism suggested by a variety of environmental researchers is assortative mating. **Assortative mating** suggests that humans do not randomly choose partners but choose partners who are like themselves on some selected trait. If those traits could be represented by the personality characteristics of the five-factor model, then the traits would be more likely to be passed on to the couple's children. That is to say, if extraverts found themselves attracted to other extraverts, then the genetic predisposition for the

Table 13-4 Summary of hypothesized fitness benefits and costs of increasing levels of each of the big five personality dimensions (Nettle, 2006, p. 628)

Domain	Benefits	Costs
Extraversion	Mating success; social allies; exploration of environment	Physical risks; family stability
Neuroticism	Vigilance to dangers; striving and competitiveness	Stress and depression, with interpersonal and health consequences
Openness	Creativity, with effect on attractiveness	Unusual beliefs; psychosis
Conscientiousness	Attention to long-term fitness benefits; life expectancy and desirable social qualities	Missing of immediate fitness gains; obsessionality; rigidity
Agreeableness	Attention to mental states of others; harmonious interpersonal relationships; valued coalitional partner	Subject to social cheating; failure to maximize selfish advantage

temperament associated with extraversion would be passed on. The data related to what one finds attractive in others according to the five-factor model shows mainly positive correlations between one's own traits and those they find attractive in others. This supports an assortative mating model.

The actual manner in which personality develops appears to be a complicated question. Most theoretical explanations suggest that by the age of 5 or 6, personality characteristics are becoming stable. McCrae and Costa suggest that the five factors develop out of temperament and that this development is not influenced by environmental influences. An alternative model would suggest that personality is like language in that the basic predispositions are present, which carries with it a universal grammar, but that the environment influences which domains of personality become predominantly activated for a given individual. The research on attachment suggests one way in which environmental factors can lead to more enduring traits. In either case, having a variety of styles available would ensure survival in a great variety of situations. An interesting question is whether personality can also be seen in animals, as described in the box: Applying Psychological Science: Personality in Animals.

Applying Psychological Science: Personality in Animals

Is your cat agreeable like your dog, and are some cats or dogs more agreeable than others? Most of us who have had pets would say yes, we see differences within species in terms of behaviors. In the last 20 years, a number of researchers have begun to explore individual differences in animals, which is referred to as *animal personality* (Carere & Maestripieri, 2013; Pennisi, 2016; Stamps & Groothuis, 2010; Wolf & Weissing, 2010). Personality is used with animals in the same way as with humans. That is, behaviors that are consistent over time is the focus of study. Animal personality traits have been documented in many vertebrates including salamanders, fish, lizards, birds, rodents, minks, sheep, nonhuman primates, and other mammals. For example, not unlike humans in performing tasks, some bees when collecting nectar are fast and inaccurate while others are slow and accurate (Burns & Dyer, 2008).

One important question is the manner in which personality in animals is related to mating patterns (Schuett, Tregenza, & Dall, 2010). That is, does the expression of particular personality factors make one animal of a species more attractive in sexual terms to another animal? For example, female zebra finches who are exploratory prefer to mate with male finches who are highly exploratory. Female finches who are not exploratory show no preference. Likewise, male great tits showed preferences for females who showed exploration styles similar to themselves. In one review of the literature, it is suggested that the relationship between personality variables in animals that combine to represent a personality is quite convincing (Schuett, Tregenza, & Dall, 2010).

A number of researchers have sought to describe personality traits of animals including applying the five-factor model to animals (Bouchard & Loehlin, 2001; Gosling, 2001; Pennisi, 2016). One aspect of this is the value that different personality traits may have. For example, stickleback fish can be described in terms of boldness and activity level. Boldness clearly helped the fish to survive in groups as they competed for food. However, the shy fish that were alone also survived, whereas bold fish when alone became the target of predators as they were more obvious. In general, it is suggested that personality factors can play an important role in evolution.

Thought Question: How do personality factors (for example, in the five-factor model) help us understand how well an individual animal adapts to its environment? What are some differences to consider within a species? What are some differences to consider across species?

CONCEPT CHECK

1. How is an existential-humanistic approach to personality different from Freud's psychodynamic approach and from B. F. Skinner's learning approach?
2. What are the fundamental characteristics of a social cognitive theory of personality?
3. How is Julian Rotter's concept of locus of control similar to as well as different from Albert Bandura's concept of self-efficacy?
4. If *traits* are the basic units of personality, how many different traits are there? Describe the process of how psychology moved from Allport and Odbert's 17,953 to Cattell's 170 (later reduced to 16) to McCrae and Costa's 5 dimensions. What was the primary driver of this process?
5. Describe McCrae and Costa's five-factor model (FFM) of personality, including:
   a. Identify the five dimensions, including a description of the range of each dimension.
   b. How it is used to assess an individual's personality.
   c. Examples of predictive value in other areas of individual behavior.
   d. Consistency of results (1) across an individual's lifespan; (2) across generations; and (3) across cultures.
6. Daniel Nettle was interested in whether he could explain the existence of individual personalities from an evolutionary perspective.
   a. What evolutionary advantage did he conclude that personality provides?
   b. How did he explain the existence of both individuals who readily adapt to changing conditions as well as those who remain consistent in the face of change?

Genetic Factors in Personality

With the extensive research on the five-factor model of personality, the contribution of genetics has become important (Knopik, Neiderhiser, DeFries, & Plomin, 2017). Since the FFM has been shown to be stable over time, these traits could help us understand the genetics of personality (Turkheimer, Pettersson, & Horn, 2014). Over the last 40 years a number

Table 13-5 Twin, family, and adoption relationship for extraversion and neuroticism (from Loehlin, 1992)

Type of Relationship	Extraversion	Neuroticism
Identical twins reared together	.51	.46
Identical twins reared apart	.38	.38
Fraternal twins reared together	.18	.20
Fraternal twins reared apart	.05	.23
Non-adaptive parents and offspring	.16	.13
Adaptive parents and offspring	.01	.05

of studies have shown consistent results on the heritability of the major five personality traits (de Moor et al., 2012). Twin, adoption, and family studies have convincingly shown that each of the five personality traits is heritable in the range of 33% to 65%. Initial studies often focused on extraversion and neuroticism.

John Loehlin examined 24,000 pairs of twins from five different countries (Loehlin, 1992). As can be seen in **Table 13-5**, the highest correlations of about .5 are seen for twins reared together. The next highest correlations (.38) are for twins reared apart. These correlations drop to about .20 for fraternal twins reared together. The lowest correlations are for adoptive parents and their offspring, which are almost zero. These results suggest that personality is influenced by genetic factors.

At this point, every review for more than 30 years of the genetics of personality using all five factors of the FFM have concluded that identical twins are more similar for personality traits than are fraternal twins. Likewise, the personalities of adopted children are more similar to the personalities of their biological parents than to those of their adoptive parents (Turkheimer, Pettersson, & Horn, 2014). This also suggests that personality traits are less influenced by the shared family environment in which children are raised. Of course, any one child can be influenced by a number of environmental factors such as losing a parent or frequent changes in home life. Thus, environmental influence tends to be child-specific.

Physiological Factors Related to Personality

The case of Phineas Gage described previously helped professionals realize that brain changes can influence personality. Specifically, the frontal lobes were seen to play an important role in personality factors. In this century, research suggested the importance of genetic factors related to the five-factor model as shown through twin studies. Given the genetic components of the five-factor model, we might also expect that there would be particular cortical networks and brain areas involved.

Using brain-imaging techniques, an initial study examined volume of brain areas associated with each of the five factors (DeYoung et al., 2010). *Extraversion* was associated with the volume of the medial orbitofrontal cortex. This is an area associated with the reward value of events. Given that those who are high in *neuroticism* see the world in an anxious and negative manner and are sensitive to threat, it is not surprising that limbic areas show greater volume. There was also reduced volume in the dorsomedial prefrontal cortex. This area is associated with evaluation of self and emotional regulation. *Agreeableness* is associated with areas of the brain associated with socialness and understanding the actions of others. *Conscientiousness* was associated with volume in the areas involved in planned actions and guiding behavior. Similar results have been found in other studies. There were no consistent regions for *openness*.

Cultural Factors in Personality

Cultural factors in behaviors are easy to see. If you travel in different parts of this country, you quickly hear different ways of speaking English including the words that are used. If you want to order a *soft drink*, in some places you ask for a *coke*, in others a *pop*, or even a *soda pop*. Behaviors that some may see as rude, such as stepping in front of another to get into a store, would be seen as normal by others. If you watch people come to a traffic light, some will wait for the walk/don't walk sign to change while others will cross the street if no cars are coming. In some parts of the country, if you come to a four-way stop in a car, the others there may signal for you to go first, while in other parts of the country, everyone tries to be the first to go. In our popular view of the world, we see the people of some cultures such as the Southern Mediterranean of Europe as more friendly and Northern Europeans as calmer and more stoic. In Middle Eastern countries, men may hold hands with their male friends while in the West they do not. Culture also plays a role in how personality is expressed.

Cultures can be described in terms of being collective or individual oriented. Collective cultures emphasize the manner in which each person is related to the group. There are duties that you are expected to show to your family, people you work with, and your community. China and some South American countries emphasize the collective aspects of their culture. Individual cultures on the other hand place more emphasis on the individual and his or her achievements. The United States, Australia, and part of Western Europe emphasize individualism. Thus, in individualistic cultures *standing out* is important, whereas in collective cultures, *not standing out* is important. This results in different cultures describing significant personality dimensions in very different terms. These dimensions also have important implications for how personality traits are expressed.

One worldwide study of personality examined the five-factor model in 56 nations (Schmitt et al., 2007). This study of 17,837 individuals sought to determine whether any differences exist across cultures. One important result of this study was that individuals across the world give similar answers to the same question when asked on different occasions. This suggests that the five-factor model can be understood worldwide. Further, the five factors are related to one another in similar ways around the world.

In terms of *extraversion*, there was similarity of levels in major regions except East Asia, South Asia, and South America, which had lower levels of extraversion. *Neuroticism* also was found at similar levels except for South America, Southern Europe, and South Asia, which had higher levels. Those in Africa reported lower levels of neuroticism. *Openness* was also similar in all regions except for South America in which it was higher, Africa in which it was slightly lower, and East Asia in which openness was much lower. As shown in **Figure 13-5**, *agreeableness* varied by region. This was also true for *conscientiousness* (**Figure 13-6**).

In another study, Robert McCrae and his colleagues examined the five-factor model in 51 countries with 12,156 individuals (McCrae et al., 2005). These researchers conclude that their results were not related to the economic development of each country. Looking at the five factors by country, there is a similarity of results. However, some regions show differences, as found in other studies. One type of analysis performed shows the relationship between items used in the five-factor model by country. **Figure 13-7** shows how similar the countries are on two factors, extraversion and emotional stability (neuroticism). For

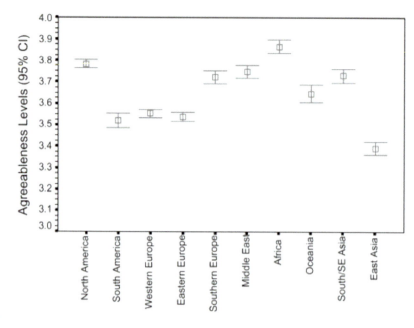

Figure 13-5 Agreeableness by world region.
Source: Schmitt, Allik, Mccrae, and Benet-Martínez (2007).

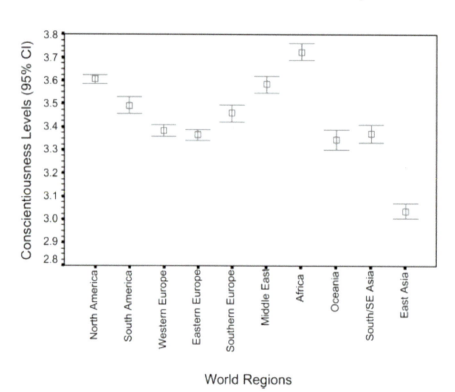

Figure 13-6 Conscientiousness by world region.
Source: Schmitt, Allik, Mccrae, and Benet-Martínez (2007).

example, the African countries cluster on introversion, whereas the European countries and America cluster on extraversion.

Both studies of personality around the world show striking similarities in the responses on the five-factor model. Within these similarities, it is possible to mathematically highlight the differences between countries as was the case with the circular placement of countries.

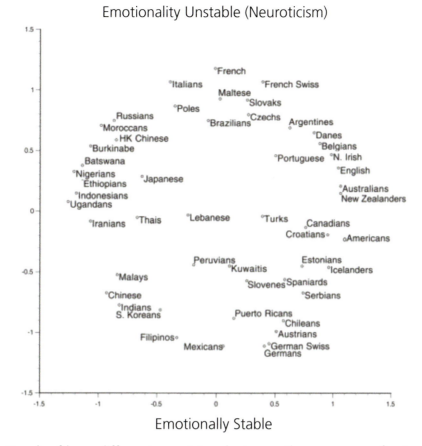

Figure 13-7 Graph of how different countries cluster on the measures of extraversion and neuroticism.
Source: McCrae, Terracciano, and Personality Profiles of Cultures Project (2005).

Overall, this suggests that personality is part of the human condition worldwide. If personality is part of the human condition, then we should see it expressed in other ways than answering questions on a personality test. An alternative approach is described in the box: The World Is Your Laboratory: Knowing Personality by What You See.

The World Is Your Laboratory: Knowing Personality by What You See

Personality as measured by psychologists typically is determined by how you respond to items on a questionnaire. "I like to be with lots of people." "I avoid difficult situations." "People don't take care of each other." These types of questions ask how we experience ourselves. However, what if there was a personality test based on your bathroom or bedroom? Sam Gosling and his colleagues asked this very question (Gosling, Ko, Mannarelli, & Morris, 2002).

These researchers described their research in an article titled "A Room with a Cue: Personality Judgments Based on Offices and Bedrooms." In two separate studies, the researchers first examined the perceptions of participants concerning their own office space and another set of participants in terms of their own bedrooms. Besides participants, a team of observers who did not know the participants made personality ratings based entirely on the occupants' personal environments. The observers could note whether the person had an organized office or bedroom, were there lots of books available, what was the nature of the color of the décor, and so forth. From that, one could also note a personality dimension. For example, if there were lots of memorabilia in the room, you might guess the person to be sentimental. Organization would suggest more conscientiousness. A snowboard in the room might suggest sensation seeking. Since each of the five factors is made up of underlying dimensions, it was also possible to obtain a rating for each of the factors—extraversion, agreeableness, consciousness, emotional stability, and openness to experience. Further, the observer's ratings could also be correlated with the participant's actual score on a measure of the five-factor model.

What did they find? Sam Gosling and his colleagues found that indeed one's environment does reflect one's personality. Although the results were similar, bedrooms revealed more information about the person than did offices. The observers showed the most agreement in terms of openness and conscientiousness. Openness was reflected in terms of the use of space and decoration and the variety of books and CDs. Conscientiousness was reflected in the use of space, being clean, organized, and not cluttered. In bedrooms, agreeableness was associated with the room being cheerful, colorful, clean, organized, neat, comfortable, and inviting. Overall, this research suggests that the five-factor model reflects not only how you see yourself, but also how you organize your world.

Thought Question: Take the opportunity to be a personality researcher: Invite other students to rate your personality by looking at your bedroom using the dimensions listed above. How much do the others agree? Do they agree with your own rating of your personality?

CONCEPT CHECK

1. What can we say about the influence of genetics and environment on personality? What kinds of studies are used to tease out these influences?
2. What have we learned from brain-imaging studies about different areas in the brain being associated with specific personality factors from the five-factor model?
3. A number of research studies have looked at personality across cultures. List three important findings from this research on the similarities and differences in personality traits in different cultures.
4. How has research characterized our ability to judge the personality of others? In what ways does this surprise you?

Self

The self has been an important concept in psychology. Yet, the term has been used in a number of different ways. In his *Principles of Psychology* published in 1890, William James points out a number of these. One of these is to distinguish between "I" and "me." Me is that part of ourselves that we observe and describe. I, on the other hand, is more difficult to comprehend since it is the process that does the observing and describing. When you are asked to describe yourself on a personality measure such as the five-factor model, it is the "me" that you are describing.

At times, we do not like what we see when we look at ourselves. Karen Horney made a distinction between the "real self" and the "ideal self." The real self is who we actually are. It is this real self that Maslow saw as capable of self-actualization. The ideal self is who we believe we should be or want to be. This could include the idea that everyone should love us, that we should not make mistakes, and so forth. Horney suggested that it required considerable psychic energy to keep this ideal world intact and thus would limit growth of the real self. Jung also suggested that acting or believing that one was different from their true self could cause distress.

Self-Concept

Social psychology adopted the "I" and "me" distinction as it developed a theory of *self-concept* (Gecas, 1982; Markus & Kitayama, 2010). Self was seen as a process that develops as we relate to others in social interactions. We see ourselves with our friends, playing sports, walking in the woods, and all the other experiences you had as you grew up. As such, our self-concept includes our body, our emotions, and our thoughts. These "me" aspects typically include our experienced gender, physical appearance, how we relate with others as well as the types of music, movies, and books we like. It is my "me," which is at the center of my experiences.

The self is seen as an adapting process that develops in terms of the social environment in which one lives. As such, the self requires a larger social context that includes values, practices, and social interactions. Social psychologists see the self-involved in all aspects of human behavior (Markus & Kitayama, 2010). It even has a special place in our attentional world. For example, if you are at a party, you tend to ignore others that you are not directly interacting with. However, if your name is mentioned in another conversation across the room, you quickly notice it.

Our self-concept is storied in network memory systems that reflect our past experiences, as shown in **Figure 13-8**. This information is referred to as our *self-schema*. Some of these characteristics can have very strong connections with the idea of self, while others may be less strongly connected. You can ask yourself which characteristics strongly describe you at this moment. New experiences such as going to college can produce changes in our self-concept.

The self has also been studied in different cultures (Markus & Kitayama, 2010). There are different expectations of the self in different cultures. The nail that sticks out is likely to be hammered down in Japan, whereas the squeaky wheel attracts grease and attention in the United States. Likewise, American students are expected to speak out in class in comparison to Korean students who are not. Those who compete for Olympic medals in Japan are more likely to describe their failures than are

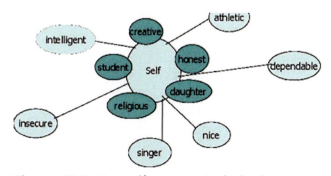

Figure 13-8 Our self-concept includes how we see our self, which involves our memories of our past interactions.

American Olympic medalists. Further, Western Europeans are less likely to associate happiness with personal achievement than are North Americans.

A related term is ***self-esteem,*** which relates to the evaluation of the self. That is, self-esteem refers to the way we value and accept ourselves. Aspects of self-esteem are thus more affective than cognitive. As humans, we want to be told we are good—a good student, a good person, a good romantic partner. A desire for self-esteem has been seen as a motivating factor in humans, as noted by both philosophers and psychologists (Greenberg, 2008).

Self-esteem involves the subjective feelings of self-acceptance and self-respect. However, individuals seeing themselves as superior to others just because they have high self-esteem *is not* part of the concept of self-esteem. Seeing oneself as superior and much better than others is better described as *narcissism*. Narcissism includes having a grandiose view of one's self and one's talents.

Ulrich Orth and his colleagues conducted two long-term studies examining the development of self-esteem (Orth, Robins, & Widaman, 2012; Orth, Maes, & Schmitt, 2015). These studies suggest self-esteem increases beginning at about 16 years of age and peaks in a person's 50s to 60s. It then decreases into old age, although not every study finds a decline (Orth & Robins, 2014). The increase in self-esteem from adolescence to middle age is seen for both males and females. Further, in the lifespan studies, self-esteem is more of a variable trait in that individual scores appear to remain stable in relation to others over time (Trzesniewski, Donnellan, & Robins, 2003).

What are the advantages of having self-esteem? This question has been asked in a number of studies. Overall, self-esteem is predictive of a person's success in a number of critical domains (Orth & Robins, 2014). These experiences include satisfaction in marriage and close relationships as well as job success and job satisfaction. Higher self-esteem is also predictive of physical and mental health.

Not only are there advantages to having higher self-esteem, but there are disadvantages associated with lower self-esteem. In three different studies involving participants from both New Zealand and the United States, low self-esteem was associated with aggression, antisocial behavior, and delinquency (Donnellan, Trzesniewski, Robins, Moffitt, & Caspi, 2005). Further, a meta-analysis of 77 studies of depression and 18 studies of anxiety showed a relationship of low self-esteem with these affective problems (Sowisto & Orth, 2013).

The positive and negative consequences related to self-esteem have created a self-help industry. There are numerous books on how to boost your self-esteem. As such, the concept of self-esteem has developed a life of its own (Orth & Robins, 2014), and the development of self-esteem has been implemented in the classroom, sports competitions, the workplace, and a number of other life situations. However, these endeavors have been largely untested.

Neuroscience of Self

Paying attention to ourselves has raised a number of questions for those interested in neuroscience (Heatherton, 2011; Sui & Gu, 2017). How can we understand what it means for "I" to watch "me," and is this different from watching other processes? Further, how does watching our relations with others lead to changes in behaviors and brain processes? Clearly, we must both regulate ourselves and inhibit certain processes.

From an evolutionary perspective, the brain has evolved distinct mechanisms for knowing ourselves, knowing how others respond to us, detecting threats from within the social group, and regulating actions in order to avoid being excluded from those groups (Krendl

& Heatherton, 2009). Knowing ourselves is a critical process. This relates to our self-concept, which draws on memory systems and prior learning.

One important brain area for self-knowledge is the medial prefrontal cortex (mPFC). Increased activation is seen in the mPFC when individuals think about themselves as opposed to other people (Goldberg et al., 2006; Sui & Gu, 2017). This was also true for remembering what happened to them in the past (Cabeza et al., 2004).

This research also helps us understand cultural perspectives as to whether the self is seen as just belonging to me or whether my definition of self involves others. In one fMRI study, Chinese participants who are more collective in orientation showed mPFC activation when thinking about themselves and significant others in their lives. American participants who are more individualistic only showed mPFC activation when thinking of themselves (Zhu et al., 2007).

Additional research focusing on self-esteem has shown different parts of the frontal areas involved in terms of type of social processes (Yang, Xu, Chen, Shi, & Han, 2016). In particular, feedback concerning social relationships shows fMRI activation in the mPFC, whereas self-reflection involves the orbitofrontal cortex. Further, activity in these areas was positively correlated with self-esteem.

The Characteristics of a Healthy Self

In the next chapter, you will learn about personality disorders. In the process of creating definitions of personality disorders, the American Psychiatry Association sought to define what a healthy personality would look like. That is, what is a *healthy self*? One conceptualization suggested in *DSM-5* (APA, 2013) is to consider the healthy self in terms of a "Self and Interpersonal Functioning Continuum."

The first aspect of this continuum is *identity*. In terms of identity, the healthy person would see herself as a unique person with stable boundaries between herself and others. The self would have a history that the person understands. The person would also have an accurate sense of who she is and what she can do.

Another aspect of the self is *self-direction*. Healthy self-direction reflects the ability to have both meaningful short-term and long-term goals consistent with one's identity. Self-direction also includes a sense of what would be productive for society and how to interact with others. Internally, healthy self-direction also includes the ability to reflect on one's life in a productive manner.

The healthy personality also suggests the ability to have *positive interpersonal relationships*. One aspect of this is *empathy*. This includes understanding how another person experiences his life and what that person might want to accomplish. It also includes the ability to experience and accept different perspectives toward life and goals and how one's own behavior may influence others. In healthy relationships, *intimacy* is also critical. Intimacy includes having a relationship with another person that includes mutual connectedness and a valuing of that other person. The healthy personality values closeness and seeks it when appropriate.

Thus, a person can develop a stable self that has an identity and has the ability for self-direction and the fulfillment of goals. This person can also have positive interpersonal relationships in which she relates to others in an intimate and empathetic manner. This person we would describe as healthy.

Not having a stable self and the ability to have intimate and empathetic relationships with others is a significant part of a personality disorder (Kernberg, 1984). One consideration for a future version of *DSM* is to place personality disorders on a continuum in terms of the person's disturbance of self and others as just described (Bender, Morey, & Skodol, 2011). That is, you could rate the person's level of identity, self-direction, empathy, and intimacy on four scales. This would more clearly reflect those areas in which there are fundamental personality disturbances.

Another way to consider these relationships is from an evolutionary perspective by viewing personality disorders as a failure to solve adaptive life tasks relating to identity or self, intimacy and attachment, and prosocial behavior (see Livesley, 2007; Millon & Strack, 2015, for overviews). From this perspective, it has been the evolutionary task of a human to perform on three levels. The first level is the individual level and the development of a self. The second level is the interpersonal level, which reflects attachment processes. And the third is the group level and involves prosocial behavior, altruism, and the cooperation needed for the functioning of society.

CONCEPT CHECK

1. What can we say about the influence of genetics and environment on personality? What kinds of studies are used to tease out these influences?
2. What have we learned from brain-imaging studies about different areas in the brain being associated with specific personality factors from the five-factor model?
3. A number of research studies have looked at personality across cultures. List three important findings from this research on the similarities and differences in personality traits in different cultures.
4. How has research characterized our ability to judge the personality of others? In what ways does this surprise you?
5. The self has been an important concept in psychology. Yet, the term has been used in a number of different ways. What contributions did the following researchers make to the evolving concept of the *self*:
    a. William James?
    b. Karen Horney?
    c. Markus and Kitayama?
    d. Ulrich Orth and colleagues?
6. Neuroscience is just beginning to study how the brain is involved in focusing on the self. Briefly describe three findings that begin the process of understanding the connections between the brain and the self.
7. Describe the five characteristics of a *healthy self* as defined by the American Psychiatry Association. What led them to develop a definition of a *healthy self*?

Summary

Learning Objective 1: Describe the historical influences on the early study of personality.
The study of *personality* is the study of internal dispositions or ways of being.

The Greeks suggested that all things in the world, including personality and temperament, can be understood in terms of just four elements—earth, air, fire, and water. In the body, they thought that these four elements were connected with the humors—yellow bile (fire), blood (air), phlegm (water), and black bile (earth). About 100 years after Hippocrates, Theophrastus wrote a series of personality sketches he referred to as "characters." Each of the characters described one or more psychological traits. These included the flatterers, the garrulous, the penurious, the tactless, the boors, and the surly.

In the early part of the 20th century, Carl Jung invented the terms *introversion* and *extraversion* to describe a person's approach to the world. Extraversion was seen as a flow of energy outward to the world, whereas introversion was seen as a flow inward toward a person's inner world. Also in the 20th century, Ernst Kretschmer in Germany and later William Sheldon in the United States sought to develop a personality system that combined physical body type with temperament. Sheldon suggested that an individual could be described in terms of three types. The *endomorph* body type is soft and round with a relaxed and sociable temperament. The *mesomorph* body type is muscular, strong, and low fat with an energetic and assertive temperament. The *ectomorph* body type is long and thin with more of a cerebral and introverted temperament. Later in the 20th century, Hans Eysenck translated the idea of Greek humors into modern psychological language in terms of two dimensions.

Learning Objective 2: Summarize the main ideas of the psychodynamic perspective on the development of personality.

Freud divides the mind into three parts: *id*, *ego*, and *superego*. The *id* is present at birth. It represents those instinctual processes that help us to obtain our basic needs. Beginning at about 3 years of age, the child learns to mediate his or her desires. This reflects the development of an *ego*. The ego is seen to be part of personality, which helps us navigate the demands between external requirements and our internal experiences. At a later point, an individual develops a moral sense, which directs our behaviors with one another. The structure is referred to as the *superego* and reflects perspectives we learn from our parents and our culture as well as our own moral development.

Freud also suggested there are stages of development that are often referred to as *psychosexual development*. At each of these stages there is a physical focus and a psychological theme. The first stage is referred to as the *oral* stage. The second stage is referred to as the *anal* stage of development. The third stage is referred to as the *phallic* stage, which lasts from 3 and a half to 7 years of age. This is followed by the *latency* phase, which lasts from 7 years of age to puberty. The final stage is the *genital* phase and represents an understanding of one's sexuality and the development of mature relationships.

During Freud's time, there were a number of professionals who took a *psychodynamic approach* and adopted or modified Freud's ideas in their theories and the treatment of their patients. Alfred Adler emphasized social processes, especially in childhood, as important for personality development. Anna Freud placed more emphasis on the ability of the ego to live life and adapt to the demands of life. John Bowlby believed that early relationships with significant people in one's life constituted a powerful role in relation to many personality factors. Two others who expanded the psychodynamic perspective were Carl Jung, who emphasized the evolutionary aspects of development, and Karen Horney, who emphasized social aspects of personality development.

Projective testing techniques were formally introduced in the first half of the 1900s as a means of detecting primary process types of thinking and feeling including instinctual and motivational processes. Two of the most well-known projective techniques are the *Rorschach Inkblot* and the *Thematic Apperception Test (TAT)*.

Learning Objective 3: Summarize the main ideas of the existential-humanistic approach to personality.

The major focus of *existentialism* was the nature of human nature and the meaning of life. One important aspect of the *humanistic* tradition was an emphasis on choice. Throughout our lives, we all make critical choices that determine who we are and how we live our lives. In this way, we express our personality by the choices we make. For the humanistic psychologists, these choices can lead to positive as well as negative outcomes. One critical aspect of these choices according to the *existential-humanistic approach* is our ability to be true to one's self.

Learning Objective 4: Summarize the main ideas of the social cognitive theories of personality.

Social cognitive theories of personality are also referred to as *social learning theories*. These theories emphasize a person's view of the world, that is, the person's cognitive understanding of their environment. The social aspect is that many of these beliefs are the result of our interactions with others. In this sense, they are learned through our interactions. The research related to the social cognitive theory of personality typically focuses on how a person's cognitive views of the world interact with situational variables to produce different behaviors.

Learning Objective 5: Summarize the main ideas of the current perspectives on personality.

Current perspectives on personality have tended to focus on the stability of personality traits. This is not to suggest that we do not act differently in very different situations. What personality does focus on is our long-term ways of relating to the world. As individuals move into adulthood and become employed, for example, there are changes in approaches to one's environment. However, like intelligence, we can note differences between individuals as these changes take place.

Gordon Allport identified *traits* as the basic units of personality. He saw traits as "generalized and personalized determining tendencies—consistent and stable modes of an individual's adjustment to his environment." McCrae and Costa used a factor analytic approach to personality, which suggested five major personality dimensions. This is referred to as the *five-factor model (FFM), often called the Big 5*. These five dimensions include *extraversion, neuroticism, openness, agreeableness,* and *conscientiousness*.

Over the last 40 years, a number of studies have shown consistent results on the heritability of the major five personality traits. Twin, adoption, and family studies have convincingly shown that each of the five personality traits is heritable in the range of 33% to 65%.

Using brain-imaging techniques, an initial study examined volume of brain areas associated with each of the five factors (DeYoung et al., 2010). *Extraversion* was associated with the volume of the medial orbitofrontal cortex. This is an area associated with the reward value of events. Given that those who are high in *neuroticism* see the world in an anxious and negative manner and are sensitive to threat, it is not surprising that limbic areas show greater volume. There was also reduced volume in the dorsomedial prefrontal cortex. This area is associated with evaluation of self and emotional regulation. *Agreeableness* is associated with areas of the brain associated with socialness and understanding the actions of others. *Conscientiousness* was associated with volume in the areas involved in planned actions and guiding behavior.

Culture plays a role in how personality is expressed. Cultural factors in behaviors are easy to see. If you travel in different parts of this country, you quickly hear different ways of speaking English, including the words that are used. Behaviors that some may see as rude, such as stepping in front of another to get into a store, would be seen as normal by others. In our popular view of the world, we see the people of some cultures such as the Southern Mediterranean of Europe as more friendly and Northern Europeans as calm and stoic. Cultures can be described in terms of being collective or individual oriented. Collective cultures emphasize the manner in which each person is related to the group. There are duties that you are expected to show to your family, people you work with, and your community. China and some South American countries emphasize the collective aspects of their culture. Individual cultures, on the other hand, place more emphasis on the individual and his or her achievements. The United States, Australia, and part of Western Europe emphasize individualism.

A recent development in the consideration of personality from an evolutionary perspective is the idea that humans have evolved an ability to judge the personality of others. Part of this idea is based on the variety of social psychological research studies that have shown that humans are able to make quick judgments concerning the attributes of other humans. Not only are humans able to make quick judgments but these judgments reflect an accuracy of processing that one would not expect given the limited experience with the person and the complex possibilities available.

Learning Objective 6: Define the concept of self.

The self is seen as an adapting process that develops in terms of the social environment in which one lives. As such, the self requires a larger social context, which includes values, practices, and social interactions. Social psychologists see the self as involved in all aspects of human behavior. Self-esteem relates to the evaluation of the self and refers to the way we value and accept ourselves.

Paying attention to ourselves has raised a number of questions for those interested in neuroscience. From an evolutionary perspective, the brain has evolved distinct mechanisms for knowing ourselves, knowing how others respond to us, detecting threats from within the social group, and regulating actions in order to avoid being excluded from those groups. Knowing ourselves is a critical process. This relates to our self-concept, which draws on memory systems and prior learning.

The healthy person would see herself with *identity*, *self-direction*, and *positive interpersonal relationships*.

Study Resources

Review Questions

1. The definition of personality has been conceptualized differently across human history. This chapter has discussed a number of different historical conceptions of personality. Describe the historical timeline of the study of personality.
2. Three different perspectives or approaches in understanding personality were presented in this chapter: (1) psychodynamic, (2) existential-humanistic, and (3) social cognitive. Answer the following questions from each of the three perspectives:
   a. What are some core research questions researchers from this perspective would want to answer?

b. What are some research methods researchers from this perspective would choose to study those questions?
c. What population would researchers from this perspective focus on in their studies?
d. How would researchers from this perspective characterize a healthy personality? An unhealthy personality?
e. How would researchers from this perspective approach treatment for personality problems?
3. Traits are said to be the basic units of personality. Dimensions are also proposed as an approach to define personality.
   a. What are some differences between the two approaches?
   b. What are some similarities between the two approaches?
   c. What are the advantages and disadvantages of each approach?
   d. Is there a way to integrate them into a single perspective? If so, how would you do that?
4. Describe our current understanding of the concept of personality from the perspective of the following seven levels: cultural, social, individual, cognitive/emotional, physiological, brain, and genetic?
5. What is *personality*? How has your concept of the term changed from your study of this chapter?
6. The self has been an important concept in psychology. Yet, the term has been used in a number of different ways. How do the following terms—or sets of terms—expand our understanding of the self:
   a. *I* and *me*
   b. *Real self* and *ideal self*
   c. *Self-concept*
   d. *Self-schema*
   e. *Self-esteem*
7. What is *self*? How has your concept of the term changed from your study of this chapter?

For Further Reading

Dumont, F. (2010). *A History of Personality Psychology.* New York: Cambridge University Press.
Sulloway, F. (1983). *Freud Biologist of the Mind.* New York: Basic Books.

Web Resources

Flow—https://www.ted.com/talks/mihaly_csikszentmihalyi_on_flow

Key Terms and Concepts

agreeableness
animal personality
assortative mating
conscientiousness
defense mechanisms
existential-humanistic approach
existentialism
extraversion
five-factor model (FFM) or the Big 5
healthy self
humanistic
neuroticism
openness
personality
projective technique
psychodynamic approach
real self
Rorschach inkblots
self-concept
self-esteem
self-realization
self-schema
social cognitive theories of personality
Thematic Apperception Test (TAT)
traits

14 Psychological Disorders

LEARNING OBJECTIVES

14.1 Explain how psychological disorders are classified and diagnosed.

14.2 Describe the various types of anxiety, obsessive-compulsive, and mood disorders.

14.3 Discuss the dissociative disorders of depersonalization, dissociative amnesia, and dissociative identity disorder.

14.4 Describe the main features and causes of schizophrenia.

14.5 Discuss the basic characteristics of personality disorders.

14.6 Discuss the neurodevelopmental disorders that begin early in a child's life.

The book A Beautiful Mind *describes the life and experiences of John Nash (Nasar, 1998). The book tells a powerful story and was made into a major Hollywood film that won the Academy Award for Best Picture of 2001. John Nash was a remarkable figure, who received a PhD in mathematics from Princeton University and taught at both the Massachusetts Institute of Technology (MIT) and Princeton. In 1994, Nash won the Nobel Prize in economics for his work on game theory.*

From what you just read, you probably assume that John Nash had a very productive career. However, there was another aspect to John Nash's life that caused considerable distress to him and puzzlement to others. One day he walked into a room full of others in his university department and held up a copy of The New York Times. *He said to no one in particular that the story in the upper-left corner contained an encrypted message that had been put there by inhabitants of another galaxy and that he knew how to decode it (Nasar, 1998, p. 16). He was 30 years old at the time.*

In the film, John Nash is contacted by the United States Department of Defense to help decipher codes sent by enemy nations. The defense department asks him to search patterns of Soviet plots placed in American magazines and newspapers. You see a large number of magazines and papers with notations. As you watch the film, everything seems reasonable, for indeed during the Cold War era after World War II many in the American government felt that there was a Soviet plot to overthrow the United States government. It is only later that you realize that the story is being told from John Nash's perspective. What you discover is that you are seeing the world as John Nash saw it and it is not reality. John Nash created a world that did not exist.

After Nash won the Nobel Prize in 1994, there were times when he was productive, but there were also times where he had disordered thoughts, mumbled to himself without thought of those around him, and experienced delusions of situations that did not exist. He felt there were individuals around him who put him in danger. He even wrote letters to officials in the United States government to suggest that these individuals were setting up alternative governments. John Nash suffered from a serious mental illness called schizophrenia.

Psychological Disorders

As you have moved through the chapters in this book, one theme has been apparent and that is the manner in which we are in close connection with our environment including friends and others. An important part of our relationship with our environment is our ability to reflect on ourselves and our world. In this way, a layer of thought can be injected between the person and the environment. This allows for expectation and even imagination to play a role in human behavior and experience.

We can imagine our lives with very different outcomes. For example, you can tell yourself you are wonderful or you are stupid. Whatever you say internally, there is no one there to dispute it. One positive aspect of this is that your inner world allows you to plan future actions and reflect on past ones. A negative aspect of this is that it can also be experienced as distress when your internal thoughts reflect such states as anxiety or hopelessness. This chapter begins with a discussion of psychological disorders and then looks at several major forms of mental disorder: anxiety, obsessive-compulsive disorder, mood disorders, dissociative disorders, schizophrenia, and neurodevelopmental disorders.

It should be noted that psychological disorders are referred to by a number of different terms depending on the historical tradition. These include the terms *abnormal psychology*, *mental disorders, mental illness*, and *psychopathology*. Psychopathology is the most common term used in neuroscience research. In legal considerations, the term *insanity* is often used. Of course, there is slang in which people are referred to as crazy or nuts. Additionally, some individuals self-diagnose or make an emotional statement such as, "I am so schizo" or "I am so OCD." As you will see, there are technical definitions of mental disorders presented in this chapter that have specified criteria. Before presenting these, let's consider some of the general characteristics of psychopathology.

What is psychopathology? Although there is no one single definition of what represents abnormal processes in general, four ideas have been critical, as shown in **Table 14-1**. One important characteristic of psychological disorders is the lack of control over one's experience. This can also be described as a loss of freedom or an inability to consider alternative ways of thinking, feeling, or doing. Some individuals show this loss mainly in terms of emotional processes. Others show the loss in terms of cognitive processes, such as the experiences of John Nash.

Another common theme seen in psychopathology is the loss of honest personal contact. Individuals with depression or schizophrenia often find it difficult to experience social interactions as experienced by other people. Just having a simple conversation or talking to clerks in stores may seem impossible. Mental illness not only affects individuals' interpersonal relationships with others but also their relationship with themselves, their *intrapersonal* relationship. When individuals with schizophrenia or depression talk to themselves, they often think negative thoughts about who they are and what will happen to them in the future.

Additionally, in most cases, the experience of a mental disorder results in personal distress. Not being able to get out of bed, or feeling that a voice in your head is telling you that you are evil, or worrying that even a rice cake or an apple will make you fat all represent different degrees of distress. Distress represents one important aspect of psychological disorders also referred to as psychopathology. In fact, for most disorders, distress is the key ingredient.

Thus, we can consider four important personal components in **psychopathology**: first, a loss of freedom or ability to consider alternatives; second, a loss of honest personal contact; third, a loss of one's connection with one's self and ability to live in a productive manner;

Table 14-1 Key personal components of psychopathology.

Four Key Personal Components of Psychopathology
1. Loss of freedom and ability to consider alternatives
2. Loss of honest personal contact
3. Loss of one's connections with one's self and ability to live in a productive manner
4. Personal distress

and fourth, personal distress. In many psychological disorders, personal distress for a period of time is one of the criteria required for a diagnosis to be made. There is also a more global component in which the person's behavior and experiences are considered to be different from cultural and statistical norms.

The National Institute of Mental Health (NIMH) estimates that at least 20.6% of adults in America experience a diagnosable mental disorder during a given year (see **Figure 14-1**). This would be more than 51.5 million people over the age of 18 who experienced a mental disorder in 2019 (https://www.nimh.nih.gov/health/statistics/mental-illness.shtml).

With mental illness being so common, you might think that we as humans would have a complete understanding of the factors involved. However, this is not the case. We are not even sure how to refer to individuals with mental disorders. Are they abnormal? Depending on the reference group one uses, one can be normal or abnormal. Many famous artists such as the Impressionists in France had their work initially rejected because it did not fit into the standards of what was considered good art at the time. However, today we appreciate that these artists showed us another way of viewing the world. Likewise, many movies and edgy YouTube videos today would be rejected as not representing mainstream values at a previous time. Further, what would be acceptable in one culture might be seen

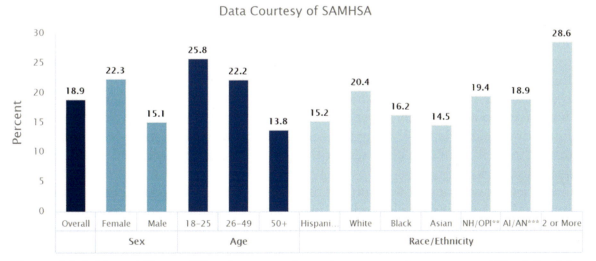

Figure 14-1 Mental illness differs in terms of gender, age, and race among US adults. More females than males experience mental illness. Those aged 50 and older experience less mental illness. Native Americans show the most mental illness often in relation to disorders of substance abuse.

as completely "crazy" in another. However, many individuals with mental illness experience stigma.

Stigma and Mental Disorders

Experiencing a mental illness does not mean that one has to live a limited life. Individuals like John Nash not only have had a productive career but have enjoyed successful personal relationships. However, many children, adolescents, and young adults with a mental illness report being told they could never perform in a high-level profession or have the types of relationships that others have.

There is often a *stigma* experienced by those with a mental disorder. Historically, stigma has been defined as a mark of disgrace associated with a particular person. In psychological terms, stigma involves negative attitudes and beliefs that cause the general public to avoid others including those with a mental illness. Throughout the world, those with mental illness experience stigma. In many cultures, they are seen as different. When they are thus stigmatized, they are no longer treated as an individual person, but only as part of a group that is different. It becomes an "us versus them" way of thinking.

Part of the stigma comes from inaccurate information concerning those with mental illness. For example, many people think that anyone with a mental illness is violent. In 2012, there was a killing of 20 children and 6 teachers at the Sandy Hook Elementary School in Newtown, Connecticut. Immediately, it was suggested that the killer had a mental illness. Officials of the National Rifle Association immediately claimed that this could not have been done by a sane person. The same was true with the Parkland Florida shooting in 2018 in which 17 people were killed. People have talked about "red flag" laws and placing more individuals in institutions. However, the data do not support a strong relationship between mental disorders and violence.

The MacArthur Foundation followed hospitalized individuals with mental illness after their release from the hospital and found that only 2% to 3% of these individuals were involved with violence with a gun. As a general rule, individuals with mental illness do not show more violence than that seen in the general population. There are, however, particular disorders such as psychopathy associated with serial killers in which individuals are violent. Also, substance abuse can increase violence in some individuals. With these exceptions, having a mental illness does not increase violence toward others.

Stigma can be seen on a number of levels. If a society believes that mental illness is the fault of the person—and that the person can change himself or herself by willpower—then it is less likely to spend the money necessary to set up clinics and train professionals. Society may also be less likely to set up school-based programs to help adolescents with bullying or suicide. As well, companies may not be willing to include mental health treatment in their insurance coverage, or they may place limits on benefits for treatment of these disorders.

As a society, Americans show a number of different values when considering individuals with mental illness. On the one hand, we may want to help those who experience distress. Many communities, for example, have developed programs for the homeless, especially those with mental disorders. On the other hand, we may feel it is their own responsibility to take care of themselves.

In the United States, attitudes are moving toward less stigma. In 1996, for example, 54% of the US population viewed depression as related to neurobiological causes. During the next 10 years, this increased to 67%. With a better understanding of mental disorders, it is possible to have a more compassionate as well as intellectual understanding of those with mental disorders.

Understanding Psychopathology

The modern study of psychopathology is generally dated to the late 1700s. As with the move toward experimentation and empiricism in physics and chemistry, the study of psychopathology initially began with careful description. There was also a shift away from external mechanisms such as possession by spirits toward an explanation in terms of natural processes. With this shift came a differentiation between patients in mental hospitals who experienced mental disorders from those who were just misfits in their society. Marquis de Sade, who wrote novels of a sexual nature, was released by the director of a mental hospital in Paris during this period with the statement, "… is not mad. His only madness is vice" (Pires, 2008, p. 430).

The difference between vice and madness is one of many dichotomies that has plagued the study of psychopathology over the centuries and continues to this day as larger intellectual and societal questions. For example, should we consider drug addiction as a pleasure-seeking mechanism that is being overused and under someone's control? If so, we would not consider it a disorder, but only the result of lack of will on the part of an individual. It was only at the end of the 20th century that addictions such as alcoholism were officially viewed by the US Federal Government as a physiological disorder rather than a problem of will. This allowed it to be treated in Veterans Administration Hospitals. As you have learned throughout this book, it is important to move beyond simple dichotomies such as "is it mind or body that produces the disorder." It is also important to realize that psychological disorders can be understood on a variety of levels ranging from cultural influences to genetic ones.

One of the major contributions of the 20th century toward understanding psychopathology was the creation of a reliable diagnosis and classification system. This system in the United States, referred to as the *Diagnostic and Statistical Manual of Mental Disorders* (*DSM*), made it easier for different mental health workers to label a disorder in the same way. For example, generalized anxiety disorder (GAD) was described in terms of "Excessive anxiety and worry (apprehensive expectation), occurring more days than not for at least 6 months, about a number of events or activities (such as work or school performance)." In this way, the particular symptoms of the disorder were specified as well as the requirement that these symptoms had existed for at least 6 months. The next requirement was that "The person finds it difficult to control the worry."

The experience of anxiety and worry was further differentiated in terms of specific symptoms. These include:

1. restlessness or feeling keyed up or on edge
2. being easily fatigued
3. difficulty concentrating or mind going blank
4. irritability
5. muscle tension
6. sleep disturbance (difficulty falling or staying asleep, or restless unsatisfying sleep)

To be diagnosed with GAD, the person would have to experience at least three of the six symptoms. Further, the anxiety must be experienced as distressing by the person and cannot be the result of another disorder or drug use. By the end of the 20th century, mental health facilities in the United States used the *DSM* system to diagnose and classify mental disorders.

At the end of the 20th century and the beginning of the 21st century, neuroscience techniques such as brain imaging and genetic analysis had been developed and were available in the research and clinical community. For many in the field, this suggests that there will be another level of analysis from which to understand psychopathology. These techniques will not only allow one to note the particular symptoms present as seen with *DSM*, but it will also be possible to ask how the brain is involved in the disorder.

Currently, the United States National Institute of Mental Health (NIMH) is asking whether multiple levels (from genomics and neural circuits to behavior and self-reports) can also be used to help in the diagnosis of psychopathology (Clark, Cuthbert, Lewis-Fernández, Narrow, & Reed, 2017; Cuthbert & Insel, 2013; Hyman, 2010; Miller & Rockstroh, 2017). This approach is referred to as Research Domain Criteria (RDoC) (https://www.nimh.nih.gov/research/research-funded-by-nimh/rdoc/index.shtml).

Other researchers have sought to determine the genetic components involved in particular disorders. We have discovered in children that attention deficit hyperactivity disorder (ADHD) is heritable, but that aggressive and disruptive conduct is not. The critical question is the manner in which genes and behavior are related. A variety of genetic studies suggest that genetic factors account for about 82% of the variance in schizophrenia, suggesting that environmental factors are less critical in the development of schizophrenia (Rutter, 2006). Further, adopted children from families with schizophrenia show a similar rate to those raised with their natural families, also suggesting rearing factors per se are not related to its development.

In terms of depression, genetic studies suggest that depression is equally influenced by genetic and environmental factors (Rutter, 2006). In one set of studies, monkeys with a genetic risk for depression were raised by either a highly responsive or less-responsive foster mother (Suomi, 1999). In this situation, it was the mothers that determined the outcome, with more-responsive foster mothers having less-depressed infants.

Creating a System to Understand Mental Disorders

As science progressed in the 1800s, there was an attempt to bring a classification system to psychological disorders. For example, Emil Kraepelin (1856–1926) who was a student of Wilhelm Wundt's began to study symptoms of mental illness. It was his ability to observe and describe the symptoms his patients presented that helped to establish Kraepelin's success. In particular, he was able to describe a set of symptoms that go together. Today, we refer to a collection of symptoms that occur together and have a particular course of development over time as a **syndrome**. By describing disorders in terms of patterns of symptoms, Kraepelin set the stage for diagnostic systems in both the United States and Europe.

As noted, the current diagnostic system used in the United States and some other countries is the *Diagnostic and Statistical Manual of Mental Disorders*. This is commonly referred to as *DSM* followed by a number to denote which edition it is. The initial *DSM* was released in 1952. *DSM-5* was released in 2013. In Europe, psychological disorders are included with medical disorders in *International Classification of Diseases*, which is referred to as *ICD*. *ICD 11* was released in 2018 and takes effect in 2022. Although similar, there are some differences between *DSM* and *ICD*.

One advantage of the *DSM* system is that it helps to improve the reliability of diagnosis. That is, since mental health workers from different locations use the same criteria for making a diagnosis, the agreement between professionals is higher. Another advantage is that *DSM* helps interviewers know which questions to ask and ensures that relevant information is not left out. Thus, there is emphasis on reliability of diagnosis such that mental health professionals in one location would diagnose the same individual in the same manner as professionals in another location. As part of this emphasis, there has been a push for observable characteristics that would define a specific disorder. Such characteristics as depressed mood over the day, diminished interest in activities, weight loss, insomnia, fatigue, feelings of worthlessness, difficulty thinking, and thoughts of suicide would be considered in the diagnosis of depression.

The *DSM* approach also helps to make a decision concerning which disorder is present. What if an individual appears with rapid speech, saying grandiose things, and talking about that they need to protect themselves? You might ask yourself if this person was experiencing a psychosis, or a manic episode? However, if you were to discover this person was using a drug that makes them high such as an amphetamine, then you would know it was drug-related. Neither schizophrenia nor bipolar disorder would be the appropriate diagnosis.

In the development of *DSM-5*, a variety of questions were asked. One of these is how do we define a mental disorder? One answer that was given was that a **mental disorder** contains five features (Stein et al., 2010). These are:

A. A behavioral or psychological syndrome or pattern that occurs in an individual
B. That reflects an underlying psychobiological dysfunction
C. The consequences of which are clinically significant distress (for example, a painful symptom) or disability (that is, impairment in one or more important areas of functioning)
D. Must not be merely an expectable response to common stressors and losses (for example, the loss of a loved one) or a culturally sanctioned response to a particular event (for example, trance states in religious rituals)
E. That is not primarily a result of social deviance or conflicts with society

As you read these, you may note that from the *DSM-5* standpoint, a mental disorder is more than a difference in cultural traditions or experience. It is also more than our common human experiences in terms of grief over a loved one or day-to-day anxiety or loneliness. A mental disorder is a pattern of symptoms that are distressing and keep the individual from engaging in his or her full functioning in life. A mental disorder also reflects underlying differences in physiological and psychological functioning. This is another way of saying that the brain is involved in all mental disorders. Finally, each disorder described in *DSM* is defined as a discrete disorder. **Table 14-2** shows the major disorder categories in *DSM*. Currently, *DSM* plays an important role in our society since it are used in psychological, medical, and legal settings. As you see, legal definitions of psychological disorders are different than that found in *DSM*. This is described in the box: The World Is Your Laboratory: Legal Understanding of Mental Illness.

Comorbidity

Although each disorder described in *DSM-5* is presented as a discrete disorder, it is possible for an individual to show characteristics of more than one disorder. Technically, when an individual is seen to have more than one disorder at the same time, the disorders are referred to as **comorbid**. In the National Comorbidity Survey, a large number of individuals with one disorder were found to have one or more additional diagnoses (Kessler et al., 2005).

Table 14-2 Major *DSM-5* disorder categories.

Neurodevelopmental Disorder
Conditions that begin in childhood such as autism spectrum disorder or attention-deficit/hyperactivity disorder (ADHD).

Schizophrenia Spectrum
Conditions in which individuals show hallucinations, delusions, disordered thought, and flat affect.

Bipolar and Related Disorders
Conditions in which individuals show changes in mood, such as alternations between mania and depression or periods of mania.

Depressive Disorders
Conditions such as depression in which the person feels sad, empty, and without energy to accomplish tasks.

Anxiety Disorders
Conditions in which anxiety, worry, or fear are present such as generalized anxiety disorder or phobias.

Obsessive-compulsive and Related Disorders
Conditions in which a person has recurrent thoughts and the desire to engage in certain behaviors.

Trauma and Stressor Related Disorders
Conditions that involve exposure to traumatic events such as posttraumatic stress disorder (PTSD).

Dissociative Disorders
Conditions that show changes in experiences related to one's self, such as not experiencing one's self as real or dissociative identity disorder (previously called multiple personality disorder).

Somatic Symptom and Related Disorders
Conditions that focus on one's bodily experiences such as excessive concern about bodily sensations or imagining that one or another person has a medical condition they do not have.

Feeding and Eating Disorders
Conditions involving eating too much or too little to maintain optimal health along with psychological concerns about weight such as anorexia nervosa and bulimia nervosa.

Elimination Disorders
Conditions such as bed-wetting that involve urinary and fecal processes.

Sleep-Wake Disorders
Conditions that involve problems with normal sleep–wake cycles such as insomnia or narcolepsy.

Sexual Dysfunctions
Conditions that involve problems with arousal or ability to perform sexually.

Gender Dysphoria
Conditions in which there is a difference in one's experienced gender and the one assigned at birth.

Table 14-2 (Continued).

Disruptive, Impulse-Control, and Conduct Disorder
Conditions involving children and adolescents that breaks norms of society such as conduct disorder or stealing.

Substance Related and Addictive Disorders
Conditions that involve addiction to various drugs such alcohol or drug addiction.

Neurocognitive Disorders
Conditions involving a decline in cognitive and other abilities such as Alzheimer's disease.

Personality Disorders
Conditions involving problems in one's relationship with others, such as borderline personality disorder or antisocial disorder.

Paraphilic Disorders
Conditions related to sexuality such as voyeurism or fetishism.

For example, individuals with generalized anxiety disorder will often also show symptoms of depression. Further, these two disorders have overlapping genetic and environmental risk factors (Kendler et al.,, 2012). The number of diagnoses found in the National Comorbidity Survey was associated with the severity of the symptoms. This has suggested to researchers that there exists a general underlying vulnerability to psychopathology that may be independent of the particular symptoms expressed (Pittenger & Etkin, 2008; Lahey, Krueger, Rathouz, Waldman, & Zald, 2017; Marshall, 2020; Smith et al., 2020).

The World Is Your Laboratory: Legal Understanding of Mental Illness

It is important to understand that mental health professionals and the legal system see psychopathology from very different perspectives. In fact, the legal system often uses the word *insanity* rather than the term *psychopathology*. Think for a second—what are courts and juries required to do? They determine if a person is innocent or guilty. In doing this they determine if a person is responsible for an action. Often, they further ask if a person performed an action of his or her own free will. The basic idea in the legal system is that it would be unfair to hold someone responsible and punish them for an action that was beyond their control. For example, courts would treat a situation in which someone who was driving had a heart attack and hit another car differently than if a person purposely hit another car. The same is true if mental disorders are involved. This has come to be known as the *insanity defense*.

The American system of justice in relation to insanity was initially influenced by an event that happened in England some 150 years ago. An individual named Daniel M'Naghten (pronounced McNaughton) believed that he was being persecuted by one of the political parties of England, the Tory party. In response to this belief, M'Naghten planned to kill the British Prime Minister, Sir Robert Peel. However, he ended up attacking and killing the prime minister's secretary rather than the prime minister himself. When M'Naghten was tried for the crime, medical experts said he was psychotic. Today, he would be described as someone with paranoid schizophrenia. The court found M'Naghten not guilty by reason of insanity. There was some concern about the verdict on the part of the public, which resulted in a more formal definition of mental insanity. Mental insanity could be used as a defense only if

> at the time of the committing of the act, the party accused was labouring under such a defect of reason, from a disease of the mind, as not to know the nature and quality of the act he was doing; or, if he did know it, that he did not know he was doing what was wrong.
> (*Queen v. M'Naghten*, 8 Eng. Rep. 718 [1843])

This came to be known as the *M'Naghten rule*.

In the United States a number of variations based on capacity and knowledge have been applied in determining sanity. In the 1880s, the State of Alabama found an individual not guilty by reason of insanity because mental illness made the person unable to control himself even though he knew the difference between right and wrong. This came to be known as the *volitional test*. In the 1950s, a decision based on an 1871 New Hampshire ruling became known as the *Durham rule*. The basic idea is that an individual is not "criminally responsible if his unlawful act is the product of a mental disease or defect."

The insanity defense was changed drastically by an event on March 30, 1981. On that day in Washington, DC, John Hinckley tried to kill the President of the United States, Ronald Reagan. John Hinckley wanted to have a relationship with an actress named Jodie Foster. Hinckley believed that if he acted like one of the characters in one of her movies, she would notice him and be impressed. He wrote a letter to her a few hours before he shot the president saying, "I would abandon this idea of getting Reagan in a second if I could only win your heart and live out the rest of my life with you…" He further said "I am doing all of this for your sake! By sacrificing my freedom and possibly my life, I hope to change your mind about me…" At his trial, John Hinckley was found not guilty by reason of insanity. This upset the American public and resulted in four changes to the law.

1. *Twelve states changed the insanity plea to guilty but mentally ill.*
2. *Some states abolished the insanity defense.*
3. *Expert witness testimony was limited in terms of ability to express an opinion.*
4. *Burden of proof was increased to require clear and convincing evidence.*

Additional legal information concerning this case can be found at *http://law2.umkc.edu/faculty/projects/ftrials/hinckley/hinckleytrial.html*

At present there is no one rule that determines legal sanity in all 50 states. The insanity defense is largely misunderstood by the lay public. It is often said that someone got off by pleading insanity. Actually, the loss of freedom is generally greater in these cases since the person is usually placed in a facility for the criminally insane for an indefinite period of time. Being convicted for a crime on the other hand carries with it a sentence for a specified period of time. The actual number of insanity pleas is much smaller than public perception and few of these individuals are set free without going to a mental hospital or other facility.

> **Thought Question:** How has the concept of "not guilty by reason of insanity" changed in the US over the last 150 years? What is the rule that determines legal sanity in your state? Should there be one rule that determines legal sanity in all 50 US states as well as at the Federal level?

Universal Psychopathology

If psychopathology is part of our human makeup, then we expect to see similar manifestations of it worldwide. One classic study in this regard was performed by Jane Murphy of Harvard University (Murphy, 1976). It dates from the 1970s when mental illness was seen to be related to learning and the social construction of norms. In fact, some suggested that mental illness was just a myth developed by Western societies.

This perspective suggests that neither the individual nor his acts are abnormal in an objective sense. It depends on the situation. What would be seen as mental illness in a Western industrial culture might be very different than what was seen in a less-developed rural culture. That is to say, mental illness in this perspective was viewed as a social construction of the society. The alternative to this perspective is more similar to that we saw with human processes, such as emotionality, in which humans throughout the world show similar expression of the basic emotions.

If mental illness is part of our human history, as evolutionary psychologists would suggest, then we would expect to find similar manifestations across a variety of cultures. Dr. Murphy first studied two geographically separate and distinct non-Western groups, the Inuits of northwest Alaska and the Yorubas of rural tropical Nigeria. Although many researchers of that time would have expected to find that the conceptions of normality and abnormality were very different in the two cultures, this is not what she found.

What she found was that these cultures were well acquainted with processes in which a person was said to be "out of their mind." This included doing strange things as well as hearing voices. Dr. Murphy concluded that processes of disturbed thought and behavior similar to schizophrenia is found in most cultures and that most cultures have a distinct name in their language for these processes. Additionally, she reported that these cultures had a variety of words for what traditionally is referred to as neurosis, although today we would refer to these as affective disorders such as anxiety and depression. Affective disorders include feeling anxious, tense, fearful of being with others, as well as being troubled and not able to sleep. One Eskimo term was translated as worrying too much until it makes the person sick.

Overall, it appears that most cultures have a word for what has been called psychosis such as schizophrenia, what has been called affective disorders such as anxiety and depression, and what has been called being sane. What is also interesting is that many cultures also have words for describing people who are out of their mind but not crazy. These would include witch doctors, shamans, and artists. Volition appears to be an important distinction for this concept.

To add evidence to her argument that psychopathology is indeed part of our human nature, Murphy also reviewed a large variety of studies conducted by others that looked at how common mental illness was in different cultures. The suggestion here is that if its prevalence is similar in cultures across the world then it is more likely to be part of the human condition rather than culturally derived. Overall, this research established mental illness was not a created concept by a given culture but rather part of the human condition in both its recognition and its prevalence. This set the stage for a development that came to be known as evolutionary psychopathology or Darwinian psychiatry.

Thinking about Psychopathology from an Evolutionary Perspective

An evolutionary perspective on psychopathology goes beyond the traditional psychological considerations. For example, we could ask how long in terms of our human history has a particular psychopathology existed. Let's take schizophrenia as an example. A World Health Organization (WHO) study examined the presence of schizophrenia in a number of countries with very different racial and cultural backgrounds (Sartorius et al., 1986). If schizophrenia was largely related to the society or family in which you lived, then we would expect to see different rates and manifestations of the disorder in different cultures.

What these authors found was that despite the different cultural and racial backgrounds surveyed, the experience of schizophrenia was remarkably similar across countries. Likewise, the risk of developing schizophrenia was similar in terms of total population presence—about 1%. Further, the disorder had a similar time course in its occurrence with its characteristics first being seen in young adults. If you put these facts together, it was possible to suggest that schizophrenia is not directly related to environmental factors such as culture or family patterns. Because it develops at a similar age and follows a similar pattern across cultures, this suggests a genetic component to the disorder.

The next question that might be asked is how long has schizophrenia existed? Because it is found throughout the world in strikingly similar ways, this suggests that it existed before humans migrated out of Africa. The genes related to schizophrenia were carried by early humans who migrated from Africa and thus its presence is equally likely throughout the world. Given these estimates as to the history of the disorder, one might ask why does schizophrenia continue to exist? We know that individuals with schizophrenia tend to have fewer children than individuals without the disorder. Thus, we might assume that schizophrenia would have disappeared over evolutionary time in that it reduces reproductive success and has a genetic component. However, this is not the case.

This creates a mystery for evolutionary psychologists to solve. In order to answer this question, we can draw on many of the considerations seen in relation to human health and disease. Perhaps, in the same way that sickle cell anemia is associated with a protection against malaria, schizophrenia protects the person from another disorder. Or, perhaps like the reaction of rats to stress, which results in depression-like symptoms, the symptoms seen in schizophrenia are the result of a long chain of stressful events in which the organism breaks down in its ability to function. Psychopathology could even go in a more positive direction and be associated with creative and nontraditional views of the world. For example, there are a variety of accounts that have noted greater creativity in families of individuals with schizophrenia. Thus, the genetic components associated with creativity and intelligence may also make the individual with a variant form susceptible to schizophrenia.

Overall, the evolutionary perspective helps us ask questions such as what function a disorder might serve, as well as how it came about. In the same way that pain can be seen as a warning system in the body to protect from tissue damage, anxiety may have evolved to protect the person from other types of potential threats. For example, many of the outward expressions of social anxiety parallel what is seen in dominance interactions in primates. Submissive monkeys avoid contact with most dominant ones as do individuals experiencing social anxiety.

Developmentally, there is some suggestion that the excessive scanning of the environment seen in some individuals with generalized anxiety disorder is associated with being required as children to prematurely play a responsible parental role for others. That is, if your mother was disorganized when you were a child, you may have needed to watch out for your own needs and maybe even those of younger siblings and your mother. The evolutionary perspective can also help us to think about solutions to how psychopathology should be classified and treated.

CONCEPT CHECK

1. One way to define psychopathology is to consider its four important personal components. What are these four components?
2. What are four advantages of having a classification system, like *DSM*, to define psychological disorders?
3. There is often a stigma experienced by those with a mental disorder. What are three examples of this stigmatizing? What can be done to reduce stigmatizing?
4. What does the term comorbid refer to?
5. The modern study of psychopathology is generally dated to the late 1700s. What major changes have occurred in our understanding of psychopathology since that time?
6. Is psychopathology universal? List three pieces of evidence in support of this position.
7. What new kinds of questions does taking an evolutionary perspective allow us to ask in gaining a better understanding of psychopathology?

Common Disorders Involving Emotions or Moods

Our emotions and moods influence our behaviors and experiences. Most of the time they are consistent with our environmental conditions. We hear bad news and feel sad. Something startles us and we feel afraid. We win an award and feel happy. These tend to be short-term events. However, other times the feelings may persist without environmental conditions that would support them. When the experience of anxiety or depression persists without such external stimuli, then these conditions can be classified as psychological disorders. In this section, we will describe such conditions.

Anxiety Disorders

Anxiety is to be afraid of what might happen. What if I don't do well when I give a presentation to a room full of important people? Will I get the job I want? What if a snake bites me when I am in the woods? What if the plane I am on crashes? What if I get germs on my hands when I go into a public restroom? What if others do not like me?

Anxiety is about the future, whereas *fear* typically has a stimulus in the present. With fear, we see a snake and become apprehensive. We look down from a tall building and feel unease. With anxiety, there is often no stimulus in front of us. With anxiety, the stimulus is in our mind. However, our cognitive and emotional consideration of a negative possibility does not make it any less real. Our body, mind, and emotions experience our ideas as real possibilities. We show the same autonomic nervous systems responses such as a higher heart rate as described in the chapter on stress. In anxiety, we increase the probability in our mind that an undesirable event will happen. Performers such as Ariana Grande and the British performer Adele have spoken openly about their experience with anxiety.

What we do know is that fear and anxiety involve high-level as well as more primitive brain processes. Cognitively, we can make ourselves feel more anxious by thinking of all the terrible things that can happen in a given situation. We get on an airplane feeling somewhat anxious. We then hear a sound from the engine that we interpret to be a problem. This, in turn, results in our being even more vigilant and listening for every sound. The plane begins to move down the runway, and we tell ourselves it is not going to make it. This allows for emotional reactions that our body normally keeps in check to increase and we feel anxious.

Limbic system processes, as you learned about in the coverage of stress, can also respond to stimuli on their own. For example, our amygdala can respond to an angry face in a manner that begins an autonomic nervous system reaction. From an evolutionary perspective, to be fearful in the presence of dangerous situations would be adaptive. However, extreme anxiety can hurt our performance. Thus, anxiety can both help us and hurt us, depending on the situation and the extent of the anxiety. One scientific aspect of this is the question of where these anxieties and fears come from. From research, we know that certain phobias run in families, suggesting a genetic component. However, not everyone has exactly the same fears, suggesting that fears can be learned during development.

The development of anxiety and fear follows a trajectory that is part of the human condition. Children and adolescents show similar profiles of anxiety and fear across cultures; however, cultures that favor inhibition, compliance, and obedience also show increased levels of fear (Ollendick, Yang, King, Dong, & Akande, 1996). Fears are traditionally seen in relation to immediate experiences. Young children during their first year of life, usually about 9 months, will react to strangers. After that, they will react to separation. Infants of other species also show distress vocalizations when separated from their mothers. Human infants also begin to display distress to specific stimuli, such as insects or flying bees, or animals. By adolescence, the fear turns to anxiety in that the object of concern is not present. Social anxiety about a future situation is common among adolescents. The normal expression of fear and anxiety only becomes pathological when it interferes with the child's or adolescent's ability to function or causes distress.

A number of epidemiology studies have shown that 2.5% to 5% of children and adolescents meet criteria for anxiety disorders at any one time (see Rapee, Schniering, & Hudson, 2009, for an overview). The earliest anxiety disorder to develop is *separation anxiety disorder*. The next is *specific phobias*, which begin in early to middle childhood. Next comes *social phobia*, which begins in early to middle adolescence. *Panic disorder* appears in early adulthood. Given the nature of adolescence, anxiety disorders at this time have an influence on popularity and social competence. They are also associated with victimization.

Although fear and anxiety are often studied together, research suggests that different brain areas are involved. Specifically, the areas involved in anxiety are not those directly responsible for the expression of fear. Rather, anxiety is related to the areas of the brain that regulate the fear system. These include the prefrontal cortex (PFC), the amygdala, and the hippocampus. These are systems involved in cognitions, emotional reactivity, and memory—all important components in the social and cognitive aspects of anxiety. These systems are also seen in humans to be the ones involved in increased vigilance and attention to threat (Robinson et al., 2014).

Normally, the amygdala shows lower firing rates of neurons than other areas. With threat, this silence is broken. With increased neural activity, its connections with other threat networks are activated (Möhler, 2012). Thus, activation of the amygdala and its networks is associated with feeling anxious. The amygdala is also involved in the formation and storage of fear memories and fear conditioning.

One of the major neurotransmitters involved in anxiety is *gamma-aminobutyric acid (GABA)* (see Kalueff & Nutt, 2007; Millan, 2003; Möhler, 2012, for overviews). GABA is the major inhibitory neurotransmitter in the brain. Although GABA is involved in a variety of processes, it is thought to play a major role in anxiety. The basic idea is that individuals with anxiety have reduced GABA activity, which in turn results in less inhibition of the brain structures, such as the amygdala, that are involved in threat responses. That is, with reduced GABA activity, the amygdala becomes more active and the person experiences increased anxiety. It should also be noted that GABA receptors are densely located in the PFC, the amygdala, and the hippocampus.

One way to reduce anxiety is to use medications that contain *benzodiazepines*, for example, Valium. These are common drugs used in the treatment of anxiety disorders. One way benzodiazepines work is to influence the GABA system. Specifically, benzodiazepines reduce the amount of serotonin available to the brain. Animal models of anxiety have shown increased GABA activity in the amygdala and a reduction of fear with the introduction of serotonin in the hippocampus and amygdala. There are also developmental processes that influence GABA activity. An adult rat that was nurtured and licked as an infant will have greater expression of GABA activity in the amygdala with fewer signs of fearfulness and stress responses (Fries, Moragues, Caldji, Hellhammer, & Meaney, 2004).

In reviewing studies with both humans and other animals, Gross and Hen (2004) suggested that anxiety should be seen as a developmental problem involving both environmental and genetic factors. From twin studies, it is apparent that the genetic contribution to anxiety is moderate (30%–40%). Genetic studies of individuals with anxiety disorders show the highest concordance for monozygotic (MZ) versus dizygotic (DZ) twin pairs as would be expected if there were a genetic component. Family interviews also suggest the presence of GAD in first-degree relatives. Other anxiety disorders show higher genetic contribution. Panic disorder was associated with a heritability of 48% (Hettema, Neale, & Kendler, 2001). Similar heritability numbers were found for specific phobias, such as animal (47%), blood injury (59%), and situational (46%). Social phobia was found to be 51%. Overall, this strongly suggests genetic contributions to the development of certain anxiety disorders.

Generalized anxiety disorder (GAD) is characterized by excessive anxiety and worry. Its diagnosis in a clinical setting requires that anxiety and worry have been present for more than 6 months. GAD is one of the most commonly diagnosed mental disorders in the United States. It is more commonly seen in women than men. With GAD, there are both physiological and psychological symptoms. The physiological symptoms may include problems sleeping, muscle tension, and feeling fatigued. In fact, one of the more consistent physiological patterns seen in GAD is high muscle tension. The psychological symptoms may include feeling on edge, irritability, and difficulty in concentration as well as decision making (Bishop & Gagne, 2018).

Worry is an important component of GAD. In terms of frequency, those with GAD also report that they worry a larger percentage of each day and tend to have a larger set of domains such as family, money, and friends that they worry about than those without GAD. Those with GAD also reported that they worry about minor things (100%) versus those with other types of anxiety disorders (50%) (Barlow, 2002). Not only do individuals with GAD worry, but they also find it difficult to control their worry. Bodily symptoms such as feeling on edge and muscle tension also accompany the worry.

Social Anxiety Disorder (SAD)

Most of us can think of a time that we were concerned about meeting someone or giving a talk in front of a group. *Perhaps I will say the wrong thing. Perhaps others will think I am foolish. Perhaps I will spill my food on my shirt when I am eating.* These are all common reactions and are part of our human condition. However, when these feelings are severe and last for more than 6 months, it would be considered a **social anxiety disorder (SAD)**. Previously, social anxiety disorder was referred to as *social phobia*.

Social anxiety disorder is characterized by marked fear or anxiety about one or more social situations in which the individual is exposed to possible scrutiny by others. Those with social anxiety are often concerned that they will humiliate or embarrass themselves. Approximately 8% of US citizens will experience a social anxiety disorder during their lifetime (Kessler et al., 2010). It is more common in women than men. The disorder is also associated with later mood disorders and substance abuse.

Theoretically, it has been suggested that individuals with social anxiety process their world differently from those without the disorder. Specifically, they process social situations with evolutionarily older alarm systems such as the amygdala, whereas non-anxious individuals process the same situations with newer cognitive–analytic processes using the prefrontal cortex (PFC). It has also been suggested that social anxiety can be seen as part of the larger dominance and submission system seen across other primate species (Öhman, 1986, 2009; Öhman & Mineka, 2001). This view is supported by research revealing that individuals with social anxiety show enhanced amygdala activation to images of hostile faces. Further, the degree of amygdala activity is positively correlated with the severity of social anxiety, but not with general anxiety (Phan, Fitzgerald, Nathan, & Tancer, 2006).

Panic Disorder

A **panic disorder** is an anxiety disorder that comes quickly and carries with it an intense feeling of apprehension, anxiety, or fear (see Craske et al., 2010; Fava & Morton, 2009, for overviews). It happens without an actual situation that would suggest danger. Physiological symptoms can include shortness of breath, trembling, heart palpitations, dizziness, faintness, and hot or cold flashes. The person can also experience the world as if it were not real and can be concerned about dying. The symptoms usually peak within the first 10 minutes of the attack. The experience of one's heart pounding (97%) and dizziness (96%) are reported by almost all individuals who experience panic attacks.

A **panic attack** is a frequent cause of individuals going to a hospital emergency room. The person may think there are heart problems since the symptoms can include a pounding heart, chest pains, feeling dizzy, nausea, shaking, chills, fear of dying, and a number of other bodily sensations. There is some suggestion that panic is more common during periods of stress. Although many individuals experience an episode of panic-like symptoms at some point in their lives, it is necessary for these symptoms to be recurrent and followed by a month of concern or change in lifestyle to be diagnosed with a panic disorder.

Once individuals experience a panic attack, they often become concerned about having another attack. They may also try to change their behavior as a way to prevent panic attacks. For example, some individuals will not exercise or do other tasks that would raise their heart rates. Although presented as a separate anxiety disorder, panic attacks can occur within the context of any of the other anxiety disorders. It is often comorbid with the fear of being in public, referred to as agoraphobia. Lifetime prevalence rates are 4.7% for panic disorder (Kessler et al., 2006). The common age of onset for panic disorder is from 21 to 23 years of age, although children and adolescents may experience panic attacks along with other anxiety disorders. Studies have shown that twice as many women as men have panic disorder.

On a brain level, it is suggested that panic and anxiety involve different areas of the brain (Graeff & Del-Ben, 2008). Anxiety is integrated in the forebrain, whereas panic is organized in the midbrain, especially the basal ganglia and limbic structures. Decreased gray matter in individuals with panic disorder has also been reported in these areas (Lai, 2011). The idea of different areas for anxiety and panic is consistent with the suggestion that there are two defense systems in the brain (Gray & McNaughton, 2000; McNaughton & Corr, 2004). The basic model suggests that fear and anxiety are involved in different approach-and-avoidance systems that utilize distinct brain networks.

Agoraphobia

Agoraphobia is the condition in which a person experiences fear or anxiety when in public. These situations can involve public transportation, open spaces such as parking lots or marketplaces, or places with a large number of individuals such as theaters or shops, as well as being in a crowd or just being outside the home. One characteristic of agoraphobia is that the person is concerned that escape from the situation would be difficult. In some individuals, panic disorder and agoraphobia go together and in others they do not. Age of onset in both agoraphobia and panic disorder is about 21 to 23 years of age. Agoraphobia is seen more frequently in women than men. Some studies have shown that negative experiences in childhood, such as the death of a parent, are associated with both agoraphobia and panic disorder. With *DSM–5*, agoraphobia is considered a separate disorder, although it may occur with any other disorder, especially the anxiety disorders.

Specific Phobia

A **specific phobia** is an anxiety disorder in which an individual experiences fear or anxiety to a particular situation or object. Common phobias are fear of snakes, spiders, flying, heights, blood, injections, and the dark. Although almost all individuals have experiences such as driving in bad weather in which they feel concern from time to time, these fears tend not to be long-lasting or result in major changes in lifestyle. To be diagnosed with a specific phobia, the individual must actively avoid the condition or object, and the fear or anxiety must have lasted for 6 months or more. Further, the fear or anxiety causes distress and is out of proportion to the actual danger posed by the situation.

Obsessive-Compulsive and Related Disorders

Some individuals hoard their possessions even if they are of no value. Others are always thinking about their body and particular flaws they believe they have. Still others pick at their skin or pull their hair. Other individuals refuse to step on sidewalk cracks, often wash their hands to prevent germs, or experience unwelcome thoughts coming into their minds. In *DSM-5*, these conditions are referred to as **obsessive-compulsive and related disorders**.

Obsessive-Compulsive Disorder (OCD)

Have you ever been concerned about walking under a ladder or felt you needed to do a ritual before you played a sport? Do you have specific numbers you play in a lottery? Most of us have superstitions. However, when the thoughts and behaviors become extreme in producing distress and last for a period of time, they can be a part of obsessive-compulsive disorder. **Obsessive-compulsive disorder (OCD)** is characterized by repetitive thoughts and feelings usually followed by behaviors in response to them (Hirschtritt, Bloch, & Mathews, 2017). The thoughts are usually perceived as unpleasant and not wanted.

A distinction is made between *obsessions* and *compulsions*. **Obsessions** are generally unwelcome thoughts that come into our heads. Will I get sick from using a public toilet? I feel I want to hit that person. Did I put my campfire out? I am thinking of touching another person sexually. That picture frame is crooked. In studies examining these thoughts in patients with OCD, they involve a limited number of categories. The main categories are avoiding contamination, aggressive impulses, sexual content, somatic concerns, religious concerns, and the need for order.

Obsessions can also be defined in terms of how they are experienced by the person (Abramowitz & Jacoby, 2013). The two classes are *autogenous obsessions* and *reactive obsessions*. Autogenous obsessions are thoughts or images that come into a person's mind. They are generally expressed as distressing and may appear without any stimulus in the environment. Some examples would include urges to perform unacceptable acts of an aggressive, sexual, or immoral nature. Reactive obsessions, on the other hand, are evoked by an actual environmental situation. These types of obsessions could result from seeing a dirty bathroom, having a stranger touch you, or seeing a crooked picture. This type of obsession may lead to an action such as making the crooked picture straight.

Compulsions are the behaviors that individuals use to respond to their distressing thoughts. Overall, these behaviors are performed in order to reduce anxiety, gain control, or resist unwanted thoughts. Some behaviors, like cleaning or placing objects in order, reflect a desire to respond to the obsessions. Other compulsions, such as hand washing, are more avoidant in nature for fear of what one might say, do, or experience in a particular situation.

Often individuals with OCD will constantly check to see if they performed a particular behavior such as turning off the stove or unplugging an iron. Interestingly, individuals with OCD may be aware that their thoughts and actions may seem bizarre to others, but they cannot dismiss the thoughts or the need to perform the action. For example, one person checked his window locks every 30 minutes even though each time he found them locked.

Traditionally, compulsions have been seen as a mechanism for reducing the anxiety or distress caused by the obsession. Not being allowed to engage in these behaviors results in distress and anxiety. More than 90% of those with OCD show both obsessions and behavioral rituals. OCD has an adulthood prevalence of 2% to 3% and a child and adolescence prevalence of 1% to 2%. Approximately 40% of those with childhood OCD report continuing symptoms into adulthood. There is not a gender difference in rates.

There is clearly a parallel between the themes found in OCD and concerns expressed by those without the disorder. Most individuals naturally avoid contamination or express concern when they experience unusual bodily sensations. On a societal level, there are often rituals concerned with health and success in the world. Tribal cultures would perform rituals to dispel evil spirits or bring in the good ones. Most modern societies have a variety of rituals including not walking under a ladder, not stepping on sidewalk cracks, or not partaking in other behaviors as ways of avoiding bad luck. Sports teams also have rituals for how to prepare for an important game. Not performing any of these rituals may result in a feeling of anxiety for many individuals.

CONCEPT CHECK

1. What is *anxiety*? What is *fear*? In what ways are they similar? In what ways are they different?
2. What are the defining characteristics of the following anxiety disorders:
   a. Generalized anxiety disorder (GAD)?
   b. Social anxiety disorder (SAD)?
   c. Panic disorder?
   d. Agoraphobia?
   e. Specific phobia?
3. What evidence can you cite that anxiety disorders have a genetic component?
4. In obsessive-compulsive disorder (OCD), what are obsessions? What are compulsions? What are some examples of each?

Mood Disorders

Emotional experiences and moods are an important part of our world. Sometimes we feel happy; other times we feel sad. We have all experienced ourselves as having different moods. Our thoughts are often consistent with our moods as when we feel sad and think we are not doing things well. Likewise our behaviors match our moods. To want to stay in bed in the morning or not to want to be with others is often the outcome of feeling blue. Other times we go in the opposite direction and feel full of energy. Our thoughts when we are in a positive mood influence what activities we can engage in or what accomplishments we can achieve. Behaviorally, we tend to seek social interactions and start new projects.

Neither positive nor negative moods as most of us experience them interfere with our daily life or separate us from ourselves or others. However, the mood disorders discussed in this chapter do. Not only do these disorders separate us; they also last for a long time and, in some cases, are experienced throughout one's life. The Russian writer Leo Tolstoy who wrote the novel *War and Peace* wrote, "The truth was that life is meaningless. I had as it were lived, lived, and walked, walked, till I had come to a precipice and saw clearly that there was nothing ahead of me but destruction" (Tolstoy, 1882, p. 402). Tolstoy experienced depression, which influenced his artistic life (Anargyros-Klinger, 2002).

Both depression and mania have been described for more than 2,000 years. The ancient Greek writers Hippocrates, Aretaeus, and Galen each described a condition they referred to as *melancholia*, which today we call *depression*. Melancholia was described in terms of despondency, dissatisfaction with life, problems sleeping, restlessness, irritability, difficulties in decision-making, and a desire to die. *Mania*, on the other hand, was described in terms of euphoria, excitement, cheerfulness, grandiosity, and at times anger. There was also a realization that mania and melancholia could exist in the same person.

Characteristics and Symptoms of Major Depressive Disorder (MDD)

When depression is severe, it is referred to as **major depressive disorder (MDD)**. With major depressive disorder, a person feels sad and empty and may display an irritable mood. These feelings may include hopelessness and be experienced over a number of days. The person may seeing himself or herself as worthless in a world with little support. If asked to remember their past, unlike healthy individuals, individuals with depression tend to remember more negative than positive events (Dillon & Pizzagalli, 2018). Body experiences, such as difficulty sleeping and eating, are also common.

Those who experience depression describe both psychological and physical symptoms. They feel sad much of the time and may even be close to tears for no apparent reason. If you talk with these individuals, they will tell you that they feel worthless. Not only will you notice their negative affect, but you may also notice a lack of any positive affect. They may even say that they just do not feel like being involved in activities or being with others. They may also think of dying. In terms of physical symptoms, you might notice that the person has had weight changes. They will also describe problems with sleeping almost every night. They will report a loss of energy and feeling tired. This loss of energy may also be associated with an inability to concentrate. MDD is seen when the majority of these symptoms last for at least two weeks.

Depression has been related to a variety of physiological, psychological, economic, family, and social components. In 2018, the World Health Organization (WHO) has ranked depression as the leading cause of disability worldwide with women being affected by depression more than men (https://www.who.int/news-room/fact-sheets/detail/depression). It is also estimated to be one of the most economically costly mental disorders worldwide. MDD has been shown to take individuals out of their normal roles or jobs for a number of lost days equal to that due to medical disorders. In fact, MDD is second only to chronic back or neck pain in terms of disability days lost. Part of this is related to the fact that only one-third of those with depression seek help in the first year of onset. The median delay for seeking treatment among those who did not seek treatment in the first year was five years. Even with treatment, the chance of another episode of depression is high. Most patients experience a recurrence within five years (see Boland & Keller, 2009, for an overview). Historical figures such as President Abraham Lincoln have described their own experiences of mood disorders (Shenk, 2005). "I am now the most miserable man living," Lincoln wrote when he was a state senator to his friend John T. Stuart in 1841. "If what I feel were equally distributed to the whole human family, there would not be one cheerful face on the earth."

A number of performers have spoken of their personal struggles with depression. Brian Wilson of The Beach Boys said that he would go for long periods without being able to do anything. The actor and singer Ashley Judd describes herself as depressed and isolated. The singer Sheryl Crow has also documented her own experiences of depression and said there were periods she thought about suicide every day. For completeness, it should be noted that many performers and artists have consulted with mental health professionals and reflect this experience in their statements. However, some information presented on the Internet may be just the person saying, "That sounds like me, so I must have this or that disorder," which may not be the case.

Today, major depressive disorder (MDD) is one of the most commonly diagnosed mental disorders among adults and is estimated to be found in about 13 million adult Americans during the preceding 12 months (see Kessler & Wang, 2009). There is a gender difference in that over the course of a lifetime, about one in four females and one in ten males experience a major depressive episode (Rutter, 2006; see also Ryba & Hopko, 2012). Genetic studies suggest that depression is equally influenced by environmental and genetic factors (Rutter, 2006).

There is a difference between factors related to initial episodes and later episodes of depression. Research suggests that the initial episode of depression has a strong environmental component, whereas later episodes are thought to be related to internal physiological changes (Kendler, Thornton, & Gardner, 2000). Thus, major life stress such as loss of a close relationship is highly associated with the development of depression. Individuals with depression are 2.5 to 10 times more likely to have experienced a recent major life event than nondepressive individuals (see Slavich, O'Donovan, Epel, & Kemeny, 2010, for an overview).

From a variety of studies, chronic severe depression has been shown to be familial (Otte et al., 2016 Peterson & Weissman, 2011). Offspring of individuals with MDD have a threefold to fivefold increased risk of developing MDD themselves. From longitudinal studies over three generations, individuals initially show elevated anxiety disorders before puberty, which then become MDD in mid to late adolescence. Further, familial MDD tends to have an earlier onset and to be more severe, more recurrent, and less responsive to treatment than is nonfamilial MDD.

Types and Characteristics of Bipolar Disorder

Bipolar disorder was previously referred to as *manic-depressive disorder*. Changes in mood are an important aspect of bipolar disorders. These include the intense sense of well-being along with high energy seen in mania and its opposite seen in depression. Changes in cognition and perception also accompany these states. In mania, thoughts seem to flow easily, and many individuals find themselves very productive during mania. Perceptions and sensations may also be heightened. However, mania can also increase a feeling of pressure with racing thoughts and ideas that do not make sense. Sometimes, this includes a feeling of "I can do anything" and the sense that nothing will not work out. Individuals in a manic state may buy expensive items they cannot afford, place large bets, and engage in all types of risky sexual behavior. It is as if there is nothing to worry about.

Terri Cheney, an attorney who has represented such performers as Michael Jackson and Quincy Jones, described her experiences of bipolar disorder in her book *Manic* (Cheney, 2008).

> The mania came in four-day spurts. Four days of not eating, not sleeping, barely sitting in one place for more than a few minutes at a time. Four days of constant shopping . . .
>
> And four days of indiscriminate, nonstop talking: first to everyone I knew on the West Coast, then to anyone still awake on the East Coast, then to Santa Fe itself, whoever would listen. The truth was, I didn't just need to talk. I was afraid to be alone.

The depressive episodes show the opposite picture with the person experiencing a bleak outlook, low energy in a world of black-and-white, and a wish to do little. Kay Jamison received her PhD in clinical psychology from UCLA and is a professor of psychiatry at Johns Hopkins University. She has written significant books describing the scientific and clinical aspects of bipolar disorders (for example, Goodwin & Jamison, 2007) as well as her own experiences in *An Unquiet Mind* (Jamison, 1996). She describes the depressive aspect of bipolar disorder as follows:

> Every day I awoke deeply tired, a feeling as foreign to my natural self as being bored or indifferent to life. Those were next. Then a gray, bleak preoccupation with death, dying, decaying, that everything was born but to die, best to die now and save the pain while waiting.

One characteristic experienced in both mania and depression by many individuals is a sense of irritability. Today we call these alternating periods of depression and mania *bipolar disorder*. This is in contrast to *unipolar depression*, which is the experience of depression without mania.

DSM–5 classifies bipolar disorder in terms of the manic and the depressive symptoms. *Bipolar I disorder* requires the presence of one or more manic episodes. Bipolar I does not require any depressive symptoms for the diagnosis. In fact, some individuals with bipolar disorder never report depression (see Johnson, Cuellar, & Miller, 2009, for an overview). However, the majority of individuals with bipolar disorder do experience depression during their lifetime. *Bipolar II disorder*, on the other hand, requires an episode of a major depressive disorder along with a hypomanic episode. A *hypomanic episode* is similar to mania but shorter in duration and less severe. Further, an individual with bipolar II disorder cannot have had a full manic episode.

Research over the past 40 years suggests a genetic predisposition for bipolar disorder (see Craddock & Sklar, 2009; Goodwin & Jamison, 2007; Harrison, Geddes, & Tunbridge, 2018). For bipolar disorders, heritability is about 5% to 10% for first-degree relatives and 40% to 70% for monozygotic (MZ) twins compared with only 14% for fraternal twins. That is to say, a first-degree relative of someone with bipolar disorder has approximately ten times the risk of having the disorder compared with a random person. This is much higher than first-degree relatives of a person with depression, which is about three times higher. Further, relatives of individuals with MDD do not appear to be at risk for mania, whereas relatives of those with bipolar disorder are at risk for depression.

Suicide

The term **suicide** has been dated to 1642 in a work *Religio Medici* written by Sir Thomas Browne. It comes from the Latin meaning to kill oneself. Suicidal behaviors can be seen as existing on a continuum ranging from thinking about suicide to attempting suicide to an act that leads to death. However, some individuals think often about suicide—referred to as *suicidal ideation*—without actually attempting to harm themselves.

Suicidal ideation begins at about the time of puberty (Nock et al., 2013). Having a plan for committing suicide is associated with attempting suicide for the adolescent age group. Beginning at about puberty, suicide ideation begins to increase. Actual suicide plans and attempts increase somewhat, too, but with significantly less frequency than ideation.

Mental illness has a strong connection with suicide (see Goldsmith, 2001, for an overview). Of those suicide attempts that lead to death, it is estimated that 90% of adults and 67% of youth would meet diagnostic criteria for a mental disorder. The most common disorders associated with suicide are depression, bipolar disorder, substance use disorders, personality disorders, and schizophrenia, in that order. In bipolar and personality disorders, suicide is often associated with impulsiveness. With schizophrenia, it is more associated with active manifestation of the disorder. The rate of suicide among those with psychological disorders is highest in the three months following hospitalization (Chung et al., 2017).

To put suicide in perspective, more people die annually from suicide than from homicide and even war. In 2016, there were 793,000 people from around the world who died from suicide (https://www.who.int/gho/mental_health/suicide_rates/en/). This represents a one-year prevalence rate of approximately 11 people per 100,000. This makes suicide the 13th leading cause of death worldwide. It becomes the second leading cause of death

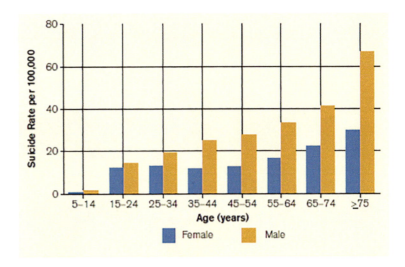

Figure 14-2 Suicide rates worldwide in terms of gender and age.

among those 15 to 29 years of age. In all age groups, worldwide suicide rates increase with age (see **Figure 14-2**). This graph also shows that males commit suicide more often than females.

One theory related to suicide is the *interpersonal-psychological theory of suicide (IPTS)* (Joiner, 2005). This theory suggests there are two important components for an individual to engage in suicidal behaviors. The first is a suicidal desire to die. According to the theory, part of this is the sense that the person experiences herself as a burden to others and the feeling that she is isolated from others and not important to them. The second important component is the capability to act to commit suicide. This is also associated with a lowered fear of death. Studies based on this theory have shown that factors such as feeling to be a burden is associated with greater suicidal ideation as well as attempts.

As shown in **Figure 14-3**, there are cultural differences in the rate of suicide. Hungary has the highest national suicide rate in the world, followed by Finland and Austria. Their rates are 66, 43, and 42 per 100,000 compared with 11.3 in the United States. Countries with low rates of suicide such as Mexico tend to be predominantly Catholic or Muslim, have strong family ties, and have a younger population. There are also psychological differences related to suicide worldwide. In the United States and Europe, suicide is associated with depression and alcohol use disorder, whereas in Asia, impulsiveness plays an important role. There are also cultural differences in gender ratios. The rate is more similar in Asia but higher for males in Chile and Puerto Rico. Further, the suicide rate of Caucasians is approximately twice that observed in other races.

In the United States, the suicide rate is about in the middle of all countries (Miller, Azrael, & Barber, 2012). According to the Centers for Disease Control and Prevention (CDC) the US rate increased from 29,199 deaths in 1996 to 47,173 in 2017 (https://www.cdc.gov/nchs/data/hestat/suicide/rates_1999_2017.htm). Among adults aged 18 or older in 2019, 4.8% (or 12 million people) thought seriously about trying to kill themselves in 2019. Further, 1.4% (or 3.5 million people) made a suicide plan (Substance Abuse and Mental Health Services Administration, 2020). In the United States, firearm-related suicide for those under 15 is some 11 times higher. A strong risk factor for attempting suicide is the presence of a mental illness or substance use disorder. During the COVID-19 pandemic in 2020, suicidal ideation increased along with mental health problems especially among younger adults (https://www.cdc.gov/mmwr/volumes/69/wr/mm6932a1.htm).

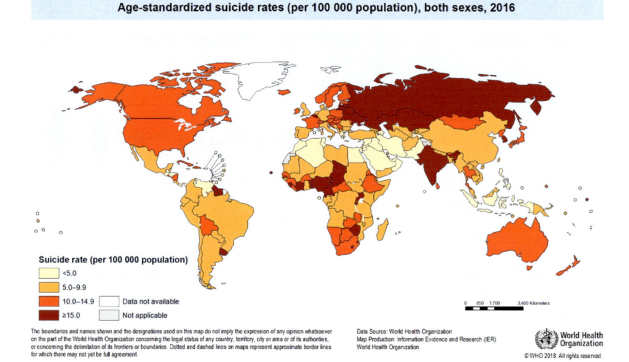

Figure 14-3 Map of suicide rates worldwide per 100,000 people for 2016.
Source: https://www.who.int/teams/mental-health-and-substance-use/suicide-data

Worldwide, religion plays a protective role in preventing suicide. However, in a recent meta-analysis, the protective aspect of religion was stronger in some cultures than others (Wu, Wang, & Jia, 2015). The authors of this meta-analysis suggest that culturally end of life is understood differently in countries of Africa and South America as compared to India and Vietnam. Overall, Eastern cultures have historically viewed suicide as an act of nobility and selflessness, whereas Western values have typically associated it with shame and cowardice. Religious practices in all cultures have a strong social support aspect that have been associated with less stress and depression.

Although females attempt suicide more often than males, males are three to four times more likely to die because the methods they use are more lethal (see Miller et al., 2012, for an overview). For example, men are more likely to use firearms or hanging as opposed to drug overdose. Among men, firearms account for about 62% of all suicide deaths in the United States.

In older adults, mental disorders are often comorbid with physical disorders. However, a physical disorder alone is not highly associated with suicide. In older adults, hopelessness along with depression was associated with suicidal ideation. Suicide attempts among the US military is highest in those units who had another person attempt suicide during the previous year (Ursano et al., 2017).

College Students and Suicide

Each year, hundreds of thousands of new students begin their undergraduate education at colleges around the United States. For most, their lifestyle changes in many ways. They often meet people who are different from those with whom they went to high school. Competition increases. Those who made perfect grades or were editors of their school newspapers discover that they are no longer unique. Most students find themselves working harder. Some believe that they are the only ones who feel stressed and are working constantly. For a number of these students, every setback is experienced as an extreme failure. Social comparisons leave them feeling inadequate. Some think of suicide.

In response to concern over suicide, many colleges and universities are setting up programs to help identify and treat those at risk. Collecting data from mental health centers at more than 140 colleges and universities around the US gives us a picture of who is seeking help. Data from more than 80,000 students who went to their local mental health center for all types of distress in 2018 shows that anxiety and depression are the two most common presenting problems. More than 30% of all students in this sample have considered suicide (see **Figure 14-4**).

Seriously considered attempting suicide (how many times)

	Overall (%) n=105,951	Female (%) n=67,860	Male (%) n=36,135
Never	65.5	65.2	68.0
1 time	12.3	12.5	11.8
2-3 times	12.4	12.9	11.1
4-5 times	2.6	2.7	2.2
More than 5 times	7.1	6.7	6.9

Figure 14-4 Seriously considered attempting suicide from students who visit campus mental health centers (how many times).

Preventing Suicide

Suicide-prevention programs seek to reduce the factors that increase the risk for suicidal thoughts and behaviors. These programs seek to work on at least four levels: the individual, the individual's relationships, the community, and the society. Suicide prevention began in the United States in the 1950s and has continued through to the present day. Many communities have hotlines for people to call 24 hours a day. There has also been a national focus on groups that are at higher risk for suicide including Native Americans and members of the armed forces and veterans. Friends and relatives of individuals who show signs described in **Table 14-3** should help them find a mental health professional or suicide-prevention center in their community. Interestingly, those who tried to commit suicide but did not succeed tend to feel relieved. This makes it possible for those individuals to receive help.

Follow-up studies of suicide-prevention programs suggest they are effective. One such study examined youth prevention programs across 46 states and 12 tribal communities in the US (Garraza, Walrath, Goldston, Reid, & McKeon, 2015). These programs included

Table 14-3 The warning signs of suicide.

Talking about wanting to die
Looking for a way to kill oneself
Talking about feeling hopeless or having no purpose
Talking about feeling trapped or being in unbearable pain
Talking about being a burden to others
Increasing the use of alcohol or drugs
Acting anxious, agitated, or reckless
Sleeping too little or too much
Withdrawing or feeling isolated
Showing rage or talking about seeking revenge
Displaying extreme mood swings

education and mental health awareness, screening activities, gatekeeper training events, improved community partnerships and linkages to services, programs for suicide survivors, and crisis hotlines. Some 57,000 youth aged 16 to 23 years were involved in the suicide-prevention programs. These individuals were compared with some 84,000 youth who were not involved in these prevention programs. In the year following the program, there were 4.9 fewer suicide attempts per 1,000 youth in the treatment group compared to the control group. This suggests that thousands of suicide attempts can be averted by such prevention programs.

CONCEPT CHECK

1. What is the impact of depression from a number of perspectives:
   a. Worldwide prevalence?
   b. Lifetime prevalence?
   c. Gender prevalence?
   d. Costs to economy, society, family, and individual?
   e. Other psychological disorders?
2. Changes in mood are an important aspect of bipolar disorders. How would you describe these changes in each of the different types of bipolar disorder?
3. What evidence can you cite on whether there is a scientific basis for the association between creativity and bipolar disorder?
4. In what ways are different types of mental illness related to suicide?
5. How do the following factors influence the rate of suicide:
   a. Culture?
   b. Religion?
   c. Gender?
   d. Age?
6. What are the four levels that suicide-prevention programs work on?

Dissociative Disorders

Most of us have had the experience of sitting in a lecture and realizing that we have not been listening for a period of time. Most of us also have had the experience of driving down a highway and all of a sudden realizing that 30 minutes has passed with no awareness of what we had been doing. Sometimes while watching a movie, people become so absorbed in the film that they forget they are in a theater. These are common experiences of dissociation, or *spacing out*, shared by most people. Overall, this is the situation in which there is a disruption in our normal ability to integrate information from our sensory and psychological processes such as memory and awareness.

The term *dissociation* (*désaggregation* in French) was introduced by Pierre Janet in 1889 to describe symptoms such as repetitive behaviors triggered by distressful memory, presentation of different incongruous personality characteristics (for example, shy, flirtatious) after a triggering event, and limb paralysis under hypnosis. Janet saw these as representing amnesic processes (memory loss from shock or trauma) where patients "forgot" the ability to receive external stimulation, their own personality, and the ability to move limbs. The common thread in these experiences according to Janet was a traumatic event. That is, a traumatic event or talk of a traumatic event preceded the dissociative experiences. For Janet, dissociation resulted from a weak ego that could not tolerate the overwhelming trauma. Freud, on the other hand, saw dissociation resulting from a strong ego that sought to wall off the experience of trauma as something separate and not part of the self.

Many researchers see **dissociation** as a normal experience to a difficult situation. In times of stress, it is a mechanism that protects the individual and allows her to survive (see Steinberg & Schnall, 2000, for an overview). In one study using a community sample of 1,055 individuals from Winnipeg, Canada, it was suggested that more than 25% of the individuals reported dissociative experiences, and some 5% showed symptoms consistent with a clinical diagnosis (Ross, Joshi, & Currie, 1990). Overall, Ross and colleagues concluded that *dissociative experiences* are common in the general population; do not differ in terms of socioeconomic status, gender, education, or religion of the respondent; and are reported less by older respondents.

In order to better understand dissociative experiences as seen in normal populations, Lukens and Ray (1995) interviewed college students who scored high on a common measure of dissociation. These young adults reported a variety of dissociative experiences. Three of these are presented here:

- One person reported that she would walk through town and the next moment she would "wake up" standing in line at a store's cash register with unfamiliar store items in her hands. She also reported feeling embarrassed at having no explanation for her actions.
- Another individual reported, "While I was sitting in my room, I zoned out, and then as a third person or camera, I watched myself, my body, leave the room to visit a friend. I then returned to my room whereupon I snapped out of it. An hour had passed."
- Another person said, "I have episodes where I see everything differently, everything starts blending . . . things look more fluid. I snap out of it on purpose because it is a disturbing experience. I can't tell what is real and what is not."

Other studies of college students suggest that slightly over 11% of those 31,905 students studied would qualify for a dissociative disorder (Kate, Hopwood, & Jamieson, 2020). Dissociative experiences can last for a few minutes or hours but reoccur. They can also last for a longer period of time. Some of these experiences are severe and represent significant disruptions in the organization of identity, memory, perception, or consciousness (see Maldonado & Spiegel, 2015; Spiegel et al., 2013, for overviews). More pathological symptoms of dissociation are often connected with trauma and experiences greatly beyond the individual's control.

In one study of individuals who had been subject to torture, all of the individuals who had been tortured showed signs of *post-traumatic stress disorder (PTSD)* but varied in terms of their level of dissociation (Ray et al., 2006). This suggests that dissociation is a separate process from PTSD, which was discussed in the chapter on stress and health. Additionally, the number of dissociative experiences in these individuals directly and positively correlated with magnetoencephalography (MEG) activity in the left frontal cortex and negatively correlated with MEG activity in the right frontal cortex. This suggests that brain changes associated with not experiencing the overwhelming nature of torture become permanent and result in a disruption of networks involved in integrating emotional experience with the language features and executive control associated with the left hemisphere.

Pathological dissociative symptoms are generally experienced as involuntary disruption of the normal integration of consciousness, memory, identity, or perception. These can range from not having a sense of who one is or not remembering large parts of one's past to having no memory of one's personal history or to experiencing a lack of a developmental self. *DSM–5* describes three major dissociative disorders. These are depersonalization—derealization disorder, dissociative amnesia, and dissociative identity disorder (DID).

Depersonalization–Derealization Disorder

Depersonalization is the perception of not experiencing the reality of one's self. This experience can include feeling detached or observing one's self as if you were an outside observer. **Derealization**, on the other hand, is the experience that the external world is not solid. One's world is experienced with a sense of detachment or as if in a fog or a dream, or in other ways distorted or unreal. Immediately following an automobile accident, for example, many individuals report feeling as if the world and what is occurring is not real. Unlike psychotic experiences, reality testing is still available to individuals experiencing **depersonalization-derealization disorder**. It is estimated that at least 50% of all adults in the United States have experienced depersonalization–derealization symptoms sometime in their life (APA, 2013).

Depersonalization and derealization are seen as normal responses to many types of acute stress. However, when they cause distress or impairment in important areas of one's life, they qualify as a *DSM* disorder. The lifetime prevalence for the disorder is approximately 2%, and there are no gender differences.

Let's look at one case study (Simeon et al., 1997). This case study describes a 43-year-old woman who was living with her mother and working at a clerical job. She reports a trauma history of her mother fondling her and frequently giving her enemas until the time she was 10 years old. From the earliest times, this person reports having depersonalization experiences. She explains them this way: "It is as if the real me is taken out and put on a shelf or stored somewhere inside of me. Whatever makes me me is not there. It is like an opaque curtain . . . like going through the motions and having to exert discipline to keep the unit together." Each year, she experiences several such depersonalization episodes.

Dissociative Amnesia

The main diagnostic element of **dissociative amnesia** is an inability to recall important autobiographical information. *Dissociative fugue*, which was listed as a separate disorder in *DSM-IV*, now falls under the diagnosis of dissociative amnesia in *DSM-5*. Dissociative fugue is a sudden, unexpected travel away from one's home or place of work with an inability to recall one's past.

Memory loss in terms of dissociative amnesia appears to be of a particular first-person nature rather than a global memory disorder. In fact, interacting with these individuals would seem like nothing out of the ordinary until they are asked about personal history. At that point, they are unable to remember any of their historical experiences. However, our memory of events is different than our memory of how to do things, such as riding a bike. This type of memory referred to as procedural memory is not lost nor is the ability to create new long-term memories. Dissociative amnesia may last for a few days to years. Unlike the other dissociative disorders, dissociative amnesia occurs most often when someone is in his or her 30s or 40s. Twelve-month prevalence is estimated to be about 1.8% with a 2.6-to-1 female-to-male ratio (APA, 2013).

One case of dissociative amnesia reported in the media concerned Michael Boatwright. Michael Boatwright was taken to the emergency room of the Desert Regional Medical Center in Palm Springs, California. He had been found unconscious in his motel room. When he awoke in the hospital, he said his name was Johan Ek and he only spoke Swedish. He had with him five tennis rackets, two cell phones, a duffel bag filled with casual athletic clothes, some money, photos, and identification cards. Each of the cards—including a passport, a US Department of Veterans Affairs (VA) card, and a social security card—said he was Michael Boatwright. When asked by a translator about the identification cards, the man reported that he was Johan and did not know Michael. The hospital determined it would be unsafe to release this person without any memory who only spoke Swedish. He remained in a nursing facility for a few weeks to evaluate his condition. He had nightmares almost every night. During this time hospital personnel sought to determine his past through his ID cards. They discovered that he recently flew in from China where he had taught English and was a graphic designer for the previous four years. Before that, he had worked in Japan for ten years. The hospital staff also found that he did live in Sweden when he was younger. Through contacts in these countries, they were able to obtain some pictures of him with others. He reported that although he did not recognize the pictures, they gave him a sense of comfort and security. The hospital staff also sought to determine whether he showed any signs of faking, which he did not. He was diagnosed with dissociative amnesia (based on Pelham, 2013).

Dissociative Identity Disorder

Dissociative identity disorder (DID) has received considerable attention from the media and popular press with such films as the *Three Faces of Eve* released in 1957 and the book *Sybil* released in 1973. Previously referred to as *multiple personality disorder*, there is a large amount of misinformation concerning its existence. Most television and film depictions of DID are not true to life and there is evidence that the book *Sybil* was more storytelling than an accurate picture of a person with a dissociative disorder.

Current views suggest that DID is less the case of a person having multiple personalities than it is a developmental disorder where one consistent sense of self does not occur. That is, the person does not experience his or her thoughts, feelings, or actions in terms of a well-developed "I" or sense of self. Rather, the person experiences different "personalities" at different times. DID is seen as a complex disorder related to the experience of trauma occurring before the age of 5 or 6. This is the time at which a sense of self is in development.

Epidemiological studies suggest the prevalence of DID to be from 1% to 3% with slightly more males than females showing the disorder (see Vermetten, Schmahl, Lindner, Loewenstein, & Bremner, 2006, for an overview). Although the prevalence is similar in males and females, the manner of presentation is different (American Psychiatric Association, 2013). Females with DID are more likely to be seen in adult clinical settings. Males, on the other hand, tend to deny their symptoms and trauma history. However, the symptoms can be seen following children experiencing combat conditions or acts of physical or sexual assault. Cultural differences are also seen. In developing countries or rural communities, the fragmented identities can become part of religious or other experiences. For example, possessions by gods or spirits are described in a number of cultures.

In *DSM-5*, an important feature of dissociative identity disorder is the presence of two or more distinct personality states or an experience of possession. The experience or the expression of these distinct personality states can be influenced by a number of factors. These factors include the person's psychological state such as his or her current experience of stress, ability to cope, internal conflicts, as well as cultural factors.

Disruptions in memory are also an important part of DID. These memory problems can appear in three different ways. First, the person may not remember significant parts of his or her life such as what occurred from 12 to 14 years of age or an event that would be considered significantly important to most people. Second, the person may not remember how to perform an act or well-learned skills such as driving or using a computer. And third, there may be discovery of the evidence of actions that the person does not remember doing. For example, individuals may find notes written in their handwriting that they do not remember writing or clothes in their closet they do not remember buying. These disruptions may occur without any significant psychologically stressful event taking place.

Schizophrenia

Schizophrenia is one of the most debilitating of the mental disorders. It affects one's ability to express oneself clearly, to have close social relationships, and to express and experience positive emotions (see Andreasen, 2001 Walker, Kestler, Bollini, & Hochman, 2004 for reviews). Some individuals with schizophrenia also hear voices, see images not seen by others, or believe that others wish to harm or control them. It affects about 1% of the population. It is seen throughout the world with similar symptoms regardless of culture or geographical location. In general, the onset of schizophrenia occurs in the late teens or early twenties. It also more often affects males than females.

The course of schizophrenia generally first becomes evident in adolescence or young adulthood (see Tandon, Nasrallah, & Keshavan, 2009, for an overview). The course of the disorder is shown in **Figure 14-5**. The initial phase is referred to as the *premorbid phase*. During this phase, only subtle or nonspecific problems with cognition, motor, or social functioning can be detected. These are accompanied by poor academic achievement and social functioning. This is followed by a *prodromal phase* in which initial positive symptoms along with declining functioning can be seen. From prospective studies, this phase can last from a few months to years with the mean duration being about five years. The next phase is the *psychotic phase*, where the positive psychotic symptoms are apparent. For

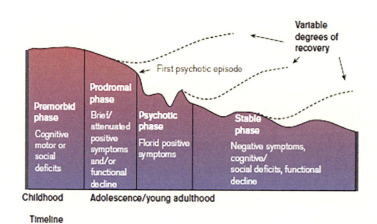

Figure 14-5 Phases in the development of schizophrenia.

most individuals, this phase occurs between 15 and 45 years of age with the onset being about five years earlier in males than females. This phase is marked by repeated episodes of psychosis with remission in between. The greatest decline in functioning is generally seen during the first five years after the initial episode. This phase is followed by a *stable phase* characterized by fewer positive symptoms and an increase in negative ones. Stable cognitive and social deficits also characterize this phase. The actual course of the disorder varies greatly across individuals.

Schizophrenia is part of a broad category of disorders referred to as **schizophrenia spectrum and other psychotic disorders**. **Psychotic disorders** involve a loss of being in touch with reality and are characterized by abnormal thinking and sensory processes. Individuals with a psychotic disorder may show delusions, hallucinations, disorganized thinking and speech, abnormal motor behaviors, and negative symptoms. People who do not have schizophrenia may show psychotic symptoms for a brief period of time or for a longer duration. They may also show delusions, affective problems outside the normal range, or simply seem odd to those around them. Psychotic symptoms not part of schizophrenia can be induced through drugs, lack of sleep, and other medical conditions. Also, it should be noted that although the term schizophrenia comes from the Greek meaning *to split the mind*, it is a very different disorder from dissociation disorders, such as dissociative identity disorder.

Individuals with schizophrenia can display problems in terms of cognitive processes, emotional processes, and motor processes. Cognitive problems can be seen as a disorganization of thinking and behavior. In listening to a person with schizophrenia, you may note a speech style that, although detailed, does not seem to have a coherent focus and does seem to constantly change themes. Technically, these are referred to as *circumstantiality* and *tangentiality*. In more severe cases, the speech is actually incoherent and contains a stream of words that are unrelated to one another, which is referred to as *word salad*.

Mood symptoms include impairments in affective experience and expression. Depression is a common experience with schizophrenia along with thoughts of suicide. A number of individuals with schizophrenia hear voices that tell them to kill themselves. Ken Steele wrote about his experiences with schizophrenia in his book *The Day the Voices Stopped*. Ken Steele's voices told him "Hang yourself. The world will be better off. You're no good, no good at all" (Steele & Berman, 2001). Motor symptoms can range from repetitive behaviors such as rocking to total stiffness or lack of change in posture referred to as *catatonia*.

Different individuals with schizophrenia may show very different symptoms. For example, some individuals may hear voices but never see a visual hallucination. Others show a still different presentation of symptoms. This has led some researchers to conclude that there exist a variety of similar disorders that are currently described by the term schizophrenia. This would suggest that schizophrenia is not a single disorder but a number of related disorders that are described by the name schizophrenia.

The symptoms of schizophrenia are not constantly present. There are examples of individuals with schizophrenia who are able to finish college and maintain jobs, even high-level jobs. Elyn R. Saks, who you will meet in the next chapter is a professor of law, psychology, and psychiatry and the behavioral sciences at the University of Southern California's law school. She describes her experiences with schizophrenia in a memoir, *The Center Cannot Hold: My Journey Through Madness*. Thus, individuals with schizophrenia may show periods in which they are able to function in terms of external realities. Symptoms for some people tend to appear in times of change or stress.

Positive and Negative Symptoms

Based on initial descriptions used by Hughlings Jackson in the 1800s, schizophrenia symptoms are referred to as *positive* or *negative* (Jackson, 1932). The more familiar **positive symptoms** are hallucinations, delusions, disorganized thinking, and disorganized behavior. The more familiar **negative symptoms** include lack of affect in situations that call for it, poor motivation, and social withdrawal. Jackson saw positive symptoms as reflecting a lack of high cortical control over more primitive brain processes. Negative symptoms, on the other hand, were the result of loss of function—what today we would refer to as a dysfunctional network of the brain. It should be noted that positive or negative are not evaluative terms when applied to symptoms of schizophrenia. Instead, they indicate either the presence of something unusual such as hearing voices or seeing hallucinations, which would be positive symptoms, or the lack of a normal human process, such as poor motivation or social withdrawal, which would be negative symptoms.

Positive Symptoms

Hallucinations are sensory experiences that can involve any of the senses, although auditory hallucinations are the ones most commonly reported by individuals with schizophrenia. Ken Steele, while listening to music on the radio, heard it tell him to kill himself. Richard McLean in his book *Recovered not Cured: A Journey through Schizophrenia* reported that he picked up a phone to hear voices tell him that they were following his every move (McLean, 2003). These auditory hallucinations were experienced as coming from outside the person. Other individuals experience the voices or thoughts as coming from within their head. Individuals with schizophrenia report that they may hear voices throughout the day and on more than one day.

Delusions are beliefs without support for their occurrence and that are at odds with the individual's current environment. One hospitalized patient believed that the Central Intelligence Agency (CIA) had cameras in the drawer pulls of her dresser. John Hinckley, who tried to kill President Ronald Reagan, believed that Jodie Foster, the actress, would be impressed by this event. Another patient believed that God spoke to her when the dogs outside her house barked.

The most common delusions can be organized into categories. The first is *persecution*. This is the belief that other people or groups such as the CIA are plotting against the individual. John Nash wrote letters to the US government describing attempts of others to take over the world. The second category is *grandeur*. This is the belief that one is really a very famous person. The individual with schizophrenia may tell everyone that he is Jesus or some other famous figure. The third delusion is *control*. For example, the delusion is that someone or some entity such as aliens can put thoughts into one's mind. A related delusion is that others can hear or understand your thoughts without being told what they are. Finally, one common delusion is that one is special and that God or important individuals are speaking directly to the person.

Negative Symptoms

Negative symptoms seen in schizophrenia tend to be more constant and stable than positive symptoms. Several studies have linked negative symptoms with a poorer prognosis (see Foussias & Remington, 2010, for a review). Whereas it is usually the positive symptoms that result in a diagnosis of schizophrenia, it is the negative symptoms that tend to persist over time. Many individuals with schizophrenia have little interest in doing simple day-to-day activities such as taking a bath or shopping for food. This lack of will or volition is technically referred to as *avolition*. Individuals with schizophrenia also show a lack of interest in talking with others or answering questions with more than a one- or two-word answer. This is referred to as *alogia*. They also show a flattening of affect or difficulty expressing emotion. Another symptom is referred to as *anhedonia* or the inability to experience pleasure. One interesting finding is that those with schizophrenia do not experience visual illusions in the same way as others. This is described in the box: Applying Psychological Science: Charlie Chaplin Illusion.

Applying Psychological Science: Charlie Chaplin Illusion

One surprising finding is that those with schizophrenia tend to respond to visual illusions differently than individuals without schizophrenia. This has included the Rubin vase and Schroeder stairs illusions (see **Figure 14-6** and **Figure 14-7**). In one study, those with schizophrenia showed more reversals in the Rubin's vase and saw the Schroeder stairs from underneath rather than from above (Keil, Elbert, Rockstroh, & Ray, 1998). Another example of differential brain processing in individuals with schizophrenia is the Charlie Chaplin illusion. If healthy individuals look at a mask of Charlie Chaplin as it rotates, they will see the reverse side of the mask not as hollow but as convex. That is, even though the mask from behind should appear to go in, those without schizophrenia see it pop out as you would with a normal face. A video of the rotating mask can be seen online (http://www.richardgregory.org/experiments/). As you can see in the video, as the mask turns, an individual initially sees the hollow mask, but this changes into a normal face. Individuals with schizophrenia do not see the illusion and view the reverse side of the mask as hollow.

The Charlie Chaplin illusion has been studied with fMRI (Dima et al., 2009). What these researchers found was that individuals with schizophrenia and those without schizophrenia showed different types of connectivity in the brain. Specifically, individuals without schizophrenia showed more top-down processing when perceiving the illusion. This suggests that part of the illusion is the sensory expectation of how a face should appear. Thus, in individuals without schizophrenia, the brain creates the face as it should appear and not hollow as it actually is. Individuals with schizophrenia, on the other hand, show weakened top-down processes and stronger bottom-up processes. As a result, they see the sensory stimuli as they are without expectation. Overall, this is consistent with other research that suggests that individuals with schizophrenia

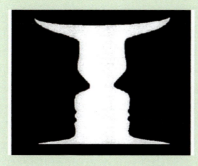

Figure 14-6 Rubin vase.

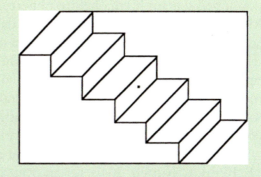

Figure 14-7 Schroeder stairs.

lack the top-down expectations necessary to predict future events (for example, Allen et al., 2008).

Thought Question: After reading this feature, how do you respond to the statement that the individual with a psychological disorder sees the "real" visual stimulus, whereas the "normal" individual sees "something that is not really there" based on expectations?

Factors in the Development of Schizophrenia

Schizophrenia typically is first noted during the transition from late adolescence to adulthood. However, theories related to its development generally see its onset at this time as the manifestation of a process that may have begun before the individual was born (see Uhlhaas, 2011, for an overview). In a review of birth cohort studies in which individuals are followed from birth, there is evidence to suggest that children who later develop schizophrenia show different profiles from those who do not (Welham, Isohanni, Jones, & McGrath, 2009). These data from seven different countries show subtle deficits in terms of behavioral disturbances, intellectual and language deficits, and early motor delays.

The current research literature suggests that schizophrenia is a disorder that begins early in life. This has led some researchers to suggest that we consider schizophrenia as a *neurodevelopmental disorder* (Insel, 2010). A variety of negative events can happen to a fetus, including infections and malnutrition. It has been shown, for example, that vitamin D deficiency during pregnancy can be seen as a risk for developing schizophrenia (see McGrath, Burne, Féron, Mackay-Sim, & Eyles, 2010, for a review). Likewise, maternal infection is now regarded as a potential risk factor for schizophrenia (see Brown & Patterson, 2011, for an overview).

Overall, the theory that the development of schizophrenia involves events experienced during pregnancy is referred to as the *neurodevelopmental hypothesis*. The basic idea is that during the time the fetus is in utero an insult happens that influences the changes to the brain that later take place during adolescence.

We know that adolescence is a time of great reorganization of cortical networks. What can be described about the reorganization of brain processes during adolescence in relation to schizophrenia? Gogtay, Vyas, Testa, Wood, and Pantelis (2011) reviewed two longitudinal studies with this question in mind. The first data set is composed of individuals who developed schizophrenia before puberty and has been studied at the National Institute of Mental Health (NIMH). The second data set is from Melbourne, Australia, and includes adolescents who are ultra-high risk for schizophrenia. Imaging studies showed larger ventricles and greater gray matter loss in the parietal and frontal areas in children who developed schizophrenia before puberty as compared with those who developed schizophrenia in adulthood. The data set from Australia showed that those adolescents who developed schizophrenia showed greater gray matter loss especially in the prefrontal cortex (PFC) as compared with those who did not develop the disorder.

Environmental factors can also play a role in the development of schizophrenia (see van Os, Kenis, & Rutten, 2010, for an overview). The basic idea is that environmental factors can influence the developing social brain and lead to the development of schizophrenia in those at risk. Such factors as early life adversity, growing up in an urban environment, and cannabis use have been associated with the development of schizophrenia. Being part of an ethnic group is not associated with schizophrenia per se if the ethnic group lives together, but if one is a minority in a larger ethnic group, then there is an association. Also, if one moves from an urban environment to a rural one, then the chance of having schizophrenia goes down. Overall, greater amounts of stress are associated with greater chances of developing schizophrenia. However, environmental factors continue to reflect an interaction with genetic influences and are not a sole condition in themselves for developing schizophrenia (Sariaslan et al., 2016).

Genetic Factors in Schizophrenia

Since schizophrenia tends to run in families and is seen throughout the world, it is assumed to have a genetic component. As can be seen in **Figure 14-8**, schizophrenia has a strong genetic component. The more similar the genes between two individuals, one of whom has schizophrenia, the more likely the other person will also develop its characteristics. That is, if you are an identical twin (MZ) and your twin has schizophrenia, you have a 48% chance of experiencing schizophrenia. If you are a fraternal twin, the risk drops to 18%. If one of your first-degree relatives, such as a parent or sibling, had schizophrenia, you would have a 9% risk. The risk would be even lower (4%) if you had a grandparent or aunt or uncle with schizophrenia. However, the genetic underpinnings of schizophrenia are not simple. It is clearly not the result of a single gene as with some other neurological disorders such as Huntington's disease.

Research suggests that the number of genetic variants seen in individuals with schizophrenia is very large. There may be 1,000 different genes contributing to the disorder, which also include rare genetic variants (Cannon, 2015; Keller, 2018; Walker, Shapiro, Esterberg, & Trotman, 2010; Wray & Visscher, 2010). These genes may act in an additive or interactive manner to produce the disorder. That is to say, there may be a variety of genetic combinations that are associated with schizophrenia. For example, heritable traits such as white matter connections and the thickness of gray matter in the brain are reduced in individuals with schizophrenia. Those with schizophrenia show both fewer connections that link different parts of the brain and a reduction of dendrite connections at the level of the neuron. Adolescence and early adulthood bring extensive elimination of synapses in regions of the cerebral cortex, such as the prefrontal cortex. An impairment of this process takes place in those with schizophrenia.

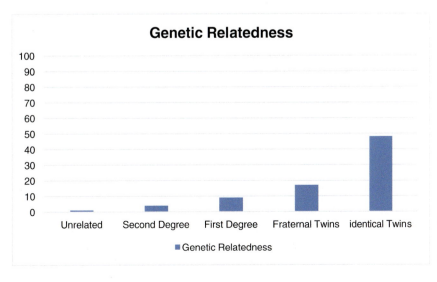

Figure 14-8 Risk for schizophrenia increases with genetic relatedness.
Source: Gottesman (1991).

Psychological Disorders

Brain Changes Seen in Schizophrenia

Exactly when brain changes take place in those with schizophrenia is an important question. In order to better understand the role of timing in terms of brain structure, John Gilmore and his colleagues (2010) performed imaging studies before and after birth. These researchers used ultrasound scans prior to birth and magnetic resonance imaging (MRI) scans after birth while the babies slept. They compared children whose mothers had schizophrenia with a matched control group whose mothers did not have the disorder. Using ultrasound prior to birth, they found no differences between the two groups. After birth, males whose mothers had schizophrenia showed more gray matter in the brain, increased cerebrospinal fluid, and larger ventricles. Female infants did not show any differences. This suggests that at least the genetic setup for schizophrenia in males can be seen early in life.

Neuroimaging studies of those with schizophrenia have included both structural and functional approaches (see Giraldo-Chica, Rogers, Damon, Landman, & Woodward, 2018; Karlsgodt et al., 2010; Shenton & Turetsky, 2011, for overviews). Structural approaches have focused on gray matter and white matter differences as well as the size of the ventricles (Cannon, 2015; Thompson et al., 2001). In a variety of reviews, both general and specific reductions in gray matter have been reported for individuals with schizophrenia. Specifically, reductions have been in the temporal cortex, especially the hippocampus, the frontal lobe, and the parietal lobe. Additionally, the striatum part of the basal ganglia has been shown to be reduced (Shenton et al., 2001). Gray matter reductions have also been seen in cases when one identical twin has schizophrenia and the other does not.

What might be at the heart of this gray matter reduction? One possibility is that the neurons actually die. However, a number of studies suggest this is not the case. What has been found is that the neurons in the brains of individuals with schizophrenia are more densely packed. This suggests that the substance found between neurons, *neuropil*, was reduced, resulting in a greater density of neurons. Further, gray matter abnormalities have been shown to be partly hereditary and also related to trauma during pregnancy (see Karlsgodt et al., 2010, for an overview). Those individuals with schizophrenia show a reduction of gray matter over a five-year period (Thompson et al., 2001). **Figure 14-9** shows the differences in gray matter between individuals with schizophrenia and normal controls.

White matter changes have also been observed in individuals with schizophrenia. One study compared 114 individuals with schizophrenia with 138 matched controls in terms

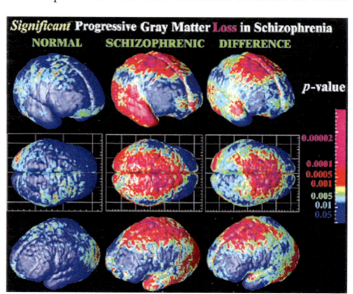

Figure 14-9 Annual loss of gray matter in those with schizophrenia.

Ventricles in the Brain

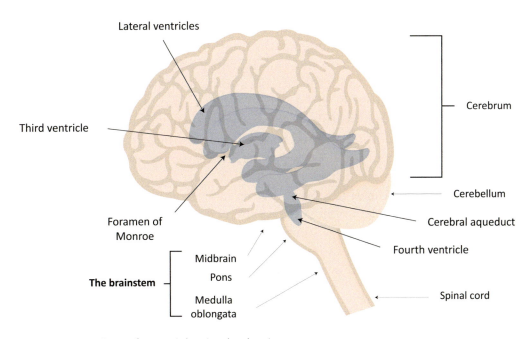

Figure 14-10 Location of ventricles in the brain.

of white matter (White et al., 2011). Using a brain-imaging technique—diffusion tensor imaging (DTI)—sensitive to white matter, individuals with chronic schizophrenia, individuals with first episode schizophrenia, and matched controls were compared. Measures of white matter were lower for individuals with chronic schizophrenia in the four lobes of the brain but not in the cerebellum or brain stem. Individuals experiencing their first episode of schizophrenia did not show significant differences from controls, which suggests that white matter reduction is part of the progression of the disorder over time.

There are four ventricles in the brain (see **Figure 14-10**). These ventricles contain cerebrospinal fluid. From a number of studies, it has been shown that individuals with schizophrenia have larger ventricles (see Vita, de Peri, Silenzi, & Dieci, 2006, for a meta-analysis). Since the walls of the ventricles are not rigid, it is assumed that larger ventricles result from a decrease in volume in other areas of the brain. Some of the other areas that have been shown to be smaller in individuals with schizophrenia are the frontotemporal cortices, the anterior cingulate cortex (ACC), and the right insular cortex. One question is whether this reduction could be related to the medications that individuals with schizophrenia take. To answer this question, one study examined individuals with first episode schizophrenia and compared their brain structure with that of matched healthy controls (Rais et al., 2012). These researchers found brain volume loss in the individuals with schizophrenia. This suggests that the brain volume loss is present when symptoms begin. They found reduced volume in the temporal and insular cortex. Brain-imaging studies have shown a larger ventricle in an MZ twin who had schizophrenia and a smaller one in the twin who did not.

In summary, gray matter and white matter changes along with differences in ventricles have been found in schizophrenia in a large number of studies. In addition to these changes in the brains of individuals with schizophrenia, researchers have sought to study cortical networks in schizophrenia.

Myths and Misconceptions: Those Who Have Hallucinations Have Serious Mental Disorders

If someone were to tell you that he hears voices or sees people you do not see, you might think that he had a serious mental disorder such as psychosis or schizophrenia. While that may be true, it is also the case that just hearing voices or having visual hallucinations is not always the result of a serious mental disorder. In fact, visual hallucinations can be produced by the medication that some people with Parkinson's disease take. Further, people who have lost some of their vision may have visual hallucinations. This is a condition referred to as Charles Bonnet syndrome. Overall, those who take Parkinson's medication or have Charles Bonnet syndrome know that what they are seeing is not actual reality.

What about hearing voices? It is now increasingly recognized that many individuals in the general population hear voices in the absence of distress or psychiatric disorder (Hill & Lindon, 2013). One survey found that 10% to 15% of the people in the United States reported either visual or auditory hallucinations (Tien, 1991). Of all the people who hear voices, only a small percentage seek help and would be diagnosed with a serious mental disorder.

Albert Powers and his colleagues at Yale University sought to study those who claim to hear voices but would not be diagnosed with a psychological disorder (Powers, Kelley, & Corlett, 2017). To do this, they studied self-identified psychics. They compared the psychics with three other groups of individuals. These were (1) people with a serious mental disorder who hear voices; (2) people without a serious mental disorder who hear voices (psychics); (3) those with a serious mental disorder who do not hear voices; and (4) those without a serious mental disorder and do not hear voices. These individuals were given a number of questionnaires designed to measure psychological symptoms, delusions, and agreement with religious beliefs. In terms of hearing voices, these researchers found the hallucinatory experiences of psychic voice-hearers to be very similar to those of patients who were diagnosed with a mental disorder. Further, they found that this sample of non-help-seeking voice hearers were able to control the onset and offset of their voices and that they were less distressed by their voice-hearing experiences. Those with a serious mental disorder had much more negative voice-hearing experiences.

How should we understand hallucinations in those without a serious mental disorder? The first conclusion is that hallucinations use similar brain networks as those involved in vision and hearing. Thus, hallucinations are not totally different from normal vision and hearing and use the same circuits. The second conclusion is that hallucinations in non-clinical populations tend to be more positive and more under the control of the individual. And third, hallucinations in non-clinical populations may offer a way to understand the components that underlie more serious disorders (Baumeister, Sedgwick, Howes, & Peters, 2017). Although visual and auditory hallucinations can be a part of serious mental disorders, they can also exist in other situations. Oliver Sacks describes one of these individuals in a TED Talk (https://www.ted.com/talks/oliver_sacks_what_hallucination_reveals_about_our_minds).

Thought Question: Clearly, we can no longer say that just because a person has visual or auditory hallucinations, he or she has a mental disorder. What does processing the world "normally" mean? What might be the value of processing the world "differently"?

CONCEPT CHECK

1. In what ways are dissociative disorders similar to the types of dissociative experiences common to most people? In what ways are they different?
2. What are the defining characteristics of the following dissociative disorders:
    a. Depersonalization–derealization?
    b. Dissociative amnesia?
    c. Dissociative identity disorder (DID)?
3. How are the four stages of the course of schizophrenia defined, and when do they typically occur? Is the course the same for each individual? If not, how does it differ?
4. The symptoms of schizophrenia are characterized as positive symptoms and negative symptoms.
    a. What is the definition of each symptom type?
    b. What are primary examples of each type?
    c. What role does each type play in the course of schizophrenia?
5. Schizophrenia typically is first noted during the transition from late adolescence to adulthood, but current research suggests that the disorder begins early in life. What evidence points to this characterization?
6. What evidence can you cite that schizophrenia has a genetic component?
7. What structural brain changes in white matter and gray matter are characteristic of those with schizophrenia?

Personality Disorders and Personality

Am I completely selfish? Is that what all this is about? I must be because the one thing that scares me more than living, more than death, is surviving another suicide attempt. Then I would have to face up to my actions. Then I would have to try and mend the relationships that my selfishness has destroyed. So why do it? Why do I have such strong suicidal urges? Why have I had these urges all these years? Why does it seem to bear no relation to what is actually going on in my life? Why won't the God damn shrinks tell me that one? Have I got too much of the suicidal gene in my DNA? Are there too many suicidal chemicals in my brain? Can't they give me a pill that deals with that? They can't can they? They send me to therapy with three different people and not one of them has been able to touch on just why. Why a kid from the country village of Wymondley grew up from catching newts and making camps to slashing his wrists and taking overdoses. Surely there is something in between those two events that has made me this way? . . . But no one can help me and I have always been meant to kill myself, so that's what will have to happen. It is my unwritten destiny. It gets to the point where I feel that I really have to do it. It is not even a choice anymore. I must obey.

You might ask how I can do it to my family. How I can do this to the girl I love. Well, the guilt I feel about my plans to die is just as strong as my urge to carry them out. It is as if someone else, the other me, made those plans for me. When Ashley comes home from work I usually put that other me aside and I am there for her, but sometimes he stays like a great dark cloud smothering my thoughts. Living for the sake of someone else is not easy. I wish that I wanted to live for myself, but I probably never will.

(From Westwood, 2007, p. 5)

As you read the self-report from Stephen Westwood above, you probably had a number of reactions. You might have thought of others you know who react in similar ways. You might have thought about how you would react and what upsets you. You might have wondered why some people seem to be so dramatic in everything they do. Some people will tell you that they cut themselves or burn themselves when they experience psychological pain. Steven Westwood tells you that all he thinks about is suicide. However, he also tells you that he can have a relationship with a girlfriend. People who have these types of relationships with themselves and others are described in terms of personality disorders.

What Is a Personality Disorder?

The basic definition of a ***personality disorder*** is that it represents an enduring pattern of inner experience and behavior that deviates markedly from the expectations of the individual's culture (APA, 2013, p. 645). Further, the pattern is inflexible, stable, and generally begins in adolescence, and leads to distress or impairment. The characteristics of these disorders are especially apparent when these individuals find themselves in situations that are beyond their ability to cope. *DSM-5* identifies ten personality disorders that form separate categories. These ten disorders can be organized into three clusters, which are presented in **Table 14-4**.

Table 14-4 Three clusters of personality disorder.

Disorder	Characteristics	Prevalence
Cluster A	*Odd or eccentric disorders*	5.7%
Paranoid	Pervasive distrust and suspiciousness of others; sees others as having malevolent intentions	2.3–4.4%
Schizoid	Detachment from social relationships and restriction of the expression of emotions in interpersonal settings.	3.1–4.9%
Schizotypal	Discomfort with close relationships; Cognitive and perceptual distortions and eccentricities of behavior	3.3–3.9%
Cluster B	*Dramatic, emotional, or erratic disorders*	1.5%
Antisocial	Disregard for and violation of the rights of others	0.2–3.3%
Borderline	Instability of interpersonal relationships and impulsivity	1.6–5.9%
Histrionic	Excessive emotionality and attention seeking	1.8%
Narcissistic	Grandiosity, need for admiration, and lack of empathy	6.2%
Cluster C	*Anxious or fearful disorders*	6%
Avoidant	Social inhibition, feelings of inadequacy, and hypersensitivity to negative evaluation	2.4–5.2%
Dependent	Need to be taken care of, clinging behaviors, and fear of separation	0.49–0.6%
Obsessive-compulsive	Preoccupation with orderliness, perfectionism, and control at the expense of flexibility, openness, and efficiency	2.1–7.9%

Note: Prevalence based on APA (2013) and Lenzenweger et al. (2007).

The first cluster is referred to as *Cluster A* and includes *odd or eccentric disorders*. These include *schizoid personality disorder, paranoid personality disorder*, and *schizotypal personality disorder*. Individuals with these disorders typically feel uncomfortable or suspicious of others or restrict their relationships. Schizoid personality disorder is characterized by a pervasive pattern of detachment from social relationships and a restricted range of emotional expression. Paranoid personality disorder is characterized by a pervasive distrust and suspiciousness of others. Schizotypal personality disorder is characterized by odd beliefs and behaviors.

The second cluster is referred to as *Cluster B* and includes *dramatic, emotional, or erratic disorders*. These include *antisocial personality disorder, borderline personality disorder (BPD), histrionic personality disorder*, and *narcissistic personality disorder*. Individuals with these disorders show a wide diversity of patterns of social and emotional interactions with others. Antisocial personality disorder is characterized by a disregard for the other person. BPD is characterized by instability in relationships. Histrionic personality disorder is characterized by excessive emotional responding and the seeking of attention. Narcissistic personality disorder is characterized by grandiosity in terms of one's abilities and a lack of empathy.

The third cluster is referred to as *Cluster C* and includes *anxious or fearful disorders*. These include *avoidant personality disorder, dependent personality disorder*, and *obsessive-compulsive personality disorder*. Avoidant personality disorder is characterized by a pattern of social inhibition, feelings of inadequacy, and hypersensitivity to negative evaluation. Dependent personality disorder is characterized by an excessive need to be taken care of, including clinging behavior. Obsessive-compulsive personality disorder is characterized by a preoccupation with orderliness, perfectionism, and interpersonal control.

In a number of community samples, personality disorders are found in 9% to 13% of the population (see Lawton, Shields, & Oltmanns, 2011; Lenzenweger, 2008; Tyrer, Reed, & Crawford, 2015 for overviews). This suggests that one in ten people suffers from a personality disorder. Overall, similar numbers of males and females are seen in each personality disorder. The only exception is antisocial personality disorder, which is seen more frequently in men.

In terms of the three clusters, Cluster A shows a prevalence of 5.7%, Cluster B shows a prevalence of 1.5%, and Cluster C shows a prevalence of 6% in a community sample (Lenzenweger, Lane, Loranger, & Kessler, 2007), although prevalence rates vary by a few percent in different studies. Estimates from World Health Organization (WHO) surveys of 13 countries suggest a worldwide prevalence of about 6.1% for having any one personality disorder and 3.6% for Cluster A, 1.5% for Cluster B, and 2.7% for Cluster C (Huang et al., 2009).

Personality Disorders and Typical Personality Traits

Not only do the ten separate personality disorders show considerable overlap with other mental disorders, they also show considerable overlap with traits found in typical personality patterns (see Bagby & Widiger, 2018; Costa & Widiger, 2002; Krueger & Markon, 2014; Samuel & Widiger, 2008; South, Oltmanns, & Krueger, 2011, for overviews). In one study, measures of typical personality functioning and pathological personality functioning showed a shared dimensional structure (Samuel, Simms, Clark, Livesley, & Widiger, 2010). That is to say, personality characteristics reflected in personality disorders can be seen as an extreme version of typical personality characteristics.

Initially, the studies concerning typical personality factors and personality disorders were conducted separately. In the development of *DSM*, scales were conducted and analyzed in terms of the symptoms of personality disorder. These separate studies have found a five-factor structure of personality disorder characteristics (see DeYoung, Carey, Krueger,

& Ross, 2016 for an overview). These five factors emphasize the opposite poles of typical personality dimensions. These factors have been labeled *detachment, negative affectivity, antagonism, disinhibition, and psychoticism*. Detachment, for example, can be seen as the extreme and opposite version of extraversion.

Thus, there can be both healthy and maladaptive personality styles. An individual can be extraverted in a healthy manner by seeking relationships with others and developing warm and meaningful relationships. He can also enjoy large parties and feel fulfilled by meeting new people. This could also occur in a maladaptive manner in which the individual has a need to always be with others and to value himself only when in a relationship. An individual can also be introverted in a healthy way by valuing his inner experiences such as writing poetry or enjoying walks alone or with a friend. One could also be introverted in a maladaptive manner by avoiding or distrusting others and living a life without meaningful contact with others and one's self.

Antisocial Personality Disorder

The diagnostic criteria in *DSM–5* for **antisocial personality disorder** describe a person who shows a pattern of disregard for the rights of others. A person with this disorder must be 18 years old, and the personality style should have been present since 15 years of age. Before age 15, the person should meet criteria for a conduct disorder. Child conduct disorder includes aggression toward animals or people, destruction of property, deception or stealing, and serious rule violations. Three specific characteristics should also currently be present for a diagnosis of antisocial personality disorder. These characteristics include (1) a failure to observe social norms that can result in legal arrest, (2) a deceitfulness including lying to and using others, (3) a failure to plan ahead, (4) an irritability and aggressiveness that lead to physical fights, (5) a reckless disregard for the safety of others, (6) an irresponsibility, such as a failure to pay debts or perform duties at work, and (7) a lack of remorse when another person is hurt.

The prevalence rate for antisocial personality disorder is about 3%, with more males than females having the disorder. Those with antisocial disorder also show a high comorbidity (80%) with the use of drugs (see Patrick, 2007, for an overview). However, the opposite is not the case. That is, those who use drugs do not necessarily have an antisocial personality disorder. The prevalence of antisocial personality disorder also tends to be higher in correctional and forensic settings. In prisons, the base rates have been recorded between 50% and 80% of the population (Hare, 2003). Often those who are mandated by the courts for treatment of sexual offences would qualify for an antisocial personality disorder.

Borderline Personality Disorder (BPD)

Borderline personality disorder (BPD) is characterized by an instability in mood, interpersonal relationships, and a sense of self (see Bradley, Conklin, & Westen, 2007, for an overview). These three factors interact with one another in such a manner that the person with BPD experiences a changing world without a solid sense of self. At one point, the person may feel rejected and abandoned due to a misinterpretation of an event and lash out in anger. At other times, they may see another person as perfect and form an intense relationship only to have that go to its opposite without warning. The movie *Fatal Attraction* released in 1987 and the 2015–2019 TV series *Crazy Ex-Girlfriend* show this type of intense relationship seen in people with BPD.

In her book *Borderline Traits*, Arlene Roberson describes the experiences of a person with BPD: "I go from feeling panicked and angry to feeling depressed and hurt to feeling

Table 14-5 Functions of self-injurious behavior.

Feel pain	60%
Punish self	50%
Control feelings	40%
Exert control	22%
Express anger	22%
Feel	20%

Source: Shearer, Peters, Quaytman, and Wadman (1988).

anxious" (Roberson, 2010). It continues: "I have to react to this pain by lashing out at everything and everyone around me." This lashing out includes not only angry outbursts at others but also self-mutilating behaviors and suicide attempts. It is estimated that 75% of those with BPD engage in self-injurious behavior. Two common behaviors are to cut or burn themselves. Some say that the external pain from burning or cutting gives them an experience that they are alive compared with feeling that they do not exist. For those with BPD, feelings of emptiness and boredom are common as well as feelings of being special or having exceptional talents. **Table 14-5** shows some of the common functions of self-injurious behavior as reported by female inpatients.

Self-harm is closely related to attempts to regulate one's emotions. One review of the literature suggests three aspects of this relationship (Klonsky, 2007). The first aspect is that acute negative affect precedes self-injury. The second aspect is that after self-injury, individuals report relief. The third aspect is that individuals engage in self-injury as a means to reduce their experience of negative affect. Although many studies involve self-report, similar findings were seen in research studies performed in the lab.

Although self-harm is different from suicide, successful suicide is estimated to be about 9% in clinical samples with BPD. Also, suicide threats or gestures are estimated to occur in 90% of clinical samples with BPD (Gunderson & Ridolfi, 2001). Their view of self and others is sometimes described in terms of *splitting* or having things be all good or all bad without the nuance most individuals experience in their relationships. Thus, people with BPD have a sense of self that is fluid and can change quickly.

The conceptualization of BPD has been greatly influenced by the work of Kernberg (1984, 1995), who viewed these individuals as using immature ways of dealing with impulses and emotions. Historically, the term *borderline,* as the name implies, denoted individuals who were neither neurotic nor psychotic. Although not out of touch with reality, when under stress, these individuals can become disorganized in their view of self and others. On the other hand, their experiences go beyond those seen in anxiety or depression where the tendency is to withdraw when experiencing psychological distress.

One term that has been used to describe individuals with BPD is *fearful preoccupation* (Levy, 2005). This reflects an intense need for attention and closeness on the one hand and a deep fear of rejection and abandonment on the other. Thus, these individuals want to be close but become fearful and then angry when they experience closeness. Anger is also seen whenever individuals perceive they are being rejected.

Although genetic factors may play a role in terms of the trait of impulsivity, environmental factors play an important role. About 70% of these individuals report some type of physical, emotional, or sexual abuse. Overall, there is evidence to suggest that the development of BPD is related to heightened risk from chaotic family life, increased stress experienced by the parents, and disruptive communications between the caregiver and the child.

The disorder is also related to attachment (see Levy, 2005, for an overview). In general, individuals with BPD show an insecure pattern of attachment. Only some 6% to 8% show secure attachment patterns. Studies that used dimensional measures of BPD show an inverse relationship between secure attachment and BPD. Further, studies that have looked at early loss or separation in children found that it occurred in 37% to 64% of individuals with BPD.

The diagnostic criteria in *DSM–5* for BPD describe a person who shows a pattern of instability and impulsivity in social relationships and his or her self-image. This personality style should begin in early adulthood. Five specific characteristics should also be present. These characteristics include (1) a frantic effort to avoid abandonment, whether real or imagined; (2) a pattern of unstable and intense interpersonal relationships characterized by alternating idealization and devaluation; (3) an unstable self-image and sense of self; (4) impulsivity in areas that can be damaging such as sexual relations, substance abuse, reckless driving, and binge eating; (5) recurrent suicidal behaviors or self-mutilating behaviors; (6) emotional instability lasting only a few hours; (7) chronic feelings of emptiness; (8) inappropriate anger and ability to control anger; and (9) short-term stress-related dissociative experiences or paranoid ideation. The current *DSM–5* criteria for BPD can be met in a variety of ways. Given the nine criteria, there are at least 150 different ways that a person can receive the diagnosis based on various combinations of the criteria. This suggests that the instability of the self and its functioning can be manifested in a number of ways.

One way the instability manifests for society is that individuals with BPD are high consumers of emergency room services, crisis lines, and referrals from health professionals to mental health services (see Bradley et al., 2007). It is estimated that individuals with BPD represent 20% of inpatients and 10% of outpatients in mental health clinics. Prevalence rates in community samples are about 1.6%, as found in the National Comorbidity Survey Replication (Lenzenweger et al., 2007).

CONCEPT CHECK

1. What is the basic definition of a personality disorder?
2. *DSM-5* has organized personality disorders into three clusters—A, B, and C. What are the defining characteristics that run through the personality disorders in each cluster? What is an example of a disorder in each cluster?
3. What is the relationship between the five-factor model of personality you read about in the chapter on personality and what you have read in this chapter on personality disorders?
4. What are the three defining characteristics of borderline personality disorder (BPD)?
5. What role do self-mutilating behaviors and suicide attempts play in individuals with BPD?
6. What environmental factors play a role in the development of BPD?

Neurodevelopmental Disorders

Neurodevelopmental disorders are those disorders that begin early in a child's life. These can include problems in the development of language, as well as cognitive, emotional, and motor problems. Two of these disorders are autism spectrum disorder and attention deficit hyperactivity disorder (ADHD).

Autism Spectrum Disorder (ASD)

Autism was initially described by Leo Kanner (1943) as an innate disorder in which children do not show normal development in emotional contact with others. Autism spectrum disorder (ASD) has achieved a significant place in clinical and research programs. Individuals with **autism spectrum disorder (ASD)** have difficulty in three separate areas. The first is *social interactions*. Children with autism do not connect with other children or adults in the manner that other children do. They do not look others in the eye or may appear to ignore others while being more interested in other aspects of their environment. The second area is *communication*. The communication patterns of those with autism spectrum disorder do not usually show the give-and-take of most conversations. The third area is *behavioral processes*. Individuals with autism spectrum disorder often engage in the same behavior in a repetitive manner (Baron-Cohen & Belmonte, 2005; Kamio, Tobimatsu, & Fukui, 2011). About 30% of children with ASD may also show additional complications such as seizure disorders, intellectual disabilities of various kinds, and gastrointestinal problems.

DSM–5 uses ASD as the new single disorder "umbrella" term for what were previously separate disorders—*autistic disorder*, *Asperger's disorder*, and a *general pervasive developmental disorder*—to be evaluated and specified on a continuum (spectrum). In *DSM-5*, the term *Asperger's syndrome*, which had been added to the *DSM* in 1994, is no longer used. Historically, Asperger's disorder was the diagnostic term for a milder form of autism in which developmental language delays may not be present. Also, compared with many others with autism, individuals identified with Asperger's are high-functioning in social processes, and show average to above average cognitive skills. General pervasive developmental disorder was characterized in *DSM–IV* as a disorder in which the full criteria for autism were not met, and the individuals exhibited a much lower level of functioning.

Some researchers suggest that autism spectrum disorder offers us a way to study brain development that takes a non-normal route (Wicker & Gomot, 2011), and acknowledges a sharp gradation of functioning level among those with the disorder. *ICD-11* combined autism spectrum disorder and **Asperger's syndrome** as a single disorder. Those with the Asperger's side of autism spectrum disorder report that they do not see the world as others do.

An example of a person who would have been diagnosed with Asperger's syndrome is Temple Grandin. Temple Grandin described her experiences of being a person who experienced an autism spectrum disorder (Grandin, 2009, 2010). She described how at age 2 and a half she did not speak and performed actions in a repetitive manner. She was also very sensitive to certain sounds and would respond to these by rocking or staring at sand dribbling through her fingers. Later as a child, she had no understanding of how people relate to one another. She would watch others, trying to understand how she should behave.

Figure 14-11 Temple Grandin has experienced a special relationship with animals.
Source: Associated Press.

Temple Grandin became very productive. She received her PhD and is a professor of animal sciences at Colorado State University. She has consulted with many companies concerning how to design environments that treat livestock in a humane manner. She, herself, describes individuals with autism as *specialized thinkers* (Grandin, 2009). For her, they are specialized in one of three types of thinking. The first is *visual thinking,* which allows one to view the world and even words in terms of images. The second is *pattern thinking,* in which the thinking is in terms of patterns such as those seen in music and mathematics. The third is *word and fact thinking,* in which the individual displays an ability to know a large number of facts such as baseball scores or the names of films and who their stars were. More formal research articles have also shown that hypersensitivity to sensory information along with strong logical reasoning ability may be at the basis of talent seen in individuals with autism spectrum disorder (Baron-Cohen, Ashwin, Ashwin, Tavassoli, & Chakrabarti, 2009). An exception to sensory sensitivity is found with odors. Children with autism spectrum disorder show little reaction to strong unpleasant odors such as sour milk or rotten fish (Rozenkrantz et al., 2015).

Causes of Autism Spectrum Disorder

Autism was initially thought to be largely influenced by environmental factors. In the 1960s and 1970s, individuals with autism were considered to have a form of psychosis similar to childhood schizophrenia. Consistent with the historical view at that time, environmental factors such as bad parenting were suggested to be a cause of the disorder. Often, the mother was seen as the cause of the disorder. Another study suggested that measles, mumps, and rubella (MMR) vaccinations produced changes in the infant that led to autism. Not only has this been shown to be false; it was discovered that the original research was fraudulent. Today parenting or social factors are seen to play little role at all with genetic factors being more important.

Autism has been shown to have a strong genetic component (see Dawson et al., 2009, for an overview). Concordance rates from numerous studies of twins in terms of autism show a range from 69% to 95% for monozygotic (MZ) twins and 0% to 24% for dizygotic (DZ) twins. Also, relatives of those with autism show higher rates of autism-like symptoms. The farther a relative is from the person with autism, the fewer symptoms that are seen. This suggests that autism involves a genetic pathway involving a number of genes in a complex manner. In fact, hundreds of genetic differences have been associated with autism but each of these represents a small percentage of cases (see Klin, Shultz, & Jones, 2015, for an overview).

There is also some suggestion that autism spectrum disorder shares common genetic processes with schizophrenia (Chisholm, Lin, Abu-Akel, & Wood, 2015). There is also a connection with *attention deficit hyperactivity disorder* (ADHD) (Lord & Bishop, 2015). A large-scale study of more than 10,000 twin pairs in Sweden reported that an MZ twin with autism spectrum disorder had a 44% chance of also being diagnosed with ADHD, whereas a DZ twin had only a 15% chance (Lichtenstein, Carlstrom, Råstam, Gillberg, & Anckarsäter, 2010).

In addition, genetic factors show a complex relationship involving environmental factors such as the age of the mother (see Waterhouse, 2012, for an overview). Younger mothers have the lowest risk for having children with ASD, and older mothers have the highest risk. There is also some suggestion that the mother's health during pregnancy is associated with ASD, although the exact factors remain ambiguous. Fathers more than 50 years of age have four times the risk of having a child with autism. Whether this is related to the older males having a different quality of sperm is not known.

Brain Contributions to Autism Spectrum Disorder

In terms of the brain, it is suggested that ASD reflects dysfunction in areas associated with the social brain (see Minshew & Williams, 2007, for an overview). Briefly, these are the amygdala, specific areas of the frontal lobes, and areas of the temporal lobe. Further, those with autism were shown to have less activity in the mirror neuron system when viewing emotional expressions of faces (Dapretto et al., 2006). In those with autism, there was a negative correlation between cortical activity during this task and the severity of symptoms in the social domain. Another characteristic of autism is the desire to have a stable set of routines, which results in problems shifting attention.

Adolescents with ASD show fewer whole-brain connections than a control group (Moseley et al., 2015). This was particularly true in networks involved in visual processing and the default network. However, those with ASD show more connections between the primary sensory areas and subcortical areas such as the thalamus and basal ganglia (Cerliani et al., 2015). This can help to explain why those with ASD focus more on sensory stimuli rather than social processes.

Attention Deficit Hyperactivity Disorder (ADHD)

Attention deficit hyperactivity disorder (ADHD) is a disorder of childhood that tends to develop before the age of 12 and is seen worldwide (Hinshaw, 2018). Although the conceptualization of ADHD has changed over the years, it currently includes two major dimensions (see Adler, Spencer, & Wilens, 2015; Frick & Nigg, 2012, for overviews). The first dimension is *inattention*. Children and adults with inattention problems tend to exhibit these in a cognitive realm such as letting their mind wander or not paying attention. As shown with the inattention diagnostic criteria, these individuals may have difficulty paying close attention to details or focusing on activities such as schoolwork or lectures, appear disorganized, be unwilling to engage in activities that require mental effort, and be easily distracted. Individuals with this type of ADHD may also show learning problems.

The second dimension is *hyperactivity and impulsivity*. Children with hyperactivity and impulsivity tend to show these symptoms in a behavioral or motor realm. As shown in the hyperactivity and impulsivity diagnostic criteria, these individuals may have difficulty waiting their turn, waiting to respond, keeping still, and remaining in their seat. Children with this type of ADHD may also show conduct problems. There is some suggestion that hyperactivity problems may lessen as a child grows older, whereas attentional problems may increase, resulting in increasing difficulty with schoolwork. It is also possible that individuals with ADHD show characteristics of both inattention and hyperactivity.

ADHD is reported to be the most common emotional–behavioral disorder treated in youth (see Wilens, Biederman, & Spencer, 2002, for an overview). Epidemiological studies suggest a prevalence rate of 4% to 5% of children in the United States, New Zealand, Australia, Germany, and Brazil. Of those with ADHD, some 20% to 30% have the inattentive subtype, less than 15% have the hyperactive-impulsive subtype, and 50% to 75% have a combination of both. Although long-term studies show different rates, it is assumed that more than 50% of the children with ADHD will show continued ADHD into adolescence. A smaller proportion will show ADHD symptoms in adulthood.

Adults with ADHD show more symptoms related to inattention as compared with hyperactivity and impulsivity (Kessler et al., 2010). Specifically, almost half (45.7%) of the individuals studied who had childhood ADHD continued to meet full *DSM–IV* criteria for current adult ADHD, with 94.9% of these cases having attention deficit disorder and 34.6% hyperactivity disorder. According to the Centers for Disease Control and Prevention (CDC), boys are more likely (13.2%) than girls (5.6%) to be diagnosed with ADHD (www.cdc.gov/ncbddd/adhd/data.html).

CONCEPT CHECK

1. Individuals with autism spectrum disorder (ASD) have difficulty in three separate areas. What are those areas and what specific types of difficulty do these individuals encounter in each area?
2. Some researchers suggest that autism spectrum disorder (ASD) offers us a way to study brain development that takes a non-normal route. Temple Grandin, who is on the spectrum, describes individuals with ASD as *specialized thinkers*. Give a brief description of the three types of thinking she describes.
3. What are the primary genetic, environmental, and neurological factors related to autism spectrum disorder (ASD)?
4. Describe the two (2) primary dimensions of attention deficit hyperactivity disorder (ADHD) and give an example of each.

Summary

Learning Objective 1: Explain how psychological disorders are classified and diagnosed.

We can consider four important personal components in *psychopathology*: first, a loss of freedom or ability to consider alternatives; second, a loss of honest personal contact; third, a loss of one's connection with one's self and ability to live in a productive manner; and fourth, personal distress. In many psychological disorders, personal distress for a period of time is one of the criteria required for a diagnosis to be made. There is also a more global component in which the person's behavior and experiences are considered to be different from cultural and statistical norms.

Stigma involves negative attitudes and beliefs that cause the general public to avoid others including those with a mental illness. Throughout the world, those with mental illness experience stigma. In many cultures, they are seen as different. When they are thus stigmatized, these individuals are no longer treated as an individual person, but only as part of a group that is different.

One of the major contributions of the 20th century toward understanding psychopathology was the creation of a reliable diagnosis and classification system. This system in the United States, referred to as *Diagnostic and Statistical Manual of Mental Disorders (DSM)*, made it easier for different mental health workers to label a disorder in the same way. For example, generalized anxiety disorder (GAD) was described in terms of "Excessive anxiety and worry (apprehensive expectation), occurring more days than not for at least 6 months, about a number of events or activities (such as work or school performance)."

Neuroscience techniques such as brain imaging and genetic analysis have been developed and are available in the research and clinical community. These techniques not only allow one to note the particular symptoms present as seen with *DSM*, but also to ask how the brain is involved in the disorder. Researchers have sought to determine the genetic components involved in particular disorders. We have discovered in children that ADHD (attention deficit hyperactivity disorder) is heritable, but that aggressive and disruptive conduct is not. A variety of genetic studies suggest that genetic factors account for about 82% of the variance in schizophrenia, suggesting that environmental factors are less critical in the development of schizophrenia.

We refer to a collection of symptoms that occur together and have a particular course of development over time as a *syndrome*. By describing disorders in terms of patterns of symptoms, Emil Kraepelin set the stage for diagnostic systems in both the United States and Europe.

A *mental disorder* contains five features: (a) a behavioral or psychological syndrome or pattern that occurs in an individual; (b) reflects an underlying psychobiological dysfunction; (c) the consequences are clinically significant distress; (d) must not be merely an expectable response to common stressors and losses or a culturally sanctioned response to a particular event; (e) is not primarily a result of social deviance or conflicts with society.

Research established mental illness was not a created concept by a given culture but rather part of the human condition in both its recognition and its prevalence. This set the stage for a development that came to be known as evolutionary psychopathology or Darwinian psychiatry.

Learning Objective 2: Describe the various types of anxiety, obsessive-compulsive, and mood disorders.

Anxiety is to be afraid of what might happen. Anxiety is about the future, whereas *fear* typically has a stimulus in the present. *Generalized anxiety disorder (GAD)* is characterized by excessive anxiety and worry. Its diagnosis in a clinical setting requires that anxiety and worry have been present for more than 6 months. GAD is one of the most commonly diagnosed mental disorders in the United States. It is more commonly seen in women than men. *Social anxiety disorder* is characterized by marked fear or anxiety about one or more social situations in which the individual is exposed to possible scrutiny by others. A *panic disorder* is an anxiety disorder that comes quickly and carries with it an intense feeling of apprehension, anxiety, or fear.

A *panic attack* is a frequent cause of individuals going to a hospital emergency room. *Agoraphobia* is the condition in which a person experiences fear or anxiety when in public. A *specific phobia* is an anxiety disorder in which an individual experiences fear or anxiety to a particular situation or object. Common phobias are fear of snakes, spiders, flying, heights, blood, injections, and the dark.

Obsessive-compulsive disorder (OCD) is characterized by repetitive thoughts and feelings usually followed by behaviors in response to them. The thoughts are usually perceived as unpleasant and not wanted. A distinction is made between *obsessions* and *compulsions*. *Obsessions* are generally unwelcome thoughts that come into our heads. *Compulsions* are the behaviors that individuals use to respond to their distressing thoughts. Overall, these behaviors are performed in order to reduce anxiety, gain control, or resist unwanted thoughts. Other compulsions, such as hand washing, are more avoidant in nature for fear of what one might say, do, or experience in a particular situation.

When depression is severe, it is referred to as *major depressive disorder (MDD)*. With major depressive disorder, a person feels sad and empty and may display an irritable mood. These feelings may include hopelessness and be experienced over a number of days. Body experiences, such as difficulty sleeping and eating, are also common.

Bipolar disorder was previously referred to as *manic-depressive disorder.* Changes in mood are an important aspect of bipolar disorders. These include the intense sense of well-being along with high energy seen in mania and its opposite seen in depression. Changes in cognition and perception also accompany these states. In mania, thoughts seem to flow easily, and many individuals find themselves very productive during mania. The depressive episodes show the opposite picture with the person experiencing a bleak outlook, low energy in a world of black-and-white, and a wish to do little.

Mental illness has a strong connection with suicide (see Goldsmith, 2001, for an overview). Of those suicide attempts that lead to death, it is estimated that 90% of adults and 67% of youth would meet diagnostic criteria for a mental disorder. The most common disorders associated with suicide are depression, bipolar disorder, substance use disorders, personality disorders, and schizophrenia, in that order. In bipolar and personality disorders, suicide is often associated with impulsiveness. With schizophrenia, it is more associated with active manifestation of the disorder. The rate of suicide among those with psychological disorders is highest in the three months following hospitalization.

Learning Objective 3: Discuss the dissociative disorders of depersonalization, dissociative amnesia, and dissociative identity disorder.

Dissociate disorders involve problems with memory. The dissociative experiences can last for a few minutes or hours but reoccur. They can also last for a longer period of time. Some of these experiences are severe and represent significant disruptions in the organization of identity, memory, perception, or consciousness. More pathological symptoms of dissociation are often connected with trauma and experiences greatly beyond the individual's control.

The main types include depersonalization–derealization disorder, dissociative amnesia, and dissociative identity disorder.

Learning Objective 4: Describe the main features and causes of schizophrenia.
Schizophrenia is part of a broad category of disorders referred to as *schizophrenia spectrum and other psychotic disorders*. *Psychotic disorders* involve a loss of being in touch with reality and are characterized by abnormal thinking and sensory processes. Individuals with a psychotic disorder may show delusions, hallucinations, disorganized thinking and speech, abnormal motor behaviors, and negative symptoms.

The course of schizophrenia generally first becomes evident in adolescence or young adulthood. The initial phase is referred to as the *premorbid phase*. This is followed by a *prodromal phase* in which initial positive symptoms along with declining functioning can be seen. The next phase is the *psychotic phase*, where the positive psychotic symptoms are apparent. For most individuals, this phase occurs between 15 and 45 years of age with the onset being about five years earlier in males than females. This phase is marked by repeated episodes of psychosis with remission in between. The greatest decline in functioning is generally seen during the first five years after the initial episode. This phase is followed by a *stable phase* characterized by fewer positive symptoms and an increase in negative ones. Stable cognitive and social deficits also characterize this phase. The actual course of the disorder varies greatly across individuals.

The current research literature suggests that schizophrenia is a disorder that begins early in life. This has led some researchers to suggest that we consider schizophrenia as a *neurodevelopmental disorder*. A variety of negative events can happen to a fetus, including infections and malnutrition. It has been shown, for example, that vitamin D deficiency and maternal infection during pregnancy can be seen as a risk for developing schizophrenia.

Environmental factors can also play a role in the development of schizophrenia. The basic idea is that environmental factors can influence the developing social brain and lead to the development of schizophrenia in those at risk. Greater amounts of stress are associated with greater chances of developing schizophrenia. Since schizophrenia tends to run in families and is seen throughout the world, it is assumed to have a genetic component. The risk of developing schizophrenia is much higher if someone else in your family also has the disorder.

Learning Objective 5: Discuss the basic characteristics of personality disorders.
The basic definition of a *personality disorder* is that it represents an enduring pattern of inner experience and behavior that deviates markedly from the expectations of the individual's culture. Further, the pattern is inflexible, stable, and generally begins in adolescence, and leads to distress or impairment. The characteristics of these disorders are especially apparent when these individuals find themselves in situations that are beyond their ability to cope. *DSM-5* identifies ten personality disorders that form separate categories.

These ten disorders can be organized into three clusters. The first cluster is referred to as *Cluster A* and includes *odd or eccentric disorders*. These include *schizoid personality disorder*, *paranoid personality disorder*, and *schizotypal personality disorder*. The second cluster is referred to as *Cluster B* and includes *dramatic, emotional, or erratic disorders*. These include *antisocial personality disorder, borderline personality disorder (BPD), histrionic personality disorder*, and *narcissistic personality disorder*. The third cluster is referred to as *Cluster C* and includes *anxious or fearful disorders*. These include *avoidant personality disorder, dependent personality disorder*, and *obsessive-compulsive personality disorder*.

The diagnostic criteria in *DSM–5* for *antisocial personality disorder* describe a person who shows a pattern of disregard for the rights of others. A person with this disorder must be 18 years old, and the personality style should have been present since 15 years of age. Before age 15, the person should meet criteria for a conduct disorder. Child conduct disorder includes aggression toward animals or people, destruction of property, deception or stealing, and serious rule violations.

Individuals who display signs of *psychopathy* show emotional detachment with a lack of empathy for the experiences of others (see Patrick, 2010, for an overview). They also show impulsive behavior and a callousness concerning their actions. These patterns are stable and difficult to change. Although individuals with this condition take a real toll on society, there is also a fascination by many with these individuals.

Borderline personality disorder (BPD) is characterized by an instability in mood, interpersonal relationships, and a sense of self. These three factors interact with one another in such a manner that the person with BPD experiences a changing world without a solid sense of self.

Learning Objective 6: Discuss the neurodevelopmental disorders that begin early in a child's life.

Neurodevelopmental disorders are those disorders that begin early in a child's life. These can include problems in the development of language and cognitive, emotional, and motor problems. Two of these disorders are autism spectrum disorder and attention deficit hyperactivity disorder (ADHD).

Individuals with *autism spectrum disorder (ASD)* have difficulty in three separate areas. The first is *social interactions*. Children with autism do not connect with other children or adults in the manner that other children do. They do not look others in the eye or may appear to ignore others while being more interested in other aspects of their environment. The second area is *communication*. The communication patterns of those with autism spectrum disorder do not usually show the give-and-take of most conversations. The third area is *behavioral processes*. Individuals with autism spectrum disorder often display stereotypical behaviors and the desire to engage in the same behavior in a repetitive manner.

Attention deficit hyperactivity disorder (ADHD) is a disorder of childhood that tends to develop before the age of 12. Although the conceptualization of ADHD has changed over the years, it currently includes two major dimensions. The first dimension is *inattention*. The second dimension is *hyperactivity and impulsivity*. There is some suggestion that hyperactivity problems may lessen as a child grows older whereas, attentional problems may increase, resulting in increasing difficulty with schoolwork. It is also possible that individuals with ADHD show characteristics of both inattention and hyperactivity.

Study Resources

Review Questions

1. What is the contribution of each of these to our understanding of psychopathology today:
    a. The move toward experimentation and empiricism in science?
    b. The move beyond simple dichotomies in terms of causes?
    c. The development of the *Diagnostic and Statistical Manual of Mental Disorders (DSM)*?
    d. The use of neuroscience techniques?
    e. The use of genetic studies?

2. How are anxiety and fear related? When is our experience of anxiety and fear a normal part of the human condition? What turns it into a psychopathology?
3. What are the functions of obsessions and compulsions in obsessive-compulsive disorder (OCD)? How are they different from similar concerns and behaviors in individuals who do not have OCD?
4. Mental illness has a strong connection with suicide. This is especially true of depression and bipolar disorder. With what you've learned in this chapter, design a suicide-prevention program that targets a specific population of individuals with depression or bipolar disorder.
    a. What cultural, gender, and age factors would you consider?
    b. How would your program focus on the following levels: the individual, the individual's relationships, the community, and the society?
5. "In times of stress, [dissociation] is a mechanism that protects the individual and allows her to survive." Considering all of the dissociative disorders, how do they protect the individual? What are they protecting her from? What are some of the costs of that protection?
6. This chapter states that "individuals with schizophrenia have a variety of different symptoms and show an inconsistent picture of the disorder. This has led some to suggest that there is not a single schizophrenia disorder but rather a variety of syndromes." What do you think: Is schizophrenia one disorder? What evidence would you cite to support your position?
7. Are the prevalence rates and patterns the same for the three clusters of personality disorders? If not, how are they different? What are the prevalence rates and patterns specifically for antisocial personality disorder and borderline personality disorder (BPD)?
8. Historically, the term *borderline,* as the name implies, denoted individuals who were neither neurotic nor psychotic. From what you have read in this chapter, what additional meanings do you think the term *borderline* implies about that personality disorder?
9. What is the significance of "spectrum" in the term *autism spectrum disorders*? Why did *DSM–5* group previously separate disorders under this one characterization? How does it help us better understand the disorders in terms of causes, diagnostic criteria, and treatments? What are the disadvantages of grouping the disorders as a spectrum?
10. Describe the typical course of attention deficit hyperactivity disorder (ADHD) and presentation of symptoms across different age groups and ADHD subtypes.

For Further Reading

Jamison, Kay (2006). *An Unquiet Mind.* New York: Random House.
Lowe, J. (2017). *Mental, Lithium, Love, and Losing My Mind.* New York: Blue Rider Press.
McLean, R. (2003). *Recovered, Not Cured: A Journey through Schizophrenia.* Australia: Allen Unwin.
Mukherjee, S. (2016). Runs in the family: New findings about schizophrenia rekindle old questions about genes and identity. *The New Yorker* (March 28).
Nasar, S. (1998). *A Beautiful Mind.* New York: Simon & Schuster.
Sacks, Oliver (2012). *Hallucinations.* New York: Alfred Knopf.
Saks, Elyn (2007). *The Center Cannot Hold: My Journey Through Madness.* New York: Hyperion.
Steele, K., & Berman, C. (2001). *The Day the Voices Stopped.* New York: Basic Books.
Torrey, E. (1997). *Out of the Shadows: Confronting America's Mental Illness Crisis.* New York: Wiley.

Web Resources

NIMH mental health statistics—https://www.nimh.nih.gov/health/statistics/mental-illness.shtml

RDoC—https://www.nimh.nih.gov/research/research-funded-by-nimh/rdoc/index.shtml

WHO and depression—https://www.who.int/news-room/fact-sheets/detail/depression

Suicide—https://www.who.int/gho/mental_health/suicide_rates/en/

Charlie Chaplin—www.richardgregory.org/experiments.

Oliver Sacks—https://www.ted.com/talks/oliver_sacks_what_hallucination_reveals_about_our_minds

CDC ADHD—www.cdc.gov/ncbddd/adhd/data.html

Key Terms and Concepts

agoraphobia
antisocial personality disorder
anxiety
Asperger's syndrome
attention deficit hyperactivity disorder (ADHD)
autism spectrum disorder (ASD)
bipolar disorder
borderline personality disorder (BPD)
comorbid
compulsions
delusions
depersonalization
depersonalization-derealization disorder
derealization
dissociation
dissociative amnesia
dissociative identity disorder (DID)
fear
generalized anxiety disorder (GAD)
hallucinations
major depressive disorder (MDD)
mental disorder
negative symptoms
obsessions
obsessive-compulsive and related disorders
obsessive-compulsive disorder (OCD)
panic attack
panic disorder
pathological dissociative symptoms
personality disorder
positive symptoms
psychopathology
psychotic disorders
schizophrenia
schizophrenia spectrum and other psychotic disorders
social anxiety disorder (SAD)
specific phobia
stigma
suicide
syndrome

15 Treatment

LEARNING OBJECTIVES

15.2 Discuss the history of psychopathology and its treatments.

15.3 Describe the psychological treatment perspectives for the treatment of mental disorders.

15.4 Summarize the biological approaches to treating mental disorders.

15.5 Summarize the effective treatment options for mental disorders.

My students filled the room. They were interested and eager, unusually so, given that they were second- and third-year law students for whom the fear and trembling that came with the first year had long since faded. The course was "Advanced Mental Health Law." The day's topic: Billie Boggs. A street person who lived over a hot air vent in midtown Manhattan, she threw food at people who wanted to help her and chased them across the street. Her rantings and ravings seemed crazy to most of the students, and we were discussing whether she should be sent to a psychiatric hospital.

I heard myself speak, surprising myself by the steady sound of my voice as I tried to restore my attention to the group before me: *"What if Billie Boggs were your sister—would you put her in a psychiatric hospital then?" Up shot the hands.*

Concentrate. These are your students. You have an obligation to them. Canceling class would be admitting defeat. But there are explosions in my head. They're testing nuclear devices on my brain. They're very little and they can get inside. They are powerful.

I pulled myself together, enough to point to a young woman who spoke often in class. *"I couldn't let my sister live like that," she said from across the classroom, which held the students in curved rows, like a giant palm before me. "I know my sister. That wouldn't be her. There's one and only one of her—and that's the one before she got sick."*

Is she trying to kill me? No, she's a student. But what about the others? The voices inside my head, the explosions. What do they want? Are they trying to interdict me, to hit me with the Kramer device? I went to the store and they said "interdiction." Interdiction, introduction, exposition, explosion. Voicemail is the issue.

I knew not to say those thoughts out loud. Not because they were crazy thoughts—they were every bit as real as the students sitting right in front of me—but I kept silent because others would think them crazy. People would think me as deranged as Billie Boggs. But I'm not crazy. I simply have greater access to the truth.

"Good," I replied. "But why isn't it the case that your sister has two selves, the sick one you see now and the healthy one you've known all your life? Why should you get to pick which is real? Shouldn't your sister make that choice?" Up shot more hands.

My brain is on fire! My head is going to explode right here, right in front of my class!

"But isn't health always preferred to illness?" a bright-eyed young man countered. "We should prefer the healthy self." Mercifully, the class ended. A law-school dean spotted me as I walked back to my office. He said I looked as if I were in pain. "Just a lot on my mind," I heard myself reply as I continued quickly down the hall. Keys out, door open, door shut. I crumpled into my chair and buried my face in my hands.

That was in September of 1991, and it was one of my worst such incidents. Ten years before, in my mid-20s, during my third psychiatric hospitalization, I had been given the diagnosis "chronic paranoid schizophrenia with acute exacerbation." My prognosis? "Grave." I was, in other words, expected to be unable to live independently, let alone work. At best I would be in a board-and-care, holding a minimum-wage job—perhaps flipping burgers—when my symptoms had become less severe.

That has not turned out to be my life. I am the Orrin B. Evans professor of law, psychology, and psychiatry and the behavioral sciences at the University of Southern California's law school; adjunct professor of psychiatry at the University of California at San Diego's medical school; and an assistant faculty member at the New Center for Psychoanalysis, where I am also a research clinical associate.

My schizophrenia has not gone away. I still become psychotic, as happened in class that day in 1991. Today my symptoms, while not as severe, still recur and I struggle to stay in the world, so to speak, doing my work. I have written about my illness in a memoir and much of the narrative takes place after I had accepted a tenure-track appointment at USC.

Barring a medical breakthrough of Nobel-Prize-winning proportions, I will never fully recover from schizophrenia. I will remain on antipsychotic medication and in talk therapy for the rest of my life. Yet I have learned to manage my illness.

Some are steps that everyone with mental illness should take. First, learn about the illness you have—the typical signs, symptoms, and course. Many excellent sources are available. Second, understand how your illness affects you. What are your triggers? What are your early warning signs? What can you do to minimize your symptoms when they worsen—e.g., call your therapist, increase your medication, listen to music, exercise? Try to devise some techniques for your own situation. Some colleagues and I are studying how a group of high-functioning people with schizophrenia manage their symptoms. You are in the best position to determine what works for you.

Put a good treatment team in place. You need a therapist you can trust and can turn to in times of difficulty. Does he or she respond if you call in crisis? The same is true of a psychopharmacologist. Make friends and family members part of your team.

Sometimes your team can see early warning signs before you can. For instance, my closest friend, Steve, and my husband, Will, often identify when I am slipping. Will says I become quieter in a particular way that signals all is not well. It's a blessing to have such people in your life. Seek them out.

We also need to put a face on mental illness. Being open about one's own illness will probably do more good than all the laws we can pass.

My own "outing" of myself was a bit of a risk, but has turned out well. I am glad and relieved I no longer have to hide. And my story seems to be meaningful to people—it has helped people understand mental illness more and perhaps has led to a decrease in the stigma. I was lucky in that my law school accommodated my teaching needs without my having to invoke the ADA. My colleagues are supportive, and I no longer feel ashamed about needing their help.

Perhaps most important: Seek help when you need it. Mental illness is a no-fault disease like any other, such as cancer or diabetes. Help is available, but you need to ask for it. Don't let the threat of stigma deter you. You shouldn't have to suffer.

And you shouldn't allow mental illness to stand in the way of the wonderful contributions you are poised to make to your students and to your field.

From *Chronicle of Higher Education,* November 25, 2009 (edited part of a larger article). Elyn R. Saks is a professor of law, psychology, and psychiatry and the behavioral sciences at the University of Southern California's law school. She is the author of a memoir, *The Center Cannot Hold: My Journey Through Madness* (Hyperion, 2007).

You just read the description of one person's experience with mental illness. In describing her experiences, she also gives you a quick history of how mental illness has been conceptualized in the past and what the future may offer. When Elyn Saks initially went to the hospital, she was told that her prognosis was "grave." She was also told that she would never live independently, hold a job, find a loving partner, or get married. Her future was described as one in which she would live in a board-and-care facility, spending her days watching TV in a dayroom with other people debilitated by mental illness. For work, she would work at menial jobs when her symptoms were quiet.

Following her last psychiatric hospitalization at the age of 28, she was encouraged by a doctor to work as a cashier making change. Similar to people with cancer who were told in the last century to not expect a long life, individuals with mental illness were not given the possibility of real change. However, Elyn Saks was able to complete her law degree at Yale University and become a professor of law, psychology, and psychiatry at the University of Southern California. You can see her Ted Talk on her experience with mental illness online (https://www.ted.com/talks/elyn_saks_seeing_mental_illness).

This chapter will examine the treatments for mental illness over time. As we developed new scientific techniques for understanding human processes, our conceptualizations of mental illness and its treatment have also changed. We have gone from a worldview hundreds of years ago in which magic, including the idea that you could be possessed by spirits or demons, produced mental illness to a time in which our scientific understanding describes a complex set of processes on many levels that contribute to mental illness. During the current historical period, we have also come to see those with mental illness as whole people with both abilities and difficulties. In terms of the future, Elyn Saks described a movement to allow people with mental disorders to have a say in their treatment. A person's high functioning and the ability to make decisions is not totally taken away by having a mental disorder. The person is still able to describe her experiences and, in the best of conditions, to ask others for help.

Historical Understanding of Psychopathology and Its Treatment

Although the Greek and Roman periods saw individuals who attempted to understand psychopathology in a more humane way, this disappeared as their civilizations declined. As the Middle Ages approached, disease and especially mental illness was seen from the standpoint of a religious perspective with the devil being a major player. One of the classic books in this genre was the *Malleus Maleficarum* published in the 1480s. "The Hammer of the Witches" was written by two German priests and approved by the Pope. It went through a number of editions and became the handbook of the inquisition. As such, it explained how witches existed and flew through the air as well as how they should be tortured if they did not confess.

In a "catch-22," the witches were tied to a device and lowered into cold water. If they floated, they were seen to be possessed by the devil and most likely killed by hanging or fire. If they went to the bottom and drowned, then they were innocent. During the interrogations, witches were not to be left alone or given clothes since the devil would visit them or hide in their clothing. Although the writers did not understand the nature of psychopathology, they did describe in some detail particular characteristics of different disorders including bipolar disorder, depression, and psychotic processes such as hallucinations and delusions.

In 1330, a convent of the order of St. Mary of Bethlehem became the first institution for the mentally ill in England. Two hundred years later, King Henry VIII gave the institution a royal charter. Over the years, the word "Bethlehem" became "Bedlam," and the institution was referred to as "Old Bedlam." The English word "bedlam" comes from this institution. Various reports suggested that the inmates were often chained and treated cruelly without proper food or clothing. As depicted in novels of the day, people of the 1700s would go to Bedlam to see the inmates as a form of an outing as we today would go to a zoo. This is depicted in a 1796 illustration (**Figure 15-1**). In 1814, some 96,000 people visited the asylum.

Another common occurrence of that time is depicted in an illustration of a seaman James Norris who was shackled for 14 years (see **Figure 15-2**).

In the 1800s, there was a campaign in England to change the conditions of the patients, which led to the establishment of the Committee on Madhouses in 1815. This issued in a period of concern for the patients rather than seeing them as objects of curiosity as in the previous century. Treatment for patients during the 1800s brought new practices including the therapeutic value of work.

During this period, there was a spirit throughout the world to adopt a "moral treatment of the insane." Three important individuals were Benjamin Rush (1745–1813) in the United States, Philippe Pinel (1745–1826) in France, and Vincenzo Chiarugi (1759–1820) in Italy (see Gerard, 1997). In the United States, Rush, who had signed the Declaration of Independence, later established a wing at the Pennsylvania Hospital in Philadelphia for the treatment of mental illness. He is often seen as the father of American psychiatry and saw mental illness as a problem of the mind. He developed a tranquilizing chair that he believed would change the flow of the blood. Modern professionals tend to view this invention as neither helpful nor hurtful to the patient. He also wrote the first psychiatric textbook published in America.

In France, Pinel sought to change the way the insane were treated in France. Pinel supported the idea that mental illness could be studied by the methods of the natural sciences. In 1793, Pinel became the director of the Bicêtre Asylum in Paris. As director, he reviewed the commitment papers of the inmates, toured the building, and met with each patient individually. The building was in bad shape and the patients were chained to walls. Pinel himself wrote "everything presented to me the appearance of chaos and confusion." Pinel petitioned the government and received permission to remove the chains. He also abandoned the practice of bloodletting.

Pinel began to carefully observe patients and to interact with them. In these discussions, he attempted to create a detailed case history and to better understand the development of the disorder. This led to a classification system, which he published in his *Nosographie*

Figure 15-1 The English word *bedlam* comes from the name of the first institution for the mentally ill in 14th-century England.
Source: Wellcome Library London.

philosophique ou méthode de l'analyse appliquée à la médecine in 1789, which sorted mental diseases into five categories: melancholia, mania without delirium, mania with delirium, dementia, and idiocy. In 1795, Pinel became the chief physician at the Hospice de la Salpêtrière where he remained for the rest of his life. For many, Pinel is seen as the father of scientific psychiatry.

Vincenzo Chiarugi had been less well known outside of Italy until a paper in the middle of the last century brought his name to the attention of Americans (Mora, 1959). Some eight years earlier than Pinel, Chiarugi began removing chains from his patients. Early in his career, Chiarugi became the director of a large hospital in Florence that included special facilities for the mentally ill. This resulted from the passage of a law in 1774 in Italy that allowed individuals seen as mentally ill to be hospitalized. As director of the hospital, Chiarugi created guidelines concerning how patients were to be treated. One of these rules suggested that patients were to be treated with respect. He also suggested that if restraints were required, they should be applied in a manner to protect the patient from sores and be made of leather rather than chains. He also used psychopharmacological agents such as opium for treatment.

In addition to mental health professionals, the humane care of individuals with mental illness was moved forward by a variety of other individuals. William Tuke (1732–1822) was a successful merchant of tea, coffee, and cocoa in England. He was a Quaker philanthropist and friends had told him of being turned away from an asylum in York when they had tried to visit a fellow Quaker who had been confined there. Within a few days, the patient was reported dead.

Tuke visited the asylum and found the conditions deplorable. Having retired, he decided to devote his life to creating alternative places where "the unhappy might find refuge." In 1796, near York, England, he created a Retreat for Persons Afflicted with Disorders of the Mind. This Quaker retreat carried with it the idea that the individuals who were there should be given respect as well as good food and exercise. There were to be no chains or manacles. The model for the retreat was that of a farm and the patients performed farm duties as part of their treatment. Others visited to learn of its operation. In 1813, the Quakers of Philadelphia founded the Friends Asylum for the Use of Persons Deprived of the Use of Their Reason, which was the first private psychiatric hospital in the US. Both the retreat in York and the Friend's Hospital of Philadelphia continue to function as places for mental health treatment.

Figure 15-2 James Norris was kept in a harness in 1814. He has been confined for more than ten years.

Source: Wellcome Library London.

Another individual who contributed to the American mental health movement was Dorothea Dix (1802–1887). Dix became a schoolteacher but contracted tuberculosis and needed to find a less than full-time position. She found a job teaching women at the East Cambridge House of Correction in Massachusetts. This position opened her eyes to the terrible conditions these women faced. Dix also realized that a number of these women had some type of mental illness. From this experience, she devoted her life to crusading for the improved treatment of the mentally ill. As part of this crusade, she visited every state east of the Mississippi River and testified before local and national legislatures. She encouraged the American congress to give federal land to the states to establish mental hospitals in the same way they created land grant colleges in the 1860s. Both houses of congress passed the bill only to be vetoed by President Franklin Pierce. Although this bill was not passed, it is estimated that her work led to the establishment of some 40 mental hospitals in the US and Europe.

CONCEPT CHECK

1. What were the unique contributions of the following individuals and groups to our current understanding of the treatment of mental illness—include dates and locations as well in your response:

a. Convent of the order of St. Mary of Bethlehem?
b. Committee on Madhouses?
c. Benjamin Rush?
d. Philippe Pinel?
e. Vincenzo Chiarugi?
f. William Tuke?
g. Quakers of Philadelphia?
h. Dorothea Dix?

The Psychological Treatment Perspectives in the 20th Century

This section will discuss three approaches for the psychological treatment of mental disorders. These are the psychodynamic approach, the existential-humanistic approach, and the cognitive behavioral approach. These approaches were developed somewhat independently and are often seen in opposition to one another. For that reason, they will initially be discussed independently, which will include a historical understanding of each approach, including its broad principles, and then present specific treatments that have been tested in a scientific manner. In addition, many current approaches represent an integration of these three approaches.

Psychodynamic Perspectives on Treatment

The **psychodynamic perspective** is based on the idea that psychological problems are manifestations of inner mental conflicts and that conscious awareness of those conflicts is a key to recovery. Historically, Sigmund Freud laid the foundation for this perspective. By the beginning of the 20th century, there was an understanding that psychological processes were an important source of information concerning mental illness. Sigmund Freud had worked with Jean-Martin Charcot in Paris. Charcot has been called the founder of modern neurology and is known for his study of hypnosis. He observed individuals with *hysteria*. In this disorder, the experience, such as not feeling pain in a limb or difficulty hearing, did not match the underlying physiology. For example, with *glove amnesia* the person would not feel pain in the area of the fingers covered by a glove even when pricked with a pin. However, the nerves related to this pain followed a different pattern, which meant that the pain experience could not have a totally physiological cause. These types of experiences led Freud to seek psychological explanations for the cause and treatment of mental disorders. Psychodynamic therapy is based on Freud's ideas. Psychoanalysis was the first psychodynamic therapy to develop, and we look at that next.

Psychoanalysis

For Freud, treatment was based on the search for ideas and emotions that are in conflict and the manner in which an individual has relationships with other people. His specific treatment came to be called **psychoanalysis**. One basic procedure was *free association* in which an individual lay on a couch with the therapist behind him and said whatever came to mind. It was the therapist's job to help the client connect ideas and feelings of which he was not aware. One thing Freud was searching for was connections within the person's psyche when external stimulation was reduced as with free association or during sleep. Dreams were also analyzed in this way since they are produced outside of daily life.

One purpose of psychoanalysis was to examine *resistance*, or what the client is unwilling to say or experience. That is, clients may not fully say what is coming into their minds or faithfully report what they experienced in a dream. *Transference* is the manner in which an individual imagines how another person thinks about him or her. For example, a person may expect the therapist to treat him or her just like a parent did. Since the job of the therapist is to only ask a few questions or make interpretations during a session, the client knew little of how the therapist actually felt. Thus, the client's view of the therapist such as "he is critical of me" or "does not like my ideas" were seen to come from the client's psyche.

One critical aspect of psychodynamic therapy is the relationship between the therapist and client, which continues to be emphasized in current approaches. The therapeutic relationship that develops between the client and the therapist offers an opportunity to see disturbed relationships in a safe environment. Transference is an important mechanism in which the client tends to see the therapist in terms of significant others in his or her life. As the client talks with the therapist, he or she will replay prior conflicts and enact maladaptive patterns. For example, if one of your parents was very critical of your ideas, then you may initially find it difficult to tell the therapist feelings or thoughts that are very important to you or related to how you see yourself. You could have another situation in which a parent never allowed you to engage in tasks in which you could fail or would save you whenever you encountered problems. These past situations would leave you with unrealistic expectations as to what to expect from the world and others. In these situations, the person has never really learned what the world has to offer and may act as a child expecting someone to protect her and thus miss out on new experiences and learning.

In the last 50 years, a number of dynamically orientated therapies have been shown to be effective (Barber, Muran, McCarthy, & Keefe, 2013). One empirically supported therapy based on dynamic principles was developed by Hans Strupp and his colleagues. Strupp was a researcher who throughout his career sought to understand the important components of successful therapy and how to perform therapy outcome research (Strupp, 1971). He was particularly interested in the psychoanalytic or psychodynamic perspective as it is sometimes called. Strupp demonstrated changes could be seen in a therapy of a few-months duration (Strupp & Binder, 1984). The focus of this therapy is the relationship between the client and other individuals in his or her life. It is assumed that the client's problems are based on disturbed prior relationships.

Strupp and Binder illustrate how they might initially discuss interpersonal transactions with a client.

> Therapist: How do you feel about yourself at those times?
> Client: I feel like I don't have anything to offer.
> Therapist: That you have nothing to offer. What do you imagine people are thinking about you then? What's their attitude toward you when you're with them and you feel like you have nothing to say?
> Client: Really, that I'm present and that's about all.
> Therapist: Really, that I'm present. They're not attracted to you or they have negative feelings toward you. They just don't feel about you one way or the other?
> Client: Right.
> Therapist: Like you're invisible.
> Client: Just like I'm not there. It doesn't really matter whether I'm there or not.
> (Strupp & Binder, 1984, p. 115)

The role of the therapist from this approach is mainly to listen. As the therapist listens to a client, the therapist seeks to understand what the client is saying and how he or she feels as the client describes their world. The therapist would note when she or he finds talking to the therapist difficult or experiences distress as she or he talks about their life. On a broader level, the therapist is looking for themes and patterns that came from one's past. In a relaxed, nonjudgmental manner, it is the task of the therapist to help the client understand the patterns and to see how they interfere with living and having rewarding relationships with others. Different versions of dynamic psychotherapy have been shown to be effective for a number of disorders, especially the personality disorders (Barber, Muran, McCarthy, & Keefe, 2013).

Existential-Humanistic Perspectives

The ***existential-humanistic perspective*** begins by asking what is the nature of human existence? This includes both the positive experiences of intimacy and the negative experiences of loss. As the existential-humanistic movement grew, a number of themes became critical. The first is an emphasis on human growth and the need for a positive psychology that moves beyond the discussion of stress and neurosis seen in the psychodynamic approaches. A second emphasis is that psychological health is more than just the absence of pathology. Not having a problem is not the same as finding meaning in one's life. The third theme stresses the importance of not only considering the external world and a person's relationship to it but also the internal world. In the existential-humanistic perspective, the internal world of a person and his or her experiences are valued. With the emphasis on *experience*, you will also see the therapies that developed from this approach referred to as humanistic-experiential therapies. One well-known humanistic therapy is client-centered therapy.

Client-Centered Therapy

Carl Rogers brought the humanistic movement to the forefront by creating **client-centered therapy**, also referred to as **person-centered therapy**. He was also one of the first psychologists to record therapy sessions so that they could be used for research. Rogers continued on the theme of potential by saying that psychotherapy is a releasing of an already existing capacity in a potentially competent individual. In fact, it was the interaction with the therapist that allowed for the person to experience himself and come to understand his potential. In this way, Rogers emphasized the relationship between the therapist and client as a critical key to effective therapy.

There are three key characteristics of the client-centered approach. The first is *empathic understanding*. As the therapist reflects back what the client says, the client begins to experience his innermost thoughts and feelings. The second is what Rogers referred to as *unconditional positive regard*. That is, the therapist accepts what the client says without trying to change the client. For some individuals who had experienced significant others in their lives as critical of them, to be accepted by the therapist is a new experience. The third characteristic is for the therapist to show *genuineness* and *congruence*. In this way, the therapist models what interactions between two real people could be like.

As a person continues in therapy, Rogers suggested that the client goes through seven stages. These stages begin with an unwillingness to share one's internal world. This is followed by blaming things on others and accepting one's own experiences. The next set of stages begins with a freer description of feeling and ends with the client's being comfortable with himself. The stages are:

1. Unwillingness to reveal self, feeling not recognized
2. Externalizes
3. Wants to be different (not accepting past feelings)
4. Freer description of feelings
5. Recognition of conflict between feelings and thoughts
6. Experience feelings without denial, more willing to risk in relationships
7. Comfortable with self and with having new feelings

One individual who helped to form early ideas of what became the existential humanistic approach was Karen Horney, a German-born psychoanalyst who was introduced to you in Chapter 13. She influenced the movement by emphasizing growth as well as suggesting that Freud's approach did not fully present a psychology that applied to women. Overall, for both men and women she differentiated between *healthy growth* in which a person developed to her full potential and *neurotic growth* in which a person limited her development by unrealistic ideas and feelings. These unrealistic ideas would include the idea that "everyone should love me," "I should never make mistakes," or "the world should always give me what I want." Horney's final book, *Neurosis and Human Growth*, describes how these types of unrealistic ideas, along with an idealized self-image, leave the person feeling out of touch with herself and others.

In contrast to an idealized self-image in which one is always perfect and loved by everyone, Karen Horney created the concepts of **self-realization** and a **real self**. A real self includes who one is and what one appreciates. It is the alienation from the real self that is seen to constitute a key process of neurotic development. It also requires energy to present a false self, which leaves few resources for developing healthy human growth. Her ideas were echoed later in the century by Abraham Maslow.

One of the best known of the humanistic psychologists is Abraham Maslow. Maslow is well known for his *hierarchy of needs* described in the chapter on motivation and emotion. Although there are few empirical studies examining the hierarchy, it has remained an important theoretical concept for understanding the nature of human needs. The first level is physiological needs such as hunger and thirst. Before one can seek higher level psychological needs, physiological needs must be met. The second level needs are safety, which includes the desire for safety, and the avoidance of pain and anxiety. The third level of needs includes belongingness and love. These needs are related to intimacy, affection, and being part of a peer group. The fourth level is esteem. It is at this level that one seeks self-respect, adequacy, and mastery of one's skills. The fifth and highest level is a search for self-actualization.

Self-actualization, according to Maslow, is the situation in which one lives one's life to the fullest. At times, one may experience peak experiences or flow states in which everything appears to go perfectly with little effort, but this is not a constant state. In general, self-actualized individuals are reality- and problem-centered. It is not their desire to blame others but rather to solve the problem at hand. They also accept others as well as themselves. In their actions, they tend to be spontaneous and live a fairly simple life.

Emotional Focused Therapy

A number of humanistic-experiential oriented therapies have been shown to be effective (Elliott, Greenberg, Watson, Timulak, & Freire, 2013). One of these empirically supported therapies based on humanistic principles was developed by Leslie Greenberg and his colleagues. This approach is known as **emotion-focused therapy** or **process experiential therapy**

(Greenberg, 2002; Greenberg & Watson, 2006). In this therapy, emotion is viewed as centrally important in the experience of self. Emotion can be either adaptive or maladaptive. However, in either case, emotion is the crucial element that brings about change in therapy. In therapy, clients are helped to identify and explore their emotions. The aim is to both manage and transform emotional experiences.

Greenberg describes five principles that relate emotion-focused therapy to a humanist approach concerning human nature (Pos & Greenberg, 2006). These principles are:

1. Experiencing is the basis of thought, feeling, and action.
2. Human beings are fundamentally free to choose how to construct their worlds.
3. People function holistically while at the same time are made up of many parts, or self-organizations, each of which may be associated with quite distinctive thoughts, feelings, and self-experiences.
4. People function best and are best helped by a therapist who is psychologically present and who establishes an interpersonal environment that is empathic, unconditionally accepting, and authentic.
5. People grow and develop to the best of their abilities in supportive environments.

Emotion-focused therapy can be thought of in three phases (Greenberg & Watson, 2006). The first phase is one of *bonding and awareness* in which it is the job of the therapist to create a safe environment in which emotional experience can take place. Empathy and positive regard are part of the way the client is helped to feel safe. In the early part of therapy, the client is not only helped to experience an emotion but also to put words to it as illustrated below.

> Therapist: So can you pay attention to what you feel inside in that place where you feel your feelings?
> Client: I just feel this heaviness inside. I feel the weight of all the things I have to do just pushing down on me.
> Therapist: Can you put words to that feeling?
> Client: "I have no choice."

The second phase is *evocation and exploration*. At this point, emotions are evoked and even intensified. The therapist also helps the client understand how she might be interfering with her own experience of emotion. Such examples of interference would include changing the subject, beginning to talk about the emotion in a cognitive manner as a way to distance one's self from the experience. The third phase is *transformation and generation of alternatives*. It is at this point that the therapist helps the client construct alternative ways of thinking, feeling, and doing that are more consistent with her real self. Empirical studies have shown that emotion-focused therapy is effective with depression and emotional trauma (Greenberg & Watson, 2006).

Another therapeutic technique that has gained popularity and been empirically shown to be effective is **mindfulness** (Creswell, 2017). Mindfulness techniques were originally meditation techniques developed in Theravada Buddhism. These techniques involve an increased focused purposeful awareness of the present moment. The idea is to relate to one's thoughts and experiences in an open, non-judgmental, and accepting manner (Kabit-Zinn, 1990). The basic technique is to observe thoughts without reacting to them in the present. This increases sensitivity to important features of the environment and one's internal reactions. This leads to better self-management and awareness as an alternative to ruminating about the past or worrying about the future. This reduces self-criticism.

Non-judgmental observing allows for a reduction in stress, reduction in reactivity, and more time for interaction with others and the world. Also, feelings of compassion for another person become possible. This broadens attention and alternatives. Meta-analysis performed by Hofmann and his colleagues examined 39 studies of mindfulness (Hofmann, Sawyer, Witt, & Oh, 2010). He found significant reductions in anxiety and depression following mindfulness techniques. Grossman and his colleagues examined 20 studies and found overall positive changes following mindfulness approaches (Grossman, Niemann, Schmidt, & Walach, 2010; see also Hofmann, Grossman, & Hinton, 2011). Empirical evidence using mindfulness techniques has shown positive change with a number of disorders including anxiety, depression, chronic pain, and stress. Mindfulness is also a component of *dialectical behavior therapy,* which is an effective treatment of borderline personality disorder.

Overall, the existential-humanistic perspective emphasizes the emotional level. There is also an emphasis on the value of internal processes and the manner in which the exploration and experiencing of these internal processes can lead to changes in behavior and experience.

Behavioral and Cognitive Behavioral Perspectives

Behavioral therapy focused on changing behaviors through conditioning principles, whereas cognitive behavioral therapy examined the manner in which thoughts influence behaviors. The cognitive behavioral movement seeks to understand how cognitions are disordered or disrupted in mental disorders. Whereas humanistic therapies emphasize emotional processing, cognitive behavioral approaches emphasize thoughts and the manner in which a person thinks about her life and experiences. The basic idea is that psychological disturbances often involve errors in thinking. One real value of many cognitive behavioral approaches is that they have been tested empirically and presented in books and manuals that describe the steps involved in therapy. Cognitive behavioral therapy (CBT) has been developed for a variety of disorders, which will be described later in this chapter.

The **behavioral perspective**, as the name implies, has focused on the level of actions and behaviors. Most histories of behaviorism begin with a discussion of Ivan Pavlov, the Russian physiologist who won the Nobel Prize in 1904 for his work on the physiology of digestion. Pavlov noted in his Nobel Prize speech that the sight of tasty food makes the mouth of a hungry man water. However, what became of interest to behavioral psychologists was not the salivary reflex itself, but the fact that other objects associated with the presentation of food could also produce salivation. For example, in his work with dogs, the sound of the door of the lab being opened preceding the dogs being presented with food would also produce the reflex. In a variety of studies it was shown that any sensory process such as sound that was paired with the food would produce salivation. After a number of pairings, the sound alone without the food could produce this reflex. This came to be known as *classical conditioning*, as described in the chapter on learning.

John Watson is often described as America's first behaviorist. His work set psychology on the course of emphasizing environmental explanations for behavior and rejecting the theoretical value of internal concepts. Watson saw the goal of psychology as identifying environmental conditions that direct behavior. In this perspective, psychological disorders are considered to be under the rules of learning. Watson created a psychology based on observable behaviors alone. This position allowed for and supported the development of a strong stimulus–response psychology. Watson's statement emphasizing the role of the environment in development is well known.

> Give me a dozen healthy infants, well-formed, and my own specified world to bring them up in and I'll guarantee to take any one at random and train him to become any type of specialist I might select – doctor, lawyer, artist, merchant-chief, and yes, even beggar-man and thief, regardless of his talents, penchants, tendencies, abilities, vocations, and race of his ancestors.
>
> (Watson, 1924)

As the quote implies, Watson assumed that there existed "talents, penchants, tendencies, abilities," which were part of an individual but that these could be overridden by environmental factors. In fact, as described in the chapter on learning, Watson demonstrated that a 9-month-old infant named Little Albert could be conditioned to fear an animal such as a lab rat that the infant had previously enjoyed playing with (Watson & Rayner, 1920). The procedure (which would be considered unacceptable and unethical today) was to create a loud noise while the infant was observing the animal. A loud noise will produce a startle response. In a classical conditioning manner, the pairing of the aversive noise and the animal led to conditioned fear. Behaviorists used classical conditioning as a mechanism for understanding phobias and other processes seen in mental illness.

B. F. Skinner became the 20th century's most vocal proponent of behaviorism. Beginning with his 1938 book, *The Behavior of Organisms,* Skinner played a significant role in experimental psychology until his death in 1990. His exemplar experimental procedure was to demonstrate that an animal, generally a laboratory rat or pigeon, could be taught to make specific responses if, after the occurrence of the desired response, the animal was given a reward, generally food. This procedure came to be known as operant conditioning. These techniques were applied to the management of individuals with psychological disorders. In institutional settings this approach was called *token economies*. Individuals with schizophrenia, for example, were rewarded with products they sought for behaviors such as cleaning their room or taking a bath.

Both Skinner and Watson left us with a psychology that emphasized the environment and ignored any discussion of internal processes or mechanisms for understanding life. Their real contribution for understanding mental illness was not their mechanisms per se since it is difficult for learning theory to adequately describe psychopathology across the lifespan, but their emphasis on experimental research and the necessity to evaluate treatment procedures in a scientific manner.

In the middle of the last century, a number of psychologists began to see the limitation of strict behaviorism in that it ignored internal processes. Simple demonstrations such as offering a 6-year-old a candy bar if he would do a particular task showed that the idea of a reward was enough to motivate behavior. Also, behaviorally oriented psychologists such as Albert Bandura showed that humans would imitate the behaviors of others even without reinforcement. This type of learning was called **observational learning** or **modeling**. One classic set of studies involved children hitting a Bobo doll after seeing cartoon characters being aggressive. In another study, children watched an adult interact with the Bobo doll in an aggressive or non-aggressive manner. Those children who watched the aggressive adult later showed more aggression than those who watched a non-aggressive adult.

The **cognitive behavioral perspective** suggests that dysfunctional thinking is common to all psychological disturbances. By learning in therapy how to understand one's thinking,

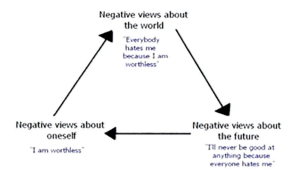

Figure 15-3 Beck's cognitive triad.

it is possible to change the way one thinks as well as one's emotional state and behaviors. One basic feature of our thinking is that it is automatic. Ideas just pop into our mind such as, "I can't solve this," or "It is all my fault." A number of therapies based on cognitive principles along with behavioral interventions have been shown to be effective (Hollon & Beck, 2013). David Barlow at Boston University and Tom Borkovec at Penn State University used cognitive and behavioral research to develop empirically supported treatments for anxiety (Barlow, 2002; Borkovec, 2006).

Aaron Beck developed a cognitive therapy for depression in the early 1960s (Beck, 1967, 2019; see also Judith Beck, 2011 for an overview and update). The model is described in terms of a *cognitive triad* related to depression (see **Figure 15-3**).

The first component of the triad is the *individual's negative view of self*. This is when the individual attributes unpleasant experiences to his own mental, physical, and moral defects. When something negative happens, the person says, "This is my fault." In therapy, the client can become aware of the content of his thinking. The second component is the *individual's tendency to interpret experiences in a negative manner*. That is, the person tailors the facts to fit negative conclusions. The basic idea is that thinking influences emotion and behavior. The third component is that the *individual regards the future in a negative way*. He envisions a life of only hardships and anticipates failure in all tasks. In therapy, the basic idea is that the individual can modify his cognitive and behavioral responses. Overall, the therapy is directed at the automatic thoughts in relation to *catastrophizing*—believing that nothing will work out; *personalization*—believing that everything relates to you; *overgeneralization*—believing that one event is how it always is; and *dichotomous thinking*—believing that things are either good or bad. The following is an example of a **Cognitive Behavioral Therapy (CBT)** therapy session:

> Therapist: Okay, Sally, you said you wanted to talk about a problem with finding a part-time job?
> Patient: Yeah. I need the money . . . but I don't know.
> Therapist: (*noticing that Sally looks more dysphoric*) What's going through your mind right now?
> Patient: [automatic thought] I won't be able to handle a job.
> Therapist: [labeling her idea as a thought and linking it to her mood] And how does that thought make you feel?
> Patient: [emotion] Sad. Really low.
> Therapist: [beginning to evaluate the thought] What's the evidence that you won't be able to work?
> Patient: Well, I'm having trouble just getting through my classes.
> Therapist: Okay. What else?
> Patient: I don't know . . . I'm still so tired. It's hard to make myself even go and *look* for a job, much less go to work every day.
> Therapist: In a minute we'll look at that. [suggesting an alternative view] Maybe it's actually harder for you at this point to go out and *investigate* jobs than it

would be for you to go to a job that you already had. In any case, is there any other evidence that you couldn't handle a job, assuming that you can get one?
Patient: . . . No, not that I can think of.
Therapist: Any evidence on the other side? That you *might* be able to handle a job?
Patient: I did work last year. And that was on top of school and other activities. But this year . . . I just don't know.
Therapist: Any other evidence that you could handle a job?
Patient: I don't know. . . . It's possible I could do something that doesn't take much time. And that isn't too hard.
Therapist: What might that be?
Patient: A sales job, maybe. I did that last year.
Therapist: Any ideas of where you could work?
Patient: Actually, maybe the [university] bookstore. I saw a notice that they're looking for new clerks.
Therapist: Okay. And what would be the *worst* that could happen if you did get a job at the bookstore?
Patient: I guess if I couldn't do it.
Therapist: And if that happened, how would you cope?
Patient: I guess I'd just quit.
Therapist: And what would be the *best* that could happen?
Patient: Uh . . . that I'd be able to do it easily.
Therapist: And what's the most realistic outcome?
Patient: It probably won't be easy, especially at first. But I might be able to do it.
Therapist: Sally, what's the effect of believing your thought, "I won't be able to handle a job"?
Patient: Makes me feel sad. . . . Makes me not even try.
Therapist: And what's the effect of changing your thinking, of realizing that possibly you could work in the bookstore?
Patient: I'd feel better. I'd be more likely to apply for the job.
Therapist: So what do you want to do about this?
Patient: Go to the bookstore. I could go this afternoon.
Therapist: How likely are you to go?
Patient: Oh, I guess I will. I will go.
Therapist: And how do you feel now?
Patient: A little better. A little more nervous, maybe. But a little more hopeful, I guess.

(Beck 2011, p. 23–5)

As with other perspectives, cognitive behavioral approaches have been expanded to include a number of other techniques including those drawn from other perspectives. Some of these approaches are mindfulness approaches and dialectical behavior therapy (DBT) as will be discussed, as well as Acceptance and Commitment Therapy (ACT) and Acceptance-Based Behavioral Therapy (ABBT). ACT and ABBT combine mindfulness with an emphasis of accepting inner experiences without judgment, along with awareness and resilience. These approaches have been referred to as the *new wave* or *third wave of CBT* (Hofmann, Sawyer, & Fang, 2010). One common theme in these approaches is the role of acceptance. In each approach, clients are encouraged to not react to negative thoughts and feelings.

CONCEPT CHECK

1. Describe the following three aspects of psychoanalysis including their role in treatment: *free association*, *resistance*, and *transference*.
2. In what ways did the work of Karen Horney expand on Sigmund Freud's theories of psychopathology and treatment?
3. Identify and describe the three primary themes of the existential-humanistic movement.
4. Identify and describe the three key characteristics of Carl Rogers's client-centered approach.
5. Describe the three phases of Leslie Greenberg's emotion-focused therapy and the role that each plays in the therapy process.
6. What is *mindfulness*? In what ways is it effective in treating mental illness?
7. List three kinds of evidence used by a number of psychologists to point out the limitations of a strict behaviorist perspective and pave the way to a cognitive behavioral perspective.
8. What are the primary characteristics of the cognitive behavioral perspective?
9. Describe the three components of Aaron Beck's model of a cognitive triad for depression.

Biological Approaches to Treating Mental Illness

Throughout our history as humans, we have used natural substances to treat illness. Often treatment was a hit-or-miss procedure as people learned which substances were more effective than others. With the development of better chemical methods in the last 100 years, scientists began to modify the substances and create them as drugs. Today, we refer to these as **psychotropic medications**. Psychotropic medications are those that are used to treat mental disorders. The study of these drugs is the domain of psychopharmacology (Evans, 2019).

As you will see, introduction of medications directed at mental illness allowed individuals to live in more independent settings. In the middle part of the 20th century, this led to the closing of mental hospitals throughout the US. The closing of hospitals is described in the box: The World Is Your Laboratory: Closing Mental Hospitals in America. Today, medication plays an important role in the treatment of mental illness. In addition to medication, there are other treatment approaches that seek to directly change physiological processes. Today, treatments range from the widespread prescribing of drugs to deal with psychological disorders to the less-often used but significant measures involving shock or electrical stimulation of the brain to the rarer use of neurosurgery.

Biological approaches play an important role in the treatment of mental disorders. Treatment effectiveness is not an either/or question of psychological and biological approaches but an attempt to combine treatments that work together in an effective way. For example, research from 2015 shows that psychotherapy along with lower levels of psychotropic medication are very effective for treating schizophrenia (Insel, 2016, Kane et al., 2016).

Psychotropic Medications

During the US Civil War, a textbook by Union Army Surgeon General William Hammond suggested that lithium bromide be used to treat manic patients (see Perlis & Ostacher, 2016, for an overview). However, it was not until 1949 that the Australian John Cade reported that lithium had a calming effect on animals and humans with mania. As you will see, lithium is still used to treat mania, which we refer to as bipolar disorder today. Drugs that came to be called antidepressants for the treatment of depression such as monoamine oxidase inhibitors (MAOIs) and the tricyclic antidepressants (TCAs) were discovered by serendipity in the 1950s (Fava & Papakostas, 2016). Some common MAOIs are Nardil and Parnate. Common tricyclics are Elavil and Tofranil. SSRIs (selective serotonin re-uptake inhibitors) such as Prozac and Paxil were developed later. These are typically used for the treatment of mood disorders. Benzodiazepines such as Valium have been used for the treatment of anxiety for at least 50 years.

One significant event came in 1952 when a French naval surgeon was attempting to find medications to give before an operation to reduce stress (see Freudenreich, Goff, & Henderson, 2016 for an overview). What he discovered was that an antihistamine substance, called chlorpromazine, left individuals feeling indifferent about their operation. Noticing its calming effect, he suggested that this might be useful in treatment of mental disorders. In particular, it was discovered that chlorpromazine [Thorazine] helped to reduce the symptoms of schizophrenia and initially became an important antipsychotic medication. This, in turn, led to the reduction in the number of patients in mental hospitals, as noted in the box: The World Is Your Laboratory: Closing Mental Hospitals in America.

Also, in the 1950s, drugs were introduced and accepted by the public, which were designed to treat milder forms of anxiety and stress. These were referred to as minor tranquilizers and included meprobamate (Miltown), chlordiazepoxide (Librium), and diazepam (Valium). In the 1990s, popular press books such as *Listening to Prozac* suggested that these drugs can help you feel "better than well" (Kramer, 1993).

Although the public accepted medication as safe, it should be noted that some of the early antipsychotic medications had problematic side effects, such as weight gain, tiredness, trouble sleeping, and involuntary movements (tardive dyskinesia). Newer drugs used today have fewer of these side effects but are not totally free of problems.

As you learned in chapter 3, the brain is a complex organ that processes information through chemical and electrical signals. Most of the drugs used in the treatment of mental disorders influence information processing in the brain by influencing neurotransmitters at the level of the synapse. Since the 1970s, benzodiazepines have been used to treat anxiety. Benzodiazepines are thought to influence the neurotransmitter GABA. Individuals with anxiety have reduced GABA activity, which in turn results in less inhibition of those brain structures that are involved in threat responses. A second class of medication referred to as azapirones were introduced in the 1990s. Buspirone (Buspar and Wellbutrin) is a common azapirone that influences serotonin receptors in the brain. Depression is treated with drugs that also influence the neurotransmitter serotonin. These are referred to as serotonin reuptake inhibitors (SSRIs), such as paroxetine (Paxil). SSRIs block the reuptake of serotonin at the synapse. Specific psychotropic medications will be described in greater detail later in this chapter in terms of the treatment of particular mental disorders.

The World Is Your Laboratory: Closing Mental Hospitals in America

During the first half of the 20th century, state mental hospitals were the main source of treatment and care for those with serious mental disorders in the United States (see Fisher, Geller, & Pandiani, 2009; Torrey, 1997, for overviews). By the 1950s, there were more than a half million individuals in these hospitals. However, during the 1950s and 1960s, a number of events occurred that changed the way individuals with mental disorders were treated in the United States. One significant event was the introduction of antipsychotic medication. Prior to this, individuals with serious mental disorders such as schizophrenia needed a high level of care and protection. With the introduction of medications that would help treat the disorder, it was possible for some of these individuals to live outside the hospital.

The Community Mental Health Act of 1963, signed into law by President John F. Kennedy, reflected the growing understanding that all but a small portion of those in mental hospitals could be treated in the community. The basic idea was that community mental health centers would offer a variety of programs to those with mental illness.

Although the population of the United States increased by 100 million between 1955 and 1994, the number of individuals in mental hospitals decreased from 550,239 to 71,619. The process of moving individuals from mental hospitals to the community was known as *deinstitutionalization*. **Figure 15-4** shows this drastic change.

For some of the individuals today who would have been placed in a hospital in the 1950s, their quality of life in the community is much better than it would have been.

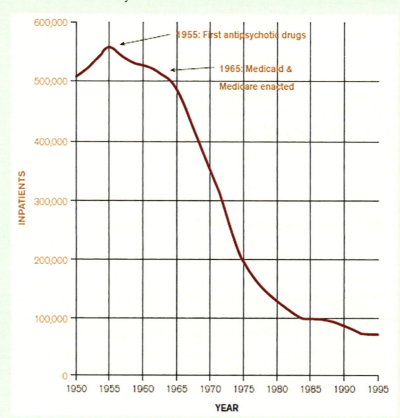

Figure 15-4 Beginning in the 1960s, the number of individuals in a mental hospital in the US began to decline.

Source: Fuller Torrey (1997).

However, for many individuals, the ideals of the community mental health movement were never fulfilled. The community facilities for those with mental illness were never fully funded or were not even built. This left many individuals not receiving the type of treatment they needed. Some of these individuals have found themselves homeless and on the streets. Others, who were disruptive or concerned the community, found themselves in jails and prisons with little mental health treatment and care. Similar deinstitutionalization occurred in the United Kingdom and other developed countries.

Thought Question: Our history has shown us that neither institutionalizing nor deinstitutionalizing all individuals with serious mental disorders has been effective. What do you think some characteristics of a workable solution are?

Electroconvulsive Therapy

Other current treatment approaches seek to influence the individual's brain by changing the underlying electrical activity. Some of these treatments are seen as *noninvasive* (see Camprodon, Kaur, Rauch, & Dougherty, 2016 for overviews). That is, there is no requirement that electrodes or other devices be placed inside the brain itself. The oldest of these techniques is **electroconvulsive therapy (ECT)** in which electrical activity disrupts the normal brain activity and produces convulsions (see Welch, 2016 for an overview). This electrical activity triggers a brief seizure of less than a minute, which most likely influences changes in brain chemistry and specific networks of the cortex. ECT has changed over the years with a reduction in motor convulsions and a reduction in the number of brain areas affected. It is seen as an effective treatment for those with severe depression that does not respond to other types of medication or psychotherapy (Haq et al., 2015; Ross, Zivin, & Maixner, 2018).

Brain Simulation

An alternative to ECT, **transcranial magnetic stimulation (TMS)** disrupts the brain activity using magnetic stimulation to treat mental disorders, including depression. It has been known for a long time that electromagnetic activity can induce electrical changes in various materials. In transcranial magnetic stimulation, an electromagnetic coil is placed on the scalp (see Pitcher, Parkin, & Walsh, 2021, for an overview). From the coil, a magnetic field induces a small electrical current in the first few centimeters of the brain, which depolarizes the neurons. One advantage is that TMS is a noninvasive method for stimulating cortical cells in fully awake and responsive individuals.

Initial research used single-pulse TMS to study underlying motor processes by placing the TMS coil above the motor cortex. One of these studies showed a relationship between motor responses and a measure of depression (Oathes & Ray, 2006). More recently, it was found that repetitive TMS (rTMS) where multiple pulses are generated in rapid succession is effective in the treatment of depression (cf. Loo & Mitchell, 2005). A study from 42 different locations in the United States with 307 outpatients showed significant changes in depression scores following rTMS treatment (Carpenter et al., 2012). In humans who do not respond to antidepressant medication, rTMS has shown similar results to ECT. The advantage of rTMS in comparison with ECT is that no anesthetic is required and no side effects such as memory loss have been reported. Like ECT, rTMS is recommended for those who do not show changes in depression from medication.

More invasive treatments require that electrodes be placed in the brain that change the existing brain networks. The technique has been referred to as ***deep brain stimulation (DBS)*** and has been used for the treatment of motor disorders such as Parkinson's disease, as well as obsessive compulsive disorder (OCD) and depression. Stimulating electrodes are placed deep in the brain and these electrodes are connected to a pulse generator that is placed under the person's skin, typically below the neck. Current devices allow health care professionals to adjust the stimulation from wireless devices outside the skin. The NPR podcast Invisibilia describes the treatment of a woman for OCD (https://www.npr.org/2019/03/28/707639854/the-remote-control-brain).

The most invasive procedures are surgical procedures in which different areas of the brain are removed or their connections disrupted. Severe epilepsy, in which a person has numerous seizures and cannot work or function in a normal life, has been treated in this manner. Today, surgical procedures of the brain are limited to very small areas. In fact, gamma rays rather than a surgical knife are used to make the small cuts. Such small cuts in the brain are used with individuals who show no improvement in epilepsy, depression, or anxiety using standard treatments.

Not all of the biological treatments have been successful. In the first half of the 1900s, as a treatment for mental illness, the frontal areas of the brain were disconnected from the rest of the brain. This procedure was used until the 1950s and then discontinued. This procedure, which was referred to as *frontal lobotomy*, left the person with limited emotional and cognitive abilities. Even during its time, there were serious debates as to its ethics and effectiveness.

As you will also learn in the Applying Psychological Science feature, psychotherapy and biological approaches work through different brain mechanisms and at different levels of the brain.

Applying Psychological Science: Mechanisms of Action with Psychotherapy and Medication

Brain-imaging techniques are now allowing scientists to better understand how a particular psychological disorder affects the brain and how various treatments work. For example, with mood disorders, there are changes in the brain in those areas that are involved in emotional regulation (DeRubeis, Siegle, & Hollon, 2008). In particular, individuals with depression often have negative thoughts about themselves and their future that they keep repeating to themselves. These thoughts are associated with increased activity in the limbic areas including the amygdala and decreased activity in the prefrontal cortex. The decreased activity of the prefrontal areas would allow for increased activity in the limbic processes associated with emotionality.

How about treatments for depression? What brain changes would be seen? One possibility is that cognitive therapy and medication work through different pathways in the brain (DeRubeis, Siegle, & Hollon, 2008). As noted previously, brain-imaging studies show greater amygdala activity and less prefrontal cortex activity in those with depression compared to those without depression. After successful treatment for depression, amygdala activity is decreased and prefrontal activity increases.

Different pathways in the brain may be involved in successful treatment of depression. Before treatment, those with depression show more amygdala activity and less prefrontal cortex activity. Cognitive therapy (CT) increases prefrontal cortex activity, which in turn decreases limbic reactivity. Antidepressant medication (ADM) decreases the amygdala activity directly. Thus, as suggested by DeRubeis and his colleagues, cognitive therapy with its focus on cognitive processing may increase prefrontal activity, which in turn is able to inhibit amygdala activity. Antidepressant medication, on the other hand, decreases amygdala activation directly. Thus, neuroscience techniques and findings may help to explain the mechanisms of action as well as the value of utilizing more than one treatment approach.

Thought Question: How might you use brain-imaging techniques to know whether a treatment is effective?

CONCEPT CHECK

1. Psychotropic medications play an important role in the treatment of mental illness. Describe the circumstances that led to the discovery of three of these medications as well as their current uses in treating mental illness.
2. Some treatment approaches to mental illness seek to influence the individual's brain by changing the underlying electrical activity. Briefly describe how each of these techniques works and indicate current applications in the treatment of mental illness:
    a. Electroconvulsive therapy (ECT)
    b. Transcranial magnetic stimulation (TMS)
    c. Deep brain stimulation (DBS)
    d. Frontal lobotomy

Effective Treatment of Mental Disorders

Before the middle of the 20th century, very little formal research was performed to see how effective psychological interventions were. This was also true of traditional medical procedures. Beginning in the 1950s and 1960s, there were the beginnings of a movement to determine the effectiveness of both medical and psychological treatments in a scientific manner. In medicine, this came to be known as *evidence-based medicine*. In psychology, the terms **empirically based treatments** or **empirically based principles** refer to treatments and their aspects for which there is scientific evidence that the treatment is effective.

Three websites have been developed that list treatments for specific mental disorders. The first is maintained by the Clinical Psychology section of the American Psychological Association (https://www.div12.org/psychological-treatments/). The second is maintained by the US Substance Abuse and Mental Health Services Administration (SAMHSA), which is part of the US Department of Health and Human Services. This website contains a searchable online registry of mental health and substance abuse interventions that have been evaluated (https://www.samhsa.gov/find-treatment). The third website is devoted to effective treatments for children and adolescents (http://effectivechildtherapy.com/). This site is maintained by the Society of Clinical Child and Adolescent Psychology section of the American Psychological Association.

As researchers and clinicians began to focus more on approaches and principles for which there was scientific evidence that they were effective, there began a movement to develop effective treatments for particular disorders that used both biological and psychological treatment approaches. There has also been more willingness to integrate techniques from the different psychological approaches as well as from other perspectives. For example, in the discussion on personality disorders treatment, you will see that one of the most researched treatments—dialectical behavior therapy (DBT)—is based on techniques from each of the three approaches described in this chapter. This effective treatment uses aspects of cognitive behavioral techniques, dynamic techniques, and existential-humanistic techniques.

Treatment for Anxiety Disorders

Anxiety is a common experience of many individuals that they may report to many types of health professionals including psychologists, psychiatrists, and even their family physician. These individuals are often given medications such as benzodiazepines or offered one of the types of psychotherapy described previously. Studies using psychodynamic, existential-humanistic, and cognitive behavioral approaches have all reported reductions in anxiety. At this point, both medications and psychological treatments show similar reductions in generalized anxiety disorder (GAD) in the short term. However, only about 40% to 60% of those treated with either medication or psychological treatments show full improvement. This is in comparison with other anxiety disorders such as phobias, which show higher rates of improvement after treatment.

Psychological Treatment of GAD

The best-studied psychological interventions have involved cognitive behavioral approaches and behavioral approaches with GAD although dynamic approaches have also been shown to be effective (Barber, Muran, McCarthy, & Keefe, 2013). The behavioral approaches include relaxation training and other such techniques. The cognitive behavioral techniques focus on *automatic thinking*. Typical approaches train clients to detect internal and external anxiety cues and to apply new coping skills that focus on both psychic and somatic symptoms (Borkovec & Ruscio, 2001). Initially, clients are asked to pay close attention to those factors in their daily life that trigger anxiety responses. They are also asked to pay attention to physiological and cognitive responses experienced as anxiety develops. In the therapy itself, the client is asked to imagine a situation that would increase stress or anxiety or choose a topic that he or she would worry about and notice the associated thoughts, feelings, and images. Overall, the major cognitive behavioral approaches are designed to be offered for a specific period of time. These techniques help the client learn how to reduce anxiety and worry, which is a major component of GAD.

Some important components of a cognitive behavioral therapy (CBT) approach are as follows:

1. Identifying the anxiety-associated thoughts, images, beliefs, and so forth
2. Discussing these to bring out their causal role
3. Leading clients to question the validity of thoughts or beliefs, and to search for evidence
4. Helping clients develop alternative, less anxiety-arousing assumptions or interpretations
5. Testing alternative viewpoints in homework assignments or experiments
6. Teaching the above methods as self-helping coping devices to be used in real life

These components were developed by Tom Borkovec and his colleagues, who tested the effectiveness of therapy components in a variety of outcome studies. Additionally, Borkovec and Ruscio (2001) reviewed outcome research from 13 randomized controlled GAD studies that involved a CBT component. As a whole, these CBT studies showed decreases in anxiety and depression following treatment, which was maintained in a 6- to 12-month follow-up. This suggests that CBT is effective not only for GAD but also for some of the comorbid conditions. Successful treatment was also associated with specific psychophysiological changes such as EEG activity in the gamma band (Oathes et al., 2008).

Another effective treatment for GAD is mindfulness (Hoge et al., 2013). Mindfulness-based treatments have the person with GAD focus on the present moment. This attention to the present is performed with openness and a nonjudgmental manner. This allows for better emotional regulation and reduction of anxiety symptoms. In randomized control trials for the treatment of GAD, mindfulness-based treatment has been shown to be more effective than one involving stress-reduction techniques (Hoge et al., 2013). Further, functional magnetic resonance imaging (fMRI) changes were seen following mindfulness training in those with GAD in the amygdala and the connections between the frontal areas and the amygdala (Hölzel et al., 2013). These cortical changes were also associated with symptom reduction.

Mindfulness approaches have also been integrated into traditional CBT. One of these is Acceptance and Commitment Therapy (ACT) (Hayes, 2004; Hayes, Strosahl, & Wilson, 2011). This approach suggests that those with GAD attempt to control their internal experiences, which often does not work. Based on this failure to control such thoughts and feelings, these individuals avoid internal processes. ACT uses acceptance and mindfulness to regain connections with one's internal processes including thoughts, feelings, memories, and physical sensations.

Another therapy that has integrated mindfulness with CBT is referred to as acceptance-based behavioral therapy (ABBT) (for example, Hayes-Skelton, Roemer, & Orsillo, 2013; Orsillo & Roemer, 2016; Roemer & Orsillo, 2002; Roemer, Orsillo, & Salters-Pednault, 2008). This treatment involves educating individuals with GAD about their relationship with internal experiences, especially negative reactions to these. The second part of the treatment includes mindfulness exercises. A third component emphasizes behavioral changes rather than reacting to internal processes.

Biological Treatment of GAD

Since the 1970s, benzodiazepines such as Xanax and Klonopin have been used to treat anxiety (Wilson & Stein, 2019). Benzodiazepines are thought to influence the neurotransmitter GABA. Individuals with anxiety have reduced GABA activity, which in turn results in less inhibition of those brain structures that are involved in threat responses. Unlike antidepressant medications, benzodiazepines show their effect within a week. A large number of studies have shown anxiety reductions in approximately 65% to 70% of GAD clients when given benzodiazepines (see Roemer, Orsillo, & Barlow, 2002, for an overview). A smaller percentage shows a full remission of anxiety symptoms. However, when a person discontinues benzodiazepines, GAD symptoms will reappear.

A second class of medication referred to as azapirones (BuSpar) was introduced in the 1990s. Buspirone (Buspar and Wellbutrin) is a common azapirone that influences serotonin receptors in the brain. This drug influences more of the cognitive components of GAD and has fewer side effects than benzodiazepines. A third class of drugs for GAD is antidepressants. Both tricyclic antidepressants, such as imipramine (Tofranil), and serotonin reuptake inhibitors (SSRIs), such as paroxetine (Paxil), have been shown to be effective with GAD.

Treatment for Social Anxiety Disorder

There are a number of psychological therapies that have been developed for treating social anxiety disorder (SAD) (see Hofmann & Barlow, 2002; Rodebaugh, Holaway, & Heimberg, 2004; Weiss, Hope, & Cohn, 2010, for overviews). These therapies include CBT, exposure therapy, social skills training, and group CBT. These different approaches may also be combined in different ways. Both CBT-type therapies and medication have been shown to be effective with SAD. CBT-type therapies show larger changes with fewer side effects than medications (Mayo-Wilson et al., 2014). Medications appear to show a faster reduction in anxiety initially. However, following treatment when no additional medication or psychotherapy is offered, there is a greater relapse with medication treatment than with CBT therapy.

Exposure therapy places a client in a feared situation despite the experience of distress. One technique is for clients to create a hierarchy of situations that they would fear or avoid. They can rank this hierarchy in terms of the level of anxiety they would expect to experience. These situations can then be used in the therapy. Typically, the person begins with the least anxiety-producing situation, such as talking to the staff at the coffee shop. The person then moves to more anxiety-producing situations, such as talking to someone you want to impress. At the top of the hierarchy would be the most anxiety-producing situation, such as giving a talk to an audience evaluating you. The situation can be experienced by either role-playing or actually being in the feared environment. Although the underlying mechanisms leading to change have not been determined precisely, exposure therapy has been shown to reduce anxiety in social situations for individuals with SAD (see Abramowitz, Deacon, & Whiteside, 2011, for an overview).

Social skills training is based on the idea that individuals with social anxiety have inadequate social interaction skills. Social skills training teaches the individual practical social skills through modeling, corrective feedback, reinforcement, and other such techniques. Since this type of training involves trying out new behaviors, it is difficult to separate it completely from exposure therapy in outcome studies.

CBT, as described previously, assumes that social anxiety is produced by the person's automatic thoughts in the social situation or the expectation of the social situation. The task is to help the person detect and restructure these thoughts and expectations. In the treatment of social anxiety, it has been offered in both individual and group therapy.

Psychopharmacological approaches have been shown to be useful in the treatment of social anxiety (Leichsenring & Leweke, 2017). One of the earliest drugs used was a monoamine oxidase (MAO) inhibitor, phenelzine sulfate (Nardil), which was seen as the drug of choice. More recent medications have included the SSRIs, paroxetine (Paxil) and sertraline (Zoloft). The norepinephrine-SSRI venlafaxine (Effexor) has also been used. The choice of medication is often left with the individual health professional based on a specific person's side effects.

Treatment for Specific Phobias

It is commonly accepted that phobias are best treated by exposure to the feared object (see Antony & Barlow, 2002; Böhnleina et al., 2020, for overviews). Lars Öst has shown in a number of studies that a phobia such as fear of snakes or spiders can be significantly reduced after a single three-hour session, although similar results are found in a larger number of shorter sessions (Davis, Ollendick, & Öst, 2019; and Öst, 1989, 1996). The basic procedure would be for the client to describe her fears as well as catastrophic expectations and the situations that evoke these in a session with her therapist. This would be followed by the therapist slowly introducing the feared object such as a snake from a distance. The therapist checks with the client as this is happening to determine the magnitude of fear. In general, it is the client who directs the speed of the introduction of the feared object. During the session, the therapist would bring the feared object closer to the person until she was able to touch it with reduced fear.

Using the rapid gradual exposure techniques of Lars Öst, Thomas Straube and his colleagues measured brain changes prior to and following therapy (Straube, Glauer, Dilger, Mentzel, & Miltner, 2006). They studied a group of individuals with spider phobia. These individuals received two sessions of therapy with a duration of four to five hours. Gradual exposure started with the presentation of spider pictures. Then, the individuals were shown the skin of a tarantula, followed by an actual tarantula. Once the actual tarantula was introduced, the goals of the therapy were fourfold. These were (1) to hold a living tarantula for about 10 minutes, (2) to catch moving and non-moving spiders at least ten times with a glass at different locations within the therapy room, (3) to catch any species of spider in the basement of the institute at least three times, and (4) to touch a rapidly moving house spider. By the completion of the therapy, all of the individuals with spider phobia were able to fulfill the four treatment goals without strong feelings of anxiety.

An fMRI session was conducted prior to the beginning of any therapy in which the individuals with spider phobia and a control group were shown pictures of spiders as well as neutral pictures. As expected, individuals with spider phobia showed greater activation in the insula and ACC, which is part of the fear network. Following therapy, this activation was reduced.

Treatment for Panic Disorder

The currently preferred medication treatments for panic disorder are SSRIs, which have been shown to be more effective than placebo treatments. Benzodiazepines have also been shown to be effective. The best-studied psychological treatment for panic disorder is CBT, which has been shown to be effective. In general, CBT approaches educate the individual concerning the nature of panic symptoms and reduce misconceptions. Internal exposure techniques can also be employed. For example, the person could be asked to exercise to increase his or her heart rate or spin around in a chair to feel dizzy. In this way, the person is exposed to the internal situation associated with a panic attack. More global aspects of CBT, such as cognitive restructuring in terms of distortions in thinking, are also used. This helps to reduce the catastrophic expectations, such as thinking that one is going to die when one's heart rate increases. Meta-analyses have shown that combining CBT and antidepressant medication is more effective than either one alone (Mitte, 2005; Watanabe, Churchill, & Furukawa, 2009).

Treatment for Obsessive-Compulsive Disorder

Both psychopharmacological and behavioral therapies have been shown to be effective for OCD (Hirschtritt, Bloch, & Mathews, 2017). The most common medications are SSRIs and the tricyclic antidepressant clomipramine. Meta-analysis of randomized control trials shows SSRIs effective compared to placebos (Abramowitz & Jacoby, 2014). Changes with CBT have been shown to be greater when CBT is compared to SSRIs. However, both together show the best effects (see Pauls, Abramovitch, Rauch, & Geller, 2014, for an overview). These have been shown to be effective for about 60% of people with the disorder. OCD has been less well studied with randomized control trials in terms of psychotropic medications. For those disorders, CBT is considered the treatment of choice at this point.

The psychosocial treatment that has the best empirical support is exposure and response prevention (EX/RP), which is largely based on the work of Foa and Kozak (1986; see also Franklin & Foa, 2008, 2011, for overviews). One component includes discussions with the client concerning beliefs related to the outcome of feared behaviors. For example, the client may think that he or she would get germs from being in public bathrooms. Discussions can also be focused on what the person needs to do to prevent the expected negative outcome. Another component of this approach includes prolonged exposure to obsessional cues. For example, if the person finds it distressing to go into public restrooms, then he or she would be exposed to that actual situation. By prolonged exposure, rituals can be blocked. In addition to the actual situation, imagery can be used to repeat the situation without the ritual until the anxiety is lessened. Thus, the initial inability to conduct rituals produces distress. The basic idea, according to Foa and Kozak, is that repeated, prolonged exposure to feared thoughts and situations will provide information to the person concerning his or her mistaken beliefs and in turn allow for habituation (Foa & Kozak, 1986).

In February 2009, the US Food and Drug Administration (FDA) approved the use of a device for deep brain stimulation to treat OCD. As with deep brain stimulation for severe depression, an electrode is implanted in the brain along with a generator and battery placed under the person's skin. Currently, there are a number of clinical trials examining this treatment. One study showed that deep brain stimulation disrupts the maladaptive pathways in OCD between the frontal areas of the brain and subcortical structures and restores normal function (Figee et al., 2013).

Treatment for Depression

Given the prevalence of depression, its treatment has been studied over a number of years (Beck & Bredemeier, 2016). Both medication and a number of different psychological approaches have been shown to be effective. Additionally, the combination of both is also very effective. This section will describe both medications and psychological treatment for the depression. The best treatment results rely on both, as described in the box: Myths and Misconceptions: Medication Shows More Long-Term Effects for Treating Depression.

Myths and Misconceptions: Medication Shows More Long-Term Effects for Treating Depression

Although drugs such as Prozac are often discussed in the popular press, clinical trials suggest that only about 50% of those who take medication for depression are helped (Fava, 2003). Another problem in the treatment of depression is that even in situations in which symptoms are reduced, individuals are at risk for a relapse of the symptoms. This is especially true when medication is used alone. For this reason, professionals have searched for a combination of treatments that might help prevent relapse by involving more than one underlying depressive mechanism. For example, antidepressant medication and a form of psychotherapy such as cognitive behavioral therapy (CBT) have been shown to each be effective in comparison to a placebo treatment (DeRubeis, Siegle, & Hollon, 2008).

In **Figure 15-5**, you can see that an antidepressant medication shows greater progress in reducing symptoms of depression at eight weeks of therapy as compared to CBT. Both medication and CBT are better than a placebo pill. It should also be noted that giving individuals with depression a placebo that is described as fast-acting will itself cause brain changes associated with a reduction in depression (Peciña et al., 2015). After 16 weeks of treatment, CBT and medication show equal effectiveness.

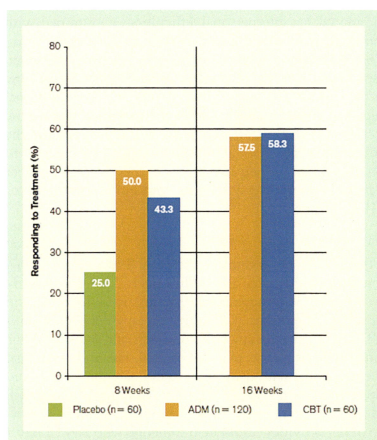

Figure 15-5 Cognitive behavioral therapy (CBT) and antidepressant medication (ADM) have comparable short-term effects.

Source: DeRubeis et al. (2008, p. 781).

With equal effectiveness of CBT and an antidepressant medication, what do you think would happen if they were both discontinued? What happened was that in both groups symptoms of depression began to reappear. However, there were fewer symptoms of depression in the CBT condition than in the drug condition. Thus, what was learned in CBT could continue to be effective although the therapy itself had been stopped. The medication on the other hand showed no lingering positive effects when it was no longer given. Other studies have shown that the combination of CBT with an antidepressant medication is more effective than either alone. Thus, although medication may initially be more effective for the treatment of depression, CBT shows more long-term effects. Of course, both together will give you the most effective treatment.

Thought Question: Write a brief explanation to give one of your friends if she asked you why a treatment for depression that combined medication and psychotherapy was more effective than providing either one alone.

Psychological Treatments for Depression

All of the three major psychological therapy approaches—dynamic, cognitive behavioral, and existential-humanistic—have empirically supported therapies for the treatment of depression. Emotion-focused therapy for depression, which is based on existential-humanistic techniques, has been shown to be useful for someone with mild to moderate depression (Greenberg & Watson, 2006). As noted previously, whereas the dynamic approach focuses on insight, the cognitive behavioral approach emphasizes the importance of action. That is to say, in dynamic approaches interpersonal difficulties are examined, with some focus on where thoughts and behaviors that did not work in the past came from. This often leads to discussion of early and significant relationships. Cognitive behavioral approaches, on the other hand, spend less time on past relationships and more on how to deal effectively with events in the future. The session itself is more of an educational process in which the client is helped to consider alternative explanations and learn how to cope. In CBT, there is little discussion of the relationship between the therapist and the client as there would be in dynamic approaches. Both approaches examine the manner in which individuals with depression distort and misperceive events in their lives. A number of studies have shown similar changes in depressive symptoms with either a dynamic or CBT approach (Goldfried et al., 1997; Shapiro et al., 1994).

Cognitive Therapy for Depression

Aaron Beck created a cognitive therapy for depression in the early 1960s (Beck, 1967; 2019; Beck & Alford, 2009; Hollon & Beck, 2013; see also Judith Beck, 2011, for an overview and update). The cognitive therapy model suggests that dysfunctional thinking and negative information processing maintain depression. Cognitive therapy for depression is structured and problem focused. By learning in therapy how to understand one's thinking, it is possible to change the way one thinks as well as one's emotional state and behaviors. Thus, the therapy process helps the individual with depression to evaluate the validity and utility of her thoughts. For example, if a person says, "It is all my fault," or "No one will ever hire me," the therapist would help the client consider ways to test these ideas empirically. Having a person fill out a log of her activities would help someone who says, "I never do anything," determine the validity of the statement. The client might also be assigned homework to move beyond inertia and create potentially positive experiences.

The cognitive model is described in terms of a cognitive triad related to depression. The first component of the triad is the individual's negative view of self. This is when the individual attributes unpleasant experiences to her own mental, physical, and moral defects. When something negative happens, the person says this is my fault. In therapy, clients can become aware of the content of their thinking. The second component is the individual's tendency to interpret experiences in a negative manner. That is, the person tailors the facts to fit negative conclusions. The basic idea is that thinking influences emotion and behavior. The third component is that the person regards the future in a negative way. She envisions a life of only hardships and anticipates failure in all tasks. In therapy, the basic idea is that individuals can modify their cognitive and behavioral responses. Overall, the therapy is directed at the automatic thoughts in relation to *catastrophizing*—believing that nothing will work out; *personalization*—believing that everything relates to you; *overgeneralization*—believing that one event is how it always is; and *dichotomous thinking*—believing that things are either good or bad.

A number of researchers and clinicians have further developed the classic approaches of Aaron Beck and others. These cognitive behavioral treatments are referred to as "new wave" or "third wave" approaches (Cristea, Montgomery, Szamoskozi, & David, 2013; Hayes, 2004). These new wave approaches focus less on changing the contents of a person's thoughts and more on the person's relationship to them and how they influence the person's functioning. The goals of these new wave therapies include creating flexibility and a willingness to experience one's thoughts and emotions rather than avoiding them. It is assumed that this experiential avoidance lies at the heart of psychological difficulties. Some examples of these new wave treatment approaches are *acceptance and commitment therapy* (ACT) and *mindfulness-based cognitive therapy* (MBCT), which have been shown to be effective for the treatment of depression (Kuyken et al., 2016). In other studies, it has been suggested that mindfulness meditation works through the default mode network to help regulate emotional reactions (Barnhofer, Huntenburg, Lifshitz, Wild, Antonova, & Margulies, 2016).

Emotion-Focused Therapy for Depression

Emotion-focused therapy (EFT) for depression is an empirically supported therapy developed by Leslie Greenberg and his colleagues (Greenberg & Watson, 2006). EFT promotes the individual experiencing and processing emotional aspects of his experience. This may involve bringing past emotional experiences and memories into the present. As part of therapy, the client is able to identify his maladaptive emotions and understand emotional needs in the present. This, in turn, allows the person to discover new ways of satisfying his current needs.

In terms of depression, the treatment begins with the person experiencing the weak or bad sense of self, which lies at the core of depression. Often a sense of shame and fear is associated with this maladaptive sense of self. In EFT, the client must do more than just name the maladaptive sense of self. They must fully experience it so change can take place. The role of the therapist is to empathetically be with the person and help the person regulate these negative emotional states without the fear of being overwhelmed. Thus, EFT works on the level of emotionality rather than the cognitive level as seen in CBT, although they both emphasize the meaning a client gives to his or her experiences. Like dynamic therapy, EFT would also consider the relationship between the therapist and the client on an emotional level. Further, where CBT may be seen as helping the person develop a logic and intelligence for dealing with his thoughts, EFT seeks to develop *emotional intelligence.*

In their empirical research to study the efficacy of EFT (see Greenberg & Watson, 2006, for an overview), Greenberg and his colleagues found that it worked best in individuals with depression who were not completely immobile. The clients that it worked best with were those who were able to parent, work, or go to school, although all of these individuals reported difficulty and found little satisfaction in their activities. EFT emphasizes tailoring the therapy to the client since depression can manifest on a number of levels. Although all of the clients in the study were diagnosed with depression according to *DSM,* their depression symptoms differed. Some were highly critical and felt like failures while others had lost relationships and felt abandoned and sad. Still others felt empty, confused, and aimless. Their interpersonal relationships with the therapist also differed greatly. In testing the effects of EFT against other therapies, EFT was shown to be effective in reducing the symptoms of depression.

Psychodynamic Therapy for Depression

One important aspect of dynamic therapy is the search for insight. One focus would be an understanding of how the depressive symptoms developed. Do they relate to the experience of losses in one's life? Do they relate to previous negative relationships, including critical parents who leave the child with little ability to accomplish life's goals? Do they relate to confusions concerning one's role in a job or relationship? Most short-term psychodynamic therapy would then focus on this theme.

In addition to past experiences, an additional focus would be on current relationships, including the relationship with the therapist. Like the Strupp and Binder (1984) approach, most psychodynamic approaches in relation to depression would begin with an understanding of the client's behavior and relationships and how these contribute to the continuation of the depressive symptoms. Some common themes with depression include a feeling of being helpless and the dependent feeling associated with this, an overdeveloped sense of responsibility, and a feeling of anger for one's situation, which becomes internalized.

The therapeutic relationship between the client and the therapist offers an opportunity to see disturbed relationships in a safe environment. Transference is an important mechanism in which the client tends to see the therapist in terms of significant others in his life. As the client talks with the therapist, he will replay prior conflicts and enact maladaptive patterns. For example, if one of his parents was very critical of his ideas, then he may initially find it difficult to tell the therapist feelings or thoughts that are very important to him or related to how he sees himself. Another situation would be one in which a parent never allowed him to engage in tasks that he could fail at or would save him whenever he encountered problems. These past situations would leave him with unrealistic expectations as to what to expect from the world and from others. In these situations, the person has never really learned what the world has to offer and may act as a child expecting someone to protect him and thus miss out on new experiences and learning. By understanding one's life, it is possible to gain insight into how to avoid moving into old, unhealthy patterns in new situations, which would maintain depressive symptoms.

Medications for Depression

The first effective medications for depression were introduced in the 1950s and 1960s (Gitlin, 2009; Hantsoo & Mathews, 2019). Two of these were imipramine (Tofranil), a tricyclic antidepressant, and iproniazid (Marsilid, Rivivol, Euphozid, Iprazid, Ipronid, Ipronin), a monoamine oxidase (MAO) inhibitor. The term *tricyclic* refers to the three-ring chemical structure of the drug. *MAO inhibitor* refers to the focus of action at the synapse. One problem with these initial medications was side effects such as weight gain, sleep problems, and irregular cardiovascular functioning. Additionally, MAO inhibitors can interact with certain foods, such as cheese, that contain the amino acid tyramine to increase blood pressure to dangerous levels.

In the late 1980s, a second generation of medications was released with fewer side effects. One of the most well-known was fluoxetine (Prozac). Prozac became an instant hit and was given to a large number of individuals worldwide, although the popular press suggested it was overprescribed. One problem with Prozac is that it is connected with thoughts of suicide in those under 18 years of age. It has also been associated with less sexual desire and symptoms such as headache and joint pain. Prozac is one of a number of drugs referred to as selective serotonin reuptake inhibitors (SSRIs) because of their effects at the synapse. SSRIs prevent the presynaptic reuptake of serotonin, which in turn increases the level of serotonin at the synapse. Newer antidepressant medications alter the central nervous system by influencing serotonin or norepinephrine or both. These are referred to as SNRIs. It general, it takes more than four weeks for antidepressant medications to have an effect.

One faster acting medication for depression that is being researched is Ketamine (Andrade, 2017; Hirota & Lambert, 2018; Nemeroff, 2018). It is generally administered as a slow intravenous infusion, although in 2019 a nasal spray related to Ketamine was approved by the FDA, which also must be administered in a medical setting. With Ketamine, changes in depression are seen within hours but decrease after 3 to 12 days. It has also been shown to reduce suicidal tendencies in individuals with major depressive disorder.

Overall, the effectiveness of antidepressant medication is found to be about 50% in clinical trials with adults (Fava, 2003). There have been a number of concerns when antidepressant medication is used with children and adolescents. In particular, some studies have suggested, as noted above, a risk for increased suicide among adolescents on these medications (Bridge et al., 2007). In children, these drugs may interact with normal processes such as exercise to lead to problems. However, for millions of Americans, a range of antidepressant medications have provided significant relief from depression.

Treatment for Bipolar Disorder

Until the middle of the last century, there was no effective treatment for bipolar disorder. Even today, it remains a complex disorder to treat. The main treatment goals are to optimize function and minimize symptoms and to establish mood stability. There is no accepted treatment for bipolar disorder that does not involve some form of medication. Because its symptoms may vary from depression to mania and this occurs in an irregular manner, there are fewer medications available for bipolar disorder. Further, a large number of individuals with bipolar disorder report a history of being misdiagnosed. This is partly because it is difficult to diagnose bipolar disorder without a clear picture of its course. Young adults who first show the symptoms in college, for example, may experience the symptoms as part of their lifestyle. It is often during a treatment for a depressive episode when mania appears that it is realized that bipolar disorder is the correct diagnosis.

Even with treatment, as just noted, those individuals with bipolar disorder who live in a negative emotional environment are more likely to relapse. Further, some people with bipolar disorder will discontinue their medication on their own, which leads to relapse. They may discontinue the medication because they miss the "highs" they experienced during mania, or want a wider range of emotional experience. Thus, most professionals recommend a combination of medication and psychotherapy and other types of support including family involvement for those with bipolar disorder. The nature of the disorder and the various psychosocial factors experienced by the person with bipolar disorder make performing research on a single medication or psychotherapy difficult.

Psychological Treatments for Bipolar Disorder

Most psychological therapies that have been used with bipolar disorders focus on both an educational and a psychological perspective. Specifically, techniques related to stress reduction and ways to reduce negative interactions with others are emphasized. Additionally, the client is also taught about bipolar disorder, its symptoms, the manner in which it may occur over time, and the importance of the use of medication. Family members and significant others in the client's life may also be involved in the education and stress-reduction aspects of therapy.

Monica Basco and John Rush (2005) have developed a 20-session CBT for use with individuals with bipolar disorder. The initial therapy sessions focus on the symptoms of bipolar disorder and the medications that are used to treat them. The next sessions focus on the client's particular symptoms, how to systematically monitor them, and factors related to treatment compliance. Following this, sessions are devoted to understanding one's cognitions including biased thinking and acting in both mania and depression. The final sessions emphasize an understanding of social relationships and ways to problem solve and resolve difficult situations.

Medications for Bipolar Disorder

It is important to keep in mind that there are different stages of treatment that require different processes (Goodwin & Jamison, 2007). These can be described as acute treatment, continuation treatment, and maintenance treatment. Acute treatment refers to the period from the beginning of a manic or depressive episode to remission of the symptoms. This period usually lasts from 6 to 12 weeks. Continuation treatment is the period from the remission of the symptoms to the time that they would not be expected to recur. This time has been determined from noting spontaneous recovery times in individuals who have not been treated. This period is about 6 months for a depressive episode and 4 months for a manic episode. Maintenance treatment is designed to prevent or reduce future episodes of mania and depression.

Psychopharmacological treatments for bipolar disorder involve a treatment for episodes of depression, a treatment for episodes of mania, and drugs to reduce relapse (Rosenblat & McIntyre, 2019; Thase & Denko, 2008). Lithium (Eskalith, Lithobid) is the most common treatment for bipolar disorder. Lithium is a salt found in nature. It was first used in the 1800s to treat mental disorders, although real interest in its use for the treatment of bipolar disorder began in the 1950s (Malhi, 2009). Lithium is more effective for the mania aspect of bipolar than the depressive aspect, and it is seen as a mood stabilizer. Although lithium has been used for a number of years, a major review suggested it is not as effective as commonly believed (Geddes, Burgess, Hawton, Jamison, & Goodwin, 2004). However, this review suggests its use is warranted in those individuals who respond to the drug. One group of individuals who do not respond to lithium are those who show rapid cycling.

Because lithium is not useful with certain groups, drugs referred to as anticonvulsants have been tried and shown to be effective such as lamotrigine (Lamictal). Another two of these anticonvulsants are sodium valproate (Depalote, Epival) and carbamazepine (Tegretol, Carbartol). Other classes of drugs such as antipsychotics have also been used in the treatment of bipolar disorder. One might think that antidepressants would work, but in some individuals these cause a switch to mania and rapid cycling.

Treatment for Dissociative Disorders

Although some dissociative disorders such as dissociative amnesia may resolve on their own, others such as dissociative identity disorder (DID) require long-term treatment. The basic procedure for treating DID is typically long-term psychotherapy. In therapy, a focus on the relationship between the client and the therapist is important. The emphasis is on developing a safe place where individuals can experience and integrate the various parts of themselves. At present, there are no empirically supported principles that have been tested in terms of dissociation. However, techniques from cognitive behavioral therapy (CBT), existential-humanistic, and dynamic approaches have been used in various combinations (see Ross, 1997). There are also no established medications directed solely for DID.

Treatment for Schizophrenia

Until about the 1960s, individuals with schizophrenia were placed in mental hospitals, often with little real treatment other than controlling them. With the advent of medications in the middle of the past century, it became possible for individuals with schizophrenia to live within community or home settings. In fact, individuals with schizophrenia tend to show more positive mental health behaviors when living within a community. In some cultures, small towns saw it as their duty to take care of these individuals. Today, after initial hospitalizations to gain control over symptoms, many individuals with schizophrenia return to their family. Other individuals continue their education or work. Some individuals are able to be productive and succeed in high-level jobs with appropriate support. However, some individuals with schizophrenia become homeless and are at the mercy of their community. In many communities, it becomes the role of the police and others to help protect these individuals.

Over the past 100 years, there has been a shift in viewing schizophrenia as a disorder with inevitable deterioration to one in which recovery is possible (see Frese, Knight, & Saks, 2009, for an overview). Recovery includes having a career. Living with schizophrenia depends on the resources of the individual in terms of intellectual abilities, coping techniques, and willingness to accept the advice of professionals.

Treatment for schizophrenia involves addressing the specific stage of the illness. These stages include the premorbid (before onset), prodromal (initial symptoms), first psychotic symptoms, a possible relapse even with treatment, and recovery. One major focus of treatment and research is the manner in which early intervention at each stage can reduce the severity of that stage. There are studies currently underway that are seeking to identify reliable indicators as to who will develop schizophrenia later in life (for example, Dixon, Goldman, Srihari, & Kane, 2018). However, at this point the research is not definitive. Thus, knowing with whom and how to intervene remains a future possibility, although a number of programs are testing this possibility. Once signs of schizophrenia develop, early intervention becomes important. With signs of a psychotic episode, antipsychotic medication and psychological treatments become important. Following this, supportive mechanisms such as family therapy and the creation of living and work conditions that help to reduce relapse are critical.

The Internet offers access to local and national groups that offer support for those with schizophrenia as well as the caregivers who offer support. In order to help individuals with schizophrenia cope in the community, a number of support procedures have been developed. These include antipsychotic medications as well as educational procedures to help the individual with schizophrenia and his or her family understand the course of the illness and the types of support necessary. As with other mental health disorders, specific psychotherapies for the person himself have been developed. Research suggests that the most effective treatment of schizophrenia should involve both medication and psychological approaches (Beck & Rector, 2005; Kane et al., 2015).

Psychological Interventions for Schizophrenia

Psychosocial factors play an important role in the overall treatment of individuals with schizophrenia. It has been estimated that more than 60% of people with a first episode of a major mental illness return to live with relatives. Thus, families play an important role in supporting these individuals. In fact, *family interventions* for schizophrenia reduce relapse and hospitalizations. A number of meta-analyses looked at evidence supporting family interventions (see Barrowclough & Lobban, 2008, for an overview). In general, family interventions involve the following key components:

1. Provide practical emotional support to family members.
2. Provide information about schizophrenia, what mental health services are available in the community, and nationwide support services (such as those found on the Internet).
3. Help the family develop a model of schizophrenia (including not blaming themselves).
4. Modify beliefs about schizophrenia that are unhelpful or inaccurate.
5. Increase coping for all family members.

6. Enhance problem-solving skills.
7. Enhance positive communications.
8. Involve everyone in a relapse-prevention plan.

A number of manuals involving *cognitive behavioral therapy (CBT) approaches* to schizophrenia are available (for example, Kingdon & Turkington, 1994; Smith, Nathan, Juniper, Kingsep, & Lim, 2003). The basic model suggests that what is important is the manner in which individuals interpret psychotic phenomena (see Beck & Rector, 2005; A. Morrison, 2008, for overviews). The overall model suggests that neurocognitive impairment in the premorbid state makes the individual vulnerable to difficulties in school or work, which lead to nonfunctional beliefs such as "I am inferior," maladaptive cognitive appraisals, and in turn nonfunctional behavior such as social withdrawal (Beck & Rector, 2005). The cognitive approach is aimed at helping the client understand the psychotic experience as well as cope with the experience and reduce distress. One key feature of schizophrenia is the disruption of thought processes, and one part of the treatment is directed at these illogical associations. Another focus of the treatment is directed at interpersonal relationships and success at work. This approach may also involve skills training such as self-monitoring and activity scheduling. Since individuals with schizophrenia may also show mood and anxiety problems, CBT aimed at these processes can also be utilized. The key features of CBT for schizophrenia can be summarized as follows (Beck & Rector, 2005; Turkington, Kingdon, & Weiden, 2006):

1. Develop a therapeutic alliance based on the client's perspective.
2. Understand the client's interpretation of past and present events.
3. Develop alternative explanations of schizophrenia symptoms.
4. Normalize and reduce the impact of positive and negative symptoms.
5. Educate the client in terms of the role of stress.
6. Teach the client about the cognitive model, including the role between thoughts, feelings, and behaviors.
7. Offer alternatives to the medical model to address medication adherence.

Developing a therapeutic alliance, that is, a relationship between the therapist and client who helps the work of therapy, is an initial task of therapy. Part of this may include talking with the client about his delusional beliefs. For example, if a client says that he invented a machine to solve the world's problems, then the therapist might ask when the person had this idea and what he has done to create the machine. The therapist might also ask him about others who had helped him with his ideas. As with CBT for other disorders, the basic idea is to look for inconsistent thoughts and conclusions that do not follow logically. For example, if no one would help the person with his machine, it does not follow logically that everyone is out to get him.

Another major task of therapy is helping the individual develop an alternative understanding of his or her symptoms. For example, some individuals with schizophrenia experience the voices that they hear as coming from outside of them. One goal of therapy would be to help the client reinterpret the source of the voices. Part of this may also include a cognitive assessment of alternatives to obeying the voices.

The role of stress in increasing symptoms of schizophrenia is an important concept for clients to understand. It is also important for them to understand the problems associated with not taking medication to control the symptoms of schizophrenia. Keeping individuals with schizophrenia on their medications is a difficult problem. In studies involving active medication alone versus a placebo alone, the relapse rates are about one half with medication compared with a placebo (32% versus 72%) (Hogarty & Goldberg, 1973). Based on current studies, treating individuals with schizophrenia with both CBT and psychotropic medication appears to be the most effective approach (see Beck & Rector, 2005, for outcome studies).

In the 1950s, George Brown in London, England sought to understand why some individuals with schizophrenia were readmitted soon after their hospital discharge with their symptoms reoccurring (see Brown, 1985 for an overview). What was found was that one important factor was the emotional environment in the home. This came to be referred to as *expressed emotion*. That is, homes in which the person experienced critical comments, hostility, and angry arguments were associated with relapse, whereas homes with warmth and positive remarks were not. Since that time, a number of intervention programs have been developed involving caregivers and others who live with those with schizophrenia (Amaresha & Venkatasubramanian, 2012).

A new approach is being tried in the treatment of schizophrenia—*early intervention* (see Fisher, Loewy, Hardy, Schlosser, & Vinogradov, 2013, for an overview). This approach seeks individuals who are at high risk for developing schizophrenia. The basic approach is to help these individuals develop cognitive skills as a way to increase attention, memory, executive control, and other cognitive processes. In addition, cognitive therapy is being used to reduce the reactivity to stress seen in the period prior to the development of psychosis and to better understand their thoughts and feelings. Although some success has been reported, this approach for the prevention of schizophrenia is still early in its development.

Another new approach referred to as *NAVIGATE* has been designed for the treatment of first-episode psychosis (Kane et al., 2015). NAVIGATE is a multidisciplinary, team-based approach that emphasizes low-dose antipsychotic medications, cognitive-behavioral psychotherapy, family education and support, and vocational and educational support. The program also helps the person engage in his or her community. One advantage of this approach is that the individual with first-episode psychosis receives all of these different treatment approaches. In a randomized control study involving 34 community mental health centers in 21 US states, the NAVIGATE program was shown to be more effective than the standard care found in the community health center. Further, the earlier the person entered treatment after the first psychotic episode, the better his or her outcome measures were. Based on these types of results, the National Institute of Mental Health has announced the Early Psychosis Intervention Network (EPINET) (http://www.nimh.nih.gov/ and search for EPINET).

Many professionals involved in the treatment of schizophrenia have come to realize that people are more likely to accept treatment and follow directions if they are involved in their own treatment. A number of states have coordinated treatment approaches such as NAVIGATE that use a multidisciplinary team as well as input from the person with schizophrenia. This is critical since many youths in the early stages of schizophrenia drop out of conventional medication-alone treatment.

Antipsychotic Medications

A variety of medications have been used in the treatment of schizophrenia (see Gopalakrishna, Ithman, & Lauriello, 2016; Hyman & Cohen, 2013; Kutscher, 2008; Minzenberg, Yoon, & Carter, 2010; Serper & Wang, 2019, for overviews). The treatment of schizophrenia changed drastically in 1954 with the discovery of chlorpromazine (Thorazine). When effective, this drug reduces agitation, hostility, and aggression. It also reduces the positive symptoms such as hallucinations and delusions and increases the time between hospitalizations associated with schizophrenia. However, negative symptoms and cognitive deficits are not changed by the drug.

One problem of this and other initial drugs were side effects such as *tardive dyskinesia*, which is a movement disorder resulting in involuntary movement of the lower face and at times the limbs. These purposeless movements include sucking, smacking the lips, and making tongue movements. These and other movement side effects are difficult to reverse if the medication was given over a period of time. Weight gain is also seen with antipsychotic medications. In subsequent years, new and different classes of *neuroleptic* medications have been developed with different or fewer side effects (Gopalakrishna, Ithman, & Lauriello, 2016). These newer drugs tend to reduce the positive symptoms of schizophrenia such as hallucinations and delusions. They also help the individual think more clearly and remain calmer. Not all medications work for all individuals. There is also some suggestion that different ethnic groups respond differently to neuroleptics, although it is less clear whether it is genetic factors or diet that influences these differences.

Overall, medications for schizophrenia have been referred to as first-generation or second-generation antipsychotics. Second-generation antipsychotics are also known as *atypical antipsychotics*. First-generation antipsychotics influence dopamine receptors (D_2), although the exact mechanism by which they work is still being studied. One example of a first-generation antipsychotic medication is haloperidol, which has a number of trade names worldwide, one being Haldol. Second-generation or atypical antipsychotic medications influence the dopamine receptors differently. Both first- and second-generation antipsychotics are successful in treating the positive symptoms seen in schizophrenia. One advantage of the second-generation antipsychotics is that they are also able to treat the negative symptoms. Initially, it was thought that the second-generation antipsychotics had fewer motor side effects, although this has not always been shown to be the case (Peluso, Lewis, Barnes, & Jones, 2012). In fact, large-scale studies suggest that second-generation drugs are no more effective than the older ones (Hyman & Cohen, 2013).

One large-scale study of effectiveness of antipsychotic medication was conducted at 57 clinical sites in the United States in the early 2000s involving almost 1,500 individuals with schizophrenia (see Lieberman & Stroup, 2011, for an overview and update). This is referred to as the CATIE (Clinical Antipsychotic Trials of Intervention Effectiveness) study. Individuals with schizophrenia were randomly assigned to one of five antipsychotic medications—olanzapine (Zyprexa), quetiapine (Seroquel), risperidone (Risperdal), ziprasidone (Geodon) and perphenazine (Trilafon)—and followed for 18 months. One important aspect of the study was to compare first- and second-generation antipsychotic medications. One surprising result was that the second-generation medications did not show greater effectiveness than the first-generation medication, perphenazine. This included greater effectiveness in terms of negative symptoms and cognitive impairment. These results had implications not only for treatment effectiveness, but also for economic considerations since first-generation medications are less expensive. The CATIE study brought forth much controversy in the years following its publication (Lieberman & Stroup, 2011).

Treatment for Personality Disorders

Personality disorders are difficult to treat. This is in part related to the fact that one individual with a personality disorder may show different signs and symptoms than another. Additionally, individuals with personality disorders find it difficult to maintain a close intimate relationship with their therapist. Because of this, psychotherapy for personality disorders is more individual focused than that for other disorders. At this point, research studies have shown that treatments based on both cognitive behavioral and dynamic perspectives have been effective. Medications have not been used as a direct treatment, but only as an adjunct (Bateman, Gunderson, & Mulder, 2015).

Although psychosocial treatment approaches come from different traditions, the effective approaches show many common factors (Bateman, Gunderson, & Mulder, 2015; Cuijers, Reijnders, & Huibers, 2019). Borderline personality disorder (BPD) has been the focus of most empirical treatment studies. The common factors seen in the treatment of BPD are:

1. A structured manualized approach is used that focuses on the commonly seen problems.
2. Clients are encouraged to assume control of themselves.
3. The therapist helps the clients to understand the connections of their feelings to events and actions. The therapist helps the client to consider the situation rather than just experiencing anxiety.
4. Therapists are active, responsive, and validating.
5. Therapists are willing to discuss their own reactions in the therapy session. For example, the therapist might say, "I misunderstood."

Let us now discuss specific treatment approaches.

Dialectical Behavior Therapy

One of the first researched treatment approaches for BPD is **dialectical behavior therapy (DBT)**. DBT was developed by Marsha Linehan, based on her work with suicidal clients and then expanded to those with BPD (Linehan, 1993; Linehan & Dexter-Mazza, 2008). Numerous studies have shown DBT to be effective in reducing suicide and increasing positive changes. This is especially true when a group skills training component is included (Linehan et al., 2015).

DBT therapy begins with the acceptance of the fact that individuals with BPD experience extreme emotional reactions and are particularly sensitive to changes in the environment. Anger toward the therapist is not uncommon. Individuals with BPD take longer to return to baseline conditions after their emotional reactivity. They may be impulsive. Suicidal considerations are common. This makes these clients difficult to work with and therapy sessions are often very challenging.

DBT is described by Marsha Linehan and her colleagues as a blend of behavioral science, dialectical philosophy, and Zen practice. The cornerstone of DBT is based on problem solving and acceptance of the experience of the moment. That is, the therapist acknowledges and accepts that a person felt rejected at the moment but not that the response to the rejection would be to hurt herself. The therapy itself is conceptualized in terms of a number of stages.

The *pretreatment stage* is a time when the client and the therapist arrive at a mutually informed decision to work together. This includes an understanding of the person's history and decisions concerning which processes should receive high priority. This pretreatment stage also includes a discussion concerning what can reasonably be expected from therapy and the roles of the therapist and the client. One emphasis is on the therapist and the client as a team, whose goal it is to help the client create a life worth living. In the service of creating a productive life, the individual will develop problem-solving skills for her own life.

The *first stage of therapy* is directed at helping the client develop a stable life. This includes reducing suicide-related behaviors and other behaviors that interfere with therapy and life. This stage typically lasts for one year. During this stage, dialectical thinking encourages clients to see reality as complex and not something that can be reduced to a single idea. This includes developing the ability to experience thoughts and feelings, which are experienced as contradictory. This is a difficult task for those with BPD. Four specific goals of Stage 1 include reducing suicidal ideation, reducing behavior that interferes with therapy, achieving a stable lifestyle, and developing skills in emotional regulation such as mindfulness. Stage 1 has been most researched in terms of empirically supported procedures.

The *second stage of therapy* moves to processing previously experienced traumatic events. One approach is to have the person re-experience prior trauma inside the therapy session. This stage can only occur once the person's life is stable and her emotional responding is under her control. The four specific goals of this stage include remembering and accepting the facts of earlier trauma, reducing any self-blame involving the earlier trauma, reducing the intrusive material associated with the earlier trauma as well as any denial associated with it, and resolving dialectical tensions associated with blame for the trauma.

The *third stage of therapy* is directed at helping the person develop a sense of self that allows her to live independently. The goal is to help the person experience both happiness and unhappiness with the ability to trust in her experiences. The *fourth and final stage of therapy* focuses on the ability to sustain joy and be part of an ever-changing world.

Other Effective Therapies for Treating Borderline Personality Disorder

In addition to DBT, there are also a number of dynamic-oriented therapies that are empirically supported. One of these is dynamic deconstructive psychotherapy (DDP). DDP was developed for clients who find therapy difficult, as well as for those who may also have substance abuse problems (Gregory & Remen, 2008). This approach is partly based on neuroscience research, which shows that individuals with BPD show difficulties with memory, emotional regulation, and decision making. This is seen as preventing these individuals from building a coherent self-system independent of other people. DDP is designed to help individuals with BPD develop a coherent sense of self.

DDP is divided into four distinct stages. The *first stage* is for the client and the therapist together to identify the client's difficulties and establish a series of goals and tasks for working on these difficulties. They also create an agreement as to how the client will keep himself safe. By the end of this stage, the relationship between the therapist and client should be stable and give the client comfort. This stage is similar in both dynamic and cognitive behavioral approaches.

The *second stage* involves the development of the client's ability to maintain complex ideas related to his relationships with others. For example, when a relationship with another ended, he would be able to say, "I felt both horrified and relieved." As this stage ends, the client begins to give up an idealized image of himself. As his idealized image of himself and his abilities is given up, there can be a better understanding of self-limitations, which is the focus of the *third stage*. During this third stage, the client can learn to verbalize his or her disappointments and experience the loss associated with this. This can also lead to fears of personal incompetence. The *fourth and final stage* moves to the relationship between the client and therapist and how the person will experience the termination of therapy.

Another empirically supported therapy is transference-focused psychotherapy (TFP). This is a twice-weekly therapy based on Otto Kernberg's object relations model (Clarkin, Yeomans, & Kernberg, 2006; see also Levy & Scala, 2012). As with other approaches, TFP seeks to reduce symptoms of BPD, especially self-destructive behaviors. The technique involves an exploration of how the person views herself and may combine her identity with that of another. That is, she does not have a stable view of self. During the first year of treatment, behaviors involved with self-harm are limited and a therapy contract is developed. In the sessions, the therapist follows the affect that the client brings to the session. The emphasis is on the relationship between the client and therapist. Questions of whether this relationship can also be seen in the client's other relationships can be addressed. Many of these techniques are similar to those of Hans Strupp described previously.

Treatment of Other Personality Disorders

Most of our knowledge of the treatment of personality disorders other than BPD is based on the experience of health care professionals, case studies, or simple descriptions of treatments. These include treatment approaches described in terms of borderline personality disorder. The individuals with other personality disorders about whom we have information present problems with their self and in their behavior toward—or relationships with—others in a number of different ways. This requires the mental health professional to pay attention to the specific way in which an individual is interacting with his or her world. Thus, manualized, empirically validated treatments for disorders other than BPD are less available.

Treatment for Neurodevelopment Disorders

As noted in the last chapter, neurodevelopmental disorders are those disorders that begin early in a child's life. These can include problems in the development of language, cognitive, emotional, and motor problems. Much of the treatment of these disorders takes place in the school that the child attends. In addition to programs in the school, both psychological treatments and medications have been used with two of these disorders, which are autism spectrum disorder and attention deficit hyperactivity disorder (ADHD).

Treatment for Autism Spectrum Disorder

Since autism spectrum disorder appears early in a child's life, parents turn to a number of different professionals for help. Depending on the initial problems of development noted, these professionals can include kindergarten teachers, special education teachers, speech pathologists, child clinical psychologists and psychiatrists, and pediatricians.

The first empirically supported treatments were developed by Lovaas and his colleagues in the 1960s (Lovaas & Smith, 2003). This approach, which was based on behavioral principles, was referred to as the UCLA Young Autism Project. This project has reported about 50% "recovery" rates for young children with autism, and these principles have been supported in other studies (Rogers & Vismara, 2008). Besides the success with individual children, this approach helped the field to understand that children with autism can learn important new skills.

The UCLA Project accepts children with autism under 4 years of age with the average age being 2 years 10 months. These children also need not to show major medical problems such as hearing or vision loss. These children then receive 40 hours a week of one-to-one interventions. This treatment lasts for about three years, depending on the individual child. Based on behavioral principles, the treatment was designed to maximize positive outcomes and reduce failure experiences. This includes giving the child short and clear instructions and immediate reinforcement for each correct response. Parents are also an important part of the process.

There are five major stages of treatment in the Lovaas treatment program. The first is establishing a teaching relationship, which lasts from two to four weeks. Since many of these children have previously avoided situations through tantrums and other means, the therapist works with the child in following simple directions. The second stage, which lasts from one to four months, involves teaching foundational skills related to following directions, imitating behaviors, and identifying objects. The third stage lasts for about six months and focuses on beginning communication. This includes initial speech processes and identifying objects and actions. The fourth stage, which lasts for about a year, continues communication processes such as labeling colors and shapes and developing the basic concepts of language. The fifth stage, which also lasts about a year, is designed to continue communication processes and help the child adjust to school situations, including peer interactions. The program ends as the child becomes part of a school situation.

In addition to psychosocial treatment approaches, medications have been used to address specific disruptive behaviors seen in ASD. These behaviors include hyperactivity, inattention, repetitive thoughts and behaviors, and aggressive behaviors against others and the self. Medications include antidepressants, stimulants, and antipsychotic medications. These medications are typically given to older rather than younger children with ASD. Those randomized control trials that do exist suggest improvement in irritability and hyperactivity resulting from a number of different medications (Friedman, Politte, Nowinski, & McDougle, 2015). At this point, there are no US Food and Drug Administration (FDA) approved drugs that have demonstrated significant changes in the core autism spectrum symptoms (Matson & Burns, 2019).

Treatment for ADHD

The major treatment for ADHD is medications that are stimulants. The benefit of stimulants for this purpose was found by accident in the last century. Although initially given to children as a treatment for headaches following an invasive brain X-ray technique, the stimulant amphetamine was also shown to help the children in the hospital to be calmer and more organized in their thinking (Adler et al., 2015). Although it may seem paradoxical to give a stimulant to a person who is hyperactive, these medications have been shown to be effective (Bidwell, McClernon, & Kolins, 2011; Fredriksen, Halmøy, Faraone, & Haavik, 2013). Stimulants appear to improve functioning by changing neurotransmitters in the brain.

The most common medications used in ADHD treatment are methylphenidates, which include the trade name Ritalin, and amphetamines including dextroamphetamine, which are known as Adderall and Dexedrine. These drugs reduce the symptoms of ADHD, such as disruptive and noncompliant behavior. They also increase the ability to focus attention. These medications may also improve physical coordination. It has been estimated that 70% of children with ADHD will show symptom reduction with stimulant medications.

Psychosocial methods are also used for the treatment of ADHD. These are often used in combination with medication, with the best treatment results seen with a combination of both (Hoza, Kaiser, & Hurt, 2008; Newcorn, Ivanov, & Chacko, 2015). Reviews of the treatment literature show that psychosocial interventions can have a positive impact beyond that of the medication alone (Watson, Richels, Michalek, & Raymer, 2015). With older adolescents and adults, psychological therapies may be useful in allowing the person to talk about the experience of having ADHD and to create cognitive and behavioral strategies for managing his or her environment. For example, reducing distraction allows the person to function more effectively.

CONCEPT CHECK

1. What is the importance of the concept of *empirically based treatments* or *empirically based principles* to the treatment of mental disorders?
2. What medications and psychological therapies are recommended for treating generalized anxiety disorder (GAD)? What aspects of GAD does each type of treatment target?
3. What do we know about how specific phobias are treated?
4. What medication and psychological approaches are available for the treatment of panic disorders? Is there one approach that is the most effective?
5. If a friend or family member asked you for a recommendation of the best treatment for OCD, what would you include in your answer?
6. Currently, what are the primary classes of antidepressant medications? How does each work? What are the advantages and disadvantages of each?
7. All of the three psychological therapy approaches—cognitive behavioral, existential-humanistic, and dynamic—described previously have empirically supported therapies for the treatment of depression. Considering each of these approaches, what is the primary focus of the therapy in regard to depression and what course does the therapy typically follow in providing an effective treatment?
8. What is currently available for the assessment and treatment of individuals with dissociative disorders?
9. What are three critical shifts in the past 60 years that have transformed the treatment of schizophrenia from one that was institution-based to one that is community-based?
10. A variety of classes of medications have been used in the treatment of schizophrenia. What are they, and what are the advantages and disadvantages of each?
11. What is it about personality disorders that makes them difficult to treat? What factors do effective treatments have in common to address those difficulties?
12. What are the major treatments for autism spectrum disorder and ADHD?

Summary

Learning Objective 1: Discuss the history of psychopathology and its treatments. Although the Greek and Roman periods saw individuals who attempted to understand psychopathology in a more humane way, this disappeared as their civilizations declined. As the Middle Ages approached, disease and especially mental illness was seen from the standpoint of a religious perspective with the devil being a major player. In 1330, a convent of the order of St. Mary of Bethlehem became the first institution for the mentally ill in England. Two hundred years later, King Henry VIII gave the institution a royal charter.

In the 1800s, there was a campaign in England to change the conditions of the patients, which led to the establishment of the Committee on Madhouses in 1815. This issued in a period of concern for the patients rather than seeing them as objects of curiosity as in the previous century. Treatment for patients during the 1800s brought new practices, including the therapeutic value of work. During this period, there was a spirit throughout the world to adopt a "moral treatment of the insane." Three important individuals were Benjamin Rush (1745–1813) in the United States, Philippe Pinel (1745–1826) in France, and Vincenzo Chiarugi (1759–1820) in Italy. In the United States, Rush, who had signed the Declaration of Independence, is often seen as the father of American psychiatry and saw mental illness as a problem of the mind.

William Tuke (1732–1822) was a Quaker philanthropist. In 1796, near York, England, he created a *Retreat for Persons Afflicted with Disorders of the Mind*. This Quaker retreat carried with it the idea that the individuals who were there should be given respect as well as good food and exercise. Another individual who contributed to the American mental health movement was Dorothea Dix (1802–1887). She encouraged the American congress to give federal land to the states to establish mental hospitals in the same way they created land grant colleges in the 1860s. Although this bill was not passed, it is estimated that her work led to the establishment of some 40 mental hospitals in the US and Europe.

Learning Objective 2: Describe the psychological treatment perspectives for the treatment of mental disorders.

There are three approaches for the psychological treatment of mental disorders: psychodynamic approach, existential-humanistic approach, and the cognitive behavioral approach.

The *psychodynamic perspective* is based on the idea that psychological problems are manifestations of inner mental conflicts and that conscious awareness of those conflicts is a key to recovery. Historically, Sigmund Freud laid the foundation for this perspective. By the beginning of the 20th century, there was an understanding that psychological processes were an important source of information concerning mental illness. Psychodynamic therapy is based on Freud's ideas and psychoanalysis was the first psychodynamic therapy to develop. Psychoanalysis treatment was based on the search for ideas and emotions that are in conflict and the manner in which an individual has relationships with other people. His specific treatment came to be called *psychoanalysis*.

The *existential-humanistic perspective* focuses on three themes: The first is an emphasis on human growth and the need for a positive psychology that moves beyond the discussion of stress and neurosis seen in the psychodynamic approaches. A second emphasis is that psychological health is more than just the absence of pathology. Not having a problem is not the same as finding meaning in one's life. The third theme stresses the importance of not only considering the external world and a person's relationship to it but also the internal world.

With the emphasis on *experience*, one well-known humanistic therapy is client-centered therapy.

Carl Rogers brought the humanistic movement to the forefront by creating *client-centered therapy*, also referred to as *person-centered therapy*. He was also one of the first psychologists to record therapy sessions so that they could be used for research. Rogers emphasized the relationship between the therapist and client as a critical key to effective therapy. There are three key characteristics of the client-centered approach: (1) *empathic understanding*, (2) *unconditional positive regard*, and (3) for the therapist to show *genuineness* and *congruence*.

The cognitive behavioral movement seeks to understand how cognitions are disordered or disrupted in mental disorders. Whereas humanistic therapies emphasize emotional processing, cognitive behavioral approaches emphasize thoughts and the manner in which a person thinks about her life and experiences. The basic idea is that psychological disturbances often involve errors in thinking. One real value of many cognitive behavioral approaches is that they have been tested empirically and presented in books and manuals that describe the steps involved in therapy. Cognitive behavioral therapy (CBT) has been developed for a variety of disorders. Overall, behavioral therapy focused on changing behaviors through conditioning principles, whereas cognitive behavioral therapy examined the manner in which thoughts influence behaviors. The behavioral perspective, as the name implies, has focused on the level of actions and behaviors.

Learning Objective 3: Summarize the biological approaches to treating mental disorders.
Medication plays an important role in the treatment of mental illness. In addition to medication, there are other treatment approaches that seek to directly change the physiological processes. These treatments range from the widespread prescribing of drugs to deal with psychological disorders to the less-often used but significant measures involving shock or electrical stimulation of the brain to the rarer use of neurosurgery.

Psychotropic Medications. Drugs that came to be called antidepressants for the treatment of depression such as monoamine oxidase inhibitors (MAOIs) and the tricyclic antidepressants (TCAs) were discovered by serendipity in the 1950s. SSRIs (selective serotonin re-uptake inhibitors) such as Prozac were developed later. These are typically used for the treatment of mood disorders. Benzodiazepines such as Valium have been used for the treatment of anxiety for at least 50 years. One significant event came in 1952 when a French naval surgeon was attempting to find medications to give before an operation to reduce stress. What he discovered was that an antihistamine substance, called chlorpromazine, left individuals feeling indifferent about their operation. Noticing its calming effect, he suggested that this might be useful in treatment of mental disorders. In particular, it was discovered that chlorpromazine (Thorazine) helped to reduce the symptoms of schizophrenia and became an important antipsychotic medication.

Electroconvulsive Therapy. Other current treatment approaches seek to influence the individual's brain by changing the underlying electrical activity. Some of these treatments are seen as *noninvasive*. That is, there is no requirement that electrodes or other devices be placed inside the brain itself. The oldest of these techniques is *electroconvulsive therapy (ECT)* in which electrical activity disrupts the normal brain activity and produces convulsions. This electrical activity triggers a brief seizure of less than a minute, which most likely influences changes in brain chemistry and specific networks of the cortex. ECT has changed over the years with a reduction in motor convulsions and a reduction in the number of brain areas affected. It is seen as an effective treatment for those with severe depression that does not respond to other types of medication or psychotherapy.

Brain Stimulation. An alternative to ECT, referred to as *transcranial magnetic stimulation (TMS)*, disrupts the brain activity using magnetic stimulation to treat mental disorders, including depression. It has been known for a long time that electromagnetic activity can induce electrical changes in various materials.

Learning Objective 4: Summarize the effective treatment options for mental disorders.

Anxiety is a common experience of many individuals that they may report to many types of health professionals. These individuals are often given medications such as benzodiazepines or offered one of the types of psychotherapy described previously. Studies using psychodynamic, existential-humanistic, and cognitive behavioral approaches have all reported reductions in anxiety. At this point, both medications and psychological treatments show similar reductions in generalized anxiety disorder (GAD) in the short term.

Social Anxiety Disorder. There are a number of psychological therapies that have been developed for treating social anxiety disorder (SAD). These therapies include CBT, exposure therapy, social skills training, and group CBT. These different approaches may also be combined in different ways. Both CBT-type therapies and medication have been shown to be effective with SAD. CBT-type therapies show larger changes with fewer side effects than medications. Medications appear to show a faster reduction in anxiety initially. However, following treatment when no additional medication or psychotherapy is offered, there is a greater relapse with medication treatment than with CBT therapy.

Specific Phobias. It is commonly accepted that phobias are best treated by exposure to the feared object. Lars Öst has shown in a number of studies that a phobia such as fear of snakes or spiders can be significantly reduced after a single three-hour session, although similar results are found in a larger number of shorter sessions. During the session, the therapist would bring the feared object closer to the person until she was able to touch it with reduced fear.

Panic Disorder. The currently preferred medication treatments for panic disorder are SSRIs, which have been shown to be more effective than placebo treatments. Benzodiazepines have also been shown to be effective. The best-studied psychological treatment for panic disorder is CBT, which has been shown to be effective.

Obsessive-Compulsive Disorder. Both psychopharmacological and behavioral therapies have been shown to be effective for OCD. The most common medications are SSRIs and the tricyclic antidepressant clomipramine.

Depression. Both medication and a number of different psychological approaches have been shown to be effective. Additionally, the combination of both is also very effective.

Bipolar Disorder. The main treatment goals are to optimize function and minimize symptoms and to establish mood stability. There is no accepted treatment for bipolar disorder that does not involve some form of medication. Because its symptoms may vary from depression to mania and this occurs in an irregular manner, there are fewer medications available for bipolar disorder. Most professionals recommend a combination of medication and psychotherapy and other types of support, including family involvement, for those with bipolar disorder.

Dissociative Disorders. Although some dissociative disorders such as dissociative amnesia may resolve on their own, others such as dissociative identity disorder (DID) require long-term treatment. The basic procedure for treating DID is typically long-term psychotherapy. In therapy, a focus on the relationship between the client and the therapist is important. Cognitive behavioral therapy (CBT), existential-humanistic, and dynamic approaches have been used in various combinations.

Schizophrenia. Until about the 1960s, individuals with schizophrenia were placed in mental hospitals, often with little real treatment other than controlling them. With the advent of medications in the middle of the past century, it became possible for individuals with schizophrenia to live within community or home settings. In fact, individuals with schizophrenia tend to show more positive mental health behaviors when living within a community. Today, after initial hospitalizations to gain control over symptoms, many individuals with schizophrenia return to their family. Other individuals continue their education or work. Some individuals are able to be productive and succeed in high-level jobs with appropriate support. However, some individuals with schizophrenia become homeless and are at the mercy of their community. In many communities, it becomes the role of the police and others to help protect these individuals.

Personality Disorders. Personality disorders are difficult to treat. This is in part related to the fact that one individual with a personality disorder may show different signs and symptoms than another. Additionally, individuals with personality disorders find it difficult to maintain a close intimate relationship with their therapist. Because of this, psychotherapy for personality disorders is more individual focused than that for other disorders. At this point, research studies have shown that treatments based on both cognitive behavioral and dynamic perspectives have been effective. Medications have not been used as a direct treatment, but only as an adjunct.

Study Resources

Review Questions

1. "During the current historical period, we have also come to see those with mental illness as whole people with both abilities and difficulties." How does viewing mental illness from the perspective of the individual change our views of appropriate treatment?
2. This chapter introduced three primary psychological treatment perspectives—dynamic, existential-humanistic, and behavioral and cognitive behavioral. For each perspective, describe:
   a. Its historical understanding
   b. Its broad principles
   c. Examples of specific treatments that have been tested in a scientific manner
3. Many current therapy approaches represent an integration of the three primary psychological treatment perspectives—dynamic, existential-humanistic, and behavioral and cognitive behavioral—as well as from other perspectives. Describe two examples that illustrate this integration, including the perspectives from which it draws.
4. What are the respective roles of therapist and client in each of these treatment approaches based on the three primary psychological treatment perspectives—dynamic, existential-humanistic, and behavioral and cognitive behavioral:
   a. Psychoanalysis, the dynamic treatment approach developed by Sigmund Freud?
   b. The dynamic treatment approach developed by Hans Strupp and colleagues?
   c. Client-centered or person-centered therapy, an existential-humanistic treatment approach developed by Carl Rogers?
   d. Emotion-focused or process experiential therapy, a humanistic-experiential treatment approach developed by Leslie Greenberg and colleagues?
   e. Cognitive triad for depression model, a cognitive behavioral approach developed by Aaron Beck?
5. In what ways are generalized anxiety disorder (GAD), social anxiety disorder (SAD), specific phobias, and panic disorder similar in terms of their treatment? How are they different?

6. What are three examples of effective treatment approaches for borderline personality disorder (BPD)? What is the overall approach of each therapy as well as the goals for each of the therapy's stages? How are the therapies similar, and how are they different?
7. Construct a table that lists all of the specific disorders included in this chapter on treatment of mental disorders. For each disorder, make a column for its empirically supported biological and medication treatments and psychological treatments.
    a. What patterns of treatment similarities—and differences—do you see across the different disorders?
    b. What are two or three insights on the current state of treatment for psychological disorders that this analysis gives you?

Web Resources

Elyn Saks—https://www.ted.com/talks/elyn_saks_seeing_mental_illness
Deep brain treatment of OCD—https://www.npr.org/2019/03/28/707639854/the-remote-control-brain
Treatment APA—https://div12.org/psychological-treatments/
SAMHSA substance abuse interventions—https://www.samhsa.gov/find-treatment
Effective treatments for children and adolescents—http://effectivechildtherapy.com/
Early Psychosis Intervention Network (EPINET)—https://www.nimh.nih.gov/index.shtml

Key Terms and Concepts

behavioral perspective
client-centered therapy or person-centered therapy
cognitive behavioral perspective
cognitive behavioral therapy (CBT)
deep brain stimulation (DBS)
electroconvulsive therapy (ECT)
emotion-focused therapy (ETF)
empirically based treatments or empirically based principles
existential-humanistic perspective
mindfulness
modeling
observational learning
process experiential therapy
psychoanalysis
psychodynamic perspective
psychotropic medications
real self
self-actualization
self-realization
transcranial magnetic stimulation (TMS)

References

Abbott, A. (2003). Restless nights, listless days. *Nature, 425*, 896–898.

Abramowitz, J., Deacon, B., & Whiteside, S. (2011). *Exposure Therapy for Anxiety*. New York: Guilford Press.

Abramowitz, J. S., & Jacoby, R. J. (2013). Obsessive-compulsive and related disorders: A critical review of the new diagnostic class. *Annual Review of Clinical Psychology, 11*(1), 150112144717005. http://doi.org/10.1146/annurev-clinpsy-032813-153713

Abutalebi, J., & Green, G. (2007). Bilingual language production: The neurocognition of language representation and control. *Journal of Neurolinguistics, 20*, 242–275.

Adamantidis, A. R., Gutierrez Herrera, C., & Gent, T. C. (2019). Oscillating circuitries in the sleeping brain. *Nature Reviews. Neuroscience, 20*(12), 746–762. https://doi.org/10.1038/s41583-019-0223-4

Adelson, E., & Fraiberg, S. (1974). Gross motor development in infants blind from birth. *Child Development, 45*(1), 114–126.

Ader, R. (2003). Conditioned immunomodulation: Research needs and directions. *Brain, Behavior, and Immunity, 17 Suppl 1*, S51–S57. https://doi.org/10.1016/s0889-1591(02)00067-3

Adian, E. (1928). *The Basis of Sensation*. New York: Norton.

Adler, A. (1924). *The Practice and Theory of Individual Psychology*. London: Routledge

Adler, L, Spencer, T., & Wilens, T. (2015). *Attention-Deficit Hyperactivity Disorder in Adults and Children*. Cambridge: Cambridge University Press.

Adolphs, R. (2003). Cognitive neuroscience of human social behaviour. *Nature Reviews. Neuroscience, 4*(3), 165–178. https://doi.org/10.1038/nrn1056

Adolphs, R. (2017). How should neuroscience study emotions? By distinguishing emotion states, concepts, and experiences. *Social Cognitive and Affective Neuroscience, 12*(1), 24–31. https://doi.org/10.1093/scan/nsw153

Adolphs, R., & Anderson, D. (2018). *The Neuroscience of Emotion*. Princeton, NJ: Princeton University Press.

Adolphs, R., & Tusche, A. (2017). From faces to prosocial behavior: Cues, tools, and mechanisms. *Current Directions in Psychological Science, 26*(3), 282–287. https://doi.org/10.1177/0963721417694656

Adolphs, R., Tranel, D., Damasio, H., & Damasio, A. (1994). Impaired recognition of emotion in facial expressions following bilateral damage to the human amygdala. *Nature, 372*(6,507), 669–672. https://doi.org/10.1038/372669a0

Adolphs, R., Gosselin, F., Buchanan, T. W., Tranel, D., Schyns, P., & Damasio, A. R. (2005). A mechanism for impaired fear recognition after amygdala damage. *Nature, 433*(7,021), 68–72. https://doi.org/10.1038/nature03086

Adrian, E. (1928). *The Basis of Sensation*. New York: W. W. Norton.

Ahima, R., & Lazar, M. (2013). The health risk of obesity—better metrics imperative. *Science, 341*, 856–858.

Ahmed, F. (2010). Tales of adversity. *Nature, 468,* 520.

Ainsworth, M., Blehar, M., Waters, E., & Wall, S. (1978). *Patterns of Attachment: A Psychological Study of the Strange Situation*. Hillsdale, NJ: Lawrence Erlbaum.

Albright, T. (2009). On the perception of probable things: Neural substrates of associative memory. *Neuron, 74*, 227–245.

Alexander, R. (1979). *Darwinism and Human Affairs*. Seattle, WA: University of Washington Press.

Allen, M., & Friston, K. J. (2018). From cognitivism to autopoiesis: Towards a computational framework for the embodied mind. *Synthese, 195*(6), 2,459–2,482. https://doi.org/10.1007/s11229-016-1288-5

Allen, M., Dietz, M., Blair, K. S., van Beek, M., Rees, G., Vestergaard-Poulsen, P., Lutz, A., & Roepstorff, A. (2012). Cognitive-affective neural plasticity following active-controlled mindfulness intervention. *The Journal of Neuroscience, 32*(44), 15,601–15,610. https://doi.org/10.1523/JNEUROSCI.2957-12.2012

Allen, P., Larøi, F., McGuire, P., & Aleman, A. (2008). The hallucinating brain: A review of structural and functional neuroimaging studies of hallucinations. *Neuroscience and Biobehavioral Reviews, 32*, 175–191.

Allison, T., & Cicchetti, D. V. (1976). Sleep in mammals: Ecological and constitutional correlates. *Science (New York, N.Y.), 194*(4,266), 732–734. https://doi.org/10.1126/science.982039

Allman, J. (2001). *Evolving Brains*. New York: Scientific American Library.

Allport, G. W., & Odbert, H. S. (1936). Trait-names: A psycho-lexical study. *Psychological Monographs, 47*, 592.

Alt, D. (2015). College students' academic motivation, media engagement and fear of missing out. *Computers in Human Behavior, 49*, 111–119. https://doi.org/10.1016/j.chb.2015.02.057

Amanzio, M., Pollo, A., Maggi, G., & Benedetti, F. (2001). Response variability to analgesics: A role for non-speci® c activation of endogenous opioids. *Pain, 90*, 205–215.

Amaresha, A., & Venkatasubramanian, G. (2012). Expressed emotion in schizophrenia: An overview. *Indian Journal of Psychological Medicine, 34*, 12–20.

American Academy of Sleep Medicine (2016). *AASM Manual for the Scoring of Sleep and Associated Events Version 2.3*. Darien, IL: American Academy of Sleep Medicine.

American Psychiatric Association (2013). *Diagnostic and Statistical Manual of Mental Disorders* (5th ed.). Washington, DC: American Psychiatric Association.

Amodio, D. M. (2014). The neuroscience of prejudice and stereotyping. *Nature Reviews. Neuroscience, 15*(10), 670–682. https://doi.org/10.1038/nrn3800

Amodio, D. M., & Cikara, M. (2021). The social neuroscience of prejudice. *Annual Review of Psychology, 72*(1), 1–31. https://doi.org/10.1146/annurev-psych-010419-050928

Anafi, R. C., Kayser, M. S., & Raizen, D. M. (2019). Exploring phylogeny to find the function of sleep. *Nature Reviews. Neuroscience, 20*(2), 109–116. https://doi.org/10.1038/s41583-018-0098-9

Anargyros-Klinger, A. (2002). The thread of depression throughout the life and works of Leo Tolstoy. *International Journal of Psychoanalysis, 83*(2), 407–418. https://doi.org/10.1516/2M6C-51NQ-W7N5-AYT2

Andersen, B. L., Cyranowski, J. M., & Espindle, D. (1999). Men's sexual self-schema. *Journal of Personality and Social Psychology, 76*(4), 645–661. https://doi.org/10.1037//0022-3514.76.4.645

Anderson, M. C., & Hulbert, J. C. (2021). Active forgetting: Adaptation of memory by prefrontal control. *Annual Review of Psychology, 72*(1), 1–36. https://doi.org/10.1146/annurev-psych-072720-094140

Andics, A., Gábor, A., Gácsi, M., Faragó, T., Szabó, D., & Miklósi, Á. (2016). Neural mechanisms for lexical processing in dogs. *Science (New York, N.Y.), 353*(6,303), 1,030–1,032. https://doi.org/10.1126/science.aaf3777

Andrade, C. (2017). Ketamine for depression, 1: Clinical summary of issues related to efficacy, adverse effects, and mechanism of action. *Journal of Clinical Psychiatry, 78,* e415–e419. doi.org/10.4088/JCP.17f11567

Andreasen, N. (2001). *Brave New Brain.* New York: Oxford University Press.

Antony, M. M., & Barlow, D. H. (2002). Specific phobia. In D. H. Barlow (ed.), *Anxiety and Its Disorders: The Nature and Treatment of Anxiety and Panic* (2nd ed., pp. 380–417). New York: Guilford Press.

Apfel, B., Ross, J., Hlavin, J., Meyerhoff, D., Metzler, T., Marmar, C., Weiner, M., Schuff, N., & Neylan, T. (2011). Hippocampal volume differences in Gulf War veterans with current versus lifetime posttraumatic stress. *Biological Psychiatry, 69,* 541–548.

Arendt, H. (1958). What was authority? In C. J. Friedrich (ed.), *Authority* (pp. 81–112). Cambridge: Harvard University Press, 1958.

Ariely, D. (2009). *Predictably Irrational.* Revised and expanded edition. London: HarperCollins.

Aronson, J., Quinn, D. M., & Spencer, S. J. (1998). Stereotype threat and the academic underperformance of minorities and women. In *Prejudice* (pp. 83–103). Cambridge, MA: Academic Press.

Asbury, K., & Plomin, R. (2013). *G is for Genes: The Impact of Genetics on Education and Achievement.* Somerset, NJ: Wiley-Blackwell, 2013.

Asch, S. (1946). Forming impressions of personality. *Journal of Abnormal and Social Psychology, 41,* 258–290.

Asch, S. (1956). Studies of independence and conformity: 1. A minority of one against a unanimous majority. *Psychological Monographs, 70,* 1–70.

Aserinsky, E., & Kleitman, N. (1953/2003). Regularly occurring periods of eye motility, and concomitant phenomena, during sleep. *The Journal of Neuropsychiatry and Clinical Neurosciences, 15*(4), 454–455. https://doi.org/10.1176/jnp.15.4.454

Asma, S., & Gabriel, R. (2019). *The Emotional Mind: The Affective Roots of Culture and Cognition.* Cambridge, MA: Harvard University Press.

Aubert, M., Lebe, R., Oktaviana, A. A., Tang, M., Burhan, B., Hamrullah, Jusdi, A., Abdullah, Hakim, B., Zhao, J. X., Geria, I. M., Sulistyarto, P. H., Sardi, R., & Brumm, A. (2019). Earliest hunting scene in prehistoric art. *Nature, 576*(7,787), 442–445. https://doi.org/10.1038/s41586-019-1806-y

Avis, N. E., Coeytaux, R. R., Isom, S., Prevette, K., & Morgan, T. (2016). Acupuncture in menopause (AIM) study: A pragmatic, randomized controlled trial. *Menopause (New York, N.Y.), 23*(6), 626–637. https://doi.org/10.1097/GME.0000000000000597

Awh, E., & Gehring, W. J. (1999). The anterior cingulate cortex lends a hand in response selection. *Nature Neuroscience, 2*(10), 853–854.

Axelrod, R. (1984). *The Evolution of Cooperation.* New York: Basic Books.

Axelrod, R., & Hamilton, W. D. (1981). The evolution of cooperation. *Science (New York, N.Y.), 211*(4,489), 1,390–1,396. https://doi.org/10.1126/science.7466396

Axtell, R. (1993). *Do's and Taboos around the World.* New York: John Wiley & Sons.

Azevedo, F. A. C., Carvalho, L. R. B., Grinberg, L. T., Farfel, J. M., Ferretti, R. E. L., Leite, R. E. P., …, & Herculano-Houzel, S. (2009). Equal numbers of neuronal and non-neuronal cells make the human brain an isometrically scaled-up primate brain. *Journal of Comparative Neurology, 513*(5), 532–541. https://doi.org/10.1002/cne.21974

Bach, D. R., & Dayan, P. (2017). Algorithms for survival: A comparative perspective on emotions. *Nature Reviews. Neuroscience, 18*(5), 311–319. https://doi.org/10.1038/nrn.2017.35

Baddeley A. (2010). Working memory. *Current Biology: CB, 20*(4), R136–R140. https://doi.org/10.1016/j.cub.2009.12.014

Baden, T., Euler, T., & Berens, P. (2020). Understanding the retinal basis of vision across species. *Nature Reviews. Neuroscience, 21*(1), 5–20. https://doi.org/10.1038/s41583-019-0242-1

Bagby, R. M., & Widiger, T. A. (2018). Five factor model personality disorder scales: An introduction to a special section on assessment of maladaptive variants of the five factor model. *Psychological Assessment, 30*(1), 1–9. http://dx.doi.org/10.1037/pas0000523

Bagot, R., Labonté, B., Peña, C., & Nestler, E. (2014). Epigenetic signaling in psychiatric disorders: Stress and depression. *Dialogues in Clinical Neuroscience, 16*, 281–295.

Bagot, R. C., Parise, E. M., Peña, C. J., Zhang, H.-X., Maze, I., Chaudhury, D., …, & Nestler, E. J. (2015). Ventral hippocampal afferents to the nucleus accumbens regulate susceptibility to depression. *Nature Communications, 6*(May), 7,062. https://doi.org/10.1038/ncomms8062

Baillargeon, R. (2004). Infants' reasoning about hidden objects: Evidence for event-general and event-specific expectations. *Developmental Science, 7*, 391–424.

Baillargeon, R., Scott, R. M., & He, Z. (2010). False-belief understanding in infants. *Trends in Cognitive Sciences, 14*(3), 110–118. https://doi.org/10.1016/j.tics.2009.12.006

Baldauf, D., & Desimone, R. (2014). Neural mechanisms of object-based attention. *Science, 344*, 42.

Bálint, A., Andics, A., Gácsi, M., Gábor, A., & Czeibert, K. (2020). Dogs can sense weak thermal radiation. *Scientific Reports*, 1–9. https://doi.org/10.1038/s41598-020-60439-y

Balsters, J. H., & Ramnani, N. (2011). Cerebellar plasticity and the automation of first-order rules. *The Journal of Neuroscience: The Official Journal of the Society for Neuroscience, 31*(6), 2,305–2,312. https://doi.org/10.1523/JNEUROSCI.4358-10.2011

Bandura, A. (1977). Self-efficacy: Toward a unifying theory of behavioral change. *Psychological Review, 84*(2), 191.

Bandura, A. (2019). Applying theory for human betterment. *Perspectives on Psychological Science, 14*(1), 12–15.

Bandura, A., Adams, N. E., Hardy, A. B., & Howells, G. N. (1980). Tests of the generality of self-efficacy theory. *Cognitive Therapy and Research, 4*(1), 39–66.

Bandura, A., Ross, D., & Ross, S. A. (1961). Transmission of aggression through imitation of aggressive models. *Journal of Abnormal and Social Psychology, 63*, 575–582. https://doi.org/10.1037/h0045925

Bar, M. (ed.). (2011). *Predictions in the Brain: Using Our Past to Generate a Future.* New York: Oxford University Press.

Bar, M., & Bubic, A. (2014). Top-down effects in visual perception. In K. Ochsner, & S. Kosslyn (eds.), *The Oxford Handbook of Cognitive Neuroscience.* New York: Oxford University Press.

Barber, J., Muran, J., McCarthy, K., & Keefe, J. (2013). Research on dynamic therapies. In M. Lambert (ed.), *Handbook of Psychotherapy and Behavior Change* (6th ed.). Hoboken, NJ: Wiley.

Bardin, J. (2012). Unlocking the brain. *Nature, 487*, 24–26.

Barlow, D. (2002). *Anxiety and Its Disorders: The Nature and Treatment of Anxiety and Panic* (2nd ed.). New York: Guilford Press.

Barnard, N., & Kaufman, S. (1997). Animal research is wasteful and misleading. *Scientific American, 276*, 80–82.

Barnhofer, T., Huntenburg, J. M., Lifshitz, M., Wild, J., Antonova, E., & Margulies, D. S. (2015). How mindfulness training may help to reduce vulnerability for recurrent depression: A neuroscientific perspective. *Clinical Psychological Science, 4*, 328–343. http://doi.org/10.1177/2167702615595036

Baron, A., & Banaji, M. (2006). The development of implicit attitudes: Evidence of race evaluations from ages 6 and 10 and adulthood. *Psychological Science, 17*, 53–58.

Baron-Cohen, S. (2005). The empathizing system. In B. Ellis, & D. Bjorklund (eds.), *Origins of the Social Mind: Evolutionary Psychology and Child Development*. New York: Guilford Press.

Baron-Cohen, S., & Belmonte, M. (2005). Autism: A window onto the development of the social and the analytic brain. *Annual Review of Neuroscience, 28*, 109–126.

Baron-Cohen, S., Ashwin, E., Ashwin, C., Tavassoli, T., & Chakrabarti, B. (2009). Talent in autism: Hyper-systemizing, hyper-attention to detail and sensory hypersensitivity. *Philosophical Transactions of the Royal Society of London. Series B, Biological Sciences, 364*(1,522), 1,377–1,383. https://doi.org/10.1098/rstb.2008.0337

Barrett L. F. (2017). Categories and their role in the science of emotion. *Psychological Inquiry, 28*(1), 20–26. https://doi.org/10.1080/1047840X.2017.1261581

Barrett, L. F., Adolphs, R., Marsella, S., Martinez, A. M., & Pollak, S. D. (2019). Emotional expressions reconsidered: Challenges to inferring emotion from human facial movements. *Psychological Science in the Public Interest: A Journal of the American Psychological Society, 20*(1), 1–68. https://doi.org/10.1177/1529100619832930

Barrett, L. F., Mesquita, B., Ochsner, K. N., & Gross, J. J. (2007). The experience of emotion. *Annual. Review of Psychology, 58*, 373–403.

Barrlett, L., Lewis, M., & Haviland-Jones, J. (eds.) (2016). *Handbook of Emotions* (4th ed.). New York: Guilford Press.

Barron, A. B., Hebets, E. A., Cleland, T. A., Fitzpatrick, C. L., Hauber, M. E., & Stevens, J. R. (2015). Embracing multiple definitions of learning. *Trends in Neurosciences, 38*(7), 405–407. https://doi.org/10.1016/j.tins.2015.04.008

Barrowclough, C., & Lobban, F. (2008). Family intervention. In K. Meser, & D. Jeste (eds.), *Clinical Handbook of Schizophrenia* (pp. 214–225). New York: Guilford Press.

Bartlett, F. C. (1932). *Remembering*. Cambridge: Cambridge University Press.

Basbaum, A., & Jessell, T. (2013). Pain. In Kandel, E. R., Schwartz, J. H., Jessell, T. M., Siegelbaum, S., & Hudspeth, A. J. (eds.), *Principles of Neural Science* (5th ed.). New York: McGraw-Hill.

Basco, N., & Rush, A. (2005). *Cognitive-behavioral Therapy for Bipolar Disorder* (2nd ed.). New York: Guilford Press.

Bass, A. H., Gilland, E. H., & Baker, R. (2008). Evolutionary origins for social vocalization in a vertebrate hindbrain-spinal compartment. *Science (New York, N.Y.), 321*(5,887), 417–421. https://doi.org/10.1126/science.1157632

Bassett, D. S., & Mattar, M. G. (2017). A network neuroscience of human learning: Potential to inform quantitative theories of brain and behavior. *Trends in Cognitive Sciences, 21*(4), 250–264. https://doi.org/10.1016/j.tics.2017.01.010

Bassett, D. S., & Sporns, O. (2017). Network neuroscience. *Nature Neuroscience, 20*(3), 353. https://doi.org/10.1038/nn.4502

Bateman, A., Gunderson, J., & Mulder, R. (2016). Treatment of personality disorders. *Lancet, 385,* 735–743.

Baucom, L. B., Wedell, D. H., Wang, J., Blitzer, D. N., & Shinkareva, S. V. (2012). Decoding the neural representation of affective states. *Neuroimage, 59*(1), 718–727.

Bauer, I. M., & Baumeister, R. F. (2011). Self-regulatory strength. In K. D. Vohs, & R. F. Baumeister (eds.), *Handbook of Self-Regulation: Research, Theory, and Applications* (pp. 64–82). New York: Guilford Press.

Baumeister, D., Sedgwick, O., Howes, O., & Peters, E. (2017). Auditory verbal hallucinations and continuum models of psychosis: A systematic review of the healthy voice-hearer literature. *Clinical Psychology Review, 51,* 125–141. https://doi.org/10.1016/j.cpr.2016.10.010

Baumeister, R. F. (2000). Gender differences in erotic plasticity: The female sex drive as socially flexible and responsive. *Psychological Bulletin, 126*(3), 347–389. https://doi.org/10.1037/0033-2909.126.3.347

Bavelier, D., & Hirshorn, E. (2010). I see where you're hearing: How cross-modal plasticity may exploit homologous brain structures. *Nature Neuroscience, 13,* 1,309–1,311.

Bayne, T., Hohwy, J., & Owen, A. M. (2016). Are there levels of consciousness? *Trends in Cognitive Sciences, xx,* 1–9. https://doi.org/10.1016/j.tics.2016.03.009

Beason-Held, L. L., Hohman, T. J., Venkatraman, V., An, Y., & Resnick, S. M. (2017). Brain network changes and memory decline in aging. *Brain Imaging and Behavior, 11*(3), 859–873. https://doi.org/10.1007/s11682-016-9560-3

Beck, A. T. (1967). *Depression: Clinical, Experimental, and Theoretical Aspects.* New York: Harper & Row.

Beck, A. T. (2019). A 60-year evolution of cognitive theory and therapy. *Perspectives on Psychological Science, 14,* 16–20. https://doi.org/10.1177/1745691618804187

Beck, A. T., & Alford, B. A. (2009). *Depression: Causes and Treatments* (2nd ed.). Philadelphia: University of Pennsylvania Press.

Beck, A. T., & Bredemeier, K. (2016). A unified model of depression: Integrating clinical, cognitive, biological, and evolutionary perspectives. *Clinical Psychological Science, 4,* 596–619. https://doi.org/10.1177/2167702616628523

Beck, A. T., & Rector, N. A. (2005). Cognitive approaches to schizophrenia: Theory and therapy. *Annual Review of Clinical Psychology, 1,* 577–606.

Beck, J. (2011). *Cognitive Behavioral Therapy* (2nd ed.). New York: Guilford Press.

Begola, M. J., & Schillerstrom, J. E. (2019). Hallucinogens and their therapeutic use: A literature review. *Journal of Psychiatric Practice, 25*(5), 334–346. https://doi.org/10.1097/PRA.0000000000000409

Bell, J. A., Kivimäki, M., Bullmore, E. T., Steptoe, A., MRC ImmunoPsychiatry Consortium, & Carvalho, L. A. (2017). Repeated exposure to systemic inflammation and risk of new depressive symptoms among older adults. *Translational Psychiatry, 7*(8), e1208. https://doi.org/10.1038/tp.2017.155

Bell, J. T., & Spector, T. D. (2011). A twin approach to unraveling epigenetics. *Trends in Genetics: TIG 27*(3), 116–125. https://doi.org/10.1016/j.tig.2010.12.005

Bender, D. S., Morey, L. C., & Skodol, A. E. (2011). Toward a model for assessing level of personality functioning in DSM–5, part I: A review of theory and methods. *Journal of Personality Assessment, 93*(4), 332–346.

Benedetti, F. (2009). *Placebo Effects: Understanding the Mechanisms in Health and Disease.* New York: Oxford University Press.

Benjamin, L. T., Henry, K. D., & Mcmahon, L. R. (2005). Inez Beverly Prosser and the education of African Americans. *Journal of the History of the Behavioral Sciences, 41*(1), 42–62. https://doi.org/10.1002/jhbs.20058

Bennett, M. R., & Hacker, P. M. (2005). Emotion and cortical-subcortical function: conceptual developments. *Progress in Neurobiology, 75*(1), 29–52. https://doi.org/10.1016/j.pneurobio.2004.11.002

Bennett, M. R., & Hacker, P. M. S. (2005). Emotion and cortical-subcortical function: Conceptual developments. *Progress in Neurobiology, 75*(1), 29–52.

Berger, H. (1929–1969). Über das Elektrekephalogramm des Menschen. *Electroencephalography and Clinical Neurophysiology* (Supp. 28). (Reprinted from *Archive für Psychiatrie und Nervenkrankheiten, 87,* 527–570, 1929.)

Berger, J. M., Singh, P., Khrimian, L., Morgan, D. A., Chowdhury, S., Arteaga-Solis, E., Horvath, T. L., Domingos, A. I., Marsland, A. L., Yadav, V. K., Rahmouni, K., Gao, X. B., & Karsenty, G. (2019). Mediation of the acute stress response by the skeleton. *Cell Metabolism, 30*(5), 890–902.e8. https://doi.org/10.1016/j.cmet.2019.08.012

Bergsieker, H. B., Leslie, L. M., Constantine, V. S., & Fiske, S. T. (2012). Stereotyping by omission: Eliminate the negative, accentuate the positive. *Journal of Personality and Social Psychology, 102*(6), 1,214.

Bernard, C. (1927). *An Introduction to the Study of Experimental Medicine.* Translated by H. C. Greene. New York: Macmillan.

Bernhard, H., Fischbacher, U., & Fehr, E. (2006). Parochial altruism in humans. *Nature, 442*(7,105), 912–915. https://doi.org/10.1038/nature04981

Berns, G., Chappelow, J., Zink, C. Pagnoni, G., Martin-Skurski, M., & Richards, J. (2005). Neurobiological correlates of social conformity and independence during mental rotation. *Biological Psychiatry, 58,* 245–253.

Berntson, G. G., Cacioppo, J. T., & Quigley, K. S. (1991). Autonomic determinism: The modes of autonomic control, the doctrine of autonomic space, and the laws of autonomic constraint. *Psychological Review, 98*(4), 459–487. https://doi.org/10.1037/0033-295x.98.4.459

Berridge, K. C. (2003). Pleasures of the brain. *Brain and Cognition, 52*(1), 106–128. https://doi.org/10.1016/s0278-2626(03)00014-9

Berry, R. B., Brooks, R., Gamaldo, C. E., Harding, S. M., Lloyd, R. M., Marcus, C. L., & Vaughn, B. V. (2015). *The AASM Manual for the Scoring of Sleep and Associated Events: Rules, Terminology and Technical Specifications, Version 2.2.* www.aasmnet.org. Darien, IL: American Academy of Sleep Medicine.

Berthoud, H. R., & Morrison, C. (2008). The brain, appetite, and obesity. *Annual Review of Psychology, 59,* 55–92.

Berwick, R. C., Friederici, A. D., Chomsky, N., & Bolhuis, J. J. (2013). Evolution, brain, and the nature of language. *Trends in Cognitive Sciences, 17*(2), 89–98. https://doi.org/10.1016/j.tics.2012.12.002

Beyerstein, B. L. (1999) Whence cometh the myth that we only use ten percent of our brains? In S. Della Sala (ed.), *Mind Myths: Exploring Everyday Mysteries of the Mind and Brain* (pp. 1–24). Chichester, UK: John Wiley and Sons, Ltd.

Bialystok, E. (2017). The bilingual adaptation: How minds accommodate experience. *Psychological Bulletin, 143*(3), 233–262. https://doi.org/10.1037/bul0000099

Bialystok, E., Craik, F., & Luk, G. (2012). Bilingualism: Consequences for mind and brain. *Trends in Cognitive Sciences, 16,* 240–250.

Bian, L., Leslie, S. J., & Cimpian, A. (2017). Gender stereotypes about intellectual ability emerge early and influence children's interests. *Science (New York, N.Y.), 355*(6,323), 389–391. https://doi.org/10.1126/science.aah6524

Bidwell, L., McClernon, F., & Kolins, S. (2011). Cognitive enhancers for the treatment of ADHD. *Pharmacology, Biochemistry and Behavior, 99*, 262–274.

Bilbo, B. S., & Stevens, B. (2017). Microglia: The brain's first responders. *Cerebrum: The Dana Forum on Brain Science* (November), 1–14.

Bishop, S. J., & Gagne, C. (2018). Anxiety, depression, and decision making: A computational perspective. *Annual Review of Neuroscience, 41*, 371–388.

Blaak, E. (2001). Gender differences in fat metabolism. *Current Opinion in Clinical Nutrition & Metabolic Care, 4*(6), 499–502.

Blakemore, S. (2019). The art of medicine. Adolescence and mental health. *The Lancet, 393*(10,185), 2,030–2,031. https://doi.org/10.1016/S0140-6736(19)31013-X

Blakemore, S., & Mills, K. (2014). Is adolescence a sensitive period for sociocultural processing? *Annual Review of Psychology, 65*, 187–207.

Blanke, O., & Arzy, S. (2005). The out-of-body experience: Disturbed self-processing at the temporo-parietal junction. *Neuroscientist, 11,* 16–24.

Blanke, O., Landis, T., Spinelli, L., & Seeck, M. (2004). Out-of-body experience and autoscopy of neurological origin. *Brain, 127*(2), 243–258. https://doi.org/10.1093/brain/awh040

Bleidorn, W., Klimstra, T. A., Denissen, J. J., Rentfrow, P. J., Potter, J., & Gosling, S. D. (2013). Personality maturation around the world: A cross-cultural examination of social-investment theory. *Psychological Science, 24*(12), 2,530–2,540. https://doi.org/10.1177/0956797613498396

Blinkov, S. M., & Glezer, I. I. (*1968*) *The Human Brain in Figures and Tables: A Quantitative Handbook.* New York: Basic Books, Plenum.

Böhnleina, J., Altegoera, L., Muck, N., Roesmann, Redlich, B., Dannlowski, U., & Leehr, E. (2020). Factors influencing the success of exposure therapy for specific phobia: A systematic review. *Neuroscience and Biobehavioral Reviews, 108,* 796–820.

Boland, R. J., & Keller, M. B. (2009). Course and outcome of depression. In I. H. Gotlib, & C. L. Hammen (eds.), *Handbook of Depression* (2nd ed.). New York: Guilford Press.

Bolhuis, J., Okanoya, K., & Scharff, C. (2010). Twitter evolution: Converging mechanisms in birdsong and human speech. *Nature Neuroscience, 11,* 747–759.

Bolles, R., & Fanselow, M. (1982). Endorphins and behavior. *Annual Review of Psychology, 33,* 87–101.

Bonnefon, J., Shariff, A., & Rahwan, I. (2016). The social dilemma of autonomous vehicles. *Science, 352,* 1,573–1,576.

Boring, E., (1950). *A History of Experimental Psychology* (2nd ed.). New York: Appleton-Century-Crofts.

Borkovec, T. D. (2006). Treatment of generalized anxiety disorder and its central worry process. In S. Sassaroli, & G. Ruggerio (eds.), *Worry, Need of Control, and Other Core Cognitive Constructs in Anxiety and Eating Disorders.* New York: Wiley.

Borkovec, T. D., & Ruscio, A. (2001). Psychotherapy for generalized anxiety disorder. *Journal of Clinical Psychiatry, 62,* 37–42.

Bossaerts, P., & Murawski, C. (2015). From behavioural economics to neuroeconomics to decision neuroscience: The ascent of biology in research on human decision making. *Current Opinion in Behavioral Sciences, 5,* 37–42.

Botting, J., & Morrison, A. (1997). Animal research is vital to medicine. *Scientific American, 276,* 83–85.

Bouchard, T. J. (2013). The Wilson Effect: The increase in heritability of IQ with age. *Twin Research and Human Genetics: The Official Journal of the International Society for Twin Studies, 16*(5), 923–930. https://doi.org/10.1017/thg.2013.54

Bouchard, T. J., Jr., & Loehlin, J. C. (2001). Genes, evolution, and personality. *Behavior Genetics, 31*(3), 243–273. https://doi.org/10.1023/a:1012294324713

Bouchard, T. J., Jr., Lykken, D. T., McGue, M., Segal, N. L., & Tellegen, A. (1990). Sources of human psychological differences: The Minnesota Study of Twins Reared Apart. *Science (New York, N.Y.), 250*(4,978), 223–228. https://doi.org/10.1126/science.2218526

Bowlby, J. (1951). *Maternal Care and Mental Health.* World Health Organization, Monograph Series No. 2.

Bowlby, J. (1961). Childhood mourning and its implications for psychiatry. The Adolf Meyer lecture. *American Journal of Psychiatry, 118,* 481–497.

Bowlby, J. (1969). *Attachment and Loss: Vol 1. Attachment.* London: Hogarth.

Bowlby, J. (1980). *Attachment and Loss: Vol. 3. Loss.* New York: Basic Books.

Bowlby, J. (1982). Attachment and loss: Retrospect and prospect. *American Journal of Orthopsychiatry, 52,* 664–678.

Bowlby, J. (1988). *A Secure Base: Clinical Applications of Attachment Theory.* London: Routledge.

Bradley, R., Conklin, C. Z., & Westen, D. (2007). Borderline personality disorder. In W. O'Donohue, K. Fowler, & S. Lilienfeld (eds.), *Sage Handbook of Personality Disorders.* Thousand Oaks, CA: Sage.

Bransford, J. D., & Johnson, M. K. (1972). Contextual prerequisites for understanding: Some investigations of comprehension and recall. *Journal of Verbal Learning and Verbal Behavior, 11,* 717–726.

Branstetter, B. K., Finneran, J. J., Fletcher, E. A., Weisman, B. C., & Ridgway, S. H. (2012). Dolphins can maintain vigilant behavior through echolocation for 15 days without interruption or cognitive impairment. *PLoS One, 7*(10), e47478. https://doi.org/10.1371/journal.pone.0047478

Brant, A. M., Munakata, Y., Boomsma, D. I., DeFries, J. C., Haworth, C. M., Keller, M. C., . . . & Hewitt, J. K. (2013). The nature and nurture of high IQ: An extended sensitive period for intellectual development. *Psychological Science, 24*(8), 1,487–1,495.

Breuer, J., & Freud, S. (1955) Studies on hysteria (1893–95). In *The Standard Edition of the Complete Psychological Works of Sigmund Freud* (pp. 2: 1–311). London: Hogarth.

Bridge, J., Iyengar, S., Salary, C., Barbe, R., Birmaher, B., Pincus, H., Ren, L., & Brent, D. (2007). Clinical response and risk for reported suicidal ideation and suicide attempts in pediatric antidepressant treatment: A meta-analysis of randomized controlled trials. *JAMA, 297,* 1,683–1,696.

Brodin, P., & Davis, M. M. (2017). Human immune system variation. *Nature Reviews. Immunology, 17*(1), 21–29. https://doi.org/10.1038/nri.2016.125

Brothers, L. (1990). The social brain: A project for integrating primate behaviour and neurophysiology in a new domain. *Concepts in Neuroscience, 1,* 27–51.

Brown, A., & Patterson, P. (2011). Maternal infection and schizophrenia: Implications for prevention. *Schizophrenia Bulletin, 37,* 284–290.

Brown, G. (1985) The discovery of expressed emotion: Induction or deduction? In J. Leff, & C. Vaughn (eds.), *Expressed Emotion in Families.* New York: Guilford Press.

Brown, J. (1958). Some tests of the decay theory of immediate memory. *The Quarterly Journal of Experimental Psychology, 10*, 12–21. DOI:10.1080/17470215808416249.

Brownley, K. A., Berkman, N. D., Peat. C. M., Lohr, K. N., Cullen, K. E., Bann, C. M., & Bulik, C. M. (2016) Binge-eating disorder in adults: A systematic review and meta-analysis. *Ann Intern Med., 165*(6), 409–420. DOI:10.7326/M15–2455. Epub 2016 Jun 28. PMID: 27367316; PMCID: PMC5637727.

Brucker, R., & DiNicola, L. (2019). The brain's default network: Updated anatomy, physiology, and evolving insights. *Nature Reviews. Neuroscience, 20*, 593–608.

Bruine de Bruin, W., Parker, A. M., & Fischhoff, B. (2007). Individual differences in adult decision-making competence. *Journal of Personality and Social Psychology, 92*(5), 938–956. https://doi.org/10.1037/0022-3514.92.5.938

Buchman, A. S., Boyle, P. A., Yu, L., Shah, R. C., Wilson, R. S., & Bennett, D. A. (2012). Total daily physical activity and the risk of AD and cognitive decline in older adults. *Neurology, 78*(17), 1,323–1,329. https://doi.org/10.1212/WNL.0b013e3182535d35

Buchman, A. S., Yu, L., Boyle, P. A., Shah, R. C., & Bennett, D. A. (2012). Total daily physical activity and longevity in old age. *Archives of Internal Medicine, 172*(5), 444–446. https://doi.org/10.1001/archinternmed.2011.1477

Buck, L., & Bargmann, C. (2013). Smell and taste: The chemical senses. In Kandel, E. R., Schwartz, J. H., Jessell, T. M., Siegelbaum, S., & Hudspeth, A. J. (eds.), *Principles of Neural Science* (5th ed.). New York: McGraw-Hill.

Buckner, R. L., Andrews-Hanna, J. R., & Schacter, D. L. (2008). The brain's default network: Anatomy, function, and relevance to disease. *Annals of the New York Academy of Sciences, 1,124*, 1–38. https://doi.org/10.1196/annals.1440.011

Buglass, S. L., Binder, J. F., Betts, L. R., & Underwood, J. D. M. (2017). Motivators of online vulnerability: The impact of social network site use and FOMO. *Computers in Human Behavior, 66*, 248–255. https://doi.org/10.1016/j.chb.2016.09.05

Bullmore, E. (2019). *The Inflamed Mind: A Radical New Approach to Depression.* New York: Picador.

Burger, J. M. (2009). Replicating Milgram: Would people still obey today? *American Psychologist, 64*(1), 1–11. https://doi.org/10.1037/a0010932

Burghardt, G. (2005). *The Genesis of Animal Play: Testing the Limits.* Cambridge, MA: MIT Press.

Burhan, N. A. S., Yunus, M. M., Tovar, M. E. L., & Burhan, N. M. G. (2017). Why are cognitive abilities of children so different across countries? The link between major socioeconomic factors and PISA test scores. *Personality and Individual Differences, 105*(September 2016), 95–106. https://doi.org/10.1016/j.paid.2016.09.043

Burnett, S., Sebastian, C., Cohen Kadosh, K., & Blakemore, S. J. (2011). The social brain in adolescence: Evidence from functional magnetic resonance imaging and behavioural studies. *Neuroscience and Biobehavioral Reviews, 35*(8), 1,654–1,664. https://doi.org/10.1016/j.neubiorev.2010.10.011

Burnette, M. L., & Cicchetti, D. (2012). Multilevel approaches toward understanding antisocial behavior: Current research and future directions. *Development and Psychopathology, 24*(3), 703–704. https://doi.org/10.1017/S0954579412000314

Burns, J. G., & Dyer, A. G. (2008). Diversity of speed-accuracy strategies benefits social insects. *Current Biology: CB, 18*(20), R953–R954. https://doi.org/10.1016/j.cub.2008.08.028

Bushdid, C., Magnasco, M. O., Vosshall, L. B., & Keller, A. (2014). Humans can discriminate more than 1 trillion olfactory stimuli. *Science (New York, N.Y.), 343*(6,177), 1,370–1,372. https://doi.org/10.1126/science.1249168

Buss, D. M. (2018). Sexual and emotional infidelity: Evolved gender differences in jealousy prove robust and replicable. *Perspectives on Psychological Science, 13*(2), 155–160. https://doi.org/10.1177/1745691617698225

Buss, D. M., Larsen, R. J., Westen, D., & Semmelroth, J. (1992). Sex differences in jealousy: Evolution, physiology, and psychology. *Psychological Science, 3*(4), 251–256.

Byrge, L., Sporns, O., & Smith, L. B. (2014). Developmental process emerges from extended brain-body-behavior networks. *Trends in Cognitive Sciences, 18*(8), 395–403. https://doi.org/10.1016/j.tics.2014.04.010

Cabeza, R., Daselaar, S. M., Dolcos, F., Prince, S. E., Budde, M., & Nyberg, L. (2004). Task-independent and task-specific age effects on brain activity during working memory, visual attention and episodic retrieval. *Cerebral Cortex (New York, N.Y.: 1991), 14*(4), 364–375. https://doi.org/10.1093/cercor/bhg133

Calkins, M. (1901). *An Introduction to Psychology.* London: Macmillan.

Camerer, C. F. (2014). Behavioral economics. *Current Biology, 24*(18), R867–R871.

Campbell A. (1999). Staying alive: Evolution, culture, and women's intrasexual aggression. *The Behavioral and Brain Sciences, 22*(2), 203–252. https://doi.org/10.1017/s0140525x99001818

Campbell, D. (1983) The two distinct routes beyond kin selection to ultrasociality. In D. Bridgeman (ed.), *The Nature of Prosocial Development* (pp. 11–39). New York: Academic Press.

Campbell, D. T. (1957). Factors relevant to the validity of experiments in social settings. *Psychological Bulletin, 54*, 297–312.

Campbell, D. T., & Stanley, J. C. (1963). *Experimental and Quasi-experimental Designs for Research.* Chicago: Rand McNally.

Campbell, S. S., & Tobler, I. (1984). Animal sleep: A review of sleep duration across phylogeny. *Neuroscience and Biobehavioral Reviews, 8*(3), 269–300. https://doi.org/10.1016/0149-7634(84)90054-x

Campos, J., Bertenthal, B., & Kermoian, R. (1992). Early experience and emotional development: The emergence of wariness of heights. *Psychological Science, 3*, 61–64.

Camprodon, J., Kaur, N., Rsauch, S., & Dougherty, D. (2016). Neurotherapeutics. In T. Stern, M. Fava, T. Wilens, & J. Rosenbaum (eds), *Massachusetts General Hospital Comprehensive Clinical Psychiatry* (2nd ed.). New York: Elsevier.

Cannon, T. D. (2015). How schizophrenia develops: Cognitive and brain mechanisms underlying onset of psychosis. *Trends in Cognitive Sciences, 19*, 744–756. http://doi.org/10.1016/j.tics.2015.09.009

Cannon, W. (1932). *The Wisdom of the Body.* New York: W. W. Norton.

Cannon, W. B. (1929). Organization for physiological homeostasis. *Physiological Reviews, 9*, 399.

Carere, C., & Maestripieri, D. (eds.). (2013). *Animal Personalities: Behavior, Physiology, and Evolution.* Chicago: University of Chicago Press.

Carey, N. (2012). *The Epigenetics Revolution: How Modern Biology Is Rewriting Our Understanding of Genetics, Disease and Inheritance.* New York: Columbia University Press.

Carone, B., Fauquier, L., Habib, N., Shea, J., Hart, C., Li, R., . . . & Rando, O. (2010). Paternally induced transgenerational environmental reprogramming of metabolic gene expression in mammals. *Cell, 143,* 1,084–1,096.

Carpenter, L. Janicak, P., Aaronson, S., Boyadjis, T., Brock, D., Cook, I., . . . & Demitrack, M. (2012). Transcranial magnetic stimulation (TMS) for major depression: A multi-site, naturalistic, observational study of acute treatment outcomes in clinical practice. *Depression and Anxiety, 29*, 587–596.

Carver, C. S., & Connor-Smith, J. (2010). Personality and coping. *Annual Review of Psychology, 61,* 679–704. https://doi.org/10.1146/annurev.psych.093008.100352

Cassia, V. M., Turati, C., & Simion, F. (2004). Can a nonspecific bias toward top-heavy patterns explain newborns' face preference? *Psychological Science, 15*(6), 379–383. DOI:10.1111/j.0956–7976.2004.00688.x

Cassina, M., Salviati, L., Di Gianantonio, E., & Clementi, M. (2012). Genetic susceptibility to teratogens: State of the art. *Reproductive Toxicology (Elmsford, N.Y.), 34*(2), 186–191. https://doi.org/10.1016/j.reprotox.2012.05.004

Cattell, R. (1971). *Abilities: Their Structure, Growth, and Action.* Boston, MA: Houghton Mifflin.

Cerliani, L., Mennes, M., Thomas, R. M., Di Martino, A., Thioux, M., & Keysers, C. (2015). Increased functional connectivity between subcortical and cortical resting-state networks in autism spectrum disorder. *JAMA Psychiatry, 72*(8), 767–777. https://doi.org/10.1001/jamapsychiatry.2015.0101

Cerminara, N. L., Lang, E. J., Sillitoe, R. V., & Apps, R. (2015). Redefining the cerebellar cortex as an assembly of non-uniform Purkinje cell microcircuits. *Nature Reviews. Neuroscience, 16*(2), 79–93. https://doi.org/10.1038/nrn3886

Cerny, J., & Janssen, E. (2011). Patterns of sexual arousal in homosexual, bisexual, and heterosexual men. *Archives of Sexual Behavior, 40,* 687–697.

Chabris, C., & Simons, D. J. (2010). *The Invisible Gorilla: And Other Ways Our Intuitions Deceive Us.* New York: Crown

Chabris, C. F. (1999). Prelude or requiem for the "Mozart effect"? *Nature, 400*(6,747), 826–828. https://doi.org/10.1038/23608

Chambers, A., & Payne, J. (2015). The memory function of sleep. In D. Addis, M. Barense, & A. Duarte (eds.), *The Wiley Handbook on the Cognitive Neuroscience of Memory.* New York: John Wiley & Sons.

Charmandari, E., Tsigos, C., & Chrousos, G. (2005). Endocrinology of the stress response. *Annual Review of Physiology, 67,* 259–284.

Charpentier, C. J., Martino, B. D., Sim, A. L., Sharot, T., & Roiser, J. P. (2016). Emotion-induced loss aversion and striatal-amygdala coupling in low-anxious individuals. *Social Cognitive and Affective Neuroscience, 11*(4), 569–579.

Chartrand, T. L., & Bargh, J. A. (1999). The chameleon effect: The perception–behavior link and social interaction. *Journal of Personality and Social Psychology, 76*(6), 893–910. https://doi.org/10.1037//0022-3514.76.6.893

Chase, W. G., & Simon, H. A. (1973). Perception in chess. *Cognitive Psychology, 4*(1), 55–81.

Chein, J., Albert, D., O'Brien, L., Uckert, K., & Steinberg, L. (2011). Peers increase adolescent risk taking by enhancing activity in the brain's reward circuitry. *Developmental Science, 14*(2), F1–F10. https://doi.org/10.1111/j.1467-7687.2010.01035.x

Cheney, T. (2008). *Manic.* New York: William Morrow.

Chess, S., & Thomas, A. (1977). Temperamental individuality from childhood to adolescence. *Journal of the American Academy of Child Psychiatry, 16*(2), 218–226. https://doi.org/10.1016/s0002-7138(09)60038-8

Chi, R. P., & Snyder, A. W. (2011). Facilitate insight by non-invasive brain stimulation. *PLoS One, 6*(2). https://doi.org/10.1371/journal.pone.0016655

Chi, R. P., & Snyder, A. W. (2012). Brain stimulation enables the solution of an inherently difficult problem. *Neuroscience Letters, 515*(2), 121–124.

Chiao, J. Y. (2018). Developmental aspects in cultural neuroscience. *Developmental Review, 50,* 77–89.

Chisholm, K., Lin, A., Abu-Akel, A., & Wood, S. J. (2015). The association between autism and schizophrenia spectrum disorders: A review of eight alternate models of co-occurrence. *Neuroscience & Biobehavioral Reviews, 55*, 173–183. https://doi.org/10.1016/j.neubiorev.2015.04.012

Chivers, M. L., Seto, M. C., Lalumière, M. L., Laan, E., & Grimbos, T. (2010). Agreement of self-reported and genital measures of sexual arousal in men and women: A meta-analysis. *Archives of Sexual Behavior, 39*(1), 5–56. https://doi.org/10.1007/s10508-009-9556-9

Chomsky, N. (1959). A review of Skinner's *Verbal Behavior. Language, 35*, 26–58.

Christensen, J. S., Wild, H., Kenzie, E. S., Wakeland, W., Budding, D., & Lillas, C. (2020). Diverse autonomic nervous system stress response patterns in childhood sensory modulation. *Frontiers in Integrative Neuroscience, 14*, 6. https://doi.org/10.3389/fnint.2020.00006

Christie, R., & Geis, F. (1970). *Studies in Machiavellianism,* New York: Academic Press.

Chung, D. T., Ryan, C. J., Hadzi-Pavlovic, D., Singh, S. P., Stanton, C., & Large, M. M. (2017). Suicide rates after discharge from psychiatric facilities: a systematic review and meta-analysis. *JAMA Psychiatry, 74*(7), 694–702. https://doi.org/10.1001/jamapsychiatry.2017.1044

Cialdini, R. B., Vincent, J. E., Lewis, S. K., Catalan, J., Wheeler, D., & Darby, B. L. (1975). Reciprocal concessions procedure for inducing compliance: The door-in the-face technique. *Journal of Personality and Social Psychology, 31*, 206–215.

Clark, L. A., Cuthbert, B., Lewis-Fernández, R., Narrow, W. E., & Reed, G. M. (2017). Three approaches to understanding and classifying mental disorder: ICD-11, DSM-5, and the National Institute of Mental Health's Research Domain Criteria (RDoC). *Psychological Science in the Public Interest: A Journal of the American Psychological Society, 18*(2), 72–145. https://doi.org/10.1177/1529100617727266

Clark, R., & Hatfield, E. (1989). Gender differences in receptivity to sexual offers. *Journal of Psychology & Human Sexuality, 2*, 39–55.

Clarkin, J. F., Yeomans, F. E., & Kernberg, O. F. (2006). *Psychotherapy for Borderline Personality: Focusing on Object Relations.* Washington, DC: American Psychiatric Publishing, Inc.

Cohen, M. X. (2017). Where does EEG come from and what does it mean? *Trends in Neurosciences, 40*(4), 208–218. https://doi.org/10.1016/j.tins.2017.02.004

Colby, A., Kohlberg, L., Gibbs, J., Lieberman, M., Fischer, K., & Saltzstein, H. D. (1983). A longitudinal study. *Monographs of the Society for Research, 48*(1), 1–124.

Colcombe, S. J., Erickson, K. I., Scalf P. E., et al. (2006). Aerobic exercise training increases brain volume in aging humans. *J Gerontol A Biol Sci Med Sci, 61*(11), 1,166–1,170. DOI:10.1093/gerona/61.11.1166

Collin, G., & van den Heuvel, M (2013). The ontogeny of the human connectome: Development and dynamic changes of brain connectivity across the life span. *The Neuroscientist, 19*, 616–628.

Collins, A. M., & Loftus, E. F. (1975). A spreading-activation theory of semantic processing. *Psychological Review, 82*(6), 407–428. https://doi.org/10.1037/0033-295X.82.6.407

Conduct Problems Prevention Research Group (2010). The effects of a multiyear universal social-emotional learning program: The role of student and school characteristics. *Journal of Consulting and Clinical Psychology, 78*(2), 156–168. https://doi.org/10.1037/a0018607

Constantinidis, C., & Klingberg, T. (2016). The neuroscience of working memory capacity and training. *Nature Reviews. Neuroscience, 17*(7), 438–449. https://doi.org/10.1038/nrn.2016.43

Cook, G, (2014). *The Best American Infographics, 2014.* Boston, MA: Mariner Books.

Corballis M. C. (2017). Language evolution: A changing perspective. *Trends in Cognitive Sciences, 21*(4), 229–236. https://doi.org/10.1016/j.tics.2017.01.013

Corbett, J. E. (2017). The whole warps the sum of its parts. *Psychological Science, 28*(1), 12–22. https://doi.org/10.1177/0956797616671524

Corkin, S. (2002). What's new with the amnesic patient HM? *Nature Reviews Neuroscience, 3*(2), 153–160.

Correll, J., Hudson, S., Guillermo, S., & Ma, S. (2014). The police officer's dilemma: A decade of research on racial bias in the decision to shoot. *Social and Personality Psychology Compass, 8*, 201–213

Correll, J., Park, B., Judd, C., & Wittenbrink, B. (2002). The police officer's dilemma: Using ethnicity to disambiguate potentially threatening individuals. *Journal of Personality and Social Psychology, 83*, 1,314–1,329.

Costa, A., & Sebastián-Gallés, N. (2014). How does the bilingual experience sculpt the brain? *Nature Reviews. Neuroscience, 15*(5), 336–345. https://doi.org/10.1038/nrn3709

Costa, P. T., & Widiger, T. (eds.) (2002). *Personality Disorders and the Five Factor Model of Personality* (2nd ed.). Washington, DC: American. Psychological Association.

Costa, P. T., Jr., & McCrae, R. R. (1995). Primary traits of Eysenck's P-E-N system: Three- and five-factor solutions. *Journal of Personality and Social Psychology, 69*(2), 308–317. https://doi.org/10.1037//0022-3514.69.2.308

Couzin-Frankel, J. (2020). Rethinking anorexia. *Science, 368*, 124–127. DOI:10.1126/science.368.6487.124. PMID: 32273451.

Cowan, N. (2008). What are the differences between long-term, short-term, and working memory? *Progress in Brain Research, 169*, 323–338. https://doi.org/10.1016/S0079-6123(07)00020-9

Cowen, A., Sauter, D., Tracy, J. L., & Keltner, D. (2019). Mapping the passions: Toward a high-dimensional taxonomy of emotional experience and expression. *Psychological Science in the Public Interest: A Journal of the American Psychological Society, 20*(1), 69–90. https://doi.org/10.1177/1529100619850176

Cowen, A. S., & Keltner, D. (2017). Self-report captures 27 distinct categories of emotion bridged by continuous gradients. *Proceedings of the National Academy of Sciences of the United States of America, 114*(38), E7900–E7909. https://doi.org/10.1073/pnas.1702247114

Cowen, A. S., & Keltner, D. (2019). What the face displays: Mapping 28 emotions conveyed by naturalistic expression. *American Psychologist, 75*, 349–364. https://doi.org/10.1037/amp0000488

Cowen, A. S., & Keltner, D. (2020). What the face displays: Mapping 28 emotions conveyed by naturalistic expression. *The American Psychologist, 75*(3), 349–364. https://doi.org/10.1037/amp0000488

Cox, J. J., Reimann, F., Nicholas, A. K., Thornton, G., Roberts, E., Springell, K., Karbani, G., Jafri, H., Mannan, J., Raashid, Y., Al-Gazali, L., Hamamy, H., Valente, E. M., Gorman, S., Williams, R., McHale, D. P., Wood, J. N., Gribble, F. M., & Woods, C. G. (2006). An SCN9A channelopathy causes congenital inability to experience pain. *Nature, 444*(7,121), 894–898. https://doi.org/10.1038/nature05413

Craddock, N., & Sklar, P. (2009). Genetics of bipolar disorder: Successful start to a long journey. *Trends in Genetics, 25*, 95–105.

Craig, A. (2016). Interoception and emotion. In L. Barrlett, M. Lewis, & J. Haviland-Jones (eds.), *Handbook of Emotions* (4th ed.). New York: Guilford Press.

Craik, F. I., & Lockhart, R. S. (1972). Levels of processing: A framework for memory research. *Journal of Verbal Learning and Verbal Behavior, 11*(6), 671–684.

Craske, M. G., Kircanski, K., Epstein, A., Wittchen, H. U., Pine, D. S., Lewis-Fernández, R., Hinton, D., . . . & Posttraumatic and Dissociative Disorder Work Group. (2010). Panic disorder: A review of DSM-IV panic disorder and proposals for DSM-V. *Depression and Anxiety, 27*, 93–112.

Crean, R., Crane, N., & Mason, B. (2011). An evidence based review of acute and long-term effects of cannabis use on executive cognitive functions. *Journal of Addiction Medicine, 5*, 1–8.

Creswell, J. D. (2017). Mindfulness interventions. *Annual Review of Psychology, 68*, 491–516. https://doi.org/10.1146/annurev-psych-042716-051139

Crick F. (1970). Central dogma of molecular biology. *Nature, 227*(5,258), 561–563. https://doi.org/10.1038/227561a0

Crick, F., & Koch, C. (2003). A framework for consciousness. *Nature Neuroscience, 6*(2), 119–126.

Cristea, I., Montgomery, G., Szamoskozi, S., & David, D. (2013). Key constructs in "classical" and "new wave" cognitive behavioral psychotherapies: Relationships among each other and with emotional distress. *Journal of Clinical Psychology, 69*, 584–599.

Csikszentmihalyi, M. (1990). *Flow: The Psychology of Optimal Experience.* New York: Harper & Row, 1990.

Cuddy, A., Fiske, S., & Glick, P. (2007). The BIAS map: Behaviors from intergroup affect and stereotypes. *Journal of Personality and Social Psychology, 92*, 631–648.

Cuijpers, P., Clignet, F., van Meijel, B., van Straten, A., Li, J., & Andersson, G. (2011). Psychological treatment of depression in inpatients: A systematic review and meta-analysis. *Clinical Psychology Review, 31*, 353–360.

Cuijpers, P., Reijnders, M., & Huibers, M. (2019). The role of common factors in psychotherapy outcomes. *Annual Review of Clinical Psychology, 15*, 207–231. https://doi.org/10.1146/annurev-clinpsy-050718-095424

Cuthbert, B., & Insel, T. (2013). Towards the future of psychiatric diagnosis: The seven pillars of RDoC. *BMC Medicine, 11*, 126.

Cytowic, R., & Eagleman, D. (2009). *Wednesday Is Indigo Blue: Discovering the Brain of Synesthesia.* Cambridge, MA: MIT Press.

da Cruz, L., Coley, B. F., Dorn, J., Merlini, F., Filley, E., Christopher, P., …, & Dagnelie, G. (2013). The Argus II epiretinal prosthesis system allows letter and word reading and long-term function in patients with profound vision loss. *The British Journal of Ophthalmology, 97*(5), 632–636. https://doi.org/10.1136/bjophthalmol-2012-301525

Dallman, M. (2009). Stress-induced obesity and the emotional nervous system. *Trends in Endocrinology and Metabolism, 21*, 159–165.

Dallman, M. F., Pecoraro, N., Akana, S. F., La Fleur, S. E., Gomez, F., Houshyar, H., Bell, M. E., Bhatnagar, S., Laugero, K. D., & Manalo, S. (2003). Chronic stress and obesity: A new view of "comfort food." *Proceedings of the National Academy of Sciences of the United States of America, 100*(20), 11,696–11,701. https://doi.org/10.1073/pnas.1934666100

Damasio, H., Grabowski, T., Frank, R., Galaburda, A. M., & Damasio, A. (1994). The return of Phineas Gage: Clues about the brain from the skull of a famous patient. *Science, 264*, 51–62.

Đapo, N., & Kolenović-Đapo, J. (2012). Sex differences in fluid intelligence: Some findings from Bosnia and Herzegovina. *Personality and Individual Differences, 53*(7), 811–815.

Dapretto, M., Davies, M. S., Pfeifer, J. H., Scott, A. A., Sigman, M., Bookheimer, S. Y., & Iacoboni, M. (2006). Understanding emotions in others: Mirror neuron dysfunction in children with autism spectrum disorders. *Nature Neuroscience, 9*(1), 28–30. https://doi.org/10.1038/nn1611

Darwin, C. (1859). *On the Origin of Species by Means of Natural Selection.* London: J Murray.

Darwin, C. (1872/1998). *The Expression of Emotions in Man and Animals* (3rd ed.). New York: Oxford University Press.

Darwin, C. (1874). *The Descent of Man, and Selection in Relation to Sex.* Chicago: Rand, McNally.

Darwin, C. (1877). A biographical sketch of an infant. *Mind, 7,* 285–294.

Davachi, L., & Preston, A. (2014). The medial temporal love and memory. In M. Gazzaniga, & G. Mangun (eds.), *The Cognitive Neurosciences* (5th ed.). Cambridge, MA: MIT Press.

Davis, C. (1939) Results of the self-selection of diets by young children. *Canadian Medical Association Journal, 41,* 257–261.

Davis, K., Christodoulou, J., Seider, S., & Gardner, H. (2011). The theory of multiple intelligences. In R. Sternberg, & S. Kaufman (eds.), *The Cambridge Handbook of Intelligence.* New York: Cambridge University Press.

Davis, T., Ollendick, T., & Öst, L. (2019). One-session treatment of specific phobias in children: Recent developments and a systematic review. *Annual Review of Clinical Psychology, 15,* 233–256. doi.org/10.1146/annurev-clinpsy-050718-095608

Dawson, G., Sterling, L., & Faja, S. (2009). Autism. In M. De Haan, & M. Gunnar (eds.), *Handbook of Developmental Social Neuroscience* (pp. 435–458). New York: Guilford Press.

De Araujo, I., Schatzker, M., & Small, D. (2020). Rethinking food reward. *Annual Review of Psychology, 71,* 139–164.

De Gelder B. (2010). Uncanny sight in the blind. *Scientific American, 302*(5), 60–65. https://doi.org/10.1038/scientificamerican0510-60

De Gelder, B. (2016). *Emotions and the Body.* New York: Oxford University Press.

De Martino, B., Camerer, C. F., & Adolphs, R. (2010). Amygdala damage eliminates monetary loss aversion. *Proceedings of the National Academy of Sciences, 107*(8), 3,788–3,792.

De Martino, B., Fleming, S. M., Garrett, N., & Dolan, R. J. (2013). Confidence in value-based choice. *Nature Neuroscience, 16*(1), 105–110.

de Moor, M. H., Costa, P. T., Terracciano, A., Krueger, R. F., de Geus, E. J., Toshiko, T., Penninx, B. W., Esko, T., Madden, P. A., Derringer, J., Amin, N., Willemsen, G., Hottenga, J. J., Distel, M. A., Uda, M., Sanna, S., Spinhoven, P., Hartman, C. A., Sullivan, P., Realo, A., ..., & Boomsma, D. I. (2012). Meta-analysis of genome-wide association studies for personality. *Molecular Psychiatry, 17*(3), 337–349. https://doi.org/10.1038/mp.2010.128

de Waal, F. (2008). Putting the altruism back into altruism: The evolution of empathy. *Annual Review of Psychology, 59,* 279–300.

Deary, I. (2012). Intelligence. *Annual Review of Psychology, 63,* 453–482.

Deary, I. (2014). The stability of intelligence from childhood to old age. *Current Directions in Psychological Sciences, 23,* 239–245.

Deary, I., Penke, L., & Johnson, W. (2010). The neuroscience of human intelligence differences. *Nature Reviews Neuroscience, 11,* 201–211.

Deary, I., Whiteman, M., Starr, J., Whalley, L., & Fox, H. (2004). The impact of childhood intelligence on later life: Following up the Scottish mental surveys of 1932 and 1947. *Journal of Personality and Social Psychology, 86,* 130–147.

Deary, I. J., Thorpe, G., Wilson, V., Starr, J. M., & Whalley, L. J. (2003). Population sex differences in IQ at age 11: The Scottish mental survey 1932. *Intelligence, 31*(6), 533–542. https://doi.org/10.1016/S0160-2896(03)00053-9

Deary, I. J., Whalley, L. J., & Starr, J. M. (2009). *A Lifetime of Intelligence: Follow-Up Studies of the Scottish Mental Surveys of 1932 and 1947.* Washington, DC: American Psychological Association.

Deary, I. J., Whiteman, M. C., Starr, J. M., Whalley, L. J., & Fox, H. C. (2004). The impact of childhood intelligence on later life: Following up the Scottish mental surveys of 1932 and 1947. *Journal of Personality and Social Psychology, 86*(1), 130–147. https://doi.org/10.1037/0022-3514.86.1.130

DeCasper, A. J., & Spence, M. J. (1986). Prenatal maternal speech influences newborns' perception of speech sounds. *Infant Behavior and Development, 9*, 133–150.

DeCasper, A., Lecanuet, J., Busnel, M., Granier-Deferre, C., & Maugeais, R. (1994). Fetal reactions to recurrent maternal speech. *Infant Behavior and Development, 17*, 159–164.

Decety, J., & Yoder, K. J. (2016). Empathy and motivation for justice: Cognitive empathy and concern, but not emotional empathy, predict sensitivity to injustice for others. *Social Neuroscience, 11*(1), 1–14. https://doi.org/10.1080/17470919.2015.1029593

Dehaene, S. (2014). *Consciousness and the Brain: Deciphering How the Brain Codes Our Thoughts*. New York: Penguin.

Dehaene, S., & Dehaene-Lambertz, G. (2016). Is the brain prewired for letters? *Nature Neuroscience, 19*, 1,192–1,193.

Dehaene, S., Lau, H., & Kouider, S. (2017). What is consciousness, and could machines have it? *Science, 358*(6,362), 486–492. https://doi.org/10.1126/science.aan8871

de-Magistris, T., & Gracia, A. (2017). Does hunger matter in consumer purchase decisions? An empirical investigation of processed food products. *Food Quality and Preference, 55*, 1–5.

DeMartino, B., Kumaran, D., Seymour, B., & Dolan, R. (2006). The neurobiology of reference-dependent value computation. *The Journal of Neuroscience, 29*, 3,833–3,842.

Demertzi, A., Tagliazucchi, E., Dehaene, S., Deco, G., Barttfeld, P., Raimondo, F., ..., & Sitt, J. D. (2019). Human consciousness is supported by dynamic complex patterns of brain signal coordination. *Science Advances, 5*(2), 1–12. https://doi.org/10.1126/sciadv.aat7603

Dennis, E., & Thompson, P. (2013). Mapping connectivity in the developing brain. *International Journal of Developmental Neuroscience, 31*, 525–542.

Department of Justice. (2001). *Policing and Homicide, 1976–98: Justifiable Homicide by Police, Police Officers Murdered by Felons (NCJ 180987)*. Washington, DC: Bureau of Justice Statistics.

DeRubeis, R., Siegle, G., & Hollon, S. (2008). Cognitive therapy versus medication for depression: Treatment outcomes and neural mechanisms. *Nature Reviews. Neuroscience, 9*, 788–796.

DeSalle, R. (2018). *Our Senses*. New Haven, CT: Yale University Press.

Devos, T. (2014). Stereotypes and intergroup attitudes. In F. Leong (ed.), *APA Handbook of Multicultural Psychology, Vol. 1*. Washington, DC: APA Books.

DeYoung, C. G., Carey, B. E., Krueger, R. F., & Ross, S. R. (2016). Ten aspects of the big five in the personality inventory for DSM–5. *Personality Disorders: Theory, Research, and Treatment, 7*(2), 113–123. https://doi.org/10.1037/per0000170

DeYoung, C., Hirsh, J., Shane, M., Papademetris, X., Rajeevan, N., & Gray, J. (2010). Testing predictions from personality neuroscience: Brain structure and the big five. *Psychological Science, 21*, 820–828. DOI:10.1177/0956797610370159

Diamond, A. (1985). Development of the ability to use recall to guide action, as indicated by infants' performance on AB. *Child Development, 56*, 868–883.

Diamond, L. M., Fagundes, C. P., & Butterworth, M. R. (2010). Intimate relationships across the life span. In M. E. Lamb, A. M. Freund, & R. M. Lerner (eds.), *The Handbook of Life-span Development, Vol. 2. Social and Emotional Development* (pp. 379–433). John Wiley & Sons, Inc. https://doi.org/10.1002/9780470880166.hlsd002011

Dickens, W. T., & Flynn, J. R. (2006). Black Americans reduce the racial IQ gap: Evidence from standardization samples. *Psychological Science, 17*(10), 913–920.

Diekelmann, S., & Born, J. (2010). The memory function of sleep. *Nature Reviews. Neuroscience, 11*(2), 114–126. https://doi.org/10.1038/nrn2762

Dietrich, M., & Horvath, T. (2013). Hypothalamic control of energy balance: Insights into the role of synaptic plasticity. *Trends in Neuroscience, 36,* 66–73.

Dillon, D. G., & Pizzagalli, D. A. (2018). Mechanisms of memory disruption in depression. *Trends in Neurosciences, 41,* 137–149. https://doi.org/10.1016/j.tins.2017.12.006

Dima, D., Roiser, J. P., Dietrich, D. E., Bonnemann, C., Lanfermann, H., Emrich, H. M., & Dillo, W. (2009). Understanding why patients with schizophrenia do not perceive the hollow-mask illusion using dynamic causal modelling. *NeuroImage, 15,* 1,180–1,186.

Dingman, M. (2019). *Your Brain, Explained.* Boston, MA: Nicholas Brealey Publishing.

Dionne, G., Tremblay, R., Boivin, M., Laplante, D., & Perusse, D. (2003). Physical aggression and expressive vocabulary in 19-month-old twins. *Developmental Psychology, 39*(2), 261.

Dixon, L., Goldman, H., Srihari, V., & Kane, J. (2018). Transforming the treatment of schizophrenia in the United States: The RAISE initiative. *Annual Review of Clinical Psychology, 14,* 237–258.

Dolder, D. Van, & Assem, M. J. Van Den (2018). The wisdom of the inner crowd in three large natural experiments. *Nature Human Behaviour, 2*(January). https://doi.org/10.1038/s41562-017-0247-6

Dolensek, N., Gehrlach, D. A., Klein, A. S., & Gogolla, N. (2020). Facial expressions of emotion states and their neuronal correlates in mice. *Science, 368,* 89–94. https://doi.org/10.1126/science.aaz9468

Domitrovich, C. E., Cortes, R. C., & Greenberg, M. T. (2007). Improving young children's social and emotional competence: A randomized trial of the preschool "PATHS" curriculum. *The Journal of Primary Prevention, 28*(2), 67–91. https://doi.org/10.1007/s10935-007-0081-0

Donnellan, M. B., Trzesniewski, K. H., Robins, R. W., Moffitt, T. E., & Caspi, A. (2005). Low self-esteem is related to aggression, antisocial behavior, and delinquency. *Psychological Science, 16*(4), 328–335. https://doi.org/10.1111/j.0956-7976.2005.01535.x

Dooley, L. N., Kuhlman, K. R., Robles, T. F., Eisenberger, N. I., Craske, M. G., & Bower, J. E. (2018). The role of inflammation in core features of depression: Insights from paradigms using exogenously-induced inflammation. *Neuroscience and Biobehavioral Reviews, 94*(July), 219–237. https://doi.org/10.1016/j.neubiorev.2018.09.006

Dosil, J. (2008). *Eating Disorders in Athletes.* New York: John Wiley & Sons.

Draper, D, and Klemm, W (1967). Behavioral responses associated with animal hypnosis. *The Psychological Record, 17,* 13–21.

Drewnowski, A. (1997). Taste preferences and food intake. *Annual Review of Nutrition, 17,* 237–253.

Dumont, F. (2010). *A History of Personality Psychology: Theory, Science, and Research from Hellenism to the Twenty-First Century.* New York: Cambridge University Press.

Dunbar, I. (2014). The social brain: Psychological underpinnings and implications for the structure of organizations. *Current Directions in Psychological Science, 23,* 109–114.

Dunbar, R. (1996). *Grooming, Gossip and the Evolution of Language.* London: Faber & Faber.

Dunbar, R. (2003). The social brain: Mind, language and society in evolutionary perspective. *Annual Review of Anthropology, 32,* 161–181.

Dunbar, R. (2004). *The Human Story: A New History of Mankind's Evolution.* London: Faber & Faber.

Dunbar R. I. (2012). The social brain meets neuroimaging. *Trends in Cognitive Sciences*, *16*(2), 101–102. https://doi.org/10.1016/j.tics.2011.11.013

Dunbar, R. I. (2014). The social brain: Psychological underpinnings and implications for the structure of organizations. *Current Directions in Psychological Science*, *23*(2), 109–114.

Dunbar, R., Marriott, A., & Duncan, N. (1997). Human conversational behavior. *Human Nature, 8*, 231–246.

Duncan, J. R., Paterson, D. S., Hoffman, J. M., Mokler, D. J., Borenstein, N. S., Belliveau, R. A., Krous, H. F., Haas, E. A., Stanley, C., Nattie, E. E., Trachtenberg, F. L., & Kinney, H. C. (2010). Brainstem serotonergic deficiency in sudden infant death syndrome. *JAMA*, *303*(5), 430–437. https://doi.org/10.1001/jama.2010.45

Duncker, K. (1945). On problem solving. *Psychological Monographs, 58*, 1–113.

Dunsmoor, J. E., & Murphy, G. L. (2015). Categories, concepts, and conditioning: How humans generalize fear. *Trends in Cognitive Sciences*, *19*(2), 73–77. https://doi.org/10.1016/j.tics.2014.12.003

Dykas, M., & Cassidy, J. (2011). Attachment and the processing of social information across the life span: Theory and evidence. *Psychological Bulletin, 137*, 19–46.

Dykiert, D., Gale, C. R., & Deary, I. J. (2009). Are apparent sex differences in mean IQ scores created in part by sample restriction and increased male variance? *Intelligence, 37*(1), 42–47.

Dziura, S. L., & Thompson, J. C. (2014). Social-network complexity in humans is associated with the neural response to social information. *Psychological Science*, *25*(11), 2,095–2,101. https://doi.org/10.1177/0956797614549209

Eagleman D. M. (2001). Visual illusions and neurobiology. *Nature Reviews Neuroscience*, *2*(12), 920–926. https://doi.org/10.1038/35104092

Edlund, J. E., & Sagarin, B. J. (2017). Sex differences in jealousy: A 25-year retrospective. In *Advances in Experimental Social Psychology* (Vol. 55, pp. 259–302). New York: Academic Press.

Eichenbaum, H. (2017a). Memory: Organization and control. *Annual Review of Psychology*, *68*(1), 19–45. https://doi.org/10.1146/annurev-psych-010416-044131

Eichenbaum, H. (2017b). Prefrontal–hippocampal interactions in episodic memory. *Nature Reviews. Neuroscience*, *18*(9), 547–558. https://doi.org/10.1038/nrn.2017.74

Eisenberg, D., & Berman, K. (2010). Executive function, neural circuitry, and genetic mechanisms in schizophrenia. *Neuropsychopharmacology, 35*, 258–277.

Eisenberg, D. M., Kessler, R. C., Foster, C., Norlock, F. E., Calkins, D. R., & Delbanco, T. L. (1993). Unconventional medicine in the United States. Prevalence, costs, and patterns of use. *The New England Journal of Medicine*, *328*(4), 246–252. https://doi.org/10.1056/NEJM199301283280406

Eisenberg, N. (2000). Emotion, regulation, and moral development. *Annual Review of Psychology*, *51*, 665–697. https://doi.org/10.1146/annurev.psych.51.1.665

Eisenberger N. I. (2015). Social pain and the brain: controversies, questions, and where to go from here. *Annual Review of Psychology*, *66*, 601–629. https://doi.org/10.1146/annurev-psych-010213-115146

Eisenberger, N. I., Lieberman, M. D., & Williams, K. D. (2003). Does rejection hurt? An FMRI study of social exclusion. *Science (New York, N.Y.)*, *302*(5,643), 290–292. https://doi.org/10.1126/science.1089134

Eisner, M. (2001). Modernization, self-control and lethal violence. *British Journal of Criminology, 41*, 618–638.

Ekman, P. (1957). A methodological discussion of nonverbal behavior. *The Journal of psychology, 43*(1), 141–149.

Ekman, P. (1973). *Darwin and Facial Expression: A Century of Research in Review.* New York: Academic Press.

Ekman, P. (1999a). Basic emotions. In T. Dalgleish, & M. Power (eds.), *Handbook of Cognition and Emotion.* Sussex, UK: John Wiley & Sons.

Ekman, P. (1999b). Facial expressions. In T. Dalgleish, & M. Power (eds.), *Handbook of Cognition and Emotion.* Sussex, UK: John Wiley & Sons.

Ekman, P., & Friesen, W. (1971). Constants across cultures in the face and emotion. *Journal of Personality and Social Psychology, 17,* 124–129.

Ekman, P., Campos, J. J., & de Waal, F. (eds.). (2003). *Emotions Inside Out: 130 Years after Darwin's The Expression of the Emotions in Man and Animals* (Vol. 1,000). New York: Academy of Sciences.

Elbert, T., Pantev, C., Wienbruch, C., Rockstroh, B., & Taub, E. (1995). Increased cortical representation of the fingers of the left hand in string players. *Science, 270,* 305–307.

Elfenbein, H. A., & Ambady, N. (2002). Is there an in-group advantage in emotion recognition? *Psychological Bulletin, 128*(2), 243–249. https://doi.org/10.1037/0033-2909.128.2.243

Elkins, G. R., Barabasz, A. F., Council, J. R., & Spiegel, D. (2015). Advancing research and practice: The revised APA Division 30 definition of hypnosis. *The International Journal of Clinical and Experimental Hypnosis, 63*(1), 1–9. https://doi.org/10.1080/00207144.2014.961870

Ellenberger, H. F. (1970). *The Discovery of the Unconscious: The History and Evolution of Dynamic Psychiatry.* New York: Basic Books.

Elliott, R., Greenberg, L., Watson, J., Timulak, L., & Freire, E. (2013). Humanistic-experiential psychotherapies. In M. Lambert (ed.), *Handbook of Psychotherapy and Behavior Change* (6th ed.). Hoboken, NJ: Wiley.

Ellis, B. J., & Del Giudice, M. (2019). Developmental adaptation to stress: An evolutionary perspective. *Annual Review of Psychology, 70,* 111–139. https://doi.org/10.1146/annurev-psych-122216-011732

Ellis, H. (1921). *Studies in the Psychology of Sex.* Philadelphia, PA: F A Davis.

Elwood, P., Galante, J., Pickering, J., Palmer, S., Bayer, A. Ben-Shlomo, Y., Longley, M., & Gallacher, J. (2013). Healthy lifestyles reduce the incidence of chronic diseases and dementia: Evidence from the Caerphilly cohort study. *PLoS One, 8,* e81877.

Encyclopedia of Human Behavior, pages 218–224, https://www.sciencedirect.com/science/article/pii/B978012809324506538X

Engel, G. (1977). The need for a new medical model: A challenge for biomedicine. *Science, 196,* 129–136.

English, H. (1929). Three cases of the "conditioned fear response." *Journal of Abnormal Psychology, 24,* 221–225.

Epel, E., Jimenez, S., Brownell, K., Stroud, L., Stoney, C., & Niaura, R. (2004). Are stress eaters at risk for the metabolic syndrome? *Annals of the New York Academy of Sciences, 1,032,* 208–210. https://doi.org/10.1196/annals.1314.022

Erdelyi, M. H. (1985). *Psychoanalysis: Freud's Cognitive Psychology.* New York: Henry Holt & Co.

Ericsson, K. A., Delaney, P. F., Weaver, G., & Mahadevan, R. (2004). Uncovering the structure of a memorist's superior "basic" memory capacity. *Cognitive Psychology, 49*(3), 191–237. https://doi.org/10.1016/j.cogpsych.2004.02.001

Ertel, K. A., Glymour, M. M., & Berkman, L. F. (2008). Effects of social integration on preserving memory function in a nationally representative US elderly population. *American Journal of Public Health, 98*(7), 1,215–1,220. https://doi.org/10.2105/AJPH.2007.113654

Espay, A. J., Norris, M. M., Eliassen, J. C., Dwivedi, A., Smith, M. S., Banks, C., Allendorfer, J. B., Lang, A. E., Fleck, D. E., Linke, M. J., & Szaflarski, J. P. (2015). Placebo effect of medication cost in Parkinson disease: A randomized double-blind study. *Neurology, 84*(8), 794–802. https://doi.org/10.1212/WNL.0000000000001282

Estabrook, B. (2015). *Pig Tales*. New York: W. W. Norton & Co.

Estreicher, S. K. (2017). The beginning of wine and viticulture. *Physica Status Solidi (C) Current Topics in Solid State Physics, 14*(7). https://doi.org/10.1002/pssc.201700008

Euston, D., & Steenland, H. (2014). Memories—getting wired during sleep. *Science, 344*, 1,087–1,088.

Evans, J. S. B., & Over, D. E. (2013). *Rationality and Reasoning*. East Sussex, UK: Psychology Press.

Evans, S. (ed.) (2019). *APA Handbook of Psychopharmacology*. Washington, DC: American Psychological Association.

Exner, J. E. (1993). *The Rorschach: A Comprehensive System: Basic Foundations, Vol. 1*. New York: John Wiley & Sons.

Falk, E. B., & Bassett, D. S. (2017). Brain and social networks: Fundamental building blocks of human experience. *Trends in Cognitive Sciences, 21*(9), 674–690. https://doi.org/10.1016/j.tics.2017.06.009

Fancher, R. (1996). *Pioneers of Psychology* (3rd ed.). New York: W.W. Norton & Co.

Fava, G. (2003). Can long-term treatment with antidepressant drugs worsen the course of depression? *Journal of Clinical Psychiatry, 64*, 123–133.

Fava, L., & Morton, J. (2009). Causal modeling of panic disorder theories. *Clinical Psychology Review, 29*, 623–637.

Fava, M., & Papakostas, G. (2016). Antidepressants. In T. Stern, M. Fava, T. Wilens, & J. Rosenbaum (eds), *Massachusetts General Hospital Comprehensive Clinical Psychiatry* (2nd ed.). New York: Elsevier.

Fazekas, P., & Overgaard, M. (2016). Multidimensional models of degrees and levels of consciousness. *Trends in Cognitive Sciences, 20*(10), 715–716. https://doi.org/10.1016/j.tics.2016.06.011

Fechner, G. (1860) *Elements of Psychophysics*. New York: Holt, Rinehart and Winston.

Fedorenko, E., & Thompson-Schill, S. (2014). Reworking the language network. *Trends in Cognitive Sciences, 18*, 120–126.

Fehr, E., & Gächter, S. (2002). Altruistic punishment in humans. *Nature, 415*(6,868), 137–140. https://doi.org/10.1038/415137a

Feinstein, J. S., Adolphs, R., & Tranel, D. (2016). A tale of survival from the world of patient S. M. In D. G. Amaral, & R. Adolphs (eds.), *Living without an Amygdala* (pp. 1–38). New York: The Guilford Press.

Felitti, V. J., Anda, R. F., Nordenberg, D., Williamson, D. F., Spitz, A. M., Edwards, V., Koss, M. P., & Marks, J. S. (1998). Relationship of childhood abuse and household dysfunction to many of the leading causes of death in adults. The Adverse Childhood Experiences (ACE) Study. *American Journal of Preventive Medicine, 14*(4), 245–258. https://doi.org/10.1016/s0749-3797(98)00017-8

Felson, R. B. (2002). *Violence & Gender Reexamined*. Washington, DC: American Psychological Association.

Felton, A., Vazquez, D., Ramos-Nunez, A. I., Greene, M. R., Macbeth, A., Hernandez, A. E., & Chiarello, C. (2017). Bilingualism influences structural indices of interhemispheric organization. *Journal of Neurolinguistics*, *42*, 1–11. https://doi.org/10.1016/j.jneuroling.2016.10.004

Fernandes, J., Arida, R., & Gomez-Pinilla, F. (2017). Physical exercise as an epigenetic modulator of brain plasticity. *Neuroscience and Biobehavioral Review*, *80*, 443–456.

Ferrand, M., Ruffault, A., Tytelman, X., Flahault, C., & Négovanska, V. (2015). A cognitive and virtual reality treatment program for the fear of flying. *Aerospace Medicine and Human Performance*, *86*(8), 723–727.

Festinger, L. (1957). *A Theory of Cognitive Dissonance* (Vol. 2). Palo Alto, CA: Stanford University Press.

Festinger, L., & Carlsmith, J. M. (1959). Cognitive consequences of forced compliance. *The Journal of Abnormal and Social Psychology*, *58*(2), 203.

Field, M., & Behrman, R. (2004). *The Ethical Conduct of Clinical Research Involving Children*. Washington, DC: National Academies Press.

Figee, M., Luigjes, J., Smolders, R., Valencia-Alfonso, C.-E., van Wingen, G., de Kwaasteniet, B., Mantione, M., Ooms, P., de Koning, P., Vulink, N., Levar, N., Droge, L., van den Munckhof, P., Schuurman, P. R., Nederveen, A., van den Brink, W., Mazaheri, A., Vink, M., & Denys, D. (2013). Deep brain stimulation restores frontostriatal network activity in obsessive-compulsive disorder. *Nature Neuroscience*, *16*(4), 386–387. https://doi.org/10.1038/nn.3344

Finger, S. (2000). *Minds Behind the Brain: A History of the Pioneers and Their Discoveries*. New York: Oxford University Press.

Fisher, M., Loewy, R., Hardy, K., Schlosser, D., & Vinogradov, S. (2013). Cognitive interventions targeting brain plasticity in the prodromal and early phases of schizophrenia. *Annual Review of Clinical Psychology*, *9*, 435–463.

Fisher, S. E., & Marcus, G. F. (2006). The eloquent ape: genes, brains and the evolution of language. *Nature reviews. Genetics*, *7*(1), 9–20. https://doi.org/10.1038/nrg1747

Fisher, T., Moore, Z., & Pittenger, M. (2012). Sex on the brain?: An examination of frequency of sexual cognitions as a function of gender, erotophilia, and social desirability. *Journal of Sex Research*, *49*, 69–77.

Fisher, W., Geller, J., & Pandiani, J. (2009). The changing role of state psychiatric hospital. *Health Affairs*, *28*, 676–684.

Flavell, J. H. (2000) Development of children's knowledge about the mental world. *International Journal of Behavioral Development*, *24*(1), 15–23, DOI:10.1080/016502500383421

Flynn, J. (2011). Secular changes in intelligence. In R. Sternberg, & S. Kaufman (eds.), *The Cambridge Handbook of Intelligence*. New York: Cambridge University Press.

Flynn, K. (1999). The focus of Diallo murder trial: Testimony of four police officers. *The New York Times*, CXLIX 51732, A1.

Foa, E., & Kozak, M. (1986). Emotional processing of fear: Exposure to corrective information. *Psychological Bulletin*, *99*, 20–35.

Foa, E., Gillihan, S., & Bryant, R. (2013). Challenges and successes in dissemination of evidence-based treatments for posttraumatic stress: Lessons learned from prolonged exposure therapy to PTSD. *Psychological Science in the Public Interest*, *14*, 65–111.

Foussias, G., & Remington, G. (2010). Negative symptoms in schizophrenia: Avolition and Occam's razor. *Schizophrenia Bulletin*, *36*, 359–369.

Frank, M. & Cantera, R. (2014). Sleep, clocks, and synaptic plasticity. *Trends in Neuroscience*, *37*, 491–501.

Franklin, M., & Foa, E. (2008). Obsessive-compulsive disorder. In D. Barlow (ed.), *Clinical Handbook of Psychological Disorders: A Step-by-step Treatment Manual* (4th ed., pp. 164–215). New York: Guilford Press.

Franklin, M., & Foa, E. (2011). Treatment of obsessive-compulsive disorder. *Annual Review of Clinical Psychology, 7,* 229–243.

Frederick, S. (2005). Cognitive reflection and decision making. *Journal of Economic Perspectives, 19*(4), 25–42.

Fredriksen, M., Halmøy, A., Faraone, S., & Haavik, J. (2013). Long-term efficacy and safety of treatment with stimulants and atomoxetine in adult ADHD: A review of controlled and naturalistic studies. *European Neuropsychopharmacology, 23,* 508–527.

Freedman, J. L., & Fraser, S. C. (1966). Compliance without pressure: The foot-in-the-door technique. *Journal of Personality and Social Psychology, 4*(2), 195–202. https://doi.org/10.1037/h0023552

Frenda, S., Knowles, E., Saletan, W., & Loftus, E. (2013). False memories of fabricated political events. *Journal of Experimental Social Psychology, 49,* 280–286.

Frese, F., Knight, E., & Saks, E. (2009). Recovery from schizophrenia: With views of psychiatrists, psychologists, and others diagnosed with this disorder. *Schizophrenia Bulletin, 35,* 370–380.

Freud, S. (1900, 2020). *The Interpretation of Dreams.* New York: Capstone (Wiley).

Frick, P., & Nigg, J. (2012). Current issues in the diagnosis of attention deficit hyperactivity disorder, oppositional defiant disorder, and conduct disorder. *Annual Review of Clinical Psychology, 8,* 77–107.

Frick, P., Barry, C., & Kamphaus, R. (2010). *Clinical Assessment of Child and Adolescent Personality and Behavior.* New York: Springer.

Fried, I., Rutishauser, U., Cerf, M., & Kreiman, G. (2014). *Single Neuron Studies of the Human Brain.* Cambridge, MA: MIT Press.

Friedman, N., Politte, L., Nowinski, L., & McDougle, C. (2015). Autism spectrum disorder. In A. Tasman, J. Kay, J. Lieberman, M. First, & M. Riba (eds.), *Psychiatry* (4th ed.). New York: John Wiley & Sons.

Fries, E., Moragues, N., Caldji, C., Hellhammer, D. H., & Meaney, M. J. (2004). Preliminary evidence of altered sensitivity to benzodiazepines as a function of maternal care in the rat. *Annals of the New York Academy of Science, 1,032,* 320–324.

Friston, K. (2018). Does predictive coding have a future? *Nature Neuroscience, 21*(August), 1,019–1,021.

Frith, U., & Frith, C. (2010). The social brain: Allowing humans to boldly go where no other species has been. *Philosophical Transactions of the Royal Society B: Biological Sciences, 365*(1,537), 165–176.

Fritsch, J. (2000). The Diallo verdict: The overview; 4 officers in Diallo shooting are acquitted of all charges. *The New York Times,* CXLIX 51310, A1–B6.

Gage, F., & Muoti, A. (2012). What makes each brain unique. *Scientific American,* (March), 26–31.

Galati, D., Scherer, K. R., & Ricci-Bitti, P. E. (1997). Voluntary facial expression of emotion: Comparing congenitally blind with normally sighted encoders. *Journal of Personality and Social Psychology, 73*(6), 1,363–1,379. https://doi.org/10.1037//0022-3514.73.6.1363

Galland, B., Taylor, B., Elder, D., & Herbison, P. (2012). Normal sleep patterns in infants and children: A systematic review of observational studies. *Sleep Medicine Reviews, 16,* 213–222.

Gallese, V. (2014). Mirror neurons and the perception–action link. In K. Ochsner, & S. Kosslyn (eds.), *The Oxford Handbook of Cognitive Neuroscience.* New York: Oxford University Press.

Gallup, G. (1972). Opinion polling in a democracy. In J. Tanur (ed.), *Statistics: A Guide to the Unknown.* San Francisco: Holden-Day.

Galton, F. (1907). Vox Populi (The Wisdom of Crowds). *Nature, 75,* 450–451.

Galván, A. (2013). The teenage brain: Sensitivity to rewards. *Current Directions in Psychological Science, 22,* 88–93.

Galván, A. (2020). The need for sleep in the adolescent brain. *Trends in Cognitive Sciences, 24*(1), 79–89. https://doi.org/10.1016/j.tics.2019.11.002

Gansberg, M. (1964, March 27). 37 who saw murder didn't call the police. *The New York Times.* https://timesmachine.nytimes.com/timesmachine/1964/03/27/97175042.html?pageNumber=1

Garb, H. N., Wood, J. M., Lilienfeld, S. O., & Nezworski, M. T. (2005). Roots of the Rorschach controversy. *Clinical Psychology Review, 25*(1), 97–118.

Garcia, J., Kimeldorf, D. J., & Koelling, R. A. (1955). Conditioned aversion to saccharin resulting from exposure to gamma radiation. *Science, 122*(3,160), 157–158.

Gardner, E. & Johnson, K. (2013). Touch. In Kandel, E. R., Schwartz, J. H., Jessell, T. M., Siegelbaum, S., & Hudspeth, A. J. (eds.), *Principles of Neural Science* (5th ed.). New York: McGraw-Hill.

Gardner, H. (1993). *Multiple Intelligences: The Theory in Practice.* New York: Basic Books.

Gardner, H., Kornhaber, M., & Wake, W. (1996). *Intelligence, Multiple Perspectives.* New York: Harcourt Brace.

Gardner, R., Gardner, B., & van Cantfort, T. (1989). *Teaching Sign Language to Chimpanzees.* Albany, NY: State University of New York Press.

Garm, A., Oskarsson, M., & Nilsson, D. (2011). Box jellyfish use terrestrial visual cues for navigation. *Current Biology, 21,* 798–803.

Garraza. L., Walrath, C., Goldston, D., Reid, H., & McKeon, R. (2015). Effect of the Garrett Lee Smith Memorial Suicide Prevention Program on suicide attempts among youths. *JAMA Psychiatry, 72,* 1,143–1,149.

Garrett-Bakelman, F., et al. (2019). The NASA twin study: A multidimensional analysis of a year-long human spaceflight. *Science, 364,* eaau8650. DOI:10.1126/science.aau8650

Gaudio, S., & Quattrocchi, C. C. (2012). Neural basis of a multidimensional model of body image distortion in anorexia nervosa. *Neurosci Biobehav Rev., 36*(8), 1,839–1,847. DOI:10.1016/j.neubiorev.2012.05.003. Epub 2012 May 18. PMID: 22613629.

Gazzaniga, M. S., & LeDoux, J. E. (1978). *The Integrated Mind.* New York: Plenum Press.

GBD 2015 Obesity Collaborators. (2017). Health effects of overweight and obesity in 195 countries over 25 years. *New England Journal of Medicine, 377*(1), 13–27.

Gecas, V. (1982). The self-concept. *Annual Review of Sociology, 8*(1), 1–33.

Geddes, J., Burgess, S., Hawton, K., Jamison, K., & Goodwin, G. (2004). Long-term lithium therapy for bipolar disorder: Systematic review and meta-analysis of randomized controlled trials. *American Journal of Psychiatry, 161,* 217–222.

Genzel, L., Kroes, M. C., Dresler, M., & Battaglia, F. P. (2014). Light sleep versus slow wave sleep in memory consolidation: A question of global versus local processes? *Trends in Neurosciences, 37*(1), 10–19. https://doi.org/10.1016/j.tins.2013.10.002

Gerard, D. (1997). Chiarugi and Pinel considered: Soul's brain.person's mind. *Journal of the History of the Behavioral Sciences, 33,* 381–403.

Gervain, J., & Mehler, J. (2010). Speech perception and language acquisition in the first year of life. *Annual Review of Psychology, 61,* 191–218. https://doi.org/10.1146/annurev.psych.093008.100408

Getov, S., Kanai, R., Bahrami, B., & Rees, G. (2015). Human brain structure predicts individual differences in preconscious evaluation of facial dominance and trustworthiness. *Social Cognitive and Affective Neuroscience, 10*(5), 690–699.

Geuter, S., Koban, L., & Wager, T. D. (2017). The cognitive neuroscience of placebo effects: Concepts, predictions, and physiology. *Annual Review of Neuroscience, 40*(1), 167–188. https://doi.org/10.1146/annurev-neuro-072116-031132

Ghazanfar A. A. (2008). Language evolution: Neural differences that make a difference. *Nature Neuroscience, 11*(4), 382–384. https://doi.org/10.1038/nn0408-382

Giedd, J. N. (2015). The amazing teen brain. *Scientific American, 312*(6), 32–37.

Gigerenzer, G. (2008a). Why heuristics work. *Perspectives on Psychological Science, 3*(1), 20–29.

Gigerenzer, G. (2008b). *Rationality for Mortals: How People Cope with Uncertainty.* New York: Oxford University Press.

Gilboa, A., & Marlatte, H. (2017). Neurobiology of schemas and schema-mediated memory. *Trends in Cognitive Sciences, 21*(8), 618–631. https://doi.org/10.1016/j.tics.2017.04.013

Gilmore, J. H., Kang, C., Evans, D. D., Wolfe, H. M., Smith, J. K., Lieberman, J. A., . . . & Gerig, G. (2010). Prenatal and neonatal brain structure and white matter maturation in children at high risk for schizophrenia. *American Journal of Psychiatry, 167,* 1,083–1,091.

Gilmore, J. H., Knickmeyer, R. C., & Gao, W. (2018). Imaging structural and functional brain development in early childhood. *Nature Reviews. Neuroscience, 19*(3), 123–137. https://doi.org/10.1038/nrn.2018.1

Gingerich, A. C., & Lineweaver, T. T. (2014). OMG! Texting in class = u fail: (Empirical evidence that text messaging during class disrupts comprehension). *Teaching of Psychology, 41*(1), 44–51. https://doi.org/10.1177/0098628313514177

Giraldo-Chica, M., Rogers, B. P., Damon, S. M., Landman, B. A., & Woodward, N. D. (2018a). Archival report prefrontal-thalamic anatomical connectivity and executive cognitive function in schizophrenia. *Biological Psychiatry, 83*(6), 509–517. https://doi.org/10.1016/j.biopsych.2017.09.022

Giraldo-Chica, M., Rogers, B. P., Damon, S. M., Landman, B. A., & Woodward, N. D. (2018b). Prefrontal-thalamic anatomical connectivity and executive cognitive function in schizophrenia. *Biological Psychiatry, 83*(6), 509–517. https://doi.org/10.1016/j.biopsych.2017.09.022

Giromini, L., Porcelli, P., Viglione, D., Parolin, L., & Pineda, J. (2010). The feeling of movement: EEG evidence for mirroring activity during the observations of static, ambiguous stimuli in the Rorschach cards. *Biological Psychology, 85,* 233–241.

Gitlin, M. (2009). Pharmacotherapy and other somatic treatments for depression. In I. Gotlib, & C. Hammen (eds.), *Handbook of Depression* (2nd ed.). New York: Guilford Press.

Glorioso, C. A., Pfenning, A. R., Lee, S. S., Bennett, D. A., Sibille, E. L., Kellis, M., & Guarente, L. P. (2019). Rate of brain aging and APOE 4 are synergistic risk factors for Alzheimer's disease. *Life Science Alliance, 2*(3), 1–12. https://doi.org/10.26508/lsa.201900303

Glucksberg, S. (1962). The influence of strength of drive on functional fixedness and perceptual recognition. *Journal of Experimental Psychology, 63*(1), 36–41. https://doi.org/10.1037/h0044683

Gobet, F., Lane, P., Croker, S., Cheng, P., Jones, G., Oliver, I., & Pine, J. (2001). Chunking mechanisms in human learning. *Trends in Cognitive Sciences, 5,* 236–243.

Gogtay, N., Vyas, N., Testa, R., Wood, S., & Pantelis, C. (2011). Age of onset of schizophrenia perspectives from structural neuroimaging studies. *Schizophrenia Bulletin, 37,* 504–513.

Goldberg, I. I., Harel, M., & Malach, R. (2006). When the brain loses its self: Prefrontal inactivation during sensorimotor processing. *Neuron, 50*(2), 329–339. https://doi.org/10.1016/j.neuron.2006.03.015

Goldenberg, A., & Gross, J. (2020). Digital emotion contagion. *Trends in Cognitive Sciences, 24,* 316–328.

Goldfried, M., Castonguay, L., Hayes, A., Drozd, J., & Shapiro, D. (1997). A comparative analysis of the therapeutic focus in cognitive-behavioral and psychodynamic-interpersonal sessions. *Journal of Consulting and Clinical Psychology, 65,* 740–748.

Goldsmith, S. (2001). *Rick Factors for Suicide.* Washington, DC: National Academy Press.

Goldstein, A. N., & Walker, M. P. (2014). The role of sleep in emotional brain function. *Annual Review of Clinical Psychology, 10,* 679–708.

Goldstone, R. L., Kersten, A., & Cavalho, P. F. (2012). Concepts and categorization. In A. F. Healy, & R. W. Proctor (eds.), *Comprehensive Handbook of Psychology, Volume 4: Experimental Psychology.* New Jersey: Wiley.

Golombek, D., & Rosenstein, R. (2010). Physiology of circadian entrainment. *Physiological Reviews, 90,* 1,063–11,02.

Goncu, A., & Gaskins, S. (eds.) (2007). *Play and Development: Evolutionary, Sociocultural, and Functional Perspectives.* East Sussex, UK: Psychology Press.

Goodall, J. (1990). *Through a Window: My Thirty Years With the Chimpanzees of Gombe.* New York: Houghton Mifflin Harcourt

Goodman, A. (2007). Neurobiology of addiction. An integrative review. *Biochemical Pharmacology, 75,* 266–322.

Goodwin, F., & Jamison, K. (2007). *Manic Depressive Illness* (2nd ed.). New York: Oxford University Press.

Gopalakrishna, G., Ithman, M. H., & Lauriello, J. (2016). Update on new and emerging treatments for schizophrenia. *Psychiatric Clinics of North America, 39,* 217–238. https://doi.org/10.1016/j.psc.2016.01.005

Gordon, B.E. (1949). The physiology of hypnosis. *Psychiatric Quarterly, 23,* 317–343.

Gosling S. D. (2001). From mice to men: What can we learn about personality from animal research? *Psychological Bulletin, 127*(1), 45–86. https://doi.org/10.1037/0033-2909.127.1.45

Gosling, S. D., Ko, S. J., Mannarelli, T., & Morris, M. E. (2002). A room with a cue: Personality judgments based on offices and bedrooms. *Journal of Personality and Social Psychology, 82*(3), 379–398. https://doi.org/10.1037//0022-3514.82.3.379

Gosseries, O., Di, H., Laureys, S., & Boly, M. (2014). Measuring consciousness in severely damaged brains. *Annual Review of Neuroscience, 37,* 457–478.

Gottesman, I. (1991). *Schizophrenic Genetics: The Origin of Madness.* New York: Freeman.

Gottfredson, L. S., & Deary, I. J. (2004). Intelligence predicts health and longevity, but why? *Current Directions in Psychological Science, 13*(1), 1–4.

Gottlieb, D. A., & Begej, E. L. (2014). Principles of Pavlovian conditioning: Description, content, function. In F. K. McSweeney, & E. S. Murphy (eds.), *The Wiley Blackwell Handbook of Operant and Classical Conditioning* (pp. 3–25). Hoboken, NJ: John Wiley & Sons, Ltd.

Graeff, F. G., & Del-Ben, C. M. (2008). Neurobiology of panic disorder: From animal models to brain neuroimaging. *Neuroscience and Biobehavioral Reviews, 32*(7), 1,326–1,335. https://doi.org/10.1016/j.neubiorev.2008.05.017

Grandin, T. (2009). How does visual thinking work in the mind of a person with autism? A personal account. *Philosophical Transactions of the Royal Society B, 364,* 1,437–1,442.

Grandin, T. (2010). *Thinking in Pictures, Expanded Edition: My Life with Autism.* New York: Vintage.

Grant, J. A., & Rainville, P. (2005). Hypnosis and meditation: Similar experiential changes and shared brain mechanisms. *Medical Hypotheses, 65*(3), 625–626. https://doi.org/10.1016/j.mehy.2005.04.013

Gray, J. A., & McNaughton, N. (2000). *The Neuropsychology of Anxiety* (2nd ed.). Oxford: Oxford University Press.

Greenberg, J. (2008). Understanding the vital human quest for self-esteem. *Perspectives on Psychological Science, 3*(1), 48–55.

Greenberg, L. (2002). *Emotion-focused Therapy: Coaching Clients to Work through Their Feelings.* Washington, DC: American Psychological Association.

Greenberg, L. S., & Watson, J. C. (2006). *Emotion-focused Therapy for Depression.* Washington, DC: American Psychological Association.

Greenberg M. T. (2018). A science-driven model of community collaboration to improve youth outcomes. *American Journal of Public Health, 108*(5), 592–593. https://doi.org/10.2105/AJPH.2018.304380

Greenberg, M. T., & Lippold, M. A. (2013). Promoting healthy outcomes among youth with multiple risks: innovative approaches. *Annual Review of Public Health, 34*, 253–270. https://doi.org/10.1146/annurev-publhealth-031811-124619

Greenwald, A., McGhee, D., & Schwartz, J. (1998). Measuring individual differences in implicit cognition: The implicit association test. *Journal of Personality and Social Psychology, 74*, 1,464–1,480.

Greenwald, A. G., Poehlman, T. A., Uhlmann, E. L., & Banaji, M. R. (2009). Understanding and using the Implicit Association Test: III. Meta-analysis of predictive validity. *Journal of Personality and Social Psychology, 97*(1), 17–41. https://doi.org/10.1037/a0015575

Gregory, R. & Wallace, J. (1963) *Recovery from Early Blindness: A Case Study. Experimental. Society Monograph.* No. 2. Cambridge: Heffers.

Gregory, R. J., & Remen, A. L. (2008). A manual-based psychodynamic therapy for treatment-resistant borderline personality disorder. *Psychotherapy Theory, Research, Practice, Training, 45*, 15–27.

Gregory, R. L., & Wallace, J. G. (1963). Recovery from early blindness: A case study. *Experimental Psychology Society Monograph No. 2.*

Griggs, R. A. (2014). Coverage of the Stanford Prison Experiment in introductory psychology textbooks. *Teaching of Psychology, 41*(3), 195–203.

Griggs, R. A. (2017). Milgram's obedience study: A contentious classic reinterpreted. *Teaching of Psychology, 44*(1), 32–37. https://doi.org/10.1177/0098628316677644

Grimm, D. (2015). The scientist behind the "personhood2" chimps. *Science, 348,* 1,187–1,188.

Grosjean, F. (2010) *Bilingual: Life and Reality.* Cambridge, MA: Harvard University Press.

Gross, C., & Hen, R. (2004). The developmental origins of anxiety. *Nature Reviews. Neuroscience, 5*, 545–552.

Grossman, P., Niemann, L., Schmidt, S., & Walach, H. (2004). Mindfulness-based stress reduction and health benefits: A meta-analysis. *Journal of Psychosomatic Research, 57*, 35–43.

Gu, S., Wang, F., Cao, C., Wu, E., Tang, Y. Y., & Huang, J. H. (2019). An integrative way for studying neural basis of basic emotions with fMRI. *Frontiers in Neuroscience, 13*(June), 1–12. https://doi.org/10.3389/fnins.2019.00628

Gunderson, J., & Ridolfi, M. (2001). Borderline personality disorder: Suicidality and self-mutilation. *Annals of the New York Academy of Science, 932,* 61–77.

Gunnar, M., & Quevedo, K. (2007). The neurobiology of stress and development. *Annual Review of Psychology, 58,* 145–173. https://doi.org/10.1146/annurev.psych.58.110405.085605

Haas, R., Watson, J., Buonasera, T., Southon, J., Chen, J. C., Noe, S., . . . & Parker, G. (2020). Female hunters of the early Americas. *Science Advances, 6*(45), eabd0310.

Hagoort, P. (2019). The neurobiology of language beyond single-word processing. *Science, 366*(6,461), 55–58. https://doi.org/10.1126/science.aax0289

Hahn, G., Zamora-López, G., Uhrig, L., Tagliazucchi, E., Laufs, H., Mantini, D., …, & Deco, G. (2021). Signature of consciousness in brain-wide synchronization patterns of monkey and human fMRI signals. *NeuroImage, 226*(May 2020), 117470. https://doi.org/10.1016/j.neuroimage.2020.117470

Hallgrímsson, B., & Hall, B. (eds.) (2011). *Epigenetics: Linking Genotype and Phenotype in Development and Evolution.* Berkeley: University of California Press.

Halpern, D. F., Beninger, S. A., & Straight, C. A. (2011). Sex differences in intelligence. In R. J. Sternberg, & S. B. Kaufman (eds.), *The Cambridge Handbook of Intelligence* (pp. 253–272). Cambridge: Cambridge University Press.

Hamann, S., Herman, R. A., Nolan, C. L., & Wallen, K. (2004). Men and women differ in amygdala response to visual sexual stimuli. *Nature Neuroscience, 7*(4), 411–416. https://doi.org/10.1038/nn1208

Hameroff, S., & Penrose, R. (2014). Consciousness in the universe: A review of the "Orch OR" theory. *Physics of Life Reviews, 11*(1), 39–78.

Haney, C., Banks, C., & Zimbardo, P. (1973). A study of prisoners and guards in a simulated prison. *International Journal of Criminology & Penology, 1,* 69–97.

Hanslmayr, S., Staresina, B. P., & Bowman, H. (2016). Oscillations and episodic memory: Addressing the synchronization/desynchronization conundrum. *Trends in Neurosciences, 39*(1), 16–25. https://doi.org/10.1016/j.tins.2015.11.004

Hantsoo, L., & Mathews, S. (2019). Pharmacological treatment of depressive disorders. In S. M. Evans, & K. M. Carpenter (eds.), *APA Handbooks in Psychology® Series. APA Handbook of Psychopharmacology* (pp. 141–164). American Psychological Association.

Happé, F., Cook, J. L., & Bird, G. (2017). The structure of social cognition: In(ter)dependence of sociocognitive processes. *Annual Review of Psychology, 68*(1), 243–267. https://doi.org/10.1146/annurev-psych-010416-044046

Haq, A., Sitzmann, A., Goldman, M., Maixner, D., & Mickey, B. (2015). Response of depression to electroconvulsive therapy. *Journal of Clinical Psychiatry, 76,* 1,374–1,384.

Harden, K. P. (2021). "Reports of my death were greatly exaggerated": Behavior genetics in the postgenomic era. *Annual Review of Psychology, 72*(1), 1–24. https://doi.org/10.1146/annurev-psych-052220-103822

Hare, R. (2003). *The Hare Psychopathy Checklist-Revised.* Toronto, ON: Multi-Health System.

Harlow, H. F. (1958). The nature of love. *American Psychologist, 13*(12), 673–685. https://doi.org/10.1037/h0047884

Harlow, H., McGaught, J., & Thompson, R. (1971). *Psychology.* San Francisco: Albion Publishing.

Harlow, J. (1868). Recovery from the passage of an iron bar passing through the head. *Publications of the Massachusetts Medical Society, 2,* 327–347.

Harris, L., Todorov, A., & Fiske, S. (2005). Attributions on the brain: Neuro-imaging dispositional inferences, beyond theory of mind. *Neuroimage, 28,* 763–769.

Harris S. E., & Deary, I. J. (2011). The genetics of cognitive ability and cognitive ageing in healthy older people. *Trends Cognitive Sciences, 15*(9), 388–394. DOI:10.1016/j.tics.2011.07.004

Harrison, P. J., Geddes, J. R., & Tunbridge, E. M. (2018). The emerging neurobiology of bipolar disorder. *Trends in Neurosciences, 41*(1), 18–30. https://doi.org/10.1016/j.tins.2017.10.006

Harrison, T. M., Weintraub, S., Mesulam, M.-M., & Rogalski, E. (2012). Superior memory and higher cortical volumes in unusually successful cognitive aging. *Journal of the International Neuropsychological Society: JINS, 18*(6), 1,081–1,085. https://doi.org/10.1017/S1355617712000847

Hartline, H. (1938). The responses of single optic nerve fibers of the vertebrate eye to illumination of the retina. *American Journal of Physiology, 121,* 400–415.

Hartshorne, J. K., & Germine, L. T. (2015). When does cognitive functioning peak? The asynchronous rise and fall of different cognitive abilities across the life span. *Psychological Science, 26*(4), 433–443.

Haslam, S. A., Reicher, S., & Birney, M. E. (2016). Questioning authority: New perspectives on Milgram's "obedience" research and its implications for intergroup relations. *Current Opinion in Psychology, 11,* 6–9. DOI:10.1016/j.copsyc.2016.03.007

Haworth C. M., Wright, M. J., Luciano, M., et al. (2010). The heritability of general cognitive ability increases linearly from childhood to young adulthood. *Molecular Psychiatry, 15*(11), 1,112–1,120. DOI:10.1038/mp.2009.55

Hayden, B., Canuel, N., & Shanse, J. (2013). What was brewing in the Natufian? An archaeological assessment of brewing technology in the Epipaleolithic. *Journal of Archaeological Method and Theory, 20,* 102–150.

Hayes, S., Hirsch, C., & Mathews, A. (2008). Restriction of working memory capacity during worry. *Journal of Abnormal Psychology, 117*(3), 712–717. https://doi.org/10.1037/a0012908

Hayes, S. C. (2004). Acceptance and commitment therapy, relational frame theory, and the third wave of behavioral and cognitive therapies. *Behavior Therapy, 35,* 639–665.

Hayes, S. C., Strosahl, K. D., & Wilson, K. G. (2011) *Acceptance and Commitment Therapy: The Process and Practice of Mindful Change* (2nd ed.). New York: Guilford Press.

Hayes-Skelton, S. A., Roemer, L., & Orsillo, S. M. (2013). A randomized clinical trial comparing an acceptance-based behavior therapy to applied relaxation for generalized anxiety disorder. *Journal of Consulting and Clinical Psychology, 81*(5), 761–773. https://doi.org/10.1037/a0032871

Hazan, C., & Shaver, P. R. (1987). Romantic love conceptualized as an attachment process. *Journal of Personality and Social Psychology, 52,* 511–524.

Heatherton T. F. (2011). Neuroscience of self and self-regulation. *Annual Review of Psychology, 62,* 363–390. https://doi.org/10.1146/annurev.psych.121208.131616

Hebb, D. (1949). *The Organization of Behavior.* New York: Wiley.

Heckman, J. (2006). Investing in disadvantaged young children is an economically efficient policy. Presented at the Committee for Economic Development/The Pew Charitable Trusts/PNC Financial Services Group Forum on "Building the economic case for investment in preschool." New York, 10 January.

Hehman, E., Ingbretsen, Z., & Freeman, J. (2014). The neural basis of stereotypic impact on multiple social categorization. *Neuroimage, 101,* 704–711.

Heider, F. (1958). *The Psychology of Interpersonal Relations.* New York: Wiley

Held, R. & Heim, A. (1963). Movement-produced stimulation in the development of visually guided behavior. *Journal of Comparative and Physiological Psychology, 56,* 872–876.

Henrich, J., & Muthukrishna, M. (2021). The origins and psychology of human cooperation. *Annual Review of Psychology, 72*(1), 1–34. https://doi.org/10.1146/annurev-psych-081920-042106

Herrnstein, R., & Murray, C. (1994). *The Bell Curve: Intelligence and Class Structure in American Life*. New York: Free Press.

Hettema, J., Neale, M., & Kendler, K. (2001). A review and meta-analysis of the genetic epidemiology of anxiety disorders. *American Journal of Psychiatry, 158*, 1,568–1,578.

Heywood, C., & Zihl, J. (1999). Motion blindness. In G. Humphreys (ed.), *Case Studies in the Neuropsychology of Vision*. East Sussex: Psychology Press.

Hill, K., & Linden, D. E. (2013). Hallucinatory experiences in non-clinical populations. In R. Jardri, A. Cachia, P. Thomas, & D. Pine (eds.), *The Neuroscience of Hallucinations* (pp. 21–41). New York: Springer.

Hill, K., Reilly, J. L., Keefe, R. S. E., Gold, J. M., Bishop, J. R., Gershon, E. S., Tamminga, C. A., Pearlson, G. D., Keshavan, M. S., & Sweeney, J. A. (2013). Neuropsychological impairments in schizophrenia and psychotic bipolar disorder: Findings from the Bipolar-Schizophrenia Network on Intermediate Phenotypes (B-SNIP) study. *American Journal of Psychiatry, 170*(11), 1,275–1,284. https://doi.org/10.1176/appi.ajp.2013.12101298

Hinshaw, S. P. (2018). Attention Deficit Hyperactivity Disorder (ADHD): Controversy, developmental mechanisms, and multiple levels of analysis. *Annual Review of Clinical Psychology, 14*, 291–316.

Hippocrates, trans. Francis Adams (400 B.C.E.). *On the Sacred Disease*, http://classics.mit.edu/Hippocrates/sacred.html

Hirota, K., & Lambert, D. G. (2018). Ketamine and depression. *British Journal of Anaesthesia, 121*(6), 1,198–1,202. https://doi.org/10.1016/j.bja.2018.08.020

Hirschtritt, M., Bloch, M., & Mathews, C. (2017). Obsessive-compulsive disorder advances in diagnosis and treatment. *JAMA, 317*(13), 1,358–1,367. https://doi.org/10.1001/jama.2017.2200

Hirst, W., & Phelps, E. A. (2016). Flashbulb memories. *Current Directions in Psychological Science, 25*(1), 36–41. https://doi.org/10.1177/0963721415622487

Hobson, J. (1989). *Sleep*. New York: Scientific American Library.

Hobson, J. (2009). REM sleep and dreaming: Towards a theory of protoconsciousness. *Nature Reviews. Neuroscience, 10*, 803–813.

Hobson, J., & Pace-Schott, E. (2002). The cognitive neuroscience of sleep: Neuronal systems, consciousness and learning. *Nature Reviews. Neuroscience, 3*, 679–693.

Hoeft, F., Gabrieli, J. D., Whitfield-Gabrieli, S., Haas, B. W., Bammer, R., Menon, V., & Spiegel, D. (2012). Functional brain basis of hypnotizability. *Archives of General Psychiatry, 69*(10), 1,064–1,072. https://doi.org/10.1001/archgenpsychiatry.2011.2190

Hofman, M. (2001). Brain evolution in hominids: Are we at the end of the road? In D. Falk, & K. Gibson (eds.), *Evolutionary Anatomy of the Primate Cerebral Cortex*. New York: Cambridge University Press.

Hofman, M., & Swaab, D. (1992). The human hypothalamus: Comparative morphometry and photoperiodic influences. *Progress in Brain Research, 93*, 133–147.

Hofman, M. A. (2014). Evolution of the human brain: When bigger is better. *Frontiers in Neuroanatomy, 8*, 1–12. https://doi.org/10.3389/fnana.2014.00015

Hofmann, S., Grossman, P., & Hinton, D. (2011). Loving-kindness and compassion meditation: Potential for psychological interventions. *Clinical Psychology Review, 31*, 1,126–1,132.

Hofmann, S., Sawyer, A., Witt, A., & Oh, D. (2010). The effect of mindfulness-based therapy on anxiety and depression: A meta-analytic review. *Journal of Consulting and Clinical Psychology, 78*, 169–183.

Hofmann, S. G., & Barlow, D. H. (2002). Social phobia (social anxiety disorder). In D. H. Barlow (ed.), *Anxiety and Its Disorders: The Nature and Treatment of Anxiety and Panic* (2nd ed.). New York: Guilford Press.

Hogan, M., Staff, R., Bunting, B., Murray, A., Ahearn, T., Deary, I., & Whalley, L. (2011). Cerebellar brain volume accounts for variance in cognitive performance in older adults. *Cortex, 47,* 441.

Hogarty, G., & Goldberg, S. (1973). Drugs and sociotherapy in the after care of schizophrenic patients: One year relapse rates. *Achieves of General Psychiatry, 28,* 54–64.

Hoge, E. A., Bui, E., Marques, L., Metcalf, C. A., Morris, L. K., Robinaugh, D. J., . . ., & Simon, N. M. (2013). Randomized controlled trial of mindfulness meditation for generalized anxiety disorder: Effects on anxiety and stress reactivity. *Journal of Clinical Psychiatry, 74.*

Holliday, B. G. (2009). The history and visions of African American psychology: Multiple pathways to place, space, and authority. *Cultural Diversity & Ethnic Minority Psychology, 15*(4), 317–337. https://doi.org/10.1037/a0016971

Hollister, L. E. (1984). Effects of hallucinogens in humans. In B. L. Jacobs (ed.), *Hallucinogens: Neurochemical, Behavioral, and Clinical Perspectives* (pp. 19–33). New York: Raven Press.

Hollon, S., & Beck, A. (2013). Cognitive and cognitive-behavioral therapies. In M. Lambert (ed.), *Handbook of Psychotherapy and Behavior Change* (6th ed.). Hoboken, NJ: Wiley.

Holmes, S. E., Scheinost, D., Finnema, S. J., Naganawa, M., Davis, M. T., DellaGioia, N., Nabulsi, N., Matuskey, D., Angarita, G. A., Pietrzak, R. H., Duman, R. S., Sanacora, G., Krystal, J. H., Carson, R. E., & Esterlis, I. (2019). Lower synaptic density is associated with depression severity and network alterations. *Nature Communications, 10*(1), 1–10. https://doi.org/10.1038/s41467-019-09562-7

Holtzheimer, P., Kosel, M., & Schlaepfer, T. (2012). Brain stimulation therapies for neuropsychiatric disease. In M. Aminoff, F. Boller, & D. Swaab (eds.), *Handbook of Clinical Neurology* (pp. 681–695). New York: Elsevier.

Hölzel, E., Hoge, D., Greve, D., Gard, T., Creswell, J., Brown, L., . . . Lazar, S. (2013). Neural mechanisms of symptom improvements in generalized anxiety disorder following mindfulness training. *NeuroImage: Clinical, 2,* 448–458.

Horney, K (1951). *Neurosis and Human Growth.* New York: Routledge.

Horovitz, S. G., Braun, A. R., Carr, W. S., Picchioni, D., Balkin, T. J., Fukunaga, M., & Duyn, J. H. (2009). Decoupling of the brain's default mode network during deep sleep. *Proceedings of the National Academy of Sciences of the United States of America, 106*(27), 11,376–11,381. https://doi.org/10.1073/pnas.0901435106

Howe, L. C., & Krosnick, J. A. (2017). Attitude strength. *Annual Review of Psychology, 68,* 327–351. https://doi.org/10.1146/annurev-psych-122414-033600

Howley, M. M., Carter, T. C., Browne, M. L., Romitti, P. A., Cunniff, C. M., Druschel, C. M., & National Birth Defects Prevention Study (2016). Fluconazole use and birth defects in the National Birth Defects Prevention Study. *American Journal of Obstetrics and Gynecology, 214*(5), 657.e1–657.e6579. https://doi.org/10.1016/j.ajog.2015.11.022

Hoza, B., Kaiser, N., & Hurt, E. (2008). Evidence-based treatments for attention-deficit/hyperactivity disorder (ADHD). In R. Steele, T. Elkin, & M. Roberts (eds.), *Handbook of Evidence-based Therapies for Children and Adolescents: Bridging Science and Practice.* New York: Springer.

Huang, Y., Kotov, R., de Girolamo, G., Preti, A., Angermeyer, M., Benjet, C., . . ., & Kessler, R. (2009). DSM-IV personality disorders in the WHO World Mental Health Surveys. *British Journal of Psychiatry, 195,* 46–53.

Huentelman, M. J., Talboom, J. S., Lewis, C. R., Chen, Z., & Barnes, C. A. (2020). Reinventing neuroaging research in the digital age. *Trends in Neurosciences, 43*(1), 17–23. https://doi.org/10.1016/j.tins.2019.11.004

Humphreys, G., & Riddoch, J (2014). *A Case Study in Visual Agnosia Revisited: To See But Not to See* (2nd ed.). New York: Psychology Press.

Hung, L. W., Neuner, S., Polepalli, J. S., Beier, K. T., Wright, M., Walsh, J. J., Lewis, E. M., Luo, L., Deisseroth, K., Dölen, G., & Malenka, R. C. (2017). Gating of social reward by oxytocin in the ventral tegmental area. *Science, 357*(6,358), 1,406–1,411. https://doi.org/10.1126/science.aan4994

Hunsley, J., & Mash, E. J. (2007). Evidence-based assessment. *Annual Review of Clinical Psychology, 3*, 29–51. https://doi.org/10.1146/annurev.clinpsy.3.022806.091419

Huth, A. G., de Heer, W. A., Griffiths, T. L., Theunissen, F. E., & Gallant, J. L. (2016). Natural speech reveals the semantic maps that tile human cerebral cortex. *Nature, 532*(7,600), 453–458. https://doi.org/10.1038/nature17637

Huxley, J. (1942) Evolution, the Modern Synthesis. London: Allen and Unwin.

Hyman, S. (2010). The diagnosis of mental disorders: The problem of reification. *Annual Review of Clinical Psychology, 6*, 155–179.

Hyman, S., & Cohen, J. (2013). Disorders of thought and volition: Schizophrenia. In E. Kandel, J. Schwartz, T. Jessell, S. Siegelbaum, & A. Hudspeth (eds.), *Principles of Neural Science* (5th ed.). New York: McGraw-Hill.

Hyman, S., Malenka, R., & Nester, E. (2006). Neural mechanisms of addiction: The role of reward-related learning and memory. *Annual Review of Neuroscience, 29*, 565–598.

Iacoboni M. (2009). Imitation, empathy, and mirror neurons. *Annual Review of Psychology, 60*, 653–670. https://doi.org/10.1146/annurev.psych.60.110707.163604

Ikeda, M., Tanaka, S., Saito, T., Ozaki, N., Kamatani, Y., & Iwata, N. (2018). Re-evaluating classical body type theories: Genetic correlation between psychiatric disorders and body mass index. *Psychological Medicine, 48*(10), 1,745–1,748. https://doi.org/10.1017/S0033291718000685

Imagery, and perception. In S. M. Evans, & K. M. Carpenter (eds.), *APA Handbooks in Psychology® Series. APA Handbook of Psychopharmacology* (pp. 141–164). Washington, DC: American Psychological Association. https://doi.org/10.1037/0000133-007

Impett, E. A., & Peplau, L. A. (2003). Sexual compliance: gender, motivational, and relationship perspectives. *Journal of Sex Research, 40*(1), 87–100. https://doi.org/10.1080/00224490309552169

Ingalhalikar, M., Smith, A., Parker, D., Satterthwaite, T. D., Elliott, M. A., Ruparel, K., Hakonarson, H., Gur, R. E., Gur, R. C., & Verma, R. (2014). Sex differences in the structural connectome of the human brain. *Proceedings of the National Academy of Sciences of the United States of America, 111*(2), 823–828. https://doi.org/10.1073/pnas.1316909110

Insel, T. (2010). Rethinking schizophrenia. *Nature, 468*, 187–193.

Insel, T. R. (2016). RAISE-ing our expectations for first-episode psychosis. *American Journal of Psychiatry, 173*(4), 311–312. https://doi.org/10.1176/appi.ajp.2015.15091204

Ionta, S., Martuzzi, R., Salomon, R., & Blanke, O. (2014). The brain network reflecting bodily self-consciousness: A functional connectivity study. *Social Cognitive and Affective Neuroscience*, 1–10. https://doi.org/10.1093/scan/nst185

Ison, M. J., Quian Quiroga, R., & Fried, I. (2015). Rapid encoding of new memories by individual neurons in the human brain. *Neuron, 87*(1), 220–230. https://doi.org/10.1016/j.neuron.2015.06.016

Ito, T., Hearne, L., Mill, R., Cocuzza, C., & Cole, M. W. (2020). Discovering the computational relevance of brain network organization. *Trends in Cognitive Sciences, 24*(1), 25–38. https://doi.org/10.1016/j.tics.2019.10.005

Iversen, L. (2006). Neurotransmitter transporters and their impact on the development of psychopharmacology. *British Journal of Pharmacology, 147*, S82–S88.

Izard, C. E. (2007). Emotion feelings stem from evolution and neurobiological development, not from conceptual acts: Corrections for Barrett et al. *Perspectives on Psychological Science: A Journal of the Association for Psychological Science, 2*(4), 404–405. https://doi.org/10.1111/j.1745-6916.2007.00053.x

Jack, R. E., & Schyns, P. G. (2017). Toward a social psychophysics of face communication. *Annual Review of Psychology, 68*(1), 269–297. https://doi.org/10.1146/annurev-psych-010416-044242

Jackson, J. (1932). Evolution and dissolution of the nervous system. In J. Taylor (ed.), *Selected Writing of John Hughlings Jackson* (Vol. 2). London: Hodder & Stroughton.

Jackson, J. C., Watts, J., Henry, T. R., List, J., Forkel, R., Mucha, P. J., …, & Lindquist, K. A. (2019). Emotion semantics show both cultural variation and universal structure. *Science, 366*(December), 1,517–1,522.

James, W. (1890, 1981). *The Principles of Psychology.* Cambridge, MA: Harvard University Press.

Jameson, K. A., Highnote, S. M., & Wasserman, L. M. (2001). Richer color experience in observers with multiple photopigment opsin genes. *Psychonomic Bulletin & Review, 8*(2), 244–261.

Jamieson, J. P. (2010). The home field advantage in athletics: A meta analysis. *Journal of Applied Social Psychology, 40*(7), 1,819–1,848.

Jamison, K. (1996). *An Unquiet Mind.* New York: Random House.

Janssen E. (2011). Sexual arousal in men: A review and conceptual analysis. *Hormones and Behavior, 59*(5), 708–716. https://doi.org/10.1016/j.yhbeh.2011.03.004

Jarvis, E. D. (2019). Evolution of vocal learning and spoken language. *Science, 366*(6,461), 50–54. https://doi.org/10.1126/science.aax0287

Jensen, A. R. (1969). How much can we boost IQ and scholastic achievement? *Harvard Educational Review, 39*(1), 1–123.

Johnson, E., & Goldstein, D. (2003). Do defaults save lives. *Science, 302,* 1,338–1,339.

Johnson, S., Cuellar, A., & Miller, C. (2009). Bipolar and unipolar depression: A comparison of clinical phenomenology, biological vulnerability and psychosocial predictors. In I. Gotlib, & C. Hammen (eds.), *Handbook of Depression* (2nd ed., pp. 142–160). New York: Guilford Press.

Johnson, W., Turkheimer, E., Gottesman, I. I., & Bouchard, T. J., Jr (2010). Beyond heritability: Twin studies in behavioral research. *Current Directions in Psychological Science, 18*(4), 217–220. https://doi.org/10.1111/j.1467-8721.2009.01639.x

Joiner, T. (2005). *Why People Die by Suicide.* Cambridge, MA: Harvard University Press.

Jones, D. (2008) Killer instincts. *Nature, 451,* 512–515.

Jones, E., & Nisbett, R. (1971). *The Actor and the Observer: Divergent Perceptions of the Causes of Behavior.* Morristown, NJ: General Learning Press.

Jordon, G., Deeb, S., Costen, J., & Mollon, J. (2010). The dimensionality of color vision in carriers of anomalous trichromacy. *Journal of Vision, 10,* 1–19.

Josselyn, S. A., & Tonegawa, S. (2020). Memory engrams: Recalling the past and imagining the future. *Science, 367*(6,473). https://doi.org/10.1126/science.aaw4325

Jung, C. G. (1989). *Memories, Dreams, Reflections.* New York: Vintage.

Jung-Beeman, M., Bowden, E. M., Haberman, J., Frymiare, J. L., Arambel-Liu, S., Greenblatt, R., Reber, P. J., & Kounios, J. (2004). Neural activity when people solve verbal problems with insight. *PLoS Biology, 2*(4), E97. https://doi.org/10.1371/journal.pbio.0020097

Kabat-Zinn, J. (1990). *Full Catastrophe Living.* New York: Delta Publishing.

Kagan J. (2003). Biology, context, and developmental inquiry. *Annual Review of Psychology, 54,* 1–23. https://doi.org/10.1146/annurev.psych.54.101601.145240

Kahn, D., & Gover, T. (2010). Consciousness in dreams. *International Review of Neurobiology, 91,* 181–195.

Kahneman, D. (2011). *Thinking, Fast and Slow.* New York: Farrar, Straus, & Giroux.

Kalisch, R., Müller, M. B., & Tüscher, O. (2015). Advancing empirical resilience research. *The Behavioral and Brain Sciences, 38,* e128. https://doi.org/10.1017/S0140525X15000023

Kalueff, A., & Nutt, D. (2007). Role of GABA in anxiety and depression. *Depression and Anxiety, 24,* 495–517.

Kamio, Y., Tobimatsu S., & Fukui, H. (2011). Developmental disorders. In J. Decety, & J. Cacioppo (eds.), *The Handbook of Social Neuroscience.* New York: Oxford University Press.

Kandel, E., & Tauc, L. (1964) Mechanism of prolonged heterosynaptic facilitation. *Nature, 202,* 145–147.

Kandel E. R. (1998). A new intellectual framework for psychiatry. *The American Journal of Psychiatry, 155*(4), 457–469. https://doi.org/10.1176/ajp.155.4.457

Kandel E. R. (1999). Biology and the future of psychoanalysis: a new intellectual framework for psychiatry revisited. *The American Journal of Psychiatry, 156*(4), 505–524. https://doi.org/10.1176/ajp.156.4.505

Kandel, E. (2005). *Psychiatry, Psychoanalysis, and the New Biology of Mind.* Washington, DC: American Psychiatric Publishing.

Kandel, E. R. (2006). In Search of Memory: The Emergence of a New Science of Mind. New York: W. W. Norton.

Kandel, E. R. (2012). *The Age of Insight: The Quest to Understand the Unconscious in Art, Mind, and Brain, from Vienna 1900 to the Present.* New York: Random House Incorporated.

Kandel, E. R., Schwartz, J. H., Jessell, T. M., Siegelbaum, S., & Hudspeth, A. J. (eds.) (2013). *Principles of Neural Science* (5th ed.). New York: McGraw-Hill.

Kane, J. M., Robinson, D. G., Schooler, N. R., Mueser, K. T., Penn, D. L., Rosenheck, R. a., Addington, J., Brunette, M. F., Correll, C. U., Estroff, S. E., Marcy, P., Robinson, J., Meyer-Kalos, P. S., Gottlieb, J. D., Glynn, S. M., Lynde, D. W., Pipes, R., Kurian, B. T., Miller, A. L., …, & Heinssen, R. K. (2015). Comprehensive versus usual community care for first-episode psychosis: 2-year outcomes from the NIMH RAISE early treatment program. *American Journal of Psychiatry, 173,* 362–372. https://doi.org/10.1176/appi.ajp.2015.15050632

Kang, S. K., & Bodenhausen, G. V. (2015). Multiple identities in social perception and interaction: Challenges and opportunities. *Annual Review of Psychology, 66,* 547–574. https://doi.org/10.1146/annurev-psych-010814-015025

Kanner L. (1943). Autistic disturbances of affective contact. *Nervous Child, 2,* 217–250.

Kano, F., & Tomonaga, M (2010). Face scanning in chimpanzees and humans: Continuity and discontinuity. *Animal Behavior, 79,* 227–235.

Kanwisher, N., & Yovel, G. (2006). The fusiform face area: A cortical region specialized for the perception of faces. *Philosophical Transactions of the Royal Society, B, 361,* 2,109–2,128.

Kaplan, J. T., Aziz-Zadeh, L., Uddin, L. Q., Iacoboni, M. (2008). The self across the senses: An fMRI study of self-face and self-voice recognition. *Social Cognition and Affective Neuroscience, 3*(3): 218–223. DOI:10.1093/scan/nsn014

Kaptchuk, T., & Miller, F. (2018). Open label placebo: Can honestly prescribed placebos evoke meaningful therapeutic benefits? *BMJ.* DOI:10.1136/bmj.k3889

Karlsgodt, K. H., Sun, D., & Cannon, T. D. (2010). Structural and functional brain abnormalities in schizophrenia. *Current Directions in Psychological Science, 19,* 226–231.

Kate, M., Hopwood, T., & Jamieson, G. (2020). The prevalence of dissociative disorders and dissociative experiences in college populations: A meta-analysis of 98 studies. *Journal of Trauma & Dissociation, 21,* 16–61.

Katsnelson, A. (2010). Epigenome effort makes its mark. *Nature, 467*(7,316), 646. https://doi.org/10.1038/467646a

Katz, L., & Lambert, W. (2016). A happy and engaged class without cell phones? It's easier than you think. *Teaching of Psychology, 43*(4), 340–345. https://doi.org/10.1177/0098628316662767

Kaviani, S., & Cooper, J. A. (2017). Appetite responses to high-fat meals or diets of varying fatty acid composition: A comprehensive review. *European Journal of Clinical Nutrition, 71*(10), 1,154–1,165. https://doi.org/10.1038/ejcn.2016.250

Keel, P. K., Brown, T. A., Holland, L. A., & Bodell, L. P. (2012). Empirical classification of eating disorders. *Annual Review of Clinical Psychology, 8,* 381–404. https://doi.org/10.1146/annurev-clinpsy-032511-143111.

Keil, A., Elbert, T., Rockstroh, B., & Ray, W. J. (1998). Dynamical aspects of motor and perceptual processes in schizophrenic patients and healthy controls. *Schizophrenia Research, 33*(3), 169–178. https://doi.org/10.1016/S0920-9964(98)00069-3

Keller, M. C. (2018). Evolutionary perspectives on genetic and environmental risk factors for psychiatric disorders. *Annual Review of Clinical Psychology, 14*(1), 471–493. https://doi.org/10.1146/annurev-clinpsy-050817-084854

Kelman, H. C. (1968). *A Time to Speak.* San Francisco: Jossey-Bass.

Keltner, D., & Buswell, B. N. (1997). Embarrassment: Its distinct form and appeasement functions. *Psychological Bulletin, 122*(3), 250–270. https://doi.org/10.1037/0033-2909.122.3.250

Keltner, D., Sauter, D., Tracy, J., & Cowen, A. (2019). Emotional expression: Advances in basic emotion theory. *Journal of Nonverbal Behavior, 43*(2), 133–160. https://doi.org/10.1007/s10919-019-00293-3

Kemeny, M., & Schedlowski, M. (2007). Understanding the interaction between psychosocial stress and immune-related diseases: A stepwise progression. *Brain, Behavior, and Immunity, 21,* 1,009–1,018.

Kemmerer, D. (2015) *Cognitive Neuroscience of Language.* New York: Psychology Press.

Kendler, K., Thornton, L., & Gardner, C. (2000). Stressful life events and previous episodes in the etiology of major depression in women: An evaluation of the "kindling" hypothesis. *American Journal of Psychiatry, 157,* 1243–1251.

Keng, S., Smoski, M., & Robins, C. (2011). Effects of mindfulness on psychological health: A review of empirical studies. *Clinical Psychology Review, 31,* 1,041–1,056.

Kernberg, O. (1984). *Severe Personality Disorders: Psychotherapeutic Strategies.* New Haven, CT: Yale University Press.

Kernberg, O. (1995). *Love Relations: Normality and Pathology.* New Haven, CT: Yale University Press.

Kessler, R., Berglumd, P., Demier, O., Jin, R., Merikangas, K., & Walters, E. (2005) Lifetime prevalence and age-of-onset distributions of DSM-IV disorders in the National Comorbidity Survey Replication. *Arch. Gen. Psychiatry, 62,* 593–602.

Kessler, R., Chiu, W., Jin, R., Ruscio, A., Shear, K., & Walters, E. (2006). The epidemiology of panic attacks, panic disorder, and agoraphobia in the National Comorbidity Survey Replication. *Archives of General Psychiatry, 63,* 415–424.

Kessler, R. C., Berglund, P., Demler, O., Jin, R., Merikangas, K. R., & Walters, E. E. (2005). Lifetime prevalence and age-of-onset distributions of DSM-IV disorders in the National Comorbidity Survey Replication. *Archives of General Psychiatry, 62,* 593–602.

Kessler, R. C., Green, J. G., Gruber, M. J., Sampson, N. A., Bromet, E., Cuitan, M., . . . & Zaslavsky, A. M. (2010). Screening for serious mental illness in the general population with the K6 screening scale: Results from the WHO World Mental Health (WMH) survey initiative. *International Journal of Methods in Psychiatric Research, 19*(S1), 4–22.

Kessler, R. C., Petukhova, M., Sampson, N., Zaslavsky, A., & Wittchen, H. (2012). Twelve-month and lifetime prevalence and lifetime morbid risk of anxiety and mood disorders in the United States. *International Journal of Methods in Psychiatric Research, 21*, 169–184.

Khandaker, G. M., Pearson, R. M., Zammit, S., Lewis, G., & Jones, P. B. (2014). Association of serum interleukin 6 and C-reactive protein in childhood with depression and psychosis in young adult life: a population-based longitudinal study. *JAMA Psychiatry, 71*(10), 1,121–1,128. https://doi.org/10.1001/jamapsychiatry.2014.1332

Kiecolt-Glaser, J. K., Marucha, P. T., Atkinson, C., & Glaser, R. (2001). Hypnosis as a modulator of cellular immune dysregulation during acute stress. *Journal of Consulting and Clinical Psychology, 69*(4), 674–682. https://doi.org/10.1037//0022-006x.69.4.674

Kiecolt-Glaser, J. K., McGuire, L., Robles, T. F., & Glaser, R. (2002). Psychoneuroimmunology: psychological influences on immune function and health. *Journal of Consulting and Clinical Psychology, 70*(3), 537–547. https://doi.org/10.1037//0022-006x.70.3.537

Kim, K., Ekstrom, A. D., & Tandon, N. (2016). A network approach for modulating memory processes via direct and indirect brain stimulation: Toward a causal approach for the neural basis of memory. *Neurobiology of Learning and Memory, 134*(A), 162–177. https://doi.org/10.1016/j.nlm.2016.04.001

King, M. (1968) The role of the behavioral scientist in the civil rights movement. *American Psychologist, 23*, 180–186.

King, M., Hernandez-Castillo, C. R., Poldrack, R. A., Ivry, R. B., & Diedrichsen, J. (2019). Functional boundaries in the human cerebellum revealed by a multi-domain task battery. *Nature Neuroscience, 22*(8), 1,371–1,378. https://doi.org/10.1038/s41593-019-0436-x

Kingdon, D., & Turkington, D. (1994). Cognitive behaviour therapy of schizophrenia. The amenability of delusions and hallucinations to reasoning. *British Journal of Psychiatry, 164*, 581–587.

Kinsey, A. (1948). *Sexual Behavior in the Human Male.* Bloomington: Indiana University Press.

Kinsey, A. (1953). *Sexual Behavior in the Human Female.* Bloomington: Indiana University Press.

Kipnis, J. (2018). Immune system: The "seventh sense." *Journal of Experimental Medicine, 215*(2), 397–395. https://doi.org/10.1084/jem.20172295

Kirsch, I., Montgomery, G., & Sapirstein, G. (1995). Hypnosis as an adjunct to cognitive-behavioral psychotherapy: A meta-analysis. *Journal of Consulting and Clinical Psychology, 63*(2), 214–220. https://doi.org/10.1037//0022-006x.63.2.214

Kitayama, S., Chua, H. F., Tompson, S., & Han, S. (2013). Neural mechanisms of dissonance: An fMRI investigation of choice justification. *NeuroImage, 69*, 206–212. https://doi.org/10.1016/j.neuroimage.2012.11.034

Kleinman, D., & Gollan, T. H. (2016). Speaking two languages for the price of one: Bypassing language control mechanisms via accessibility-driven switches. *Psychological Science, 27*(5), 700–714. https://doi.org/10.1177/0956797616634633

Kleinspehn-Ammerlahn, A., Kotter-Grühn, D., & Smith, J. (2008). Self-perceptions of aging: Do subjective age and satisfaction with aging change during old age? *The Journals of Gerontology. Series B, Psychological Sciences and Social Sciences*, 63(6), P377–P385. https://doi.org/10.1093/geronb/63.6.p377

Klin, A., Shultz, S., & Jones, W. (2014). Social visual engagement in infants and toddlers with autism: Early developmental transitions and a model of pathogenesis. *Neuroscience & Biobehavioral Reviews*, 50, 189–203. http://doi.org/10.1016/j.neubiorev.2014.10.006

Klonsky, E. (2007). The functions of deliberate self-injury: A review of the evidence. *Clinical Psychology Review*, 27, 226–239.

Knoblich, G., & Oellinger, M. (2006). The eureka moment. *Scientific American Mind*, 17(5), 38–43.

Knopik, V., Neiderhiser, J., DeFries, J., & Plomin, R. (2017). *Behavioral Genetics* (7th ed.). New York: Worth Publishers.

Knox, S. S., & Uvnäs-Moberg, K. (1998). Social isolation and cardiovascular disease: An atherosclerotic pathway? *Psychoneuroendocrinology*, 23(8), 877–890. https://doi.org/10.1016/s0306-4530(98)00061-4

Knutson, K. M., Mah, L., Manly, C. F., & Grafman, J. (2007). Neural correlates of automatic beliefs about gender and race. *Human Brain Mapping*, 28(10), 915–930. https://doi.org/10.1002/hbm.20320

Koch, C., & Greenfield, S. (2007). How does consciousness happen? *Scientific American*, 297(4), 76–83.

Koch, C., & Tsuchiya, N. (2007). Attention and consciousness: Two distinct brain processes. *Trends in Cognitive Sciences*, 11(1), 16–22. https://doi.org/10.1016/j.tics.2006.10.012

Koenigs, M., Huey, E. D., Calamia, M., Raymont, V., Tranel, D., & Grafman, J. (2008). Distinct regions of prefrontal cortex mediate resistance and vulnerability to depression. *The Journal of Neuroscience*, 28(47), 12,341–12,348. https://doi.org/10.1523/JNEUROSCI.2324-08.2008

Kohlberg, L. (1963). Development of children's orientation toward a moral order (part 1), sequencing the development of moral thought. *Vita Humana*, 6, 11–36.

Köhler, W. (1925). *The Mentality of Apes*. Trans., from 2nd rev. ed. by Ella Winter. New York: Harcourt, Brace.

Konrad, K., & Eickhoff, S. B. (2010). Is the ADHD brain wired differently? A review on structural and functional connectivity in attention deficit hyperactivity disorder. *Human Brain Mapping*, 31(6), 904–916. https://doi.org/10.1002/hbm.21058

Koob, A. (2009). *The Roots of Thought: Unlocking Glia*. Upper Saddle River, NJ: FT Press.

Koob, G., Kandel, D., & Volkow, N. (2008). Pathophysiology of addiction. In A. Tasman, J. Kay, J. Lieberman, M. First, & M. Maj (eds.), *Psychiatry* (3rd ed.). New York: Wiley.

Koole, S. L., Tjew A Sin, M., & Schneider, I. K. (2014). Embodied terror management. *Psychological Science*, 25(1), 30–37. https://doi.org/10.1177/0956797613483478

Kopelman, S. (2020). Tit for tat and beyond: The legendary work of Anatol Rapoport. *Negotiation and Conflict Management Research*, 13(1), 60–84.

Kounios, J., & Beeman, M. (2009). The Aha! moment: The cognitive neuroscience of insight. *Current Directions in Psychological Science*, 18(4), 210–216.

Kovacs, B., & Kleinbaum, A. M. (2020). Language-style similarity and social networks. *Psychological Science*, 31(2), 202–213. https://doi.org/10.1177/0956797619894557

Kragel, P. A., & LaBar, K. S. (2016). Decoding the nature of emotion in the brain. *Trends in Cognitive Sciences*, 20(6), 444–455. https://doi.org/10.1016/j.tics.2016.03.011

Kragel, P. A., Knodt, A. R., Hariri, A. R., & LaBar, K. S. (2016). Decoding spontaneous emotional states in the human brain. *PLoS Biology*, 14(9), e2000106. https://doi.org/10.1371/journal.pbio.2000106

Kramer, A. F., & Erickson K. I. (2007) Capitalizing on cortical plasticity: Influence of physical activity on cognition and brain function. *Trends Cogn Sci.*, *11*(8), 342–348. DOI:10.1016/j.tics.2007.06.009. Epub 2007 Jul 12. PMID: 17629545.

Krapohl, E., Rimfeld, K., Shakeshaft, N. G., Trzaskowski, M., McMillan, A., Pingault, J. B., ... & Plomin, R. (2014). The high heritability of educational achievement reflects many genetically influenced traits, not just intelligence. *Proceedings of the National Academy of Sciences*, *111*(42), 15,273–15,278.

Krause, A. J., Simon, E. B., Mander, B. A., Greer, S. M., Saletin, J. M., Goldstein-Piekarski, A. N., & Walker, M. P. (2017). The sleep-deprived human brain. *Nature Reviews. Neuroscience*, *18*(7), 404–418. https://doi.org/10.1038/nrn.2017.55

Krendl A, & Heatherton T. (2009). Self versus others/self-regulation. In G. Berntson, & J Cacioppo (eds.), *Handbook of Neuroscience for the Behavioral Sciences* (pp. 859–878). Hoboken, NJ: Wiley.

Kring, A. M., & Elis, O. (2013). Emotion deficits in people with schizophrenia. *Annual Review of Clinical Psychology*, *9*, 409–433. https://doi.org/10.1146/annurev-clinpsy-050212-185538

Krueger, R. F., & Markon, K. E. (2014). The role of the DSM-5 personality trait model in moving toward a quantitative and empirically based approach to classifying personality and psychopathology. *Annual Review of Clinical Psychology*, *10*, 477–501. https://doi.org/10.1146/annurev-clinpsy-032813-153732

Kryklywy, J. H., Ehlers, M. R., Anderson, A. K., & Todd, R. M. (2020). From architecture to evolution: Multisensory evidence of decentralized emotion. *Trends in Cognitive Sciences*, *24*(11), 916–929. https://doi.org/10.1016/j.tics.2020.08.002

Kudielka, B. M., & Kirschbaum, C. (2005). Sex differences in HPA axis responses to stress: a review. *Biological Psychology*, *69*(1), 113–132. https://doi.org/10.1016/j.biopsycho.2004.11.009

Kuhl P. K. (2004). Early language acquisition: Cracking the speech code. *Nature Reviews. Neuroscience*, *5*(11), 831–843. https://doi.org/10.1038/nrn1533

Kuhl, P. K. (2010). Brain mechanisms in early language acquisition. *Neuron*, *67*(5), 713–727. https://doi.org/10.1016/j.neuron.2010.08.038

Kuhn, T. (1970). *The Structure of Scientific Revolutions* (2nd ed.). Chicago: University of Chicago Press.

Kulig, T. C., Pratt, T. C., & Cullen, F. T. (2017). Revisiting the Stanford Prison Experiment: A case study in organized skepticism. *Journal of Criminal Justice Education*, *28*(1), 74–111.

Kulka, R. A., Schlenger, W. E., Fairbank, J. A., Hough, R. L., Jordan, B. K., Marmar, C. R., & Weiss, D. S. (1990). *Trauma and the Vietnam Generation: Report of findings from the National Vietnam Veterans Readjustment Study*. New York: Brunner/Mazel.

Kuppens, P., Tuerlinckx, F., Russell, J. A., & Barrett, L. F. (2013). The relation between valence and arousal in subjective experience. *Psychological Bulletin*, *139*(4), 917.

Kusnecov, A. W. (2014). Behavioral conditioning of immune responses: An overview and consideration of clinical applications. In F. K. McSweeney, & E. S. Murphy (eds.), *The Wiley Blackwell Handbook of Operant and Classical Conditioning* (pp. 143–163). New York: Wiley Blackwell. https://doi.org/10.1002/9781118468135.ch7

Kutscher, E. (2008). Antipsychotics. In K. Meser, & D. Jeste (eds.), *Clinical Handbook of Schizophrenia* (pp. 159–167). New York: Guilford Press.

Kuyken, W., Warren, F., Taylor, R., Whalley, B., Crane, C., Bondolfi, G., Hayes, R., Huijbers, M., Ma, H., Schweizer, S., Segal, Z., Speckens, A., et al. (2016). Efficacy of mindfulness-based cognitive therapy in prevention of depressive relapse: An individual patient data meta-analysis from randomized trials. *JAMA Psychiatry, 73,* 565–574. http://doi.org/10.1001/jamapsychiatry.2016.0076

Labonte, B., & Turecki, G. (2010). The epigenetics of suicide: explaining the biological effects of early life environmental adversity. *Archives of Suicide Research: Official Journal of the International Academy for Suicide Research, 14*(4), 291–310. https://doi.org/10.1080/13811118.2010.524025

Lahey, B. B., Krueger, R. F., Rathouz, P. J., Waldman, I. D., & Zald, D. H. (2017a). Supplemental material for a hierarchical causal taxonomy of psychopathology across the life span. *Psychological Bulletin, 143*(2), 142–186. https://doi.org/10.1037/bul0000069.supp

Lahey, B. B., Krueger, R. F., Rathouz, P. J., Waldman, I. D., & Zald, D. H. (2017b). A hierarchical causal taxonomy of psychopathology across the life span. *Psychological bulletin, 143*(2), 142–186. https://doi.org/10.1037/bul0000069

Lai, C. (2011). Gray matter deficits in panic disorder. *Journal of Clinical Psychopharmacology, 31,* 287–293.

Lai, C., Altavilla, D., Ronconi, A., & Aceto, P. (2016). Fear of missing out (FOMO) is associated with activation of the right middle temporal gyrus during inclusion social cue. *Computers in Human Behavior, 61,* 516–521.

Laker, M. (2012). Specific phobia: flight. *Activitas Nervosa Superior, 54*(3–4), 108–117.

Lander, E. S., Linton, L. M., Birren, B., Nusbaum, C., Zody, M. C., Baldwin, J., Devon, K., Dewar, K., Doyle, M., FitzHugh, W., Funke, R., Gage, D., Harris, K., Heaford, A., Howland, J., Kann, L., Lehoczky, J., LeVine, R., McEwan, P., McKernan, K., ..., & International Human Genome Sequencing Consortium (2001). Initial sequencing and analysis of the human genome. *Nature, 409*(6,822), 860–921. https://doi.org/10.1038/35057062

Lane, M., & Cha, S. (2009). Effect of glucose and fructose on food intake via malonyl-CoA signaling in the brain. *Biochemical and Biophysical Research Communications, 382,* 1–5.

Långsjö, J. W., Alkire, M. T., Kaskinoro, K., Hayama, H., Maksimow, a., Kaisti, K. K., ..., & Scheinin, H. (2012). Returning from oblivion: Imaging the neural core of consciousness. *Journal of Neuroscience, 32*(14), 4,935–4,943. https://doi.org/10.1523/JNEUROSCI.4962-11.2012

Latane, B., Williams, K., & Harkins, S. (1979). Many hands make light the work: Causes and consequences of social loafing. *Journal of Personality and Social Psychology, 37,* 822–832.

Latané, B., & Darley, J. (1969). Bystander "apathy." *American Scientist, 57,* 244–268.

Laughlin, S., & Sejnowski, T. (2003). Communication in neuronal networks. *Science, 301,* 1,870–1,874.

Laukka, P., & Elfenbein, H. A. (2020). Cross-cultural emotion recognition and in-group advantage in vocal expression: A meta-analysis. *Emotion Review,* 1754073919897295.

Laureys, D. (2005). The neural correlate of (un)awareness: Lessons from the vegetative state. *Trends in Cognitive Sciences, 8,* 556–559.

Lawton, E., Shields, A., & Oltmanns, T. (2011). Five-factor model personality disorder prototypes in a community sample: Self- and informant-reports predicting interview-based DSM diagnoses. *Personality Disorders, 2,* 279–292.

LeDoux, J. E. (1994). Emotion, memory and the brain. *Scientific American, 270*(6), 50–57.

Lee, J. L. C., Nader, K., & Schiller, D. (2017). An update on memory reconsolidation updating. *Trends in Cognitive Sciences, 21*(7), 531–545. https://doi.org/10.1016/j.tics.2017.04.006

Leichsenring, F., & Leweke, F. (2017). Social anxiety disorder. *New England Journal of Medicine, 376,* 2,255–2,264. https://doi.org/10.1056/NEJMcp1614701

Lenoir, M., Serre, F., Cantin, L., & Ahmed, S. H. (2007). Intense sweetness surpasses cocaine reward. *PLoS One, 2*, e698.

Lenzenweger, M. (2008). Epidemiology of personality disorders. *Psychiatric Clinics of North America, 31*, 395–403.

Lenzenweger, M., Lane, M., Loranger, A., & Kessler, R. (2007). DSM-IV personality disorders in the National Comorbidity Survey Replication. *Biological Psychiatry, 62*, 553–564.

Leong, F. (2014). *APA Handbook of Multicultural Psychology, Vol 1 & 2*. Washington, DC: American Psychological Association.

LePort, A. K., Mattfeld, A. T, Dickinson-Anson, H., Fallon, J. H., Stark, C. E., Kruggel, F., Cahill, L., & McGaugh, J. L. (2012) Behavioral and neuroanatomical investigation of Highly Superior Autobiographical Memory (HSAM). *Neurobiol Learn Mem., 98*(1), 78–92. DOI: 10.1016/j.nlm.2012.05.002. Epub 2012 May 29. PMID: 22652113; PMCID: PMC3764458.

Lerner, R. M., & Overton, W. F. (eds.). (2010). *The Handbook of Life-Span Development, Volume 1: Cognition, Biology, and Methods* (Vol. 1). Hoboken, NJ: John Wiley & Sons.

LeVay, S. & Baldwin, J. (2012). *Human Sexuality* (4th ed.). Sunderland, MA: Sinauer.

Levine, J. D., Gordon, N. C., & Fields, H. L. (1978). The mechanism of placebo analgesia. *Lancet (London, England), 2*(8,091), 654–657. https://doi.org/10.1016/s0140-6736(78)92762-9

Levy, K. N. (2005). The implications of attachment theory and research for understanding borderline personality disorder. *Development and Psychopathology, 17*, 959–986.

Levy, K. N., & Scala, J. W. (2012). Transference, transference interpretations, and transference-focused psychotherapies. *Psychotherapy, 49*, 391–403.

Lewis, D., Al-Shawaf, L., Conroy-Beam, D., Asao, K., & Buss, D. M. (2017). Evolutionary psychology: A how-to guide. *The American Psychologist, 72*(4), 353–373. https://doi.org/10.1037/a0040409

Lewontin, R. (1976). The fallacy of biological determinism. *The Sciences*, 16, 6–10. https://doi.org/10.1002/j.2326-1951.1976.tb01213.x

Li, P., Legault, J., & Litcofsky, K. A. (2014). Neuroplasticity as a function of second language learning: Anatomical changes in the human brain. *Cortex; A Journal Devoted to the Study of the Nervous System and Behavior, 58*, 301–324. https://doi.org/10.1016/j.cortex.2014.05.001

Liberman, Z., Woodward, A. L., & Kinzler, K. D. (2017). The origins of social categorization. *Trends in Cognitive Sciences, 21*(7), 556–568. https://doi.org/10.1016/j.tics.2017.04.004

Lichtenstein, P., Carlstrom, E., Råstam, M., Gillberg, C., & Anckarsäter, H. (2010). The genetics of autism spectrum disorders and related neuropsychiatric disorders in childhood. *Archives of General Psychiatry, 167*, 1,357–1,363.

Lieberman, J., & Stroup, T. (2011). The NIMH-CATIE schizophrenia study: What did we learn? *American Journal of Psychiatry, 168*, 770–778.

Lieberman, M., & Eisenberger, N. (2009). Pains and pleasures of social life. *Science, 323*, 890–891.

Lieberman M. D. (2007). Social cognitive neuroscience: A review of core processes. *Annual Review of Psychology, 58*, 259–289. https://doi.org/10.1146/annurev.psych.58.110405.085654

Lieberman, P. (2000). *Human Language and our Reptilian Brain: The Subcortical Bases of Speech, Syntax, and Thought.* Cambridge, MA.: Harvard University Press.

Lieberman, P. (2006). *Toward an Evolutionary Biology of Language.* Cambridge, MA: Harvard University Press.

Linehan, M. M. (1993). *Cognitive-behavioral Treatment of Borderline Personality Disorder.* New York: Guilford Press.

Linehan, M. M., & Dexter-Mazza, E. T. (2008). Dialectical behavior therapy for borderline personality disorder. In D. H. Barlow (ed.), *Clinical Handbook of Psychological Disorders: A Step-by-step Treatment Manual* (pp. 365–420). New York: The Guilford Press.

Linehan, M. M., Korslund, K. E., Harned, M. S., Gallop, R. J., Lungu, A., Neacsiu, A. D., …, & Murray-Gregory, A. M. (2015). Dialectical behavior therapy for high suicide risk in individuals with borderline personality disorder. *JAMA Psychiatry, 72*(5), 475–482. http://doi.org/10.1001/jamapsychiatry.2014.3039

Little, A., Jones, B., & DeBruine, L. (2011). Facial attractiveness: Evolutionary based research. *Philosophical Transactions of the Royal Society, B, 366,* 1,638–1,659.

Livesley, W. J. (2007). A framework for integrating dimensional and categorical classifications of personality disorder. *Journal of Personality Disorders, 21*(2), 199–224.

Livingstone, M. (2000). Is it warm? Is it real? Or just low spatial frequency? *Science, 290,* 1,299.

Locke, J. L., & Bogin, B. (2006). Language and life history: A new perspective on the evolution and development of linguistic communication. *The Behavioral and Brain Sciences, 29,* 259–325.

Lodi-Smith, J., & Roberts, B. W. (2007). Social investment and personality: A meta-analysis of the relationship of personality traits to investment in work, family, religion, and volunteerism. *Personality and Social Psychology Review, 11*(1), 68–86. https://doi.org/10.1177/1088868306294590

Loehlin, J. C. (1992). *Genes and Environment in Personality Development.* Thousand Oaks: Sage Publications, Inc.

Loewenstein, G., Rick, S., & Cohen, J. D. (2008). Neuroeconomics. *Annual. Review of Psychology, 59,* 647–672.

Loftus E. F. (2003). Make-believe memories. *The American Psychologist, 58*(11), 867–873. https://doi.org/10.1037/0003-066X.58.11.867

Loftus, E. F., & Palmer, J. C. (1974). Reconstruction of automobile destruction: An example of the interaction between language and memory. *Journal of Verbal Learning and Verbal Behavior, 13*(5), 585–589.

Logothetis, N. K. (2015). Neuronal-event-triggered fMRI of large-scale neural networks. *Current Opinion in Neurobiology, 31,* 214–222. https://doi.org/10.1016/j.conb.2014.11.009

Loo, C., & Mitchell, P. (2005). A review of the efficacy of transcranial magnetic stimulation (TMS) treatment for depression, and current and future strategies to optimize efficacy. *Journal of Affective Disorders, 88,* 255–267.

Lord, C., & Bishop, S. L. (2015). Recent advances in autism research as reflected in DSM-5 criteria for autism spectrum disorder. *Annual Review of Clinical Psychology, 11*(1), 150112144717005. http://doi.org/10.1146/annurev-clinpsy-032814-112745

Lovaas, O., & Smith, T. (2003). Early and intensive behavioral intervention in autism. In A. Kazdin, & J. Weisz (eds.), *Evidence-based Psychotherapies for Children and Adolescents.* New York: Guilford Press.

Lukens, S., & Ray, W. (1995) Dissociative experiences and their relation to psychopathology. Paper presented at the Society for Psychopathology Research annual meeting, Iowa City, IA.

Luo, Y., & Baillargeon, R. (2005). When the ordinary seems unexpected: Evidence for incremental physical knowledge in young infants. *Cognition*, *95*(3), 297–328. https://doi.org/10.1016/j.cognition.2004.01.010

Luria, A (1968). *The Mind of a Mnemonist.* New York: Basic Books

Lutz, A., Slagter, H. A., Dunne, J. D., & Davidson, R. J. (2008). Attention regulation and monitoring in meditation. *Trends in Cognitive Sciences*, *12*(4), 163–169. https://doi.org/10.1016/j.tics.2008.01.005

Lykins, A., Meana, M., & Kambe, G. (2006). Detection of differential viewing patterns to erotic and non-erotic stimuli using eye-tracking methodology. *Archives of Sexual Behavior, 35,* 569–575.

Lynn, R., & Kanazawa, S. (2011). A longitudinal study of sex differences in intelligence at ages 7, 11 and 16 years. *Personality and Individual Differences*, *51*(3), 321–324.

Ma, F., Zeng, D., Xu, F., Compton, B. J., & Heyman, G. D. (2020). Delay of gratification as reputation management. *Psychological Science*, *31*(9), 1,174–1,182. https://doi.org/10.1177/0956797620939940

Machiavelli, N. (1513/1947). *The Prince.* New York: Appleton-Century-Crofts.

Mack, K. J., & Mack, P. A. (1992). Induction of transcription factors in somatosensory cortex after tactile stimulation. *Brain Research. Molecular Brain Research*, *12*(1–3), 141–147. https://doi.org/10.1016/0169-328X(92)90077-O

Mackintosh, N. (2011). History of theories and measurement of intelligence. In R. Sternberg, & S. Kaufman (eds.), *The Cambridge Handbook of Intelligence.* New York: Cambridge University Press.

MacLean, P. (1973). *A Triune Concept of the Brain and Behaviours.* Toronto: University of Toronto Press.

MacLean, P. D. (*1990*) *The Triune Brain in Evolution (Role in Paleocerebral Functions).* New York: Plenum Press.

MacLeod, C., Jonker, T., & James, G. (2014). Individual differences in remembering. In T. Perfect, & D. Lindsay (eds.), *The Sage Handbook of Applied Memory.* Los Angeles, CA: SAGE.

Macrae. C., & Quadflieg, S. (2010). Perceiving people. In S. Fiske, D. Gilbert, & G. Lindzey (eds.), *Handbook of Social Psychology.* New York: John Wiley & Sons.

Maeda, Y., Kim, H., Kettner, N., Kim, J., Cina, S., Malatesta, C., Gerber, J., McManus, C., Ong-Sutherland, R., Mezzacappa, P., Libby, A., Mawla, I., Morse, L. R., Kaptchuk, T. J., Audette, J., & Napadow, V. (2017). Rewiring the primary somatosensory cortex in carpal tunnel syndrome with acupuncture. *Brain: A Journal of Neurology*, *140*(4), 914–927. https://doi.org/10.1093/brain/awx015

Maffei, C., Capasso, R., Cazzolli, G., Colosimo, C., Dell'Acqua, F., Piludu, F., Catani, M., & Miceli, G. (2017). Pure word deafness following left temporal damage: Behavioral and neuroanatomical evidence from a new case. *Cortex; A Journal Devoted to the Study of the Nervous System and Behavior*, *97*, 240–254. https://doi.org/10.1016/j.cortex.2017.10.006

Magistretti, P. J. (2009). Neuroscience. Low-cost travel in neurons. *Science (New York, N.Y.)*, *325*(5,946), 1,349–1,351. https://doi.org/10.1126/science.1180102

Mahoney, J. L., Weissberg, R. P., Greenberg, M. T., Dusenbury, L., Jagers, R. J., Niemi, K., Schlinger, M., Schlund, J., Shriver, T. P., VanAusdal, K., & Yoder, N. (2020). Systemic social and emotional learning: Promoting educational success for all preschool to high school students. *The American Psychologist*, 10.1037/amp0000701. Advance online publication. https://doi.org/10.1037/amp0000701

Mahowald, M., & Schenck, C. (2005). Insights from studying human sleep disorders. *Nature, 437*, 1,279–1,285.

Maier, N. R. F. (1930). Reasoning in humans. I. On direction. *Journal of Comparative Psychology, 10*(2), 115–143. https://doi.org/10.1037/h0073232

Maier, N. R. F. (1931). Reasoning in humans. II. The solution of a problem and its appearance in consciousness. *Journal of Comparative Psychology, 12*(2), 181–194. https://doi.org/10.1037/h0071361

Main, M., & Solomon, J. (1990). Procedures for identifying infants as disorganized/disoriented during the Ainsworth strange situation. In M. Greenberg, D. Cicchetti, & E. M. Cummings (eds.), *Attachment in the Preschool Years: Theory, Research and Intervention* (pp. 121–160). Chicago, IL: University of Chicago Press.

Ma-Kellams, C. (2020). Cultural variation and similarities in cognitive thinking styles versus judgment biases: A review of environmental factors and evolutionary forces. *Review of General Psychology, 24*(3), 238–253.

Maldonado, J. R., & Spiegel, D. (2015). Dissociative disorders. In A. Tasman, J. Kay, J. Lieberman, M. First, & M. Riba (eds.), *Psychiatry* (4th ed.). New York: John Wiley & Sons.

Malhi, G. (2009). The impact of lithium on bipolar disorder. *Bipolar Disorders*, Supplement, 2, 1–3.

Malle, B. (2006). The actor–observer asymmetry in attribution: A (surprising) meta-analysis. *Psychological Bulletin, 132*, 895–919.

Malle, B. F. (2021). Moral judgments. *Annual Review of Psychology, 72*(1), 1–26. https://doi.org/10.1146/annurev-psych-072220-104358

Mamede, S., Schmidt, H. G., Rikers, R. M., Custers, E. J., Splinter, T. A., & van Saase, J. L. (2010). Conscious thought beats deliberation without attention in diagnostic decision-making: At least when you are an expert. *Psychological Research, 74*(6), 586–592.

Maras, P. M., & Baram, T. Z. (2012). Sculpting the hippocampus from within: Stress, spines, and CRH. *Trends in Neuroscience, 35*, 315–324.

Markant, J., Cicchetti, D., Hetzel, S., & Thomas, K. M. (2014). Relating dopaminergic and cholinergic polymorphisms to spatial attention in infancy. *Developmental Psychology, 50*(2), 360–369. https://doi.org/10.1037/a0033172

Markus, H. (1977). Self-schemas and processing information about the self. *Journal of Personality and Social Psychology, 35*, 63–78.

Markus, H. R., & Kitayama, S. (2010). Cultures and selves: A cycle of mutual constitution. *Perspectives on Psychological Science: A Journal of the Association for Psychological Science, 5*(4), 420–430. https://doi.org/10.1177/1745691610375557

Marshall, J., & O'Dell, S. (2012). Methamphetamine influences on brain and behavior: Unsafe at any speed? *Trends in Neurosciences, 35*, 536–545.

Marshall, M. (2020). The hidden links between mental disorders. *Nature, 581*(7,806), 19–21. https://doi.org/10.1038/d41586-020-00922-8

Martin, A., & Caramazza, A. (2003). Neuropsychological and neuroimaging perspectives on conceptual knowledge: An introduction. *Cognitive Neuropsychology, 20*(3–6), 195–212.

Martin, J., Rychlowska, M., Wood, A., & Niedenthal, P. (2017). Smiles as multipurpose social signals. *Trends in Cognitive Sciences, 21*(11), 864–877. https://doi.org/10.1016/j.tics.2017.08.007

Mascheretti, S., Bureau, A., Trezzi, V., Giorda, R., & Marino, C. (2015). An assessment of gene-by-gene interactions as a tool to unfold missing heritability in dyslexia. *Human Genetics, 134*(7), 749–760. https://doi.org/10.1007/s00439-015-1555-4

Maslow, A. (1970). *Motivation and Personality* (2nd ed.). New York: Harper & Row.

Masters, W., & Johnson, V. (1979). *Homosexuality in Perspective.* New York: Little, Brown.

Masters, W., Johnson, V., & Kolodny, R. (1986). *Masters and Johnson on Sex and Human Loving.* New York: Little, Brown.

Masuda, T. P. C., & Nisbett, R. E. (2001). Attending holistically versus analytically: Comparing the context sensitivity of Japanese and Americans. *Journal of Personality and Social Psychology, 81*(5), 922–934.

Matson, J., & Burns, C. (2019). Pharmacological treatment of autism spectrum disorders. In S. Evans (ed.), *APA Handbook of Psychopharmacology.* Washington, DC: American Psychological Association.

Matsumoto, D., Yoo, S. H., & Fontaine, J. (2008). Mapping expressive differences around the world: The relationship between emotional display rules and individualism versus collectivism. *Journal of Cross-Cultural Psychology, 39*, 55–74. DOI:10.1177/0022022107311854

Mayo, E., 1933. *The Human Problems of an Industrial Civilization.* New York: Macmillan Co.

Mayo-Wilson, E., Dias, S., Mavranezouli, I., Kew, K., Clark, D. M., Ades, A. E., & Pilling, S. (2014). Psychological and pharmacological interventions for social anxiety disorder in adults: A systematic review and network meta-analysis. *The Lancet Psychiatry, 1*(October), 368–376. http://doi.org/10.1016/S2215-0366(14)70329-3

Mayr, E. (1942). *Systematics and the Origin of Species.* New York: Columbia University Press.

Mazzoni, A., Whittingstall, K., Brunel, N., Logothetis, N., & Panzeri, S. (2010). Understanding the relationships between spike rate and delta/gamma frequency bands of LFPs and EEGs using a local cortical network model. *Neuroimage, 52,* 956–972.

Mazzoni, G., & Memon, A. (2003). Imagination can create false autobiographical memories. *Psychological Science, 14*(2), 186–188. https://doi.org/10.1046/j.1432-1327.2000.01821.x

McAdams, D. P., & Olson, B. D. (2010). Personality development: Continuity and change over the life course. *Annual Review of Psychology, 61,* 517–542.

McAuley, E., Szabo, A. N., Mailey, E. L., Erickson, K. I., Voss, M., White, S. M., Wójcicki, T. R., Gothe, N., Olson, E. A., Mullen, S. P., & Kramer, A. F. (2011). Non-exercise estimated cardiorespiratory fitness: Associations with brain structure, cognition, and memory complaints in older adults. *Mental Health and Physical Activity, 4*(1), 5–11. https://doi.org/10.1016/j.mhpa.2011.01.001

McCormick, D., & Westbrook, G. (2013). Sleep and dreaming. In E. Kandel, J. Schwartz, T. Jessell, S. Siegelbaum, & A. Hudspeth (eds.), *Principles of Neural Science* (5th ed.). New York: McGraw Hill.

McCrae, R., & Coasta, P. (1985). Openness to experience. In R Hogan, & W. Jones (eds.), *Perspectives in Personality, Vol 1.* Greenwich, CT: JAI Press.

McCrae, R., & Costa, P. (1987). Validation of the five-factor model of personality across instruments and observers. *Journal of Personality and Social Psychology, 52,* 81–90.

McCrae, R., & Costa, P. (1996). Toward a new generation of personality theories: Theoretical contexts for the five-factor model. In J. S. Wiggins (ed.), *The Five-factor Model of Personality.* New York: Guilford Press.

McCrae, R., Gaines, J., & Wellington, M. (2013). The five-factor model in fact and fiction. In I. Weiner (ed.), *Handbook of Psychology* (2nd ed.). New York: Wiley.

McCrae, R. R., & Costa, P. T., Jr. (1999). A five-factor theory of personality. In L. A. Pervin, & O. P. John (eds.), *Handbook of Personality: Theory and Research* (2nd ed., pp. 139–153). New York: Guilford Press.

McCrae, R. R., Terracciano, A., & Personality Profiles of Cultures Project (2005). Personality profiles of cultures: Aggregate personality traits. *Journal of Personality and Social Psychology, 89*(3), 407–425. https://doi.org/10.1037/0022-3514.89.3.407

McCullough, M. E., Kilpatrick, S. D., Emmons, R. A., & Larson, D. B. (2001). Is gratitude a moral affect? *Psychological Bulletin, 127*(2), 249–266. https://doi.org/10.1037/0033-2909.127.2.249

McEwen, B. S. (1998). Protective and damaging effects of stress mediators. *New England Journal of Medicine, 338,* 171–179.

McEwen, B. S. (2013). The brain on stress: Toward an integrative approach to brain, body, and behavior. *Perspectives on Psychological Science, 8*(6), 673–675. http://doi.org/10.1177/1745691613506907

McEwen, B. S., Bowles, N. P., Gray, J. D., Hill, M. N., Hunter, R. G., Karatsoreos, I. N., & Nasca, C. (2015). Mechanisms of stress in the brain. *Nature Neuroscience, 18,* 1,353–1,363. http://doi.org/10.1038/nn.4086

McFarland, D. J., & Wolpaw, J. R. (2017). EEG-based brain–computer interfaces. *Current Opinion in Biomedical Engineering, 4,* 194–200. https://doi.org/10.1016/j.cobme.2017.11.004

McGann J. P. (2017). Poor human olfaction is a 19th-century myth. *Science (New York, N.Y.), 356*(6,338), eaam7263. https://doi.org/10.1126/science.aam7263

McGaugh, J. L. (2004). The amygdala modulates the consolidation of memories of emotionally arousing experiences. *Annu. Rev. Neurosci., 27,* 1–28.

McGaugh, J. L. (2013). Making lasting memories: Remembering the significant. *Proceedings of the National Academy of Sciences, 110*(Supplement 2), 10,402–10,407.

McGaugh J. L. (2015). Consolidating memories. *Annual Review of Psychology, 66,* 1–24. https://doi.org/10.1146/annurev-psych-010814-014954

McGaugh, J. L., & LePort, A. (2014). Remembrance of all things past. *Scientific American, 310*(2), 40–45. https://doi.org/10.1038/scientificamerican0214-40

McGovern, P., Jalabadze, M., Batiuk, S., Callahan, M. P., Smith, K. E., Hall, G. R., ..., & Lordkipanidze, D. (2017). Early Neolithic wine of Georgia in the South Caucasus. *Proceedings of the National Academy of Sciences of the United States of America, 114*(48), E10309–E10318. https://doi.org/10.1073/pnas.1714728114

McGrath, J., Burne, T., Féron, F., Mackay-Sim, A., & Eyles, D. (2010). Developmental vitamin D deficiency and risk of schizophrenia: A 10 year update. *Schizophrenia Bulletin, 36,* 1,073–1,078.

McGraw, M. (1935). *Growth: A Study of Johnny and Jimmy.* New York: Appleton-Century Company.

McGuagh, J., & LePort, A. (2014). Remembrance of all things past. *Scientific American* (February), 41–45.

McKelvie, P., & Low, J. (2002). Listening to Mozart does not improve children's spatial ability: Final curtains for the Mozart effect. *British Journal of Developmental Psychology, 20*(2), 241–258. https://doi.org/10.1348/026151002166433

McLean, R. (2003). *Recovered, Not Cured: A Journey through Schizophrenia.* Crows Nest, NSW, Australia: Allen Unwin.

McLean, S. A., & Paxton, S. J. (2019). Body image in the context of eating disorders. *Psychiatric Clinics of North America, 42*(1), 145–156. https://doi.org/10.1016/j.psc.2018.10.006

McNaughton, N., & Corr, P. J. (2004). A two-dimensional neuropsychology of defense: Fear/anxiety and defensive distance. *Neuroscience and Biobehavioral Reviews, 28,* 285–305.

Meaney M. J. (2010). Epigenetics and the biological definition of gene x environment interactions. *Child Development, 81*(1), 41–79. https://doi.org/10.1111/j.1467-8624.2009.01381.x

Medin, D. L., & Schaffer, M. M. (1978). Context theory of classification learning. *Psychological Review, 85*(3), 207–238.

Mendelson, W. (2017). *The Science of Sleep: What It Is, How It Works, and Why It Matters.* Chicago, IL: University of Chicago Press.

Méndez-Bértolo, C., Moratti, S., Toledano, R., Lopez-Sosa, F., Martínez-Alvarez, R., Mah, Y. H., . . . & Strange, B. A. (2016). A fast pathway for fear in human amygdala. *Nature neuroscience, 19*(8), 1,041–1,049.

Mennella, J. A., & Beauchamp, G. K. (1998). Early flavor experiences: Research update. *Nutrition Reviews, 56*(7), 205–211. DOI:10.1111/j.1753–4887.1998.tb01749.x

Menon, V. (2011). Large scale brain networks and psychopathology: A unifying triple network model. *Trends in Cognitive Sciences, 15,* 483–506.

Meyer, G. (2001). Introduction to the final special section in the special series on the utility of the Rorschach for clinical assessment. *Psychological Assessment, 13,* 419–422.

Meyer, G., & Archer, R. (2001). The hard science of Rorschach research: What do we know and where do we go? *Psychological Assessment, 13,* 486–502.

Meyer, G. J., Erdberg, P., & Shaffer, T. W. (2007). Toward international normative reference data for the comprehensive system. *Journal of Personality Assessment, 89 Suppl 1,* S201–S216. https://doi.org/10.1080/00223890701629342

Meyer-Lindenberg, A. (2010). From maps to mechanisms through neuroimaging of schizophrenia. *Nature, 468,* 194–202.

Michaelson, L. E., & Munakata, Y. (2020). Same data set, different conclusions: Preschool delay of gratification predicts later behavioral outcomes in a preregistered study. *Psychological Science, 31*(2), 193–201. https://doi.org/10.1177/0956797619896270

Milgram, S. (1963). Behavioral study of obedience. *The Journal of Abnormal and Social Psychology, 67*(4), 371–378. https://doi.org/10.1037/h0040525.

Milgram, S. (1965). Some conditions of obedience and disobedience to authority. *Human Relations, 18,* 57–76.

Milgram, S. (1974). *Obedience to Authority,* New York: Harper & Row.

Milinski M. (2016). Reputation, a universal currency for human social interactions. *Philosophical Transactions of the Royal Society of London. Series B, Biological Sciences, 371*(1,687), 20150100. https://doi.org/10.1098/rstb.2015.0100

Millan, M. (2003). The neurobiology and control of anxious states. *Progress in Neurobiology, 70,* 83–244.

Miller, D., & Halpern, D. (2014). The new science of cognitive sex differences. *Trends in Cognitive Sciences, 18,* 37–45.

Miller, G. (2005). The dark side of glia. *Science, 308,* 778–781.

Miller, G. (2008). The roots of morality. *Science, 320,* 734–737.

Miller, G. (2010). The seductive allure of behavioral epigenetics. *Science, 329,* 24–27.

Miller, G., & Rockstroh, B. (2017). Progress and prospects for endophenotypes for schizophrenia in the time of genomics, epigenetics, oscillatory brain dynamics, and the research domain criteria. In T. Nickl-Jockschat, & T. Abel (eds.), *The Neurobiology of Schizophrenia.* New York: Elsevier.

Miller, M., Azrael, D., & Barber, C. (2012). Suicide mortality in the United States: The importance of attending to method in understanding population-level disparities in the burden of suicide. *Annual Review of Public Health, 33,* 393–408.

Miller, N. E., & Dollard, J. (1941). *Social Learning and Imitation.* New Haven, CT: Yale University Press.

Miller, V., Mente, A., Dehghan, M., Rangarajan, S., Zhang, X., Swaminathan, S., . . . & Lopez, P. C. (2017). Fruit, vegetable, and legume intake, and cardiovascular disease and deaths in 18 countries (PURE): A prospective cohort study. *The Lancet, 390*(10,107), 2,037–2,049.

Millon T. (2012). On the history and future study of personality and its disorders. *Annual Review of Clinical Psychology, 8,* 1–19. https://doi.org/10.1146/annurev-clinpsy-032511-143113

Millon, T., & Strack, S. (2015). An integrating and comprehensive model of personality pathology based on evolutionary theory. In S. Huprich (ed.), *Personality Disorders: Toward Theoretical and Empirical Integration in Diagnosis and Assessment*, Washington, DC: American Psychological Association, 367–393.

Milner, A., & Goodale, M. (2006). *The Visual Brain in Action* (2nd ed.). New York: Oxford University Press.

Milner, B., Corkin, S., & Teuber, H. L. (1968). Further analysis of the hippocampal amnesic syndrome: 14-year follow-up study of HM. *Neuropsychologia, 6*(3), 215–234.

Minshew, N., & Williams, D. (2007). The new neurobiology of autism. *Archives of Neurology, 64,* 945–950.

Minzenberg, M., Yoon, J., & Carter, C. (2010). Schizophrenia and other psychotic disorders. In R. Hales, & S. Yudofsky (eds.), *Essentials of Psychiatry.* Arlington, VA: American Psychiatric Press.

Mischel, W. (2014). *The Marshmallow Test: Mastering Self-control.* Little, Brown and Co.

Mitte, K. (2005). A meta-analysis of the efficacy of psycho- and pharmacotherapy in panic disorder with and without agoraphobia. *Journal of Affective Disorders, 88,* 27–45.

Moffitt, T. E. (1993). Adolescence-limited and life-course-persistent antisocial behavior: A developmental taxonomy. *Psychological Review, 100,* 674–701.

Möhler, H. (2012). Neuropharmacology: The GABA system in anxiety and depression and its therapeutic potential. *Neuropharmacology, 62*(1), 42–53. https://doi.org/10.1016/j.neuropharm.2011.08.040

Monteleone, P., & Maj, M. (2013). Dysfunctions of leptin, ghrelin, BDNF and endocannabinoids in eating disorders: Beyond the homeostatic control of food intake. *Psychoneuroendocrinology, 38*(3), 312–330.

Mook, D. (2004). *Classic Experiments in Psychology.* Westport, CT: Greenwood Press.

Mora, G. (1959). Vincenzo Chiarugi (1759–1820) and his psychiatric reform in Florence in the late 18th century. *Journal of the History of Medicine and Allied Sciences, 14,* 424–433.

Morales, M., & Margolis, E. B. (2017). Ventral tegmental area: Cellular heterogeneity, connectivity and behaviour. *Nature Reviews. Neuroscience, 18*(2), 73–85. https://doi.org/10.1038/nrn.2016.165

Moran, J., Kelley, W., & Heatherton, T. (2014). Self-knowledge. In K. Ochsner, & S. Kosslyn (eds), *Oxford Handbook of Cognitive Neuroscience.* New York: Oxford University Press.

Moriarity, J. L., Boatman, D., Krauss, G. L., Storm, P. B., & Lenz, F. A. (2001). Human "memories" can be evoked by stimulation of the lateral temporal cortex after ipsilateral medial temporal lobe resection. *Journal of Neurology, Neurosurgery, and Psychiatry, 71*(4), 549–551. https://doi.org/10.1136/jnnp.71.4.549

Morrison, A. (2008). Cognitive-behavioral therapy. In K. Meser, & D. Jeste (eds.), *Clinical Handbook of Schizophrenia* (pp. 226–239). New York: Guilford Press.

Morrison, J., & Baxter, M. (2012). The ageing cortical synapse: Hallmarks and implications for cognitive decline. *Nature Reviews. Neuroscience, 13,* 240–250.

Moruzzi, G., & Magoun, H. W. (1949). Brain stem reticular formation and activation of the EEG. *Electroencephalography and Clinical Neurophysiology, 1*(4), 455–473.

Moseley, R. L., Ypma, R. J. F., Holt, R. J., Floris, D., Chura, L. R., Spencer, M. D., …, & Rubinov, M. (2015). Whole-brain functional hypoconnectivity as an endophenotype of autism in adolescents. *NeuroImage: Clinical, 9,* 140–152. http://doi.org/10.1016/j.nicl.2015.07.015

Mota, N. B., Weissheimer, J., Ribeiro, M., de Paiva, M., Avilla-Souza, J., Simabucuru, G., et al. (2020) Dreaming during the Covid-19 pandemic: Computational assessment of dream reports reveals mental suffering related to fear of contagion. *PLoS One, 15*(11), e0242903. https://doi.org/10.1371/journal.pone.0242903

Murphy, J. (1976). Psychiatric labeling in cross-cultural perspective. *Science, 191,* 1,019–1,028.

Murthy, S., & Gould, E. (2020). How early life adversity influences defensive circuitry. *Trends in Neurosciences, 43*(4), 200–212. https://doi.org/10.1016/j.tins.2020.02.001

Nagamatsu, L. S., Chan, A., Davis, J. C., Beattie, B. L., Graf, P., Voss, M. W., Sharma, D., & Liu-Ambrose, T. (2013). Physical activity improves verbal and spatial memory in older adults with probable mild cognitive impairment: A 6-month randomized controlled trial. *Journal of Aging Research,* 861893. https://doi.org/10.1155/2013/861893

Namkung, H., Kim, S. H., & Sawa, A. (2017). The insula: An underestimated brain area in clinical neuroscience, psychiatry, and neurology. *Trends in Neurosciences, 40*(4), 200–207. https://doi.org/10.1016/j.tins.2017.02.002

Nantsoo, L., & Mathews, S. (2019). Pharmacological treatment of depressive disorders. In Evans, S. (ed.), *APA Handbook of Psychopharmacology.* Washington, DC: American Psychological Association.

Napolitan, D. A., & Goethals, G. R. (1979). The attribution of friendliness. *Journal of Experimental Social Psychology, 15*(2), 105–113.

Naranjo, C., & Ornstein, R. (1971). *On the Psychobiology of Meditation.* New York: Viking Press.

Nasar, S. (1998). *A Beautiful Mind.* New York: Simon & Schuster

Nash, M. R., & Benham, G. (2005). The truth and the hype of hypnosis. *Scientific American Mind, 16*(2), 46–53.

Nasser, M., Katzman, M., & Gordon, R. A. (Eds.). (2001). *Eating Disorders and Cultures in Transition:* East Sussex: Psychology Press.

National Academy of Sciences (2019). *Reproducibility and Replicability in Science.* Washington, DC: National Academies Press.

Nature of Prosocial Development. New York: Academic Press

Nedergaard M. (2013). Neuroscience. Garbage truck of the brain. *Science, 340*(6,140), 1,529–1,530. https://doi.org/10.1126/science.1240514

Neisser, U. (1967). *Cognitive Psychology.* Englewood Cliffs: Prentice-Hall.

Nelson, E. E., Leibenluft, E., McClure, E. B., & Pine, D. S. (2005). The social re-orientation of adolescence: A neuroscience perspective on the process and its relation to psychopathology. *Psychological Medicine, 35*(2), 163–174. DOI:10.1017/s0033291704003915

Nemeroff, C. (2018) Ketamine: Quo Vadis. *American Journal of Psychiatry, 175,* 297–299.

Nesse, R. (2019). *Good Reasons for Bad Feelings.* New York: Dutton.

Nestler, E. (2011). Hidden switches in the mind. *Scientific American, 305,* 76–83.

Nestler, E., & Malenka, R. (2004). The addictive brain. *Scientific American, 290,* 78–85.

Nettle, D. (2006). The evolution of personality variation in humans and other animals. *American Psychologist, 61*(6), 622.

Newcorn, J. H., Ivanov, I., & Chacko, A. (2015). Recent progress in psychosocial and psychopharmacologic treatments for ADHD. *Current Treatment Options in Psychiatry, 2,* 14–27. https://doi.org/10.1007/s40501-015-0030-0

Newton, I. (1729/1969). *Mathematical Principles.* Translated by F. Cajori. New York: Greenwood.

Ng, S., Lin, R., Laybutt, D., Barres, R., Owens, J., & Morris, M. (2010). Chronic high-fat diet in fathers programs β-cell dysfunction in female rat offspring. *Nature, 467,* 963–966.

Nichols, D. (2004) Hallucinogens. *Pharmacology & Therapeutics, 101,* 131–181.

Nickerson, R., & Adams, M. (1979). Long term memory for a common object. *Cognitive Psychology, 11,* 287–307.

Niedenthal, P. M., & Brauer, M. (2012). Social functionality of human emotion. *Annual Review of Psychology, 63,* 259–285. https://doi.org/10.1146/annurev.psych.121208.131605

Nielsen, T. (2020). Infectious dreams. *Scientific American, 323,* 30–34 (October). DOI:10.1038/scientificamerican1020-30

Nock, Matthew K., Greif Green, Jennifer, Hwang, Irving, McLaughlin, Katie A., Sampson, Nancy A., Zaslavsky, Alan M., Kessler, R. C. (2013). Prevalence, correlates, and treatment of lifetime suicidal behavior among adolescents: Results from the national comorbidity survey replication adolescent supplement: Lifetime suicidal behavior among adolescents. *JAMA Psychiatry, 70*(3), 300–310. https://doi.org/10.1001/2013.jamapsychiatry.55

Northcutt, R. G., & Kaas, J. H. (1995). The emergence and evolution of mammalian neocortex. *Trends in Neuroscience, 18,* 373–379.

Nowak, M. A., & Sigmund, K. (1998). The dynamics of indirect reciprocity. *Journal of Theoretical Biology, 194*(4), 561–574. https://doi.org/10.1006/jtbi.1998.0775

Nunez, P., & Srinivasan, R. (2006). *Electric Fields of the Brain: The Neurophysics of EEG.* New York: Oxford University Press.

O'Connor, D. B., Thayer, J. F., & Vedhara, K. (2021). Stress and health: A review of psychobiological processes. *Annual Review of Psychology, 72*(1), 1–26. https://doi.org/10.1146/annurev-psych-062520-122331

O'Connor, E., Bureau, J., McCartney, K., & Lyons-Ruth, K. (2011). Risks and outcomes associated with disorganized/controlling patterns of attachment at age three in the NICHD Study of Early Child Care and Youth Development. *Infant Mental Health Journal, 32,* 450–472.

O'Donnell, K., & Meaney, M. (2020). Epigenetics. Development and psychopathology. *Annual Review of Clinical Psychology, 16,* 327–350. https://doi.org/10.1146/annurev-clinpsy-050718-095530

O'Keefe, J. (1978). *The Hippocampus as a Cognitive Map.* Oxford: Clarendon Press.

O'Keefe, P. (2016). The detectives who never forget a face. *The New Yorker,* 22 August 2016, http://www.newyorker.com/magazine/2016/08/22/londons-super-recognizer-police-force

Oakes, M., & Bor, R. (2010). The psychology of fear of flying (part I): A critical evaluation of current perspectives on the nature, prevalence and etiology of fear of flying. *Travel Medicine and Infectious Disease, 8*(6), 327–338. https://doi.org/10.1016/j.tmaid.2010.10.001

Oakley, D. A., & Halligan, P. W. (2009). Hypnotic suggestion and cognitive neuroscience. *Trends in Cognitive Sciences, 13*(6), 264–270. https://doi.org/10.1016/j.tics.2009.03.004

Oathes, D. J., & Ray, W. J. (2006). Depressed mood, index finger force, and motor cortex stimulation: A transcranial magnetic stimulation (TMS) study. *Biological Psychology, 72*, 278–290.

Oathes, D. J., Ray, W. J., Yamasaki, A. S., Borkovec, T. D., Newman, M. G., & Castonguay, L. G. (2008). Worry, generalized anxiety disorder, and emotion: Evidence from the EEG gamma band. *Biological Psychology, 79*, 165–170.

Oberauer, K., Süß, H. M., Wilhelm, O., & Wittmann, W. W. (2008). Which working memory functions predict intelligence? *Intelligence, 36*(6), 641–652.

Oberst, U., Wegmann, E., Stodt, B., Brand, M., & Chamarro, A. (2017). Negative consequences from heavy social networking in adolescents: The mediating role of fear of missing out. *Journal of Adolescence, 55*, 51–60. https://doi.org/10.1016/j.adolescence.2016.12.008

Öhman, A. (1986). Face the beast and fear the face: Animal and social fears as prototypes for evolutionary analyses of emotion. *Psychophysiology, 23*, 123–145.

Öhman, A. (1999). Distinguishing unconscious from conscious emotional processes: Methodological considerations and theoretical implications. In T. Dalgleish, & M. Power (eds), *Handbook of Cognition and Emotion* (pp. 321–352). New York: Wiley.

Öhman, A. (2009). Of snakes and faces: An evolutionary perspective on the psychology of fear. *Scandinavian Journal of Psychology, 50*, 543–552.

Öhman, A., & Mineka, S. (2001). Fears, phobias, and preparedness: Toward an evolved module of fear and fear learning. *Psychological Review, 108*, 483–522.

Oliver, M. B., & Hyde, J. S. (1993). Gender differences in sexuality: A meta-analysis. *Psychological bulletin, 114*(1), 29–51. https://doi.org/10.1037/0033-2909.114.1.29

Olivola, C., Funk, F., & Todorov, A. (2014). Social attributions from faces bias human choices. *Trends in Cognitive Sciences, 18*, 566–570.

Ollendick T., Yang, B., King, N., Dong, Q., & Akande, A. (1996). Fears in American, Australian, Chinese, and Nigerian children and adolescents: A cross-cultural study. *Journal of Child Psychology and Psychiatry, 37*, 213–220.

Olszak, T., An, D., Zeissig, S., Vera, M. P., Richter, J., Franke, A., Glickman, J. N., Siebert, R., Baron, R. M., Kasper, D. L., & Blumberg, R. S. (2012). Microbial exposure during early life has persistent effects on natural killer T cell function. *Science (New York, N.Y.), 336*(6,080), 489–493. https://doi.org/10.1126/science.1219328

Ong, J. C., Manber, R., Segal, Z., Xia, Y., Shapiro, S., & Wyatt, J. K. (2014). A randomized controlled trial of mindfulness meditation for chronic insomnia. *Sleep, 37*(9), 1,553–1,563. https://doi.org/10.5665/sleep.4010

Orsillo, S., & Roemer, L., (2016). *Worry Less, Live More.* New York: Guilford.

Orth, U., & Robins, R. W. (2014). The development of self-esteem. *Current Directions In Psychological Science, 23*(5), 381–387.

Orth, U., Maes, J., & Schmitt, M. (2015). Self-esteem development across the life span: A longitudinal study with a large sample from Germany. *Developmental Psychology, 51*(2), 248–259. https://doi.org/10.1037/a0038481

Orth, U., Robins, R. W., & Widaman, K. F. (2012). Life-span development of self-esteem and its effects on important life outcomes. *Journal of Personality and Social Psychology, 102*(6), 1,271–1,288. https://doi.org/10.1037/a0025558

Ortony, A., & Turner, T. J. (1990). What's basic about basic emotions? *Psychological Review, 97*(3), 315–331. https://doi.org/10.1037/0033-295x.97.3.315

Öst, L., (1989). One-session treatment for specific phobias. *Behavior Research and Therapy, 27*, 1–7.

Öst, L., (1996). One-session treatment for specific phobias. *Behavior Research and Therapy, 34*, 707–715.

Ostafin, B. D., & Kassman, K. T. (2012). Stepping out of history: Mindfulness improves insight problem solving. *Consciousness and Cognition, 21*(2), 1,031–1,036.

Otte, C., Gold, S. M., Penninx, B. W., Pariante, C. M., Etkin, A., Fava, M., Mohr, D. C., & Schatzberg, A. F. (2016). Major depressive disorder. *Nature Reviews. Disease Primers, 2*, 16,065. https://doi.org/10.1038/nrdp.2016.65

Ozer, D. J., & Benet-Martínez, V. (2006). Personality and the prediction of consequential outcomes. *Annual Review of Psychology, 57*, 401–421. https://doi.org/10.1146/annurev.psych.57.102904.190127

Page, K., Chan, O., Arora, J., Belfort-Deaguiar, R., Dzuira, J., Roehmholdt, B., Cline, G., Naik, S., Sinha, R., Constable, R., & Sherwin R. (2013). Effects of fructose vs glucose on regional cerebral blood flow in brain regions involved with appetite and reward pathways. *JAMA, 309*, 63–70.

Paller, K, & Suzuki, S. (2014). The source of consciousness. *Trends in Cognitive Sciences, 18*(8), 387–389. https://doi.org/10.1016/j.tics.2014.05.012

Paller, K. A., Creery, J. D., & Schechtman, E. (2021). Memory and sleep: How sleep cognition can change the waking mind for the better. *Annual Review of Psychology, 72*(1), 1–28. https://doi.org/10.1146/annurev-psych-010419-050815

Paluck, E. L., Porat, R., Clark, C. S., & Green, D. P. (2021). Prejudice reduction: Progress and challenges. *Annual Review of Psychology, 72*, 533–560. https://doi.org/10.1146/annurev-psych-071620-030619.

Panksepp, J. (1998). *Affective Neuroscience: The Foundations of Human and Animal Emotions.* New York: Oxford University Press.

Panksepp, J. (Ed.). (2004). *Textbook of Biological Psychiatry.* New York: Wiley.

Panksepp J. (2017). The psycho-neurology of cross-species affective/social neuroscience: Understanding animal affective states as a guide to development of novel psychiatric treatments. *Current Topics in Behavioral Neurosciences, 30*, 109–125. https://doi.org/10.1007/7854_2016_458

Panksepp, J., & Biven, L. (2012). *The Archaeology of Mind: Neuroevolutionary Origins of Human Emotions.* New York: Norton.

Papez, J. W. (*1937*). A proposed mechanism of emotion. *Archives of Neurology & Psychiatry, 38*, 725–743. https:// https://doi.org/10.1001/archneurpsyc.

Paré, W. P. (1990). Pavlov as a psychophysiological scientist. *Brain Research Bulletin, 24*(5), 643–649.

Park, D. C., & Reuter-Lorenz, P. (2009). The adaptive brain: Aging and neurocognitive scaffolding. *Annual Review of Psychology, 60*, 173–196. https://doi.org/10.1146/annurev.psych.59.103006.093656

Parker, E. S., Cahill, L., & McGaugh, J. L. (2006). A case of unusual autobiographical remembering. *Neurocase, 12*(1), 35–49. https://doi.org/10.1080/13554790500473680

Parkin, J., & Cohen, B. (2001). An overview of the immune system. *Lancet (London, England), 357*(9,270), 1,777–1,789. https://doi.org/10.1016/S0140-6736(00)04904-7

Patrick, C. J. (2007). Antisocial personality disorder and psychopathy. In W. O'Donohue, K. A. Fowler, & S. O. Lilienfeld (eds.), *Personality Disorders: Toward the DSM-V* (pp. 325–352). Thousand Oaks, CA: Sage.

Patrick, C. J. (2010). Conceptualizing psychopathic personality: Disinhibited, bold, or just plain mean? In R. J. Salekin, & D. R. Lynam (eds.), *Handbook of Child and Adolescent Psychopathy* (pp. 15–48). New York: Guilford Press.

Patterson, P. D., Ghen, J. D., Antoon, S. F., Martin-Gill, C., Guyette, F. X., Weiss, P. M., Turner, R. L., & Buysse, D. J. (2019). Does evidence support "banking/extending sleep" by shift workers to mitigate fatigue, and/or to improve health, safety, or performance? A systematic review. *Sleep Health*, *5*(4), 359–369. https://doi.org/10.1016/j.sleh.2019.03.001

Pauls, D. L., Abramovitch, A., Rauch, S. L., & Geller, D. a. (2014). Obsessive-compulsive disorder: An integrative genetic and neurobiological perspective. *Nature Reviews. Neuroscience*, *15*(6), 410–424. http://doi.org/10.1038/nrn3746

Paus, T., Keshavan, M., & Giedd, J. N. (2008). Why do many psychiatric disorders emerge during adolescence? *Nature Reviews. Neuroscience*, *9*(12), 947–957. https://doi.org/10.1038/nrn2513

Pavlov, I. (1927; 1960). *Conditioned Reflexes: An Investigation of the Physiological Activity of the Cerebral Cortex*. Translated by G. V. Anrep. Dover: New York.

Pavlova, M., & Abdennadher, M. (2013) Sleep terrors and confusional arousals in adults. In S. Kothare, & A. Ivanenko (eds.), *Parasomnias*. New York: Springer. https://doi.org/10.1007/978-1-4614-7627-6_7

Payne, J. D., Chambers, A. M., & Kensinger, E. A. (2012). Sleep promotes lasting changes in selective memory for emotional scenes. *Frontiers in Integrative Neuroscience*, *6*, 108. https://doi.org/10.3389/fnint.2012.00108

Payne, J. D., Tucker, M. A., Ellenbogen, J. M., Wamsley, E. J., Walker, M. P., Schacter, D. L., & Stickgold, R. (2012). Memory for semantically related and unrelated declarative information: The benefit of sleep, the cost of wake. *PLoS ONE*, *7*(3), 1–7. https://doi.org/10.1371/journal.pone.0033079

Peciña, M., Bohnert, A. S. B., Sikora, M., Avery, E. T., Langenecker, S. a., Mickey, B. J., & Zubieta, J.-K. (2015). Association between placebo-activated neural systems and antidepressant responses. *JAMA Psychiatry*, 1. https://doi.org/10.1001/jamapsychiatry.2015.1335

Pelham, V. (2013, July 7). Michael Boatwright awakes in Palm Springs with apparent amnesia. *The Desert Sun*. http://www.mydesert.com/

Pellman, B. A., & Kim, J. J. (2016). What can ethobehavioral studies tell us about the brain's fear system? *Trends in Neurosciences*, *39*(6), 420–431. https://doi.org/10.1016/j.tins.2016.04.001

Peluso, M., Lewis, S., Barnes, T., & Jones, P. (2012). Extrapyramidal motor side-effects of first- and second-generation antipsychotic drugs. *British Journal of Psychiatry, 200*, 387–392.

Pembrey, M., Bygren, L., Kaati, G., et al. (2006). Sex-specific, male-line transgenerational responses in humans. *European Journal of Human Genetics*, 14, 159–166. https://doi.org/10.1038/sj.ejhg.5201538

Penfield W. (1952). Memory mechanisms. *A.M.A. Archives of Neurology and Psychiatry*, *67*(2), 178–198. https://doi.org/10.1001/archneurpsyc.1952.02320140046005

Pennisi, E. (2016). The power of personality. *Science, 352*, 644–647.

Perea, G., Sur, M., & Araque, A. (2014). Neuron-glia networks: Integral gear of brain function. *Frontiers in Cellular Neuroscience, 8*. DOI:10.3389/fncel.2014.00378

Perlis, R. H., Ostacher, M. J., & Mmsc, M. P. H. (n.d.). Lithium and its role in psychiatry. In *Massachusetts General Hospital Comprehensive Clinical Psychiatry* (2nd ed.). Elsevier Inc. https://doi.org/10.1016/B978-0-323-29507-9.00047-0

Peterson, B., & Weissman, M. (2011). A brain-based endophenotype for major depressive disorder. *Annual Review of Medicine, 62*, 461–474.

Peterson, L. R., & Peterson, M. J. (1959). Short-term retention of individual verbal items. *Journal of Experimental Psychology, 58*, 193–198. https://doi.org/10.1037/h0049234

Pfungst, O. (1911). *Clever Hans*. New York: Henry Holt and Co.

Phan, K. L., Fitzgerald, D. A., Nathan, P. J., & Tancer, M. E. (2006). Association between amygdala hyperactivity to harsh faces and severity of social anxiety in generalized social phobia. *Biological Psychiatry, 59*, 424–429.

Phan, K. L., Wager, T., Taylor, S. F., & Liberzon, I. (2002). Functional neuroanatomy of emotion: A meta-analysis of emotion activation studies in PET and fMRI. *Neuroimage, 16*(2), 331–348.

Phelps, E. A. (2006). Emotion and cognition: insights from studies of the human amygdala. *Annual Review of Psychology, 57*, 27–53. https://doi.org/10.1146/annurev.psych.56.091103.070234

Picchioni, D., Duyn, J. H., & Horovitz, S. G. (2013). Sleep and the functional connectome. *NeuroImage, 80*, 387–396. https://doi.org/10.1016/j.neuroimage.2013.05.067

Picchioni, D., Pixa, M., Fukunaga, M., Carr, W., Horovitz, S., Braun, A., & Duyn, J. (2014). Decreased connectivity between the thalamus and the neocortex during human non-rapid eye movement sleep. *Sleep, 37*, 387–397.

Pietschnig, J., & Voracek, M. (2015). One century of global IQ gains: A formal meta-analysis of the Flynn effect (1909–2013). *Perspectives on Psychological Science, 10*(3), 282–306. DOI:10.1177/1745691615577701

Pinker, S. (1994). *The Language Instinct*. New York: William Morrow.

Pinker, S. (2014). The moral instinct. In H. Putnam, S. Neiman, & J. Schloss (eds), *Understanding Moral Sentiments*. London: Transaction Publishers.

Pinker, S. & Bloom, P. (1990). Natural language and natural selection. *Behavioral and Brain Sciences, 13*, 707–784. https://doi.org/10.1017/S0140525X00081061

Pires, E. (2008). Sade's delectation morosa and the erotic sovereignty. *Revista filosófica de Coimbra, 17(34)*, 427–460.

Pitcher, D., Parkin, B., & Walsh, V. (2021). Transcranial magnetic stimulation and the understanding of behavior. *Annual Review of Psychology, 72*(1), 1–25. https://doi.org/10.1146/annurev-psych-081120-013144

Pittenger, C., & Etkin, A (2008). Are there biological commonalities among different psychiatric disorders? In A. Tasman, J. Kay, J. Lieberman, M. First, & M. Maj (eds.), *Psychiatry* (3rd ed.). New York: John Wiley & Sons.

Platt, J. M., Keyes, K. M., McLaughlin, K. A., & Kaufman, A. S. (2019). The Flynn effect for fluid IQ may not generalize to all ages or ability levels: A population-based study of 10,000 US adolescents. *Intelligence*, 77 (February), 101,385. https://doi.org/10.1016/j.intell.2019.101385

Plihal, W., & Born, J. (1997). Effects of early and late nocturnal sleep on declarative and procedural memory. *Journal of Cognitive Neuroscience, 9*(4), 534–547. https://doi.org/10.1162/jocn.1997.9.4.534

Plomin, R. (2018). *Blueprint: How DNA Makes Us Who We Are*. Cambridge, MA: MIT Press.

Plomin, R., & Deary, I. J. (2015). Genetics and intelligence differences: Five special findings. *Molecular Psychiatry, 20*(1), 98–108.

Plomin, R., & Spinath, F. (2002). Genetics and general cognitive ability (g). *Trends in Cognitive Sciences, 6*, 169–176.

Plomin, R., Plomin, R., & Deary, I. (2014). Genetics and intelligence differences: Five special findings. *Molecular Psychiatry, 20*(1), 98–108.

Pluvinage, J., & Wyss-Coray, T. (2020). Systemic factors as mediators of brain homeostasis, ageing and neurodegeneration. *Nature Reviews. Neuroscience, 21*, 93–102.

Pos, A., & Greenberg, L. (2007). Emotion-focused therapy: The transforming power of affect. *Journal of Contemporary Psychotherapy, 37*, 25–31.

Posner, J., Russell, J. A., & Peterson, B. S. (2005). The circumplex model of affect: An integrative approach to affective neuroscience, cognitive development, and psychopathology. *Development and Psychopathology, 17*(3), 715–734. DOI:10.1017/S0954579405050340

Powell, K., Paluch, A., & Blair, S. (2011). Physical activity for health: What kind? How much? How intense? On top of what? *Annual Review of Public Health, 32*, 349–365.

Power, M. L., & Schulkin, J. (2008). Sex differences in fat storage, fat metabolism, and the health risks from obesity: possible evolutionary origins. *British Journal of Nutrition, 99*(5), 931–940.

Powers, A. R., Kelley, M. S., & Corlett, P. R. (2017). Varieties of voice-hearing: Psychics and the psychosis continuum. *Schizophrenia Bulletin, 43*(1), 84–98. https://doi.org/10.1093/schbul/sbw133

Pressman, S. D., Jenkins, B. N., & Moskowitz, J. T. (2019). Positive affect and health: What do we know and where next should we go? *Annual Review of Psychology, 70*(1), 627–650. https://doi.org/10.1146/annurev-psych-010418-102955

Preston, S. D. (2017). The rewarding nature of social contact. *Science, 357*(6,358), 1,353–1,354. https://doi.org/10.1126/science.aao7192

Preuss, T., & Kaas, J. (1999). Human brain evolution. In F. Bloom, S. Landis, J. Roberts, L. Squire, & M. Zigmond (eds.). *Fundamental Neuroscience*. New York: Academic Press.

Pribram, Karl H., & Gill, Merton M. (1976). *Freud's "Project" Reassessed*. London: Hutchinson.

Price, D., Finniss, D., & Benedetti, F. (2008). A comprehensive review of the placebo effect: Recent advances and current thought. *Annual Review of Psychology, 59*, 565–590.

Prince, M. (1913). *The Dissociation of a Personality: A Biographical Study in Abnormal* Prince *Psychology*. New York: Longmans, Green.

Protzko, J. (2020). Kids these days! Increasing delay of gratification ability over the past 50 years in children. *Intelligence, 80*(March), 101,451. https://doi.org/10.1016/j.intell.2020.101451

Puce, A. (2014). Perception of nonverbal cues. In K. N. Ochsner, & S. M. Kosslyn (eds.), *Oxford Library of Psychology. The Oxford Handbook of Cognitive Neuroscience, Vol. 2. The Cutting Edges* (pp. 148–164). New York: Oxford University Press.

Purves, D., Cabeza, R., Huettel, S., LaBar, K., Platt, M., & Woldorff, M. (2013). *Principles of Cognitive Neuroscience* (2nd ed.). Sunderland, MA: Sinauer Associates.

Pylkkänen, L. (2019). The neural basis of combinatory syntax and semantics. *Science, 366*(6,461), 62–66. https://doi.org/10.1126/science.aax0050

Qu, C., Ligneul, R., Van der Henst, J. B., & Dreher, J. C. (2017). An integrative interdisciplinary perspective on social dominance hierarchies. *Trends in Cognitive Sciences, 21*(11), 893–908. https://doi.org/10.1016/j.tics.2017.08.004

Raebhausen, O. M., & Brim, O. G. (1967). Privacy and behavioral research. *American Psychologist, 22*, 423–437.

Raevuori, A., Keski-Rahkonen, A., & Hoek, H. W. (2014). A review of eating disorders in males. *Current Opinion in Psychiatry, 27*(6), 426–430. https://doi.org/10.1097/YCO.0000000000000113

Raichle, M. E. (2015). The brain's default mode network. *Annual Review of Neuroscience*, (April), 413–427. https://doi.org/10.1146/annurev-neuro-071013-014030

Raichlen, D. A., & Alexander, G. E. (2017). Adaptive capacity: An evolutionary neuroscience model linking exercise, cognition, and brain health. *Trends in Neurosciences, 40*(7), 408–421. https://doi.org/10.1016/j.tins.2017.05.001

Rainville, P., Duncan, G. H., Price, D. D., Carrier, B., & Bushnell, M. C. (1997). Pain affect encoded in human anterior cingulate but not somatosensory cortex. *Science (New York, N.Y.), 277*(5,328), 968–971. https://doi.org/10.1126/science.277.5328.968

Rainville, P., Streff, A., Chen, J. I., Houzé, B., Desmarteaux, C., & Piché, M. (2019). Hypnotic Automaticity in the Brain at Rest: An Arterial Spin Labelling Study. *The International Journal of Clinical and Experimental Hypnosis, 67*(4), 512–542. https://doi.org/10.1080/00207144.2019.1650578

Rais, M., Cahn, W., Schnack, H. G., Hulshoff Pol, H. E., Kahn, R. S., & van Haren, N. E. (2012). Brain volume reductions in medication-naïve patients with schizophrenia in relation to intelligence quotient. *Psychosomatic Medicine, 42*, 1,847–1,856.

Rajsic, J., Wilson, D., & Pratt, J. (2015). Investigating confirmation bias in overt visual selection. *Journal of Vision, 15*(12), 1,356–1,356.

Raju, D., & Radtke, R. (2012). Sleep/Wake electroencephalography across the lifespan. *Sleep Medicines Reviews, 7*, 13–22.

Rakison, D. (2005). Infant perception and cognition: An evolutionary perspective on early learning. In B. Ellis, & D. Bjorklund (eds.), *Origins of the Social Mind*. New York: Guilford Press.

Ralls, F., & Grigg-Damberger, M. (2013) Sleepwalking and its variants in adults. In S. Kothare, & A. Ivanenko (eds.), *Parasomnias*. New York: Springer. https://doi.org/10.1007/978-1-4614-7627-6_5

Ramachandran, V. S. (1998). Consciousness and body image: Lessons from phantom limbs, Capgras syndrome and pain asymbolia. *Transitions of the Royal Society of London, B, 353*, 1,851–1,859.

Ramachandran, V. S., & Blakeslee, S. (1998). *Phantoms in the Brain*. New York: William Morrow and Company.

Ramon, M., Miellet, S., Dzieciol, A. M., Konrad, B. N., Dresler, M., & Caldara, R. (2016). Super-memorizers are not super-recognizers. *PLoS One, 11*(3), e0150972. https://doi.org/10.1371/journal.pone.0150972

Rampon, C., Tang, Y. P., Goodhouse, J., Shimizu, E., Kyin, M., & Tsien, J. Z. (2000). Enrichment induces structural changes and recovery from nonspatial memory deficits in CA1 NMDAR1-knockout mice. *Nature Neuroscience, 3*(3), 238–244. https://doi.org/10.1038/72945

Ramsden, S., Richardson, F. M., Josse, G., Thomas, M. S., Ellis, C., Shakeshaft, C., . . . & Price, C. J. (2011). Verbal and non-verbal intelligence changes in the teenage brain. *Nature, 479*(7,371), 113–116.

Rapee, R., Schniering, C., & Hudson, J. (2009). Anxiety disorders during childhood and adolescence: Origins and treatment. *Annual Review of Clinical Psychology, 5*, 311–341.

Rauscher, F. H., Shaw, G. L., & Ky, K. N. (1993). Music and spatial task performance. *Nature, 365*(6,447), 611. https://doi.org/10.1038/365611a0

Rauscher, F. H., Shaw, G. L., Levine, L. J., Wright, E. L., Dennis, W. R., & Newcomb, R. L. (1997). Music training causes long-term enhancement of preschool children's spatial-temporal reasoning. *Neurological Research, 19*(1), 2–8. https://doi.org/10.1080/01616412.1997.11740765

Ray, W. (2022). *Research Methods in Psychological Science*. Thousand Oaks, CA: SAGE.

Ray, W., J., (2007). The experience of agency and hypnosis from an evolutionary perspective. In G. Jamieson (ed.), *Hypnosis and Conscious States: The Cognitive-Neuroscience Perspective*. Oxford: Oxford University Press.

Ray, W. J. (2010). *Dreams. The Corsini Encyclopedia of Psychology*. Hoboken, NJ: Wiley.

Ray, W. J., Keil, A., Mikuteit, A., Bongartz, W., & Elbert, T. (2002). High resolution EEG indicators of pain responses in relation to hypnotic susceptibility and suggestion. *Biological Psychology, 60*(1), 17–36. https://doi.org/10.1016/s0301-0511(02)00029-7

Ray, W., Odenwald, M., Neuner, F., Schauer, M., Ruf, M., Wienbruch, C., . . ., & Elbert, T. (2006). Decoupling neural networks from reality: Dissociative experiences in torture victims are reflected in abnormal brain waves in left frontal cortex. *Psychological Science, 17*, 825–829.

Ray, W. J., & Tucker, D. (2003). Evolutionary approaches to understanding the hypnotic experience. *International Journal of Clinical and Experimental Hypnosis, 51*, 256–281.

Reid, V. M., Dunn, K., Young, R. J., Amu, J., Donovan, T., & Reissland, N. (2017). The human fetus preferentially engages with face-like visual stimuli. *Current Biology: CB, 27*(13), 2,052. https://doi.org/10.1016/j.cub.2017.06.036

Renoult, L., Irish, M., Moscovitch, M., & Rugg, M. D. (2019). From knowing to remembering: The semantic–episodic distinction. *Trends in Cognitive Sciences, 23*(12), 1,041–1,057.

Repetti R. L. (1989). Effects of daily workload on subsequent behavior during marital interaction: the roles of social withdrawal and spouse support. *Journal of Personality and Social Psychology, 57*(4), 651–659. https://doi.org/10.1037//0022-3514.57.4.651

Reuben, A., Caspi, A., Belsky, D. W., Broadbent, J., Harrington, H., Sugden, K., …, & Moffitt, T. E. (2017). Association of childhood blood lead levels with cognitive function and socioeconomic status at age 38 years and with IQ change and socioeconomic mobility between childhood and adulthood. *JAMA—Journal of the American Medical Association, 317*(12), 1,244–1,251. https://doi.org/10.1001/jama.2017.1712

Reuter-Lorenz, P. A., & Park, D. C. (2010). Human neuroscience and the aging mind: A new look at old problems. *The Journals of Gerontology. Series B, Psychological Sciences and Social Sciences, 65*(4), 405–415. https://doi.org/10.1093/geronb/gbq035

Reverberi, C., Toraldo, A., D'Agostini, S., & Skrap, M. (2005). Better without (lateral) frontal cortex? Insight problems solved by frontal patients. *Brain: A Journal of Neurology, 128*(12), 2,882–2,890. https://doi.org/10.1093/brain/awh577

Ricard, M., Lutz, A., & Davidson, R. J. (2014). Mind of the meditator. *Scientific American, 311*(5), 38–45. https://doi.org/10.1038/scientificamerican1114-38

Richards, W. (1973). Visual processing in scotomata. *Experimental Brain Research, 17*, 333–347.

Richeson, J. A., & Shelton, J. N. (2003). When prejudice does not pay: Effects of interracial contact on executive function. *Psychological Science, 14*(3), 287–290. https://doi.org/10.1111/1467-9280.03437

Richeson, J. A., & Sommers, S. R. (2016). Toward a social psychology of race and race relations for the twenty-first century. *Annual Review of Psychology, 67*, 439–463. https://doi.org/10.1146/annurev-psych-010213-115115

Richeson, J., & Trawalter, S. (2005). Why do interracial interactions impair executive function? A resource depletion account. *Journal of Personality and Social Psychology, 88*, 934–947.

Rieke, F., Warland, D., van Steveninck, R., & Bialek, W. (1999). *Spikes: Exploring the Neural Code*. Cambridge, MA: The MIT Press.

Rilling, J. K., Glasser, M. F., Preuss, T. M., Ma, X., Zhao, T., Hu, X., & Behrens, T. E. (2008). The evolution of the arcuate fasciculus revealed with comparative DTI. *Nature Neuroscience, 11*(4), 426–428. https://doi.org/10.1038/nn2072

Rizzolatti, G., & Craighero, L. (2004). The mirror-neuron system. *Annual Review of Neuroscience, 27*, 169–192. https://doi.org/10.1146/annurev.neuro.27.070203.144230

Rizzolatti, G., & Fogassi, L. (2007). Mirror neurons and social cognition. In *The Oxford Handbook of Evolutionary Psychology* (pp. 179–195). Oxford: Oxford University Press.

Rizzolatti, G., & Fogassi, L. (2014). The mirror mechanism: recent findings and perspectives. *Philosophical Transactions of the Royal Society of London. Series B, Biological sciences, 369*(1,644), 20130420. https://doi.org/10.1098/rstb.2013.0420

Rizzolatti, G., Alberto Semi, A., & Fabbri-Destro, M. (2014). Linking psychoanalysis with neuroscience: The concept of ego. *Neuropsychologia, 55*(1), 143–148. https://doi.org/10.1016/j.neuropsychologia.2013.10.003

Roberson, A., (2010). *Borderline Traits: Her Life with Borderline Personality Disorder*. Bloomington, IN: Xlibris Corporation.

Roberts, J. A., & David, M. E. (2020). The social media party: Fear of missing out (FoMO), social media intensity, connection, and well-being. *International Journal of Human–Computer Interaction, 36*(4), 386–392. https://doi.org/10.1080/10447318.2019.1646517

Robinson, O. J., Krimsky, M., Lieberman, L., Allen, P., Vytal, K., & Grillon, C. (2014). Towards a mechanistic understanding of pathological anxiety: The dorsal medial prefrontal-amygdala "aversive amplification" circuit in unmedicated generalized and social anxiety disorders. *The Lancet. Psychiatry, 1*(4), 294–302. http://doi.org/10.1016/S2215-0366(14)70305-0

Rodebaugh, T., Holaway, R., & Heimberg, R. (2004). The treatment of social anxiety disorder. *Clinical Psychology Review, 24*, 883–908.

Roediger, H. L., & McDermott, K. B. (1995). Creating false memories: Remembering words not presented in lists. *Journal of Experimental Psychology: Learning, Memory, and Cognition, 21*(4), 803.

Roemer, L., Orsillo, S. M., & Barlow, D. H. B. (2002). Generalized anxiety disorder. In D. Barlow (ed.), *Anxiety and Its Disorders: The Nature and Treatment of Anxiety and Panic* (2nd ed., pp. 477–515). New York: Guilford Press.

Roemer, L., Orsillo, S. M., & Salters-Pedneault, K. (2008). Efficacy of an acceptance-based behavior therapy for generalized anxiety disorder: Evaluation in a randomized controlled trial. *Journal of Consulting and Clinical Psychology, 76*(6), 1,083–1,089. https://doi.org/10.1037/a0012720

Rogers, C. R. (1951). *Client-centered Therapy*. Boston: Houghton Mifflin

Rogers, S., & Vismara, L. (2008). Evidence-based comprehensive treatments for early autism. *Journal of Clinical Child & Adolescent Psychology, 37*, 8–38.

Ronfani, L., Brumatti, L. V., Mariuz, M., Tognin, V., Bin, M., Ferluga, V., . . . & Barbone, F. (2015). The complex interaction between home environment, socioeconomic status, maternal IQ and early child neurocognitive development: A multivariate analysis of data collected in a newborn cohort study. *PloS One, 10*(5), e0127052.

Roper, S. D., & Chaudhari, N. (2017). Taste buds: Cells, signals and synapses. *Nature Reviews. Neuroscience, 18*(8), 485–497. https://doi.org/10.1038/nrn.2017.68

Rorschach, H. (1942). *Psychodiagnostics*. New York: Grune and Stratton.

Rosch, E. (1975). Cognitive representations of semantic categories. *Journal of Experimental Psychology: General, 104*(3), 192–233.

Rosch, E., & Mervis, C. B. (1975). Family resemblances: Studies in the internal structure of categories. *Cognitive Psychology, 7*(4), 573–605.

Rosenberg, M. D., Finn, E. S., Scheinost, D., Constable, R. T., & Chun, M. M. (2017). Characterizing attention with predictive network models. *Trends in Cognitive Sciences*, *21*(4), 290–302. https://doi.org/10.1016/j.tics.2017.01.011

Rosenblat, J., & McIntye, R. (2019). Pharmacological treatment of bipolar disorder. In S. Evans (ed.), *APA Handbook of Psychopharmacology*. Washington, DC: American Psychological Association. https://doi.org/10.1037/0000133-008

Rosenblum, L. A., & Andrews, M. W. (1994). Influences of environmental demand on maternal behavior and infant development. *Acta paediatrica (Oslo, Norway: 1992). Supplement*, *397*, 57–63. https://doi.org/10.1111/j.1651-2227.1994.tb13266.x

Ross, C. (1997). *Dissociative Identity Disorder: Diagnosis, Clinical Features, and Treatment of Multiple Personality Disorder*. New York: Wiley.

Ross, C., Joshi, S., & Currie, R. (1990). Dissociative experiences in the general population. *American Journal of Psychiatry, 147*, 1,547–1,552.

Ross, E. L., Zivin, K., & Maixner, D. F. (2018). Cost-effectiveness of electroconvulsive therapy vs pharmacotherapy/psychotherapy for treatment-resistant depression in the United States. *JAMA Psychiatry, 75*, 713–722. https://doi.org/10.1001/jamapsychiatry.2018.0768

Ross, J. J. (1965). Neurological findings after prolonged sleep deprivation. *Archives of Neurology*, *12*, 399–403. https://doi.org/10.1001/archneur.1965.00460280069006

Roth, G., & Dicke, U. (2005). Evolution of brain and intelligence. *Trends in Cognitive Sciences, 9*, 250–257.

Rotter, J. (1954). *Social Learning and Clinical Psychology*. Englewood Cliffs, NJ: Prentice-Hall.

Rouse, B. T., & Sehrawat, S. (2010). Immunity and immunopathology to viruses: what decides the outcome?. *Nature Reviews. Immunology*, *10*(7), 514–526. https://doi.org/10.1038/nri2802

Rovec, C, & Luciano, D (1973). Rearing influences on tonic immobility in three day old chicks (*Gallus gallus*). *Journal of Comparative and Physiological Psychology, 83*, 351–354.

Rowe, J., & Kahn, R. (1997). Successful aging. *The Gerontologist, 37*, 433–440.

Roy, M., Shohamy, D., & Wager, T. D. (2012). Ventromedial prefrontal-subcortical systems and the generation of affective meaning. *Trends in Cognitive Sciences*, *16*(3), 147–156. https://doi.org/10.1016/j.tics.2012.01.005

Rozenkrantz, L., Zachor, D., Heller, I., Plotkin, A., Weissbrod, A., Snitz, K., . . ., & Sobel, N. (2015). A mechanistic link between olfaction and autism spectrum disorder. *Current Biology, 25*(14), 1,904–1,910. http://doi.org/10.1016/j.cub.2015.05.048

Rozin, P., & Schull, J. (1988). The adaptive-evolutionary point of view in experimental psychology. In R. C. Atkinson, R. J. Herrnstein, G. Lindzey, & R. D. Luce (eds.), *Handbook of Experimental Psychology* (pp. 503–546). New York: Wiley lnterscience.

Rupp, H., & Wallen, M. (2007). Sex differences in viewing sexual stimuli: An eye-tracking study in men and women. *Hormones and Behavior, 51*, 524–533.

Rupp, T. L., Wesensten, N. J., Bliese, P. D., & Balkin, T. J. (2009). Banking sleep: Realization of benefits during subsequent sleep restriction and recovery. *Sleep, 32*(3), 311–321. https://doi.org/10.1093/sleep/32.3.311

Russell, G. (1979). Bulimia nervosa: An ominous variant of anorexia nervosa. *Psychological Medicine, 9*, 429–448.

Russell, J. A. (1980). A circumplex model of affect. *Journal of Personality and Social Psychology, 39*(6), 1,161.

Russell, J. A. (2003). Core affect and the psychological construction of emotion. *Psychological Review, 110*(1), 145.

Russell, J. A. (2009). Emotion, core affect, and psychological construction. *Cognition and Emotion, 23*(7), 1,259–1,283.

Russell, J. A. (2017). Mixed emotions viewed from the psychological constructionist perspective. *Emotion Review, 9*(2), 111–117.

Russell, R., Duchaine, B., & Nakayama, K. (2009). Super-recognizers: People with extraordinary face recognition ability. *Psychonomic Bulletin & Review, 16*(2), 252–257. https://doi.org/10.3758/PBR.16.2.252

Rutter, M. (2006). *Genes and Behavior: Nature-nurture Interplay Explained.* Malden, MA: Blackwell Publishing.

Ryba, M. M., & Hopko, D. R. (2012). Gender differences in depression: Assessing mediational effects of overt behaviors and environmental reward through daily diary monitoring. *Depression Research and Treatment*, 865679. http://doi.org/10.1155/2012/865679

Saah, T. (2005). The evolutionary origins and significance of drug addiction. *Harm Reduction Journal, 2*, 2–8.

Sachs, B. D. (2007). A contextual definition of male sexual arousal. *Hormones and Behavior, 51*, 569–578.

Sackeim, H. A., & Gur, R. C. (1979). Self-deception, other-deception, and self-reported psychopathology. *Journal of Consulting and Clinical Psychology, 47*(1), 213–215. https://doi.org/10.1037//0022-006x.47.1.213

Sackett, P. R., Hardison, C. M., & Cullen, M. J. (2005). On interpreting research on stereotype threat and test performance. *American Psychologist, 60*(3), 271–272.

Sacks, Oliver (2007). The abyss. *The New Yorker* (24 September).

Saks, E. (2007). *The Center Cannot Hold: My Journey through Madness.* New York: Hyperion.

Salthouse T. A. (2004). Localizing age-related individual differences in a hierarchical structure. *Intelligence, 32*(6), 10.1016/j.intell.2004.07.003. https://doi.org/10.1016/j.intell.2004.07.003

Samuel, D. B., Simms, L. J., Clark, L. A., Livesley, W. J., & Widiger, T. A. (2010). An item response theory integration of normal and abnormal personality scales. *Personality Disorders: Theory, Research, and Treatment, 1*, 5–21.

Sandoval, D., Cota, D., & Seeley, R. J. (2008). The integrative role of CNS fuel-sensing mechanisms in energy balance and glucose regulation. *Annual Review of. Physiology, 70*, 513–535.

Sandrini, M., Cohen, L. G., & Censor, N. (2015). Modulating reconsolidation: A link to causal systems-level dynamics of human memories. *Trends in Cognitive Sciences, 19*(8), 475–482. https://doi.org/10.1016/j.tics.2015.06.002

Sanefuji, W., Wada, K., Yamamoto, T., Mohri, I., & Taniike, M. (2014). Development of preference for conspecific faces in human infants. *Developmental Psychology, 50*(4), 979–985. https://doi.org/10.1037/a0035205

Sanfey, A. G., Rilling, J. K., Aronson, J. A., Nystrom, L. E., & Cohen, J. D. (2003). The neural basis of economic decision-making in the Ultimatum Game. *Science (New York, N.Y.), 300*(5,626), 1,755–1,758. https://doi.org/10.1126/science.1082976

Sapolsky, R. M. (2003). Stress and plasticity in the limbic system. *Neurochemical Research, 28*(11), 1,735–1,742.

Sapolsky, R. M., & Share, L. J. (2004). A pacific culture among wild baboons: Its emergence and transmission. *PLoS Biology, 2*(4), E106. https://doi.org/10.1371/journal.pbio.0020106

Schacter, D., & Wagner, A. (2013). Learning and memory. In E. R. Kandel, J. H. Schwartz, T. M. Jessell, S. Siegelbaum, & A. J. Hudspeth (eds.), *Principles of Neural Science* (5th ed.). New York: McGraw-Hill.

Schmahmann, J. D., Guell, X., Stoodley, C. J., & Halko, M. A. (2019). The theory and neuroscience of cerebellar cognition. *Annual Review of Neuroscience, 42*(1), 337–364. https://doi.org/10.1146/annurev-neuro-070918-050258

Schacter D. L. (2012). Constructive memory: Past and future. *Dialogues in Clinical Neuroscience, 14*(1), 7–18. https://doi.org/10.31887/DCNS.2012.14.1/dschacter

Schacter, D. L., & Loftus, E. F. (2013). Memory and law: What can cognitive neuroscience contribute? *Nature Neuroscience, 16*(2), 119–123. https://doi.org/10.1038/nn.3294

Schacter, D. L., Addis, D. R., & Buckner, R. L. (2007). Remembering the past to imagine the future: The prospective brain. *Nature Reviews. Neuroscience, 8*(9), 657–661. https://doi.org/10.1038/nrn2213

Schmitt, D. P., Allik, J., McCrae, R. R., & Benet-Martínez, V. (2007). The geographic distribution of big five personality traits: Patterns and profiles of human self-description across 56 nations. *Journal of Cross-Cultural Psychology, 38*(2), 173–212. https://doi.org/10.1177/0022022106297299 13–22

Schneider, R. H., Grim, C. E., Rainforth, M. V., Kotchen, T., Nidich, S. I., Gaylord-King, C., Salerno, J. W., Kotchen, J. M., & Alexander, C. N. (2012). Stress reduction in the secondary prevention of cardiovascular disease: Randomized, controlled trial of transcendental meditation and health education in Blacks. *Circulation. Cardiovascular Quality and Outcomes, 5*(6), 750–758. https://doi.org/10.1161/CIRCOUTCOMES.112.967406

Schnupp, J., Nelken, I., & King, A. (2011). *Auditory Neuroscience: Making Sense of Sound.* Cambridge, MA: MIT press.

Schott, G. (2011). Freud's Project and its diagram: Anticipating the Hebbian synapse. *Journal of Neurology, Neurosurgery, and Psychiatry, 82*(2), 122–125. https://doi.org/10.1136/jnnp.2010.220400

Schreiner, T., & Rasch, B. (2015). Boosting vocabulary learning by verbal cueing during sleep. *Cerebral Cortex (New York, N.Y.: 1991), 25*(11), 4,169–4,179. https://doi.org/10.1093/cercor/bhu139

Schuett, W., Tregenza, T., & Dall, S. R. (2010). Sexual selection and animal personality. *Biological Reviews of the Cambridge Philosophical Society, 85*(2), 217–246. https://doi.org/10.1111/j.1469-185X.2009.00101.x

Schulkin, J., & Sterling, P. (2019). Allostasis: A brain-centered, predictive mode of physiological regulation. *Trends in Neurosciences, 42*(10), 740–752. https://doi.org/10.1016/j.tins.2019.07.010

Schulz, L. (2015). Infants explore the unexpected. *Science, 348*(6,230), 42–43.

Scott, S. K. (2019). From speech and talkers to the social world: The neural processing of human spoken language. *Science (New York, N.Y.), 366*(6,461), 58–62. https://doi.org/10.1126/science.aax0288

Scott-Phillips, T. C., & Blythe, R. A. (2013). Why is combinatorial communication rare in the natural world, and why is language an exception to this trend? *Journal of the Royal Society, Interface, 10*(88), 20130520. https://doi.org/10.1098/rsif.2013.0520

Seamon, J. G., Blumenson, C. N., Karp, S. R., Perl, J. J., Rindlaub, L. A., & Speisman, B. B. (2009). Did we see someone shake hands with a fire hydrant?: Collaborative recall affects false recollections from a campus walk. *The American Journal of Psychology, 122*(2), 235–247.

Segal, N. (2012). *Born Together—Reared Apart.* Cambridge, MA: Harvard University Press.

Segal, N. L., & Johnson, W. (2009). Twin studies of general mental ability. In Y.-K. Kim (ed.), *Handbook of Behavior Genetics* (pp. 81–99). Springer Science + Business Media. https://doi.org/10.1007/978-0-387-76727-7_6

Selye, H. (1956). *The Stress of Life*. New York: McGraw-Hill.

Shafto, M. A., & Tyler, L. K. (2014). Language in the aging brain: The network dynamics of cognitive decline and preservation. *Science (New York, N.Y.)*, *346*(6,209), 583–587. https://doi.org/10.1126/science.1254404

Shalev, A., Liberzon, I., & Marmar, C. (2017). Post-traumatic stress disorder. *New England Journal of Medicine*, *376*(25), 2,459–2,469.

Shea, N., Boldt, A., Bang, D., Yeung, N., Heyes, C., & Frith, C. D. (2014). Supra-personal cognitive control and metacognition. *Trends in Cognitive Sciences*, *18*(4), 186–193.

Shenk, J. (2005). Lincoln's great depression. *The Atlantic* (October). https://www.theatlantic.com/magazine/archive/2005/10/lincolns-great-depression/304247/

Sheppes, G., Suri, G., & Gross, J. J. (2015). Emotion regulation and psychopathology. *Annual Review Of Clinical Psychology*, *11*, 379–405. https://doi.org/10.1146/annurev-clinpsy-032814-112739

Sheskin, M., Chevallier, C., Lambert, S., & Baumard, N. (2014). Life-history theory explains childhood moral development. *Trends in Cognitive Sciences*, *18*(12), 613–615. https://doi.org/10.1016/j.tics.2014.08.004

Shotland, R. L., & Straw, M. K. (1976). Bystander response to an assault: When a man attacks a woman. *Journal of Personality and Social Psychology*, *34*(5), 990.

Shrout, P. E., & Rodgers, J. L. (2018). Psychology, science, and knowledge construction: Broadening perspectives from the replication crisis. *Annual Review of Psychology*, *69*, 487–510.

Siegel J. M. (2008). Do all animals sleep? *Trends in Neurosciences*, *31*(4), 208–213. https://doi.org/10.1016/j.tins.2008.02.001

Siegel, S. (2001). Pavlovian conditioning and drug overdose: When tolerance fails. *Addiction Research & Theory*, *9*(5), 503–513.

Siegel, S. (2008). Learning and the wisdom of the body. *Learning & Behavior*, *36*(3), 242–252.

Siegel, S., & Allan, L. G. (1998). Learning and homeostasis: Drug addiction and the McCollough effect. *Psychological Bulletin*, *124*, 230–239.

Simões-Franklin, C., Whitaker, T. A., & Newell, F. N. (2011). Active and passive touch differentially activate somatosensory cortex in texture perception. *Human Brain Mapping*, *32*(7), 1,067–1,080. https://doi.org/10.1002/hbm.21091

Simon, H. A. (1990). A mechanism for social selection and successful altruism. *Science*, *250*(4,988), 1,665–1,668.

Singer, W. (2009). Distributed processing and temporal codes in neuronal networks. *Cognitive Neurodynamics*, *3*, 189–196.

Singer, W., & Gray, C. (1995). Visual feature integration and the temporal correlation hypothesis. *Annual Review of Neuroscience*, *18*, 555–586.

Singleton, O., Hölzel, B. K., Vangel, M., Brach, N., Carmody, J., & Lazar, S. W. (2014). Change in brainstem gray matter concentration following a mindfulness-based intervention is correlated with improvement in psychological well-being. *Frontiers in Human Neuroscience*, *8*, 33. https://doi.org/10.3389/fnhum.2014.00033

Sinigaglia, C., & Rizzolatti, G. (2011). Through the looking glass: Self and others. *Consciousness and Cognition*, *20*(1), 64–74. https://doi.org/10.1016/j.concog.2010.11.012

Sisk, C. L., & Foster, D. L. (2004). The neural basis of puberty and adolescence. *Nature Neuroscience*, *7*(10), 1,040–1,047.

Skeide, M. A., & Friederici, A. D. (2016). The ontogeny of the cortical language network. *Nature Reviews. Neuroscience*, *17*(5), 323–332. https://doi.org/10.1038/nrn.2016.23

Skinner, M. (2010). Fathers' nutritional legacy. *Nature*, *467*, 922–923.

Slavich, G. M., & Irwin, M. R. (2014). From stress to inflammation and major depressive disorder: A social signal transduction theory of depression. *Psychological Bulletin*, *140*(3), 774–815. https://doi.org/10.1037/a0035302

Sleek, S. (2018). The bias beneath: Two decades of measuring implicit associations. *APS Observer*, *31*(2).

Slovic, P., & Peters, E. (2006). Risk perception and affect. *Current Directions in Psychological Science*, *15*(6), 322–325.

Smetana, J., Schlagman, N., & Adams, P. (1993). Preschool children's judgments about hypothetical and actual transgressions. *Child Development*, *64*(1), 202–214. DOI:10.2307/1131446

Smetana, J. G., Schlagman, N., & Adams, P. W. (1993). Preschool children's judgments about hypothetical and actual transgressions. *Child Development*, *64*(1), 202–214.

Smith, A. M., & Messier, C. (2014). Voluntary out-of-body experience: an fMRI study. *Frontiers in Human Neuroscience*, *8*(February), 1–10. https://doi.org/10.3389/fnhum.2014.00070

Smith, L. B., & Thelen, E. (2003). Development as a dynamic system. *Trends in Cognitive Sciences*, *7*(8), 343–348. https://doi.org/10.1016/s1364-6613(03)00156-6

Snyder, C. R. (1974). Why horoscopes are true: The effects of specificity on acceptance of astrological interpretations. *Journal of Clinical Psychology*, *30*(4), 577–580.

Snyder, C. R., & Larson, G. R. (1972). A further look at student acceptance of general personality interpretations. *Journal of Consulting and Clinical Psychology*, *38*(3), 384–388. https://doi.org/10.1037/h0032899

Sowislo, J. F., & Orth, U. (2013). Does low self-esteem predict depression and anxiety? A meta-analysis of longitudinal studies. *Psychological Bulletin*, *139*(1), 213–240. https://doi.org/10.1037/a0028931

Spain, S. L., Pedroso, I., Kadeva, N., Miller, M. B., Iacono, W. G., McGue, M., Stergiakouli, E., Davey Smith, G., Putallaz, M., Lubinski, D., Meaburn, E. L., Plomin, R., & Simpson, M. A. (2016). A genome-wide analysis of putative functional and exonic variation associated with extremely high intelligence. *Molecular Psychiatry*, *21*(8), 1145–1151. https://doi.org/10.1038/mp.2015.108

Spencer, S. J., Steele, C. M., & Quinn, D. M. (1999). Stereotype threat and women's math performance. *Journal of Experimental Social Psychology*, *35*, 4–28.

Sperling, G. (1960). The information available in brief visual presentations. *Psychological Monographs: General and Applied*, *74*, (Whole #48).

Springer, S. P., & Deutsch, G. (1998). *A Series of Books in Psychology. Left Brain, Right Brain: Perspectives from Cognitive Neuroscience* (5th ed.). W H Freeman/Times Books/Henry Holt & Co.

Squire L. R. (2004). Memory systems of the brain: A brief history and current perspective. *Neurobiology of Learning and Memory*, *82*(3), 171–177. https://doi.org/10.1016/j.nlm.2004.06.005

Squire, L. R. (2009). The legacy of patient HM for neuroscience. *Neuron*, *61*(1), 6–9.

Stamps, J., & Groothuis, T. G. (2010). The development of animal personality: relevance, concepts and perspectives. *Biological Reviews of the Cambridge Philosophical Society*, *85*(2), 301–325. https://doi.org/10.1111/j.1469-185X.2009.00103.x

Stahl, A. E., & Feigenson, L. (2015). Cognitive development. Observing the unexpected enhances infants' learning and exploration. *Science (New York, N.Y.)*, *348*(6,230), 91–94. https://doi.org/10.1126/science.aaa3799

Stanovich, K. E., & Toplak, M. E. (2012). Defining features versus incidental correlates of Type 1 and Type 2 processing. *Mind & Society, 11*(1), 3–13.

Steele, C. M. (1997). A threat in the air: How stereotypes shape intellectual identity and performance. *American Psychologist, 52*(6), 613–629. https://doi.org/10.1037/0003-066X.52.6.613

Steele, C. M., & Aronson, J. (1995). Stereotype threat and the intellectual test performance of African Americans. *Journal of Personality and Social Psychology, 69*(5), 797–811. https://doi.org/10.1037/0022-3514.69.5.797

Steele, K., & Berman, C. (2001). *The Day the Voices Stopped.* New York: Basic Books.

Steinberg, L. (2007). Risk taking in adolescence: New perspectives from brain and behavioral science. *Current Directions in Psychological Science, 16*(2), 55–59.

Stephens, D. W., McLinn, C. M., & Stevens, J. R. (2002). Discounting and reciprocity in an Iterated Prisoner's Dilemma. *Science (New York, N.Y.), 298*(5,601), 2,216–2,218. https://doi.org/10.1126/science.1078498

Steptoe, A., de Oliveira, C., Demakakos, P., & Zaninotto, P. (2014). Enjoyment of life and declining physical function at older ages: A longitudinal cohort study. *CMAJ: Canadian Medical Association journal = journal de l'Association medicale canadienne, 186*(4), E150–E156. https://doi.org/10.1503/cmaj.131155

Striedter, G. F. (2005). Principles of Brain Evolution. Sunderland, MA: Sinauer Associates.

Stuart, D., (2004). *Dangerous Garden.* Cambridge, MA: Harvard University Press.

Strupp, H. H. & Binger. J. L. (1984). *A Guide to Time-Limited Dynamic Psychotherapy.* New York: Basic Books.

Sturman, D. A., & Moghaddam, B. (2011). The neurobiology of adolescents: Changes in brain architecture, functional dynamics, and behavioral tendencies. *Neuroscience and Behavioral Reviews, 35,* 1,704–1,712.

Substance Abuse and Mental Health Services Administration. (2020). *Key substance use and mental health indicators in the United States: Results from the 2019 National Survey on Drug Use and Health* (HHS Publication No. PEP20-07-01-001, NSDUH Series H-55). Rockville, MD: Center for Behavioral Health Statistics and Quality, Substance Abuse and Mental Health Services Administration.

Sulloway, F. (1979). *Freud, Biologist of the Mind.* New York: Basic Books.

Sundgot-Borgen, J., & Torstveit, M. K. (2004). Prevalence of eating disorders in elite athletes is higher than in the general population. *Clinical Journal of Sport Medicine: Official Journal of the Canadian Academy of Sport Medicine, 14*(1), 25–32. https://doi.org/10.1097/00042752-200401000-00005

Takashima, A., Petersson, K. M., Rutters, F., Tendolkar, I., Jensen, O., Zwarts, M. J., …, & Fernández, G. (2006). Declarative memory consolidation in humans: A prospective functional magnetic resonance imaging study. *Proceedings of the National Academy of Sciences of the United States of America, 103*(3), 756–761. https://doi.org/10.1073/pnas.0507774103

Talarico, J. M., & Rubin, D. C. (2003). Confidence, not consistency, characterizes flashbulb memories. *Psychological Science, 14*(5), 455–461. https://doi.org/10.1111/1467-9280.02453

Talarico, J. M., & Rubin, D. C. (2007). Flashbulb memories are special after all; in phenomenology, not accuracy. *Applied Cognitive Psychology: The Official Journal of the Society for Applied Research in Memory and Cognition, 21*(5), 557–578.

Tallon-Baudry, C., & Bertrand, O. (1999). Oscillatory gamma activity in humans and its role in object representation. *Trends in Cognitive Sciences, 3,* 151–162.

Tambini, A., Rimmele, U., Phelps, E. A., & Davachi, L. (2017). Emotional brain states carry over and enhance future memory formation. *Nature Neuroscience, 20*(2), 271–278.

Tan, Q. (2019). The epigenome of twins as a perfect laboratory for studying behavioural traits. *Neuroscience and Biobehavioral Reviews, 107*(August), 192–195. https://doi.org/10.1016/j.neubiorev.2019.09.022

Taylor, S. E., & Stanton, A. L. (2007). Coping resources, coping processes, and mental health. *Annual Review of Clinical Psychology, 3*, 377–401. https://doi.org/10.1146/annurev.clinpsy.3.022806.091520

Taylor, S. E., Gonzaga, G. C., Klein, L. C., Hu, P., Greendale, G. A., & Seeman, T. E. (2006). Relation of oxytocin to psychological stress responses and hypothalamic-pituitary-adrenocortical axis activity in older women. *Psychosomatic Medicine, 68*(2), 238–245. https://doi.org/10.1097/01.psy.0000203242.95990.74

Taylor, S. E., Klein, L. C., Lewis, B. P., Gruenewald, T. L., Gurung, R. A., & Updegraff, J. A. (2000). Biobehavioral responses to stress in females: Tend-and-befriend, not fight-or-flight. *Psychological Review, 107*(3), 411.

Thomas, M. S., Kovas, Y., Meaburn, E. L., & Tolmie, A. (2015). What can the study of genetics offer to educators? *Mind, Brain, and Education, 9*(2), 72–80.

Tishkoff, S. A., Reed, F. A., Ranciaro, A., Voight, B. F., Babbitt, C. C., Silverman, J. S., Powell, K., Mortensen, H. M., Hirbo, J. B., Osman, M., Ibrahim, M., Omar, S. A., Lema, G., Nyambo, T. B., Ghori, J., Bumpstead, S., Pritchard, J. K., Wray, G. A., & Deloukas, P. (2007). Convergent adaptation of human lactase persistence in Africa and Europe. *Nature Genetics, 39*(1), 31–40. https://doi.org/10.1038/ng1946

Todorov A. (2008). Evaluating faces on trustworthiness: An extension of systems for recognition of emotions signaling approach/avoidance behaviors. *Annals of the New York Academy of Sciences, 1124*, 208–224. https://doi.org/10.1196/annals.1440.012

Todorov, A., Olivola, C. Y., Dotsch, R., & Mende-Siedlecki, P. (2015). Social attributions from faces: Determinants, consequences, accuracy, and functional significance. *Annual Review of Psychology, 66*, 519–545. https://doi.org/10.1146/annurev-psych-113011-143831

Tomasello M. (2014). The ultra-social animal. *European Journal of Social Psychology, 44*(3), 187–194. https://doi.org/10.1002/ejsp.2015

Tomkins, S. (1965). *Affect, Cognition, and Personality: Empirical Studies.* New York: Springer Publishing.

Tomkins, S. S. (1984). Affect theory. *Approaches to Emotion, 163*(163–195).

Toomey, T., Richardson, D., & Hammock, G. (2017). Introductory psychology: How student experiences relate to their understanding of psychological science. *Teaching of Psychology, 44*(3), 246–249. https://doi.org/10.1177/0098628317712749

Torrey, E., Kennard, A., Eslinger, D., Lamb, R., & Pavle, J. (2010). More mentally ill persons are in jails and prisons than hospitals: A survey of the states. *Report for National Sheriffs Association, & Treatment Advocacy Center.*

Tottenham, N. (2017, July). The brain's emotional development. In *Cerebrum: The Dana Forum on Brain Science* (Vol. 2017). Dana Foundation.

Towbin, K. E., & Showalter, J. E. (2008). Adolescent development. *Psychiatry*, 161–180.

Trivers, R. (1985). *Social Evolution.* Menlo Parak, CA: Benjamin/Cummings Publishing.

Trivers, R. L. (1971). The evolution of reciprocal altruism. *The Quarterly Review of Biology, 46*(1), 35–57.

Trivers, T. (2002). *National Selection and Social Theory.* New York: Oxford University Press.

Trzesniewski, K. H., Donnellan, M. B., & Robins, R. W. (2003). Stability of self-esteem across the life span. *Journal of Personality and Social Psychology, 84*(1), 205.

Turati, C., Simion, F., Milani, I., & Umiltà, C. (2002). Newborns' preference for faces: What is crucial? *Developmental Psychology, 38*(6), 875–882.

Turkheimer, E., Pettersson, E., & Horn, E. E. (2014). A phenotypic null hypothesis for the genetics of personality. *Annual Review of Psychology, 65*, 515–540. https://doi.org/10.1146/annurev-psych-113011-143752

Tversky, A., & Kahneman, D. (1973). Availability: A heuristic for judging frequency and probability. *Cognitive Psychology, 5*(2), 207–232.

Tversky, A., & Kahneman, D. (1974). Judgment under uncertainty: Heuristics and biases. *Science, 185*(4,157), 1,124–1,131.

Tversky, A., & Kahneman, D. (1981). The framing of decisions and the psychology of choice. *Science (New York, N.Y.), 211*(4,481), 453–458. https://doi.org/10.1126/science.7455683

Ubel, P. A. (2009). *Free Market Madness: Why Human Nature Is at Odds with Economics—And Why It Matters.* Cambridge, MA: Harvard Business Press.

Underwood, E. (2014) Starting young, *Science, 346*, 568–571.

United Nations Office on Drugs and Crime (2011) *Amphetamines and Ecstasy.* New York: United Nations. www.unodc.org/documents/ATS/ATS_Global_Assessment_2011.pdf

Upshur, C., Wenz-Gross, M., & Reed, G. (2013). A pilot study of a primary prevention curriculum to address preschool behavior problems. *The Journal of Primary Prevention, 34*(5), 309–327. https://doi.org/10.1007/s10935-013-0316-1

Ursano, R. J., Fullerton, C. S., Weisaeth, L., & Raphael, B. (Eds.). (2017). *Textbook of Disaster Psychiatry.* New York: Cambridge University Press.

Vaillant, G. (2002). *Aging Well.* Boston, MA: Little, Brown and Company.

van den Heuvel, M. I., & Thomason, M. E. (2016). Functional connectivity of the human brain in utero. *Trends in Cognitive Sciences, 20*(12), 931–939. https://doi.org/10.1016/j.tics.2016.10.001

van der Lely, H. K., & Pinker, S. (2014). The biological basis of language: Insight from developmental grammatical impairments. *Trends in Cognitive Sciences, 18*(11), 586–595. https://doi.org/10.1016/j.tics.2014.07.001

van Dolder, D., & van den Assem, M. J. (2018). The wisdom of the inner crowd in three large natural experiments. *Nature Human Behaviour, 2*(1), 21–26. https://doi.org/10.1038/s41562-017-0247-6

Van Horn, J. D., Irimia, A., Torgerson, C. M., Chambers, M. C., Kikinis, R., & Toga, A. (2012). Mapping connectivity damage in the case of Phineas Gage. *PLoS One, 7*(5), e37454. DOI:10.1371/journal.pone.0037454

van Praag H. (2009). Exercise and the brain: Something to chew on. *Trends in Neurosciences, 32*(5), 283–290. https://doi.org/10.1016/j.tins.2008.12.007

Váša, F., Romero-Garcia, R., Kitzbichler, M. G., Seidlitz, J., Whitaker, K. J., Vaghi, M. M., ..., & Bullmore, E. T. (2020). Conservative and disruptive modes of adolescent change in human brain functional connectivity. *Proceedings of the National Academy of Sciences of the United States of America, 117*(6), 3,248–3,253. https://doi.org/10.1073/pnas.1906144117

Vignal, J. P., Maillard, L., McGonigal, A., & Chauvel, P. (2007). The dreamy state: Hallucinations of autobiographic memory evoked by temporal lobe stimulations and seizures. *Brain: A Journal of Neurology, 130*(1), 88–99. https://doi.org/10.1093/brain/awl329

Völgyesi, F. (1966). *Hypnosis of Man and Animals.* Baltimore: Williams & Wilkins Co.

Volkow, N., & Li, T. (2005). The neuroscience of addiction. *Nature, 8*, 1,429–1,430.

Volkow, N., Wang, G., Fowler, J., & Tomasi, D. (2012). Addiction circuitry in the human brain. *Annual Review of Pharmacology and Toxicology, 52,* 321–336.

Voss, U., Holzmann, R., Hobson, A., Paulus, W., Koppehele-Gossel, J., Klimke, A., & Nitsche, M. a. (2014). Induction of self-awareness in dreams through frontal low current stimulation of gamma activity. *Nature Neuroscience, 17*(6), 810–812. https://doi.org/10.1038/nn.3719

Wager, T. D., & Atlas, L. Y. (2015). The neuroscience of placebo effects: Connecting context, learning and health. *Nature Reviews. Neuroscience, 16*(7), 403–418. https://doi.org/10.1038/nrn3976

Wamsley, E. J., & Stickgold, R. (2019). Dreaming of a learning task is associated with enhanced memory consolidation: Replication in an overnight sleep study. *Journal of Sleep Research, 28*(1), e12749. https://doi.org/10.1111/jsr.12749

Watkins, L. R., & Maier, S. F. (2002). Beyond neurons: Evidence that immune and glial cells contribute to pathological pain states. *Physiological Reviews, 82*(4), 981–1,011. https://doi.org/10.1152/physrev.00011.2002

Watson, J., & Rayner, R. (1920). Conditioned emotional reactions. *Journal of Experimental Psychology, 3,* 1–14.

Wearing, Deborah (2005). *Forever Today: A Memoir of Love and Amnesia.* New York: Random House

Wehrwein, E. A., Orer, H. S., & Barman, S. M. (2016). Overview of the anatomy, physiology, and pharmacology of the autonomic nervous system. *Comprehensive Physiology, 6*(3), 1,239–1,278. https://doi.org/10.1002/cphy.c150037

Wei, M., Joshi, A. A., Zhang, M., Mei, L., Manis, F. R., He, Q., Beattie, R. L., Xue, G., Shattuck, D. W., Leahy, R. M., Xue, F., Houston, S. M., Chen, C., Dong, Q., & Lu, Z. L. (2015). How age of acquisition influences brain architecture in bilinguals. *Journal of Neurolinguistics, 36,* 35–55. https://doi.org/10.1016/j.jneuroling.2015.05.001

Weiskrantz, L. (1996). Blindsight revisited. *Current Opinion in Neurobiology, 6*(2), 215–220.

Weiss, J. M., Goodman, P. A., Losito, B. G., Corrigan, S., Charry, J. M., & Bailey, W. H. (1981). Behavioral depression produced by an uncontrollable stressor: Relationship to norepinephrine, dopamine, and serotonin levels in various regions of rat brain. *Brain Research Reviews, 3*(2), 167–205.

Weiss, S. K. (2013). Sleep starts and sleep talking. In *Parasomnias* (pp. 139–154). New York: Springer.

Welham, J., Isohanni, M., Jones, P., & McGrath, J. (2009). The antecedents of schizophrenia: A review of birth cohort studies. *Schizophrenia Bulletin, 35*(3), 603–623. https://doi.org/10.1093/schbul/sbn084

Westen, D. (1998). The scientific legacy of Sigmund Freud: Toward a psychodynamically informed psychological science. *Psychological Bulletin, 124*(3), 333.

Whelan, R., Conrod, P. J., Poline, J.-B., Lourdusamy, A., Stephens, D., & Al, E. (2012). Adolescent impulsivity phenotypes characterized by distinct brain networks, *15*(6). https://doi.org/10.1038/nn.3092

White, T., Magnotta, V., Bockholt, H., Williams, S., Wallace, S., Ehrlich, S., . . ., & Lim, K. (2011). Global white matter abnormalities in schizophrenia: A multisite diffusion tensor imaging study. *Schizophrenia Bulletin, 37,* 222–232.

Wilson, M. L., & Wrangham, R. W. (2003). Intergroup relations in chimpanzees. *Annual Review of Anthropology, 32*(1), 363–392.

Wincze, J., & Carey, M. (2001). *Sexual Dysfunction: A Guide for Assessment and Treatment* (2nd ed.). New York: Guilford Press.

Wittgenstein, L. (1953). *Philosophical Investigations*. London: Blackwell Publishing.

Wolpe, J. (1958). *Psychotherapy by Reciprocal Inhibition*. Palo Alto, CA: Stanford University. Press.

Wolz, I., Sauvaget, A., Granero, R., Mestre-Bach, G., Baño, M., Martín-Romera, V., Veciana de Las Heras, M., Jiménez-Murcia, S., Jansen, A., Roefs, A., & Fernández-Aranda, F. (2017). Subjective craving and event-related brain response to olfactory and visual chocolate cues in binge-eating and healthy individuals. *Scientific Reports*, 7, 41,736. https://doi.org/10.1038/srep41736

Woollett, K., & Maguire, E. A. (2011). Acquiring "the Knowledge" of London's layout drives structural brain changes. *Current Biology*, 21(24), 2,109–2,114. https://doi.org/10.1016/j.cub.2011.11.018

Woolley, A. W., Chabris, C. F., Pentland, A., Hashmi, N., & Malone, T. W. (2010). Evidence for a collective intelligence factor in the performance of human groups. *Science (New York, N.Y.)*, 330(6,004), 686–688. https://doi.org/10.1126/science.1193147

Wrangham, R. W., Koops, K., Machanda, Z. P., Worthington, S., Bernard, A. B., Brazeau, N. F., Donovan, R., Rosen, J., Wilke, C., Otali, E., & Muller, M. N. (2016). Distribution of a chimpanzee social custom is explained by matrilineal relationship rather than conformity. *Current Biology: CB*, 26(22), 3,033–3,037. https://doi.org/10.1016/j.cub.2016.09.005

Wulff, D. U., De Deyne, S., Jones, M. N., Mata, R., Austerweil, J. L., Harald Baayen, R., …, & Veríssimo, J. (2019). New perspectives on the aging lexicon. *Trends in Cognitive Sciences*, 23(8), 686–698. https://doi.org/10.1016/j.tics.2019.05.003

Wundt, W. (1894/1998). *Lectures on Human and Animal Psychology* (translated from the 1892 ed. of Vorlesungen über die Menschen- und Thierseele by J. E. Creighton, & E. B. Titchener). Bristol, UK: Theommes Press.

Wundt, W. (1896). *Grundriss der Psychologie* [Outlines of Psychology]. Leibzig: Engelma.

Wundt, W. (1896/1897). *Outlines of Psychology* (translated with the cooperation of the author by C. H. Judd). Leipzig, Germany: Wilhelm Engelmann.

Wyman, A. J., & Vyse, S. (2008). Science versus the stars: A double-blind test of the validity of the NEO Five-Factor Inventory and computer-generated astrological natal charts. *The Journal of General Psychology*, 135(3), 287–300. https://doi.org/10.3200/GENP.135.3.287-300

Yang, J., Xu, X., Chen, Y., Shi, Z., & Han, S. (2016). Trait self-esteem and neural activities related to self-evaluation and social feedback. *Scientific Reports*, 6, 20,274. https://doi.org/10.1038/srep20274

Yonelinas, A. P., & Ritchey, M. (2015). The slow forgetting of emotional episodic memories: An emotional binding account. *Trends in Cognitive Sciences*, 19(5), 259–267. https://doi.org/10.1016/j.tics.2015.02.009

Zadra, A., & Stickgold, R. (2021). *When Brains Dream*. New York: Norton.

Zebrowitz, L. A. (2017). First impressions from faces. *Current Directions in Psychological Science*, 26(3), 237–242.

Zelazo, P. D., & Lee, W. S. C. (2010). Brain development: An overview: Handbook of life-span development. In R. M. Lerner (ed.), *Cognition, Biology, and Methods across the Lifespan: Handbook of Life-Span Development* (pp. 89–114). Hoboken, NJ: Wiley.

Zeltser, L. M., & Madra, M. (2018). A framework for elucidating causes and consequences of malnutrition in anorexia nervosa. In *Neurobiology of Abnormal Emotion and Motivated Behaviors* (pp. 92–118). Cambridge, MA: Academic Press.

Zheng, Y., Manson, J. E., Yuan, C., Liang, M. H., Grodstein, F., Stampfer, M. J., Willett, W. C., & Hu, F. B. (2017) Associations of weight gain from early to middle adulthood with major health outcomes later in life. *JAMA*, *318*(3), 255–269. DOI: 10.1001/jama.2017.7092. PMID: 28719691; PMCID: PMC5817436.

Zhu, Y., Zhang, L., Fan, J., & Han, S. (2007). Neural basis of cultural influence on self-representation. *NeuroImage*, *34*(3), 1,310–1,316. https://doi.org/10.1016/j.neuroimage.2006.08.047

Zimmer, C. (2001). *Evolution: The Triumph of an Idea.* New York: HarperCollins.

Intro Glossary

A

accommodation: accommodation is the process by which existing schemas are modified or new ones created.

acquisition: in classical conditioning, the process of pairing a UCS and a CS

action potential: as more electrical changes add together, the size of the electrical potential is increased. At a critical point, an electrical signal—called an action potential—is produced at a location near the cell body. The brain receives, analyzes, and conveys information by using action potentials. When you see something, hear something, feel something, and even smell something, action potentials are involved

addiction: dependence on a substance (or process) in which an individual experiences a strong motivation that results in an active wanting and seeking of the substance, which may be experienced as compulsive

adoption study: research into the phenomenon where dizygotic (DZ) and monozygotic (MZ) twins have been raised apart, providing insights into the environmental and genetic influences on human development and behavior

affect heuristic: the basic idea is that people make a decision based not only on what they think but also on what they feel

aggression: using a life-span perspective with humans, aggression has been studied from infancy to adulthood. Aggression is composed of hostile behavior or attitudes toward another. This includes the aggressive biting seen in children to the aggressive behaviors seen in adults

agoraphobia: the condition in which a person experiences fear or anxiety when in public

agreeableness: as a personality trait it is associated with being sympathetic, trusting, cooperative, modest, and straightforward; as a dimension in the five-factor model (FFM), this dimension ranges from being friendly and compassionate to being competitive and outspoken

alcohol: a liquid created through a process of fermentation; in most humans, the experience of alcohol intake includes pleasant subjective experiences, which are partly related to the effects of alcohol on such neurotransmitters as serotonin, endorphins, and dopamine; alcohol will also decrease inhibition by reducing the effects of the GABA system, which is associated with anxiety

allele: the alternative molecular form of the same gene

allostasis: refers to the body's ability to achieve stability through an active process of change, often involving the brain. This is in contrast to the older term stress in which responses to change were seen as passive and fixed

allostatic load: cumulative wear and tear on the body from responding to stressful conditions

allostatic systems: allostatic systems are designed to adapt to change. The overall stress response involves two tasks for the body: (1) turn on the allostatic response that initiates a complex adaptive pathway; and (2) once the danger has passed, turning off these responses

altruism: behaviors that appear not to benefit the individual. Altruistic behavior is seen across all species. Why would individuals engage in behaviors that did not benefit themselves in terms of survival or passing on their genes?

altruistic punishment: altruistic punishment is when an individual forgoes a personal gain to punish another

amphetamines: stimulants produced in the laboratory that result in positive feelings, a burst of energy, and alertness

anesthesia: a common procedure that is designed to change the level of a person's consciousness. Combining the ability to control anesthesia with current brain-imaging techniques has opened up new ways to study levels of consciousness

animal personality: recently, a number of researchers have begun to explore individual differences in animals, which is referred to as animal personality. Personality is used with animals in the same way as with humans. That is, behaviors that are consistent over time is the focus of study. A number of researchers have sought to describe personality traits of animals including applying the five-factor model to animals. In general, it is suggested that personality factors can play an important role in evolution

anonymity: a principle that requires that the personal identity of a given participant in a research study be kept separate from his or her data

anorexia nervosa: a serious eating disorder involving the restriction of food, a weight that is below normal, a fear of gaining weight, a lack of recognition of the seriousness of current body weight, and a distorted perception of one's body

anterograde amnesia: a type of amnesia in which the person is not able to form new memories

antisocial personality disorder: one of the dramatic emotional personality disorders (Cluster B); typically involving repeated participation in illegal acts, deceitfulness, impulsiveness, hostility and aggression, engagement in dangerous acts, irresponsible behavior, and absence of remorse

anxiety: anxiety is to be afraid of what might happen. It is about the future whereas fear typically has a stimulus in the present. With anxiety, there is often no stimulus in front of us. With anxiety, the stimulus is in our mind. However, our cognitive and emotional consideration of a negative possibility does not make it any less real. Our body, mind, and emotions experience our ideas as real possibilities. Fear and anxiety involve high-level as well as more primitive brain processes

aphasia: the loss of ability to understand or express certain aspects of speech related to damage in the brain

Asperger's syndrome: diagnosis (no longer used in DSM–5) given to those individuals with ASD who tend to be more intelligent and display higher functioning in terms of social processes

assimilation: assimilation is the process by which new experiences are made part of existing schemas

assortative mating: assortative mating suggests that humans do not randomly choose partners but choose partners like themselves on some selected trait. It is one possible mechanism suggested by researchers to explain what leads to the stability of personality traits across generations

attachment: the quality of the relationship between an infant and parent or primary caregiver

attention deficit hyperactivity disorder (ADHD): a disorder of childhood that includes two major dimensions: inattention, and hyperactivity and impulsivity

attributions: an attribution is how we explain events in the world. In this way, we create causal explanations for what we experience and do

autism spectrum disorder (ASD): the DSM–5 diagnosis for a neurodevelopmental disorder in which individuals have difficulty in three separate areas: (1) social interactions, (2) communication, and (3) behavioral processes

autonomic nervous system (ANS): a division of the nervous system that innervates a variety of organs including the adrenal medulla that results in the release of catecholamines (norepinephrine and epinephrine) from the terminal of sympathetic nerves

availability heuristic: this bias is simply our tendency to use information that we can quickly access in our minds

axon: underlying the gray matter are the axons which transfer information throughout the brain

B

behavior: simply the way we act. Behavior includes our actions and those of others in a variety of situations. We see behavior all around us and make inferences about its meaning

behavioral and experiential perspective: examines the behavior and experience observed in psychopathology, especially the manner in which the signs and symptoms of a particular disorder are seen in a similar manner throughout the world

behavioral economics: a primary focus of economics is the consideration of decision and choice. Unlike traditional economics, which suggests that humans optimize their choice in a rational manner, behavioral economics uses behavioral and neuroscience research to understand the factors involved. That is, people do not make decisions in isolation, but in relation to other choices as well how these choices are framed and the effort required

behavioral genetics: the study of genetic and environmental contributions to behavior. A fundamental question addressed is the manner in which genes and the environment work together to shape behavior

behavioral perspective: a psychological approach focused only on actions and behaviors, not internal processes or aspects of consciousness

behaviorism: at the beginning of the 1900s, behaviorism adopted a strict form of empiricism, the idea that knowledge should be derived through our sensory processes. The idea was that psychology could become a science like physics, but all that should be studied is observable behavior. This was in direct opposition to the use of introspection

binge-eating disorder: characterized by the consumption of large amounts of food and the sense that one cannot control his or her eating behavior

biopsychosocial: in 1977 in the scientific journal Science, George Engel introduced the term biopsychosocial which refers to biological, psychological, and social variables. An integrative perspective that includes all three of these domains can offer a fuller picture of human behavior and experience

bipolar disorder: previously referred to as manic-depressive disorder; a mood disorder characterized by the experience of both depression and mania

blind controls: research participants who do not know whether they are in the experimental group or the control (placebo) group

bodily kinesthetic intelligence: one of Gardner's multiple intelligences, bodily kinesthetic intelligence entails the potential of using one's whole body or parts of the body to solve problems. It is the ability to use mental abilities to coordinate bodily movements

body mass index (BMI): a measure of obesity; an indirect measure of body fat based on a person's height and weight

borderline personality disorder (BPD): one of the dramatic emotional personality disorders (Cluster B); characterized by an instability in mood, interpersonal relationships, and sense of self

brain stem: the brain stem includes the midbrain, pons, and medulla. These structures are involved in basic life functions, including breathing, digestion, levels of arousal, pleasure, and physiological processes such as heart rate and blood pressure. Movements controlled by the brain stem tend to be whole body movements rather than the finer hand movements connected with neocortical control. Across species, movements related to the brain stem tend to be more of an instinctual nature, such as those seen in a startled organism

bulimia nervosa: an eating disorder involving periods of overeating in which the person feels out of control, followed by purging

bystander intervention: understanding the factors involved in helping led to a series of studies examining bystander intervention. Bystander intervention research predicts the likelihood that someone will actively address a situation they view as problematic. In general, it has focused on the situational factors that influence whether a person will intervene or not

C

cannabis: a plant species also referred to as marijuana; the resin is referred to as hashish; the main psychoactive ingredient in cannabis is THC

case study: a research method that typically focuses on recording the experiences and behaviors of one individual

cell assembly: core element of Donald Hebb's model of learning and memory: The basic model suggests that when one neuron in the brain excites another one nearby repeatedly, then the connection between the two is strengthened. This came to be described as "cells that fire together wire together." One implication of this is that even if only a few cells of a well-established cell assembly are activated, this has the potential to activate the other neurons in the entire cell assembly. Thus, being able to remember one aspect of an event may lead to your remembering of the entire event. One implication of Donald Hebb's work is that memories of related items are associated with one another, and these associations appear not only in our cognitions but also in our brain

cell body: an aspect of a neuron. The cell body contains a nucleus, which includes deoxyribonucleic acid (DNA) and other substances, and also mitochondria that are involved in supplying energy

central executive network: the neural network involved in performing such tasks as planning, goal setting, directing attention, performing, inhibiting the management of actions, and the coding of representations in working memory

central nervous system (CNS): the central nervous system, which includes the brain and spinal cord, develops during the first month of pregnancy to form the spinal cord and the brain

cerebellum: Involved in the coordination of movement, the cerebellum (little brain) is located at the base of the skull. It receives inputs from almost all areas of the cortex and allows for the smooth movement of our bodies

chromosomes: thread-like structures located inside the nucleus of animal and plant cells. Each chromosome is made of protein and a single molecule of deoxyribonucleic acid (DNA). Passed from parents to offspring, DNA contains the specific instructions that make each type of living creature unique

chunking: Chase and Simon studied chess players. They discovered that the expert chess players were better able than novices to reproduce the location of pieces in the middle of a game or at the end of a game. The experts did this by chunking the chess pieces into meaningful patterns. That is, they organized the chess pieces into groups. it was not the experts' memory ability that made the difference, but their ability to chunk the material into meaningful group

circadian: comes from Latin and can be translated as "about a day." A circadian rhythm is a cycle that happens each day as with adult sleep patterns

circadian rhythm disorders: these disorders result in the person being unable to sleep at the desired time. However, once the person falls asleep, they experience the normal sleeping pattern

classical conditioning: the pairing of the unconditioned stimulus with a neutral stimulus eventually causing the neutral stimulus to produce the same response

client-centered therapy or person-centered therapy: a treatment approach in psychology characterized by the therapist's empathic understanding, unconditional positive regard, and genuineness

clinical psychology: although humans have created theories of mental disorders for centuries, it was Sigmund Freud (1856–1939) who influenced early thinking in clinical psychology. Clinical psychologists assess and treat mental, emotional, and behavioral disorders. They may focus on a particular disorder such as anxiety or schizophrenia. They may also focus on particular groups such as adolescents who consider suicide, or older individuals who are seeking new experiences, or groups that feel left out by society

cocaine: a stimulant that comes from the naturally occurring coca plant largely grown in South America; its psychoactive effects include a mental alertness, heightening sensory experiences, and increased heart rate

cognitive behavioral perspective: a treatment perspective that suggests that dysfunctional thinking is common to all psychological disturbances; by learning in therapy how to understand one's thinking, it is possible to change the way one thinks as well as one's emotional state and behaviors

cognitive behavioral therapy (CBT): a therapy based on the cognitive behavioral perspective, directed at changing the individual's faulty logic and maladaptive behaviors

cognitive development: Piaget is considered to have created the study of cognitive development which refers to the way we reason and use language, as well as traditional intellectual abilities such as memory and problem solving

cognitive dissonance: according to Festinger, cognitive dissonance is an unpleasant state that occurs when a person realizes that attitudes, actions, or beliefs are inconsistent

cognitive neuroscience: the addition of cognitive psychology with brain imaging and other physiological techniques came to be called cognitive neuroscience

cognitive psychology: by the 1960s, a number of psychologists sought to understand how thinking, attention, perception, problem solving, and other such internal processes influence both human reasoning and action. The cognitive perspective offered a broader approach to understanding human behavior and experience

color blind: some individuals use only two of the three light sources to match colors. These individuals are commonly called color blind. Some color-blind individuals match colors to a standard color by using only green and blue light while others use only blue and red light. These individuals are called dichromats. Color blindness is found more often in males than females, since it is caused by a recessive allele on the X chromosome

comorbid: descriptive term used when an individual has more than one disorder at the same time

compensation: in order to solve problems, older individuals use their brains differently. In order to optimize their performance on tasks, older adults use additional neural circuitry. When older adults use just the brain areas that are activated in younger individuals, they do not perform the tasks as well as younger adults

compulsions: repetitive behaviors that one uses to respond to obsessive thoughts with the goal of decreasing anxiety

concrete operations: in Piaget's third stage of development, children can move their thinking beyond themselves and deal with the nature of concrete objects. With the schema to perform abstract operations comes the fourth stage—formal operations

conditioned response (CR): after a number of times of pairing, the conditioned stimulus alone will produce the natural response. This response is referred to as a conditioned response (CR)

conditioned stimuli (CS): events that happen at about the same time as an unconditioned stimulus could themselves produce a response after a number of pairings

cones: photoreceptors related to daytime vision. In each type of cone, the chemical sensitive to light is sensitive to a different frequency. This gives us the ability to experience color. Cones also allow you to see with high-spatial acuity, which gives you the ability to see detail. Cones are located in a more central region of the retina called the fovea.

confidentiality: (1) a principle that requires that the scientist not release data of a personal nature to other scientists or groups without the participant's consent; (2) the principle that the health care professional is not to discuss information learned in a therapy session in any other context

confirmation bias: if we have a strongly held belief, we are more likely to see information that supports our views

confound: a factor that systematically biases the results of experimental research

confound hypothesis: a conceptual question that asks if results of an experiment could have been influenced by a factor other than the independent variable (IV)

confounding variables: unintended factors not chosen by the experimenter, but which influence the independent variable (IV)

conscientiousness: as a personality trait, it is associated with being diligent, disciplined, well-organized, punctual, and dependable; as a dimension in the five-factor model (FFM), this dimension ranges from being efficient and organized to being easygoing and careless

consciousness: psychologists define consciousness as being aware and knowing that you are involved in a particular event. A change in the scientific study of consciousness began with the advent of a scientific psychology. Individuals such as William James began to ask questions concerning the function of consciousness rather than its physical properties. Freud described three types of consciousness: (1) conscious awareness, (2) latent consciousness or pre-consciousness, and (3) unconscious processes. More recently, with the development of neuroscience techniques for understanding brain function, consciousness has become a more popular topic of scientific study

consolidation: psychologists describe long-term memory processes in terms of four separate steps: encoding, storage, consolidation, and retrieval. The process by which the information stored becomes more stable, consolidation takes place in the brain on two levels: (1) the first level involves structural changes at the synapse, and (2) the second level involves a reorganization of long-term memories over brain networks. Sleep improves memory consolidation

continuous reinforcement: if reinforcement follows every operant response, it is referred to as continuous reinforcement. Typically, continuous reinforcement is used to shape and train the animal to perform the desired response

control group: in a research experiment, the group that is treated exactly like the experimental group except for not experiencing the independent variable (IV) being studied

cooperation: cooperation is helping others even when it does not help ourselves. With extensive research on bees, ants, and humans, it became clear that, in addition to self-preservation and sexuality, there were also instinctual programs for social processes related to cooperation. Understanding cooperation has been a daunting task for evolutionary psychology and there has been a lot of research in the evolution of cooperation and non-cooperation

corpus callosum: the fiber tract that connects the left and right hemispheres of the brain

correlation coefficient: a statistic ranging from -1 to +1 that indicates the degree of association between two variables

correlational research: a research method designed to measure how specific factors are associated with one another

correspondence bias: the tendency for individuals to see that how another person acts reflects their internal thoughts and feelings

critical or sensitive periods: the fact that the lock and key only work for a limited temporal period in imprinting and other similar phenomena

crystallized intelligence: the second factor of intelligence for Cattell was crystallized intelligence which reflects the ability of a person to acquire knowledge available in his or her culture, for example, the ability to use tools, know the meaning of words, or understand cultural practices

D

debriefing: the process of informing a participant after the experiment about the nature of the experiment, clarifying any misunderstanding, and answering any questions that the participant may have concerning the experiment; a necessary and important aspect of deception experiments

deception: although we don't usually think of cheating as being pervasive, Robert Trivers suggests that deception is a wide-spread feature of communication within many social species. Deception in this case is to make things seem as they not

deception research: research in which participants are led to believe that the purpose of the study or their performance in the experiment is something different from the actual case

deep brain stimulation (DBS): a treatment for depression in which electrodes are placed in the brain and connected to a pulse generator in the chest, which influences electrical activity in certain parts of the brain

deep structure: the meaning of speech is called deep structure. There are a variety of ways (surface structure) of saying something that would convey the same meaning (deep structure)

default or intrinsic network: neural network that is active during internal processing

defense mechanisms: their purpose is to reduce neurotic anxiety. Thus, repression, or the process of inhibiting anxiety-producing ideas, underlies all defense mechanisms

delusions: beliefs without support for their occurrence and which are at odds with the individual's current environment

demand characteristics: bias that occurs when a participant's response is influenced more by the research setting than by the independent variable (IV)

dendrites: a part of a neuron. The dendrites (from the Greek word for tree) are attached to the soma and receive information from other cells

deoxyribonucleic acid (DNA): a molecule that provides information necessary to produce proteins, which are involved in growth and functioning

dependent variable (DV): bias that occurs when a participant's response is influenced more by the research setting than by the independent variable (IV)

depersonalization: the perception of not experiencing the reality of one's self; this experience can include feeling detached or observing one's self as an outside observer

depersonalization-derealization disorder: depersonalization and derealization are seen as normal responses to many types of acute stress. However, when they cause distress or impairment in important areas of one's life, they qualify as a DSM disorder

derealization: the experience that the external world is not solid; one's world is experienced with a sense of detachment or as if in a fog or a dream, or in other ways distorted or unreal

descriptive statistics: statistics that define the nature of the number that we are examining. You use descriptive statistics all the time in terms of your weight, your grades, and the amount of money you spend. Descriptive statistics allow us to characterize numbers in terms of frequency and variability

dialectical behavior therapy (DBT): treatment approach for borderline personality disorders developed by Marsha Linehan; the cornerstone of DBT therapy is based on problem solving and acceptance of the experience of the moment

diffusion tensor imaging (DTI): procedure that uses the magnetic resonance imaging (MRI) magnet to measure fiber tracts (white matter) in the brain

dissociation: experiencing a disruption in our normal ability to integrate information from our sensory and psychological processes such as memory and awareness

dissociative amnesia: an inability to recall important autobiographical information

dissociative identity disorder (DID): a developmental disorder where one consistent sense of self does not occur—that is, the person does not experience her thoughts, feelings, or actions in terms of a well-developed "I" or sense of self and instead experiences different "personalities" at different times; previously referred to as multiple personality disorder

dizygotic (DZ) twins: twins who arise from the situation in which two different eggs are fertilized by two different spermatozoa; these are called fraternal twins since their shared genes are approximately 50%—the same as that between any two siblings

door-in-the-face technique: a technique used to bring about compliance. It is also called reciprocal concessions. The situation in which a small request is more likely to be accepted if it follows a larger one that has been rejected

dopamine: a type of neurotransmitter, dopamine is released in the brain and was initially thought to be the neurobiological correlate of reward or pleasure. Recent research suggests that the presence of dopamine signals to the person that something good is about to happen. Thus, dopamine is not so much associated with pleasure as with the expectation of pleasure. On a neuroscience level, studies show the rewarding effect of drugs is their ability to increase dopamine

double-blind experiment: research procedure in which participants do not know whether they are in the experimental group or the control (placebo) group, and the researchers involved in the study also do not know which participants are in which group

doubt: to question ideas and research and ask whether factors other than the ones that were originally considered might have influenced the results

dreams: are experienced during sleep and reflect mainly involuntary images, ideas, feelings, and sensations. In dreams, we are aware of the unfolding situation in front of us; we experience ourselves being part of the action unlike our daydreams or mind-wandering when we are awake; we participate in the experiences of the dream; we have emotional reactions and experience it as real, however, we would not say it was reality

dynamic system theory: Esther Thelen sought to integrate an understanding of motor movement with advances in the neurosciences, biomechanics, and the study of perception and action. The emphasis for the dynamic system approach is to ask how all of our different body parts work together to produce stability and change

E

electroconvulsive therapy (ECT): a treatment for depression in which electrical current is passed through the brain for a brief period

electroencephalography (EEG): a technique for recording electrical activity from the scalp, which measures the electrical activity of the brain at the level of the synapse

emotion-focused therapy (EFT): also known as process-experiential therapy; in this therapy, emotion is viewed as centrally important in the experience of self, as either adaptive or maladaptive, and as the crucial element that brings about change and management of emotional experiences

emotions: emotion is defined as a subjective or internal experience that is accompanied by physiological changes

empirically based treatments or empirically based principles: these terms refer to treatments and their aspects for which there is scientific evidence that the treatment is effective

empiricism: the idea that knowledge should be derived through our sensory processes. That is, it is better to learn from observation than to just believe what one has been told

encode: to lay out the process by which a particular protein is made; this is the job of a gene

encoding: psychologists describe long-term memory processes in terms of four separate steps: encoding, storage, consolidation, and retrieval. The first step, encoding, is the process by which information is attended to and connected with other information in memory

endocrine system: a system of glands located throughout our body

endorphin: our brains contain receptors that are sensitive to the actual drugs of addiction. Our brains make a substance, called endorphins, that is actually like morphine. Endorphin is a combination of the word for internally produced—endogenous—and the ending syllable of morphine

epigenetic inheritance: a form of inheritance by which factors largely influenced by the environment of the organism that turn the genes on and off can be passed on to the next generation without influencing DNA itself

episodic memory: a type of long-term memory in which we remember events that we have personally experienced. Episodic memory is also called autobiographical memory

ethics: the study of proper action

evolution of cooperation: using the prisoners' dilemma game, Axelrod and Hamilton looked at the evolution of cooperation. That is, how did cooperation evolve over evolutionary time. They suggested that the evolution of cooperation can be conceptualized in terms of three separate questions related to robustness, stability, and initial viability

existential-humanistic approach: one critical aspect of the choices we make according to the existential-humanistic approach is our ability to be true to one's self. One emphasis was how to live in the present and consider one's choices

existential-humanistic perspective: psychological therapy that focuses on the experience of the person in the moment and the manner in which he or she interprets the experiences; it emphasizes processing and understanding both internal and external experiences of human life

existentialism: the existential movement began in Europe in the 1800s and gained followers after World War II. The major focus of existentialism was the nature of human nature and the meaning of life. One critical question of existentialism focused on the basic experience of being alive and living life

experience: experiences are related to our internal thoughts and feelings. Some of our experiences are similar to those of others. Other experiences are rare but still can be understood through the scientific methods available to psychologists. Unlike actions that we can observe, experiences are internal and take many forms

experimental design: Somewhat like a blueprint, the experimental design directs the procedures and gives form to the experiment. In essence, an experimental design is a plan for how a study is to be structured. In an outline form, a design tells us what will be done to whom and when

experimental group: a group that receives the independent variable (IV) in a study using the experimental method

experimental method: scientific research technique in which the influence of an independent variable (IV) on a dependent variable (DV) is determined, using carefully structured conditions

experimenter effects: bias that occurs due to the experimenter's expectations

explicit memory: information that we can consciously bring forth from memory. Episodic memory and semantic memory are grouped under the larger heading of explicit memory. Explicit memory is also referred to as declarative memory

external or situational attribution: the case where a person's behavior is attributed to external factors. If you said your grade on a test was low because you were not given enough time, you would be attributing your behavior to an external or situational factor

external validity: also known as generalizability, the ability to apply the results from an internally valid experiment to other situations and other research participants

extinction: the process by which, after a period of time, the conditioned stimulus, when presented alone, will no longer produce the response

extraversion: as a personality trait, it is associated with sociability, cheerfulness, energy, and a sense of fun; as a dimension in the five-factor model (FFM), this dimension ranges from being passive, quiet, and inner-directed to being active, talkative, and outer-directed

extrinsic motivation: to perform behaviors for the seeking of rewards

F

facts: general conclusions drawn from observations

false memory: a false memory is one that is experienced as any other memory and you believe it to be true

falsification: the philosophical position that the goal of science is to falsify hypotheses. A major proponent of this position is Karl Popper. It is further suggested that, to be scientific, a hypothesis must be stated so that it can be falsified through research

fear: fear typically has a stimulus in the present. With fear, we see a snake and become apprehensive. We look down from a tall building and feel unease. Fear and anxiety involve high-level as well as more primitive brain processes

fear of missing out (FOMO): when not connected, some individuals feel left out and experience the fear of missing out (FOMO). That is, they are concerned that an event is happening without being a part of it. This fear has been seen in adolescents and young adults around the world

fight or flight response: the overall stress reaction in which the body prepares you either to fight or to leave the scene

figure–ground relationship: our perceptual system organizes ambiguous stimuli in a definite manner. The famous Rubin's vase image clearly demonstrates that given this ambiguous set of stimuli, our perceptual system will organize it in one of two ways, either as two faces or as a vase. When we see faces, the vase becomes the ground and is no longer viewed as a vase. The opposite is true when we see the vase

five-factor model (FFM) or the Big 5: a model of personality based on a factor analytic approach to personality developed by Robert McCrae and Paul Costa, which suggested five major personality dimensions: extraversion, neuroticism, openness, agreeableness, and conscientiousness

fixed-interval schedule: in operant conditioning, using a fixed interval schedule, the animal receives a reinforcement after a certain amount of time

fixed-ratio schedule: in operant conditioning, using a fixed ratio schedule, the animal receives a reinforcement every certain number of times

fluid intelligence: Cattell suggested that general intelligence is made up of two separate factors. The first factor is referred to as fluid intelligence which reflects the ability to perceive relationships with previous specific experience

Flynn Effect: IQ has changed in different groups of individuals over time. If you were to look at just the score that a group of people received on IQ tests across generations, you would see an increase in IQ. That is, people today perform much better on IQ tests than did those of earlier generations. This has been referred to as the Flynn Effect after James Flynn who studied this effect using the major IQ tests in the United States. At this point no single answer to the Flynn Effect has been demonstrated

foot-in-the-door technique: a technique used to bring about compliance. This technique is based on the fact that if you can get someone to agree to a small request, then that person is more likely to agree to a larger request

framed: a critical factor in terms of how we make decisions is the way it is presented or framed

free-gift technique: a technique used to bring about compliance. This is a situation in which you are given a small gift from an organization, such as a calendar, address labels, or even a dollar in the solicitation, requesting that you give money to the organization or if you do an unexpected favor for someone, they are more likely to comply with your requests

frontal lobe: the frontal lobe, located at the front of the cortex, is involved in planning, higher order cognitive processes such as thinking and problem solving, as well as moral and social judgments

functional fixedness: to be fixed on a limited view of how an object is used is referred to as functional fixedness. Although functional fixedness may hurt our ability to solve insight problems, it does have the evolutionary value of helping us limit our alternatives. This saves us valuable energy and time

functional magnetic resonance imaging (fMRI): a brain imaging technique that measures increased blood flow in active areas of the cortex by determining the ratio of hemoglobin with and without oxygen

functionalism: William James was particularly interested in the functional aspects of psychological processes, asking the question what purposes specific psychological processes serve. He distinguished between the more long-term cause or function of the behavior and an immediate cause of a behavior

fundamental attribution error or person bias: individuals tend to see the behavior of others as internally directed even when there might be evidence for external influences. It is also known as correspondence bias since there is a tendency for individuals to see that how another person acts reflects their internal thoughts and feelings

G

"g" or general intelligence: Spearman's global factor of intelligence. He saw "g" as an energy or power that was available to the entire brain. In essence, "g" refers to the situation in which someone who does well in one domain tends to perform well in others

General Adaptation Syndrome (GAS): Selye's model of how the body reacts similarly to a variety of different stressors in three stages: the alarm stage, the resistance stage, and the exhaustion stage

generalizability: also known as external validity, the ability to apply the results from an internally valid experiment to other situations and other research participants

generalization: in fear conditioning, initially, Little Albert was conditioned by pairing a white rat and a loud noise. After this, any furry animal such as a rabbit would produce the same fear response. This is referred to as generalization, first noted by Pavlov. The less the stimulus is like the original conditioned one, the less intense the conditioned response will be, and the more similar the new stimulus is to the original conditioned one, the stronger the response. Since then it has been determined that fear conditioning works better with evolutionarily relevant objects

generalized anxiety disorder (GAD): a disorder characterized by excessive anxiety and worry that has been present for more than 3 months

generative: language is generative, that is, we can generate sentences we have never uttered before as well as understand sentences we have never heard before

genotype: the set of observable characteristics of an individual resulting from the interaction of its genotype with the environment

Gestalt psychology: the German word Gestalt refers to such English terms as pattern, form, structure, and a sense of the whole perception. Gestalt psychology suggested that the whole is always greater than the sum of its parts

gustatory system: the taste system determines the chemical makeup of foods and beverages in terms of nutrient content, agreeableness, and potential toxicity. By definition, taste refers to the five qualities processed by our gustatory system—sweet, bitter, salty, sour, and umami

H

habituation: the situation in which a reflexive action decreases with repeated presentation of the stimulus

hallucinations: sensory experiences that can involve any of the senses and that are at odds with the individual's current environment

hallucinogens: drugs such as mescaline, LSD, and ecstasy that are able to alter perception, mood, and cognitive processes in often unpredictable ways; also called psychedelics

healthy self: in DSM–5, the healthy self is described in terms of a Self and Interpersonal Functioning Continuum, which includes the aspects of identity, self-direction, empathy, and intimacy

hearing or audition: the manner in which we detect sounds. The auditory system is not only able to detect whether a sound is present but also where the sound is coming from

hemispheric specialization: the left and right hemispheres of the human brain are specialized for different tasks. The left hemisphere is involved in language processing and other serial processes. The right hemisphere processes spatial tasks and other global processes

heritability: heritability is about individual differences. In each generation genetic factors would result in some individuals being taller than others and these individuals would have come from the same family. In the next generation that family would also have even taller children as compared to others. The technical estimate of heritability is a statistic that describes the proportion of a given trait's variation within a group of people that is attributable to variations in the genes

heuristic: the procedures for arriving at a decision are called heuristics. Developed by Simon, a heuristic is a set of rules that help us to understand how people make decisions. Heuristics help humans perform a task with reduced effort

homeostasis: a concept that reflects the manner in which a physiological system tends to center around a set point, like a thermostat that regulates temperature in a building

hormones: endocrine glands release biochemical substances into the bloodstream called hormones that change the physiology and behavior of specific organs as they move throughout the body. These hormones can stimulate our immune system, influence male and female sex characteristics, affect blood sugar levels, and perform a number of other functions

HPA (hypothalamic pituitary adrenal) pathway: the brain has two major pathways in which it influences peripheral physiology. These pathways are distinct but interrelated. The second pathway activated in times of stress is slower and referred to as the HPA which includes the hypothalamus, pituitary, and adrenal

human origins and historical cultural perspective: in adopting this perspective for examining psychological processes, we can think about how certain ways of behaving and seeing the world might be adaptive. We can think about how the experiences of those who came before us might have influenced how our nervous system functions. The human origins and historical cultural perspective gives us a way to think about cultural factors. We can also think about how humans are both similar and different to other animals with whom we share a variety of genetic and physiological mechanisms. The human origins and historical cultural perspective leads to some interesting questions related to psychology. For example, given the evolutionary process of survival of the fittest, we ask why particular mental disorders continue to exist

humanistic: one important aspect of the humanistic tradition was an emphasis on choice. Throughout our lives, we all make critical choices that determine who we are and how we live our lives. In this way, we express our personality by the choices we make. For the humanistic psychologists, these choices can lead to positive as well as negative outcomes

humanistic perspective: in the 1950s, Carl Rogers brought the humanistic perspective to the forefront. He emphasized the theme of human potential by saying that psychotherapy is a releasing of an already existing capacity in a potentially competent individual. He emphasized the relationship between the therapist and client as a critical key to effective therapy

hypersomnia: a class of sleep disorders that is characterized by a lack of sufficient sleep

hypothesis: a statement or expectation developed in relation to an explicit or implicit theory concerning potential outcomes of an experiment (that is, the relationship between the independent and dependent variable)

I

Illusions: in some ways all of what we "see" is an illusion or construction of our nervous system because vision is based both on a top-down process in which our expectations help to form what we see and on a bottom-up process by which our sensory system puts together the individual features into a coherent scene.

imitation learning: a brain system response to observing an action that leads to a motor representation of the observed action, essentially turning a visual image into a motor plan

Implicit Association Test (IAT): the Implicit Association Test (IAT) measures attitudes and beliefs that people may be unwilling or unable to report, that is, implicit attitudes. The IAT may be especially interesting if it shows that you have an implicit attitude that you do not know about

implicit memory: implicit memory has the ability to influence our behavior and experiences without our being aware of the learning taking place. We can perform a number of motor tasks without consciously remembering how to perform them. This type of memory is referred to as procedural memory which is a type of implicit memory. Implicit memory also includes classical conditioning and priming

imprinting: a built-in pattern in which birds follow an object, usually their mother, which moves in front of them during the first 18-36 hours after birth. Imprinting and similar phenomena work like a lock and key. Once in place, it is almost irreversible and cannot be changed

independent variable (IV): the variable that is defined by the experimenter and thus is outside the experimental situation (and therefore is independent)

indirect reciprocity: a form of reciprocity where help is given to individuals based on their reputation

inference: the process by which we look at the evidence available and then use logic to reach a conclusion

inferential statistics: a method of analysis that concerns the relationship between the statistical characteristics of the population and those of the experimental sample

informed consent: a prospective participant in psychological research must be given complete information on which to base a decision, including information about what will be required of him or her during the study, and about any potential harm that may come from participation

insight problems: a problem that requires a person to shift his or her perspective and view the problem in a different way. The answer is often a reorganization of the information available and seeing the situation in a new light

insomnia: the most common sleep disorder seen by professionals. It is described in terms of the inability to obtain enough sleep to leave one feeling rested

intelligence: overall, intelligence is defined as the ability to learn from and adapt to our environment by solving problems and predicting what might happen next. This is a broad understanding of intelligence. There is also a narrower definition that refers to how we perform on tests of intelligence and compare to others

internal or dispositional attribution: the situation in which observed behaviors are attributed to the internal state of the person. Saying someone is lazy when they do not get a job would be an example of internal attributions

internal validity: the ability to make valid inferences between the independent variables (IVs) and dependent variables (DVs)

interneurons: neurons that relay information from other neurons are referred to as interneurons, which create circuits to process information in the brain

interpersonal intelligence: one of Gardner's multiple intelligences, interpersonal intelligence is concerned with the capacity to understand the intentions, motivations, and desires of other people. It allows people to work effectively with others

intrapersonal intelligence: one of Gardner's multiple intelligences, intrapersonal intelligence entails the capacity to understand oneself and to appreciate one's feelings, fears, and motivations

intrinsic motivation: to perform behaviors because we enjoy it; being a curious and interested explorer of the world rather than a passive recipient of environmental influences; seeking new information on a variety of levels, including motor, emotional, and cognitive responses; feeling happy when solving a problem or learning something new

introspection: the examination of one's own mental state, which Wilhelm Wundt referred to as internal perception

J

just-noticeable difference or JND: refers to just how much physical difference is needed for you to detect a change in any of our sensory processes including, vision, hearing, and touch

K

kin selection or inclusive fitness: a property can be measured by considering the reproductive success of the individual plus the effects of an individual's actions on the reproductive success of one's relatives

L

law of effect: formulated by Edward Thorndike, it says that, for example, when a cat made a response that led to the opening of the door and food (the satisfying effect), then the cat would be more likely to perform that same response again. The opposite is also true. If the response produces discomfort, then those responses will be reduced

levels of analysis: examination of psychopathology ranging from culture and society at a higher level to the individual at a middle level and physiology and genetics at the lower levels

levels of consciousness: these levels can be discussed in terms of coma, vegetative state, and wakefulness and awareness and represent how well a person is connected with his or her environment at a given time

lifespan development: following an individual across his or her lifespan in a theoretically integrated manner using psychological research

limbic system: Papez believed that in the same way that the occipital lobe processes visual information, the limbic system processes emotional processes. Today, scientists see this system involved in emotion, motivation, memory, and other related processes

linguistic intelligence: one of Gardner's multiple intelligences, linguistic intelligence involves sensitivity to spoken and written language, the ability to learn languages, and the capacity to use language to accomplish certain goals

logic: is the systematic study of valid rules of inference, i.e. the relations that lead to the acceptance of one proposition (the conclusion) on the basis of a set of other propositions (premises). More broadly, logic is the analysis and appraisal of arguments

logical-mathematical intelligence: one of Gardner's multiple intelligences, logical-mathematical intelligence consists of the capacity to analyze problems logically, carry out mathematical operations, and investigate issues scientifically

long-term memory: to have a memory available to us in the future, the information needs to be converted from short-term memory into long-term memory. Information available to us through long-term memory can be relatively permanent

M

magnetic resonance imaging (MRI): brain imaging technique that offers a static image of brain structure

magnetoencephalography (MEG): brain imaging technique that measures the small magnetic field gradients exiting and entering the surface of the head that are produced when neurons are active

major depressive disorder (MDD): a mood disorder characterized by depressed mood for at least 2 weeks in which one feels sad or empty without any sense of pleasure in one's activities

mean: the average of a set of scores

measures of central tendency: there are three measures of central tendency, which is simply a single summary measure that describes a number of scores. These central tendency measures are known as the mean, median, and mode

median: the middle score in a distribution

meditation: historically, it has been a part of religious and spiritual traditions worldwide. In general, meditative techniques can be thought of in terms of three broad approaches: (1) an attempt to reduce awareness as normally experienced; (2) more of an expressive experience as might be seen in free dancing; (3) awareness of all activity is allowed without the attempt to reduce, modify, or react to what is being experienced (called mindfulness in current-day psychology)

memory: learning and memory are processes that go together. Traditionally, they have focused on different aspects of behavior and experience. Memory traditionally has focused on how information is stored and later retrieved

mental disorder: a mental disorder contains five features: (1) a behavioral or psychological syndrome or pattern that occurs in an individual; (2) that reflects an underlying psychobiological dysfunction; (3) the consequences of which are clinically significant distress or disability; (4) must not be merely an expectable response to common stressors and losses or a culturally sanctioned response to a particular event; and (5) that is not primarily a result of social deviance or conflicts with society

meta-analysis: statistical examination of the results of studies taken together and treated as one study. One can also examine the psychological experiences and internal states related to various forms of meditation.

meta-awareness: we can be aware of our awareness. I can experience myself watching something else. In conversations, meta-awareness lets us experience ourselves talking as well as having awareness of the other person at the same time. As such we use our awareness systems as a way to plan and direct our actions and cooperate with others

metacognition: having cognition about our cognition. Shea and his colleagues suggest that metacognition is composed of two systems. The first metacognition system functions out of awareness whereas the second system is able to accomplish a richer number of tasks. System one works quicker and in parallel whereas system two performs action in a serial form

mindfulness: a therapeutic technique involving an increased, focused, nonjudgmental, purposeful awareness of the present moment to observe thoughts without immediately reacting to them

mirror neurons: neurons in your brain that fire as if you had performed the same actions as you observe

mode: the score that occurs with the greatest frequency

modeling: also known as observational learning; when humans imitate the behaviors of others even without reinforcement

monozygotic (MZ) twins: identical twins resulting from the zygote (fertilized egg) dividing during the first 2 weeks of gestation

moral development: based on the idea of stages of cognitive development suggested by Piaget, Kohlberg asked if there are similar stages in moral development. As such, an individual's way of solving a moral dilemma would be different at different ages. The type of reasoning given at one stage would be self-contained and different from that at another stage. Further, with development these stages become more complex and differentiated. He outlined 3 levels of moral development: (1) preconventional morality; (2) conventional morality; and (3) post-conventional morality

moral emotions: research suggests that individuals' shame experiences are more painful and intense than guilt experiences. Since guilt and shame involve transgression against the conventions of the group, these have been called moral emotions

moral judgments: judgments that involve values related to human functioning such as life and death. Pinker suggests that there are two important hallmarks of moral judgments: (1) these judgments are felt to be universal, and (2) the belief that committing immoral acts should be followed by punishment

morpheme: the smallest meaningful unit of a language. A common example would be "ed," which would signal past tense as in talked, or "s," which would signal plural, as in books, or "un," which would signal not, as in unbelievable

motivations: motivation is defined as the process that makes a person move toward a goal-directed behavior

motor neurons: are involved in moving our muscles, which allows us to walk, throw a ball, or send a text

motor strip: in the area of the frontal lobe along the central sulcus is a strip of cortex referred to as the motor strip. Different parts of this strip correspond to movements of different parts of the body

musical intelligence: one of Gardner's multiple intelligences, musical intelligence involves skill in the performance, composition, and appreciation of musical patterns

N

naturalistic intelligence: one of Gardner's multiple intelligences, naturalistic intelligence entails the ability to identify and distinguish aspects of the natural world. This would include weather patterns, types of plants, animals, or rock structure

naturalistic observation: research method based on observing and describing the phenomenon occurring naturally, without manipulating any variables

negative correlation: an association between two variables where a decrease in one variable correlates to a decrease in the other

negative punishment: negative punishment occurs when the likelihood of a behavior is decreased by the removal of an event

negative reinforcement: negative reinforcement occurs when the likelihood of a behavior is increased by the removal of an event

negative symptoms: in schizophrenia, lack of affect in situations that call for it, poor motivation, and social withdrawal. Positive or negative are not evaluative terms when applied to symptoms of schizophrenia. Instead, they indicate either the presence of something unusual such as hearing voices or seeing hallucinations, which would be positive symptoms, or the lack of a normal human process, such as poor motivation or social withdrawal, which would be negative symptoms

network: our brains are not static. A network is simply a group of neurons that becomes active under certain conditions. Networks allow basic human processes such as learning, memory, thinking, planning, feeling, and decision making to take place

networks: there are also connections between the brain areas involved in different sensory processes that give us an integration of sensory processes. Putting these together gives us the feeling of a single event. These specific connections are referred to as pathways and networks. These pathways and networks allow us to see, hear, and feel the world as if it is a coherent whole

neurons: single nerve cells that can transmit information to other neurons. Neurons are central to all brain processes, and are the basis for the brain's communication with the rest of the body

neuroscience perspective: examines what we know about particular psychopathological experience from the standpoint of neuroscience, including the structure and function of the brain, the autonomic nervous system, and a genetic and epigenetic consideration as it relates to psychopathology

neuroticism: as a personality trait, it is associated with a tendency to express distressing emotions and difficulty experiencing stressful situations; as a dimension in the five-factor model (FFM), this dimension ranges from being calm, even-tempered, and comfortable to being worried, temperamental, and self-conscious

neurotransmitters: chemicals released into the synaptic space that are involved in increasing or decreasing the likelihood for action potentials to be produced; they also maintain the communication across the synapse. Their presence or lack is related to particular psychopathological disorders

nociceptors: the cells related to the experience of pain outside of the brain. The brain itself cannot feel pain as it contains no nociceptors

null hypothesis: a statistical hypothesis that is tested to determine if there are differences between the experimental and control groups; the null hypothesis states that there is no difference

O

obedience: in the 1960s, Stanley Milgram conducted a set of obedience experiments to determine how far a participant would go in obeying the instructions of the experimenter to cause harm to a second participant. The second participant was never harmed, but the original participant did not know that during the experiment. The results of the studies were disturbing as to how far participants would go in obeying the experimenter. Subsequently, there has been criticism of the manner in which the Milgram study was conducted and reported

object permanence: in Piaget's theory of development, initially, the child understands something exists only while that object is experienced. When he begins to understand that an object still exists even if it is covered with a cloth or placed in a drawer, this is the beginning of what is referred to as object permanence. We now know that object permanence develops as memory develops

observational learning: also known as modeling; when humans imitate the behaviors of others even without reinforcement

obsessions: persistent, generally unwelcome thoughts or images that come into one's head, which the person experiences as disturbing

obsessive-compulsive and related disorders: some individuals hoard their possessions even if they are of no value. Others are always thinking about their body and particular flaws they believe they have. Still others pick at their skin or pull their hair. Other individuals refuse to step on sidewalk cracks, often wash their hands to prevent germs, or experience unwelcome thoughts coming into their minds. In DSM-5, these conditions are referred to as obsessive-compulsive and related disorders

obsessive-compulsive disorder (OCD): a disorder characterized by repetitive, intrusive thoughts and feelings (obsessions) usually followed by behaviors in response to them (compulsions)

occipital lobe: the occipital lobe is near the back of the brain and toward the bottom. It is involved with the processing of visual information and receives information from our eyes

olfaction: refers to your sense of smell. In your nose are sensory neurons that are responsive to chemicals that we experience as odors

openness: as a personality trait, it is associated with curiosity, flexibility, and an artistic sensitivity, including imaginativeness and the ability to create a fantasy world; as a dimension in the five-factor model (FFM), this dimension ranges from inventive and curious to cautious and conservative

operant behavior: Skinner coined the term operant behavior to refer to the behavior that an organism produces that influences its environment

operant conditioning: Skinner's exemplar experimental procedure. The basic procedure noted that behavior could be elicited or shaped if reinforcement followed its occurrence. This procedure came to be known as operant conditioning

operational definition: a definition that presents a construct in terms of observable operation that can be measured and utilized in research

opioids: psychoactive substances derived from the opium poppy used to control pain and bring on euphoric feelings; more common opioids are heroin, opium, morphine, methadone, and oxycodone

opponent-process theory of color vision: an alternative theory of color vision to the Young–Helmholtz trichromatic theory of color. This theory holds that certain colors result in opposite responses in the visual system.

optic disk or blind spot: the place where visual information leaves the eye. Although there are no receptors in this part of the eye to respond to light, the brain fills in the missing information by using information from the other eye and eye movement. Thus, you see a complete scene without a hole in the image

P

panic attack: a sudden, intense feeling of apprehension, anxiety, or fear; happens without an actual situation that would suggest danger

panic disorder: an anxiety disorder defined by recurrent and unpredictable panic-like symptoms followed by at least 1 month of concern or change in lifestyle

paradigm: Kuhn has pointed out that at any moment in the history of science some questions are overemphasized and others ignored. The topics we study and the types of questions we ask Kuhn called a paradigm

paradigm shift: a paradigm is a set of assumptions that guides the activity until a new revolution (a paradigm shift) takes place. Psychology and the neurosciences have gone through a number of these revolutions

parasomnias: a category of sleep disorders representing a variety of conditions that may leave the person feeling distressed or bring distress to others. In general, these disorders are not related to one another from an underlying physiological or psychological standpoint. Examples include sleep paralysis, night or sleep terrors, sleep walking, sleep talking, and sleep jerks or starts

parasympathetic nervous system: the branch of the autonomic nervous system involved in the restoration of bodily reserves and the elimination of bodily waste

parietal lobe: the parietal lobe, which is toward the back and at the top of the cortex, is involved in spatial processes such as knowing where you are in space and performing spatial problems

partial reinforcement: if reinforcement only sometimes follows the operant response, it is referred to as partial reinforcement

pathological dissociative symptoms: pathological dissociative symptoms are generally experienced as involuntary disruption of the normal integration of consciousness, memory, identity, or perception. These can range from not having a sense of who one is or not remembering large parts of one's past to having no memory of one's personal history or to experiencing a lack of a developmental self. DSM–5 describes three major dissociative disorders: (1) depersonalization—derealization disorder, (2) dissociative amnesia, and (3) dissociative identity disorder (DID)

patterns of attachment styles: attachment patterns can be seen as an internal roadmap or schema through which the person interprets his or her social experiences. Ainsworth described three patterns of attachment styles describing the mother-infant relationship: (1) secure attachment pattern, (2) avoidant attachment pattern, and (3) anxious/ambivalent attachment pattern. A fourth pattern was later added: (4) disorganized/controlling attachment pattern

peer review: scientists pay particular attention to research that has been evaluated by other scientists before it is published. This process is called peer review, and journals that follow this procedure are peer-reviewed journals

perception: the manner in which our brain and nervous system take energy that exists around us and turns it into an experience is a critical aspect of sensation and perception. Sensation refers to the manner in which our receptor system transforms energy into activity that can be interpreted by the brain. Perception is the manner in which the brain makes sense of this activity

peripheral nervous system (PNS): a major division of our nervous system. It includes the somatic nervous system, which sends and receives information to and from the brain. This system also permits our brains to send information to and receive information from internal organs.

person perception: person perception is simply how we categorize others. These categories are processed spontaneously and effortlessly. Traditional categories of person perception include age, gender, and race

personality: the study of personality is the study of internal dispositions or ways of being. Another way of thinking about personality is to consider what we value. Psychologists focus on those aspects of ourselves that can be seen across a number of different situations

personality disorder: an enduring pattern of inner experience and behavior that deviates markedly from the expectations of the individual's culture; the pattern is inflexible, stable, and generally begins in adolescence, and it leads to distress or impairment; characteristics of these disorders are especially apparent when these individuals find themselves in situations that are beyond their ability to cope

phenotype: the phenotype represents the observed traits of the individual including morphology, physiology, and behavior. The focus of psychology has largely been the study of the phenotype

phoneme: the basic sound of a language. There are approximately 100 different phonemes used in all languages around the world. English uses approximately 40 of these phonemes. A phoneme has no meaning other than the sound we process

phonology: the study of the ways phonemes can be combined in a language is called phonology

photoreceptor: a cell that responds when light hits it. One type of photoreceptor was sensitive to low light. These light-sensitive cells, which later evolved as *rods*, allow us to see in dim light. Another type of photoreceptor was produced that required greater illumination. Over time, the receptors of this system differentially became sensitive to different frequencies in the visual spectrum. These were the forerunners of the *cones* in our visual system that allow us to experience colors

pituitary gland: the pituitary gland is a pea-sized gland located at the base of the brain, just below the hypothalamus. The hypothalamus controls the glandular system by affecting the pituitary. The pituitary gland is sometimes called the master gland since it affects other glands of the endocrine system

placebo effect: the phenomenon that some people show psychological and physiological changes just from the suggestion that a change will take place

plasticity: the term that is often used to describe conditions in which processes are open to modification is plasticity

population: in a research study, the larger group of individuals to which the results can be generalized

positive correlation: an association between two variables where an increase in one variable correlates to an increase in the other

positive punishment: positive punishment decreases the likelihood that a particular response will be repeated. The meaning of positive refers to something being added that changes the likelihood of a response

positive reinforcement: giving a reinforcement following a particular behavior that increases the likelihood that the behavior just produced will reoccur. The meaning of positive refers to something being added that changes the likelihood of a response

positive symptoms: in schizophrenia, the presence of such characteristics as hallucinations, delusions, disorganized thinking, and disorganized behavior. Positive or negative are not evaluative terms when applied to symptoms of schizophrenia. Instead, they indicate either the presence of something unusual such as hearing voices or seeing hallucinations, which would be positive symptoms, or the lack of a normal human process, such as poor motivation or social withdrawal, which would be negative symptoms

positron emission tomography (PET): a brain imaging technique that measures the blood flow in the brain that is correlated with brain activity

post-traumatic stress disorder (PTSD): a long-term reaction to traumatic events that lasts longer than 1 month

preoperational stage: Piaget's second stage of development which shows the beginning of symbolic thought

private personality: the private thoughts of a person

proactive interference: proactive interference is the case in which old information inhibits your ability to remember new information

probability: the likelihood that a set of results in an experiment differed from what would be expected by chance

procedural memory: we can perform a number of motor tasks without consciously remembering how to perform them. You ride a bicycle, drive a car, play a musical instrument, or type a text-message without consciously remembering every step. This type of memory is referred to as procedural memory. Procedural memory is a type of implicit memory

process experiential therapy: also known as emotion-focused therapy (EFT); in this therapy, emotion is viewed as centrally important in the experience of self, as either adaptive or maladaptive, and as the crucial element that brings about change and management of emotional experiences

projective technique: a technique is called projective since the person projects onto an image certain ideas and emotions

proteins: the job of a gene is to lay out the process by which a particular protein is made. In other words, each gene is able to encode a protein. Proteins are involved in a variety of processes. Proteins do the work of the body and genes influence their production

pseudoscience: the phenomenon of presenting information as if it is based on science when it is not is referred to as pseudoscience. Pseudoscience is false science

psychoactive substances: there are some plants referred to as psychoactive substances, which change our brain in a manner that influences our consciousness, including thoughts and feelings. Examples include betel nuts, for its nicotine-like effects, cocaine naturally available in coca leaves, and morphine from poppy plants

psychoanalysis: treatment developed by Freud based on the search for ideas and emotions that are in conflict on an unconscious level

psychodynamic approach: psychodynamic psychology is based on the idea that thoughts and emotions basically learned in childhood can influence your behavior and experiences. Others adopted or modified Freud's ideas in their theories and the treatment of their patients

psychodynamic perspective: approach to psychological therapy that emphasizes how behaviors and experience may be influenced by internal processes that are out of awareness, often due to internal conflicts

psychology: the study of behavior and experience. Behavior is what we do. Experiences are related to our internal thoughts and feelings. Behavior and experience always take place within a context.

psychopathology: the scientific study of mental illness and its causes

psychophysics: psychophysics is the study of the relationship between the physical characteristics of a stimulus and the manner in which we experience it

psychosocial stages: one of the first theorists to present a map of lifespan development was Erik Erikson. He suggested that people throughout the world experience eight major psychosocial stages. During each of these stages there is a major conflict or question that must be answered

psychotic disorders: disorders that involve a loss of being in touch with reality and are characterized by abnormal thinking and sensory processes

psychotropic medications: psychotropic medications are those that are used to treat mental disorders. The study of these drugs is the domain of psychopharmacology

purging: an aspect of bulimia where a person eliminates food from the body by such means as vomiting, taking laxatives, diuretics, or enemas

R

random sampling: the selection of participants in an unbiased manner so that each potential participant has an equal possibility of being selected for the experiment

randomization: in an experiment, selection of participants solely by chance to either the experimental group or the control group

range: the measure of dispersion reflecting the difference between the largest and smallest scores in a set of data

rapid eye movement or REM sleep: periods during sleep in which a person's eyes—although closed—move quickly. When individuals were wakened during REM sleep, they were more likely to report having a dream than if wakened during quiet sleep. During REM sleep, EEG looks very different than during quiet sleep. The EEG actually looked more like that seen in wakefulness. Because of this, REM sleep is also referred to as paradoxical sleep

real self: concept developed by Karen Horney that includes who one is and what one appreciates. It is the alienation from the real self that is seen to constitute a key process of neurotic development. It also requires energy to present a false self, which leaves few resources for developing healthy human growth

reciprocal altruism: theory that we help unrelated individuals if we expect them to help us in turn. Our own fitness, in an evolutionary sense, is increased because we have greater chance of surviving and passing on the genes related to these processes

reconstructive memory: we learn information that helps us to adapt, that protects us, that feeds us, that involves our friends, and helps us to find mates. That is, we remember things that have meaning to us. Remembering is a constructive process that allows each recall of information to be a constructive event. We actually recreate each memory as we recall this. This is referred to as reconstructive memory

reinforcement: Skinner's basic procedure of operant conditioning noted that behavior could be elicited or shaped if reinforcement followed its occurrence. Consequently, if these behaviors ceased to be rewarded, the occurrence would decrease

replication: the process whereby a study is performed in different laboratories with different participants and obtains the same results

research hypothesis: the formal statement of the manner in which the dependent variable (DV) is related to the independent variable (IV)

reserve: concept that suggests that the brain can compensate for problems in neural functioning; high functioning or intelligence is often associated with greater reserve

resilience: resilience research seeks to understand how some individuals are able to encounter severe psychological or physical adversity without showing traditional stress effects. One key finding suggests that resilience is associated with the ability to reinterpret both internal and external events in a more positive manner

retina: a part of the eye; light reaches the cornea where it is bent and the lens where it is focused. Both are located at the front of the eye. The object we see is focused on the retina at the back of the eye

retrieval: psychologists describe long-term memory processes in terms of four separate steps: encoding, storage, consolidation, and retrieval. This stage is what we think of when we say we recalled something. Typically, retrieval involves different types of information stored in different places throughout the brain. This information can include sensory, emotional, and cognitive information

retroactive interference: the case in which new information inhibits your ability to remember old information

retrograde amnesia: a type of amnesia in which a person cannot remember events prior to trauma to the brain

ribonucleic acid (RNA): DNA information is carried as RNA, which determines the sequence of amino acids, the building blocks of proteins; it is made up of single strands rather than the dual strands in DNA

right to privacy: in an experiment, this means that information given by a participant to a scientist should be considered a private event, not a public one

rods: photoreceptors related to nighttime vision. Rods allow you to see in dim light. They are much more sensitive than cones to the few photons of light energy available on dark nights. There are many more rods in the peripheral parts of the retina

Rorschach inkblots: a projective test using inkblots; an individual's interpretation of the ambiguous ink patterns is evaluated to identify patterns in underlying thoughts and feelings

S

salience network: the neural network involved in monitoring and noting important changes in biological and cognitive systems

SAM (sympathetic adrenal medullary) system: the brain has two major pathways in which it influences peripheral physiology. These pathways are distinct but interrelated. The first pathway activated in times of stress is more fast acting and is referred to as SAM which involves the sympathetic division of the autonomic nervous system

satiety: the experience of feeling full

scatterplot: a scatterplot is a graph on which the data from each person is plotted

schedules of reinforcement: partial reinforcement can be programmed in relation to the number of responses (ratio) the animal makes or the amount of time (interval) between responses. Skinner examined a number of these patterns, which came to be called schedules of reinforcement. The ratio and interval schedules of reinforcement can be either fixed or variable resulting in four major categories

schema: Piaget introduced the term schema, which refers to how the child sees the world. Although schemas influence our actions, it typically works outside of our awareness. These schemas can be changed as the child interacts with the world and takes in new information

schemas: one traditional view of the self in social psychology is that it is made up of schemas or beliefs about oneself. These schemas help us define who we are and how we see ourselves. Schemas differ for different people

schizophrenia: a debilitating psychotic disorder in which individuals may hear voices, see images not seen by others, believe that others wish to harm or control them, and have bizarre thoughts

schizophrenia spectrum and other psychotic disorders: schizophrenia is part of a broad category of disorders referred to as schizophrenia spectrum and other psychotic disorders. Psychotic disorders involve a loss of being in touch with reality and are characterized by abnormal thinking and sensory processes. Individuals with a psychotic disorder may show delusions, hallucinations, disorganized thinking and speech, abnormal motor behaviors, and negative symptoms. People who do not have schizophrenia may show psychotic symptoms for a brief period of time or for a longer duration. They may also show delusions, affective problems outside the normal range, or simply seem odd to those around them. Psychotic symptoms not part of schizophrenia can be induced through drugs, lack of sleep, and other medical conditions

science: a process of understanding the world through observation and research, which includes developing theories

scientific knowledge: the known facts about a particular subject derived from the scientific method

scientific method: in its simplest form, the scientific method consists of asking a question about the world and then experiencing the world to determine the answer

scripts: we all have ideas of what to expect in different relationships. In social interactions, there are scripts for what we say to one another. These scripts have both a cultural and a universal level

secure base: Bowlby considered the process of attachment as a social-emotional behavior equally as important as mating behavior and parental behavior. For him, attachment was a process in which the mother was able to reduce fear by direct contact with the infant and provide support, called a secure base

self-actualization: Abraham Maslow suggested that beyond basic needs humans also have the need to be recognized by others as well as to acknowledge their own self. He referred to the desire to express one's self in the context of humanity as self-actualization. However, he suggested that self-actualization would only come after basic needs were satisfied

self-concept: social psychology adopted the "I" and "me" distinction as it developed a theory of self-concept. Self was seen as a process that develops as we relate to others in social interactions. It is my "me," which is at the center of my experiences. The self is seen as an adapting process that develops in terms of the social environment in which one lives

self-esteem: self-esteem relates to the evaluation of the self. That is, self-esteem refers to the way we value and accept ourselves. Aspects of self-esteem are thus more affective than cognitive. A desire for self-esteem has been seen as a motivating factor in humans, as noted by both philosophers and psychologists

self-realization: concept developed by Karen Horney related to the process of an individual's realizing, or developing a real self

self-schema: our self-concept is stored in network memory systems that reflect our past experiences. This information is referred to as our self-schema. Some of these characteristics can have very strong connections with the idea of self, while others may be less strongly connected

self-scripts: most people think that they do know themselves and can accurately predict how they would act in a given situation using their self-scripts. However, research in social psychology suggests that that may not be the case. There is clearly some information that is available to us that we refer to as explicit. However, there are other attitudes and stereotypes that are formed outside of awareness, referred to as implicit

self-serving bias: the tendency to see positive events as our making and negative events as situational

semantic memory: a type of long-term memory that relates to impersonal facts and everyday knowledge, that is, information about people, places, and things

semantics: the study of meaning in language—how we understand what is being said. A critical question has been the way in which humans are able to move between the levels of meaning and syntax

sensation: the manner in which our brain and nervous system take energy that exists around us and turns it into an experience is a critical aspect of sensation and perception. Sensation refers to the manner in which our receptor system transforms energy into activity that can be interpreted by the brain. Perception is the manner in which the brain makes sense of this activity

sensitization: the opposite of habituation. For example, if you receive a painful shock, then the next shock would result in a greater response in a number of different systems. The shock could, for example, make a noise seem louder

sensorimotor stage: Piaget's first stage of development is the sensorimotor stage which is characterized by the use of motor actions and the senses

sensory memory: if you were to listen to someone talk, you would retain the words said for just a few seconds as you processed the next words. This is referred to as sensory memory. Sensory memory lasts only a few seconds and takes place in all of our senses. If it involves the auditory system, it is referred to as echoic memory. If it involves the visual system, it is referred to as iconic memory. This is the first step of how we remember information. Sensory memory lasts just long enough for the information to be processed by the brain

sensory neurons: help us to see, feel, and hear the world. Other senses, such as taste and smell, also involve sensory neurons. These neurons send information to the brain that allows us to experience the world

sexuality: a driving force in many species including humans. The way people experience and express themselves sexually. This involves biological, erotic, physical, emotional, social, or spiritual feelings and behaviors. Because it is a broad term, which has varied with historical contexts over time, it lacks a precise definition

shaping: a process by which the animal is led to make the desired response in small steps. It is a common procedure used to train animals to perform any new task. Even a complex performance can be broken down into discrete steps that can be learned through reinforcement

short-term memory: the second step in remembering information is to transform the sensory information and work with it for a short period of time, that is, less than a minute

sleep patterns: evolved in terms of sensory systems. Humans and other animals that use vision as the primary way of finding food and interacting with the world sleep at night. On the other hand, animals such as rats that use nonvisual systems for dealing with the world tend to sleep in the day and look for food at night

small world framework: a model of brain connectivity based on the idea that the ability to socially contact any two random individuals in the world can be accomplished in a limited number of connections

social anxiety disorder (SAD): a disorder characterized by marked fear or anxiety about one or more social situations in which the individual is exposed to possible scrutiny by others

social brain hypothesis: developed in the 1980s, the social brain hypothesis suggests that humans and other primates differ from non-primates principally in the size of their brain as compared to their body size. The basic idea is that complexity of social skills requires a large brain. In our social reactions, we need to be able to interact with a number of individuals. With some of these people we have close relationships and with others we need to pay attention to what they want or expect of us. All of this requires cognitive and emotional effort

social categorizing: an aspect of stereotyping when we place the person in a certain group

social cognitive theories of personality: also referred to social learning theories. These theories emphasize a person's view of the world, that is, the person's cognitive understanding of their environment. The social aspect is that many of these beliefs are the result of our interactions with others. In this sense, they are learned through our interactions. The research related to the social cognitive theory of personality typically focuses on how a person's cognitive views of the world interact with situational variables to produce different behaviors

social emotion: social emotions are those emotions that involve our interactions with other people in a social context. Examples include embarrassment, shame, guilt, jealousy, envy, and pride

social facilitation: social facilitation is defined as an improvement in performance when working with or being accompanied by others as opposed to being alone

social inhibition: social psychologists understand social inhibition in which a person does not act to be a general phenomenon that can be observed across a number of situations even outside the laboratory. In terms of helping, safety in numbers does not apply. Even if a person is alone, the context of the situation can play a role

social loafing: the phenomenon where some individuals do less work than others in a group setting

social shaping hypothesis: this hypothesis developed by Taylor and Gonzaga suggests that early social relationships can shape the manner in which a person's biological, social, and behavioral processes respond to a variety of situations including stressful ones

somatosensory cortex: behind the central sulcus is a strip of cortex in the parietal lobe referred to as the somatosensory cortex. It is this strip that is associated with receiving sensations from various parts of the body

spatial intelligence: one of Gardner's multiple intelligences, spatial intelligence involves the potential to recognize and use the patterns of wide space as well as more confined areas

specific phobia: an anxiety disorder in which an individual experiences fear of or anxiety about a particular situation or object

spinal cord: as the second structure of the central nervous system (the brain is the first) the spinal cord contains fiber tracts within a cavity surrounded by bone through which information from all parts of the body is taken to the brain. Information is also taken from the brain to the muscles and internal organs

split-brain: term to describe people with severe epilepsy whose corpus callosum has been cut to sever connections between the left and right hemispheres of the brain. Overall, following the operation these patients showed a drastic reduction in seizures, but surprisingly, the operation did not appear to cause any changes in the everyday behavior or experience of these patients

spontaneous recovery: in classical conditioning, after a period of presenting the CS without the UCS, resulting in extinction of the CR, after a subsequent delay of a day or two, presenting the CS will once again elicit the CR in what is referred to as spontaneous recovery

standard deviation: a measure of variability calculated by taking the square root of the variance

stereotype activation: an aspect of stereotyping where once we have stereotyped another person, then a series of opinions about the person come into our mind

stereotype application: an aspect of stereotyping where we use the information to understand the situation we have observed or what to expect in an interaction

stereotype bias: stereotype bias reflects negative stereotypes about one's group. The basic idea is that a negative stereotype can influence one's performance

stereotyping: occurs when we make inferences about a group of individuals that share similar characteristics

stigma: negative attitudes and beliefs that cause the general public to avoid others including those with a mental illness

stimulus generalization: the less a stimulus is like the original conditioned one, the less intense the conditioned response will be, and the more similar the new stimulus is to the original conditioned one, the stronger the response.

storage: psychologists describe long-term memory processes in terms of four separate steps: encoding, storage, consolidation, and retrieval. Following encoding, the information must be stored. Storage involves those areas of the brain and neural mechanisms by which memories are retained over time

strange situation: based on infants' reactions to their caregiver, Mary Ainsworth developed the strange situation to research attachment patterns experimentally

stress: commonly defined as a response that is brought on by any situation that threatens a person's ability to cope

stress response: a response to a critical situation that allows an organism to avoid danger or reduce other types of threat

strong altruism: a situation where if someone asks you to help them, and it costs you something, you have to determine whether helping is going to cost you more than the benefit you would receive

structuralism: Edward Titchener's idea that human processes can be broken down into their component parts. The first task for psychology was to ask what the basic elements of experience are. The second task is to determine how these elements combine. And, third, the task is to understand the causal relationships

successful aging: individuals who continue to be productive well into their eighties and nineties; characterized by (1) freedom from disability and disease, (2) high cognitive and physical functioning, and (3) social activity including both having friends and being productive

suicide: the term comes from the Latin meaning to kill oneself

superordinate goals: superordinate goals come into play in the expectation that by getting two groups to work together in meeting those goals, then prior conflict between the groups would decrease

surface structure: the actual spoken words with their grammatical structure is called surface structure. There are a variety of ways (surface structure) of saying something that would convey the same meaning (deep structure)

sympathetic nervous system: the branch of the autonomic nervous system that connects with its target organs through the middle part of the spinal cord, responsible for the fight-or-flight response

synapse: dendrites receive information from other neurons via a biochemical connection through a small gap filled with fluid which is referred to as a synapse

syndrome: a collection of symptoms that occur together and have a particular course of development over time

synesthesia: the condition in which the experience of one sense automatically produces experience in another. For example, some people see a color when they look at numbers or words. Synesthesia is present in about 1% of the population.

syntax: the structure of a sentence and the rules that govern it

T

temperament: we all come into the world with bodily emotional responses all our own. The emotional responses seen early in one's life remain fairly stable. This constellation of emotional and behavioral responses is referred to as temperament

temporal lobe: the temporal lobe is near the front of the brain and toward the bottom. The temporal lobe receives information from our ears and is involved in hearing as well as aspects of language. Other parts of the temporal lobe are involved in the naming of objects from visual information processed in the occipital lobes

tend and befriend response: a response to stress associated with the tendency of females to take care of others and form social connections in times of stress, as opposed to the fight-or-flight response by most males

Thematic Apperception Test (TAT): a projective testing instrument composed of black-and-white drawings of various scenes and people; by evaluating the individual's interpretive responses to the ambiguous drawings, it is possible to gain insight into his or her thoughts, emotions, and motivations including areas of conflict

theory of mind: included in theory of mind is the capacity to infer another's mental state from his or her behavior. Mental state can include purpose, intention, knowledge, belief, thinking, doubt, pretending, liking, and so forth

theory of multiple intelligences: Howard Gardner's theory sought to define intelligence within the context of different domains. His idea was that there exist separate intelligences and a person can be excellent in one ability such as dancing or music and less proficient in another such as mathematics. Gardner suggested there are eight separate intelligences

traits: Allport emphasized traits as the basic units of personality. He saw traits as "generalized and personalized determining tendencies—consistent and stable modes of an individual's adjustment to his environment". He further suggested that traits are based in the nervous system. Although Allport studied personality traits, he also emphasized the uniqueness of the individual

transcranial magnetic stimulation (TMS): a treatment for depression in which an electromagnetic coil is placed on the scalp; from the coil, a magnetic field induces a small electrical current in the first few centimeters of the brain, which depolarizes the neurons

transducers: each of our sensory systems uses different biological processes referred to as transducers to initiate the sensory process. The transducer in the auditory system turns sound waves into mechanical and then electrical impulses. The transducers in our eye turn light energy into electrical impulses

triune brain: MacLean suggested that our current brain can be viewed as having the features of three basic evolutionary formations—reptiles, early mammals, and recent mammals. Through rich interconnections our brains process information in three somewhat independent, although not autonomous, ways

t-test: a technique for determining whether a set of results is different from what would be expected. One of the common statistical techniques used for this is the t-test. A t-test determines the size of the association between two variables in relation to the number of participants in the study

twin studies: a major paradigm of behavioral genetics involving examination and understanding of critical factors related to genetic influences by studying twins

U

unconditioned response (UCR): a naturally occurring response to a naturally occurring stimulus, for example an animal salivating when food is presented

unconditioned stimulus (UCS): a naturally occurring stimulus which will consistently produce a response, for example a food stimulus presented to an animal

uncontrollable stress: a negative experience that the organism cannot influence or control. Research with animals has shown that uncontrollability produced both health problems (for example, gastric ulcers) and depressive symptoms

universal grammar: Noam Chomsky suggested that all humans have a set of innate principles and parameters which he called universal grammar

V

validity: the accuracy of our ideas and our research; the degree to which these are true and capable of support

variability: the manner in which measurements vary within an experimental condition. The statistical measurements of variability are those of standard deviation and variance

variable-interval schedule: in operant conditioning, using a variable interval schedule, each reinforcement would vary such that the average amount of time would be constant

variable-ratio schedule: in operant conditioning, using a variable ratio schedule, the animal receives a reinforcement in a manner that averages out to a certain number

variance: a measure of variability of how much each score varies from the mean

vestibular system: a system that is contained in the inner ear. It contributes to your experience of movement, head position, and where you are in space in relation to gravity. It also functions as an internal guidance device

visual field: nothing more than what you see in front of you without moving your head or eyes. Drawing an imaginary vertical line down the middle of this field creates a right visual field and a left visual field

voluntary participation: a principle stating that a person should participate in an experiment only by free choice, and should be free to leave an experiment at any time, whether or not the experiment has been completed

W

weak altruism: a situation where if someone asks you to help them do something, and it really does not cost you anything, then you will most likely say "yes"

well-defined problems: a type of problem that has a possible or correct solution and that solution can be determined given that there are known constraints with a specific outcome

working memory: the concept of working memory evolved from short-term memory to reflect the systems required to keep things in mind while performing tasks. That is, working memory is all the information you keep in mind while you pay attention to the task you are doing

Y

Young–Helmholtz trichromatic theory of color: the idea that variations in three different light colors lies at the bottom of our experience of color. An alternative theory is referred to as the opponent-process theory of color vision

Index

Note: Locators in *italic* indicate figures, in **bold** tables and in ***bold-italic*** boxes.

A Beautiful Mind 553
acceptance and commitment therapy (ACT) 621, 629
acceptance-based behavioral therapy (ABBT) 621, 629
acquisition, learning 310, 312, 344, 458, *459*
action potential, neural impulses 85–86, *85*, *86*; conditioning 316; EEG 99; myelin sheath 86, 90, *102*, 131, 138, *139*; senses, perception **190**, 195, 209, *213*, 223; synaptic gap 87–89, *88*
actor–observer hypothesis 471, 472–473, 513
Adams, Patricia W. 511–512
addiction 263–265, *265*, 271, 274; causes (first-use age, genetics, environmental) 264; conditioning: addictive drug reaction ***313–314***; dopamine release 264–265, *265*; *DSM-5* disorder 557, ***561***; pattern 263–264, *263*; *see also* psychoactive substances
Ader, Robert 344–345, 449
adolescence, development 165–170, 177–178; brain development 137, 138–139, 140, 167; definition 166; developmental changes 165–170; fear of missing out (FOMO) 479, *479*; hormones 166; moral 168–170, *169*; peers 167; physical changes, puberty 166; risk-taking, impulsivity 166–167, *167*; sexual activity 407–408, *408*; types of learning 139
adrenaline (epinephrine) 87, **87**, 292–293, 429, 446–447, 446–447, *446*, 466
Adrian, Edgar 89
adulthood; *see* lifespan/adulthood, development

affect heuristic 355, 358
African American psychologists 24
aging 173–175, *174*, 381–382, ***382–383***
agoraphobia 569, 602; *see also* phobias
Ainsworth, Mary 161, 177
alcohol 138, 263, 264, 265, 266–267, 274, ***313–314***
Alexander 493
allostasis, allostatic systems/load 442–443, *443*, 467
Allport, Gordon 533–534, 550
alogia 585
alternative/complementary medicine 465
altruism: altruistic punishment 494; kin selection theory, inclusive fitness 490; reciprocal 490, 491; weak/strong altruism 490
American Academy of Sleep Medicine 240
American Psychological Association (APA): African American psychologists 24, 38; career fields 35; female psychologists 23; research guidelines, ethics 73, 74, 79; treatment mental disorders 75, 627, 628
American Psychological Society (APS) 60
amnesia: anterograde 299, 307; Clive Wearing case 277, 278; dissociative 580–581, 602; posthypnotic 258, ***259***; retrograde 299, 307
amphetamines 266, 268–269
An Unquiet Mind 573
anhedonia 274, 585
animal personality ***538–539***
animal research, ethics 75–76, 79
Anna O. case study (Sigmund Freud) 50
antidepressants 623, 629, 639, 646, 649

antisocial personality disorder 593, 594, 604; *see also* personality disorders
anxiety defence mechanism (Freud) 525–526, **526**
anxiety disorders **560**, 565–569; attachment styles, influence 87; deception studies 76; generalized anxiety disorder (GAD) 567–568, 601, 601–602, 628–629, 651; heritability 567; panic disorder 566, 568–569, 602, 631, 651; phobias: specific phobias 569, 602, 630–631, 651; physiological mechanisms 566–567; social anxiety disorder (SAD) 568, 602, 630, 651; treatment 86, 87, 567, 628–631, 651
aphasia 339
APOE gene and intelligence 379–381
arachnophobia 631, 651
Aristotle 6, 7
artificial intelligence (AI) 18–19, 227
Asch experiment/Solomon Ash 470, 502–504, *502, 504*
Aserinsky, Eugene 240, 253
Asperger 597–598
assortative mating 379, 537–538
astrology, astrological traits 520–522
attachment: Bowlby World War II orphan study 159, 161; measuring 161; pattern: disorganized/controlling 162; pattern: secure, avoidant, anxious/ambivalent 161; phases 159; primate studies 160, *160*; Romania adoption study **162–164**, *163–164*; secure base 163–*164*; separation anxiety 161, 566
attention, consciousness and attention 227–230, *229, 230*
attention deficit hyperactivity disorder (ADHD) 558, **560**, 599, 599–600, 601, 604, 646
attribution 472–474; brain functions, research 473–474; cultural differences 473; external/situational attribution 472; fundamental attribution error/correspondence bias 471, 472–473, 513; information types (consensus, consistency, distinctiveness) 514; internal/dispositional 472; self-serving bias 472–473; theory of mind 158–159, 484

audition; *see* hearing, audition
authority ranking, social relationship 499–500
autism spectrum disorder (ASD) 53, 597–599, 604; Asperger 597–598; brain contributions, social brain dysfunctions 599; causes/heritability 598–599; childhood MMR vaccination **53–54**, *54*, 599; definition, characteristics 597, 598; thinking styles (visual, pattern, word/fact) 598; treatment 645
autogenous obsessions 570
automatic thinking 628
autonomic nervous system (ANS) *83*, 444–451, 467; anxiety disorder 565–566; branches: sympathetic/parasympathetic NS 430, 442, 444–445, *445*, 446, 447, 448, 467; emotional responses 426, 430; nervous system, part of *83*; physiology control function, homeostasis 441, 444–445; smell 214; stress/fight-or-flight response 41, 444–446, *445*
availability heuristic, availability bias 354, 355
avolition 584–585
awareness 229–231, 272; blindsight 232; conscious awareness 236; meditation 261, 273; meta-awareness 230–231, 272; metacognition 231, 272; split-brain patients 233, 234, 236; types 230–231
Axelrod, Robert *491*, 492
axon, axon terminals 83–84, *84*, 86, 90, 109, 131, 194, 222
azapirones 623, 629

Baillargeon, Renée 143
Bandura, Albert 326, 533, 619
Barry, Christopher T. 530
Bartlett, Frederic 286, **295**
Basco, Monica 636
basic emotions; *see* emotions, basic emotions
BBC prison study 509; *see also* Stanford Prison Study
Beck, Aaron 620, 620–621, *620*, 634
Beck cognitive triad 620, *620*, 634
Bedlam 610, *611*

behavior genetics 127–128, *127*, **128–129**; *see also* heritability–behavior–experience link; twins, behavioral genetics/epigenetics

Behavior of Organisms, The 619

behavioral economics, decision making 356–358, *356*, *357*, 500; framing (gain, loss) 356–357, *357*; *see also* decision making

behavioral therapy 618–619; *see also* cognitive behavioral therapy (CBT)

behaviorism 16–17, 18, 37–38, 148, 310, 618–619

benzodiazepines **87**, 567, 623, 629, 649, 651

Bernard, Claude 395, 441, 466

Bernhard, Helen 494

Berns experiment/Gregory Berns 503–504, *503*

Bernstein, Nikolai 146

Beyerstein, Barry **28**

bias; *see* heuristics, bias

Bicêtre Asylum, Paris 610

Big 5 (five-factor model (FFM)) **521**, 534–536, **536**, 537–538, **538–539**, 539, 541–543, *543*, 550

Binder, Jeffrey L. 614, 635–636

Binet, Alfred 149, 366–367, 391; Binet–Simon Intelligence Scale 366, 391; Stanford–Binet Intelligence Scales 367, 391

Binet–Simon Intelligence Scale 366, 391

binocular clues 198, 222

biopsychosocial perspective 21, 460

bipolar disorder 573–574, *574*, 602, 637–638, 651

blind control/double-blind experiment 71, 78

blindsight 232–233

Boatwright, Michael 581

Bobo doll experiment 326–327, 619

bodily kinesthetic intelligence 373

borderline personality disorder (BPD) **561**, 594–596, **595**, 604, 642–644

Borderline Traits 594–595

Borkovec, Tom 620, 629

bounded rationality 352, 390

Bowlby, John 159, 161, 162

Braid, James 257

brain, development/evolution: 10%-usage myth **28**; critical or sensitive periods 140–141; electrical impulses 10, 84–86, *85*, 99–100 (*see also* electroencephalography (EEG)); fetal alcohol syndrome (FAS) 138; information processing areas, brain size variations 109, 110–111, *140*; learning stages by age *139*; localized functions, brain areas 10–11, *11*; magnetic activities: magnetoencephalography (MEG) 56, 100, *100*, **105**, 106, 480, 579; mammal specifics 109; necessity-based timeliness 110–111; neocortex 109–110, *110*, *111* (*see also* neocortex); neural tube to brain, prenatal 108–109, *109*, 132, 137; neuron/neural connections 109–110, *110*; plasticity 140, 262; teratogens 137–138; 'triune brain' model (MacLean) 111–112, *111*, 132

brain, measuring activity/structure: blood flow changes: functional magnetic resonance imaging (fMRI) (*see* functional magnetic resonance imaging (fMRI)); blood flow changes: positron emission tomography (PET) 104–105, *105*, 106, 231, 260, 293, 410; brain activity: electroencephalography (EEG) (*see* electroencephalography (EEG)); brain activity: magnetoencephalography (MEG) 100, *100*, **105**, 106, 480, 579; brain structure: magnetic resonance imaging (MRI) 100–103, *101–102*, *105*, 138, 376; brain–machine interface (BMI) **106–108**, *107*; cortial connections: diffusion tensor imaging (DTI) 100–101, 102–103, *103*, 589; electrical activities 99–100; magnetic activities 99–100; neuroscience techniques, evaluation **105**, 106

brain, structure 91–98; arteries and vesicles 84; brain stem 96, *97*, 111, 131, 215, *215*, 218, 224, 256, 429–430; cerebellum 96–98, *96*; glia cells 84; gray matter (*see* gray matter); limbic system ("emotional brain") 92–94, *94*; neocortex 92, *92*,

93; neurons (*see* neurons); social brain hypothesis, size/volume variations 471, 483–484, *483*; spinal cord 98, *98*; white matter 90, 100, *102*, 131–132, 138, *139*, 342, 587, 588–589; *see also* central nervous system (CNS)
brain stem 97, 111, 131, 215, *215*, 218, 224, 256, 429–430
brain-imaging techniques **626–627**
brain–machine interface (BMI) **106–108**, *107*
Bransford, John 287, *287*
Brazil World Cup (2014) **106**, *107*, **108**
Broca, Paul 10–11, *11*, **213–214**, 339–340, 347
Broca's aphasia 339
Brown, Michael **481**
Brown v Board of Education (1933) 24
Buchman, Aron 175, 381
Burger, Jerry 508
Burghardt, Gordon 325, **325**
bystander intervention, experiment/research 488–489; *see also* prosocial behavior, influences

Cajal, Santiago Ramón y 83
Calkins, Mary 23, 38
Campbell, Donald
Campos, Joe 138
cannabis (THC), cannabinoids 267
Cannon, Walter 395, 396, 428, 441, 444, 447, 466
Cannon–Bard theory 428, 437
Capgras syndrome 41–42, 50
Carnegie, Dale **28**
case studies: depersonalization-derealization disorder 580; dreaming, involved brain areas 256; infant motor development, Darwin 144–145; Little Albert, emotional conditioning 314–315, *314*; Phineas Gage, brain damage effects 81–82, *82*; research method 49–50, 78; SM (Urbach–Wiethe disease) **432–434**, *433*; sport, weight issues, coach influence **405**
Cat in the Hat, The 141–142, 329
catastrophizing 634
categorization 474–477
category, cognition 351

CATIE (Clinical Antipsychotic Trials of Intervention Effectiveness) study 642
Cattell, Raymond 370–371, 534, **535–536**
Cattell's 16 personality factors 534, **535**
cave allegory (Plato) 6–7
cave art, Lascaux, France 5, *5*
cell assembly 288–289
cell body, neuron part 83, *84*
Center Cannot Hold: My Journey Through Madness, The 583, 608–609
Center for Disease Control and Prevention (CDC) 138, 400, 402, 407, *408*, 436, 575, 600
central executive network 90–91, 132
central nervous system (CNS): antidepressants 636; brain–spinal cord division 32, *32*, 82–83, *83* (*see also* brain; spinal cord); pain, reception/reaction 1, 27–28, 219, 219, 219–220, 219–221, 220, *220*, 225; peripheral nervous system (PNS). 32, *32*, 82–83, *83*; prenatal development 108–109, *109*, 132; psychoactive substances, effects 266, 267, 271, 274
central tendency: frequency distribution (normal, skewed) 63, *64*; measures (mean, median, mode) 63–64, *64*; *see also* descriptive statistics
cerebellum 50, 96–98, *96*, 108, *109*, 187
Chabris, Christopher **154**
Charcot, Jean-Martin 19, 613
Charles Bonnet syndrome **590**
Charlie Chaplin illusion 585–586, *585*
Chein, Jason 167, *167*
chemical senses; *see* smell, taste; touch, pain (somatosenzation)
Cheney, Terri 573
Chiarugi, Vincenzo 610, 611–612, 648
childhood, developmental processes 176; cognitive 148–155 (*see also* cognitive development, childhood); learning stages by age *139*; Marshmallow Test 135–136; memory 152–154; moral 168–170, *169*; physical 136–148 (*see also* physical development, childhood); social (self/others) 156–165 (*see also* social development, childhood);
chlorpromazine (Thorazine) 623, 642, 649

Chomsky, Noam 18, 329, 334, 335
chromosomes 114, *115*, 118, *118*, 119, 120, 132–133, 133; chromosome 7, language and genes 343; gender differences, X/Y chromosomes 114, *115*, 120, 133
cingulate gyrus 91
circadian rhythm, circadian rhythm disorders 242, 243, 247, 250, 272, 273
circadian rhythm disorders 250, 273
Clark, Kenneth 24, 38
Clark, Mamie Phipps 24, 38
classical conditioning, learning; *see* conditioning, classical
classical conditioning, long-term memory 17, 18, 283, 305, 311–312, *312*
Clever Hans, horse 45–46
client-centered/person-centered therapy 20
client/person-centered therapy 20, 38, 615–616, 648
clinical psychology 19–21, 38
cocaine 265, 268
cochlear 207–210, *207*, *211*
cochlear implant, sound restoration *210*
cognition 349–360; category 351, 390; concept/family resemblance 351, 390; decision making 352–360 (*see also* decision making); exemplar approach 351–352; fast and slow thinking/decision making 350–351, 354, 390; France Flight 447, disaster 349; Miracle on the Hudson, plane emergency 349; prototype 351–352
cognition, "g" and cognitive factors 374–376
cognitive behavioral therapy (CBT) 618, 619–621, *620*, 649; bipolar disorder 639; depression 620–621, *620*, **632–633**, *633*, 634, 635; vs emotion-focused therapy (EFT) 635; generalized anxiety disorder (GAD) 628–629; obsessive-compulsive disorder 631; panic disorder 631, 651; schizophrenia 640–641; social anxiety disorder (SAD) 630, 651
cognitive development, childhood 149–155, 176, 177; definition 149; memory 152–154; Piaget stages *152*; Piaget stages: accommodation 150; Piaget stages: assimilation 149–150; Piaget stages: concrete operations 151; Piaget stages: formal operations 151; Piaget stages: preoperational stage 150–151, *150*; Piaget stages: sensorimotor stage 150; sociocultural perspective (Lev Vygotsky) 151–152, *152*, 177; temperament 154–155; tools of intellectual adaptation 151; zone of proximal development 152
cognitive dissonance 473–474
cognitive psychology/neuroscience 18–19, 31, 38, 44, 103, 362
Collins, Allan 289, *290*
color vision 191–194, 222; cones, light wavelengths sensitivity 191; opponent-process theory of color vision 192; theory of color 191–192, *192*; Young–Helmholtz trichromatic theory of color 192–193, 222
color-blindness 120, *121*, 193–194, *193*, 222
Committee on Madhouses (1815) 610, 648
communal sharing, social relationship 499
Community Mental Health Act (1963) **22**, **624**
comorbidity, psychological disorders 458, 559, 561, 569, 576, 594
compulsions 570, 602; *see also* obsessive-compulsive disorder (OCD)
concept, cognition 351, 390
Condillac, Étienne Bonnot de 332
conditioned response (CR) 283, 312, 314, 344
conditioned stimulus (CS) 283, 312, **313**, 315, 317, 344
conditioning, classical 311–319; acquisition/learning (UCS–CS pairing) 310, 312, 344; addictive drug reaction **313–314**; brain processes (glutamate release) 316–317; conditioned response (CR) 283, 312, 314, 344; conditioned stimulus (CS) 283, 312, **313**, 315, 317, 344; daily life conditioning *459*; definition 311; emotional conditioning (Little Albert study) 314–315, *314*, 328, 344, 619; evolutionary aspects 315, 317; extinction of responses

312, ***317–318***, 322, 458, *459*; fear of flying ***317–318*** (*see also* fear); food aversion (Garcia effect) 315–316, 344; generalization 314–315, 344; habituation 316, 345; immune system conditioning 344–345; Pavlov, Ivan 311–312, *312*, 314, 315, 344; Pavlov's psychic secretions, dog experiments 311–312, *312*; sensitization ***95–96***, 316, 345; spontaneous recovery 312; unconditioned response (UCR) 311, 344; unconditioned stimulus (UCS) 283, 311, 312, *313*, 315, 317, 344

conditioning, operant (instrumental conditioning) 319–324; consequences as frequency control 319, 345; law of effect 319–320, 345; operant behavior (operate, environment) 319, 320, 345; punishment (positive/negative) 321, *322*, 345; reinforcement (continuous, partial) 322; reinforcement (positive/negative) 319, 320, 321–322, ***322***; reinforcement schedules (fixed/variable interval) 322–323, *323*; reinforcement schedules (fixed/variable ratio) 322–323, *323*; shaping 321 (*see also* social shaping hypothesis); Skinner box experiments 17, 320–322, *320*, 345; Thorndike's puzzle box experiments 17, 319–321, 345

cones (red, blue, green) 186–187, 189–191, *189*, 221–222

confirmation bias 355

conformity, social influences 502–505; Asch experiment 470, 502–504, *502*, *504*; Berns experiment 503–504, *503*

confounding variables/hypothesis 56, 67, 68, 69–70, 79

congruence, client-centered therapy 20, 615, 648

connectomes 102–103, *103*

conscientiousness, personality trait 534, ***536***, ***537***, 540–541, *542*, ***544***, 550

conscious awareness 236, 523, 613

consciousness 227–274; consciousness and attention 227–230, *229*, 230, *230*; dreams 252–256 (*see also* dreams); hypnosis, meditation 257–262, ***258–259***, 260–261, 273; psychoactive substances, addiction 262–271; sleep 238–250 (*see also* sleep); types of awareness 230–231; variations (blindsight, split brain, conscious awareness) 232–237

control group, experiment 55–56, 56, *66*, 67, 68, 70, ***95***, 175, 296, 502

Convent of the order of St. Mary of Bethlehem (1330) 610, 647

cooperation, non-cooperation 490–498; altruistic punishment 494; Chimpanzees intergroup relations study 496–497; definition 490; evolution of 490, 492; indirect reciprocity 493; motivation, game study research 491–493, ***491***, 494; non-cooperation research: intergroup conflict 495–496; non-cooperation research: interpersonal/group aggression/violence 496–498; non-cooperation research: social punishing 493–495; reputation, indirect reciprocity 493; Robbers cave experiment 495–496

correlational research 50–54, *50*; causation misconception: MMR vaccination–autism ***53–54***, *54*; correlation coefficient (direction, degree) 51–52, *51*; correlation–causation 52–54, *52*; data visualization 50–51, *50*; *see also* descriptive research

cortisol 124, 248, *248*, 446, *446*, 447

Costa, Paul 534, 536, ***536***, 538, 541, 550

COVID-19 48, *48*, 167, 252, 449, 575

Crazy Ex-Girlfriend 594

Crick, Francis 117, 122–123, 228

Csikszentmihalyi, Mihalyi 532

cultural influences, psychological thinking 21–23

da Vinci, Leonardo 7, *8*, 190, 197

Damasio, Antonio 415

dance of neurons, brain 82, *82*; *see also* neurons

Darley, John 469, 488–489

Darwin, Charles: Darwinian psychiatry 601; dreaming 253; embarrassment, social psychology 487; emotions 416,

417–418, 419–422, *420*, *421*, 436–437; evolution, natural selection 12–13, *12*, 37, 119, 490, 536; *The Expression of the Emotions in Man and Animals* 419–421, 419–422, *420*, 436; heredity, behavior, experience 113–114; influence on Sigmund Freud 19, 522; instincts, motivation 394–395, 406; intrinsic motivation 141; motor development 144–145; observation studies, scientific technique 48; reflex action 144–145; stress response 440

data, evaluation and analysis 59–66; descriptive statistics 62–66 (*see also* descriptive statistics); frequency distribution, data 61–62, *62*, *63*, *64*; inferential statistics 59, 69; measurement, analysis 61–62, *62*, *62*; reliability 60–61; validity 59–60, 78, 528, 530

Day the Voices Stopped, The 583

de Sade, Marquis 557

decision making 352–360; analogies 352; behavioral economics 356–358, 500; bounded rationality, information-limiting factors 352, 390; conditions (necessary, sufficient) 353; framing (gain, loss) 355–357, *357*, **358–359**; heuristics, bias 354–356; logic, rationality 352–354, **358–359**; reasoning (deductive, inductive) 353

declarative memory 283, *283*, 284–285, *293*, 305–306, 432

deductive reasoning 353

deep brain stimulation (DBS) 279, 625–626, 632, 651

deep structure. language 334

Deese–Roediger–McDermott (DRM) procedure 300, **300**

default or intrinsic network, brain 90, 132, 248, 273, 375

dendrites 84, *84*, 85, 86, 90, 109, 131, 137, 245, 453

Department of Health and Human Services 75, 400, 627

dependent variable (DV) 55–56, 61, 66, 68, 69, 79

depersonalization 580

depersonalization–derealization disorder 580, 603; *see also* dissociative disorders

depression **560**, 571, 583; genetics/epigenetic causes 125, 455, 558; inter-/intrapersonal relationship 554; major depressive disorder (MDD) 571–573, 602; onset, initial episode 572–573; physiological causes/mechanisms 449–450, 623; physiological mechanisms **87**, **626–627**; symptoms 572; treatment: brain stimulation 625; treatment: cognitive behavioral therapy (CBT) 620–621, *620*, **627**, **632–633**, *633*, 634–635; treatment: emotion-focused therapy (EFT) 635; treatment: medication, antidepressants 623, **627**, **632–633**, *633*, 636–637; treatment: psychodynamic therapy 635–636

depth perception, vision 187, 197–198, 202

derealization 580

Descartes, René 7–8, *9*, 39

Descent of Man, The 253

descriptive research 47–54, *48*; case studies 49–50, 78, 81–82, *82*, 144–145, 256, 314–315, *314*, **405**, **432–434**, *433*, 580; correlational research *50*, 51–54 (*see also* correlational research); observation studies/naturalistic observation 48–49, *49*; *see also* science, scientific method

descriptive statistics 62–66, 78; central tendency, measures (mean, median, mode) 63–64, *64*, 78; variability, measures 64–66, *65*, *65*, 78; *see also* data, evaluation and analysis

developmental processes: adolescence 137, 138–139, 140, 165–170, 479, *479*; childhood, cognitive 148–156 (*see also* cognitive development, childhood); childhood, moral 168–170, *169*; childhood, physical 136–148, *139* (*see also* physical development, childhood); childhood, social 156–165 (*see also* social development, childhood); lifespan, adulthood 170–174

developmental prosopagnosia 297

developmental psychology 136, 176; *Mind* (Darwin) 144–145; Piaget, Jean

149–152, *152*, 177, 310; theory of mind 158–159, 484
Diagnostic and Statistical Manual of Mental Disorders DSM) 455–456, 557–558, 558–559, 601; agoraphobia 569; attention deficit hyperactivity disorder (ADHD) 600; autism spectrum disorder (ASD) 597; bipolar disorder 574; dissociative disorders 580, 582; healthy self, *DSM-5* 547, 547–548; vs *International Classification of Diseases (ICD)* 558–559; mental disorder, definition/categories, *DSM-5* 558–559, **560**; obsessive-compulsive and related disorders 569; personality disorders 592, *592*, 594, 596, 603, 604
dialectical behavior therapy (DBT) 621, 628, 643
Diallo, Amadou **480–481**
dichotomous thinking 620, 634
diffusion tensor imaging (DTI) 100–101, 102–103, *103*, 589
display rules, emotionality 423, *424*
dissociation 578–579
Dissociation of a Personality, The 50
dissociative amnesia 580–581, 602, 639, 650
dissociative disorders **560**, 578–582, 602–603, 650; depersonalization–derealization disorder 580, 603; dissociation experience vs pathological dissociative symptoms 578–580; dissociative amnesia 580–581, 602, 639, 650; dissociative identity disorder (DID) 50, 581–582, 583, 638, 650; vs PTSD 579; treatment 638, 650
dissociative experience 579, 596, 602
dissociative fugue 580
dissociative identity disorder (DID) 50, 581–582, 583, 638, 651
dissonance 473–474
Dix, Dorothea 612, 648
Dollard, John 326
door-in-the-face technique, compliance 502
dopamine **87**, 96, 264–265, *265*, 268, 270, 292, 306, **461–462**, 642
double-blind experiment 71, 78
Dr. Seuss 141–142

dreaming; *see* sleep and dreams
dreams 252–256, 273, 524; Aserinsky and Kleitman studies 253; dream analysis 527–528; external event and 252; historical understanding (Lucretius, Darwin, Jung) 252; lucid dreams 254, **254–255**, *254*, *255*; neuroscience research 256; REM sleep and dreams (*see* rapid eye movement (REM) sleep);
drugs; *see* psychoactive substances
DSM; *see Diagnostic and Statistical Manual of Mental Disorders (DSM)*
du Bois-Reymond, Emil 10
Dunbar, Robin 333, 483, *483*
Dutch hongerwinter study (1944), epigenetic study 125–126
dynamic deconstructive psychotherapy (DDP) 644

ear, structure/function 207–208, *207*, *208*, 223–224; *see also* hearing, audition
eating disorders 403–405; anorexia nervosa 403–404, **404**, **560**; binge-eating disorder 404; bulimia nervosa 404; frequency, male vs female **404–405**; purging 404; *see also* addiction
Ebbinghaus, Hermann 285–286, *286*
Edwin Smith Papyrus 5–6
Eichmann, Adolf 505
eidetic memory 297
Ekman, Paul 419, 421–422, **422**, 423, 426, 427, 436–437, 487
Elbert, Thomas 56–57, *57*, 60
electrical impulses, brain and body 10, 84–86, *85*, 99–100; *see also* magnetic activities, brain
electroconvulsive therapy (ECT) 625, 649
electrodermal activity (EDA) 41
electroencephalography (EEG) 99–100; artificial limb control **106–108**, *107*; dreaming 253–254, **254–255**, *254*, *255*; electrical activity (synapse level) 99; function 99, *99*; hypnosis 257–258, 260; insight problem, solving 363–364; perception, consciousness 229–230, *230*, 272; sleep pattern/stages 240, *241*, 243–244, *244*, 247, *247*; technique development/evaluation 99, **105**; temporal resolution 106, *106*

electromagnetic spectrum 185, 221
Elements of Psychophysics 184
Ellis, Havelock 406, 436
embarrassment 487
emotional-focused therapy (EFT)/process experiential therapy 616–617, 621, 635
emotions 415–434, *416*; affect 426; approaches: categorical (Darwin) 417–418; approaches: dimensional (valence, arousal, power) (Wundt) 417–418, 427; basic emotions, common characteristics/lists of 415, 425–426, 425–427; definition debate 415–416; display rules across cultures 423, *424*; emotion universality–cultural expression shaping 417, 419, 420, 421, 427; emotionality, dimensions (pleasure/displeasure, activation/deactivation) 427–428, *427*; evolutionary perspective 418, 420–421, 421–425, **422–423**, *424*; facial expressions (innateness, physiological changes) 417, 418, 419, 420–421, 422 *420*, **422–423**, 427; fundamental life tasks response 423–425; vs mood 426
emotions, physiological systems 429–432, *429*, *430*, 437; amygdala (fear) 431–432, **432–433**; amygdala (fear, emotional imagery response) 437; autonomic nervous system (ANS) 426, 430; brain stem level 429–430; cognitive processes: emotion inhibition/creation 432; discrete emotions, brain areas *429*; emotionality as "total body" response 430; hippocampus (emotional memory) 430, 431, 437; insula and anterior cingulate (memory) 431, 437; limbic system: "emotional brain" 430, *430*; medial prefrontal cortex (emotional tasks) 431, 437; occipital lobe (emotional imagery) 437; subcallosal cingulate 431, 437; Urbach–Wiethe disease, amygdala damage **432–433**
emotions, research/scientific understanding: Cannon–Bard theory (behavioral response) 428, 437; current trends 416–419; definition debate 416–417; emotion expression, universality/cultural determination (Ekman studies) 419, 421–422, **422**, 423, 426, 427, 436–437, 487; emotions as basic life task response (Panksepp) 423–425; *Expression of the Emotions in Man and Animals, The* (Darwin) 419–421, 419–422, *420*, 436; historical theories, emotionality 428–429; James-Lange theory (physiological response) 428–429, 437; Schachter–Singer theory (emotional experience) 428, 429, 437; Urbach–Wiethe disease (SM) case study **433–434**, *433*
empathic understanding, client-centered therapy 20, 615, 648
empathy 156–157, 177, 547, **592**, 593, 604
empiricism 7, 16, 38, 46, 557
enchanted loom, brain 82
endocrine system 91, *91*; see also hormones
endorphins 71, 87, **87**, 271, 274, 462
Engel, George 21
engram, memory trace 288
envy 488
epigenetic system/epigenetic modifications 122–125, *123*, 124; DNA–environment relationship 123; Dutch hongerwinter study (1944) 125–126; epigenetic inheritance 123; epigenetic marks/tags *123*; function 123–124; NASA twin, study (2019) 113; phenotype influence (non-Mendelian) 125; rat offspring study 124, *124*; stress influence 440; as stress reaction 125, 498; twin behavior differences 337
epilepsy 87, 233, 237, 279, 289, 626
epinephrine (adrenaline) 87, **87**, 292–293, 429, 446–447, 446–447, *446*, 466
episodic memory (autobiographical) memory 27, 152, 282–283, *283*, 292, **295–296**, 315; see also long-term memory
equality matching (tit for tat), social relationship 499, 500
Erickson, Kirk I. 175, 381
Erikson, Erik 171–172, *172*, **172**
estrogen 166
ethics; see research, ethics

exemplar approach, cognition 351–352
existential-humanistic perspective (personality, therapy) 20, 526–527, 531–532, 550, 615–618, 633, 648
expectations 25–26, *25*
experimental group 55–56, 68, 71, 502
experimental research/method 55–56; *see also* science, scientific method
experimenter effects, research results 71, 78
explicit memory 283, *283*, 284–285, *293*, 305–306, 432
Expression of the Emotions in Man and Animals, The 419–421, 419–422, *420*, 436
extraversion, personality trait 128, 519, *520*, 534, **536**, **537**, **540**, *543*
eye, structure/function 187–189, *187*, *188*; bionic eye implants **190–191**; photoreceptors: rods, cones 186–187, 189–191, *189*, 221–222
Eysenck, Hans 519, *520*, 549

face and person perception 477–482; baby-face preference 477–478; face processing, brain 480, *480*; face–character/intention inferences 478; fear of missing out (FOMO) 479, *479*
face processing/recognition 298, 480, *480*, 484, *485*; developmental prosopagnosia 297
false memories, memory manipulation 299–304; altering political memories, (Slate.com experiment, 2010) 302–303, *303*; Deese–Roediger–McDermott (DRM) procedure 300, **300**; eye-witness testimony 303; false crime-committing memories (Shaw and Porter study, 2015) **303–304**; imagination: adding false autobiographical memories (Mazzoni/Memon study, 2003) 300–301; imagination: false recollections (Seamon et al. study, 2009) 301; Larry Henderson trial (2003), false witness 302; reconstructive nature of memory 300
fast thinking/decision making 354, 390
Fatal Attraction 594

fear: *agoraphobia* 569, 602; anxiety and (similarities and differences) 565–567, 569, 601–602, 630; brain development 138; conditioning, observational learning 314–315, *314*, **317–318**, 326, 344, 619; cortical networks 431, 432–434, *433*, 437, 458, *459*; *The Expression of Emotions* (Darwin) 419–421, *421*; Little Albert case study 314–315, *314*, 328, 344, 619; monkeys' fear of snakes study 309, 310; *The Project for a Scientific Psychology* (Darwin) 524; specific phobia 569, 602, 630–631, 651; temperament and 154–155; Urbach–Wiethe disease 432–434, *433*
fear of missing out (FOMO 479, *479*
fearful preoccupation (borderline personality disorder) 595
Fechner, Gustav 183–184
Fehr, Ernst 494
Feigenson, Lisa 143–144, *144*
female psychologists 23–24
fetal alcohol syndrome (FAS) 138
fight-or-flight response; *see* response (fight or flight/tend to befriend)
figure–ground relationship *18*, 200, *585*
Fiske, Alan 499
five-factor model (FFM) (Big 5) **521**, 534–536, **536**, 537–538, **538–539**, 539, 541–543, *543*, 550
flashbulb memories 293, 306
Flavell, John 153
flavor 215
Flynn effect 384, 385
Fogassi, Leonardo 156, 327
Food and Drug Administration (FDA) 190, 210, 269, 632, 636, 646
foot-in-the-door technique, compliance 501–502
forebrain 108; anxiety 569; neural tube 108, *109*, 132; sleep, dreaming 132, 247, *247*, 256
Fox, Nathan A. 162–163, *163*
FoxP2 gene, language 343
framing, decision making 355–356, 356–357, *357*, **358–359**
France Flight 447 disaster 349
Frederick, Shane 351

free association, psychoanalysis (Freud) 20, 261, 528, 613
free-gift technique, compliance 502
frequency distribution, data 61–62, *62*, 63, *64*
Freud, Sigmund: clinical psychology, development 19–20; conditioning, fear 315; consciousness, dreams 228, 231, 253, 528; dissociation 579; free association 261, 528; life drive 532; *Project for a Scientific Psychology, The* 19–20, 253, 524–525; psychoanalysis 20, 613–615, 648; psychodynamic perspective on personality (*see* psychodynamic perspective on personality); psychopathology research 50; sexuality 406, 436
Frick, Paul J. 530
Friederici, Angela D. 329
Friedman, Meyer 455
frontal lobe 92, *93*; cognition/social functions 10, 483; development 137, 167, 375; frontal lobe tasks/executive tasks 90–91; insight problems, solving 362; memory 293, *293*, 306; prefrontal cortex (PFC), medial prefrontal cortex (mPFC), ventromedial prefrontal cortex (vmPFC) 92, 458, *459*, 485, 511, 547
functional magnetic resonance imaging (fMRI) 103–104, *104*, 743; adolescence, risk taking 167; Charlie Chapin illusion response, schizophrenia **585–586**; hypnosis 260; language, dogs *337*; meditation 464; Parkinson, medical expectations test 461; phobias 631; pro/con evaluation **105**, 106; sleep 248; social pressure/stress 503–504, 547
functionalism 15, *15*, 37
fundamental attribution error 471, 472–473, 513
fusiform face area (FFA) 343, 431, 437, 480, *480*, 484, *485*

"g" (general intelligence) 370, 371, 374–375, *374*, **382–383**, 391
GABA; *see* gamma-aminobutyric acid (GABA)
Gächter, Simon 494

Gage case study, brain damage effects 81–82, *82*
Galen 7, 267, 571
Galileo 8, 37
Gall, Franz Josef 10, *11*
Gallup, George 67, 75
gamma-aminobutyric acid (GABA) 87, **87**, 266–267, 567, 623, 629
Garcia effect/John Garcia 315–316, 344
Gardner, Allen and Beatrix 333–334, 336
Gardner, Howard 24, 372–373, 391
Gardner, Randy 239
Gazzaniga, Michael S. 235
General Adaptation Syndrome (GAS) 441–441, 467
general adaptation syndrome (GAS), stress response 441–442, 467
generalized anxiety disorder (GAD) 567–568, 601, 601–602, 628–629, 651; *see also* anxiety disorders
genetic inheritance (Mendelian genetics)
Genetics and the Origins of Species (1937) 119
gene-trait relationship 113
genotype 113, 116, 133
Genovese, Kitty 469, 471, 488
Gestalt psychology 17–18, *18*, 38, 199–203, *200–202*, 223, 282, 363
Gilmore, John 588
glove amnesia 19, 613
glutamate 86–87, **87**, **95–96**, 316
Gogtay, Nitin 586
Goodall, Jane 48, 326
Gosling, Sam **543–544**
Gosset, William 69
Gottesman, Irving I. 128, 587
Grandin, Temple 597–598, *598*
Grant, William T. 173–174, *174*
grasping reflex 144
gray matter, brain 90, 131; abnormalities: panic disorder 569; abnormalities: schizophrenia 586, 587, 588, *588*; heritable traits 587; intelligence and 389, 97389; memory abilities 296; volume: changes by age 138, *139*; volume: changes by learning (London

taxi test) 262; volume: learning effect (London taxi test) **95**
Greenberg, Leslie 616–617, 635
Greenberg, Mark **157–158**
Greenberg, Martin 469
Gregory, Richard **203–204**
guilt 487, 514
Gur 500
gustatory system 214–215, *215*, 224

habituation **95–96**, *95*, 143, 316, 345
hallucinogens (LSD, MDMA, MDA, PCP) 266, 269–270, *270*, 274
Hamilton, William D. 280, 490, *491*, 492
Harlow, Harry 81, 160–162, *161*
Hawthorne effect 69–70
health 460–466; alternative/complementary medicine 465; behavior, impact 460, 468; biopsychosocial perspective 21, 460; expectations and health outcome 461–462, 467; life expectancy 171, *172*, 460, *461*; meditation, midfulness, influence (*see* mindfulness); meditation, mindfulness, influence 464–465; physical activity, influence 462–463, *463*, *464*; resilience 459–460; risk factors, death 462; statistics 460, *460*; stress management, influence 462
healthy vs neurotic growth 527, 616
hearing 205–211
hearing (auditory) 205–211
hearing, audition 205–211, 223–224; brain: sound creation (pathway) 209–210, *209*, 223; cochlear implant, sound restoration 210, *210*; definition *205*; ear, anatomy/working 207–208, *207*, *208*; ear, structure/function 223–224; sound waves (amplitude, frequency, timbre/complexity) 205–207, *205*, *206*, 223; vestibular system 210–211, *211*, 224
Hebb, Donald 89, 288–289, 525
Heider, Fritz 472
Helmholtz, Hermann 13–14, *14*, 192–193, 222
Hering, Ewald 192–193

heritability–behavior–experience link 112–129; behavior genetics 127–128, *127*, **128–129** (*see also* twins, behavioral genetics/epigenetics); chromosomes (*see* chromosomes); DNA and RNA 116–118, *117*, *118*; evolutionary changes, genetic explanation 113–118; evolutionary changes: natural selection, Darwin 113–114; gene expression, influence: behavior and environment 121–122; gene expression, influence: epigenetic 113–118 (*see also* epigenetic system/epigenetic modifications); genes, protein encoding 114–116; genotype 113, 116, 133; inheritance variations, patterns 118–121; karyotype 114, *115*; phenotype 113, 116, 125, 133, 377; sex-linked inheritance 120, *121*, 133, 193–194, *193*, 222, 343
heuristics, bias 354–356; affect heuristic 355; availability heuristic, availability bias 354, 355; confirmation bias 355; implicit association test (IAT) **476–477**; social relationships 471, 472
Heyward, Jr., Nicholas **481**
Highly Superior Autobiographical Memory (HSAM) 1, **295–296**, *296*; *see also* memory
Hinckley, John **562**, 584
hindbrain 108, *109*, 132
hippocampus *279*, *430*; aging 375, 381; damage: H.M. (Henry Molaison) memory study 289–291, *290*, *291*, 299; function 124; London Taxi test study **95–96**; memory 94, 247, 282, 292, 306, 317, 430, 431, 437; physical changes by experience/exercise **95–96**, 175, 453; post-traumatic stress disorder (PTSD) 94, 458; *see also* limbic system
Hippocrates 6, 518–519, 571
history of psychology; *see* psychology, history
H.M. (Henry Molaison) research 289–291, *290*, *291*, 299, 305, 306
hormones 91; endocrine system 91, *91*; function 91; hunger/satiety: leptin, ghrelin 398, 400, 435; level changes puberty: estrogen 166, 177; level

changes puberty: testosterone 166, 177, 448; levels: sleep 238, 248, 250; neurotransmitters comparison *87*, 447; pituitary gland *91*, 921; stress response: cortisol 124, 248, *248*, 447; stress response: epinephrine *87*; stress response: norepinephrine *87*, 447; stress response: oxytocin 448, 480
Horney, Karen 526, 527
Hospice de la Salpêtrière, Paris 611
How to Win Friends and Influence People 28
Howard (Beckman), Ruth Winifred 24, 38
Human Genome Project 118
Huth, Alexander 340–341
hypersomnia 250, 273
hypnosis 257–262, 273; animal hypnosis, studies 260–261; brain function 260; definition 257; hypnotic effect 257–262; misconceptions *258–259*; posthypnotic amnesia 258; psychological treatment 257; scientific understanding 257
hypothalamus 94, *94*, 108, 215, 430; hunger/satiety 398–399, *399*, 400, 435; sleep 246–247, 248, *248*, 273; stress 446, *446*, 447
hysteria 19, 50, 613

ideal self 545
imitation learning, mirror neurons 156–157, 177, 327, 346, 599, 617
immune system 449–452; conditioning 344–345; emotions 449–450; hypnosis, meditation 258, 273; immunity, types (innate, learned) 450; pathogen exposure and strength *451–452*; physiological mechanisms 91, 450–451
immunity, types 450
implicit association test (IAT) *476–477*
implicit memory 283, *283*, 291, 305–306
imprinting 161, 324, 346, 352
independent variable (IV) 55–56, 61, 66, 68, 69, 79
indirect reciprocity, cooperation 493
inductive reasoning 353
inference: behavior interpretation/attribution, conditioning 2; behaviour interpretation/attribution, conditioning 37, 315, 471, 472, 474 (*see also* fundamental attribution error); research methods 59, 66, 78, 79; unconscious 13–14
inferential statistics 59, 69
inferiority complex 526
inheritance, genetic: epigenetic 122–125, *123*, *124*; Mendelian genetics 119–120, 122, 125; mitochondrial *118*
insanity, legal term/legal defence 554, *561–563*
insomnia 250, **465**, **560**
intelligence: age: brain/ability changes, intelligence maintenance 374, *374*, 380–381; age-related brain changes, intelligence maintenance 375–376; APOE gene and 379–381; cognitive domains and 374, *374*; defining (broad, narrow) 365, *369*; fluid/crystallized intelligence 370, 370–371, 375, 378; Flynn effect 384, 385; "g" (general intelligence) 370, 371, 374–375, *374*, **382–383**, 391; group differences (socioeconomic, race, gender) 384, *385*, *386*; heritability 129, 377–379, *378*, *379*, **382**, 391–392; intelligence quotient (IQ) 367; IQ-inconstancy, malleability **383–384**; mental age 366–367, 369, 391; multiple intelligences, theory of 372–373; psychometric theories 369–371; Raven Matrices Test 370, *370*, 374, 378; Scottish Mental Survey Study 375–376, *376*
intelligence, measuring: Binet–Simon Intelligence Scale 366, 391; crowd wisdom, collective intelligence **371–372**, *371*; Galton, intelligence research, testing 365; heritability 365–389; Stanford–Binet Intelligence Scales 367, 391; Stern intelligence quotient (IQ) test 391; WAIS elements: perceptual reasoning 368, *368*; WAIS elements: processing speed 368; WAIS elements: verbal comprehension 368; WAIS elements: working memory 368; WAIS: IQ normal curve *369*; WAIS structure *367*; Wechsler Adult Intelligence Scale

(WAIS) *367, 368, 369*, 391; Wechsler Intelligence Scale for Children (WISC) 367, 391
interneurons 84
interpersonal intelligence 373
interpersonal-psychological theory of suicide (IPTS) 575
intrapersonal intelligence 373
intrinsic motivation 141
intrinsic or default network, brain 90, 132, 248, 273, 375
introspection 14, 16, 19
introversion, personality trait 519, 527, 528, 542, *543*, 549
Izard, Carrol 415–416, 427

Jackson, Hughlings 11–12, 19, 233, 432, 522, 584
Jacob, François 117
James, William 14–16, *15*, **28**, 37, 90, 227–228, 395, 415, 428–429, 437, 501, 544–545
James-Lange theory 428–429, 437
Jamison, Kay 573
Janet, Pierre 578–579
Johnson, Marcia 287, *287*
Johnson, Virginia 410–412, 411–412, *411*, 436
jumping gene **129**
Jung, Carl 171, 253, 261, 519, 526–527, 528, 545, 549
just-noticeable difference (JND), sensation 184, 221

Kagan, Jerome 155, 177
Kahneman, Daniel 350, 354, 355–356
Kamphaus, Randy W. 530
Kandel, Eric **95–96**, 310, 316, 525
Kanner, Leo 597
Kellogg, John 406
Kennedy, John F. 22
Ketamine 636
Kinsey, Alfred 407, 436
Kitayama, Shinobu 545
Kitty Genovese 469, 471, 488
Kleitman, Nathaniel 240, 253
Koch, Christof 228
Koenigs, Michael 511

Koffka, Kurt 201, *201*
Kohlberg, Lawrence 168–170, *169*
Köhler, Wolfgang 201, *201*, 363
Kraepelin, Emil 558, 601
Kramer, Arthur F. 175, 381
Kretschmer, Ernst 519, 549
Kuhn, Thomas **57–58**
Kuppens, Peter 428

lactose tolerance 122
Ladd-Franklin, Christine 23, 38
language/speech, anatomical requirements (speech), vocal cord 338–339
language/speech, defining/learning 329–343, 334; anatomical requirements, vocal cord 338–339; animals, language learning (chimpanzee Washoe, bonobo Kanzi, dogs) 332–333, 336, **337–338**; aphasia 339; brain: semantic system/areas related to 10–11, 339–341, *339*, *340*, **341–342**, *342*; Broca's areas/Werrnicke's area 11, *11*, *339*; definition, evolutionary stages, function 331, 333, 334–337; generative nature 334–335; genes–language relationship 343; infants: speech processing, vocalization 329, *329*; language evolution 332–333, 343; larynx and human vocalization 337–338; McGurk effect 27, 340; reading 343; second language **341–342**, *342*; Skinner's enforcement principles 329; universal grammar 334; vocal cords 330, 337–338
language/speech, structure 331–332, *332*; deep structure 334; definition 331; generative structure 334–335; morpheme 332, *332*, 347; phonemes 140, 329, 330, 331–332, *332*, **341**, 346–347, *347*; phonology 331–332; semantics 332, 347; surface structure 334; syntax 332, *332*, 340, 347; universal grammar 334
Lashley, Karl 288
Latané, Bibb 469, 488–489
law of effect 319–320, 345
learning: definition 310; ethology 324–328; language learning 329–343; mechanism: classical conditioning

312–318; mechanism: operant conditioning 319–324; during sleep 244–246, *246*, **327–328**; strategies **33–34**

learning, ethology view 324–328; Bobo doll experiment 326–327, 617; fear learning (monkeys–snakes study) 309, 310; Goodall, Jane (chimpanzee studies) 48, 326; imitation learning, mirror neurons 156–157, 177, 327, 346, 599; imprinting 161, 324, 346, 352; Lorenz, Conrad 161, 324, 346; observational learning 326–327, 346; play as learning, characteristics 324–325, 325, **325**; understanding of learning 324

learning/long-term memory process, steps: consolidation 285; encoding 284, *284*, 305; retrieval 285, 306; storage 285, 305

LeDoux, Joseph 235, 426
Levinson, Daniel 171
Liberman, Alvin 336
libido, sexual energy 20, 524
Lieberman, Philip 333, 340
life expectancy 171, *172*, 460, *461*
lifespan approach, psychological science 36
lifespan/adulthood, development 136, 170–175, 170–176, 178; aging 173–175, *174*, 381–382, **382–383**; cognitive ability, brain changes *374*, 375–376, *376* (see also plasticity, brain); intelligence, maintaining 379, *379*, 381–382; personality traits, five- factor model (FFM) 535, 536, 546; psychosocial stages (Erik Erikson) 171–173; rite of passage, commemorating 165; Scottish Mental Survey 375–376, *376*; sexual activity 407, *408*; sleep changes 242, *242*; weight, BMI 402

light/energetic energy 184–187, *186*
limbic system 93–94, *94*; amygdala (*see* amygdala, emotional processing); anxiety disorders 566; cingulate gyrus 94; function 94; hippocampus (*see* hippocampus); hypothalamus 94; thalamus 94, *94*

Lincoln, Abraham 572
Linehan, Marsha 643
linguistic intelligence 373
Listening to Prozac 623
lithium 623, 638
Little Albert case study, emotional conditioning 314–315, *314*, 328, 344, 619
Livingstone, Margaret 190
locus of control 532–533
Loehlin, John 540, **540**
Loftus, Elizabeth 289, *290*, 299–300, 302, *302*
logical-mathematical intelligence 373
long-term memory 282–285; classical conditioning 17, 18, 283, *283*, 305, 311–312, *312*; episodic/semantic 27, 152, 282–283, *283*, 292; explicit/implicit 283, *283*, 291, 305–306, 432; hippocampus: H.M. (Henry Molaison) research 289–291, *290*, *291*, 299, 305, 306; priming 283, *283*, 305–306; procedural memory 283, *283*, *293*, 305, 580; steps: consolidation 285; steps: encoding 284, *284*, 305; steps: retrieval 285, 306; steps: storage 285, 305
Lorenz, Konrad 161, 324, 346
Lovaas, Ivar 645
Lovaas treatment 645
lucid dreams 254, **254–255**, *254*, *255*
Lucretius 253
Lukens, Sarah 579
Luria, Alexander R. 296

Macbeth 477
Machiavelli, Niccolò di Bernardo dei 517
MacLean, Paul 93–94, 111–112, 132
MacLean, Richard 584
madness vs vice, difference 557
magnetic resonance imaging (MRI) 100, *101*
magnetoencephalography (MEG) 56, 100, *100*, **105**, 106, 480, 579
Magoun, Horace 246
Maie, Steven F. 449
Maier, Norman 361
major depressive disorder (MDD); *see* depression

Malleus Maleficarum (Hammer of Witches) 609–610
mania **560**, 571, 573, 574, 602, 611, 623, 638–639; *see also* bipolar disorder
manic-depressive disorder; *see* bipolar disorder
market pricing, social relationship 499, 500
Markus, Hazel R. 501, 545
Marshmallow Test 135–136
Martino, Benedetto De 356–357
Maslow, Abraham 20, 395–396, *396*, 435, 532, 545, 616
Maslow's hierarchy of needs pyramid *396*, 435, 616
Masters, William 410–412, *411*, 436
Matsumoto, David 423, *424*
Mazzoni, Giuliana 300
McClintock, Barbara **129**
McCrae, Robert 534, 536, **536**, 538, 541, 550
McEwen, Bruce 442–443, *443*, 467
McGaugh, James 292–293, **295–296**
McGraw, Myrtle 146
McGurk effect 27, 340
McLinn, Colleen M. 492–493
mean 63–64, *64*, 78
median 63–64, *64*, 78
meditation/mindfulness 261–262, 272, 464–465, 617; definition, functioning 261, 273–274, 464; meta-analysis studies 262, 618; mindfulness-based cognitive therapy (MBCT) 635; psychological health effect and therapeutic use 262, 274, 464, 617–618, 621, 629
Meissner corpuscles, tactile receptors 217, *217*
melancholia 571, 611; *see also* depression
Memon, Amina 300
memory 277–307; childhood development 152–154; development in infants 152–153; false memories (*see* false memories); Highly Superior Autobiographical Memory (HSAM) 1, **295–296**, *296*; interference (proactive, retroactive) 285–286; Penfield electrical stimulation treatment 279; reconstructive nature of memory 286, 300–303; role of meaning 285–287
memory, brain processes 288–293, *293*; amygdala: emotional arousal 292–293; brain area activation (remembering, initial event) 306; cell assembly 288–289; engram, memory trace 288; flashbulb memories 293, 306; frontal lobe 292, 293; hippocampus 289, 291, 292, 293, 306; H.M. (Henry Molaison) case, research conclusions 289–291, *290*, *291*, 292, 299, 305, 306; memory (information) network model 289, *290*; temporal lobe 289, 291, 292, 293, 306; tip-of-the-tongue phenomenon 294; working memory 90, 280–281, 292, 305, 306, *367*, 368, 375
memory abilities, variations 294–299; highly superior autobiographical memory (HSAM) 1, **295–296**, *296*; mnemonists 296–297; photographic or eidetic memory 297; super-recognizers **297–298**
memory disorders 299; anterograde amnesia 299, 307; Clive Wearing case 277, 278; dissociative amnesia 580–581, 602; H.M. (Henry Molaison) research 289–291, *290*, *291*, 299, 305, 306; retrograde amnesia 299, 307
memory types: episodic (autobiographical) 27, 152, 282–283, *283*, 292, **295–296**, 315; explicit (declarative) 283, *283*, 284–285, *293*, 305–306, 432; implicit *283*, 291, *293*, 305–306; long-term (*see* long-term memory); procedural 283, *283*, *293*, 305, 580; semantic 282–283, *283*; sensory 280; short-term 277–278, 280–282, *280*, 285, 290, 305, 306; working memory 90, 280–281, 292, 305, 306, *367*, 368, 375
Mendel, Gregor 119–120
Mendelian genetics, inheritance: first and second law or the law of segregation 119–120, 122, 125
mental age 366–367, 369, 391
mental hospitals, closures **624–625**, *625*
Merkel receptors 217, *217*

meta-analysis 61, 164, *379*, 413, 427, 449, **476**, 576
meta-awareness 230–231, 272
metacognition 231, 272
midbrain: brain stem 96, 131; neural tube 108, *109*, 132; panic, integration 132
Milgram, Stanley 89–90, 505–508
Milgram Shock Experiment 505–508, *507*; *see also* Stanford Prison Study
Milinski, Manfred 493
Miller, George 281
Miller, Neal 326
Milner, Brenda 289–291, 305
Mind of a Mnemonist, The 296
mindfulness and meditation 261–262, 272, 464–465, 617; definition, functioning 261, 273–274, 464; meta-analysis studies 262, 618; mindfulness-based cognitive therapy (MBCT) 635; psychological health effect and therapeutic use 262, 274, 464, 617–618, 621, 629
Mineka, Susan 309
Miracle on the Hudson, plane emergency 349
mirror neurons, imitation learning 156–157, 177, 327, 599
Mischel, Walter 135, 136
mitochondrial DNA (mtDNA) *118*
mitochondrial inheritance
MMR vaccination–autism, causation misconception **53–54**, *54*
M'Naghten rule/M'Naghten Daniel **561–562**
mnemonists 296–297
mode 63–64, *64*, 78
Mona Lisa 190
monoamine oxidase inhibitors (MAOIs) 623, 649
monoamine oxidase (MAO) inhibitor 623, 630, 636
monocular cues 197, 222
Monod, Jacques 117
moral development stages, childhood/adolescence *167*, 168–170, *170*
moral emotions (guilt, shame) 487, 514
moral judgements 509, *510*, *511*, 512; children studies, moral and conventional transgressions 511–512; definition 509; low/high-conflict situation 511; vs preferences 509; self-driving cars, crash rule judgements **512**; Trolley problems, studies 509–511, *510*, *511*, 549; universality, cultural shaping 509
Morgan, Christiana 529
morpheme 332, *332*, 347
Moruzzi, Giuseppe 246
motivations 394–414; basic motivations: Maslow's hierarchy of needs 395–396, *396*; basic needs, Maslow 395–396, *396*; goal 395; intrinsic/extrinsic 141, 396; motivation, emotions: definition, conceptualization 395; move (action) 395; needs (instincts, drives) 394–395; self-actualization 395–396, *396*, 435, 532, 545, 616
motivations, food 397–405, *399*, *401*, **401**, *402*, **404–405**; appetite regulation: blood-glucose/leptin levels 398; appetite regulation: brain mechanisms 398–399, *399*; body image distortion 403; body mass index (BMI) 402; eating disorders (*see* eating disorders); eating pattern (evolutionary shaping vs modern food availability) 400; gastrointestinal hormones 400; hunger, satiety experiences 398–400; motivation levels 398; obesity/overweight (global, gender) 400–401, *401*, **401**, 402; obesity/overweight, health effects 402–403
motor cortex 218, *218*, 225
motor development: Darwin, studies on 144–145; development milestones by age 147–148; directions 145; dynamic system theory 146–147; infant reflexes (grasping, rooting, sucking) 144–145; stages 144–148, *145*, *146*, **147–148**; swimming reflex 146; vestigial structures 145–146
motor neurons 84, 95, 316
Mozart effect **153–154**
Murphy, Jane 563–564
Murray, Henry 529, *530*
musical intelligence 373
myelin sheath 86, 90, *102*, 131, 138, *139*

Nagamatsu, Lindsay 175, 381
narcissism, narcissistic personality disorder 36, 546, **592**, 593, 603
NASA twin, study (2019) 113
Nash, John 553, 554, 556, 584
National Center for Complementary and Alternative Medicine (NCCAM) 465
National Center for Complementary and Integrative Health (NCCIH) 465
natural selection 12–13, *12*, 19, 113–114, 335, 419, 421, 436, 490–491
naturalistic intelligence 373
NAVIGATE, schizophrenia treatment approach 641
negative punishment, conditioning 321, *322*, 345
Nelson, Charles A. 162–163, *163*
neocortex 92, *92*; central sulcus 92; frontal lobe (*see* frontal lobe); motor strip 92–93, *93*; occipital lobe ("visual brain") 92, 93, 131, *195*, 222, 431, 437, 480; parietal lobe *92*, 93, 131, 218, 375; somatosensory cortex 93, 131, 218, 224–225; temporal lobe (*see* temporal lobe);
nervous system and behavior/experience 82–91, 403; central nervous system (CNS) 82–83, *83*, 108–109, *109*, 132, 220, 225; peripheral nervous system (PNS) 82–83, *83*
Nettle, Daniel 536–537, **537**
neural impulses, synapses 84–86, *86*, 87–88, *88*
neural tube, prenatal brain development 108–109, *109*, 132, 137
neural/cortical networks 89–91, 111, 131–132, 235, 248, 272, 291–292, 306, 457, *459*; central executive network 90–91, 132; default or intrinsic network 90, 132, 248, 273, 375; salience network 90–91, 132, 260, 454
neuronal activity, measuring 56–57, *57*, **105**, 106, 131; electroencephalography (EEG) 99–100, *99*; functional magnetic resonance imaging (fMRI) 103, *103*, *104*; magnetic resonance imaging (MRI) 102, *102*; magnetoencephalography (MEG) 100, *100*; positron emission tomography (PET) 104, 105

neurons 32, *32*, 82, 91, 99; amygdala 94; circadian rhythm 247–248; definition, structure, function *82*, 83–84, *83*, *84*, 130; development, post/postnatal 109–110, *109*, *110*, 132, 137, 138, 139–140; by function: interneurons 84; by function: motor neurons 84, 95, 316; by function: sensory neurons 84, 95, 212, 224, 316; habituation, conditioning, learning **95–96**, 316; hypothalamus, appetite control 94, 398, 399, *399*, 435; memory forming 288–289, 306; mirror neurons, imitation learning 156–157, 177, 327, 599; neocortex layers 109–110, *110*, 132; networks (*see* neural/cortical networks); neural impulses, synapses/synaptic gap 84–86, *85*, *86*, 87–88, *88*; neurotransmission (*see* neurotransmitter); psychoactive substances, effects 265, *265*; schizophrenia, neuron density 588; sleep and learning 245, 246, *246*, 247; smelling sense 212, **214**, 224; sound perception, cochlea neurons/auditory cortex 209, *209*, 223; spike trains 89; structure: axons, axon terminals 83–84, *84*, 86, 90, 109, 131, 194, 222; structure: cell body 84, *84*; structure: dendrites (*see* dendrites); types 84
neuropeptides 87, **87**
neuroscience, techniques, electroencephalography (EEG) 99–100, *99*, **105**
Neurosis and Human Growth 527, 545, 616
neurotic vs healthy growth 527, 616
neuroticism, personality trait 519, 534, 536–537, **536**, **537**, 540, **540**, 541, *543*, 550
neurotransmitter 86–89, *87*, *88*; anxiety, gamma-aminobutyric acid (GABA) 567; emotion, oxytocin 415; habituation processes/conditioning, glutamate **95**, 316; hormones and 91; measuring, PET 105, **105**; memory, dopamine 292, 306; Parkinson's disease, dopamine 96, **461**; psychoactive

substances, effect 266, 267, 270; psychotropic medications 623; structure, types, function 86–89, *87*, 447; synaptic gap 87–88, *88*
Newton, Isaac 9, 37, 191, 191–192
norepinephrine *87*, 447
Norris, James 610, *612*
Nosographie philosophique ou méthode de l'analyse appliquée à la médecine 610–611
Nowak, Martin 493
null hypothesis 68, 79

obedience, social influences 505–509; Milgram Shock Experiment 505–508; Stanford Prison Study 508–509
observation studies/naturalistic observation 48–49, *49*; *see also* descriptive research
observational learning, modeling 326–327, 346, 619
obsessions 570, 602
obsessive-compulsive disorder (OCD) 569–570, 602, 626, 631–632, 651
occipital lobe ("visual brain") *92*, 93, 131, *195*, 222, 431, 437, 480
Odbert, Henry 533, 534
Öhman, Arne 419
olfaction 212–213, *213*, 224
open-hidden paradigm 70
openness, personality trait 534, **536**, **537**, 541, **544**, 550
operant conditioning; *see* conditioning, operant
operational definition, research 55
opioids 268
Orth, Ulrich 546
Öst, Lars 630–631, 651
overgeneralization 620, 634

Pacinian corpuscles, tactile receptors 217, *217*
pain 219–221, 225; assessment 219, *220*; reception pathway 219–220; touch, pain (somatosensory) 1, 27–28, 219, 220, 225
panic disorder 566, 568–569, 602, 631, 651
Panksepp, Jaak 423–425

Pantelis, Christos 586
paraplegia **106**, *107*
parasomnias 250–251, 273
parasympathetic nervous systems 430, 444–445, *445*, 448, 467; *see also* autonomic nervous system (ANS); nervous system and behavior/experience
parietal lobe *92*, 93, 131, 218, 375
Parkinson's disease 96, **461–462**, **590**, 626
PATHS curriculum **157–158**
Pavlov, Ivan: behaviorism 17; behaviourism 618; conditioning 311–312, *312*, 314, 315, 344; sleep, hypnosis 257, 261
peer review 44
Penfield electrical stimulation treatment/ Penfield, Wilder 279
pep pills 269
perception 183; constructive process 13–14, *13*; Gestalt psychology 17–18, *18*, 38; hearing (*see* hearing); internal perception, introspection 14, 16, 19; vs sensation 183; smell, taste 212–215; tactile (touch, pain) (*see* touch, pain (somatosenzation)); visual (*see* vision);
peripheral nervous system (PNS) *32*, *32*, 82–83, *83*
person bias 471, 472–473, 513
personality **358–359**, 517–551; animals **538–539**; astrology, astrological traits 520–522; cultural influences and variability 541, *542*, *543*, 551; evolutionary perspectives 536–538, **537**; existential-humanistic approach 531–532, 550; genetic factors 539, **540**; historical conceptions *518*, **520–521**, *520*, 548–549; personal environment as trait identifier **543–544**; physiological factors 540–541; projective techniques (Rorschach Inkblots, TAT) 527–530, *529*, *530*; psychodynamic perspective (*see* psychodynamic perspective on personality (Sigmund Freud)); self 544–548, *545*; social cognitive/social learning theories 532–533; traits 533–536, **536**, 550 (*see also* five-factor model (FFM) (Big 5));

personality disorders 591–596; antisocial personality disorder 593, 594, 604; borderline personality disorder (BPD) *561*, 594–596, ***595***, 604, 643–644; characteristics 593–594; definition, classification (cluster) 592–593, ***592***; treatment 642–644

personality traits 533, 533–536, ***536***, 550

personalization 620, 634

Pfungst, Oskar 45–46

phantom limb 1, 27–28, 219, 220, 225; *see also* pain

phenotype 113, 116, 125, 133, 377

pheromones 213

phi phenomenon 18, 200

Phineas Gage case study, brain damage effects 81–82, *82*

phobias ***560***; agoraphobia 569, 602; conditioning/heritability 314–315, *314*, 344, 567, 619; development 566; specific phobias 569, 602, 630–631; treatment 630–631, 651 (*see also* anxiety disorders);

phonemes 140, 329, 330, 331–332, *332*, *341*, 346–347, *347*

photographic memory 297

photoreceptors (rods, cones) 186–187

photoreceptors: rods, cones 186–187, 189–191, *189*, 221–222

physical development, childhood 136–148; brain 138–141, *139–140*; learning from environment, habituation 143–144, *144*; milestones by age ***147–148***; motor 144–147, *145*, *146*; prenatal 137–138; sensory 141–143, *142*

Piaget, Jean 149–152, *152*, 177, 310

Piaget stages of cognitive development 150–152, *152*, 177

Pinel, Phillipe 610–611, 648

Pinker, Steven 335–336, 509, 515

pituitary gland 91, *91*

placebo response, placebo treatment 70, 76, 78, 641; depression treatment ***632–633***; endorphins 71; expectations and health outcome ***461–462***; external/internal factors 70; research: experimenter effect, blind/double-blind setup 71; research: open-hidden paradigm 70

plasticity, brain 140, 262

Plato 6–7

Popper, Karl 43

Porter, Steven ***303–304***

positive punishment, conditioning 321, *322*, 345

positron emission tomography (PET) 104–105, ***105***, 106, 231, 260, 293, 410

post-traumatic stress disorder (PTSD) 456–459, ***560***; brain structure and 94, 458–459, *459*; dissociation and 579; flashback, trauma event 456; "hot" vs "cold" associations/memory 457–458, *458*; stressors ***214***, ***457***; therapy approach 458; US army veterans 457

Powers, Albert ***590***

prefrontal cortex (PFC), medial prefrontal cortex (mPFC), ventromedial prefrontal cortex (vmPFC) 92, 458, *459*, 485, 511, 547

Premack, David 158–159

prenatal development 108–109, *109*, 132, 137, 137–138

Price, Jill 295–296

primary visual cortex 195–197, *195*, 209, 222, 232

priming, long-term memory 283, *283*, 305–306

Prince, Morton 50

Prince, The 517

Principia 9

Principles of Psychology 544–545

prisoners' dilemma, game studies 485, 491–493, ***491***

proactive interference, memory 285

problem solving, insight 360–364; brain, temporal lobe 362, ***363–364***; functional fixedness 362, 390; insight, improving 363–364, *364*; insight, nature of 361–363; insight problems 360–362; insight problems (9-dot problem), candle problem) *360*, *361*, 390; well-defined problems 360

procedural memory 283, *283*, *293*, 305, 580

Project for a Scientific Psychology, The 19–20, 253, 524–525; associationism 524; "Q," libido or sexual energy 524; reflex processes 524

Index

projective techniques (Rorschach Inkblots, TAT) 527–530

Promoting Alternative Thinking Strategies (PATHS) curriculum **157–158**

prosocial behavior, influences 498–509; altruism/helping, human origin perspectives 490–491, 494; bystander intervention, experiment/research 488–489; cooperation (*see* cooperation, non-cooperation); social inhibition 489, **592**, 593

Prosser, Inez 24, 38

proteins, gene encoding 114–116

prototype, cognition 351–352

Prozac 623, 636, **637**, 649

psychoactive substances 262–271; addiction (*see* addiction); alcohol 138, 263, 264, 265, 266–267, 274, **313–314**; cannabis (THC), cannabinoids 267; depressants (alcohol, barbiturates) 266–267, 274; hallucinogens (LSD, MDMA, MDA, PCP) 266, 269–270, *270*, 274; medical use 268, 270; stimulants (amphetamines, cocaine, opioids) 268–269; usage, statistics 269; β-endorphin (beta-endorphin) 271

psychoanalysis 20, 613–615, 648; *see also* psychodynamic perspective, Sigmund Freud

psychodynamic perspective on personality 19–20, 38, 522–525, 526, 527, 549, 613, 648; Freud: anxiety defense mechanism 525–526, **526**; Freud: associationism 524; Freud: personality structure (id, ego, superego) 523, 549; Freud: pleasure principle, reality principle 523; Freud: psychosexual development stages (oral, phallic, latency, genital) 523–524, 549; Freud: "Q," libido or sexual energy 524; Freud: reflex processes 524; Freud: types of consciousness 523, 524; Freud-influenced approaches (Adler, Anna Freud, "object relations," Horney, Jung) 526–527, 549; projective techniques (Rorschach Inkblots, TAT) 528–530, *530*, 549–550

psychological disorders, dissociative disorders; *see* dissociative disorders

psychological disorders, emotions/mood disorders 565–578; anxiety disorders 565–569; mood disorders (depressions, bipolar) 571–574; obsessive-compulsive disorders (OCD) 569–570, 602, 626, 631–632, 651; suicide 125, 574–578, *575*, *577*, **577**, 595, 602

psychological disorders, heredity: anxiety 567; attention deficit hyperactivity disorder (ADHD) 558, 599, 601; autism 599; bipolar disorder 574; depression 125, 455, 558; schizophrenia 587, *587*, 588, 589

psychological disorders, neurodevelopmental disorders 597–601; attention deficit hyperactivity disorder (ADHD) 558, **560**, 599–600, 601, 604, 646; autism spectrum disorder (ASD) 53, **53–54**, *54*, 597–598, *598*, 604, 645–646; treatment 645–646

psychological disorders, personality disorders; *see* personality disorders

psychological disorders, schizophrenia; *see* schizophrenia

psychological disorders/psychopathology 553–604; comorbidity 458, 559, 561, 569, 576, 594; definition/personal components 554–555, **555**; evolutionary perspectives 564–565; extend/statistics 555, *555*; legal understanding, insanity 554, **561–563**; mental disorder, *DSM-5* definition/categories 558–559, **560–561**; stigma 556–557, 601; studying/classifying, *DSM* 557–561, **560–561**

psychological treatment, by disorder; *see individual disorders*

psychological treatment, perspectives 607–648; behavioral/cognitive behavioral 20, 618–622, *620*, 639; biological/biopsychosocial 21, 622–627, **624–625**, *624*; existential-humanistic 20, 526–527, 531–532, 550, 615–618, 633, 649; historical 609–612, *611*, *612*, 648; psychodynamic 19–20, 38, 522–525, 526, 527, 549, 613–615, 648

psychological treatment, techniques: behavioral therapy 618–619; brain stimulation (TMS/DBS) 279, 625–626, 632, 651; client/person-centered therapy 20, 38, 615–616, 648; cognitive behavioral therapy (CBT) 619–621, 620; effectiveness research 38, 627–628; electroconvulsive therapy (ECT) 625, 650–651; emotional focused therapy(EFT)/process experiential therapy 616–617, 621, 635; mindfulness/dialectical behavior therapy 617–618; psychoanalysis 20, 613–615, 648; psychotropic medications 622–624, 631, 649

psychology: definition, scope (behavior, experience) 2–5, 37; scientific methods, neuroscience 4; social psychology (*see* social psychology);

psychology, history 4, 5–16, *5*, 35–36, 38; 1700s–1900s (Gall, Broca, Wernicke, Jackson, Darwin, Helmholtz) 9–14, *11*, *12*, *13*, 37; 1900s onwards, **20**h century major approaches 16–23, 37–38; African American psychologists 24, 38; Ancient Greece, Roman Empire 6–7, 37; cultural context **21–23**; early modern philosophy (Descartes) 7–8, *9*; early Western science (Galileo, Newton) 8–9, 37; female psychologists 23–24, 38; psychological treatment, perspectives 609–612, *611*, *612*, 648; Renaissance to 1700s (da Vinci) 7, *8*; scientific psychology, beginnings (James, Wundt) 14–16, *15*

psychology, levels of analysis 31–32, **31**, *32*–*33*, 35–36

psychology, perspectives: behavioral and experiential 25–26, *25*, 38; human origins, historical cultural 28–31, *29*, *30*, 38–39; neuroscientific 26–28, *27*, 38

psychopathology; *see* psychological disorders/psychopathology

psychopathy 556, 604

psychophysics 183–184, 183–185, 221

psychosocial stages (Erik Erikson) 171–173, *172*, **172**

psychotic disorders 583

psychotropic medications 622–624, 631, 641–642

puberty 42, 165–166, 177, 242, 424, 574
public goods game, game study research 494
purging 404
puzzle box experiment 17, 319–321, 345
Pythagoras 6

Quakers of Philadelphia (Friends Asylum for the Use of Persons Deprived of the Use of Their Reason, 1813) 612
qualitative/quantitative research 46, 61

race, black suspect police shootings **480–482**, *482*
Ramachandran, Vilayanur Subramanian 41–42
randomization, experiment design 67, 629, 631, 641, 646
Rapaport, Anatol 492
rapid eye movement (REM) sleep: dreaming 253–254, **254**, *254*, 256; narcolepsy 250; neuroscience studies 246–247, *247*, *249*; sleep pattern 240–243, *241*, *242*, 272; sleepwalking 251
Ray, William J. 579
reactive obsessions 570
real self 527, 545, 616
reconstructive memory 286–287, *287*
Recovered not Cured: A Journey through Schizophrenia 584
reflexes: conditioning and habituation 311–312, 316, 618; historical views 7, 15, 19, 82; imune system 450; infants (grasping, rooting, sucking, swimming) 144–145, 146, *146*, 159; motor development and (Darwin) 144–145; reflex processes, associationism (Freud) 19, 525
reinforcement, conditioning: continuous, partial 322, 345; fixed/variable interval 322–323, *323*; fixed/variable ratio 322–323, *323*; positive/negative 319, 321–322, **322**, 345
reliability 60–61; *see also* data, evaluation and analysis
REM sleep; *see* rapid eye movement (REM) sleep
Repetti, Rena L. 448

replication/research replicability 60–61, 79; *see also* data, evaluation and analysis

research, design 66–71, *66*, 78–79; experimental design, structure planning 67–68; participant selection/assignment 66, 67; result interpretation (IV–DV relationship) 61, 68–71

research, ethics 72–77, 79; animal research 75–76, 79; anonymity 74, 79; APA guidelines 73; confidentiality 74, 79; deception studies 75–77; empirically based treatments, effectiveness **74–75**; informed consent 73–74, 77, 79; Nuremberg Code 72; Tuskegee experiment 73; voluntary participation 73–74, 79

research, methods; *see* science, scientific method

research hypothesis 68, 79

resilience 459–460

resistance examination, psychoanalysis (Freud) 614

reticular activating system (RAS) 246

Retreat for Persons Afflicted with Disorders of the Mind, York (Quaker retreat, 1796) 612, 648

retroactive interference, memory 285–286

rhodopsin 190

Ritalin 646

Rizzolatti, Giacomo 156, 327

Robbers cave experiment 495–496

Roberson, Arlene 594–595

rods 186–187, 189–191, *189*, 221–222

Rogers, Carl 20, 38, 532, 615–616, 648

Romania adoption study 162–164, *163*, *164*

rooting reflex 144–145

Rorschach Inkblots 528–529, *529*

Rosch, Eleanor 351

Rosenhand, Ray 455

Ross, Colin A. 579

Rotter, Julian 532, 533

Rubin, Edgar 200–201, **585**

Rubin vase illusion 18, *18*, 200–201, **585**, *586*

Ruffini endings, tactile receptors 217, *217*

Rush, Benjamin 610, 639, 648

Rush, John 637, 648

Russell, James 427, *427*

Sackeim 500

Saks, Elyn R. 583

salience network 90–91, 132, 260, 454

Salthouse, Timothy 374–375

Sandy Hook Elementary School, shooting 556

S.B. study/treatment (sight restoration) **203–204**, *204*

Schachter–Singer theory 428, 429, 437

Schacter, Daniel L. 302

schadenfreude 488

schemas 500

schizophrenia 30, 582–590, *582*, 603; brain changes 588–589, *588*, *589*; delusions (persecution, grandeur, control) 584, 603; development factors 586–587; evolutionary context 564; hallucinations 584, **590**; heritability 120, 128, *128*, 564, 587, *587*, 588, 589; John Nash 553, 554, 556, 584; neurotransmitter **87**; optical illusions, response **585–586**, *585*; phases (onset, development) 582, *582*; symptoms 583–585; treatment 608, 638–642, 652

Schlagman, Naomi 511–512

Schroeder stairs illusion **585**, *586*

science, scientific method: combination research 56–58; culture of science, paradigm shifts **57–58**; definition, scope 42–43, *43*, 78; descriptive research 47–54 (*see also* descriptive research); doubt, falsification 43–44; experimental research/method 55–56; qualitative/quantitative research 46, 61; stages (hypothesis, experiment design/ execution, result interpretation) 46–47, *47*, 78; superstition, pseudoscience, unintended influence 43–46, **53–54**, *54*, 78

Scottish Mental Survey Study 375–376, *376*

scripts (cultural, universal), self-scripts 498–500, 501, 514

self 501, 544–548, *545*, 551; healthy self, *DSM-5* 547, 547–548; "I" and

"me" distinction 501, 523, 544–545; neuroscience research 546–547
self-actualization 395–396, *396*, 435, 532, 545, 616
self-concept 501, 514, 545–546, *545*
self-efficacy 533
self-esteem 546–547
self-harm/injury 595, 645
self-realization 527, 616
self-schemas 501, 514, 545, *545*
self-scripts, scripts (cultural, universal) 498–500, 501, 514
self-serving bias 473–474
Selye, Hans 441–442, 466–467
semantic memory 282–283, *283*; *see also* long-term memory
semantics, language 332, 347
Semon, Richard 288
sensation: cerebral cortex *93*; vs perception 183; sensory thresholds 184, 221
sensitization **95–96**, 316, 345
sensory memory 280
sensory neurons 84, 95, 212, 224, 316
sensory thresholds 184
separation anxiety disorder 566
serotonin 87, *87*, 96, 270, 567, 623, 629, 636
sexuality 406–414, *408*, **409**, *411*; adolescence 165, 166, 173; basic needs/motivations (Darwin, Maslow)) 394, 395, 406; brain activity 410, 444; Center for Sexual Health Promotion study (2010) 406, 436; Centers for Disease Control and Prevention (CDC) survey (2006) 407, *408*, 436; Freud: "Q," libido or sexual energy 20, 524; gender differences 408, 410, 412–413; historical perspective 406–407; homosexuality, bisexuality 406, 407, 410, 413, 436; Masters/Johnson studies 411–412, *411*, 436; masturbation 406, 407; sex as peace making (bonobo study) 48; sexual activities, Americans (statistics) 407–408, **409**; sexual arousal, levels 408, 436; *Sexual Behavior in the Human Female*, Kinsey survey (1953) 407, 436; *Sexual Behavior in the Human Male*, Kinsey survey (1948) 407, 436; sexual energy, libido 20, 524; sexual orientation 410; sexual response, phases (excitement, plateau, orgasm, resolution) 411–412, *411*, 436; sexual selection, evolution (Darwin, Freud) 12–13, *12*, 19, 406; *Studies in the Psychology of Sex*, Ellis research studies 406, 436
Shakespeare, William 477
shame 487, 514
shaping 341; *see also* social shaping hypothesis
Shaw, Julia **303–304**
Sheldon, William 519, 549
Shereshevsky, Solomon 296, 297
Sherif, Carolyn 495–496
Sherif, Muzafar 495–496
Sherrington, Charles 82
short-term memory 277–278, 280–282, *280*, 285, 290, 305, 306
Shotland, Lance 489
Sigmund, Karl 493
Simon, Théodore/Binet–Simon Intelligence Scale 366, 391
Simpsons, The 44, 255
situational explanations (self-attributing) 471, 513
Skeide, Micheal A. 329
Skinner, B. F. 17, 309–310, 320–322, *320*, *322*, 329, 345, 531, 619
Skinner box experiment 17, 320–322, *320*, 345
sleep 238–256; deprivation, effects 239; disorders 250–252, 273; learning during sleep 244–246, *246*, **327–328**; needs, species variations 244, *244*; neuroscience studies 246–249, *247*, *248*, *249*; pattern (*see* sleep pattern); ; *see also* consciousness; dreams
sleep jerks, starts 251–252
sleep paralysis 251
sleep pattern 240–246; changes by age 242, *242*; circadian rhythm 242, 243, 247, 250, 272, 273; cycle/night 241–242, *241*; non-REM sleep 240; REM sleep (*see* rapid eye movement (REM) sleep); species variations 243–244, *244*; stability of sleep cycles, environmental impact 243, *243*; stages 240–241, *241*

sleep talking 251
sleep terror, night terror 251
sleepwalking 251
slow thinking/decision making 354, 390
SM (Urbach–Wiethe disease) case study **432–434**, *433*
small world framework 90, 131
smell, taste 212–215; definition 224; flavor experience 215; gustatory system 214–215, *215*, 224; human-vs-other animals, smell ability research **213–214**; olfaction 212–213, *213*, 224; pheromones 213; taste signal pathway *215*; see also smell, taste
Smetana, Judith G. 511–512
social behavior influences 498–509; compliance techniques 501–502; conformity 502–505, *503*, *504*; group-level (social loafing/facilitation) 500; persuasion/obedience 505–509, *507*; relationship types: authority ranking 499–500; relationship types: communal sharing 499; relationship types: equality matching (tit for tat) 499, 500; relationship types: market pricing 499, 500; scripts (cultural, universal), self-scripts 498–500, 501, 514; self-level (self-scripts, schemas) 500–501
social brain hypothesis 482–483, *483*
social cognition 471–486, 514–515; attribution 158–159, 471, 472–474, 484, 513; brain systems for social relations 484–485, *485*; brain systems, social relations 484–486; face and person perception 477–482, 484; gaming as real-world experience, brain response 485; social brain hypothesis 482–483, *483*; stereotyping, categorizing 385–387, *386*, 389, 474–476, 480–482, 495, 514
social cognitive/social learning personality, theories 532–533
social development, childhood 156–164, 177; empathy 156–157; imitation learning, mirror neurons 156–157, 177; PATHS curriculum **157–158**; theory of attachment 159–164, *160*, **162–163**, *163–164*; theory of mind 158–159, 484

social emotions: definition 487; embarrassment 484, 487, 514; envy 488; morel emotions (guilt, shame) 168, 487, 514; schadenfreude 488
social facilitation 500
social inhibition 489, **592**, 593
social loafing 500
social processing 1
social psychology 469–512; behavior, social influences 498–509; moral judgements 509, *510*, *511*, 512; race, black suspect police shootings **480–482**, *482*; social cognition 471–486; social emotions 486–498
social shaping hypothesis 454, 467
somatic nervous system 82–83, *83*
somatosensory cortex 93, 131, 218, *218*, 224, 224–225
sound: creation, brain 209–210, *209*, *210*, 223; waves (amplitude, frequency, timbre/complexity) 205–207, *205*, *206*, 223; see also hearing, audition
spacing out 272, 578
spatial intelligence 373
Spearman, Charles 369–370, 391
speech; see language/speech
Sperling, George 280, *280*
spider phobia 631, 651
spike trains 88–89, 99
spinal cord 82, 98, *98*, 108, *109*, 132, 137, 338, 444, *445*; see also central nervous system (CNS)
SSRIs (selective serotonin re-uptake inhibitors) 623, 629, 630, 631, 636, 649, 651
Stahl, Aimee 143–144, *144*
Stanford Prison Study 508–509; see also Milgram Shock Experiment
Stanford–Binet Intelligence Scales 367, 391
Steele, Claude 385–386, *386*, 389
Steele, Ken 583, 584
Stephens, David William 492–493
Stephens, Jeffrey R. 492–493
stereotype bias 385, 387
stereotyping, categorizing 474–476, 480–482, 495, 514; acquisition process 474–475; bias research: implicit association test (IAT) **476–477**; brain

aspects 475; corporate training 474; gender stereotypes, influence 389; in-group/out-group 474; mechanism (social categorization, stereotype activation/application) 475, 514; person perception 474; race, black suspect police shootings **480–482**, *482*; stereotype bias 385–387, *386*
stereotyping/stereotype bias 385–387, *386*, 389, 474–476, 480–482, 495, 514
Stern, William 367, 391
stigma 556–557, 601
stimulants (amphetamines, cocaine, opioids)) 268–269
Straube, Thomas 631
Straw, Margaret 489
stream of consciousness 15, 90, 227
stress 439–467; allostasis (allostatic systems/load) 442–443, *443*, 467; alternative/complementary medicine **465**; autonomic nervous system (ANS) (*see* autonomic nervous system (ANS)); definition, concept 440–441, 466; expectations and health outcome **461–462**; historical research approaches 441–443, *443*; immune system 91, 258, 273, 344–345, 449, 449–451, **451–452**; meditation, mindfulness, influence 464–465 (*see also* mindfulness); physical activity, influence 462–463, **463**, *464*; PTSD (*see* post-traumatic stress disorder (PTSD)); social support and stress response, research 452–456, *454*
stress physiology 41, 444–446, *445*, *446*; acute stress: SAM (sympathetic adrenal medullary) system 446–447, *446*; cardiovascular system effects (type A/B) 455; chronic stress: HPA (hypothalamic pituitary adrenal) pathway 446–447, *447*; fight-or-flight response 41, 444–446, *445*; hormonal response 447–449; oxytosis, gender variations 448–449; rest-and-digest response 444
stress response (fight or flight/tend to befriend) 440, 446; allostasis response 441, 442, 467; autonomic nervous system (ANS) 41, 444–446, *445*; definition, evolutionary link 439–440, 453, 466; gender differences, tend-to-befriend response 447–448; general adaptation syndrome (GAS) 441–442, 467; vs PTSD 456; SAM/HPA pathways *446*, 447, *447*, 453; social shaping hypothesis 454, 467; stress eating 454–455
Stroop color interference task/effect **482**, *482*
structuralism 14, *15*, 17–18, 37, 38
Strupp, Hans 614, 635–636, 645
Substance Abuse and Mental Health Services Administration (SAMHSA) 75, 627
sucking reflex 145
suicidal ideation 530, 574, 575, 576
suicide 125, 574–578, *575*, *577*, **577**, 595, 602
Sullenberger, Chesley (Sully) 349
Summer, Francis Cecil 24, 38
superordinate goals, cooperation 495–496
super-recognizers, memory **297–298**
suprachiasmatic nucleus (SCN) 247–248
surface structure, language 334
Susskind, Joshua M. 420, *420*
Sybil 581
sympathetic nervous system 430, 442, 444–445, *445*, 446, 447, 448, 467; *see also* autonomic nervous system (ANS); nervous system and behavior/experience
synapses/synaptic gap 84–86, *86*, **95–96**, 95–99, 245, 316
synesthesia 181–182
syntax, language 332, *332*, 340, 347

tactile receptors, tactile image creation 216–218, *217*, *218*, 224
taste; *see* smell, taste
taste, smell (chemical senses) 212–215
Taylor, Shelley 447–448
temperament: classification by reactivity (inhibited, uninhibited) 155; definition 154; development 154–155; endomorph, mesomorph, ectomorph personalities 519, 549; genetic predisposition 129, 155, 537; historical characteristics 518, *518*
temporal lobe *92*, 93, 131, 375, 483; amygdala, emotional processing 293,

375, 432, 437; hippocampus, memory 279, *279*, 282, 291, 292, 306; language 11, 343; problem solving, insight 362, **363–364**

tend-to-befriend response; *see* response (fight or flight/tend to befriend)

teratogens 137–138

Testa, Renee 586

testosterone 166, 448

thalamus 94, *94*, 108, 215, 218, 219, 246, 247, *430*

The Witness 488

Thelen, Esther 146

thematic apperception test (TAT) 529–530, *530*

Theophrastus 519, 549

theory of mind 158–159, 484

Thorndike, Edward L. 17, 315, 319–321, 345

Three Faces of Eve 581

Titchener, Edward 14

tit-for-tat, game study 492, 500

token economies 619

Tolstoy, Leo 571

Tomkins, Silvan 426

tools of intellectual adaptation 151

touch, pain (somatosenzation) 216–221; motor cortex 218, *218*, 225; nociceptors 219; pain 219–221, 225; pain assessment 219, *220*; pain reception pathway 219–220; phantom limb 1, 27–28, 219, 220, 225; somatosensory cortex 93, 131, 218, *218*, 224, 224–225; tactile receptors types, tactile image creation 216–218, *217*, *218*, 224; touch, active/passive 216

trait characteristics (attributing others) 471, 513

transcranial magnetic stimulation (TMS) 279, 625–626, 632, 651

transducers 183, 221

transference, psychoanalysis (Freud) 614, 636

transference-focused psychotherapy (TFP) 645

Travis 492

tricyclic antidepressants (TCAs) 623, 649

'triune brain' model (MacLean) 111–112, *111*, 132

Trivers, Robert 490, 492, 494

Trolley problem 509–511, *510*, *511*, 549

trust game, game study research 493

t-test 69

Tuke, William 612, 648

Turing, Alan 227, 228

Turner, Alberta Banner 24

Tuskegee experiment 73

Tversky, Amos 350, 354, 355–356

Twain, Mark 165

twin studies, motor development 146

twin studies, psychological disorders, heredity: anorexia nervosa/bulimia 403; anxiety 567; attention deficit hyperactivity disorder (ADHD) 599; autism 599; bipolar disorder 574; schizophrenia 128, *128*, 587, *587*, 588, 589

twins, behavioral genetics/epigenetics: brain development variations **128–129**; inter-personal/group violence and aggression, studies 497–498; IQ-development, variations 129, 377–379, *378*, *379*, **382**, 391–392; monozygotic (MZ)/dizygotic (DZ) twins 127, *128*; NASA twin, study (2019) 113, 116; personality traits 540, **540**, 550

type A/B behavior 455

UCLA Young Autism Project 645

ultimatum, game study 485–486

unconditional positive regard, client-centered therapy 615, 648

unconditioned response (UCR) 311, 344

unconditioned stimulus (UCS) 283, 311, 312, **313**, 315, 317, 344

United States National Institutes of Health (NIH) 465

universal grammar, language 334

Urbach–Wiethe disease (SM) case study **432–434**, *433*

validity: internal/external 59–60, *60*, 78; projective techniques (Rorschach Inkblots, TAT) 528, 530

variability, measures 64–66, *65*, **65**; *see also* descriptive statistics

variables: confounding variables/
hypothesis 56, 67, 68, 69–70, 79;
dependent (DV)/independent (IV)
55–56, 61, 66, 68, 69, 79; IV–DV
relationship (research interpretation) 61,
66, 68–71, 79
ventral tegmental area (VTA) 264, 265,
265, 410, 415, *479*, 480
Verbal behavior 329
vestigial structures 145–146
vision 184–204; bionic eye implants
190–191; blindsight 232–233; color,
color blindness (*see* color blindness;
color vision); depth 187, 197–198, 222;
evolutionary changes 186–187; eye,
structure/function 187–189, *187*, *188*;
eye–brain connection 194–195, *194*,
195; Gestalt psychology, organizational
principles 199–202, *200*; light/energetic
energy, sensitivity 184–187, *186*;
photoreceptors: rods, cones 186–187,
189–191, *189*, 221–222; primary visual
cortex 195–197, *195*, 209, 222, 232; sight
restoration (S.B. case) *200*, 204; visual
field 194–195, *195*; visual pathway *196*
visual acuity 142, 187, 189, 221
visual illusions 198–199, *199*, 203, *204*,
222–223, 585–586, *585*
visual word form area (VWFA) *340*, 343
vocal cords 330, 337–338
Vyas, Nora S. 586
Vygotsky, Lev 149, 151–152, 177

Wakefield, Andrew **54**
Wannerton, James 181–182, *182*
Washburn, Margaret Floy 14, 23, 38
Watkins, Linda R. 449
Watson, James 117
Watson, John 17, 148–149, 314–315, *314*,
344, 618–619
Wearing, Clive 277, 278
Weber's law/Weber, Ernst 184
Wechsler, David: Wechsler Adult
Intelligence Scale (WAIS) 367–369, *367*,
368, *369*, 391; Wechsler Intelligence
Scale for Children (WISC) 367, 391

Wechsler Adult Intelligence Scale (WAIS)
367–369, *367*, *368*, *369*, 391
Wechsler Intelligence Scale for Children
(WISC) 367, 391
Weiss, Jay 455–456, *456*
Wernicke, Carl 10–11, *11*
Wertheimer, Max 200, 201, *201*
Westwood, Stephen 591–592
white coat syndrome 440
white matter, brain 90, 131–132, 342;
abnormalities: schizophrenia 588–589;
heritable traits 587; increase by age 138,
139; mapping, diffusion tensor imaging
(DTI) 100, *102*
White Men Can't Jump 474
Wilson, Michael L. 496–497
wisdom of the body 395, 441
witches 609–610
Wittgenstein, Ludwig 351
Wolf 537
Wolpe, Joseph **317–318**
Wood, Stephen J. 586
Woodruff, Guy 158–159
Woolley, Anita **371–372**, *371*
working memory 90, 280–281, 292, 305,
306, *367*, 368, 375
World Health Organization (WHO) 161,
460, *461*, 462–463, 564, 572, 593
World War II: epigenetic study: Dutch
Hongerwinter (1944) **125–126**, 129;
ethics, concentration camp experiments
72; obedience, following-order argument
505
Wrangham, Richard W. 496–497
Wundt, Wilhelm 14–15, *15*, 37, 417–418,
427

yoked-control experiment 455–456
Young, Thomas 192–193, 222
Young–Helmholtz trichromatic theory of
color 192–193, 222

Zeanah, Charles H. 162–163, *163*
zeitgeber 243
Zimbardo, Philip 508–509
zone of proximal development 152